OCA: Oracle®
Database 12c Administrator
Certified Associate
Study Guide

Biju Thomas

SYBEX®
A Wiley Brand

Senior Acquisitions Editor: Jeff Kellum
Development Editor: Lisa Bishop
Technical Editors: Arup Nanda and Syed Jaffar Hussain
Production Editor: Dassi Zeidel
Copy Editor: Kathy Grider-Carlyle
Editorial Manager: Pete Gaughan
Vice President and Executive Group Publisher: Richard Swadley
Associate Publisher: Chris Webb
Media Project Manager 1: Laura Moss-Hollister
Media Associate Producer: Shawn Patrick
Media Quality Assurance: Marilyn Hummel
Book Designer: Judy Fung
Compositor: Craig Woods, Happenstance Type-O-Rama
Proofreader: Kathy Pope
Indexer: Ted Laux
Project Coordinator, Cover: Todd Klemme
Cover Designer: Wiley
Cover Image: © Getty Images Inc./Jeremy Woodhouse

Dear Reader,

Thank you for choosing *OCA: Oracle Database 12c Administrator Certified Associate Study Guide*. This book is part of a family of premium-quality Sybex books, all of which are written by outstanding authors who combine practical experience with a gift for teaching.

Sybex was founded in 1976. More than 30 years later, we're still committed to producing consistently exceptional books. With each of our titles, we're working hard to set a new standard for the industry. From the paper we print on, to the authors we work with, our goal is to bring you the best books available.

I hope you see all that reflected in these pages. I'd be very interested to hear your comments and get your feedback on how we're doing. Feel free to let me know what you think about this or any other Sybex book by sending me an email at contactus@sybex.com. If you think you've found a technical error in this book, please visit http://sybex.custhelp.com. Customer feedback is critical to our efforts at Sybex.

Best regards,

Chris Webb
Associate Publisher
Sybex, an Imprint of Wiley

*To the ladies in my family: my lovely wife, loving mom, and lovable sisters.
Thanks for always being there for me.*

To my children: Joshua and Jeanette. You brighten my day, every day!

Acknowledgments

I thank the great publishing team at Wiley for helping me throughout the writing process. I am grateful to Jeff Kellum, acquisitions editor at Wiley, for initiating this project and having faith in me. I am indebted to Lisa Bishop, developmental editor, for offering valuable suggestions to improve the readability and organization of the book. Thank you both for your patience and hard work throughout this project.

Thank you Kathy Grider-Carlyle, copy editor, for meticulously going through the chapters and making sure there is no ambiguity and that all the pieces tie together. I thank Dassi Zeidel, production editor, for ensuring consistency and accuracy and coordinating the production process. I would like to thank Pete Gaughan, Connor O'Brien, Jenni Housh, Rayna Erlick, and everyone at Wiley who helped in the making of this book.

A technical book is judged by not only who wrote it, but also who reviewed it. I am much honored to have two great Oracle experts as technical reviewers, both Oracle ACE Directors and recipients of the DBA of the Year award. I thank Arup Nanda for reviewing each paragraph of every chapter and for the invaluable comments, tips, and edits. I thank Syed Jaffar Hussain for reading and ensuring the technical accuracy. The input from two Oracle stalwarts certainly improved the content and reliability of the book.

I sincerely thank Gavin Powell for initially signing up as a coauthor to this book. Due to unforeseen events, Gavin could complete only one chapter. I thank Gavin for working with me and helping with the book.

I have many friends to thank at OneNeck IT Solutions for their friendship and encouragement. My heartfelt thanks to Chuck Vermillion (SVP & General Manager) for his support and confidence in me. Thank you Danny Carrizosa for the motivation and your willingness to help out wherever needed. I thank Phil Pearson and the entire team for their trust in my technical abilities. It sure is great working with you all.

Last but not least, no words can express the ceaseless support and encouragement given by my dear wife. Thank you, Shiji. You are the best. I owe my kids several weekends and thank them for their patience and tolerance of so much of my attention being given to this book.

About the Author

Biju Thomas is an Oracle ACE, Oracle Certified Professional, and Certified Oracle Database SQL Expert. Biju has been developing and administering Oracle databases since 1993. He now spends time mentoring DBAs, performance tuning, and designing Oracle solutions. He is Principal Solutions Architect at OneNeck IT Solutions (http://www.oneneck.com). He is a frequent presenter at Oracle conferences and a contributor to Oracle technical journals. He blogs at http://www.bijoos.com/oraclenotes, and you can follow his tweets @biju_thomas.

About the Contributor

Gavin Powell spent 25 years as an IT professional in positions such as Oracle DBA, performance tuner, data architect, and developer. In the last 10 years, he has branched out into technical writing (many titles in print) in between contract and consulting jobs. He also enjoys music, songwriting, performing, singing, playing too many instruments, home recording/producing, and studying music at Berklee.

About the Technical Reviewers

Arup Nanda has been an Oracle DBA for the last 20 years, working on all aspects of Oracle technology from modeling to performance tuning to disaster recovery. He has written over 500 published articles, presented over 300 sessions in 22 countries, and coauthored 5 books. He is an Oracle ACE Director, Oak Table Network member, editor for *SELECT Journal*, and a board member of Exadata SIG of IOUG. In recognition, Oracle conferred on him the coveted DBA of the Year and Architect of the Year awards in 2003 and 2012, respectively. He lives in Danbury, CT.

Syed Jaffar Hussain has over 21 years IT experience that includes more than 14 years of production Oracle database administration. Oracle has honored him with the prestigious Oracle ACE Director role and named him DBA of the Year for 2011, both for his excellent knowledge and contributions to the Oracle community. He is an Oracle Certified Master (OCM) for Oracle Database 10g, a status granted only after passing extensive challenges in a hands-on environment. He is also an Oracle Database 10g RAC Certified Expert. Syed Jaffar is a well-known Oracle speaker, and he coauthored *Expert Oracle RAC12* and *Oracle 11g R1/R2 Real Application Clusters Essentials*. He blogs regularly at http://jaffardba.blogspot.com.

Contents at a Glance

Contents

Table of Exercises

Introduction

There is high demand for professionals in the information technology (IT) industry, and Oracle certifications are the hottest credential in the database world. You have made the right decision to pursue certification, because being certified in the latest version of Oracle, Oracle Database 12c, will give you a distinct advantage in this highly competitive market.

Many readers may already be familiar with Oracle and do not need an introduction to Oracle databases. For those who aren't familiar with the company, Oracle, founded in 1977, sold the first commercial relational database and is now the world's leading database company and second-largest independent software company with revenues of more than $37 billion, and is headquartered in Redwood City, California.

Oracle databases are the de facto standard for large Internet sites, mission-critical enterprise applications, and cloud solutions. With the acquisition of Sun Microsystems, Oracle offers complete enterprise business solutions with engineered systems capable of running world-class databases and applications. Enterprise Resource Planning (ERP) application suites, data warehouses, and business applications at many large and medium-sized companies rely on Oracle. The demand for DBA resources remains higher than others during weak economic times.

This book is intended to help you on your exciting path toward becoming an Oracle Database 12c Administrator Certified Associate (OCA), which is the first step on the path toward Oracle Certified Professional (OCP) and Oracle Certified Master (OCM) certification. This book covers two of the exams required for the OCA certification. Using this book and a practice database, you can start learning Oracle Database 12c and pass the 1Z0-061 "Oracle Database 12c: SQL Fundamentals" and 1Z0-062 "Oracle Database 12c: Installation and Administration" exams.

Why Become Oracle Certified?

The number one reason to become OCA or OCP certified is to gain more visibility and greater access to the industry's most challenging opportunities. Oracle certification is the best way to demonstrate your knowledge and skills in Oracle database systems. Preparing for the certification exam may be the best time spent on your career because you learn the tasks that are necessary to be successful as a DBA.

Certification is proof of your knowledge and shows that you have the skills required to support Oracle core products. The Oracle certification program can help a company identify proven performers who have demonstrated their skills and who can support the company's investment in Oracle technology. It demonstrates that you have a solid understanding of your job role and the Oracle products used in that role.

The certification tests are scenario-based, which is the most effective way to assess your hands-on expertise and critical problem-solving skills. OCPs are among the best paid in the IT industry. Salary surveys consistently show the OCP certification to yield higher salaries than the other certifications, including Microsoft, Novell, and Cisco.

So, whether you are beginning a career, changing careers, securing your present position, or seeking to refine and promote your position, this book is for you!

Oracle Certifications

Oracle certifications follow a track that is oriented toward a job role. The primary certification tracks are Database, Applications, Java, Enterprise Management, Virtualization, and Operating Systems. Within each track, Oracle has a tiered certification program of OCA and OCP. Only the Database track has OCM. The Database track is clearly for the Database Administrator job role.

> For the latest certification information on all of Oracle certification paths, please visit the Oracle website at http://education.oracle.com/pls/web_prod-plq-dad/db_pages.getpage?page_id=39&p_org_id=1001&lang=US.

The role of database administrator (DBA) has become a key to success in today's highly complex database systems. The best DBAs work behind the scenes, but are in the spotlight when critical issues arise. They plan, create, maintain, and ensure that the database is available for the business, most importantly, DBAs troubleshoot, diagnose, and resolve issues. They have tools to proactively monitor the database for performance issues and to prevent unscheduled downtime. The DBA's job requires a broad understanding of the architecture of an Oracle database and expertise in solving problems.

Sybex has Oracle certification study guides for the Database track. The following sections will introduce you to the different tiers in the Oracle Database 12*c* certification track.

Oracle Database 12*c* Administrator Certified Associate

The Oracle Certified Associate (OCA) credential is the first step toward achieving the Oracle Certified Professional (OCP) certification. OCA shows that you have the fundamental knowledge and skills to support an Oracle Database 12*c* database. This certification requires you to pass two exams that demonstrate your Oracle basics:

- 1Z0-061: Oracle Database 12*c*: SQL Fundamentals
- 1Z0-062: Oracle Database 12*c*: Installation and Administration

If you have already passed any one of the following tests, you need not take the 1Z0-061 exam. You only need to pass the 1Z0-062.

- 1Z0-051: Oracle Database 11g SQL Fundamentals I
- 1Z0-047: Oracle Database SQL Expert

The 1Z0-061 exam can be taken at a testing location or from your home using the Internet. The 1Z0-062 test is offered at a Pearson Vue facility.

> To register for the test, visit Pearson Vue at http://www.pearsonvue.com.

Oracle Database 12*c* Administrator Certified Professional

The Oracle Certified Professional credential shows that you have the skill and technical expertise to manage and implement enterprise databases. The OCP tier challenges you to demonstrate your continuing experience and knowledge of Oracle technologies. The OCP test will measure your knowledge in setting up and managing multitenant architecture databases and in backup and recovery. The Oracle Database 12*c* Administrator Certified Professional certification requires you to have the OCA certification as well as to pass the following exam.

- 1Z0-063: Oracle Database 12*c*: Advanced Administration

In addition, the OCP candidate must take one instructor-led Oracle university hands-on requirement class.

 You should verify the list of approved hands-on courses at the Oracle Education website at http://education.oracle.com/pls/web_prod-plq-dad/db_pages.getpage?page_id=244#5.

Oracle Database 12*c* Administrator Certified Master

The highest level of certification available in any track is the Oracle Certified Master. The OCM certification credential shows that you have the highest level of expertise in an Oracle product. To become a certified master, you must first achieve OCP status and then complete two advanced instructor-led classes at an Oracle Education facility. You must also pass a hands-on examination at an Oracle Education facility. At the time of writing this book, the Oracle Database 12*c* Certified Master Exam is not released.

More Information and Resources

You can find most current information about Oracle certification at http://education .oracle.com/certification. You may be asked to choose the country of residence before being directed to the site. Follow the links under Certifications to choose the track and learn more.

Choose the Database track to view the different certification versions available. Choose Oracle Database 12*c* Administrator Certified Associate, and then click on the test to find out more about the test contents, the objectives covered in the test, the passing score, and to register for the test.

The Oracle documentation is available online at http://tahiti.oracle.com. Oracle documentation contains a wealth of information, which can be used to supplement what you learn from this book.

Oracle provides training series with step-by-step instructions to perform a variety of Oracle Database 12*c* tasks. The Oracle by Example (OBE) tutorial can be found at http://apex.oracle.com/pls/apex/f?p=44785:1.

Oracle Technology Network (http://www.oracle.com/technology/index.html) is a great resource for database administrators and developers. You can read articles; view sample code; access documentation; participate in forums; and most importantly, download Oracle Database 12*c*, Oracle Enterprise Manager Cloud Control 12*c*, and other Oracle products.

OCA/OCP Study Guides

The Oracle Database 12*c* Administration track certification consists of three tests: two for OCA and one for OCP. Sybex offers study guides to help you achieve OCA and OCP certification.

- *OCA: Oracle Database 12c Administrator Certified Associate Study Guide* (9781118643952) – Covers exams 1Z0-061: Oracle Database 12*c*: SQL Fundamentals and 1Z0-062: Oracle Database 12*c*: Installation and Administration.

- *OCP: Oracle Database 12c Administrator Certified Professional Study Guide* (9781118644072) – Covers exam 1Z0-063: Oracle Database 12*c*: Advanced Administration.

These two books are offered in a boxed set as *OCP: Oracle Certified Professional on Oracle Database 12c Certification Kit* (9781118957684).

Oracle Exam Requirements

The Oracle Database 12*c* Database Certified Associate certification tests your basic SQL skills for the SQL exam and database architecture and administration skills for the DBA exam. The SQL exam tests your knowledge of writing SQL and using the functions available in Oracle Database 12*c*. The Installation and Administration exam concentrates on the architecture and the basic administration of Oracle 12*c* databases. The following sections detail the skills needed to pass the SQL Fundamentals and the Installation and Administration exams.

OCA SQL (1Z0-061) Requirements

To pass the Oracle Database 12*c* SQL Fundamentals exam, you must have the following skills:

- Write SQL SELECT statements that display data from one or more tables
- Join tables using ANSI syntax and Oracle traditional syntax
- Restrict, sort, and aggregate data using single-row, conversion, and group functions
- Write subqueries and queries using SET operators
- Manipulate data: insert, update, delete
- Create and manage tables and other database objects

OCA Installation and Administration (1Z0-062) Requirements

To pass the Oracle Database 12*c* Installation and Administration exam, you must have the following skills:

- Understand the Oracle server architecture (database and instance)
- Install Oracle Database 12*c* software and create a database
- Use Database Configuration Assistant and Enterprise Manager tools
- Understand the physical and logical storage of the database, and be able to manage space allocation and growth

- Use the data dictionary views and set database parameters
- Manage and manipulate data, including its storage, loading, and reorganization
- Create and manage tables, constraints, and indexes
- Manage redo logs, archive logs, and automatic undo
- Configure Oracle Net on the server side and client side
- Understand backup and recovery architecture
- Secure the database and audit database usage
- Use advisors to tune and manage the database
- Upgrade the database
- Move data between databases
- Install and manage Grid Infrastructure, Oracle Restart, and Automatic Storage Management

Tips for Taking the OCA Exams

The following tips will help you prepare for and pass each exam.

- Each test consists of between 70 and 95 questions to be completed in 120 to 150 minutes (depending on the exam). Answer the questions you are sure of first, before you run out of time.

- Many questions on the exam have answer choices that at first glance look identical. Read the questions carefully. Do not jump to conclusions. Make sure you clearly understand what each question asks.

- Most questions are based on scenarios. Some of the scenarios contain nonessential information and exhibits. You need to be able to identify what's important and what's not.

- Do not leave any questions unanswered. There is no negative scoring. After selecting an answer, you can mark difficult questions or the ones you are unsure of and come back to them later.

- When answering questions you are not sure about, use a process of elimination to get rid of the obviously incorrect answers first. Doing this greatly improves your odds if you need to make an educated guess.

- If you are not sure of your answer, mark it for review and then look for other questions that may help you eliminate any incorrect answers. At the end of the test, you can review the questions you marked earlier.

 You should be familiar with the exam objectives, which are included at the beginning of each chapter. Please check the objective listing on the Oracle Education website for any changes or updates. The detail page for each exam shows the passing score, number of questions, and minutes allocated along with the exam fees and any other requirements.

What Is Covered in This Book

This book covers everything you need to pass the Oracle Database 12*c* Certified Associate exams. Part I includes the first seven chapters that cover the objectives for the Oracle Database 12*c* SQL Fundamentals exam. Part II of the book includes the remaining 11 chapters that cover the objectives for the Oracle Database 12*c* Installation and Administration exam.

Part I: Oracle Database 12*c* SQL Fundamentals

Chapter 1: Introducing Oracle Database 12*c* RDBMS introduces you to the features of Oracle Database 12*c* and the aspects of a relational database.

Chapter 2: Introducing SQL introduces you to writing simple queries using SELECT statements. It also introduces you to filtering and sorting data.

Chapter 3: Using Single-Row Functions discusses the single-row functions and conversion functions available, with details on how and where to use them.

Chapter 4: Using Group Functions explains data aggregations, Oracle's built-in group function, and nesting of functions.

Chapter 5: Using Joins and Subqueries explains how data from multiple tables can be related via joins, subqueries, and by using SET operators.

Chapter 6: Manipulating Data explores how to manipulate data: adding, removing, and updating data. The chapter also covers how transaction control works.

Chapter 7: Creating Tables and Constraints explains how to create and manage tables and constraints. It also discusses the various datatypes available in Oracle Database 12*c* to store data.

Part II: Oracle Database 12*c* Installation and Administration

Chapter 8: Introducing Oracle Database 12*c* Components and Architecture is the first chapter to start if you're reading for the Oracle Database 12*c* Installation and Administration exam. This chapter introduces you to the Oracle Database 12*c* database architecture and the relationship between logical and physical storage structures.

Chapter 9: Creating and Operating an Oracle Database 12*c* explains how you can install the Oracle Database 12*c* software and create a database. It discusses the initialization parameters, stages of database startup and shutdown, where to find log and trace files, and how to use the data dictionary.

Chapter 10: Understanding Storage and Space Management explores the logical and physical storage of the database. You will learn space management and the various types of tablespaces. This chapter also discusses monitoring space and reclaiming wasted space.

Chapter 11: Managing Data Concurrency and Undo shows you how you can add, update, and remove data from tables, as well as how transactions work. It introduces you to undo data and undo management. This chapter also discusses how Oracle manages locks to ensure data concurrency. Be sure to read Chapter 6 before you read this chapter.

Chapter 12: Understanding Oracle Network Architecture introduces you to the Oracle Net configuration and setup. You will learn to set up network architecture on the server and client.

Chapter 13: Implementing Security and Auditing shows how you can secure your database using privileges, profiles, and roles. You will also learn to audit database usage.

Chapter 14: Maintaining the Database and Managing Performance explores the tools available in Oracle Database 12*c* to manage the performance of the database. You will learn about optimizer statistics, Automatic Workload Repository, various advisors, and Automatic Memory Management.

Chapter 15: Using Backup and Recovery introduces you to the backup architecture concepts. It discusses the various backup modes and using RMAN. It also delves into the various recovery scenarios and how best to get the data back. It shows you how to use the Data Recovery Advisor, which can help find and recover the database, as well as offer advice.

Chapter 16: Controlling Resources and Jobs shows you how to manage the resources available on the database server using the Resource Manager. You will also learn about the Oracle Scheduler job management system.

Chapter 17: Upgrading to Oracle Database 12*c* familiarizes you with the process of upgrading a database to Oracle Database 12*c*. You also learn the various upgrade and migration methods.

Chapter 18: Using Grid Infrastructure and Data Movement Tools introduces you to Data Pump and SQL*Loader, the tools available in Oracle Database 12*c* to move and load data. This chapter also covers the Grid Infrastructure installation and configuration, including setting up Automatic Storage Management disks.

Each chapter ends with Review Questions that are specifically designed to help you retain the knowledge presented. To really nail down your skills, read and answer each question carefully.

What's Available Online?

The book includes a number of companion study tools, which can be downloaded from www.sybex.com/go/ocal2sg. See Appendix B, "About the Additional Study Tools," for information on how to access and install these tools:

Test Preparation Software   The test preparation software prepares you to pass both the 1Z0-061 and 1Z0-062 exams. You'll find all the review and assessment questions from the book *plus* an additional four practice exams (two for each exam) that appear exclusively from the downloadable study tools.

Electronic Flashcards   The companion study tools include over 400 flashcards specifically written to hit you hard, so don't get discouraged if you don't ace your way through them at first! They're there to ensure that you're really ready for the exam. And no worries—armed with the review questions, practice exams, and flashcards, you'll be more than prepared when exam day comes!

Author Bonus Material   I've included all of the code from the book, as well as three bonus Whitepapers that show you how to install an Oracle 12*c* database on Windows, how to create non-CDB Oracle Database 12*c* on Windows, and how to install Oracle Enterprise Manager 12*c* on Virtual Box.

Glossary   A complete glossary of common terms is available at www.sybex.com/go/ocal2sg.

How to Use This Book

This book provides a solid foundation for the serious effort of preparing for the Oracle Database 12*c* Certified Associate exams. To best benefit from the book, use the following study method:

1. Take the assessment tests immediately following this introduction. (The answers are at the end of the tests.) Carefully read the explanations for any questions you get wrong, and note in which chapters the material is covered. This information should help you plan your study strategy.

2. Study each chapter carefully, making sure you fully understand the information and the test objectives listed at the beginning of each chapter. Pay close attention to any chapter related to questions you missed in the assessment test.

3. Complete all hands-on activities in the chapter, referring to the chapter so that you understand the reason for each step you take. It is best to have an Oracle Database 12*c* database available to try out the examples and the code provided in the book. All the code is also included with the additional study tools.

4. Answer the review questions related to that chapter. Note the review questions that confuse or trick you, and study those sections of the book again.

5. The two bonus exams for each exam are included with the accompanying study tools. They will give you a complete overview of what you can expect to see on the real test.

6. Answer all the flashcard questions included with the study tools.

7. Remember to use the study tools included with this book. The electronic flash cards and the Sybex test engine exam-preparation software has been specifically designed to help you study and pass your exams.

 The additional study tools can be downloaded from www.sybex.com/go/ocal2sg.

To learn all the material covered in this book, you will need to apply yourself regularly and with discipline. Try to set the same time period every day to study, and select a comfortable and quite place to do so. If you work hard, you will be surprised at how quickly you will learn this material. You can also find supplemental reading material and Oracle documentation references on my blog that will deepen your knowledge of what you read in this book. All the best!

> Prebuilt Oracle Database 12*c* can be downloaded and set up on Virtual-Box. This is convenient, especially if you are new to Oracle. Prebuilt Oracle VMs can be downloaded from http://www.oracle.com/technetwork/community/developer-vm. You will have to install and set up Oracle VM VirtualBox to use the prebuilt VMs.

How to Contact the Author

I welcome feedback from you about this book or about books you'd like to see from me in the future. You can reach me by writing to biju.thomas.sybex@gmail.com. For more information about database administration and Oracle Database 12*c* certification, please visit my blog at www.bijoos.com/oraclenotes. You may follow me on social media through Twitter (@biju_thomas) and Facebook (Oracle Notes www.facebook.com/oraclenotes).

Sybex strives to keep you supplied with the latest tools and information you need for your work. Please check their website at www.sybex.com, where we'll post additional content, errata, and updates that supplement this book if the need arises. Enter **search terms** in the Search box (or type the book's ISBN— **9781118643952**), and click Go to get to the book's update page.

Exam Objectives

Part I: 1Z0-061 Oracle Database 12c: SQL Fundamentals Objective Map

- 1 Introduction Chapter 1
    - 1.1 Describe the features of Oracle Database 12c, Chapter 1
    - 1.2 Describe the salient features of Oracle Cloud 12c, Chapter 1
    - 1.3 Explain the theoretical and physical aspects of a relational database, Chapter 1
    - 1.4 Describe Oracle server's implementation of RDBMS and object relational database management system (ORDBMS), Chapter 1
- 2 Retrieving Data Using the SQL SELECT Statement, Chapter 2
    - 2.1 Explain the capabilities of SQL SELECT statements, Chapter 2
    - 2.2 Execute a basic SELECT statement, Chapter 2
- 3 Restricting and Sorting Data, Chapter 2
    - 3.1 Limit the rows that are retrieved by a query, Chapter 2
    - 3.2 Sort the rows that are retrieved by a query, Chapter 2
    - 3.2 Use ampersand substitution to restrict and sort output at runtime, Chapter 2
- 4 Using Single-Row Functions to Customize Output, Chapter 3
    - 4.1 Describe various types of functions available in SQL, Chapter 3
    - 4.2 Use character, number, and date functions in SELECT statements, Chapter 3
- 5 Using Conversion Functions and Conditional Expressions, Chapter 3
    - 5.1 Describe various types of conversion functions that are available in SQL, Chapter 3
    - 5.2 Use the TO_CHAR, TO_NUMBER, and TO_DATE conversion functions, Chapter 3
    - 5.3 Apply conditional expressions in a SELECT statement, Chapter 3
- 6 Reporting Aggregated Data Using the Group Functions, Chapter 4
    - 6.1 Identify the available group functions, Chapter 4
    - 6.2 Describe the use of group functions, Chapter 4
    - 6.3 Group data by using the GROUP BY clause, Chapter 4
    - 6.4 Include or exclude grouped rows by using the HAVING clause, Chapter 4

Part II: IZ0-062 Oracle Database 12*c* Installation and Administration Exam Objectives

- 1.9 Managing Data Concurrency, Chapter 11
  - 1.9.1. Describe the locking mechanism and how Oracle manages data concurrency, Chapter 11
  - 1.9.2 Monitor and resolve locking conflicts, Chapter 11
- 1.4 Configuring the Oracle Network Environment, Chapter 12
  - 1.4.1 Configure Oracle Net services, Chapter 12
  - 1.4.2 Use tools for configuring and managing the Oracle network, Chapter 12
  - 1.4.3 Configure client-side network, Chapter 12
  - 1.4.4 Understand database resident connection polling, Chapter 12
  - 1.4.5 Configure communication between databases, Chapter 12
- 1.10 Implementing Oracle Database Auditing, Chapter 13
  - 1.10.1 Explain DBA responsibilities for security and auditing, Chapter 13
  - 1.10.2 Enable standard database auditing and Unified Auditing, Chapter 13
- 1.6 Administering User Security, Chapter 13
  - 1.6.1 Create and manage database user accounts, Chapter 13
  - 1.6.2 Grant and revoke privileges, Chapter 13
  - 1.6.3 Create and manage roles, Chapter 13
  - 1.6.4 Create and manage profiles, Chapter 13
- 1.16. Performing Database Maintenance, Chapter 14
  - 1.16.1 Manage the Automatic Workload Repository (AWR), Chapter 14
  - 1.16.2 Use the Automatic Database Diagnostic Monitor (ADDM), Chapter 14
  - 1.16.3 Describe and use the advisory framework, Chapter 14
  - 1.16.4 Set alert thresholds, Chapter 14
  - 1.16.5 Use automated tasks, Chapter 14
- 1.17 Managing Performance, Chapter 14
  - 1.17.1 Use Enterprise Manager to monitor performance, Chapter 14
  - 1.17.2 Use Automatic Memory Management, Chapter 14
  - 1.17.3 Use the Memory Advisor to size memory buffers, Chapter 14
- 1.18 Managing Performance SQL Tuning, Chapter 14
  - 1.18.1 Manage optimizer statistics, Chapter 14
  - 1.18 2 Use the SQL Tuning Advisor, Chapter 14
  - 1.18.3 Use the SQL Access Advisor to tune a workload, Chapter 14
- 1.19 Managing Resources Using Database Resource Manager, Chapter 16
  - 1.19.1 Configure the Database Resource Manager, Chapter 16
  - 1.19.2 Access and create resource plans, Chapter 16
  - 1.19.3 Monitor the Resource Manager, Chapter 16

Assessment Test

Exam 1Z0-061: SQL Fundamentals

1. Which operator will be evaluated first in the following SELECT statement?

```
SELECT (2+3*4/2-5) FROM dual;
```

   A. +

   B. *

   C. /

   D. −

2. John wants to remove the values present in column SALARY in the EMPLOYEES table for all employees who belong to DEPARTMENT_ID 90. Which SQL would accomplish the task?

   A. DELETE FROM EMPLOYEES (SALARY) WHERE DEPARTMENT_ID = 90;

   B. INSERT INTO EMPLOYEES (SALARY) VALUES (NULL) WHERE DEPARTMENT_ID = 90;

   C. UPDATE EMPLOYEES SET SALARY = NULL WHERE DEPARTMENT_ID = 90;

   D. MERGE EMPLOYEES SET SALARY IS NULL WHERE DEPARTMENT_ID = 90;

3. Which function can possibly return a non-NULL value when one of the arguments is NULL?

   A. NULLIF

   B. LENGTH

   C. CONCAT

   D. INSTR

   E. TAN

4. The following statement will raise an exception on which line?

```
select dept_name, avg(all salary)
      ,count(*) "number of employees"
from emp , dept
where emp.deptno = dept.dept_no
  and count(*) > 5
group by dept_name
order by 2 desc;
```

   A. select dept_name, avg(all salary), count(*) "number of employees"

   B. where emp.deptno = dept.dept_no

   C. and count(*) > 5

D. group by dept_name

E. order by 2 desc;

5. Review the code segment.

```
1. INSERT INTO salaries VALUES (101, 23400, SYSDATE);
2. UPDATE salaries
3. SET salary = salary * 1.1
4. AND effective_dt = SYSDATE
5. WHERE empno = 333;
```

Which line has an error?

A. 2

B. 4

C. 5

D. No error

6. Review the following SQL and choose the most appropriate option.

```
SELECT job_id, COUNT(*)
FROM employees
GROUP BY department_id;
```

A. The statement will show the number of jobs in each department.

B. The statement will show the number of employees in each department.

C. The statement will generate an error.

D. The statement will work if the GROUP BY clause is removed.

7. Which datatype stores data outside the Oracle database?

A. UROWID

B. BFILE

C. BLOB

D. NCLOB

E. EXTERNAL

8. The DEPT table has the following data.

```
SQL> SELECT * FROM dept;
    DEPTNO DNAME          LOC
---------- -------------- ----------
        10 ACCOUNTING     NEW YORK
        20 RESEARCH       DALLAS
        30 SALES          CHICAGO
        40 OPERATIONS     BOSTON
```

Consider this INSERT statement:

```
INSERT INTO (SELECT * FROM dept WHERE deptno = 10)
VALUES (50, 'MARKETING', 'FORT WORTH');
```

Choose the best answer.

A. The INSERT statement is invalid; a valid table name is missing.

B. 50 is not a valid DEPTNO value, since the subquery limits DEPTNO to 10.

C. The statement will work without error.

D. A subquery and a VALUES clause cannot appear together.

9. Which two of the following queries is valid syntax that would return all rows from the EMPLOYEES and DEPARTMENTS tables, even if there are no corresponding/related rows in the other table?

A. SELECT last_name, first_name, department_nameFROM   employees e FULL JOIN departments dON   e.department_id = d.department_id;

B. SELECT last_name, first_name, department_nameFROM   employees e OUTER JOIN departments dON   e.department_id = d.department_id;

C. SELECT e.last_name, e.first_name, d.department_nameFROM   employees eLEFT OUTER JOIN departments dON   e.department_id = d.department_ idRIGHT OUTER JOIN employees fON   f.department_id = d.department_id;

D. SELECT e.last_name, e.first_name, d.department_nameFROM   employees eCROSS JOIN departments dON   e.department_id = d.department_id;

E. SELECT last_name, first_name, department_nameFROM   employeesFULL OUTER JOIN departments USING (department_id);

10. Which of the following statements could use an index on the columns PRODUCT_ID and WAREHOUSE_ID of the OE.INVENTORIES table?

A. select count(distinct warehouse_id)from oe.inventories;

B. select product_id, quantity_on_hand from oe.inventories where product_ id = 100;

C. insert into oe.inventories values (5,100,32);

D. None of these statements could use the index.

11. The following statements are executed:

```
create sequence my_seq;
select my_seq.nextval from dual;
select my_seq.nextval from dual;
rollback;
select my_seq.nextval from dual;
```

What will be selected when the last statement is executed?

A. 0

B. 1

C. 2

D. 3

E. NULL

12. Which of the following statements are true? (Choose two.)

A. Primary key constraints allow NULL values in the columns.

B. Unique key constraints allow NULL values in the columns.

C. Primary key constraints do not allow NULL values in the columns.

D. A non-unique index cannot be used to enforce primary key constraints.

13. The current time in Dubai is "04-APR-2013 08:50:00" and the time in Dallas is "03-APR-2013 23:50:00". A user from Dubai is connected to a session in the database located on a server in Dallas. What will be the result of his query?

```
SELECT TO_CHAR(SYSDATE,'DD-MON-YYYY HH24:MI:SS') FROM dual;
```

A. 04-APR-20138 08:50:00

B. 03-APR-2013 8 23:50:00

C. 03-APR-2013 2324:50:00

D. None of the above

14. The FIRED_EMPLOYEES table has the following structure.

```
EMPLOYEE_ID  NUMBER (4)
FIRE_DATE DATE
```

How many rows will be counted from the last SQL statement in the code segment?

```
SELECT COUNT(*) FROM FIRED_EMPLOYEES;
COUNT(*)
--------
     105

INSERT INTO FIRED_EMPLOYEES VALUES (104, TRUNC(SYSDATE));
SAVEPOINT A;
INSERT INTO FIRED_EMPLOYEES VALUES (106, TRUNC(SYSDATE));
SAVEPOINT B;
INSERT INTO FIRED_EMPLOYEES VALUES (108, TRUNC(SYSDATE));
ROLLBACK TO A;
```

```
INSERT INTO FIRED_EMPLOYEES VALUES (104, TRUNC(SYSDATE));
COMMIT;
SELECT COUNT(*) FROM FIRED_EMPLOYEES;
```

A. 109

B. 106

C. 105

D. 107

15. At a minimum, how many join conditions should there be to avoid a Cartesian join if there are three tables in the FROM clause?

A. 1

B. 2

C. 3

D. There is no minimum.

16. Why does the following statement fail?

```
CREATE TABLE FRUITS-N-VEGETABLES
```

```
(NAME VARCHAR2 (40));
```

A. The table should have more than one column in its definition.

B. NAME is a reserved word, which cannot be used as a column name.

C. The table name is invalid.

D. Column length cannot exceed 30 characters.

17. Which two statements are true about NULL values?

A. You cannot search for a NULL value in a column using the WHERE clause.

B. If a NULL value is returned in the subquery or if NULL is included in the list when using a NOT IN operator, no rows will be returned.

C. Only = and != operators can be used to search for NULL values in a column.

D. In an ascending order sort, NULL values appear at the bottom of the result set.

E. Concatenating a NULL value to a non-NULL string results in a NULL.

18. Table *CUSTOMERS* has a column named *CUST_ZIP* which could be NULL. Which of the following functions include the NULL rows in its result?

A. COUNT (CUST_ZIP)

B. SUM (CUST_ZIP)

C. AVG (DISTINCT CUST_ZIP)

D. None of the above

19. Using the following EMP table, you need to increase everyone's salary by 5 percent of their combined salary and bonus. Which of the following statements will achieve the desired results?

Column Name	emp_id	name	salary	bonus
Key Type	pk	pk		
NULLs/Unique	NN	NN	NN	
FK Table				
Datatype	VARCHAR2	VARCHAR2	NUMBER	NUMBER
Length	9	50	11,2	11,2

   A. `UPDATE emp SET salary = (salary + bonus)*1.05;`

   B. `UPDATE emp SET salary = salary*1.05 + bonus*1.05;`

   C. `UPDATE emp SET salary = salary + (salary + bonus)*0.05;`

   D. A, B, and C will achieve the desired results.

   E. None of these statements will achieve the desired results.

20. Which option is not available in Oracle when modifying tables?

   A. Add new columns

   B. Rename existing column

   C. Drop existing column

   D. None of the above

21. The following data is from the EMPLOYEES table:

```
DEPARTMENT_ID     EMPNO FIRST_NAME
-------------  ---------- -------------
           30        119 Karen
           50        124 Kevin
           50        135 Ki
           80        146 Karen
                     178 Kimberely
           50        188 Kelly
           50        197 Kevin
```

Which row (empno) will be returned last when the following query is executed?

```
select department_id, employee_id empno, first_name
from employees
```

order by 1, 2

A. 188

B. 178

C. 146

D. 119

22. INTERVAL datatypes store a period of time. Which components are included in the INTERVAL DAY TO SECOND datatype column? (Choose all that apply.)

A. Years

B. Quarters

C. Months

D. Days

E. Hours

F. Minutes

G. Seconds

H. Fractional seconds

23. Which components are not part of the easy connect connection string? (Choose two.)

A. hostname

B. service name

C. database sid

D. port number

E. network protocol

24. The table CUSTOMERS has the following data:

```
ID    NAME              ZIP  UPD_DATE
----  ---------------  ----------  ---------

L921  LEEZA             75252 01-JAN-00
B023  WILLIAMS          15215
K783  KATHY             75252 15-FEB-00
B445  BENJAMIN          76021 15-FEB-00
D334  DENNIS            12443
```

You issue the following command to alter the table:

```
1.   ALTER TABLE CUSTOMERS
2.   MODIFY
3.   (UPD_DATE DEFAULT SYSDATE NOT NULL,
4.    ZIP NOT NULL);
```

Which line of code will cause an error?

A. Line 2

B. Line 3

C. Line 4

D. There will be no error.

25. In ANSI SQL, a self-join can be represented by using which of the following? (Choose the best answer.)

A. NATURAL JOIN clause

B. CROSS JOIN clause

C. JOIN … USING clause

D. JOIN … ON clause

E. All of the above

26. What will be result of trunc(2916.16, -1)?

A. 2916.2

B. 290

C. 2916.1

D. 2900

E. 2910

27. The table ADDRESSES is created using the following syntax. How many indexes will be created automatically when this table is created?

```
CREATE TABLE ADDRESSES (
NAME    VARCHAR2 (40) PRIMARY KEY,
STREET VARCHAR2 (40),
CITY    VARCHAR2 (40),
STATE   CHAR     (2) REFERENCES STATE (ST_CODE),
ZIP     NUMBER   (5) NOT NULL,
PHONE  VARCHAR2 (12) UNIQUE);
```

A. 0

B. 1

C. 2

D. 3

28. Which line of the following code has an error?

```
SELECT *
FROM emp
```

```
WHERE comm = NULL
ORDER BY ename;
```

   A. SELECT *

   B. FROM emp

   C. WHERE comm = NULL

   D. There is no error in this statement.

29. How do you represent the following business rule in an ER diagram? "A customer may have one or more orders; an order must belong to one and only one customer."

   A. Single solid line.

   B. Single line that is solid at one end and dotted at another end.

   C. Single solid line with a crowfoot at one end.

   D. The business rule cannot be represented in the ER diagram.

30. What order does Oracle use in resolving a table or view referenced in a SQL statement?

   A. Table/view within user's schema, public synonym, private synonym

   B. Table/view within user's schema, private synonym, public synonym

   C. Public synonym, table/view within user's schema, private synonym

   D. Private synonym, public synonym, table/view within user's schema

31. Which two options are not true when you execute a COMMIT statement?

   A. All locks created by DML statements are released in the session.

   B. All savepoints created are erased in the session.

   C. Queries started before the COMMIT in other sessions will show the current changes after COMMIT.

   D. All undo information written from the DML statements are erased.

32. Which two operators are used to add more joining conditions in a multiple-table query?

   A. NOT

   B. OR

   C. AND

   D. Comma (,)

33. What is wrong with the following SQL?

```
SELECT  department_id, MAX(COUNT(*))
FROM employees
GROUP BY  department_id;
```

A. Aggregate functions cannot be nested.

B. GROUP BY clause should not be included when using nested aggregate functions.

C. The department_id column in the SELECT clause should not be used when using nested aggregate functions.

D. When using COUNT function cannot be nested.

34. Which types of constraints can be created on a view?

   A. Check, NOT NULL

   B. Primary key, foreign key, unique key

   C. Check, NOT NULL, primary key, foreign key, unique key

   D. No constraints can be created on a view.

35. Which two declarations define the maximum length of a CHAR datatype column in bytes?

   A. CHAR (20)

   B. CHAR (20) BYTE

   C. CHAR (20 BYTE)

   D. BYTE (20 CHAR)

   E. CHAR BYTE (20)

36. Which SELECT statement clauses can be used to limit the rows returned (say, you want to display the rows 6 through 15). (Choose two.)

   A. WHERE

   B. OFFSET

   C. FETCH

   D. FILTER

37. You query the database with the following:

```
SELECT PRODUCT_ID FROM PRODUCTS
WHERE PRODUCT_ID LIKE '%S\_J\_C' ESCAPE '\';
```

Choose the PRODUCT_ID strings from the options that will satisfy the query. (Choose two.)

   A. BTS_J_C

   B. SJC

   C. SKJKC

   D. S_J_C

38. The EMPLOYEE table is defined as follows:

```
EMP_NAME    VARCHAR2(40)
HIRE_DATE   DATE
SALARY      NUMBER (14,2)
```

Which query is most appropriate to use if you need to find the employees who were hired before 01-Jan-1998 and have a salary above 5,000 or below 1,000?

A. SELECT emp_name FROM employee WHERE hire_date > TO_
DATE('01011998','MMDDYYYY')AND SALARY < 1000 OR > 5000;

B. SELECT emp_name FROM employee WHERE hire_date < TO_
DATE('01011998','MMDDYYYY')AND SALARY < 1000 OR SALARY > 5000;

C. SELECT emp_name FROM employee WHERE hire_date < TO_
DATE('01011998','MMDDYYYY')AND (SALARY < 1000 OR SALARY > 5000);

D. SELECT emp_name FROM employee WHERE hire_date < TO_
DATE('01011998','MMDDYYYY')AND SALARY BETWEEN 1000 AND 5000;

39. What happens when you issue the following command? (Choose all correct answers.)

```
TRUNCATE TABLE SCOTT.EMPLOYEE;
```

A. All the rows in the table EMPLOYEE owned by SCOTT are removed.

B. The storage space used by the table EMPLOYEE is released (except the initial extent).

C. If foreign key constraints are defined to this table using the ON DELETE CASCADE clause, the rows from the child tables are also removed.

D. The indexes on the table are dropped.

E. You cannot truncate a table if triggers are defined on the table.

40. Which two statements will drop the primary key defined on table EMP. The primary key name is PK_EMP.

A. ALTER TABLE EMP DROP PRIMARY KEY;

B. DROP CONSTRAINT PK_EMP;

C. ALTER TABLE EMP DROP CONSTRAINT PK_EMP;

D. ALTER CONSTRAINT PK_EMP DROP CASCADE;

E. DROP CONSTRAINT PK_EMP ON EMP;

Exam 1Z0-062: Installation and Administration

1. Which database version cannot be upgraded directly to Oracle Database 12*c*?

   A. 11.2.0.2

   B. 11.2.0.1

   C. 11.1.0.7

   D. 10.2.0.5

   E. All of the above

2. The following steps might be related to relocating a data file belonging to the USERS tablespace. Pick the steps that are required for relocating the data file from /disk1 to /disk2.

   A. Copy the file '/disk1/users01.dbf' to '/disk2/users01.dbf' using an OS command.

   B. ALTER DATABASE MOVE DATAFILE '/disk1/users01.dbf' to '/disk2/users01.dbf'

   C. ALTER DATABASE RENAME FILE '/disk1/users01.dbf' to '/disk2/users01.dbf'

   D. ALTER TABLESPACE USERS OFFLINE

   E. ALTER TABLESPACE USERS ONLINE

3. Which of the following is not considered part of an Oracle database?

   A. Data files

   B. Redo logs

   C. The pfile and spfile

   D. Control files

4. The highest level at which a user can request a lock is the _____ level.

   A. Schema

   B. Table

   C. Row

   D. Block

5. To grant the SELECT privilege on the table HR.CUSTOMERS to all users in the database, which statement would you use?

   A. GRANT SELECT ON HR.CUSTOMERS TO ALL USERS;

   B. GRANT SELECT ON HR.CUSTOMERS TO ALL;

   C. GRANT SELECT ON HR.CUSTOMERS TO ANONYMOUS;

   D. GRANT SELECT ON HR.CUSTOMERS TO PUBLIC;

6. Which query can be used to find and categorize all chained jobs (only chained jobs), and includes any remote steps as applied to those chained jobs, as executed from the current database? (Choose the best answers, more than one if appropriate.)

A. `select table_name from dictionary where table_name like 'DBA_%SCHED%'`
`or table_name like 'DBA_%REMOTE%';`

B. `SELECT TABLE_NAME FROM DICTIONARY WHERE TABLE_NAME LIKE 'DBA_%CHAIN%'`
`OR TABLE_NAME LIKE 'DBA_%REMOTE%';`

C. `select table_name from dictionary where table_name like 'DBA_%CHAIN%'`
`or table_name like 'DBA_%REMOTE%';`

D. `select table_name from dictionary where table_name like 'DBA_%SCHED%'`
`or table_name like 'DBA_%CHAIN%';`

E. None of the above

7. The Automatic Workload Repository (AWR) is primarily populated with performance statistics by which Oracle Database 12c background process?

A. MMNL

B. QMN1

C. MMON

D. MMAN

8. The initialization parameter `RESUMABLE_TIMEOUT` is set to 600. Which other statements are the minimum required to enable a resumable session?

A. No other setup is required if the `RESUMABLE_TIMEOUT` is a nonzero value.

B. `ALTER SESSION ENABLE RESUMABLE`

C. `ALTER SESSION ENABLE RESUMABLE TIMEOUT 0`

D. `ALTER SESSION BEGIN RESUMABLE SESSION`

9. Which utility is used to install Oracle Database 12c?

A. DBCA

B. OUI

C. runInstaller

D. Oracle Database 12c is installed using the URL to www.oracle.com.

10. You have just made changes to the `listener.ora` file for the listener called `listener1` using Oracle Net Manager. Which of the following commands or combinations of commands would you use to put the changes into effect with the least amount of client disruption?

A. `lsnrctl stop listener1` followed by `lsnrctl start listener1`

B. `lsrnctl restart listener1`

C. `lsnrctl reload listener1`

D. `lsnrctl cycle services`

11. If a job is not running and a STOP_JOB procedure is executed, what will happen? (Choose the best answer.)

    A. An error will not occur.

    B. The job will stop running.

    C. The job will be dropped altogether.

    D. All of the above.

    E. None of the above.

12. Where does Oracle Database 12*c* record all the changes made to the database that can be used for recovery operations?

    A. Control files

    B. Redo log files

    C. Alert log file

    D. Parameter file

13. What is accomplished when you issue the following statement?

```
ALTER USER JOHN DEFAULT ROLE ALL;
```

    A. John is assigned all the roles created in the database.

    B. Any existing roles remain the same, but any future roles created will be enabled.

    C. All of John's roles are enabled except the roles with passwords.

    D. All of John's roles are enabled including the roles with passwords.

14. Which activity is a must do before upgrading a database to 12*c* using the manual upgrade method?

    A. Run dbms_stats.gather_dictionary_stats.

    B. Run $ORACLE_HOME/rdbms/admin/emremove.sql.

    C. Run dbms_stats.gather_database_stats.

    D. Run preupgrd.sql script.

15. What would you do to reduce the time required to start the instance after a database crash?

    A. Multiplex the redo log files

    B. Increase the size of the redo log files

    C. Set FAST_START_MTTR_TARGET parameter to 0

    D. All of the above

    E. None of the above

16. When you are configuring Oracle Shared Server, which initialization parameter would you likely need to modify?

A. DB_CACHE_SIZE

B. DB_BLOCK_BUFFERS

C. LARGE_POOL_SIZE

D. BUFFER_SIZE

E. None of the above

17. Which options are available in DBCA to configure recovery-related operations?

A. Data Guard

B. Standby Database

C. Fast Recovery Area

D. Archiving

18. When you started the Oracle Database 12*c* database, you got an ORA-01157: cannot identify data file … error. After invoking RMAN, which command would you first use before performing the REPAIR FAILURE?

A. RECOVER FAILURE

B. ADVISE FAILURE

C. LIST FAILURE

D. CHANGE FAILURE

19. Which of the following commands is most likely to generate an error message? (Choose two.)

A. ALTER SYSTEM SET UNDO_MANAGEMENT=AUTO SCOPE=MEMORY;

B. ALTER SYSTEM SET UNDO_MANAGEMENT=AUTO SCOPE=SPFILE;

C. ALTER SYSTEM SET UNDO_MANAGEMENT=MANUAL SCOPE=MEMORY;

D. ALTER SYSTEM SET UNDO_MANAGEMENT=MANUAL SCOPE=SPFILE;

E. ALTER SYSTEM SET UNDO_TABLESPACE=RBS1 SCOPE=BOTH;

20. You performed a SHUTDOWN ABORT on the database. What happens when you issue the STARTUP command?

A. Startup will fail, because you have not completed the instance recovery.

B. Oracle automatically performs recovery. All committed changes are written to data files.

C. During instance recovery, you have the option to selectively commit uncommitted transactions.

D. After the database starts, you have to manually clean out uncommitted transactions from the transaction table.

21. Where does the following procedure allow jobs to be created?

```
BEGIN

DBMS_SCHEDULER.CREATE_GROUP(group_name=>'things'

,group_type=>'DB_DEST',member=>'LOCAL');

END;

/
```

    A. On a remote server as a database destination

    B. On a remote server using a hostname and IP address

    C. On a local database server only

    D. On a local server using a hostname and an IP address

    E. None of the above

22. Which of the following statements is not always true? (Choose two.)

    A. Every database should have at least two tablespaces.

    B. Every database should have at least two data files.

    C. Every database should have at least three multiplexed redo logs.

    D. Every database should have at least three control files.

23. How can you prevent someone from using an all-alphabet password?

    A. Set the initialization parameter `PASSWORD_COMPLEXITY` to `ALPHANUM`.

    B. Alter that user's profile setting `PASSWORD_COMPLEXITY` to `ALPHNANUM`.

    C. Alter the user's profile to use a password-verify function that performs comparisons to validate the password.

    D. There is no mechanism that lets you prevent an all-alphabet password.

24. Which metadata view can be used to find Oracle Scheduler priorities?

    A. `DBA_CHAINS`

    B. `DBA_SCHEDULER_CHAINS`

    C. `DBA_SCHEDULER_JOBS`

    D. `DBA_SCHEDULER_DESTS`

    E. None of the above

25. Which component of the SGA has the dictionary cache?

    A. Buffer cache

    B. Library cache

    C. Shared pool

    D. Program global area

    E. Large pool

    F. Result cache

26. Which of the following advisors is used to determine if the database read-consistency mechanisms are properly configured?

    A. Undo Management Advisor

    B. SQL Access Advisor

    C. SQL Tuning Advisor

    D. Memory Advisor

27. Which storage parameter is used to make sure that each extent is a multiple of the value specified?

    A. MINEXTENTS

    B. INITIAL

    C. MINIMUM EXTENT

    D. MAXEXTENTS

28. What is (are) the name of the audit trail view(s) where audit records from Unified Auditing is (are) stored, when database auditing, RMAN, and Data Pump auditing are enabled?

    A. UNIFIED_AUDIT_TRAIL

    B. UNIFIED_AUDIT_TRAIL, COMPONENT_AUDIT_TRAIL

    C. SYS.AUD$

    D. AUDIT_TRAIL_DB, AUDIT_TRAIL_DP, AUDIT_TRAIL_RMAN

29. Which of the following is the utility that you can use to test the network connections across TCP/IP?

    A. trcasst

    B. lsnrctl

    C. namesctl

    D. ping

    E. None of the above

30. Undo data in an undo tablespace is not used for which of the following purposes?

    A. Providing users with read-consistent queries

    B. Rolling forward after an instance failure

    C. Flashback queries

    D. Recovering from a failed transaction

    E. Restoring original data when a ROLLBACK is issued

31. In which file could you tell SQL*Loader to use the direct path option?

  A. Log file

  B. Parfile

  C. Bad file

  D. Data file

32. Which of the following is false about shared servers?

  A. Shared servers can process requests from many users.

  B. Shared servers receive their requests directly from dispatchers.

  C. Shared servers place completed requests on a dispatcher response queue.

  D. The SHARED_SERVERS parameter configures the number of shared servers to start at instance startup.

33. Identify the statement that is not true about checkpoints.

  A. Instance recovery is complete when the data from the last checkpoint up to the latest SCN in the control file has been written to the data files.

  B. A checkpoint keeps track of what has already been written to the data files.

  C. The redo log group writes must occur before a commit complete is returned to the user.

  D. The distance between the checkpoint position in the redo log file and the end of the redo log group can never be more than 90 percent of the size of the largest redo log group.

  E. How much the checkpoint lags behind the SCN is controlled by both the size of the redo log groups and by setting the parameter FAST_START_MTTR_TARGET.

34. Which parameter is used to enable the Automatic Memory Management feature of the Oracle database?

  A. MEMORY_MANAGEMENT

  B. MEMORY_TARGET

  C. SGA_TARGET

  D. MEMORY_SIZE

35. When performing a Data Pump Import using impdp, which of the following options is not a valid value to the TABLE_EXISTS_ACTION parameter?

  A. SKIP

  B. APPEND

  C. TRUNCATE

  D. RECREATE

36. Two tablespaces are critical to the database. The loss of a data file in these tablespaces requires an instance shutdown to recover. Which are these tablespaces?

    A. TEMP

    B. SYSTEM

    C. UNDO

    D. SYSAUX

37. Which initialization parameter determines the location of the alert log file?

    A. DIAGNOSTIC_DEST

    B. BACKGROUND_DUMP_DEST

    C. ALERT_LOG_DEST

    D. USER_DUMP_DEST

38. Which statement regarding a global temporary table and redo generation is true?

    A. Global temporary tables generate the same amount of redo as persistent tables.

    B. Global temporary tables generate redo from undo when a DML operation is performed on them.

    C. By setting the TEMP_UNDO_ENABLED to TRUE, you turn off the undo generation for DML on temporary tables.

    D. All of the above are true.

39. Which database management tools are automatically installed and configured when Oracle Database 12*c* database is configured? (Choose two.)

    A. OEM Database Express

    B. OEM Cloud Control

    C. SQL*Plus

    D. SQL Developer

40. Which parameter is used to set up the directory for Oracle to create data files, if the DATAFILE clause does not specify a filename when you're creating or altering tablespaces?

    A. DB_FILE_CREATE_DEST

    B. DB_CREATE_FILE_DEST

    C. DB_8K_CACHE_SIZE

    D. USER_DUMP_DEST

    E. DB_CREATE_ONLINE_LOG_DEST_1

41. In Oracle Database 12*c*, which script is recommended to run for upgrading a database from 11.1.0.7?

    A. catupgrd.sql

    B. utlu121i.sql

    C. catctl.pl

    D. utlu121s.sql

42. How do you enable Database Resident Connection Pooling (DRCP)?

    A. Using listener.ora configuration.

    B. Using Oracle Net Manager configuration.

    C. Using a PL/SQL package.

    D. Depends on the application. PHP, HTTP, and SQL*Net applications have different configurations.

43. Which initialization parameter determines the location of the alert log file?

    A. LOG_ARCHIVE_DEST

    B. USER_DUMP_DEST

    C. BACKGROUND_DUMP_DEST

    D. DIAGNOSTIC_DEST

44. Which product do you install to configure an Oracle Automatic Storage Management instance?

    A. Oracle Database 12*c* database

    B. Oracle Database 12*c* Grid Infrastructure

    C. Oracle Database 12*c* Automatic Storage Management

    D. Oracle Restart

Answers to Assessment Test

Exam 1Z0-061: SQL Fundamentals

1. B. In the arithmetic operators, unary operators are evaluated first, then multiplication and division, and finally addition and subtraction. The expression is evaluated from left to right. See Chapter 2 for more information.

2. C. Except for option C, all other SQL statements are not valid syntactically. To change a value in a column for existing rows, you need to use the UPDATE statement. The DELETE statement deletes the entire row. The INSERT statement adds a new row. The MERGE statement performs kind of an upsert—it inserts if the row does not exist, and updates if the row exists. For more information, read Chapter 6.

3. C. CONCAT will return a non-NULL if only one parameter is NULL. Both CONCAT parameters would need to be NULL for CONCAT to return NULL. The NULLIF function returns NULL if the two parameters are equal. The LENGTH of a NULL is NULL. INSTR will return NULL if NULL is passed in, and the tangent (TAN) of a NULL is NULL. See Chapter 3 to learn more.

4. C. Group functions cannot appear in the WHERE clause. Read Chapter 4 to learn more about group functions.

5. B. When using multiple columns to update in a single UPDATE statement, the column assignments in the SET clause must be separated by a comma, not an AND operator. See Chapter 6 for more information.

6. C. Since job_id is used in the SELECT clause, it must be used in the GROUP BY clause also. For more information, see Chapter 4.

7. B. UROWID datatype is used ot store ROWID data. The BFILE datatype stores only the locator to an external file in the database; the actual data is stored as an operating system file. BLOB, NCLOB, and CLOB are other Large Object data types in Oracle Database 12*c*. EXTERNAL is not a valid datatype. Read Chapter 7 for more information.

8. C. The statement will work without error. Option B would be correct if you used the WITH CHECK OPTION clause in the subquery. See Chapter 5 for more information about subqueries.

9. A, E. An outer join on both tables can be achieved using the FULL OUTER JOIN syntax. The join condition can be specified by using the ON clause to specify the columns explicitly or using the USING clause to specify columns with common column names. Options B and D would result in errors. In option B, the join type is not specified; OUTER is an optional keyword. In option D, CROSS JOIN is used to get a Cartesian result, and Oracle does not expect a join condition. See Chapter 5 for more information.

10. **A, B.** The index contains all the information needed to satisfy the query in option A, and a full-index scan would be faster than a full-table scan. A subset of indexes columns is specified in the WHERE clause of option B, hence Oracle database can use the index. Read Chapter 7 to learn more about using an index.

11. **D.** The CREATE SEQUENCE statement will create an increasing sequence that will start with 1, increment by 1, and be unaffected by the rollback. A rollback will never stuff values back into a sequence. Read Chapter 7 for more information.

12. **B, C.** Primary key and unique key constraints can be enforced using non-unique indexes. Unique constraints allow NULL values in the columns, but primary keys do not. See Chapter 7 for more information.

13. **B.** The SYSDATE function returns the date and time on the server where the database instance is started. CURRENT_DATE returns local date and time. See Chapter 3 for more information.

14. **D.** The first INSERT statement and last INSERT statement will be saved in the database. The ROLLBACK TO A statement will undo the second and third inserts. For more infromation, see Chapter 6.

15. **B.** There should be at least n-1 join conditions when joining n tables to avoid a Cartesian join. See Chapter 5 for more information.

16. **C.** The table and column names can include only three special characters: #, $, and _. No other characters are allowed in the table name. You can have letters and numbers in the table name. Read Chapter 7 for more information.

17. **B, D.** You can use the IS NULL or IS NOT NULL operator to search for NULLs or non-NULLs in a column. Since NULLs are sorted higher, they appear at the bottom of the result set in an ascending order sort. See Chapter 2 for more information.

18. **D.** COUNT (<column_name>) does not include the NULL values, whereas COUNT (*) includes the NULL values. No other aggregate function takes NULL into consideration. See Chapter 4 for more information.

19. **E.** These statements don't account for possible NULL values in the BONUS column. Read Chapter 3 for more information.

20. **D.** Using the ALTER TABLE statement, you can add new columns, rename existing columns, and drop existing columns. To learn more about managing tables, read chapter 7.

21. **B.** Since DEPARTMENT_ID is NULL for employee 178, NULL will be sorted after the non-NULL values when doing an ascending order sort. Since we did not specify the sort order or NULLS FIRST clause, the defaults are ASC and NULLS LAST. Read Chapter 2 for more information.

22. **D, E, F, G.** The INTERVAL DAY TO SECOND dataype is used to store an interval between two datetime components. Read Chapter 7 for more information.

23. C, E. The easy connect syntax is @<host>:<port>/<service_name>. For databases where the sid is the same as the database unique name, the service name is the same as the sid; thus you can say option C is also part of the easy connect string. However, in reality it is the service name. Easy connect only supports TCP protocol. See Chapter 1 for more information.

24. B. When altering an existing column to add a NOT NULL constraint, no rows in the table should have NULL values. In the example, there are two rows with NULL values. Read Chapter 7 for more information.

25. D. NATURAL JOIN and JOIN … USING clauses will not allow alias names to be used. Since a self-join is getting data from the same table, you must include alias names and qualify column names. See Chapter 5 for more information.

26. E. The TRUNC function used with a negative second argument will truncate to the left of the decimal. See Chapter 3 for more information.

27. C. Oracle creates unique indexes for each unique key and primary key defined in the table. The table ADDRESSES has one unique key and a primary key. Indexes will not be created for NOT NULL or foreign key constraints. See Chapter 7 for more information.

28. D. Although there is no error in this statement, the statement will not return the desired result. When a NULL is compared, you cannot use the = or != operators; you must use the IS NULL or IS NOT NULL operator. See Chapter 2 for more information.

29. C. The solid line represents that the order must belong to a customer, and the crow-foot represents that a customer can have more than one order. See Chapter 1 for more information.

30. B. Private synonyms override public synonyms, and tables or views owned by the user always resolve first. See Chapter 7 for more information.

31. C, D. When a COMMIT is executed, all locks are released, savepoints are erased, and queries started before the COMMIT will constitute a read-consistent view using the undo information. See Chapter 6 for more information.

32. B, C. The operators OR and AND are used to add more joining conditions to the query. NOT is a negation operator, and a comma is used to separate column names and table names. For more information, see Chapter 5.

33. C. Since we are finding the aggregate of aggregate, non-aggregate columns should not be used in the SELECT clause. See Chapter 4 for more information.

34. B. You can create primary key, foreign key, and unique key constraints on a view. The constraints on views are not enforced by Oracle. To enforce a constraint, it must be defined on a table. See Chapter 7 for more information.

35. A, C. The maximum lengths of CHAR and VARCHAR2 columns can be defined in characters or bytes. BYTE is the default; the default can be changed by setting the database parameter NLS_LENGTH_SEMANTICS. See Chapter 7 for more information.

36. B, C. The row limiting feature uses OFFSET and FETCH clauses to filter the rows. To get to rows 6 through 15 here, you may use the clause OFFSET 5 ROWS FETCH NEXT 10 ROWS. See Chapter 2 for more information.

37. D. The substitution character % may be substituted for zero or many characters. The substitution character _ does not have any effect in this query because an escape character precedes it, so it is treated as a literal. See Chapter 2 for more information.

38. C. You have two main conditions in the question: one on the hire_date and the other on the salary. So an AND operator should be used. In the second part, you have two options: the salary can be either more than 5000 or less than 1000, so the second part should be enclosed in parentheses; use an OR operator. Option B is similar to option C except for the parentheses, but the difference changes the meaning completely. Option B would select the employees who were hired before 01-Jan-1998 or have a salary above 5,000 or have a salary below 1,000. Read Chapter 2 for more information.

39. A, B. The TRUNCATE command is used to remove all the rows from a table or cluster. By default, this command releases all the storage space used by the table and resets the table's high-water mark to zero. None of the indexes, constraints, or triggers on the table are dropped or disabled. If there are valid foreign key constraints defined to this table, you must disable all of them before truncating the table. Read Chapter 6 for more information.

40. A, C. Since there can be only one primary key per table, the syntax in option A works. Any constraint (except NOT NULL) can be dropped using the syntax in option C. See Chapter 7 for more information.

Exam 1Z0-062: Installation and Administration

1. B. Database Upgrade Assistant and a manual upgrade both support an upgrade from 10.2.0.5, 11.1.0.7, 11.2.0.2, and higher-version databases. For 11.2.0.1, you must upgrade to 11.2.0.2 or higher before upgrading to 12.1.0. See Chapter 17 for more information.

2. B. To rename or relocate a data file in Oracle Database 12c, you need to use only the statement specified in option B. To rename a data file in pre-12c databases, you need to take the tablespace offline so that Oracle does not try to update the data file while you are renaming. Using OS commands, copy the data file to the new location and using the ALTER DATABASE RENAME FILE command or the ALTER TABLESPACE RENAME FILE command, rename the file in the database's control file. To rename the file in the database, the new file should exist. Bring the tablespace online for normal database operation. For more information, read Chapter 10.

3. C. Although pfiles and spfiles are physical files used to configure the Oracle instance, they are not considered part of the database. For more information, see Chapter 8.

4. B. The highest level at which a user can request a lock is the table level; the only other lock level available to a user is a row-level lock. Users cannot lock at the block or schema level. Read Chapter 11 for more information.

5. D. PUBLIC is the group or class of database users where all existing and future database users belong. Read Chapter 13 for more information.

6. B, C. B and C are both the best answers. They are identical because queries in Oracle are case-insensitive. For more information, read Chapter 16.

7. C. The Manageability Monitor (MMON) process gathers performance statistics from the SGA (System Global Area) and stores them in the AWR. MMNL (Manageability Monitor Light) also does some AWR-related statistics gathering, but not to the extent that MMON does. QMN1 is the process that monitors Oracle advanced queuing features. MMAN (Memory Manager) is the process that dynamically manages the sizes of each SGA component when directed to make changes by the ADDM (Automatic Database Diagnostic Monitoring). See Chapter 14 for more information.

8. B. RESUMABLE_TIMEOUT set at the initialization parameter is used only as the default timeout value for a resumable session. The resumable session must be enabled using option B. Option C disables the resumable session. Option D is invalid. Read Chapter 10 for more information.

9. B. Use the Oracle Universal Installer (OUI) to install and configure the Oracle Database 12*c* software. The OUI is a Java-based application that provides the same installation look and feel no matter which operating system is being used for the installation. runInstaller is the executable that invokes OUI on Linux/Unix systems. See Chapter 9 for more information.

10. C. Although you can use choice A to stop and start the listener, doing so temporarily disrupts clients attempting to connect to the database. Choice D is fine if you are starting and stopping the default listener called LISTENER, but we are using a nondefault listener. Choice B is not valid because RESTART is not a valid command-line argument for lsnrctl. Therefore, the best method is C, to use the lsnrctl reload listener1 command to load the new set of values for the listener without disrupting connection service to the databases the listener is servicing. For more information, see Chapter 12.

11. E. An error will occur because the job is not running, given that a job that is not executing cannot be stopped. The error produced will be ORA-27366, including other following errors as the error trap is pushed up the stack back to the executable (something like SQL*Plus), which executed the STOP_JOB procedure. See Chapter 16 for more information.

12. B. Redo log files record all the changes made to the Oracle database, whether the change is committed or not. See Chapter 15 for more information.

13. D. Default roles are enabled when a user connects to the database, even if the roles are password protected. Read Chapter 13 for more information.

14. D. Although options A and B are recommended practices for upgrade performance, option D is a must. The Pre-Upgrade Information tool must be run, and all errors must be taken care of before upgrading the database. Option C is not required for the upgrade process. For more information, read Chapter 17.

15. E. To tune the instance recovery time, configure the FAST_START_MTTR_TARGET parameter to a nonzero value. The default is 300 seconds. A lower value will reduce the instance recovery time, but may cause frequent checkpoints. A value of 0 turns off MTTR tuning. Read Chapter 15 for more information.

16. C. Oracle Shared Server requires a shift of memory away from individual session processes to the SGA. More information has to be kept in the SGA (in the UGA) within the shared pool. A large pool is configured and is responsible for most of the SGA space allocation. The cache size and block buffers settings do not affect Oracle Shared Server. See Chapter 12 for more information.

17. C, D. Recovery options are optional when you create a database. Specify Fast Recovery Area and Enable Archiving are the options available. Read Chapter 9 for more information.

18. B. The REPAIR FAILURE command works only after an ADVISE FAILURE. Option A is invalid. LIST FAILURE displays the failures. CHANGE FAILURE can be used to lower or raise the priority of a failure. For more information, see Chapter 15.

19. A, C. You cannot dynamically change the parameter UNDO_MANAGEMENT after the instance has started. You can, however, change the UNDO_TABLESPACE parameter to switch to another undo tablespace while the instance is up and running. See Chapter 11 for more information.

20. B. Oracle automatically performs instance recovery after a database crash or SHUTDOWN ABORT. All uncommitted changes are rolled back, and committed changes are written to data files during instance recovery. Read Chapter 9 for more information.

21. C. DB_DEST implies a database instance destination identified by a TNS name. LOCAL implies the current machine only. See Chapter 16 for more information.

22. C, D. Every database must have at least two redo log files, which may or may not be multiplexed. Every database must have one control file. It is a good idea to have more than one control file for redundancy. Because SYSTEM and SYSAUX are mandatory tablespaces, there will be at least two data files. Read Chapter 8 for more information.

23. C. There are no standard password complexity settings in either the initialization parameters or profiles. A password-verify function can validate new passwords against any rules that you can code in PL/SQL, including regular expression comparisons. For more information, read Chapter 13.

24. B. DBA_CHAINS does not exist. DBA_SCHEDULER_CHAINS only shows chained groups of jobs. DBA_SCHEDULER_DESTS shows on job execution destinations. The DBA_SCHEDULER_JOBS metadata view has a JOB_PRIORITY column. For more information, read Chapter 16.

25. C. The shared pool has three components: library cache, result cache, and dictionary cache. Read Chapter 8 for more information.

26. A. You can use the Undo Management Advisor to monitor and manage the undo segments to ensure maximum levels of read consistency and minimize occurrences of ORA-01555: Snapshot Too Old error messages. For more information, see Chapter 14.

27. C. The MINIMUM EXTENT parameter is used to make sure each extent is a multiple of the value specified. This parameter is useful to reduce fragmentation in the tablespace. Read Chapter 10 for more information.

28. A. Irrespective of the components audited, all audit trail information is queried from UNIFIED_AUDIT_TRAIL. Audit records are stored in a table under the AUDSYS table. See Chapter 13 for more information.

29. D. Protocols come with tools that allow you to test network connectivity. One such utility for TCP/IP is ping. The user supplies either an IP address or a hostname to the ping utility. It then searches the network for this address. If it finds one, it displays information on data that is sent and received and on how quickly it found this address. The other choices are Oracle-supplied utilities. Read Chapter 12 for more information.

30. B. The online redo log files are used to roll forward after an instance failure; undo data is used to roll back any uncommitted transactions. See Chapter 11 for more information.

31. B. The log and bad files are written to (not read from) SQL*Loader, and the data file contains only data. The direct=y option, which tells SQL*Loader to use the direct path option, can appear on the command line or in the parfile. See Chapter 18 for more information.

32. B. Shared servers can process requests from many users. The completed requests are placed into the dispatchers' response queues. The servers are configured with the SERVERS parameter. However, shared servers do not receive requests directly from dispatchers. The requests are taken from the request queue. Read Chapter 12 for more information.

33. D. The distance between the checkpoint position in the redo log file and the end of the redo log group can never be more than 90 percent of the size of the smallest redo log group. See Chapter 15 for more information.

34. B. A nonzero value for the MEMORY_TARGET parameter enables the Automatic Memory Management. SGA_TARGET enables Automatic Shared Memory Management. Automatic Memory Management tunes both SGA and PGA components of the memory. For more information, read Chapter 14.

35. D. REPLACE is the valid value; it drops the existing table and creates the table using the definition from the dump file. SKIP leaves the table untouched. APPEND inserts rows to the existing table. TRUNCATE leaves the structure but removes all existing rows before inserting rows. Read Chapter 18 to learn more.

36. B, C. Only the SYSTEM and UNDO tablespaces require the instance to be shut down when their data files need to be recovered. See Chapter 15 for more information.

37. A. Oracle Database 12*c* uses the Automatic Diagnostic Repository to maintain the alert log and other diagnostic information. The BACKGROUND_DUMP_DEST parameter is derived from the DIAGNOSTIC_DEST. See Chapter 9 for more information.

38. B. Option A is not correct because operations on temporary tablespaces do not generate redo, and a temporary table is created in a temporary tablespace. When DML is performed on a temporary table, the undo is written by default to the active undo tablespace, which generates redo. By setting the parameter TEMP_UNDO_ENABLED, you can direct the undo writing to a temporary tablespace instead of an undo tablespace, thus eliminating redo generation. Option C is wrong. When TEMP_UNDO_ENABLED is true, the undo gets generated as usual; however, the undo gets generated in the temp tablespace, so the redo is not generated. See Chapter 11 for more information.

39. A, C. OEM Database Express is automatically configured when you create a database using DBCA. SQL*Plus is installed along with Oracle RDBMS software tools. SQLDeveloper and OEM Cloud Control must be downloaded and installed separately. Read Chapter 8 for more information.

40. B. DB_CREATE_FILE_DEST specifies the directory to use to create data files and temp files. This directory is also used for control files and redo log files if the DB_CREATE_ONLINE_LOG_DEST_1 parameter is not set. See Chapter 10 for more information.

41. C. In the previous database releases, the upgrade script was named catupgrd.sql. In Oracle Database 12*c*, the upgrade script is also catupgrd.sql, but it must be invoked using the catctl.pl perl script. This script runs the upgrade in parallel by default, thereby reducing the upgrade time. The utlu121i.sql script is replaced with the preupgrd.sql script and is used for pre-upgrade information. The utlu121s.sql script is a post-upgrade status tool. For more information, see Chapter 17.

42. C. DRCP is enabled and disabled by using the database package DBMS_CONNECTION_POOL. The procedure START_POOL starts the server pool and STOP_POOL stops it. The CONFIGURE_POOL procedure can be used to configure various parameters. Read Chapter 12 for more information.

43. D. DIAGNOSTIC_DEST determines the location of the alert log file and trace files. See Chapter 14 for more information.

44. B. Oracle Grid Infrastructure includes Oracle ASM and Oracle Restart. ASM disks are managed and controlled by a special type of instance known as the ASM instance. The ASM instance does not have any data files or database associated to it; it has only the memory structures and processes. See Chapter 18 for more information.

Oracle Database 12c: SQL Fundamentals

Chapter

1

Introducing Oracle Database 12*c* RDBMS

ORACLE DATABASE 12*c*: SQL FUNDAMENTALS EXAM OBJECTIVES COVERED IN THIS CHAPTER:

✓ **Introduction**

- ▪ Describe the features of Oracle Database 12*c*.

- ▪ Describe the salient features of Oracle Cloud 12*c*.

- ▪ Explain the theoretical and physical aspects of a relational database.

- ▪ Describe Oracle server's implementation of RDBMS and object relational database management system (ORDBMS).

Organizations and individuals collect and use a variety of information (data). A database collects data, stores and organizes data, and retrieves related data used by a business. Oracle is the world's most widely used database management system. With the release of its Database 12c, Oracle has enhanced the capabilities of its feature-rich database to include cloud architecture. The c in 12c stands for cloud computing. From Oracle version 8 onward, Oracle includes the core emphasis of the release along with the version number in its name. Versions 8 and 9 are called i to indicate Internet computing; versions 10 and 11 are called g for grid computing.

With the cloud enablement, Oracle Database 12c lets you manage many databases as one, thereby reducing overhead and valuable resource consumption.

This chapter will introduce you to the Oracle Database 12c high-level components and how the Oracle database is organized. You will also learn about the relational and object capabilities of the database, and the tools available for database administrators (DBAs) to retrieve information and manage the database.

Exam objectives are subject to change at any time without prior notice and at Oracle's sole discretion. Please visit Oracle's Training and Certification website at http://www.oracle.com/education/certification for the most current exam objectives.

Relational Database Management Systems

A *database management system* (DBMS) controls the storage, organization, and retrieval of data. In a DBMS, the kernel code is the software piece that manages the storage and memory component of the database. There is metadata in the DBMS that keeps track of all the components of the database, also known as the dictionary. The code or language used to retrieve data from the database is known as SQL, which stands for *Structured Query Language*.

Over the years, database management systems have evolved from hierarchical to network to relational database management systems (RDBMS). A *relational database management system* is an organized model of subjects and characteristics that have relationships among the subjects. A well-designed relational database provides volumes of information about a business or process. *RDBMS* is the most widely used database system, and the object structures are related. We see relationships everywhere in our daily lives: parents and children, team and players, doctor and patient, to name a few. The main advantages of RDBMS include the way it stores and retrieves information and how the data integrity is maintained. RDBMS structures are easy to understand and build. These structures are logically represented using the *entity-relationship (ER) model*. The exam will have one or two questions on the ER diagram and/or the RDBMS concept. You may already be familiar with the RDBMS concepts and ER diagrams; a brief refresher is included here.

Characteristics of a Relational Database

Relational databases have the following three major characteristics that constitute a well-defined RDBMS:

- **Structures** are objects that store or access data from the database. Tables, views, and indexes are examples of structures in Oracle.

- **Operations** are the actions that are used to define the structures or to manipulate data between the structures. SELECT statements and CREATE statements are examples of operations in Oracle.

- **Integrity rules** govern what kinds of actions are allowed on data and the database structure. These rules protect the data and the structure of the database. The primary keys and foreign keys are examples of integrity rules in Oracle.

Logical Model

In the design phase of the system development cycle, a logical model of the database is created. A logical model of an RDBMS is typically a block diagram of entities and relationships, referred to as an *entity-relationship (ER) model* or ER diagram.

An ER model has *entity*, *relationship*, and *attributes*. An ER model is visual, showing the structure, characteristics, and interactions within and around the data being modeled.

Entities and Attributes An entity in a logical model is much like a noun in grammar—a person, place, or thing. The characteristics of an entity are known as its attributes. Attributes are detailed information about an entity that serves to qualify, identify, classify, or quantify it. For example: ABC Inc. has many offices in the United States; each office has many departments, and each department may have many employees. Placing the organization of ABC Inc. in terms of the ER model, you could identify OFFICE, DEPARTMENT, and EMPLOYEE as entities. Each entity will also have its own characteristics. For instance, when you say "office," you might want to know the address and city where the office is located, the state, and how many employees work there. Similarly, you might want to know the department name, its manager, the employee's name, date of birth, hiring date, and salary grade. You might also like to know the employee's spouse's name. See Figure 1.1.

There are optional and mandatory attributes. In Figure 1.1, the spouse's name, along with the employee information, is optional; whereas the employee name, the department he/she belongs to, hire date, and date of birth are mandatory in Figure 1.2. An asterisk along with the attribute name indicates that it is mandatory. The optional attribute may be indicated with a small *o*.

FIGURE 1.1   Entities and attributes

Office	Department	Employee
Address City State ZIP	Department Name Manager	Name DOB Join Date Grade Spouse

Relationships and Unique Identifiers   In the example of ABC Inc., the relationship between the entities is described as "each office has many departments," "one department belongs to only one office," "each department has many employees," and "one employee can belong to only one department." If there is an office in one city, there should be at least one department. So it is mandatory to have at least one occurrence of department for each location. There may be many departments in one location. In the ER model, a solid line represents a mandatory relationship, and a crowfoot represents the "many." But in some departments, there may not be any employees at all. Optional occurrence is represented by a dotted line.

You should be able to identify each occurrence of an entity uniquely. Now what happens if there are two employees with the same name? How do you distinguish them? For office location, the city and state uniquely identify each office; for department, the department name identifies it uniquely. For employee, you can introduce a unique identifier (UID) called employee number. Figure 1.2 is a refined version of Figure 1.1, and it shows the entities, attributes, relationships, optional and mandatory attributes, and UIDs. UID is represented in the diagram using a pound (#) symbol.

FIGURE 1.2   An entity-relationship (ER) model

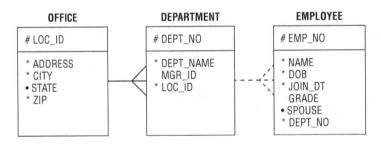

Three types of relationships can be defined between the entities. (Figure 1.3):

One-to-One   A one-to-one relationship is one in which each occurrence of one entity is represented by a single occurrence in another entity. For example, product and patent—one product might have a patent, and one patent corresponds to only one product.

One-to-Many   A one-to-many relationship is one in which an occurrence of one entity can be represented by many occurrences in another entity. For example, department and employees—one department has one or more employees, and an employee belongs to only one department.

Many-to-Many   A many-to-many relationship is one in which an occurrence from one entity can be represented by one or more occurences in another entity, and an occurrence from the second entity may be represented by one or many occurences in the first entity. Many-to-many relationships should not exist in RDBMS because they cannot be properly joined to represent a single row correctly. To solve this, create another entity that has an one-to-many relationship with the first entity and an one-to-many relationship with the second entity. For example, doctor and patient—a patient can visit many doctors, and a doctor can have many patients.

FIGURE 1.3   Types of relationships

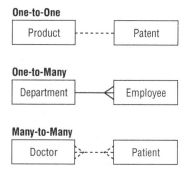

The logical model also provides information known as *access paths*. They are the common ways you usually query the database in order to retreive information. For example, you would always query the employee records with the Dept_No or Emp_No. Think of the access paths as an index to the data; they help us locate data just as the index of a book helps us quickly find the information we need.

When you have established the relationships between entities, it's time to normalize the design. *Normalization* is the process of eliminating redundant information from the entities until you can uniquely identify each occurrence of the entity. This may not always be practical due to performance and implementation issues. In such cases, you can denormalize to some extent.

Physical Model

The physical model is created by taking the logical model and creating a database and database objects to represent the entities and relationships. In the physical model, each entity becomes a *table* and attributes of the entity become *columns* of the table. The relationship between the entities is part of one or more *constraints* between the tables. Physical implementations might force you to combine, separate, or create completely new entities in order to best realize the logical model. The unique identifiers of an entity become the *primary key* of the table. Stored procedures, functions, and triggers may be created to enforce business rules.

NOTE   In RDBMS, the physical database storage is independent of the logical model.

Oracle's Implementation of RDBMS and ORDBMS

A database server is the key to information management. An Oracle database satisfies all three major characteristics of the relational model. Oracle lets you define tables, columns, column characteristics such as datatype, length, whether the values are mandatory, and default values. Defining *foreign key* ensures the *referential integrity* of the data. You can define *primary keys* and indexes on the data. The primary key of a relational table uniquely identifies each record in the table; it may consist of a single attribute (column) or multiple attributes in combination. A foreign key is a column (or collection of columns) in one table that uniquely identifies a row of another table, defining the relationship between the tables.

Records in a database table can be seen as instances of the entity. Each occurrence of an entity is differentiated by the values of the attributes. Oracle stores these records as *rows* of the table and the attributes as *columns* in each row. In the most generic form, a database table can be seen as a single spreadsheet with unlimited numbers of columns and rows. The columns are not defined until the user names them and gives them a datatype. Oracle extends the concept of spreadsheets by defining relationships between multiple spreadsheets, constraints on columns, and providing mechanisms for multiple users to access the same database table(s) at the same time.

The data access path is implemented in Oracle using indexes. Indexing allows us to predefine to the relational database system the most common access paths that will be used. These indexes decrease the time required to search for data in a table using a number of algorithms such as B-tree, bitmap, etc.

Oracle implements the RDBMS characteristics using the following set of structures:

- Tables are used for data storage.
- Views and synonyms are created for data access.
- Indexes are used to speed up data retrieval.
- Primary keys, foreign keys, and unique keys are called *constraints* and are created to enforce data integrity.
- Triggers are created to satisfy the business rules.
- Roles and privileges are used for security.
- Procedures, functions, and packages are used to code the application.

Oracle, since version 8i, is also an Object Relational DBMS. An RDBMS that implements object-oriented features such as user-defined types, inheritance, and polymorphism is called ORDBMS. It lets you create user-defined object types in the relational database system. Object types are structures that consist of built-in or user-defined data types. For example, Address can be defined as an object type and can be referenced in tables.

Here's an example where STREET_TYPE is defined as:

STREET_TYPE
```
STREET_NUMBER NUMBER    (6)
STREET_NAME1  VARCHAR2 (40)
STREET_SUFFIX VARCHAR2 (10)
APARTMENT_NO  VARCHAR2 (5)
```

Here's an example where ADDRESS_TYPE is an object type defined using another object type as:

ADDRESS_TYPE
```
STREET        STREET_TYPE
CITY          VARCHAR2 (30)
STATE         CHAR (2)
ZIP           NUMBER (5)
```

In this example for CUSTOMER_TABLE, the object CUST_ADDR is a type.

CUSTOMER_TABLE
```
CUST_NAME     VARCHAR2 (40)
CUST_ADDR     ADDRESS_TYPE
CUST_PHONE    VARCHAR2 (12)
CUST_FAX      VARCHAR2 (12)
```

Now that the ADDRESS_TYPE is defined, it can be used in any number of tables, where ADDRESS needs to be stored. This is a small example to show you how objects can be reused and how the functionality of the RDBMS can be extended to include built-in complex business rules.

The Oracle Database 12*c*

An Oracle Database 12*c* server is a feature-rich RDBMS that extends its capabilities beyond any other RDBMS in the market, with object relational and cloud capabilities. In this section, we will discuss the capabilities and features of Oracle Database 12*c*.

Oracle Database 12*c* Implementations

Let's start with the architecture of the database server at a very high level. Detailed architecture and components are discussed in various chapters in Part II of this book.

The physical structure of an Oracle Database 12*c* server consists of two major components: the *database* and the *instance*. The database is a set of physical files saved on the disk that store information. The instance is a set of memory structures and processes that uses the physical components to manipulate and retrieve data.

Figure 1.4 shows the database architecture. The host machine is where the Oracle instance is running. It has the memory structures and processes. The storage array, or disk, is where the database resides.

FIGURE 1.4   An Oracle database server

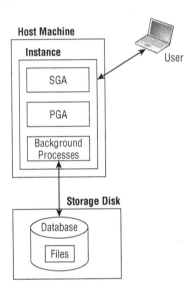

In the architecture shown in Figure 1.4, one instance communicates with one database. The host machine is where users and applications connect and interact. If the machine goes down for some reason, the database will be unavailable. Oracle alleviates this issue by introducing an architecture named the *Real Application Clusters* (RAC).

Figure 1.5 shows RAC architecture. In this architecture, more than one instance communicates to a single database. Oracle RAC takes reliability a step further by removing the database server as a single point of failure. If an instance fails, the remaining instances in the RAC pool remain open and active; and connections from failed instances can be failed-over to active instances. The RAC load balancer directs the user connection request to the appropriate instance.

With RAC, high availability and CPU/memory capacity available to the database is increased. Oracle manages the connection load balancing and failover automatically.

Many organizations have several hundreds or thousands of Oracle databases. Imagine if the policy were to have one instance per server, then you would have as many servers as the number of instances to manage. If you have a high-capacity server or if the database resource requirements are minimal, you can have more than one instance on the same host machine. Figure 1.6 shows an architecture in which more than one database is hosted on the same machine.

FIGURE 1.5   An Oracle database server — RAC

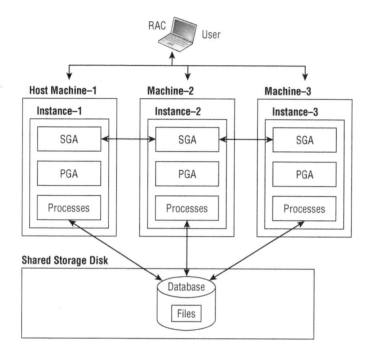

FIGURE 1.6   Multiple Oracle databases on same machine

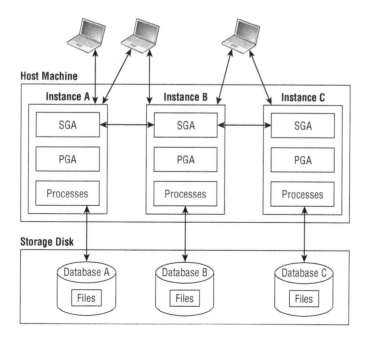

Figure 1.6 clearly shows that even though you consolidated multiple database servers to one host, you still have the same overhead of managing the database. You need instance memory structures, processes, and management activities such as backup for each instance or database.

With Oracle 12c, a new architecture feature is introduced known as the *multitenant archi-tecture*. The multitenant architecture enables an Oracle database to function as a multitenant container database (CDB) that includes zero, one, or many *pluggable databases* (PDBs). All databases created prior to Oracle Database 12c are non-CDB; a pluggable database appears as a non-CDB to the application, so existing code and application need not be changed when you move to Oracle Database 12c.

The PDBs belonging to a CDB share the database overhead such as redo, undo, and memory. Oracle RDBMS is responsible for keeping the pluggable databases separate, private for the application, and secure. The instance and SGA are assigned to a container database. Figure 1.7 shows the *multitenant database* architecture. The databases that are part of the CDB are known as pluggable databases.

FIGURE 1.7 Oracle Database 12c — Multitenant architecture with pluggable databases

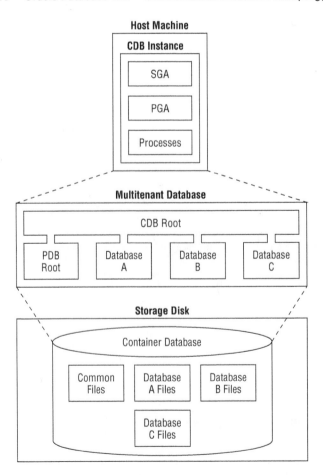

Pluggable databases in the multitenant architecture, as the name suggests, can be unplugged and plugged to another CDB easily. With the pluggable databases and multitenant architecture, Oracle Database 12*c* offers the following benefits:

- **Increased server utilization:** Because the overhead associated with each database is now shared among all databases, you can consolidate more databases with the same resources.

- **Cost reduction:** By consolidating hardware and sharing database memory and files, the cost of hardware is less.

- **Application transparency:** Although the architecture changed, each PDB acts and works as a traditional pre-12*c* Oracle database. There is no need to change application code or architecture to start using Oracle Database 12*c*.

- **Manage many databases as one:** Administrative activities such as patching and upgrade are performed on the container database so they do not need to be repeated for each database in the CDB. This drastically reduces the administrative time required.

- **Less backup configuration:** With multiple databases consolidated into one server, you still have to back up each database separately. With container and pluggable databases, you only need to back up one multitenant container database.

- **Easier provisioning:** In the container database architecture, it is very easy to clone and provision pluggable databases.

- **Less time to upgrade:** When you upgrade the container database, all the pluggable databases are automatically upgraded.

- **Move databases:** It is also possible to move a pluggable database from one container database to another. This is especially useful if you plan to upgrade all but a few databases to the next release. Before upgrading the container database, you may move a few pluggable databases to another container database, or move pluggable databases to another CDB of higher release.

- **Separation of duties:** Database administrators can be defined as a CDB administrator (common user with administrative privileges on all CDB and PDBs) or a PDB administrator (local user in PDB with administrative privilege only on the PDB).

In the next section, you will learn about users and schema in the database, which is the basis for connecting to the database.

Connecting to Oracle Database

Before you can connect to an Oracle database, you must create a user. When you create a new Oracle database, several default users are automatically created. (The preferred method for creating a database is to use the Database Configuration Assistant [DBCA], which is discussed in Chapter 9, "Creating and Operating Oracle Database 12*c*.")

SYS is the data dictionary or metadata dictionary owner for the database. Using this account for day-to-day operations is not recommended. You connect to SYS to start and stop database and other key administrative tasks. SYSTEM is a powerful administrative user in the database. Initially, you use this user connection to create database users and other administrators in the database. Along with SYS and SYSTEM, several other database users are also created based on the options you choose during the installation and on the components installed in the database.

In a container database, the users are either common or local. Common users are visible on the container as well as in all pluggable databases; they have the same username and password across all pluggable databases and in the container database. The schema for common user is still local to each pluggable database and the container database.

A *schema* is a collection of database objects owned by a user account in the database. The objects in the schema may be related to support a business application. A schema and user have a one-to-one relationship in a database. A schema is created as a user in the database, but when the user owns database objects, it is called a schema. Schema objects are discussed in Chapter 7, "Creating Tables and Constraints."

When an object is created under someone's schema, the user has full privilege on the object by default. Using Oracle's roles and privileges, a schema owner or administrator can grant privilege on his or her object (such as a table) to another user in the same database. This is known as object-level privilege. For certain users, you may want to grant privileges on all the objects in the database; this is accomplished by using the system privileges. Privileges and system security are discussed in Chapter 13, "Implementing Security and Auditing."

The next section will introduce you to the tools available to manage and administer Oracle Database 12*c*.

Database Management Tools

Oracle Database 12*c* comes with multiple feature-rich tools to help administrators manage and monitor the database and all of its components. In this section, you will review the tools that are used for everyday administration of Oracle database. Let's start with the tool that is equally beneficial to DBAs, developers, and power users.

SQL Developer

SQL Developer is a graphical tool used to perform everyday activities in the Oracle database. It has several predefined menu functions; therefore, there is no need to remember the syntax or SQL command to perform basic functions. In addition to Oracle (database versions higher than 9i Release 2), SQL Developer can also connect to Microsoft Access, Microsoft SQL Server, MySQL, IBM DB2, and Sybase Adaptive Server databases to view data and metadata.

SQL Developer is installed along with Oracle Database 12*c* on Windows platforms. For Linux, you must download and install it outside of an Oracle Database 12*c* installation. The distribution usually included in the database software distribution might not be the current version. It is better to always download the latest version and install SQL Developer from http://www.oracle.com/technetwork/developer-tools/sql-developer/downloads. As instructed on the download page, you will also need Java JRE installed for SQL Developer to work.

Once it is installed, you can invoke SQL Developer from /usr/local/bin directory on Linux or from the Oracle Installation program group on Windows. Figure 1.8 shows the initial SQL Developer screen. To get started and learn more about SQL Developer, click the choices available in the screen.

FIGURE 1.8   The initial SQL Developer screen

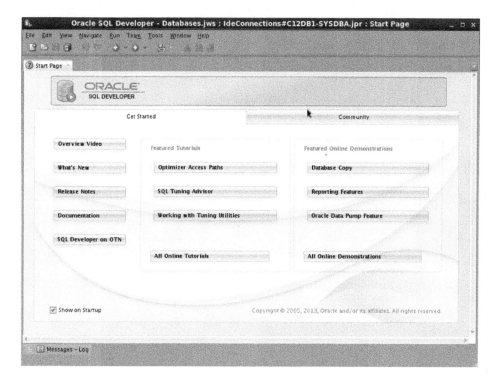

The Connections navigation pane is the most commonly used pane, which navigates through the database objects providing you with information and options to modify the objects. In Figure 1.9, you can see the various sections and navigations in SQL Developer. The section marked 1 shows various database connections and the objects in those databases. Section 2 provides you with a set of predefined reports. If you know how to write SQL, you can define your own reports as well. Section 3 shows the DBA navigation screen, showing you various DBA tasks.

Section 4 is the SQL worksheet. You use this section to interact directly with the database using SQL language. Output from the SQL commands is listed in section 5; both query output and script output are visible. Section 6 is the logging pane. This is useful when you are debugging code.

For simplicity and ease of results capture, the SQL statements used in this book are using SQL*Plus. All of the SQL commands can also run using the SQL Worksheet in SQL Developer.

FIGURE 1.9 SQL Developer navigation windows

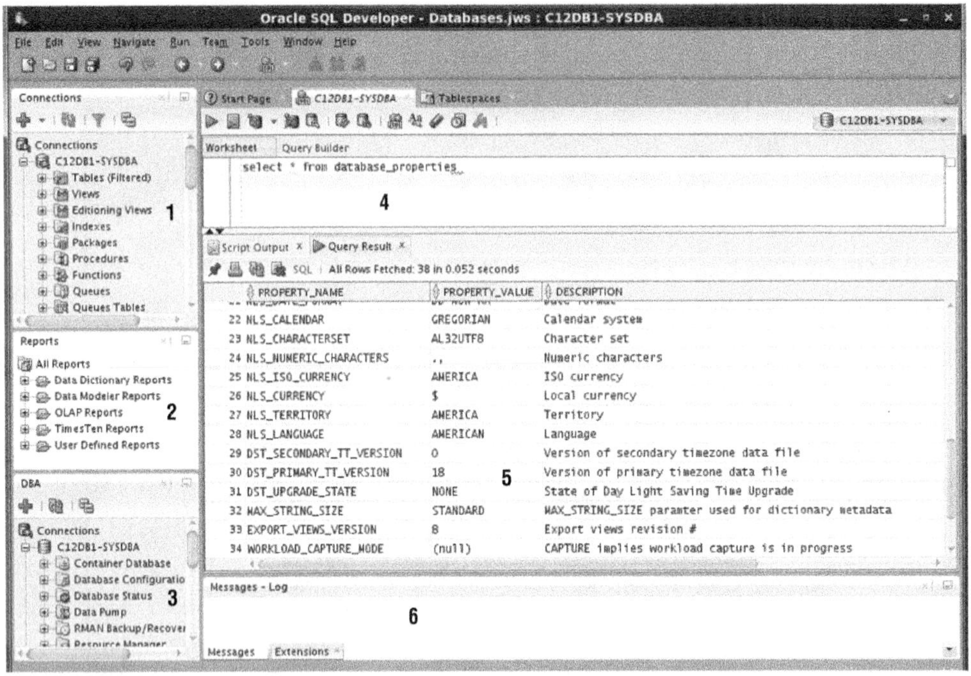

SQL*Plus

*SQL*Plus* is Oracle's command-line interface to the Oracle database. You run SQL commands to query the database or to manage the database. SQL*Plus is packaged with the Oracle software and can be installed using the client software installation routine on any machine. This tool is automatically installed when you install the Oracle Database 12*c* server software.

On Unix/Linux platforms, you can invoke SQL*Plus using the sqlplus executable found in the $ORACLE_HOME/bin directory. On Windows, SQL*Plus is under the Oracle Home Group menu. On Windows and Unix/Linux platforms, when you start SQL*Plus, you will be prompted for a username and password, as shown in Figure 1.10.

Once you are in SQL*Plus, you can connect to another database or change your connection by using the CONNECT command, with this syntax:

```
CONNECT <username>/<password>@<connect_string>
```

The slash separates the username and password. The connect string following @ is the database alias name known as the net service name. If you omit the password, you will be prompted to enter it. If you omit the connect string, SQL*Plus tries to connect you to the local database defined in the ORACLE_SID variable (or the net service name defined by TWO_TASK variable). You will not be prompted for the <connect_string>. Include <connect_string> along with <username> as in bthomas@myowndb.

FIGURE 1.10 A SQL*Plus screen

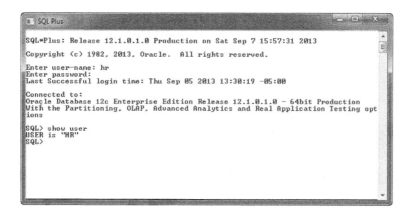

You may replace the connect string with a construct called the easy connect. The syntax is [//]*Host*[:*Port*]/<*service_name*>]. For example, to connect to database service named C12DB1 on machine BTLNX63, where the listener is running in port 1521, use

```
sqlplus system@"btlnx63:1521/C12DB1"
```

You can invoke and connect to SQL*Plus using the `sqlplus` command, with this syntax:

```
sqlplus <username>/<password>@<connectstring>
```

If you invoke the tool with just `sqlplus`, you will be prompted for a username and password, as in Figure 1.10. If you invoke SQL*Plus with a username, you will be prompted for a password. See Figure 1.11 for an example.

FIGURE 1.11 A SQL*Plus screen with a password prompt

```
[samuel@btlnx63 ~]$ echo $ORACLE_HOME
/u01/app/oracle/product/12.1.0/dbhome_1
[samuel@btlnx63 ~]$ echo $ORACLE_SID
C12DB1
[samuel@btlnx63 ~]$ echo $TWO_TASK
C12PDB1
[samuel@btlnx63 ~]$ sqlplus system

SQL*Plus: Release 12.1.0.1.0 Production on Wed Nov 20 16:17:17 2013

Copyright (c) 1982, 2013, Oracle.  All rights reserved.

Enter password:
Last Successful login time: Wed Nov 20 2013 16:16:58 -06:00

Connected to:
Oracle Database 12c Enterprise Edition Release 12.1.0.1.0 - 64bit Production
With the Partitioning, OLAP, Advanced Analytics and Real Application Testing options

SQL> show user
USER is "SYSTEM"
SQL>
```

Once you are connected to SQL*Plus, you will get the SQL> prompt. This is the default prompt, which can be changed using the SET SQLPROMPT command. Type the command you want to execute at this prompt. With SQL*Plus, you can enter, edit, and execute SQL statements; perform database administration; and execute statements interactively by accepting user input. You can also format query results and perform calculations.

To exit from SQL*Plus, use the EXIT command. On platforms where a return code is used, you can provide a return code while exiting. You can also use the QUIT command to complete the session. EXIT and QUIT are synonymous.

The command sqlplus -help displays a help screen to show the various options available when starting SQL*Plus. Multiple administrative connections such as SYSDBA, SYSOPER, SYSBACKUP, SYSASM, SYSKM, and SYSDG are also available. They are discussed in this book in various chapters.

Oracle Enterprise Manager Database Express 12*c*

Oracle Enterprise Manger (OEM) Database Express 12*c* is a web-based tool that can be configured using default by Database Configuration Assistant (DBCA, the tool you use to create and configure databases) when you create an Oracle database. OEM Database Express by default uses port 5500, hence is invoked using URL https:// database_host_machine:5500/em.

OEM Database Express is designed to manage only one database, and is intended for database administrators. When you invoke Database Express, you will be prompted for a username and password to connect to the database. You should provide a user account that has administrative privileges.

For the SQL section of this book, you will not be using this tool, so we will not discuss it in more detail here. You can read more information about OEM Database Express in Chapter 3, "Getting Started with Database Administration," of "Oracle Database 2 Day DBA 12*c* Release 1 (Part E17643-12)," found at http://docs.oracle.com/.

Oracle Enterprise Manager Cloud Control 12*c*

Oracle Enterprise Manager Cloud Control 12c (OEM 12c) is Oracle's integrated enterprise management administrative tool, providing complete cloud management solutions. With OEM 12*c*, you can manage multiple databases and all products under the Oracle stack. It is a complete cloud lifecycle management answer to quickly set up, administer, and support enterprise clouds and Oracle environments from applications to storage.

OEM 12*c* is not part of the Oracle Database 12*c* software install; it must be downloaded and installed separately. To read more about OEM 12*c*, please check out "Oracle Enterprise Manager Cloud Control Introduction 12*c* Release 3 (Part E25353-14)" at http://docs .oracle.com/.

Oracle Database 12*c* in the Cloud

Cloud architecture emphasizes sharing resources and maximizing the effectiveness of shared resources. Cloud resources are shared not only by multiple users, but are also capable of reallocation based on demand. Cloud computing allows organizations to provision resources and applications rapidly, with improved manageability and less administrative overhead.

By enabling customers to efficiently use their information technology infrastructure, Oracle Database 12*c* was designed for the cloud. The following are the benefits of having Oracle Database 12*c* in the cloud architecture:

- It consolidates multiple Oracle databases into multitenant container databases.
- With multitenant architecture, DBAs can manage multiple databases as one database for many administrative tasks on the database. DBAs need to perform fewer patches and upgrades and will not need to configure many backups.
- It automatically optimizes database storage and performance based on usage.
- Oracle Database 12*c* supports smart compression and storage tier. The heat map feature tracks data usage information; administrators can create appropriate policies to automatically move and compress data based on age and activity of data.
- Oracle RAC supports deployment of database instances across a pool of servers, helping to avoid downtime caused by unplanned server outages.
- With Oracle Enterprise Manager Cloud Control 12*c*, the provisioning and cloning of databases are simplified.

Oracle Database 12*c* helps customers reduce IT complexity and cost through private database cloud deployments by consolidation. Cloud computing offers an opportunity for IT organizations to be more responsive to changes in application workloads and business demands.

Because the test is on SQL and the tool used throughout the book for executing SQL is SQL*Plus, the next section will discuss some fundamentals of SQL*Plus.

Becoming Familiar with SQL*Plus

SQL*Plus, widely used by DBAs and developers to interact with a database, is a powerful tool from Oracle. Using SQL*Plus, you can execute all SQL statements and PL/SQL programs, format results from queries, and administer the database.

Earlier in this chapter, you learned how to connect to the database using SQL*Plus. In this section, you will learn about entering SQL commands, understanding the difference between SQL commands and SQL*Plus commands, editing the SQL*Plus buffer, and running commands in a script.

Entering SQL Statements

A SQL statement can spread across multiple lines, and the commands are not case sensitive. The previously executed SQL statement will always be available in the *SQL buffer.*

The buffer can be edited or saved to a file. You can terminate a SQL statement in any of the following ways:

- End with a semicolon (;): The statement is completed and executed.
- Enter a slash (/) on a new line by itself: The statement in the buffer is executed.
- Enter a blank line: The statement is saved in the buffer.

You can use the RUN command instead of a slash to execute a statement in the buffer. The SQL prompt returns when the statement has completed execution. You can enter your next command at the prompt.

 Only SQL statements and PL/SQL blocks are stored in the SQL buffer; SQL*Plus commands are not stored in the buffer.

Entering SQL*Plus Commands

SQL*Plus has its own commands to perform specific tasks on the database, as well as to format the query results. Unlike SQL statements, which are terminated with a semicolon or a blank line, SQL*Plus commands are entered on a single line. Pressing Enter executes the SQL*Plus command.

When you log in to the SQL*Plus session, you get the SQL prompt. By default, the prompt is SQL>. You can change this prompt using the SET SQLPROMPT SQL*Plus command. When you continue a SQL command to the next line, a line number appears at the beginning of the line. As shown here, when you type SELECT USERNAME in the first line (the SQL prompt line) and press Enter, line number 2 appears where you continue the SQL command FROM DBA_USERS.

```
SQL> SELECT USERNAME
  2 FROM DBA_USERS
```

SQL statements can span multiple lines. If you want to continue a SQL*Plus command onto the next line, you must end the current line with a hyphen (-), which indicates command continuation. When a command continuation character is entered, SQL*Plus will not show the line number next, but instead displays the greater than symbol (>). This is in contrast to SQL statements, which can be continued to the next line without a continuation operator. For example, the following SQL statement gives an error, because SQL*Plus treats the hyphen operator (-) as a continuation character instead of a minus operator:

```
SQL> SELECT 800 -
> 400 FROM dual;
SELECT 800  400 FROM dual
             *
ERROR at line 1:
ORA-00923: FROM keyword not found where expected
SQL>
```

You need to put the hyphen in the next line for the query to succeed:

```
SQL> SELECT 800
  2  - 400 FROM dual;

   800-400
----------
       400
SQL>
```

Getting Structural Information with the DESCRIBE Command

You can use the DESCRIBE command to obtain information about the database objects. Using DESCRIBE on a table or view shows the columns, its datatypes, and whether each column can be NULL. Using DESCRIBE on a stored program, such as procedure or function, shows the parameters that need to be passed in/out, their datatype, and whether there is a default value. You can abbreviate this command to the first four characters or more—DESC, DESCR, and DESCRIB are all valid.

If you're connected to the HR schema and need to see the tables and views in this schema, use the following query:

```
SQL> SELECT * FROM tab;

TNAME                           TABTYPE CLUSTERID
------------------------------- ------- ----------
COUNTRIES                       TABLE
DEPARTMENTS                     TABLE
EMPLOYEES                       TABLE
EMP_DETAILS_VIEW                VIEW
JOBS                            TABLE
JOB_HISTORY                     TABLE
LOCATIONS                       TABLE
REGIONS                         TABLE

8 rows selected.
```

To see the columns or definition of the EMPLOYEES table, execute:

```
SQL> DESCRIBE employees
 Name                                      Null?    Type
 ----------------------------------------- -------- --------------------

 EMPLOYEE_ID                               NOT NULL NUMBER(6)
 FIRST_NAME                                         VARCHAR2(20)
```

LAST_NAME	NOT NULL VARCHAR2(25)
EMAIL	NOT NULL VARCHAR2(25)
PHONE_NUMBER	VARCHAR2(20)
HIRE_DATE	NOT NULL DATE
JOB_ID	NOT NULL VARCHAR2(10)
SALARY	NUMBER(8,2)
COMMISSION_PCT	NUMBER(2,2)
MANAGER_ID	NUMBER(6)
DEPARTMENT_ID	NUMBER(4)

If there are invisible columns in the table, they are not displayed by the DESCRIBE command unless you use SET COLINVISIBLE ON.

Invisible columns are newly introduced in Oracle Database 12c, where a column in the table can be hidden from the application. Invisible columns help to remove a column from the table quickly without actually dropping the column. Invisible columns are discussed in Chapter 7.

Editing the SQL Buffer

The most recent SQL statement executed or entered is stored in the SQL buffer of SQL*Plus. You can run the command in this buffer again by simply typing a slash or using the RUN command.

SQL*Plus provides a set of commands to edit the buffer. Suppose you want to add another column or add an ORDER BY condition to the statement in the buffer. You do not need to type the entire SQL statement again. Instead, just edit the existing statement in the buffer.

One way to edit the SQL*Plus buffer is to use the EDIT command to write the buffer to an operating-system file named afiedt.buf (this is the default filename, which can be changed) and then use a system editor to make changes.

You can use your favorite text editor by defining it in SQL*Plus. For example, to make Notepad your favorite editor, just issue the command DEFINE _EDITOR = NOTEPAD.

To view the editor defined, just execute DEFINE _EDITOR as shown here.

```
SQL> define _editor
DEFINE _EDITOR         = "Notepad" (CHAR)
```
Provide the entire path if the program is not available in the search path.

Another way to edit the buffer is to use the SQL*Plus editing commands. You can make changes, delete lines, add text, and list the buffer contents using the commands described in the following sections. Most editing commands operate on the current line. You can change the current line simply by typing the line number. All commands can be abbreviated, except DEL (which is already abbreviated).

LIST

The LIST command lists the contents of the buffer. The asterisk indicates the current line. The abbreviated command for LIST is L.

```
SQL> L
  1  SELECT empno, ename
  2* FROM emp
SQL> LIST LAST
  2* FROM emp
SQL>
```

The command LIST *n* displays line *n*, and LIST * displays the current line. The command LIST *m n* displays lines from *m* through *n*. If you substitute * for *m* or *n*, it implies from or to the current line. The command LIST LAST displays the last line.

APPEND

The APPEND *text* command adds text to the end of a line. The abbreviated command is A.

```
SQL> A  WHERE empno <> 7926
  2* FROM emp WHERE empno <> 7926
SQL>
```

CHANGE

The CHANGE /*old*/*new* command changes an old entry to a new entry. The abbreviated command is C. If you omit *new*, *old* will be deleted.

```
SQL> C /<>/=
  2* FROM emp WHERE empno = 7926
SQL> C /7926
  2* FROM emp WHERE empno =
SQL>
```

The ellipses (…) can be used as wildcard characters. The following example changes everything in the line from "fro" to the new value.

```
SQL> l
  1* select name from v$instance
SQL> c/fro.../from v$database
  1* select name from v$database
SQL>
```

The next example shows the substitution of a string in the middle of the line using ellipses.

```
SQL> l
  1* select owner from dba_tables where table_name like 'HR%'
SQL> c/dba...table/dba_views where view
  1* select owner from dba_views where views where table_name like 'HR%'
SQL>
```

INPUT

The INPUT *text* command adds a line of text. Its abbreviation is I. If *text* is omitted, you can add as many lines as you want.

```
SQL> I
  3  7777 AND
  4  empno = 4354
  5
SQL> I ORDER BY 1
SQL> L
  1  SELECT empno, ename
  2  FROM emp WHERE empno =
  3  7777 AND
  4  empno = 4354
  5* ORDER BY 1
SQL>
```

DEL

The DEL command used alone or with * deletes the current line. The DEL *m n* command deletes lines from *m* through *n*. If you substitute * for *m* or *n*, it implies the current line. The command DEL LAST deletes the last line.

```
SQL> 3
  3* 7777 AND
SQL> DEL
SQL> L
  1  SELECT empno, ename
  2  FROM emp WHERE empno =
  3  empno = 4354
  4* ORDER BY 1
SQL> DEL 3 *
```

```
SQL> L
  1  SELECT empno, ename
  2* FROM emp WHERE empno =
SQL>
```

CLEAR BUFFER

The CLEAR BUFFER command (abbreviated CL BUFF) clears the buffer. This deletes all lines from the buffer.

```
SQL> L
  1  SELECT empno, ename
  2* FROM emp WHERE empno =
SQL> CL BUFF
buffer cleared
SQL> L
No lines in SQL buffer.
SQL>
```

Using Script Files

SQL*Plus provides commands to save the SQL buffer to a file, as well as to run SQL statements from a file. SQL statements saved in a file are called a *script file*.

You can work with script files as follows:

- To save the SQL buffer to an operating-system file, use the command SAVE *filename*. If you do not provide an extension, the saved file will have the extension .sql.

- By default, the SAVE command will not overwrite an existing file. If you want to overwrite an existing file, you need to use the keyword REPLACE.

- To add the buffer to the end of an existing file, use the SAVE *filename* APPEND command.

- You can edit the saved file using the EDIT *filename* command.

- You can bring the contents of a *script file* to the SQL buffer using the GET *filename* command.

- If you want to run a script file, use the command START *filename*. You can also run a script file using @*filename*.

- An @@*filename* used inside a script file looks for the filename in the directory where the parent *script file* is saved and executes it.

Exercise 1.1 will familiarize you with the script file commands, as well as the other topics covered so far.

EXERCISE 1.1

Practicing SQL*Plus File Commands

In this exercise, you will learn how to edit the SQL*Plus buffer using various buffer edit commands.

1. Enter the following SQL code; the third line is a blank line so that the SQL code is saved in the buffer:

```
SQL> SELECT employee_id, first_name, last_name
  2  FROM    employees
  3
SQL>
```

2. List the SQL buffer:

```
SQL> L
  1  SELECT employee_id, first_name, last_name
  2* FROM    employees
SQL>
```

3. Save the buffer to a file named myfile; the default extension will be .sql:

```
SQL> SAVE myfile
Created file MYFILE.sql
SQL>
```

4. Choose to edit the file:

```
SQL> EDIT myfile
SQL>
```

5. Add WHERE EMPLOYEE_ID = 106 as the third line to the SQL statement.

6. List the buffer:

```
SQL> LIST
  1  SELECT employee_id, first_name, last_name
  2* FROM    employees
SQL>
```

The buffer listed is still the old buffer. The edited changes are not reflected because you edited the file MYFILE, which is not yet loaded to the buffer.

7. Bring the file contents to the buffer:

```
SQL> GET myfile
  1  SELECT employee_id, first_name, last_name
  2  FROM    employees
  3* WHERE employee_id = 106
SQL>
```

8. List the buffer to verify its contents:

```
SQL> LI
  1  SELECT employee_id, first_name, last_name
  2  FROM    employees
  3* WHERE employee_id = 106
SQL>
```

9. Change the employee number from 106 to 110:

```
SQL> C/106/110
  3* WHERE employee_id = 110
SQL>
```

10. Save the buffer again to the same file:

```
SQL> SAVE myfile
SP2-0540: File "MYFILE.sql" already exists.
Use "SAVE filename[.ext] REPLACE".
SQL>
```

An error is returned, because SAVE will not overwrite the file by default.

11. Save the file using the REPLACE keyword:

```
SQL> SAVE myfile REPLACE
Wrote file MYFILE.sql
SQL>
```

12. Execute the file:

```
SQL> START myfile
```

```
EMPLOYEE_ID FIRST_NAME           LAST_NAME
----------- -------------------- ---------
        110 John                 Chen
SQL>
```

13. Change the employee number from 110 to 106, and append this SQL code to the file; then execute it using @:

```
SQL> C/110/106
  3* WHERE employee_id = 106
SQL> SAVE myfile APPEND
Appended file to MYFILE.sql
SQL> @MYFILE
EMPLOYEE_ID FIRST_NAME           LAST_NAME
----------- -------------------- ---------
        110 John                 Chen


EMPLOYEE_ID FIRST_NAME           LAST_NAME
----------- -------------------- ---------
        106 Valli                Pataballa
SQL>
```

Saving Query Results to a File

You can use the SPOOL *filename* command to save the query results to a file. By default, the SPOOL command creates a .lst file extension. SPOOL overwrites an existing file by default. If you include the APPEND option—as in SPOOL *filename* APPEND—the results are added to an existing file. A new file will be created if the file does not exist already.

SPOOL OFF stops writing the output to the file. SPOOL OUT stops the writing of output and sends the output file to the printer. SPOOL with no clauses lists the current spooling status.

Adding Comments to a Script File

Comments in the script file can improve readability and make the code more understandable. You can enter comments in SQL*Plus using the REMARKS (abbreviated REM) command. Lines in the script file beginning with the keyword REM are comments and are not executed. You can also enter a comment between /* and */. Comments can also be entered following -- (double hyphen); all characters following -- in the line are treated as comments by Oracle.

While a script file with comments is being executed, the remarks entered using the REMARKS command are not displayed on the screen, but the comments within /* and */ are displayed on the screen with the prefix DOC> when there is more than one line between /* and */. You can turn this off by using SET DOCUMENT OFF.

Now that you understand the concepts of RDBMS and how Oracle Database 12*c* helps organizations achieve the cloud architecture, let's move on to the core of the Oracle Database 12*c* SQL Fundamentals OCA exam in the coming chapters. Before moving on to Chapter 2, "Introducing SQL," please make sure you have an Oracle Database 12*c* to practice on and try out the examples.

You may perform a quick default install of the database after downloading the software from OTN (www.technet.oracle.com).

 **Real World Scenario**

Install Oracle Database 12*c* for SQL Practice

To be able to practice the examples provided in this book and to familiarize yourself with Oracle Database 12*c* SQL, an Oracle Database 12*c* database must be available to you. If you do not have such a database, you can follow these instructions to install software and create databases on a Windows machine.

Download and Install Software

You may download Oracle Database 12*c* software from Oracle Technology Network (OTN) or from Oracle Cloud Delivery service (edelivery.oracle.com). After downloading the software, you can invoke the setup.exe to install software. For detailed instructions on downloading and installing Oracle software, refer to www.bijoos.com/certify/db12csw.pdf. You can also refer to Chapter 9 to install database software.

Create Oracle Database

Databases are created using the Database Configuration Assistant tool. You can choose the Create Database With Default Configuration option to create a database quickly. For detailed instructions on creating a database, refer to www.bijoos.com/certify/db12c_ndb.pdf. You can also refer to Chapter 9 to create a database.

Create Sample Schema

The sample schema provided by Oracle includes HR, OE, PM, SH, and IX. For the majority of the SQL used in the book, the HR schema is used. If you did not install the sample schema during database creation, you can do so using the following procedure.

When you install Oracle software, you can choose the Create Database With Default Configuration option, but this will not include the sample schemas. The account SYS is the Oracle dictionary owner, and SYSTEM is a database administrator (DBA) account. Initially, the sample schema user accounts are locked. You need to log in to the database using SQL*Plus as the SYSTEM user and then unlock the account using the ALTER USER statement. To unlock the HR schema, use ALTER USER hr IDENTIFIED BY hrpassword ACCOUNT UNLOCK;. Now you can log in to the database using the hr user with the password hrpassword. Remember, the password is case sensitive by default.

To install the sample schemas in an existing Oracle Database 12*c*, follow the instructions in the Oracle document "Oracle Database Sample Schemas 12*c* Release 1 (12.1) Part E15979-04" at http://docs.oracle.com/. Chapter 2 of this document provides instructions on how to install the sample schemas using Database Configuration Assistant (DBCA) as well as on running scripts. The same chapter also gives you steps to reinitialize the sample schema data.

The manual installation of HR and OE sample data on Linux-based Oracle Database 12*c* databases can be quickly summarized as:

Change the directory to $ORACLE_HOME/demo/schema/human_resources.

Connect to database using SQL*Plus as SYSDBA (sqlplus sys@mydb as sysdba).

Run the schema and objects creation script (@hr_main.sql).

Change the directory to $ORACLE_HOME/demo/schema/order_entry.

Connect to the database using SQL*Plus as SYSDBA (sqlplus sys@mydb as sysdba).

Run the schema and objects creation script (@oe_main.sql).

Summary

This chapter reviewed the concepts of relational database systems and Object RDBMS. You also learned how Oracle implements the RDBMS and relational theory into the Oracle database. The entity-relationship diagram is a modeling tool used in the beginning stages or application development.

You also learned about the high-level architecture and various implementations of Oracle, such as single database, RAC database, and container database.

Oracle Database 12*c* is cloud enabled. The multitenant architecture of the database helps to consolidate multiple Oracle databases (pluggable databases) into a single container database.

Various tools are available for the DBA to connect to the Oracle database and administer it. SQL*Plus is Oracle's SQL command-line interface tool. SQL Developer is a graphical tool, with ease of navigation and predefined tasks. You also saw an overview of SQL*Plus in this chapter, including how to connect to the database using SQL*Plus and basic editing commands.

SQL*Plus supports all SQL statements and has its own formatting and enhancement commands. Using this tool, you can produce interactive SQL statements and formatted reports. SQL*Plus is the command-line interface to the database widely used by DBAs. SQL*Plus has its own buffer where SQL statements are buffered. You can edit the buffer using SQL*Plus editing commands. The DESCRIBE command is used to get information on a table, view, function, or procedure. Multiple SQL and SQL*Plus commands can be stored in a file and can be executed as a unit. Such files are called script files.

Exam Essentials

Know RDBMS Concepts.   Review the RDBMS concepts. Understand entities and relationships.

Understand what structures make Object RDBMS.   Learn how Oracle implements the object relational database management system.

Know the tools.   Have an understanding of what tools are available for database management in Oracle and their purposes.

Learn the various architectures Oracle Database 12c can implement.   Oracle database can be installed as a single instance single database, multiple instance RAC database, or multitenant container database.

Identify Oracle Database 12c cloud features.   Know the features of Oracle Database 12c that make cloud implementation easier.

Review Questions

1. Look at the diagram. What kind of relationship exists between MOVIES and CHARACTERS?

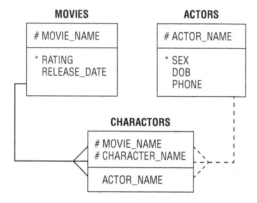

   A. Each movie may have one or more characters.

   B. Each movie must have one or more characters.

   C. Many movies may have many characters.

   D. One movie can have only one character.

2. When the physical model is being designed from the logical model, which element may be attributed as a table from the ER diagram?

   A. Relationship

   B. Attribute

   C. Unique identifier

   D. Entity

3. Which statement about the object type is true?

   A. They are structures that consist of built-in or user-defined data types.

   B. They are structures that consist of only built-in data types.

   C. They are structures that consist of only user-defined data types.

   D. Only one column in a table can be object type.

4. Which of the following is not a benefit of Oracle Database 12c?

   A. Manage multiple databases as one

   B. Fast provisioning of cloned databases

   C. Plug and unplug databases

   D. Patch each pluggable database separately

5. Which one of the following Oracle SQL*Plus command lines is not valid?

   A. `sqlplus <username>`

   B. `sqlplus @<connect_string>`

   C. `sqlplus <username>@<connect_string>`

   D. `sqlplus`

6. Which database tools are parts of Oracle Database 12*c*? Choose two.

   A. Oracle Enterprise Manager Cloud Control 12*c*

   B. Oracle Enterprise Manager Database Express 12*c*

   C. SQL Developer

   D. TOAD (Tool for Oracle Application Developers)

7. In the physical implementation of RDBMS, which database object is used to represent unique identifiers?

   A. Any constraint

   B. Index

   C. Primary key

   D. Foreign key

8. SQL Developer is a tool primarily for whom?

   A. Database administrators

   B. End users

   C. Application developers

   D. All of the above

9. Which architecture in the Oracle Database 12*c* implementation guards against unplanned machine downtime?

   A. Multitenancy Container Database

   B. Real Application Clusters

   C. Consolidate multiple databases and instances to one server

   D. None of the above

10. Which connection method to the Oracle database is known as the easy connect?

   A. `<username>@<connect_string>`

   B. `<username>@<host>:<port>/<service_name>`

   C. Both A and B

   D. Neither A or B

Chapter

2

Introducing SQL

ORACLE DATABASE 12*c*: SQL FUNDAMENTALS EXAM OBJECTIVES COVERED IN THIS CHAPTER:

✓ **Retrieving Data Using the SQL SELECT Statement**

- ▪ Explain the capabilities of SQL SELECT statements.

- ▪ Execute a basic SELECT statement.

✓ **Restricting and Sorting Data**

- ▪ Limit the rows that are retrieved by a query.

- ▪ Sort the rows that are retrieved by a query.

- ▪ Use ampersand substitution to restrict and sort output at runtime.

Oracle Database 12*c* is a very powerful and feature-rich relational database management system (RDBMS). SQL has been adopted by most RDBMSs for the retrieval and management of data, schema creation, and access control. The American National Standards Institute (ANSI) has been refining standards for the SQL language for more than 25 years. Oracle, like many other companies, has taken the ANSI standard of SQL and extended it to include much additional functionality.

SQL is the basic language used to manipulate and retrieve data from Oracle Database 12*c*. SQL is a nonprocedural language, meaning it does not have programmatic constructs such as loop structures. PL/SQL is Oracle's procedural extension of SQL, and SQLJ allows embedded SQL operations in Java code. The scope of the Oracle Database 12*c* SQL Fundamentals test includes only SQL.

In this chapter, we will discuss Oracle SQL fundamentals such as the various types of SQL statements, introduce SQL*Plus and a few SQL*Plus commands, and discuss SELECT statements.

You will learn how to write basic SQL statements to retrieve data from tables. This will include coverage of SQL SELECT statements, which are used to query data from the database-storage structures, such as tables and views. You will also learn how to limit the information retrieved and to display the results in a specific order.

SQL Fundamentals

SQL is the standard language used to query and modify data as well as manage databases. SQL is the common language used by programmers, database administrators, and users to access and manipulate data as well as to administer databases. To get started with SQL in this chapter, we will use the sample HR schema supplied with Oracle Database 12*c*.

SQL statements are like plain English but with specific syntax. SQL is a simple, yet powerful language used to create, access, and manipulate data and structures in the database. SQL statements can be categorized as listed in Table 2.1.

TABLE 2.1 SQL Statement Categories

SQL Category	Description
Data Manipulation Language (DML)	Used to access, insert, modify, or delete data in the existing structures of the database. DML statements include those used to query information (SELECT), add new rows (INSERT), modify existing rows (UPDATE), delete existing rows (DELETE), perform a conditional update or insert operation (MERGE), see an execution plan of SQL (EXPLAIN PLAN), and lock a table to restrict access (LOCK TABLE). Including the SELECT statement in the DML group is debatable within the SQL community, because SELECT does not modify data.
Data Definition Language (DDL)	Used to define, alter, or drop database objects and their privileges. DDL statements include those used to create, modify, drop, or rename objects (CREATE, ALTER, DROP, RENAME), remove all rows from a database object without dropping the structure (TRUNCATE), manage access privileges (GRANT, REVOKE), audit database use (AUDIT, NOAUDIT), and add a description about an object to the dictionary (COMMENT).
Transaction Control	Used to group a set of DML statements as a single transaction. Using these statements, you can save the changes (COMMIT) or discard the changes (ROLL-BACK) made by DML statements. Also included in the transaction-control statements are statements to set a point or marker in the transaction for possible roll-back (SAVEPOINT) and to define the properties for the transaction (SET TRANSACTION).
Session Control	Used to control the properties of a user session. (A session is the point from which you are connected to the database until you disconnect.) Session-control statements include those to control the session properties (ALTER SESSION) and to enable/disable roles (SET ROLE).
System Control	Used to manage the properties of the database. There is only one statement in this category (ALTER SYSTEM).

Table 2.1 provides an overview of all the statements that will be covered in this book. Do not worry if you do not understand certain terms, such as *role*, *session*, *privilege*, and so on. We will cover all the statements in the coming chapters and include many examples. In this chapter, we will begin by writing simple statements to query the database (SELECT statements), but we'll go over some fundamentals first.

This section provided an overview of SQL*Plus, the tool you will be using to enter and execute SQL statements in Oracle Database 12c. In the next sections, we will discuss some of the Oracle Database 12c SQL fundamentals before showing you how to write your first SQL query (a SELECT statement).

Oracle Datatypes

The basic structure of data storage in Oracle Database 12c is a table. A table can be considered as a spreadsheet with columns and rows. Data is stored in the table as rows. Each column in the table has storage characteristics such as the type of data contained in the column. Oracle has several built-in datatypes to store different kinds of data. In this section, we will go over the built-in datatypes available in Oracle Database 12c. Chapter 7, "Creating Tables and Constraints," includes a detailed discussion of datatypes and how to create and maintain tables.

When you create a table to store data in the database, you need to specify a datatype for all the columns you define in that table. Oracle has many datatypes to suit application requirements. Oracle Database 12c also supports ANSI and DB2 datatypes. The Oracle built-in datatypes can be broadly classified as shown in Table 2.2.

TABLE 2.2   Oracle Built-in Datatypes

Category	Datatypes
Character	CHAR, NCHAR, VARCHAR2, NVARCHAR2
Number	NUMBER, FLOAT, BINARY_FLOAT, BINARY_DOUBLE
Long and raw	LONG, LONG RAW, RAW
Date and time	DATE, TIMESTAMP, TIMESTAMP WITH TIME ZONE, TIMESTAMP WITH LOCAL TIME ZONE, INTERVAL YEAR TO MONTH, INTERVAL DAY TO SECOND
Large object	CLOB, NCLOB, BCLOB, BFILE
Row ID	ROWID, UROWID

In the following sections, we will discuss only a few of the built-in datatypes to get you started with SQL. We discuss all the datatypes and their usage in detail in Chapter 7.

CHAR(<size>) and VARCHAR2(<size>)

The *CHAR* datatype is a fixed-length alphanumeric string, which has a maximum length in bytes (to specify length in characters, use the CHAR keyword inside parentheses along with a size; see Chapter 7). Data stored in CHAR columns is space-padded to fill the maximum length. Its size can range from a minimum of 1 byte to a maximum of 2,000 bytes. The default size is 1.

When you create a column using the CHAR datatype, the database will ensure that all data placed in this column has the defined length. If the data is shorter than the defined length, it is space-padded on the right to the specified length. If the data inserted is longer than the column length, an error is raised.

The *VARCHAR2* datatype is a variable-length alphanumeric string, which has a maximum length in bytes (to specify the length in characters, use the CHAR keyword inside parentheses along with a size; see Chapter 7). VARCHAR2 columns require only the amount of space needed to store the data and can store up to 32KB (32,767 bytes). There is no default size for the VARCHAR2 datatype. An empty VARCHAR2(2000) column takes up as much room in the database as an empty VARCHAR2(1) column.

VARCHAR2 columns by default allow only 4,000 bytes or characters. To be able to store more than 4,000 bytes or characters, the MAX_STRING_SIZE database parameter needs to be set to EXTENDED. The default value of this parameter is STANDARD, which allows only 4,000 bytes in a VARCHAR2 column.

 The default size of a CHAR datatype is 1. For a VARCHAR2 datatype, you must always specify the size.

The VARCHAR2 and CHAR datatypes have different comparison rules for trailing spaces. With the CHAR datatype, trailing spaces are ignored. With the VARCHAR2 datatype, trailing spaces are not ignored, and they sort higher than no trailing spaces. Here's an example:

CHAR datatype: 'Yo' = 'Yo   '

VARCHAR2 datatype: 'Yo' < 'Yo   '

NUMBER (<p>, <s>)

The *NUMBER* datatype stores numbers with a precision of <p> digits and a scale of <s> digits. The precision and scale values are optional. Numeric datatypes are used to store negative and positive integers, fixed-point numbers, and floating-point numbers. The precision can be between 1 and 38, and the scale has a range between −84 and 127. If the precision and scale are omitted, Oracle assumes the maximum of the range for both values.

You can have precision and scale digits in the integer part. The scale rounds the value after the decimal point to <s> digits. For example, if you define a column as NUMBER(5,2), the range of values you can store in this column is from −999.99 to 999.99—that is, 5 − 2 = 3 for the integer part, and the decimal part is rounded to two digits. Even if you do not include the decimal part for the value inserted, the maximum number you can store in a NUMBER(5,2) definition is 999.

Oracle will round numbers inserted into numeric columns with a scale smaller than the inserted number. For example, if a column were defined as NUMBER(4,2) and you specified a value of 12.125 to go into that column, the resulting number would be rounded to 12.13 before it was inserted into the column. If the value exceeds the precision, however, an Oracle error is returned. You cannot insert 123.1 into a column defined as NUMBER(4,2). Specifying the scale and precision does not force all inserted values to be a fixed length.

If the scale is negative, the number is rounded to the left of the decimal. Basically, a negative scale forces <s> number of zeros just to the left of the decimal.

If you specify a scale that is greater than the precision value, the precision defines the maximum number of digits to the right of the decimal point after the zeros. For example, if a column is defined as NUMBER(3,5), the range of values you can store is from −0.00999 to 0.00999—that is, it requires two zeros (<s>-<p>) after the decimal point and rounds the decimal part to three digits (<p>) after zeros. Table 2.3 shows several examples of how numeric data is stored with various definitions.

TABLE 2.3   Precision and Scale Examples

Value	Datatype	Stored Value	Explanation
123.2564	NUMBER	123.2564	The range and precision are set to the maximum, so the datatype can store any value.
1234.9876	NUMBER(6,2)	1234.99	Because the scale is only 2, the decimal part of the value is rounded to two digits.
12345.12345	NUMBER(6,2)	Error	The range of the integer part is only from −9999 to 9999.
123456	NUMBER(6,2)	Error	The precision is larger than specified; the range is only from −9999 to 9999.
1234.9876	NUMBER(6)	1235	The decimal part is rounded to the next integer.
123456.1	NUMBER(6)	123456	The decimal part is rounded.
12345.345	NUMBER(5,-2)	12300	The negative scale rounds the number <s> digits left to the decimal point. −2 rounds to hundreds.
1234567	NUMBER(5,-2)	1234600	Rounded to the nearest hundred.
12345678	NUMBER(5,-2)	Error	Outside the range; can have only five digits, excluding the two zeros representing hundreds, for a total of seven digits: $(s - (-p)) = s + p = 5 + 2 = 7$.

Value	Datatype	Stored Value	Explanation
123456789	NUMBER(5,-4)	123460000	Rounded to the nearest 10,000.
1234567890	NUMBER(5,-4)	Error	Outside the range; can have only five digits, excluding the four trailing zeros.
12345.58	NUMBER(*, 1)	12345.6	The use of * in the precision specifies the default limit (38).
0.1	NUMBER(4,5)	Error	Requires a zero after the decimal point (5 − 4 = 1).
0.01234567	NUMBER(4,5)	0.01235	Rounded to four digits after the decimal point and zero.
0.09999	NUMBER(4,5)	0.09999	Stored as it is; only four digits after the decimal point and zero.
0.099996	NUMBER(4,5)	Error	Rounding this value to four digits after the decimal and zero results in 0.1, which is outside the range.

DATE

The *DATE* datatype is used to store date and time information. This datatype can be converted to other forms for viewing, but it has a number of special functions and properties that make date manipulation and calculations simple. The time component of the DATE datatype has a resolution of one second—no less. The DATE datatype occupies a storage space of 7 bytes. The following information is contained within each DATE datatype:

- Century
- Year
- Month
- Day
- Hour
- Minute
- Second

DATE datatype does not have fractional seconds or time zone. Date values are inserted or updated in the database by converting either a numeric value or a character value into a DATE datatype using the function TO_DATE. Oracle defaults the format to display the date as *DD-MON-YY* (the format is determined by parameter NLS_DATE_FORMAT). This format shows that the default date must begin with a two-digit day, followed by a three-character abbreviation for the month, followed by a two-digit year. If you specify the date without including a time component, the time is defaulted to midnight, or 00:00:00 in military time. The SYSDATE function returns the current system date and time from the database server to which you're currently connected.

TIMESTAMP [<precision>]

The *TIMESTAMP* datatype stores date and time information with fractional precision for seconds. The only difference between the DATE and TIMESTAMP datatypes is the ability to store fractional seconds up to a precision of nine digits. The default precision is 6 and can range from 0 to 9. Similar to the SYSDATE function, the SYSTIMESTAMP function returns the current system date and time, with fractional precision for seconds.

Operators and Literals

An *operator* is a manipulator that is applied to a data item in order to return a result. Special characters represent different operations in Oracle (+ represents addition, for example). Operators are commonly used in all programming environments, and you should already be familiar with the following operators, which may be classified into two types:

Unary Operator   A unary operator has only one operand. It has the format *<operator><operand>*. Examples are +2 and −5.

Binary Operator   A binary operator has two operands. It has the format *<operand1><operator><operand2>*. You can insert spaces between the operand and operator to improve readability. Examples are 5 + 4 and 7 × 5.

We'll now discuss the various types of operators available in Oracle.

Arithmetic Operators

Arithmetic operators operate on numeric values. Table 2.4 shows the various arithmetic operators in Oracle and how to use them.

TABLE 2.4   Arithmetic Operators

Operator	Purpose	Example
+ −	Unary operators: Used to represent positive or negative data item. For positive items, the + is optional.	−234.44
+	Addition: Used to add two data items or expressions.	2+4
−	Subtraction: Used to find the difference between two data items or expressions.	20.4−2
*	Multiplication: Used to multiply two data items or expressions.	5*10
/	Division: Used to divide a data item or expression with another.	8.4/2

WARNING | Do not use two hyphens (--) to represent double negation; use a space or parentheses in between, as in -(-20). Two hyphens represent the beginning of a comment in SQL.

Concatenation Operator

The *concatenation operator* is used to concatenate or join two character (text) strings. The result of concatenation is another character string. Concatenating a zero-length string ('') or a NULL with another string results in a string, not a NULL (NULL in Oracle Database 12*c* represents unknown or missing data). Two vertical bars (||) are used as the concatenation operator.

Here are two examples:

```
'Oracle12c' || 'Database' results in 'Oracle12cDatabase'.

'Oracle12c ' || 'Database' results in 'Oracle12c Database'.
```

Operator Precedence

If multiple operators are used in the same expression, Oracle evaluates them in the *order of precedence* set in the database engine. Table 2.5 lists the precedence. Operators with higher precedence are evaluated before operators with lower precedence. Operators with the same precedence are evaluated from left to right.

TABLE 2.5 SQL Operator Precedence

Precedence	Operator	Purpose
1	- +	Unary operators, negation
2	* /	Multiplication, division
3	+ - ||	Addition, subtraction, concatenation

Using parentheses changes the order of precedence. The innermost parenthesis is evaluated first. In the expression 1+2*3, the result is 7, because 2×3 is evaluated first and the result is added to 1. In the expression (1+2)*3, 1+2 is evaluated first, and the result is multiplied by 3, giving 9.

Literals

A *literal* is a value that represents a fixed value (constant). There are four types of literals:

- Text (or character)
- Numeric (integer and number)

- Datetime

- Interval

You can use literals within many of the SQL functions, expressions, and conditions.

Text Literals

A *text literal* must be enclosed in single quotation marks. Any character between the quotation marks is considered part of the text value. Oracle treats all text literals as though they were CHAR datatypes for comparison (blank padded). The maximum length of a text literal is 4,000 bytes if the database parameter MAX_STRING_SIZE is STANDARD. Single quotation marks can be included in the literal text value by preceding it with another single quotation mark. Here are some examples of text literals:

```
'The Quick Brown Fox'
'That man''s suit is black'
'And I quote: "This will never do." '
'12-SEP-2011'
```

Alternatively, you can use Q or q quoting, which provides a range of delimiters. The syntax for using the Q/q quoting with a quote-delimiter text literal is as follows:

```
[Q|q]' <quote_delimiter> <text literal> <quote_delimiter>'
```

<quote_delimiter> is any character except a space, tab, or carriage return. The quote delimiter can be a single quotation mark, but make sure inside the text literal a single quotation mark is not immediately followed by another single quotation mark. If the opening quote delimiter is [or { or < or (, then the closing quote must be the corresponding] or } or > or). For all other quote delimiters, the opening quote delimiter must be the same as the closing quote delimiter. Here are some examples of text literals using the alternative quoting mechanism:

```
q'<The Quick Brown Fox>'
Q'#The Quick Brown Fox#'
q'{That man's suit is black}'
Q'(And I quote: "This will never do." )'
Q'"And I quote: "This will never do." "'
q'[12-SEP-2001]'
```

Numeric Literals

Integer literals can be any number of numerals, excluding a decimal separator and up to 38 digits long. Here are two examples:

- 24

- −456

Number literals and *floating-point literals* can include scientific notation, as well as digits and the decimal separator. E or e represents a number in scientific notation; the exponent can be in the range of −130 to 125. If the literal is followed by an F or f, it is treated as a BINARY_FLOAT datatype. If the literal is followed by a D or d, it is treated as a BINARY_DOUBLE datatype. Here are some examples:

- 24.0
- −345.65
- 23E-10
- 1.5f
- −34.567D
- −4d
- −4.0E+0

Datetime Literals

You can specify a date value as a string literal using the *datetime literals*. The most common methods to represent the datetime values are to use the conversion function TO_DATE or TO_TIMESTAMP with the appropriate format mask. To complete this discussion of literals, we will discuss the datetime literals briefly.

The DATE literal uses the keyword DATE followed by the date value in single quotes, and the value must be specified in *YYYY-MM-DD* format with no time component. The time component will be defaulted to midnight (00:00:00). The following are examples of the DATE literal:

```
DATE '2008-03-24'
DATE '1999-12-31'
```

Similar to the TIMESTAMP datatype, the TIMESTAMP literal can be used to specify the year, month, date, hour, minute, second, and fractional second. You can also include time-zone data along with the TIMESTAMP literal. The time zone information can be specified using the UTC offset or using the time-zone region name. The literal must be in the format *YYYY-MM-DD HH24:MI:SS TZ*.

Here are some examples of the TIMESTAMP literal:

```
TIMESTAMP '2008-03-24 03:25:34.123'
TIMESTAMP '2008-03-24 03:25:34.123 -7:00'
TIMESTAMP '2008-03-24 03:25:34.123 US/Central'
TIMESTAMP '2008-03-24 03:25:34.123 US/Central CDT'
```

Interval Literals

Interval literals specify a period of time in terms of years and months or in terms of days and seconds. These literals correspond to the Oracle datatypes INTERVAL YEAR TO MONTH and INTERVAL DAY TO SECOND. We'll discuss these datatypes in more detail in Chapter 7.

Writing Simple Queries

A *query* is a request for information from the database tables. Queries do not modify data; they read data from database tables and views. Simple queries are those that retrieve data from a single table or view. A table is used to store data and is stored in rows and columns. The basis of a query is the SELECT statement. The SELECT statement can be used to get data from a single table or from multiple tables. Queries using multiple tables are discussed in later chapters.

Using the SELECT Statement

The SELECT statement is the most commonly used statement in SQL. It allows you to retrieve information already stored in the database. The statement begins with the keyword SELECT, followed by the names of the columns with data you want to query. You can select information either from all the columns (denoted by *) or from name-specific columns in the SELECT clause to retrieve data. When * is used in the column projection, it lists the columns in the same order as they are defined in the table definition. The FROM clause provides the name of the table, view, or materialized view to use in the query. These objects are discussed in detail in later chapters. For simplicity, we will use tables for the rest of this chapter.

The simple SELECT statement at a high level is of the form:

```
SELECT column_list
FROM table
WHERE filtering_conditions
ORDER BY column_list
OFFSET n_rows
FETCH row_limiting_conditions
```

The SELECT clause lists the columns from the table you are interested in reading. The FROM clause identifies the table name. The SELECT and FROM clauses are mandatory, and the rest of the clauses are optional. The FETCH clause is used to limit rows; the OFFSET clause is used to skip rows; the WHERE clause is used for filtering; and the ORDER BY clause is for sorting. We will discuss all of these clauses in detail in the coming sections of this chapter.

Let's use the JOBS table defined in the HR schema of Oracle Database 12*c*. You can use the SQL*Plus tool to connect to the database as discussed earlier in the chapter. The JOBS table definition is provided in Table 2.6.

TABLE 2.6 JOBS Table Definition

Column Name	Datatype	Length
JOB_ID	VARCHAR2	10
JOB_TITLE	VARCHAR2	35

Column Name	Datatype	Length
MIN_SALARY	NUMBER	6,0
MAX_SALARY	NUMBER	6,0

The simple form of a SELECT statement to retrieve all the columns and rows from the JOBS table is as follows (only part of output result set is shown here):

```
SQL> SELECT * FROM jobs;

JOB_ID     JOB_TITLE                       MIN_SALARY MAX_SALARY
---------- ------------------------------- ---------- ----------
AD_PRES    President                            20080      40000
AD_VP      Administration Vice President        15000      30000
AD_ASST    Administration Assistant              3000       6000
FI_MGR     Finance Manager                       8200      16000
FI_ACCOUNT Accountant                            4200       9000
... ... ... ... ...
IT_PROG    Programmer                            4000      10000
MK_MAN     Marketing Manager                     9000      15000
MK_REP     Marketing Representative              4000       9000
HR_REP     Human Resources Representative        4000       9000
PR_REP     Public Relations Representative       4500      10500

19 rows selected.
```

> The keywords, column names, and table names are not case sensitive. Only literals enclosed in single quotation marks are case sensitive in Oracle.

How do you list only the job title and minimum salary from this table? If you know the column names and the table name, writing the query is simple. Here, the column names are JOB_TITLE and MIN_SALARY, and the table name is JOBS. Execute the query by ending the query with a semicolon. In SQL*Plus, you can execute the query by entering a slash on a line by itself or by using the RUN command.

```
SQL> SELECT job_title, min_salary FROM jobs;

JOB_TITLE                          MIN_SALARY
---------------------------------- ----------
President                               20080
Administration Vice President           15000
```

```
Administration Assistant                      3000
Finance Manager                               8200
Accountant                                    4200
Accounting Manager                            8200
Public Accountant                             4200

... ... ... ... ...
Programmer                                    4000
Marketing Manager                             9000
Marketing Representative                      4000
Human Resources Representative                4000
Public Relations Representative               4500

19 rows selected.
```

Notice that the numeric column (MIN_SALARY) is aligned to the right, and the character column (JOB_TITLE) is aligned to the left. If you want the column heading MIN_SALARY to be more meaningful, you can provide a *column alias* to appear in the query results.

Column Alias Names

The column alias name is defined next to the column name with a space or by using the keyword AS. If you want a space in the column alias name, you must enclose it in double quotation marks. The case is preserved only when the alias name is enclosed in double quotation marks; otherwise, the display will be uppercase. The following example demonstrates using an alias name for the column heading in the previous query:

```
SELECT job_title AS Title, min_salary AS "Minimum Salary"
FROM jobs;
```

```
TITLE                                 Minimum Salary
----------------------------------    --------------
President                                      20080
Administration Vice President                  15000
Administration Assistant                        3000
Finance Manager                                 8200
Accountant                                      4200
Accounting Manager                              8200

... ... ... ... ...
Programmer                                      4000
Marketing Manager                               9000
Marketing Representative                        4000
Human Resources Representative                  4000
```

```
Public Relations Representative                 4500
```

```
19 rows selected.
```

In this listing, the column alias name `Title` appears in all capital letters because it was not enclosed in double quotation marks.

 The asterisk (*) is used to select all columns in the table. This is useful when you do not know the column names or when you are too lazy to type all the column names. The invisible columns and pseudo columns are not included in *.

Ensuring Uniqueness

The `DISTINCT` keyword (or `UNIQUE` keyword) following `SELECT` ensures that the resulting rows are unique. Uniqueness is verified against the complete row, not the first column. If you need to find the unique departments in the `EMPLOYEES` table, issue this query:

```
SELECT DISTINCT department_id
FROM employees;
```

```
DEPARTMENT_ID
-------------
          100
           30

           90
           20
           70
          110
           50
           80
           40
           60
           10
```

```
12 rows selected.
```

To demonstrate that uniqueness is enforced across the row, let's do one more query using the `SELECT DISTINCT` clause. Notice `DEPARTMENT_ID` repeating for each `JOB_ID` value in the following example:

```
SELECT DISTINCT department_id, job_id
FROM employees;
```

```
DEPARTMENT_ID JOB_ID
------------- ----------
          110 AC_ACCOUNT
           90 AD_VP
           50 ST_CLERK
           80 SA_REP
          110 AC_MGR
...  ...  ...
           10 AD_ASST
           20 MK_REP
           40 HR_REP
           30 PU_MAN

20 rows selected.
```

> SELECT * FROM TAB; shows all the tables and views in your schema. Don't be alarmed if you see a table name similar to BIN$PJV23QpwQfu0zPN9uaX w+w==$0. These are tables that belong to the Recycle Bin (or dropped tables). The tasks of creating tables and managing tables are discussed in Chapter 7.

The DUAL Table

The DUAL table is a special table available to all users in the database. It has one column and one row. Oracle optimized the database so that it no longer performs physical or logical input/output on the DUAL table. The DUAL table is mostly used to select system variables or to evaluate an expression. Here are a few examples. The first query is to show the contents of the DUAL table.

```
SQL> SELECT * FROM dual;

D
-
X

SQL> SELECT SYSDATE, USER FROM dual;

SYSDATE   USER
--------- -----------------------------
13-JUL-13 HR
```

```
SQL> SELECT 'I''m ' || user || ' Today is ' || SYSDATE
  2  FROM dual;


'I''M'||USER||'TODAYIS'||SYSDATE
-------------------------------------------------------
I'm HR Today is 13-JUL-13


SQL>
```

SYSDATE and USER are built-in functions that provide information about the environment. These functions are discussed in Chapter 3, "Using Single-Row Functions."

Filtering Rows

You can use the WHERE clause in the SELECT statement to restrict the number of rows processed. Any logical conditions of the WHERE clause use the comparison operators. Rows are returned or operated upon where the data satisfies the logical condition(s) of the WHERE clause. You can use column names or expressions in the WHERE clause, but not column alias names. The WHERE clause follows the FROM clause in the SELECT statement.

How do you list the employees who work for department 90? The following example shows how to limit the query to only the records belonging to department 90 by using a WHERE clause:

```
SELECT first_name || ' ' || last_name "Name", department_id
FROM    employees
WHERE   department_id = 90;


Name                                       DEPARTMENT_ID
------------------------------------------ -------------
Steven King                                           90
Neena Kochhar                                         90
Lex De Haan                                           90
```

You need not include the column names in the SELECT clause to use them in the WHERE clause.

You can use various operators in Oracle Database 12c in the WHERE clause to limit the number of rows.

Comparison Operators

Comparison operators compare two values or expressions and give a Boolean result of TRUE, FALSE, or NULL. The comparison operators include those that test for equality, inequality, less than, greater than, and value comparisons.

= (Equality)

The = operator tests for equality. The test evaluates to TRUE if the values or results of an expression on both sides of the operator are equal. The following shows an example of finding all the employees belonging to department 90—that is, the department ID is equal to 90:

```
SELECT first_name || ' ' || last_name "Name", department_id
FROM    employees
WHERE   department_id = 90;
```

```
Name                                        DEPARTMENT_ID
------------------------------------------- --------------
Steven King                                            90
Neena Kochhar                                          90
Lex De Haan                                            90
```

!=, <>, or ^= (Inequality)

You can use any one of these three operators to test for inequality. The test evaluates to TRUE if the values on both sides of the operator do not match. The following shows an example of querying employees whose commission is not the default 35 percent—that is, to find all employees with a commission percent that is not 35:

```
SELECT first_name || ' ' || last_name "Name", commission_pct
FROM    employees
WHERE   commission_pct != .35;
```

```
Name                                        COMMISSION_PCT
------------------------------------------- --------------
John Russell                                            .4
Karen Partners                                          .3
Alberto Errazuriz                                       .3
Gerald Cambrault                                        .3
... ... ... ... ... ...
Jack Livingston                                         .2
Kimberely Grant                                        .15
Charles Johnson                                         .1

32 rows selected.
```

< (Less Than)

The < operator evaluates to TRUE if the left side (expression or value) of the operator is less than the right side of the operator. The following shows an example of employees with a commission percent less than 15:

```
SELECT first_name || ' ' || last_name "Name", commission_pct
FROM    employees
WHERE   commission_pct < .15;
```

```
Name                                     COMMISSION_PCT
---------------------------------------- --------------
Mattea Marvins                                       .1
David Lee                                            .1
Sundar Ande                                          .1
Amit Banda                                           .1
Sundita Kumar                                        .1
Charles Johnson                                      .1

6 rows selected.
```

> (Greater Than)

The > operator evaluates to TRUE if the left side (expression or value) of the operator is greater than the right side of the operator. The following shows an example of employees with a commission percent over 35:

```
SELECT first_name || ' ' || last_name "Name", commission_pct
FROM    employees
WHERE   commission_pct > .35;
```

```
Name                                     COMMISSION_PCT
---------------------------------------- --------------
John Russell                                         .4
```

<= (Less Than or Equal To)

The <= operator evaluates to TRUE if the left side (expression or value) of the operator is less than or equal to the right side of the operator. The following shows an example similar to the one for less than, but here we include all employees who have a commission percent less than 15 or equal to 15:

```
SELECT first_name || ' ' || last_name "Name", commission_pct
FROM    employees
WHERE   commission_pct <= .15;
```

Name	COMMISSION_PCT
Oliver Tuvault	.15
Danielle Greene	.15
Mattea Marvins	.1
David Lee	.1
Sundar Ande	.1
Amit Banda	.1
William Smith	.15
Elizabeth Bates	.15
Sundita Kumar	.1
Kimberely Grant	.15
Charles Johnson	.1

11 rows selected.

>= (Greater Than or Equal To)

The >= operator evaluates to TRUE if the left side (expression or value) of the operator is greater than or equal to the right side of the operator. The following shows an example of employees with commission percent at or over 35:

```
SELECT first_name || ' ' || last_name "Name", commission_pct
FROM    employees
WHERE   commission_pct >= .35;
```

Name	COMMISSION_PCT
John Russell	.4
Janette King	.35
Patrick Sully	.35
Allan McEwen	.35

ANY or SOME

You can use the ANY or SOME (both are the same and can be used interchangeably) operator to compare a value to each value in a list or subquery. The ANY and SOME operators always must be preceded by one of the following comparison operators: =, !=, <, >, <=, or >=. Consider the following SQL with ANY operator:

```
SELECT first_name || ' ' || last_name "Name", department_id
FROM    employees
WHERE   department_id <= ANY (10, 15, 20, 25);
```

Name	DEPARTMENT_ID
Jennifer Whalen	10
Michael Hartstein	20
Pat Fay	20

Oracle in fact expands the ANY condition to department_id <= 10 OR department_id <= 15 OR department_id <= 20 OR department_id <= 25. The behavior of ANY with each comparison operator is

X = ANY (*list*): Evaluates to TRUE if value of X matches at least one value in the list.

X != ANY (*list*): Evaluates to TRUE if value of X does not match one or more value in the list.

X > ANY (*list*): Evaluates to TRUE if value of X is higher than the smallest value in the list.

X < ANY (*list*): Evaluates to TRUE if value of X is lower than the biggest value in the list.

X >= ANY (*list*): Evaluates to TRUE if value of X is higher than or equal to the smallest value in the list.

X <= ANY (*list*): Evaluates to TRUE if value of X is lower than or equal to the biggest value in the list.

ALL

You can use the ALL operator to compare a value to every value in a list or subquery. The ALL operator must always be preceded by one of the following comparison operators: =, !=, <, >, <=, or >=. The following shows an example of using the ALL operator:

```
SELECT first_name || ' ' || last_name "Name", department_id
FROM    employees
WHERE   department_id >= ALL (80, 90, 100);
```

Name	DEPARTMENT_ID
Nancy Greenberg	100
Daniel Faviet	100
John Chen	100
Ismael Sciarra	100
Jose Manuel Urman	100
Luis Popp	100
Shelley Higgins	110
William Gietz	110

8 rows selected.

The SQL code is evaluated by Oracle as `department_id >= 80 AND department_id >= 90 AND department_id >= 100`. The behavior of `ALL` with each comparison operator is

X = `ALL` (*list*): Evaluates to TRUE if value of X matches all of the values in the list.

X != `ALL` (*list*): Evaluates to TRUE if value of X does not match any value in the list.

X > `ALL` (*list*): Evaluates to TRUE if value of X is higher than the biggest value in the list.

X < `ALL` (*list*): Evaluates to TRUE if value of X is lower than the smallest value in the list.

X >= `ALL` (*list*): Evaluates to TRUE if value of X is higher than or equal to the highest value in the list.

X <= `ALL` (*list*): Evaluates to TRUE if value of X is lower than or equal to the smallest value in the list.

The `ANY`, `SOME`, and `ALL` operators make more sense when used with subqueries rather than a list of known values. Subqueries are discussed in Chapter 5, "Using Joins and Subqueries."

For all the comparison operators discussed, if one side of the operator is NULL, the result is NULL. At least one question with the ANY, ALL operator will be on the OCA test, so make sure you understand these operators thoroughly.

Logical Operators

Logical operators are used to combine the results of two comparison conditions (compound conditions) to produce a single result or to reverse the result of a single comparison. NOT, AND, and OR are the logical operators. When a logical operator is applied to NULL, the result is UNKNOWN. UNKNOWN acts similarly to FALSE; the only difference is that NOT FALSE is TRUE, whereas NOT UNKNOWN is also UNKNOWN.

NOT

You can use the NOT operator to reverse the result. It evaluates to TRUE if the operand is FALSE, and it evaluates to FALSE if the operand is TRUE. NOT returns NULL if the operand is NULL. The following shows an example of employees that do not belong to department number greater or equal to 30—that is, it basically evaluates to department number less than 30:

```
SELECT first_name, department_id
FROM   employees
WHERE  not (department_id >= 30);


FIRST_NAME           DEPARTMENT_ID
-------------------- --------------
Jennifer                        10
```

```
Michael                    20
Pat                        20
```

AND

The AND operator evaluates to TRUE if both operands are TRUE. It evaluates to FALSE if either operand is FALSE. Otherwise, it returns NULL. The following shows an example of employees with the last name Smith and a salary over $7,500. Both conditions must evaluate to TRUE:

```
SELECT first_name, salary
FROM   employees
WHERE  last_name = 'Smith'
AND    salary    > 7500;


FIRST_NAME                SALARY
-------------------- ----------
Lindsey                     8000
```

OR

The OR operator evaluates to TRUE if either operand is TRUE. It evaluates to FALSE if both operands are FALSE. Otherwise, it returns NULL. The following shows an example of employees whose last name is Smith or whose first name is Kelly. Either one condition must evaluate to TRUE:

```
SELECT first_name, last_name
FROM   employees
WHERE  first_name = 'Kelly'
OR     last_name  = 'Smith';


FIRST_NAME           LAST_NAME
-------------------- -------------------------
Kelly                Chung
Lindsey              Smith
William              Smith
```

Logical Operator Truth Tables

The following tables are the truth tables for the three logical operators.

Table 2.7 is a truth table for the AND operator.

TABLE 2.7 AND Truth Table

AND	TRUE	FALSE	UNKNOWN
TRUE	TRUE	FALSE	UNKNOWN
FALSE	FALSE	FALSE	FALSE
UNKNOWN	UNKNOWN	FALSE	UNKNOWN

Table 2.8 is the truth table for the OR operator.

TABLE 2.8 OR Truth Table

OR	TRUE	FALSE	UNKNOWN
TRUE	TRUE	TRUE	TRUE
FALSE	TRUE	FALSE	UNKNOWN
UNKNOWN	TRUE	UNKNOWN	UNKNOWN

Table 2.9 is the truth table for the NOT operator.

TABLE 2.9 NOT Truth Table

NOT	
TRUE	FALSE
FALSE	TRUE
UNKNOWN	UNKNOWN

Other Operators

In the following sections, we will discuss the operators that can be used in the WHERE clause of the SQL statement that were not discussed earlier.

IN and NOT IN

You can use the IN and NOT IN operators to test a membership condition. IN is equivalent to the =ANY operator, which evaluates to TRUE if the value exists in the list or the result set from a subquery. The NOT IN operator is equivalent to the !=ALL operator, which evaluates to TRUE if the value does not exist in the list or the result set from a subquery. The following examples demonstrate how to use these two operators:

```
SELECT first_name, last_name, department_id
FROM    employees
WHERE   department_id IN (10, 20, 90);
```

FIRST_NAME	LAST_NAME	DEPARTMENT_ID
Jennifer	Whalen	10
Michael	Hartstein	20
Pat	Fay	20
Steven	King	90
Neena	Kochhar	90
Lex	De Haan	90

6 rows selected.

FIRST_NAME	LAST_NAME	DEPARTMENT_ID
Hermann	Baer	70
Pat	Fay	20
Michael	Hartstein	20

SQL>

WARNING   When using the NOT IN operator, if any value in the list or the result returned from the subquery is NULL, the NOT IN condition is evaluated to FALSE. For example, last_name not in ('Smith', 'Thomas', NULL) evaluates to last_name != 'Smith' AND last_name != 'Thomas' AND last_name != NULL. Any comparison on a NULL value results in NULL. So the previous condition does not return any row even though there may be some rows with LAST_NAME as Smith or Thomas.

BETWEEN

You can use the BETWEEN operator to test a range. BETWEEN *A* AND *B* evaluates to TRUE if the value is greater than or equal to *A* and less than or equal to *B*. If NOT is used, the result is the reverse. The following example lists all the employees whose salary is between $5,000 and $6,000:

```
SELECT first_name, last_name, salary
FROM    employees
```

```
WHERE  salary BETWEEN 5000 AND 6000;
```

FIRST_NAME	LAST_NAME	SALARY
Bruce	Ernst	6000
Kevin	Mourgos	5800
Pat	Fay	6000

EXISTS

The EXISTS operator is always followed by a subquery in parentheses. EXISTS evaluates to TRUE if the subquery returns at least one row. The following example lists the employees who work for the administration department. Here is an example of using EXISTS:

```
SELECT last_name, first_name, department_id
FROM    employees e
WHERE   EXISTS (select 1 FROM departments d
        WHERE  d.department_id = e.department_id
        AND    d.department_name = 'Administration');
```

LAST_NAME	FIRST_NAME	DEPARTMENT_ID
Whalen	Jennifer	10

```
SQL>
```

 NOTE   Don't worry if you do not understand the SQL examples now; subqueries are discussed in detail in Chapter 5.

IS NULL and IS NOT NULL

To find the NULL values or NOT NULL values, you need to use the IS NULL operator. The = or != operator will not work with NULL values. IS NULL evaluates to TRUE if the value is NULL. IS NOT NULL evaluates to TRUE if the value is not NULL. To find the employees who do not have a department assigned, use this query:

```
SELECT last_name, department_id
FROM    employees
WHERE   department_id IS NULL;
```

LAST_NAME	DEPARTMENT_ID
Grant	

```
SQL>
SELECT last_name, department_id
FROM employees
WHERE department_id = NULL;
```

```
No rows selected.
```

LIKE

Using the LIKE operator, you can perform pattern matching. The pattern-search character % is used to match any character and any number of characters. The pattern-search character _ is used to match any single character. If you are looking for the actual character % or _ in the pattern search, you can include an escape character in the search string and notify Oracle using the ESCAPE clause.

The following query searches for all employees whose first name begins with *Su* and whose last name does not begin with *S*:

```
SELECT first_name, last_name
FROM    employees
WHERE   first_name LIKE 'Su%'
AND     last_name NOT LIKE 'S%';
```

```
FIRST_NAME           LAST_NAME
-------------------- -------------------------
Sundar               Ande
Sundita              Kumar
Susan                Mavris
```

The following example looks for all JOB_ID values that begin with *AC_*. Because _ is a pattern-matching character, you must qualify it with an escape character. Oracle does not have a default escape character.

```
SELECT job_id, job_title
FROM    jobs
WHERE   job_id like 'AC\_%' ESCAPE '\';
```

```
JOB_ID     JOB_TITLE
---------- ----------------------------------
AC_MGR     Accounting Manager
AC_ACCOUNT Public Accountant
```

Table 2.10 shows more examples of pattern matching.

TABLE 2.10 Pattern-Matching Examples

Pattern	Matches	Does Not Match
%SONI_1	SONIC1, ULTRASONI21	SONICS1, SONI315
_IME	TIME, LIME	IME, CRIME
\%SONI_1 ESCAPE '\'	%SONIC1, %SONI91	SONIC1, ULTRASONIC1
%ME_ _ _LE ESCAPE '\'	CRIME_FILE, TIME_POLE	CRIMESPILE, CRIME_ALE

Sorting Rows

The SELECT statement may include the ORDER BY clause to sort the resulting rows in a specific order based on the data in the columns. Without the ORDER BY clause, there is no guarantee that the rows will be returned in any specific order. If an ORDER BY clause is specified, by default the rows are returned in ascending order of the columns specified. If you need to sort the rows in descending order, use the keyword DESC next to the column name. You can specify the keyword ASC to explicitly state to sort in ascending order, although it is the default. The ORDER BY clause follows the FROM clause and the WHERE clause in the SELECT statement.

To retrieve all employee names of department 90 from the EMPLOYEES table ordered by last name, use this query:

```
SELECT first_name || ' ' || last_name "Employee Name"
FROM    employees
WHERE   department_id = 90
ORDER BY last_name;


Employee Name
---------------------------------------------
Lex De Haan
Steven King
Neena Kochhar
SQL>
```

You can specify more than one column in the ORDER BY clause. In this case, the result set will be ordered by the first column in the ORDER BY clause, then the second, and so on. Columns or expressions not used in the SELECT clause can also be used in the ORDER BY clause. The following example shows how to use DESC and multiple columns in the ORDER BY clause:

```
SELECT first_name, hire_date, salary, manager_id mid
FROM    employees
```

```
WHERE   department_id IN (110,100)
ORDER BY mid ASC, salary DESC, hire_date;

FIRST_NAME              HIRE_DATE    SALARY         MID
--------------------    ---------    ----------    ----------

Shelley                 07-JUN-02     12008         101
Nancy                   17-AUG-02     12008         101
Daniel                  16-AUG-02      9000         108
John                    28-SEP-05      8200         108
Jose Manuel             07-MAR-06      7800         108
Ismael                  30-SEP-05      7700         108
Luis                    07-DEC-07      6900         108
William                 07-JUN-02      8300         205


8 rows selected.
SQL>
```

   You can use column alias names in the ORDER BY clause.

If the DISTINCT keyword is used in the SELECT clause, you can use only those columns listed in the SELECT clause in the ORDER BY clause. If you have used any operators on columns in the SELECT clause, the ORDER BY clause also should use them. Here is an example:

```
SELECT DISTINCT 'Region ' || region_id
FROM    countries
ORDER BY region_id;

ORDER BY region_id
         *
ERROR at line 3:
ORA-01791: not a SELECTed expression

SELECT DISTINCT 'Region ' || region_id
FROM    countries
ORDER BY 'Region ' || region_id;

'REGION'||REGION_ID
---------------------------------------------

Region 1
Region 2
```

Region 3
Region 4

Not only can you use the column name or column alias to sort the result set of a query, but you can also sort the results by specifying the position of the column in the SELECT clause. This is useful if you have a lengthy expression in the SELECT clause and you need the results sorted on this value. The following example sorts the result set using positional values:

```
SELECT first_name, hire_date, salary, manager_id mid
FROM    employees
WHERE   department_id IN (110,100)
ORDER BY 4, 2, 3;
```

```
FIRST_NAME              HIRE_DATE   SALARY        MID
--------------------    ---------   ----------    ----------
Shelley                 07-JUN-02   12008         101
Nancy                   17-AUG-02   12008         101
Daniel                  16-AUG-02   9000          108
John                    28-SEP-05   8200          108
Ismael                  30-SEP-05   7700          108
Jose Manuel             07-MAR-06   7800          108
Luis                    07-DEC-07   6900          108
William                 07-JUN-02   8300          205

8 rows selected.
```

 The ORDER BY clause cannot have more than 255 columns or expressions.

Sorting NULLs

By default, in an ascending-order sort, the NULL values appear at the bottom of the result set—that is, NULLs are sorted higher. For descending-order sorts, NULL values appear at the top of the result set—again, NULL values are sorted higher. You can change the default behavior by using the NULLS FIRST or NULLS LAST keyword, along with the column names (or alias names or positions). The following examples demonstrate how to use NULLS FIRST in an ascending sort:

```
SELECT last_name, commission_pct
FROM    employees
WHERE   last_name LIKE 'R%'
ORDER BY commission_pct ASC, last_name DESC;
```

```
LAST_NAME                    COMMISSION_PCT
------------------------     --------------
Russell                                  .4
Rogers
Raphaely
Rajs


SELECT last_name, commission_pct
FROM    employees
WHERE   last_name LIKE 'R%'
ORDER BY commission_pct ASC NULLS FIRST, last_name DESC;


LAST_NAME                    COMMISSION_PCT
------------------------     --------------
Rogers
Raphaely
Rajs
Russell                                  .4
SQL>
```

 Real World Scenario

Why Do You Limit and Sort Rows?

The power of an RDBMS and SQL lies in getting exactly what you want from the database. The sample tables you considered under the HR schema are small, so even if you get all the information from the table, you can still find the specific data you're seeking. But what if you have a huge transaction table with millions of rows?

You know how easy it is to look through a catalog in the library to find a particular book or to search through an alphabetical listing to find your name. When querying a large table, make sure you know what you want.

The WHERE clause lets you query for exactly what you're seeking. The ORDER BY clause lets you sort rows. The following steps can be used as an approach to query data from a single table:

1. Know the columns of the table. You can issue the DESCRIBE command to get the column names and datatype. Understand which column has what information.

2. Pick the column names you are interested in including in the query. Use these columns in the SELECT clause.

3. Identify the column or columns where you can limit the rows, or the columns that can show you only the rows of interest. Use these columns in the WHERE clause of the query, and supply the values as well as the appropriate operator.

4. If the query returns more than a few rows, you may be interested in having them sorted in a particular order. Specify the column names and the sorting order in the ORDER BY clause of the query.

Let's consider a table named PURCHASE_ORDERS. First, use the DESCRIBE command to list the columns:

```
SQL> DESCRIBE purchase_orders
```

Name	Null?	Type
ORDER#	NOT NULL	NUMBER (16)
ORDER_DT	NOT NULL	DATE
CUSTOMER#	NOT NULL	VARCHAR2 (12)
BACK_ORDER		CHAR (1)
ORD_STATUS		CHAR (1)
TOTAL_AMT	NOT NULL	NUMBER (18,4)
SALES_TAX		NUMBER (12,2)

The objective of the query is to find the completed orders that do not have any sales tax. You want to see the order number and total amount of the order. The corresponding columns that appear in the SELECT clause are ORDER# and TOTAL_AMT. Because you're interested in only the rows with no sales tax in the completed orders, the columns to appear in the WHERE clause are SALES_TAX (checking for zero sales tax) and ORD_STATUS (checking for the completeness of the order, which is status code C). Because the query returns multiple rows, you want to order them by the order number. Notice that the SALES_TAX column can be NULL, so you want to make sure you get all rows that have a sales tax amount of zero or NULL.

```
SELECT order#, total_amt
FROM    purchase_orders
WHERE   ord_status = 'C'
AND     (sales_tax IS NULL
OR       sales_tax = 0)
ORDER BY order#;
```

An alternative is to use the NVL function to deal with the NULL values. This function is discussed in Chapter 3.

Limiting Rows

The row-limiting clause in the SELECT statement follows the ORDER BY clause, if used. Use the OFFSET and FETCH clauses to limit the number of rows retrieved by specifying a certain number of rows or certain percent of rows to be retrieved. The WHERE clause and FETCH clause are used to restrict the amount of rows returned in the query. WHERE is used for filtering the rows; FETCH is used for limiting the rows.

The OFFSET clause is optional and used to skip a specified number of rows before the retrieval begins. If the offset is higher than the number of rows retrieved or is NULL, no rows are returned. The ROW and ROWS keywords are optional and used only for readability. You need not provide the ROW or ROWS keyword when using the FETCH and OFFSET clauses.

The FETCH clause can specify the number of rows to return or a percentage of rows to return. The FIRST and NEXT keywords can be used interchangeably and are for semantic clarity only. Either one must be used.

The following examples clarify the use of the row-limiting clauses in SELECT. First, show the top five salary-earned employees:

```
SELECT first_name, department_id, salary
FROM employees
ORDER BY salary DESC
FETCH FIRST 5 ROWS ONLY;
```

FIRST_NAME	DEPARTMENT_ID	SALARY
Steven	90	24000
Neena	90	17000
Lex	90	17000
John	80	14000
Karen	80	13500

If there is a tie in the last row, using the WITH TIES clause instead of the ONLY clause will retrieve all rows with ties. The ONLY or WITH TIES keyword must always be used with the FETCH clause. In the following example, the top two salaried employees are queried. Because there is a tie for the second position, all tied records are retrieved:

```
SELECT first_name, department_id, salary
FROM employees
ORDER BY salary DESC
FETCH FIRST 2 ROWS WITH TIES;
```

FIRST_NAME	DEPARTMENT_ID	SALARY
Steven	90	24000
Neena	90	17000
Lex	90	17000

The OFFSET clause is used to skip rows before the limiting begins. The following example shows the third through fifth position in salary:

```
SELECT first_name, department_id, salary
FROM employees
ORDER BY salary DESC
OFFSET 2 ROWS
FETCH NEXT 3 ROWS WITH TIES;
```

```
FIRST_NAME            DEPARTMENT_ID    SALARY
--------------------  -------------- ----------

Lex                              90     17000
John                             80     14000
Karen                            80     13500
```

There are 107 rows in the EMPLOYEES table; instead of number of rows, you may limit using a PERCENT. The ONLY or WITH TIES keyword is a must whether using ROWS or PERCENT in the FETCH clause. The following example shows using PERCENT to retrieve 5 percent rows from the EMPLOYEES table:

```
SELECT first_name, salary
FROM employees
FETCH FIRST 5 PERCENT ROWS ONLY;
```

```
FIRST_NAME                SALARY
--------------------  ----------

Steven                     24000
Neena                      17000
Lex                        17000
Alexander                   9000
Bruce                       6000
David                       4800
type="tip"
```

Using the ORDER BY clause with the FETCH clause is not mandatory but is highly recommended to achieve a consistent result set.

Using Expressions

An *expression* is a combination of one or more values, operators, and SQL functions that result in a value. The result of an expression generally assumes the datatype of its components.

The simple expression 5 + 6 evaluates to 11 and assumes a datatype of NUMBER. Expressions can appear in the following clauses:

- The SELECT clause of queries
- The WHERE clause, ORDER BY clause, and HAVING clause
- The VALUES clause of the INSERT statement
- The SET clause of the UPDATE statement

 We will review the syntax of using a HAVING clause and INSERT, UPDATE statements in later chapters.

You can include parentheses to group and evaluate expressions and then apply the result to the rest of the expression. When parentheses are used, the expression in the innermost parentheses is evaluated first. Here is an example of a compound expression:

```
((2*4)/(3+1))*10.
```

The result of 2*4 is divided by the result of 3+1. Then the result from the division operation is multiplied by 10.

The CASE Expression

You can use the CASE expression to derive the IF…THEN…ELSE logic in SQL. Here is the syntax of the simple CASE expression:

```
CASE <expression>
WHEN <compare value> THEN <return value> … … …
[ELSE <return value>]
END
```

The CASE expression begins with the keyword CASE and ends with the keyword END. The ELSE clause is optional. The maximum number of arguments in a CASE expression is 255. The following query displays a description for the REGION_ID column based on the value:

```
SELECT country_name, region_id,
       CASE region_id WHEN 1 THEN 'Europe'
                      WHEN 2 THEN 'America'
                      WHEN 3 THEN 'Asia'
                      ELSE 'Other' END Continent
FROM    countries
WHERE   country_name LIKE 'I%';
```

```
COUNTRY_NAME          REGION_ID CONTINE
-------------------- ---------- -------
Israel                        4 Other
India                         3 Asia
Italy                         1 Europe
SQL>
```

The other form of the CASE expression is the searched CASE, where the values are derived based on a condition. Oracle evaluates the conditions top to bottom; when a condition evaluates to true, the rest of the WHEN clauses are not evaluated. This version has the following syntax:

```
CASE
WHEN <condition> THEN <return value> … … …
[ELSE <return value>]
END
```

The following example categorizes the salary as Low, Medium, and High using a searched CASE expression:

```
SELECT first_name, department_id, salary,
       CASE WHEN salary < 6000 THEN 'Low'
            WHEN salary < 10000 THEN 'Medium'
            WHEN salary >= 10000 THEN 'High' END Category
FROM   employees
WHERE department_id <= 30
ORDER BY first_name;
```

```
FIRST_NAME           DEPARTMENT_ID    SALARY CATEGO
-------------------- ------------- ---------- ------
Alexander                       30       3100 Low
Den                             30      11000 High
Guy                             30       2600 Low
Jennifer                        10       4400 Low
Karen                           30       2500 Low
Michael                         20      13000 High
Pat                             20       6000 Medium
Shelli                          30       2900 Low
Sigal                           30       2800 Low

9 rows selected.
```

Oracle uses the ampersand (&) character to substitute values at runtime. In the next section, we will discuss how to create SQL statements that can be used to get a different set of results based on values passed during execution time.

Real World Scenario

Finding the Current Sessions and Program Name

As a DBA, you may have to query the V$SESSION dictionary view to find the current sessions in the database. This view has several columns that provide information about the session; often the DBA is interested in finding out the username and which program is connecting to the database. If the DBA wants to find out what SQL is executed in the session, the SID and SERIAL# columns can be queried to enable tracing using the DBMS_TRACE package.

This example will review how to query the V$SESSION view using the simple SQL statements you learned in this chapter.

The following query may return several rows depending on the activity and number of users connected to the database:

```
SELECT username, sid, serial#, program
FROM v$session;
```

If you're using SQL*Plus, you may have to adjust the column width to fit the output in one line:

```
COLUMN program FORMAT a20
COLUMN username FORMAT a20
SELECT username, sid, serial#, program
FROM v$session;
```

```
USERNAME                    SID     SERIAL# PROGRAM
-------------------- ---------- ---------- -----------------
                            118       6246 ORACLE.EXE (W000)
BTHOMAS                     121        963 sqlplus.exe
DBSNMP                      124      23310 emagent.exe
DBSNMP                      148        608 emagent.exe
                            150          1 ORACLE.EXE (FBDA)
                            152          7 ORACLE.EXE (SMCO)
                            155          1 ORACLE.EXE (MMNL)
                            156          1 ORACLE.EXE (DIA0)
```

```
                         158           1 ORACLE.EXE  (MMON)
                         159           1 ORACLE.EXE  (RECO)
                         164           1 ORACLE.EXE  (MMAN)
... ... ...  (Output truncated)
```

As you can see, the background processes do not have usernames. To find out only the user sessions in the database, you can filter out the rows that do not have valid usernames:

```
SELECT username, sid, serial#, program
FROM v$session
WHERE username is NOT NULL;
```

If you're looking for specific information, you may want to add more filter conditions such as looking for a specific user or a specific program. The following SQL code returns the rows in order of their session login time, with the most recent session on the top:

```
SELECT username, sid, serial#, program
FROM v$session
WHERE username is NOT NULL
ORDER BY logon_time;
```

```
USERNAME                    SID     SERIAL# PROGRAM
-------------------- ---------- ---------- ---------------

DBSNMP                      148        608 emagent.exe
DBSNMP                      124      23310 emagent.exe
BTHOMAS                     121        963 sqlplus.exe
SCOTT                       132         23 TOAD.EXE
SJACOB                      231         32 discoverer.exe
```

Accepting Values at Runtime

To create an interactive SQL statement, you can define variables in the SQL statement. This allows the user to supply values at runtime, further enhancing the ability to reuse the SQL scripts. An ampersand (&) followed by a variable name prompts for and accepts values at runtime. For example, the following SELECT statement queries the DEPARTMENTS table based on the department number supplied at runtime:

```
SELECT department_name
FROM    departments
```

```
WHERE  department_id = &dept;

Enter value for dept: 10
old    3: WHERE  DEPARTMENT_ID = &dept
new    3: WHERE  DEPARTMENT_ID = 10


DEPARTMENT_NAME
---------------
Administration


1 row selected.
```

Using Ampersand Substitution Variables

Suppose that you have defined DEPT as a variable in your script, but you want to avoid the prompt for the value at runtime. SQL*Plus prompts you for a value only when the variable is undefined. You can define a *substitution variable* in SQL*Plus using the DEFINE command to provide a value. The variable will always have the CHAR datatype associated with it. Here is an example of defining a substitution variable:

```
SQL> DEFINE DEPT = 20
SQL> DEFINE DEPT
DEFINE DEPT            = "20" (CHAR)
SQL> LIST
  1  SELECT department_name
  2  FROM   departments
  3* WHERE  department_id = &DEPT
SQL> /
old    3: WHERE  DEPARTMENT_ID = &DEPT
new    3: WHERE  DEPARTMENT_ID = 20


DEPARTMENT_NAME
---------------
Marketing


1 row selected.
SQL>
```

 Using the DEFINE command without any arguments shows all the defined variables.

```
SQL> define
DEFINE _DATE             = "13-JUL-13" (CHAR)
DEFINE _CONNECT_IDENTIFIER = "o12c01" (CHAR)
DEFINE _USER             = "HR" (CHAR)
DEFINE _PRIVILEGE        = "" (CHAR)
DEFINE _SQLPLUS_RELEASE = "1201000100" (CHAR)
DEFINE _EDITOR           = "Notepad" (CHAR)
DEFINE _O_VERSION        = "Oracle Database 12c Enterprise Edition Release 12.1.0.
1.0 - 64bit Production
With the Partitioning, OLAP, Advanced Analytics and Real Application Testing opt
ions" (CHAR)
DEFINE _O_RELEASE        = "1201000100" (CHAR)
DEFINE _RC               = "0" (CHAR)
DEFINE DEPT              = "20" (CHAR)
SQL>
```

A dot (.) is used to append characters immediately after the substitution variable. The dot separates the variable name and the literal that follows immediately. If you need a dot to be part of the literal, provide two dots continuously. For example, the following query appends _REP to the user input when seeking a value from the JOBS table:

```
SQL> SELECT job_id, job_title FROM jobs
  2* WHERE   job_id = '&JOB._REP'
SQL> /
Enter value for job: MK
old    2: WHERE   JOB_ID = '&JOB._REP'
new    2: WHERE   JOB_ID = 'MK_REP'

JOB_ID     JOB_TITLE
---------- ------------------------
MK_REP     Marketing Representative

1 row selected.
SQL>
```

The following example shows the use of a dot as part of the literal.

```
SQL> SELECT file_name
  2  FROM    mytraces
  3  WHERE   file_name like '&DB.%&PROCID..trc';
Enter value for db: C12DB1
```

```
Enter value for procid: 25285
old   3: WHERE   file_name like '&DB.%&PROCID..trc'
new   3: WHERE   file_name like 'C12DB1%25285.trc'


FILE_NAME
------------------------------
C12DB1_aqpc_25285.trc
```

The old line with the variable and the new line with the substitution are displayed. You can turn off this display by using the command SET VERIFY OFF.

Saving a Variable for a Session

Consider the following SQL code, saved to a file named ex01.sql. When you execute this script file, you will be prompted for the COL1 and COL2 values multiple times:

```
SQL> SELECT &COL1, &COL2
  2   FROM     &TABLE
  3   WHERE    &COL1 = '&VAL'
  4   ORDER BY &COL2
  5
SQL> SAVE ex01
Created file ex01.sql
SQL> @ex01
Enter value for col1: FIRST_NAME
Enter value for col2: LAST_NAME
old   1: SELECT &COL1, &COL2
new   1: SELECT FIRST_NAME, LAST_NAME
Enter value for table: EMPLOYEES
old   2: FROM     &TABLE
new   2: FROM     EMPLOYEES
Enter value for col1: FIRST_NAME
Enter value for val: John
old   3: WHERE   &COL1 = '&VAL'
new   3: WHERE   FIRST_NAME = 'John'
Enter value for col2: LAST_NAME
old   4: ORDER BY &COL2
new   4: ORDER BY LAST_NAME
```

```
FIRST_NAME           LAST_NAME
-------------------- ---------
John                 Chen
John                 Russell
John                 Seo

3 rows selected.
SQL>
```

The user can enter different or wrong values for each prompt. To avoid multiple prompts, use a double ampersand (&&), where the variable is saved for the session.

To clear a defined variable, you can use the UNDEFINE command. Let's edit the ex01.sql file to make it look like this:

```
SELECT &&COL1, &&COL2
FROM    &TABLE
WHERE   &COL1 = '&VAL'
ORDER BY &COL2
/
Enter value for col1: first_name
Enter value for col2: last_name
old   1: SELECT &&COL1, &&COL2
new   1: SELECT first_name, last_name
Enter value for table: employees
old   2: FROM &TABLE
new   2: FROM employees
Enter value for val: John
old   3: WHERE &COL1 = '&VAL'
new   3: WHERE first_name = 'John'
old   4: ORDER BY &COL1
new   4: ORDER BY first_name

FIRST_NAME           LAST_NAME
-------------------- -------------------------
John                 Chen
John                 Russell
John                 Seo


UNDEFINE COL1 COL2
```

Using Positional Notation for Variables

Instead of variable names, you can use positional notation, where each variable is identified by &1, &2, and so on. The values are assigned to the variables by position. Do this by putting an ampersand (&), followed by a numeral, in place of a variable name. Consider the following query:

```
SQL> SELECT department_name, department_id
  2  FROM    departments
  3  WHERE   &1 = &2;
Enter value for 1: DEPARTMENT_ID
Enter value for 2: 10
old   3: WHERE   &1 = &2
new   3: WHERE   DEPARTMENT_ID = 10


DEPARTMENT_NAME                 DEPARTMENT_ID
------------------------------- -------------
Administration                             10


1 row selected.
SQL>
```

If you save the SQL as a script file, you can submit the substitution-variable values while invoking the script (as command-line arguments). Each time you run this command file, START replaces each &1 in the file with the first value (called an *argument*) after START *filename*, then replaces each &2 with the second value, and so forth. Here is an example of saving and running the previous query:

```
SQL> SAVE ex02
Created file ex02.sql
SQL> SET VERIFY OFF
SQL> @ex02 department_id 20


DEPARTMENT_NAME                 DEPARTMENT_ID
------------------------------- -------------
Marketing                                  20


1 row selected.
SQL>
```

Although we did not specify two ampersands for positional substitution variables, SQL*Plus keeps the values of these variables for the session (because we passed the values as parameters to a script file). The next time you run any script with positional substitution variables, Oracle will use these values to execute the script.

Summary

This chapter started off by reviewing the fundamentals of SQL. You got a quick introduction to the Oracle datatypes, operators, and literals. You learned to write simple queries using the SELECT statement. You also learned to use the WHERE clause and the ORDER BY clause in this chapter.

The CHAR and VARCHAR2 datatypes are used to store alphanumeric information. The NUMBER datatype is used to store any numeric value. Date values can be stored using the DATE or TIMESTAMP datatypes. Oracle has a wide range of operators: arithmetic, concatenation, comparison, membership, logical, pattern matching, range, existence, and NULL checking. The CASE expression is used to bring conditional logic to SQL.

Data in the Oracle database is managed and accessed using SQL. A SELECT statement is the basic form of querying or reading records from the database table. You can limit the rows using the FETCH clause and filter the rows using the WHERE clause. You can use the AND and OR logical operators to join multiple filter conditions. The ORDER BY clause is used to sort the result set in a particular order. You can use an ampersand (&) character to substitute a value at runtime.

Exam Essentials

Understand the operators.   Know the various operators that can be used in queries. The parentheses around an expression change the precedence of the operators.

Understand the WHERE clause.   The WHERE clause specifies a condition by which to filter the rows returned. You cannot use column alias names in this clause.

Understand the ORDER BY clause.   The ORDER BY clause is used to sort the result set from a query. You can specify ascending order or descending order for the sort. Ascending order is the default. Also know that column alias names can be used in the ORDER BY clause. You can also specify columns by their position.

Know how to specify string literals using the Q/q operator.   You can use the Q or q operator to specify the quote delimiters in string literals. Understand the difference between using the (, <, {, and [characters and other delimiters.

Know the order of clauses in the SELECT statement.   The SELECT statement must have a FROM clause. The WHERE clause, if it exists, should follow the FROM clause and precede the ORDER BY clause. OFFSET and FETCH clauses should follow ORDER BY.

Know the use of the DUAL table.   The DUAL table is a special table in Oracle with one column and one row. This table is commonly used to get the values of system variables such as SYSDATE or USER.

Know the characters used for pattern matching.   The % character is used to match zero or more characters. The _ character is used to match one, and only one, character. The SQL operator used with a pattern-matching character is LIKE.

Know the sort order of NULL values in queries with an ORDER BY clause.   By default, in an ascending-order sort, the NULL values appear at the bottom of the result set—that is, NULLs are sorted higher. For descending-order sorts, NULL values appear at the top of the result set—again, NULL values are sorted higher.

Understand the FETCH clause.   The FETCH clause specifies a value to limit the number or rows returned. The OFFSET clause may be used along with FETCH to skip a certain number of rows before returning the result set.

Review Questions

1. You issue the following query:

```
SELECT salary "Employee Salary"
FROM employees;
```

How will the column heading appear in the result?

A. EMPLOYEE SALARY

B. EMPLOYEE_SALARY

C. Employee Salary

D. employee_salary

2. The EMP table is defined as follows:

Column	Datatype	Length
EMPNO	NUMBER	4
ENAME	VARCHAR2	30
SALARY	NUMBER	14,2
COMM	NUMBER	10,2
DEPTNO	NUMBER	2

You perform the following two queries:

```
1. SELECT empno enumber,  ename    FROM emp ORDER BY 1;
2. SELECT empno,  ename    FROM emp ORDER BY  empno ASC;
```

Which of the following is true?

A. Statements 1 and 2 will produce the same result in data.

B. Statement 1 will execute; statement 2 will return an error.

C. Statement 2 will execute; statement 1 will return an error.

D. Statements 1 and 2 will execute but produce different results.

3. You issue the following SELECT statement on the EMP table shown in question 2.

```
SELECT (200+((salary*0.1)/2)) FROM emp;
```

What will happen to the result if all the parentheses are removed?

A. No difference, because the answer will always be NULL.

B. No difference, because the result will be the same.

C. The result will be higher.

D. The result will be lower.

4. In the following SELECT statement, which component is a literal? (Choose all that apply.)

```
SELECT 'Employee Name: ' || ename
FROM emp WHERE deptno = 10;
```

A. 10

B. ename

C. Employee Name:

D. ||

5. What will happen if you query the EMP table shown in question 2 with the following?

```
SELECT empno, DISTINCT ename, salary
FROM emp;
```

A. EMPNO, unique values of ENAME, and then SALARY are displayed.

B. EMPNO and unique values of the two columns, ENAME and SALARY, are displayed.

C. DISTINCT is not a valid keyword in SQL.

D. No values will be displayed because the statement will return an error.

6. Which clause in a query restricts the rows selected?

A. ORDER BY

B. WHERE

C. SELECT

D. FROM

7. The following listing shows the records of the EMP table:

EMPNO	ENAME	SALARY	COMM	DEPTNO
7369	SMITH	800		20
7499	ALLEN	1600	300	30
7521	WARD	1250	500	30
7566	JONES	2975		20
7654	MARTIN	1250	1400	30
7698	BLAKE	2850		30
7782	CLARK	2450	24500	10
7788	SCOTT	3000		20
7839	KING	5000	50000	10
7844	TURNER	1500	0	30
7876	ADAMS	1100		20
7900	JAMES	950		30
7902	FORD	3000		20
7934	MILLER	1300	13000	10

When you issue the following query, which value will be displayed in the first row?

```
SELECT empno
FROM emp
WHERE deptno = 10
ORDER BY ename DESC;
```

A. MILLER

B. 7934

C. 7876

D. No rows will be returned because ename cannot be used in the ORDER BY clause.

8. Refer to the listing of records in the EMP table in question 9. How many rows will the following query return?

```
SELECT * FROM emp WHERE ename BETWEEN 'A' AND 'C'
```

A. 4

B. 2

C. A character column cannot be used in the BETWEEN operator.

D. 3

9. Refer to the EMP table in question 2. When you issue the following query, which line has an error?

```
1. SELECT empno "Enumber", ename "EmpName"
2. FROM emp
3. WHERE deptno = 10
4. AND  "Enumber" = 7782
5. ORDER BY "Enumber";
```

A. 1

B. 5

C. 4

D. No error; the statement will finish successfully.

10. You issue the following query:

```
SELECT empno, ename
FROM emp
WHERE empno = 7782
OR empno = 7876;
```

Which other operator can replace the OR condition in the WHERE clause?

A. IN

B. BETWEEN ... AND ...

C. LIKE

D. <=

E. >=

11. Which statement searches for PRODUCT_ID values that begin with DI_ from the ORDERS table?

   A. SELECT * FROM ORDERS

   WHERE PRODUCT_ID = 'DI%';

   B. SELECT * FROM ORDERS

   WHERE PRODUCT_ID LIKE 'DI_' ESCAPE '\';

   C. SELECT * FROM ORDERS

   WHERE PRODUCT_ID LIKE 'DI_%' ESCAPE '\';

   D. SELECT * FROM ORDERS

   WHERE PRODUCT_ID LIKE 'DI_' ESCAPE '\';

   E. SELECT * FROM ORDERS

   WHERE PRODUCT_ID LIKE 'DI_%' ESCAPE '\';

12. COUNTRY_NAME and REGION_ID are valid column names in the COUNTRIES table. Which one of the following statements will execute without an error?

   A. SELECT country_name, region_id,CASE region_id = 1 THEN 'Europe', region_id = 2 THEN 'America', region_id = 3 THEN 'Asia', ELSE 'Other' END ContinentFROM   countries;

   B. SELECT country_name, region_id,CASE (region_id WHEN 1 THEN 'Europe', WHEN 2 THEN 'America', WHEN 3 THEN 'Asia', ELSE 'Other') ContinentFROM countries;

   C. SELECT country_name, region_id,CASE region_id WHEN 1 THEN 'Europe' WHEN 2 THEN 'America' WHEN 3 THEN 'Asia' ELSE 'Other' END ContinentFROM countries;

   D. SELECT country_name, region_id,CASE region_id WHEN 1 THEN 'Europe' WHEN 2 THEN 'America' WHEN 3 THEN 'Asia' ELSE 'Other' ContinentFROM countries;

13. The EMPLOYEE table has the following data:

EMP_NAME	HIRE_DATE	SALARY
SMITH	17-DEC-90	800
ALLEN	20-FEB-91	1600
WARD	22-FEB-91	1250
JONES	02-APR-91	5975
WARDEN	28-SEP-91	1250
BLAKE	01-MAY-91	2850

What will be the value in the first row of the result set when the following query is executed?

`SELECT hire_date FROM employee ORDER BY salary, emp_name;`

A. 02-APR-91

B. 17-DEC-90

C. 28-SEP-91

D. The query is invalid, because you cannot have a column in the ORDER BY clause that is not part of the SELECT clause.

14. Which SQL statement will query the EMPLOYEES table for FIRST_NAME, LAST_NAME, and SALARY of all employees in DEPARTMENT_ID 40 in the alphabetical order of last name?

A. SELECT first_name last_name salary FROM employees ORDER BY last_name WHERE department_id = 40;

B. SELECT first_name, last_name, salaryFROM employees ORDER BY last_name ASC WHERE department_id = 40;

C. SELECT first_name last_name salary FROM employees WHERE department_id = 40 ORDER BY last_name ASC;

D. SELECT first_name, last_name, salary FROM employees WHERE department_id = 40 ORDER BY last_name;

E. SELECT first_name, last_name, salary FROM TABLE employees WHERE department_id IS 40 ORDER BY last_name ASC;

15. Column alias names cannot be used in which clause?

A. SELECT clause

B. WHERE clause

C. ORDER BY clause

D. None of the above

16. What is wrong with the following statements submitted in SQL*Plus?

```
DEFINE V_DEPTNO = 20
SELECT LAST_NAME, SALARY
FROM    EMPLOYEES
WHERE DEPARTMENT_ID = V_DeptNo;
```

    A. Nothing is wrong. The query lists the employee name and salary of the employees who belong to department 20.

    B. The DEFINE statement declaration is wrong.

    C. The substitution variable is not preceded with the & character.

    D. The substitution variable in the WHERE clause should be V_DEPTNO instead of V_DeptNo.

17. Which two statements regarding substitution variables are true?

    A. &*variable* is defined by SQL*Plus, and its value will be available for the duration of the session.

    B. &&*variable* is defined by SQL*Plus, and its value will be available for the duration of the session.

    C. &*n* (where *n* is any integer) variables are defined by SQL*Plus when values are passed in as arguments to the script, and their values will be available for the duration of the session.

    D. &&*variable* is defined by SQL*Plus, and its value will be available only for every reference to that variable in the current SQL.

18. Look at the data in table PRODUCTS. Which SQL statements will list the items on the
BL shelves? (Show the result with the most available quantity at the top row.)

```
PRODUCT_ID PRODUCT_NAME              SHELF   AVAILABLE_QTY
---------- --------------------      ------  -------------
      1001 CREST                     BL36              354
      1002 COLGATE                   BL36               54
      1003 AQUAFRESH                 BL37               43
      2002 SUNNY-D                   LA21               53
      2003 CAPRISUN                  LA22               45
```

A. SELECT * FROM products

WHERE shelf like '%BL'

ORDER BY available_qty SORT DESC;

B. SELECT * FROM products

WHERE shelf like 'BL%';

C. SELECT * FROM products

WHERE shelf = 'BL%'

ORDER BY available_qty DESC;

D. SELECT * FROM products

WHERE shelf like 'BL%'

ORDER BY available_qty DESC;

E. SELECT * FROM products

WHERE shelf like 'BL%'

ORDER BY available_qty SORT;

19. The EMP table has the following data:

EMPNO	ENAME	SAL	COMM
7369	SMITH	800	
7499	ALLEN	1600	300
7521	WARD	1250	500
7566	JONES	2975	
7654	MARTIN	1250	1400
7698	BLAKE	2850	
7782	CLARK	2450	
7788	SCOTT	3000	
7839	KING	5000	
7844	TURNER	1500	0
7876	ADAMS	1100	
7900	JAMES	950	
7902	FORD	3000	
7934	MILLER	1300	

Consider the following two SQL statements:

```
1. SELECT empno, ename, sal, comm
   FROM emp WHERE comm IN (0, NULL);
2. SELECT empno, ename, sal, comm
   FROM emp WHERE comm = 0 OR comm IS NULL;
```

A. 1 and 2 will produce the same result.

B. 1 will error; 2 will work fine.

C. 1 and 2 will produce different results.

D. 1 and 2 will work but will not return any rows.

20. Consider the EMP table in the previous question. Which SQL code will retrieve the names of employees whose salary is at the fourth position from top?

A. SELECT ename, sal FROM emp ORDER BY 2 DESC OFFSET 3 ROWS FETCH NEXT 1 ROW WITH TIES;

B. SELECT ename, sal FROM emp ORDER BY 2 OFFSET 3 ROWS FETCH NEXT 1 ROW;

C. SELECT ename, sal FROM emp ORDER BY 2 DESC OFFSET 4 ROWS FETCH NEXT 1 ROW ONLY;

D. SELECT ename, sal FROM emp ORDER BY 2 FETCH FIRST 4 ROWS ONLY;

Chapter

3

Using Single-Row Functions

ORACLE DATABASE 12c: SQL FUNDAMENTALS EXAM OBJECTIVES COVERED IN THIS CHAPTER:

✓ **Using Single-Row Functions to Customize Output**

  ▪ Describe various types of functions available in SQL.

  ▪ Use character, number, and date functions in SELECT statements.

✓ **Using Conversion Functions and Conditional Expressions**

  ▪ Describe various types of conversion functions that are available in SQL.

  ▪ Use the TO_CHAR, TO_NUMBER, and TO_DATE conversion functions.

  ▪ Apply conditional expressions in a SELECT statement.

Functions are programs that take zero or more arguments and return a single value. Oracle has built a number of functions into SQL, and these functions can be called from SQL statements. The functions can be classified into many groups:

- Single-row functions
- Aggregate functions (also known as *group functions*)
- Analytical functions and regular expression functions
- National-language functions
- Object-reference functions
- Programmer-defined functions

The certification exam focuses on single-row and aggregate functions, so only those types are covered in this book. Single-row functions are covered in this chapter, and aggregate functions are covered in Chapter 4, "Using Group Functions."

Single-row functions operate on expressions derived from columns or literals, and they are executed once for each row retrieved. In this chapter, we will cover which single-row functions are available, the rules for how to use them, and what to expect on the exam regarding them.

Single-row functions also include conversion functions. Conversion functions are used to convert the datatype of the input value to a different datatype. The Oracle database has conditional expressions and functions. We discussed the conditional expression CASE in Chapter 2, "Introducing SQL." In this chapter, we will also discuss the conditional function DECODE.

Single-Row Function Fundamentals

Many types of single-row functions are built into SQL. They include character, numeric, date, conversion, and miscellaneous single-row functions, as well as programmer-written stored functions.

All single-row functions can be incorporated into SQL (and PL/SQL). You can use these single-row functions in the SELECT, WHERE, and ORDER BY clauses of SELECT statements. For example, the following query includes the TO_CHAR, UPPER, and SOUNDEX single-row functions:

```
SELECT first_name, TO_CHAR(hire_date,'Day, DD-Mon-YYYY')
FROM employees
```

```
WHERE UPPER(first_name) LIKE 'AL%'
ORDER BY SOUNDEX(first_name);
```

Single-row functions also can appear in other types of statements, such as the SET clause of an UPDATE statement, the VALUES clause of an INSERT statement, and the WHERE clause of a DELETE statement. The certification exam tends to focus on using functions in SELECT statements, so we will use examples of SELECT statements in this chapter. For completeness, many functions are discussed in this chapter, but the certification exam tends to focus on NULL functions, date functions, and conversion functions.

The built-in functions presented in this chapter are grouped by topic (character functions, date functions, and so on), and within each topic they appear in alphabetical order. Before we get into the different types of functions, let's start with the functions that are used to handle NULL values.

 Functions can be nested so that the output from one function is used as input to another. Nested functions can include single-row functions nested within group functions or group functions nested within either single-row functions or other group functions.

Functions for NULL Handling

One area in which beginners frequently have difficulty and where even veterans sometimes stumble is the treatment of NULLs. You can expect at least one question on the exam to address the use of NULLs, but it probably won't look like a question on the use of NULLs.

NULL values represent unknown data or a lack of data. Any operation on a NULL results in a NULL. This NULL-in/NULL-out model is followed for most functions as well. Oracle Database 12c has six NULL-handling functions; we'll give special attention to the NVL, NVL2, and COALESCE functions because these are commonly used.

NVL

The NVL function is used to replace a NULL value with a literal value. NVL takes two arguments, NVL(*x1*, *x2*), where *x1* and *x2* are expressions. The NVL function returns *x2* if *x1* is NULL. If *x1* is not NULL, then *x1* is returned. The arguments *x1* and *x2* can be of any datatype. If *x1* and *x2* are not of the same datatype, Oracle tries to convert them to the same datatype before performing the comparison.

For example, suppose you need to calculate the total compensation in the EMPLOYEES table, which contains SALARY and COMMISSION_PCT columns (NULL values are displayed with a question mark (?) for readability using the SET NULL ? command of SQL*Plus):

```
SELECT first_name, salary, commission_pct,
       salary + (salary * commission_pct) compensation
FROM employees
WHERE first_name LIKE 'T%';
```

FIRST_NAME	SALARY	COMMISSION_PCT	COMPENSATION
Tayler	9600	.2	11520
Timothy	2900 ?	?	
TJ	2100 ?	?	
Trenna	3500 ?	?	

As you can see in the table, the total compensation is being calculated only on Tayler; all others have their total compensation as NULL. This is because any operation on NULL results in a NULL.

You can use the NVL function to substitute a zero in place of any NULL you encounter, like this:

```
SELECT first_name, salary, commission_pct,
       salary + (salary * NVL(commission_pct,0)) compensation
FROM employees
WHERE first_name LIKE 'T%';
```

FIRST_NAME	SALARY	COMMISSION_PCT	COMPENSATION
Tayler	9600	.2	11520
Timothy	2900 ?		2900
TJ	2100 ?		2100
Trenna	3500 ?		3500

When you used the NVL function to substitute zero for NULL, the total compensation was calculated correctly. For the employees who do not have a commission, the salary and compensation are the same.

NVL2

The function NVL2 is a variation of NVL. NVL2 takes three arguments, NVL2($x1, x2, x3$), where $x1$, $x2$, and $x3$ are expressions. NVL2 returns $x3$ if $x1$ is NULL, and $x2$ if $x1$ is not NULL.

For the example presented in the previous section, you could also use the NVL2 function and write the code a bit differently:

```
SELECT first_name, salary, commission_pct, NVL2(commission_pct,
       salary + salary * commission_pct, salary) compensation
FROM employees
WHERE first_name LIKE 'T%';
```

FIRST_NAME	SALARY	COMMISSION_PCT	COMPENSATION
TJ	2100		2100

Trenna	3500		3500
Tayler	9600	.2	11520
Timothy	2900		2900

Using the NVL2 function, if COMMISSION_PCT is not NULL, then salary + salary * commission_pct is returned. If COMMISSION_PCT is NULL, then just SALARY is returned.

The NVL function allows you to perform some value substitution for NULLs. The NVL2 function, on the other hand, allows you to implement an IF…THEN…ELSE construct based on the nullity of data. Both are useful tools to deal with NULL values.

 Be prepared for a possible exam question that tests your knowledge of when to use an NVL function in a calculation. Such a question probably won't mention NVL and may not look like it is testing your knowledge of NULLs. If sample data is given as an exhibit, be sure to look for data columns with NULL values and whether they are used in the SQL code presented to you.

COALESCE

COALESCE is a generalization of the NVL function. COALESCE(*exp_list*) takes more than one argument, where *exp_list* is a list of arguments separated by commas. This function returns the first non-NULL value in *exp_list*. If all expressions in *exp_list* are NULL, then NULL is returned. Each expression in *exp_list* should be the same datatype, or else Oracle tries to convert them implicitly.

For example, COALESCE(x1, x2, x3) would be evaluated as the following:

If x1 is not NULL, then
  Return x1
Else
      Check x2
  If x2 is not NULL, then
    Return x2
     Else
    Check x3
       If x3 is not NULL, then
         Return x3
    Else
     Return NULL
    End If
  End If
End If

Consider the following example. The objective is to find the total salary based on COMMISSION_PCT. If COMMISSION_PCT is not NULL, calculate SALARY using COMMISSION_PCT.

If COMMISSION_PCT is NULL, then give $100 as commission. If SALARY is not defined (NULL) for an employee, give the minimum salary of $900.

```
SELECT last_name, salary, commission_pct AS comm,
       COALESCE(salary+salary*commission_pct,
                salary+100, 900) compensation
FROM employees
WHERE last_name like 'T%';
```

```
LAST_NAME                     SALARY       COMM COMPENSATION
------------------------- ---------- ---------- ------------
Taylor                          8600         .2        10320
Taylor                          3200                    3300
Tobias                                                   900
Tucker                         10000         .3        13000
Tuvault                         7000        .15         8050
```

As you can see in the example, using the COALESCE function helps you avoid writing several IF...THEN conditions, as well as avoid writing several nested NVL functions. You could write the same SQL using the CASE statement you learned about in Chapter 2 as follows:

```
SELECT last_name, salary, commission_pct AS comm,
       (CASE WHEN salary IS NULL THEN 900
          WHEN commission_pct IS NOT NULL
              THEN salary+salary*commission_pct
          WHEN commission_pct IS NULL THEN salary+100
          ELSE 0 END) AS compensation
 FROM employees
 WHERE last_name like 'T%';
```

```
LAST_NAME                     SALARY       COMM COMPENSATION
------------------------- ---------- ---------- ------------
Tayler                          8600         .2        10320
Tayler                          3200                    3300
Tobias                                                   900
Tucker                         10000         .3        13000
Tuvault                         7000        .15         8050
```

Try using WHEN salary IS NULL as the third condition in the CASE statement (instead of the first condition), and find out whether you see any difference in the result.

Using Single-Row Character Functions

Single-row character functions operate on character data. Most have one or more character arguments, and most return character values. Character functions take the character input value and return a character or numeric value. If the input to the function is a literal, be sure to enclose it in single quotes. The exam focuses on many commonly used character functions such as SUBSTR, INSTR, and LENGTH. When reading about these functions, pay particular attention to the commonly used functions. Even experienced programmers get confused with the REPLACE and TRANSLATE functions. In the following sections, we will review the single-row character functions in detail.

Character Function Overview

Table 3.1 summarizes the single-row character functions. We will cover each of these functions in the "Character Function Descriptions" section.

TABLE 3.1 Character Function Summary

Function	Description
ASCII	Returns the ASCII decimal equivalent of a character
CHR	Returns the character given the decimal equivalent
CONCAT	Concatenates two strings; same as the operator ||
INITCAP	Returns the string with the first letter of each word in uppercase
INSTR	Finds the numeric starting position of a string within a string
INSTRB	Same as INSTR but counts bytes instead of characters
LENGTH	Returns the length of a string in characters
LENGTHB	Returns the length of a string in bytes
LOWER	Converts a string to all lowercase
LPAD	Left-fills a string to a set length using a specified character
LTRIM	Strips leading characters from a string
REPLACE	Performs substring search and replace

TABLE 3.1   Character Function Summary *(continued)*

Function	Description
RPAD	Right-fills a string to a set length using a specified character
RTRIM	Strips trailing characters from a string
SOUNDEX	Returns a phonetic representation of a string
SUBSTR	Returns a section of the specified string, specified by numeric character positions
SUBSTRB	Returns a section of the specified string, specified by numeric byte positions
TRANSLATE	Performs character search and replace
TRIM	Strips leading, trailing, or both leading and trailing characters from a string
UPPER	Converts a string to all uppercase

The functions ASCII, INSTR, LENGTH, and REGEXP_INSTR return number values, although they take character datatype as the input.

Character Function Descriptions

Over the years, Oracle has added several functions to its library to make the lives of developers easy so that they do not have to write built-in functions. Oracle has a function for most of the day-to-day programming needs. Before you write your own custom-developed piece of code, it is always a good idea to scan the Oracle documentation on built-in functions.

The character functions in the following sections are arranged in alphabetical order, with descriptions and examples of each one.

ASCII

ASCII(*c1*) takes a single argument, where *c1* is a character string. This function returns the ASCII decimal equivalent of the first character in *c1*.

See also CHR() for the inverse operation.

```
SELECT ASCII('A') Big_A, ASCII('z') Little_Z, ASCII('AMER')
FROM dual;

   BIG_A   LITTLE_Z ASCII('AMER')
---------- ---------- -------------
       65        122            65
```

CHR

CHR(*i* [USING NCHAR_CS]) takes a single argument, where *i* is an integer. This function returns the character equivalent of the decimal (binary) representation of the character. If the optional USING NCHAR_CS is included, the character from the national character set is returned. The default behavior is to return the character from the database character set.

```
SELECT CHR(65), CHR(122), CHR(223)
FROM dual;

CHAR65 CHAR122 CHAR233
------ ------- -------
A      z       ß
```

CONCAT

CONCAT(*c1*,*c2*) takes two arguments, where *c1* and *c2* are both character strings. This function returns *c2* appended to *c1*. If *c1* is NULL, then *c2* is returned. If *c2* is NULL, then *c1* is returned. If both *c1* and *c2* are NULL, then NULL is returned. CONCAT returns the same results as using the concatenation operator: *c1*//*c2*. In the following example, notice the use of the nested function—a function inside a function—as an argument:

```
SELECT CONCAT(CONCAT(first_name, ' '), last_name) employee_name,
       first_name || ' ' || last_name AS alternate_method
FROM employees
WHERE department_id = 30;

EMPLOYEE_NAME            ALTERNATE_METHOD
------------------------ ------------------
Den Raphaely             Den Raphaely
Alexander Khoo           Alexander Khoo
Shelli Baida             Shelli Baida
Sigal Tobias             Sigal Tobias
Guy Himuro               Guy Himuro
Karen Colmenares         Karen Colmenares
```

INITCAP

INITCAP(*c1*) takes a single argument, where *c1* is a character string. This function returns *c1* with the first character of each word in uppercase and all others in lowercase. Words are delimited by white space or characters that are not alphanumeric.

```
SELECT data_value, INITCAP(data_value) initcap_example
FROM sample_data;
```

```
DATA_VALUE           INITCAP_EXAMPLE
-------------------- --------------------
THE three muskETeers The Three Musketeers
ali and*41*thieves   Ali And*41*Thieves
mississippi          Mississippi
mister INDIA         Mister India
```

INSTR

INSTR(*c1*,*c2*[,*i*[,*j*]]) takes four arguments, where *c1* and *c2* are character strings and *i* and *j* are integers. This function returns the numeric character position in *c1* where the *j* occurrence of *c2* is found. The search begins at the *i* character position in *c1*. INSTR returns a 0 when the requested string is not found. If *i* is negative, the search is performed backward, from right to left, but the position is still counted from left to right. Both *i* and *j* default to 1, and *j* cannot be negative.

The following example finds the first occurrence of *i* in the string starting from the fourth position of the string:

```
SELECT data_value, INSTR(data_value,'i',4,1) instr_example
FROM sample_data;
```

```
DATA_VALUE           INSTR_EXAMPLE Comment
-------------------- ------------- --------------------------------------------
THE three muskETeers             0 There is no "i" in the data value; so "0"
ali and*41*thieves              14 The first "i" is skipped, since we start
                                    at the 4th position. So the "i" in the 14th
                                    position is picked
mississippi                      5 the first "i" in 2nd position is skipped
mister INDIA                     0 INDIA has an "I" (upper case); so no
                                    match for "i"
```

Here is another example using a negative argument for the beginning character position. The search for the *is* string will start at the fourth position from the end and move to the left.

```
SELECT data_value, INSTR(data_value,'is',-4,1) instr_example
FROM sample_data;
```

DATA_VALUE	INSTR_EXAMPLE
THE three muskETeers	0
ali and*41*thieves	0
mississippi	5
mister INDIA	2

INSTRB

INSTRB($c1,c2[,i[,j]]$) is the same as INSTR(), except it returns bytes instead of characters. For single-byte character sets, INSTRB() is equivalent to INSTR().

LENGTH

LENGTH(c) takes a single argument, where c is a character string. This function returns the numeric length in characters of c. If c is NULL, a NULL is returned.

```
SELECT data_value, LENGTH(data_value) length_example
FROM sample_data;
```

DATA_VALUE	LENGTH_EXAMPLE
THE three muskETeers	20
ali and*41*thieves	18
mississippi	11
mister INDIA	12

LENGTHB

LENGTHB(c) is the same as LENGTH(), except it returns bytes instead of characters. For single-byte character sets, LENGTHB() is equivalent to LENGTH().

LOWER

LOWER(c) takes a single argument, where c is a character string. This function returns the character string c with all characters in lowercase.

 See also UPPER for the inverse operation.

```
SELECT data_value, LOWER(data_value) lower_example
FROM sample_data;
```

```
DATA_VALUE            LOWER_EXAMPLE
--------------------  --------------------
THE three muskETeers  the three musketeers
ali and*41*thieves    ali and*41*thieves
mississippi           mississippi
mister INDIA          mister india
```

LPAD

LPAD(*c1*, *i* [,*c2*]) takes three arguments, where *c1* and *c2* are character strings and *i* is an integer. This function returns the character string *c1* expanded in length to *i* characters, using *c2* to fill in space as needed on the left side of *c1*. If *c1* is more than *i* characters, it is truncated to *i* characters. *c2* defaults to a single space.

    See also RPAD.

The following example adds * to the SALARY column toward the left side. Because it does not specify a fill-in character when LPAD is applied to last_name, Oracle uses the default space as the fill-in character.

```
SELECT LPAD(last_name,10) lpad_lname,
       LPAD(salary,8,'*') lpad_salary
FROM employees
WHERE last_name like 'J%';


LPAD_LNAME LPAD_SAL
---------- --------
   Johnson ****6200
     Jones ****2800
```

LTRIM

LTRIM(*c1* [,*c2*]) takes two arguments, where *c1* and *c2* are character strings. This function returns *c1* without any leading characters that appear in *c2*. If no *c2* characters are leading characters in *c1*, then *c1* is returned unchanged. *c2* defaults to a single space.

    See also RTRIM and TRIM.

```
SELECT LTRIM('Mississippi','Mis') test1
      ,LTRIM('Rpadded          ') test2
      ,LTRIM('        Lpadded') test3
      ,LTRIM('       Lpadded', 'Z') test4
FROM dual;


TES TEST2            TEST3   TEST4
--- ---------------- ------- ------------
ppi Rpadded          Lpadded Lpadded
```

In the previous example, all occurrences of the trimmed characters M, i, and s are trimmed from the input string Mississippi, beginning on the left (with M) and continuing until the first character that is not an M, i, or s is encountered. Note that the trailing i is not trimmed; only the leading characters are removed. In TEST4, there is no occurrence of Z, so the input string is returned unchanged.

REPLACE

REPLACE($c1$, $c2$ [,$c3$]) takes three arguments, where $c1$, $c2$, and $c3$ are character strings. This function returns $c1$ with all occurrences of $c2$ replaced with $c3$. $c3$ defaults to NULL. If $c3$ is NULL, all occurrences of $c2$ are removed. If $c2$ is NULL, then $c1$ is returned unchanged. If $c1$ is NULL, then NULL is returned.

```
SELECT REPLACE('uptown','up','down') FROM dual;


REPLACE(
--------
downtown
```

This function can come in handy when you need to perform some dynamic substitutions. For example, suppose you have a number of indexes that were created in the _DATA tablespace instead of in the _INDX tablespace:

```
SELECT index_name, tablespace_name
FROM user_indexes
WHERE tablespace_name like '%DATA%';


INDEX_NAME        TABLESPACE_NAME
---------------- ----------------
PK_DEPT          HR_DATA
PK_PO_MASTER     PO_DATA
```

You can generate the Data Definition Language (DDL) to rebuild these misplaced indexes in the correct location. In this scenario, you know your tablespace naming convention has an INDX tablespace for every DATA tablespace. You use the REPLACE function to generate the new tablespace name, replacing DATA with INDX. So, the HR index is rebuilt in the HR_INDX tablespace, and the PO index is rebuilt in the PO_INDX tablespace.

```
SELECT 'ALTER INDEX '||index_name||
                   ' rebuild tablespace '||
REPLACE(tablespace_name, 'DATA', 'INDX')|| '; ' DDL
FROM user_indexes
WHERE tablespace_name LIKE '%DATA%';


DDL
----------------------------------------------------
ALTER INDEX PK_DEPT rebuild tablespace HR_INDX;
ALTER INDEX PK_PO_MASTER rebuild tablespace PO_INDX;
```

RPAD

RPAD(*c1*, *i* [, *c2*]) takes three arguments, where *c1* and *c2* are character strings and *i* is an integer. This function returns the character string *c1* expanded in length to *i* characters, using *c2* to fill in space as needed on the right side of *c1*. If *c1* is more than *i* characters, it is truncated to *i* characters. *c2* defaults to a single space.

 See also LPAD.

```
SELECT RPAD(first_name,15,'.') rpad_fname, lpad(job_id,12,'.') lpad_jid
FROM employees
WHERE first_name like 'B%';


RPAD_FNAME        LPAD_JID
---------------   -------------
Bruce..........   .....IT_PROG
Britney........   ....SH_CLERK
```

RTRIM

RTRIM(*c1* [,*c2*]) takes two arguments, where *c1* and *c2* are character strings. This function returns *c1* without any trailing characters that appear in *c2*. If no *c2* characters are trailing characters in *c1*, then *c1* is returned unchanged. *c2* defaults to a single space.

See also LTRIM and TRIM.

```
SELECT RTRIM('Mississippi','ip') test1
      ,RTRIM('Rpadded          ') test2
      ,RTRIM('Rpadded     ', 'Z') test3
      ,RTRIM('          Lpadded') test4
FROM dual;


TEST1   TEST2   TEST3        TEST4
------- ------- ------------ ----------------
Mississ Rpadded Rpadded                Lpadded
```

SOUNDEX

SOUNDEX($c1$) takes a single argument, where $c1$ is a character string. This function returns the Soundex phonetic representation of $c1$. The SOUNDEX function is usually used to locate names that sound alike. The example returns the records with first names that sound like "Stevan."

```
SELECT first_name, last_name
FROM employees
WHERE SOUNDEX(first_name) = SOUNDEX('Stevan');


FIRST_NAME           LAST_NAME
-------------------- -------------------------
Steven               King
Steven               Markle
Stephen              Stiles
```

SUBSTR

SUBSTR($c1$, x [, y]) takes three arguments, where $c1$ is a character string and both x and y are integers. This function returns the portion of $c1$ that is y characters long, beginning at position x. If x is negative, the position is counted backward (that is, right to left). This function returns NULL if y is 0 or negative. y defaults to the remainder of string $c1$.

```
SELECT SUBSTR('The Three Musketeers',1,3) Part1
      ,SUBSTR('The Three Musketeers',5,5) Part2
      ,SUBSTR('The Three Musketeers',11)  Part3
      ,SUBSTR('The Three Musketeers',-5)  Part4
FROM dual;
```

```
PAR PART2 PART3      PART4
--- ----- ---------- -----
The Three Musketeers teers
```

 Real World Scenario

Parsing the Filename from the Whole Path

Let's look at a real example from the life of a DBA. Suppose you want to extract only the filename from dba_data_files without the path name; you could use the following SQL code. Here the INSTR function is nested inside a SUBSTR function. Single-row functions can be nested to any level. When functions are nested, the innermost function is evaluated first. The INSTR function is used to find the character position where the last backslash (\) appears in the filename string (looking for the first occurrence from the end). This position is passed into the SUBSTR function as the start position.

```
SELECT file_name,
       SUBSTR(file_name, INSTR(file_name,'\', -1,1)+1) name
FROM dba_data_files;

FILE_NAME                                NAME
---------------------------------------- -------------
C:\ORACLE\ORADATA\W11GR1\USERS01.DBF     USERS01.DBF
C:\ORACLE\ORADATA\W11GR1\UNDOTBS01.DBF   UNDOTBS01.DBF
C:\ORACLE\ORADATA\W11GR1\SYSAUX01.DBF    SYSAUX01.DBF
C:\ORACLE\ORADATA\W11GR1\SYSTEM01.DBF    SYSTEM01.DBF
C:\ORACLE\ORADATA\W11GR1\EXAMPLE01.DBF   EXAMPLE01.DBF
```

To perform the same operation on Unix or Linux databases, replace the backslash (\) in the INSTR function with a regular slash (/), because a regular slash (/) is used on Linux/Unix to separate directories.

Let's review another example using the Linux or Unix platform. Suppose you want to find all the file systems (mount points) used by your database; you could use the following SQL:

```
SELECT DISTINCT
       SUBSTR(file_name, 1, INSTR(file_name,'/', 1,2)-1) fs_name
FROM dba_data_files;
```

```
FS_NAME
----------------------------
/u01
/u05
/ora_temp
/ora_undo
```

In this example, you started looking for the second occurrence of / using the INSTR function and used SUBSTR to extract only the characters from 1 through the location before the second occurrence of / in the filename (hence the –1).

SUBSTRB

SUBSTRB(c1, i[, j]) takes three arguments, where c1 is a character string and both i and j are integers. This function is the same as SUBSTR, except i and j are counted in bytes instead of characters. For single-byte character sets, they are equivalent.

TRANSLATE

TRANSLATE(c1, c2 ,c3) takes three arguments, where c1, c2, and c3 are character strings. This function returns c1 with all occurrences of characters in c2 replaced with the positionally corresponding characters in c3. A NULL is returned if any of c1, c2, or c3 is NULL. If c3 has fewer characters than c2, the unmatched characters in c2 are removed from c1. If c2 has fewer characters than c3, the unmatched characters in c3 are ignored. TRANSLATE is similar to the REPLACE function. REPLACE substitutes a single string from another string, whereas TRANSLATE makes several single-character one-to-one substitutions.

The following example substitutes the asterisk (*) for a, pound sign (#) for e, and dollar sign ($) for i; and it removes o and u from the last_name column:

```
SELECT last_name, TRANSLATE(last_name, 'aeiou', '*#$') no_vowel
FROM employees
WHERE last_name like 'S%';


LAST_NAME                    NO_VOWEL
--------------------------   --------------
Sarchand                     S*rch*nd
Sciarra                      Sc$*rr*
Seo                          S#
Smith                        Sm$th
Sullivan                     Sll$v*n
Sully                        Slly
```

Here is another example where the case is reversed; uppercase letters are converted to lowercase, and lowercase letters are converted to uppercase:

```
SELECT data_value, TRANSLATE(data_value,
'abcdefghijklmnopqrstuvwxyzABCDEFGHIJKLMNOPQRSTUVWXYZ',
'ABCDEFGHIJKLMNOPQRSTUVWXYZabcdefghijklmnopqrstuvwxyz')
FROM sample_data;


DATA_VALUE           TRANSLATE(DATA_VALUE
-------------------- --------------------
THE three muskETeers the THREE MUSKetEERS
ali and*41*thieves   ALI AND*41*THIEVES
mississippi          MISSISSIPPI
mister INDIA         MISTER india
```

TRIM

TRIM([[c1] c2 FROM] c3) can take three arguments, where c2 and c3 are character strings. If present, c1 can be one of the following literals: LEADING, TRAILING, or BOTH. This function returns c3 with all c1 (leading, trailing, or both) occurrences of characters in c2 removed. A NULL is returned if any of c1, c2, or c3 is NULL. c1 defaults to BOTH. c2 defaults to a space character. c3 is the only mandatory argument. If c2 or c3 is NULL, the function returns a NULL. It is equivalent to applying both LTRIM and RTRIM on the string c3.

```
SELECT TRIM('   fully padded   ') test1
      ,TRIM('   left padded') test2
      ,TRIM('right padded   ') test3
FROM dual;


TEST1        TEST2        TEST3
------------ ------------ ------------
fully padded left padded right padded
```

Another example of using the TRIM function is shown here. It removes (trims) character "a" from the leading position and the trailing position. For the names Alana and Alyssa, both the leading and the trailing "a" are removed; notice for the name Aalberto, both occurrences of the leading "a" are removed.

```
SELECT first_name, TRIM('a' FROM LOWER(first_name)) A_TRIMMED
FROM employees
WHERE first_name like 'A%';
```

```
FIRST_NAME           A_TRIMMED
-------------------- --------------------
Amit                 mit
Alexis               lexis
Anthony              nthony
Aalberto             lberto
Adam                 dam
Alexander            lexander
Alyssa               lyss
Alexander            lexander
Allan                llan
Alana                lan
```

UPPER

UPPER(c) takes a single argument, where c is a character string. This function returns the character string c with all characters in uppercase. UPPER frequently appears in WHERE clauses when you're not sure of the case of the data in the table.

See also LOWER.

```
SELECT first_name, last_name
FROM employees
WHERE UPPER(first_name) = 'JOHN';
```

```
FIRST_NAME           LAST_NAME
-------------------- -------------------------
John                 Chen
John                 Russell
John                 Seo
```

```
SELECT data_value, UPPER(data_value) upper_data
FROM sample_data;
```

```
DATA_VALUE           UPPER_DATA
-------------------- --------------------
THE three muskETeers THE THREE MUSKETEERS
ali and*41*thieves   ALI AND*41*THIEVES
```

```
mississippi          MISSISSIPPI
mister INDIA         MISTER INDIA
```

Using Single-Row Numeric Functions

When you think of numeric functions, the tasks that come to mind are finding a total, finding the average, counting the number of records, and so on. These numeric functions are group functions that operate on one or more rows. We'll discuss group functions in Chapter 4.

In the following sections, we will review the numeric functions used on single rows. Single-row numeric functions operate on numeric data and perform some kind of mathematical or arithmetic manipulation. When using a literal in a numeric function, do not enclose it in single quotes. Literals in single quotes are treated as a character datatype.

Numeric Function Overview

Table 3.2 summarizes the single-row numeric functions in Oracle Database 12*c*. We will cover each of these functions in the "Numeric Function Descriptions" section.

TABLE 3.2 Numeric Function Summary

Function	Description
ABS	Returns the absolute value
ACOS	Returns the arc cosine
ASIN	Returns the arc sine
ATAN	Returns the arc tangent
ATAN2	Returns the arc tangent; takes two inputs
BITAND	Returns the result of a bitwise AND on two inputs
CEIL	Returns the next higher integer
COS	Returns the cosine
COSH	Returns the hyperbolic cosine
EXP	Returns the base of natural logarithms raised to a power

Function	Description
FLOOR	Returns the next smaller integer
LN	Returns the natural logarithm
LOG	Returns the logarithm
MOD	Returns the modulo (remainder) of a division operation
NANVL	Returns an alternative number if the value is Not a Number (NaN) for BINARY_FLOAT and BINARY_DOUBLE numbers
POWER	Returns a number raised to an arbitrary power
REMAINDER	Returns the remainder in a division operation
ROUND	Rounds a number
SIGN	Returns an indicator of sign: negative, positive, or zero
SIN	Returns the sine
SINH	Returns the hyperbolic sine
SQRT	Returns the square root of a number
TAN	Returns the tangent
TANH	Returns the hyperbolic tangent
TRUNC	Truncates a number
WIDTH_BUCKET	Creates equal-width histograms

Numeric Function Descriptions

Numeric functions have numeric arguments and return numeric values. The trigonometric functions all operate on radians, not degrees.

The numeric functions are arranged in alphabetical order, with descriptions and examples of each one.

SIGN, ROUND, and TRUNC are most commonly used numeric functions—pay particular attention to them. FLOOR, CEIL, MOD, and REMAINDER are also important functions that can appear on the test. TRUNC and ROUND functions can take numeric input or datetime input.

These two functions are discussed in the "Using Single-Row Date Functions" section to illustrate their behavior with a datetime datatype input.

ABS

ABS(n) takes a single argument, where n is a numeric datatype (NUMBER, BINARY_FLOAT, or BINARY_DOUBLE). This function returns the absolute value of n.

```
SELECT ABS(-52) negative, ABS(52)  positive
FROM dual;

  NEGATIVE    POSITIVE
---------- ----------
        52          52
```

ACOS

ACOS(n) takes a single argument, where n is a numeric datatype between –1 and 1. This function returns the arc cosine of n expressed in radians, accurate to 30 digits of precision.

```
SELECT ACOS(-1) PI, ACOS(0) ACOSZERO,
       ACOS(.045) ACOS045, ACOS(1) ZERO
FROM dual;

        PI    ACOSZERO    ACOS045        ZERO
---------- ---------- ---------- ----------
3.14159265 1.57079633 1.52578113          0
```

ASIN

ASIN(n) takes a single argument, where n is a numeric datatype between –1 and 1. This function returns the arc sine of n expressed in radians, accurate to 30 digits of precision.

```
SELECT ASIN(1) high, ASIN(0) middle, ASIN(-1) low
FROM dual;

      HIGH     MIDDLE        LOW
---------- ---------- ----------
1.57079633          0 -1.5707963
```

ATAN

ATAN(*n*) takes a single argument, where *n* is a numeric datatype. This function returns the arc tangent of *n* expressed in radians, accurate to 30 digits of precision.

```
SELECT ATAN(9E99) high, ATAN(0) middle, ATAN(-9E99) low
FROM dual;
```

```
      HIGH      MIDDLE        LOW
---------- ---------- ----------
1.57079633          0 -1.5707963
```

ATAN2

ATAN2(*n1*, *n2*) takes two arguments, where *n1* and *n2* are numbers. This function returns the arc tangent of *n1* and *n2* expressed in radians, accurate to 30 digits of precision. ATAN2(*n1,n2*) is equivalent to ATAN(*n1/n2*) if *n1* and *n2* are positive integers.

```
SELECT ATAN2(9E99,1) high, ATAN2(0,3.1415) middle, ATAN2(-9E99,1) low
FROM dual;
```

```
      HIGH      MIDDLE        LOW
---------- ---------- ----------
1.57079633          0 -1.5707963
```

BITAND

BITAND(*n1*, *n2*) takes two arguments, where *n1* and *n2* are NUMBER datatypes. This function performs a bitwise AND operation on the two input values and returns the results, also integers. It is used to examine bit fields.

Here are two examples of BITAND. The first one performs a bitwise AND operation on 6 (binary 0110) and 3 (binary 0011). The result is 2 (binary 0010). Similarly, the bitwise AND between 8 (binary 1000) and 2 (binary 0010) is 0 (0000).

```
SELECT BITAND(6,3) T1, BITAND(8,2) T2
FROM dual;
```

```
        T1         T2
---------- ----------
         2          0
```

CEIL

CEIL(*n*) takes a single argument, where *n* is a numeric datatype. This function returns the smallest integer that is greater than or equal to *n*. CEIL rounds up to a whole number.

 NOTE   See also FLOOR.

```
SELECT CEIL(9.8), CEIL(-32.85), CEIL(0), CEIL(5)
FROM dual;

CEIL(9.8)  CEIL(-32.85)   CEIL(0)    CEIL(5)
---------- ------------ ---------- ----------
       10          -32          0          5
```

COS

COS(*n*) takes a single argument, where *n* is a numeric datatype in radians. This function returns the cosine of *n*, accurate to 36 digits of precision.

```
SELECT COS(-3.14159) FROM dual;

COS(-3.14159)
-------------
          -1
```

COSH

COSH(*n*) takes a single argument, where *n* is a numeric datatype. This function returns the hyperbolic cosine of *n*, accurate to 36 digits of precision.

```
SELECT COSH(1.4) FROM dual;

 COSH(1.4)
----------
2.15089847
```

EXP

EXP(*n*) takes a single argument, where *n* is a numeric datatype. This function returns e (the base of natural logarithms) raised to the *n* power, accurate to 36 digits of precision.

```
SELECT EXP(1) "e" FROM dual;
```

```
         e
----------
2.71828183
```

FLOOR

FLOOR(*n*) takes a single argument, where *n* is a numeric datatype. This function returns the largest integer that is less than or equal to *n*. FLOOR rounds down to a whole number.

 NOTE   See also CEIL.

```
SELECT FLOOR(9.8), FLOOR(-32.85), FLOOR(137)
FROM dual;

FLOOR(9.8) FLOOR(-32.85) FLOOR(137)
---------- ------------- ----------
         9           -33        137
```

LN

LN(*n*) takes a single argument, where *n* is a numeric datatype greater than 0. This function returns the natural logarithm of *n*, accurate to 36 digits of precision.

```
SELECT LN(2.7) FROM dual;

   LN(2.7)
----------
.993251773
```

LOG

LOG(*n1*, *n2*) takes two arguments, where *n1* and *n2* are numeric datatypes. This function returns the logarithm base *n1* of *n2*, accurate to 36 digits of precision.

```
SELECT LOG(8,64), LOG(3,27), LOG(2,1024), LOG(2,8)
FROM dual;

 LOG(8,64)  LOG(3,27) LOG(2,1024)   LOG(2,8)
---------- ---------- ----------- ----------
         2          3          10          3
```

MOD

MOD(*n1*, *n2*) takes two arguments, where *n1* and *n2* are any numeric datatype. This function returns *n1* modulo *n2*, or the remainder of *n1* divided by *n2*. If *n1* is negative, the result is negative. The sign of *n2* has no effect on the result. If *n2* is zero, the result is *n1*.

 See also REMAINDER.

```
SELECT MOD(14,5), MOD(8,2.5), MOD(-64,7), MOD(12,0)
FROM dual;

 MOD(14,5) MOD(8,2.5) MOD(-64,7) MOD(12,0)
---------- ---------- ---------- ---------
         4         .5         -1        12
```

NANVL

This function is used with BINARY_FLOAT and BINARY_DOUBLE datatype numbers to return an alternative value if the input is NaN.

The following example defines the NULL display as ? to show NULL value. The TO_BINARY_FLOAT function (discussed later in the chapter) is used to convert input to a BINARY_FLOAT datatype number.

```
SET NULL ?
SELECT NANVL(TO_BINARY_FLOAT('NaN'), 0) T1,
       NANVL(TO_BINARY_FLOAT('NaN'), NULL) T2
FROM dual;

        T1         T2
---------- ----------
         0 ?
```

POWER

POWER(*n1*, *n2*) takes two arguments, where *n1* and *n2* are numeric datatypes. This function returns *n1* to the *n2* power ($n1^{n2}$).

```
SELECT POWER(2,10), POWER(3,3), POWER(5,3), POWER(2,-3)
FROM dual;
```

```
POWER(2,10) POWER(3,3) POWER(5,3) POWER(2,-3)
----------- ---------- ---------- -----------
       1024         27        125        .125
```

REMAINDER

REMAINDER(*n1*, *n2*) takes two arguments, where *n1* and *n2* are any numeric datatype. This function returns the remainder of *n1* divided by *n2*. If *n1* is negative, the result is negative. The sign of *n2* has no effect on the result. If *n2* is zero and the datatype of *n1* is NUMBER, an error is returned; if the datatype of *n1* is BINARY_FLOAT or BINARY_DOUBLE, NaN is returned.

 See also MOD.

```
SELECT REMAINDER(13,5), REMAINDER(12,5), REMAINDER(12.5, 5)
FROM dual;

REMAINDER(13,5) REMAINDER(12,5) REMAINDER(12.5,5)
--------------- --------------- -----------------
             -2               2               2.5
```

The difference between MOD and REMAINDER is that MOD uses the FLOOR function, whereas REMAINDER uses the ROUND function in the formula. If you apply the MOD function to the previous example, the results are the same except for the first column:

```
SELECT MOD(13,5), MOD(12,5), MOD(12.5, 5)
FROM dual;

 MOD(13,5)  MOD(12,5) MOD(12.5,5)
---------- ---------- -----------
         3          2         2.5
```

Here is another example of using REMAINDER with a BINARY_FLOAT number, having *n2* as zero:

```
SELECT REMAINDER(TO_BINARY_FLOAT('13.0'), 0) RBF
from dual;

       RBF
----------
       Nan
```

ROUND

ROUND(*n1* [,*n2*]) takes two arguments, where *n1* is a numeric datatype and *n2* is an integer. This function returns *n1* rounded to *n2* digits of precision to the right of the decimal. If *n2* is negative, *n1* is rounded to the left of the decimal. If *n2* is omitted, the default is zero.

 This function is similar to TRUNC.

```
SELECT ROUND(123.489), ROUND(123.489, 2),
       ROUND(123.489, -2), ROUND(1275, -2)
FROM dual;

ROUND(123.489) ROUND(123.489,2) ROUND(123.489,-2) ROUND(1275,-2)
-------------- ---------------- ----------------- --------------
           123           123.49               100           1300
```

SIGN

SIGN(*n*) takes a single argument, where *n* is a numeric datatype. This function returns –1 if *n* is negative, 1 if *n* is positive, and 0 if *n* is 0.

```
SELECT SIGN(-2.3), SIGN(0), SIGN(47)
FROM dual;

SIGN(-2.3)   SIGN(0)   SIGN(47)
----------  --------- ----------
        -1          0          1
```

SIN

SIN(*n*) takes a single argument, where *n* is a number in radians. This function returns the sine of *n*, accurate to 36 digits of precision.

```
SELECT SIN(1.57079) FROM dual;

SIN(1.57079)
------------
           1
```

SINH

SINH(*n*) takes a single argument, where *n* is a number. This function returns the hyperbolic sine of *n*, accurate to 36 digits of precision.

```
SELECT SINH(1) FROM dual;

    SINH(1)
----------
1.17520119
```

SQRT

SQRT(*n*) takes a single argument, where *n* is a numeric datatype. This function returns the square root of *n*.

```
SELECT SQRT(64), SQRT(49), SQRT(5)
FROM dual;

  SQRT(64)    SQRT(49)     SQRT(5)
---------- ---------- ----------
         8           7 2.23606798
```

TAN

TAN(*n*) takes a single argument, where *n* is a numeric datatype in radians. This function returns the tangent of *n*, accurate to 36 digits of precision.

```
SELECT TAN(1.57079633/2) "45_degrees"
FROM dual;

45_Degrees
----------
         1
```

TANH

TANH(*n*) takes a single argument, where *n* is a numeric datatype. This function returns the hyperbolic tangent of *n*, accurate to 36 digits of precision.

```
SELECT TANH( ACOS(-1) ) hyp_tan_of_pi
FROM dual;
```

```
HYP_TAN_OF_PI
-------------
   .996272076
```

TRUNC

TRUNC(*n1* [,*n2*]) takes two arguments, where *n1* is a numeric datatype and *n2* is an integer. This function returns *n1* truncated to *n2* digits of precision to the right of the decimal. If *n2* is negative, *n1* is truncated to the left of the decimal.

 See also ROUND.

```
SELECT TRUNC(123.489), TRUNC(123.489, 2),
       TRUNC(123.489, -2), TRUNC(1275, -2)
FROM dual;

TRUNC(123.489) TRUNC(123.489,2) TRUNC(123.489,-2) TRUNC(1275,-2)
-------------- ---------------- ----------------- --------------
           123           123.48               100           1200
```

WIDTH_BUCKET

You can use WIDTH_BUCKET(*n1, min_val, max_val, buckets*) to build histograms of equal width. The first argument, *n1*, can be an expression of a numeric or datetime datatype. The second and third arguments, *min_val* and *max_val*, indicate the end points for the histogram's range. The fourth argument, *buckets*, indicates the number of buckets.

The following example divides the salary into a 10-bucket histogram within the range 2,500 to 11,000. If the salary falls below 2,500, it will be in the underflow bucket (*buckets* 0), and if the salary exceeds 11,000, it will be in the overflow bucket (*buckets* + 1).

```
SELECT first_name, salary,
       WIDTH_BUCKET(salary, 2500, 11000, 10) hist
FROM employees
WHERE first_name like 'J%';

FIRST_NAME               SALARY       HIST
-------------------- ---------- ----------
Jennifer                   4400          3
John                       8200          7
Jose Manuel                7800          7
Julia                      3200          1
```

```
James            2400          0
James            2500          1
Jason            3300          1
John             2700          1
Joshua           2500          1
John            14000         11
Janette         10000          9
Jonathon         8600          8
Jack             8400          7
Jean             3100          1
Julia            3400          2
Jennifer         3600          2
```

Using Single-Row Date Functions

Single-row date functions operate on datetime datatypes. A datetime is a coined word to identify datatypes used to define dates and times. The datetime datatypes in Oracle Database 12*c* are DATE, TIMESTAMP, and INTERVAL. Most have one or more date arguments, and most return a datetime value. Date data is stored internally as numbers. The whole-number portion is the number of days since January 1, 4712 B.C., and the decimal portion is the fraction of a day (for example, 0.5=12 hours).

Date Format Conversion

National-language support (NLS) parameters and arguments allow you to internationalize your Oracle database system. NLS internationalizations include date representations, character sets, alphabets, and alphabetical ordering.

Oracle will implicitly or automatically convert its numeric date data to and from character data using the format model specified with NLS_DATE_FORMAT. The default format is *DD-MON-RR* (see Table 3.7). You can change this date format model for each session with the ALTER SESSION SET NLS_DATE_FORMAT command. Here's an example:

```
SQL> SELECT SYSDATE FROM dual;

SYSDATE
---------
13-JUL-13

SQL> ALTER SESSION SET NLS_DATE_FORMAT='DD-Mon-YYYY HH24:MI:SS';
```

```
Session altered.

SQL> SELECT SYSDATE FROM dual;

SYSDATE
--------------------
13-Jul-2013 16:01:22
```

This ALTER SESSION command will set the *implicit conversion* mechanism to display date data in the format specified, such as 12-Dec-2002 15:45:32. This conversion works both ways. If the character string '30-Nov-2002 20:30:00' were inserted, updated, or assigned to a date column or variable, the correct date would be entered.

If the format model were *DD/MM/YY* or *MM/DD/YY*, there could be some ambiguity in the conversion of some dates, such as 12 April 2000 (04/12/00 or 12/04/00). To avoid problems with implicit conversions, Oracle provides explicit date/character-conversion functions: TO_DATE, TO_CHAR, TO_TIMESTAMP, TO_TIMESTAMP_TZ, TO_DSINTERVAL, and TO_YMINTERVAL. These explicit conversion functions are covered in the "Using Single-Row Conversion Functions" section later in this chapter.

Date Function Overview

Table 3.3 summarizes the single-row date functions. We will cover each of these functions in the "Date Function Descriptions" section.

TABLE 3.3 Date Function Summary

Function	Description
ADD_MONTHS	Adds a number of months to a date
CURRENT_DATE	Returns the current date and time in a DATE datatype
CURRENT_TIMESTAMP	Returns the current date and time in a TIMESTAMP datatype
DBTIMEZONE	Returns the database's time zone
EXTRACT	Returns a component of a date/time expression
FROM_TZ	Returns a timestamp with time zone for a given timestamp
LAST_DAY	Returns the last day of a month
LOCALTIMESTAMP	Returns the current date and time in the session time zone

Function	Description
MONTHS_BETWEEN	Returns the number of months between two dates
NEW_TIME	Returns the date/time in a different time zone
NEXT_DAY	Returns the next day of a week following a given date
ROUND	Rounds a date/time
SESSIONTIMEZONE	Returns the time zone for the current session
SYS_EXTRACT_UTC	Returns the UTC (GMT) for a timestamp with a time zone
SYSDATE	Returns the current date and time in the DATE datatype
SYSTIMESTAMP	Returns the current timestamp in the TIMESTAMP datatype
TRUNC	Truncates a date to a given granularity
TZ_OFFSET	Returns the offset from UTC for a time zone name

Date Function Descriptions

The date functions are arranged in alphabetical order except the first three, with descriptions and examples of each one. SYSDATE, SYSTIMESTAMP, and LOCALTIMESTAMP are used in many examples, so we'll discuss them first.

SYSDATE

SYSDATE takes no arguments and returns the current date and time to the second for the operating-system host where the database resides. The value is returned in a DATE datatype. The format that the value returned is based on NLS_DATE_FORMAT, which can be altered for the session using the ALTER SESSION SET NLS_DATE_FORMAT command. The format mask for dates and timestamps are discussed later in the chapter.

```
ALTER SESSION SET NLS_DATE_FORMAT='DD-MON-YYYY HH:MI:SS AM';
Session altered.

SELECT SYSDATE FROM dual;

SYSDATE
---------------------
13-JUL-2013 04:01:22 PM
```

SYSDATE is one of the most commonly used Oracle functions. There's a good chance you'll see it on the exam. Because the SYSDATE value is returned based on the time of the host server where the database resides, the result will be the same for a user sitting in New York or one in Hong Kong.

SYSTIMESTAMP

SYSTIMESTAMP takes no arguments and returns a TIMESTAMP WITH TIME ZONE for the current database date and time (the time of the host server where the database resides). The fractional second is returned with six digits of precision. The format of the value returned is based on NLS_TIMESTAMP_TZ_FORMAT, which can be altered for the session using the ALTER SESSION SET NLS_TIMESTAMP_TZ_FORMAT command.

```
SQL> SELECT SYSDATE, SYSTIMESTAMP FROM dual;


SYSDATE
SYSTIMESTAMP
------------------------------------
13-JUL-13
13-JUL-13 04.01.22.362000 PM -05:00


ALTER SESSION SET NLS_DATE_FORMAT='DD-MON-YYYY HH24:MI:SS';
Session altered.

ALTER SESSION SET
     NLS_TIMESTAMP_TZ_FORMAT='YYYY-MON-DD HH:MI:SS.FF TZR';
Session altered.

SELECT SYSDATE, SYSTIMESTAMP FROM dual;

SYSDATE
SYSTIMESTAMP
------------------------------------
13-JUL-2013 16:01:22
2013-JUL-13 04:01:22.368000 -05:00
```

LOCALTIMESTAMP

LOCALTIMESTAMP([p]) returns the current date and time in the session's time zone to p digits of precision. p can be 0 to 9 and defaults to 6. This function returns the value in the datatype TIMESTAMP. You can set the client time zone using the ALTER SESSION SET TIME_ZONE command.

The following example illustrates LOCALTIMESTAMP and how to change the time zone for the session. The database is in the U.S./Central time zone, and the client is in the U.S./Eastern time zone.

 See also CURRENT_TIMESTAMP.

```
SQL> SELECT SYSTIMESTAMP, LOCALTIMESTAMP FROM dual;

SYSTIMESTAMP
LOCALTIMESTAMP
-----------------------------------------------
12-OCT-13 01.30.44.605577 PM -05:00
12-OCT-13 02.30.44.605584 PM


SQL> ALTER SESSION SET TIME_ZONE = '-8:00';

Session altered.

SQL> SELECT SYSTIMESTAMP, LOCALTIMESTAMP FROM dual;

SYSTIMESTAMP
LOCALTIMESTAMP
-----------------------------------------------
12-OCT-13 01.30.56.507508 PM -05:00
12-OCT-13 10.30.56.507516 AM
```

ADD_MONTHS

ADD_MONTHS(*d*, *i*) takes two arguments, where *d* is a date and *i* is an integer. This function returns the date *d* plus *i* months. If *i* is a decimal number, the database will implicitly convert it to an integer by truncating the decimal portion (for example, 3.9 becomes 3). If <*d*> is the last day of the month or the resulting month has fewer days, then the result is the last day of the resulting month.

```
SELECT SYSDATE, ADD_MONTHS(SYSDATE, -1) PREV_MONTH,
       ADD_MONTHS(SYSDATE, 12) NEXT_YEAR
FROM dual;
```

```
SYSDATE                PREV_MONTH            NEXT_YEAR
-------------------- -------------------- --------------------
13-JUL-2013 16:01:22 13-JUN-2013 16:01:22 13-JUL-2014 16:01:22
```

CURRENT_DATE

CURRENT_DATE takes no arguments and returns the current date in the Gregorian calendar for the session's (client) time zone. This function is similar to SYSDATE, whereas SYSDATE returns the current date for the database's (host's) time zone. You can set the client time zone using the ALTER SESSION SET TIME_ZONE command.

The following example illustrates CURRENT_DATE and how to change the time zone for the session. The database is in the U.S./Central time zone, and the client is in the U.S./Mountain time zone.

```
ALTER SESSION SET NLS_DATE_FORMAT='DD-Mon-YYYY HH24:MI:SS';
Session altered.

SELECT SYSDATE, CURRENT_DATE FROM dual;

SYSDATE              CURRENT_DATE
-------------------- --------------------
13-Jul-2013 16:01:22 13-Jul-2013 13:01:22

ALTER SESSION SET TIME_ZONE = 'US/Eastern';
Session altered.

SELECT SYSDATE, CURRENT_DATE FROM dual;

SYSDATE              CURRENT_DATE
-------------------- --------------------
13-Jul-2013 16:01:22 13-Jul-2013 17:01:22
```

CURRENT_TIMESTAMP

CURRENT_TIMESTAMP([p]) returns the current date and time in the session's time zone to p digits of precision. p can be an integer 0 through 9 and defaults to 6.

See also LOCALTIMESTAMP.

This function is similar to CURRENT_DATE. CURRENT_DATE returns the result in the DATE datatype, whereas CURRENT_TIMESTAMP returns the result in the TIMESTAMP WITH TIME ZONE datatype.

```
SQL> SELECT CURRENT_DATE, CURRENT_TIMESTAMP FROM dual;


CURRENT_DATE
CURRENT_TIMESTAMP
-------------------------------------
13-Jul-2013 17:01:22
2013-JUL-13 05:01:22.386000 US/EASTERN
```

DBTIMEZONE

DBTIMEZONE returns the database's time zone, as set by the latest CREATE DATABASE or ALTER DATABASE SET TIME_ZONE statement. Note that after changing the database time zone with the ALTER DATABASE statement, the database must be bounced (restarted) for the change to take effect. The time zone is a character string specifying the hours and minutes offset from UTC (Coordinated Universal Time, also known as GMT, or Greenwich mean time) or a time zone region name. The valid time zone region names can be found in the TZNAME column of the view V$TIMEZONE_NAMES. The default time zone for the database is UTC (00:00) if you do not explicitly set the time zone during database creation.

```
SQL> SELECT DBTIMEZONE FROM dual;


DBTIME
------
-05:00
```

EXTRACT

EXTRACT(c FROM dt) extracts and returns the specified component c of date/time or interval expression dt. The valid components are YEAR, MONTH, DAY, HOUR, MINUTE, SECOND, TIMEZONE_HOUR, TIMEZONE_MINUTE, TIMEZONE_REGION, and TIMEZONE_ABBR. The specified component must exist in the expression. So, to extract a TIMEZONE_HOUR, the date/time expression must be a TIMESTAMP WITH TIME ZONE datatype.

Although HOUR, MINUTE, and SECOND exist in the DATE datatype, you can extract only YEAR, MONTH, and DAY from the DATE datatype expressions.

```
SELECT SYSDATE, EXTRACT(YEAR FROM SYSDATE) year_d
FROM dual;
```

```
SYSDATE                    YEAR_D
--------------------    ----------
13-Jul-2013 16:01:22       2013
```

You can extract YEAR, MONTH, DAY, HOUR, MINUTE, and SECOND from the TIMESTAMP datatype expression. You can extract all the components from the TIMESTAMP WITH TIMEZONE datatype expression.

```
SELECT LOCALTIMESTAMP,
       EXTRACT(YEAR FROM LOCALTIMESTAMP) YEAR_TS,
       EXTRACT(DAY FROM LOCALTIMESTAMP) DAY_TS,
       EXTRACT(SECOND FROM LOCALTIMESTAMP) SECOND_TS
FROM dual;
```

```
LOCALTIMESTAMP                 YEAR_TS DAY_TS  SECOND_TS
----------------------------  ------- ------- ---------
13-JUL-13 05.01.22.391000 PM     2013      13    22.391
```

You will be able to get the same result using the TO_CHAR function as well, as shown here.

```
SELECT LOCALTIMESTAMP,
       TO_CHAR(LOCALTIMESTAMP, 'YYYY') YEAR_TS,
       TO_CHAR(LOCALTIMESTAMP, 'DD') DAY_TS,
       TO_CHAR(LOCALTIMESTAMP, 'SSXFF') SECOND_TS
FROM dual;
```

```
LOCALTIMESTAMP                 YEAR_TS DAY_TS  SECOND_TS
----------------------------  ------- ------- ---------
13-JUL-13 05.11.54.777891 PM     2013      13 54.777891
```

FROM_TZ

FROM_TZ(*ts, tz*) returns a TIMESTAMP WITH TIME ZONE for the timestamp *ts* using time zone value *tz*. The character string *tz* specifies the hours and minutes offset from UTC or is a time zone region name. The valid time zone region names can be found in the TZNAME column of the view V$TIMEZONE_NAMES.

```
SELECT LOCALTIMESTAMP, FROM_TZ(LOCALTIMESTAMP, 'Japan') Japan,
FROM_TZ(LOCALTIMESTAMP, '-5:00') Central
FROM dual;
```

```
LOCALTIMESTAMP
JAPAN
```

```
CENTRAL
------------------------------------
13-JUL-13 05.01.22.393000 PM
2013-JUL-13 05:01:22.393000 JAPAN
2013-JUL-13 05:01:22.393000 -05:00
```

LAST_DAY

LAST_DAY(*d*) takes a single argument, where *d* is a date. This function returns the last day of the month for the date *d*. The return datatype is DATE.

```
SELECT SYSDATE,
       LAST_DAY(SYSDATE)  END_OF_MONTH,
       LAST_DAY(SYSDATE)+1 NEXT_MONTH
FROM dual;
```

```
SYSDATE              END_OF_MONTH         NEXT_MONTH
-------------------- -------------------- --------------------
13-Jul-2013 16:01:22 31-Jul-2013 16:01:22 01-Aug-2013 16:01:22
```

MONTHS_BETWEEN

MONTHS_BETWEEN(*d1*, *d2*) takes two arguments, where *d1* and *d2* are both dates. This function returns the number of months that *d2* is later than *d1*. A whole number is returned if *d1* and *d2* are the same day of the month or if both dates are the last day of a month.

```
SELECT MONTHS_BETWEEN('31-MAR-08', '30-SEP-08') E1,
       MONTHS_BETWEEN('11-MAR-08', '30-SEP-08') E2,
       MONTHS_BETWEEN('01-MAR-08', '30-SEP-08') E3,
       MONTHS_BETWEEN('31-MAR-08', '30-SEP-07') E4
FROM dual;
```

```
        E1         E2         E3         E4
---------- ---------- ---------- ----------
        -6 -6.6129032 -6.9354839          6
```

NEW_TIME

NEW_TIME(*d>*, *tz1*, *tz2*) takes three arguments, where *d* is a date and both *tz1* and *tz2* are one of the time zone constants. This function returns the date in time zone *tz2* for date *d* in time zone *tz1*.

```
SELECT SYSDATE Dallas, NEW_TIME(SYSDATE, 'CDT', 'HDT') Hawaii
FROM dual;
```

```
DALLAS               HAWAII
-------------------- --------------------
13-Jul-2013 16:01:22 13-Jul-2013 12:01:22
```

Table 3.4 lists the time zone constants.

TABLE 3.4   Time Zone Constants

Code	Time Zone
GMT	Greenwich mean time
NST	Newfoundland standard time
AST	Atlantic standard time
ADT	Atlantic daylight time
BST	Bering standard time
BDT	Bering daylight time
CST	Central standard time
CDT	Central daylight time
EST	Eastern standard time
EDT	Eastern daylight time
MST	Mountain standard time
MDT	Mountain daylight time
PST	Pacific standard time
PDT	Pacific daylight time
YST	Yukon standard time
YDT	Yukon daylight time
HST	Hawaii-Alaska standard time
HDT	Hawaii-Alaska daylight time

NEXT_DAY

NEXT_DAY(*d*, *dow*) takes two arguments, where *d* is a date and *dow* is a text string containing the full or abbreviated day of the week in the session's language. This function returns the next *dow* following *d*. The time portion of the return date is the same as the time portion of *d*.

```
SELECT SYSDATE, NEXT_DAY(SYSDATE,'Thu') NEXT_THU,
       NEXT_DAY('31-OCT-2014', 'Tue') Election_Day
FROM dual;


SYSDATE            NEXT_THU           ELECTION_DAY
------------------ ------------------ ------------------
13-JUL-13 16:48:04 18-JUL-13 16:48:04 04-NOV-14 00:00:00
```

ROUND

ROUND(<*d*> [, *fmt*]) takes two arguments, where *d* is a date and *fmt* is a character string containing a date format string. This function returns *d* rounded to the granularity specified in *fmt*. If *fmt* is omitted, *d* is rounded to the nearest day.

```
SELECT SYSDATE, ROUND(SYSDATE,'HH24') ROUND_HOUR,
       ROUND(SYSDATE) ROUND_DATE, ROUND(SYSDATE,'MM') NEW_MONTH,
       ROUND(SYSDATE,'YY') NEW_YEAR
FROM dual;


SYSDATE              ROUND_HOUR           ROUND_DATE
NEW_MONTH            NEW_YEAR
-------------------- -------------------- --------------------
13-Jul-2013 16:01:22 13-Jul-2013 16:00:00 14-Jul-2013 00:00:00
01-Jul-2013 00:00:00 01-Jan-2014 00:00:00
```

SESSIONTIMEZONE

SESSIONTIMEZONE takes no arguments and returns the database's time zone offset as per the last ALTER SESSION statement. SESSIONTIMEZONE will default to DBTIMEZONE if it is not changed with an ALTER SESSION statement.

```
SELECT DBTIMEZONE, SESSIONTIMEZONE
FROM dual;


DBTIMEZONE  SESSIONTIMEZONE
----------- ---------------
-05:00      US/Eastern
```

SYS_EXTRACT_UTC

SYS_EXTRACT_UTC(*ts*) takes a single argument, where *ts* is a TIMESTAMP WITH TIME ZONE. This function returns the UTC (GMT) time for the timestamp *ts*.

```
SELECT CURRENT_TIMESTAMP local,
       SYS_EXTRACT_UTC(CURRENT_TIMESTAMP) GMT
FROM dual;


LOCAL
GMT
----------------------------------------
2013-JUL-13 05:01:22.420000 US/EASTERN
13-JUL-13 09.01.22.420000 PM
```

TRUNC

TRUNC(*d* [, *fmt*]) takes two arguments, where *d* is a date and *fmt* is a character string containing a date format string. This function returns *d* truncated to the granularity specified in *fmt*.

    See also ROUND.

```
SELECT SYSDATE, TRUNC(SYSDATE,'HH24') CURR_HOUR,
       TRUNC(SYSDATE) CURR_DATE, TRUNC(SYSDATE,'MM') CURR_MONTH,
       TRUNC(SYSDATE,'YY') CURR_YEAR
FROM dual;


SYSDATE              CURR_HOUR            CURR_DATE
CURR_MONTH           CURR_YEAR
-------------------- -------------------- --------------------
13-Jul-2013 16:01:22 13-Jul-2013 16:00:00 13-Jul-2013 00:00:00
01-Jul-2013 00:00:00 01-Jan-2013 00:00:00
```

TZ_OFFSET

TZ_OFFSET(*tz*) takes a single argument, where *tz* is a time zone offset or time zone name. This function returns the numeric time zone offset for a textual time zone name. The valid time zone names can be obtained from the TZNAME column in the V$TIMEZONE_NAMES view.

```
SELECT TZ_OFFSET(SESSIONTIMEZONE) NEW_YORK,
       TZ_OFFSET('US/Pacific') LOS_ANGELES,
```

```
        TZ_OFFSET('Europe/London') LONDON,
        TZ_OFFSET('Asia/Singapore') SINGAPORE
FROM dual;


NEW_YOR LOS_ANG LONDON  SINGAPO
------- ------- ------- -------
-04:00  -07:00  +01:00  +08:00
```

Using Single-Row Conversion Functions

Single-row *conversion functions* operate on multiple datatypes. The TO_CHAR and TO_NUMBER functions have a significant number of formatting codes that can be used to display date and number data in a wide assortment of representations.

You can use the conversion functions to convert a numeric value to a character or a character value to a numeric or datetime value. Character datatypes in Oracle Database 12*c* are CHAR, VARCHAR2, NCHAR, NVARCHAR2, and CLOB. Numeric datatypes in Oracle Database 12*c* are NUMBER, BINARY_DOUBLE, and BINARY_FLOAT. Datetime datatypes in Oracle Database 12*c* are DATE, TIMESTAMP, and INTERVAL.

Datatype conversions are required and used extensively in day-to-day SQL use. When a user enters data, it may be in character format, which you may need to convert to a date or number. Sometimes the data is in a specific format, and you have to tell Oracle how to treat the data using conversion functions and format codes. In the following sections, you will learn the various conversions and how to use them.

> The exam may include a question that tests your recollection of some of the nuances of these formatting codes. General usage in a professional setting would afford you the opportunity to look them up in a reference. In the test setting, however, you must recall them on your own.

Conversion Function Overview

Table 3.5 summarizes the single-row conversion functions. We will cover each of these functions in the "Conversion Function Descriptions" section.

TABLE 3.5 Conversion Function Summary

Function	Description
ASCIISTR	Converts characters to ASCII
BIN_TO_NUM	Converts a string of bits to a number
CAST	Converts datatypes
CHARTOROWID	Casts a character to the ROWID datatype
COMPOSE	Converts to Unicode
CONVERT	Converts from one character set to another
DECOMPOSE	Decomposes a Unicode string
HEXTORAW	Casts a hexadecimal to a raw
NUMTODSINTERVAL	Converts a number value to an interval day to second literal
NUMTOYMINTERVAL	Converts a number value to an interval year to month literal
RAWTOHEX	Casts a raw to a hexadecimal
ROWIDTOCHAR	Casts a ROWID to a character
SCN_TO_TIMESTAMP	Converts an SCN to corresponding timestamp of the change
TIMESTAMP_TO_SCN	Converts timestamp to an SCN
TO_BINARY_DOUBLE	Converts input into a BINARY_DOUBLE number
TO_BINARY_FLOAT	Converts input into a BINARY_FLOAT number
TO_CHAR	Converts and formats a date into a string
TO_CLOB	Converts character input or NCLOB input to CLOB
TO_DATE	Converts a string to a date, specifying the format
TO_DSINTERVAL	Converts a character string value to an interval day to second literal
TO_LOB	Converts LONG or LONG RAW values to CLOB or BLOB datatype

Function	Description
TO_MULTIBYTE	Converts a single-byte character to its corresponding multibyte equivalent
TO_NUMBER	Converts a string to a number, specifying the format
TO_SINGLE_BYTE	Converts a multibyte character to its corresponding single-byte equivalent
TO_TIMESTAMP	Converts a character string to a TIMESTAMP value
TO_TIMESTAMP_TZ	Converts a character string to a TIMESTAMP WITH TIME ZONE value
TO_YMINTERVAL	Converts a character string value to an interval year to month literal
UNISTR	Converts UCS2 Unicode

Conversion Function Descriptions

The conversion functions are arranged in alphabetical order, with descriptions and examples of each one. Oracle Database 12*c* includes functions to convert from one datatype to another datatype. Most of the functions have only one argument. Many functions used to convert to/from numeric or datetime datatypes have three arguments; the second argument will tell Oracle what format the input given in the first argument should be. The third argument may be to specify an NLS string. You can use NLS parameters to tell Oracle what character set or language should be used when performing the conversion. The format mask and NLS parameters are always optional.

Pay particular attention to the TO_CHAR, TO_NUMBER, and TO_DATE functions. The format codes associated with numbers and dates are always a favorite on OCP certification exams.

ASCIISTR

ASCIISTR(*c1*) takes a single argument, where *c1* is a character string. T is function returns the ASCII equivalent of all the characters in *c1*. This function leaves ASCII characters unchanged, but non-ASCII characters are returned in the format *xxxx* where *xxxx* represents a UTF-16 code unit.

```
SELECT ASCIISTR('cañon') E1, ASCIISTR('fa⇓') E2
FROM dual;
```

```
E1        E2
--------- -------
ca\00F1on fa\00DF
```

BIN_TO_NUM

BIN_TO_NUM(*b*) takes a single argument, where *b* is a comma-delimited list of bits. This function returns the numeric representation of all the bit-field set *b*. It essentially converts a base 2 number into a base 10 number. Bit fields are the most efficient structure to store simple yes/no and true/false data. You can combine numerous bit fields into a single numeric column. Using bit fields departs from a normalized relational model, because one column represents more than one value, but this encoding can enhance performance and/or reduce disk-space usage.

 See also BITAND.

To understand the number returned from the BIN_TO_NUM function, recall from base 2 (binary) counting that the rightmost digit counts the 1s, the next counts the 2s, the next counts the 4s, then the 8s, and so on. Therefore, 13 is represented in binary as 1101. There are one 1, zero 2s, one 4, and one 8, which add up to 13 in base 10.

```
SELECT BIN_TO_NUM(1,1,0,1) bitfield1,
       BIN_TO_NUM(0,0,0,1) bitfield2,
       BIN_TO_NUM(1,1) bitfield3
FROM dual;

BITFIELD1  BITFIELD2  BITFIELD3
---------- ---------- ----------
       13          1          3
```

CAST

CAST(*c* AS *t*) takes two arguments, where *c* is an expression, subquery, or MULTISET clause and *t* is a datatype. This function converts the expression *c* into the datatype *t*. The *CAST* function is most frequently used to convert data into programmer-defined datatypes, but it can also be used to convert data to built-in datatypes. No translation is performed; only the datatype is converted. Table 3.6 shows the datatypes that can be converted using CAST.

TABLE 3.6 CAST Datatype Conversions

Convert From/To	BINARY_FLOAT, BINARY_DOUBLE	CHAR, VARCHAR2	NCHAR, NVARCHAR2	DATE, TIMESTAMP, INTERVAL	NUMBER	RAW	ROWID, UROWID
BINARY_FLOAT BINARY_DOUBLE	Yes	Yes	Yes	No	Yes	No	No
CHAR, VARCHAR2	Yes	Yes	No	Yes	Yes	Yes	Yes
NCHAR, NVARCHAR2	Yes	No	Yes	Yes	Yes	Yes	Yes
DATE, TIMESTAMP, INTERVAL	No	Yes	No	Yes	No	No	No
NUMBER	Yes	Yes	No	No	Yes	No	No
RAW	No	Yes	No	No	No	Yes	No
ROWID, UROWID	No	Yes	No	No	No	No	Yes

The following example shows datatype conversion using the CAST function.

```
SELECT CAST(SYSDATE AS TIMESTAMP WITH LOCAL TIME ZONE) DT_2_TS
FROM dual;

DT_2_TS
-----------------------------
13-JUL-13 04.01.22.000000 PM
```

CHARTOROWID

CHARTOROWID(c) takes a single argument, where c is a character string. This function returns c as a ROWID datatype. No translation is performed; only the datatype is converted.

```
SELECT rowid, first_name
FROM employees
WHERE first_name = 'Sarath';

ROWID              FIRST_NAME
------------------ --------------------
AAAWWqAAKAAAADNAA9 Sarath

SELECT first_name, last_name
FROM employees
WHERE rowid = CHARTOROWID('AAARAgAAFAAAABYAA9');

FIRST_NAME          LAST_NAME
------------------- -------------------------
Sarath              Sewall
```

 Each row in the database is uniquely identified by a ROWID. ROWID shows the physical location of the row stored in the database. The pseudocolumn ROWID shows the address of the row.

COMPOSE

COMPOSE(c) takes a single argument, where c is a character string. This function returns c as a Unicode string in its fully normalized form, in the same character set as c. The COMPOSE and DECOMPOSE functions support Unicode 3.0. The Unicode 3.0 standard allows you to combine, or *compose*, a valid character from a base character and a modifier.

CONVERT

CONVERT(*c*, *dset* [,*sset*]) takes three arguments, where *c* is a character string and *dset* and *sset* are character-set names. This function returns the character string *c* converted from the source character set *sset* to the destination character set *dset*. No translation is performed. If the character does not exist in both character sets, the replacement character for the character set is used. *sset* defaults to the database character set.

```
select convert ('vis-à-vis','AL16UTF16','AL32UTF8')
from dual;


CONVERT('VIS-?-VIS','AL16UTF
------------------------------------------
 v i s -?? - v i s
```

DECOMPOSE

DECOMPOSE(*c*) takes a single argument, where *c* is a character string. This function returns *c* as a Unicode string after canonical decomposition in the same character set as *c*. The COMPOSE and DECOMPOSE functions support Unicode 3.0.

HEXTORAW

HEXTORAW(*x*) takes a single argument, where *x* is a hexadecimal string. This function returns the hexadecimal string *x* converted to a RAW datatype. No translation is performed; only the datatype is changed.

NUMTODSINTERVAL

NUMTODSINTERVAL(*x* , *c*) takes two arguments, where *x* is a number and *c* is a character string denoting the units for *x*. This function converts the number *x* into an INTERVAL DAY TO SECOND datatype. Valid units are DAY, HOUR, MINUTE, and SECOND. *c* can be uppercase, lowercase, or mixed case.

```
SELECT SYSDATE,
       SYSDATE+NUMTODSINTERVAL(2,'HOUR') "2 hours later",
       SYSDATE+NUMTODSINTERVAL(30,'MINUTE') "30 minutes later"
FROM dual;


SYSDATE             2 hours later        30 minutes later
------------------- -------------------- --------------------
13-Jul-2013 16:01:22 13-Jul-2013 18:01:22 13-Jul-2013 16:31:22
```

NUMTOYMINTERVAL

NUMTOYMINTERVAL(x , c) takes two arguments, where x is a number and c is a character string denoting the units for x. This function converts the number x into an INTERVAL YEAR TO MONTH datatype. Valid units are YEAR and MONTH. c can be uppercase, lowercase, or mixed case.

```
SELECT SYSDATE,
       SYSDATE+NUMTOYMINTERVAL(2,'YEAR') "2 years later",
       SYSDATE+NUMTOYMINTERVAL(5,'MONTH') "5 months later"
FROM dual;


SYSDATE             2 years later        5 months later
------------------- -------------------- --------------------
13-Jul-2013 16:01:22 13-Jul-2015 16:01:22 13-Dec-2013 16:01:22
```

RAWTOHEX

RAWTOHEX(x) takes a single argument, where x is a raw string. This function returns the raw string x converted to a hexadecimal. No translation is performed; only the datatype is changed.

ROWIDTOCHAR

ROWIDTOCHAR(x) takes a single argument, where x is a character string in the ROWID datatype. This function returns the ROWID string x converted to a VARCHAR2 datatype. No translation is performed; only the datatype is changed. The resulting string is always 18 characters long.

```
SELECT ROWIDTOCHAR(ROWID) Char_RowID, first_name
FROM employees
WHERE first_name = 'Sarath';


CHAR_ROWID         FIRST_NAME
------------------ --------------------
AAAWWqAAKAAAADNAA9 Sarath
```

SCN_TO_TIMESTAMP

SCN_TO_TIMESTAMP (n) takes a single argument, where n is a numeric datatype representing a system change number (SCN) in the database. This function returns the timestamp associated with the SCN. The return datatype is TIMESTAMP.

```
SELECT SCN_TO_TIMESTAMP(8569432113130) UPD_TIME
from dual;
```

```
UPD_TIME
--------------------------------------------------------
25-MAR-08 12.16.49.000000000 PM
```

An SCN is a number that gets incremented when a commit occurs in the database. The SCN identifies the state of the database uniquely, is recorded in the redo log files, and will be used in case instance recovery is needed. Please see Chapter 8, "Introducing Oracle Database 12*c* Components and Architecture," for more information.

Oracle provides the ORA_ROWSCN pseudocolumn to identify the SCN when the block containing the row was last modified. Using the ORA_ROWSCN pseudocolumn, you can identify the approximate time when the row was last modified. The time is *approximate* because the SCN is associated with a block, and all the rows in the block will have the same SCN associated with them. This is useful in identifying the last modified time of a table, because a block can belong to only one table. Please see Chapter 10, "Understanding Storage and Space Management," for more information on blocks.

```
SELECT SCN_TO_TIMESTAMP(ORA_ROWSCN) mod_time, last_name
FROM employees
WHERE first_name = 'Lex';


MOD_TIME                             LAST_NAME
---------------------------------- -----------
28-JUN-13 11.30.39.000000000 AM     De Haan
```

TIMESTAMP_TO_SCN

TIMESTAMP_TO_SCN (<ts>) is used to identify the SCN associated with a particular timestamp. The function takes one argument, *ts*, which is of datatype TIMESTAMP. The return datatype is NUMBER.

```
SELECT TIMESTAMP_TO_SCN(SYSTIMESTAMP) DB_SCN
FROM dual;


      DB_SCN
--------------
  8569432102308
```

TO_BINARY_DOUBLE

TO_BINARY_DOUBLE(<*expr*> [,<*fmt*> [,<*nlsparm*>]]) takes three arguments, where *expr* is a character or numeric string, *fmt* is a format string specifying the format that *c* appears in, and *nlsparm* specifies language- or location-formatting conventions. This function returns a binary double-precision floating-point number of datatype BINARY_DOUBLE represented by *expr*. The *fmt* and *nlsparm* arguments are valid only if *expr* is a character expression. You can also use `'INF'`, `'-INF'`, and `'NaN'` to represent positive infinity, negative infinity, and NaN in *expr*.

The valid *fmt* numeric format conventions are listed in Table 3.9.

```
SELECT TO_BINARY_DOUBLE('1234.5678','999999.9999') CHR_FMT_DOUBLE,
       TO_BINARY_DOUBLE('1234.5678') CHR_DOUBLE,
       TO_BINARY_DOUBLE(1234.5678) NUM_DOUBLE,
       TO_BINARY_DOUBLE('INF') INF_DOUBLE
FROM dual;
```

CHR_FMT_DOUBLE	CHR_DOUBLE	NUM_DOUBLE	INF_DOUBLE
1.2345678E+003	1.2345678E+003	1.2345678E+003	Inf

TO_BINARY_FLOAT

TO_BINARY_FLOAT(<*expr*> [,<*fmt*> [,<*nlsparm*>]]) takes three arguments, where *expr* is a character or numeric string, *fmt* is a format string specifying the format that *c* appears in, and *nlsparm* specifies language- or location-formatting conventions. This function returns a binary single-precision floating-point number of datatype BINARY_FLOAT represented by *expr*. The *fmt* and *nlsparm* arguments are valid only if *expr* is a character expression. You can also use `'INF'`, `'-INF'` and `'NaN'` to represent positive infinity, negative infinity, and NaN in *expr*.

```
SELECT TO_BINARY_FLOAT('1234.5678','999999.9999') CHR_FMT_FLOAT,
       TO_BINARY_FLOAT('1234.5678') CHR_FLOAT,
       TO_BINARY_FLOAT(1234.5678) NUM_FLOAT,
       TO_BINARY_FLOAT('INF') INF_FLOAT
FROM dual;
```

CHR_FMT_FLOAT	CHR_FLOAT	NUM_FLOAT	INF_FLOAT
1.23456775E+003	1.23456775E+003	1.23456775E+003	Inf

Converting from a character or NUMBER to BINARY_FLOAT and BINARY_DOUBLE may not be exact because BINARY_FLOAT and BINARY_DOUBLE use binary precision, whereas NUMBER uses decimal precision. Converting from BINARY_FLOAT to BINARY_DOUBLE is always exact; converting BINARY_DOUBLE to BINARY_FLOAT may lose precision if BINARY_DOUBLE uses more bits of precision.

TO_CHAR

TO_CHAR(*<expr>* [,*<fmt >*[,*<nlsparm>*]]) takes three arguments, where *expr* is a date or a number or a character datatype, *fmt* is a *format model* specifying the format that *expr* will appear in, and *nlsparm* specifies language- or location-formatting conventions. This function returns *expr* converted into a character string (the VARCHAR2 datatype).

You can use the TO_CHAR function to convert a datetime or numeric datatype value to character. When the input is not in the default format expected by the database, you have to provide the format of the input data as the second argument. In this section, we'll demonstrate how a datetime datatype value and a numeric datatype value can be converted to a character datatype.

Date Conversion

If *expr* is a date or timestamp value, *fmt* is a date format code, and *nlsparm* is an NLS_DATE_LANGUAGE specification, if included. Note that the spelled-out numbers always appear in English, while the day or month may appear in the NLS language.

```
SELECT TO_CHAR(SYSDATE,'Day Ddspth,Month YYYY'
             ,'NLS_DATE_LANGUAGE=German') Today_Heute
FROM dual;


TODAY_HEUTE
----------------------------------------
Samstag    Thirteenth,Juli     2013


SELECT TO_CHAR(SYSDATE
             ,'"On the "Ddspth" day of "Month, YYYY') Today
FROM dual;


TODAY
-------------------------------------------
On the Thirteenth day of July    , 2013
```

Table 3.7 lists the date format codes.

TABLE 3.7   Date Format Codes

Date Code	Format Code Description
AD or BC	Epoch indicator.
A.D. or B.C.	Epoch indicator with periods.
AM or PM	Meridian indicator.

TABLE 3.7 Date Format Codes *(continued)*

Date Code	Format Code Description
A.M. or P.M.	Meridian indicator with periods.
DY	Day of week abbreviated.
DAY	Day of week spelled out.
D	Day of week (1–7).
DD	Day of month (1–31).
DDD	Day of year (1–366).
DL	Long date format.
DS	Short date format.
TS	Time in short format.
FF	Fractional seconds.
J	Julian day (days since 4712 B.C.).
W	Week of the month (1–5).
WW, IW	Week of the year, ISO week of the year.
MM	Two-digit month.
MON	Month name abbreviated.
MONTH	Month name spelled out.
Q	Quarter.
RM	Roman numeral month (I–XII).
YYYY, YYY, YY, Y	Four-digit year; last 3, 2, 1 digits in the year.
YEAR	Year spelled out.
SYYYY	If B.C., year is shown as negative.

Date Code	Format Code Description
RR	Used for data input with only two digits for the year to store twentieth-century dates in the twenty-first century.
RRRR	Used for data input. If a two-digit year is entered, this works like RR. If a four-digit year is entered, it works like YYYY.
CC, SCC	Century.
HH, HH12	Hour of the half-day (1–12).
HH24	Hour of the day (0–23).
MI	Minutes of the hour (0–59).
SS	Seconds of the minute (0–59).
SSSSS	Seconds of the day (0–86399).
TZD	Time zone daylight savings; must correspond to TZR.
TZH	Time zone hour, together with TZM, is time zone offset.
TZM	Time zone minute, together with TZH, is time zone offset.
TZR	Time zone region.
, . / - ; :	Punctuation.
'text'	Quoted text.
FM	Returns value with no leading or trailing blanks (fill mode).
FX	Requires exact match for the format model.

The RR code is used for data input with only two digits for the year. It is intended to deal with two-digit years before and after 2000. It rounds the century based on the current year and the two-digit year, entered as follows:

- If the current year is greater than or equal to 50 and the two-digit year is less than 50, the century is rounded up to the next century.

- If the current year is greater than or equal to 50 and the two-digit year is greater than or equal to 50, the century is unchanged.

- If the current year is less than 50 and the two-digit year is less than 50, the century is unchanged.

- If the current year is less than 50 and the two-digit year is greater than or equal to 50, the century is rounded down to the previous century.

So, if the current year is 2009 (less than 50) and the two-digit year is entered as 62 (greater than or equal to 50), the year is interpreted as 1962.

For any of the numeric codes, the ordinal and/or spelled-out representation can be displayed with the modifier codes th (for ordinal) and sp (for spelled out). Here is an example:

```
SELECT SYSDATE,
       TO_CHAR(SYSDATE,'Mmspth') Month,
       TO_CHAR(SYSDATE,'DDth') Day,
       TO_CHAR(SYSDATE,'Yyyysp') Year
FROM dual;


SYSDATE              MONTH    DAY  YEAR
-------------------- -------- ---- ------------------------
13-Jul-2013 16:01:22 Seventh  13TH Two Thousand Thirteen
```

For any of the spelled-out words or ordinals, case follows the pattern of the first two characters in the code. If the first two characters are uppercase, the spelled-out words are all uppercase. If the first two characters are lowercase, the spelled-out words are all lowercase. If the first two characters are uppercase and then lowercase, the spelled-out words have the first letter in uppercase and the remaining characters in lowercase.

```
SELECT TO_CHAR(SYSDATE,'MONTH') upperCase,
       TO_CHAR(SYSDATE,'Month') mixedCase,
       TO_CHAR(SYSDATE,'month') lowerCase
FROM dual;


UPPERCASE MIXEDCASE LOWERCASE
--------- --------- ---------
APRIL     April     april
```

Table 3.8 shows several examples of using the different date format models with the TO_CHAR function. Please pay close attention to the format model and result to understand the format-model characteristics. The format model is applied to the date Tuesday 01-APR-2008.

TABLE 3.8 Date Format Examples for Tuesday 01-APR-2008

Format Model	Result
`'CCth "Century" BC'`	21ST Century AD
`'"On the "DDSpth" Day of "MONTH", "YYYY'`	On the FIRST Day of APRIL, 2008
`'"On the "DdSpth" Day of "FMMonth", "YYYY'`	On the First Day of April, 2008
`'DS TS'`	4/1/2008 01:41:32 PM
`'"Today is week" WW "and day" DDD'`	Today is week 14 and day 092
`'Year'`	Two Thousand Eight
`'W WW WW D DD DDD Y YY YYY YYYY'`	1 14 14 3 01 092 8 08 008 2008

Number Conversion

If *expr* is a number, *fmt* is a numeric format code. Table 3.9 lists these codes.

TABLE 3.9 Numeric Format Codes

Numeric Code	Format-Code Description
9	Numeric digits with a leading space if positive and a leading – (minus) if negative.
0	Leading and/or trailing zeros.
,	Comma, for use as a group separator. It cannot appear after a period or decimal code.
G	Local group separator; could be comma (,) or period (.).
.	Period, for use as the decimal character. It cannot appear more than once or to the left of a group separator.
D	Local decimal character; could be comma (,) or period (.). Only one D is allowed in the format model.
$	Dollar-sign currency symbol.

TABLE 3.9 Numeric Format Codes *(continued)*

Numeric Code	Format-Code Description
C	ISO currency symbol (USD for $).
L	Local currency symbol.
FM	No leading or trailing blanks.
EEEE	Scientific notation.
MI	Negative as a trailing minus. Can appear only in the last position of the format model.
PR	Negative in angle brackets (< >). Can appear only in the last position of the format model.
S	Negative as a leading minus. Can appear only in the first or last position of the format model.
RN	Uppercase Roman numeral.
rn	Lowercase Roman numeral.
X	Hexadecimal.
V	Returns value multiplied by 10^n, where n is the number of 9s after the V.
B	Returns blanks for a fixed-point number if the integer part is zero.

nlsparm can include `NLS_NUMERIC_CHARACTERS` for specifying decimal and grouping symbols (format symbols D and G, respectively), `NLS_CURRENCY` for specifying the currency symbol (format symbol L), and `NLS_ISO_CURRENCY` for specifying the ISO international currency symbol (format symbol C). The `NLS_CURRENCY` symbol and the `NLS_ISO_CURRENCY` mnemonic are frequently different. For example, the `NLS_CURRENCY` symbol for U.S. dollars is $, but this symbol is not uniquely American, so the ISO symbol for U.S. dollars is USD.

```
SELECT TO_CHAR(-1234.56,'L099G999D99MI',
               'NLS_NUMERIC_CHARACTERS='',.''
               NLS_CURRENCY=''DM''
               NLS_ISO_CURRENCY=''GERMANY''
               ')  Balance
FROM dual;
```

```
BALANCE
------------------
DM001.234,56-
```

Table 3.10 shows several examples of using the different numeric format models. To understand the format-model characteristics, pay close attention to the format model and result.

TABLE 3.10 Numeric Format Examples

Numeric Format	Source Value	Result Value
'C099G999D99'	-1234.56	-USD001,234.56
'099.99'	1234.56	#######
'09G999V99'	1234.56	01,23456
'09G999D99'	1234.56	01,234.56
'09G999D99PR'	-1234.56	<01,234.56>
'999.99EEEE'	-1234.56	-1.23E+03
'$9999.999S'	-1234.56	$1234.560-
'$9999.999S'	1234.56	$1234.560+
'RN'	141	CXLI
'L99G999D99MI'	1234	$1,234.00

TO_CLOB

TO_CLOB ('<x>') converts input value to a CLOB datatype value. The argument *x* can be of type CHAR, VARCHAR2, NCLOB, NCHAR, NVARCHAR2, or CLOB. CLOB datatypes are discussed in Chapter 7, "Creating Tables and Constraints."

TO_DATE

TO_DATE(<c> [,<fmt> [,<nlsparm>]]) takes three arguments, where *c* is a character string, *fmt* is a format string specifying the format that *c* appears in (refer to Table 3.7, "Date Format Codes"), and *nlsparm* specifies language- or location-formatting conventions. This function returns *c* converted into the DATE datatype.

If you omit *fmt*, *c* should be in the default date format (as defined in NLS_DATE_FORMAT or derived from NLS_TERRITORY). It is always a good practice to specify the format mask when using the TO_DATE function.

```
alter session set nls_date_format = 'DD-MON-RR HH24:MI:SS';
Session altered.

SELECT TO_DATE('30-SEP-2007', 'DD/MON/YY') DateExample
FROM dual;

DATEEXAMPLE
-------------------
30-SEP-07 00:00:00

SELECT TO_DATE('SEP-2007 13', 'MON/YYYY HH24') DateExample
FROM dual;

DATEEXAMPLE
-------------------
01-SEP-07 13:00:00
```

When you use the TO_DATE function and specify a format mask, Oracle will try some additional formats if the data in the input string does not match the original format. For the MM format, Oracle will try the MON and MONTH formats. The MON or MONTH formats can be used interchangeably. For the YY and RR formats, Oracle will try YYYY and RRRR.

Adding the FX format model to the TO_DATE function will require the input be given in the exact format, including spaces and punctuation characters.

Table 3.11 shows examples of the TO_DATE function and their resulting dates.

TABLE 3.11 Date Conversion Examples

Function	Resulting Date
TO_DATE('01-01-08','DD-MM-RR')	01-JAN-2008
TO_DATE('01-01-1908','DD-MM-RR')	01-JAN-1908
TO_DATE('01-MAR-1998','DD-MONTH-YY')	01-MAR-1998
TO_DATE('01-01-98','DD-MM-YY')	01-JAN-2098
TO_DATE('01-01-98','DD-MM-YYYY')	01-JAN-0098

Function	Resulting Date
TO_DATE('01-01-98','DD-MM-RRRR')	01-JAN-1998
TO_DATE('01-MARCH-98','DD-MM-RRRR')	01-MAR-1998
TO_DATE('01-MAR-08','DD-MONTH-RRRR')	01-MAR-2008
TO_DATE('01-MAR-1998','fxDD/MON/YYYY')	ORA-01861 error
TO_DATE('13 MAY 2003','fxDD MON YYYY')	ORA-01841 error

Real World Scenario

Converting Numbers to Words

Once we had to debug a PL/SQL function developed by a programmer to convert numeric input to words. His program unit was very lengthy; basically, it defined the numbers from one through twenty, tens, hundreds, thousands, and millions in words. He used a complicated logic to split each digit from the input and assigned a word for each digit. We told him there is a neat, single-line SQL function that could replace his tens of lines of PL/SQL code. When he saw the SQL code, he was amazed by the power of simple SQL functions.

Using the J format along with the TO_CHAR and TO_DATE functions, you can display any number between 1 and 5,373,484 in words. The limit is because Oracle supports dates between January 1, 4712 B.C., and A.D. December 31, 9999.

The J format is used to display the date in Julian numbers.

```
SELECT SYSDATE, TO_CHAR(SYSDATE, 'J') Julian
FROM dual;

SYSDATE            JULIAN
------------------ -------
13-JUL-13 16:01:22 2456487
```

The SP format will spell the date. By combining the J and JSP formats, you can spell a number. Notice the use of & in the SQL code. You run the SQL multiple times to input different values. Negative numbers cannot be converted to Julian dates.

```
SQL> SET VERIFY OFF
SQL> SELECT TO_CHAR(TO_DATE(&NUM, 'J'), 'jsp') num_to_spell
     FROM dual;
Enter value for num: 3456

NUM_TO_SPELL
-------------------------------------
three thousand four hundred fifty-six

SQL> /
Enter value for num: 5023456

NUM_TO_SPELL
--------------------------------------------------------
five million twenty-three thousand four hundred fifty-six

SQL> /
Enter value for num: -456
SELECT TO_CHAR(TO_DATE(-456, 'J'), 'jsp') num_to_spell
                          *
ERROR at line 1:
ORA-01854: julian date must be between 1 and 5373484
```

TO_DSINTERVAL

TO_DSINTERVAL(<*c*> [,<*nlsparm*>]) takes two arguments, where *c* is a character string and *nlsparm* specifies the decimal and group separator characters. This function returns *c* converted into an INTERVAL DAY TO SECOND datatype.

```
SELECT SYSDATE,
       SYSDATE+TO_DSINTERVAL('007 12:00:00') "+7 1/2 days",
       SYSDATE+TO_DSINTERVAL('030 00:00:00') "+30 days"
FROM dual;
```

```
SYSDATE              +7 1/2 days         +30 days
-----------------    ------------------  ------------------
13-JUL-13 16:01:32   21-JUL-13 04:01:32  12-AUG-13 16:01:32
```

TO_LOB

TO_LOB (<long>) converts a LONG or LONG RAW datatype to a CLOB or BLOB datatype. LONG values are converted to a CLOB datatype, and LONG RAW values are converted to a BLOB datatype.

To learn more about CLOB and BLOB datatypes, see Chapter 7.

TO_MULTI_BYTE

TO_MULTI_BYTE(<c>) takes a single argument, where c is a character string. This function returns a character string containing c, with all single-byte characters converted to their multibyte counterparts. This function is useful only in databases using character sets with both single-byte and multibyte characters.

See also TO_SINGLE_BYTE.

TO_NUMBER

TO_NUMBER(<expr> [,<fmt> [,<nlsparm>]]) takes three arguments, where expr is a character or numeric string, fmt is a format string specifying the format that expr appears in, and nlsparm specifies language- or location-formatting conventions. This function returns the numeric value represented by expr. Table 3.9 lists all the format models that can be used with the TO_NUMBER function. The return datatype is NUMBER.

```
SELECT TO_NUMBER('234.89'), TO_NUMBER(1E-3) FROM dual;

TO_NUMBER('234.89')  TO_NUMBER(1E-3)
-------------------  ---------------
             234.89             .001
```

TO_SINGLE_BYTE

TO_SINGLE_BYTE(<c>) takes a single argument, where c is a character string. This function returns a character string containing c with all multibyte characters converted to their single-byte counterparts. This function is useful only in databases using character sets with both single-byte and multibyte characters.

See also TO_MULTI_BYTE.

TO_TIMESTAMP

TO_TIMESTAMP(<*c*> [,<*fmt*> [,<*nlsparm*>]]) takes three arguments, where *c* is a character string, *fmt* is a format string specifying the format that *c* appears in, and *nlsparm* specifies language- or location-formatting conventions. If *c* is in default timestamp format (as defined in NLS_TIMESTAMP_FORMAT or derived from NLS_TERRITORY), then *fmt* need not be specified. The return value is of the TIMESTAMP datatype.

```
SELECT TO_TIMESTAMP('30-SEP-2007 08:51:23.456',
                    'DD-MON-YYYY HH24:MI:SS.FF')
FROM dual;


TO_TIMESTAMP('30-SEP-200708:51:23.456','DD-MON-YYYYHH24:MI:SS.FF')
-----------------------------------------------------------------------
30-SEP-07 08.51.23.456000000 AM
```

TO_TIMESTAMP_TZ

TO_TIMESTAMP(<*c*> [,<*fmt*> [,<*nlsparm*>]]) takes three arguments, where *c* is a character string, *fmt* is a format string specifying the format that *c* appears in, and *nlsparm* specifies language- or location-formatting conventions. This function has the same behavior as the TO_TIMESTAMP function, except you can specify a time zone. The return datatype is TIMESTAMP WITH TIME ZONE.

```
SELECT TO_TIMESTAMP_TZ('30-SEP-2007 08:51:23.456',
                    'DD-MON-YYYY HH24:MI:SS.FF') TS_TZ_Example
FROM dual;


TS_TZ_EXAMPLE
-----------------------------------------------------------------------
2007-SEP-30 08:51:23.456000000 US/EASTERN
```

TO_YMINTERVAL

TO_YMINTERVAL(<*c*>) takes a single argument, where *c* is a character string. This function returns *c* converted into an INTERVAL YEAR TO MONTH datatype.

```
SELECT SYSDATE,
       SYSDATE+TO_YMINTERVAL('01-03') "+15 months",
```

```
        SYSDATE-TO_YMINTERVAL('00-03') "-3 months"
FROM dual;

SYSDATE             +15 months          -3 months
------------------ ------------------- -------------------
13-JUL-13 16:01:32 13-OCT-14 16:01:32 13-APR-13 16:01:32
```

Table 3.12 shows examples to demonstrate the difference between using the ADD_MONTHS function and the TO_YMINTERVAL function.

TABLE 3.12   Compare ADD_MONTHS and TO_YMINTERVAL

Expression	Result
TO_DATE('28-FEB-2007')+ TO_YMINTERVAL('01-00')	28-FEB-2008
ADD_MONTHS('28-FEB-2007',12)	29-FEB-2008
TO_DATE('29-FEB-2008')+ TO_YMINTERVAL('01-00')	Error: ORA-01839
ADD_MONTHS('29-FEB-2008',12)	28-FEB-2009
TO_DATE('30-APR-2008')+ TO_YMINTERVAL('00-04')	30-AUG-2008
ADD_MONTHS('30-APR-2008',04)	31-AUG-2008
TO_DATE('31-JAN-2008')+ TO_YMINTERVAL('00-03')	Error: ORA-01839

UNISTR

UNISTR(<c>) takes a single argument, where c is a character string. This function returns c in Unicode in the database Unicode character set. Include UCS2 characters by prepending a backslash (\) to the character's numeric code. Include the backslash character by specifying two backslashes (\\).

```
SELECT UNISTR('\00A3'), UNISTR('\00F1'), UNISTR('ca\00F1on')
FROM dual;

UN UN UNISTR('CA
-- -- ----------
 £  ñ  c a ñ o n
```

Using Other Single-Row Functions

This is the catchall category to include all the single-row functions that don't fit into the other categories. Some are incredibly useful, such as DECODE. DECODE is a very special function and the most widely used function. Most likely, you'll see a question on the certification exam about the DECODE function.

The NULLIF function is included in this category and not with other NULL-related functions. The NULLIF function returns a NULL value, whereas the NULL-related functions we discussed earlier take NULL as one of the inputs and give a value as a result.

Miscellaneous Function Overview

Table 3.13 summarizes the single-row miscellaneous functions. We will cover each of these functions in the "Miscellaneous Function Descriptions" section.

TABLE 3.13   Miscellaneous Function Summary

Function	Description
BFILENAME	Returns the BFILE locator for the specified file and directory
DECODE	Acts as an inline CASE statement (emulating IF…THEN…ELSE logic)
DUMP	Returns a raw substring in the specified encoding (octal/hex/character/decimal)
EMPTY_BLOB	Returns an empty BLOB locator
EMPTY_CLOB	Returns an empty CLOB locator
GREATEST	Sorts the arguments and returns the largest
LEAST	Sorts the arguments and returns the smallest
NULLIF	Returns NULL if two expressions are equal
ORA_HASH	Returns the hash value for an expression
SYS_CONTEXT	Returns various session attributes, such as IP address, terminal, and current user
SYS_GUID	Generates a globally unique identifier as a RAW value
UID	Returns the numeric user ID for the current session

Function	Description
USER	Returns the username for the current session
USERENV	Returns information about the current session
VSIZE	Returns the internal size in bytes for an expression

Miscellaneous Function Descriptions

These miscellaneous functions are arranged in alphabetical order, with descriptions and examples of each one.

BFILENAME

BFILENAME(*dir*, *file*) takes two arguments, where *dir* is a directory and *file* is a filename. This function returns an empty BFILE locator. This function is used to initialize a BFILE variable or BFILE column in a table. When this function is used, the BFILE is instantiated. Neither *dir* nor *file* needs to exist at the time BFILENAME is called, but both must exist when the locator is used. We'll discuss the BFILE datatype in Chapter 7.

DECODE

DECODE is a conditional function. We discussed the CASE conditional expression in Chapter 2.

DECODE(*x* ,*m1*, *r1* [,*m2* ,*r2*]…[,*d*]) can use multiple arguments. *x* is an expression. *m1* is a matching expression to compare with *x*. If *m1* is equivalent to *x*, then *r1* is returned; otherwise, additional matching expressions (*m2*, *m3*, *m4*, and so on) are compared, if they are included, and the corresponding result (*r2*, *r3*, *r4*, and so on) is returned. If no match is found and the default expression *d* is included, then *d* is returned. This function acts like a case statement in C, Pascal, or Ada. DECODE is a powerful tool that can make SQL very efficient—or very dense and nonintuitive. Let's look at some examples to help clarify its use.

The following example queries the COUNTRIES table and displays a region name based on the region_id column value. If the region_id column value does not match the values in the list, you want to display Other. To limit the rows in the output, you use the SUBSTR function to identify the country codes that begin with I or end with R.

```
SELECT country_id, country_name, region_id,
       DECODE(region_id, 1, 'Europe',
                         2, 'Americas',
                         3, 'Asia',
                            'Other') Region
```

```
FROM countries
WHERE SUBSTR(country_id,1,1) = 'I'
   OR SUBSTR(country_id,2,1) = 'R';


CO COUNTRY_NA        REGION_ID REGION
-- ----------  ---------------- --------
AR Argentina            2 Americas
BR Brazil               2 Americas
FR France               1 Europe
IL Israel               4 Other
IN India                3 Asia
IT Italy                1 Europe
```

DECODE does not have to return a value; it can return NULL if the optional *d* argument is not provided. In the previous example, if Other is omitted, the region name for Israel will be NULL.

```
SELECT country_id, country_name, region_id,
       DECODE(region_id, 1, 'Europe',
                         2, 'Americas',
                         3, 'Asia') Region
FROM countries
WHERE SUBSTR(country_id,1,1) = 'I'
   OR SUBSTR(country_id,2,1) = 'R';
```

In the DECODE function, Oracle treats two NULL values as equal. Hence, you can represent the NVL function using DECODE, as in DECODE(<string>, NULL, <new_value>, <string>).

DUMP

DUMP(*x* [,*fmt* [,*n1* [,*n2*]]]) can take four arguments, where *x* is an expression. *fmt* is a format specification for octal (8), decimal (10), hexadecimal (16), or single characters (17). Decimal is the default. If you add 1000 to the format specification, the character set name is also returned (for example, 1008 for octal). *n1* is the starting byte offset within *x*, and *n2* is the length in bytes to dump. This function returns a character string containing the datatype of *x* in numeric notation (for example, 2=number, 12=date), the length in bytes of *x*, and the internal representation of *x*. This function is mainly used for troubleshooting data problems.

```
SELECT last_name, DUMP(last_name) DUMP_EX
FROM employees
WHERE last_name like 'J%';
```

```
LAST_NAME    DUMP_EX
------------ -------------------------------------------------
Johnson      Typ=1 Len=7: 74,111,104,110,115,111,110
Jones        Typ=1 Len=5: 74,111,110,101,115

SELECT last_name, DUMP(last_name, 1017, 3, 3) DUMP_EX
FROM employees
WHERE last_name like 'J%';

LAST_NAME    DUMP_EX
------------ -------------------------------------------------
Johnson      Typ=1 Len=7 CharacterSet=WE8MSWIN1252: h,n,s
Jones        Typ=1 Len=5 CharacterSet=WE8MSWIN1252: n,e,s
```

EMPTY_BLOB

EMPTY_BLOB() takes no arguments. This function returns an empty BLOB locator. This function is used to initialize a BLOB variable or BLOB column in a table. When used, the BLOB is instantiated but not populated.

EMPTY_CLOB

EMPTY_CLOB() takes no arguments. This function returns an empty CLOB locator. This function is used to initialize a CLOB variable or CLOB column in a table. When used, the CLOB is instantiated but not populated.

GREATEST

GREATEST(*exp_list*) takes one argument, where *exp_list* is a list of expressions. This function returns the expression that sorts highest in the datatype of the first expression. If the first expression is any of the character datatypes, a VARCHAR2 is returned, and the comparison rules for VARCHAR2 are used for character-literal strings. A NULL in the expression list results in a NULL being returned.

The following example shows you that the list was treated as a character list and not a date, even though you had all date values as input:

```
SELECT GREATEST('01-ARP-08','30-DEC-01','12-SEP-09')
FROM dual;

GREATEST(
---------
30-DEC-01
```

In the following example, because the first argument is numeric, Oracle tries to convert the rest of the list to numeric and encounters an error:

```
SELECT GREATEST(345, 'XYZ', 2354) FROM dual;
ERROR at line 1:
ORA-01722: invalid number
```

In the next example, we changed the order to have the character string as the first entry in the list; hence, Oracle considers the rest of the list to be characters and does not produce an error:

```
SELECT GREATEST('XYZ', 345, 2354) FROM dual;


GRE
---
XYZ
```

LEAST

LEAST(*exp_list*) takes one argument, where *exp_list* is a list of expressions. This function returns the expression that sorts lowest in the datatype of the first expression. If the first expression is any of the character datatypes, a VARCHAR2 is returned.

```
SELECT LEAST(SYSDATE,'15-MAR-2002','17-JUN-2002') oldest
FROM dual;


OLDEST
---------
15-MAR-02
```

The following SQL is used to calculate a bonus of 15 percent of salary to employees, with a maximum bonus at 500 and a minimum bonus at 400:

```
SELECT last_name, salary,
       GREATEST(LEAST(salary*0.15, 500), 400) bonus
FROM employees
WHERE department_id IN (30, 10)
ORDER BY last_name;


LAST_NAME          SALARY           BONUS
------------ ---------------- ----------------
Baida                 2900              435
Colmenares            2500              400
Himuro                2600              400
```

```
Khoo                    3100            465
Raphaely               11000            500
Whalen                  4400            500
```

The comparison rules used by GREATEST and LEAST on character literals order trailing spaces higher than no spaces. This behavior follows the nonpadded comparison rules of the VARCHAR2 datatype. Note the ordering of the leading and trailing spaces: trailing spaces are greatest and leading spaces are least.

```
SELECT GREATEST(' Yes','Yes','Yes ')
       ,LEAST(' Yes','Yes','Yes ')
FROM dual;


GREA LEAST
---- -----
Yes  Yes
```

To remember the comparison rules for trailing and leading space in character literals, think "leading equals least."

NULLIF

NULLIF($x1$, $x2$) takes two arguments, where $x1$ and $x2$ are expressions. This function returns NULL if $x1$ equals $x2$; otherwise, it returns $x1$. If $x1$ is NULL, NULLIF returns NULL.

To facilitate visualizing a NULL, the following example has the NULL indicator set to ?. So, a ? in the query results that follow represents a NULL:

```
SET NULL ?
SELECT ename, mgr, comm,
       NULLIF(comm,0) test1,
       NULLIF(0,comm) test2,
       NULLIF(mgr,comm) test3
FROM scott.emp
WHERE empno IN (7844,7839,7654,7369);
```

ENAME	MGR	COMM	TEST1	TEST2	TEST3
SMITH	7902	?	?	0	7902
MARTIN	7698	1400	1400	0	7698
KING	?	?	?	0	?
TURNER	7698	0	?	?	7698

ORA_HASH

ORA_HASH (expr [,max_bucket [,seed]]) can take three arguments. The first argument, *expr*, is an expression whose hash value will be calculated and assigned to a bucket. The maximum bucket value is determined by the second argument, *max_bucket*; the default and maximum is 4,294,967,295. The *seed* argument enables Oracle to generate many different results for the same sets of data. The hash function is applied to *expr* and *seed*. The *seed* can be between 0 and 4,294,967,295.

This function is useful for getting a random sample of rows from a table. In the following example, you can get a few random rows from the EMPLOYEES table. Notice the difference in result for each run and with different seed values. The rows in the table are divided into 20 buckets (0 through 19) based on the hash value, and you are selecting the rows from bucket 0.

```
SELECT department_id, last_name, salary
FROM employees
WHERE ORA_HASH(last_name || first_name, 19, 2) = 0;
```

```
DEPARTMENT_ID LAST_NAME                        SALARY
------------- ------------------------- ----------
          100 Greenberg                     12008
           30 Himuro                         2600
           50 Nayer                          3200
           80 Banda                          6200
           80 Fox                            9600
?             Grant                          7000
           10 Whalen                         4400
          110 Gietz                          8300
```

```
SELECT department_id, last_name, salary
FROM employees
WHERE ORA_HASH(last_name || first_name, 19, 5) = 0;
```

```
DEPARTMENT_ID LAST_NAME                        SALARY
------------- ------------------------- ----------
           30 Tobias                         2800
```

```
SELECT department_id, last_name, salary
FROM employees
WHERE ORA_HASH(last_name || first_name, 19) = 0;
```

```
DEPARTMENT_ID LAST_NAME                      SALARY
------------- ------------------------- ----------
           60 Austin                          4800
          100 Greenberg                      12008
           80 Vishney                        10500
?               Grant                         7000
           50 Geoni                           2800
```

SYS_CONTEXT

SYS_CONTEXT(*n* , *p* [, *length*]) can take three arguments, where *n* is a namespace, *p* is a parameter associated with namespace *n*, and *length* is the length of the return value in bytes. *length* defaults to 256. The built-in namespace in Oracle is called USERENV, which describes the current session. The return datatype is VARCHAR2.

```
SELECT SYS_CONTEXT('USERENV','IP_ADDRESS')
FROM dual;

SYS_CONTEXT('USERENV','IP_ADDRESS')
-----------------------------------
192.168.1.100
```

Table 3.14 lists the parameters available in the USERENV namespace for the SYS_CONTEXT function.

TABLE 3.14 Parameters in the USERENV Namespace

Parameter	Description
ACTION	Returns the position in the module (application).
AUDITED_CURSORID	Returns the cursor ID of the SQL code that triggered the auditing.
AUTHENTICATED_IDENTITY	Returns the identity used in the authentication.
AUTHENTICATION_DATA	Returns the data used to authenticate a logged-in user.
AUTHENTICATION_METHOD	Returns the method used to authenticate a user. The return value can be DATABASE for database-authenticated accounts, OS for externally identified accounts, NETWORK for globally identified accounts, and so on.

TABLE 3.14 Parameters in the USERENV Namespace *(continued)*

Parameter	Description
BG_JOB_ID	Returns the job ID (that is, DBA_JOBS) if the session was created by a background process. Returns NULL if the session is a foreground session. See also FG_JOB_ID.
CLIENT_IDENTIFIER	Returns the client session identifier in the global context. It can be set with the DBMS_SESSION built-in package.
CLIENT_INFO	Returns the 64 bytes of user session information stored by DBMS_APPLICATION_INFO.
CURRENT_BIND	Returns bind variables for fine-grained auditing.
CURRENT_SCHEMA	Returns the current schema as set by ALTER SESSION SET CURRENT_SCHEMA or, by default, the login schema/ID.
CURRENT_SCHEMAID	Returns the numeric ID for CURRENT_SCHEMA.
CURRENT_SQL	Returns the SQL that triggered fine-grained auditing (use only within scope inside the event handler for fine-grained auditing).
CURRENT_SQL_LENGTH	Returns the length of the current SQL that triggered fine-grained auditing.
DB_DOMAIN	Returns the contents of the DB_DOMAIN init.ora parameter.
DB_NAME	Returns the contents of the DB_NAME init.ora parameter.
DB_UNIQUE_NAME	Returns the contents of the DB_UNIQUE_NAME init.ora parameter.
ENTRYID	Returns the auditing entry identifier.
ENTERPRISE_IDENTITY	Returns OID DN for enterprise users, for local users NULL.
FG_JOB_ID	Returns the job ID of the current session if a foreground process created it. Returns NULL if the session is a background session. See also BG_JOB_ID.
GLOBAL_CONTEXT_MEMORY	Returns the number in the SGA by the globally accessible context.
GLOBAL_UID	Returns the global user ID from OID.

Parameter	Description
HOST	Returns the hostname of the machine from where the client connected. This is not the same terminal in V$SESSION.
IDENTIFICATION_TYPE	Returns how the user is set to authenticate in the database: LOCAL, EXTERNAL, or GLOBAL.
INSTANCE	Returns the instance number for the instance to which the session is connected. This is always 1 unless you are running Oracle Real Application Clusters.
INSTANCE_NAME	Returns the name of the instance.
IP_ADDRESS	Returns the IP address of the machine from where the client connected.
ISDBA	Returns TRUE if the user connected AS SYSDBA.
LANG	Returns the ISO abbreviation for the language name.
LANGUAGE	Returns a character string containing the language and territory used by the session and the database character set in the form language_territory.characterset.
MODULE	Returns the application name set through DBMS_APPLICATION_INFO.
NETWORK_PROTOCOL	Returns the network protocol being used as specified in the PROTOCOL= section of the connect string or tnsnames.ora definition.
NLS_CALENDAR	Returns the calendar for the current session.
NLS_CURRENCY	Returns the currency for the current session.
NLS_DATE_FORMAT	Returns the date format for the current session.
NLS_DATE_LANGUAGE	Returns the language used for displaying dates.
NLS_SORT	Returns the binary or linguistic sort basis.
NLS_TERRITORY	Returns the territory for the current session.
OS_USER	Returns the operating-system username for the current session.

TABLE 3.14 Parameters in the USERENV Namespace *(continued)*

Parameter	Description
POLICY_INVOKER	Returns the invoker of row-level security-policy functions.
PROXY_ENTERPRISE_IDENTITY	Returns OID DN when the proxy user is an enterprise user.
PROXY_GOLBAL_UID	Returns the global user ID from OID for Enterprise User Security proxy users.
PROXY_USER	Returns the name of the database user who opened the current session for the session user.
PROXY_USERID	Returns the numeric ID for the database user who opened the current session for the session user.
SERVER_HOST	Returns the hostname of the machine where the instance is running.
SERVICE_NAME	Returns the name of the service where the session is connected.
SESSION_USER	Returns the database username for the current session.
SESSION_USERID	Returns the numeric database user ID for the current session.
SESSIONID	Returns the auditing session identifier AUDSID. This parameter is out of scope for distributed queries.
SID	Returns the session number (same as the SID from V$SESSION).
STATEMENT_ID	Returns the auditing statement identifier.
TERMINAL	Returns the terminal identifier for the current session. This is the same as the terminal in V$SESSION.

Here are few more examples of SYS_CONTEXT in the USERENV namespace:

```
SELECT SYS_CONTEXT('USERENV', 'OS_USER'),
       SYS_CONTEXT('USERENV', 'CURRENT_SCHEMA'),
       SYS_CONTEXT('USERENV', 'HOST'),
       SYS_CONTEXT('USERENV', 'NLS_TERRITORY')
FROM dual;
```

```
SYS_CONTEXT('USERENV','OS_USER')
SYS_CONTEXT('USERENV','CURRENT_SCHEMA')
SYS_CONTEXT('USERENV','HOST')
SYS_CONTEXT('USERENV','NLS_TERRITORY')
-------------------------------------------
oracle
HR
linux04.mycompany.corp
AMERICA
```

SYS_GUID

SYS_GUID() generates a globally unique identifier as a RAW value. This function is useful for creating a unique identifier to identify a row. SYS_GUID() returns a 32-bit hexadecimal representation of the 16-byte RAW value.

```
SELECT SYS_GUID() FROM DUAL;

SYS_GUID()
--------------------------------
CDA78A020D6E43A6AB743A5CE8CB8C55

SELECT SYS_GUID() FROM DUAL;

SYS_GUID()
--------------------------------
DC7C19A3AD264CE184C64194E65F83E5
```

UID

UID takes no parameters and returns the integer user ID for the current user connected to the session. The user ID uniquely identifies each user in a database and can be selected from the DBA_USERS view.

```
SQL> SHOW USER
USER is "BTHOMAS"

SELECT username, account_status
FROM dba_users
WHERE user_id = UID;
```

```
USERNAME          ACCOUNT_STATUS
----------------  ----------------
BTHOMAS           OPEN
```

USER

USER takes no parameters and returns a character string containing the username for the current user.

```
SELECT default_tablespace, temporary_tablespace
FROM dba_users
WHERE username = USER;
```

```
DEFAULT_TABLESPACE              TEMPORARY_TABLESPACE
------------------------------  ----------------------
USERS                           TEMP
```

USERENV

USERENV(*opt*) takes a single argument, where *opt* is one of the following options:

- ISDBA returns TRUE if the SYSDBA role is enabled in the current session.
- SESSIONID returns the AUDSID auditing session identifier.
- ENTRYID returns the auditing entry identifier if auditing is enabled for the instance (the init.ora parameter AUDIT_TRAIL is set to TRUE).
- INSTANCE returns the instance identifier to which the session is connected. This option is useful only if you are running the Oracle Parallel Server and have multiple instances.
- LANGUAGE returns the language, territory, and database character set. The delimiters are an underscore (_) between language and territory and a period (.) between the territory and character set.
- LANG returns the ISO abbreviation of the session's language.
- TERMINAL returns a VARCHAR2 string containing information corresponding to the operating system identifier for the current session's terminal.

The option can appear in uppercase, lowercase, or mixed case. The USERENV function has been deprecated since Oracle 9*i*. It is recommended to use the SYS_CONTEXT function with the built-in USERENV namespace instead.

VSIZE

VSIZE(*x*) takes a single argument, where *x* is an expression. This function returns the size in bytes of the internal representation of the *x*.

```
SELECT last_name, first_name,
       VSIZE(last_name) ln_size, VSIZE(first_name) fn_size
```

```
FROM employees
WHERE last_name like 'K%';

LAST_NAME    FIRST_NAME            LN_SIZE    FN_SIZE
------------ -------------------- ---------- ----------
Kaufling     Payam                        8          5
Khoo         Alexander                    4          9
King         Janette                      4          7
King         Steven                       4          6
Kochhar      Neena                        7          5
Kumar        Sundita                      5          7
```

Because the database character set is single-byte, the byte used for each character is 1; hence, the size shown here is actually the number of characters in the input. For multibyte characters, this would be different.

Summary

This chapter introduced single-row functions. It started by discussing the functions available in Oracle Database 12*c* to handle NULLs. Then it discussed the single-row functions available in Oracle Database 12*c* by grouping them into character, numeric, date, and conversion functions.

You learned that single-row functions return a value for each row as it is retrieved from the table. You can use single-row functions to interpret NULL values, format output, convert datatypes, transform data, perform date arithmetic, give environment information, and perform trigonometric calculations.

You can use single-row functions in the SELECT, WHERE, and ORDER BY clauses of SELECT statements. We covered the rich assortment of functions available in each datatype category and some functions that work on any datatype.

The NVL, NVL2, and COALESCE functions interpret NULL values.

The single-row character functions operate on character input. The INSTR function returns the position of a substring within the string. The SUBSTR function returns a portion of the string. INSTR and SUBSTR are great for extracting part of the input string. REPLACE and TRANSLATE transform the input.

Single-row numeric functions operate on numeric input. FLOOR, CEIL, ROUND, and TRUNC get the nearest number. FLOOR, CEIL, and ROUND return the nearest integer, whereas ROUND returns a value rounded to certain digits of precision. REMAINDER and MOD are similar functions.

Date functions operate on datetime values. SYSDATE and SYSTIMESTAMP values return the current date and time. MONTHS_BETWEEN finds the number of months between two date values. ADD_MONTHS is a commonly used function and can add months to or subtract months from a date. You can use ROUND and TRUNC on datetime values to find the nearest date, month, or year.

Of the conversion functions, TO_CHAR and TO_DATE are the most commonly used. We also reviewed the format codes that can be used with numeric and datetime values.

The DECODE function evaluates a condition, and you can easily build IF...THEN...ELSE logic into SQL using the DECODE function.

Exam Essentials

Understand where single-row functions can be used.   Single-row functions can be used in the SELECT, WHERE, and ORDER BY clauses of SELECT statements.

Know the effects that NULL values can have on arithmetic and other functions.   Any arithmetic operation on a NULL results in a NULL. This is true of most functions as well. Use the NVL, NVL2, and COALESCE functions to deal with NULLs.

Review the character-manipulation functions.   Understand the arguments and the results of using character-manipulation functions such as INSTR, SUBSTR, REPLACE, and TRANSLATE.

Understand the numeric functions.   Know the effects of using TRUNC and ROUND with -n as the second argument. Also practice using LENGTH and INSTR, which return numeric results, inside SUBSTR and other character functions.

Know how date arithmetic works.   When adding or subtracting numeric values from a DATE datatype, whole numbers represent days. Also, the date/time intervals INTERVAL YEAR TO MONTH and INTERVAL DAY TO SECOND can be added or subtracted from date/time datatypes. You need to know how to interpret and create expressions that add intervals to or subtract intervals from dates.

Know the datatypes for the various date/time functions.   Oracle has many date/time functions to support the date/time datatypes. You need to know the return datatypes for these functions. SYSDATE and CURRENT_DATE return a DATE datatype. CURRENT_TIMESTAMP and SYSTIMESTAMP return a TIMESTAMP WITH TIME ZONE datatype. LOCALTIMESTAMP returns a TIMESTAMP datatype.

Know the format models for converting dates to/from character strings.   In practice, you can simply look up format codes in a reference. For the certification exam, you must have them memorized.

Understand the use of the DECODE function.   DECODE acts like a case statement in C, Pascal, or Ada. Learn how this function works and how to use it.

Learn the COALESCE and the NVL2 functions.   All the NULL-related functions are important. Pay particular attention to COALESCE and NVL2. Try out various examples.

Review Questions

1. You want to display each project's start date as the day, week, number, and year. Which statement will give output like the following?

   ```
   Tuesday  Week 23, 2008
   ```

   A. SELECT proj_id, TO_CHAR(start_date, 'DOW Week WOY YYYY')
      FROM projects;

   B. SELECT proj_id, TO_CHAR(start_date,'Day'||' Week'||' WOY, YYYY')
      FROM projects;

   C. SELECT proj_id, TO_CHAR(start_date, 'Day" Week" WW, YYYY')
      FROM projects;

   D. SELECT proj_id, TO_CHAR(start_date, 'Day Week# , YYYY') FROM projects;

   E. You can't calculate week numbers with Oracle.

2. What will the following statement return?

   ```
   SELECT last_name, first_name, start_date
   FROM employees
   WHERE hire_date < TRUNC(SYSDATE) - 5;
   ```

   A. Employees hired within the past five hours

   B. Employees hired within the past five days

   C. Employees hired more than five hours ago

   D. Employees hired more than five days ago

3. Which assertion about the following statements is most true?

   ```
   SELECT name, region_code||phone_number
   FROM customers;
   SELECT name, CONCAT(region_code,phone_number)
   FROM customers;
   ```

   A. If REGION_CODE is NULL, the first statement will not include that customer's PHONE_NUMBER.

   B. If REGION_CODE is NULL, the second statement will not include that customer's PHONE_NUMBER.

   C. Both statements will return the same data.

   D. The second statement will raise an error if REGION_CODE is NULL for any customer.

4. Which single-row function could you use to return a specific portion of a character string?

   A. INSTR

   B. SUBSTR

   C. LPAD

   D. LEAST

5. The data in the PRODUCT table is as described here. The bonus amount is calculated as the lesser of 5 percent of the base price or 20 percent of the surcharge.

sku	name	division	base_price	surcharge
1001	PROD-1001	A	200	50
1002	PROD-1002	C	250	
1003	PROD-1003	C	240	20
1004	PROD-1004	A	320	
1005	PROD-1005	C	225	40

   Which of the following statements will achieve the desired results?

   A. SELECT sku, name, LEAST(base_price * 1.05, surcharge * 1.2)FROM products;

   B. SELECT sku, name, LEAST(NVL(base_price,0) * 1.05, surcharge * 1.2)FROM products;

   C. SELECT sku, name, COALESCE(LEAST(base_price*1.05, surcharge * 1.2), base_price * 1.05)FROM products;

   D. A, B, and C will all achieve the desired results.

   E. None of these statements will achieve the desired results.

6. Which function(s) accept arguments of any datatype? (Choose all that apply.)

   A. SUBSTR

   B. NVL

   C. ROUND

   D. DECODE

   E. SIGN

7. What will be returned by SIGN(ABS(NVL(-32,0)))?

   A. 1

   B. 32

   C. -1

   D. 0

   E. NULL

8. The SALARY table has the following data:

LAST_NAME	FIRST_NAME	SALARY
Mavris	Susan	6500
Higgins	Shelley	12000
Tobias	Sigal	
Colmenares	Karen	2500
Weiss	Matthew	8000
Mourgos	Kevin	5800
Rogers	Michael	2900
Stiles	Stephen	3200

Consider the following SQL instructions, and choose the best option:

```
SELECT last_name, NVL2(salary, salary, 0) N1,
       NVL(salary,0) N2
FROM salary;
```

A. Column N1 and N2 will have different results.

B. Column N1 will show zero for all rows, and column N2 will show the correct salary values, and zero for Tobias.

C. The SQL will error out because the number of arguments in the NVL2 function is incorrect.

D. Columns N1 and N2 will show the same result.

9. Which two functions could you use to strip leading characters from a character string? (Choose two.)

A. LTRIM

B. SUBSTR

C. RTRIM

D. INSTR

E. STRIP

10. What is the result of MOD(x1, 4) if x1 is 11?

A. -1

B. 3

C. 1

D. REMAINDER(11,4)

11. Which SQL statement will replace the last two characters of *last_name* with 'XX' in the employees table when executed?

A. SELECT RTRIM(last_name, SUBSTR(last_name, LENGTH(last_name)-1)) || 'XX' new_col FROM employees;

B. SELECT REPLACE(last_name, SUBSTR(last_name, LENGTH(last_name)-1), 'XX') new_col FROM employees;

C. SELECT REPLACE(SUBSTR(last_name, LENGTH(last_name)-1), 'XX') new_col FROM employees;

D. SELECT CONCAT(SUBSTR(last_name, 1,LENGTH(last_name)-2), 'XX') new_col FROM employees;

12. Which date components does the CURRENT_TIMESTAMP function display?

A. Session date, session time, and session time zone offset

B. Session date and session time

C. Session date and session time zone offset

D. Session time zone offset

13. Using the SALESPERSON_REVENUE table described here, which statements will properly display the TOTAL_REVENUE (CAR_SALES + WARRANTY_SALES) of each salesperson?

Column Name	salesperson_id	car_sales	warranty_sales
Key Type	Pk		
NULLs/Unique	NN	NN	
FK Table			
Datatype	NUMBER	NUMBER	NUMBER
Length	10	11,2	11,2

A. SELECT salesperson_id, car_sales, warranty_sales, car_sales + warranty_sales total_salesFROM salesperson_revenue;

B. SELECT salesperson_id, car_sales, warranty_sales, car_sales + NVL2(warranty_sales,0) total_salesFROM salesperson_revenue;

C. SELECT salesperson_id, car_sales, warranty_sales, NVL2(warranty_sales, car_sales + warranty_sales, car_sales) total_salesFROM salesperson_revenue;

D. SELECT salesperson_id, car_sales, warranty_sales, car_sales + COALESCE(car_sales, warranty_sales, car_sales + warranty_sales) total_salesFROM salesperson_revenue;

14. What would be the result of executing the following SQL, if today's date were February 28, 2009?

```
SELECT ADD_MONTHS('28-FEB-09', -12) from dual;
```

A. 28-FEB-10

B. 28-FEB-08

C. 29-FEB-08

D. 28-JAN-08

15. Consider the following two SQL statements, and choose the best option:

```
1. SELECT TO_DATE('30-SEP-07','DD-MM-YYYY')  from dual;
2. SELECT TO_DATE('30-SEP-07','DD-MON-RRRR') from dual;
```

A. Statement 1 will error; 2 will produce results.

B. The resulting date value from the two statements will be the same.

C. The resulting date value from the two statements will be different.

D. Both statements will generate an error.

16. What will the following SQL statement return?

```
SELECT COALESCE(NULL,'Oracle ','Certified') FROM dual;
```

A. NULL

B. Oracle

C. Certified

D. Oracle Certified

17. Which expression will always return the date one year later than the current date?

A. SYSDATE + 365

B. SYSDATE + TO_YMINTERVAL('01-00')

C. CURRENT_DATE + 1

D. NEW_TIME(CURRENT_DATE,1,'YEAR')

E. None of the above

18. Which function will return a TIMESTAMP WITH TIME ZONE datatype?

A. CURRENT_TIMESTAMP

B. LOCALTIMESTAMP

C. CURRENT_DATE

D. SYSDATE

19. Which statement would change all occurrences of the string `'IBM'` to the string `'SUN'` in the DESCRIPTION column of the VENDOR table?

A. SELECT TRANSLATE(description, 'IBM', 'SUN') FROM vendor

B. SELECT CONVERT(description, 'IBM', 'SUN') FROM vendor

C. SELECT EXTRACT(description, 'IBM', 'SUN') FROM vendor

D. SELECT REPLACE(description, 'IBM', 'SUN') FROM vendor

20. Which function implements IF…THEN…ELSE logic?

A. INITCAP

B. REPLACE

C. DECODE

D. IFELSE

Chapter

4

Using Group Functions

ORACLE DATABASE 12*c*: SQL FUNDAMENTALS EXAM OBJECTIVES COVERED IN THIS CHAPTER:

✓ **Reporting Aggregated Data Using the Group Functions**

- Identify the available group functions.

- Describe the use of group functions.

- Group data by using the GROUP BY clause.

- Include or exclude the grouped rows by using the HAVING clause.

As explained in the previous chapter, *functions* are programs that take zero or more arguments and return a single value. The certification exam focuses on two types of functions: single-row and aggregate (group) functions. Single-row functions were covered in Chapter 3, "Using Single-Row Functions." Group functions are covered in this chapter.

Group functions differ from single-row functions in how they are evaluated. Single-row functions are evaluated once for each row retrieved. Group functions are evaluated on groups of one or more rows at a time.

In this chapter, you will explore which group functions are available in SQL, the rules for how to use them, and what to expect on the exam about aggregating data and group functions. You will also explore nesting function calls together. SQL allows you to nest group functions within calls to single-row functions, as well as nest single-row functions within calls to group functions.

Group Function Fundamentals

Group functions are sometimes called *aggregate functions* and return a value based on a number of inputs. The exact number of inputs is not determined until the query is executed and all rows are fetched. This differs from single-row functions, in which the number of inputs is known at parse time before the query is executed. Because of this difference, group functions have slightly different requirements and behavior than single-row functions.

Group functions do not consider NULL values, except the COUNT(*) and GROUPING functions. You may apply the NVL function to the argument of the group function to substitute a value for NULL and hence be included in the processing of the group function. If the dataset contains all NULL values or there are no rows in the dataset, the group function returns NULL (the only exception to this rule is COUNT—it returns zero).

Most of the group functions can be applied either to ALL values or to only the DISTINCT values for the specified expression. When ALL is specified, all non-NULL values are applied to the group function. When DISTINCT is specified, only one of each non-NULL value is applied to the function. If you do not specify ALL or DISTINCT, the default is ALL.

To better understand the difference between ALL and DISTINCT, let's look at a few rows from the EMPLOYEES table:

```
SELECT first_name,  salary
FROM employees
WHERE first_name LIKE 'D%'
```

```
ORDER BY salary;

FIRST_NAME               SALARY
-------------------- ----------
Donald                     2600
Douglas                    2600
Diana                      4200
David                      4800
David                      6800
Daniel                     9000
David                      9500
Danielle                   9500
Den                       11000
```

The SALARY column contains nine values. Two employees have $2,600 and $9,500 each. When you count unique entries in the SALARY column, there are seven, because two are duplicates. The following SQL code shows a few examples. The COUNT function is used to get a count, and the SUM function is used to find the total. (We'll discuss these functions later in the chapter.) When the UNIQUE keyword is used, the 2,600 and 9,500 are included in the result only once.

```
SELECT COUNT(salary) cnt_nu, COUNT(DISTINCT salary) cnt_uq,
       SUM(salary) sum_nu, SUM(DISTINCT salary) sum_uq
FROM employees
WHERE first_name LIKE 'D%';

    CNT_NU     CNT_UQ     SUM_NU     SUM_UQ
---------- ---------- ---------- ----------
         9          7      60000      47900
```

Unlike with single-row functions, you cannot use programmer-written functions on grouped data.

Utilizing Aggregate Functions

As with single-row functions, Oracle offers a rich variety of aggregate functions. These functions can appear in the SELECT, ORDER BY, or HAVING clauses of SELECT statements. When used in the SELECT clause, they usually require a GROUP BY clause as well. If no GROUP BY clause is specified, the default grouping is for the entire result set. Group functions cannot appear in the WHERE clause of a SELECT statement. The GROUP BY and HAVING clauses of SELECT statements are associated with grouping data. We'll discuss the GROUP BY clause before you learn about the various group functions.

> You almost certainly will encounter a certification exam question that tests whether you will incorrectly put a group function in the WHERE clause.

Grouping Data with GROUP BY

As the name implies, group functions work on data that is grouped. You tell the database how to group or categorize the data with a GROUP BY clause. Whenever you use a group function in the SELECT clause of a SELECT statement, you must place all nongrouping/nonconstant columns in the GROUP BY clause. If no GROUP BY clause is specified (only group functions and constants appear in the SELECT clause), the default grouping becomes the entire result set. When the query executes and the data is fetched, it is grouped based on the GROUP BY clause, and the group function is applied.

The basic syntax of using a group function in the SELECT statement is as follows:

```
SELECT [column names], group_function (column_name), … … …
FROM table
[WHERE condition]
[GROUP BY column names]
[ORDER BY column names]
```

In the following example, you find the total number of employees from the EMPLOYEES table:

```
SELECT COUNT(*) FROM employees;

  COUNT(*)
----------
       107
```

Because you did not have any other column in the SELECT clause, you did not need to specify the GROUP BY clause. Suppose you want to find out the number of employees in each department; you can include department_id in the SELECT clause:

```
SELECT department_id, COUNT(*) "#Employees"
FROM employees;
SELECT department_id, COUNT(*) "#Employees"
      *
```

```
ERROR at line 1:
ORA-00937: not a single-group group function
```

Because you used an aggregate function and nonaggregated column, Oracle generated an error and is telling you to group the data. Here you have to use the GROUP BY clause. If you include a group function in the SELECT clause, you cannot select individual results unless you use the GROUP BY clause. Make sure all the columns in the SELECT clause that are not part of a group function are included in the GROUP BY clause. The following SQL code lists the number of employees by their department:

```
SELECT department_id, COUNT(*) "#Employees"
FROM employees
GROUP BY department_id;


DEPARTMENT_ID #Employees
------------- ----------
          100          6
           30          6
                       1
           20          2
           70          1
           90          3
          110          2
           50         45
           40          1
           80         34
           10          1
           60          5
```

Notice that the rows are returned in no specific order. If you want the rows to be arranged in the order of the number of employees, you can either specify the aggregate function in the ORDER BY clause or use the position of the column, like so:

```
SELECT department_id, COUNT(*) "#Employees"
FROM employees
GROUP BY department_id
ORDER BY count(*) DESC, department_id;


SELECT department_id, COUNT(*) "#Employees"
FROM employees
GROUP BY department_id
ORDER BY 2 DESC, department_id;
```

```
DEPARTMENT_ID #Employees
------------- ----------
           50         45
           80         34
           30          6
          100          6
           60          5
           90          3
           20          2
          110          2
           10          1
           40          1
           70          1
                       1
```

You cannot use a column alias name or column position in the GROUP BY clause (as you can in the ORDER BY clause). The following SQL instructions use the column position in the GROUP BY clause and hence generate an error:

```
SELECT department_id, COUNT(*) "#Employees"
FROM employees
GROUP BY 1;
SELECT department_id, COUNT(*) "#Employees"
        *
ERROR at line 1:
ORA-00979: not a GROUP BY expression
```

The following is another invalid SQL statement. In this example, the GROUP BY clause uses a column alias, which is not supported. Pay particular attention to GROUP BY questions on the certification exam, because you might see one with a column alias or column position used.

```
SELECT department_id di, COUNT(*) emp_cnt
FROM employees
GROUP BY di;
GROUP BY di
         *
ERROR at line 3:
ORA-00904: "DI": invalid identifier
```

The GROUP BY column does not have to be in the SELECT clause. In most cases, the result may not make much sense, but you might need it. In the following example, you are calculating the average salary of employees in each department; you do not want to share which department the average salary belongs to, and you are only interested in knowing the average salaries in the company by department:

```
SELECT AVG(salary) average_salary
FROM employees
GROUP BY department_id;
```

```
AVERAGE_SALARY
--------------
   8601.33333
         4150
         7000
   19333.3333
         9500
        10000
        10154
   3475.55556
   8955.88235
         6500
         5760
         4400
```

If you have more than one column in the GROUP BY clause, Oracle creates groups within groups. The order of columns in the GROUP BY clause determines the grouping. Multiple columns in the GROUP BY clause are required when you have more than one nonaggregate column in the SELECT clause. In the following example, the rows are grouped by the department_id, and within each department they are grouped by the job_id. The SQL shows the number of different jobs within each department:

```
SELECT department_id, job_id, COUNT(*)
FROM employees
GROUP BY department_id, job_id
ORDER BY 1, 2;
```

```
DEPARTMENT_ID JOB_ID      COUNT(*)
------------- ----------  ----------
           10 AD_ASST            1
           20 MK_MAN             1
           20 MK_REP             1
           30 PU_CLERK           5
           30 PU_MAN             1
           40 HR_REP             1
```

```
 50  SH_CLERK          20
 50  ST_CLERK          20
 50  ST_MAN             5
 60  IT_PROG            5
 70  PR_REP             1
 80  SA_MAN             5
 80  SA_REP            29
 90  AD_PRES            1
 90  AD_VP             2
100  FI_ACCOUNT         5
100  FI_MGR             1
110  AC_ACCOUNT         1
110  AC_MGR             1
     SA_REP             1
```

The GROUP BY clause groups data, but Oracle does not guarantee the order of the result set by the grouping order. To order the data in any specific order, you must use the ORDER BY clause. ORDER BY clause follows the GROUP BY clause and if the ORDER BY clause is used, it is the last clause in the SELECT statement.

Group Function Overview

Tables 4.1 and 4.2 summarize the group functions discussed in this chapter. We will cover each of these functions in the "Group Function Descriptions" sections. Table 4.1 summarizes the group functions that are most likely to appear on the OCP certification exam.

TABLE 4.1   Group Function Summary: Part 1

Function	Description
AVG	Returns the statistical mean
COUNT	Returns the number of non-NULL rows
MAX	Returns the largest value
MEDIAN	Returns a middle value
MIN	Returns the smallest value

Function	Description
STDDEV	Returns the standard deviation
SUM	Adds all values and returns the result
VARIANCE	Returns the sample variance, or 1 for sample size 1
LISTAGG	Returns multiple rows of data in a single row based for each group

Table 4.2 summarizes the group functions available in Oracle Database 12*c* that are not included in Table 4.1. Although they are less likely to appear on the certification exam, they are still important to review.

TABLE 4.2   Group Function Summary: Part 2

Function	Description
CORR	Returns the coefficient of correlation of number pairs
COVAR_POP	Returns the population covariance of number pairs
COVAR_SAMP	Returns the sample covariance of number pairs
CUME_DIST	Returns the cumulative distribution of values within groupings
DENSE_RANK	Returns the ranking of rows within an ordered group, without skipping ranks on ties
FIRST	Modifies other aggregate functions to return expressions based on the ordering of the second-column expression
GROUP_ID	Returns a group identifier used to uniquely identify duplicate groups
GROUPING	Returns 0 for nonsummary rows or 1 for summary rows
GROUPING_ID	Helps determine group by levels when CUBE or ROLLUP is used
KEEP	Modifies other aggregate functions to return the first or last value in a grouping

TABLE 4.2 Group Function Summary: Part 2 *(continued)*

Function	Description
LAST	Modifies other aggregate functions to return expressions based on ordering of the second-column expression
PERCENTILE_CONT	Returns the interpolated value that would fall in the specified percentile position using a continuous model
PERCENTILE_DISC	Returns the interpolated value that would fall in the specified percentile position using a discrete model
PERCENT_RANK	Returns the percentile ranking of the specified value
RANK	Returns the ranking of rows within an ordered group, skipping ranks when ties occur
STDDEV_POP	Returns the population standard deviation
STDDEV_SAMP	Returns the sample standard deviation
VAR_POP	Returns the population variance
VAR_SAMP	Returns the sample variance

Group Function Descriptions: Part 1

We divided the group functions into two sections. The group functions included in the following sections are commonly used in everyday SQL and are most likely to appear on the OCP certification exam. We discuss each of these functions and include descriptions and examples of each.

 For the certification exam, concentrate more on the group functions covered in the Part 1 discussion than those in the Part 2 discussion.

AVG

AVG function has the syntax AVG([{DISTINCT | ALL}] *n*), where *n* is a numeric expression. The AVG function returns the average of the expression *n*. The following example finds the average salary of employees by job, whose job name begins with AC:

```
SELECT job_id, AVG(salary)
FROM employees
```

```
WHERE job_id like 'AC%'
GROUP BY job_id;


JOB_ID      AVG(SALARY)
----------  -----------

AC_ACCOUNT       8300
AC_MGR          12000
```

You can use an expression or formula in the group functions. In the following example, the average compensation including commission is calculated for department 30 from the SCOTT.EMP table. The expression will be evaluated first, and its result will be used to calculate the mean. To help you better understand the example, the data in department 30 is listed.

```
SELECT deptno, sal, comm
FROM scott.emp
WHERE deptno = 30;


    DEPTNO        SAL       COMM
----------  ---------- ----------
        30       1600        300
        30       1250        500
        30       1250       1400
        30       2850
        30       1500          0
        30        950
```

```
SELECT deptno, AVG(sal + NVL(comm,0)) avg_comp
FROM scott.emp
WHERE deptno = 30
GROUP BY deptno;


    DEPTNO    AVG_COMP
----------  ----------
        30  1933.33333
```

Remember that group functions ignore NULL values. If the NVL function is not used, the employees with no commission are not included in the mean calculation. See the result difference in the following example without the NVL use:

```
SELECT deptno, AVG(sal + comm) avg_comp
FROM scott.emp
WHERE deptno = 30
GROUP BY deptno;
```

```
    DEPTNO   AVG_COMP
---------- ----------
        30       1950
```

COUNT

The *COUNT* function has the syntax COUNT({* | [DISTINCT | ALL] <x>}), where x is an expression. The COUNT function returns the number of rows in the query. If an expression is given and neither DISTINCT nor ALL is specified, the default is ALL. The asterisk (*) is a special quantity; it counts all rows in the result set, regardless of NULLs.

In the example that follows, you can count the number of rows in the EMPLOYEES table (the number of employees), the number of departments that have employees in them (DEPT_COUNT), and the number of employees that have a department (NON_NULL_DEPT_COUNT). You can see from the results that one employee is not assigned to a department, and the other 106 are assigned to one of 11 departments.

```
SELECT COUNT(*) emp_count,
       COUNT(DISTINCT department_id) dept_count,
       COUNT(ALL department_id) non_null_dept_count
FROM hr.employees;
```

```
EMP_COUNT  DEPT_COUNT  NON_NULL_DEPT_COUNT
---------- ----------  -------------------
       107          11                  106
```

This next example looks at the number of employees drawing a commission, as well as the distinct number of commissions drawn. You can see that 35 out of 107 employees draw a commission and that seven different commission levels are in use.

```
SELECT COUNT(*),
       COUNT(commission_pct) comm_count,
       COUNT(DISTINCT commission_pct) distinct_comm
FROM hr.employees;
```

```
  COUNT(*) COMM_COUNT DISTINCT_COMM
---------- ---------- -------------
       107         35             7
```

MAX

The *MAX* function has the syntax MAX([{DISTINCT | ALL}] <x>), where x is an expression. This function returns the highest value in the expression x. x can be a datetime, numeric, or character value. The results of the MAX operation on the three groups of datatypes are as follows:

- If the expression *x* is a datetime datatype, it returns a DATE. For dates, the maximum is the latest date.

- If the expression *x* is a numeric datatype, it returns a NUMBER. For numbers, the maximum is the largest number.

- If the expression is a character datatype, it returns a VARCHAR2. For character strings, the maximum is the one that sorts highest based on the database character set.

Although the inclusion of either DISTINCT or ALL is syntactically acceptable, their use does not affect the calculation of a MAX function; the largest distinct value is the same as the largest of all values. The following example finds information from the employees table: the latest hire date, highest salary, and employee whose last name is last when sorted in ascending order:

```
SELECT MAX(hire_date),
       MAX(salary),
       MAX(last_name)
FROM hr.employees;


MAX(HIRE_ MAX(SALARY) MAX(LAST_NAME)
--------- ----------- ------------------------
21-APR-08       24000 Zlotkey
```

MIN

The *MIN* function has the syntax MIN([{DISTINCT | ALL}] <*x*>), where *x* is an expression. This function returns the lowest value in the expression *x*. Similar to the MAX function, the *x* in MIN can also be a numeric, datetime, or character datatype.

- If the expression *x* is a datetime datatype, it returns a DATE. For dates, the minimum is the earliest date.

- If the expression *x* is a numeric datatype, it returns a NUMBER. For numbers, the minimum is the smallest number.

- If the expression is a character datatype, it returns a VARCHAR2. For character strings, the minimum is the one that sorts lowest based on the database character set.

Although the inclusion of either DISTINCT or ALL is syntactically acceptable, their use does not affect the calculation of a MIN function; the smallest distinct value is the same as the smallest value. The following example finds the oldest hired employee, and the lowest salary and highest salary for each job category. The rows are filtered for jobs ending with CLERK:

```
SELECT job_id, MIN(hire_date) oldest, MIN(salary) low_sal,
       MAX(salary) high_sal
FROM hr.employees
```

```
WHERE job_id like '%CLERK'
GROUP BY job_id;


JOB_ID      OLDEST       LOW_SAL    HIGH_SAL
----------  ---------  ----------  ----------
PU_CLERK    18-MAY-03      2500        3100
SH_CLERK    27-JAN-04      2500        4200
ST_CLERK    14-JUL-03      2100        3600
```

SUM

The *SUM* function has the syntax SUM([{DISTINCT | ALL}] <x>), where *x* is a numeric expression. This function returns the sum of the expression *x*. The following example finds the total salary and average salary of employees by their phone number area code. Notice the use of group functions and a single-row function in the same SQL instructions:

```
SELECT SUBSTR(phone_number, 1,3) area_code,
      SUM(salary) total_sal, ROUND(AVG(salary)) avg_sal
FROM employees
GROUP BY SUBSTR(phone_number, 1,3);


AREA_CODE     TOTAL_SAL    AVG_SAL
------------  ----------  ----------
515              188716       8986
590               28800       5760
603                6000       6000
011              311500       8900
650              156400       3476
```

MEDIAN

MEDIAN (<x>) is an inverse distribution function that returns a middle value after the values in the expression are sorted. The argument *x* is an expression of numeric or datetime value. The following example finds the median, average, low, and high salary of employees by job category. To limit the rows returned, a filter condition is used:

```
SELECT job_id, MEDIAN(Salary) median, AVG(salary) average,
      MIN(salary) low_sal, MAX(salary) high_sal
FROM hr.employees
WHERE job_id like '%CLERK'
GROUP BY job_id;
```

JOB_ID	MEDIAN	AVERAGE	LOW_SAL	HIGH_SAL
PU_CLERK	2800	2780	2500	3100
SH_CLERK	3100	3215	2500	4200
ST_CLERK	2700	2785	2100	3600

STDDEV

This function has the syntax STDDEV([{DISTINCT | ALL}] <x>), where x is a numeric expression. The STDDEV function returns the numeric standard deviation of the expression x.

The standard deviation is calculated as the square root of the variance:

```
SELECT department_id,
       COUNT(salary) emp_cnt,
       MIN(salary) minimum,
       MAX(salary) maximum,
       AVG(salary) mean,
       STDDEV(salary) deviation
FROM employees
GROUP BY department_id
ORDER BY department_id;
```

DEPARTMENT_ID	EMP_CNT	MINIMUM	MAXIMUM	MEAN	DEVIATION
10	1	4400	4400	4400	0
20	2	6000	13000	9500	4949.74747
30	6	2500	11000	4150	3362.58829
40	1	6500	6500	6500	0
50	45	2100	8200	3475.55556	1488.00592
60	5	4200	9000	5760	1925.61678
70	1	10000	10000	10000	0
80	34	6100	14000	8955.88235	2033.6847
90	3	17000	24000	19333.3333	4041.45188
100	6	6900	12008	8601.33333	1804.13155
110	2	8300	12008	10154	2621.95194
	1	7000	7000	7000	0

VARIANCE

This function has the syntax VARIANCE([{DISTINCT | ALL}] <x>), where x is a numeric expression. This function returns the variance of the expression x. The following example finds the total number of employees in each department and their variance in salary by department:

```
SELECT department_id,
       COUNT(*),
       VARIANCE(salary)
FROM hr.employees
GROUP BY department_id
ORDER BY department_id;
```

```
DEPARTMENT_ID   COUNT(*) VARIANCE(SALARY)
------------- ---------- ----------------
           10          1                0
           20          2         24500000
           30          6         11307000
           40          1                0
           50         45       2214161.62
           60          5          3708000
           70          1                0
           80         34       4135873.44
           90          3        16333333.3
          100          6       3254890.67
          110          2          6874632
                       1                0
```

LISTAGG

The *LISTAGG* function aggregates data from multiple rows into one row per group. LISTAGG can be used as an aggregate function or analytic function. The aggregate function syntax is

```
LISTAGG(<expression> [, '<delimiter>']) WITHIN GROUP ( ORDER BY <columns>)
```

where *expression* is a numeric expression or string expression, usually the column you want to concatenate. The *delimiter* is optional, with default value NULL. If a delimiter is provided, the values returned in the expression are separated by this delimiter. The WITHIN GROUP clause is mandatory and it tells Oracle to produce one row per each distinct value of the GROUP BY columns, and within that group to sort the results according to the ORDER BY clause. The ORDER BY clause determines the order in which the aggregated values are ordered. The ORDER BY clause is mandatory; if you do not want to specify any column order, specify ORDER BY NULL. Let's review with an example to help you understand the LISTAGG function.

The following SQL code displays the first names of employees in each department concatenated and delimited with a comma.

```
SQL> col employee_names format a60 word
SQL> SELECT LISTAGG(first_name, ', ') WITHIN GROUP (
```

```
 2          ORDER BY first_name) Employee_Names,
 3          department_id
 4  FROM employees
 5  WHERE department_id > 75
 6* GROUP BY department_id;
```

```
EMPLOYEE_NAMES                                                DEPARTMENT_ID
------------------------------------------------------------- -------------
Alberto, Allan, Alyssa, Amit, Charles, Christopher, Clara,               80
Danielle, David, David, Eleni, Elizabeth, Ellen, Gerald,
Harrison, Jack, Janette, John, Jonathon, Karen, Lindsey,
Lisa, Louise, Mattea, Nanette, Oliver, Patrick, Peter,
Peter, Sarath, Sundar, Sundita, Tayler, William
Lex, Neena, Steven                                                      90
Daniel, Ismael, John, Jose Manuel, Luis, Nancy                         100
Shelley, William                                                       110
```

```
SQL>
```

If the GROUP BY clause is not used, one row result will be returned, similar to any other group function. The following example shows employee names and their hire date, in the order of hire date concatenated for department ID over 85. The filtering for this SQL is done only to restrict the number of rows. This example also shows using an expression as the first parameter for the LISTAGG function.

```
SQL> col employee_hire_dates format a60 word
SQL> SELECT LISTAGG(first_name || '('||hire_date||')', '; ')
 2          WITHIN GROUP (ORDER BY hire_date) Employee_Hire_Dates
 3  FROM employees
 4* WHERE department_id > 85;
```

```
EMPLOYEE_HIRE_DATES
-----------------------------------------------------------
Lex(13-JAN-01); Shelley(07-JUN-02); William(07-JUN-02);
Daniel(16-AUG-02); Nancy(17-AUG-02); Steven(17-JUN-03);
Neena(21-SEP-05); John(28-SEP-05); Ismael(30-SEP-05); Jose
Manuel(07-MAR-06); Luis(07-DEC-07)
```

```
SQL>
```

⊕ **Real World Scenario**

Exploring DBA Queries Using Aggregate Functions

As a DBA, you often need to find out how much space is allocated for a schema and how much is free. You might not be interested in seeing the space used by all the tables or indexes in the schema, but it would be nice to have the summary broken down into tablespace-wise schema storage space. Let's write a few SQL statements using the group functions that you can use to calculate space usage in a database.

The DBA_SEGMENTS dictionary view shows the segments allocated in the database—each table or index created in the database must have at least one segment created. The columns you are interested in for the query are tablespace_name, owner (or the schema name), and bytes (allocated space in bytes).

This first SQL code just gives the total space used by all the objects in the database. This is a simple SQL statement on all the rows in the view:

```
SELECT SUM(bytes)/1048576 size_mb
FROM dba_segments;


    SIZE_MB
----------
 1564.8125
```

Now, let's break down this space into the next level to see the space used in each tablespace. Because you are not interested in any aggregate function over the entire database but want to break it down by tablespaces, you must have the GROUP BY clause:

```
SELECT tablespace_name, SUM(bytes)/1048576 size_mb
FROM dba_segments
GROUP BY tablespace_name;

TABLESPACE_NAME                     SIZE_MB
------------------------------- ----------
SYSAUX                              716.375
UNDOTBS1                             48.25
USERS                                21.25
SYSTEM                              701.625
EXAMPLE                             77.3125
```

To find the amount of space allocated to each schema owner within the tablespaces, all you have to do is add the owner column to the query. Remember, because you are not performing an aggregate function on owner, that column also should be part of the GROUP BY clause. You also need to include an ORDER BY clause so that the rows returned are in the order of tablespace name.

```
SELECT tablespace_name, owner, SUM(bytes)/1048576 size_mb
FROM dba_segments
GROUP BY tablespace_name, owner
ORDER BY 1, 2;
```

TABLESPACE_NAME	OWNER	SIZE_MB
EXAMPLE	HR	1.5625
EXAMPLE	IX	1.625
EXAMPLE	OE	6.25
EXAMPLE	PM	11.875
EXAMPLE	SH	56
SYSAUX	CTXSYS	5.4375
... ...		
USERS	HR	.1875
USERS	OE	2.625
USERS	SCOTT	.375
USERS	SH	2

If you want to know the amount of space allocated to the objects owned by each schema, you can run the following query:

```
SELECT owner, SUM(bytes)/1048576 size_mb
FROM dba_segments
GROUP BY owner
ORDER BY 1;
```

OWNER	SIZE_MB
BTHOMAS	16.0625
CTXSYS	5.4375
DBSNMP	1.5
EXFSYS	3.875

```
FLOWS_030000                  100.6875
FLOWS_FILES                      .4375
HR                               1.75
... ... ...
```

Group Function Descriptions: Part 2

The group functions discussed in the following sections are included in this chapter for completeness of the group functions discussion. The likelihood of these appearing in the OCP certification exam is minimal, but knowing these functions will help you write better SQL queries.

Many group functions discussed in this group (and AVG, COUNT, MAX, MIN, STDDEV, SUM, and VARIANCE) can be used as analytic functions. Analytic functions are commonly used in data warehouse environments. They compute an aggregate based on a group of rows, called a *window*. Because the OCP certification exam does not include analytic functions, we won't discuss them in this chapter.

CORR

CORR(y, x) takes two arguments, where y and x are numeric expressions representing the dependent and independent variables, respectively. This function returns the coefficient of the correlation of a set of number pairs.

The coefficient of correlation is a measure of the strength of the relationship between the two numbers. CORR can return a NULL. The coefficient of the correlation is calculated from those x, y pairs that are both not NULL using the formula COVAR_POP(y,x) / (STDDEV_POP(y) * STDDEV_POP(x)).

```
SELECT CORR(list_price,min_price) correlation,
       COVAR_POP(list_price,min_price) covariance,
       STDDEV_POP(list_price) stddev_popy,
       STDDEV_POP(min_price) stddev_popx
FROM oe.product_information
WHERE list_price IS NOT NULL
AND  min_price IS NOT NULL;


CORRELATION   COVARIANCE STDDEV_POPY STDDEV_POPX
----------- ------------ ----------- -----------
  .99947495   206065.903  496.712198  415.077696
```

The previous output shows that there is a 99.947 percent chance that the list price depends on the minimum price. So, when the minimum price moves by x percent, there is a 99.947 percent chance that the list price will also move by x percent.

COVAR_POP

COVAR_POP(*y*, *x*) takes two arguments, where *y* and *x* are numeric expressions. This function returns the population covariance of a set of number pairs, which can be NULL.

The covariance is a measure of how two sets of data vary in the same way. The population covariance is calculated from those *y*, *x* pairs that are both not NULL using the formula (SUM(*y**x) − SUM(*y*) * SUM(*x*) / COUNT(*x*)) / COUNT(*x*).

```
SELECT category_id,
       COVAR_POP(list_price,min_price) population,
       COVAR_SAMP(list_price,min_price) sample
FROM oe.product_information
GROUP BY category_id;
```

```
CATEGORY_ID POPULATION     SAMPLE
----------- ---------- ----------
         25   27670.25 31623.1429
         22         45       67.5
         11 92804.9883 98991.9875
         13  25142.125 26465.3947
         29    3446.75 3574.40741
         14 17982.9924 18800.4012
         31 1424679.17    1709615
         21 21.5306122 25.1190476
         24 109428.285 114639.156
         32    4575.06 4815.85263
         17 5466.14286    5739.45
         33        945       1134
         15 7650.84375     8160.9
         16     431.38 479.311111
         19 417343.887 426038.551
         12 26472.3333  29781.375
         39 1035.14059 1086.89762
```

COVAR_SAMP

COVAR_SAMP(*y*, *x*) takes two arguments, where *y* and *x* are numeric expressions representing the dependent and independent variables, respectively. This function returns the sample covariance of a set of number pairs, which can be NULL.

The covariance is a measure of how two sets of data vary in the same way. The sample covariance is calculated from those *x*, *y* pairs that are both not NULL using the formula (SUM(*y**x) − SUM(*y*) * SUM(*x*) / COUNT(*x*)) / (COUNT(*x*)−1).

```
SELECT SUM(list_price*min_price) sum_xy,
       SUM(list_price) sum_y,
       SUM(min_price) sum_x,
       COVAR_SAMP(list_price,min_price) COVARIANCE
FROM oe.product_information;


    SUM_XY       SUM_Y      SUM_X COVARIANCE
---------- ---------- ---------- ----------

  73803559       71407      60280 206791.488
```

CUME_DIST

This function has the syntax

```
CUME_DIST(<val_list>) WITHIN GROUP (ORDER BY col_list
[ASC|DESC] [NULLS {first|last}])
```

where *val_list* is a comma-delimited list of expressions that evaluate to numeric constant values and *col_list* is the comma-delimited list of column expressions. CUME_DIST returns the cumulative distribution of a value in *val_list* within a distribution in *col_list*.

The cumulative distribution is a measure of ranking within the ordered group and will be in the range 0 < CUME_DIST <= 1. See also PERCENT_RANK.

```
SELECT department_id,
       COUNT(*) emp_count,
       AVG(salary) mean,
       PERCENTILE_CONT(0.5) WITHIN GROUP
           (ORDER BY salary DESC) Median,
       CUME_DIST(10000) WITHIN GROUP
           (ORDER BY salary DESC) Cume_Dist_10K
FROM hr.employees
GROUP BY department_id;
```

DEPARTMENT_ID	EMP_COUNT	MEAN	MEDIAN	CUME_DIST_10K
10	1	4400	4400	.5
20	2	9500	9500	.666666667
30	6	4150	2850	.285714286
40	1	6500	6500	.5
50	45	3475.55556	3100	.02173913
60	5	5760	4800	.166666667
70	1	10000	10000	1
80	34	8955.88235	8900	.342857143

```
 90        3 19333.3333      17000              1
100        6 8601.33333       8000     .285714286
110        2       10154      10154    .666666667
           1        7000       7000             .5
```

DENSE_RANK

This function has the syntax

```
DENSE_RANK(val_list) WITHIN GROUP (ORDER BY col_list
[ASC|DESC] [NULLS {first|last}])
```

where *val_list* is a comma-delimited list of numeric constant expressions (expressions that evaluate to numeric constant values) and *col_list* is the comma-delimited list of column expressions. DENSE_RANK returns the row's rank within an ordered group. The ranks are consecutive integers starting with 1. The rank values are the number of unique values returned by the query. When there are ties, ranks are not skipped. For example, if three items are tied for first, then the second and third will not be skipped. See also RANK. The following example finds the number of employees in each department along with their low and high salary. Use the DENSE_RANK function to figure out the ranking of a $10,000 salary within each department:

```
SELECT department_id,
       COUNT(*) emp_count,
       MAX(salary) highsal,
       MIN(salary) lowsal,
       DENSE_RANK(10000) WITHIN GROUP
          (ORDER BY salary DESC) dense_rank_10K
FROM hr.employees
GROUP BY department_id;
```

```
DEPARTMENT_ID EMP_COUNT    HIGHSAL    LOWSAL DENSE_RANK_10K
------------- ---------- ---------- ---------- ---------------
           10         1       4400       4400              1
           20         2      13000       6000              2
           30         6      11000       2500              2
           40         1       6500       6500              1
           50        45       8200       2100              1
           60         5       9000       4200              1
           70         1      10000      10000              1
           80        34      14000       6100              7
           90         3      24000      17000              3
          100         6      12008       6900              2
          110         2      12008       8300              2
```

To understand this ranking, let's look closer at department 80. You can see that $10,000 is the seventh-highest salary in department 80. Even though there are 11 employees that make $10,000 or more, the duplicates are not counted for ranking purposes.

```
SELECT salary, COUNT(*)
FROM hr.employees
WHERE department_id=80
GROUP BY salary
ORDER BY salary DESC;

    SALARY   COUNT(*)
---------- ----------
     14000          1
     13500          1
     12000          1
     11500          1
     11000          2
     10500          2
     10000          3
      9600          1
... ... ... (output truncated)
```

See also RANK.

FIRST

See KEEP.

GROUP_ID

GROUP_ID( ) takes no arguments and requires a GROUP BY clause. GROUP_ID returns a numeric identifier that can be used to uniquely identify duplicate groups. For i duplicate groups, GROUP_ID will return values 0 through i-1.

GROUPING

GROUPING(x) takes a single argument, where x is an expression in the GROUP BY clause of the query. The GROUPING function is applicable only for queries that have a GROUP BY clause and a ROLLUP or CUBE clause. The ROLLUP and CUBE clauses create summary rows (sometimes called *superaggregates*) containing NULL in the grouped expressions. The GROUPING function returns a 1 for these summary rows and a 0 for the nonsummary rows, and it is used to distinguish the summary rows from the nonsummary rows.

GROUPING is discussed in detail in the "Creating Superaggregates with CUBE and ROLLUP" section later in this chapter.

GROUPING_ID

This function has the syntax GROUPING_ID (<col_list>) and is applicable only in SELECT statements with a GROUP BY clause with CUBE or ROLLUP. If the query contains many expressions in the GROUP BY clause, determining the GROUP BY level will require many GROUPING functions. The GROUPING_ID eliminates such a need. For a more detailed discussion on GROUPING_ID, see the section "Creating Superaggregates with CUBE and ROLLUP" later in this chapter.

KEEP

The KEEP function has the syntax

```
agg_function KEEP(DENSE_RANK {FIRST|LAST}
ORDER BY col_list [ASC|DESC] [NULLS {first|last}]))
```

where *agg_function* is an aggregate function (COUNT, SUM, AVG, MIN, MAX, VARIANCE, or STDDEV) and *col_list* is a list of columns to be ordered for the grouping.

This function is sometimes referred to as either the FIRST or LAST function, and it is actually a modifier for one of the other group functions, such as COUNT or MIN. The KEEP function returns the first or last row of a sorted group. It is used to avoid the need for a self-join, looking for the minimum or maximum

```
SELECT department_id,
       MIN(hire_date) earliest,
       MAX(hire_date) latest,
       COUNT(salary) KEEP
           (DENSE_RANK FIRST ORDER BY hire_date) FIRST,
       COUNT(salary) KEEP
           (DENSE_RANK LAST ORDER BY hire_date) LAST
FROM hr.employees
GROUP BY department_id;
```

DEPARTMENT_ID	EARLIEST	LATEST	FIRST	LAST
10	17-SEP-03	17-SEP-03	1	1
20	17-FEB-04	17-AUG-05	1	1
30	07-DEC-02	10-AUG-07	1	1
40	07-JUN-02	07-JUN-02	1	1
50	01-MAY-03	08-MAR-08	1	1
60	25-JUN-05	21-MAY-07	1	1
70	07-JUN-02	07-JUN-02	1	1

```
     80  30-JAN-04  21-APR-08            1              2
     90  13-JAN-01  21-SEP-05            1              1
    100  16-AUG-02  07-DEC-07            1              1
    110  07-JUN-02  07-JUN-02            2              2
         24-MAY-07  24-MAY-07            1              1
```

You can see from the previous query that department 80's earliest and latest anniversary dates are 30-Jan-2004 and 21-Apr-2008. The FIRST and LAST columns show us that one employee was hired on the earliest anniversary date (30-Jan-2004) and two were hired on the latest anniversary date (21-Apr-2008). Likewise, you can see that department 110 has two employees hired on the earliest anniversary date (07-Jun-2002) and two on the latest anniversary date (07-Jun-2002). If you look at the following detailed data, this becomes clearer:

```
SELECT department_id,hire_date
FROM hr.employees
WHERE department_id IN (80,110)
ORDER BY 1,2;

DEPARTMENT_ID HIRE_DATE
------------- ---------
           80 30-JAN-04
           80 04-MAR-04
           80 11-MAY-04
           80 01-AUG-04
           80 01-OCT-04
           80 05-JAN-05
           80 30-JAN-05
... ... ... (output truncated)
           80 21-APR-08
           80 21-APR-08
          110 07-JUN-02
          110 07-JUN-02
```

LAST

See KEEP.

PERCENT_RANK

The PERCENT_RANK function has the syntax

```
PERCENT_RANK(<val_list>) WITHIN GROUP (ORDER BY col_list
[ASC|DESC] [NULLS {first|last}])
```

where *val_list* is a comma-delimited list of expressions that evaluate to numeric constant values and *col_list* is the comma-delimited list of column expressions. PERCENT_RANK returns the percent ranking of a value in *val_list* within a distribution in *col_list*. The percent rank x will be in the range $0 <= x <= 1$.

The main difference between PERCENT_RANK and CUME_DIST is that PERCENT_RANK will always return a 0 for the first row in any set, while the CUME_DIST function cannot return a 0. You can use the PERCENT_RANK and CUME_DIST functions to examine the rankings of employees with salaries of more than $10,000 in the HR.EMPLOYEES table. Notice the different results for departments 40 and 70.

```
SELECT DEPARTMENT_ID DID,
       COUNT(*) emp_count,
       AVG(salary) mean,
       PERCENTILE_CONT(0.5) WITHIN GROUP
           (ORDER BY salary DESC) median,
       PERCENT_RANK(10000) WITHIN GROUP
           (ORDER BY salary DESC)*100 pct_rank_10K,
       CUME_DIST(10000) WITHIN GROUP
           (ORDER BY salary DESC)*100 cume_dist_10K
FROM hr.employees
GROUP BY department_id;
```

DID	EMP_COUNT	MEAN	MEDIAN	PCT_RANK_10K	CUME_DIST_10K
10	1	4400	4400	0	50
20	2	9500	9500	50	66.6666667
30	6	4150	2850	16.6666667	28.5714286
40	1	6500	6500	0	50
50	45	3475.55556	3100	0	2.17391304
60	5	5760	4800	0	16.6666667
70	1	10000	10000	0	100
80	34	8955.88235	8900	23.5294118	34.2857143
90	3	19333.3333	17000	100	100
100	6	8601.33333	8000	16.6666667	28.5714286
110	2	10154	10154	50	66.6666667
	1	7000	7000	0	50

PERCENTILE_CONT

PERCENTILE_CONT has the syntax

```
PERCENTILE_CONT(<x>) WITHIN GROUP (ORDER BY col_list
[ASC|DESC])
```

where x is a percentile value in the range $0 < x < 1$ and *col_list* is the sort specification. PERCENTILE_CONT returns the interpolated value that would fall in percentile position x within the sorted group *col_list*.

This function assumes a continuous distribution and is most useful for obtaining the median value of an ordered group. The median value is defined to be the midpoint in a group of ordered numbers—half of the values are greater than the median, and half of the values are less than the median.

 The median together with the mean or average are the two most common measures of a central tendency used to analyze data. See the AVG function for more information on calculating the mean.

For this example, you will use the SCOTT.EMP table, ordered by department number:

```
SELECT ename ,deptno ,sal
FROM scott.emp
ORDER BY deptno ,sal;
```

ENAME	DEPTNO	SAL
MILLER	10	1300
CLARK	10	2450
KING	10	5000
SMITH	20	800
ADAMS	20	1100
JONES	20	2975
SCOTT	20	3000
FORD	20	3000
JAMES	30	950
WARD	30	1250
MARTIN	30	1250
TURNER	30	1500
ALLEN	30	1600
BLAKE	30	2850

You can see that for department 10, there are three SAL values: 1300, 2450, and 5000. The median would be 2450, because there is one value greater than this number and one value less than this number. The median for department 30 is not so straightforward, because there are six values and the middle value is actually between the two data points 1250 and 1500. To get the median for department 30, you need to interpolate the midpoint.

Two common techniques are used to interpolate this median value: one technique uses a continuous model, and one uses a discrete model. In the continuous model, the midpoint is assumed to be the value halfway between the 1250 and 1500, which is 1375. Using the discrete model, the median must be an actual data point, and depending on whether the data is ordered ascending or descending, the median would be 1250 or 1500.

```
SELECT deptno,
       PERCENTILE_CONT(0.5) WITHIN GROUP
             (ORDER BY sal DESC) "CONTINUOUS",
       PERCENTILE_DISC(0.5) WITHIN GROUP
             (ORDER BY sal DESC) "DISCRETE DESC",
       PERCENTILE_DISC(0.5) WITHIN GROUP
             (ORDER BY sal ASC) "DISCRETE ASC",
       AVG(sal) mean
FROM scott.emp
GROUP BY deptno;
```

DEPTNO	CONTINUOUS	DISCRETE DESC	DISCRETE ASC	MEAN
10	2450	2450	2450	2916.66667
20	2975	2975	2975	2175
30	1375	1500	1250	1566.66667

PERCENTILE_DISC

PERCENTILE_DISC has the syntax

```
PERCENTILE_DISC(<x>) WITHIN GROUP (ORDER BY col_list
[ASC|DESC])
```

where x is a percentile value in the range $0 < x < 1$ and col_list is the sort specification. PERCENTILE_DISC returns the smallest cumulative distribution value from the col_list set that is greater than or equal to value x.

This function assumes a discrete distribution. Sometimes data cannot be averaged in a meaningful way. Date data, for example, cannot be averaged, but you can calculate the median date in a group of dates. For example, to calculate the median hire date for employees in each department, you could run the following query:

```
SELECT department_id did,
       COUNT(*) emp_count,
       MIN(HIRE_DATE) first,
       MAX(HIRE_DATE) last,
       PERCENTILE_DISC(0.5) WITHIN GROUP
             (ORDER BY HIRE_DATE) median
FROM hr.employees
GROUP BY department_id;
```

```
     DID  EMP_COUNT  FIRST      LAST       MEDIAN
---------- ---------- ---------- ---------- ----------
        10          1 17-SEP-03 17-SEP-03 17-SEP-03
        20          2 17-FEB-04 17-AUG-05 17-FEB-04
        30          6 07-DEC-02 10-AUG-07 24-JUL-05
        40          1 07-JUN-02 07-JUN-02 07-JUN-02
        50         45 01-MAY-03 08-MAR-08 15-MAR-06
        60          5 25-JUN-05 21-MAY-07 05-FEB-06
        70          1 07-JUN-02 07-JUN-02 07-JUN-02
        80         34 30-JAN-04 21-APR-08 23-MAR-06
        90          3 13-JAN-01 21-SEP-05 17-JUN-03
       100          6 16-AUG-02 07-DEC-07 28-SEP-05
       110          2 07-JUN-02 07-JUN-02 07-JUN-02
                    1 24-MAY-07 24-MAY-07 24-MAY-07
```

RANK

RANK function is similar to DENSE_RANK and has the syntax

```
RANK(<val_list>) WITHIN GROUP (ORDER BY col_list
[ASC|DESC] [NULLS {first|last}])
```

where *val_list* is a comma-delimited list of numeric constant expressions (expressions that evaluate to numeric constant values) and *col_list* is the comma-delimited list of column expressions. RANK returns the row's rank within an ordered group.

When there are ties, ranks of equal value are assigned equal rank, and the number of tied rows is skipped before the next rank is assigned. For example, if three items are tied for first, the second and third items will be skipped, and the next will be the fourth. Whereas when DENSE_RANK is used, ranks are not skipped and only unique values are considered for ranking. The following example shows the same example we used for DENSE_RANK, but includes RANK function as well to show the difference in behavior for these functions.

```
SELECT department_id,
       MAX(salary) highsal,
       MIN(salary) lowsal,
       DENSE_RANK(10000) WITHIN GROUP
           (ORDER BY salary DESC) dense_rank_10K,
       RANK(10000) WITHIN GROUP
           (ORDER BY salary DESC) rank_10K
FROM hr.employees
GROUP BY department_id;
```

DEPARTMENT_ID	HIGHSAL	LOWSAL	DENSE_RANK_10K	RANK_10K
10	4400	4400	1	1
20	13000	6000	2	2
30	11000	2500	2	2
40	6500	6500	1	1
50	8200	2100	1	1
60	9000	4200	1	1
70	10000	10000	1	1
80	14000	6100	7	9
90	24000	17000	3	4
100	12008	6900	2	2
110	12008	8300	2	2

To help you understand this ranking, let's look again at department 80. You can see that 10,000 is the seventh-highest salary in department 80. But because there are eight employees who make more than $10,000, the rank of 10,000 is 9. The duplicates are counted for ranking purposes when using RANK, but not for DENSE_RANK. Refer to the "DENSE_RANK" section to see the distinct salaries in department 80.

STDDEV_POP

STDDEV_POP(<x>) takes a single argument, where x is a numeric expression. This function returns the numeric population standard deviation of the expression x. The population standard deviation is calculated as the square root of the population variance VAR_POP.

```
SET NULL ?
SELECT department_id DID,
       STDDEV(salary) STD,
       STDDEV_POP(salary) STDPOP,
       STDDEV_SAMP(salary) STDSAMP
FROM hr.employees
GROUP BY department_id;
```

DID	STD	STDPOP	STDSAMP
100	1804.13155	1646.93925	1804.13155
30	3362.58829	3069.6091	3362.58829
?	0	0	?
90	4041.45188	3299.83165	4041.45188

```
 20 4949.74747       3500 4949.74747
 70          0          0 ?
110 2621.95194       1854 2621.95194
 50 1488.00592 1471.37963 1488.00592
 80  2033.6847 2003.55437  2033.6847
 40          0          0 ?
 60 1925.61678 1722.32401 1925.61678
 10          0          0 ?
```

STDDEV_SAMP

STDDEV_SAMP(<x>) takes a single argument, where x is a numeric expression. This function returns the numeric sample standard deviation of the expression x.

The sample standard deviation is calculated as the square root of the sample variance VAR_SAMP. *STDDEV* is similar to the STDDEV_SAMP function, except STDDEV will return 1 when there is only one row of input, while STDDEV_SAMP will return NULL.

See the description of STDDEV_POP for an example.

VAR_POP

VAR_POP(<x>) takes a single argument, where x is a numeric expression. This function returns the numeric population variance of x. The population variance is calculated with the formula (SUM($x*x$) - SUM(x) * SUM(x) / COUNT(x)) / COUNT(x).

```
SELECT department_id,
       VARIANCE(salary),
       VAR_POP(salary),
       VAR_SAMP(salary)
FROM hr.employees
GROUP BY department_id;
```

DEPARTMENT_ID	VARIANCE(SALARY)	VAR_POP(SALARY)	VAR_SAMP(SALARY)
100	3254890.67	2712408.89	3254890.67
30	11307000	9422500	11307000
?	0	0	?
90	16333333.3	10888888.9	16333333.3
20	24500000	12250000	24500000
70	0	0	?
110	6874632	3437316	6874632
50	2214161.62	2164958.02	2214161.62
80	4135873.44	4014230.1	4135873.44

```
    40              0              0 ?
    60        3708000        2966400        3708000
    10              0              0 ?
```

VAR_SAMP

VAR_SAMP(`<x>`) takes a single argument, where x is a numeric expression. This function returns the numeric sample variance of x. The sample variance is calculated with the formula (SUM(x*x) - SUM(x) * SUM(x) / COUNT(x)) / (COUNT(x)-1). When the number of expressions (COUNT(x)) = 1, VARIANCE returns a 0, whereas VAR_SAMP returns NULL. When (COUNT(x)) = 0, they both return NULL. See the description of VAR_POP for an example.

Limiting Grouped Data with HAVING

A SELECT statement includes a HAVING clause to filter the grouped data. We discussed the GROUP BY clause and various group functions earlier in this chapter. The group functions cannot be used in the WHERE clause. For example, if you wanted to query the total salary by department, excluding department 50, and return only those rows with more than $10,000 in the total salary column, you would have trouble with the following query:

```
SELECT department_id, sum(salary) total_sal
FROM employees
WHERE department_id != 50
AND SUM(salary) > 10000
GROUP BY department_id;
```

The database doesn't know what the sum is when extracting the rows from the table—remember that the grouping is done after all the rows have been fetched. You get an exception when you try to use SUM in the WHERE clause. The correct way to get the requested information is to instruct the database to group all the rows and then limit the output of those grouped rows. You can do this by using the HAVING clause. The HAVING clause is used to restrict the groups of returned rows to those groups where the specified condition is satisfied.

```
SELECT department_id, sum(salary) total_sal
FROM employees
WHERE department_id != 50
GROUP BY department_id
HAVING SUM(salary) > 10000;

DEPARTMENT_ID  TOTAL_SAL
-------------  ----------
          100       51608
           30       24900
```

```
        90      58000
        20      19000
       110      20308
        80     304500
        60      28800
```

As you can see in the previous query, a SQL statement can have both a WHERE clause and a HAVING clause. WHERE filters data before grouping; HAVING filters data after grouping.

> If the SELECT statement includes a WHERE clause and a GROUP BY clause, the GROUP BY (and HAVING) clause should come after the WHERE clause. HAVING and GROUP BY clauses can appear in any order.

Creating Superaggregates with CUBE and ROLLUP

The CUBE and ROLLUP modifiers to the GROUP BY clause allow you to create aggregations of aggregates, or *superaggregates*. These superaggregates, or summary rows, are included with the result set in a way similar to using the COMPUTE statement on control breaks in SQL*Plus—that is, they are included in the data and contain NULL values in the aggregated columns:

- ROLLUP creates hierarchical aggregates.

- CUBE creates aggregates for all combinations of columns specified.

The key advantages of CUBE and ROLLUP are that they will allow more robust aggregations than COMPUTE and they work with any SQL-enabled tool.

These superaggregations can be visualized with a simple example using the OE.CUSTOMERS table. For this example, say you are interested in two columns—MARITAL_STATUS, which has the value single or married, and GENDER, which has the value M or F. Let's write some SQL instructions to find the total number of rows by GENDER and MARITAL_STATUS:

```
SELECT gender, marital_status, count(*) num_rec
FROM oe.customers
GROUP BY gender, marital_status;
```

```
G MARITAL_STATUS          NUM_REC
- -------------------- ----------
M married                    117
M single                      92
F single                      47
F married                     63
```

But suppose you want subtotals for each gender—a count of all female customers regardless of marital status and a count of all male customers regardless of marital status.

You could remove the MARITAL_STATUS column from the previous query, which would give you the desired result, but what if you want to display the subtotals along with the original query? Oracle introduced the ROLLUP modifier to accomplish this task.

Using ROLLUP

ROLLUP is used in SELECT statements with GROUP BY clauses to calculate multiple levels of subtotals. It also provides a grand total. The ROLLUP extension adds only minimal overhead to the overall query performance. ROLLUP creates subtotals from the most detailed level to a grand total based on the grouping list provided with the ROLLUP modifier. It creates subtotals moving left to right using the columns provided in ROLLUP. The grand total is provided only if the ROLLUP modifier includes all the columns in the GROUP BY clause.

Using the previous example, you could use the ROLLUP modifier to roll up the MARITAL_STATUS column, leaving subtotals on the grouped column GENDER. Here we have not included GENDER in the ROLLUP; hence, the grand total is not provided:

```
SELECT gender, marital_status, count(*) num_rec
FROM oe.customers
GROUP BY gender, ROLLUP(marital_status);


G MARITAL_STATUS            NUM_REC
- -------------------- ----------

F single                     47
F married                    63
F                           110    <- Subtotal
M single                     92
M married                   117
M                           209    <- Subtotal
```

In the previous example, you do not have any NULL values in the MARITAL_STATUS column. If you added another record with GENDER = 'F' and a NULL value for MARITAL_STATUS, the result would be as follows:

```
SELECT gender, marital_status, count(*) num_rec
FROM oe.customers
GROUP BY gender, ROLLUP(marital_status);


G MARITAL_STATUS            NUM_REC
- -------------------- ----------

F single                     47
F married                    63
F                             1    <- Null Marital_Status
F                           111    <- Subtotal
```

```
M single                    92
M married                   117
M                           209    <- Subtotal
```

On the OCA certification exam, this can appear as a trick question to confuse you about which line is the subtotal. You may use an NVL function to display meaningful data in the result.

Now, if you want to add an aggregation for all genders as well, you put the GENDER column into the ROLLUP modifier, as follows:

```
SELECT gender, marital_status, count(*) num_rec
FROM oe.customers
GROUP BY ROLLUP(gender, marital_status);


G MARITAL_STATUS         NUM_REC
- -------------------- ----------
F single                     47
F married                    63
F                           110    <- Subtotal
M single                     92
M married                   117
M                           209    <- Subtotal
                            319    <- Grand total
```

The order of the columns in the ROLLUP modifier is significant, because this order determines where Oracle produces subtotals. ROLLUP creates hierarchical aggregations, so the order of the expressions in the ROLLUP clause is significant. The ordering follows the same conventions used in the GROUP BY clause—most general to most specific. When you reverse the order in the example, you get different subtotals:

```
SELECT gender, marital_status, count(*) num_rec
FROM oe.customers
GROUP BY ROLLUP(marital_status, gender);


G MARITAL_STATUS         NUM_REC
- -------------------- ----------
F single                     47
M single                     92
  single                    139    <- Subtotal
F married                    63
M married                   117
  married                   180    <- Subtotal
                            319    <- Grand total
```

Suppose you want all these subtotals, both by GENDER and by MARITAL_STATUS. This requirement calls for the CUBE modifier, which will produce all possible aggregations, not just those in the hierarchy of columns specified.

Using CUBE

The CUBE modifier in the GROUP BY clause creates subtotals for all possible combinations of grouping columns. Let's try the previous example using the CUBE modifier:

```
SELECT gender, marital_status, count(*) num_rec
FROM oe.customers
GROUP BY CUBE(gender, marital_status);
```

```
G MARITAL_STATUS           NUM_REC
- -------------------- ----------
                           319    <- Grand total
  single                   139    <- Subtotal Marital_Status
  married                  180    <- Subtotal Marital_Status
F                          110    <- Subtotal Gender
F single                    47
F married                   63
M                          209    <- Subtotal Gender
M single                    92
M married                  117
```

The number of aggregations created by the CUBE modifier is the number of distinct combinations of data values in all the columns that appear in the CUBE clause. CUBE creates aggregations for all combinations of columns, so unlike ROLLUP, the order of expressions in a CUBE is not significant. As you can see, the result set is the same, but the order of rows (grouping) is different (Note: a question mark in the result indicates a NULL value, due to the SET NULL ? setting):

```
SELECT gender, marital_status, count(*) num_rec
FROM oe.customers
GROUP BY CUBE(marital_status, gender);
```

```
G MARITAL_STATUS           NUM_REC
- -------------------- ----------
? ?                        319
F ?                        110
M ?                        209
? single                   139
F single                    47
```

```
M single                   92
? married                 180
F married                  63
M married                 117
```

 Real World Scenario

More DBA Queries

In the "Exploring DBA Queries Using Aggregate Functions" sidebar, you saw some queries written to determine the space allocated by tablespace, the space allocated by schema, and the space allocated by tablespace and schema. The queries were written using three different SQL statements. In the following SQL instructions, you can see the power of CUBE. The results from all three of the SQL statements you tried before are in this summary report, showing the different levels of aggregation.

```
SELECT tablespace_name, owner, SUM(bytes)/1048576 size_mb
FROM dba_segments
GROUP BY CUBE (tablespace_name, owner);


TABLESPACE_NAME   OWNER            SIZE_MB
----------------- ---------------- ----------
                                   1564.8125  <- Grand Total
                  HR                    1.75  <- Subtotal HR schema
                  IX                   1.625  <- Subtotal IX schema
                  OE                   8.875
... ... ...
                  FLOWS            100.6875    <- Subtotal FLOWS schema
USERS                                 21.25   <- Subtotal USERS tablespace
USERS             HR                  .1875    <- HR schema in USERS tablespace
USERS             OE                  2.625    <- OE schema in USERS tablespace
USERS             SH                      2
USERS             SCOTT                .375
USERS             BTHOMAS           16.0625
SYSAUX                              716.375    <- Subtotal SYSAUX tablespace
... ... ...
SYSAUX            FLOWS            100.6875
SYSTEM                              701.625    <- Subtotal SYSTEM tablespace
SYSTEM            SYS              685.1875
```

```
SYSTEM          OUTLN              .5625
SYSTEM          SYSTEM           15.875
EXAMPLE                          77.3125
EXAMPLE         HR                1.5625
... ... ...
```

As you can see in the result, the space used by each schema in each tablespace is shown as well as the total space used in each tablespace and the total space used by each schema. The total space used in the database (including all tablespaces) is also shown in the very first line.

Three functions (GROUPING, GROUP_ID, and GROUPING_ID) can come in very handy when you're using the ROLLUP and CUBE modifiers of the GROUP BY clause.

In the examples you have seen using the ROLLUP and CUBE modifiers, there was no way of telling which row was a subtotal and which row was a grand total. You can use the GROUPING function to overcome this problem. Review the following SQL example:

```
SELECT gender, marital_status, count(*) num_rec,
       GROUPING (gender) g_grp, GROUPING (marital_status) ms_grp
FROM oe.customers
GROUP BY CUBE(marital_status, gender);
```

```
G MARITAL_STATUS          NUM_REC       G_GRP      MS_GRP
- -------------------- ----------- ----------- -----------
                            319           1           1
F                           110           0           1
M                           209           0           1
  single                    139           1           0
F single                     47           0           0
M single                     92           0           0
  married                   180           1           0
F married                    63           0           0
M married                   117           0           0
```

The G_GRP column has a 1 for NULL values generated by the CUBE or ROLLUP modifier for GENDER column. Similarly, the MS_GRP column has a 1 when NULL values are generated in the MARITAL_STATUS column. By using a DECODE function on the result of the GROUPING function, you can produce a more meaningful result set, as in the following example:

```
SELECT DECODE(GROUPING (gender), 1, 'Multi-Gender',
              gender) gender,
       DECODE(GROUPING (marital_status), 1,
```

```
                  'Multi-MaritalStatus', marital_status) marital_status,
         count(*) num_rec
FROM oe.customers
GROUP BY CUBE(marital_status, gender);
```

GENDER	MARITAL_STATUS	NUM_REC
Multi-Gender	Multi-MaritalStatus	319
F	Multi-MaritalStatus	110
M	Multi-MaritalStatus	209
Multi-Gender	single	139
F	single	47
M	single	92
Multi-Gender	married	180
F	married	63
M	married	117

 You can use the GROUPING function in the HAVING clause to filter out rows. You can display only the summary results using the GROUPING function in the HAVING clause.

The GROUPING_ID function returns the exact level of the group. It is derived from the GROUPING function by concatenating the GROUPING levels together as bits, and it gives the GROUPING_ID. To help you understand this, closely review the following example:

```
SELECT gender, marital_status, count(*) num_rec,
       GROUPING (gender) g_grp, GROUPING (marital_status) ms_grp,
       GROUPING_ID (gender, marital_status) groupingid
FROM oe.customers
GROUP BY CUBE(gender, marital_status);
```

G	MARITAL_STATUS	NUM_REC	G_GRP	MS_GRP	GROUPINGID
		319	1	1	3
	single	139	1	0	2
	married	180	1	0	2
F		110	0	1	1
F	single	47	0	0	0
F	married	63	0	0	0
M		209	0	1	1
M	single	92	0	0	0
M	married	117	0	0	0

In this example, you can clearly identify the level of grouping using the GROUPING_ID function. The GROUP_ID function is used to distinguish the duplicate groups. In the following example, the GROUP_ID() value is 1 for duplicate groups. When writing complex aggregates, you can filter out the duplicate rows by using the HAVING GROUP_ID = 0 clause in the SELECT statement.

```
SELECT gender, marital_status, count(*) num_rec,
       GROUPING_ID (gender, marital_status) groupingid,
       GROUP_ID() groupid
FROM oe.customers
GROUP BY gender, CUBE(gender, marital_status);
```

G	MARITAL_STATUS	NUM_REC	GROUPINGID	GROUPID
F	single	47	0	0
F	married	63	0	0
M	single	92	0	0
M	married	117	0	0
F	single	47	0	1
F	married	63	0	1
M	single	92	0	1
M	married	117	0	1
F		110	1	0
M		209	1	0
F		110	1	1
M		209	1	1

Nesting Functions

Functions can be *nested* so that the output from one function is used as input to another. Operators have an inherent precedence of execution such as * before +, but function precedence is based on position only. Functions are evaluated innermost to outermost and left to right. This nesting technique is common with some functions, such as DECODE (covered in Chapter 3), where it can be used to implement limited IF…THEN…ELSE logic within a SQL statement.

For example, the V$SYSSTAT view contains one row for each of three interesting sort statistics. If you want to report all three statistics on a single line, you can use DECODE combined with SUM to filter out data in the SELECT clause. This filtering operation is usually done in the WHERE or HAVING clause, but if you want all three statistics on one line, you can issue this command:

```
SELECT SUM (DECODE
        (name,'sorts (memory)',value,0)) in_memory,
```

```
    SUM (DECODE
      (name,'sorts (disk)',  value,0)) on_disk,
    SUM (DECODE
      (name,'sorts (rows)',  value,0)) rows_sorted
FROM v$sysstat;

IN_MEMORY ON_DISK ROWS_SORTED
--------- ------- -----------
    728      12       326714
```

What happens in the previous statement is a single pass through the V$SYSSTAT table. The presummary result set would have the same number of rows as V$SYSSTAT (232, for instance). Of these 232 rows, all rows and columns have zeros, except for one row in each column that has the data of interest. Table 4.3 shows the data that was used in this example. The summation operation then adds all the zeros to your interesting data and gives you the results you want.

TABLE 4.3 Presummarized Result Set

in_memory	on_disk	rows_sorted
0	0	0
0	12	0
0	0	0
0	0	326714
728	0	0
0	0	0

Nesting Single-Row Functions with Group Functions

Nested functions can include single-row functions nested within group functions, as you've just seen, or group functions nested within either single-row functions or other group functions. For example, suppose you need to report on the departments in the EMP table, showing either the number of jobs or the number of managers, whichever is greater. You would enter the following:

```
SELECT deptno, GREATEST(
       COUNT(DISTINCT job),
```

```
        COUNT(DISTINCT mgr)) cnt,
        COUNT(DISTINCT job) jobs,
        COUNT(DISTINCT mgr) mgrs
FROM scott.emp
GROUP BY deptno;
```

```
    DEPTNO         CNT        JOBS        MGRS
---------- ---------- ---------- ----------
        10           3           3           2
        20           4           3           4
        30           3           3           2
```

Nesting Group Functions

You can also nest group functions within group functions. Only one level of nesting is allowed when nesting a group function within a group function. To report the maximum number of jobs in a single department, you would query the following:

```
SELECT MAX(COUNT (DISTINCT job_id))
FROM employees
GROUP BY department_id;
```

```
MAX(COUNT(DISTINCTJOB_ID))
--------------------------
                         3
```

Group functions can be nested only one level. If you try to nest more than one level of group functions, you will encounter an error. Also, there is no reason to do so. Here is an example to show the error, though the SQL does not mean much:

```
SELECT MIN (MAX (COUNT (DISTINCT job_id)))
FROM employees
GROUP BY department_id;
```

```
SELECT MIN (MAX (COUNT (DISTINCT job_id)))
            *
ERROR at line 1:
ORA-00935: group function is nested too deeply
```

Summary

Although this is a small chapter in terms of OCA certification exam content, this chapter is very important for the test. It is important to understand the concept of grouping data, where GROUP BY and HAVING clauses can be used, and the rules associated with using these clauses. We began this chapter by discussing the group function fundamentals and reviewed the group functions by concentrating on the functions that are important for the test.

We also discussed how group functions can be used in the SELECT, HAVING, and ORDER BY clauses of SELECT statements. Most group functions can be applied to all data values or only to the distinct data values. Except for COUNT(*), group functions ignore NULLs. Programmer-written functions cannot be used as group functions. COUNT, SUM, and AVG are the most commonly used group functions.

When group functions or aggregate functions are being used in a query, the columns that do not have any aggregate function applied to them must appear in the GROUP BY clause of the query. The HAVING clause is used to filter out data after the aggregates are calculated. Group functions cannot be used in the WHERE clause.

You can create superaggregates using the CUBE and ROLLUP modifiers in the GROUP BY clause.

Exam Essentials

Understand the usage of DISTINCT in group functions.   When DISTINCT is specified, only one of each non-NULL value is applied to the function. To apply all non-NULL values, the keyword ALL should be used.

Know where group functions can be used.   Group functions can be used in GROUP BY, ORDER BY, and HAVING clauses. They cannot be used in WHERE clauses.

Know how MIN and MAX sort date and character data.   Older dates evaluate to lower values, while newer dates evaluate to higher values. Character data, even if it contains numbers, is sorted according to the NLS_SORT specification.

Know which expressions in a SELECT list must appear in a GROUP BY clause.   If any grouping is performed, all nongroup function expressions and nonconstant expressions must appear in the GROUP BY clause.

Know the order of precedence for evaluating nested functions.   You may need to evaluate an expression containing nested functions. Make sure you understand the left-to-right order of precedence used to evaluate these expressions.

Review Questions

1. How will the results of the following two statements differ?

   ```
   Statement 1:
   SELECT MAX(longitude), MAX(latitude)
   FROM zip_state_city;

   Statement 2:
   SELECT MAX(longitude), MAX(latitude)
   FROM zip_state_city
   GROUP BY state;
   ```

   A. Statement 1 will fail because it is missing a GROUP BY clause.

   B. Statement 2 will return one row, and statement 1 may return more than one row.

   C. Statement 2 will fail because it does not have the columns used in the GROUP BY clause in the SELECT clause.

   D. Statement 1 will display one row, and statement 2 will display two columns for each state.

2. Using the SALES table described here, you need to report the following:

   ▪ Gross, net, and earned revenue for the second and third quarters of 1999

   ▪ Gross, net, and earned revenue for sales in the states of Illinois, California, and Texas (codes IL, CA, and TX)

Column Name	state_code	sales_date	gross	net	earned
Key Type	PK	PK			
Nulls/Unique	NN	NN	NN	NN	NN
FK Table					
Datatype	VARCHAR2	DATE	NUMBER	NUMBER	NUMBER
Length	2		11,2	11,2	11,2

   Will all the requirements be met with the following SQL statement?

   ```
   SELECT state_code, SUM(ALL gross), SUM(net), SUM(earned)
   FROM sales_detail
   WHERE TRUNC(sales_date,'Q') BETWEEN
   ```

```
                        TO_DATE('01-Apr-1999','DD-Mon-YYYY')
                  AND TO_DATE('01-Sep-1999','DD-Mon-YYYY')
  AND  state_code IN ('IL','CA','TX')
GROUP BY state_code;
```

A. The statement meets all three requirements.

B. The statement meets two of the three requirements.

C. The statement meets one of the three requirements.

D. The statement meets none of the three requirements.

E. The statement will raise an exception.

3. Which line in the following SQL has an error?

```
1  SELECT department_id, SUM(salary)
2  FROM employees
3  WHERE department_id <> 40
4  ORDER BY department_id;
```

A. 1

B. 3

C. 4

D. No errors in SQL

4. John is trying to determine the average salary of employees in each department. He noticed that the SALARY column can have NULL values, and he does not want the NULLs included when the average is calculated. Identify the correct SQL statements that will produce the desired results.

A. `SELECT department_id, AVG(salary)`

      `FROM employees`

      `GROUP BY department_id;`

B. `SELECT department_id, AVG(NVL(salary,0))`

      `FROM employees`

      `GROUP BY department_id;`

C. `SELECT department_id, NVL(AVG(salary), 0)`

      `FROM employees`

      `GROUP BY department_id;`

D. `SELECT department_id, AVG(salary)`

      `FROM employees`

      `GROUP BY department_id`

      `HAVING salary IS NOT NULL;`

5. Review the following two SQL statements, and choose the appropriate option.

```
1.    SELECT department_id, COUNT(*)
FROM employees
HAVING COUNT(*) > 10
GROUP BY department_id;
2.    SELECT department_id, COUNT(*)
FROM employees
WHERE COUNT(*) > 10
GROUP BY department_id;
```

- **A.** Statement 1 and statement 2 will produce the same results.
- **B.** Statement 1 will succeed, and statement 2 will fail.
- **C.** Statement 2 will succeed, and statement 1 will fail.
- **D.** Both statements fail.

6. Carefully read the following SQL instructions, and choose the appropriate option. The JOB_ID column shows the various jobs.

```
SELECT  MAX(COUNT(*))
FROM employees
GROUP BY job_id, department_id;
```

- **A.** Aggregate functions cannot be nested.
- **B.** The columns in the GROUP BY clause must appear in the SELECT clause for the query to work.
- **C.** The GROUP BY clause is not required in this query.
- **D.** The SQL code will produce the highest number of jobs within a department.

7. Choose the SQL statement that has no syntax error and is valid.

A. SELECT department_id, SUM(salary)

        FROM employees

        WHERE department_id <> 50

        GROUP BY department_id

        HAVING COUNT(*) > 30;

B. SELECT department_id, SUM(salary) sum_sal

        FROM employees

        WHERE department_id <> 50

        GROUP BY department_id

        HAVING sum_sal > 3000;

C. SELECT department_id, SUM(salary) sum_sal

        FROM employees

        WHERE department_id <> 50

        AND sum_sal > 3000

        GROUP BY department_id;

D. SELECT department_id, SUM(salary)

        FROM employees

        WHERE department_id <> 50

        AND SUM(salary) > 3000

        GROUP BY department_id;

8. Consider the following SQL code, and choose the most appropriate option.

```
SELECT COUNT(DISTINCT SUBSTR(first_name, 1,1))
FROM employees;
```

A. A single-row function nested inside a group function is not allowed.

B. The GROUP BY clause is required to successfully run this query.

C. Removing the DISTINCT qualifier will fix the error in the query.

D. The query will execute successfully without any modifications.

9. The sales order number (ORDER_NO) is the primary key in the table SALES_ORDERS. Which query will return the total number of orders in the SALES_ORDERS table?

   A. `SELECT COUNT(ALL order_no) FROM sales_orders;`

   B. `SELECT COUNT(DISTINCT order_no) FROM sales_orders;`

   C. `SELECT COUNT(order_no) FROM sales_orders;`

   D. `SELECT COUNT(NVL(order_no,0) FROM sales_orders;`

   E. All of the above

   F. A and C

10. Sheila wants to find the highest salary within each department of the EMPLOYEES table. Which query will help her get what she wants?

   A. `SELECT MAX(salary) FROM employees;`

   B. `SELECT MAX(salary BY department_id) FROM employees;`

   C. `SELECT department_id, MAX(salary) max_sal FROM employees;`

   D. `SELECT department_id, MAX(salary) FROM employees GROUP BY department_id;`

   E. `SELECT department_id, MAX(salary) FROM employees USING department_id`

11. Which assertion about the following queries is true?

```
SELECT COUNT(DISTINCT mgr), MAX(DISTINCT salary)
FROM emp;

SELECT COUNT(ALL mgr), MAX(ALL salary)
FROM emp;
```

   A. They will always return the same numbers in columns 1 and 2.

   B. They may return different numbers in column 1 but will always return the same number in column 2.

   C. They may return different numbers in both columns 1 and 2.

   D. They will always return the same number in column 1 but may return different numbers in column 2.

12. Which clauses in the SELECT statement can use single-row functions nested in aggregate functions? (Choose all that apply.)

   A. SELECT

   B. ORDER BY

   C. WHERE

   D. GROUP BY

13. Consider the following two SQL statements. Choose the most appropriate option.

1. `select substr(first_name, 1,1) fn, SUM(salary) FROM employees GROUP BY first_name;`

2. `select substr(first_name, 1,1) fn, SUM(salary) FROM employees GROUP BY substr(first_name, 1,1);`

A. Statement 1 and 2 will produce the same result.

B. Statement 1 and 2 will produce different results.

C. Statement 1 will fail.

D. Statement 2 will fail, but statement 1 will succeed.

14. How will the results of the following two SQL statements differ?

```
Statement 1:
SELECT COUNT(*), SUM(salary)
FROM hr.employees;
```

```
Statement 2:
SELECT COUNT(salary), SUM(salary)
FROM hr.employees;
```

A. Statement 1 will return one row, and statement 2 may return more than one row.

B. Both statements will fail because they are missing a GROUP BY clause.

C. Both statements will return the same results.

D. Statement 2 might return a smaller COUNT value than statement 1.

15. Why does the following SELECT statement fail?

```
SELECT colorname Colour, MAX(cost)
FROM itemdetail
WHERE UPPER(colorname) LIKE '%WHITE%'
GROUP BY colour
HAVING COUNT(*) > 20;
```

A. A GROUP BY clause cannot contain a column alias.

B. The condition COUNT(*) > 20 should be in the WHERE clause.

C. The GROUP BY clause must contain the group functions used in the SELECT list.

D. The HAVING clause can contain only the group functions used in the SELECT list.

16. What will the following SQL statement return?

```
select max(prod_pack_size)
from sh.products
where min(prod_weight_class) = 5;
```

  A. An exception will be raised.

  B. The largest PROD_PACK_SIZE for rows containing PROD_WEIGHT_CLASS of 5 or higher.

  C. The largest PROD_PACK_SIZE for rows containing PROD_WEIGHT_CLASS of 5.

  D. The largest PROD_PACK_SIZE in the SH.PRODUCTS table.

17. Why will the following query raise an exception?

```
select dept_no, avg(distinct salary),
       count(job) job_count
from emp
where mgr like 'J%'
   or  abs(salary) > 10
having count(job) > 5
order by 2 desc;
```

  A. The HAVING clause cannot contain a group function.

  B. The GROUP BY clause is missing.

  C. ABS() is not an Oracle function.

  D. The query will not raise an exception.

18. Which clause will generate an error when the following query is executed?

```
SELECT department_id, AVG(salary) avg_sal
FROM employees
GROUP BY department_id
HAVING TRUNC(department_id) > 50;
```

  A. The GROUP BY clause, because it is missing the group function.

  B. The HAVING clause, because single-row functions cannot be used.

  C. The HAVING clause, because the AVG function used in the SELECT clause is not used in the HAVING clause.

  D. None of the above. The SQL statement will not return an error.

19. Which statements are true? (Choose all that apply.)

   A. A group function can be used only if the GROUP BY clause is present.

   B. Group functions along with nonaggregated columns can appear in the SELECT clause as long as a GROUP BY clause and a HAVING clause are present.

   C. The HAVING clause is optional when the GROUP BY clause is used.

   D. The HAVING clause and the GROUP BY clause are mutually exclusive; you can use only one clause in a SELECT statement.

20. Read the following two statements, and choose the best option.

   1. A HAVING clause should always appear after the GROUP BY clause.

   2. A GROUP BY clause should always appear after the WHERE clause.

   A. Statement 1 and 2 are false.

   B. Statement 1 is true, and statement 2 is false.

   C. Statement 1 is false, and statement 2 is true.

   D. Statements 1 and 2 are true.

Chapter

5

Using Joins and Subqueries

ORACLE DATABASE 12c: SQL FUNDAMENTALS EXAM OBJECTIVES COVERED IN THIS CHAPTER:

✓ **Displaying Data from Multiple Tables Using Joins**

- Write SELECT statements to access data from more than one table using equijoins and nonequijoins.

- Join a table to itself by using a self-join.

- View data that generally does not meet a join condition by using outer joins.

- Generate a Cartesian product of all rows from two or more tables.

✓ **Using Subqueries to Solve Queries**

- Define subqueries.

- Describe the types of problems that the subqueries can solve.

- List the types of subqueries.

- Write single-row and multiple-row subqueries.

- Use the set operators.

- Describe set operators.

- Use a set operator to combine multiple queries into a single query.

- Control the order of rows returned.

A database has many tables that store data. In Chapter 2, "Introducing SQL," you learned how to write simple queries that select data from one table. Although this information is essential to passing the certification exam, the ability to join two or more related tables and access information is the core strength of relational databases. Using the SELECT statement, you can write advanced queries that satisfy end-user requirements.

This chapter focuses on querying data from more than one table using table joins and subqueries. When you use two or more tables or views in a single query, it is a *join query*. You'll need to understand how the various types of joins and subqueries work, as well as the proper syntax, for the certification exam.

Set operators in Oracle let you combine results from two or more SELECT statements. The results of each SELECT statement are considered a set, and Oracle provides UNION, INTERSECT, and MINUS operators to get the desired results. You will learn how these operators work in this chapter.

Writing Multiple-Table Queries

In relational database management systems (RDBMSs), related data can be stored in multiple tables. You use the power of SQL to relate the information and query data. A SELECT statement has a mandatory SELECT clause and FROM clause. The SELECT clause can have a list of columns, expressions, functions, and so on. The FROM clause tells you in which table(s) to look for the required information. In Chapter 2, you learned to query data using simple SELECT statements from a single table. In this chapter, you will learn how to retrieve data from more than one table.

To query data from more than one table, you need to identify common columns that relate the two tables. Here's how you do it:

1. In the SELECT clause, you list the columns you are interested in from all the related tables. If the same column name exist in more than one table, such columns must be qualified with the table name or table alias.

2. In the FROM clause, you include all the table names separated by commas.

3. In the WHERE clause, you define the relationship between the tables listed in the FROM clause using comparison operators.

You can also specify the relationship using a JOIN clause instead of the WHERE clause. The JOIN clause introduced by Oracle in Oracle 9*i* was added to conform to the ANSI/ISO SQL1999 standard. Throughout this section, you'll see examples of queries using the Oracle native syntax as well as the ANSI/ISO SQL1999 standard. A query from multiple tables without a relationship or common column is known as a *Cartesian join* or *cross join* and is discussed later in this chapter.

A *join* is a query that combines rows from two or more tables or views. Oracle performs a join whenever multiple tables appear in the query's FROM clause. The query's SELECT clause can have the columns or expressions from any or all of these tables.

 If multiple tables have the same column names, the duplicate column names should be qualified in the queries with their table name or table alias.

Inner Joins

Inner joins return only the rows that satisfy the join condition. The most common operator used to relate two tables is the equality operator (=). If you relate two tables using an equality operator, it is an *equality join*, also known as an *equijoin*. This type of join combines rows from two tables that have equivalent values for the specified columns.

Simple Inner Joins

A simple inner join has only the join condition specified, without any other filtering conditions. For example, let's consider a simple join between the DEPARTMENTS and LOCATIONS tables of the HR schema. The common column in these tables is LOCATION_ID. You will query these tables to get the location ID, city name, and department names in that city:

```
SELECT locations.location_id, city, department_name
FROM   locations, departments
WHERE  locations.location_id = departments.location_id;
```

Here, you are retrieving data from two tables—two columns from the LOCATIONS table and one column from the DEPARTMENTS table. These two tables are joined in the WHERE clause using an equality operator on the LOCATION_ID column. It is not necessary for the column names in both tables to have the same name to have a join. Notice that the LOCATION_ID column is qualified with its table name for every occurrence. This is to avoid ambiguity; it is not necessary to qualify each column, but it increases the readability of the query. If the same column name appears in more than one table used in the query, you must qualify the column name with the table name or table alias.

To execute a join of three or more tables, Oracle takes these steps:

1. Oracle joins two of the tables based on the join conditions, comparing their columns.

2. Oracle joins the result to another table, based on join conditions.

3. Oracle continues this process until all tables are joined into the result.

Complex Inner Joins

Apart from specifying the join condition in the WHERE clause, you may have another condition to limit the rows retrieved. Such joins are known as *complex joins*. For example, to continue with the example in the previous section, if you are interested only in the departments that are outside the United States, use this query:

```
SELECT locations.location_id, city, department_name
FROM   locations, departments
WHERE  locations.location_id = departments.location_id
AND    country_id != 'US';
```

```
LOCATION_ID CITY                 DEPARTMENT_NAME
----------- -------------------- -----------------
       1800 Toronto              Marketing
       2400 London              Human Resources
       2700 Munich              Public Relations
       2500 Oxford              Sales
```

Using Table Aliases

Like columns, tables can have alias names. Table aliases increase the readability of the query. You can also use them to shorten long table names with shorter alias names. Specify the *table alias name* next to the table, separated with a space. You can rewrite the query in the previous section using alias names, as follows:

```
SELECT l.location_id, city, department_name
FROM   locations l, departments d
WHERE  l.location_id = d.location_id
AND    country_id != 'US';
```

When tables (or views or materialized views) are specified in the FROM clause, Oracle looks for the object in the schema (or user) connected to the database. If the table belongs to another schema, you must qualify it with the schema name. (You can avoid this by using synonyms, which are discussed in Chapter 7, "Creating Tables and Constraints.") You can use the schema owner to qualify a table; you can also use the table owner and schema owner to qualify a column. Here is an example:

```
SELECT locations.location_id, hr.locations.city,
       department_name
FROM   hr.locations, hr.departments
WHERE  locations.location_id = departments.location_id;
```

Keep in mind that you can qualify a column name with its schema and table only when the table name is qualified with the schema. In the previous SQL, you qualified the column CITY with the schema HR. This is possible only if you qualify the LOCATIONS table with the schema. The following SQL will produce an error:

```
SELECT locations.location_id, hr.locations.city
       ,department_name
FROM   locations, hr.departments
WHERE  locations.location_id = departments.location_id;


SELECT locations.location_id, hr.locations.city
                              *
ERROR at line 1:
ORA-00904: "HR"."LOCATIONS"."CITY": invalid identifier
```

When you use table alias names, you must qualify the column names with the alias name only; qualifying the columns with the table name will produce an error, as in this example:

```
SELECT locations.location_id, city, department_name
FROM   locations l, hr.departments d
WHERE  locations.location_id = d.location_id;


WHERE  locations.location_id = d.location_id
       *
ERROR at line 3:
ORA-00904: "LOCATIONS"."LOCATION_ID": invalid identifier
```

The correct syntax is to replace locations.location_id with l.location_id in the SELECT and WHERE clauses.

If there are no common column names between the two tables used in the join (the FROM clause), you don't need to qualify the columns. However, if you qualify the columns, you are telling the Oracle database engine where exactly to find the column; hence, you are improving the performance of the query.

If there are column names common to multiple tables used in a join query, you must qualify the column name with a table name or table alias. This is true for column names appearing in SELECT, WHERE, ORDER BY, GROUP BY, and HAVING clauses. When using the ANSI syntax, the rule is different. The ANSI syntax is discussed in the next section.

When joining columns using the traditional syntax or ANSI syntax, if the column datatypes are different, Oracle tries to perform an implicit datatype conversion. This may affect your query performance. It is better if the columns used in the join condition have the same datatype or if you use the explicit conversion functions you learned in Chapter 3, "Using Single-Row Functions."

Using the ANSI Syntax

The difference between traditional Oracle join syntax and the ANSI/ISO SQL1999 syntax is that in ANSI, the join type is specified explicitly in the FROM clause. Using the ANSI syntax is clearer and is recommended over the traditional Oracle syntax. Simple joins can have the following forms:

```
<table name> NATURAL [INNER] JOIN <table name>
```

```
<table name> [INNER] JOIN <table name> USING (<columns>)
```

```
<table name> [INNER] JOIN <table name> ON <condition>
```

The following sections discuss each of the syntax forms in detail. In all three syntaxes, the keyword INNER is optional and is the default.

NATURAL JOIN

The NATURAL keyword indicates a *natural join*, where the join is based on all columns that have the same name in both tables. In this type of join, you should not qualify the column names with the table name or table alias name. Let's return to the example of querying the DEPARTMENTS and LOCATIONS tables using LOCATION_ID as the join column. The new Oracle syntax is as follows:

```
SELECT location_id, city, department_name
FROM   locations NATURAL JOIN departments;
```

The common column in these two tables is LOCATION_ID, and that column is used to join the tables. When specifying NATURAL JOIN, the columns with the same name in both tables should also have the same datatype. The following query will return the same results:

```
SELECT location_id, city, department_name
FROM   departments NATURAL JOIN locations;
```

Notice that even though the LOCATION_ID column is in both tables, you did not qualify this column in the SELECT clause. You cannot qualify the column names used for the join when using the NATURAL JOIN clause. The following query will result in an error:

```
SELECT l.location_id, city, department_name
FROM   departments NATURAL JOIN locations l;
SELECT l.location_id, city, department_name
       *
ERROR at line 1:
ORA-25155: column used in NATURAL join cannot have qualifier
```

The following query will not return an error because the qualifier is used on a column that's not part of the join condition:

```
SELECT location_id, city, d.department_name
FROM    departments d NATURAL JOIN locations l;
```

If you use SELECT *, common columns are listed only once in the result set. The following example demonstrates this. The common column in the COUNTRIES table and the REGIONS table is the REGION_ID.

```
SQL> DESCRIBE regions
Name                        Null?    Type
----------------------      -------- ------------
REGION_ID                   NOT NULL NUMBER
REGION_NAME                          VARCHAR2(25)


SQL> DESCRIBE countries
Name                        Null?    Type        .
----------------------      -------- ------------
COUNTRY_ID                  NOT NULL CHAR(2)
COUNTRY_NAME                         VARCHAR2(40)
REGION_ID                            NUMBER


SELECT *
FROM    regions NATURAL JOIN countries;


REGION_ID REGION_NAME               CO COUNTRY_NAME
---------- ------------------------ -- --------------------
        2 Americas                  AR Argentina
        3 Asia                      AU Australia
        1 Europe                    BE Belgium
        2 Americas                  BR Brazil
        2 Americas                  CA Canada
... ... ...
```

Here is another example, which joins three tables:

```
SELECT region_id, region_name, country_id, country_name,
       location_id, city
FROM    regions
NATURAL JOIN countries
NATURAL JOIN locations;
```

When you're specifying more than two tables using NATURAL JOIN syntax, it is a good idea to use parentheses to increase readability. The previous SQL can be interpreted in two ways:

- Join the REGIONS table and the COUNTRIES table, and join the result to the LOCATIONS table.

- Join the COUNTRIES table to the LOCATIONS table, and join the result to the REGIONS table.

If you do not use parentheses, Oracle uses left associativity by pairing the tables from left to right (as in the first scenario). By using parentheses, you can make the query less ambiguous, as shown here:

```
SELECT region_id, region_name, country_id, country_name,
       location_id, city
FROM   locations
NATURAL JOIN (regions
NATURAL JOIN countries);
```

The same query written in traditional Oracle syntax is as follows:

```
SELECT regions.region_id, region_name, countries.country_id, country_name,
       location_id, city
FROM   regions, countries, locations
WHERE  regions.region_id = countries.region_id
AND    countries.country_id = locations.country_id;
```

NATURAL JOIN syntax is easy to read and use; however, its usage should be discouraged in good coding practice. Because NATURAL JOIN joins the tables by all the identical column names, you could end up having a wrong join condition if you're not careful. It is always better to explicitly specify the join condition using the syntaxes available.

JOIN...USING

If the tables you are joining have columns with the same name but not all are used in the join condition between tables or if they do not have the same datatype, you can specify the columns that should be considered for an equijoin using the JOIN...USING syntax. The USING clause specifies the column names that should be used to join the tables. Here is an example:

```
SELECT location_id, city, department_name
FROM   locations JOIN departments USING (location_id);
```

The column names used in the USING clause should not be qualified with a table name or table alias. The column names not appearing in the USING clause can be qualified. If there are other common column names in the tables and if those column names are used in the query, they must be qualified.

Let's consider this syntax with joining more than two tables:

```
SELECT region_name, country_name, city
FROM   regions
JOIN   countries USING (region_id)
JOIN   locations USING (country_id);
```

Here, the REGIONS table is joined with the COUNTRIES table using the REGION_ID column, and its result is joined with the LOCATIONS table using the COUNTRY_ID column.

The following query will result in an error because there is no common column between the REGIONS and LOCATIONS tables:

```
SELECT region_name, country_name, city
FROM   regions
JOIN   locations USING (country_id)
JOIN   countries USING (region_id);


JOIN   locations USING (country_id)
                        *
ERROR at line 3:
ORA-00904: "REGIONS"."COUNTRY_ID": invalid identifier
```

You can add a WHERE clause to limit the number of rows and an ORDER BY clause to sort the rows retrieved along with any type of join operation:

```
SELECT region_name, country_name, city
FROM   regions
JOIN   countries USING (region_id)
JOIN   locations USING (country_id)
WHERE  country_id = 'US'
ORDER BY 1;
```

When you're using the NATURAL JOIN or JOIN USING syntax, you can't use alias or table names to qualify the column names on the columns used in the join operation anywhere in the query. You may see questions in the certification exam testing this rule.

JOIN...ON

When you do not have common column names between tables to make a join or if you want to specify arbitrary join conditions, you can use the JOIN...ON syntax. This syntax specifically defines the join condition using the column names. You can qualify column names with a table name or an alias name. If the column name is common to multiple tables involved in the query, those column names must be qualified.

Using the JOIN ON syntax over the traditional join method separates the table joins from the other conditions. Because this syntax explicitly states the join condition, it is easier to read and understand. Here is the three-table example you used in the previous section, written using the JOIN...ON syntax. Notice the use of a qualifier on the COUNTRY_ID column; this is required because COUNTRY_ID appears in COUNTRIES and LOCATIONS tables.

```
SELECT region_name, country_name, city
FROM   regions r
JOIN   countries c ON r.region_id = c.region_id
JOIN   locations l ON c.country_id = l.country_id
WHERE  c.country_id = 'US';
```

Multitable Joins

A *multitable join* is a join of more than two tables. In the ANSI syntax, joins are performed from left to right. The first join condition can reference columns from only the first and second tables; the second join condition can reference columns from the first, second, and third tables; and so on. Consider the following example:

```
SELECT first_name, department_name, city
FROM   employees e
JOIN   departments d
ON (e.department_id = d.department_id)
JOIN   locations l
ON (d.location_id = l.location_id);
```

The first join to be performed is EMPLOYEES and DEPARTMENTS. The first join condition can reference columns in EMPLOYEES and DEPARTMENTS but cannot reference columns in LOCATIONS. The second join condition can reference columns from all three tables.

 Real World Scenario

How Do You Specify Join Conditions When You Have More Than One Column to Join?

Company XYZ keeps detailed information about customer geography in its purchase-orders database. Consider the tables and data shown here. For simplicity, only the interesting columns in the tables are used for this example. For this demonstration, you are interested in three tables: COUNTRY, STATE, and CITY.

```
SQL> SELECT * FROM country;
```

```
  CNT_CODE CNT_NAME                CONTINENT
---------- ---------------------- ----------
         1 UNITED STATES          N.AMERICA
        91 INDIA                  ASIA
        65 SINGAPORE              ASIA

SQL> SELECT * FROM state;

  CNT_CODE ST ST_NAME
---------- -- ---------------
         1 TX TEXAS
         1 CA CALIFORNIA
         1 TN TENNESSE
        91 TN TAMIL NADU
        91 KL KERALA

SQL> SELECT * FROM city;

  CNT_CODE ST   CTY_CODE CTY_NAME
---------- -- ---------- --------------------
         1 TX       1001 DALLAS
         1 CA       8099 LOS ANGELES
        91 TN       2243 CHENNAI

SQL>
```

The CNT_CODE column relates the COUNTRY table and the STATE table. The ST_CODE and CNT_CODE columns relate the STATE table and CITY table. The following examples show how to join the STATE and CITY tables to get information on the country code, state name, and city name.

Traditional Oracle Join

```
SQL> SELECT s.cnt_code, st_name, cty_name
    FROM   state s, city c
    WHERE  s.cnt_code = c.cnt_code
    AND    s.st_code  = c.st_code
    AND    s.cnt_code = 1;
```

```
   CNT_CODE ST_NAME              CTY_NAME
---------- -------------------- -------------
         1 CALIFORNIA           LOS ANGELES
         1 TEXAS                DALLAS
SQL>
```

ANSI Natural Join

```
SQL> SELECT cnt_code, st_name, cty_name
     FROM   state NATURAL JOIN city
     WHERE  cnt_code = 1;

   CNT_CODE ST_NAME              CTY_NAME
---------- -------------------- --------------
         1 TEXAS                DALLAS
         1 CALIFORNIA           LOS ANGELES
SQL>
```

ANSI Using JOIN...USING

```
SQL> SELECT cnt_code, st_name, cty_name
     FROM   state JOIN city USING (cnt_code, st_code)
     WHERE  cnt_code = 1;

   CNT_CODE ST_NAME              CTY_NAME
---------- -------------------- ----------------
         1 TEXAS                DALLAS
         1 CALIFORNIA           LOS ANGELES
SQL>
```

ANSI Using JOIN...ON

```
SQL> SELECT s.cnt_code, s.st_name, c.cty_name
     FROM   state s
     JOIN   city c ON s.cnt_code = c.cnt_code
     AND    s.st_code  = c.st_code
     WHERE  s.cnt_code = 1;

   CNT_CODE ST_NAME              CTY_NAME
---------- -------------------- ------------------
         1 CALIFORNIA           LOS ANGELES
         1 TEXAS                DALLAS
SQL>
```

Cartesian Joins

A *Cartesian product* occurs when data is selected from two or more tables and no common relationship is specified in the WHERE clause. If you do not specify a join condition for the tables listed in the FROM clause, Oracle joins each row from the first table to every row in the second table. If the first table has 3 rows and the second table has 4 rows, the result will have 12 rows. If you add another table with 2 rows without specifying a join condition, the result will have 24 rows.

For the most part, Cartesian joins happen when there are many tables in the FROM clause and developers forget to include the join condition or they specify a wrong join condition. You should, therefore, avoid them. To avoid a Cartesian join, there should be at least $n-1$ join conditions when joining n tables. Sometimes you intentionally use Cartesian joins to generate large amounts of data, especially when testing applications.

Consider the following example:

```
SELECT region_name, country_name
FROM   regions, countries
WHERE  countries.country_id LIKE 'I%';


REGION_NAME                 COUNTRY_NAME
--------------------------  -------------
Europe                      Israel
Americas                    Israel
Asia                        Israel
Middle East and Africa      Israel
Europe                      India
Americas                    India
Asia                        India
Middle East and Africa      India
Europe                      Italy
Americas                    Italy
Asia                        Italy
Middle East and Africa      Italy
```

Although there is a WHERE clause, you did not specify a join condition between the COUNTRIES and REGIONS tables. The query returns all the matching rows from the COUNTRIES table based on the WHERE clause and retrieves one row from the REGIONS table for every row from the COUNTRIES table. There are four rows in the REGIONS table and three rows in the COUNTRIES table with a country name beginning with *I*.

If a Cartesian join is made between a table having *m* rows and another table having *n* rows, the resulting query will have *m* × *n* rows.

Using the ANSI Syntax

A Cartesian join in ANSI syntax is known as a *cross join*. A cross join is represented in ANSI/ISO SQL1999 syntax using the CROSS JOIN keywords. You can code the previous example using the ANSI syntax as follows:

```
SELECT region_name, country_name
FROM    countries
CROSS JOIN regions
WHERE   countries.country_id LIKE 'I%';
```

```
REGION_NAME                  COUNTRY_NAME
-----------------------      -------------
Europe                       Israel
Americas                     Israel
Asia                         Israel
Middle East and Africa       Israel
Europe                       India
Americas                     India
Asia                         India
Middle East and Africa       India
Europe                       Italy
Americas                     Italy
Asia                         Italy
Middle East and Africa       Italy
```

Outer Joins

So far, you have seen only inner joins, which return just the matched rows. Sometimes, however, you might want to see the data from one table, even if there is no corresponding row in the joining table. Oracle provides the *outer join* mechanism for this. An outer join returns results based on the inner join condition, as well as the unmatched rows from one or both of the tables.

In traditional Oracle syntax, the plus symbol surrounded by parentheses, (+), denotes an outer join in the query. Enter (+) beside the column name of the table in the WHERE clause where there may not be a corresponding row. For example, to write a query that performs an outer join of tables A and B and returns all rows from A, apply the outer join operator (+) to all columns of B in the join condition. For all rows in A that have no matching rows in B, the query returns NULL values for the columns in B.

Consider an example using the COUNTRIES and LOCATIONS tables. Say you want to list the country name and location city, and you also want to see all the countries in the COUNTRIES table. To perform this outer join, place an outer join operator beside all columns referencing LOCATIONS in the WHERE clause:

```
SELECT c.country_name, l.city
FROM   countries c, locations l
WHERE  c.country_id = l.country_id (+);
```

```
COUNTRY_NAME                             CITY
---------------------------------------- --------------------
Australia                                Sydney
Brazil                                   Sao Paulo
Canada                                   Toronto
Canada                                   Whitehorse
Switzerland                              Geneva
Switzerland                              Bern
China                                    Beijing
Germany                                  Munich
India                                    Bombay
Italy                                    Rome
Italy                                    Venice
Japan                                    Tokyo
Japan                                    Hiroshima
Mexico                                   Mexico City
Netherlands                              Utrecht
Singapore                                Singapore
United Kingdom                           London
United Kingdom                           Oxford
United Kingdom                           Stretford
United States of America                 Southlake
United States of America                 South San Francisco
United States of America                 South Brunswick
United States of America                 Seattle
Argentina
Israel
Nigeria
Egypt
Kuwait
France
Hong Kong
Belgium
Zimbabwe
Zambia
Denmark
```

The order of tables in the query's FROM clause determines whether the join is a left outer join or a right outer join. In the previous example, you are selecting all the rows from the table appearing on the left (COUNTRIES); therefore, this query is using a left outer join.

If tables A and B are outer-joined (FROM A, B) and you need all rows from B, the outer join operator is placed beside all columns of A. This is a right outer join, because you are retrieving all rows from the table on the right side (table B). In outer-join syntax using the (+) operator, the placement of the outer join operator, (+), is what determines the table from where all the rows are retrieved, not the order of tables; the order of tables determines whether it is a left or right outer join. When using the ANSI syntax, the left outer join and right outer join syntaxes depend on the table order.

The outer join operator, (+), can appear only in the WHERE clause. If there are multiple join conditions between the tables, the outer join operator should be used against all the conditions. Consider the following query:

```
SELECT c.country_name, l.city
FROM   countries c, locations l
WHERE  c.country_id = l.country_id (+)
AND    l.city LIKE 'B%';
```

```
COUNTRY_NAME                        CITY
----------------------------------- --------
China                               Beijing
India                               Bombay
Switzerland                         Bern
```

Even though you included the outer join operator, Oracle just ignored it, and did not provide unmatched rows in the query result. This is because you did not place the outer join operator beside all the columns from the LOCATIONS table. The following query will return the desired result:

```
SELECT c.country_name, l.city
FROM   countries c, locations l
WHERE  c.country_id = l.country_id (+)
AND    l.city (+) LIKE 'B%';
```

An outer join (containing the (+) operator) cannot be combined with another condition using the OR or IN logical operators. For example, the following query is not valid:

```
SELECT c.country_name, l.city
FROM   countries c, locations l
WHERE  c.country_id = l.country_id (+)
OR     l.city (+) LIKE 'B%';
```

```
OR     l.city (+) LIKE 'B%'
                 *
ERROR at line 4:
ORA-01719: outer join operator (+) not allowed in operand of OR or IN
```

The following query works because the outer join operator is used on the LOCATIONS table and the IN condition is used on the column from the COUNTRIES table:

```
SELECT c.country_name, l.city
FROM   countries c, locations l
WHERE  c.country_id = l.country_id (+)
AND    c.country_name IN ('India','Israel');


COUNTRY_NAME                        CITY
---------------------------------- --------
Israel
India                               Bombay
```

Using the ANSI Syntax

The ANSI syntax allows you to specify three types of outer joins:

- Left outer join
- Right outer join
- Full outer join

Left Outer Joins

A *left outer join* is a join between two tables that returns rows based on the matching condition, as well as unmatched rows from the table to the left of the JOIN clause. For example, the following query returns the country name and city name from the COUNTRIES and LOCATIONS tables, as well as the entire country name from the COUNTRIES table.

```
SELECT c.country_name, l.city
FROM   countries c LEFT OUTER JOIN locations l
ON  c.country_id = l.country_id;
```

The keyword OUTER between LEFT and JOIN is optional. LEFT JOIN will return the same result, as in the following example:

```
SELECT country_name, city
FROM   countries LEFT JOIN locations
USING (country_id);
```

The same query can be written using a NATURAL JOIN, because COUNTRY_ID is the only column common to both tables.

```
SELECT country_name, city
FROM   countries NATURAL LEFT JOIN locations;
```

In traditional Oracle outer join syntax, the query is written as follows:

```
SELECT c.country_name, l.city
FROM   countries c, locations l
WHERE  l.country_id (+) = c.country_id;
```

Right Outer Joins

A *right outer join* is a join between two tables that returns rows based on the matching condition, as well as unmatched rows from the table to the right of the JOIN clause. Let's rewrite the previous example using RIGHT OUTER JOIN:

```
SELECT country_name, city
FROM   locations NATURAL RIGHT OUTER JOIN countries;
```

  or:

```
SELECT c.country_name, l.city
FROM   locations l RIGHT JOIN countries c
ON  c.country_id = l.country_id;
```

WARNING   You cannot specify the traditional outer join operator, (+), in a query when the ANSI JOIN syntax is used.

Full Outer Joins

A *full outer join* is possible when using the ANSI syntax. It is not available using the (+) operator. This is a join between two tables that returns rows based on the matching condition, as well as unmatched rows from the table on the right and left of the JOIN clause. Suppose you want to list all the employees' last names with their department names. You want to include all the employees, even if they have not been assigned a department. You also want to include all the departments, even if no employees are working for that department. Here's the query:

```
SELECT e.employee_id, e.last_name,
       d.department_id, d.department_name
FROM   employees e FULL OUTER JOIN departments d
ON     e.department_id = d.department_id;
```

Trying to perform a similar query with the outer join operator will produce an error:

```
SELECT e.employee_id, e.last_name, d.department_name
FROM   employees e, departments d
WHERE  e.department_id (+) = d.department_id (+);


WHERE  e.department_id (+) = d.department_id (+)
                               *
ERROR at line 3:
ORA-01468: a predicate may reference only one outer-joined table
```

You can achieve the full outer join using the UNION operator and the outer join operator, as in the following query:

```
SELECT e.employee_id, e.last_name, d.department_name
FROM   employees e, departments d
WHERE  e.department_id (+) = d.department_id
UNION
SELECT e.employee_id, e.last_name, d.department_name
FROM   employees e, departments d
WHERE  e.department_id = d.department_id (+);
```

 If you do not specify a join type before the JOIN keyword, Oracle assumes the default value of INNER. To specify an outer join, you must use the LEFT, RIGHT, or FULL keyword.

Other Multiple-Table Queries

In this section, you will consider other methods used to retrieve data from more than one table. These methods include using self-joins and using nonequality joins. Using set operators in queries can also retrieve rows from multiple tables. Set operators are discussed in the next section.

Self-Joins

A *self-join* joins a table to itself. The table name appears in the FROM clause twice, with different alias names. The two aliases are treated as two different tables, and they are joined as you would join any other tables, using one or more related columns. The following example lists the employees' names and their manager names from the EMPLOYEES table:

```
SELECT e.last_name Employee, m.last_name Manager
FROM   employees e, employees m
WHERE  m.employee_id = e.manager_id;
```

When performing self-joins in the ANSI syntax, you must always use the JOIN...ON syntax. You cannot use NATURAL JOIN and JOIN...USING. In the following example, the keyword INNER is optional. The certification example also includes an additional WHERE clause to filter the records.

```
SELECT e.last_name Employee, m.last_name Manager
FROM    employees e INNER JOIN employees m
ON      m.employee_id = e.manager_id
WHERE   e.last_name like 'R%';
```

```
EMPLOYEE                  MANAGER
------------------------  -------------------------
Russell                   King
Raphaely                  King
Rogers                    Kaufling
Rajs                      Mourgos
```

Nonequality Joins

If the query is relating two tables using an equality operator (=), it is an equality join, also known as an *inner join* or an *equijoin*, as discussed earlier in this chapter. If any other operator is used to join the tables in the query, it is a *nonequality join*. Let's consider an example of a nonequality join. The EMPLOYEES table has a column named SALARY; the GRADES table has the range of salary values that correspond to each grade.

```
SELECT * FROM grades;
```

```
GRADE  LOW_SALARY HIGH_SALARY
------ ---------- -----------
P5              0        3000
P4           3001        5000
P3           5001        7000
P2           7001       10000
P1          10001
```

To find out which grade each employee belongs to, use the following query. You limit the rows returned by using last_name LIKE 'R%'.

```
SELECT last_name, salary, grade
FROM    employees, grades
WHERE   last_name LIKE 'R%'
AND     salary >= low_salary
AND     salary <= NVL(high_salary, salary);
```

```
LAST_NAME                 SALARY GR
------------------------- ---------- --
Russell                    14000 P1
Raphaely                   11000 P1
Rajs                        3500 P4
Rogers                      2900 P5
```

You can write the same query using the ANSI syntax as follows:

```
SELECT last_name, salary, grade
FROM   employees JOIN grades
ON     salary >= low_salary
AND    salary <= NVL(high_salary, salary)
WHERE  last_name LIKE 'R%';
```

Using Set Operators

You can use *set operators* to select data from multiple tables. Set operators basically combine the results of two queries into one. These queries are known as *compound queries*. All set operators have equal precedence. When multiple set operators are present in the same query, they are evaluated from left to right, unless another order is specified by using parentheses. The datatypes of the resulting columns, as well as the number of columns, should match in both queries. Oracle has four set operators, which are listed in Table 5.1.

TABLE 5.1 Oracle Set Operators

Operator	Description
UNION	Returns all unique rows selected by either query
UNION ALL	Returns all rows, including duplicates selected by either query
INTERSECT	Returns rows selected from both queries
MINUS	Returns unique rows selected by the first query but not the rows selected from the second query

We'll discuss all of these in a bit, but let's first consider the EMPLOYEE table and the following two queries to illustrate the use of set operators:

```
SELECT last_name, hire_date
FROM   employees
WHERE  department_id = 90;
```

```
LAST_NAME                HIRE_DATE
------------------------ ---------
King                     17-JUN-03
Kochhar                  21-SEP-05
De Haan                  13-JAN-01
```

```
SELECT last_name, hire_date
FROM   employees
WHERE  last_name LIKE 'K%';
```

```
LAST_NAME                HIRE_DATE
------------------------ ---------
Kaufling                 01-MAY-03
Khoo                     18-MAY-03
King                     30-JAN-04
King                     17-JUN-03
Kochhar                  21-SEP-05
Kumar                    21-APR-08
```

The UNION Operator

The UNION operator is used to return rows from either query, without any duplicate rows.

```
SELECT last_name, hire_date
FROM   employees
WHERE  department_id = 90
UNION
SELECT last_name, hire_date
FROM   employees
WHERE  last_name LIKE 'K%';
```

```
LAST_NAME                HIRE_DATE
------------------------ ---------
De Haan                  13-JAN-01
```

Kaufling	01-MAY-03
Khoo	18-MAY-03
King	17-JUN-03
King	30-JAN-04
Kochhar	21-SEP-05
Kumar	21-APR-08

Notice that even though there is a total of nine rows in both queries, the UNION query returned only unique values. The employees with the last name King appear twice, but their hire dates are different.

The UNION ALL Operator

The UNION ALL operator does not sort or filter the result set; it returns all rows from both queries. Let's consider this SQL code:

```
SELECT last_name, hire_date
FROM    employees
WHERE   department_id = 90
UNION ALL
SELECT last_name, hire_date
FROM    employees
WHERE   last_name LIKE 'K%';
```

LAST_NAME	HIRE_DATE
King	17-JUN-03
Kochhar	21-SEP-05
De Haan	13-JAN-01
Kaufling	01-MAY-03
Khoo	18-MAY-03
King	30-JAN-04
King	17-JUN-03
Kochhar	21-SEP-05
Kumar	21-APR-08

UNION Operator reads data from both queries and sorts them to get unique rows. If you are joining queries that produce unique results, using UNION ALL instead of UNION operator avoids unnecessary sort operation and thus improves the performance of the query.

The INTERSECT Operator

The INTERSECT operator is used to return the rows returned by both queries. Let's find the employees common to both queries:

```
SELECT last_name, hire_date
FROM    employees
WHERE   department_id = 90
INTERSECT
SELECT last_name, hire_date
FROM    employees
WHERE   last_name LIKE 'K%';
```

```
LAST_NAME                   HIRE_DATE
------------------------    ---------
King                        17-JUN-03
Kochhar                     21-SEP-05
```

The MINUS Operator

Now, let's find the employees from the first query but not in the second query. You can use the MINUS operator here:

```
SELECT last_name, hire_date
FROM    employees
WHERE   department_id = 90
MINUS
SELECT last_name, hire_date
FROM    employees
WHERE   last_name LIKE 'K%';
```

```
LAST_NAME                   HIRE_DATE
------------------------    ---------
De Haan                     13-JAN-01
```

Putting It All Together

Each query appearing with the set operators is an independent query and will work by itself. You can have join conditions and all the SQL options and functions in these independent queries. There can be only one ORDER BY clause in the query at the very end; you cannot specify an

ORDER BY clause for each query appearing with the set operators. For example, the following query will produce an error:

```
SELECT last_name, hire_date
FROM   employees
WHERE  department_id = 90
ORDER BY last_name
UNION ALL
SELECT first_name, hire_date
FROM   employees
WHERE  first_name LIKE 'K%'
ORDER BY first_name;


UNION ALL
*
ERROR at line 5:
ORA-00933: SQL command not properly ended
```

You can use the column name or alias name used in the first query or positional notation in the ORDER BY clause. Here are two examples (the result is the same for both queries):

```
SELECT last_name, hire_date "Join Date"
FROM   employees
WHERE  department_id = 90
UNION ALL
SELECT first_name, hire_date
FROM   employees
WHERE  first_name LIKE 'K%'
ORDER BY last_name, "Join Date";

SELECT last_name, hire_date "Join Date"
FROM   employees
WHERE  department_id = 90
UNION ALL
SELECT first_name, hire_date
FROM   employees
WHERE  first_name LIKE 'K%'
ORDER BY 1, 2;

LAST_NAME                Join Date
------------------------ ---------
De Haan                  13-JAN-01
Karen                    05-JAN-05
```

Karen	10-AUG-07
Kelly	14-JUN-05
Kevin	23-MAY-06
Kevin	16-NOV-07
Ki	12-DEC-07
Kimberely	24-MAY-07
King	17-JUN-03
Kochhar	21-SEP-05

When using set operators, the number of columns in the SELECT clause of the queries appearing on either side of the set operator should be the same. The column datatypes should be compatible. If the datatypes are different, Oracle tries to do an implicit conversion of data.

Using Subqueries

A *subquery* is a query within a query. A subquery answers the queries that have multiple parts; the subquery answers one part of the question, and the parent query answers the other part. When you nest several subqueries, the innermost query is evaluated first. Subqueries can be used with all Data Manipulation Language (DML) statements.

Using subqueries in the FROM clause of a top-level query is known as an *inline view*. You can nest any number of such queries; Oracle does not have a limit. Using the inline view, you can write queries to find top-*n* values. This is possible because Oracle allows an ORDER BY clause in the inline view.

There are three types of subqueries:

- A subquery in the WHERE clause of a query is called a *nested subquery*. You can have 255 levels of nested subqueries.

- When a column from the table used in the parent query is referenced in the subquery, it is known as a *correlated subquery*. For each row processed in the parent query, the correlated subquery is evaluated once.

- A *scalar subquery* returns a single row and a single column value. Scalar subqueries can be used anywhere a column name or expression can be used.

If the columns in the subquery have the same name as the columns in the containing SQL statement, it is a good idea to qualify the column names with table names or table aliases to avoid ambiguity. A subquery must be enclosed in parentheses and must be placed on the right side of the comparison operator when used in the WHERE clause.

Single-Row Subqueries

Single-row subqueries return only one row of results. A single-row subquery uses a single-row operator; the common operator is the equality operator (=). Consider an example using the tables from the HR schema. To find the name of the employee with the highest salary, you first need to find the highest salary using a subquery. Then you can execute the parent query with the result from the subquery.

```
SELECT last_name, first_name, salary
FROM    employees
WHERE   salary = (SELECT MAX(salary) FROM employees);
```

```
LAST_NAME                 FIRST_NAME             SALARY
------------------------  --------------------  ----------
King                      Steven                  24000
```

The parent query of a single-row subquery can return more than one row. For example, to find the names and salaries of employees who work in the accounting department, you need to find the department number for accounting in a subquery and then execute the parent query:

```
SELECT last_name, first_name, salary
FROM    employees
WHERE   department_id = (SELECT department_id
        FROM    departments
        WHERE   department_name = 'Accounting');
```

```
LAST_NAME                 FIRST_NAME             SALARY
------------------------  --------------------  ----------
Higgins                   Shelley                 12008
Gietz                     William                  8300
```

All single-row comparison operators can be used in the single-row subquery (=, >, >=, <, <=, or <>). The following example uses two subqueries. So, there are three query blocks in total. The two inner query blocks (subqueries) are executed first, and their result is passed on to the outer query (parent query) to complete its processing.

```
SELECT last_name, first_name, department_id
FROM employees
WHERE department_id < (SELECT MAX(department_id)
                       FROM departments
                       WHERE location_id = 1500)
AND hire_date >= (SELECT MIN(hire_date)
                  FROM employees
                  WHERE department_id = 30);
```

Similar to the WHERE clause, a subquery can be used in the HAVING clause. The following query lists the latest hire dates by departments that have hired an employee after the first employee was hired in department 80:

```
SELECT department_id, MAX(hire_date)
FROM employees
GROUP BY department_id
HAVING MAX(hire_date) > (SELECT MIN(hire_date)
                         FROM employees
                         WHERE department_id = 80);
```

```
DEPARTMENT_ID MAX(HIRE_
------------- ---------
          100 07-DEC-07
           30 10-AUG-07
              24-MAY-07
           90 21-SEP-05
           20 17-AUG-05
           50 08-MAR-08
           80 21-APR-08
           60 21-MAY-07
```

Multiple-Row Subqueries

Multiple-row subqueries return more than one row of results from the subquery. It is safer to provide the multiple-row operators in the subqueries if you are not sure of the results. In the previous query, if there is more than one department ID with the name accounting, the query will fail.

The following query returns three rows from the subquery. It lists all the employees who work for the same department as John does.

```
SELECT last_name, first_name, department_id
FROM   employees
WHERE  department_id = (SELECT department_id
       FROM    employees
       WHERE   first_name = 'John');


WHERE  department_id = (SELECT department_id
                        *
ERROR at line 3:
ORA-01427: single-row subquery returns more than one row
```

The query failed because you used a single-row operator with a multiple-row subquery. Change the = to a multiple-row operator to make the query work:

```
SELECT last_name, first_name, department_id
FROM   employees
WHERE  department_id IN (SELECT department_id
       FROM    employees
       WHERE   first_name = 'John');
```

IN is the most commonly used multiple-row subquery operator. Other operators are EXISTS, ANY, SOME, and ALL. You may use NOT with the IN and EXISTS operators.

ANY and SOME are synonymous operators. ANY, SOME, and ALL operators must always be preceded by any of the single-row conditional operators (=, >, >=, <, <=, or <>) and are used to compare a value to each value returned by the subquery. Table 5.2 lists the meanings of the ANY and ALL operators when used with different conditional operators.

TABLE 5.2 ANY and ALL Operator Meanings

Operation	Meaning
<ANY	Less than the maximum
<=ANY	Less than or equal to the maximum
>ANY	More than the minimum
=ANY	Equivalent to the IN operator
<ALL	Less than the minimum
>ALL	More than the maximum
<>ALL	Equivalent to the NOT IN operator

Let's review the ANY and ALL operators using examples. The following query will be used in the next subquery using the ANY operator. The subquery returns the 12000 and 8300 values. The minimum is 8300. The second query returns salaries equal to or above 8300 that do not belong to department 80.

```
SELECT salary FROM employees WHERE department_id = 110;

    SALARY
----------
     12008
      8300
```

```
SELECT last_name, salary, department_id
FROM employees
WHERE salary >= ANY (SELECT salary FROM employees
                     WHERE department_id = 110)
AND department_id != 80;
```

```
LAST_NAME                        SALARY DEPARTMENT_ID
------------------------- ---------- -------------
King                              24000            90
De Haan                           17000            90
Kochhar                           17000            90
Hartstein                         13000            20
Higgins                           12008           110
Greenberg                         12008           100
Raphaely                          11000            30
Baer                              10000            70
Faviet                             9000           100
Hunold                             9000            60
Gietz                              8300           110
```

The following example lists only the salaries that are more than the maximum (12008) returned from the subquery:

```
SELECT last_name, salary, department_id
FROM employees
WHERE salary > ALL (SELECT salary FROM employees
                    WHERE department_id = 110)
AND department_id != 80;
```

```
LAST_NAME                        SALARY DEPARTMENT_ID
------------------------- ---------- -------------
Hartstein                         13000            20
De Haan                           17000            90
Kochhar                           17000            90
King                              24000            90
```

You can use the DISTINCT keyword in the subquery when using ANY or ALL operators to prevent rows from being selected multiple times.

Subquery Returns No Rows

If the subquery returns no rows, a NULL value is returned to the parent query. Because NULL is not equal to another NULL, the parent query may not return any row even if there are NULL values in the column used in the WHERE clause of the subquery.

As shown in the following SQL, there is one record in the EMPLOYEES table where you have a NULL DEPARTMENT_ID:

```
SQL> SELECT last_name, first_name, salary
     FROM employees
     WHERE department_id IS NULL;
```

```
LAST_NAME                FIRST_NAME           SALARY
------------------------ -------------------- ----------
Grant                    Kimberely              7000
```

Let's use this column in the subquery and see what happens:

```
SQL> SELECT last_name, first_name, salary
     FROM employees
     WHERE department_id = (SELECT department_id
                            FROM departments
                            WHERE department_name = 'JustDummy');
```

```
no rows selected
```

```
SQL>
```

In the previous example, the outer query will return a value only if the DEPARTMENT_ID column matches some value. Although the inner query returned NULL, the outer query will not match for NULL, since NULL ≠ NULL. Let's review another example. In the following query, only Tobias has a NULL salary value:

```
SQL> SELECT last_name, salary
     FROM employees
     WHERE department_id = 30;
```

```
LAST_NAME                SALARY
------------------------ ----------
Raphaely                  11000
Khoo                       3100
Baida                      2900
Tobias
Himuro                     2600
Colmenares                 2500
```

When you use this subquery, you expect to see some results, because you know the EMPLOYEES table has more than five different salary values:

```
SQL> SELECT first_name, last_name, salary
     FROM employees
```

```
    WHERE salary NOT IN (
        SELECT salary
        FROM employees
        WHERE department_id = 30);
```

```
no rows selected
```

```
SQL>
```

The SQL code does not return any rows because one of the rows returned by the inner query is NULL. So, be careful when using NOT IN conditions with subqueries that could have a NULL value. This is not a problem when you use the IN operator. The IN operator is equivalent to =ANY, and the NOT IN operator is equivalent to <> ALL. If you include one more condition in the WHERE clause of the inner query, the SQL would work as expected:

```
SELECT first_name, last_name, salary
FROM employees
WHERE salary NOT IN (
        SELECT salary
        FROM employees
        WHERE department_id = 30
        AND salary is NOT NULL);
```

> If the subquery used with the ANY operator returns no rows, the condition evaluates to False. If the query used with the ALL operator returns no rows, the condition evaluates to True.

Correlated Subqueries

Oracle performs a *correlated subquery* when the subquery references a column from a table referred to in the parent statement. A correlated subquery is evaluated once for each row processed by the parent statement. The parent statement can be a SELECT, UPDATE, or DELETE statement. In the following example, the highest-paid employee of each department is selected. The subquery is executed for each row returned in the parent query. Notice that the parent table column is used inside the subquery.

```
SELECT department_id, last_name, salary
FROM    employees e1
WHERE   salary = (SELECT MAX(salary)
        FROM employees e2
        WHERE e1.department_id = e2.department_id)
ORDER BY 1, 2, 3;
```

DEPARTMENT_ID	LAST_NAME	SALARY
10	Whalen	4400
20	Hartstein	13000
30	Raphaely	11000
40	Mavris	6500
50	Fripp	8200
60	Hunold	9000
70	Baer	10000
80	Russell	14000
90	King	24000
100	Greenberg	12008
110	Higgins	12008

The following example shows a correlated subquery using the EXISTS operator. The EXISTS operator checks for the existence of a row in the subquery based on the condition. The column results of the SELECT clause in the subquery are ignored when using the EXISTS operator. The query lists the names of employees who work with John (in the same department). The subquery selects a dummy value of 'x', which is ignored.

```
SELECT last_name, first_name, department_id
FROM   employees e1
WHERE  EXISTS (SELECT 'x'
       FROM   employees e2
       WHERE  first_name = 'John'
       AND    e1.department_id = e2.department_id);
```

NOTE The column names in the parent queries are available for reference in subqueries. The column names from the tables in the subquery cannot be used in the parent queries. The scope is only the current query level and its subqueries.

Scalar Subqueries

A *scalar subquery* returns exactly one column value from one row. You can use scalar subqueries in most places where you would use a column name or expression, such as in a single-row function as an argument, in the VALUES clause of an INSERT statement, in an ORDER BY clause, in a WHERE clause, and in a SELECT clause. You can also use scalar subqueries in CASE expressions. Scalar subqueries cannot be used in GROUP BY or HAVING clauses. The following sections review a few examples of using scalar subqueries.

A Scalar Subquery in a CASE Expression

To list the city name, the country code, and whether the city is in India, you use a CASE expression with a subquery to return the country code for India from the COUNTRIES table. To limit the rows, let's select only the cities that begin with *B*:

```
SELECT city, country_id, (CASE
        WHEN country_id IN (SELECT country_id
                 FROM   countries
                 WHERE  country_name = 'India')
        THEN 'Indian'
        ELSE 'Non-Indian'
        END) "INDIA?"
FROM    locations
WHERE   city LIKE 'B%';


CITY                          CO INDIA?
----------------------------- -- ----------
Beijing                       CN Non-Indian
Bombay                        IN Indian
Bern                          CH Non-Indian
```

A Scalar Subquery in a SELECT Clause

To report the employee name, the department, and the highest salary in that department, you use a subquery in the SELECT clause. This is also a correlated subquery.

```
SELECT last_name, department_id,
     (SELECT MAX(salary)
      FROM   employees sq
      WHERE  sq.department_id = e.department_id) HSAL
FROM    employees e
WHERE   last_name like 'R%';


LAST_NAME                DEPARTMENT_ID       HSAL
------------------------ ------------- ----------
Raphaely                            30      11000
Rogers                              50       8200
Rajs                                50       8200
Russell                             80      14000
```

A Scalar Subquery in SELECT and WHERE Clauses

The following query may be confusing, but pay close attention to the flexibility of using subqueries to solve your queries. A scalar subquery is used in the SELECT clause as well as in the WHERE clause. A multiple-row subquery is also used in the WHERE clause, after the IN operator. The purpose of the query is to find the department names and their manager names for all departments that are in the United States or Canada. Because the country information is not available in the DEPARTMENTS table, you need to get this information from the LOCATIONS table. Also, you do not know the country IDs of the United States and Canada, so you use a subquery to get them. The query also limits the number of rows retrieved by checking whether a manager is assigned to the department (d.manager_id IS NOT NULL).

```
SELECT department_name, manager_id, (SELECT last_name
    FROM employees e
    WHERE e.employee_id = d.manager_id) MGR_NAME
FROM   departments d
WHERE ((SELECT country_id FROM locations l
    WHERE   d.location_id = l.location_id)
    IN (SELECT country_id FROM countries c
    WHERE   c.country_name = 'United States of America'
    OR      c.country_name = 'Canada'))
AND    d.manager_id IS NOT NULL;
```

```
DEPARTMENT_NAME       MANAGER_ID MGR_NAME
-------------------- ---------- --------------

Administration              200 Whalen
Marketing                   201 Hartstein
Purchasing                  114 Raphaely
Shipping                    121 Fripp
IT                          103 Hunold
Executive                   100 King
Finance                     108 Greenberg
Accounting                  205 Higgins
```

A Scalar Subquery in an ORDER BY Clause

You can also use scalar subqueries in the ORDER BY clause. The following example sorts the city names by their country name order. Notice that the country name is not included in the SELECT clause.

```
SELECT country_id, city, state_province
FROM   locations l
```

```
ORDER BY (SELECT country_name
          FROM   countries c
          WHERE  l.country_id = c.country_id);
```

If the scalar subquery returns more than one row, the query will fail. If the scalar subquery returns no rows, the value is NULL.

Finding Total Space and Free Space Using Dictionary Views

The following dictionary views are best friends of a DBA. They show the most critical aspect of the database from the user perspective—the space allocated and free. If the DBA is not monitoring the growth and free space available in the database, they will probably get calls from the user community saying they ran out of space in the tablespace. Let's build a query using four dictionary views (you may need the SELECT_CATALOG_ROLE privilege to query these views).

- DBA_TABLESPACES: Shows the tablespace name, type, and so on.

- DBA_DATA_FILES: Shows the data files associated with a permanent or undo tablespace and the size of the data file. The total size of all data files associated with a tablespace gives the total size of the tablespace.

- DBA_TEMP_FILES: Shows the temporary files associated with a temporary tablespace and their sizes.

- DBA_FREE_SPACE: Shows the unallocated space (free space) in each tablespace.

The query to get the tablespace names and type of tablespace would be as follows:

```
column tablespace_name format a18
SELECT tablespace_name, contents
FROM dba_tablespaces;


TABLESPACE_NAME     CONTENTS
------------------  ---------
SYSTEM              PERMANENT
SYSAUX              PERMANENT
UNDOTBS1            UNDO
TEMP                TEMPORARY
USERS               PERMANENT
EXAMPLE             PERMANENT
```

To find the total space allocated to each tablespace, you need to query DBA_DATA_FILES and DBA_TEMP_FILES. Because you are using a group function (SUM) along with a nonaggregated column (tablespace_name), the GROUP BY clause is a must. Notice the use of an arithmetic operation on the aggregated result to display the bytes in megabytes.

```
SELECT tablespace_name, SUM(bytes)/1048576 MBytes
FROM dba_data_files
GROUP BY tablespace_name;


TABLESPACE_NAME       MBYTES
------------------ ----------
UNDOTBS1                  730
SYSAUX              800.1875
USERS                201.75
SYSTEM                   710
EXAMPLE                  100


SELECT tablespace_name, SUM(bytes)/1048576 MBytes
FROM dba_temp_files
GROUP BY tablespace_name;


TABLESPACE_NAME       MBYTES
------------------ ----------
TEMP                 50.0625
```

You can find the total amount of free space in each tablespace using the DBA_FREE_SPACE view. Notice that the free space from temporary tablespace is not shown in this query.

```
SELECT tablespace_name, SUM(bytes)/1048576 MBytesFree
FROM dba_free_space
GROUP BY tablespace_name;


TABLESPACE_NAME     MBYTESFREE
------------------ ----------
SYSAUX                  85.25
UNDOTBS1            718.6875
USERS               180.4375
SYSTEM                8.3125
EXAMPLE               22.625
```

Let's try to display the total size of the tablespaces and their free space side-by-side using a UNION ALL query. UNION ALL is used to avoid sorting. UNION will produce the same result.

```
SELECT tablespace_name, SUM(bytes)/1048576 MBytes, 0 MBytesFree
FROM dba_data_files
GROUP BY tablespace_name
UNION ALL
SELECT tablespace_name, SUM(bytes)/1048576 MBytes, 0
FROM dba_temp_files
GROUP BY tablespace_name
UNION ALL
SELECT tablespace_name, 0, SUM(bytes)/1048576
FROM dba_free_space
GROUP BY tablespace_name;
```

TABLESPACE_NAME	MBYTES	MBYTESFREE
UNDOTBS1	730	0
SYSAUX	800.1875	0
USERS	201.75	0
SYSTEM	710	0
EXAMPLE	100	0
TEMP	50.0625	0
SYSAUX	0	85.25
UNDOTBS1	0	718.6875
USERS	0	180.4375
SYSTEM	0	8.3125
EXAMPLE	0	22.625

The result is not exactly what you expected. You want to see the free-space information beside each tablespace. Let's join the results of the total space with the free space and see what happens. Here you are creating two subqueries (inline views totalspace and freespace) and joining them together using the tablespace_name column.

```
SELECT tablespace_name, MBytes, MBytesFree
FROM
 (SELECT tablespace_name, SUM(bytes)/1048576 MBytes
  FROM dba_data_files
  GROUP BY tablespace_name
```

```
  UNION ALL
  SELECT tablespace_name, SUM(bytes)/1048576 MBytes
  FROM dba_temp_files
  GROUP BY tablespace_name) totalspace
JOIN
 (SELECT tablespace_name, 0, SUM(bytes)/1048576 MBytesFree
  FROM dba_free_space
  GROUP BY tablespace_name) freespace
USING (tablespace_name);


TABLESPACE_NAME        MBYTES MBYTESFREE
------------------ ---------- ----------

SYSAUX                800.1875      85.25
UNDOTBS1                   730   718.6875
USERS                  201.75   180.4375
SYSTEM                    710     8.3125
EXAMPLE                   100     22.625
```

You are almost there; the only item missing is information about the temporary tablespace. Because the temporary-tablespace free-space information is not included in the freespace subquery and you used an INNER join condition, the result set did not include temporary tablespaces. Now if you change the INNER JOIN to an OUTER JOIN, you'll get the desired result:

```
SELECT tablespace_name, MBytes, MBytesFree
FROM
 (SELECT tablespace_name, SUM(bytes)/1048576 MBytes
  FROM dba_data_files
  GROUP BY tablespace_name
  UNION ALL
  SELECT tablespace_name, SUM(bytes)/1048576 MBytes
  FROM dba_temp_files
  GROUP BY tablespace_name) totalspace
LEFT OUTER JOIN
 (SELECT tablespace_name, 0, SUM(bytes)/1048576 MBytesFree
  FROM dba_free_space
  GROUP BY tablespace_name) freespace
USING (tablespace_name)
ORDER BY 1;
```

```
TABLESPACE_NAME        MBYTES MBYTESFREE
------------------- ---------- ----------
EXAMPLE                   100     22.625
SYSAUX               800.1875    85.0625
SYSTEM                    710     8.3125
TEMP                  50.0625
UNDOTBS1                  730   718.6875
USERS                  201.75   180.4375
```

Another method to write the same query would be to use the query you built earlier and aggregate its result using an outer query, as shown here:

```
SELECT tsname, sum(MBytes) MBytes, sum(MBytesFree) MBytesFree
FROM (
  SELECT tablespace_name tsname, SUM(bytes)/1048576 MBytes, 0 MBytesFree
  FROM dba_data_files
  GROUP BY tablespace_name
  UNION ALL
  SELECT tablespace_name, SUM(bytes)/1048576 MBytes, 0
  FROM dba_temp_files
  GROUP BY tablespace_name
  UNION ALL
  SELECT tablespace_name, 0, SUM(bytes)/1048576
  FROM dba_free_space
  GROUP BY tablespace_name)
GROUP BY tsname
ORDER BY 1;

TSNAME                        MBYTES MBYTESFREE
----------------------------- ---------- ----------
EXAMPLE                          100     22.625
SYSAUX                      800.1875    85.0625
SYSTEM                           710     8.3125
TEMP                         50.0625          0
UNDOTBS1                         730   718.6875
USERS                         201.75   180.4375
```

Multiple-Column Subqueries

A subquery is multiple-column when you have more than one column in the SELECT clause of the subquery. *Multiple-column subqueries* are generally used to compare column conditions or in an UPDATE statement. Let's consider a simple example using the STATE and CITY tables shown here:

```
SQL> SELECT * FROM state;

 CNT_CODE  ST_CODE    ST_NAME
---------- -------    ------------
        1  TX         TEXAS
        1  CA         CALIFORNIA
       91  TN         TAMIL NADU
        1  TN         TENNESSE
       91  KL         KERALA

SQL> SELECT * FROM city;

 CNT_CODE ST_CODE    CTY_CODE CTY_NAME
---------- -------    -------- --------------
        1 TX             1001 DALLAS
       91 TN             2243 MADRAS
        1 CA             8099 LOS ANGELES
```

List the cities in Texas using a subquery on the STATE table:

```
SELECT cty_name
FROM   city
WHERE  (cnt_code, st_code) IN
       (SELECT cnt_code, st_code
        FROM   state
        WHERE  st_name = 'TEXAS');

CTY_NAME
----------

DALLAS
```

Subqueries in Other DML Statements

You can use subqueries in DML statements such as INSERT, UPDATE, DELETE, and MERGE. DML statements and their syntax are discussed in Chapter 6, "Manipulating Data." The following are some examples of subqueries in DML statements:

▪ To update the salary of all employees to the maximum salary in the corresponding department (correlated subquery), use this:

```
UPDATE employees e1
SET   salary = (SELECT MAX(salary)
      FROM  employees e2
      WHERE e1.department_id = e2.department_id);
```

▪ To delete the records of employees whose salary is less than the average salary in the department (using a correlated subquery), use this:

```
DELETE FROM employees e
WHERE salary < (SELECT AVG(salary) FROM employees
      WHERE  department_id = e.department_id);
```

▪ To insert records to a table using a subquery, use this:

```
INSERT INTO employee_archive
SELECT * FROM employees;
```

▪ To specify a subquery in the VALUES clause of the INSERT statement, use this:

```
INSERT INTO departments
      (department_id, department_name)
VALUES ((SELECT MAX(department_id)
        +10 FROM departments), 'EDP');
```

You can also have a subquery in the INSERT, UPDATE, and DELETE statements in place of the table name. Here is an example:

```
DELETE FROM
(SELECT * FROM departments
 WHERE department_id > 200)
WHERE department_id = 280;
```

The subquery can have an optional WITH clause. WITH READ ONLY specifies that the subquery cannot be updated. WITH CHECK OPTION specifies that if the subquery is used in place of a table in an INSERT, UPDATE, or DELETE statement, Oracle will not allow any changes to the table that would produce rows that are not included in the subquery. Let's look at an example:

```
INSERT INTO (SELECT department_id, department_name
      FROM departments
```

```
      WHERE department_id < 20)
VALUES (35, 'MARKETING');

1 row created.

INSERT INTO (SELECT department_id, department_name
      FROM departments
      WHERE department_id < 20 WITH CHECK OPTION)
VALUES (45, 'EDP')
SQL> /
      FROM departments
           *
ERROR at line 2:
ORA-01402: view WITH CHECK OPTION where-clause violation
SQL>
```

Summary

In this chapter, you learned to retrieve data from multiple tables. We began by discussing table joins. You also learned how to use subqueries and set operators.

Joins are used to relate two or more tables (or views). In a relational database, it is common to have a requirement to join data. The tables are joined by using a common column in the tables in the WHERE clause of the query. Oracle supports ANSI/ISO SQL1999 syntax for joins. Using this syntax, the tables are joined using the JOIN keyword, and a condition can be specified using the ON clause.

If the join condition uses the equality operator (= or IN), it is known as an equality join. If any other operator is used to join the tables, it is a nonequality join. If you do not specify any join condition between the tables, the result will be a Cartesian product: each row from the first table joined to every row in the second table. To avoid Cartesian joins, there should be at least *n*-1 join conditions in the WHERE clause when there are *n* tables in the FROM clause. A table can be joined to itself. If you want to select the results from a table, even if there are no corresponding rows in the joined table, you can use the outer join operator: (+). In the ANSI syntax, you can use the NATURAL JOIN, CROSS JOIN, LEFT JOIN, RIGHT JOIN, and FULL JOIN keywords to specify the type of join.

A subquery is a query within a query. Writing subqueries is a powerful way to manipulate data. You can write single-row and multiple-row subqueries. Single-row subqueries must return zero or one row; multiple-row subqueries return zero or more rows. IN and EXISTS are the most commonly used subquery operators. Subqueries can appear in the WHERE clause or in the FROM clause. They can also replace table names in SELECT, DELETE, INSERT, and UPDATE statements. Subqueries that return one row and one column result are known as scalar subqueries. Scalar subqueries can be used in most places where you would use an expression.

Set operators are used to combine the results of more than one query into one. Each query is separate and will work on its own. Four set operators are available in Oracle: UNION, UNION ALL, MINUS, and INTERSECT.

Exam Essentials

Understand joins.   Make sure you know the different types of joins. Understand the difference between natural, cross, simple, complex, and outer joins.

Know the different outer join clauses.   You can specify outer joins using LEFT, RIGHT, or FULL. Know the syntax of each type of join.

Be sure of the join syntax.   Spend time practicing each type of join using the ANSI syntax. Understand the restrictions of using each ANSI keyword in the JOIN and their implied column-naming conventions.

Know how to write subqueries.   Understand the use and flexibility of subqueries. Practice using scalar subqueries and correlated subqueries.

Understand the use of the ORDER BY clause in the subqueries.   You can use the ORDER BY clause in all subqueries, except the subqueries appearing in the WHERE clause of the query. You can use the GROUP BY clause in the subqueries.

Know the set operators.   Understand the set operators that can be used in compound queries. Know the difference between the UNION and UNION ALL operators.

Understand where you can specify the ORDER BY clause when using set operators.   When using set operators to join two or more queries, the ORDER BY clause can appear only at the very end of the query. You can specify the column names as they appear in the top query or use positional notation.

Review Questions

1. Which line of code has an error?

   A. SELECT dname, ename

   B. FROM   emp e, dept d

   C. WHERE emp.deptno = dept.deptno

   D. ORDER BY 1, 2;

2. What will be the result of the following query?

```
SELECT c.cust_id, c.cust_name, o.ord_date, o.prod_id
FROM    customers c, orders o
WHERE   c.cust_id = o.cust_id (+);
```

   A. List all the customer names in the CUSTOMERS table and the orders they made from the ORDERS table, even if the customer has not placed an order.

   B. List only the names of customers from the CUSTOMERS table who have placed an order in the ORDERS table.

   C. List all orders from the ORDERS table, even if there is no valid customer record in the CUSTOMERS table.

   D. For each record in the CUSTOMERS table, list the information from the ORDERS table.

3. The CUSTOMERS and ORDERS tables have the following data:

```
SQL> SELECT * FROM customers;

CUST_ CUST_NAME              PHONE            CITY
----- --------------------  ---------------  -----------
A0101 Abraham Taylor Jr.                     Fort Worth
B0134 Betty Baylor          972-555-5555     Dallas
B0135 Brian King                             Chicago


SQL> SELECT * FROM orders;

ORD_DATE     PROD_ID CUST_ID   QUANTITY       PRICE
---------- ---------- -------  ----------  ----------
20-FEB-00       1741 B0134            5        65.5
02-FEB-00       1001 B0134           25     2065.85
02-FEB-00       1001 B0135            3       247.9
```

When the following query is executed, what will be the value of PROD_ID and ORD_DATE for the customer Abraham Taylor, Jr.?

```
SELECT c.cust_id, c.cust_name, o.ord_date, o.prod_id
FROM   customers c, orders o
WHERE  c.cust_id = o.cust_id (+);
```

A. NULL, 01-JAN-01

B. NULL, NULL

C. 1001, 02-FEB-00

D. The query will not return customer Abraham Taylor, Jr.

4. When using ANSI join syntax, which clause is used to specify a join condition?

    A. JOIN

    B. USING

    C. ON

    D. WHERE

5. The EMPLOYEES table has EMPLOYEE_ID, DEPARTMENT_ID, and FULL_NAME columns. The DEPARTMENTS table has DEPARTMENT_ID and DEPARTMENT_NAME columns. Which two of the following queries return the department ID, name, and employee name, listing department names even if there is no employee assigned to that department? (Choose two.)

    A. SELECT d.department_id, d.department_name, e.full_name FROM departments d NATURAL LEFT OUTER JOIN employees e;

    B. SELECT department_id, department_name, full_name FROM   departments NATURAL LEFT JOIN employees;

    C. SELECT d.department_id, d.department_name, e.full_name FROM departments d LEFT OUTER JOIN employees eUSING (d.department_id);

    D. SELECT d.department_id, d.department_name, e.full_name FROM departments d LEFT OUTER JOIN employees eON (d.department_id = e.department_id);

6. Which two operators are not allowed when using an outer join operator in the query? (Choose two.)

    A. OR

    B. AND

    C. IN

    D. =

7. Which SQL statements do not give an error? (Choose all that apply.)

A.
```
SELECT last_name, e.hire_date, department_id
FROM employees e
JOIN (SELECT max(hire_date) max_hire_date
      FROM employees ORDER BY 1) me
ON (e.hire_date = me.max_hire_date)
```

B.
```
SELECT last_name, e.hire_date, department_id
FROM employees e
WHERE hire_date =
(SELECT max(hire_date) max_hire_date
      FROM employees ORDER BY 1)
```

C.
```
SELECT last_name, e.hire_date, department_id
FROM employees e
WHERE (department_id, hire_date) IN
(SELECT department_id, max(hire_date) hire_date
      FROM employees GROUP BY department_id)
```

D.
```
SELECT last_name, e.hire_date, department_id
FROM employees e JOIN
(SELECT department_id, max(hire_date) hire_date
FROM employees GROUP BY department_id) me
USING (hire_date)
```

8. The columns of the EMPLOYEES, DEPARTMENTS, and JOBS tables are shown here:

Table	Column Names	Datatype
EMPLOYEES	EMPLOYEE_ID	NUMBER (6)
	FIRST_NAME	VARCHAR2 (25)
	LAST_NAME	VARCHAR2 (25)
	SALARY	NUMBER (8,2)
	JOB_ID	VARCHAR2 (10)
	MANAGER_ID	NUMBER (6)
	DEPARTMENT_ID	NUMBER (2)
DEPARTMENTS	DEPARTMENT_ID	NUMBER (2)
	DEPARTMENT_NAME	VARCHAR2 (30)
	MANAGER_ID	NUMBER (6)
	LOCATION_ID	NUMBER (4)
JOBS	JOB_ID	VARCHAR2 (10)
	JOB_TITLE	VARCAHR2 (30)

Which assertion about the following query is correct?

```
1  SELECT e.last_name, d.department_name, j.job_title
2  FROM   jobs j
3  INNER JOIN employees e
4  ON (e.department_id = d.department_id)
5  JOIN departments d
6  ON (j.job_id = e.job_id);
```

A. The query returns all the rows from the EMPLOYEE table, where there is a corresponding record in the JOBS table and the DEPARTMENTS table.

B. The query fails with an invalid column name error.

C. The query fails because line 3 specifies INNER JOIN, which is not a valid syntax.

D. The query fails because line 5 does not specify the keyword INNER.

E. The query fails because the column names are qualified with the table alias.

9. The columns of the EMPLOYEES and DEPARTMENTS tables are shown in question 8. Consider the following three queries using those tables.

```
1. SELECT last_name, department_name
   FROM    employees e, departments d
   WHERE   e.department_id = d.department_id;
2. SELECT last_name, department_name
   FROM    employees NATURAL JOIN departments;
3. SELECT last_name, department_name
   FROM    employees JOIN departments
   USING (department_id);
```

Which of the following assertions best describes the results?

A. Queries 1, 2, and 3 produce the same results.

B. Queries 2 and 3 produce the same result; query 1 produces a different result.

C. Queries 1, 2, and 3 produce different results.

D. Queries 1 and 3 produce the same result; query 2 produces a different result.

10. The data in the STATE table is shown here:

```
SQL> SELECT * FROM state;

CNT_CODE ST_CODE ST_NAME
---------- ------- ------------
       1 TX       TEXAS
       1 CA       CALIFORNIA
      91 TN       TAMIL NADU
       1 TN       TENNESSE
      91 KL       KERALA
```

Consider the following query.

```
SELECT cnt_code
FROM    state
WHERE   st_name = (SELECT st_name FROM state
                   WHERE   st_code = 'TN');
```

Which of the following assertions best describes the results?

A. The query will return the CNT_CODE for the ST_CODE value 'TN'.

B. The query will fail and will not return any rows.

C. The query will display 1 and 91 as CNT_CODE values.

D. The query will fail because an alias name is not used.

11. The data in the STATE table is shown in question 10. The data in the CITY table is as shown here:

```
SQL> SELECT * FROM city;

CNT_CODE ST_CODE    CTY_CODE CTY_NAME
---------- ------- ---------- -------------
       1    TX         1001 DALLAS
      91    TN         2243 MADRAS
       1    CA         8099 LOS ANGELES
```

What is the result of the following query?

```
SELECT st_name "State Name"
FROM    state
WHERE  (cnt_code, st_code) =
       (SELECT cnt_code, st_code
        FROM   city
        WHERE  cty_name = 'DALLAS');
```

A. TEXAS

B. The query will fail because CNT_CODE and ST_CODE are not in the WHERE clause of the subquery.

C. The query will fail because more than one column appears in the WHERE clause.

D. TX

12. Which line of the code has an error?

```
1   SELECT department_id, count(*)
2   FROM    employees
3   GROUP BY department_id
4   HAVING COUNT(department_id) =
5   (SELECT max(count(department_id))
6    FROM employees
7    GROUP BY department_id);
```

A. Line 3

B. Line 4

C. Line 5

D. Line 7

E. No error

13. Which of the following is a correlated subquery?

A. `select cty_name from city where st_code in (select st_code from state where st_name = 'TENNESSEE' and city.cnt_code = state.cnt_code);`

B. `select cty_name from city where st_code in (select st_code from state where st_name = 'TENNESSEE');`

C. `select cty_name from city, state where city.st_code = state.st_code and city.cnt_code = state.cnt_code and st_name = 'TENNESSEE';`

D. `select cty_name from city, state where  city.st_code = state.st_code (+) and city.cnt_code = state.cnt_code (+) and st_name = 'TENNESSEE';`

14. The `COUNTRY` table has the following data:

```
SQL> SELECT * FROM country;

  CNT_CODE CNT_NAME           CONTINENT
---------- ------------------ ----------
         1 UNITED STATES      N.AMERICA
        91 INDIA              ASIA
        65 SINGAPORE          ASIA
```

What value is returned from the subquery when you execute the following?

```
SELECT CNT_NAME
FROM    country
WHERE   CNT_CODE =
(SELECT MAX(cnt_code) FROM country);
```

A. INDIA

B. 65

C. 91

D. SINGAPORE

15. Which line in the following query contains an error?

```
1   SELECT deptno, ename, sal
2   FROM    emp e1
3   WHERE   sal = (SELECT MAX(sal) FROM emp
4                  WHERE   deptno = e1.deptno
5                  ORDER BY deptno);
```

A. Line 2

B. Line 3

C. Line 4

D. Line 5

16. Consider the following query:

```
SELECT deptno, ename, salary salary, average,
       salary-average difference
FROM   emp,
(SELECT deptno dno, AVG(salary) average FROM emp
 GROUP BY deptno)
WHERE  deptno = dno
ORDER BY 1, 2;
```

Which of the following statements is correct?

A. The query will fail because no alias name is provided for the subquery.

B. The query will fail because a column selected in the subquery is referenced outside the scope of the subquery.

C. The query will work without errors.

D. GROUP BY cannot be used inside a subquery.

17. The COUNTRY table has the following data:

```
SQL> SELECT * FROM country;
```

CNT_CODE	CNT_NAME	CONTINENT
1	UNITED STATES	N. AMERICA
91	INDIA	ASIA
65	SINGAPORE	ASIA

What will be result of the following query?

```
INSERT INTO (SELECT cnt_code FROM country
        WHERE continent = 'ASIA')
VALUES (971, 'SAUDI ARABIA', 'ASIA');
```

A. One row will be inserted into the COUNTRY table.

B. WITH CHECK OPTION is missing in the subquery.

C. The query will fail because the VALUES clause is invalid.

D. The WHERE clause cannot appear in the subqueries used in INSERT statements.

18. Review the SQL code, and choose the line number that has an error.

```
1   SELECT DISTINCT department_id
2   FROM employees
3   ORDER BY department_id
4   UNION ALL
5   SELECT department_id
6   FROM departments
7   ORDER BY department_id
```

A. 1

B. 3

C. 6

D. 7

E. No error

19. Consider the following queries:

```
1. SELECT last_name, salary,
        (SELECT (MAX(sq.salary) - e.salary)
        FROM    employees sq
        WHERE   sq.department_id = e.department_id) DSAL
FROM    employees e
WHERE   department_id = 20;
2. SELECT last_name, salary, msalary - salary dsal
FROM    employees e,
        (SELECT department_id, MAX(salary) msalary
         FROM    employees
         GROUP BY department_id) sq
WHERE e.department_id = sq.department_id
AND    e.department_id = 20;
3. SELECT last_name, salary, msalary - salary dsal
FROM    employees e INNER JOIN
        (SELECT department_id, MAX(salary) msalary
         FROM    employees
         GROUP BY department_id) sq
ON      e.department_id = sq.department_id
WHERE   e.department_id = 20;
4. SELECT last_name, salary, msalary - salary dsal
FROM    employees INNER JOIN
        (SELECT department_id, MAX(salary) msalary
         FROM    employees
         GROUP BY department_id) sq
USING   (department_id)
WHERE   department_id = 20;
```

Which of the following assertions best describes the results?

A. Queries 1 and 2 produce identical results, and queries 3 and 4 produce identical results, but queries 1 and 3 produce different results.

B. Queries 1, 2, 3, and 4 produce identical results.

C. Queries 1, 2, and 3 produce identical results; query 4 will produce errors.

D. Queries 1 and 3 produce identical results; queries 2 and 4 will produce errors.

E. Queries 1, 2, 3, and 4 produce different results.

F. Queries 1 and 2 are valid SQL; queries 3 and 4 are not valid.

20. The columns of the EMPLOYEES and DEPARTMENTS tables are shown in question 8. Which query will show you the top five highest-paid employees in the company?

A. SELECT last_name, salaryFROM employeesWHERE ROWNUM <= 5ORDER BY salary DESC;

B. SELECT last_name, salaryFROM (SELECT *FROM employeesWHERE ROWNUM <= 5ORDER BY salary DESC)WHERE ROWNUM <= 5;

C. SELECT * FROM(SELECT last_name, salaryFROM employeesORDER BY salary) WHERE ROWNUM <= 5;

D. SELECT * FROM(SELECT last_name, salaryFROM employeesORDER BY salary DESC)WHERE ROWNUM <= 5;

Chapter

6

Manipulating Data

ORACLE DATABASE 12c: SQL FUNDAMENTALS EXAM OBJECTIVES COVERED IN THIS CHAPTER:

✓ **Managing Tables Using DML Statements**

  ▪ Truncate data.

  ▪ Insert rows into a table.

  ▪ Update rows in a table.

  ▪ Delete rows from a table.

  ▪ Control transactions.

In this chapter, we will cover how to manipulate data in the Oracle 12*c* database; this means we'll be using SQL Data Manipulation Language (DML) statements. You will also learn how to coordinate multiple changes using transactions. We will discuss how to insert new data into a table, update existing data, and delete existing data from a table.

Because Oracle is a multiuser database and more than one user or session can change data at the same time, we will cover locks and how they are used to control this concurrency. We will also cover another effect of a multiuser database, which is that data can change during the execution of statements. You can exercise some control over the consistency or visibility of these changes within a transaction, which is covered later in the chapter.

The certification exam will assess your knowledge of how to change data and control these changes. This chapter will solidify your understanding of these concepts in preparation for the certification exam.

Using DML Statements

DML is a subset of SQL that is employed to change data in a database table. Because SQL is English-like, meaning it's not cryptic like C or Perl, the statements used to perform data manipulation are easy to remember. The *INSERT* statement is used to add new rows to a table. The *UPDATE* statement is used to modify existing rows in a table, and the *DELETE* statement is used to remove rows from a table.

Oracle also has the *MERGE* statement to perform an insert or update on the table from an existing source of data (table or view). MERGE also can include an optional clause to delete rows when certain conditions are met. Table 6.1 summarizes the DML statements that Oracle supports.

TABLE 6.1 DML Statements Supported by Oracle

Statement	Purpose
INSERT	Adds rows to a table
UPDATE	Changes the value stored in a table
DELETE	Removes rows from a table
MERGE	Updates or inserts rows from one table into another

Table 6.1 lists the SQL statements that alter data in the database. LOCK TABLE, CALL, and EXPLAIN PLAN statements are also classified as DML statements.

Inserting Rows into a Table

The *INSERT* statement is used to add rows to one or more tables. The syntax for a simple INSERT statement is as follows:

```
INSERT INTO [schema.]table_name [(column_list)]
VALUES (data_values)
```

In the syntax, *table_name* is the name of the table where you want to add new rows. *table_name* may be qualified with the schema name. *column_list* is the name of the columns in the table, separated by commas, that you want to populate. *data_values* represents the corresponding values separated by commas. Using this syntax, you can add only one row at a time.

column_list is optional. If *column_list* is not included, Oracle includes all columns in the order specified when the table was created. *data_values* in the VALUES clause must match the number of columns and datatype in *column_list* (or the number of columns and datatype in the table if *column_list* is omitted). For clarity, it is a good practice to include *column_list* when using the INSERT statement.

If you omit columns in *column_list*, those columns will have NULL values if no default value is defined for the column. If a default value is defined for the column, the column will get the default value. You can insert the default value using the DEFAULT keyword. The SQL statements in the following example show two methods to insert the default value into the MYACCOUNTS table if a default value of C is defined on the DR_CR column:

```
DESCRIBE MYACCOUNTS
Name          Null?    Type
------------- -------- --------------------
ACC_NO        NOT NULL NUMBER(5)
ACC_DT        NOT NULL DATE
DR_CR                  CHAR
AMOUNT                 NUMBER(15,2)

INSERT INTO myaccounts (acc_no, acc_dt, amount)
VALUES (120003, TRUNC(SYSDATE), 400);

INSERT INTO myaccounts (acc_no, acc_dt, dr_cr, amount)
VALUES (120003, TRUNC(SYSDATE), DEFAULT, 400);
```

When you're specifying *data_values*, enclose character and datetime values in single quotes. For date values, if the value is not in the default date format, you may have to use the TO_DATE function. When you enclose a value in single quotes, Oracle considers it character data and performs an implicit conversion if the column datatype is not a character; therefore, do not enclose numeric values in single quotes.

You can determine the order of columns in a table by using the USER_TAB_ COLUMNS view. The COLUMN_ID column shows the order of columns in the table. When you use the DESCRIBE command to list the table columns, the columns are listed in that order.

We'll use the ACCOUNTS table to demonstrate the INSERT statements. The column names, their order, and their datatype can be displayed using the DESCRIBE statement, as shown here:

```
SQL> DESCRIBE accounts
Name                    Null?    Type
----------------------- -------- -------------

CUST_NAME                        VARCHAR2(20)
ACC_OPEN_DATE                    DATE
BALANCE                          NUMBER(15,2)
```

To insert rows into the ACCOUNTS table, you can use the INSERT statement in its simplest form, as shown here:

```
SQL> INSERT INTO accounts VALUES ('John', '13-MAY-68', 2300.45);
1 row created.
```

The following are some more examples of using INSERT statements. When you use the column list, they can appear in any order. If the DATE value is not in the default date format specified by the NLS_DATE_FORMAT parameter, you should use the TO_DATE function with the format mask. To help you understand the statement rules, the examples also include some errors generated from INSERT. Notice that you can explicitly insert a NULL value, or if you omit a column in the column list, a NULL value is inserted into that column, provided the column is nullable—in other words, a NOT NULL constraint is not defined on the column.

```
SQL> INSERT INTO hr.accounts (cust_name, acc_open_date)
  2  VALUES (Shine, 'April-23-2001');
VALUES (Shine, 'April-23-2001')
        *
ERROR at line 2:
ORA-00984: column not allowed here

SQL> INSERT INTO hr.accounts (cust_name, acc_open_date)
  2  VALUES ('Shine', 'April-23-2001');
```

```
VALUES ('Shine', 'April-23-2001')
              *
ERROR at line 2:
ORA-01858: a non-numeric character was found where a numeric was expected

SQL> INSERT INTO hr.accounts (cust_name, acc_open_date)
  2  VALUES ('Shine', TO_DATE('April-23-2001','Month-DD-YYYY'));
1 row created.


SQL> INSERT INTO accounts VALUES ('Jishi', '4-AUG-72');
INSERT INTO accounts VALUES ('Jishi', '4-AUG-72')
            *
ERROR at line 1:
ORA-00947: not enough values
```

You can also use functions like SYSDATE or USER in the INSERT statement. See these examples:

```
SQL> SHOW USER
USER is "HR"
SQL> INSERT INTO accounts VALUES (USER, SYSDATE, 345);
1 row created.


SQL> SELECT * FROM accounts;
CUST_NAME            ACC_OPEN_    BALANCE
-------------------- ---------   ----------
John                 13-MAY-68    2300.45
Shine                23-APR-01
Jishi                12-SEP-99
HR                   23-APR-08        345
```

You can add rows with specific data values, as you have seen in the examples, or you can create rows from existing data using a subquery.

Inserting Rows from a Subquery

You can insert data into a table from an existing table or view using a subquery. To perform the subquery insert, replace the VALUES clause with the subquery. You cannot have both a VALUES clause and a subquery. The columns in the column list should match the number of columns selected in the subquery as well as their datatype. Here are a few examples:

```
SQL> INSERT INTO accounts
  2  SELECT first_name, hire_date, salary
  3  FROM hr.employees
```

```
   4  WHERE first_name like 'R%';
3 rows created.

SQL> INSERT INTO accounts (cust_name, balance)
   2  SELECT first_name, hire_date, salary
   3  FROM hr.employees
   4  WHERE first_name like 'T%';
INSERT INTO accounts (cust_name, balance)
            *
ERROR at line 1:
ORA-00913: too many values

SQL> INSERT INTO accounts (cust_name, acc_open_date)
   2  SELECT UPPER(first_name), ADD_MONTHS(hire_date,2)
   3  FROM hr.employees
   4  WHERE first_name like 'T%';
4 rows created.

SQL> SELECT * FROM accounts;
CUST_NAME                ACC_OPEN_   BALANCE
--------------------     ---------   ----------
John                     13-MAY-68   2300.45
Shine                    23-APR-01
Jishi                    04-AUG-72
Renske                   14-JUL-95      3600
Randall                  15-MAR-98      2600
Randall                  19-DEC-99      2500
TJ                       10-JUN-99
TRENNA                   17-DEC-95
TAYLER                   24-MAR-98
TIMOTHY                  11-SEP-98
10 rows selected.
```

You can use SELECT * FROM if the source and destination table have the same structure, as shown in the following example:

```
INSERT INTO old_employees
SELECT * FROM employees;

107 rows created.
```

Inserting Rows into Multiple Tables

You can also use the INSERT statement to add rows to more than one table at a time. This multiple-table insert is useful for efficiently loading data, because you can add the data to multiple target tables via a single pass through the source table, with a minimum of database calls. The syntax for the multiple-table INSERT statement is shown here:

```
INSERT [ALL | FIRST] {WHEN <condition> THEN INTO <insert_clause> … … …} [ELSE
<insert_clause>}
```

The keyword ALL tells Oracle to evaluate each and every WHEN clause, whether or not any evaluate to TRUE. In contrast, the FIRST keyword tells Oracle to stop evaluating WHEN clauses after encountering the first one that evaluates to TRUE. The WHEN clause and the INTO clause can be repeated.

Suppose that your company, Sales Inc., sells books, videos, and audio CDs. You have a SALES_DETAIL table that contains information about all the sales and is used by the selling system. You need to load this information into three other tables that focus specifically on the three product categories: Book, Audio, and Video. These category-specific tables are used by the analysis systems. Here are the structure and contents of the source SALES_DETAIL table:

```
Name                          Null?    Type
----------------------------- -------- -------------
TXN_ID                        NOT NULL NUMBER
PRODUCT_ID                             NUMBER
PROD_CATEGORY                          VARCHAR2(2)
CUSTOMER_ID                            VARCHAR2(10)
SALE_DATE                              DATE
SALE_QTY                               NUMBER
SALE_PRICE                             NUMBER

SELECT * FROM sales_detail;

TXN_ID PRODUCT_ID PR CUST SALE_DATE  SALE_QTY SALE_PRICE
------ ---------- -- ---- ---------- -------- ----------
     1  304329743 B  43  17-JUN-02         2       19.1
     2  304943209 B  22  17-JUN-02         1       8.95
     3  211524098 A  16  17-JUN-02         1       11.4
     4  413354981 V  41  17-JUN-02         1      12.95
     5  304957315 B  48  17-JUN-02         1       38.5
     6  304183648 B  32  17-JUN-02         2       17.9
     7  211681559 A  32  18-JUN-02         1       11.4
     8  211944553 A  21  18-JUN-02         1       11.4
     9  304155687 B  26  18-JUN-02         1       8.95
```

```
10  304776352 B  18   18-JUN-02        3      48.45
11  413753861 V  30   18-JUN-02        1      12.95
12  413159654 V  29   18-JUN-02        1      19.99
13  304357689 B  11   18-JUN-02        2       72.3
14  211153246 A  14   18-JUN-02        2       26.4
15  304852369 B  44   18-JUN-02        1      15.95
```

The target table structures are described in the following output:

```
DESC book_sales

Name                         Null?     Type
---------------------------- --------  ------------
SALE_DATE                    NOT_NULL  DATE
PROD_ID                      NOT NULL  NUMBER
CUST_ID                      NOT NULL  VARCHAR2(10)
QTY_SOLD                     NOT NULL  NUMBER
AMT_SOLD                     NOT NULL  NUMBER
ISBN                                   VARCHAR2(24)


DESC video_sales
Name                         Null?     Type
---------------------------- --------  ------------
SALE_DATE                    NOT_NULL  DATE
PROD_ID                      NOT NULL  NUMBER
CUST_ID                      NOT NULL  VARCHAR2(10)
QTY_SOLD                     NOT NULL  NUMBER
AMT_SOLD                     NOT NULL  NUMBER
RATING                                 VARCHAR2(5)
YEAR_RELEASED                          NUMBER


DESC audio_sales
Name                         Null?     Type
---------------------------- --------  ------------
SALE_DATE                    NOT_NULL  DATE
PROD_ID                      NOT NULL  NUMBER
CUST_ID                      NOT NULL  VARCHAR2(10)
QTY_SOLD                     NOT NULL  NUMBER
AMT_SOLD                     NOT NULL  NUMBER
ARTIST                                 VARCHAR2(64)
```

The following multiple-table insert selects from the SALES_DETAIL table and, based on the value of PROD_CATEGORY, inserts a row into the BOOK_SALES, VIDEO_SALES or AUDIO_SALES table:

```
INSERT ALL
WHEN prod_category='B' THEN
  INTO book_sales(prod_id,cust_id,qty_sold,amt_sold)
      VALUES(product_id,customer_id,sale_qty,sale_price)
WHEN prod_category='V' THEN
  INTO video_sales(prod_id,cust_id,qty_sold,amt_sold)
      VALUES(product_id,customer_id,sale_qty,sale_price)
WHEN prod_category='A' THEN
  INTO audio_sales(prod_id,cust_id,qty_sold,amt_sold)
      VALUES(product_id,customer_id,sale_qty,sale_price)
SELECT prod_category ,product_id ,customer_id ,sale_qty
      ,sale_price
FROM sales_detail;
```

This multiple-table insert will create a total of 15 rows: eight rows in the BOOK_SALES table, four rows in the AUDIO_SALES table, and three rows in the VIDEO_SALES table.

WARNING   In most SQL statements, you can prefix column names with a table alias. In fact, this aids readability even if it's not strictly required for parsing. If you try to use an alias for the table name and then prefix the column names with either this alias or the schema-qualified table name in a multiple-table insert, you may raise an exception.

Updating Rows in a Table

The *UPDATE* statement is used to modify existing rows in a table. The basic syntax for the UPDATE statement is as follows:

```
UPDATE <table_name>
SET <column> = <value>
  [,<column> = <value> … … …]
[WHERE <condition>]
```

You can update more than one row at a time. If the WHERE clause is omitted, all the rows in the table are updated.

If an employee named Jennifer was transferred to another department, you can change the department_id column in the employees table for that employee. Because you know the employee ID for Jennifer, you can use the employee ID to identify Jennifer's row in the table.

```
SELECT first_name, last_name, department_id
FROM employees
WHERE employee_id = 200;
```

```
FIRST_NAME           LAST_NAME                DEPARTMENT_ID
-------------------- ------------------------ -------------

Jennifer             Whalen                              10
```

```
UPDATE employees
SET department_id = 20
WHERE employee_id = 200;
```

```
1 row updated.
```

```
SELECT first_name, last_name, department_id
FROM employees
WHERE employee_id = 200;
```

```
FIRST_NAME           LAST_NAME                DEPARTMENT_ID
-------------------- ------------------------ -------------

Jennifer             Whalen                              20
```

You can update more than one column in the same row by including the columns and values in the SET clause separated by commas. To remove a value from the column, you can update the column as NULL. The following example demonstrates how to update more than one column of the same row as well as update using NULL. Because no WHERE clause is included, all rows in the table are updated.

```
UPDATE book_sales
SET qty_sold = NULL,
    amt_sold = 0;
```

```
8 rows updated.
```

Updating Rows Using a Subquery

When a column is updated in the table, the value can be derived using a subquery. In the following example, the job_id values of all employees in department 30 are changed to match the job_id of employee 114:

```
SELECT first_name, last_name, job_id
FROM employees
```

```
WHERE department_id = 30;


FIRST_NAME              LAST_NAME                 JOB_ID
--------------------    ----------------------    ----------

Den                     Raphaely                  PU_MAN
Alexander               Khoo                      PU_CLERK
Shelli                  Baida                     PU_CLERK
Sigal                   Tobias                    PU_CLERK
Guy                     Himuro                    PU_CLERK
Karen                   Colmenares                PU_CLERK


6 rows selected.


UPDATE employees
SET job_id = (SELECT job_id
              FROM employees
              WHERE employee_id = 114)
WHERE department_id = 30;


6 rows updated.


SELECT first_name, last_name, job_id
FROM employees
WHERE department_id = 30;


FIRST_NAME              LAST_NAME                 JOB_ID
--------------------    ----------------------    ----------

Den                     Raphaely                  PU_MAN
Alexander               Khoo                      PU_MAN
Shelli                  Baida                     PU_MAN
Sigal                   Tobias                    PU_MAN
Guy                     Himuro                    PU_MAN
Karen                   Colmenares                PU_MAN


6 rows selected.
```

You may have more than one column in the SET clause to update more than one column of the same row using a subquery. If you specify more than one column, they must be enclosed in parentheses, and the subquery should have the same number of columns in the SELECT clause.

```
UPDATE book_sales a
SET (qty_sold, amt_sold) = (SELECT SUM(sale_qty), SUM(sale_price)
```

```
                   FROM sales_detail b
                   WHERE b.prod_category = 'B'
                   AND b.product_id = a.prod_id AND b.customer_id = a.cust_id
AND b.sale_date = a.sale_date
                   GROUP BY sale_date, prod_category, product_id, customer_id)
WHERE sale_date = TO_DATE('18-JUN-02','DD-MON-YY');
```

4 rows updated

 Real World Scenario

Using a Correct WHERE Clause in UPDATE

The developer had a problem. He was trying to update one row in a table, and it was taking forever. He was sure he was using the primary key of the table in the WHERE clause and expected the result to come back in seconds.

The table he was updating had the following columns (some columns have been omitted):

ORDER_HEADER

```
ORDER#   VARCHAR2 (20) – Primary Key
ORDER_DT DATE
CUSTOMER# VARCHAR2 (12)
TOTAL_AMOUNT NUMBER
```

The update was performed using the value derived from another table named ORDER_ TRANSACTIONS. It had the following structure:

ORDER_TRANSACTIONS

```
ORDER# VARCHAR2 (20) - Primary Key
ITEM# VARCHAR2 (20) - Primary Key
SHIP_DATE DATE
ITEM_AMOUNT NUMBER
```

The developer was trying to update the TOTAL_AMOUNT column in the ORDER_HEADER table with the sum of all the order items from the ORDER_TRANSACTIONS table using a subquery. This was the SQL code he used:

```
UPDATE order_header oh
SET total_amount = (SELECT SUM(item_amount)
```

```
               FROM order_transactions ot
               WHERE oh.order# = ot.order#
               AND oh.order# = 'W2H3004FU');
```

Can you see what is wrong with this statement? By the way, the table had about two million rows.

Although the developer thought he was updating only one row in the ORDER_HEADER table and querying only three rows from the ORDER_TRANSACTIONS table, Oracle was in fact updating all two million rows in the table. Why?

Look carefully at the UPDATE statement; it is missing a WHERE clause for the UPDATE statement. The WHERE clause is present as part of the correlated subquery. So, the result of this update would have been the TOTAL_AMOUNT column updated to NULL for all rows except for order W2H3004FU. When executing the correct SQL statement, the update completed in less than one second.

```
UPDATE order_header oh
SET total_amount = (SELECT SUM(item_amount)
                    FROM order_transactions ot
                    WHERE oh.order# = ot.order#
                    AND ot.order# = 'W2H3004FU')
WHERE oh.order# = 'W2H3004FU';
```

Because we are updating a specific ORDER# in the table and we are using the order number in the WHERE clause, it is safe to remove the join condition inside the subquery as in the following code.

```
UPDATE order_header oh
SET total_amount = (SELECT SUM(item_amount)
                    FROM order_transactions ot
                    WHERE ot.order# = 'W2H3004FU')
WHERE oh.order# = 'W2H3004FU';
```

The moral of this story is to be careful when you're updating tables using subqueries. Always make sure you have the correct WHERE clause for the UPDATE statement.

Deleting Rows from a Table

The *DELETE* statement is used to remove rows from a table. The syntax for a basic DELETE statement is as follows:

```
DELETE [FROM] <table>
[WHERE <condition>]
```

The FROM keyword is optional; it is included to add readability to the statement. Similar to the UPDATE statement, if the WHERE clause is omitted, all the rows in the table will be deleted.

Here are some examples of the DELETE statement. The two hyphens (--) are used to indicate comments.

```
-- Remove records from job history for start date in 2001
SELECT * FROM job_history
WHERE start_date BETWEEN TO_DATE('01JAN01','DDMONYY')
      and TO_DATE('31DEC012359','DDMONYYHH24MI')
/
DELETE FROM job_history
WHERE start_date BETWEEN TO_DATE('01JAN01','DDMONYY')
      and TO_DATE('31DEC012359','DDMONYYHH24MI');


-- Remove employee with first name Alana
-- Note FROM keyword is optional
DELETE employees
WHERE first_name = 'Alana';
```

If foreign keys are enabled in the table and child records exist for the row, you will not be able to delete rows. See the following example, where the employees table has a foreign key to itself and employee John (ID 145) is a manager with employees reporting to him.

```
SQL> SELECT employee_id, first_name, job_id, manager_id
  2  FROM employees
  3* WHERE employee_id = 145
SQL> /

EMPLOYEE_ID FIRST_NAME           JOB_ID     MANAGER_ID
----------- -------------------- ---------- ----------
        145 John                 SA_MAN            100
```

The following are the employees reporting to John.

```
SQL> SELECT employee_id, first_name, job_id, manager_id
```

```
  2  FROM employees
  3* WHERE manager_id = 145
SQL> /

EMPLOYEE_ID FIRST_NAME           JOB_ID      MANAGER_ID
----------- -------------------- ----------  ----------
        150 Peter                SA_REP             145
        151 David                SA_REP             145
        152 Peter                SA_REP             145
        153 Christopher          SA_REP             145
        154 Nanette              SA_REP             145
        155 Oliver               SA_REP             145

6 rows selected.

SQL>
```

If you try to delete employee John without deleting all the employees reporting to him, you will get an error. However, you can delete an employee who does not have any other employee reporting to him. See the following examples.

```
SQL> DELETE FROM employees
  2  WHERE employee_id = 145;
DELETE FROM employees
*
ERROR at line 1:
ORA-02292: integrity constraint (HR.DEPT_MGR_FK) violated - child record found

SQL> DELETE FROM employees
  2  WHERE employee_id = 153;

1 row deleted.

SQL>
```

Subqueries can be used in DELETE statements to identify the rows to delete. Following is a generic example to remove duplicate rows from the ALL_SALES table, where a unique row is supposed to be uniquely identified by the combination of *txn_id* and *customer_id* (imaginative primary key for this example). Here only one row of the combination (arbitrary pick) and other rows are deleted (MIN or MAX functions may be used).

```
SQL> DELETE sales_detail
  2  WHERE rowid NOT IN (SELECT MAX(rowid)
```

```
3        FROM sales_detail
4        GROUP BY txn_id, customer_id);
```

Sometimes it is required to delete all the rows from a table. You can do this by not providing any WHERE clause conditions. The following example deletes all records from the VIDEO_SALES table.

```
SQL> DELETE video_sales;
```

Removing all the rows from a large table can take a long time and can require significant rollback segment space. If you are deleting all rows from a table, consider using the TRUNCATE statement, as described in the next section.

Truncating a Table

If you're deleting all the rows from a table, truncating a table can accomplish the same task as deleting, although deleting is sometimes a better choice. If you want to empty a table of all rows, consider using the Data Definition Language (DDL) statement *TRUNCATE*. Like a DELETE statement without a WHERE clause, TRUNCATE will remove all rows from a table. However, TRUNCATE is not DML; it is DDL. Therefore, it has different characteristics from the DELETE statement. DDL is the subset of SQL that is employed to define database objects. One of the key differences between DML and DDL is that DDL statements will implicitly perform a commit, not only affecting the change in object definition but also committing any pending DML. A DDL statement cannot be rolled back; only DML statements can be rolled back.

For example, to remove all rows from the SALES_DETAIL table, truncate the table as follows:

```
SQL> TRUNCATE TABLE sales_detail;
```

TRUNCATE vs. DELETE

The TRUNCATE statement is similar to a DELETE statement without a WHERE clause, except for the following:

- TRUNCATE is very fast on both large and small tables. DELETE will generate undo information if a rollback is issued, but TRUNCATE will not generate undo information.

- TRUNCATE is DDL and, like all DDL, performs an implicit commit.

- You cannot roll back a TRUNCATE. Any uncommitted DML changes within the session will also be committed with the TRUNCATE operation.

- TRUNCATE resets the high-water mark in the table and all indexes. Because full-table scans and index fast-full scans read all data blocks up to the high-water mark, full-scan performance will not improve after a DELETE; after a TRUNCATE, it will be very fast.

- TRUNCATE does not fire any DELETE triggers.

- There is no object privilege that can be granted to allow a user to truncate another user's table. The DROP ANY TABLE system privilege is required to truncate a table in another schema. See Chapter 13, "Implementing Security and Auditing," for more information about getting around this limitation.

- When a table is truncated, the storage for the table and all indexes can be reset to the initial size. A DELETE will never shrink the size of a table or its indexes.

- By default you cannot truncate the parent table with an enabled referential integrity constraint. You must first disable the foreign key constraints that reference the parent table, and then you can truncate the parent table. If the constraint is defined with the ON DELETE CASCADE option (discussed in Chapter 7 "Creating Tables and Constraints"), then you can use CASCADE option in TRUNCATE to truncate the child tables as well.

Merging Rows

To complete the DML discussion, we will introduce you to the MERGE statement even though it is not part of the test objectives.

Available in Oracle since its *9i version*, MERGE is a very powerful statement that can insert or update rows based on a condition. The statement also has an option to delete rows when certain conditions are met. The MERGE statement has a join specification that describes how to determine whether an update or insert should be executed. MERGE is a convenient way to combine multiple operations in one statement instead of writing a complex PL/SQL program.

The basic syntax of the MERGE statement is as follows:

```
MERGE INTO <table_or_view>
USING <table_or_view_or_subquery>
ON <join_condition>
WHEN MATCHED THEN UPDATE SET <update_clause> [<where clause>] [DELETE where_
clause]
WHEN NOT MATCHED THEN INSERT <insert_columns> VALUES <insert_columns>
```

The INTO clause specifies the target table where the update/insert/delete operation will be performed. The USING clause specifies the data source. The ON clause has the join condition between the source and target tables. The WHEN MATCHED THEN UPDATE SET clause specifies which columns to update when the ON condition is matched. You can also include an optional WHERE clause. The optional DELETE clause can delete the row if the WHERE condition specified in the DELETE clause is met. The WHEN NOT MATCHED THEN INSERT clause is used to add rows to the target table from the source table.

Let's look at a few examples. Consider two tables, ORDERS1 and ORDERS2. The rows in the tables are listed using the following SQL statements:

```
SQL> SELECT * FROM orders1;

  ORDER_ID ORDER_MO CUSTOMER_ID ORDER_TOTAL
---------- -------- ----------- -----------
      2414 channel          102     10794.6
      2397 direct           102     42283.2
      2432 channel          102       10523
      2431 direct           102      5610.6
```

```
    2454 direct                103          6653.4
    2415 direct                103             310
    2433 channel               103              78
    2437 direct                103           13550
```

8 rows selected.

SQL> SELECT * FROM orders2;

```
  ORDER_ID CUSTOMER_ID ORDER_TOTAL
---------- ----------- -----------
      2414         102       35982
      2397         102      140944
      2432         102    35076.67
      2431         102           0
      2450         147        1636
      2425         147      1500.8
      2385         147      295892
      2451         148     10474.6
      2386         148     21116.9
```

9 rows selected.

SQL>

The task before you is to merge the rows in ORDERS2 into ORDERS1. If ORDER_ID and CUSTOMER_ID match between the two tables, you need to update the ORDER_TOTAL value with the value from the ORDERS2 table and update the ORDER_MODE value to modified. For the rows in ORDERS2 where ORDER_ID and CUSTOMER_ID do not match with existing rows in ORDERS1, you need to insert the values from ORDERS2 to ORDERS1. For such rows, the ORDER_MODE value should be merged. You also want to delete the row from ORDERS1 if the new order's total value is zero. The following SQL code can accomplish all these tasks using the MERGE statement:

```
MERGE INTO orders1 o1
USING orders2 o2
ON (o1.order_id = o2.order_id
    AND o1.customer_id = o2.customer_id)
WHEN MATCHED THEN UPDATE SET o1.order_total = o2.order_total,
                             o1.order_mode = 'modified'
    DELETE WHERE o2.order_total = 0
WHEN NOT MATCHED THEN INSERT
    VALUES (o2.order_id, 'merged', o2.customer_id, o2.order_total);
```

```
9 rows merged.

select * from orders1;

   ORDER_ID ORDER_MO CUSTOMER_ID ORDER_TOTAL
---------- -------- ----------- -----------
      2414 modified         102       35982
      2397 modified         102      140944
      2432 modified         102    35076.67
      2454 direct           103      6653.4
      2415 direct           103         310
      2433 channel          103          78
      2437 direct           103       13550
      2450 merged           147        1636
      2385 merged           147      295892
      2386 merged           148     21116.9
      2451 merged           148     10474.6
      2425 merged           147      1500.8

12 rows selected.
```

As you can see from the result, Oracle updated four rows that matched the ON condition and inserted five new rows that did not match the ON condition, which is why you get the "9 rows merged" feedback. Because you had the DELETE clause to delete any rows that had order total zero (of the four rows that matched the ON condition), one of them matched the DELETE condition and hence was removed from the table.

Understanding Transaction Control

Transaction control involves coordinating multiple concurrent accesses to the same data. When one session is changing data that another session is accessing, Oracle uses *transactions* to control which users have visibility to changing data and when they can see the changed data. Transactions represent an atomic unit of work. All changes to data in a transaction are applied together or rolled back (undone) together. Transactions provide data consistency in the event of a user-process failure or system failure.

A *transaction* can include one or more DML statements. A transaction ends when you save the transaction (COMMIT) or undo the changes (ROLLBACK). When DDL statements are executed, Oracle implicitly ends the previous transaction by saving the changes. It also begins a new transaction for the DDL and ends the transaction after the DDL is completed. Therefore, DDL statements cannot be undone.

A number of statements in SQL let the programmer control transactions. Using transaction-control statements, the programmer can do the following:

- Explicitly begin a transaction, choosing statement-level consistency or transaction-level consistency
- Set undo savepoints and undo changes back to a savepoint
- End a transaction by making the changes permanent or undoing the changes

Table 6.2 summarizes the transaction-control statements.

TABLE 6.2 Transaction-Control Statements

Statement	Purpose
COMMIT	Ends the current transaction, making data changes permanent and visible to other sessions.
ROLLBACK	Undoes all data changes in the current transaction.
ROLLBACK TO SAVEPOINT	Undoes all data changes in the current transactions going chronologically backward to the optionally named savepoint.
SAVEPOINT	Sets an optional marker within the transaction to be able to go back to this position if needed.
SET TRANSACTION	Enables transaction or statement consistency.
SET CONSTRAINT	Controls when deferrable constraint checking is performed for a transaction. Constraints are discussed in Chapter 7.

Throughout this section, we will use a banking example to clarify transactional concepts and the control statements used to ensure that data is changed as designed. In this example, say you have a banking customer named Sara, who has a checking account and a brokerage account with her bank.

When Sara transfers $5,000 from her checking account to her brokerage account, the balance in her checking account is reduced by $5,000, and the cash balance in her brokerage account is increased by $5,000. You cannot allow only one account to change—either both must change or neither must change.

Consider the following statements to complete the transaction. All the statements in the group must be completed, or no changes should be recorded in the database. The INSERT statements are used to log the transaction in the log table.

```
UPDATE checking
SET balance = balance - 5000
WHERE account = 'SARA1001';
```

```
INSERT INTO checking_log (action_date, action, amount)
VALUES (SYSDATE, 'Withdrawal', 5000);


UPDATE brokerage
SET balance = balance + 5000
WHERE account = 'SARA1001';


INSERT INTO brokerage_log (action_date, action, amount)
VALUES (SYSDATE, 'Deposit', 5000);
```

You issued the two UPDATE statements and the two INSERT statements in a single transaction. If there is any failure in one of these four statements (say, perhaps, the CHECKING_LOG table ran out of room in the tablespace), then none of the changes should go through. When all the previous statements are successful, you can issue a COMMIT statement to save the work to the database. The changes will be committed and made permanent only if all four statements succeed. If only part of the SQL statements were successful, you can issue a ROLLBACK statement to undo the changes.

A transaction will implicitly begin with a DML statement. The transaction will always end with either an implicit or explicit commit or rollback. A ROLLBACK TO SAVEPOINT statement will not end a transaction. The scenarios for *commit* or *rollback* of transaction are described here.

An implicit commit is issued when:

▪ You issue a DDL command.

▪ You exit out of the SQL*Plus session (with the default setting of SET EXITCOMMIT ON).

An implicit rollback is issued when:

▪ Your program is abnormally terminated.

▪ The database crashes.

▪ You exit out of the SQL*Plus session (with the setting of SET EXITCOMMIT OFF).

▪ To roll back any failed DML statement, an implicit savepoint is marked before executing an INSERT, UPDATE, or DELETE statement. If the statement fails, a rollback to this implicit savepoint is performed.

An explicit commit is issued when:

▪ You issue the COMMIT command.

An explicit rollback is issued when:

▪ You issue the ROLLBACK command.

If a DML statement fails, the transaction is not rolled back. The changes made from the successful DML statements before the failed statement are still valid. To undo those changes, you have to explicitly execute a ROLLBACK statement.

Savepoints and Partial Rollbacks

A *ROLLBACK* statement will undo all the changes made in the transaction. If you have to undo part of the changes in a transaction, you can set up savepoints or markers in the transaction and go back to a savepoint when needed. *Savepoints* are intermediate fallback positions in SQL code. The ROLLBACK TO SAVEPOINT statement is used to undo changes chronologically back to the last savepoint or to the named savepoint. Savepoints are not labels for goto statements, and ROLLBACK TO SAVEPOINT is not a goto. The code after a savepoint does not get re-executed after a ROLLBACK TO SAVEPOINT; only the data changes made since that savepoint are undone.

Savepoints are not used extensively by programmers. However, you must understand them because there will likely be a question related to savepoints on the certification exam.

Consider a transaction with various DML statements and savepoints, as in Figure 6.1.

FIGURE 6.1   Transaction control

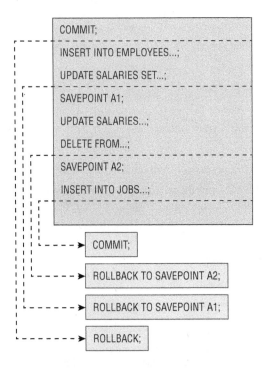

A new transaction begins after a COMMIT statement. Various DML statements are executed in the transaction. You have also set savepoints in between. After all the statements are successfully executed, the user has the option to issue the ROLLBACK TO SAVEPOINT, ROLLBACK, or COMMIT statement. The arrows in the figure show the effects of issuing the transaction-control statements.

> If you create a second savepoint with the same name as an earlier savepoint, the earlier savepoint is deleted. Oracle keeps only the latest savepoint.

Again, an example will help clarify. Sara tries to withdraw $100 from her checking account. You want to log her request in the ATM activity log, but if she has insufficient funds, you don't want to change her balance and will deny her request (part of a PL/SQL block is shown here; the IF statement is PL/SQL).

```
INSERT INTO ATM_LOG(who, when, what, where)
  VALUES('Kiesha', SYSDATE, 'Withdrawal of $100','ATM54');
SAVEPOINT ATM_logged;

UPDATE checking
  SET balance = balance - 100
  WHERE account = 'SARA1001';

SELECT balance INTO new_balance
  FROM checking
  WHERE account = 'SARA1001';

IF new_balance < 0
THEN
  ROLLBACK TO ATM_logged; -- undo update
  COMMIT; -- keep changes prior to savepoint (insert)
  RAISE insufficient_funds; -- Raise error/deny request
END IF;
COMMIT; -- keep insert and update
```

The keyword SAVEPOINT is optional, so the following two statements are equivalent:

```
ROLLBACK TO ATM_logged;
ROLLBACK TO SAVEPOINT ATM_logged;
```

> Because savepoints are not frequently used, always include the keyword SAVEPOINT in any ROLLBACK TO SAVEPOINT statement. That way, anyone reading the code will be reminded of the keyword SAVEPOINT, making it easier to recognize that a partial rollback has occurred.

Data Visibility

When DML operations are performed in a transaction, the changes are visible only to the session performing the DML operations. The changes are visible to other users in the database only when a COMMIT is issued (or a DDL statement causes an implicit commit).

All data changes made in a transaction are temporary until the transaction is committed. Oracle Database 12c has a read-consistency mechanism to ensure that each user sees the data as it existed at the last commit.

When DML operations are performed on existing rows (through UPDATE, DELETE, or MERGE operations), the affected rows are locked by Oracle; therefore, no other user can perform a DML operation on those rows. The rows updated or deleted by a transaction can be queried by another session.

When changes are committed, they are made permanent to the database. All locks on the affected rows are released, and all savepoints are removed. The previous state of the data is lost (the undo segments may be overwritten). All users can view the changed data.

When changes are rolled back, data changes are undone and the previous state of data is restored. All locks on the affected rows are released.

Oracle uses *read consistency* to make sure you do not see the changes made to data after your query is started. Also, Oracle uses a locking mechanism to make sure that two different user sessions can't modify data in the same row at the same time. Data consistency and the locking mechanism are discussed in the next sections.

Consistency and Transactions

Data consistency is one of the key concepts underlying the use of transaction-control statements. Understanding Oracle's consistency model will enable you to employ transaction control appropriately and answer exam questions about transaction control correctly. Oracle implements consistency to guarantee that the data seen by a statement or transaction does not change until that statement or transaction completes. This support is germane only to multiuser databases, where one database session can change (and commit) data that is being read by another session.

Oracle always uses statement-level consistency, which ensures that the data visible to a statement does not change during the life of that statement. Transactions can consist of one or more statements. When used, transaction-level consistency will ensure that the data visible to all statements in a transaction does not change for the life of the transaction. The banking example will help clarify.

Matt starts running a total-balance report against the checking account table at 10:00 A.M.; this report takes five minutes. During those five minutes, the data he is reporting on changes when Sara transfers $5,000 from her checking account to her brokerage account. When Matt's session gets to Sara's checking-account record, it will need to reconstruct what the record looked like at 10:00 A.M. Matt's session will examine the *undo segment* that Sara used during her account-transfer transaction and will re-create the image of what the checking-account table looked like at 10:00 A.M.

Next, at 10:05 A.M., Matt runs a total balance report on the cash in the brokerage account table. If he is using transaction-level consistency, his session will re-create what the brokerage account table looked like at 10:00 A.M. (and exclude Sara's transfer). If Matt's session is using the default statement-level consistency, his session will report on what the brokerage account table looked like at 10:05 A.M. (and include Sara's transfer).

Oracle never uses locks for reading operations, because reading operations will never block writing operations. Instead, the *undo segments* (also known as *rollback segments*) are used to re-create the image needed. Undo segments are released for reuse when the transaction writing to them commits or if undo_management is set to auto and the undo_retention period is exceeded, so sometimes a consistent image cannot be re-created. When this happens, Oracle raises a "snapshot too old" exception. Using this example, if Matt's transaction can't locate Sara's transaction in the rollback segments because it was overwritten, Matt's transaction will not be able to re-create the 10:00 A.M. image of the table and will fail.

Oracle implements consistency internally through the use of *system change numbers (SCNs)*. An *SCN* is a time-oriented, database-internal key. The SCN only increases, never decreases, and represents a point in time for comparison purposes. So, in the previous example, Oracle internally assigns Matt's first statement the current SCN when it starts reading the checking-account table. This starting SCN is compared to each data block's SCN. If the data-block SCN is higher (newer), the rollback segments are examined to find the older version of the data.

Undo segments, concurrency, and SCN are discussed in detail in Chapter 11, "Managing Data and Undo."

Locking Mechanism

Locks are implemented by Oracle Database 12c to prevent destructive interaction between concurrent transactions. Locks are acquired automatically by Oracle when a DML statement is executed; no user intervention or action is needed. Oracle uses the lowest level of restrictiveness when locking data for DML statements—only the rows affected by the DML operation are locked.

Locks are held for the duration of the transaction. A commit or rollback will release all the locks. There are two types of locks: explicit and implicit.

The locks acquired by Oracle automatically when DML operations are performed are called *implicit locks*. There is no implicit lock for SELECT statements.

If the user locks data manually, it is called *explicit locking*. The LOCK TABLE statement and SELECT...FOR UPDATE statements are used for explicitly locking the data.

The SELECT...FOR UPDATE statement is used to lock specific rows, preventing other sessions from changing or deleting those locked rows. When the rows are locked, other sessions can select these rows, but they cannot change or lock these rows. The syntax for this statement is identical to a SELECT statement, except you append the keywords FOR UPDATE to the statement. The locks acquired for a SELECT FOR UPDATE will not be released until the transaction ends with a COMMIT or ROLLBACK, even if no data changes.

```
SELECT product_id, warehouse_id, quantity_on_hand
FROM   oe.inventories
```

```
WHERE  quantity_on_hand < 5
FOR UPDATE;
```

Optional WAIT clause can be included along with FOR UPDATE clause to tell Oracle to wait a certain number of seconds if the rows in the table are locked by another session before it gives the unable to lock error.

The LOCK statement is used to lock an entire table, preventing other sessions from performing most or all DML on it. Locking can be in either shared or exclusive mode. Shared mode prevents other sessions from acquiring an exclusive lock but allows other sessions to acquire a shared lock. Exclusive mode prevents other sessions from acquiring either a shared lock or an exclusive lock. The following is an example of using the LOCK statement:

```
LOCK TABLE inventories IN EXCLUSIVE MODE;
```

Oracle employs both table and row locks. Table locks can be obtained in either share or exclusive mode. *Share locks* prevent other exclusive locks but allow other share locks on the resource. As the name indicates, this mode allows the affected resource to be shared, depending on the operation involved. Multiple sessions can perform DML operations on the same table, but on different rows. Each such session will hold a share lock on the table, to prevent someone from changing the table structure by performing a DDL on the table (DDL requires exclusive lock). Several transactions can acquire share locks on the same resource. *Exclusive locks* prevent other share locks and other exclusive locks from being used on the resource. The first transaction to lock a resource exclusively is the only transaction that can modify the resource until the exclusive lock is released through a commit or rollback. However, no DML locks prevent read access. To change data, Oracle must acquire an exclusive row-level lock on the rows that are changed. INSERT, UPDATE, DELETE, MERGE, and SELECT FOR UPDATE statements implicitly acquire the necessary exclusive locks. The LOCK TABLE x IN SHARE MODE statement acquires a share lock. Even if the DML operation affects all the rows in a table, Oracle Database 12c never escalates the row-level lock to a table-level lock; furthermore, neither users nor developers should explicitly lock unless there is a very good reason—Oracle handles it automatically 99.9% of the time.

Summary

We started this chapter discussing DML statements in Oracle. Then we reviewed the INSERT, UPDATE, DELETE, and MERGE statements to add, modify, and delete data in tables. You also learned how transactions and locking work in Oracle.

The INSERT statement is used to add new rows to a table. The VALUES clause in the INSERT statement is used to add a single row at a time. Subqueries can be used to add rows to a table from an existing row source.

The UPDATE statement is used to change existing data in a table. The DELETE statement is used to remove rows from a table. Both the UPDATE and DELETE statements can have WHERE clauses to limit the data changes to specific rows. The MERGE statement allows you to insert or update rows based on a condition.

When an update or delete operation is performed on a table, the previous state of data is written to undo segments to build a read-consistent image of data. Oracle shows only committed data to users.

DML operations lock the affected rows of the table. The locks are held until the transaction is either committed or rolled back. Until the changes are committed, data changes are not visible to other users in the database.

Exam Essentials

Know the syntax for the INSERT statement.   When a subquery is used to add rows to a table, the VALUES clause should not be used.

Practice UPDATE statements.   The UPDATE statement can update multiple columns in the same row using a subquery. Multiple subqueries can also be used to update columns in a single row.

Understand what will begin and end a transaction.   A transaction will begin with an INSERT, UPDATE, DELETE, MERGE, or SELECT FOR UPDATE statement. A COMMIT or ROLLBACK will end a transaction. A DDL statement can also end a transaction.

Know how to set and roll back to savepoints.   Savepoints are set with the SAVEPOINT statement. Data changes made after a savepoint are undone when a ROLLBACK TO SAVEPOINT statement is executed. ROLLBACK TO SAVEPOINT is a partial undo operation.

Understand the scope of data changes and consistency.   Statement-level consistency is automatic and will ensure that each SELECT will see an image of the database consistent with the beginning of the statement's execution. Transaction-level consistency will ensure that all SELECT statements within a transaction will see an image of the database consistent with the beginning of the transaction.

Review Questions

1. Jim is trying to add records from the ORDER_DETAILS table to ORDER_DETAIL_HISTORY for orders placed before the current year. Which INSERT statement would accomplish his task?

   A. INSERT INTO ORDER_DETAIL_HISTORY
   VALUES (SELECT * FROM ORDER_DETAIL
   WHERE ORDER_DATE < TRUNC(SYSDATE,'YY'));

   B. INSERT FROM ORDER_DETAIL
   INTO ORDER_DETAIL_HISTORY
   WHERE ORDER_DATE < TRUNC(SYSDATE,'YY');

   C. INSERT INTO ORDER_DETAIL_HISTORY
   FROM ORDER_DETAIL
   WHERE ORDER_DATE < TRUNC(SYSDATE,'YY');

   D. INSERT INTO ORDER_DETAIL_HISTORY
   SELECT * FROM ORDER_DETAIL
   WHERE ORDER_DATE < TRUNC(SYSDATE,'YY');

2. Which of the following statements will not implicitly begin a transaction?

   A. INSERT

   B. UPDATE

   C. DELETE

   D. SELECT FOR UPDATE

   E. None of the above; they all implicitly begin a transaction, if not started already.

3. Consider the following UPDATE statement. Which UPDATE statements from the following options will accomplish the same task? (Choose two.)

```
UPDATE ACCOUNTS
SET LAST_UPDATED = SYSDATE,
    UPDATE_USER = USER;
```

A. UPDATE ACCOUNTS
   SET (LAST_UPDATED, UPDATE_USER) =
           (SYSDATE, USER);

B. UPDATE ACCOUNTS
   SET LAST_UPDATED =
      (SELECT SYSDATE FROM DUAL),
   UPDATE_USER = (SELECT USER FROM DUAL);

C. UPDATE ACCOUNTS
   SET (LAST_UPDATED, UPDATE_USER) =
   (SELECT SYSDATE, USER FROM DUAL);

D. UPDATE ACCOUNTS
   SET LAST_UPDATED = SYSDATE
   AND UPDATE_USER = USER;

4. Which of the following statements do not end a transaction? (Choose two.)

A. SELECT

B. COMMIT

C. TRUNCATE TABLE

D. UPDATE

5. Sara wants to update the SALARY column in the OLD_EMPLOYEES table with the value from the EMPLOYEES table for employees in department 90. Which SQL code will accomplish the task?

   A. UPDATE old_employees a
   ```
   SET salary = (SELECT salary FROM employees b
                       WHERE a.employee_id = b.employee_id)
   WHERE department_id = 90;
   ```

   B. UPDATE old_employees
   ```
   SET salary = (SELECT salary FROM employees)
   WHERE department_id = 90;
   ```

   C. UPDATE old_employees a
   ```
   FROM employees b
   SET a.salary = b.salary
   WHERE department_id = 90;
   ```

   D. UPDATE old_employees a
   ```
   SET salary = (SELECT salary FROM employees b
                       WHERE a.employee_id = b.employee_id
   AND department_id = 90);
   ```

6. Review the following code snippet. Which line has an error?

   ```
   1.   UPDATE EMPLOYEES
   2.   WHERE EMPLOYEE_ID = 127
   3.   SET SALARY = SALARY * 1.25,
   4.   COMMISSION_PCT = 0
   ```

   A. 1

   B. 2

   C. 4

   D. There is no error.

7. Jim executes the following SQL statement. What will be the result?

   ```
   DELETE salary, commission_pct
   FROM employees
   WHERE department_id = 30;
   ```

   A. The salary and commission_pct columns for all records with department_id 30 will be deleted (changed to NULL).

   B. All the rows belonging to department_id 30 will be deleted from the table.

   C. The salary and commission_pct columns will be deleted from the employees table.

   D. The statement will produce an error.

8. Consider the following three SQL statements. Choose the most appropriate option.

1. `DELETE FROM CITY WHERE CNT_CODE = 1;`
2. `DELETE CITY WHERE CNT_CODE = 1;`
3. `DELETE (SELECT * FROM CITY WHERE CNT_CODE = 1);`

    A. Statements 1 and 2 will produce the same result; statement 3 will error out.

    B. Statements 1 and 2 will produce the same result; statement 3 will produce a different result.

    C. Statements 1, 2, and 3 will produce the same result.

    D. Statements 1, 2, and 3 will produce different results.

9. Consider the following code segment. How many rows will be in the CARS table after all these statements are executed?

```
SELECT COUNT(*) FROM CARS;
COUNT(*)
--------
      30

DELETE FROM CARS WHERE MAKE = 'TOYOTA';
2 rows deleted.

SAVEPOINT A;
Savepoint created.

INSERT INTO CARS VALUES ('TOYOTA','CAMRY',4,220);
1 row created.

SAVEPOINT A;

INSERT INTO CARS VALUES ('TOYOTA','COROLLA',4,180);
1 row created.

ROLLBACK TO SAVEPOINT A;
Rollback complete.
```

    A. 30

    B. 29

    C. 28

    D. 32

10. Jim noticed that the HIRE_DATE and START_DATE columns in the EMPLOYEES table had date and time values. When he tries to find employees hired on a certain date, he does not get the desired results. Which SQL statement will update all the rows in the EMPLOYEES table with no time portion in the HIRE_DATE and START_DATE columns (00:00:00)?

A. UPDATE EMPLOYEES SET HIRE_DATE = TRUNC(HIRE_DATE) AND START_DATE = TRUNC(START_DATE);

B. UPDATE TABLE EMPLOYEES SET TRUNC(HIRE_DATE) AND TRUNC(START_DATE);

C. UPDATE EMPLOYEES SET HIRE_DATE = TRUNC(HIRE_DATE), START_DATE = TRUNC(START_DATE);

D. UPDATE HIRE_DATE = TRUNC(HIRE_DATE), START_DATE = TRUNC(START_DATE) IN EMPLOYEES;

11. Sara wants to update the SALARY column in the EMPLOYEE table from the SALARIES table, based on the JOB_ID value for all employees in department 22. The SALARIES table and the EMPLOYEE table have the following structure. Which of the following options is the correct UPDATE statement?

```
DESC EMPLOYEE
EMPLOYEE_ID    NUMBER (3),
EMP_NAME       VARCHAR2 (40),
JOB_ID         VARCHAR2 (4),
DEPT_ID        NUMBER
SALARY         NUMBER

DESC SALARIES
JOB_ID         VARCHAR2 (4),
SALARY         NUMBER
```

A. UPDATE SALARIES A SET SALARY = (SELECT SALARY FROM EMPLOYEES B WHERE A.JOB_ID = B.JOB_ID WHERE DEPT_ID = 22);

B. UPDATE EMPLOYEE E SET SALARY = (SELECT SALARY FROM SALARIES S WHERE E.JOB_ID = S.JOB_IB AND DEPT_ID = 22);

C. UPDATE EMPLOYEE E SET SALARY = (SELECT SALARY FROM SALARIES S WHERE E.JOB_ID = S.JOB_IB) AND DEPT_ID = 22;

D. UPDATE EMPLOYEE E SET SALARY = (SELECT SALARY FROM SALARIES S WHERE E.JOB_ID = S.JOB_IB) WHERE DEPT_ID = 22;

12. The `FIRED_EMPLOYEE` table has the following structure:

```
EMPLOYEE_ID  NUMBER (4)
FIRE_DATE DATE
```

How many rows will be counted from the last SQL statement in the code segment?

```
SELECT COUNT(*) FROM FIRED_EMPLOYEES;
COUNT(*)
--------
     105

INSERT INTO FIRED_EMPLOYEE VALUES (104, TRUNC(SYSDATE);
SAVEPOINT A;
INSERT INTO FIRED_EMPLOYEE VALUES (106, TRUNC(SYSDATE);
SAVEPOINT B;
INSERT INTO FIRED_EMPLOYEE VALUES (108, TRUNC(SYSDATE);
ROLLBACK TO A;
INSERT INTO FIRED_EMPLOYEE VALUES (104, TRUNC(SYSDATE);
COMMIT;
SELECT COUNT(*) FROM FIRED_EMPLOYEES;
```

A. 109

B. 106

C. 105

D. 107

13. The following table describes the DEPARTMENTS table:

Column Name	dept_id	dept_name	mgr_id	location_id
Key Type	pk			
Nulls/Unique	NN			
FK Table				
Datatype	NUMBER	VARCHAR2	NUMBER	NUMBER
Length	4	30	6	4
Default Value	None	None	None	99

Which of the following INSERT statements will raise an exception?

A. INSERT INTO departments (dept_id, dept_name, location_id)
VALUES(280,'Security',1700);

B. INSERT INTO departments VALUES(280,'Security',1700);

C. INSERT INTO departments VALUES(280,'Corporate Giving',266,1700);

D. None of these statements will raise an exception.

14. Refer to the DEPARTMENTS table structure in question 13. Two SQL statements are shown here. Choose the option that best describes the SQL statements.

```
1.    INSERT INTO departments (dept_id, dept_name, mgr_id)
VALUES(280,'Security',1700);
2.    INSERT INTO departments (dept_id, dept_name, mgr_id, location_id)
VALUES(280,'Security',1700, NULL);
```

A. Statements 1 and 2 insert the same values to all columns in the table.

B. Statements 1 and 2 insert different values to at least one column in the table.

C. The location_id column must be included in the column list of statement 1.

D. A NULL value cannot be inserted explicitly in statement 2.

15. The SALES table contains the following data:

```
SELECT channel_id, COUNT(*)
FROM sales
GROUP BY channel_id;

C    COUNT(*)
-    ----------
T      12000
I      24000
```

How many rows will be inserted into the NEW_CHANNEL_SALES table with the following SQL statement?

```
INSERT FIRST
  WHEN channel_id ='C' THEN
    INTO catalog_sales (prod_id,time_id,promo_id
                      ,amount_sold)
        VALUES (prod_id,time_id,promo_id,amount_sold)
  WHEN channel_id ='I' THEN
    INTO internet_sales (prod_id,time_id,promo_id
                       ,amount_sold)
        VALUES (prod_id,time_id,promo_id,amount_sold)
  WHEN  channel_id IN ('I','T') THEN
    INTO new_channel_sales (prod_id,time_id,promo_id
                          ,amount_sold)
        VALUES (prod_id,time_id,promo_id,amount_sold)
  SELECT channel_id,prod_id,time_id,promo_id,amount_sold
  FROM sales;
```

A. 0

B. 12,000

C. 24,000

D. 36,000

16. In the following SQL code, how many rows will be counted in the last statement?

```
SELECT COUNT(*) FROM emp;
120 returned

INSERT INTO emp (emp_id)
    VALUES (140);
SAVEPOINT emp140;

INSERT INTO emp (emp_id)
    VALUES (141);
INSERT INTO emp (emp_id)
    VALUES (142);
INSERT INTO emp (emp_id)
    VALUES (143);
TRUNCATE TABLE employees;
INSERT INTO emp (emp_id)
    VALUES (144);

ROLLBACK;

SELECT COUNT(*) FROM emp;
```

    A. 121

    B. 0

    C. 124

    D. 143

17. Which of the following options best describes the following SQL statement?

```
1. UPDATE countries
2. CNT_NAME = UPPER(CNT_NAME)
3. WHERE country_code BETWEEN 1 and 99;
```

    A. The statement is missing the keyword SET, but the statement will work just fine because SET is an optional keyword.

    B. The BETWEEN operator cannot be used in the WHERE clause used in an UPDATE statement.

    C. The function UPPER(CNT_NAME) should be changed to UPPER('CNT_NAME').

    D. The statement is missing keyword SET; therefore, the statement will fail.

18. The ORDERS table has 35 rows. The following UPDATE statement updates all 35 rows. Which option best describes what will happen?

```
UPDATE orders
SET ship_date = TRUNC(ship_date)
WHERE ship_date != TRUNC(ship_date)
```

    A. When all rows in a table are updated, the LOCK TABLE orders IN EXCLUSIVE MODE statement must be executed before the UPDATE statement.

    B. No other session can query from the table until the transaction ends.

    C. Because all rows are updated, there is no need for any locking; therefore, Oracle does not lock the records.

    D. The statement locks all the rows until the transaction ends.

19. Which of the following INSERT statements will raise an exception?

    A. INSERT INTO EMP SELECT * FROM NEW_EMP;

    B. INSERT FIRST WHEN DEPT_NO IN (12,14) THEN INSERT INTO EMP SELECT * FROM NEW_EMP;

    C. INSERT FIRST WHEN DEPT_NO IN (12,14) THEN INTO EMP SELECT * FROM NEW_EMP;

    D. INSERT ALL WHEN DEPT_NO IN (12,14) THEN INTO EMP SELECT * FROM NEW_EMP;

20. After the following SQL statements are executed, what will be the salary of employee Arsinoe?

```
UPDATE emp
   SET salary = 1000
   WHERE name = 'Arsinoe';
SAVEPOINT Point_A;

UPDATE emp
   SET  salary = salary * 1.1
   WHERE name = 'Arsinoe';
SAVEPOINT Point_B;

UPDATE emp
   SET  salary = salary * 1.1
   WHERE name = 'Berenike';
SAVEPOINT point_C;

ROLLBACK TO SAVEPOINT point_b;
COMMIT;
UPDATE emp
   SET salary = 1500
   WHERE name = 'Arsinoe';
SAVEPOINT point_d;

ROLLBACK TO point_d;

COMMIT;
```

A. 1000

B. 1100

C. 1111

D. 1500

Chapter

7

Creating Tables and Constraints

ORACLE DATABASE 12*c*: SQL FUNDAMENTALS EXAM OBJECTIVES COVERED IN THIS CHAPTER:

✓ **Introduction to Data Definition Language**

- ▪ Categorize the main database objects.

- ▪ Explain the table structure.

- ▪ Describe the data types that are available for columns.

- ▪ Create a simple table.

- ▪ Explain how constraints are created at the time of table creation.

- ▪ Describe how schema objects work.

An Oracle database has many different types of objects. Related objects are logically grouped together in a schema, which consists of various types of objects. The basic types of objects in an Oracle database are tables, indexes, constraints, sequences, and synonyms. Although this chapter discusses tables and constraints, we will begin it with an overview of the main database objects in Oracle.

The table is the basic structure of data storage in Oracle. A table has columns as part of the definition and stores rows of data. In a relational database, the data in various tables may be related. A constraint can be considered as a rule or policy defined in the database to enforce data integrity and business rules. In this chapter, we will discuss creating tables and using constraints. Because the table is the most important type of object in an Oracle database, knowing how to create tables and constraints on tables is important.

Database Objects Overview

Data in an Oracle database is stored in tables. A *table* is the main database object. Many other database objects, whether or not they store data, are generally based on the tables.

Figure 7.1 shows a screenshot from SQL Developer. The left side shows the various object types available in Oracle Database 12*c*.

Let's review the main database objects in Oracle that are relevant for this certification exam:

Table A *table* is defined with columns, and it stores rows of data. A table should have at least one column. In Oracle, a table normally refers to a relational table. You can also create object tables. Object tables are created with user-defined datatypes. Temporary tables (called *global temporary tables* in Oracle) are used to hold temporary data specific to a transaction or session. A table can store a wide variety of data. Apart from storing text and numeric information, you can store date, timestamp, binary, or raw data (such as images, documents, and information about external files). A table can have *virtual columns*. As the name indicates, these types of columns do not consume storage space on disk; the database derives values in virtual columns from normal columns. Tables are discussed in the next sections of this chapter.

View A *view* is a customized representation of data from one or more tables and/or views. Views are used as windows to show information from tables in a certain way or to restrict the information. Views are queries stored in the database that select data from one or more tables. Unlike tables, views do not store data—they can be considered as stored queries.

They also provide a way to restrict data from certain users, thereby providing an additional level of security.

Sequence   A *sequence* is a way to generate continuous sequential numbers. Sequences are useful for generating unique serial numbers or key values. The sequence definition is stored in the data dictionary. Sequence numbers are generated independently of other database objects. Because a sequence can be used as part of table definition, we will discuss sequence briefly before you learn to create a table.

Synonym   A *synonym* is an alias for any table, view, sequence, or other accessible database object. Because a synonym is simply an alias, it requires no storage other than its definition in the data dictionary. Synonyms are useful because they hide the identity of the underlying object. The object can even be part of another database. A public synonym is accessible to all users of the database, and a private synonym is accessible only to its owner.

Index   An *index* is a structure associated with tables used to speed up the queries. An index is an access path to reach the desired row faster. Oracle has B-tree and bitmap indexes. Creating/dropping indexes does not affect the storage of data in the underlying tables. You can create unique or nonunique indexes. Unique indexes are created automatically by Oracle when you create a primary key or a unique key constraint in a table. A composite index has more than one column in the index.

FIGURE 7.1   SQL Developer screen showing database objects

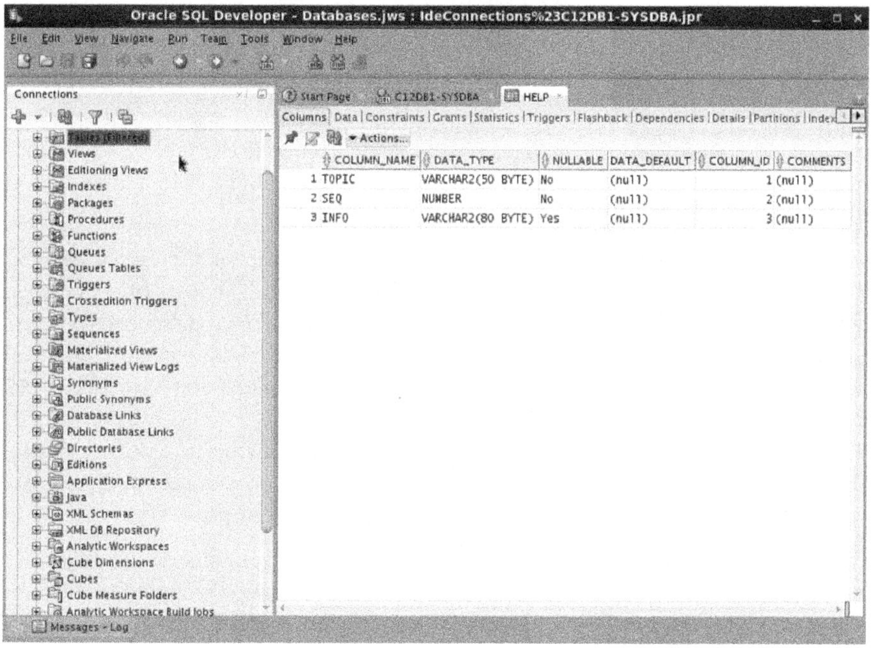

Oracle Database 12*c* has a wide array of database objects to suit various application requirements. These objects are not discussed in this book because they are not part of the certification exam at this time. Some of the other database objects that may be used in application development are clusters, dimensions, directories, functions, Java sources/classes, libraries, materialized views, and types.

Schema Objects

A *schema* is a collection of database objects owned by a single user. For example, a schema can have tables, views, triggers, synonyms, and PL/SQL programs such as procedures. A schema is owned by a database user and has the same name as the user. If the database user does not own any database objects, then no schema is associated with the user. A schema is a logical grouping of database objects.

There can be only one schema associated with a database user, and a schema is created when you create any database object under the user. A schema may include any or all of the basic database objects discussed earlier. Oracle Database 12*c* may also include the following types of structures in the schema. These objects are listed here only to give you an overview of schemas; creating and managing these objects are not part of the certification exam at this time. For the certification exam, prepare to know the schema objects discussed in this chapter.

Materialized View   *Materialized views* are objects used to summarize and replicate data. They are similar to views but occupy storage space. Materialized views are mainly used in data-warehouse environments where data needs to be aggregated and stored so that queries and reports run faster. Materialized views can also be used to replicate data from another database.

Dimension   A *dimension* is a logical structure to define the relationship between columns in a table. Dimensions are defined in the data dictionary and do not occupy any storage space. The columns in a dimension can be from a single table or from multiple tables. An example of a dimension would be the relationship between country, state, and city in a table that stores address information.

Cluster   A *cluster* is a method of storing data from related tables at a common physical location. The tables in the cluster share one or more common columns. The rows of the tables in a cluster are stored together with just one copy of the common clustered columns. You can share the storage of rows in related tables for performance reasons if the access to the rows in the tables always involves join operations on the tables. For example, if you have an ORDERS table and a CUSTOMERS table in the schema, you can query the ORDERS table always joining the CUSTOMERS table, because that's where you get the customer name associated with the customer ID. A cluster may be created for the ORDERS and CUSTOMERS tables so that the rows associated with the same customer are stored in the same physical storage area (block).

Database Links   A *database link* is a schema object that enables you to access an object from a different database. SQL queries can reference tables and views belonging to the remote database by appending @db_link_name to the table or view. For example, to access the

CUSTOMER_ORDERS table using a database link named LONDON_SALES, you would use CUSTOMER_ORDERS@LONDON_SALES.

Triggers   A *trigger* is a stored PL/SQL program that is executed when a specified condition occurs. A trigger can be defined on a table to "fire" when an insert, update, or delete operation occurs on the table. A trigger may also be defined on the database to "fire" when certain database conditions occur, such as starting the database, or when a database error occurs.

Java Objects   Oracle Database 12*c* includes *Java objects* such as Java classes, Java sources, and Java resources. Java stored programs can be created using the different Java object types.

PL/SQL Programs   *PL/SQL stored programs* include procedures, functions, and packages. A *procedure* is a PL/SQL programmatic construct. A *function* is similar to a procedure but always returns a value. A *package* is a grouping of related PL/SQL objects.

Understanding Namespaces

A *namespace* is an important concept to understand when talking about schema objects. A namespace defines a group of object types, within which all names must be uniquely identified within a schema. Objects in different namespaces can share the same name.

When you refer an object in the SQL statement, Oracle locates the object in the appropriate namespace. A table can have the same name as an index or a constraint. The namespace is simply the domain of allowable names for the set of schema objects that it serves. The following are some of the namespaces available in Oracle Database 12*c*:

- Tables, views, private synonyms, sequences, PL/SQL procedures, PL/SQL functions, PL/SQL packages, materialized views
- Constraints
- Indexes
- Clusters
- Database triggers
- Private database links
- Dimensions
- Roles
- Public synonyms
- Public database links
- Tablespaces
- Profiles

For example, if you have a view named BOOKS, you cannot name a table BOOKS (tables and views share a namespace), although you can create an index named BOOKS (indexes and tables have separate namespaces) and a constraint named BOOKS (constraints and tables have separate namespaces).

To help you understand which object types belong to the same namespace, you can use the following query in your database.

```
SQL> SELECT DISTINCT namespace, object_type
     FROM DBA_OBJECTS
     ORDER BY namespace;
```

Although it is not explicitly specified as an exam objective, we will discuss the schema object sequence in the next section, as it is possible to use the sequence values in table definition for default values of columns.

Using Sequences

An Oracle sequence is a named sequential-number generator. Sequence numbers are serial numbers incremented with a specific interval. Sequences are often used for artificial keys or to order rows that otherwise have no order. Sequences exist only in the data dictionary, and they do not take up any special storage space as tables. Sequences can be configured to increase or decrease without bounds or to repeat (cycle) upon reaching a boundary value.

Sequences are created with the CREATE SEQUENCE statement. The following statement creates a sequence in the HR schema:

```
CREATE SEQUENCE hr.employee_identity START WITH 2001;
```

To access the next number in the sequence, you simply select from it, using the pseudocolumn NEXTVAL. To get the last sequence number your session has generated, you select from it using the pseudocolumn CURRVAL. If your session has not yet generated a new sequence number, CURRVAL will be undefined.

The syntax for accessing the next sequence number is as follows:

```
sequence_name.nextval
```

Here is the syntax for accessing the last-used sequence number:

```
sequence_name.currval
```

Sequence Initialization

The sequence is initialized in the session when you select the NEXTVAL from the sequence. One problem that you may encounter using sequences involves selecting CURRVAL from the sequence before initializing it within your session by selecting NEXTVAL from it. Here is an example:

```
CREATE SEQUENCE emp_seq NOMAXVALUE NOCYCLE;

Sequence created.
```

```
SELECT emp_seq.currval FROM dual;

ERROR at line 1:
ORA-08002: sequence POLICY_SEQ.CURRVAL is not yet defined
in this session
```

Make sure your code initializes a sequence within your session by selecting its NEXTVAL before you try to reference CURRVAL:

```
SELECT emp_seq.nextval FROM dual;

   NEXTVAL
----------
         1

SELECT emp_seq.currval FROM dual;

   CURRVAL
----------
         1
```

Sequences can be used in the SET clause of the UPDATE statement to assign a value to a column in an existing row. They can be used in the VALUES clause of the INSERT statement also.

Built-in Datatypes

When creating tables, you must specify a *datatype* for each column you define. Oracle Database 12*c* is rich with various datatypes to store different kinds of information. By choosing the appropriate datatype, you will be able to store and retrieve data without compromising its integrity. A datatype associates a predefined set of properties with the column.

The built-in datatypes in Oracle Database 12*c* can be classified into five major categories. Figure 7.2 shows the categories and the datatype names.

Chapter 2, "Introducing SQL," introduced four basic datatypes: CHAR, VARCHAR2, NUMBER, and DATE. Here, we will review those datatypes and describe the other datatypes that you can specify while creating a table.

Character Datatypes

Seven character datatypes can be used to define columns in a table:

- CHAR
- NCHAR

- VARCHAR2
- NVARCHAR2
- CLOB
- NCLOB
- LONG

FIGURE 7.2 Oracle built-in datatypes

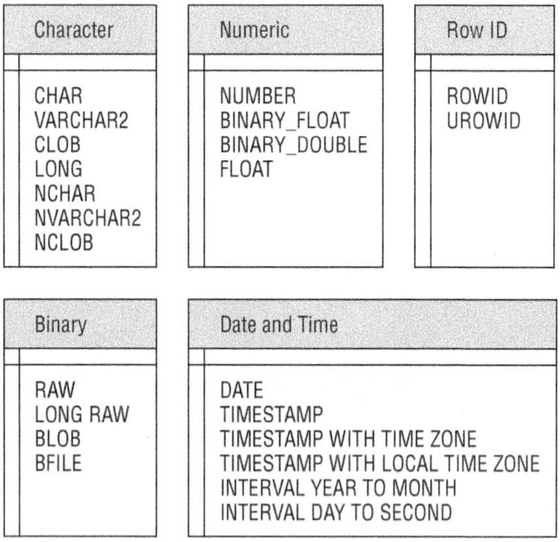

Character	Numeric	Row ID
CHAR VARCHAR2 CLOB LONG NCHAR NVARCHAR2 NCLOB	NUMBER BINARY_FLOAT BINARY_DOUBLE FLOAT	ROWID UROWID

Binary	Date and Time
RAW LONG RAW BLOB BFILE	DATE TIMESTAMP TIMESTAMP WITH TIME ZONE TIMESTAMP WITH LOCAL TIME ZONE INTERVAL YEAR TO MONTH INTERVAL DAY TO SECOND

Character datatypes store alphanumeric data in the database character set or in the Unicode character set. You define the database character set when you create the database.

The character set determines which languages can be represented in the database. For example, US7ASCII is a 7-bit ASCII character set that can represent the English language and any other language that uses the English alphabet set. WE8ISO8859P1 is an 8-bit character set that can support multiple European languages such as English, German, French, Albanian, Spanish, Portuguese, Irish, and so on, because they all use a similar writing script. Unicode, the Universal Character Set, allows you to store any language character using a single character set. The Unicode character set supported by Oracle is either 16-bit encoding (UTF-16) or 8-bit encoding (UTF-8). You can choose the Unicode datatypes to be used in the database while creating the database. The CHAR, VARCHAR2, CLOB datatype values are stored in the database default character set.

You can also define an alternative character set in the database, known as the National Character Set. This is useful when the database character set cannot accommodate multibyte languages and you need to store multibyte language in the database. The NCHAR, NVARCHAR2, and NCLOB datatype values use the National Character Set.

CHAR

The syntax for the CHAR datatype is as follows:

```
CHAR [(<size> [BYTE | CHAR ] ) ]
```

The CHAR datatype is fixed-length, with the maximum size of the column specified in parentheses. You can also include the optional keyword BYTE or CHAR inside the parentheses along with the size to indicate whether the size is in bytes or in characters. BYTE is the default.

For single-byte-database character sets (such as US7ASCII), the size specified in bytes and the size specified in characters are the same. If the column value is shorter than the size defined, trailing spaces are added to the column value. Specifying the size is optional, and the default size is 1 byte. The maximum allowed size in a CHAR datatype column is 2,000 bytes. Here are few examples of specifying a CHAR datatype column:

```
employee_id  CHAR (5)
employee_name CHAR (100 CHAR)
employee_sex CHAR
```

NCHAR

The syntax for the NCHAR datatype is as follows:

```
NCHAR [ ( <size> ) ]
```

The NCHAR datatype is similar to CHAR, but it is used to store Unicode character-set data. The NCHAR datatype is fixed-length, with a maximum size of 2,000 bytes and a default size of a character.

The size in the NCHAR datatype definition is always specified in characters. Trailing spaces are added if the value inserted into the column is shorter than the column's maximum length. Here is an example of specifying an NCHAR datatype column:

```
emp_name NCHAR (100)
```

Several built-in Oracle Database 12c functions have options to represent NCHAR data. An NCHAR string may be represented by prefixing the string with N, as in this example:

```
SELECT  emp_name FROM employee_records
WHERE emp_name = N'John Smith';
```

VARCHAR2

The syntax for the VARCHAR2 datatype is as follows:

```
VARCHAR2 (<size> [BYTE | CHAR] )
```

VARCHAR2 and VARCHAR are synonymous datatypes. VARCHAR2 specifies variable-length character data. A maximum size for the column should be defined; Oracle Database

12*c* will not assume any default value. Unlike CHAR columns, VARCHAR2 columns are not blank-padded with trailing spaces if the column value is shorter than its maximum specified length. You can specify the size in bytes or characters; by default, the size is in bytes. The range of values allowed for size is from 1 to 4,000 bytes by default. If the database parameter MAX_STRING_SIZE is set to EXTENDED, the VARCHAR2 column can store up to 32,767 bytes.

NVARCHAR2

The syntax for the NVARCHAR2 datatype is as follows:

```
NVARCHAR2 (<size>)
```

The NVARCHAR2 datatype is used to store Unicode variable-length data. The size is specified in characters, and the maximum size allowed is 4,000 bytes. Similar to VARCHAR2, if the database parameter MAX_STRING_SIZE is set to EXTENDED, then the NVARCHAR2 column can store up to 32,767 bytes.

 If you try to insert a value into a character datatype column that is larger than its maximum specified size, Oracle will return an error. Oracle will not chop or truncate the inserted value to store it in the database column.

CLOB

The syntax for the CLOB datatype is as follows:

```
CLOB
```

CLOB is one of the Large Object datatypes provided to store variable-length character data. The maximum amount of data you can store in a CLOB column is based on the block size of the database. CLOB can store up to (4GB−1)*(database block size). You do not specify a maximum size with this datatype definition.

NCLOB

The syntax for the NCLOB datatype is as follows:

```
NCLOB
```

NCLOB is one of the Large Object datatypes and stores variable-length Unicode character data. The maximum amount of data you can store in a NCLOB column is (4GB−1)*(database block size). You do not specify the size with this datatype definition.

LONG

The syntax for the LONG datatype is as follows:

```
LONG
```

Using the LONG datatype is discouraged in Oracle Database 12c. It is provided only for backward compatibility. You should use the CLOB datatype instead of LONG. LONG columns can store up to 2GB–1 of character data. There can be only one LONG column in the table definition. A LONG datatype column can be used in the SELECT clause of a query, the SET clause of the UPDATE statement, and the VALUES clause of the INSERT statement. You can also create a NOT NULL constraint on a LONG column.

LONG datatype columns cannot appear in the following:

- The WHERE, GROUP BY, or ORDER BY clauses
- A SELECT clause if the DISTINCT operator is used
- A SELECT list of subqueries used in INSERT statements
- A SELECT list of subqueries used with the UNION, INTERSECT, or MINUS operator
- A SELECT list of queries with the GROUP BY clause

Numeric Datatypes

Four built-in numeric datatypes can be used for defining numeric columns in a table:

- NUMBER
- BINARY_FLOAT
- BINARY_DOUBLE
- FLOAT

Numeric datatypes are used to store integer and floating-point numbers. The NUMBER datatype can store all types of numeric data, but BINARY_FLOAT and BINARY_DOUBLE give better performance with floating-point numbers. FLOAT is a subtype of NUMBER.

NUMBER

The syntax for the NUMBER datatype is as follows:

```
NUMBER [ (<precision> [, <scale>] )]
```

You can represent all non-Oracle numeric datatypes such as FLOAT, INTEGER, DECIMAL, DOUBLE, and so on, using the NUMBER datatype. The NUMBER datatype can store both fixed-point and floating-point numbers. Oracle Database 12c introduced two new datatypes to support floating-point numbers—specifically, BINARY_FLOAT and BINARY_DOUBLE.

BINARY_FLOAT

The syntax for the BINARY_FLOAT datatype is as follows:

```
BINARY_FLOAT
```

The BINARY_FLOAT datatype represents a 32-bit floating-point number. No precision is defined in the definition of this datatype because it uses binary precision. BINARY_FLOAT uses 5 bytes for storage.

A floating-point number can have a decimal point anywhere or can have no decimal point. Oracle stores NUMBER datatype values using decimal precision, whereas floating-point numbers (BINARY_FLOAT and BINARY_DOUBLE) are stored using binary precision. Oracle has three special values that can be used with floating-point numbers:

INF: Positive infinity

-INF: Negative infinity

NaN: Not a Number (NaN is not the same as NULL)

BINARY_DOUBLE

The syntax for the BINARY_DOUBLE datatype is as follows:

```
BINARY_DOUBLE
```

The BINARY_DOUBLE datatype represents a 64-bit floating-point number. BINARY_DOUBLE uses 9 bytes for storage. All the characteristics of BINARY_FLOAT are applicable to BINARY_DOUBLE.

FLOAT

The syntax for the FLOAT datatype is as follows:

```
FLOAT [(precision)]
```

The FLOAT datatype is a subtype of NUMBER and is internally represented as NUMBER. There is no scale for FLOAT numbers, only the precision can be optionally included. The precision can range from 1 to default binary digits. In the NUMBER datatype, the precision and scale are represented in decimal digits; whereas in FLOAT, the precision is represented in binary digits. In Oracle Database 12c, you should use BINARY_FLOAT or BINARY_DOUBLE instead of the FLOAT datatype.

Date and Time Datatypes

In pre–Oracle9i databases, the only datetime datatype available was DATE, which stores the date and time. Oracle9i Database introduced the TIMESTAMP and INTERVAL datatypes to enhance the storage and manipulation of date and time data. Six datetime datatypes in Oracle Database 12c can be used for defining columns in a table:

- DATE
- TIMESTAMP
- TIMESTAMP WITH TIME ZONE

- TIMESTAMP WITH LOCAL TIME ZONE
- INTERVAL YEAR TO MONTH
- INTERVAL DAY TO SECOND

The interval datatypes are used to represent a measure of time. They store the number of months or number of days/hours between two time points. All interval components are integers except the seconds, which may have fractional seconds represented.

DATE

The syntax for the DATE datatype is as follows:

```
DATE
```

The DATE datatype stores date and time information. You can store the dates from January 1, 4712 B.C., to A.D. December 31, 9999. If you specify a date value without the time component, the default time is 12:00 A.M. (midnight, 00:00:00 hours). If you specify a date value without the date component, the default value is the first day of the current month. The DATE datatype stores century, year, month, date, hour, minute, and seconds internally. You can display the dates in various formats using the NLS_DATE_FORMAT parameter or by specifying a format mask with the TO_CHAR function. The various date-format masks are discussed in Chapter 3, "Using Single-Row Functions."

TIMESTAMP

The syntax for the TIMESTAMP datatype is as follows:

```
TIMESTAMP [(<precision>)]
```

The TIMSTAMP datatype stores date and time information with fractional-seconds precision. The only difference between the DATE and TIMESTAMP datatypes is the ability to store fractional seconds up to a precision of nine digits. The default precision is 6 and can range from 0 to 9.

TIMESTAMP WITH TIME ZONE

The syntax for the TIMESTAMP WITH TIME ZONE datatype is as follows:

```
TIMESTAMP [(<precision>)] WITH TIME ZONE
```

The TIMESTAMP WITH TIME ZONE datatype is similar to the TIMESTAMP datatype, but it stores the *time-zone displacement*. Displacement is the difference between the local time and the Coordinated Universal Time (UTC, also known as *Greenwich mean time*). The displacement is represented in hours and minutes. Two TIMESTAMP WITH TIME ZONE values are considered identical if they represent the same time in UTC. For example, 5 P.M. CST is equal to 6 P.M. EST or 3 P.M. PST.

TIMESTAMP WITH LOCAL TIME ZONE

The syntax for the TIMESTAMP WITH LOCAL TIME ZONE datatype is as follows:

```
TIMESTAMP [(<precision>)] WITH LOCAL TIME ZONE
```

The TIMESTAMP WITH LOCAL TIME ZONE datatype is similar to the TIMESTAMP datatype; but like the TIMESTAMP WITH TIME ZONE datatype, it also includes the time-zone displacement. TIMESTAMP WITH LOCAL TIME ZONE does not store the displacement information in the database but stores the time as a normalized form of the database time zone. The data is always stored in the database time zone, but when the user retrieves data, it is shown in the user's local-session time zone.

The following example demonstrates how the DATE, TIMESTAMP, TIMESTAMP WITH TIME ZONE, and TIMESTAMP WITH LOCAL TIME ZONE datatypes store data. The NLS_xx_FORMAT parameter is explicitly set to display the values in the nondefault format. The data is inserted at Central Daylight Time (CDT), which is seven hours behind UTC. (The output shown in the example was reformatted for better readability.)

```
CREATE TABLE date_time_demo (
r_no        NUMBER (2),
c_date      DATE DEFAULT SYSDATE,
c_timezone  TIMESTAMP DEFAULT SYSTIMESTAMP,
c_timezone2 TIMESTAMP (2) DEFAULT SYSTIMESTAMP,
c_ts_wtz    TIMESTAMP (0) WITH TIME ZONE
                          DEFAULT SYSTIMESTAMP,
c_ts_wltz   TIMESTAMP (9) WITH LOCAL TIME ZONE
                          DEFAULT SYSTIMESTAMP);

Table created.

INSERT INTO date_time_demo (r_no) VALUES (1);
1 row created.

ALTER SESSION SET NLS_DATE_FORMAT = 'YYYY-MM-DD HH24:MI:SS';
Session altered.

ALTER SESSION SET NLS_TIMESTAMP_FORMAT  = 'YYYY-MM-DD HH24:MI:SS.FF';
Session altered.

ALTER SESSION SET NLS_TIMESTAMP_TZ_FORMAT = 'YYYY-MM-DD HH24:MI:SS.FFTZH:TZM';
Session altered.

SELECT * FROM date_time_demo;
```

```
R_NO C_DATE              C_TIMEZONE
-------------------      ---------------------------
1 2013-08-18 16:05:52    2013-08-18 16:05:52.188000


C_TIMEZONE2              C_TS_WTZ
-------------------      ---------------------------
2013-08-18 16:05:52.19   2013-08-18 16:05:52.-05:00


C_TS_WLTZ
---------------------------
2013-08-18 16:05:52.188000000
```

INTERVAL YEAR TO MONTH

The syntax for the INTERVAL YEAR TO MONTH datatype is as follows:

```
INTERVAL YEAR [(precision)] TO MONTH
```

The INTERVAL YEAR TO MONTH datatype is used to represent a period of time as years and months. The *precision* value specifies the precision needed for the year field, and its default is 2. Valid precision values are from 0 to 9. This datatype can be used to store the difference between two datetime values, where the only significant portions are the year and month.

INTERVAL DAY TO SECOND

The syntax for the INTERVAL DAY TO SECOND datatype is as follows:

```
INTERVAL DAY [(precision)] TO SECOND
```

The INTERVAL DAY TO SECOND datatype is used to represent a period of time as days, hours, minutes, and seconds. The *precision* variable specifies the precision needed for the day field, and its default is 6. Valid precision values are from 0 to 9. Larger precision values allow a greater difference between the dates; for example, a precision of 2 allows values from 0 through 99, and a precision of 4 allows values from 0 through 9,999. This datatype can be used to store the difference between two datetime values, including seconds.

The following example demonstrates the INTERVAL datatypes. It creates a table with the INTERVAL datatype, inserts data into it, and selects data from the table.

```
CREATE TABLE interval_demo (
ts1    TIMESTAMP (2),
iy2m   INTERVAL YEAR (3) TO MONTH,
id2s   INTERVAL DAY (4) TO SECOND);
Table created.

INSERT INTO interval_demo VALUES (
```

```
TO_TIMESTAMP('080101-102030.45', 'YYMMDD-HH24MISS.FF'),
TO_YMINTERVAL('3-7'),
TO_DSINTERVAL('4 02:20:30.30'));
1 row created.

SELECT * FROM interval_demo;
TS1                      IY2M     ID2S
------------------------ -------- --------------------
2008-01-01 10:20:30.45   +003-07  +0004 02:20:30.300000
```

Date Arithmetic

Datetime datatypes can be used in expressions with the plus (+) or minus (−) operator. You can use the +, −, *, and / operators with the INTERVAL datatypes. Dates are stored in the database as Julian numbers with a fraction component for the time. A *Julian date* refers to the number of days since January 1, 4712 B.C. Because of the time component of the date, comparing dates can result in fractional differences, even though the date is the same. Oracle provides a number of functions, such as TRUNC, that help you remove the time component when you want to compare only the date portions.

Adding 1 to the date simply moves the date ahead one day. You can add time to the date by adding a fraction of a day. One day equals 24 hours, or 24×60 minutes, or $24 \times 60 \times 60$ seconds. Table 7.1 shows the numbers used to add or subtract time for a datetime datatype.

TABLE 7.1   Date Arithmetic

Time to Add or Subtract	Fraction	Date Difference
1 day	1	1
1 hour	1/24	1/24
1 minute	$1/(24 \times 60)$	1/1440
1 second	$1/(24 \times 60 \times 60)$	1/86400

Subtracting two dates gives you the difference between the dates in days. This usually results in a fractional component that represents the time difference. If the time components are the same, there will be no fractional results.

A datetime value operation using a numeric value results in a datetime value. The following example adds two days and 12 hours to a date value:

```
ALTER SESSION SET NLS_DATE_FORMAT = 'YYYY-MM-DD HH24:MI:SS';
```

```
SELECT TO_DATE('2013-10-24 13:09:14') + 2.5 EXAMP
FROM dual;


EXAMP
-------------------
2013-10-27 01:09:14
```

This example subtracts six hours from a timestamp value:

```
SELECT TO_TIMESTAMP('2013-10-24 13:09:14.05') - 0.25 EXAMP
FROM dual;


EXAMP
-------------------
2013-10-24 07:09:14
```

A datetime value subtracted from another datetime value results in a numeric value (the difference in days). You cannot add two datetime values. Here is an example that results in the difference between dates as a fraction of a day:

```
SELECT SYSDATE,
       SYSDATE - TO_DATE('2012-10-24 13:09:14')
FROM dual;


SYSDATE             SYSDATE-TO_DATE('2012-10-2413:09:14')
------------------- ------------------------------------
2013-08-18 16:05:52                        298.122662
```

This example converts the fraction of days to hours, minutes, and seconds using the NUMTODSINTERVAL function:

```
SELECT SYSDATE,
       NUMTODSINTERVAL(SYSDATE - TO_DATE('2012-10-24 13:09:14'), 'DAY')
FROM DUAL;


SYSDATE             NUMTODSINTERVAL(SYSDATE
------------------- ----------------------------
2013-08-18 16:05:52  + 000000298 02:56:38.000000000
```

A datetime value operation using an interval value results in a datetime value. The following example adds one year and three months to today's date:

```
SELECT TRUNC(SYSDATE),
       TRUNC(SYSDATE) + TO_YMINTERVAL('1-3')
FROM dual;
```

```
TRUNC(SYSDATE)       TRUNC(SYSDATE) + TO_Y
------------------- -------------------
2013-08-18 00:00:00 2014-11-18 00:00:00
```

An interval datatype operation on another interval or numeric value results in an interval value. You can use + and – between two interval datatypes and use * and / between interval and numeric values. The following example converts a string (which represents 1 day, 3 hours, and 30 minutes) to an INTERVAL DAY TO SECOND datatype and multiplies that value by 2, which results in 2 days and 7 hours:

```
SELECT TO_DSINTERVAL('1 03:30:00.0') * 2 FROM dual;


TO_DSINTERVAL('103:30:00.0')*2
-------------------------------
+000000002 07:00:00.000000000
```

The following example shows arithmetic between two INTERVAL DAY TO SECOND datatype values. The interval value of 3 hours and 30 minutes is subtracted from 1 day, 3 hours, and 30 minutes, resulting in 1 day.

```
SELECT TO_DSINTERVAL('1 03:30:00.0')
          - TO_DSINTERVAL('0 03:30:00.0')
FROM dual;


TO_DSINTERVAL('103:30:00.0') - TO_DSINTERVAL('003:30:00.0')
-----------------------------------------------------------
+000000001 00:00:00.000000000
```

Binary Datatypes

Binary datatypes store information without converting it to the database's character set. This type of storage is required to store images, audio/video, executable files, and similar data. Four datatypes are available to store binary data:

- RAW
- LONG RAW
- BLOB
- BFILE

RAW

The syntax for the RAW datatype is as follows:

```
RAW (<size>)
```

RAW is used to store binary information up to 2,000 bytes. You must specify the maximum size of the column in bytes. RAW is a variable-length datatype.

LONG RAW

The syntax for the LONG RAW datatype is as follows:

```
LONG RAW
```

It's the same as RAW, but with up to 2GB of storage, and you can't specify a maximum size. LONG RAW is supported in Oracle Database 12*c* for backward compatibility. Use BLOB instead. You can have only one LONG RAW or LONG column in a table.

BLOB

The syntax for the BLOB datatype is as follows:

```
BLOB
```

BLOB can store binary data up to 4GB. There is no size specification for this datatype.

BFILE

The syntax for the BFILE datatype is as follows:

```
BFILE
```

BFILE is used to store information on external files. The external file size can be up to 4GB. Oracle stores only the file pointer in the database. The actual file is stored on the operating system. Of the four Large Object datatypes (CLOB, BLOB, NCLOB, and BFILE), only BFILE stores actual data outside the Oracle database.

Row ID Datatypes

Physical storage of each row in a table can be represented using a unique value called the ROWID. Every table has a pseudocolumn called the ROWID. To store such values, Oracle provides two datatypes:

- ROWID
- UROWID

ROWID

The syntax for the ROWID datatype is as follows:

```
ROWID
```

ROWID can store the physical address of a row. Physical ROWIDs store the addresses of rows in ordinary tables (excluding index-organized tables), clustered tables, table partitions and subpartitions, indexes, and index partitions and subpartitions. Logical ROWIDs store the addresses of rows in index-organized tables. Physical ROWIDs provide the fastest possible access to a row of a given table.

UROWID

The syntax for the UROWID datatype is as follows:

```
UROWID
```

UROWID can store the logical ROWIDs of index-organized tables or non-Oracle database tables. Oracle creates logical ROWIDs based on an index-organized table's primary key. The logical ROWIDs do not change as long as the primary key does not change.

Creating Tables

Now that you have learned about the various datatypes you can use to store table data, you are ready to create a table. You can think of a table as a spreadsheet with columns and rows. It is a structure that holds data in a relational database. The table is created with a name to identify it and columns defined with valid column names and column attributes, such as the datatype and size. CREATE TABLE is a comprehensive statement with many options. The certification exam only covers creating and managing a simple relational table. Here is the simplest format to use to create a table:

```
CREATE TABLE products
( prod_id    NUMBER (4),
  prod_name  VARCHAR2 (20),
  stock_qty  NUMBER (15,3)
);
```

```
Table created.
```

You specify the table name following the keywords CREATE TABLE. The previous example creates a table named PRODUCTS under the user (schema) connected to the database. The table name can be qualified with the username; you must qualify the table when creating a table in another user's schema. Table and column names are discussed in more detail in the next section.

The column definitions are enclosed in parentheses. The table created by the previous code has three columns, each identified by a name and datatype. Commas separate the column definitions. This table has two columns with the NUMBER datatype and one column with the VARCHAR2 datatype. A datatype must be specified for each column.

When creating tables, you can specify the following:

- Default values for columns
- Whether the column is visible or invisible

- Constraints for the columns and/or table (discussed later in this chapter in the "Managing Constraints" section)
- The type of table: relational (heap), temporary, index-organized, external, or object (Index-organized and object tables are not covered on the certification exam.)
- Table storage, including any index storage and storage specification for the Large Object columns (LOBs) in the table
- The tablespace where the table/index should be stored
- Any partitioning and subpartitioning information

Naming Tables and Columns

Table names are used to identify each table. You should make table names as descriptive as possible. Table and column names are *identifiers* and can be up to 30 characters long. An identifier name should begin with a letter and can contain numeric digits. The only special characters allowed in an identifier name are the dollar sign ($), the underscore (_), and the number sign (#). The underscore can be used for meaningful separation of the words in an identifier name. These names are case insensitive. If, however, you enclose the identifier name in double quotation marks ("), it will be case sensitive in the Oracle dictionary.

WARNING   Creating table names enclosed in quotation marks with mixed case can cause serious problems when you query the database if you do not know the exact case of the table name.

You can use the DESCRIBE or DESC (SQL*Plus) command to list all the columns in the table, along with their datatype, size, nullity, and order. The syntax is DESCRIBE *<table name>*. The case sensitivity of names and describing tables are illustrated in the following examples:

```
CREATE TABLE MyTable (
 Column_1  NUMBER,
 Column_2  CHAR);
Table created.

DESC mytable
 Name                 Null?    Type
 ------------------- -------- --------
 COLUMN_1                      NUMBER
 COLUMN_2                      CHAR(1)

SELECT table_name FROM user_tables
WHERE  table_name = 'MyTable';
no rows selected
```

```
CREATE TABLE "MyTable" (
 "Column1" number,
 "Column2" char);
Table created.

DESC "MyTable"
 Name                  Null?    Type
 ------------------- -------- --------
 Column1                        NUMBER
 Column2                        CHAR(1)


SELECT table_name FROM user_tables
WHERE  upper(table_name) = 'MYTABLE';


TABLE_NAME
------------------------------

MYTABLE
MyTable
```

It is a good practice to give the other objects directly related to a table a name that reflects the table name. For example, consider the EMPLOYEE table. The primary key of the table may be named PK_EMPLOYEE, indexes might be named EMPLOYEE_NDX1 and EMPLOYEE_NDX2, a check constraint could be named CK_EMPLOYEE_STATUS, a trigger could be named TRG_EMPLOYEE_HIRE, and so on.

Creating a Temporary Table

When you create a table without any specific keywords to indicate the type of the table, the table created is a relational table that is permanent. If you include the keywords GLOBAL TEMPORARY, Oracle creates a temporary relational table known as the *global temporary table* (GTT); its definition is available to all sessions in the database; however, the data is available only to the session that inserted data into it. The GTT is truly a temporary table. On other flavors of RDBMS, a permanent table created to hold temporary data is called a *temporary table*. You can do the same with Oracle, but Oracle provides true temporary tables with GTT.

The data inserted by a session is visible only to that session. Normally, when you commit the data changes or new rows added to a table, the data is visible to all other sessions. When you're using GTTs, the data is truly temporary—it is not written permanently anywhere. The ON COMMIT clause can be included to specify whether the data in the temporary table is session-specific (ON COMMIT PRESERVE ROWS) or transaction-specific (ON COMMIT DELETE ROWS). ON COMMIT DELETE ROWS is the default. If the definition is for session-specific data, the inserted data will be available throughout the session. If the GTT is defined as transaction-specific, then when a COMMIT or ROLLBACK is performed, the data in the table is cleared. Here is an example of creating a temporary table with inserted data that will be available throughout the session:

```
CREATE GLOBAL TEMPORARY TABLE emp_bonus_temp  (
emp_id   NUMBER (10),
bonus    NUMBER (15,2))
ON COMMIT PRESERVE ROWS;
```

Specifying Default Values for Columns

When creating or altering a table, you can specify *default values* for columns. The default value specified will be used when you do not specify any value for the column while inserting data. The default value specified in the definition should satisfy the datatype and length of the column. If a default value is not explicitly set, the default for the column is implicitly set to NULL. If you want to substitute another value for the explicitly set NULL value, you can use the DEFAULT ON NULL clause. The following is the syntax to use the DEFAULT clause in column definition.

```
column datatype   [ DEFAULT [ ON NULL ] expr | identity_clause ]
```

The expr should be an expression or constant that is of the same data type as the column. The identity_clause is discussed under "Using Sequence Values as Default Values."

Default values cannot refer to another column, and they cannot have the pseudocolumns LEVEL, ROWNUM, or PRIOR. The default values can include SYSDATE, USER, USERENV, and UID. The DEFAULT expression can include any SQL function as long as the function does not return a literal argument, a column reference, or a nested function invocation.

In the following example, the table ORDERS is created with a column STATUS that has a default value of PENDING:

```
CREATE TABLE orders (
order_number NUMBER (8),
status       VARCHAR2 (10) DEFAULT 'PENDING');
```

```
Table created.

INSERT INTO orders (order_number) VALUES (4004);

1 row created.

SELECT * FROM orders;

ORDER_NUMBER STATUS
------------ ----------
        4004 PENDING
```

Here is an example of creating a table that includes default values for two columns:

```
CREATE TABLE emp_punch (
emp_id       NUMBER (6) NOT NULL,
time_in      DATE,
time_out     DATE,
updated_by   VARCHAR2 (30) DEFAULT USER,
update_time  TIMESTAMP WITH LOCAL TIME ZONE
                                DEFAULT SYSTIMESTAMP
);

Table created.

DESCRIBE emp_punch
 Name                         Null?     Type
 --------------------------   --------  ------------------
 EMP_ID                       NOT NULL  NUMBER(6)
 TIME_IN                                DATE
 TIME_OUT                               DATE
 UPDATED_BY                             VARCHAR2(30)
 UPDATE_TIME                            TIMESTAMP(6) WITH
                                        LOCAL TIME ZONE

INSERT INTO emp_punch (emp_id, time_in)
VALUES (1090, TO_DATE('081813-2121','MMDDYY-HH24MI'));

1 row created.

SELECT * FROM emp_punch;
```

EMP_ID	TIME_IN	TIME_OUT	UPDATED_BY	UPDATE_TIME
1090	2013-08-18 21:21:00		HR	2013-08-18 16:05:52.349000

 NOTE   This example uses a NOT NULL constraint in the table definition. A NOT NULL constraint prevents NULL values from being entered into the column. Constraints are discussed in detail in the "Managing Constraints" section later in this chapter.

If you explicitly insert a NULL value for a column with the DEFAULT defined, the value in the DEFAULT clause will not be used. You can explicitly specify DEFAULT in the INSERT statement to use the DEFAULT value, as in the following example:

```
INSERT INTO emp_punch
VALUES (104, TO_DATE('062801-2121','MMDDYY-HH24MI'),
        DEFAULT, DEFAULT, NULL);
```

```
1 row created.
```

```
SELECT * FROM emp_punch;
```

EMP_ID	TIME_IN	TIME_OUT	UPDATED_BY	UPDATE_TIME
1090	2013-08-18 21:21:00		HR	29-JUN-01 02.55.58.000000 PM
104	2013-08-18 21:21:00		HR	

```
SQL>
```

The DEFAULT ON NULL option lets you define values when an explicit NULL value is inserted in a column, or no value is specified during INSERT. If you specify the ON NULL clause, then Oracle Database 12c assigns the DEFAULT column value when an INSERT statement attempts to assign a value that evaluates to NULL.

The following example demonstrates this.

```
SQL> CREATE TABLE orders2 (
  2   ORD_ID NUMBER,
  3   ord_date date default on null sysdate,
  4   memo  varchar2 (20));
```

```
Table created.
```

```
SQL> insert into orders2 (ord_id, ord_date, memo)
     VALUES (234, NULL, 'Test 1');
```

```
1 row created.

SQL> insert into orders2 (ord_id, memo) VALUES (345,'Test 2');

1 row created.

SQL> SELECT * FROM orders2;

    ORD_ID ORD_DATE             MEMO
---------- ------------------- --------------------
       234 2013-08-18 16:05:52 Test 1
       345 2013-08-18 16:05:52 Test 2

SQL>
```

Using Sequence Values as Default Values

The pseudocolumns NEXTVAL and CURRVAL can be used as DEFAULT [ON NULL] values for numeric columns. The sequence_name.NEXTVAL or sequence_name.CURRVAL pseudocolumns are used to retrieve the value from sequence. The sequence must exist before it can be used in the table definition. If the sequence is in some other schema, you should have read privilege on the sequence.

We will show you how to use an existing sequence generator to populate the values in a column. In the following example, a sequence is created first and is used in the table definition to populate the ID column if no value is specified for the ID column during insert. If a value is specified, that value is used. If an explicit NULL value is used, a default value is not assigned. By default, sequences start from 1 and increment by 1.

```
SQL> CREATE SEQUENCE ocaex1;

Sequence created.

SQL> CREATE TABLE ocaexample1 (
  2  ID  NUMBER DEFAULT ocaex1.NEXTVAL,
  3* NAME VARCHAR2 (20))
SQL> /

Table created.

SQL> INSERT INTO ocaexample1 (name) VALUES ('Joshua');

1 row created.
```

```
SQL> INSERT INTO ocaexample1 (id, name) VALUES (44, 'Jenna');

1 row created.

SQL> INSERT INTO ocaexample1 (name) VALUES ('Alan');

1 row created.

SQL> INSERT INTO ocaexample1 (id, name) VALUES (NULL, 'Chris');

1 row created.

SQL> SELECT * FROM ocaexample1;

        ID NAME
---------- --------------------
         1 Joshua
         4 Jenna
         2 Alan
           Chris

SQL>
```

Although using CURRVAL in the column as a default is allowed, the sequence must have initialized in the same session using the NEXTVAL for you to be able to use CURRVAL. Instead of using an existing sequence for default value, you can define a sequence generator within the column definition; this feature is called the identity column and is discussed in the next section.

Defining Identity Column

An *identity column* is used to uniquely identify each row value in a column. An implicitly defined sequence generator is used to generate the values for the column. All of the options available while defining a sequence generator are also available in defining an identity column.

The syntax of defining an identity column is as follows:

```
column datatype  GENERATED [ ALWAYS | BY DEFAULT [ ON NULL ] ]
AS IDENTITY [ ( identity_options ) ]
```

The GENERATED keyword tells Oracle that this column value is generated. ALWAYS is the default and specifies that the column value is never assigned; during INSERT/UDPATE statement execution, this column will always be evaluated to NULL—the value will be populated by Oracle based on the "identity_options."

BY DEFAULT specifies that the column value is generated by Oracle (similar to ALWAYS), but you can explicitly assign values to the column using INSERT/UPDATE statements. If you specify ON NULL with BY DEFAULT, the generated value is assigned to the column only when the column value is evaluated to NULL during INSERT/UPDATE.

The "identity_options" is basically the syntax for sequence generator, which is the same as the CREATE SEQUENCE options.

> You can have only one identity column per table. The identity column has a NOT NULL constraint automatically created.

The following example shows the SQL code used to define a table with a GENERATED BY DEFAULT identity column. The example also shows data added to the table and the results. You may also use the DEFAULT ON NULL here.

```
SQL> CREATE TABLE oca_ident1 (
  2  id NUMBER GENERATED BY DEFAULT AS IDENTITY,
  3* memo  VARCHAR2 (30));

Table created.

SQL> INSERT INTO oca_ident1 (id, memo) VALUES (454, 'Test 1');

1 row created.

SQL> INSERT INTO oca_ident1 (id, memo) VALUES (NULL, 'Test 2');
INSERT INTO oca_ident1 (id, memo) VALUES (NULL, 'Test 2')
                                          *
ERROR at line 1:
ORA-01400: cannot insert NULL into ("HR"."OCA_IDENT1"."ID")

SQL> INSERT INTO oca_ident1 (memo) VALUES ('Test 3');

1 row created.

SQL> SELECT * FROM oca_ident1;

        ID MEMO
---------- ------------------------------
       454 Test 1
         1 Test 3
```

```
SQL> UPDATE oca_ident1 SET ID = NULL where ID = 454;
UPDATE oca_ident1 SET ID = NULL where ID = 454
                     *
ERROR at line 1:
ORA-01407: cannot update ("HR"."OCA_IDENT1"."ID") to NULL


SQL> UPDATE oca_ident1 SET ID = 30 where ID = 454;

1 row updated.

SQL>
```

The next example shows the SQL code used to define a table with a GENERATED ALWAYS identity column. Here you can see that the generated value is always used, and you are not allowed to explicitly assign a value.

```
SQL> CREATE TABLE oca_ident2 (
  2  id NUMBER GENERATED ALWAYS AS IDENTITY,
  3* memo  VARCHAR2 (30));

Table created.

SQL> INSERT INTO oca_ident2 (id, memo) VALUES (454, 'Test 1');
INSERT INTO oca_ident2 (id, memo) VALUES (454, 'Test 1')
                     *
ERROR at line 1:
ORA-32795: cannot insert into a generated always identity column


SQL> INSERT INTO oca_ident2 (id, memo) VALUES (NULL, 'Test 2');
INSERT INTO oca_ident2 (id, memo) VALUES (NULL, 'Test 2')
                     *
ERROR at line 1:
ORA-32795: cannot insert into a generated always identity column


SQL> INSERT INTO oca_ident2 (memo) VALUES ('Test 3');

1 row created.
```

```
SQL> SELECT * FROM oca_ident2;

        ID MEMO
---------- ------------------------------
         1 Test 3

SQL> UPDATE oca_ident2 SET ID = 30 where ID = 1;
UPDATE oca_ident2 SET ID = 30 where ID = 1
                          *
ERROR at line 1:
ORA-32796: cannot update a generated always identity column


SQL>
```

Adding Comments

It is a good practice to document the purpose of and any information on the type of data stored in the table in the database itself so that developers and administrators working on the database know the importance of the table/data. Oracle provides the COMMENT statement to add documentation to a table or a column.

Comments on tables are added using the COMMENT ON TABLE statement, and comments on table columns are added using the COMMENT ON COLUMN statement. The following example provides comments for the sample table:

```
COMMENT ON TABLE mytable IS
   'Oracle Database 12c Study Guide Example Table';
Comment created.

COMMENT ON COLUMN mytable.column_1 is
  'First column in MYTABLE';
Comment created.
```

You can query the table and column information from the Oracle dictionary using the following views: USER_TABLES, ALL_TABLES, USER_TAB_COLUMNS, and ALL_TAB_COLUMNS.

Creating a Table from Another Table

You can create a table using a query based on one or more existing tables or views. The column datatype and width will be determined by the query result. A table created in this fashion can select all the columns from another table (you can use *) or a subset of columns or expressions and functions applied on columns (these are called *derived columns*). The syntax for creating a table using an existing table is as follows:

```
CREATE TABLE <table characteristics> AS SELECT <query>
```

This syntax is generally known as CTAS (the abbreviated form of CREATE TABLE AS SELECT). The table characteristics include the new table name and its storage properties.

For example, suppose you need to duplicate the structure and data of the EMPLOYEES table in the EMPLOYEES_COPY table. You can use CTAS, like this:

```
CREATE TABLE employees_copy
AS SELECT * FROM employees;


Table created.
```

You can have complex query statements in the CREATE TABLE statement. The table is created with no rows if the query returned no rows. If you just want to copy the structure of the table, make sure the query returns no rows:

```
CREATE TABLE employees_norows
AS SELECT * FROM employees
WHERE 1 = 2;
```

You can provide column alias names to have different column names in the newly created table. The following example shows a table structure, displays the data, and then creates a new table with the data and displays it:

```
DESCRIBE city

Name                  Null?     Type
-------------------   --------  -------------
CNT_CODE              NOT NULL  NUMBER(4)
ST_CODE               NOT NULL  VARCHAR2(2)
CTY_CODE              NOT NULL  NUMBER(4)
CTY_NAME                        VARCHAR2(20)


SELECT COUNT(*) FROM city;

  COUNT(*)
----------
         3
CREATE TABLE new_city AS
SELECT cty_code CITY_CODE, cty_name CITY_NAME
FROM city;
```

```
Table created.

SELECT COUNT(*) FROM new_city;

  COUNT(*)
----------
         3
DESC new_city
 Name                Null?    Type
 ------------------  -------  -------------
 CITY_CODE           NOT NULL NUMBER(4)
 CITY_NAME                    VARCHAR2(20)
```

The CREATE TABLE … AS SELECT … statement will not work if the query refers to columns of the LONG datatype.

When you create a table using the subquery, only the NOT NULL constraints associated with the columns are copied to the new table. Other constraints and column default definitions are not copied. This almost certainly will be an OCA certification exam question.

Modifying Tables

After you've created a table, you might want to modify it for several reasons. You can modify a table to change its column definition or default values, add a new column, rename a column, or drop an existing column. You can also drop and rename tables.

You might also modify a table if you need to change or add constraint definitions. You can make a table read-only so that no modifications are possible on the data in the table. The ALTER TABLE statement is used to change table definitions. Similar to the CREATE TABLE statement, the ALTER TABLE statement has several options. In the following sections, we will concentrate on the options that are pertinent to the OCA certification exam.

Adding Columns

Sometimes it is necessary to add a column to an existing table because enhancements were made to the application or because the developer just did not plan it well. To add a column to an existing table, you don't need to drop and re-create the table. Using the

ALTER TABLE statement, you can easily add a column to the table. All columns added to the table using the ALTER TABLE … ADD … statement are added to the end of the table definition. Here is the syntax to add a new column to an existing table:

```
ALTER TABLE [<schema>.]<table_name> ADD <column_definitions>;
```

When a new column is added, it is always at the bottom of the table. For the existing rows, the new column value will be NULL.

Let's add a new column, ORDER_AMT, to the ORDERS table. Notice that the column is added to the end of the table definition. You cannot insert a new column between other columns in a table. If you have such a requirement, the table has to be dropped and re-created.

```
DESCRIBE orders
Name                 Null?    Type
-------------------- -------- -------------
ORDER_NUMBER         NOT NULL NUMBER(8)
STATUS                        VARCHAR2(10)


SELECT * FROM orders;

ORDER_NUMBER STATUS
------------ ----------
        4004 PENDING
        5005 COMPLETED


ALTER TABLE orders ADD order_amt NUMBER (15,2);

Table altered.

DESC orders
Name                 Null?    Type
-------------------- -------- ---------------
ORDER_NUMBER         NOT NULL NUMBER(8)
STATUS                        VARCHAR2(10)
ORDER_AMT                     NUMBER (15,2)


SELECT * FROM orders;

ORDER_NUMBER STATUS     ORDER_AMT
------------ ---------- ---------
        4004 PENDING
        5005 COMPLETED
```

If you are adding more than one column, the column definitions should be enclosed in parentheses and separated by commas. If you specify a DEFAULT value for a newly added column, no value is updated in the existing rows, but value is provided from the dictionary. The following example adds two more columns to the ORDERS table:

```
ALTER TABLE orders ADD
 (quantity NUMBER (13,3),
  update_dt DATE DEFAULT SYSDATE,
  memo  VARCHAR2 (50));


Table altered.


SELECT * FROM orders;


ORDER_NUMBER STATUS     ORDER_AMT  QUANTITY UPDATE_DT
------------ ---------- --------- ---------- ---------
        4004 PENDING                         23-MAR-13
        5005 COMPLETED                       23-MAR-13
```

When adding a new column, you can specify the NOT NULL constraint even if the table already has rows, only when used with the DEFAULT clause. Here is an example:

```
ALTER TABLE orders
      ADD entered_by VARCHAR2 (30) NOT NULL;


ERROR at line 1:
ORA-01758: table must be empty to add mandatory
(NOT NULL) column


ALTER TABLE orders ADD entered_by VARCHAR2 (30)
  DEFAULT 'JOHN' NOT NULL;


Table altered.
```

In Oracle Database 12c, when you add a column with the DEFAULT value, Oracle Database 12c does not update all the existing rows in the table with the default value. Oracle Database 12c simply updates the dictionary and gets you the value from the dictionary when you query the newly added column. In Oracle Database 11g, this behavior was only applicable when the DEFAULT clause was used with the NOT NULL constraint.

Modifying Columns

On many occasions, you may need to change the table definition. The commonly used definition changes include adding or removing a NOT NULL constraint to/from a column, changing the datatype of a column, and changing the length of the column. The syntax to modify an existing column in a table is as follows:

```
ALTER TABLE [<schema>.]<table_name>
MODIFY <column_name> <new_attributes>;
```

If you omit any of the parts of the column definition (datatype, default value, or column constraint), the omitted parts remain unchanged. If you are modifying more than one column at a time, enclose the column definitions in parentheses. For example, to modify the ORDERS table, increasing the MEMO column to 25 and reducing the QUANTITY column to 10,3, do this:

```
ALTER TABLE orders MODIFY (quantity NUMBER (10,3),
                          memo VARCHAR2 (25));
```

You can add or drop constraints in the column and modify the DEFAULT values for the column. The DEFAULT value included in the MODIFY clause affects only the new rows inserted to the table; the existing rows with NULL column values are not affected. To remove the DEFAULT value for a column, redefine the DEFAULT clause with a NULL value. For example, the following statement removes the default SYSDATE value from the UPDATE_DT column of the ORDERS table:

```
ALTER TABLE orders
MODIFY update_dt DEFAULT NULL;
```

These are the rules for modifying column definitions:

- You can increase the length of the character column and precision of the numeric column. If your table has many rows, increasing the length of a CHAR column will require a lot of resources, because the column data for all the rows needs to be blank-padded with the additional length.

- You can decrease the length of a VARCHAR2 column and reduce the precision or increase the scale of a numeric column if all the data in the column fits the new length.

- You can decrease the length of a nonempty CHAR column if the parameter BLANK_TRIMMING is set to TRUE.

- The column values must be NULL to change the column's datatype. If you do not reduce the length, you can change the datatype from CHAR to VARCHAR2, or vice versa, even if the column is not empty.

When a table is modified, the dependent objects using the table could become invalid. For each dependent of an object, if a change is made to the definition of any element involved in the dependency (including dropping the element), the dependent object is invalidated. If changes are made only to definitions of elements that are not involved in the dependency, the dependent object remains valid.

Renaming Columns

Renaming a column is not a common task, but sometimes you may have to change the name of a column because there was a typo in the script or the developers decided to store different data in the column. Renaming a column does not affect its data or datatype. The syntax to rename an existing column in a table is as follows:

```
ALTER TABLE [<schema>.]<table_name>
RENAME COLUMN <column_name> TO <new_name>;
```

When renaming a column, the column name must not be the same as an existing column in the table. The following example renames the DATA_VALUE column of the SAMPLE_DATA table to SAMPLE_VALUE:

```
DESCRIBE sample_data
Name                                     Null?     Type
---------------------------------------  --------  ---------------
DATA_VALUE                                         VARCHAR2(20)
DATA_TYPE                                          VARCHAR2(10)


ALTER TABLE sample_data
RENAME COLUMN data_value to sample_value;


Table altered.


DESCRIBE sample_data
Name                                     Null?     Type
---------------------------------------  --------  ---------------
SAMPLE_VALUE                                       VARCHAR2(20)
DATA_TYPE                                          VARCHAR2(10)
```

When a column in a table is renamed, dependent views and PL/SQL programs are invalidated. You cannot rename a column that is used to define a join index. You must drop the index, rename the column, and recreate the index.

Dropping Columns

Similar to renaming columns, dropping columns is not a common activity for the DBA, but you should know how to drop a column in case you need to do it. You can drop a column that is not used, or you can mark the column as not used and drop it later. Here is the syntax for dropping a column:

```
ALTER TABLE [<schema>.]<table_name>
DROP {COLUMN <column_name> | (<column_names>)}
[CASCADE CONSTRAINTS]
```

DROP COLUMN drops the column name specified from the table. You can provide more than one column name separated by commas inside parentheses. The indexes and constraints on the column are also dropped. You must specify CASCADE CONSTRAINTS if the dropped column is part of a multicolumn constraint; the constraint will be dropped.

The syntax for marking a column as unused is as follows:

```
ALTER TABLE [<schema>.]<table_name>
SET UNUSED {COLUMN <column_name> | (<column_names>)}
[CASCADE CONSTRAINTS]
```

Because it takes a lot of resources, you will usually mark a column as unused instead of dropping it immediately, especially at peak hours, if the table is very large. In such cases, you would mark the column as unused and drop it later. Once the column is marked as unused, you will not see it as part of the table definition. Let's mark the UPDATE_DT column in the ORDERS table as unused:

```
ALTER TABLE orders SET UNUSED COLUMN update_dt;

Table altered.

DESCRIBE orders
Name                Null?     Type
------------------- --------  -------------
ORDER_NUMBER        NOT NULL  NUMBER(8)
STATUS                        VARCHAR2(15)
ORDER_DATE                    DATE
QUANTITY                      NUMBER(10,3)
```

Here is the syntax for dropping a column already marked as unused:

```
ALTER TABLE [<schema>.]<table_name>
DROP {UNUSED COLUMNS | COLUMNS CONTINUE}
```

Use the COLUMNS CONTINUE clause to continue a DROP operation that was previously interrupted. The DROP UNUSED COLUMNS clause will drop all the columns that are marked as unused. You cannot selectively drop column names after marking them as unused. The following example clears data from the UPDATE_DT column in the ORDERS table:

```
ALTER TABLE orders DROP UNUSED COLUMNS;
```

Hiding Columns from Table

Dropping columns is an expensive operation; therefore, if you just want to hide the column for now, either to test the application impact or to drop at a later time, the column can be made invisible using the ALTER TABLE statement. You can also create tables with *invisible columns*.

The following example creates a table named MYACCOUNT with the COMMENT column as not visible. Then we describe the table to view the columns and find out that the invisible column is not listed. Using the SET COLINVISIBLE option, we display the invisible column, and then use the ALTER TABLE option to make the column visible.

```
SQL> CREATE TABLE myaccount (
  2  accno  NUMBER (8) PRIMARY KEY,
  3  drcr   CHAR,
  4  openbal NUMBER (15,2),
  5  comments VARCHAR2 (20) INVISIBLE );

Table created.

SQL> desc myaccount
 Name                         Null?    Type
 --------------------------   -------- --------------------
 ACCNO                        NOT NULL NUMBER(8)
 DRCR                                  CHAR(1)
 OPENBAL                               NUMBER(15,2)

SQL> SET COLINVISIBLE ON
SQL> desc myaccount
 Name                         Null?    Type
 --------------------------   -------- --------------------
 ACCNO                        NOT NULL NUMBER(8)
 DRCR                                  CHAR(1)
 OPENBAL                               NUMBER(15,2)
 COMMENTS (INVISIBLE)                  VARCHAR2(20)

SQL> ALTER TABLE myaccount MODIFY comments VISIBLE;
```

```
Table altered.
```

```
SQL>
```

Dropping Tables

When application designs change, some tables can become orphaned or unused. You can use the DROP TABLE statement to drop an existing table. The syntax of the DROP TABLE statement is as follows:

```
DROP TABLE [schema.]table_name [CASCADE CONSTRAINTS]
```

When you drop a table, you remove the data and definition of the table. The indexes, constraints, triggers, and privileges on the table are also dropped. Once you drop a table, you cannot undo the action.

Oracle does not drop the views, materialized views, or other stored programs that reference the table, but it marks them as invalid. You must specify the CASCADE CONSTRAINTS clause if there are referential integrity constraints referring to the primary key or unique key of this table. Here's how to drop the table TEST owned by the user SCOTT:

```
DROP TABLE scott.test;
```

A method for emptying a table of all rows is to use the TRUNCATE statement. This is different from dropping and re-creating a table, because TRUNCATE does not invalidate dependent objects or drop indexes, triggers, or referential integrity constraints. See Chapter 6, "Manipulating Data," for more information about using TRUNCATE.

Renaming Tables

Tables and other database schema objects can be renamed in Oracle. The RENAME statement is used to rename a table and other database objects, such as views, private synonyms, or sequences. The syntax for the RENAME statement is as follows:

```
RENAME old_name TO new_name;
```

Here, old_name and new_name are the names of a table, view, private synonym, or sequence.

When you rename a table, Oracle automatically transfers integrity constraints, indexes, and grants on the old table to the new table. Oracle invalidates all objects that depend on the renamed table, such as views, synonyms, stored procedures, and functions.

The following example renames the ORDERS table to PURCHASE_ORDERS:

```
RENAME orders TO purchase_orders;
```

```
Table renamed.
```

```
DESCRIBE purchase_orders
```

Name	Null?	Type
ORDER_NUMBER	NOT NULL	NUMBER(8)
STATUS		VARCHAR2(15)
ORDER_DATE		DATE
QUANTITY		NUMBER(10,3)

> You can use the RENAME statement to rename only the objects you own. You cannot rename an object owned by another user.

You can also use the RENAME TO clause of the ALTER TABLE statement to rename a table. Using this technique, you can qualify the table name with the schema. You must use the ALTER TABLE statement to rename a table owned by another user (and you need the ALTER privilege on the table or the ALTER ANY TABLE system privilege). Here is an example:

```
ALTER TABLE hr.purchase_orders
RENAME TO orders;
```

```
Table altered.
```

Making Tables Read-Only

DBAs frequently receive user requests to make tables read-only. Many configuration tables can be made read-only after the initial application setup is completed so that accidental changes can be avoided. To place a table in read-only mode, use the READ ONLY clause of the ALTER TABLE statement.

The following statement makes the PRODUCTS table read-only:

```
ALTER TABLE products READ ONLY;
```

```
Table altered.
```

Once the table is marked as read-only, no operation on the table that would change its data is allowed. Many DDL operations on the table are allowed. The following operations are not allowed on a read-only table:

- INSERT, UPDATE, DELETE, or MERGE statements
- The TRUNCATE operation
- Adding, modifying, renaming, or dropping a column
- Flashing back a table
- SELECT FOR UPDATE

The following operations are allowed on a read-only table:

- SELECT
- Creating or modifying indexes

- Creating or modifying constraints
- Changing the storage characteristics of the table
- Renaming the table
- Dropping the table

The following examples demonstrate some operations that are not allowed on a read-only table:

```
TRUNCATE TABLE products;
TRUNCATE TABLE products
                *
ERROR at line 1:
ORA-12081: update operation not allowed on table "HR"."PRODUCTS"


DELETE FROM products;
DELETE FROM products
            *
ERROR at line 1:
ORA-12081: update operation not allowed on table "HR"."PRODUCTS"


INSERT INTO products VALUES (200, 'TESTING', 'X1',0);
INSERT INTO products VALUES (200, 'TESTING', 'X1',0)
             *
ERROR at line 1:
ORA-12081: update operation not allowed on table "HR"."PRODUCTS"
```

To change a read-only table to read-write, use the READ WRITE clause of the ALTER TABLE statement. The following example makes the PRODUCTS table writable:

```
ALTER TABLE products READ WRITE;

Table altered.
```

Using SQL Developer to Learn and Explore Schema Objects

SQL Developer is a good friend of developers and DBAs. SQL Developer offers complete end-to-end development of PL/SQL applications, helps run queries and scripts, acts as an administrator console for managing the database, runs various reports, and even has tools to migrate a non-Oracle database to Oracle. SQL Developer also supports a number of SQL*Plus commands. All the SQL examples you see in this book can be performed using SQLDeveloper in the Worksheet screen.

When you are creating or modifying a database object using SQL Developer, even though it is GUI-based, you can utilize the option to see the DDL behind it. This is a great tool that can help certification candidates learn DDL and the various options to create and alter objects. Right-click on the object type on the browser, and you will be able to choose to create a new object of that type. For example, if you right-click on Tables, you will be given a choice with New Table. If you right-click on an existing table, you will see various options to modify the table properties and characteristics.

For example, the following image shows a Create Table dialog screen with the options available to create a basic table.

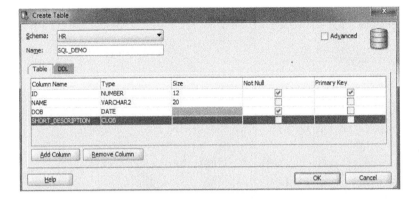

When you click on the DDL tab in the same screen, you will see the code behind the table creation, as in the following image.

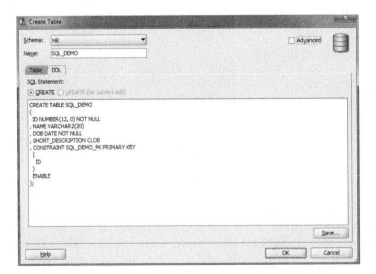

Most of the object creation dialogs also have a check box for Advanced options. In the Create Table screen, checking the Advanced box shows various options to create a table, as you can see in the following image.

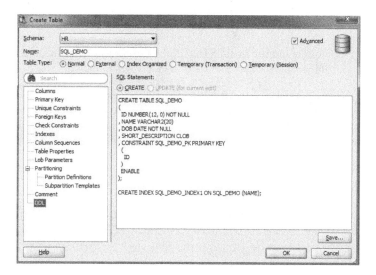

We encourage you to explore the various objects and their DDL options so that you will better understand them.

Managing Constraints

Constraints are created in the database to enforce business rules in the database and to specify relationships between various tables. You can also enforce business rules using database triggers and application code. *Integrity constraints* prevent bad data from being entered into the database. Oracle supports five types of integrity constraints, as shown in Table 7.2.

TABLE 7.2   Integrity Constraints

Constraint	Description
NOT NULL	Prevents NULL values from being entered into the column. These types of constraints are defined on a single column. By default, Oracle allows NULL values in any column.
CHECK	Checks whether the condition specified in the constraint is satisfied.

TABLE 7.2 Integrity Constraints *(continued)*

Constraint	Description
UNIQUE	Ensures that there are no duplicate values for the column(s) specified. Every value or set of values is unique within the table.
PRIMARY KEY	Uniquely identifies each row of the table and prevents NULL values. A table can have only one primary key constraint.
FOREIGN KEY	Establishes a parent-child relationship between tables by using common columns. The foreign key defined on a table refers to the primary key or unique key of another table.

Creating Constraints

Constraints are created using the CREATE TABLE or ALTER TABLE statements. You can specify the constraint definition at the column level if the constraint is defined on a single column. Multiple-column constraints must be defined at the table level; the columns should be specified in parentheses and separated by commas.

If you do not provide a name for the constraints, Oracle assigns a system-generated unique name that begins with SYS_. A name is provided for the constraint by specifying the keyword CONSTRAINT followed by the constraint name.

WARNING

You should not rely on system-generated names for constraints. If you want to compare table characteristics, such as between production and test databases, the inconsistent system-generated names will make the comparison difficult.

In the following sections, we will define the rules for each constraint type and provide examples of creating constraints.

NOT NULL Constraint

A NOT NULL constraint is defined at the column level; it cannot be defined at the table level. The syntax for a NOT NULL constraint is as follows:

```
[CONSTRAINT <constraint name>] [NOT] NULL
```

The following example creates a table with two columns that have NOT NULL constraints:

```
CREATE TABLE orders (
order_num    NUMBER (4) CONSTRAINT nn_order_num NOT NULL,
order_date   DATE NOT NULL,
product_id   NUMBER (6))
```

The example provides a name for the constraint on the ORDER_NUM column. Because no name is specified for the constraint on the ORDER_DATE column, it will get a system-generated name.

Use ALTER TABLE MODIFY to add or remove a NOT NULL constraint on the columns of an existing table. The following examples remove a constraint and add a constraint to an existing table:

```
ALTER TABLE orders MODIFY order_date NULL;
ALTER TABLE orders MODIFY product_id NOT NULL;
```

Check Constraints

You can define a *check constraint* at the column level or table level. For both the column and table levels, the syntax is as follows:

```
[CONSTRAINT <constraint name>] CHECK ( <condition> )
```

The condition specified in the CHECK clause should evaluate to a Boolean result and can refer to values in other columns of the same row; the condition cannot use queries. Environment functions (such as SYSDATE, USER, USERENV, and UID) and pseudocolumns (such as ROWNUM, CURRVAL, NEXTVAL, and LEVEL) cannot be used to evaluate the check condition. One column can have more than one check constraint defined.

The following are examples of check constraints defined at the table level:

```
CREATE TABLE bonus (
 emp_id    VARCHAR2 (40) NOT NULL,
 salary    NUMBER (9,2),
 bonus     NUMBER (9,2),
CONSTRAINT ck_bonus check (bonus > 0));
ALTER TABLE bonus
ADD CONSTRAINT ck_bonus2 CHECK (bonus < salary);
```

The check constraint can be defined at the column level if the constraint refers to only that column.

You cannot use the ALTER TABLE MODIFY clause to add or modify check constraints (only NOT NULL constraints can be modified this way). Column-level constraints can be defined when using the CREATE TABLE statement or when using the ALTER TABLE statement with the ADD clause. Here is an example:

```
ALTER TABLE orders ADD cust_id number (5)
CONSTRAINT ck_cust_id CHECK (cust_id > 0);
```

You can use the check constraint to implement a NOT NULL constraint also. This is especially useful if you need to disallow NULL values in multiple columns together. For example, the following constraint definition for the BONUS table allows a NULL value for the BONUS and SALARY columns if both column values are NULL, or else both columns should have a valid non-NULL value.

```
ALTER TABLE bonus ADD CONSTRAINT ck_sal_bonus
CHECK ((bonus IS NULL AND salary IS NULL) OR
       (bonus IS NOT NULL AND salary IS NOT NULL));
```

Unique Constraints

A *unique constraint* protects one or more columns in a table, ensuring that no two rows contain duplicate data in the protected columns. Unique constraints can be defined at the column level for single-column unique keys. Here is the column-level syntax:

```
[CONSTRAINT <constraint name>] UNIQUE
```

For a multiple-column unique key (a *composite* key; the maximum number of columns specified can be 32). The constraint should be defined at the table level. Here is the table-level syntax:

```
[CONSTRAINT <constraint name>]
UNIQUE (<column>, <column>, …)
```

Oracle creates a unique index on the unique key columns to enforce uniqueness. If a unique index or nonunique index already exists on the table with the same column-order prefix, Oracle uses the existing index. To use the existing nonunique index for enforcing uniqueness, there must not be any duplicate values in the unique key columns.

Unique constraints allow NULL values in the constraint columns. The following example defines a unique constraint with two columns:

```
ALTER TABLE employee
ADD CONSTRAINT uq_emp_id UNIQUE (dept, emp_id);
```

The next example adds a new column to the EMP table and creates a unique key at the column level:

```
ALTER TABLE employee ADD
ssn VARCHAR2 (11) CONSTRAINT uq_ssn unique;
```

Primary Key Constraints

All characteristics of the unique key are applicable to the *primary key constraint*, except that NULL values are not allowed in the primary key columns. A table can have only one primary key. The column-level syntax is as follows:

```
[CONSTRAINT <constraint name>] PRIMARY KEY
```

Here is the table-level syntax:

```
[CONSTRAINT <constraint name>]
PRIMARY KEY (<column>, <column>, …)
```

Oracle creates a unique index and NOT NULL constraints for each column in the key. The following example defines a primary key when creating the table:

```
CREATE TABLE employee (
 dept_no VARCHAR2 (2),
 emp_id  NUMBER (4),
 name    VARCHAR2 (20) NOT NULL,
 ssn     VARCHAR2 (11),
 salary  NUMBER (9,2) CHECK (salary > 0),
CONSTRAINT pk_employee primary key (dept_no, emp_id),
CONSTRAINT uq_ssn unique (ssn))
```

To add a primary key to an existing table, use the ALTER TABLE statement. Here is an example:

```
ALTER TABLE employee
ADD CONSTRAINT pk_employee PRIMARY KEY (dept_no, emp_id);
```

Indexes created to enforce unique keys and primary keys can be managed in the same way as any other index. However, these indexes cannot be dropped explicitly using the DROP INDEX statement.

Foreign Key Constraints

A *foreign key constraint* protects one or more columns in a table by ensuring that for each non-NULL value there is data available elsewhere in the database with a primary or unique key. The foreign key is the column or columns in the table (child table) where the constraint is created. The referenced key is the primary key or unique key column or columns in the table (parent table) that is referenced by the constraint. The column datatypes in the parent table and the child table should match.

You can define a foreign key constraint at the column level or table level. Here is the syntax for the column-level constraint:

```
[CONSTRAINT <constraint name>]
REFERENCES [<schema>.]<table> [(<column>, <column>, …]
[ON DELETE {CASCADE | SET NULL}]
```

Multiple-column foreign keys should be defined at the table level. Here is the table-level syntax:

```
[CONSTRAINT <constraint name>]
FOREIGN KEY (<column>, <column>, …)
```

```
REFERENCES [<schema>.]<table> [(<column>, <column>, …]
[ON DELETE {CASCADE | SET NULL}]
```

The foreign key column(s) and referenced key column(s) can be in the same table (self-referential integrity constraint). NULL values are allowed in the foreign key columns.

The following is an example of creating a foreign key constraint on the COUNTRY_CODE and STATE_CODE columns of the CITY table, which refers to the COUNTRY_CODE and STATE_CODE columns of the STATE table (the composite primary key of the STATE table).

```
ALTER TABLE city ADD CONSTRAINT fk_state
FOREIGN KEY (country_code, state_code)
REFERENCES state (country_code, state_code);
```

You can omit the column listing of the referenced table if referring to the primary key of the table. For example, if the COUNTRY_CODE and STATE_CODE columns are the primary key of the STATE table, the previous statement could be written like this:

```
ALTER TABLE city ADD CONSTRAINT fk_state
FOREIGN KEY (country_code, state_code)
REFERENCES state;
```

The ON DELETE clause specifies the action to be taken when a row in the parent table is deleted and child rows exist for the deleted parent primary key. You can delete the child rows (CASCADE) or set the foreign key column values to NULL (SET NULL). If you omit this clause, Oracle will not allow you to delete from the parent table if child records exist. You must delete the child rows first and then delete the parent row. The following are two examples of specifying the delete action in a foreign key:

```
ALTER TABLE city ADD CONSTRAINT fk_state
 FOREIGN KEY (country_code, state_code)
 REFERENCES state (country_code, state_code)
 ON DELETE CASCADE;

ALTER TABLE city ADD CONSTRAINT fk_state
 FOREIGN KEY (country_code, state_code)
 REFERENCES state (country_code, state_code)
 ON DELETE SET NULL;
```

 You can query the constraint information from the Oracle dictionary using the following views: USER_CONSTRAINTS, ALL_CONSTRAINTS, USER_CONS_COLUMNS, and ALL_CONS_COLUMNS.

Disabled Constraints

When a constraint is created, it is enabled automatically. You can create a *disabled constraint* by specifying the DISABLE keyword after the constraint definition. Here is an example:

```
ALTER TABLE city ADD CONSTRAINT fk_state
 FOREIGN KEY (country_code, state_code)
 REFERENCES state (country_code, state_code) DISABLE;


ALTER TABLE bonus
ADD CONSTRAINT ck_bonus CHECK (bonus > 0) DISABLE;
```

Dropping Constraints

Dropping a constraint defined on a table may be necessary if you find out that business data does not always meet strict data validations using constraints. In such instances, it may be necessary to drop a constraint. Constraints are dropped using the ALTER TABLE statement. Any constraint can be dropped by specifying the constraint name, as in this example:

```
ALTER TABLE bonus DROP CONSTRAINT ck_bonus2;
```

To drop the NOT NULL constraint, use the ALTER TABLE MODIFY statement, like this:

```
ALTER TABLE employee MODIFY employee_name NULL;
```

To drop unique key constraints with referenced foreign keys, specify the CASCADE clause to drop the foreign key constraints and the unique constraint. Specify the unique key column(s). Here is an example:

```
ALTER TABLE employee DROP UNIQUE (emp_id) CASCADE;
```

To drop primary key constraints with referenced foreign key constraints, use the CASCADE clause to drop all foreign key constraints and then the primary key. Here is an example:

```
ALTER TABLE bonus DROP PRIMARY KEY CASCADE;
```

Enabling and Disabling Constraints

When you create a constraint, the constraint is automatically enabled (unless you specify the DISABLE clause). You can disable a constraint by using the DISABLE clause of the ALTER TABLE statement. When you disable unique or primary key constraints, Oracle drops the associated unique index. When you re-enable these constraints, Oracle builds the index.

You can disable any constraint by specifying the DISABLE CONSTRAINT clause followed by the constraint name. Specifying UNIQUE and the column name(s) can disable unique keys, and specifying PRIMARY KEY can disable the table's primary key. You cannot disable a primary key or unique key if foreign keys that are enabled reference it. To disable all the referenced foreign keys and the primary or unique key, specify CASCADE. The following three examples demonstrate disabling constraints:

```
ALTER TABLE bonus DISABLE CONSTRAINT ck_bonus;
```

```
ALTER TABLE employee DISABLE CONSTRAINT uq_employee;
```

```
ALTER TABLE state DISABLE PRIMARY KEY CASCADE;
```

Using the ENABLE clause of the ALTER TABLE statement enables a constraint. When you enable a disabled unique or primary key, Oracle creates an index if an index with the unique or primary key columns does not already exist. You can specify storage for the unique or primary key while enabling these constraints, as in this example:

```
ALTER TABLE state ENABLE PRIMARY KEY USING INDEX
TABLESPACE user_INDEX STORAGE (INITIAL 2M NEXT 2M);
```

Validated Constraints

You have seen how to enable and disable a constraint. ENABLE and DISABLE affect only future data that will be added or modified in the table. In contrast, the VALIDATE and NOVALIDATE keywords in the ALTER TABLE statement act on the existing data. Therefore, a constraint can have four states, as shown in Table 7.3.

TABLE 7.3 Constraints

Constraint	Description
ENABLE VALIDATE	This is the default for the ENABLE clause. The existing data in the table is validated to verify that it conforms to the constraint.
ENABLE NOVALIDATE	This does not validate the existing data but enables the constraint for future constraint checking.
DISABLE VALIDATE	The constraint is disabled (any index used to enforce the constraint is also dropped), but the constraint is kept valid. No DML operation is allowed on the table because future changes cannot be verified.
DISABLE NOVALIDATE	This is the default for the DISABLE clause. The constraint is disabled, and no checks are done on future or existing data.

Suppose you have a large data-warehouse table, where bulk data loads are performed every night. The primary key of this table is enforced using a nonunique index because Oracle does not drop the nonunique index when disabling the constraint. When you do batch loads, you can disable the primary key constraint as follows:

```
ALTER TABLE wh01 MODIFY CONSTRAINT pk_wh01
DISABLE NOVALIDATE;
```

After the batch load completes, you can enable the primary key like this:

```
ALTER TABLE wh01 MODIFY CONSTRAINT pk_wh01
ENABLE NOVALIDATE;
```

 Oracle does not allow any INSERT, UPDATE, or DELETE operations on a table with a DISABLE VALIDATE constraint. This is a quick way to make a table non-updatable in releases prior to Oracle Database 11g, where the READ ONLY clause of the ALTER TABLE statement was not available.

Deferring Constraint Checks

By default, Oracle checks whether the data conforms to the constraint when the statement is executed. Oracle allows you to change this behavior if the constraint is created using the DEFERRABLE clause (NOT DEFERRABLE is the default). It specifies that the transaction can set the constraint-checking behavior.

INITIALLY IMMEDIATE specifies that the constraint should be checked for conformance at the end of each SQL statement (this is the default). INITIALLY DEFERRED specifies that the constraint should be checked for conformance at the end of the transaction.

The DEFERRABLE status of a constraint cannot be changed using ALTER TABLE MODIFY CONSTRAINT; you must drop and re-create the constraint. You can change the INITIALLY {DEFERRED|IMMEDIATE} clause using ALTER TABLE.

If the constraint is DEFERRABLE, you can set the behavior by using the SET CONSTRAINTS command or by using the ALTER SESSION SET CONSTRAINT command. You can enable or disable deferred constraint checking by listing all the constraints or by specifying the ALL keyword. The SET CONSTRAINTS command is used to set the constraint-checking behavior for the current transaction, and the ALTER SESSION command is used to set the constraint-checking behavior for the current session.

As an example, let's create a primary key constraint on the CUSTOMER table and a foreign key constraint on the ORDERS table as DEFERRABLE. Although the constraints are created as DEFERRABLE, they are not deferred because of the INITIALLY IMMEDIATE clause.

```
ALTER TABLE customer ADD CONSTRAINT pk_cust_id
PRIMARY KEY (cust_id) DEFERRABLE
INITIALLY IMMEDIATE;
```

```
ALTER TABLE orders ADD CONSTRAINT fk_cust_id
FOREIGN KEY (cust_id)
REFERENCES customer (cust_id)
ON DELETE CASCADE DEFERRABLE;
```

If you try to add a row to the ORDERS table with a CUST_ID value that is not available in the CUSTOMER table, Oracle returns an error immediately, even though you plan to add the CUSTOMER row soon. Since the constraints are verified for conformance as each SQL statement is executed, you must insert the row in the CUSTOMER table first and then add it to the ORDERS table. Because the constraints are defined as DEFERRABLE, you can change this behavior by using this command:

```
SET CONSTRAINTS ALL DEFERRED;
```

Now you can insert rows to these tables in any order. Oracle checks the constraint conformance only at commit time.

If you want deferred constraint checking as the default, create or modify the constraint by using INITIALLY DEFERRED, as in this example:

```
ALTER TABLE customer MODIFY CONSTRAINT pk_cust_id
INITIALLY DEFERRED;
```

 Real World Scenario

Creating Tables and Constraints for an Application

Here's a scenario you may find yourself in one day. You have been provided the following information to create tables and constraints for an application developed in your company to maintain geographic information:

- The COUNTRY table stores the country name and country code. The country code uniquely identifies each country. The country name must be present.

- The STATE table stores the state code, name, and its capital. The country code in this table refers to a valid entry in the COUNTRY table. The state name must be present. The state code and country code together uniquely identify each state.

- The CITY table stores the city code, name, and population. The city code uniquely identifies each city. The state and country where the city belongs are also stored in the table, which refers to the STATE table. The city name must be present.

- Each table should have a column identifying the created-on timestamp, with the system date as the default.

- The user should not be able to delete from the COUNTRY table if there are records in the STATE table for that country.

- The records in the CITY table should be automatically removed when their corresponding state is removed from the STATE table.

- All foreign and primary key constraints should be provided with meaningful names.

Let's start by creating the COUNTRY table:

```
SQL> CREATE TABLE country (
  2  code   NUMBER (4) PRIMARY KEY,
  3  name   VARCHAR2 (40));
Table created.
SQL>
```

Oops! CODE and NAME are not very descriptive column names, and you also have other columns in tables to store codes and names. Let's rename the columns to COUNTRY_CODE and COUNTRY_NAME:

```
SQL> ALTER TABLE country RENAME COLUMN
  2  code TO country_code;
Table altered.

SQL> ALTER TABLE country RENAME COLUMN
  2  name TO country_name;
Table altered.

SQL>
```

You also forgot to provide a name for the primary key constraint. Because the table was created with a system-generated name, you have to find the name first to rename the constraint:

```
SQL> SELECT constraint_name, constraint_type
  2  FROM user_constraints
  3  WHERE table_name = 'COUNTRY';

CONSTRAINT_NAME                 C
------------------------------- -
SYS_C0010893                    P


SQL> ALTER TABLE country RENAME CONSTRAINT SYS_C0010893 TO pk_country;
Table altered.

SQL>
```

Oops, again! The table should include a column to store the created-on date, and the country name cannot be NULL.

Before you continue, realize that if you have a good logical and physical design before you start creating tables, you will not have any of these problems. This is not the typical or recommended approach to creating tables for the application. The objective here is to demonstrate the various options available.

```
SQL> ALTER TABLE country MODIFY country_name NOT NULL
  2  ADD created  DATE DEFAULT SYSDATE;
Table altered.
SQL>
```

Review the table created:

```
SQL> DESCRIBE country
 Name                  Null?     Type
 ------------------- -------- ------------
 COUNTRY_CODE         NOT NULL NUMBER(4)
 COUNTRY_NAME         NOT NULL VARCHAR2(40)
 CREATED                       DATE
SQL>
```

Let's create the STATE table. Notice that multiple column constraints can be defined only at the table level.

```
SQL> CREATE TABLE state (
  2  state_code    VARCHAR2 (3),
  3  state_name    VARCHAR2 (40) NOT NULL,
  4  country_code  NUMBER (4) REFERENCES country,
  5  capital_city  VARCHAR2 (40),
  6  created       DATE DEFAULT SYSDATE,
  7  CONSTRAINT pk_state PRIMARY KEY
  8    (country_code, state_code));
Table created.
SQL>
```

Because you did not provide a name for the COUNTRY_CODE foreign key, Oracle assigns a name. To rename this constraint to provide a meaningful name, you can use the ALTER TABLE statement as you did before. To demonstrate dropping a constraint and re-creating it using ALTER TABLE, let's drop this constraint and then add it. So, find the constraint name from the USER_CONSTRAINTS view to drop and re-create it:

```
SQL> SELECT constraint_name, constraint_type
  2  FROM   user_constraints
```

```
  3  WHERE  table_name = 'STATE';

CONSTRAINT_NAME                  C
------------------------------  -
SYS_C002811                      C
PK_STATE                         P
SYS_C002813                      R

SQL> ALTER TABLE state DROP CONSTRAINT SYS_C002813;
Table altered.
SQL> ALTER TABLE state ADD CONSTRAINT fk_state
  2  FOREIGN KEY (country_code) REFERENCES country;
Table altered.
SQL>
```

Now you'll create the CITY table. Notice the foreign key constraint is created with the ON DELETE CASCADE clause:

```
SQL> CREATE TABLE city (
  2  city_code     VARCHAR2 (6),
  3  city_name     VARCHAR2 (40) NOT NULL,
  4  country_code  NUMBER (4) NOT NULL,
  5  state_code    VARCHAR2 (3) NOT NULL,
  6  population    NUMBER (15),
  7  created       DATE DEFAULT SYSDATE,
  8  constraint    pk_city PRIMARY KEY (city_code),
  9  constraint    fk_city FOREIGN KEY
 10                (country_code, state_code)
 11                REFERENCES state ON DELETE CASCADE);
Table created.
SQL>
```

Summary

Tables are the basic structure of data storage. A table comprises columns and rows, as in a spreadsheet. Each column has a characteristic that restricts and verifies the data it stores. You can use several datatypes to define columns. CHAR, NCHAR, VARCHAR2, CLOB, and NCLOB are the character datatypes. BLOB, BFILE, and RAW are the binary datatypes. DATE, TIMESTAMP, and INTERVAL are the date datatypes. TIMESTAMP datatypes can store the time-zone information also. NUMBER, BINARY_FLOAT, and BINARY_DOUBLE are the numeric datatypes.

You use the CREATE TABLE statement to create a new table. A table should have at least one column, and a datatype should be assigned to the column. The table name and column name should begin with a letter and can contain letters, numbers, or special characters. You can create a new table from an existing table using the CREATE TABLE … AS SELECT… (CTAS) statement. You can add, modify, or drop columns from an existing table using the ALTER TABLE statement.

Constraints are created in the database to enforce business rules and to specify relationships between various tables. NOT NULL constraints can be defined only with a column definition and are used to prevent NULL values (an absence of data). Check constraints are used to verify whether the data conforms to certain conditions. Primary key constraints uniquely identify a row in the table. There can be only one primary key for a table, and the columns in the primary key cannot have NULL values. A unique key is similar to a primary key, but you can have more than one unique key in a table, as well as NULL values in the unique key columns.

You can enable and disable constraints using the ALTER TABLE statement. The constraint can be in four different states. ENABLE VALIDATE is the default state.

Exam Essentials

Understand datatypes.   Know each datatype's limitations and accepted values. Concentrate on the new TIMESTAMP and INTERVAL datatypes.

Know how date arithmetic works.   Know the resulting datatype of date arithmetic, especially between INTERVAL and DATE datatypes.

Know how to modify column characteristics.   Understand how to change datatypes, add and modify constraints, and make other modifications.

Understand the rules associated with changing the datatype definitions of columns with rows in a table.   When the table is not empty, you can change a datatype only from CHAR to VARCHAR2, and vice versa. Reducing the length is allowed only if the existing data fits in the new length specified.

Understand the DEFAULT clause on the column definition.   The DEFAULT clause provides a value for the column if the INSERT statement omits a value for the column. When modifying a column to have default values, the existing rows with NULL values in the table are not updated with the default value.

Know the actions permitted on read-only tables.   Understand the various actions that are permitted on a read-only table. Any operation that changes the data in the table is not allowed on a read-only table. Most DDL statements are allowed, including DROP TABLE.

Understand constraints.   Know the difference between a primary key and a unique key constraint, and understand how to use a nonunique index for primary/unique keys.

Know how a constraint can be defined.   You can use the CREATE TABLE or ALTER TABLE statement to define a constraint on the table.

Review Questions

1. The STATE table has the following constraints (the constraint status is shown in parentheses):

Primary key	pk_state (enabled)
Foreign key	COUNTRY table: fk_state (enabled)
Check constraint	ck_cnt_code (disabled)
Check constraint	ck_st_code (enabled)
NOT NULL constraint	nn_st_name (enabled)

You execute the following SQL code:

```
CREATE TABLE STATE_NEW AS SELECT * FROM STATE;
```

How many constraints will there be in the new table?

A. 0

B. 1

C. 3

D. 5

E. 2

2. Which line of code has an error?

```
1.   CREATE TABLE FRUITS_VEGETABLES
2.   (FRUIT_TYPE VARCHAR2,
3.    FRUIT_NAME CHAR (20),
4.    QUANTITY   NUMBER);
```

A. 1

B. 2

C. 3

D. 4

3. Which statement successfully adds a new column, ORDER_DATE, to the table ORDERS?

    A. `ALTER TABLE ORDERS ADD COLUMN ORDER_DATE DATE;`

    B. `ALTER TABLE ORDERS ADD ORDER_DATE (DATE);`

    C. `ALTER TABLE ORDERS ADD ORDER_DATE DATE;`

    D. `ALTER TABLE ORDERS NEW COLUMN ORDER_DATE TYPE DATE;`

4. What special characters are allowed in a table name? (Choose all that apply.)

    A. &

    B. #

    C. @

    D. $

5. Consider the following statement:

```
CREATE TABLE MY_TABLE (
1ST_COLUMN  NUMBER,
2ND_COLUMN  VARCHAR2 (20));
```

Which of the following best describes this statement?

    A. Tables cannot be created without defining a primary key. The primary key is missing form the table definition.

    B. The reserved word COLUMN cannot be part of the column name.

    C. The column names are invalid.

    D. No maximum length is specified for the first column definition. You must always specify a length for character and numeric columns.

    E. There is no error in the statement.

6. Which dictionary view would you query to list only the tables you own?

    A. `ALL_TABLES`

    B. `DBA_TABLES`

    C. `USER_TABLES`

    D. `USR_TABLES`

7. The STATE table has six rows. You issue the following command:

```
ALTER TABLE STATE ADD UPDATE_DT DATE DEFAULT SYSDATE;
```

Which of the following is correct?

A. A new column, UPDATE_DT, is added to the STATE, table, and its contents for the existing rows are NULL.

B. Because the table is not empty, you cannot add a new column.

C. The DEFAULT value cannot be provided if the table has rows.

D. A new column, UPDATE_DT, is added to STATE, and its default value is saved in the dictionary.

8. The HIRING table has the following data:

```
EMPNO      HIREDATE
---------  ----------
1021       12-DEC-00
3400       24-JAN-01
2398       30-JUN-01
```

What will be result of the following query?

```
SELECT hiredate+1 FROM hiring WHERE empno = 3400;
```

A. 4-FEB-01

B. 25-JAN-01

C. N-02

D. None of the above

9. What is the default length of a CHAR column if no length is specified in the table definition?

A. 256

B. 1,000

C. 64

D. 1

E. You must always specify a length for CHAR columns.

10. Which statement will remove the column UPDATE_DT from the table STATE?

A. ALTER TABLE STATE DROP COLUMN UPDATE_DT;

B. ALTER TABLE STATE REMOVE COLUMN UPDATE_DT;

C. DROP COLUMN UPDATE_DT FROM STATE;

D. ALTER TABLE STATE SET UNUSED COLUMN UPDATE_DT;

E. You cannot drop a column from the table.

11. Which actions are allowed on a table that is marked as read-only? (Choose all that apply.)

    A. Truncating a table

    B. Inserting new data

    C. Dropping a constraint

    D. Dropping an index

    E. Dropping a table

12. Which of the following statements will create a primary key for the `CITY` table with the columns `STATE_CD` and `CITY_CD`?

    A. `CREATE PRIMARY KEY ON CITY (STATE_CD, CITY_CD);`

    B. `CREATE CONSTRAINT PK_CITY PRIMARY KEY ON CITY (STATE_CD, CITY_CD);`

    C. `ALTER TABLE CITY ADD CONSTRAINT PK_CITY PRIMARY KEY (STATE_CD, CITY_CD);`

    D. `ALTER TABLE CITY ADD PRIMARY KEY (STATE_CD, CITY_CD);`

    E. `ALTER TABLE CITY ADD PRIMARY KEY CONSTRAINT PK_CITY ON (STATE_CD, CITY_CD);`

13. Which of the following check constraints will raise an error? (Choose all that apply.)

    A. `CONSTRAINT ck_gender CHECK (gender IN ('M', 'F'))`

    B. `CONSTRAINT ck_old_order CHECK (order_date > (SYSDATE -30))`

    C. `CONSTRAINT ck_vendor CHECK (vendor_id IN (SELECT vendor_id FROM vendors))`

    D. `CONSTRAINT ck_profit CHECK (gross_amt > net_amt)`

14. Consider the datatypes DATE, TIMESTAMP (TS), TIMESTAMP WITH LOCAL TIME ZONE (TSLTZ), INTERVAL YEAR TO MONTH (IY2M), and INTERVAL DAY TO SECOND (ID2S). Which operations are not allowed by Oracle Database 12*c*? (Choose all that apply.)

    A. DATE+DATE

    B. TSLTZ–DATE

    C. TSLTZ+IY2M

    D. TS*5

    E. ID2S/2

    F. IY2M+IY2M

    G. ID2S+IY2M

    H. DATE–IY2M

15. A constraint is created with the `DEFERRABLE INITIALLY IMMEDIATE` clause. What does this mean?

   A. Constraint checking is done only at commit time.

   B. Constraint checking is done after each SQL statement is executed, but you can change this behavior by specifying `SET CONSTRAINTS ALL DEFERRED`.

   C. Existing rows in the table are immediately checked for constraint violation.

   D. The constraint is immediately checked in a DML operation, but subsequent constraint verification is done at commit time.

16. What is the default precision for fractional seconds in a TIMESTAMP datatype column?

   A. 0

   B. 2

   C. 6

   D. 9

17. Which datatype shows the time-zone information along with the date value?

   A. TIMESTAMP

   B. TIMESTAMP WITH LOCAL TIME ZONE

   C. TIMESTAMP WITH TIME ZONE

   D. DATE

   E. Both options B and C

18. You have a large job that will load many thousands of rows into your ORDERS table. To speed up the loading process, you want to temporarily stop enforcing the foreign key constraint FK_ORDERS. Which of the following statements will satisfy your requirement?

   A. `ALTER CONSTRAINT FK_ORDERS DISABLE;`

   B. `ALTER TABLE ORDERS DISABLE FOREIGN KEY FK_ORDERS;`

   C. `ALTER TABLE ORDERS DISABLE CONSTRAINT FK_ORDERS;`

   D. `ALTER TABLE ORDERS DISABLE ALL CONSTRAINTS;`

19. You are connected to the database as user JOHN. You need to rename a table named NORDERS to NEW_ORDERS, owned by SMITH. Consider the following two statements:

1. RENAME SMITH.NORDERS TO NEW_ORDERS;

2. ALTER TABLE SMITH.NORDERS RENAME TO NEW_ORDERS;

Which of the following is correct?

A. Statement 1 will work; statement 2 will not.

B. Statements 1 and 2 will work.

C. Statement 1 will not work; statement 2 will work.

D. Statements 1 and 2 will not work.

20. Tom executed the following SQL statement.

```
create table xx (n number, x long, y clob);
```

Choose the best option.

A. A table named xx will be created.

B. Single-character column names are not allowed in table definitions.

C. When using the LONG datatype, other LOB datatypes cannot be used in table definitions.

D. The size needs to be specified in one of the datatypes used in the column definition.

Oracle Database 12*c*: Installation and Administration

PART

II

Chapter

8

Introducing Oracle Database 12*c* Components and Architecture

ORACLE DATABASE 12*c*: OCA EXAM OBJECTIVES COVERED IN THIS CHAPTER:

✓ **Exploring the Oracle Database Architecture**

- ▪ List the architectural components of Oracle Database.

- ▪ Explain the memory structures.

- ▪ Describe the background processes.

- ▪ Explain the relationship between logical and physical storage structures.

✓ **Oracle Database Management Tools**

- ▪ Use database management tools.

With this chapter, you'll start learning Oracle Database 12*c* (Oracle 12*c*) database administration. This chapter and the remaining chapters of the book will discuss the objectives for the *Oracle Database 12c: Installation and Administration* OCA certification exam. There are two parts to the exam: *Oracle Database Administration* and *Installing, Upgrading, and Patching the Oracle Database*. The book's chapters are organized to give you a natural progression from the basics, installation, database creation, basic administration, and on to advanced topics, not necessarily organized in the order of examination objectives specified by Oracle.

With the release of Oracle Database 12*c*, the Oracle Corporation has delivered a powerful and feature-rich database that can meet the performance, availability, recoverability, multitenancy, cloud-enabled, application-testing, and security requirements of any mission-critical application. As the Oracle DBA, you are responsible for managing and maintaining the Oracle Database 12*c* environment throughout its lifecycle, from the initial installation through creation, configuration, final deployment, and its daily administration. Performing these tasks requires a solid understanding of Oracle's product offerings so that you can apply the proper tools and features to the application. You must also use relational database concepts to design, implement, and maintain the tables that store the application data. At the heart of these activities is the need for a thorough understanding of the Oracle architecture and the tools and techniques used to monitor and manage the components of this architecture.

We will begin this chapter by reviewing the Oracle database basics. You will learn what constitutes the Oracle Database 12*c* architecture. We'll provide an overview of the memory structures, the processes that manage the database, how data is stored in the database, and the many pluggable databases in a consolidated cloud database. We will also discuss the tools used to administer Oracle Database 12*c*.

In this chapter, you will see many examples of using the database to show information from the database, and you might wonder, "Why are you doing this without first showing me how to create a database?" It is a chicken-and-egg situation; we think knowing the basic components and high-level architecture will help you better understand the database and create options. So, you will learn the architecture basics in this chapter and actually create a database in the next chapter.

Exam objectives are subject to change at any time without prior notice and at Oracle's sole discretion. Please visit Oracle's Training and Certification website at `http://education.oracle.com` for the most current exam-objectives listing.

Oracle Database Fundamentals

Databases store data. The data itself is composed of related logical units of information. The *database management system* (DBMS) facilitates the storage, modification, and retrieval of this data. Some early database technologies used flat files or hierarchical file structures to store application data. Others used networks of connections between sets of data to store and locate information. The early DBMS architecture mixed the physical manipulation of data with its logical manipulation. When the location of data changed, the application referencing the data had to be updated. Relational databases brought a revolutionary change to this architecture. Relational DBMS introduced data independence, which separated the physical model of the data from its logical model. Oracle is a relational DBMS.

All releases of Oracle's database products have used a relational DBMS model to store data in the database. This relational model is based on the groundbreaking work of Dr. Edgar Codd, which was first published in 1970 in his paper "A Relational Model of Data for Large Shared Data Banks." IBM Corporation, which was then an early adopter of Dr. Codd's model, helped develop the computer language that is used to access all relational databases today—Structured Query Language (SQL). The great thing about SQL is that you can use it to easily interact with relational databases without having to write complex computer programs and without needing to know where or how the data is physically stored on disk. You saw several SQL statements in the previous chapters.

Relational Databases

The concept of a *relational database management system* (RDBMS) is that the data consists of a set of relational objects. The basic storage of data in a database is a table. The relations are implemented in tables, where data is stored in rows and columns. Figure 8.1 shows such a relationship.

The DEPT table in the lower part of the figure stores information about departments in the company. Each department is identified by the department ID. Along with the ID, the name and location of the department are also stored in the table. The EMP table stores information about the employees in the company. Each employee is identified by a unique employee ID. This table includes employee information such as hire date, salary, manager, and so on. The DEPTNO column in both tables provides a relationship between the tables. A department may have many employees, but an employee can work for only one department.

Because the user accessing this data doesn't need to know how or where the row is stored in the database, there must be a way to uniquely identify the rows in the tables. In our example, the department is uniquely identified by department number, and an employee is identified by an employee ID. The column (or set of columns) that uniquely identifies a row is known as the *primary key*. According to relational theory, each table in a relational database must have a primary key.

FIGURE 8.1   Relational tables

EMP (Employee Table)

EMPNO	ENAME	JOB	MGR	HIREDATE	SAL	COMM	DEPTNO
7369	SMITH	CLERK	7902	17-DEC -8	0800		20
7499	ALLEN	SALESMAN	7698	20-FEB-8	11600	300	30
7521	WARD	SALESMAN	7698	22-FEB-8	11250	500	30
7566	JONES	MANAGER	7839	02-APR-8	12975		20
7654	MARTIN	SALESMAN	7698	28-SEP-8	11250	1400	30
7698	BLAKE	MANAGER	7839	07-MAY-8	12850		30
7844	URNER	SALESMAN	7698	08-SEP-8	11500		30

Primary Key
Column

Foreign Key
Column

DEPT (Department Table)

DEPTNO	DNAME	LOC
10	ACCOUNTING	NEW YORK
20	RESEARCH	DALLAS
30	SALES	CHICAGO
40	OPERATIONS	BOSTON

Primary Key
Column

When relating tables together, the primary key of one table is placed in another table. For example, the primary key of the DEPT table is a column in the EMP table. In RDBMS terminology, this is known as a *foreign key*. A foreign key states that the data value in the column exists in another table and should continue to exist in the other table to keep the relationship between tables. The table where the column is a primary key is known as the *parent table*, and the table where the foreign key column exists is known as the *child table*. Oracle enforces the parent-child relationship between tables using *constraints*.

Oracle Database 12*c* Objects

Every RDBMS supports a variety of database objects. Oracle Database 12*c* supports the entire set of database objects required for a relational and object-relational database, such as tables, views, constraints, and so on. It also supports a wide range of objects specific to the Oracle database, such as packages, sequences, materialized views, and so on. Table 8.1 lists the major commonly used objects in Oracle Database 12*c*.

TABLE 8.1 Oracle Database 12c Objects

Object Type	Description
Table	A table is the basic form of data storage. A table has columns and stores rows of data.
View	A view is a stored query. No data-storage space is occupied for view data.
Index	An index is an optional structure that is useful for fetching data faster.
Materialized view	Materialized views are used to summarize and store data. They are similar to views but take up storage space to store data.
Index-organized table	An index-organized table stores the table data along with the index, instead of storing table and index separately.
Cluster	A cluster is a group of tables sharing a common column. The cluster stores the rows of the tables together with the common columns stored once.
Constraint	A constraint is a stored rule to enforce data integrity.
Sequence	A sequence provides a mechanism for the continuous generation of numbers.
Synonym	A synonym is an alias for a database schema object.
Trigger	A trigger is a PL/SQL program unit that is executed when an event occurs.
Stored function	Stored functions are PL/SQL programs that can be used to create user-defined functions to return a value.
Stored procedure	Stored procedures are PL/SQL programs to define a business process.
Package	A package is a collection of procedures, functions, and other program constructs.
Java	Stored Java procedures can be created in Oracle to define business processes.
Database link	Database links are used to communicate between databases to share data.

You use SQL to create database objects and to interact with application data. In the next section, we will discuss the tools available to access and administer Oracle Database 12*c*.

Interacting with Oracle Database 12*c*

Several Oracle database management tools are available for the DBA to interact with and manage Oracle Database 12*c*. SQL is the language used to interact with Oracle Database 12*c*. The common tools available for the DBA to administer Oracle Database 12*c* are as follows:

▪ *SQL*Plus*, which is a SQL command-line interface utility

▪ *SQL Developer*, a GUI tool to explore and manage the database using predefined menu actions and SQL statements

▪ *Oracle Enterprise Manager Database Express* 12c, a GUI tool for database administration and performance management

Using SQL*Plus and SQL Developer, you interact directly with Oracle Database 12*c* using SQL statements and a superset of commands such as STARTUP, SHUTDOWN, and so on. Using Enterprise Manager, you interact indirectly with Oracle Database 12*c*.

SQL*Plus

SQL*Plus is the primary tool for an Oracle DBA to administer the database using SQL commands. Before you can run SQL statements, you must connect to Oracle Database 12*c*. You can start SQL*Plus from a Windows command prompt using the SQLPLUS.EXE executable or using the $ORACLE_HOME/bin/sqlplus executable on the Unix/Linux platform. Figure 8.2 shows connecting to SQL*Plus from a Linux workstation.

FIGURE 8.2   SQL*Plus login in Linux

```
[samuel@btlnx63 ~]$ sqlplus system

SQL*Plus: Release 12.1.0.1.0 Production on Sun Aug 25 11:49:47 2013

Copyright (c) 1982, 2013, Oracle.  All rights reserved.

Enter password:
Last Successful login time: Sun Aug 25 2013 11:47:34 -05:00

Connected to:
Oracle Database 12c Enterprise Edition Release 12.1.0.1.0 - 64bit Production
With the Partitioning, OLAP, Advanced Analytics and Real Application Testing opt
ions

SQL> SELECT db_unique_name, cdb FROM v$database;

DB_UNIQUE_NAME                    CDB
------------------------------    ---
C12DB1                            YES

SQL> SHOW USER
USER is "SYSTEM"
SQL>
```

To get an overview of SQL*Plus and how to connect to the database using SQL*Plus, refer to Chapter 2, "Introducing SQL."

SQL Developer

SQL Developer is a GUI database-development tool. With SQL Developer, you can create and view the database objects, make changes to the objects, run SQL statements, run PL/SQL programs, create and edit PL/SQL programs, and perform PL/SQL debugging. SQL Developer also includes a migration utility to migrate Microsoft Access and Microsoft SQL Server databases to Oracle Database 12*c*. Figure 8.3 shows the object browser screen of SQL Developer.

FIGURE 8.3   The SQL Developer screen

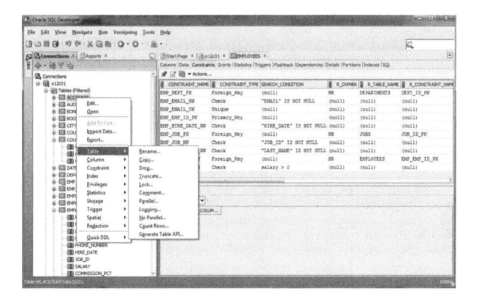

You can download and learn more about SQL Developer on the OTN website (http://www.oracle.com/technetwork/developer-tools/sql-developer). SQL Developer is installed by default with your Oracle Database 12*c* tool set.

Enterprise Manager Database Express 12*c*

Oracle Enterprise Manager (EM) Database Express is a web-based database management tool that is bundled with Oracle Database 12*c*. This is a graphical tool specifically designed to administer an Oracle database. Enterprise Manager Database Express is used to manage a single database (single instance or cluster database), whereas Enterprise Manager Cloud Control 12*c* can manage multiple databases and other services and applications, such as OAS, and even non-Oracle applications at the same time. Figure 8.4 shows the Enterprise Manager Database Express home screen, where an overview of the database is shown.

FIGURE 8.4   The Enterprise Manager home screen

EM Database Express is configured using a check box in Database Configuration Assistant when you're creating a new database. EM Database Express requires that XMLDB be installed in the database. The default port configured is 5,500, and the URL for EM Database Express is https://<hostname>:5500/em. The port can be changed using the DBMS_XDB_CONFIG.setHTTPsPort (<port>) procedure.

EM Database Express is available only when the database is open. Therefore, this tool cannot be used to start or stop a database.

Oracle Enterprise Manager (OEM) Cloud Control is installed separately, outside of the Oracle Database 12c install. Agents are installed on each server that is configured in OEM Cloud Control. To learn more about OEM Cloud Control, visit http://www.oracle.com/technetwork/oem.

For all the database-administration examples in this chapter, you can use either SQL*Plus to perform the SQL command line or use the GUI tool Enterprise Manager Database Express. All the commands you run using SQL*Plus can also be performed using SQL Developer. However, if there are any administrative tasks that can be performed using predefined menu options in SQL Developer, we will show that. Before you start learning to administer Oracle Database 12c, let's start with the basics. In the next section, you'll learn about Oracle 12c architecture.

Oracle Database 12*c* Architecture

All of the previously described database administration and development tools allow users to interact with the database. Using these tools requires that user accounts be created in the database and that connectivity to the database be in place across the network. Users must also have adequate storage capacity for the data they add, and they need recovery mechanisms for restoring the transactions they are performing in the event of a hardware failure. As the DBA, you take care of each of these tasks, as well as others, which include the following:

- Selecting the server hardware on which the database software will run
- Installing and configuring the Oracle Database 12*c* software on the server hardware
- Deciding to use Oracle Database 12*c* Container or a traditional single database (now known as non-Pluggable Database (PDB).
- Creating Oracle Database 12*c* database
- Creating and managing the tables and other objects used to manage the application data
- Creating and managing database users
- Establishing reliable backup and recovery procedure for the database
- Monitoring and tuning database performance
- Analyzing trends and forecasting resource and storage requirements

The remainder of this book is dedicated to helping you understand how to perform these and other important Oracle database-administration tasks. But first, to succeed as an Oracle DBA, you need to completely understand Oracle's underlying architecture and its mechanisms. Understanding the relationship between Oracle's memory structures, background processes, and I/O activities is critical before learning how to manage these areas.

The Oracle server architecture can be described in three categories:

- Server processes that communicate with users processes and interact with an Oracle instance to fulfill requests
- Logical memory structures that are collectively called an *Oracle instance*
- Physical file structures that are collectively called a *database*

You will also see how the physical structures map to the logical structures of the database you are familiar with, such as tables and indexes.

Database is a confusing term that is often used to represent different things on different platforms; the only commonality is that it is something related to storing data. In Oracle, however, the term *database* represents the physical files that store data. An *instance* is composed of the memory structures and background processes. Each database should have at least one instance associated with it. It is possible for multiple instances to access a single database; such a configuration is known as Real Application Clusters (RAC). In this book, however, you'll concentrate only on single-instance databases because RAC is not part of the OCA certification exam.

Figure 8.5 shows the parts of an Oracle instance and database at a high level. Although the architecture in Figure 8.5 may at first seem complex, each of these architecture components is described in more detail in the following sections, beginning with the user-related processes, and is actually fairly simple. This figure is an important piece of fundamental information when learning about the Oracle Database 12c architecture.

The key database components are memory structures, process structures, and storage structures. Process and memory structures together are called an *instance*; the storage structure is called a *database*. Taken together, the instance and the database are called an *Oracle server*.

FIGURE 8.5   The Oracle Database 12c architecture

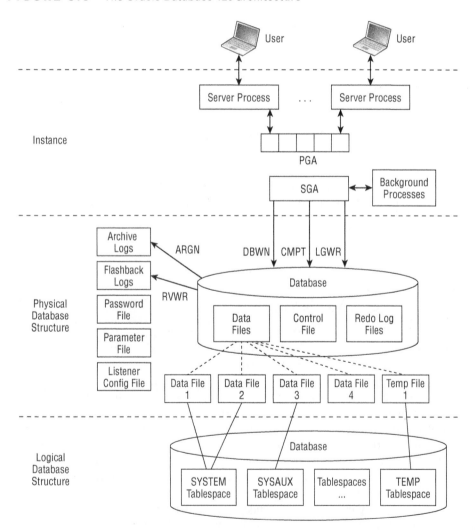

Each Oracle database consists of several schemas that reside in tablespaces. *Tablespace* is a logical storage structure at the highest level in the database. Each tablespace consists of one or more data files. The database has user data and overhead, such as database dictionary, memory, control files, archived log files, flashback files, etc. Do not worry if you do not understand these components yet; you will get to know them in the next few chapters.

Oracle Database 12c comes with a major architectural change compared to its predecessors. Oracle Database 12c allows multitenancy, meaning, you can have more than one database in a structure called a *container database*. The database overhead will be shared by all the databases in the container database. The databases in the container database are called *pluggable databases*. Administration and resource overhead are reduced by going with this architecture. Figure 8.6 shows database multitenancy.

FIGURE 8.6 Oracle Database 12c multitenancy

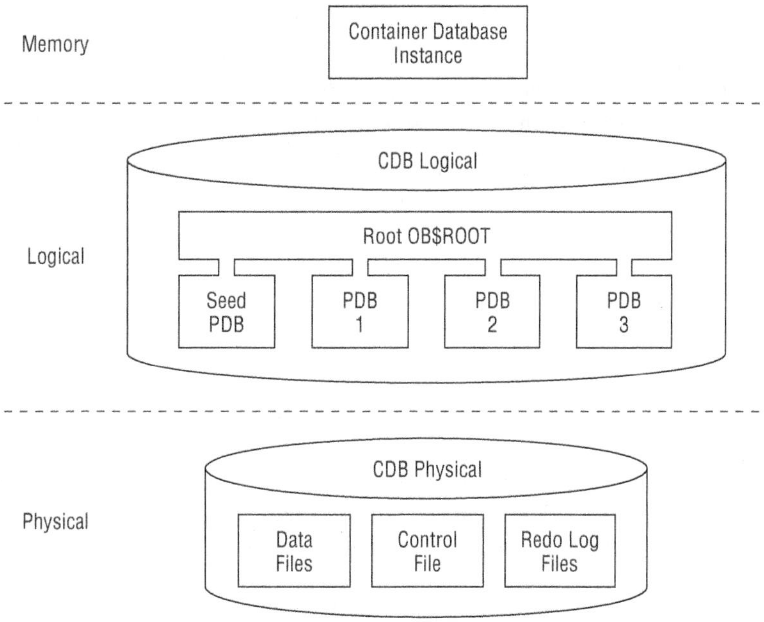

More on container and pluggable databases will be discussed in Chapter 9, "Creating and Operating Oracle Database 12c."

What Is a Schema?

When working with Oracle, you will often hear the words *schema* and *user* used interchangeably. Is there a difference between the two? Yes and no. A user is a defined database entity that has a set of abilities to perform activities based on their granted rights. A schema, which is associated with a user entity, is more appropriately defined as a collection of database objects. Some examples of database objects are tables, indexes, and views.

A schema can be related to a real person, such as a user of your Sales database who may have a user ID and password they use to access the database. This user may or may not own any schema objects.

Because a schema is a collection of objects, DBAs often define a schema to represent a collection of objects associated with an application. For example, a DBA might create a schema called SALES and create objects owned by that schema. Then, they can grant access to other database users who need the ability to access the SALES schema.

In this way, the schema becomes a logical collection of objects associated with an application and is not tied to any specific user. This ability makes it easy to logically group common objects that are related to specific applications or tasks using a common schema name.

The main difference is that users are the entities that perform work, and schemas are the collections of objects on which users perform work.

User and Server Processes

At the user level, two types of processes allow a user to interact with the instance and, ultimately, with the database: the *user process* and the *server process*.

Whenever a user runs an application, such as a human-resources or order-taking application, Oracle starts a user process to support the user's connection to the instance. Depending on the technical architecture of the application, the user process exists either on the user's own computer or on the middle-tier application server. The user process then initiates a connection to the instance. Oracle calls the process of initiating and maintaining communication between the user process and the instance a *connection*. Once the connection is made, the user establishes a *session* in the instance.

After establishing a session, each user starts a server process on the host server itself. It is this server process that is responsible for performing the tasks that actually allow the user to interact with the database. The server processes are allowed to interact with the instance, but not the user process directly.

Examples of these interactions include sending SQL statements to the database, retrieving needed data from the database's physical files, and returning that data to the user.

Server processes generally have a one-to-one relationship with user processes—in other words, each user process connects to one and only one server process. However, in some Oracle configurations, multiple user processes can share a single server process. We will discuss Oracle connection configurations in Chapter 12, "Understanding Oracle Network Architecture."

On a Unix system, it is easier to distinguish these processes. Here is an example. User initiates SQL*Plus to connect to Oracle database. You can see the process that starts SQL*Plus (user process with process ID 10604) by *samuel*. This in turn starts another process that connects to the instance (server process with process ID 10606) owned by database server user *oracle*.

```
$ ps -ef |grep sqlplus | grep -v grep
samuel   10604 10511  0 01:51 pts/2     00:00:00 sqlplus


$ ps -ef |grep 10604 | grep -v grep
samuel   10604 10511  0 01:51 pts/2     00:00:00 sqlplus
oracle   10606 10604  0 01:52 ?         00:00:00 oracleC12DB1
(DESCRIPTION=(LOCAL=YES)(ADDRESS=(PROTOCOL=beq)))
```

In addition to the user and server processes that are associated with each user connection, an additional memory structure called the *program global area* (PGA) is also created for each server process. The PGA stores user-specific session information such as bind variables and session variables. Every server process on the server has a PGA memory area. Figure 8.7 shows the relationship between a user process, server processes, and the PGA.

FIGURE 8.7   The relationship between user and server processes and the PGA

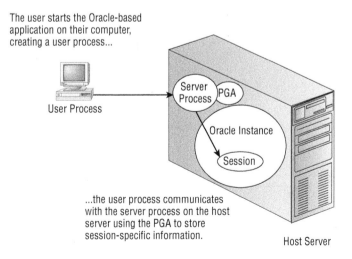

PGA memory is not shared. Each server process has a PGA associated with it and is exclusive. As a DBA, you set the total memory that can be allocated to all the PGA memory allocated to all server and background processes. The components of PGA are

SQL Work Area   Area used for memory-intensive operations such as sorting or building a hash table during join operations.

Private SQL Area   Holds information about SQL statement and bind variable values.

The PGA can be configured to manage automatically by setting the database parameter `PGA_AGGREGATE_TARGET`. Oracle then contains the total amount of PGA memory allocated across all database server processes and background processes within this target.

The server process communicates with the Oracle instance on behalf of the user. The Oracle instance is examined in the next section.

The Oracle Instance

An Oracle database instance consists of Oracle's main memory structure, called the *system global area* (SGA, also known as *shared global area*) and several Oracle background processes. When the user accesses the data in the database, it is the SGA with which the server process communicates. Figure 8.8 shows the components of the SGA.

The components of the instance are described in the following sections.

Oracle Memory Structures

The SGA is a shared memory area. All the users of the database share the information maintained in this area. Oracle allocates memory for the SGA when the instance is started and de-allocates it when the instance is shut down. The SGA consists of three mandatory components and four optional components. Table 8.2 describes the required components.

TABLE 8.2   Required SGA Components

SGA Component	Description
Shared pool	Caches the most recently used SQL statements that have been issued by database users
Database buffer cache	Caches the data that has been most recently accessed by database users
Redo log buffer	Stores transaction information for recovery purposes

FIGURE 8.8 SGA components

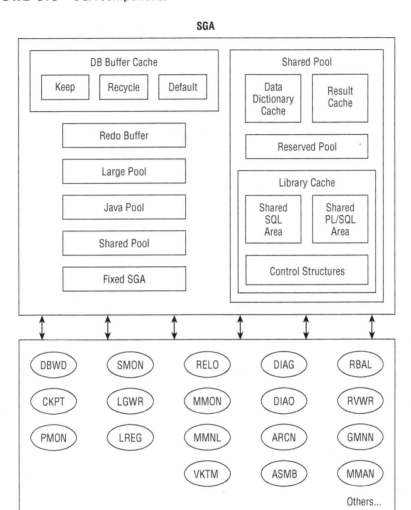

Background Processes

Table 8.3 describes the optional SGA components required, based on the database configuration and use.

TABLE 8.3 Optional SGA Components

SGA Component	Description
Java pool	Caches the most recently used Java objects and application code when Oracle's JVM option is used.
Large pool	Caches data for large operations such as Recovery Manager (RMAN) backup and restore activities and Shared Server components.
Streams pool	Caches the data associated with queued message requests when Oracle's Advanced Queuing option is used.
Result cache	This new area is introduced in Oracle Database 12c and stores results of SQL queries and PL/SQL functions for better performance.

Oracle Database 12c can manage the components of SGA and PGA automatically using the Automatic Memory Management (AMM) feature. Memory in the SGA is allocated in units of contiguous memory called *granules*. The size of a granule depends on the parameter MEMORY_MAX_TARGET. If MEMORY_MAX_TARGET is larger than 1,024MB, the granule size is either 16MB or 4MB. MEMORY_MAX_TARGET is discussed in detail in Chapter 14, "Maintaining the Database and Managing Performance." A minimum of three granules must be allocated to SGA—one each for the required components in Table 8.2.

The sizes of these SGA components can be managed in two ways: manually or automatically. If you choose to manage these components manually, you must specify the size of each SGA component and then increase or decrease the size of each component according to the needs of the application. If these components are managed automatically, the instance itself will monitor the utilization of each SGA component and adjust their sizes accordingly, relative to a predefined maximum allowable aggregate SGA size.

Oracle Database 12c provides several dynamic performance views to see the components and sizes of SGA; you can use V$SGA and V$SGAINFO, as shown here:

```
SQL> select * from v$sga;

NAME                       VALUE     CON_ID
-------------------- ---------- ----------
Fixed Size              2290368          0
Variable Size         620760384          0
Database Buffers     1694498816          0
Redo Buffers           20762624          0
```

Alternatively, you may use the SHOW SGA command from SQL*Plus, as shown here:

```
SQL> show sga
```

```
Total System Global Area 2338312192 bytes
Fixed Size                  2290368 bytes
Variable Size             620760384 bytes
Database Buffers         1694498816 bytes
Redo Buffers               20762624 bytes
SQL>
```

The output from this query shows that the total size of the SGA is 2,338,312,192 bytes. This total size is composed of the variable space that is composed of the shared pool, the large pool, and the Java pool (620,760,384 bytes); the database buffer cache (1,694,498,816 bytes); the redo log buffers (20,762,624 bytes); and some additional space (2,290,368 bytes) that stores information used by the instance's background processes. The V$SGAINFO view displays additional details about the allocation of space within the SGA, as shown in the following query:

```
SQL> SELECT * FROM v$sgainfo;

NAME                                   BYTES RES     CON_ID
------------------------------- ----------- ---  ----------
Fixed SGA Size                       2290368 No           0
Redo Buffers                        20762624 No           0
Buffer Cache Size                1694498816 Yes           0
Shared Pool Size                  570425344 Yes           0
Large Pool Size                    33554432 Yes           0
Java Pool Size                     16777216 Yes           0
Streams Pool Size                         0 Yes           0
Shared IO Pool Size               117440512 Yes           0
Data Transfer Cache Size                  0 Yes           0
Granule Size                       16777216 No           0
Maximum SGA Size                 2338312192 No           0
Startup Overhead in Shared Pool   149697048 No           0
Free SGA Memory Available                 0               0

13 rows selected.

SQL>
```

The results of this query show in detail how much space is occupied by each component in the shared pool. The components with the RESIZEABLE column with a value of Yes can be managed dynamically by Oracle Database 12*c*.

You can also use EM Database Express to view the sizes of each of the SGA components, as shown in Figure 8.9. From the home screen, go to the Server tab and click Memory Advisors to see this.

FIGURE 8.9   EM Database Express showing SGA components

You'll learn more about the components in the SGA in the next sections.

Database Buffer Cache

The *database buffer cache* is the area in SGA that caches the database data, holding blocks from the data files that have been accessed recently. The database buffer cache is shared among all the users connected to the database. There are three types of buffers:

- *Dirty buffers* are the buffer blocks that need to be written to the data files. The data in these buffers has changed and has not yet been written to the disk.

- *Free buffers* do not contain any data or are free to be overwritten. When Oracle reads data from the disk, free buffers hold this data.

- *Pinned buffers* are the buffers that are currently being accessed or explicitly retained for future use.

Oracle uses a *least recently used algorithm* (LRU algorithm) to manage the contents of the shared pool and database buffer cache. When a user's server process needs to put a SQL statement into the shared pool or copy a database block into the buffer cache, Oracle uses the space in memory that is occupied by the least recently accessed SQL statement or buffer to hold the requested SQL or block copy. Using this technique, Oracle keeps frequently accessed SQL statements and database buffers in memory longer, improving the overall performance of the server by minimizing parsing and physical disk I/O.

The background process DBW*n* writes the database blocks from the database buffer cache to the data files. Dirty buffers contain data that changed and must be written to disk.

To better manage the buffer cache better, Oracle Database 12*c* provides three buffer caches. The DEFAULT cache is the default and is required. The KEEP cache and the RECYCLE cache can be optionally configured. By default all the data read from the disk is written to the DEFAULT pool. If you want certain data not to be aged from memory, you can configure the KEEP pool and use the ALTER TABLE statement to specify which tables should use the KEEP pool. Similarly, if you do not want to age out good data from the default cache for temporary data, you may specify such tables to have the RECYCLE pool instead of the default. The blocks in the KEEP pool also follow the LRU algorithm to age out blocks when new blocks need space in the KEEP pool. By sizing the KEEP pool appropriately, you can hold frequently used blocks longer in the KEEP pool. The RECYCLE cache removes the buffers from memory as soon as they are no longer needed.

The DB_CACHE_SIZE parameter specifies the size of the database buffer cache DEFAULT pool. To configure the KEEP and RECYCLE pools, use the DB_KEEP_CACHE_SIZE and DB_RECYCLE_CACHE_SIZE parameters.

Since Oracle Database 11g Release 2, Oracle Linux and Oracle Solaris servers make use of the flash storage for additional buffer cache. *Database Smart Flash Cache* allows the database buffer cache to be expanded beyond the SGA in main memory to a second level cache on flash memory. When the block expires from the SGA buffer cache, it is evicted to the database flash cache until required again. Flash cache is configured using two database parameters. DB_FLASH_CACHE_FILE identifies the flash device, and DB_FLASH_CACHE_SIZE specifies the size of flash cache.

Redo Log Buffer

The *redo log buffer* is a circular buffer in the SGA that holds information about the changes made to the database data. The changes are known as *redo entries* or *change vectors* and are used to redo the changes in case of a failure. DML and DDL statements are used to make changes to the database data. The parameter LOG_BUFFER determines the size of the redo log buffer cache.

The background process LGWR writes the redo log information to the online redo log files.

Shared Pool

The *shared pool* portion of the SGA holds information such as SQL, PL/SQL procedures and packages, the data dictionary, locks, character-set information, security attributes, and so on. The shared pool consists of the library cache and the data dictionary cache.

The *library cache* contains the shared SQL areas, private SQL areas, PL/SQL programs, and control structures such as locks and library cache handles.

The *shared SQL area* is used for maintaining recently executed SQL statements and their execution plans. Oracle divides each SQL statement that it executes into a shared SQL area and a private SQL area. When two users are executing the same SQL, the information in the shared SQL area is used for both. The shared SQL area contains the parse tree and execution plan, whereas the private SQL area contains values for the bind variables (persistent area) and runtime buffers (runtime area). Oracle creates the runtime area as the first step of an execute request. For INSERT, UPDATE, and DELETE statements, Oracle frees the runtime area after the statement has been executed. For queries, Oracle frees the runtime area only after all rows have been fetched or the query has been canceled.

Oracle processes PL/SQL program units the same way it processes SQL statements. When a PL/SQL program unit is executed, the code is moved to the *shared PL/SQL area*, and the individual SQL commands within the program unit are moved to the shared SQL area. Again, the shared program units are maintained in memory with an LRU algorithm.

The third area in the library cache is used to store control information and is maintained internally by Oracle. Various locks, latches, and other control structures reside here, and any server process that requires this information can access it.

The *data dictionary cache* holds the most recently used database dictionary information. The data dictionary cache is also known as the *row cache* because it holds data as rows instead of buffers (which hold entire blocks of data).

The SQL query *result cache* stores the results of queries. If an application runs the same SELECT statement repeatedly and if the results are cached, then the database can return them immediately. In this way, the database avoids the expensive operation of rereading blocks to show results.

The PL/SQL function *result cache* is used to hold the SQL and PL/SQL function results. Executions of similar SQL statements can use the cached results to answer query requests. Because retrieving results from the SQL query result cache is faster than rerunning a query, frequently run queries experience a significant performance improvement when their results are cached.

The *reserved pool* is an area in the shared pool used to allocate large chunks of memory. Its size is determined by the SHARED_POOL_RESERVED_SIZE initialization parameter.

The parameter SHARED_POOL_SIZE determines the size of the shared pool.

Large Pool

The *large pool* is an optional area in the SGA that the DBA can configure to provide large memory allocations for specific database operations such as an RMAN backup or restore. The large pool allows Oracle to request large memory allocations from a separate pool to prevent contention from other applications for the same memory. The large pool does not have an LRU list; Oracle Database 12*c* does not attempt to age objects out of the large pool. The parameter LARGE_POOL_SIZE determines the size of the large pool.

Java Pool

The *Java pool* is another optional area in the SGA that the DBA can configure to provide memory for Java operations, just as the shared pool is provided for processing SQL and PL/SQL statements. The parameter JAVA_POOL_SIZE determines the size of the Java pool.

Streams Pool

The *streams pool* is exclusively used by Oracle streams. The STREAMS_POOL_SIZE parameter determines the size of the streams pool.

> If any SGA component size is set smaller than the granule size, the size of the component is rounded to the nearest granule size.

> Oracle Database 12c can manage all the components of the SGA and PGA automatically; there is no need for the DBA to configure each pool individually. You will learn more about automatic memory management in Chapter 14.

Oracle Background Process

Many types of Oracle background processes exist, designed specifically for different functions. Each process performs a specific job in helping to manage an instance. Five Oracle background processes are required by the Oracle instance, and several background processes are optional. The required background processes are found in all Oracle instances. Optional background processes may or may not be used, depending on the features that are being used in the database. Table 8.4 describes the required background processes. The database instance terminates abruptly if you terminate any of these processes (except RECO, DIA0, DIAG—these are restarted automatically if the process dies or is terminated) or if there is an error in one of these processes and Oracle had to shut down the process. The processes are started by default when the instance starts.

TABLE 8.4   Required Oracle Background Processes

Process Name	OS Process	Description
Database Writer	DBW*n* BW*nn*	Writes modified database blocks from the SGA's database buffer cache to the data files on disk.
Checkpoint	CKPT	Updates the data file headers following a checkpoint event.

TABLE 8.4   Required Oracle Background Processes *(continued)*

Process Name	OS Process	Description
Log Writer	LGWR	Writes transaction recovery information from the SGA's redo log buffer to the online redo log files on disk.
Process Monitor	PMON	Cleans up failed user database connections.
System Monitor	SMON	Performs instance recovery following an instance crash, coalesces free space in the database, and manages space used for sorting.
Listener Registration	LREG	Registers information about the database instance and dispatcher processes with the listener.
Recoverer	RECO	Recovers failed transactions that are distributed across multiple databases when using Oracle's distributed database feature.
Memory Monitor	MMON	Gathers and analyzes statistics used by the Automatic Workload Repository feature. See Chapter 14 for more information on using this feature.
Memory Monitor Light	MMNL	Gathers and analyzes statistics used by the Active Session History feature. See Chapter 14 for more information on using this feature.
Virtual Keeper of Time	VKTM	Responsible for providing a wall-clock time (updated every second) and reference-time counter.
Diagnosability	DIAG	Performs diagnostic dumps.
Diagnosability	DIA0	Diagnostic process responsible for hang detection and deadlock resolution.

Table 8.5 describes some of the optional background processes.

TABLE 8.5 Optional Oracle Background Processes

Process Name	OS Process	Description
Archiver	ARC*n*	Copies the transaction recovery information from the redo log files to the archive location. Nearly all production databases use this optional process. You can have up to 30 archival processes (ARC0–ARC9, ARCa–ARCt).
Recovery Writer	RVWR	Writes flashback data to flashback database logs in the fast recovery area.
ASM Disk	ASMB	Present on databases using Automatic Storage Management disks.
ASM Balance	RBAL	Coordinates rebalance activity of disks in an ASM disk group.
Job Queue Monitor	CJQ*n*	Assigns jobs to the job queue processes when using Oracle's job scheduling feature.
Job Queue	J*nnn*	Executes database jobs that have been scheduled using Oracle's job-scheduling feature.
Queue Monitor	QMN*n*	Monitors the messages in the message queue when Oracle's Advanced Queuing feature is used.
Event Monitor	EMNC	Process responsible for event-management coordination and notification.
Flashback Data Archive	FBDA	Archives historical records from a table when the flashback data archive feature is used.
Parallel Query Slave	Q*nnn*	Carries out portions of a larger overall query when Oracle's Parallel Query feature is used.
Dispatcher	D*nnn*	Assigns user's database requests to a queue where they are then serviced by shared server processes when Oracle's Shared Server feature is used. See Chapter 11, "Managing Data and Undo," for details on using shared servers.
Shared Server	S*nnn*	Server processes that are shared among several users when Oracle's Shared Server feature is used. See Chapter 11 for details on using shared servers.

TABLE 8.5 Optional Oracle Background Processes *(continued)*

Process Name	OS Process	Description
Memory Manager	MMAN	Manages the size of each individual SGA component when Oracle's Automatic Shared Memory Management feature is used. See Chapter 14 for more information on using this feature.
Recovery Writer	RVWR	Writes recovery information to disk when Oracle's Flashback Database feature is used. See Chapter 16, "Implementing Database Backups," for details on how to use the Flashback Database feature.
Change Tracking Writer	CTWR	Keeps track of which database blocks have changed when Oracle's incremental Recovery Manager feature is used. See Chapter 16 for details on using Recovery Manager to perform backups.
Space Management Coordinator	SMCO	Coordinates various space management tasks. Worker processes are identified with Wnnn.

On Unix systems, you can view these background processes from the operating system using the ps command, as shown here:

```
$ ps -ef |grep C12DB1
oracle     3623     1  0 Aug24 ?        00:00:05 ora_pmon_C12DB1
oracle     3625     1  0 Aug24 ?        00:00:06 ora_psp0_C12DB1
oracle     3627     1  2 Aug24 ?        00:12:21 ora_vktm_C12DB1
oracle     3631     1  0 Aug24 ?        00:00:01 ora_gen0_C12DB1
oracle     3633     1  0 Aug24 ?        00:00:01 ora_mman_C12DB1
oracle     3637     1  0 Aug24 ?        00:00:01 ora_diag_C12DB1
oracle     3639     1  0 Aug24 ?        00:00:01 ora_dbrm_C12DB1
oracle     3641     1  0 Aug24 ?        00:00:29 ora_dia0_C12DB1
oracle     3643     1  0 Aug24 ?        00:00:12 ora_dbw0_C12DB1
oracle     3645     1  0 Aug24 ?        00:00:06 ora_lgwr_C12DB1
oracle     3647     1  0 Aug24 ?        00:00:10 ora_ckpt_C12DB1
oracle     3649     1  0 Aug24 ?        00:00:12 ora_lg00_C12DB1
oracle     3651     1  0 Aug24 ?        00:00:04 ora_lg01_C12DB1
oracle     3653     1  0 Aug24 ?        00:00:01 ora_smon_C12DB1
oracle     3655     1  0 Aug24 ?        00:00:00 ora_reco_C12DB1
oracle     3657     1  0 Aug24 ?        00:00:01 ora_lreg_C12DB1
oracle     3659     1  0 Aug24 ?        00:00:23 ora_mmon_C12DB1
oracle     3661     1  0 Aug24 ?        00:00:20 ora_mmnl_C12DB1
```

```
oracle     3663     1   0 Aug24 ?        00:00:00 ora_d000_C12DB1
oracle     3679     1   0 Aug24 ?        00:01:39 ora_p000_C12DB1
oracle     3681     1   0 Aug24 ?        00:01:16 ora_p001_C12DB1
oracle     3683     1   0 Aug24 ?        00:00:00 ora_tmon_C12DB1
oracle     3685     1   0 Aug24 ?        00:00:01 ora_tt00_C12DB1
oracle     3687     1   0 Aug24 ?        00:00:00 ora_smco_C12DB1
oracle     3691     1   0 Aug24 ?        00:00:00 ora_aqpc_C12DB1
oracle     3693     1   0 Aug24 ?        00:00:03 ora_w000_C12DB1
oracle     3697     1   0 Aug24 ?        00:00:15 ora_p002_C12DB1
oracle     3699     1   0 Aug24 ?        00:00:14 ora_p003_C12DB1
oracle     3701     1   0 Aug24 ?        00:00:01 ora_p004_C12DB1
oracle     3703     1   0 Aug24 ?        00:00:01 ora_p005_C12DB1
oracle     3705     1   0 Aug24 ?        00:00:00 ora_p006_C12DB1
oracle     3707     1   0 Aug24 ?        00:00:00 ora_p007_C12DB1
oracle     3737     1   0 Aug24 ?        00:00:00 ora_qm02_C12DB1
oracle     3741     1   0 Aug24 ?        00:00:00 ora_q002_C12DB1
oracle     3743     1   0 Aug24 ?        00:00:00 ora_q003_C12DB1
oracle     3746     1   0 Aug24 ?        00:00:27 ora_cjq0_C12DB1
oracle     3951     1   0 Aug24 ?        00:00:03 ora_w001_C12DB1
oracle     4102     1   0 Aug24 ?        00:00:04 ora_w002_C12DB1
oracle     4886     1   0 Aug24 ?        00:00:00 ora_w003_C12DB1
oracle     4906     1   0 Aug24 ?        00:00:00 ora_w004_C12DB1
oracle     6504     1   0 Aug24 ?        00:00:05 ora_s000_C12DB1
oracle    11619     1   0 03:13 ?        00:00:00 ora_p00a_C12DB1
oracle    11621     1   0 03:13 ?        00:00:00 ora_p00b_C12DB1
oracle    11632     1   0 03:14 ?        00:00:00 ora_p008_C12DB1
oracle    11634     1   0 03:14 ?        00:00:00 ora_p009_C12DB1
```

This output shows that several background processes are running on the Linux server for the C12DB1 database, which is a container database.

Threaded Execution

A new parameter introduced in Oracle Database 12c allows multiple background processes to share a single OS process on Unix, similar to the model Oracle has on Windows. This behavior on Unix is controlled by the parameter THREADED_EXECUTION, which by default is set to FALSE. The multithreaded Oracle Database model enables Oracle processes to execute as operating system threads in separate address spaces. In default process models, SPID and STID columns of V$PROCESS will have the same values, whereas in multithreaded models, each SPID (process) will have multiple STID (threads) values. The EXECUTION_TYPE column in V$PROCESS will show *THREAD*.

The dynamic view V$BGPROCESS shows the background processes available. The following query may be used to list all the background processes running on the instance.

```
SQL> SELECT  min(name || ': '|| description) process_description
  2   FROM v$bgprocess
  3   group by substr(name,1,3)
  4*  ORDER BY 1
SQL> /
```

> On Windows systems, each background and server process is a thread to the oracle.exe process.

Knowing the purpose of the required background processes is a must for the OCA certification exam. We'll discuss those purposes in the next subsections.

Database Writer (DBW*n*)

The purpose of the *database writer process* (DBW*n*) is to write the contents of the dirty buffers to the data files. By default, Oracle starts one database writer process when the instance starts. For multiuser and busy systems, you can have up to 100 database writer processes to improve performance. The names of the first 36 database writer processes are DBW0–DBW9 and DBWa–DBWz. The names of the 37th through 100th database writer processes are BW36–BW99. The parameter DB_WRITER_PROCESSES determines the additional number of database writer processes to be started. Having more DBW*n* processes than the number of CPUs is normally not beneficial.

The DBW*n* process writes the modified buffer blocks to disk, so more free buffers are available in the buffer cache. Writes are always performed in bulk to reduce disk contention; the number of blocks written in each I/O is OS-dependent.

Checkpoint (CKPT)

When a change is committed to a database, Oracle identifies the transaction with a unique number called the system change number (SCN). The value of an SCN is the logical point in time at which changes are made to a database. A *checkpoint* is when the DBW*n* process writes all the dirty buffers to the data files. When a checkpoint occurs, Oracle must update the control file and each data file header to record the checkpoint. This update is done by the *checkpoint process* (CKPT); the DBW*n* process writes the actual data blocks to the data files.

Checkpoints help reduce the time required for instance recovery. If checkpoints occur too frequently, disk contention becomes a problem with the data file updates. If checkpoints occur too infrequently, the time required to recover a failed database instance can be significantly longer. Checkpoints occur automatically when an online redo log file is full (a log switch happens).

When a redo log switch happens, the checkpoint process needs to update the header of all the data files; this causes performance issues on databases with hundreds of data files. To alleviate this situation, Oracle uses incremental checkpoints. Here the responsibility of updating the data file header is given to the DBW*n* process, when it writes dirty buffers to data files. The CKPT process updates only the control file with the checkpoint position, not the data files.

When Does Database Writer Write?

The DBW*n* background process writes to the data files whenever one of the following events occurs:

- A user's server process has searched too long for a free buffer when reading a buffer into the buffer cache.

- The number of modified and committed, but unwritten, buffers in the database buffer cache is too large.

- At a database checkpoint event. See Chapter 16 for information on checkpoints.

- The instance is shut down using any method other than a shutdown abort.

- A tablespace is placed into backup mode.

- A tablespace is taken offline to make it unavailable or is changed to READ ONLY.

- A segment is dropped.

A *database checkpoint* or *thread checkpoint* is when all data file headers as well as the control file are updated with checkpoint information. At this time, the database writes all the dirty buffers to data files. This happens during normal database shutdown, online redo log switch, forced checkpoint using ALTER SYSTEM CHECKPOINT, or when the database is placed in backup mode using ALTER DATABASE BEGIN BACKUP.

Log Writer (LGWR)

The *log writer process* (LGWR) writes the blocks in the redo log buffer of the SGA to the online redo log files. When the LGWR writes log buffers to disk, Oracle server processes can write new entries in the redo log buffer. LGWR writes the entries to the disk fast enough to ensure that room is available for the server process to write the redo entries. There can be only one LGWR process in the database.

If the redo log files are multiplexed, LGWR writes simultaneously to all the members of the redo log group. Even if one of the log files in the group is damaged, LGWR writes the redo information to the available files. LGWR writes to the redo log files sequentially so that transactions can be applied in order in the event of a failure.

As soon as a transaction commits, the information is written to redo log files. By writing the committed transaction immediately to the redo log files, the change to the database is never lost. Even if the database crashes, committed changes can be recovered from the online redo log files and applied to the data files.

When Does Log Writer Write?

The LGWR background process writes to the current redo log group under any of the following conditions:

- Three seconds since the last LGWR write

- When a user commits a transaction

- When the redo log buffer is a third full

- When the redo log buffer contains 1MB worth of redo information

- Whenever a database checkpoint occurs

Process Monitor (PMON)

The *process monitor process* (PMON) cleans up failed user processes and frees up all the resources used by the failed process. It resets the status of the active transaction table and removes the process ID from the list of active processes. It reclaims all the resources held by the user and releases all locks on tables and rows held by the user. PMON wakes up periodically to check whether it is needed. Other processes can call PMON if they detect a need for a PMON process.

PMON also checks on some optional background processes and restarts them if any have stopped.

System Monitor (SMON)

The *system monitor process* (SMON) performs instance or crash recovery at database startup by using the online redo log files. SMON is also responsible for cleaning up temporary segments in the tablespaces that are no longer used and for coalescing the contiguous free space in the dictionary-managed tablespaces. If any dead transactions were skipped during instance recovery because of file-read or offline errors, SMON recovers them when the tablespace or data file is brought back online. SMON wakes up regularly to check whether it is needed. Other processes can call SMON if they detect a need for an SMON process.

In Windows environments, a Windows service called OracleService*InstanceName* is also associated with each instance. This service must be started in order to start up the instance in Windows environments.

Oracle Storage Structures

An instance is a memory structure, but the Oracle database consists of a set of physical files that reside on the host server's disk drives. The physical storage structures include three types of files. These files are called *control files*, *data files*, and *redo log files*. The additional physical files that are associated with an Oracle database but are not technically part of the database are as follows: the *password file*, the *parameter file*, and any *archived redo log files*. The Oracle Net configuration files are also required for connectivity to an Oracle database. To roll back database changes using the Database Flashback feature, the *flashback log files* are used. Table 8.6 summarizes the role that each of these files plays in the database architecture.

TABLE 8.6 Oracle Physical Files

File Type	Information Contained in Files
Control file	Locations of other physical files, database name, database block size, database character set, and recovery information. These files are required to open the database.
Data file	All application data and internal metadata.
Redo log file	Record of all changes made to the database; used for instance recovery.
Parameter (pfile or spfile)	Configuration parameters for the SGA, optional Oracle features, and background processes.
Archived redo log file	Copy of the contents of online redo logs, used for database recovery and for change capture.
Password file	Optional file used to store names of users who have been granted the SYSDBA and SYSOPER privileges. See Chapter 13, "Implementing Security and Auditing," for details on SYSDBA and SYSOPER privileges.
Oracle Net file	Entries that configure the database listener and client-to-database connectivity. See Chapter 12 for details.
Flashback log file	If the database has flashback logging enabled, files are written to the fast recovery area.

Figure 8.10 shows where to view the physical storage information of the database using OEM Database Express 12c.

Figure 8.11 shows how to access the DBA menu in SQL Developer. Under DBA menu, you can view and administer several components of the database.

The three types of critical files that make up a database—the control file, the data file, and the redo log file—are described in the following sections.

FIGURE 8.10 The OEM Database Express Storage menu

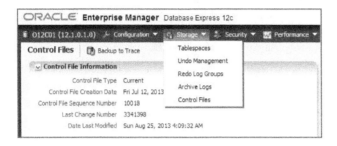

FIGURE 8.11 The SQL Developer DBA menu

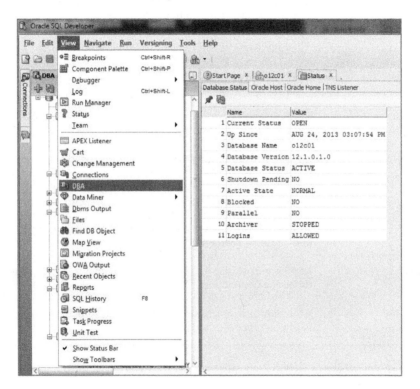

Control Files

Control files are critical components of the database because they store important information that is not available anywhere else. This information includes the following:

▪ The name of the database

▪ A database-creation timestamp

- The names, locations, and sizes of the data files and redo log files
- Tablespace information
- Redo log information used to recover the database in the case of a disk failure or user error
- Archived log information
- RMAN backup information
- Checkpoint information

The following query shows the types of information kept in the control file, indicating the importance of this file.

```
SQL> SELECT type FROM v$controlfile_record_section;

TYPE
----------------------------
DATABASE                          BACKUP SPFILE
CKPT PROGRESS                     DATABASE INCARNATION
REDO THREAD                       FLASHBACK LOG
REDO LOG                          RECOVERY DESTINATION
DATAFILE                          INSTANCE SPACE RESERVATION
FILENAME                          REMOVABLE RECOVERY FILES
TABLESPACE                        RMAN STATUS
TEMPORARY FILENAME                THREAD INSTANCE NAME MAPPING
RMAN CONFIGURATION                MTTR
LOG HISTORY                       DATAFILE HISTORY
OFFLINE RANGE                     STANDBY DATABASE MATRIX
ARCHIVED LOG                      GUARANTEED RESTORE POINT
BACKUP SET                        RESTORE POINT
BACKUP PIECE                      DATABASE BLOCK CORRUPTION
BACKUP DATAFILE                   ACM OPERATION
BACKUP REDOLOG                    FOREIGN ARCHIVED LOG
DATAFILE COPY                     PDB RECORD
BACKUP CORRUPTION                 AUXILIARY DATAFILE COPY
COPY CORRUPTION                   MULTI INSTANCE REDO APPLY
DELETED OBJECT                    PDBINC RECORD
PROXY COPY

41 rows selected.

SQL>
```

The control files are created when the database is created in the locations specified in the control_files parameter in the parameter file. Because a loss of the control files negatively impacts the ability to recover the database, most databases multiplex their control files to multiple locations. Oracle uses the CKPT background process to automatically update each of these files as needed, keeping the contents of all copies of the control synchronized. You can use the dynamic performance view V$CONTROLFILE to display the names and locations of all the database's control files. A sample query on V$CONTROLFILE is shown here:

```
SQL> SELECT name FROM v$controlfile;

NAME
--------------------------------------------------------------------------------
/u01/app/oracle/oradata/C12DB1/controlfile/o1_mf_8tx7cfnl_.ctl
/u01/app/oracle/fast_recovery_area/C12DB1/controlfile/o1_mf_8tx7cfz0_.ctl

SQL>
```

This query shows that the database has two control files, called o1_mf_8tx7cfnl_.ctl and o1_mf_8tx7cfz0_.ctl, which are stored in different directories. The control files can be stored in any directory; however, it is better if they are physically stored on different disks. You can also monitor control files using EM Database Express (on the Server tab, choose Control Files under Storage, as shown in Figure 8.12).

Control files are usually the smallest files in the database, generally a few megabytes in size. However, they can be larger, depending on the PFILE/SPFILE setting for CONTROLFILE_RECORD_KEEP_TIME when the Recovery Manager feature is used.

FIGURE 8.12   EM Database Express showing control files

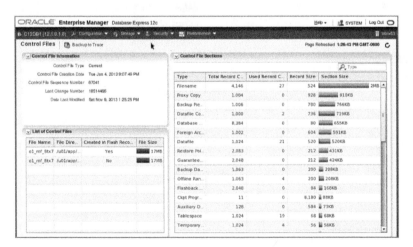

In the database, the control files keep track of the names, locations, and sizes of the database data files. Data files, and their relationship to another database structure called a *tablespace*, are examined in the next section.

Data Files

Data files are the physical files that actually store the data that has been inserted into each table in the database. The size of the data files is directly related to the amount of table data they store. Data files are the physical structure behind another database storage area called a *tablespace*. A tablespace is a logical storage area within the database. Tablespaces group logically related segments. For example, all the tables for the Accounts Receivable application might be stored together in a tablespace called AR_TAB, and the indexes on these tables might be stored in a tablespace called AR_IDX.

By default, every Oracle Database 12c must have at least three tablespaces. Table 8.7 describes these tablespaces.

TABLE 8.7   Required Tablespaces in Oracle 12c

Tablespace Name	Description
SYSTEM	Stores the data dictionary tables and PL/SQL code.
SYSAUX	Stores segments used for database options such as the Automatic Workload Repository, Online Analytical Processing (OLAP), and Spatial.
TEMP	Used for performing large sort operations. TEMP is required when the SYSTEM tablespace is created as a locally managed tablespace; otherwise, it is optional. See Chapter 10, "Understanding Storage and Space Management," for details.

In addition to these three required tablespaces, most databases have tablespaces for storing other database segments such as undo and application data. Many production databases often have many more tablespaces for storing application segments. Either you or the application vendor determines the total number and names of these tablespaces. Tablespaces are discussed in detail in Chapter 10, "Understanding Storage and Space Management."

For each tablespace in the database, there must be at least one data file. Some tablespaces may be composed of several data files for management or performance reasons. The data dictionary view DBA_DATA_FILES shows the data files associated with each tablespace in the database. The following SQL statement shows a sample query on the DBA_DATA_FILES data dictionary view:

```
SQL> SELECT tablespace_name, file_name
  2  FROM dba_data_files
  3  ORDER BY tablespace_name;
```

```
TABLESPACE_N FILE_NAME
------------ -----------------------------------------------
APPL_DATA    /u01/app/oracle/oradata/12cR1/appl_data01.dbf
APPL_DATA    /u01/app/oracle/oradata/12cR1/appl_data02.dbf
EXAMPLE      /u01/app/oracle/oradata/12cR1/example01.dbf
SYSAUX       /u01/app/oracle/oradata/12cR1/sysaux01.dbf
SYSTEM       /u01/app/oracle/oradata/12cR1/system01.dbf
UNDOTBS1     /u01/app/oracle/oradata/12cR1/undotbs01.dbf
USERS        /u01/app/oracle/oradata/12cR1/users01.dbf

7 rows selected.
SQL>
```

The output shows that the APPL_DATA tablespace is comprised of two data files; all other tablespaces have one data file. You can also monitor data files using EM, as shown in Figure 8.13.

Data files are usually the largest files in the database, ranging from megabytes to gigabytes or terabytes in size.

When a user performs a SQL operation on a table, the user's server process copies the affected data from the data files into the database buffer cache in the SGA. If the user has performed a committed transaction that modifies that data, the database writer process (DBW*n*) ultimately writes the modified data back to the data files.

FIGURE 8.13   EM Database Express showing data files

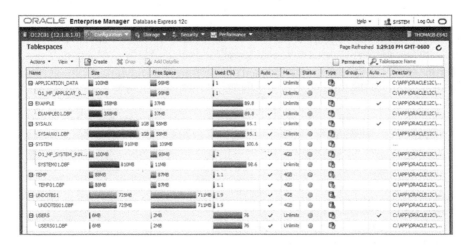

Redo Log Files

Whenever a user performs a transaction in the database, the information needed to reproduce this transaction in the event of a database failure is written to the redo log files, and the user does not get a confirmation of the commit until the transaction is successfully written to the redo log files.

Because of the important role that redo logs play in Oracle's recovery mechanism, they are usually multiplexed. This means that each redo log contains one or more copies of itself in case one of the copies becomes corrupt or is lost because of a hardware failure. Collectively, these sets of redo logs are referred to as *redo log groups*. Each multiplexed file within the group is called a *redo log group member*. Oracle automatically writes to all members of the redo log group to keep the files in sync. Each redo log group must be composed of one or more members. Each database must have a minimum of two redo log groups because redo logs are used in a circular fashion.

V$LOG dynamic performance view shows information on redo logs in the database, their size along with other information. You can use the V$LOGFILE dynamic performance view to view the names of the redo log groups and the names and locations of their members, as shown here:

```
SQL> SELECT group#, member
  2  FROM v$logfile
  3* ORDER BY group#
SQL> /

 GROUP# MEMBER
------- -----------------------------------------------
      1 C:\APP\ORACLE12C\MULTIPLEX\O12C01\REDO01.LOG
      1 D:\APP\ORACLE12C\ORADATA\O12C01\REDO01.LOG
      2 C:\APP\ORACLE12C\MULTIPLEX\O12C01\REDO02.LOG
      2 D:\APP\ORACLE12C\ORADATA\O12C01\REDO02.LOG
      3 C:\APP\ORACLE12C\MULTIPLEX\O12C01\REDO03.LOG
      3 D:\APP\ORACLE12C\ORADATA\O12C01\REDO03.LOG
      4 C:\APP\ORACLE12C\MULTIPLEX\O12C01\REDO04.LOG
      4 D:\APP\ORACLE12C\ORADATA\O12C01\REDO04.LOG

8 rows selected.
SQL>
```

This output shows that the database has a total of four redo log groups and that each group has two members. Each of the members is located in a separate directory on the server's disk drives so that the loss of a single disk drive will not result in the loss of the recovery information stored in the redo logs. You can also monitor redo logs using EM Database Express, as shown in Figure 8.14.

FIGURE 8.14 EM Database Express showing redo logs

When a user performs a DML activity on the database, the recovery information for this transaction is written to the redo log buffer by the user's server process. LGWR eventually writes this recovery information to the active redo log group until that log group is filled. Once the current log fills with transaction information, LGWR switches to the next redo log until that log group fills with transaction information, and so on, until all available redo logs are used. When the last redo log is used, LGWR wraps around and starts using the first redo log again. As shown in the following query, you can use the V$LOG dynamic performance view to display which redo log group is currently active and being written to by LGWR:

```
SQL> SELECT group#, members, status
  2  FROM v$log
  3  ORDER BY group#;


  GROUP#    MEMBERS STATUS
---------- ---------- ----------------
        1          2 CURRENT
        2          2 INACTIVE
        3          2 INACTIVE
        4          2 ACTIVE
```

This output shows that redo log group number 1 is current and being written to by LGWR. Once redo log group 4 is full, LGWR switches back to redo log group 1. The following are the statuses available for log files.

- UNUSED - Online redo log is new and never been written to.
- CURRENT - The current active redo log.

- `ACTIVE` - Log is active but is not the current log. It is needed for crash recovery.
- `CLEARING` - A short time status during `ALTER DATABASE CLEAR LOGFILE` statement. After the log is cleared, the status changes to `UNUSED`.
- `CLEARING_CURRENT` - Current log is being cleared of a closed thread. The log file may be in this status if there is an I/O error writing the new log information.
- `INACTIVE` - Log is no longer needed for instance recovery.

When LGWR wraps around from the last redo log group back to the first redo log group, any recovery information previously stored in the first redo log group is overwritten and, therefore, no longer available for recovery purposes.

However, if the database is operating in *archive log mode*, the contents of these previously used logs are copied to a secondary location before the log is reused by LGWR. If this archiving feature is enabled, it is the job of the ARC*n* background process described in the previous section to copy the contents of the redo log to the archive location. These copies of old redo log entries are called *archive logs*. Figure 8.15 shows this process graphically.

In Figure 8.15, the first redo log group has been filled, and LGWR has moved on to redo log group 2. As soon as LGWR switches from redo log group 1 to redo log group 2, the ARC*n* process starts copying the contents of redo log group 1 to the archive log file location. Once the first redo log group is safely archived, LGWR is free to wrap around and reuse the first redo log group once redo log group 3 is filled.

FIGURE 8.15 How ARC*n* copies redo log entries to disk

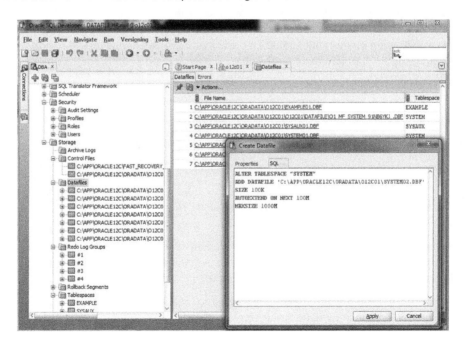

Nearly all production databases run in archive-log mode because they need to be able to redo all transactions since the last backup in the event of a hardware failure or user error that damages the database.

A database can have multiple archive processes and multiple archive destinations. We will discuss archiving and how the archived redo logs are used for database recovery in Chapter 15.

If LGWR needs to write to the redo log group that ARC*n* is trying to copy but cannot because the destination is full, the database hangs until space is cleared on the drive.

SQL Developer also has friendly menu options to manage database storage structures easily for DBAs. Figure 8.16 shows the storage menu screen from SQL Developer, giving you an overview. We encourage you to go through the menu items, modify the configuration, and use the SQL tab to view the SQL code generated by the SQL Developer tool. This will help you obtain a good understanding of the options and the syntax.

Real Application Clusters Database

Oracle *Real Application Clusters* were introduced in Oracle9*i* and have seen major enhancements in the Oracle 10g database where "grid" is the key. In the RAC architecture, there is one storage structure (database), with multiple Oracle instances (memory and processes) running on multiple nodes. This architecture gives high availability and horizontal scalability. When you need more capacity, all you need to do is add one more node to the RAC cluster.

In the RAC architecture, certain components must be shared by the instances; some can be shared by the instances and some components cannot be shared.

- Control files belong to the database, and all instances use the same control files.

- Database files belong to the database, and all instances access the same data files and permanent and temporary tablespaces.

- Each instance undo is kept separately and, therefore, requires that each instance undo its tablespace separately.

- Each instance has its own redo log buffer and redo threads and, therefore, has its own redo log files. Redo log files are not shared by the instances, but the files must reside in a shared location for recovery and backup purposes.

- It is advisable to keep the parameter file in a shared location accessible to all instances, with instance-specific parameters prefixed with the instance name.

FIGURE 8.16   The SQL Developer screen showing database storage

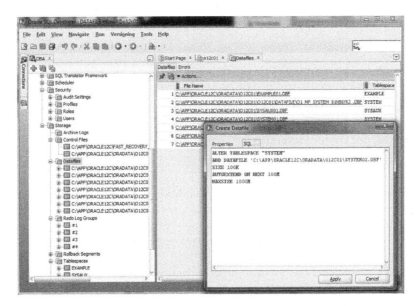

The Logical Structure

In the previous section, you saw how the Oracle database is configured physically. The obvious question is where and how your table is stored in a database. Let's try to relate the physical storage to the logical structures you know, such as tables and indexes.

Oracle logically divides the database into smaller units to manage, store, and retrieve data efficiently. The following paragraphs give you an overview of the logical structures:

Tablespaces   The database is logically divided into smaller units at the highest level, called *tablespaces*. A tablespace has a direct relationship to the physical structure—a data file can belong to one and only one tablespace. A tablespace could have more than one data file associated with it.

A tablespace commonly groups related logical structures together. For example, you might group data specific to an application in a tablespace. This will ease the management of the application from the DBA's point of view. This logical division helps administer a portion of the database without affecting the rest of it. Each Oracle Database 12c database must have at least three tablespaces: SYSTEM, SYSAUX, and TEMP. For better management and performance, it must have two more tablespaces holding the UNDO data and application data.

Tablespaces are discussed in detail in Chapter 10.

Blocks   A *block* is the smallest unit of storage in Oracle. A block is usually a multiple of the operating-system block size. A data block corresponds to a specific number of bytes of storage space. The block size is based on the parameter DB_BLOCK_SIZE and is determined when the database is created.

Extents   An *extent* is the next level of logical grouping. It is a grouping of contiguous blocks, allocated in one chunk. Because they are allocated in contiguous chunks, extents cannot spawn multiple data files.

Segments   A *segment* is a set of extents allocated for logical structures such as tables, indexes, clusters, table partitions, materialized views, and so on. Whenever you create a logical structure that stores data, Oracle allocates a segment, which contains at least one extent, which in turn has at least one block. A segment can be associated to only one tablespace; the extents of a segment may belong to more than one datafile. A segment is created when a table, index, materialized view, or a clustered table is created. When partitioned tables or partitioned indexes are created, one segment is created for each partition.

Figure 8.17 shows the relationship between data files, tablespaces, segments, extents, and blocks.

A schema is a logical structure that groups the database objects. A schema is not directly related to a tablespace or to any other logical storage structure. The objects that belong to a schema can reside in different tablespaces, and a tablespace can have objects that belong to multiple schemas. Schema objects include structures such as tables, indexes, synonyms, procedures, triggers, database links, and so on.

The DBA sees and manages the physical structure and logical structures of the database, whereas the programmer or a database user sees only the logical storage structures such as tables, indexes, and materialized views. They are not interested or not required to know to which tablespace the table belongs or where the tablespace data files are stored.

FIGURE 8.17   Logical database structure

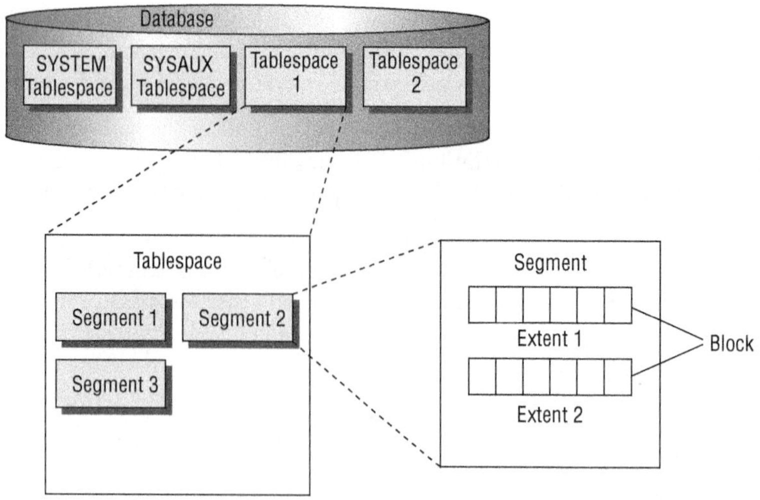

Real World Scenario

Exploring the Data Dictionary for Physical and Logical Structures

The Oracle Data Dictionary is discussed in detail in Chapter 9. You may do this exercise after the database is created, but we wanted to document the information where it is relevant.

Here are a few data dictionary objects you can use to explore and help you understand the physical and logical structures more. You can use SQL*Plus or SQL Developer to explore. However, because SQL Developer shows a spreadsheet-like output, we recommend that you use SQL Developer for improved readability; just execute SELECT * FROM <dictionary_view> in the Worksheet.

Physical Storage Structures

Use the following v$ and DBA views to explore your database's physical storage.

Control Files
V$CONTROLFILE

Redo Log Files
V$LOG

V$LOGFILE

Data Files—The tablespace number (V$) or name (DBA) links a data file to its logical storage structure

    V$DATAFILE

    V$TEMPFILE

    DBA_DATA_FILES

    DBA_TEMP_FILES

Logical Storage Structures

Use the following DBA views to explore the logical storage structures, and see how they are linked to physical storage. All of the views listed here have a file number column that ties the tablespace, segment, or extent back to its physical storage.

Tablespaces

    DBA_TABLESPACES

Segments—The tablespace name links to DBA_TABLESPACES, segment's parent in the relational model for database logical structures.

    DBA_SEGMENTS

> Extents—The tablespace name ties extents to DBA_TABLESPACES, and the segment owner, segment type, and segment name combination ties each extent to a segment in the relational model.
>
> DBA_EXTENTS

Summary

This chapter introduced you to the Oracle Database 12c architecture with the components that constitute an Oracle database server. Most popular databases today are relational databases. Relational databases consist of data composed of a set of relational objects. Data is stored in tables as rows and columns. Oracle is a relational database. SQL is the language used to manage and administer Oracle databases. Several tools are available to administer Oracle Database 12c. The most common ones used by DBAs are SQL*Plus and Oracle Enterprise Manager. SQL Developer is a GUI tool that can be used to interact with Oracle Database 12c using several DBA functions readily coded in menu items.

The Oracle Database 12c architecture consists of three major components: memory, processes, and storage. A user process initiates a connection with the Oracle database and starts a server process. The server process is responsible for performing the tasks on the database. The memory structures and background processes together are an Oracle instance. The server process communicates with the memory structure known as the system global area. The SGA consists of a shared pool, database buffer cache, and redo log buffer. The shared pool also includes components such as a Java pool, large pool, result cache, and streams pool.

There are many types of background processes, each performing a specific job to maintain and manage the database instance. All databases have at least nine background processes: the important ones are database writer, checkpoint writer, log writer, process monitor, and system monitor. Depending on the configuration of the database, there may be other background processes such as archiver, ASM balancing, and so on.

The physical data structure consists of several files stored on disk. The most important file is the control file, which keeps track of several important pieces of information, such as database name, names of data files and redo log files, backup information, and so on. The CKPT process is responsible for keeping the control file updated. Redo log files contain information from the redo log buffer. The LGWR process is responsible for writing the redo log buffer contents to the redo log files. Oracle metadata and application data are stored in data files. The DBW*n* process is responsible for writing dirty blocks from the database buffer cache to the data files.

Looking at the logical structure of the database, a tablespace is the highest level of logical unit. A tablespace consists of several segments. A segment consists of one or more extents. An extent is a contiguous allocation of blocks. A block is the smallest unit of storage in an Oracle database.

Exam Essentials

Describe common Oracle tools and their uses. Know which tools are available for connecting to and interacting with an Oracle database. Understand how these tools differ from one another.

Understand the Oracle architecture components. Be able to describe the logical and physical components of the Oracle architecture and the components that make up each. Know the relationship between segments, extents, database blocks, and operating-system blocks.

Understand the difference between a traditional Oracle database and a multitenancy database. Multitenancy databases are known as container databases and can have one or more pluggable databases. A traditional database is one database.

Know the background processes. Understand the Oracle Database 12c background processes and how they are used. The important ones to know are DBWn, CKPT, LGWR, PMON, SMON, ARCn, ASMB, RBAL.

Identify the three types of database files that constitute the database. Understand the purposes and key differences between the control files, data files, and redo log files.

Explain and categorize the SGA memory structures. Identify the SGA areas along with the subcomponents contained within each of these areas.

Review Questions

1. Choose two SGA structures that are required in every Oracle instance.

    A. Large pool

    B. Shared pool

    C. Buffer cache

    D. Java pool

2. Which statement is true?

    A. A database can have only one control file.

    B. A database must have at least two control files.

    C. A database may have zero or more control files.

    D. A database must have at least one control file.

3. Which component is configured at database startup and cannot be dynamically managed?

    A. Redo log buffer

    B. Streams pool

    C. Java pool

    D. Shared pool

    E. None of the above

4. Which component is not part of an Oracle instance?

    A. System global area

    B. Process monitor

    C. Control file

    D. Shared pool

    E. None

5. Which background process guarantees that committed data is saved even when the changes have not been recorded in data files?

    A. DBWn

    B. PMON

    C. LGWR

    D. CKPT

    E. ARCn

6. User John has updated several rows in a table and issued a commit. What does the DBW*n* (database writer) process do at this time in response to the commit event?

   A. Writes the changed blocks to data files.

   B. Writes the changed blocks to redo log files.

   C. Triggers checkpoint and thus LGWR writes the changes to redo log files.

   D. Does nothing.

7. Which of the following best describes a RAC configuration?

   A. One database, multiple instances

   B. One instance, multiple databases

   C. Multiple databases plugged in from multiple servers

   D. Multiple databases, multiple instances

8. Which component of the SGA contains the parsed SQL code?

   A. Database buffer cache

   B. Dictionary cache

   C. Library cache

   D. Parse cache

9. Which tasks are accomplished by the SMON process? (Choose all that apply.)

   A. Performs recovery at instance startup

   B. Performs cleanup after a user session is terminated

   C. Starts any server process that stopped running

   D. Coalesces contiguous free space in dictionary-managed tablespaces

10. Choose the best statement from the options related to segments.

    A. A contiguous set of blocks constitutes a segment.

    B. A nonpartitioned table can have only one segment.

    C. A segment can belong to more than one tablespace.

    D. All of the above are true.

11. From the following list, choose two processes that are optional in an Oracle Database 12*c* database.

    A. MMON

    B. MMNL

    C. ARC*n*

    D. MMAN

12. Which SGA component will you increase or configure so that RMAN tape backups do not use memory from the shared pool?

   A. Java pool

   B. Streams pool

   C. Recovery pool

   D. Large pool

13. When a user session is terminated, which processes are responsible for cleaning up and releasing locks? (Choose all that apply.)

   A. DBW*n*

   B. LGWR

   C. MMON

   D. PMON

   E. SMON

14. The LRU algorithm is used to manage what part of the Oracle architecture?

   A. Users who log on to the database infrequently and may be candidates for being dropped

   B. The data file that stores the least amount of information and will need the least frequent backup

   C. The tables that users rarely access so that they can be moved to a less active tablespace

   D. The shared pool and database buffer cache portions of the SGA

15. Two structures make up an Oracle server: an instance and a database. Which of the following best describes the difference between an Oracle instance and a database?

   A. An instance consists of memory structures and processes, whereas a database is composed of physical files.

   B. An instance is used only during database creation; after that, the database is all that is needed.

   C. An instance is started whenever the demands on the database are high, but the database is used all the time.

   D. An instance is configured using a pfile, whereas a database is configured using a spfile.

16. Which of the following is the proper order of Oracle's storage hierarchy, from smallest to largest?

A. Operating-system block, database block, segment, extent

B. Operating-system block, database block, extent, segment

C. Segment, extent, database block, operating-system block

D. Segment, database block, extent, operating-system block

17. The DBA unknowingly terminated the process ID belonging to the PMON process of Oracle Database 12*c* database using the `kill -9` command on Unix. Choose the best answer:

A. Oracle spawns another PMON process automatically.

B. The database hangs, and the DBA must manually start a PMON process.

C. If the database is in ARCHIVELOG mode, Oracle automatically starts another PMON process and recovers from the database hang.

D. The instance crashes and needs to be restarted.

18. When an incremental checkpoint happens in a database, which file(s) are updated with the checkpoint position? Choose all options that are correct.

A. Data files

B. Control files

C. Initialization Parameter Files

D. Redo log files

E. Archive log files

19. User Isabella updates a table and commits the change after a few seconds. Which of the following actions are happening in the database? Order them in the correct sequence and ignore the actions that are not relevant.

A. Oracle reads the blocks from data file to buffer cache and updates the blocks.

B. Changed blocks from the buffer cache are written to data files.

C. The user commits the change.

D. LGWR writes the changed blocks to the redo log buffer.

E. The server process writes the change vectors to the redo log buffer.

F. LGWR flushes the redo log buffer to redo log files.

G. A checkpoint occurs.

20. Querying the V$LOG file shows the following information. Which redo group files are required for instance crash recovery?

```
SQL> select GROUP#, ARCHIVED, STATUS from V$LOG;
    GROUP# ARC STATUS
---------- --- ----------------
         1 NO  CURRENT
         2 NO  INACTIVE
         3 NO  INACTIVE
         4 NO  ACTIVE
```

    A. Group 1 and 4

    B. Group 2 and 3

    C. Groups 1 through 4

    D. Group 1

    E. Group 4

Chapter

9

Creating and Operating Oracle Database 12c

ORACLE DATABASE 12c: OCA EXAM OBJECTIVES COVERED IN THIS CHAPTER:

✓ **Oracle Software Installation Basics**

- Plan for an Oracle Database software installation.

✓ **Installing Oracle Database Software**

- Install the Oracle Database software.

✓ **Creating an Oracle Database Using DBCA**

- Create a database by using the Database Configuration Assistant (DBCA).

- Generate database creation scripts by using DBCA.

- Manage database design templates by using DBCA.

- Configure database options by using DBCA.

✓ **Oracle Database Instance**

- Understand initialization parameter files.

- Start up and shut down an Oracle database instance.

- View the alert log and access dynamic performance views.

 As a DBA, you are responsible for creating and managing Oracle databases and services within your organization. Oracle provides a comprehensive and cohesive set of tools to help DBAs perform these tasks. It is important for you to understand these tools and how to use them properly.

Oracle uses Java-based tools to manage Oracle Database 12c because Java gives the same look and feel to the tools across all platforms. In this chapter, we will cover how to use the Oracle Database Configuration Assistant tool, which is used to create and delete Oracle databases, and how you can use templates to create databases. DBCA can also be used to modify the database options installed.

After the database is created using DBCA, it will be up and running. We will then cover how to shut down and restart the database for some configuration changes, apply patches, and perform server maintenance. We'll describe the various database startup and shutdown options and explain the circumstances under which you use these options.

You will also learn more about the Oracle data dictionary, including how the dictionary is created, where it is created, and so on. Finally, we will cover initialization parameter files and discuss how you can use them to manage, locate, and view the database alert log.

Oracle Database 12c Software Installation

We will begin this chapter with Oracle's software installation tool, *Oracle Universal Installer* (OUI). OUI is a Java-based graphical tool used to install Oracle software. Because it is written in Java, OUI looks and feels the same on all platforms. OUI is included with every software installation distribution media.

OUI also has the option to create an Oracle database along with the software install. Before software installation and database creation can occur, certain operating-system requirements must be met. As the DBA, you must properly plan the Oracle database software installation.

 The examples in this section are for a Linux server, but most of the concepts apply equally to Windows platforms. Any significant differences between Linux and Windows are noted.

Planning the Oracle Database 12*c* Software Install

The base release of Oracle database software and other Oracle products can be downloaded from Oracle's software delivery cloud location https://edelivery.oracle.com. You must have a valid support identification number to download patches and patch sets from My Oracle Support (MOS) location at http://support.oracle.com, widely known as Metalink.

Oracle Database 12*c* software is available on various platforms: Unix, Linux, and Windows (64-bit edition only). This chapter will show examples of downloading and installing on a Linux platform.

Reviewing the Documentation

Before beginning an installation of Oracle Database 12*c*, you need to review several documents so that you completely understand the installation requirements. These documents include the following:

- The installation guide for your operating system
- The general release notes for the version of Oracle you are installing
- The operating-system-specific release notes for the version of Oracle you are installing
- Any quick-start installation guides

Before you begin, review each of these documents so that you are thoroughly familiar with the installation process and any known associated issues.

All of these documents are available on Oracle's Documentation Library website located at http://www.oracle.com/pls/db121/homepage.

Reviewing the System Requirements

The next task is to review your server-hardware specifications to see whether they meet or exceed the specifications in the install documentation. Minimally, this means you must confirm that your server meets the installation requirements in these four areas:

- The operating system is of the proper release level.
- The server has adequate memory to perform the install and run an instance.
- The server has adequate CPU resources to perform the install and run an instance.
- The server has adequate disk storage space to perform the install and run a database.

Table 9.1 shows the recommended minimum hardware requirements for an Oracle Database 12*c* installation.

TABLE 9.1   Recommended Hardware Requirements for Oracle Database 12*c*

Hardware Component	Recommended Requirement
Memory	1GB minimum, 2GB+ recommended
Swap space	1.5GB or equal to the amount of RAM
Temp space	1GB of free space in the /tmp directory on Unix systems
Free disk space	6.4GB of disk space

The Oracle Universal Installer, which is described in the subsequent section "Using the Oracle Universal Installer," will perform a quick system check prior to starting an installation to see whether your system meets the specific requirements for your operating system. If your system does not meet the minimum requirements, the installer will return an error and abort.

On Unix systems, you must examine one critical system requirement before installation: the Unix kernel parameters. Unix kernel parameters are used to configure the Unix operating-system settings for operating-system-level operations that impact Oracle-related activities such as the following:

- The maximum size allowed for a sharable memory segment on the server, which can impact the *system global area* (SGA) size

- The maximum number of files that can be open on the server at one time, which impacts the total number of users and files in the database

- The number of processes that can run concurrently on the server, which impacts the number of users and the ability to use some optional features

The systems administrator usually makes Unix kernel changes, which may require a server reboot in order to take effect. The install guide and/or release notes provide details on the appropriate kernel setting for your operating system. In addition to kernel settings, the system administrator may have to configure the server's disk storage system and backup hardware before installing the Oracle software.

Planning Your Install

Once you review the documentation and system requirements, you are ready to begin planning your installation. This is the last step before actually running the Oracle Universal Installer.

One way to simplify the installation planning is to adopt the *Optimal Flexible Architecture* (OFA) model that Oracle recommends as a best-practice methodology for managing Oracle installations in Unix environments (and to a lesser extent, Windows environments). The OFA model was designed to produce database installations that are easier to manage, upgrade, and back up, while at the same time minimizing problems associated with database growth. The OFA model addresses four areas:

- Naming conventions for Unix file systems and mount points
- Naming conventions for directory paths
- Naming conventions for database files
- Standardized locations for Oracle-related files

In addition to using the OFA model, planning your install also means answering the following questions:

- Which operating-system user will own the installed Oracle software?
- On which disk drive and directory will the Oracle software be installed?
- What directory structure will be used to store the Oracle software, its related configuration files, and the database itself?
- How should the database files be laid out so that the maximum performance benefits will be realized?
- How should the database files be laid out so that the maximum recoverability benefits will be realized?

Creating the Oracle User Account

On Unix systems, every file is owned by an operating-system user account. Therefore, before you can install the Oracle software, you must create a Unix user account that will own the Oracle binaries. The username for this account can be anything, but common Oracle usernames include `oracle`, `ora12c`, and `ora121`. Each Unix user is also in one or more operating-system groups. Create a new operating-system group for the Oracle Unix user. This group is usually called dba, and you will be prompted for it later during the installation.

On Windows systems, you can choose an account that has administrative privileges on the server.

On Linux platforms, Oracle provides a preinstall RPM. As a root user, you can install the RPM using `yum install oracle-rdbms-server-12cR1-preinstall`. This RPM creates the required users and groups to install Oracle software as well.

Oracle Inventory

Oracle maintains an inventory of all software installed on the server using the *Oracle Inventory*. On Unix systems, the Oracle Inventory location is identified by the file /etc/oraInst.loc. The /etc/oraInst.loc file typically has two lines:

```
inventory_loc=central_inventory_location
inst_group=group
```

The central_inventory_location is the directory where the Oracle Inventory is saved. All users installing Oracle software on this server should have access to this directory. The group is the install group where the software install users belong, thus they have privilege to create and update the central inventory. The inventory group (typically named oinstall on Unix) needs to be created before the software install.

On Windows systems, the central inventory is located under C:\Program Files\Oracle\ Inventory. On Windows systems the inventory group is always named ORA_INSTALL. The ORA_INSTALL group contains all the Oracle Home Users for all the Oracle Homes on the server. The central inventory directory and group are automatically created by the installer on windows.

Job Role Separation Using OS Groups

Oracle Database 12c can use operating-system authentication to connect to a specific database, and OS groups may be configured for different job roles and separation of duties. Oracle Database 12c installation requires one mandatory group (the default group where the software install user belongs in Unix, usually named dba), which is the OSDBA group. Members belonging to this group can authenticate to the database without a password using the / AS SYSDBA login option.

Table 9.2 gives an overview of the groups identified by Oracle Database 12c. All groups are subsets of OSDBA, meaning members belonging to the OSDBA group can perform all job role functions. In Table 9.2, the <hn> indicates the home name used for software installation. The privileges are specific to the databases running under the specific Oracle Home.

TABLE 9.2 Job Role Separation Groups

Job Role	System Privilege	Windows Group	Typical Unix Group
OS DBA – OS users with DBA privileges	SYSDBA	ORA_<hn>_DBA	OSDBA (dba)
Operator – Limited administrative privileges	SYSOPER	ORA_<hn>_OPER	OSOPER (oper)
Backup and Recovery Admin	SYSBACKUP	ORA_<hn>_ SYSBACKUP	OSBACKUPDBA (backupdba)
Data Guard Admin	SYSDG	ORA_<hn>_SYSDG	OSDGDBA (dgdba)
Encryption Key Management Admin	SYSKM	ORA_<hn>_SYSKM	OSKMDBA (kmdba)

It is possible to install the Oracle Database 12*c* software without creating any additional groups on Unix. Only one group is required, typically named dba, which can be used for the software install inventory group, the OSDBA group, and the various job role authentication groups, although that is not the recommended configuration. On Windows, Oracle installer automatically creates the groups.

Naming Volumes and Mount Points

Unless Oracle's Automatic Storage Management feature or raw devices are used, almost all files on a Unix server are stored on logical storage areas called *volumes* that are attached, or *mounted*, to directories, or *mount points*, by the Unix system administrator. The OFA model suggests that these mount points be given a name that consists of a combination of a character and numeric values. Common OFA mount points for Unix systems include the following:

- /u01
- /mnt01
- /du01
- /d01

Notice that the naming convention for these mount points is generic. The mount point's name has no relationship to what type of file it will ultimately hold. The OFA model recommends this generic naming convention because it provides the greatest flexibility for future management of the server's file systems.

The concept of mount points does not apply directly to Windows environments. Windows environments assign a standard Windows drive letter (for example, C:, D:) to each volume.

Creating OFA Directory Paths

The OFA model prescribes that the directory structures under the mount points use a consistent and meaningful naming convention. In addition to this naming convention, the OFA model assigns standard operating-system environment variable names to some of these directory paths as nicknames to aid in navigation and to ensure the portability of the directory structures in the event that they need to be moved to new file systems.

Table 9.3 shows the two operating-system environment variables used in the OFA model, along with the directories with which the variables are associated, for Unix systems.

TABLE 9.3 Comparison of Unix Directory Paths and Variables

Environment Variable	Directory Path	Description
$ORACLE_BASE	/u01/app/oracle	Top-level directory for Oracle software on the host server
$ORACLE_HOME	/u01/app/oracle/product/12.1.0/dbhome_1	Directory into which the Oracle 12c software will be installed

Table 9.4 shows the variables and directories used in the OFA model for Windows systems.

TABLE 9.4 Comparison of Windows Directory Paths and Variables

Environment Variable	Directory Path	Description
%ORACLE_BASE%	C:\app\oracle12c	Top-level directory for Oracle software on the host server
%ORACLE_HOME%	C:\app\oracle12c\product\12.1.0\dbhome_1	Directory into which the Oracle 12c software will be installed

These environment variables are used extensively when Oracle systems are installed, patched, upgraded, and managed. Table 9.5 shows several examples of how these variables define the locations of other Oracle directories.

TABLE 9.5 Common Uses of ORACLE_BASE and ORACLE_HOME

Directory	Description
$ORACLE_HOME/dbs	Default location for password file and parameter file on Unix systems
%ORACLE_HOME%\database	Default location for parameter file on Windows systems
$ORACLE_BASE/admin/PROD/pfile	Location of the pfile for a database called PROD on Unix systems
%ORACLE_BASE%\admin\PROD\pfile	Location of the pfile for a database called PROD on Windows systems

Directory	Description
`$ORACLE_HOME/network/admin`	Default location for Oracle Net configuration files on Unix systems
`%ORACLE_HOME%\network\admin`	Default location for Oracle Net configuration files on Windows systems
`$ORACLE_HOME/rdbms/admin`	Location of many Oracle database-configuration scripts on Unix systems
`%ORACLE_HOME%\rdbms\admin`	Location of many database-configuration scripts on Windows systems

For Unix systems, Table 9.5 says `$ORACLE_HOME/dbs` is the default location for the pfile and spfile but then says that pfiles should be stored in `$ORACLE_BASE/admin/<instance>/pfile`. Windows systems are similar. This implies that the same file needs to be in two locations at the same time. You can accomplish this using two tricks; which one you use depends on your operating system.

The following examples use 12CR11 as the database (and instance) name. On Unix systems, you can create the pfile in the `$ORACLE_BASE/admin/12CR11/pfile` directory, and then create a symbolic link in `$ORACLE_HOME/dbs` that points to the file in `$ORACLE_BASE/admin/12CR11/pfile` using this syntax:

```
ln -s $ORACLE_BASE/admin/12CR11/pfile/init12CR11.ora
    $ORACLE_HOME/dbs/init12CR11.ora
```

On Windows systems, you can create the pfile in the `%ORACLE_BASE%\admin\12CR11\pfile` directory, and then put another pfile in `%ORACLE_HOME%\dbs` that contains a single entry that points to the other pfile in `%ORACLE_BASE%\admin\12CR11\pfile` like this:

```
ifile=D:\oracle\admin\12CR11\pfile\init12CR11.ora
```

Using these techniques allows you to put the initialization parameter files in their default locations under `$ORACLE_HOME` but also in their desired location under `$ORACLE_BASE`.

Why should the real copy of the pfiles be stored under `$ORACLE_BASE` instead of `$ORACLE_HOME`? Well, it is a good idea to keep only version-specific files under `$ORACLE_HOME`. That way, when you eventually uninstall the software from an old `$ORACLE_HOME`, you won't lose your carefully tailored initialization files.

In addition to `$ORACLE_BASE` and `$ORACLE_HOME`, you should also be aware of a few other non-OFA-related operating-system environment variables on Unix and Windows systems. These are described in Table 9.6.

TABLE 9.6   Common Non-OFA Environment Variables

Operating-System Variable	Description
$ORACLE_SID	Defines which instance a Unix user session should be connecting to on the server.
%ORACLE_SID%	Defines which instance a Windows user session should connect to on the server.
$TNS_ADMIN	Specifies where the Oracle Net configuration files are stored on Unix systems—if they are to be stored outside their default location of $ORACLE_HOME/network/admin.
%TNS_ADMIN%	Specifies where the Oracle Net configuration files are stored on Windows systems—if they are to be stored outside their default location of %ORACLE_HOME%\network\admin.
$TWO_TASK	Establishes a default Oracle Net connection string that will be used if none is specified by the user.
%LOCAL%	Establishes a default Oracle Net connection string that will be used if none is specified by the user.
$LD_LIBRARY_PATH	Specifies the locations of the Oracle shared object libraries. This variable usually points to $ORACLE_HOME/lib on Unix systems.
$PATH	Tells the operating system in which directories to look for executable files on Unix systems.
%PATH%	Tells the operating system in which directories to look for executable files on Windows systems.

There is no need to set any of these variables for an Oracle Database 12c install; setting ORACLE_BASE is recommended, but is not mandatory. These variables are important when you're ready to create a database.

Using the Oracle Universal Installer

You use the Oracle Universal Installer (OUI) to install and configure the Oracle Database 12c software. The OUI is a Java-based application that provides the same installation look and feel no matter which operating system the install is being run on. The OUI process consists of seven primary operations:

- Unzipping Software and starting the OUI
- Performing preinstallation checks

- Responding to server-specific prompts for file locations, names, and so on
- Selecting the products you want to install
- Copying the files from the install media to $ORACLE_HOME
- Compiling the Oracle binaries
- Performing post-install operations using configuration assistants

Unzipping Software and Starting the OUI

To begin the install process, unzip the software downloaded from the Oracle Software Delivery Cloud. OUI installations on Unix systems require you to set the X Windows DISPLAY environment variable; otherwise, the OUI will not appear.

Once you unzip both parts of the Oracle Database 12c Release 1 (12.1.0.1.0) software, you should see the database directory. The OUI is invoked by running the SETUP.EXE program on Windows or the runInstaller program on Unix and Linux platforms.

Performing Preinstallation Checks

Start the OUI using the runInstaller command, as shown in Figure 9.1, on the Linux platform.

FIGURE 9.1   Invoking the Oracle Database 12c install

```
[oracle@btlnx63 database]$ ./runInstaller
Starting Oracle Universal Installer...

Checking Temp space: must be greater than 500 MB.   Actual 2158 MB    Passed
Checking swap space: must be greater than 150 MB.   Actual 15857 MB   Passed
Checking monitor: must be configured to display at least 256 colors.   Actual 1
6777216     Passed
Preparing to launch Oracle Universal Installer from /tmp/OraInstall2013-09-15_02
-05-52AM. Please wait ...[oracle@btlnx63 database]$
```

Notice that the output shows that the OUI checked the server's operating-system version, available RAM, temporary and swap space, and so on.

 If necessary, you can turn off the system verification that occurs prior to the installation by using the -ignoreSysPrereqs option of the runInstaller command.

Once the preinstallation tests are completed and passed, the OUI displays the initial OUI screen shown in Figure 9.2.

Provide an email address and Oracle support password if you have one and would like to receive updates. For this install, uncheck the I Wish To Receive Security Updates check box and click Next. The second screen is also applicable if you have an Oracle support account to download software updates. Software updates are recommended; they include critical patches released for the software.

FIGURE 9.2   The initial OUI installation screen

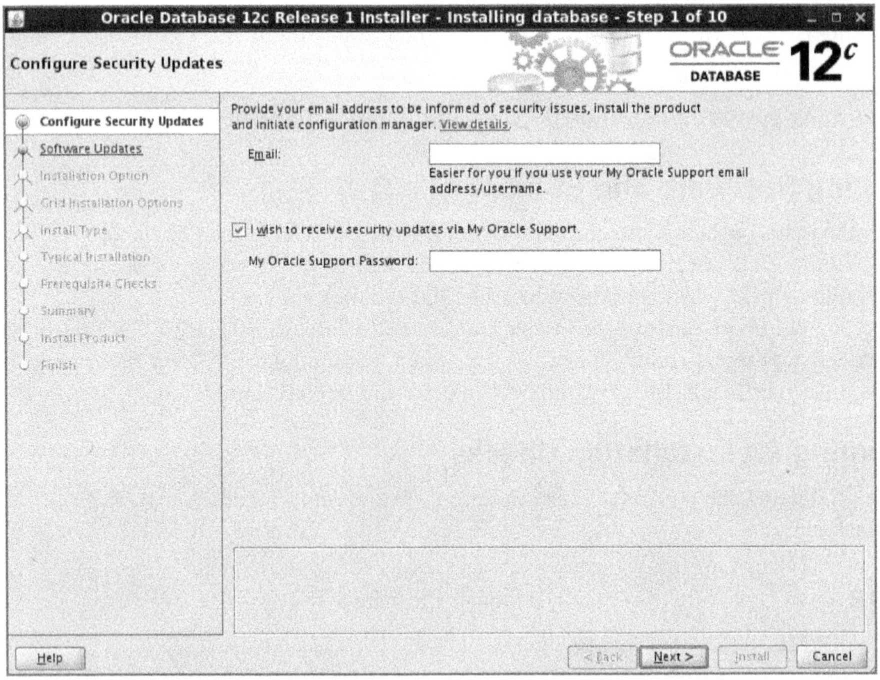

Responding to OUI Prompts

The next OUI screen, Select Installation Option, provides the various options available for the software installation. Figure 9.3 shows the installation options screen, along with the Help window display. You can click on the Help button in any screen to get context-sensitive help.

Based on the option chosen in this screen, the rest of the screens will change appropriately. The options provided in this screen are

- Create And Configure A Database: This option installs the software and creates a new database. If you choose this option, you can create a database with minimal configuration (desktop class) or opt for an advanced configuration (server class) database.

- Install Database Software Only: This option installs only the database binaries and does not create a database. Because this chapter also discusses the database creation, this section will show only the software installation.

- Upgrade An Existing Database: This option installs the database software and upgrades an existing database to Oracle Database 12c.

To create a new database in an existing software home, use the *Database Configuration Assistant* (DBCA) tool; to upgrade a previous version of the database to a current software version, use the *Database Upgrade Assistant* (DBUA) tool. The database creation screens and database upgrade screens that appear when you choose option 1 or 3 are discussed in detail later in the book. Here you will review the screens and options in option 2: Install Database Software Only. Select the Install Database Software Only option, and the next screen will prompt the grid options shown in Figure 9.4.

FIGURE 9.3   The Select Installation Option screen

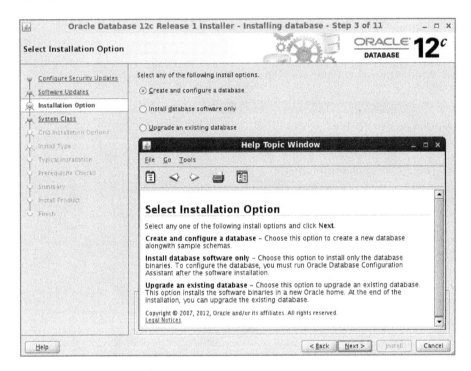

FIGURE 9.4   The Grid Installation Options screen

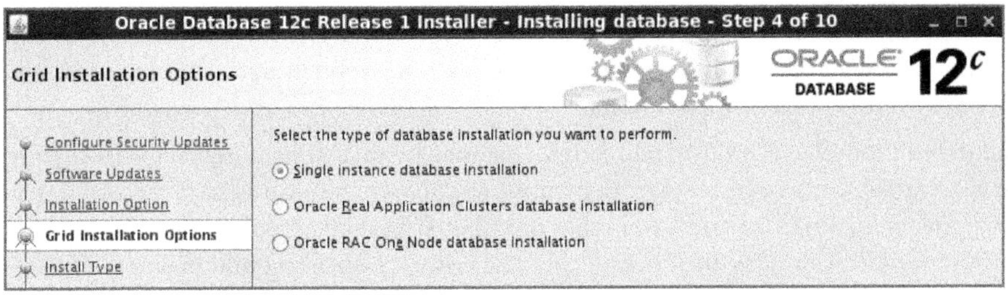

The Grid Installation screen provides the option to install software into a cluster for use with a Real Application Cluster (RAC) database. The RAC installation of Oracle Database 12*c* software is possible only if the server is part of a cluster. Because RAC is not part of the OCA exam, you should choose Single Instance Database Installation for now. When single instance installation is chosen, you have the option to install languages. By default only one language is installed (US English), but you can install as many languages as you want the product to run on. Install the supported languages used by your users.

Oracle database can be installed in one of four editions, as shown in Figure 9.5, based on the license purchased and the requirements. Figure 9.5 shows only three options, because Personal Edition is not available on Linux.

FIGURE 9.5 The Select Database Edition screen

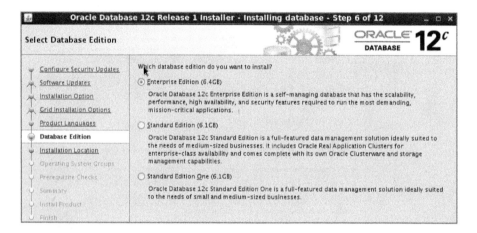

- Enterprise Edition: This installation type is designed for enterprise-level applications. It is engineered for mission-critical, high-security online transaction processing (OLTP) and data warehousing environments. If you select this installation type, then all separately licensable Enterprise Edition options are installed.

- Standard Edition: This installation type is designed for department or workgroup-level applications and for small and medium-sized enterprises (SMEs). It is engineered to provide core relational-database management services and options. It installs an integrated set of management tools, full distribution, replication, web features, and facilities for building business-critical applications.

- Standard Edition One (Desktop and Single Instance Installations Only): This installation type is designed for department, workgroup-level, or web applications. From single-server environments for small business to highly distributed branch environments, Oracle Database Standard Edition One includes all the facilities necessary to build business-critical applications.

- Personal Edition (Microsoft Windows Operating Systems Only): This installation type installs the same software as the Enterprise Edition installation type, with the exception of the management packs. However, it supports only a single-user development and deployment environment that requires full compatibility with Enterprise Edition and Standard Edition. Oracle RAC is not installed with Personal Edition.

The Specify Installation Location screen is where you specify the ORACLE_BASE and ORACLE_HOME values. If you have defined these environment variables, they will be shown here; if you haven't, platform-specific default values will be shown.

The next screen is specific to Unix installations, where you can choose the groups to identify the job roles discussed in the "Job Role Separation Using OS Groups" section. See Figure 9.6. On Windows, the groups are automatically created by the OUI with standard names.

FIGURE 9.6   The Privileged Operating System Groups screen

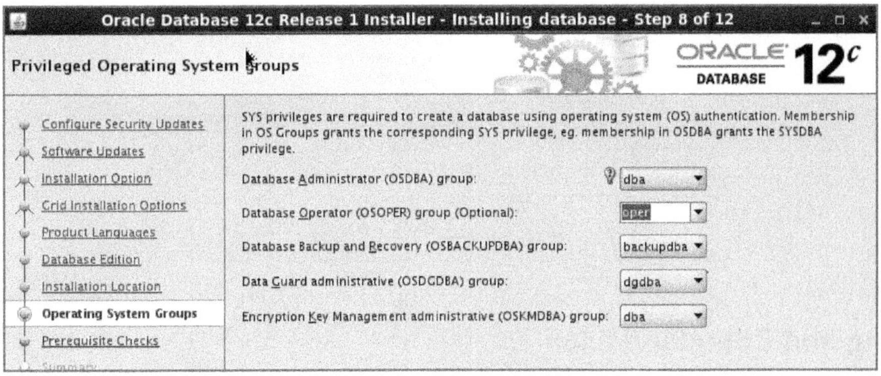

If all the prerequisite checks are successful, the Privilege Checks screen is not shown and OUI goes straight to Summary screen. If there are any prerequisite check issues, they will be displayed, and you will be given the option to fix or ignore them. Even if there are no issues, to help you better understand all of the prerequisite checks, we recommend clicking the Back button from the Summary screen to view the Prerequisite Checks screen, as shown in Figure 9.7. The bottom portion of the screen shows what is checked as part of the prerequisite. Click on each item to see the limit that the OUI checks each item against. Sometimes more information is available when you click the More Details link.

The prerequisites checks are for disk space, memory, user and groups, open file and process limits, Linux version and architecture, OS Kernel parameters, and OS Packages installed. You have the option to fix errors as well as ignore errors and warnings. Ignore errors only if you are sure ignoring will not impact the installation and ongoing operation. The Summary of installation options is shown for you to confirm before starting the installation. The same screen also has a Save Response File button to save the options chosen in the install session to a file, and it can be used to install Oracle Database 12*c* in a silent mode without going through the screens. If you are satisfied with your selections, click the Next button to start copying and linking the Oracle binaries to the $ORACLE_HOME directory.

FIGURE 9.7 The Perform Prerequisite Checks screen

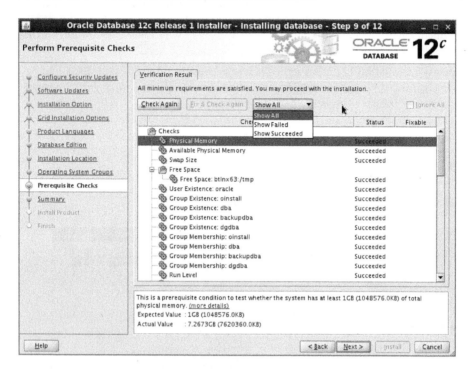

Copying and Compiling Files

The OUI displays status information while the installation and setup is in progress. Once the file-copy portion of the installation is complete, the OUI will begin linking the binaries to create the executable files needed to make the Oracle Database 12*c* software run on the server. On Unix systems, after the linking process, you are prompted to execute configuration scripts as the super-user root from the Unix command line. The orainstRoot.sh script creates the inventory location and necessary inventory directory.

> On Unix and Linux platforms, the orainstRoot.sh script creates a file named /etc/oraInst.loc, which has information about the Oracle Inventory location and the software installation owner name.

The root.sh script should be executed as root. Executing the root.sh script copies some files to a location outside $ORACLE_HOME and sets the permissions on several files inside and outside $ORACLE_HOME. Once the root.sh script executes successfully, click OK to continue the installation.

One important file created by the root.sh script is the /etc/oratab file (the /var/opt/ oracle/oratab file on Solaris). When databases are created on this server, this file will have information about the database and which Oracle Home directory is used by the database.

 If you have multiple installations to perform, you can speed up the process and minimize errors by building an OUI response file. This text file contains all the necessary responses to the OUI prompts so that an unattended, silent install is possible.

Once the root.sh script has completed, the OUI will perform some brief post-installation configuration activities before displaying the End of Installation screen. Click the Close button to exit the OUI and return to the Unix prompt.

Once the OUI is complete, you should have a completely installed and configured $ORACLE_HOME. In the next section, you'll use this software to create your first database.

Using DBCA to Create an Oracle 12*c* Database

The Oracle Database Configuration Assistant (DBCA) is a Java-based tool used to create Oracle databases. If you've been a DBA for a few years, you probably remember the days of writing and maintaining scripts to create databases. Although it is still possible to manually create a database, the DBCA provides a flexible and robust environment in which you not only can create databases but also can generate templates containing the definitions of the databases created. This provides you with the ease of using a GUI-based interface with the flexibility of Oracle-generated XML-based templates that you can use to maintain a library of database definitions.

You can also use the DBCA to add options to a running database or to remove a database. In recent years, many die-hard command-line DBAs have switched to the DBCA tool to create databases, mainly because of its flexibility and ease of use.

You can use the DBCA to create a database while the Oracle software is installed, or you can invoke the DBCA later to manually create a database. In the following sections, we will show you the steps necessary to create an Oracle database using the DBCA tool.

Invoking the Database Configuration Assistant

You can invoke the DBCA from a command line in the Unix environment or as an application in a Windows environment. If you are using the Windows environment, choose Start ➪ All Programs ➪ *Oracle Home* ➪ Configuration and Migration Tools ➪ Database Configuration Assistant.

If you are in a Unix environment or would prefer to work from the command line in Windows, type **dbca** from the $ORACLE_HOME/bin location. The ORACLE_HOME variable must be set appropriately before invoking dbca. Also, it is recommended to set the PATH variable to include $ORACLE_HOME/bin so that all Oracle Database 12c tools can be invoked without specifying or changing to the $ORACLE_HOME/bin directory.

After you invoke the DBCA, you should see the Operation screen, as shown in Figure 9.8. The Operation screen will be different on a node that belongs to Real Application Cluster, where you will have the option to create a single instance RAC database or a multinode RAC database. Because RAC is not part of the certification exam, you will be using a node that is not part of the RAC.

FIGURE 9.8   The DBCA Database Operation screen

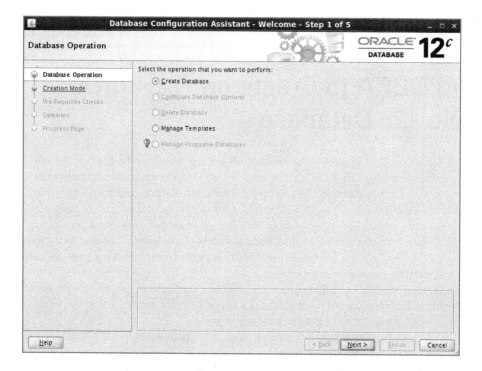

In the Database Operation screen, you can choose to create a database, configure database options, delete a database, manage templates, and manage pluggable databases. Table 9.7 lists and describes the DBCA database operation options.

Choose Create A Database, and click Next to open the Creation Mode screen. This gives you two options to create the database. The Create Database With Default Configuration option does not ask any more questions; it creates the database with minimal information collected in the screen and utilizes default configuration. See Figure 9.9 for the DBCA Creation Mode screen. (Note the number of screens on the left side; there is only one more before the summary when the default configuration is chosen.) You have to provide the database name, database file-storage location, character set, and administrative password. You can create a consolidated multitenant database by checking the Create As Container Database option; if so, you will need to provide a pluggable database name.

TABLE 9.7   DBCA Database Management Options

Option	Description
Create a Database	Allows the step-by-step creation of a database. The database can be created based on an existing template or customized for the specific needs of the organization.
Configure Database Options	Performs the necessary changes to move from a dedicated server to a shared server. You can also add database options that have not been previously configured for use with your database.
Delete a Database	Completely removes a database and all associated files.
Manage Templates	Manages database templates. The database templates are definitions of your database configuration saved in an XML file format on your local hard disk. You can choose from several predefined templates, or you can create customized templates.
Manage Pluggable Databases	This option enables you to manage pluggable databases. Pluggable or container databases allow you to consolidate multiple databases into a multitenant database. Container databases are not part of the OCA objectives at the time of writing this book.

The Advanced Mode option provides more customizable options to create the database. Choose the Advanced Mode to customize and help you learn the database creation options. Clicking Next will bring up the database template screen. In the following sections, we will discuss database templates and the various screens in the DBCA to create a database.

Database Templates

The DBCA comes with two preconfigured *database templates*. These XML-based documents contain the information necessary to create the Oracle Database 12c database. You can choose one of these predefined templates, or you can build a custom database definition. The predefined database templates are Data Warehouse and General Purpose or Transaction Processing (see Figure 9.10). These templates were designed to create databases that are optimized for a particular type of workload. When you choose Custom Database, you will have more flexibility to create tablespaces and decide which components to install. The screens that are different when choosing the Custom Database option are identified later in the section.

FIGURE 9.9 The DBCA Creation Mode screen

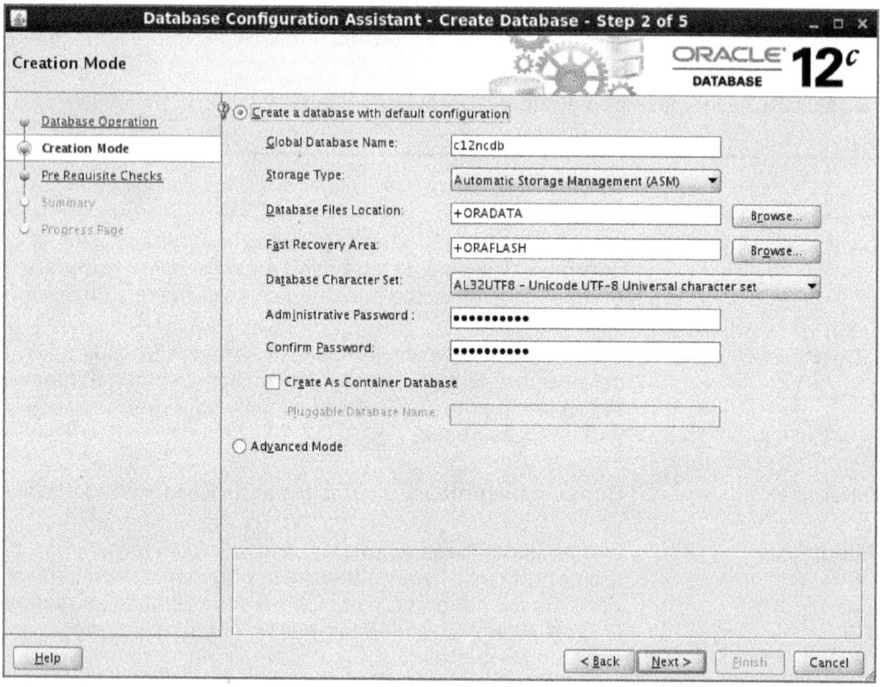

FIGURE 9.10 The DBCA Database Template screen

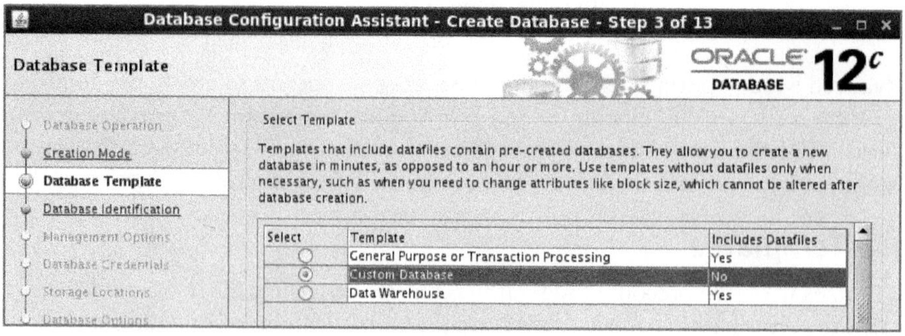

To display the configuration definitions for these preconfigured databases, click Show Details. Figure 9.11 shows the details of the General Purpose or Transaction Processing template. Using the button at the bottom-right corner, you have the option of saving the details as an HTML file. Before creating the database, you will get the summary information, and you will have the option to save the database create scripts as well as a similar HTML file with all the options and parameter values.

Table 9.8 displays information about what is contained in the template definition shown in Figure 9.11. When you scroll down, you'll see multiple sections on the page. Each section of the page gives further information about the template. For example, under the Common Options section, you will see a list of each of the database options that gets installed for the template definition you have chosen.

FIGURE 9.11   The DBCA Templates Details screen

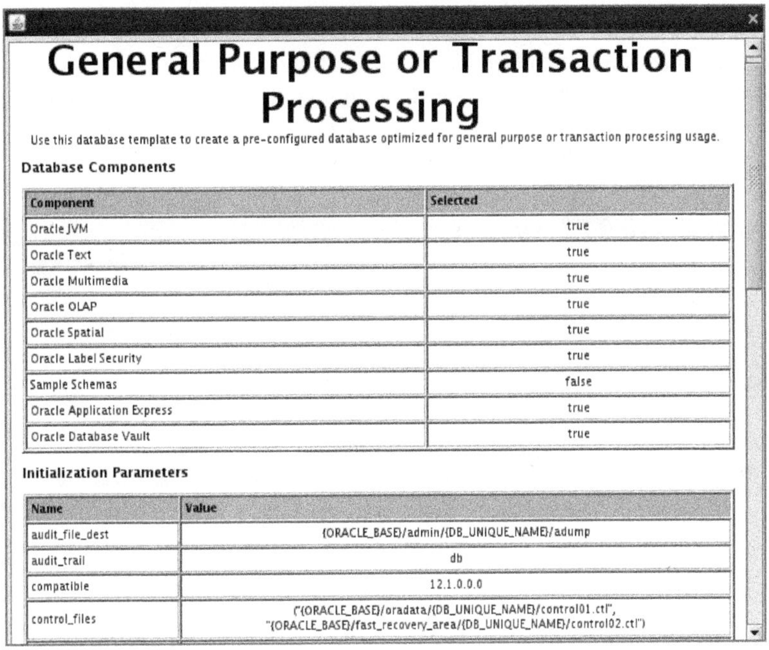

TABLE 9.8   Template Definition Details

Section	Description
Database Components	Displays which database components will be installed
Initialization Parameters	Displays the common initialization parameters and their settings
Character Sets	Displays character sets to be used
Control Files	Displays filenames and locations for control files
Data Files	Displays filenames and size for each tablespace
Redo Log Groups	Displays group number and size

Choosing the Custom Database template option on the DBCA Database Templates screen gives you the most flexibility. For other templates, the database data files are prebuilt with certain Oracle options. Also, the database block size cannot be changed from 8KB. A No value in the Includes Datafiles column in the Database Templates screen indicates which templates are fully customizable.

After you have chosen the appropriate template to use, click Next. The Database Identification screen will appear.

Database Identification

The Database Identification screen (see Figure 9.12) allows you to enter the global database name and Oracle system identification name (commonly referred to as the *Oracle SID*).

FIGURE 9.12   The DBCA Database Identification screen

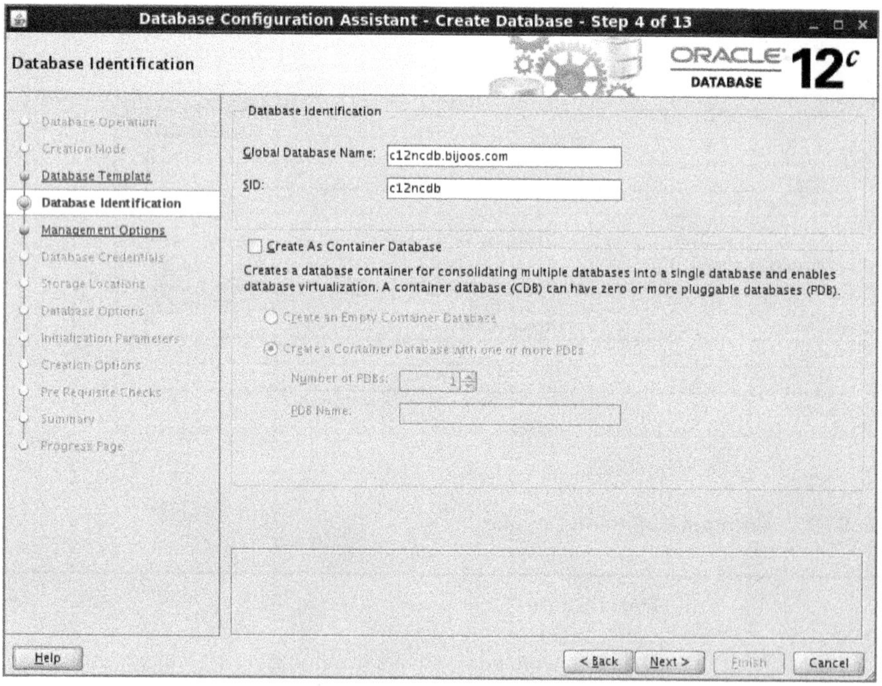

The global database name is the fully qualified name of the database in the enterprise. It is composed of a database name and a database domain, and it takes the format *database_name.database_domain*—for example, sales.company.com.

In this example, the first part of the global database name, c12ncdb, is the name of your database. Normally, the database domain is the same as the network domain within the enterprise. A global database name must be unique within a given network domain. The database name can be up to eight characters and can include letters and numbers.

The Oracle SID is the name of the instance associated with the database. Usually, this name is the same as the database name. For RAC databases where multiple instances are associated with the database, the instance name is usually different from the database name. The Oracle SID can be a maximum of eight characters and must be unique on the server. For example, you cannot have two Oracle SIDs called PROD on a single server.

The second section of the Database Identification screen is used to create the new database as a multitenant container database. If you choose this option, specify the number of pluggable databases and the pluggable database name for the CDB.

Management Options

After you provide the database name, you can configure Enterprise Manager to monitor and manage your database using the DBCA Management Options screen (see Figure 9.13).

FIGURE 9.13   The DBCA Management Options screen

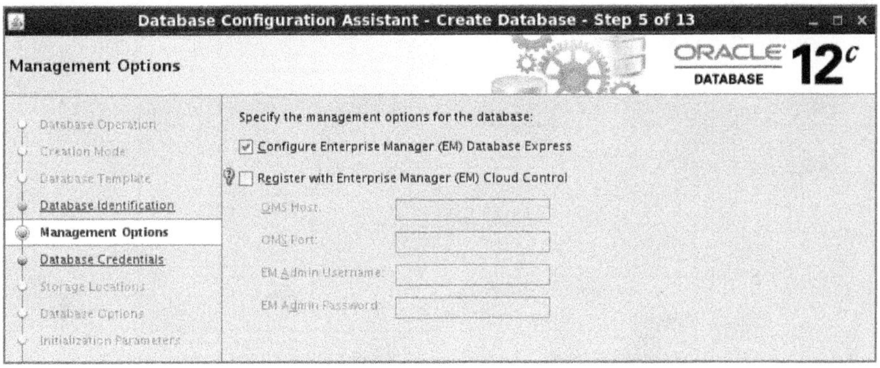

You can choose from two options: you can centrally manage all your databases from a single management console if the Management Agent for Oracle Enterprise Manager Cloud Control is installed on the database server, or you can manage each database individually using the EM Database Express.

If the *Oracle Management Agent* is installed, the DBCA detects its presence and lists the name of the agent service. You can select this name if you want this existing agent to manage this database. Your new database then becomes one of the managed targets for the existing agent.

If you don't have an agent installed or are not doing centralized database management, you can still use Enterprise Manager to monitor and maintain the database. Choose the Configure Enterprise Manager (EM) Database Express check box if you want to install Enterprise Manager and configure it locally.

Database Credentials

You use the Database Credentials screen (see Figure 9.14) to configure passwords for the various administrative accounts that are set up automatically when the database is configured. You can select the same password for all the critical accounts, or you can elect to have a different password for each of the preconfigured accounts. How you elect to set your passwords may depend on the policies of your particular organization. Typically, the same critical passwords are set for these accounts, and the accounts that you won't need to access are locked.

FIGURE 9.14   The DBCA Database Credentials screen

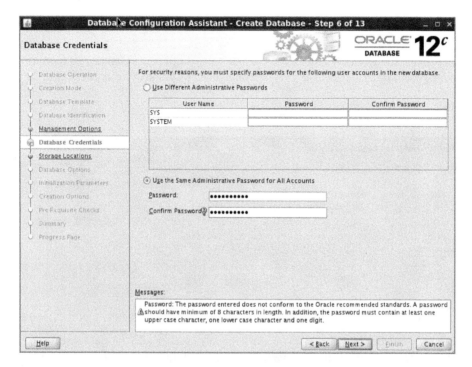

The SYS user owns all the internal Oracle tables that constitute the data dictionary. Normally, you should not perform any actions as the SYS user and should ensure that this account password is properly protected. Also, don't manually modify the underlying objects owned by the SYS user.

SYSTEM is an administrative user that contains additional administrative tables and views. Many DBAs use this account to administer the database, but ideally this account should also be locked and secured.

Once you have completed the Database Credentials page, click Next. You will be presented with the Network Configuration screen.

Network Configuration

The Network Configuration screen (shown in Figure 9.15) provides the opportunity to define and start a listener, or to associate the new database with a listener.

Click Next to go to the Storage Locations screen.

FIGURE 9.15 The DBCA Network Configuration screen

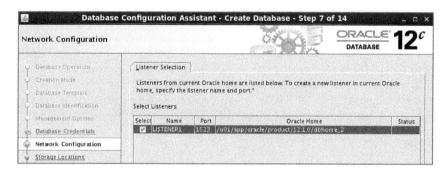

Storage Locations

The Storage Locations screen (see Figure 9.16) is used to define how you want to configure the disk storage areas used by the database. You have two choices:

- File System
- Automatic Storage Management (ASM)

Let's take a look at these options in more detail.

FIGURE 9.16 The DBCA Storage Locations screen

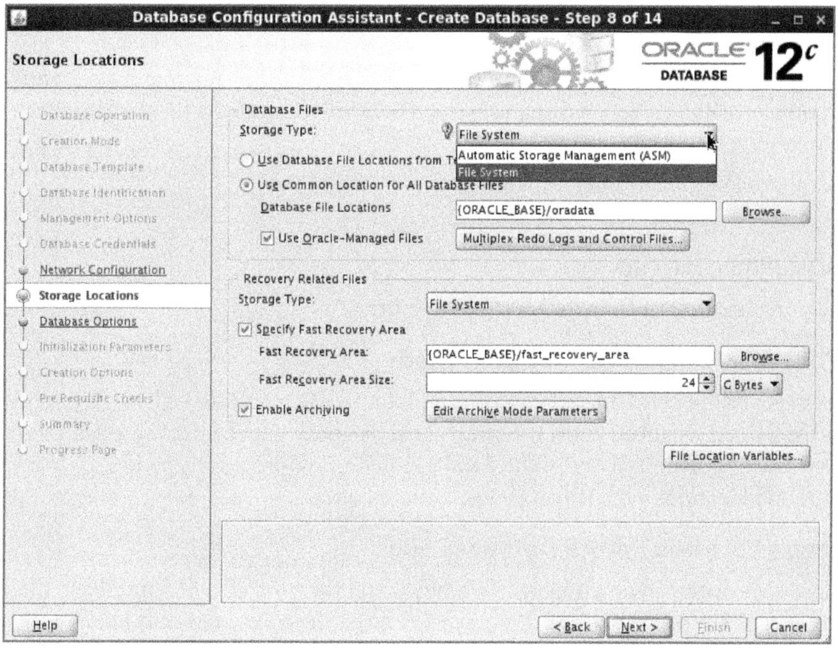

File System Storage

File system storage is a widely used type of storage configuration for many Oracle databases. This type of storage definition relies on the underlying operating system to maintain and manage the actual files you, as the DBA, define. When you choose this option, the DBCA suggests a set of data filenames and directory locations for those files. You can modify this information at the database-storage step later in the database-creation process.

The DBCA uses the Optimal Flexible Architecture (OFA) directory design for laying out the suggested file locations. The OFA is an Oracle-recommended method for designing a flexible directory structure and naming convention for your Oracle database files.

ASM Storage

Automatic Storage Management (ASM) is a type of storage mechanism available since Oracle 10g. ASM is designed to relieve the burden of disk and storage management and relies on Oracle to maintain your database storage. Instead of managing many individual database files, ASM allows you to define disk groups for file management.

Using disk groups, you can define one or more groups of disks as a logical unit that Oracle views as a single unit of storage. This concept is similar in nature to the way that some operating systems, including various versions of Unix, define volume groups.

Oracle manages the storage definitions of the database within a second instance used exclusively by ASM to keep track of the diskgroup allocations. When you create a database and select the ASM option in the Storage Locations screen, a series of screens guides you through the process of defining the secondary ASM database instance. Every server using ASM storage should be tied to an ASM instance running.

More about ASM Install and disks are discussed in Chapter 18, "Using Grid Infrastructure and Data Movement Tools." For now, choose File System on the DBCA Storage Locations screen, and specify the file locations.

Depending on the type of storage option you choose, you may have more or fewer location options available. You will be presented with three options on the Database File Locations screen:

- Use Database File Locations From Template
- Use Common Location For All Database Files
- Use Oracle-Managed Files

The following are descriptions of each of these options.

Use Database File Locations From Template

If you choose one of the predefined database templates to use for this database, Oracle uses the previously defined locations from the template as the basis for the database file locations. You still have the opportunity later in the database-definition process to review and modify the filenames and locations even if you choose this option.

Use Common Location For All Database Files

If you choose this option, you can specify a new directory for all your database files. Again, even if you choose this option, you can change the filenames and locations later in the database-definition process.

Use Oracle-Managed Files

If you choose Use Oracle-Managed Files, you let the Oracle database manage the database files. As a DBA, you just specify the location of the database files. The tasks of creating and deleting files as required by the database are automatically managed—the DBA doesn't need to specify a data file's location when creating a new tablespace or specify the size or filename. Since you will not be presented with an option to change the storage characteristics of the data files later when the Use Oracle-Managed Files option is chosen, you can have multiplexed redo log files and control files by clicking the Multiplex Redo Logs and Control Files button. In the pop-up window, specify the location of the redo log and control files.

You use the Recovery Related files section of the screen to set up database backup and recovery related files. Similar to database files, you can save the recovery related files on ASM or in a file system. You can configure several options, including specifying the flash recovery area and size. You can also enable archive-log mode for the database and specify archive-log parameters. Let's take a look at each of these options.

Fast Recovery Area

Oracle fast recovery (popularly known as FRA) has been available since Oracle 10*g*. It is the foundation of the automated disk-based recovery feature. Fast recovery is designed to simplify your life in terms of Oracle backups by providing a centralized location to maintain and manage all the files related to database backups and recovery.

The fast recovery area is an area of the disk dedicated to the storage and management of files needed for recovering an Oracle database. This area is completely separate from the other components of the Oracle database, such as the data files, redo logs, and control files.

Oracle uses the fast recovery area to store and manage the archive logs. The Oracle Recovery Manager (RMAN) uses the fast recovery area and ensures that the database is recoverable based on the files being stored in the fast recovery area. All files necessary to recover the database following a media failure are part of the fast recovery area.

 You will explore the fast recovery area in more detail in Chapter 15, "Using Backup and Recovery."

You can specify the directory location and the size of the disk area you want to dedicate to the fast recovery area. The default location of the directory provided by DBCA is $ORACLE_BASE/fast_recovery_area. You can click File Location Variables on the Recovery Configuration screen to display a summary of the Oracle file location parameters, including the current setting of the ORACLE_BASE parameter. The size of the flash recovery area defaults to 2,048MB and can be set larger or smaller by changing the Fast Recovery Size setting.

Enable Archiving

You also have the ability to enable the Oracle archive-logging option. Archive logging is the mechanism Oracle uses to enable you to perform a point-of-failure recovery of a database. To enable archive logging, select the Enable Archiving check box. By default, when the DBCA is used to create a database, the archive logs are written to Fast Recovery Area.

Once you enable the archiving checkbox, the button Edit Archive Mode Parameters will be enabled. If you click this button, you are presented with a screen that enables you to set the various parameters that are used to configure archive logging.

> We will explore archive logging in more detail in Chapter 16, "Controlling Resources and Jobs."

After completing the Storage Locations screen, click Next. The Database Options screen will appear.

Database Options

If you chose a predefined template (OLTP or Data Warehouse), you will be presented with the Database Options screen shown in Figure 9.17. You will then have the option to add sample schemas to the database, which is explored in the next section, "Sample Schemas and Custom Scripts."

FIGURE 9.17 The DBCA Database Options screen for a predefined database template

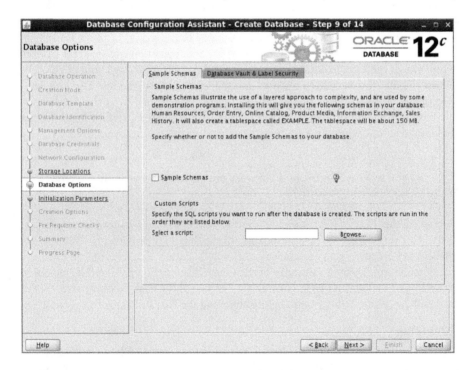

Certain options, such as Database Vault and Label Security, are not included in the predefined templates; you have the option to add them if needed. If you chose to create

a custom database on the Database Templates screen, you will be presented with the Database Options screen shown in Figure 9.18.

You use the options on this screen to specify which Oracle Database 12*c* components you want to install. Table 9.9 describes the components that can be included and configured automatically by the DBCA.

TABLE 9.9   Optional Oracle Components

Component	Description
Oracle JVM	Enables the database to run Java stored procedures, Java Database Connectivity (JDBC), and SQLJ.
Oracle Text	Provides support for multimedia content, search and analyze documents.
Oracle Multimedia	Enables you to store, manage, and retrieve images, audio, video, or other heterogeneous media data in an integrated fashion.
Oracle OLAP	Provides facilities for creating and deploying online analytical processing applications.
Oracle Spatial	Provides the components and infrastructure for Oracle to manage and maintain geographic and spatial information such as map coordinates.
Oracle Label Security	Manages and controls access to sensitive information within the database. This option will be enabled if the Label Security option is installed in the Oracle software home.
Oracle Application Express	Oracle Application Express is a rapid web application development tool using only a web browser and limited programming experience.
Oracle Database Vault	Addresses a security solution for regulatory compliance and security controls. This option will be enabled if the Database Vault option is installed in the Oracle software home.

Oracle recommends installing the standard components such as JVM, Text, multimedia, OLAP, and Application Express. You can pick the tablespace for storing the component tables; the default shown by DBCA is good to keep as is.

FIGURE 9.18 The DBCA Database Options screen for a custom database template

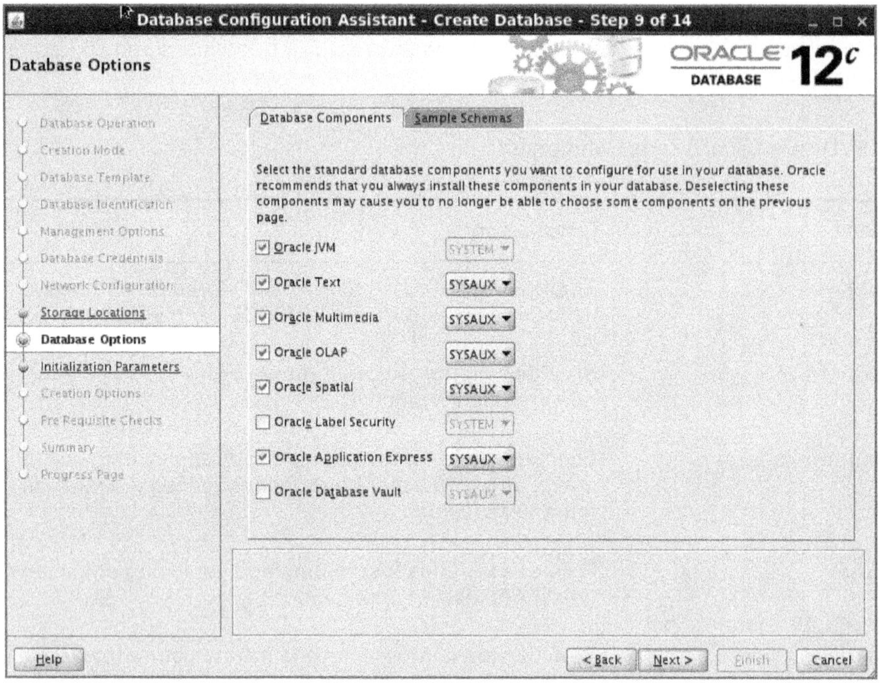

Sample Schemas and Custom Scripts

The DBCA also lets you install examples of actual working databases. Oracle provides a set of example schemas and applications that use these schemas. You can install these sample schemas now or later by running a series of SQL scripts.

These sample schemas include the following:

- Human Resources (HR)
- Order Entry (OE)
- Product Media (PM)
- Sales History (SH)
- Queued Shipping (QS)

These schemas are designed to provide you with working examples of how to use and implement a variety of features within Oracle. For example, the Product Media schema shows how to use the Oracle Intermedia option, which is used to manage binary large objects (BLOBs) such as images and sound clips.

If you choose to create the sample schemas, Oracle creates a tablespace called EXAMPLE and stores all the necessary tables within that tablespace. Be aware that this adds about 130MB to your database definition. The examples shown in Chapters 1 through 7 mostly used the tables that belonged to the sample schema HR.

You can also run custom scripts as part of the database-creation process. Click the Custom Scripts tab on the Database Options screen to enter the names and locations of the custom scripts that you want to run at database creation (see Figure 9.19).

FIGURE 9.19   The DBCA Database Options screen's Sample Schemas tab

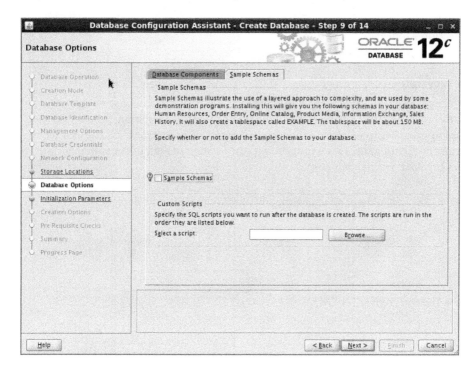

For example, you might want the DBCA to automatically create the schema and define the tables that you will use for this database. You can create a script that performs all the necessary work and have the DBCA run the script as part of the database-creation process. The custom scripts are run using the command-line utility SQL*Plus, so you will have to define a user ID and password within the body of the script. For example, your script might contain the following line:

```
connect some_userid/some_password
```

This line directs Oracle to connect to the current Oracle database, which is determined by your ORACLE_SID environment variable using the supplied user ID and password.

After completing the Database Options screen, click Next. You will then be presented with the Initialization Parameters screen.

Initialization Parameters

You use the *Initialization Parameters* screen to define the various initialization-parameter settings used to configure size and set up the characteristics of the Oracle instance. The following four tabs are categorized according to the parameters used to manage the Oracle instance:

- Memory
- Sizing
- Character Sets
- Connection Mode

Let's take a look at each of these tabs and the settings you can manage on each one.

The Memory Tab

You use the options on the Memory tab to control the size of the database parameters that configure the overall memory footprint of the Oracle instance (see Figure 9.20). There are two general approaches to managing the memory database parameters: Oracle can set and manage most of the parameters for you, or you can customize each of the initialization parameters for your specific database.

FIGURE 9.20   The Memory tab on the Initialization Parameters screen

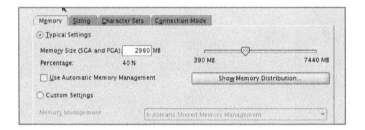

If you choose Typical Settings, Oracle allocates memory to the various components within the Oracle system global area (SGA) and process global area (PGA). This memory allocation is automatic and is a percentage of the overall physical memory available on the server. The default is 40 percent of the total memory available, but you can change this setting by specifying the memory size or by sliding the bar to the appropriate size. If you choose this setting, click the Show Memory Distribution button to see how Oracle will allocate the memory between the SGA and the PGA (see Figure 9.21).

If you choose the Use Automatic Memory Management option under Typical Settings, Oracle will manage the total memory automatically, including the SGA and PGA. The memory distribution will show differently, as in Figure 9.22, if this option is selected.

FIGURE 9.21   Memory distribution for SGA and PGA for the Typical Settings

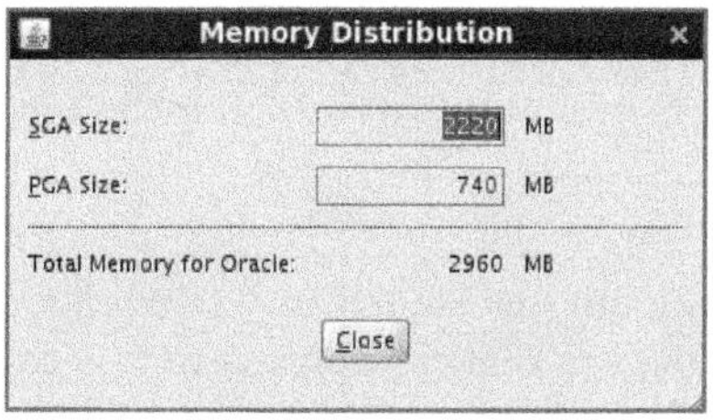

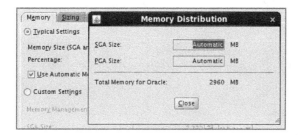

FIGURE 9.22   Memory distribution for Automatic Memory Management

   If you choose the Custom Settings option, you will again have two options: Automatic Shared Memory Management and Manual Shared Memory Management. With Automatic Shared Memory Management, you specify only the SGA size and the PGA size. Each component inside the SGA is configured automatically by Oracle. With Manual Shared Memory Management, you have full control over how much each of the specific areas of the SGA will take. The main areas that you will configure are the shared pool, buffer cache, Java pool, large pool, and PGA size. Each setting maps to a specific Oracle parameter. Figure 9.23 shows the options.

FIGURE 9.23   DBCA showing the Manual Shared Memory Management options

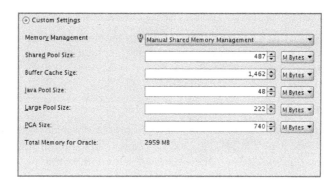

Memory management and the parameters associated with memory are discussed in detail in Chapter 14, "Maintaining the Database and Managing Performance."

The Sizing Tab

You use the options on the Sizing tab (see Figure 9.24) to configure the block size of your database and the number of processes that can connect to this database. The Block Size setting corresponds to the smallest unit of storage within the Oracle database. All storage of database objects (tables, indexes, and so on) is governed by the block size. The block size defaults to 8KB, but you can modify it in the custom template only. Once the database is created, you cannot modify the database block size.

FIGURE 9.24 The Sizing tab on the Initialization Parameters screen

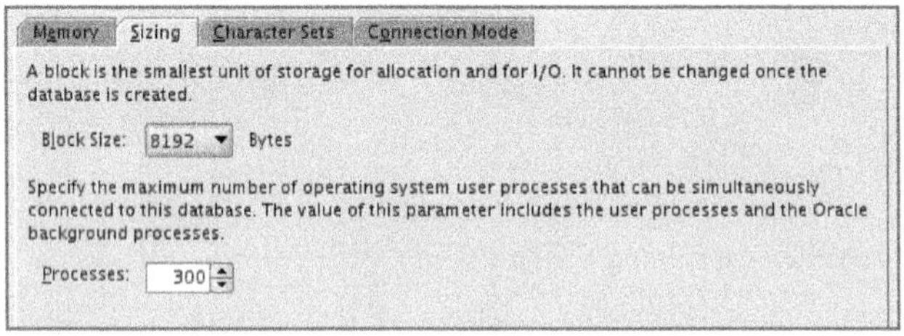

The maximum and minimum size of an Oracle block depend on the operating system. Generally, 8KB is sufficient for most transaction-oriented applications; larger block sizes, such as 16KB and higher, are used in data warehouse–type applications. The block size can be 2KB, 4KB, 8KB, 16KB, or 32KB.

The Processes setting specifies the maximum number of simultaneous operating-system processes that can be connected to this Oracle database. If you are not sure of the number of processes needed, you can start with the default value of 300. This parameter does have a bearing on the overall size of your Oracle instance. The larger you make this number, the more room Oracle must reserve in the SGA to track the processes.

The block size can be changed only for the Custom Database Template. For the other predefined templates that include data files, you cannot change the block size.

The Character Sets Tab

You use the options on the Character Sets tab to configure the character sets you will use within your database (see Figure 9.25). You will determine the database character set, the national character set, the default language, and the default date format.

FIGURE 9.25 The Character Sets tab on the Initialization Parameters screen

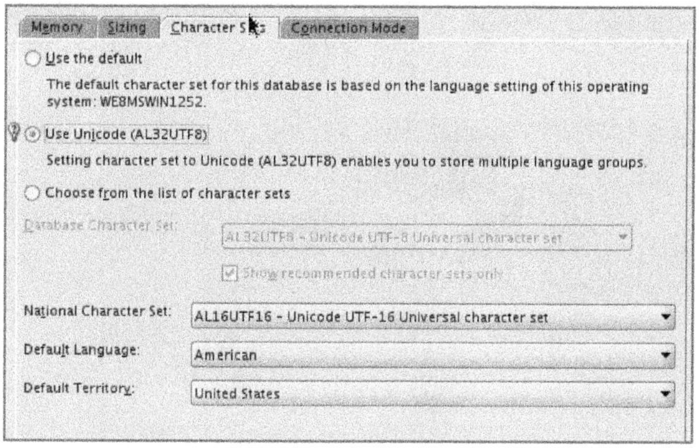

Specifying a database character set defines the type of encoding scheme that Oracle uses to determine how characters are displayed and stored within your Oracle environment. The character set you choose determines the languages that can be represented in your environment. It also controls other nuances, such as how your database interacts with your operating system and how much storage is required for your data. The default character set is based on the language setting of the operating system.

Specifying a national character set defines how your database represents Unicode characters in a database that does not use a Unicode-enabled character set. You use the Default Language setting to manage certain aspects of how your database represents information pertaining to different locales. For example, this setting determines how your database displays time and monetary values. AL16UTF16 and UTF8 are the only national character sets from which you can choose.

Use the Default Language and Default Territory setting to specify how Oracle supports certain locale-sensitive information such as day and month abbreviations, writing direction, and default sorting.

The Connection Mode Tab

You use the options on the Connection Mode tab to specify the type of connections to use for this database (see Figure 9.26). You can choose *Dedicated Server Mode* or *Shared Server Mode*. The default connection mode is Dedicated Server Mode.

> **NOTE** The Dedicated Server and Shared Server modes are covered in more detail in Chapter 12, "Understanding Oracle Network Architecture."

In the Dedicated Server Mode, each user process will have a dedicated server process. In the Shared Process Mode, many user processes share a server process.

FIGURE 9.26 The Connection Mode tab on the Initialization Parameters screen

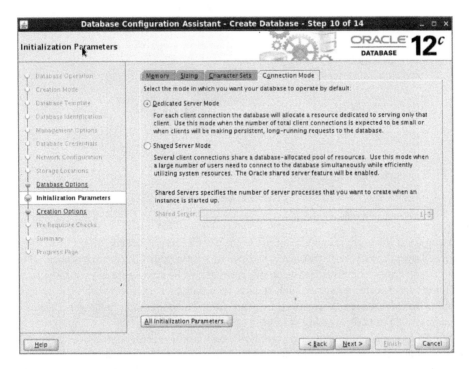

If you want to review the initialization parameters and make any changes, click the All Initialization Parameters button. The screen shown in Figure 9.27 details the basic parameters. From this screen, you can view/edit the advanced parameters using the Show Advanced Parameters button. You have the option to edit a value on this screen.

FIGURE 9.27 The DBCA Initialization Parameters screen

Name ▲	Value	Override Default	Category
cluster_database	FALSE		Cluster Database
compatible	12.1.0.0.0	✔	Miscellaneous
control_files	("/u02/oradata/{DB_UNIQUE_NAME...	✔	File Configuration
db_block_size	8	✔	Cache and I/O
db_create_file_dest			File Configuration
db_create_online_log_dest_1			File Configuration
db_create_online_log_dest_2			File Configuration
db_domain		✔	Database Identification
db_name	c12ndb1	✔	Database Identification
db_recovery_file_dest	(ORACLE_BASE)/fast_recovery_area	✔	File Configuration
db_recovery_file_dest_size	11	✔	File Configuration
db_unique_name			Miscellaneous
instance_number	0		Cluster Database
log_archive_dest_1			Archive
log_archive_dest_2			Archive
log_archive_dest_state_1	enable		Archive
log_archive_dest_state_2	enable		Archive
nls_language	AMERICAN		NLS

Help   Close   Show Advanced Parameters   Show Description

After completing the Initialization Parameters screen, click Next. You will then be presented with the Creation Options screen.

Creation Options

The Creation Options screen (see Figure 9.28) provides you with three options, and you can choose all three if needed.

FIGURE 9.28   The DBCA Creation Options screen

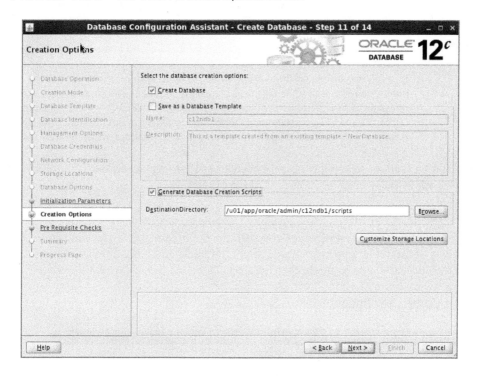

Create Database   Use this option to have the DBCA create your database.

Save as a Database Template   You can elect to save your database definition to a template and create the database at a later time, or you can have the DBCA create the template along with creating the database.

Generate Database Creation Scripts   This option will generate scripts for you to create the database at a later time without using the DBCA.

If you elect to create your database, the DBCA uses the information you provided in the previous screens to create all the necessary components of your database, populates the database with sample schemas if they were chosen, starts your database, and gets the database ready for use.

If you elect to save your database to a template definition, this definition is added to the list of database definitions that you can select on subsequent executions of the DBCA.

You can also let the DBCA create a set of scripts that you can run manually to create the database. You can choose a location to store your scripts, and then you can run the scripts manually to generate your database. If you choose a manual creation process, you will also have to manually configure several items, including the Oracle Internet Directory Service if you elect to use centralized naming and your listener. Also, depending on your operating system, you will have to configure or modify the oratab file (under /etc or /var/opt/oracle depending on the platform) on Unix or create a service in the Windows environment.

When preparing for the test, create the database using a predefined template as well as a custom template. Save the database-creation scripts, and go through the scripts so that you understand what statements are executed behind the scenes by the DBCA to create the database. When using a custom template, a new database will be created using the CREATE DATABASE statement. When using a predefined template, Oracle does not create a new database from scratch; instead, it clones an existing database from the template.

The Creation Options screen has a button to customize storage locations. Choose this if you want to adjust the storage location or data file properties.

Customizing Storage

The Customize Storage screen provides you with the opportunity to review and change the locations of the actual objects that compose the Oracle database; namely, the data files, control files, and redo logs (see Figure 9.29).

FIGURE 9.29 The DBCA Customize Storage screen

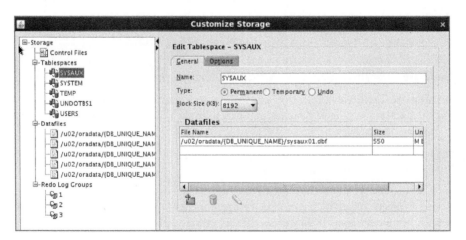

This screen displays a tree structure in the left pane. You can click the various elements within the tree to expand and display the details of each component. Selecting an element displays details about the element in the pane on the right. For example, clicking Control File displays a summary of the control filenames and locations in the right pane. You can make manual changes to the names and locations of the control files in the right pane.

If you are creating a custom database definition that does not use a template, you can add new objects to a particular group. For example, clicking the Tablespaces folder and then clicking Create lets you add new tablespaces to your database definition. If you selected a database template that included data file definitions, you cannot add or remove data files, or tablespaces, but you can modify the location of the data files, control files, and redo log groups.

 Chapter 10, "Understanding Storage and Space Management," covers configuring and managing tablespaces and data files in detail.

After completing the Database Storage screen, click Close to go back to the Database Options screen. When you click Next, DBCA performs all the prerequisite checks and skips the prerequisite screen display if there are no issues. If issues are identified, you will be provided with the Pre Requisite Checks screen as in Figure 9.30. You have the option to fix the issue and click Check Again or Ignore All and proceed with the database creation.

FIGURE 9.30   The DBCA Pre Requisite Checks screen

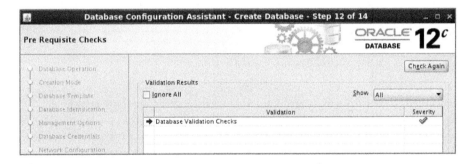

Once the prerequisites are met, the Database Summary screen appears as in Figure 9.31. You can scroll down the window to examine the following:

- Components to install into the database
- The initialization-parameter settings
- Character-set settings
- Tablespaces
- Names and locations for data files

- Names and locations for redo logs
- Names and locations for control files

FIGURE 9.31   The DBCA Summary screen

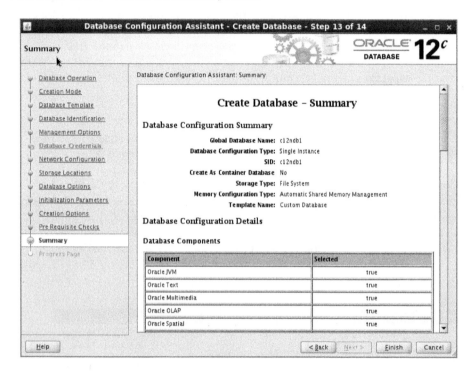

Once you click Finish to start the database-creation process, Oracle creates the database you specified. It starts the instance, creates all the necessary database components, and configures all the database options you specified. If you chose to create scripts, DBCA displays the location of the scripts. Depending on the size of database you create and how many options you are installing, the process can take anywhere from several minutes to an hour or more.

During the database creation, the summary progress is displayed. Two buttons in this screen are useful for viewing more information: Activity Log and Alert Log. Click on the Activity Log to view detailed information about the steps that are executing. Click on the Alert Log button to view the database alert log file. Figure 9.32 shows the Progress Page with alert log pop-up displaying information.

After the database is created, DBCA displays a summary screen, as shown in Figure 9.33. Note the information on this screen, especially the URL to invoke Enterprise Manager Database Express and the server parameter file location.

FIGURE 9.32 The DBCA Progress Page screen

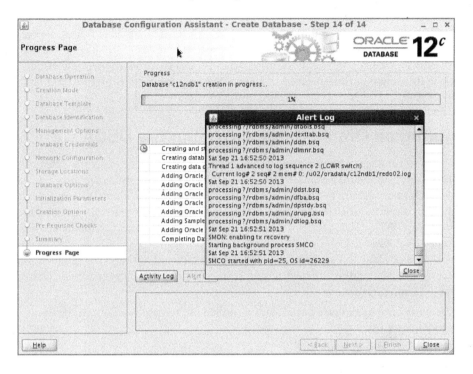

FIGURE 9.33 The DBCA result summary screen

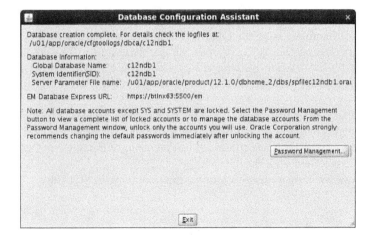

On this screen, you have the option to manage passwords (click Password Management). By default, all the accounts except SYS, SYSTEM are locked. You can change the password and unlock selective accounts.

When the creation process is complete, connect to the database with one of the tools such as SQL*Plus or Enterprise Manager to verify that all the database options and components were installed properly. Logging into Enterprise Manager will give you an overview of the new database. By using the URL specified in Figure 9.33, you can invoke the EM Database Express home page.

Configuring an Oracle Database Using the DBCA

The DBCA lets you change various aspects of an existing database. To change the database configuration, select Configure Database Options on the DBCA Operations screen, as shown in Figure 9.8. (Options that are not applicable to the particular Oracle Home are grayed out. Once a database is created, the Configure and Delete options will be visible.) If the database is not started, the DBCA starts it for you automatically. You must connect to the database as a user who has DBA authority.

Once you have selected and started the database, you can add options that may not have been previously included in the database. Using DBCA you can make the following changes to the database configuration:

- Add database options that are not already installed (no reinstall option) in the database (refer to Figure 9.18).

- Install a sample schema if not already installed (refer to Figure 9.19).

- Change the default connection mode for the database. You can change from Dedicated Server Mode to Shared Server Mode, or vice versa (refer to Figure 9.26).

Deleting an Oracle Database Using the DBCA

You can also delete a database using the DBCA. On the Operations screen (Figure 9.8), choose Delete Database, and click Next to open the Database screen. The DBCA lists all the databases available for deletion. Choose the database you want to delete. DBCA also gives you the option to deregister the database from the EM cloud control if the database is registered.

The Delete Database summary screen shows the name of the database and files associated with the database that is removed. If you click Finish, the DBCA removes all files on the disk associated with the database you have chosen. If you are using Windows, the DBCA also removes the service associated with the database.

Exercise 9.1 shows you how to delete a database manually using SQL*Plus.

EXERCISE 9.1

Manually Delete or Remove an Oracle Database

Some DBAs prefer to use a command-line interface to perform their tasks. You can delete a database using the command-line tool SQL*Plus.

To do so, first connect to SQL*Plus as an administrator who has the ability to start up the database—that is, an administrator with either the SYSOPER or the SYSDBA privilege.

Here's an example:

/u01/app/oracle>**sqlplus sys/**** as sysdba**

Once you are connected, you need to put the database in MOUNT RESTRICT mode. Issue the following command if the database is not running:

Startup mount restrict;

Next, issue the following command:

Drop database;

This command shuts down the instance and deletes all the files associated with the database, including the server parameter file. You may have to remove any archived logs from the database archive area using the appropriate operating-system command.

Managing Database Templates Using the DBCA

As explained earlier in this chapter, the DBCA can store and use XML-based templates to create your Oracle database. As the DBA, you can manage these database-definition templates. Saving a definition of your database in a template format makes it easier to perform various tasks. For example, you can copy a preexisting template to modify new database definitions. The template definition is normally stored in the $ORACLE_HOME/assistants/dbca/templates directory on Unix and in the %ORACLE_HOME%\assistants\dbca\templates directory on Windows systems.

The DBCA can use two types of templates: seed and nonseed. *Seed* templates are template definitions that contain database-definition information and the actual data files and redo log files. The advantage of a seed template is that the DBCA makes a copy of the data files and redo logs included in the definition file. These prebuilt data files include all schema information, which makes the database-creation process faster. The seed templates carry a .dbc extension. The associated predefined data files are stored as files having a .dfb extension. When you use a seed template, you can change the database name, the data file locations, the number of control files and redo log groups, and the initialization parameters.

Nonseed templates contain custom-defined database definitions. Unlike seed templates, they do not come with preconfigured data files and redo logs. Nonseed templates carry a .dbt extension.

Now let's look at the various options you have to manage templates.

Creating Template Definitions Using the DBCA

You can use the DBCA interface to create new database templates. DBCA templates are XML files that contain information required to create a new database or to clone existing databases. Templates can be copied from one machine to another, and thus can be used to create databases with a uniform standard. When you connect to the DBCA, select Manage Templates on the Database Operation screen (see Figure 9.8, shown earlier in this chapter), and click Next to open the Template Management screen, as shown in Figure 9.34.

FIGURE 9.34 The DBCA Template Management screen

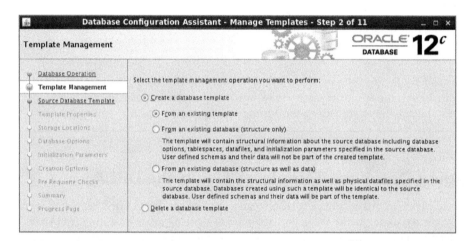

You have three choices for creating templates. Table 9.10 summarizes your options.

TABLE 9.10 Template-Creation Options

Selection	Description
From an Existing Template	Creates a new template definition from a preexisting template. This allows you to modify a variety of template settings, including parameters and data file storage characteristics.

Selection	Description
From an Existing Database (Structure Only)	Creates a new template based on the structural characteristics of an existing database. The data files are created from scratch and will not include data from the original database. Choose this option when you want a database that is structurally like another database but does not contain any data. The database you are copying from can reside anywhere in your network.
From an Existing Database (Structure As Well As Data)	Creates a new template based on the structural characteristics of an existing database. The data files and all corresponding user data are included in the new database. Choose this option when you want an exact copy of an existing database. The database you are copying must reside on the same physical server as the new database you are creating.

Depending on the option selected, you will be presented with a set of forms to save your template definition. If you elect to create a template from an existing database, you will have to connect to the database so that the DBCA can obtain information about the database. You must connect to the database as a user who has DBA credentials to perform this task.

If you are copying a definition from an existing template, you can configure the template by following a series of screens that are similar to those used to create a database. These screens allow you to configure the various aspects of the template, including initialization parameters and data file and redo log locations.

Deleting Template Definitions Using the DBCA

You can also delete an existing template definition. On the Database Operation screen (see Figure 9.8, shown earlier in this chapter), click Manage Templates. You will be presented with the Template Management screen (see Figure 9.34). Select the Delete a Database Template option. You can then select the template to delete. When you remove the template, the DBCA removes the XML file from the system.

Working with Oracle Database Metadata

In addition to tables such as DEPARTMENTS and EMPLOYEES that store important business data, Oracle databases also contain system tables that store data about the database. Examples of the type of information in these system tables include the names of all the tables in the database, the column names and datatypes of those tables, the number of rows those tables contain, and security information about which users are allowed to access those tables. This "data about the database" is referred to as *metadata*. As a DBA, you will frequently use this metadata when performing your administration tasks.

An Oracle Database 12c database contains two types of metadata views:

- Data dictionary views
- Dynamic performance views

The SYS user owns the data dictionary and dynamic performance views in the Oracle database, and they are stored in the SYSTEM tablespace. During normal database operation, Oracle frequently uses the data dictionary and updates the dictionary with the current status of the database components. The dictionary is also immediately updated when a DDL statement is executed.

Data dictionary views and dynamic performance views are described in the next section.

Data Dictionary Views

Data dictionary views provide information about the database and its objects. Depending on which features are installed and configured, an Oracle Database 12c database can contain more than 2,000 data dictionary views. Data dictionary views have names that begin with DBA_, ALL_, and USER_. For every DBA_ view a corresponding CDB_ view also exists with a container identifier. Oracle creates public synonyms on many data dictionary views so users can access the views conveniently. Data dictionary is owned by user SYS.

The difference between the DBA_, ALL_, and USER_ views can be illustrated using the DBA_OBJECTS data dictionary view as an example. The DBA_OBJECTS view shows information on all the objects in the database. The corresponding ALL_OBJECTS view, despite its name, shows only the objects that a particular database user owns or can access. For example, if you were logged into the database as a user named SCOTT, the ALL_OBJECTS view would show all the objects owned by the user SCOTT and the objects to which SCOTT has been granted access by other users or through a system privilege. The USER_OBJECTS view shows only those objects owned by a user. If the user SCOTT were to examine the USER_OBJECTS view, only those objects he owns would be displayed. In a multitenant container database, multiple pluggable databases are present. The CDB_ views are available for the CDB administrator to view information from all the databases in the CDB. Figure 9.35 shows a graphical representation of the relationship between the CDB_, DBA_, ALL_, and USER_ views.

Because the DBA_ views provide the broadest metadata information, they are generally the data dictionary views used by DBAs. Table 9.11 provides examples of a few DBA_ data dictionary views.

TABLE 9.11 Examples of Data Dictionary Views

Dictionary View	Description
DBA_TABLES	Shows the names and physical storage information about all the tables in the database
DBA_USERS	Shows information about all the users in the database

Dictionary View	Description
DBA_VIEWS	Shows information about all the views in the database
DBA_TAB_COLUMNS	Shows all the names and datatypes of the table columns in the database
DBA_TABLESPACES	Shows information on tablespaces in the database
DBA_DATA_FILES	Shows information on the data files belonging to the database

You can find a complete list of the Oracle Database 12c data dictionary views in the "Oracle Database Reference 12c Release 1 (12.1) E17615-18" document available at http://www.oracle.com/pls/db121/portal .all_books.

FIGURE 9.35　A comparison of data dictionary views

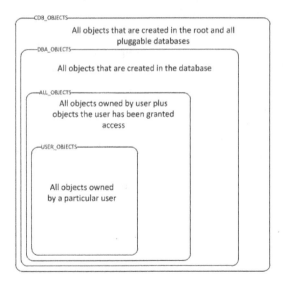

Dynamic Performance Views

Throughout database operation, Oracle updates a set of virtual tables to record the current database activity and status. These tables are called *dynamic performance tables*. Views are created on top of the dynamic performance tables so that information is grouped better and names are in a user-friendly format. The dynamic performance views are sometimes called *fixed views*, because they cannot be altered or removed by the database administrator.

The dynamic performance tables begin with X$. The dynamic performance view names begin with V_$. Public synonyms are created for these views, and they begin with V$. For example, the dynamic performance view with data file information is v_$datafile, whereas the public synonym is v$datafile.

Depending on which features are installed and configured, an Oracle database can contain over 700 dynamic performance views. Most of these views have names that begin with V$. Table 9.12 describes a few of these dynamic performance views.

TABLE 9.12   Examples of Dynamic Performance Views

Dynamic Performance View	Description
V$DATABASE	Contains information about the database, such as the database name and when the database was created
V$VERSION	Shows which software version the database is using
V$OPTION	Displays which optional components are installed in the database
V$SQL	Displays information about the SQL statements that database users have been issuing

Although the contents of the DBA_ and V$ metadata views are similar, there are some important differences between the two types. Table 9.13 compares these two types.

TABLE 9.13   Data Dictionary vs. Dynamic Performance Views

Data Dictionary Views	Dynamic Performance Views
The DBA_ views usually have plural names (for example, DBA_DATA_FILES).	The names of the V$ views are generally singular (for example, V$DATAFILE).
The DBA_ views are available only when the database is open and running.	Some V$ views are available even when the database is not fully open and running.
The data contained in the DBA_ views is static and is not cleared when the database is shut down.	The V$ views contain dynamic statistical data that is lost each time the database is shut down.

The data dictionary view DICTIONARY shows information about the data dictionary and dynamic performance views in the database. DICT is a synonym for the DICTIONARY view. The COMMENTS column shows the purpose or contents of the view. The V$FIXED_TABLE view lists the dynamic performance tables and views in the database. You can use SQL Developer to query the contents of these views so that you can better understand them.

The Oracle data dictionary and dynamic performance views are created while creating the database. The scripts to create the metadata are stored in the $ORACLE_HOME/rdbms/admin directory. Several scripts are in this directory, and the script that creates the base dictionary objects is called catalog.sql. The catproc.sql script creates the PL/SQL packages and functionality to support PL/SQL in the database.

You are not allowed to log in as SYS and modify the data dictionary views or update information directly using SQL. The only SYS-owned table you are allowed to delete records from is AUD$. This table is used to store database audit information.

Managing Initialization-Parameter Files

Oracle uses initialization-parameter files to store information about initialization parameters used when an Oracle instance starts. Oracle reads the parameter file to obtain information about how the Oracle instance should be sized and configured upon startup.

The parameter file can be a plaintext file, commonly referred to as a *pfile*, or it can be a binary parameter file, commonly referred to as an *spfile*. You can use either type of file to configure instance and database options; however, there are some important differences between the two types of configuration files, as shown in Table 9.14.

TABLE 9.14 Pfiles vs. Spfiles

Pfile	Spfile
Text file that can be edited using a text editor.	Binary file that cannot be edited directly.
When changes are made to the pfile, the instance must be shut down and restarted before it takes effect.	Parameter changes made to the database using ALTER SYSTEM are updated in the spfile.
Is called init*instance_name*.ora.	Is called spfile*instance_name*.ora.

TABLE 9.14   Pfiles vs. Spfiles *(continued)*

Pfile	Spfile
Oracle instance reads only from pfile.	Oracle instance reads and writes to the spfile.
Can be created from an spfile using the `create pfile from spfile` command.	Can be created from a pfile using the `create spfile from pfile` command.

You can specify more than 365 documented configuration parameters in the pfile or spfile. Oracle Database 12*c* divides these parameters into two categories: basic and advanced. Oracle recommends you set only the basic initialization parameters manually. Oracle also recommends you do not modify the remaining parameters unless directed to do so by Oracle Support or to meet the specific needs of your application.

Most parameters can be modified dynamically, meaning a database restart is not required for the new value to take effect. But certain parameter value changes require a database restart. Table 9.15 describes the basic initialization parameters. A "Yes" in the `Static` column indicates that the parameter is static and cannot be modified dynamically without a database restart.

TABLE 9.15   Oracle Database 12*c* Basic Initialization Parameters

Parameter Name	Static	Description
CLUSTER_DATABASE	Yes	Tells the instance whether it is part of a clustered environment.
COMPATIBLE	Yes	Specifies the release level and feature set you want to be active in the instance.
CONTROL_FILES	Yes	Designates the physical location of the database control files.
DB_BLOCK_SIZE	Yes	Specifies the default database block size. The database block size specified at database creation cannot be changed.
DB_CREATE_FILE_DEST	No	Specifies the directory location where database data files will be created if the Oracle-Managed Files feature is used.
DB_CREATE_ONLINE_LOG_DEST_*n*	No	Specifies the location(s) where the database redo log files will be created if the Oracle-Managed Files feature is used.

Parameter Name	Static	Description
DB_DOMAIN	Yes	Specifies the logical location of the database on the network.
DB_NAME	Yes	Specifies the name of the database that is mounted by the instance.
DB_RECOVERY_FILE_DEST	No	Specifies the location where recovery files will be written if the flash recovery feature is used.
DB_RECOVERY_FILE_DEST_SIZE	No	Specifies the amount of disk space available for storing flash recovery files.
DB_UNIQUE_NAME	Yes	Specifies a globally unique name for the database within the enterprise.
INSTANCE_NUMBER	Yes	Identifies the instance in a Real Application Clusters (RAC) environment.
LDAP_DIRECTORY_SYSAUTH	Yes	Enables or disables Oracle Internet Directory–based authentication for SYSDBA and SYSOPER connections to the database.
LOG_ARCHIVE_DEST_*n*	No	Specifies as many as nine locations where archived redo log files are to be written.
LOG_ARCHIVE_DEST_STATE_*n*	No	Indicates how the specified locations should be used for log archiving.
NLS_LANGUAGE	Yes	Specifies the default language of the database.
NLS_TERRITORY	Yes	Specifies the default region or territory of the database.
OPEN_CURSORS	No	Sets the maximum number of cursors that an individual session can have open at one time.
PGA_AGGREGATE_TARGET	No	Establishes the overall amount of memory that all PGA processes are allowed to consume.
PROCESSES	Yes	Specifies the maximum number of operating-system processes that can connect to the instance.
REMOTE_LISTENER	No	Specifies a network name that points to the address or list of addresses of remote Oracle Net listeners.
REMOTE_LOGIN_PASSWORDFILE	Yes	Determines whether the instance uses a password file and what type.

TABLE 9.15   Oracle Database 12*c* Basic Initialization Parameters *(continued)*

Parameter Name	Static	Description
SESSIONS	Yes	Determines the maximum number of sessions that can connect to the database.
SGA_TARGET	No	Establishes the maximum size of the SGA, within which space is automatically allocated to each SGA component when Automatic Memory Management is used.
SHARED_SERVERS	No	Specifies the number of shared server processes to start when the instance is started. See Chapter 11, "Managing Data and Undo," for details.
STAR_TRANSFORMATION_ENABLED	No	Determines whether the optimizer will consider star transformations when queries are executed. See Chapter 14 for details on the optimizer.
UNDO_TABLESPACE	No	Specifies which tablespace stores undo segments if the Automatic Undo Management option is used. See Chapter 11 for details on undo management.

The V$PARAMETER view shows the parameters that are available to use. Review the DESCRIPTION column to understand the purpose. The ISBASIC column with value TRUE identifies the basic parameters.

```
SELECT name, description
FROM   v$parameter
WHERE  isbasic = 'TRUE';
```

Any parameters not specified in the pfile or spfile take on their default values. The following is an example of the contents of a typical Oracle Database 12*c* pfile after the database was created using DBCA:

```
*.audit_file_dest='/u01/app/oracle/admin/c12ndb1/adump'
*.audit_trail='db'
*.compatible='12.1.0.0.0'
*.control_files='/u02/oradata/c12ndb1/control01.ctl','/u01/app/oracle/fast_
recovery_area/c12ndb1/control02.ctl'
*.db_block_size=8192
*.db_domain=''
*.db_name='c12ndb1'
```

```
*.db_recovery_file_dest='/u01/app/oracle/fast_recovery_area'
*.db_recovery_file_dest_size=11g
*.diagnostic_dest='/u01/app/oracle'
*.dispatchers='(PROTOCOL=TCP) (SERVICE=c12ndb1XDB)'
*.local_listener='LISTENER_C12NDB1'
*.log_archive_format='%t_%s_%r.dbf'
*.memory_target=4000m
*.open_cursors=300
*.processes=300
*.remote_login_passwordfile='EXCLUSIVE'
*.undo_tablespace='UNDOTBS1'
```

In this sample pfile, the sizes of the shared pool, database buffer cache, large pool, and Java pool are not individually specified. Instead, Oracle's Automatic Memory Management features allow you to simply set one configuration parameter—MEMORY_TARGET—to establish the total amount of memory allocated to the SGA and PGA. This parameter is discussed in Chapter 14.

On production databases, if your Oracle license is based on the number of named users, you can enforce the license compliance by setting the LICENSE_MAX_USERS parameter. The default for this parameter is 0, which means you can create any number of users in the database and the license compliance is not enforced.

 Real World Scenario

Handle with Care: Undocumented Configuration Parameters

You've just read a performance-tuning tip posted to the Oracle newsgroup at comp .databases.oracle.server. The person posting the tip suggests setting the undocumented pfile parameter _optimizer_dyn_smp_blks to a value of 200 in order to fix an issue. Should you implement this suggestion as a precaution or even if you see a similar issue?

More than 2,900 undocumented configuration parameters are available in Oracle Database 12c. Undocumented configuration parameters are distinguished from their documented counterparts by the underscore that precedes their name, as with the parameter described in the newsgroup posting.

We do not recommend utilizing undocumented pfile or spfile parameters on any of your systems because knowing the appropriate reasons to use these parameters, and the appropriate values to set these parameters to, is almost pure speculation because of their undocumented nature. Although some undocumented parameters are relatively harmless (such as _trace_files_public), using others incorrectly can cause unforeseen database problems.

You may use the following query logged in as SYSDBA to view all undocumented parameters in the database.

```
select ksppinm parameter, ksppdesc description
from x$ksppi
where substr(ksppinm,1,1) = '_'
```

One exception to this recommendation is when you are directed to use an undocumented configuration parameter by Oracle Support or an application vendor. Oracle Support occasionally uses these parameters to enhance the generation of debug information or to work around a bug in the kernel code or to enhance the performance of certain code.

Certain parameters in the spfile begin with a double underscore. These are dynamic areas managed by Oracle automatic features and are used as starting sizes when you restart the database. Here is an example:

```
$ strings spfileC12DB1.ora | head -10
C12DB1.__data_transfer_cache_size=0
C12DB1.__db_cache_size=788529152
C12DB1.__java_pool_size=16777216
C12DB1.__large_pool_size=16777216
C12DB1.__oracle_base='/u01/app/oracle'#ORACLE_BASE set from environment
C12DB1.__pga_aggregate_target=788529152
C12DB1.__sga_target=2348810240
C12DB1.__shared_io_pool_size=117440512
C12DB1.__shared_pool_size=1375731712
C12DB1.__streams_pool_size=0
```

Locating the Default Parameter File

The default location that Oracle searches to find the pfile and spfile parameter files is $ORACLE_HOME/dbs on Unix systems and %ORACLE_HOME%\database on Windows systems.

Oracle uses a search hierarchy when a startup command is issued without specifying either a pfile or an spfile. Oracle looks for files with the following names in the default directory to start the instance:

- spfile$ORACLE_SID.ora
- spfile.ora
- init$ORACLE_SID.ora

Oracle first looks for a parameter file called spfile$ORACLE_SID.ora. If it doesn't find that, it searches for spfile.ora. Finally, it searches for a traditional text pfile with the default name of init$ORACLE_SID.ora.

If the parameter files do not exist in the default location or you want to use a different parameter file to start your database, you can specify a parameter file to use when you issue a startup command to start the Oracle database. A database instance cannot start without referring to a parameter file.

 You will see examples of how database startup is performed later in this chapter in the section "Starting up and Shutting down an Oracle Instance."

Modifying Initialization-Parameter Values

In some instances, you may need to change the initialization parameters. For example, you might need to increase the number of sessions allowed to connect to the database because you are adding users. Whatever the case, you need to know how to make these changes. There are a few options to change the initialization-parameter value, based on the type of parameter file used. Here they are

- If PFILE is used, edit the pfile using an OS editor and make any appropriate changes.
- If SPFILE is used, connect to the instance and make the changes using the ALTER SYSTEM SET parameter_name = value statement.
- Use EM Database Express to make changes.

Using EM Database Express

To use the EM Database Express tool to modify existing database parameters, navigate to the Configuration menu and choose Initialization Parameters. The SPFile tab shows the parameters as set in the spfile. You can also use the filters to find the exact parameter that needs to be modified. The SPFile tab groups the parameters in various categories. Figure 9.36 shows the EM screen to change initialization parameters. You have to be logged in as SYSDBA to modify the parameters.

The Initialization Parameters screen has two tabs:

Current Tab This tab displays all the currently active settings for the initialization parameters for the database instance. If a parameter is marked Dynamic, you can modify it, and this modification immediately affects the parameter that affects the currently running instance without stopping the database. The changes you make on the Current tab are not permanent, so the next time the database is stopped and restarted, the settings will revert to their original values. Click on Set to modify the parameter values; you will have the option to change the memory value or spfile value, or both.

SPFile Tab　If you are using a server parameter file, you will see the SPFile tab. This tab also lets you change existing database parameters. The difference between changing parameters on this tab and changing parameters on the Current tab is that changes to the spfile are persistent across database startups and shutdowns because the changes are saved to the spfile definition. You can also apply your changes to the spfile only or to the spfile and the currently running instance. Click on Set to modify the parameter values. The SQL code used for set is `alter system set "<parameter>"=<value> scope=spfile sid='*'`. Click on Reset to remove the parameter from SPFile and have it default. The SQL used for reset is `alter system reset "<parameter>" scope=spfile sid='*'`.

FIGURE 9.36　The EM Database Express Initialization Parameters screen

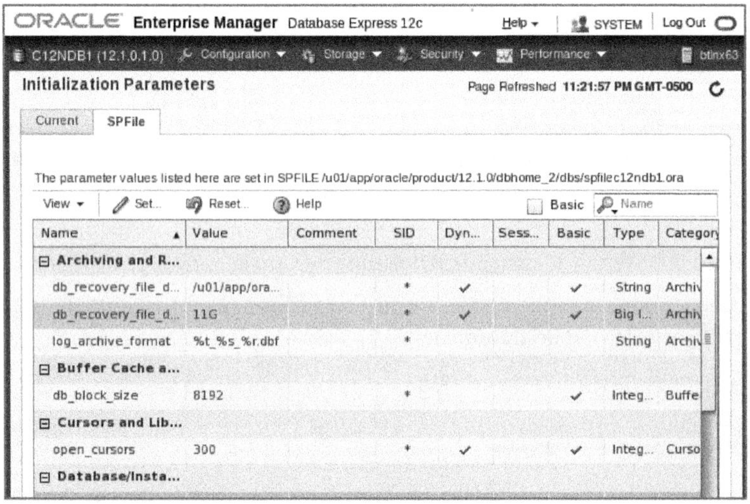

Using SQL*Plus or SQL Developer

Although EM Database Express is a handy tool to modify the initialization parameters, sometimes it is convenient to use SQL*Plus or SQL Developer and make changes to the parameters. You should know about two dynamic performance views: V$PARAMETER and V$SPPARAMETER.

V$PARAMETER

The V$PARAMETER view shows information about the initialization parameters that are currently in effect. This view has several useful columns. Table 9.16 lists some of the columns in V$PARAMETER and how they can be used in queries.

TABLE 9.16   V$PARAMETER Columns

Column Name	Description
NAME	This specifies the name of the initialization parameter.
VALUE	This specifies the current value of the parameter.
DISPLAY_VALUE	This specifies the current value in a more user-friendly format.
DESCRIPTION	This gives a short description about the parameter.
ISBASIC	TRUE indicates that the parameter is categorized as a basic parameter.
ISDEFAULT	FALSE indicates that the parameter was specified in the pfile or spfile during instance startup.
ISMODIFIED	FALSE indicates that the parameter has not been modified since the instance started.
ISSES_MODIFIABLE	TRUE indicates that the parameter can be modified using an ALTER SESSION statement.
ISSYS_MODIFIABLE	FALSE indicates that the parameter cannot be modified using an ALTER SYSTEM statement. Such parameters can be changed only using the SCOPE=SPFILE clause.

V$SPPARAMETER

The V$SPPARAMETER view shows the contents of the spfile used to start the instance. A TRUE value for the ISSPECIFIED column shows whether the parameter was specified in the spfile. If a pfile was used to start the instance, all the rows will have FALSE for the ISSPECIFIED column. Sometimes, querying the V$SPPARAMETER can produce readable output for parameters that take multiple values.

V$PARAMETER vs. V$SPPARAMETER

The following SQL example shows the difference in the result from the V$PARAMETER and V$SPPARAMETER views:

```
SQL> SELECT name, value
  2  FROM v$parameter
  3  WHERE name LIKE 'control%'
  4  AND isdefault = 'FALSE';
```

```
NAME             VALUE
---------------  ----------------------------------------------------------
control_files    /u02/oradata/c12ndb1/control01.ctl, /u01/app/oracle/fast
                 _recovery_area/c12ndb1/control02.ctl


SQL> SELECT name, value
  2  FROM v$spparameter
  3  WHERE name LIKE 'control%'
  4  AND isspecified = 'TRUE';

NAME             VALUE
---------------  ----------------------------------------------------------
control_files    /u02/oradata/c12ndb1/control01.ctl
control_files    /u01/app/oracle/fast_recovery_area/c12ndb1/control02.ctl

SQL>
```

You can use the ALTER SESSION statement to change the value of a parameter in the current session. For example, if you want to change the default date-display format for the session only, use the following statement:

```
SQL> ALTER SESSION SET NLS_DATE_FORMAT = 'DD-MON-YYYY HH24:MI:SS';

Session altered.

SQL>
```

You can use the ALTER SYSTEM statement to change the value of a parameter system-wide or in the spfile, or both. You use the SCOPE clause to define where you want to change the parameter value: MEMORY, SPFILE, and BOTH are the valid values for the SCOPE clause.

A value of DEFERRED or IMMEDIATE in the ISSYS_MODIFIABLE column shows that the parameter can be dynamically changed using ALTER SYSTEM. The DEFERRED value indicates that the change you make does not take effect until a new session is started; the existing sessions will use the current value. IMMEDIATE indicates that as soon as you change the value of the parameter, it is available to all sessions in the instance. A *session* is a job or task that Oracle manages. When you log in to the database using SQL*Plus or any other tool, you start a session.

If you want to change a parameter value for the current instance but do not want the change to persist across database shutdowns, you can specify SCOPE=MEMORY, as in the following example:

```
SQL> ALTER SYSTEM SET UNDO_RETENTION = 3600 SCOPE=MEMORY;

System altered.
SQL>
```

Some parameters values can be set only at instance startup; they are not modifiable when the instance is running. Such parameter changes can be made with the SCOPE=SPFILE clause. Oracle will make the change only to the spfile, which takes effect after you restart the database:

```
SQL> ALTER SYSTEM SET UNDO_MANAGEMENT = MANUAL;
ALTER SYSTEM SET UNDO_MANAGEMENT = MANUAL
                    *
ERROR at line 1:
ORA-02095: specified initialization parameter cannot be modified

SQL> ALTER SYSTEM SET UNDO_MANAGEMENT = MANUAL SCOPE=SPFILE;

System altered.
SQL>
```

Usually when you make a parameter change, you want it to take effect immediately in memory as well as persist the change across database shutdowns. You can use the SCOPE=BOTH clause, which is the default, for this purpose. So if you omit the SCOPE clause, Oracle will make changes to the memory and to the spfile. If a pfile is used to start the instance, the change will be in memory only for the current running instance.

```
SQL> ALTER SYSTEM SET SGA_TARGET=500M SCOPE=BOTH;

System altered.
SQL>
```

You can use the SQL*Plus command SHOW PARAMETER to view the current value of an initialization parameter. You can specify the full parameter name or part of the name. For example, to view all the parameters related to undo, you can do the following. The first one (SHOW PARAMETER) shows parameters as in memory, and the second one (SHOW SPPARAMETER) shows parameters defined in the SPFile.

```
SQL> SHOW PARAMETER undo
NAME                                 TYPE         VALUE
------------------------------------ ------------ ------------------------------
temp_undo_enabled                    boolean      FALSE
undo_management                      string       AUTO
undo_retention                       integer      900
undo_tablespace                      string       UNDOTBS1
SQL>
SQL> SHOW SPPARAMETER undo
```

SID	NAME	TYPE	VALUE
*	temp_undo_enabled	boolean	
*	undo_management	string	
*	undo_retention	integer	
*	undo_tablespace	string	UNDOTBS1

SQL>

In the next section, the options to start up and shut down a database will be discussed.

Starting Up and Shutting Down an Oracle Instance

As a DBA, you are responsible for the startup and shutdown of the Oracle instance. Oracle gives authorized administrators the ability to perform this task using a variety of interfaces. It is important to understand the options that are available to you to start up and shut down the Oracle instance and when the various options can or should be used. The stages of instance startup and the startup options appear frequently on OCA certification exams.

To start up or shut down an Oracle instance, you need to be connected to the database with the appropriate privileges. Two special connection account authorizations are available for startup and shutdown: SYSDBA and SYSOPER. The SYSDBA authorization is an all-empowering authorization that allows you to perform any database task. The SYSOPER authorization is a less powerful authorization that allows startup and shutdown abilities but restricts other administrative tasks, such as access to nonadministrative schema objects. These authorizations are managed either through a passwords file or via operating-system control.

When a database is initially installed, only the SYS schema can connect to the database with the SYSDBA authorization. You can grant this authorization and the SYSOPER authorization to give others the ability to perform these tasks without connecting as the SYS user.

Now let's look at how to perform a database startup.

The startup and shutdown discussed here are for the noncontainer databases. For container databases, the startup is the same but in addition the pluggable databases need to be opened separately. When you issue a shutdown connected to the root container of the container database, all pluggable databases are shut down before shutting down the container database.

Starting Up an Oracle Database 12*c* Instance

As described in Chapter 8, "Introducing Oracle Database 12*c* Components and Architecture," the Oracle instance is composed of a set of logical memory structures and background processes that users interact with to communicate with the Oracle database. When Oracle is started, these memory structures and background processes are initialized and started so that users can communicate with the Oracle database.

Whenever an Oracle database is started, it goes through a series of steps to ensure database consistency. When it starts up, a database passes through three modes: NOMOUNT, MOUNT, and OPEN. This section will review each of these *startup modes* and other special startup options, such as FORCE and RESTRICT, and discuss when you need to use these options. Then you'll review how to use the available interfaces to start up an Oracle instance.

STARTUP NOMOUNT   This starts the instance without mounting the database. When a database is started in this mode, the parameter file is read, and the background processes and memory structures are initiated, but they are not attached nor do they communicate with the disk structures of the database. When the instance is in this state, the database is not available for use.

If a database is started in NOMOUNT mode, the background processes are started and shared memory is allocated. The instance is not associated with any database. This state is used to create a database or to create a database control file.

At times, a database may not be able to go to the next mode (called MOUNT mode) and will remain in NOMOUNT mode. For example, this can occur if Oracle has a problem accessing the control file structures, which contain important information needed to continue with the startup process. If these structures are damaged or not available, the database startup process cannot continue until the problem is resolved.

 If STARTUP NOMOUNT fails, the most likely cause is that the parameter file cannot be read or is not in the default location. Other causes include OS resource limits that prevent memory or process allocation.

STARTUP MOUNT   This performs all the work of the STARTUP NOMOUNT option and reads the control file. At this point, Oracle obtains information from the control files that it uses to locate and attach to the physical database structures. The control file contains the name of the database, all the data filenames, and the redo log files associated with the database.

Certain administrative tasks can be performed while the database is in this mode, including renaming data files, enabling or disabling archive logging, renaming and adding redo log files, and recovering the database.

STARTUP OPEN   This is the default startup mode if no mode is specified on the STARTUP command line. STARTUP OPEN performs all the steps of the STARTUP NOMOUNT and STARTUP MOUNT options. This option makes the database available to all users.

When opening the database, you can use a couple of options. STARTUP OPEN READ ONLY opens the database in read-only mode. STARTUP OPEN RECOVER opens the database and performs a database recovery.

Although you typically use the STARTUP NOMOUNT, STARTUP MOUNT, and STARTUP OPEN options, a few other startup options are available that you can use in certain situations: STARTUP FORCE and STARTUP RESTRICT. These are discussed next.

STARTUP FORCE   You can use the STARTUP FORCE startup option if you are experiencing difficulty starting the database in a normal fashion. For example, when a database server loses power and the database stops abruptly, the database can be left in a state in which a STARTUP FORCE startup is necessary. This type of startup should not normally be required but can be used if a normal startup does not work. What is also different about STARTUP FORCE is that it can be issued no matter what mode the database is in. STARTUP FORCE does a shutdown abort and then restarts the database; therefore, it can be used to cycle a database that is in open state.

STARTUP RESTRICT   The STARTUP RESTRICT option starts up the database and places it in OPEN mode but gives access only to users who have the RESTRICTED SESSION privilege. You might want to open a database using the RESTRICTED option when you want to perform maintenance on the database while it is open but want to ensure that users cannot connect and perform work on the database. You might also want to open the database using the RESTRICTED option to perform database exports or imports and guarantee that no users access the system during these activities. After you are done with your work, you can disable the restricted session, ALTER SYSTEM DISABLE RESTRICTED SESSION, so everyone can connect to the database.

STARTUP UPGRADE / DOWNGRADE   The STARTUP UPGRADE option starts up the database in UPGRADE mode and sets system initialization parameters to specific values required to enable database upgrade scripts to be run. UPGRADE should be used only when a database is first started with a new version of the Oracle Database Server.

Similarly, the STARTUP DOWNGRADE option sets system initialization parameters to specific values required to enable database downgrade scripts to be run. Database upgrade and downgrade are discussed in Chapter 17, "Upgrading an Oracle Database."

Oracle EM Database Express is available only when the database is up and running. Hence, database instance startup and shutdown options are not available in EM Database Express. Oracle Enterprise Manager Cloud Control manages multiple databases and has an agent on the database server. You can use EM Cloud Control to start and stop the database and listener.

Starting Oracle Using SQL*Plus

You can use the command-line facility SQL*Plus to start the Oracle database. You will need to connect to SQL*Plus as a user with SYSOPER or SYSDBA privileges. Here is the syntax of the startup options available:

```
STARTUP [NOMOUNT|MOUNT|OPEN] [PFILE=] [RESTRICT] [FORCE] [QUIET]
```

Table 9.17 shows some examples of startup commands that you can use from within SQL*Plus. The QUIET option suppresses the SGA information during startup.

TABLE 9.17 SQL*Plus DB Startup-Command Examples

Command	Description
STARTUP NOMOUNT pfile=/u01/oracle/init.ora	Starts Oracle in NOMOUNT mode using a nondefault parameter file.
STARTUP MOUNT	Starts Oracle in MOUNT mode using a default spfile or pfile.
STARTUP OPEN	Starts Oracle in OPEN mode using a default spfile or pfile.
STARTUP RESTRICT	Starts Oracle in OPEN mode and allows only users with restricted session privileges to connect to the database.
STARTUP FORCE	Forces database startup using the default pfile or spfile. The running instance is shut down using the ABORT method.
STARTUP OPEN PFILE=/u01/sp01.ora	Starts Oracle in OPEN mode using a nondefault parameter file.

Here is an example of how you can use the STARTUP FORCE command with a nondefault parameter file to start an Oracle database using SQL*Plus:

```
$ sqlplus / as sysdba

SQL*Plus: Release 12.1.0.1.0 Production on Sun Sep 22 10:37:13 2013
Copyright (c) 1982, 2013, Oracle.  All rights reserved.
Enter user-name: system/**** as sysdba
```

```
Connected to:
Oracle Database 12c Enterprise Edition Release 12.1.0.1.0 - 64bit Production
With the Partitioning, OLAP, Advanced Analytics and Real Application Testing
options
SQL>
SQL> startup force pfile='/home/oracle/mypfile1.ora'

ORACLE instance started.
Total System Global Area 2505338880 bytes
Fixed Size                   2405760 bytes
Variable Size              671091328 bytes
Database Buffers          1811939328 bytes
Redo Buffers                19902464 bytes
Database mounted.
Database opened.
SQL>
```

> If you are running Oracle on Windows, you can also start the database when you start the associated Oracle service. Starting the Oracle service automatically starts the Oracle database.

Changing Database Startup States Using SQL

When the database is in the NOMOUNT or MOUNT state, you can go to the next state by using the ALTER DATABASE statement instead of shutting down the database and starting with the appropriate state option. The following SQL statements show how to perform database-availability state changes.

- To mount a database in NOMOUNT state, use ALTER DATABASE MOUNT;.
- To open a database from NOMOUNT or MOUNT state, use ALTER DATABASE OPEN;.
- To open a database in read-only mode, use ALTER DATABASE OPEN READ ONLY;.
- To enable restricted mode, use ALTER SYSTEM ENABLE RESTRICTED SESSION;.
- To disable restricted mode, use ALTER SYSTEM DISABLE RESTRICTED SESSION;.

> If the database is already open, you cannot return to the MOUNT or NOMOUNT state. You have to shut down the database and start with the appropriate state.

Shutting Down an Oracle Database 12*c* Instance

In some instances, you will need to shut down a database, such as to perform regularly scheduled cold backups of the database, to perform database upgrades, or to change a nondynamic initialization parameter. Just as with starting the database, several options as well as a variety of interfaces are available for database shutdown:

SHUTDOWN NORMAL   A normal shutdown is the default type of shutdown that Oracle performs if no shutdown options are provided. You need to be aware of the following performing a normal shutdown:

- No new Oracle connections are allowed from the time the SHUTDOWN NORMAL command is issued.
- The database will wait until all users are disconnected to proceed with the shutdown process.

Because Oracle waits until all users are disconnected before shutting down, you can find yourself waiting indefinitely for a client who may be connected but is no longer doing any work or who may have left for the day. This can require extra work, identifying which connections are still active and either notifying the users to disconnect or forcing the client disconnections by killing their sessions. This type of shutdown is also known as a *clean* shutdown because when you start Oracle again, no recovery is necessary.

SHUTDOWN TRANSACTIONAL   A transactional shutdown of the database is a bit more aggressive than a normal shutdown. The characteristics of the transactional shutdown are as follows:

- No new Oracle connections are allowed from the time the SHUTDOWN TRANSACTIONAL command is issued.
- No new transactions are allowed to start from the time the SHUTDOWN TRANSACTIONAL command is issued.
- Once all active transactions on the database have completed, all client connections are disconnected.

A transactional shutdown does allow client processes to complete prior to the disconnection. This can prevent a client from losing work and can be valuable especially if the database has long-running transactions that need to be completed prior to shutdown. This type of shutdown is also a clean shutdown and does not require any recovery on a subsequent startup.

SHUTDOWN IMMEDIATE   The immediate shutdown method is the next most aggressive option. An immediate shutdown is characterized as follows:

- No new Oracle connections are allowed from the time the SHUTDOWN IMMEDIATE command is issued.
- Any uncommitted transactions are rolled back. Therefore, a user in the middle of a transaction will lose all the uncommitted work.
- Oracle does not wait for clients to disconnect. Any unfinished transactions are rolled back, and their database connections are terminated.

This type of shutdown works well if you want to perform unattended or scripted shutdowns of the database and you need to ensure that the database will shut down without getting hung up during the process by clients who are connected. Even though Oracle is forcing transactions to roll back and disconnecting users, an immediate shutdown is still a clean shutdown. No recovery activity takes place when Oracle is subsequently restarted.

SHUTDOWN ABORT A shutdown abort is the most aggressive type of shutdown and has the following characteristics:

- No new Oracle connections are allowed from the time the SHUTDOWN ABORT command is issued.

- Any SQL statements currently in progress are terminated, regardless of their state.

- Uncommitted work is not rolled back.

- Oracle disconnects all client connections immediately upon the issuance of the SHUTDOWN ABORT command.

Do not use SHUTDOWN ABORT regularly. Use it only if the other options for database shutdown fail or if you are experiencing some type of database problem that is preventing Oracle from performing a clean shutdown. This type of shutdown is not a clean shutdown and requires instance recovery when the database is subsequently started. Instance recovery is performed automatically when you do the startup—no manual intervention required. During instance recovery the uncommitted changes are rolled back from the database, and committed changes are written to the data files. Oracle uses the redo log files and undo segments to construct the instance recovery information.

Shutting Down Oracle Using SQL*Plus

You can use the command-line facility SQL*Plus to shut down the Oracle database. You will need to connect to SQL*Plus as a user with the SYSOPER or SYSDBA privilege. Here is the syntax of the shutdown options available to you:

```
SHUTDOWN [NORMAL|TRANSACTIONAL|IMMEDIATE|ABORT]
```

Here is an example of how to use the SHUTDOWN IMMEDIATE command to shut down an Oracle database using SQL*Plus:

```
$ sqlplus / as sysdba

SQL*Plus: Release 12.1.0.1.0 Production on Sun Sep 22 10:23:33 2013
Copyright (c) 1982, 2013, Oracle.  All rights reserved.
Enter user-name: system/**** as sysdba

Connected to:
Oracle Database 12c Enterprise Edition Release 12.1.0.1.0 - 64bit Production
With the Partitioning, OLAP, Advanced Analytics and Real Application Testing
options
SQL>
```

```
SQL> shutdown immediate;
Database closed.
Database dismounted.
ORACLE instance shut down.
SQL>
```

 If you are running in a Windows environment and shut down the database using either the Database Control or SQL*Plus tool, the Oracle service will continue to run. Even though the Oracle Windows service is running, the database is not available until a subsequent startup command is issued.

Monitoring the Database Alert Log

The database *alert log*, sometimes referred to as the *alert file*, contains information about certain activities and errors that occur within your database. The alert log contains a chronological summary of the database events. The alert log contains a wealth of information that you can use to diagnose system problems and review the history of activities that have occurred on the system. This is the first location DBA must look to diagnose database issues. Some of the events and actions recorded in the alert log include the following:

- Startup and shutdown information, including a record of every time a database is started or shut down
- Certain types of administrative actions, such as the ALTER SYSTEM and ALTER DATABASE commands
- Certain types of database errors, such as internal Oracle errors (ORA-600 errors) or space errors (ORA-1542, for example)
- Messages that are errors about shared servers and dispatchers
- Errors during materialized view refreshes
- The values of initialization parameters that have values different from their default values at instance startup

Here is an excerpt from an Oracle Database 12*c* alert log. Long output is shown for you to review and understand the type of information written to alert log (the output format here is adjusted to print in two columns to conserve space):

```
Sat Sep 21 17:17:28 2013
TABLE SYS.WRP$_REPORTS: ADDED INTERVAL
PARTITION SYS_P201 (1360) VALUES LESS
THAN (TO_DATE(' 2013-09-22 01:00:00',
'SYYYY-MM-DD HH24:MI:SS', 'NLS_
CALENDAR=GREGORIAN'))

TABLE SYS.WRP$_REPORTS_DETAILS: ADDED
INTERVAL PARTITION SYS_P202 (1360)
VALUES LESS THAN (TO_DATE(' 2013-09-22
01:00:00', 'SYYYY-MM-DD HH24:MI:SS',
'NLS_CALENDAR=GREGORIAN'))
```

```
TABLE SYS.WRP$_REPORTS_TIME_BANDS:
ADDED INTERVAL PARTITION SYS_P205
(1359) VALUES LESS THAN (TO_DATE('
2013-09-21 01:00:00', 'SYYYY-MM-DD
HH24:MI:SS', 'NLS_CALENDAR=GREGORIAN'))
```

Sat Sep 21 17:17:29 2013

Thread 1 cannot allocate new log, sequence 41

Checkpoint not complete

```
  Current log# 1 seq# 40 mem# 0: /u02/
oradata/c12ndb1/redo01.log
```

Sat Sep 21 17:17:32 2013

Thread 1 advanced to log sequence 41 (LGWR switch)

```
  Current log# 2 seq# 41 mem# 0: /u02/
oradata/c12ndb1/redo02.log
```

Sat Sep 21 17:18:08 2013

Thread 1 cannot allocate new log, sequence 42

Checkpoint not complete

```
  Current log# 2 seq# 41 mem# 0: /u02/
oradata/c12ndb1/redo02.log
```

Sat Sep 21 17:18:14 2013

queuing purge of JIT compilation due to creation of d74dab20 oracle/xml/util/XMLUtil

Sat Sep 21 17:18:14 2013

Thread 1 advanced to log sequence 42 (LGWR switch)

```
  Current log# 3 seq# 42 mem# 0: /u02/
oradata/c12ndb1/redo03.log
```

… … …

Sat Sep 21 18:03:54 2013

```
****************************************
*****************************
```

LICENSE_MAX_SESSION = 0

LICENSE_SESSIONS_WARNING = 0

Initial number of CPU is 2

Number of processor cores in the system is 2

Number of processor sockets in the system is 1

CELL communication is configured to use 0 interface(s):

CELL IP affinity details:

    NUMA status: non-NUMA system

    cellaffinity.ora status: N/A

CELL communication will use 1 IP group(s):

    Grp 0:

Picked latch-free SCN scheme 3

Using LOG_ARCHIVE_DEST_1 parameter default value as USE_DB_RECOVERY_FILE_DEST

Autotune of undo retention is turned on.

IMODE=BR

ILAT =51

LICENSE_MAX_USERS = 0

SYS auditing is disabled

NOTE: remote asm mode is local (mode 0x1; from cluster type)

Starting up:

Oracle Database 12c Enterprise Edition Release 12.1.0.1.0 - 64bit Production

With the Partitioning, OLAP, Advanced Analytics and Real Application Testing options.

ORACLE_HOME = /u01/app/oracle/product/12.1.0/dbhome_2

System name:	Linux
Node name:	btlnx63
Release:	2.6.39-400.24.1.el6uek.x86_64
Version:	#1 SMP Wed May 15 11:46:52 PDT 2013
Machine:	x86_64

Using parameter settings in client-side pfile /u01/app/oracle/admin/c12ndb1/pfile/init.ora on machine btlnx63

System parameters with non-default values:

```
  processes           = 300
  sga_target          = 2224M
  control_files       = "/u02/
oradata/c12ndb1/control01.ctl"
```

```
  control_files            = "/u01/
app/oracle/fast_recovery_area/c12ndb1/
control02.ctl"
  db_block_size            = 8192
  compatible               =
"12.1.0.0.0"
  log_archive_format       = "%t_%s_%r.
dbf"
  db_recovery_file_dest    = "/u01/app/
oracle/fast_recovery_area"
  db_recovery_file_dest_size= 11G
  undo_tablespace          = "UNDOTBS1"
  remote_login_passwordfile=
"EXCLUSIVE"
  db_domain                = ""
  dispatchers              =
"(PROTOCOL=TCP) (SERVICE=c12ndb1XDB)"
  local_listener           = "LISTENER_
C12NDB1"
  audit_file_dest          = "/u01/app/
oracle/admin/c12ndb1/adump"
  audit_trail              = "DB"
  db_name                  = "c12ndb1"
  open_cursors             = 300
  pga_aggregate_target     = 740M
  diagnostic_dest          = "/u01/app/
oracle"
NOTE: remote asm mode is local (mode
0x1; from cluster type)
Starting background process PMON
Sat Sep 21 18:03:54 2013
PMON started with pid=2, OS id=26952
Starting background process PSP0

… … …
Sat Sep 21 18:03:56 2013
starting up 1 dispatcher(s) for network
address '(ADDRESS=(PARTIAL=YES)
(PROTOCOL=TCP))'...
Sat Sep 21 18:03:56 2013
MMNL started with pid=20, OS id=26990
starting up 1 shared server(s) ...
ORACLE_BASE from environment = /u01/
app/oracle
```

```
Sat Sep 21 18:03:56 2013
ALTER DATABASE   MOUNT
Sat Sep 21 18:03:58 2013
Using default pga_aggregate_limit of
2048 MB
Sat Sep 21 18:04:00 2013
Changing di2dbun from  to c12ndb1
Sat Sep 21 18:04:00 2013
Successful mount of redo thread 1, with
mount id 1855935436
Sat Sep 21 18:04:00 2013
Database mounted in Exclusive Mode
Lost write protection disabled
Ping without log force is disabled.
Completed: ALTER DATABASE   MOUNT
Sat Sep 21 18:04:01 2013
alter database archivelog
Completed: alter database archivelog
alter database open
Starting background process TMON
Sat Sep 21 18:04:01 2013
TMON started with pid=23, OS id=27006
Sat Sep 21 18:04:01 2013
LGWR: STARTING ARCH PROCESSES
Starting background process ARC0
Sat Sep 21 18:04:01 2013
ARC0 started with pid=24, OS id=27008
… … …
Sat Sep 21 18:04:03 2013
FBDA started with pid=30, OS id=27020
replication_dependency_tracking turned
off (no async multimaster replication
found)
Starting background process AQPC
Sat Sep 21 18:04:04 2013
AQPC started with pid=31, OS id=27022
Starting background process CJQ0
Completed: alter database open
Sat Sep 21 18:04:04 2013
```

This excerpt shows a successful startup of a database. Notice the section that lists the initialization parameters read from the parameter file. You can also see that Oracle is starting dispatcher processes, which indicates that Oracle Shared Server is running.

The parameter that governs the location of the alert log is DIAGNOSTIC_DEST. This parameter is set to a path that designates where Oracle should place the log. The default value for DIAGNOSTIC_DEST is the ORACLE_BASE environment value, if set when starting the database. If ORACLE_BASE is not set, DIAGNOSTIC_DEST will default to the directory of ORACLE_HOME/rdbms/log.

Oracle Database 12*c* supports two types of alert log files. The XML version of the file is located in the DIAGNOSTIC_DEST/rdbms/*dbname*/*instancename*/alert directory. The text file is in the DIAGNOSTIC_DEST/rdbms/*dbname*/*instancename*/trace directory. The alert log file is always named *alert_<instancename>.log*. For example, the alert log filename for the c12ndb1 database would be alert_c12ndb1.log.

The dictionary view V$DIAG_INFO shows the exact location of the alert log file for the instance. Here is an example from the c12ndb1 database running on a Linux server:

```
SQL> SELECT name, value FROM v$diag_info;

NAME                      VALUE
----------------------    -----------------------------------------------------
Diag Enabled              TRUE
ADR Base                  /u01/app/oracle
ADR Home                  /u01/app/oracle/diag/rdbms/c12ndb1/c12ndb1
Diag Trace                /u01/app/oracle/diag/rdbms/c12ndb1/c12ndb1/trace
Diag Alert                /u01/app/oracle/diag/rdbms/c12ndb1/c12ndb1/alert
Diag Incident             /u01/app/oracle/diag/rdbms/c12ndb1/c12ndb1/incident
Diag Cdump                /u01/app/oracle/diag/rdbms/c12ndb1/c12ndb1/cdump
Health Monitor            /u01/app/oracle/diag/rdbms/c12ndb1/c12ndb1/hm
Default Trace File        /u01/app/oracle/diag/rdbms/c12ndb1/c12ndb1/trace/c12ndb
                          1_ora_29330.trc

Active Problem Count  0
Active Incident Count 0
```

The ADR Base value is the directory specified (or derived by the instance using ORACLE_BASE or ORACLE_HOME) for DIGNOSTIC_DEST. The Diag Trace location is where the text version of the alert log file located.

The alert log is continuously appended to, so it is a good idea to periodically purge it. Many DBAs do so daily or weekly, saving a copy of the current alert log to a backup and clearing the current alert log. It is a good idea to save the log contents. You can use it to review when any initialization parameters have changed and to review database errors or problems recorded in the log. Oracle database will create the file if you remove or rename the file.

The alert log file of an Oracle Database 12*c* database is part of the advanced fault diagnostic infrastructure known as the Automatic Diagnostic Repository (ADR). ADRCI is the command interface for ADR, and the SHOW ALERT command can be used to view the contents of the alert log. Here is an example of using ADRCI.

```
$ adrci
ADRCI: Release 12.1.0.1.0 - Production on Sat Nov 9 15:16:46 2013
Copyright (c) 1982, 2013, Oracle and/or its affiliates.  All rights reserved.
ADR base = "/u01/app/oracle"

adrci> show homes
ADR Homes:
diag/rdbms/c12ndb1/c12ndb1
diag/rdbms/c12db1/C12DB1
diag/tnslsnr/btlnx63/listener1
diag/tnslsnr/btlnx63/listener

adrci> show alert

Choose the home from which to view the alert log:

1: diag/rdbms/c12ndb1/c12ndb1
2: diag/rdbms/c12db1/C12DB1
3: diag/tnslsnr/btlnx63/listener1
4: diag/tnslsnr/btlnx63/listener
Q: to quit

Please select option: 2
Output the results to file: /tmp/alert_26280_1402_C12DB1_1.ado

Please select option: q
adrci>
```

In Exercise 9.2, you'll learn how to create an Oracle Database 12*c* database without using DBCA.

EXERCISE 9.2

Creating an Oracle Database 12*c* Database

You have learned to use the DBCA to create a database, learned to start and stop a database, and learned about alert log files and the Oracle dictionary. Though the DBCA does all the background work and creates a database for you, it's good to know the stages of database creation and any relevant scripts needed if you decide to create the database manually. Here are the steps needed to create an Oracle Database 12*c* database on the Linux platform:

1. Set up the relevant environment variables before creating the database. The three important variables are ORACLE_SID, ORACLE_BASE, and ORACLE_HOME. The ORACLE_SID variable is the instance identifier, which can be up to eight characters. On Unix platforms, the instance identifier is case-sensitive. The ORACLE_BASE parameter decides where the trace file and dump file directories will be located. ORACLE_HOME is the location where the Oracle Database 12*c* software is installed.

   ```
   export ORACLE_SID=OCA12C2
   export ORACLE_BASE=/u01/app/oracle
   export ORACLE_HOME=/u01/app/oracle/product/12.1.0
   ```

2. Create a password file using the ORAPWD utility. This allows administrative logins to the Oracle Database 12*c* database using tools such as EM Database Express and SQL Developer. If the SYS password is not provided using the password parameter, orapwd will prompt for the password.

   ```
   cd $ORACLE_HOME/dbs
   orapwd file=orapwOCA12C2
   ```

3. Create an initialization-parameter file. You can create a text-based pfile, and using SQL*Plus, you can create the spfile from the pfile. The pfile must have at least DB_NAME, CONTROL_FILES, and MEMORY_TARGET parameters.

   ```
   cd $ORACLE_HOME/dbs
   sqlplus / as sysdba
   SQL> create spfile from pfile;
   ```

4. Start the instance in NOMOUNT mode:

   ```
   SQL> startup nomount;
   ```

5. Create the database using the CREATE DATABASE statement. This statement creates the database with SYSTEM, SYSAUX, TEMP, and UNDOTBS1 tablespaces. It creates control files specified in the location of the CONTROL_FILES parameter and redo log files. It also sets a password for SYS and SYSTEM users.

   ```
   CREATE DATABASE "c12ndb1"
   MAXDATAFILES 100
   DATAFILE '/u02/oradata/c12ndb1/system01.dbf' SIZE 700M REUSE AUTOEXTEND ON
   NEXT  100M MAXSIZE 32G
   EXTENT MANAGEMENT LOCAL
   SYSAUX DATAFILE '/u02/oradata/c12ndb1/sysaux01.dbf' SIZE 550M REUSE AUTOEXTEND
   ON NEXT  100M MAXSIZE 32G
   ```

EXERCISE 9.2 *(continued)*

DEFAULT TEMPORARY TABLESPACE TEMP TEMPFILE '/u02/oradata/c12ndb1/temp01.dbf'
SIZE 20M REUSE AUTOEXTEND ON NEXT 100M MAXSIZE 16G

SMALLFILE UNDO TABLESPACE "UNDOTBS1" DATAFILE '/u02/oradata/c12ndb1/
undotbs01.dbf' SIZE 200M REUSE AUTOEXTEND ON NEXT 50M MAXSIZE 16G

CHARACTER SET AL32UTF8

NATIONAL CHARACTER SET AL16UTF16

LOGFILE GROUP 1 ('/u03/oradata/c12ndb1/redo0101.log', '/u04/oradata/c12ndb1/
redo0102.log') SIZE 50M,

GROUP 2 ('/u03/oradata/c12ndb1/redo0201.log', '/u04/oradata/c12ndb1/redo0202
.log') SIZE 50M,

GROUP 3 ('/u03/oradata/c12ndb1/redo0301.log', '/u04/oradata/c12ndb1/redo0302
.log') SIZE 50M

USER SYS IDENTIFIED BY "my1Password" USER SYSTEM IDENTIFIED BY "my1Password";

6. Create additional tablespaces if any are needed:

CREATE TABLESPACE "USERS"
DATAFILE '/u02/oradata/c12ndb1/users01.dbf' SIZE 25M;

7. Build data dictionary views and public synonyms (? in SQL*Plus refers to the ORACLE_
HOME directory):

SQL> @?/rdbms/admin/catalog.sql

8. Build the PL/SQL packages:

SQL> @?/rdbms/admin/catproc.sql

9. If you want to install additional options such as JVM or Oracle Ultra Search, run the
relevant scripts:

SQL> @?/javavm/install/initjvm.sql;

Summary

In this chapter, you started off by learning how to install and create an Oracle Database 12*c*
database using the Oracle Universal Installer and Database Configuration Assistant tools.
Then you learned about the Oracle metadata dictionary and parameter files. You also learned
about database startup and shutdown as well as the alert log file.

Installing Oracle Database 12*c* software is a relatively easy task once the preinstall
checks and hardware requirements are met. Installing Oracle database software binaries

is a joint task between the system administrator and DBA, as certain scripts need to be run as root on Linux/Unix platforms.

You can use the DBCA to create databases. You can choose from preexisting database definitions stored as XML templates or create a database definition from a custom template. All aspects of the database, including database name, file location, sizing, and initialization-parameter settings, are defined within the DBCA. You can create a database after completing the database definition, or you can save the definition as a template or series of scripts to be run at a later time. You can also use the DBCA to remove databases or add options to existing databases.

You can manage and create new template definitions using the DBCA interface. This is advantageous because it serves as a way to centrally manage all your database definitions. You can also create new databases from existing databases with the DBCA by using templates.

Oracle uses a parameter file to store information about the initialization parameters used when an Oracle instance starts. Oracle reads the parameter file to obtain information about how the Oracle instance should be sized and configured upon startup. The parameter file can be either a plaintext file, commonly referred to as a pfile, or a binary file that is referred to as a spfile. You can use the EM Database Express to change database parameters when the database is running.

The data dictionary contains information about the database and database objects. The data dictionary is created when the database is created using the script catalog.sql. The data dictionary views have static data, whereas the dynamic performance views have data that does not persist across database shutdowns.

The database needs to be started in order for work to be done against it. You can start up the database in one of several modes: MOUNT, NOMOUNT, and OPEN. You can also start up the database with the RESTRICT option to restrict general access to the database. You can also start up a database using the FORCE option, which accomplishes a shutdown and startup but requires instance recovery because the shutdown is not clean.

You can shut down the database using one of several options: NORMAL, TRANSACTIONAL, IMMEDIATE, and ABORT. The NORMAL, TRANSACTIONAL, and IMMEDIATE options are considered clean shutdowns because no recovery is necessary upon a subsequent startup.

The alert log contains information about certain activities and errors that occur within your database. The alert log contains a chronological summary of these events and a wealth of information that you can use to diagnose system problems and review histories of activities that occurred on the system. The DIGNOSTIC_DEST parameter determines the location of the alert log.

Exam Essentials

Explain Oracle Database 12c system requirements.   Know what the requirements are for available server disk space and memory prior to performing an Oracle Database 12c software installation.

Describe the Optimal Flexible Architecture.   Be able to explain the concepts associated with the OFA model and how to implement an OFA-compliant installation and database directory structure.

Describe steps for installation and configuration.   Know how to set up the Oracle installation environment so that the OUI can be used to install and configure the Oracle Database 12*c* software.

Be able to create a database using the DBCA.   Describe the steps involved in creating a database using the Oracle Database Configuration Assistant (DBCA). Understand how the DBCA uses templates to store information about databases and how templates are used by the DBCA to create databases. Be familiar with the various options available to you when creating an Oracle database using the DBCA.

Know how to manage DBCA templates.   Understand how to use the DBCA to manage templates and the various options available when creating new database templates. Understand what each option is and when it should be used.

Describe the database startup modes.   Understand the various modes of database startup. Understand what each database startup option is and when you might use the option.

Recognize how to start an Oracle database.   Understand how to use the database tools to start up an Oracle Database.

Describe the database-shutdown modes.   Understand the various modes of database shutdown. Understand what each database-shutdown option is and when you might use the option.

Be able to shut down an Oracle database.   Understand how to use the database tools to shut down an Oracle database.

Know how to manage the Oracle parameter file.   Be able to identify the Oracle parameter file and the different types of parameter files. Also understand how you can change the parameter files.

View and understand the contents of the Oracle alert log.   Be able to identify the Oracle alert log and the kinds of information Oracle writes to the alert log. Be able to identify the database initialization parameter that provides the location of the alert log.

Be familiar with the data dictionary.   Understand the difference between the static data dictionary and dynamic performance views. Also understand how critical database information can be obtained from these views.

Review Questions

1. You noticed that the current value of the UNDO_RETENTION parameter is 900 and is too low for some of your transactions. The database was created using DBCA. You issue the following statement:

    ```
    ALTER SYSTEM SET UNDO_RETENTION=4800;
    ```

    Which option is true?

    A. UNDO_RETENTION is a static parameter and, therefore, cannot be changed using ALTER SYSTEM.

    B. The change will be available to the instance only after a database cycle.

    C. The value is changed in memory, and when the database restarts the next time, the new value will be preserved when using the spfile.

    D. The value is changed only in memory, and the server parameter file needs to be updated for the change to persist across database shutdowns.

2. You need to find the directory where the Oracle alert log is being written. Which initialization parameter can be best used to list the full directory path of the alert log location?

    A. ALERT_LOG_DEST

    B. BACKGROUND_DUMP_DEST

    C. DIAGNOSTIC_DEST

    D. INIT_LOG_DUMP_DEST

3. Which data dictionary view is used to view the current values of parameters?

    A. V$DATABASE

    B. V$SPPARAMETER

    C. V$PARAMETER

    D. V$SYSPARAMETER

4. Which startup options must be used to start the instance when you create a new database?

    A. STARTUP FORCE

    B. STARTUP MOUNT

    C. STARTUP RESTRICT

    D. STARTUP NOMOUNT

5. The DIAGNOSTIC_DEST parameter is not set up in the initialization-parameter file. The value of the ORACLE_HOME environment variable is /u01/app/oracle/product/12.1.0, and the value of ORACLE_BASE is /u01/app/oracle. The database and instance name is xyz. What is the location of the text-alert log file for the xyz database?

   A. /u01/app/oracle/product/12.1.0/log/rdbms/xyz/xyz/trace

   B. /u01/app/oracle/diag/rdbms/xyz/xyz/trace

   C. /u01/app/oracle/diag/rdbms/xyz/xyz/alert

   D. /u01/app/oracle/product/12.1.0/diag/rdbms/xyz/xyz/trace

   E. /u01/app/oracle/log/rdbms/xyz/xyz/trace

6. You want to create a database using the DBCA with DB_BLOCK_SIZE as 32KB. Which statement is true?

   A. A block size of 32KB is not allowed in Oracle Database 12c.

   B. You must choose the Data Warehouse template in the DBCA.

   C. You must choose the Custom template in the DBCA.

   D. You must set the environment variable DB_BLOCK_SIZE to 32,768.

7. All of the following are database-management options within the Database Configuration Assistant except which one?

   A. Change Database Initialization Parameters

   B. Create a Database

   C. Manage Templates

   D. Delete a Database

8. The Oracle Universal Installer is started by executing which program?

   A. emctl

   B. runInstaller

   C. ouistart

   D. isqlplusctl

9. You've been asked to install Oracle Database 12c on a new Linux server. You're likely to ask the Unix system administrator to do all but which one of the following for you in order to get the new server ready for Oracle?

   A. Modify the server's kernel parameters.

   B. Create a new Unix user to own the Oracle software.

   C. Create the mount points and directory structure using the OFA model.

   D. Determine which directory will be used for $ORACLE_HOME.

10. Your database name is OCA12C. The options show the files that are available in the $ORACLE_HOME/dbs directory. Which file is used to start up the database instance when you issue the STARTUP command?

A. initOCA12C.ora

B. OCA12Cspfile.ora

C. spfile.ora

D. init.ora

11. Which initialization parameter cannot be changed after the database is created?

A. DB_BLOCK_SIZE

B. DB_NAME

C. CONTROL_FILES

D. None. All parameters can be changed as and when required.

12. Which script creates the database dictionary?

A. dictionary.sql

B. catdict.sql

C. catproc.sql

D. catalog.sql

13. If your database name is PROD and your instance name is PROD1, what would be the name of the text-alert log file?

A. alertPROD.log

B. alert_PROD1.log

C. PROD1alert.log

D. PROD_alert.log

14. Your database is not responding and is in a hung state. You want to shut down and start the database to release all resources. Which statements would you use?

A. STARTUP AFTER SHUTDOWN

B. STARTUP FORCE

C. SHUTDOWN FORCE

D. SHUTDOWN ABORT and STARTUP

15. Which of the following startup options does not perform a database recovery?

A. STARTUP

B. STARTUP FORCE RESTRICT

C. STARTUP NOMOUNT

D. STARTUP OPEN

E. STARTUP RESTRICT

16. Which of the following shutdown statements does not perform a clean shutdown?

   A. SHUTDOWN ABORT

   B. SHUTDOWN TRANSACTIONAL

   C. SHUTDOWN

   D. SHUTDOWN IMMEDIATE

   E. All of these are considered clean shutdowns.

17. You would like to perform maintenance on the system and limit access to only the DBA staff during the maintenance window. Which of the following startup options should you use?

   A. STARTUP NOMOUNT RESTRICT

   B. STARTUP RESTRICT

   C. STARTUP MOUNT RESTRICT

   D. STARTUP MOUNT FORCE RESTRICT

18. You want to start up the database using a binary initialization file. What is another name for this file?

   A. Configfile

   B. Pfile

   C. Spfile

   D. init_pfile.ora

19. Under normal circumstances, which of the following actions or events is not found in the Oracle alert log?

   A. Database startup and shutdown information

   B. Nondefault initialization parameters

   C. ORA-00600 errors

   D. New columns added to a user table

20. Which of the following is true about EM Database Express? (Choose all that apply.)

   A. You can start up and shut down a database using Database Express.

   B. You can read the contents of the alert log file.

   C. You can modify static initialization parameters.

   D. The CREATE DATABASE statement creates the Database Control repository in the database.

Chapter

10

Understanding Storage and Space Management

ORACLE DATABASE 12*c*: OCA EXAM OBJECTIVES COVERED IN THIS CHAPTER:

✓ **Managing Database Storage Structures**

  ▪ Describe the storage of table row data in blocks.

  ▪ Create and manage tablespaces.

✓ **Managing Space**

  ▪ Explain how Oracle database server automatically manages space.

  ▪ Save space by using compression.

  ▪ Proactively monitor and manage tablespace space usage.

  ▪ Use the Segment Advisor.

  ▪ Reclaim wasted space from tables and indexes by using the segment shrink functionality.

  ▪ Manage resumable space allocation.

Understanding how data is stored in the database and how the space is managed are important aspects of database administration. In this chapter, you will learn more about the physical and logical storage structures. To start, you'll explore how a tablespace is the highest level of logical structure in Oracle Database 12*c*. A data file is a structure that is associated with a tablespace at the physical level. A database block is the smallest unit of logical storage. We will discuss how a table row is stored in the database block.

You will also learn about the various storage and space management aspects of Oracle Database 12*c*. With large amounts of data stored in the database, Oracle Database 12*c* has automated several space management activities and offers compression to reduce the storage footprint. Segment Advisor provides information on the tables and indexes with significant free space; a DBA can use this information to reclaim wasted space by rebuilding or utilizing the segment shrink option.

Understanding the Physical and Logical Storage

The database's data is stored logically in tablespaces and physically in data files that correspond to the tablespaces. The logical storage management is independent of the physical storage of the data files. A *tablespace* can have more than one data file associated with it, whereas one data file belongs to only one tablespace. A database has more than one tablespace. Figure 10.1 shows the relationship between the database, tablespaces, data files, and objects within the tablespace. Any object (such as a nonpartitioned table or index) created in the database is stored on a single tablespace, but the object's physical storage can be on multiple data files belonging to that tablespace. A segment is created when a table or index is created and is stored on a single tablespace.

The size of the tablespace is the total size of all the *data files* belonging to that tablespace. The size of the database is the total size of all the tablespaces in the database, which is the total size of all the data files in the database (plus redo log and control files). Changing the size of the data files belonging to a tablespace can change the size of that tablespace. You can add more space to a tablespace by adding more data files to the tablespace. You can then add more space to the database by adding more tablespaces, by adding more data files to the existing tablespaces, or by increasing the size of the existing data files.

FIGURE 10.1   Tablespaces and data files

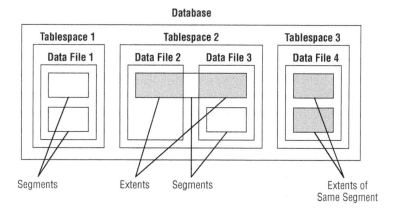

When you create a database, Oracle creates the SYSTEM tablespace. All the data dictionary objects are stored in this tablespace. You can add more space to the SYSTEM tablespace after you create the database by adding more data files or by increasing the size of the data files. The PL/SQL program units (such as procedures, functions, packages, or triggers) created in the database are also stored in the SYSTEM tablespace.

The SYSTEM tablespace is a special tablespace that must be online all the time for the database to function properly. SYSAUX is an auxiliary tablespace that is created when the Oracle Database 12c database is created. The SYSAUX and SYSTEM tablespaces cannot be renamed or dropped.

Oracle recommends against creating any objects other than the Oracle data dictionary in the SYSTEM tablespace. By having multiple tablespaces, you can do the following:

- Separate the Oracle dictionary from other database objects. Doing so reduces contention between dictionary objects and database objects for the same data file.

- Control I/O by allocating separate physical storage disks for different tablespaces.

- Manage space quotas for users on tablespaces.

- Have separate tablespaces for temporary segments (TEMP) and undo management (rollback segments). You can also create a tablespace for a specific activity; for example, you can place high-update tables in a separate tablespace. When creating the database, you can specify tablespace names for temporary tablespaces and undo tablespaces.

Make sure to group application-related or module-related data together so that when maintenance is required for the application's tablespace, you only need to take that tablespace offline, and the rest of the database will be available for users.

- Back up the database one tablespace at a time.

- Make part of the database read-only.

When you create a tablespace, Oracle creates the data files with the size specified. The space reserved for the data file is formatted but does not contain any user data. Whenever spaces for objects are needed, extents are allocated from this free space.

> The tablespace name cannot exceed 30 characters. The name should begin with an alphabetic character and can contain alphabetic characters, numeric characters, and the special characters #, _, and $.

We discussed the logical structures block, extent, and segment in Chapter 8, "Introducing Oracle Database 12c Components and Architecture." Here is a brief refresher of what you learned. The highest logical level of Oracle disk-space management are tablespaces. Drilling down, you find *segments* that can reside in only one tablespace. Each segment is constructed from one or more *extents*. Each of these extents can reside in only one *data file*. Therefore, for a segment to straddle multiple data files, it must be constructed from multiple extents that are located in separate data files. An extent is composed of a contiguous set of *data blocks*, which are at the lowest level of space management. A data block is a fixed number of bytes of disk space. You'll learn more about the data block in the next section.

Contents of a Data Block

A data block is the minimum unit of I/O in an Oracle database. A data block is a multiple of operating system block. The most commonly used data block size is 8K, but it can be at 2K, 4K, 8K, 16K, or 32K. The DB_BLOCK_SIZE initialization parameter determines the database data block size at the time of database creation. After the database is created, the data block size cannot be changed.

Every data block has an internal structure known as the *block format* to track the data stored in the block as well as the free space still available in the block. The data block can be divided into three major areas.

Data block overhead: Overhead area cannot store any user data; this portion is used to maintain the content of the block. Usually, the block overhead is between 84 to 107 bytes.

Row data: Area of the block where user data or an actual row of the table or index key is stored. Row data is stored in an internal format known as the row format.

Free space: Available space in the data block for row data.

Figure 10.2 shows how the data block is organized. The contents of data block overhead and row data are discussed next.

Oracle uses the data block overhead information to manage the block. There are three areas in the overhead area. The block header contains information about the block, such as disk address, segment type, and transaction entries. When a transaction updates a row in the block, an entry is made in the transaction list. The table directory area stores metadata about tables that have rows in the block. The row directory area identifies the location of the rows in the row data area.

FIGURE 10.2 A data block

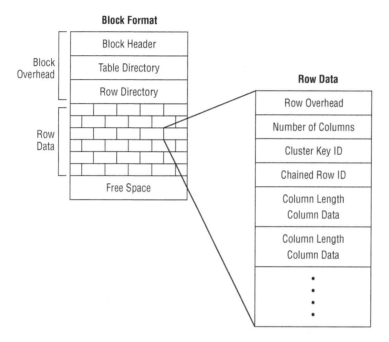

The row data part of the block contains the actual data, such as table rows or index key entries. The row format consists of row header and column data. The row header includes the columns in the row piece and if the row is chained. Column data stores the actual data in the row.

Oracle database uses *ROWID* to uniquely identify a row. Using ROWID is the fastest way to get to the row. ROWID includes the data object number, the relative file number where the block is stored, the block number in the file, and the row number.

Block storage characteristics, such as how much free space to leave in every block for row updates and how many transaction lists to create, are defined at the time a segment, such as a table, partition, or index, is created.

Defining Block Storage Characteristics

PCTFREE and PCTUSED are data block storage parameters. PCTFREE specifies the amount of free space that should be reserved in each block of the table for future updates. You specify a low PCTFREE for the ORDERS table, if there aren't many updates to the table that increase the row length. PCTUSED specifies when the block should be considered for inserting new rows once the PCTFREE threshold is reached.

INITRANS specifies the number of concurrent transactions that can update each block of the table. The default is 1 for table and 2 for index. Oracle reserves space in the block header for the INITRANS number of concurrent transactions. For each additional concurrent transaction, Oracle allocates space from the free space, which has an overhead of dynamically allocating transaction entry space. If the block is full and no space is available, the transaction waits until a transaction entry space is available.

Managing Tablespaces

Tablespaces logically group schema objects for administration convenience. Tablespaces can store zero or more segments. *Segments* are schema objects that require storage in the database. Tables and indexes are examples of segments. *Constraints* and sequences are examples of schema objects that do not store data outside the data dictionary and, therefore, do not have segments.

You can place the tables and indexes associated with an application into a set of tablespaces so that data can be managed more easily. You can take a tablespace offline and recover it (potentially to a different point in time), separate from the rest of the database. You can also move it to another database and configure it as read-only so that you do not have to make additional backups of static data.

In the following sections, you will learn how to create and manage tablespaces in your database.

Identifying Default Tablespaces

The SYSTEM tablespace is used for the data dictionary and should not be used to store schema objects other than those that are placed there during the installation. The SYSAUX tablespace stores schema objects associated with Oracle-provided features; examples are the spatial data option, Extended Markup Language Database (XMLDB), and Oracle Multimedia (formerly known as Intermedia).

The SYSTEM and SYSAUX tablespaces are always created when the database is created. One or more temporary tablespaces are usually created in a database, as well as an undo tablespace and several application tablespaces. Because SYSTEM and SYSAUX are the only tablespaces that are always created with the database, SYSTEM may be the default tablespace for temporary and user data if the database is created with SYSTEM as a dictionary-managed tablespace. You should not, however, continue to use them as the default tablespaces for your users or applications. In the following sections, you will learn how to create additional tablespaces and enable their use as better defaults.

Creating and Maintaining Tablespaces

You create tablespaces using either the CREATE DATABASE or CREATE TABLESPACE statement. When creating a tablespace, you must make several choices:

- Whether to make the tablespace bigfile or smallfile
- Whether to manage extents locally or with the dictionary
- Whether to manage segment space automatically or manually

Additionally, there are specialized tablespaces for temporary segments and undo segments.

A tablespace is created with the CREATE TABLESPACE statement. The following statement creates a tablespace named HR_DATA. The data file associated with the tablespace is physically stored on the disk at /u02/oradata/12CR11/hr_data01.dbf and has a size of 20MB.

```
SQL> CREATE TABLESPACE HR_DATA
  2  DATAFILE '/u02/oradata/12CR11/hr_data01.dbf'
  3  SIZE 20M;


Tablespace created.
SQL>
```

In the following sections, we will discuss the various options available when you create a tablespace.

Creating Bigfile and Smallfile Tablespaces

Bigfile tablespaces are built on a single data file (or temp file), which can be as many as 2^{32} data blocks in size. Therefore, a bigfile tablespace that uses 8KB data blocks can be as large as 32TB (the maximum size is 128TB for a 32KB block size). Bigfile tablespace can have only one data file.

Bigfile tablespaces are intended for very large databases. When a very large database has thousands of read-write data files, operations that must update the data file headers, such as checkpoints, can take a relatively long time. If you reduce the number of data files, these operations can complete faster.

To create a bigfile tablespace, use the keyword BIGFILE in the CREATE statement, like this:

```
CREATE BIGFILE TABLESPACE PO_ARCHIVE
DATAFILE '/u02/oradata/12CR11/po_archive.dbf' size 25G;
```

Smallfile tablespace is the new terminology for the old Oracle tablespace data file option. With a smallfile tablespace, you can have multiple data files for a tablespace. Each data file can be as many as 2^{22} data blocks in size. Therefore, data files in a smallfile tablespace that uses 8KB data blocks are limited to 32GB. The smallfile tablespace can have as many as 1,022 data files, limiting the 8KB data block tablespace to slightly less than 32TB—about the same as a bigfile tablespace.

To create a smallfile tablespace, either omit the keyword BIGFILE or explicitly use the keyword SMALLFILE, like this:

```
CREATE SMALLFILE TABLESPACE PO_DETAILS
DATAFILE '/u02/oradata/12CR11/po_details.dbf' size 2G;
```

By default, Oracle Database 12c creates SMALLFILE tablespaces. You do not have to specify SMALLFILE in the CREATE TABLESPACE statement. You can use the DATABASE_PROPERTIES dictionary to view the default tablespace type for your Oracle Database 12c database (look for the property name DEFAULT_TBS_TYPE). You can use the ALTER DATABASE statement to change the default behavior.

Working with Oracle Managed File Tablespaces

The *Oracle Managed Files* (OMF) feature can make it easier for you to administer the files used by an Oracle database. Using the OMF feature, you specify operations in terms of tablespaces and not operating-system files. You don't explicitly name data files or temp files; the database does this for you.

To enable the OMF feature, set the initialization parameter DB_CREATE_FILE_DEST to the directory where you want the database to create and manage your data and temp files, like this:

```
ALTER SYSTEM SET
  db_create_file_dest = '/u02/oradata/' SCOPE=BOTH;
```

When creating a tablespace using the OMF feature, you simply omit the filename:

```
CREATE TABLESPACE hr_data;
```

Oracle creates a tablespace using a unique filename, such as o1_mf_hr_data_46n3ck5t_. dbf under the /u02/oradata/12CR11/datafile directory. Notice that Oracle Database 12*c* adds the subdirectories <DBNAME>/datafile in the DB_CREATE_FILE_DEST directory. This data file will have autoextend enabled and be 100MB unless you specify a different size. By default, the tablespace is a smallfile tablespace, but you can specify a bigfile tablespace by including the keyword BIGFILE.

The OMF feature will be discussed later in this chapter. In the next two sections, you will learn about the automatic space management features in Oracle Database 12*c*.

Choosing Extent Management

When Oracle allocates space to an object in a tablespace, it is allocated in chunks of contiguous database blocks known as *extents*. Each object is allocated a segment, which has one or more extents. Oracle maintains the extent information such as extents free, extent size, and extents allocated, either in the data dictionary or in the tablespace itself.

If you store the *extent management* information in the dictionary for a tablespace, that tablespace is called *a dictionary-managed tablespace*. Whenever an extent is allocated or freed, the information is updated in the corresponding dictionary tables. Such updates also generate undo information.

With dictionary extent management, the database tracks free and used extents in the data dictionary, changing the FET$ and UET$ tables with recursive SQL. With local extent management, the free/used extent information is maintained in a bitmap pattern in the header of the data file. Therefore, Oracle has to check in the local bitmap instead of making trips to the UET$ or FET$ table. Local extent management is the default and is generally the preferred technique.

A simple example of a dictionary-managed tablespace creation command is as follows:

```
CREATE TABLESPACE APPL_DATA
DATAFILE '/disk3/oradata/DB01/appl_data01.dbf' SIZE 100M
EXTENT MANAGEMENT DICTIONARY;
```

This statement creates a tablespace named APPL_DATA; the data file specified is created with a size of 100MB. You can specify more than one file under the DATAFILE clause separated by commas; you may need to create more files if there are any operating-system limits on the file size. For example, if you need to allocate 6GB to the tablespace and the operating system allows only 2GB as the maximum file size, you need three data files for the tablespace. The statement will be as follows:

```
CREATE TABLESPACE APPL_DATA
DATAFILE '/disk3/oradata/DB01/appl_data01.dbf' SIZE 2000M,
         '/disk3/oradata/DB01/appl_data02.dbf' SIZE 2000M,
         '/disk4/oradata/DB01/appl_data03.dbf' SIZE 2000M
EXTENT MANAGEMENT DICTIONARY;
```

The options available when you're creating or reusing a data file are discussed in the "Managing Data Files" section, later in this chapter.

If you store the management information in the tablespace by using bitmaps in each data file, such a tablespace is known as a *locally managed tablespace*. Each bit in the bitmap corresponds to a block or a group of blocks. When an extent is allocated or freed for reuse, Oracle changes the bitmap values to show the new status of the blocks. These changes do not generate rollback information because they do not update tables in the data dictionary.

With locally managed tablespaces, you have two options for how extents are allocated: UNIFORM and AUTOALLOCATE. The UNIFORM option tells the database to allocate and deallocate extents in the tablespace with the same unvarying size that you can specify or to let extents default to 1MB. UNIFORM is the default for temporary tablespaces and cannot be specified for undo tablespaces. To create consistent 10MB extents, use the clause EXTENT MANAGEMENT LOCAL UNIFORM SIZE 10M in the CREATE TABLESPACE statement. Here is an example:

```
CREATE TABLESPACE hr_index
DATAFILE '/u02/oradata/12CR11/hr_index01.dbf' SIZE 2G
EXTENT MANAGEMENT LOCAL UNIFORM SIZE 10M;
```

   The minimum extent size for a locally managed tablespace with AUTOALLOCATE is 64KB.

AUTOALLOCATE, on the other hand, tells the database to vary the size of extents for each segment. For example, on Windows and Linux with 8KB data blocks, each segment starts out with 64KB extents for the first 16 extents, and then the extents increase in size to 1MB for the next 63 extents. The size then increases to 8MB for the next 120 extents, then 64MB, and so on, as the segment grows. This algorithm allows small segments to remain small and large segments to grow without gaining too many extents. AUTOALLOCATE is best used for a general-purpose mixture of small and large tables. Here is an example of creating a tablespace using AUTOALLOCATE:

```
CREATE TABLESPACE hr_index
DATAFILE '/u02/oradata/12CR11/hr_index01.dbf' SIZE 2G
EXTENT MANAGEMENT LOCAL AUTOALLOCATE;
```

Bigfile tablespaces are created as locally managed; you cannot specify the EXTENT MANAGEMENT DICTIONARY clause for bigfile tablespaces. You can convert a smallfile tablespace from dictionary extent management to local extent management and back with the Oracle-supplied PL/SQL package DBMS_SPACE_ADMIN.

When the SYSTEM tablespace is created as a locally managed tablespace, you cannot create dictionary-managed tablespaces in the database. The Oracle DBCA tool by default creates the SYSTEM tablespace as locally managed.

Choosing Segment Space Management

For tablespaces that have local extent management, you can use either manual or automatic *segment space management*. Manual segment space management exists for backward compatibility and uses free-block lists to identify the data blocks available for inserts together with the parameters PCTFREE and PCTUSED, which control when a block is made available for inserts.

After each INSERT or UPDATE, the database compares the remaining free space in that data block with the segment's PCTFREE setting. If the data block has less than PCTFREE free space (meaning it is almost full), it is taken off the free-block list and is no longer available for inserts. The remaining free space is reserved for update operations that may increase the size of rows in that data block. After each UPDATE or DELETE, the database compares the used space in that data block with that segment's PCTUSED setting. If the data block has less than PCTUSED used space, the data block is deemed empty enough for inserts and is placed on the free-block list.

To specify manual segment space management, use the SEGMENT SPACE MANAGEMENT MANUAL clause of the CREATE TABLESPACE statement, or simply omit the SEGMENT SPACE MANAGEMENT AUTO clause. Oracle strongly recommends AUTOMATIC segment space management for permanent locally managed tablespaces, and the default behavior of Oracle Database 12*c* is AUTO. Here is a statement that creates a tablespace with manual segment space management:

```
CREATE TABLESPACE hr_index
DATAFILE '/u02/oradata/12CR11/hr_index01.dbf'  SIZE 2G
EXTENT MANAGEMENT LOCAL AUTOALLOCATE
SEGMENT SPACE MANAGEMENT MANUAL;
```

When automatic segment space management is specified, bitmaps are used instead of free lists to identify which data blocks are available for inserts. The parameters PCTFREE and PCTUSED are ignored for segments in tablespaces with automatic segment space management. Automatic segment space management is available only on tablespaces configured for local extent management; it is not available for temporary or system tablespaces. Automatic segment space management performs better and reduces your maintenance tasks, making it the preferred technique.

To specify automatic segment space management, use the SEGMENT SPACE MANAGEMENT AUTO clause of the CREATE TABLESPACE statement like this or do not include the SEGMENT SPACE MANAGEMENT clause (it is the default):

```
CREATE TABLESPACE hr_index
DATAFILE '/u02/oradata/12CR11/hr_index01.dbf'  SIZE 2G
EXTENT MANAGEMENT LOCAL AUTOALLOCATE
SEGMENT SPACE MANAGEMENT AUTO;
```

When automatic segment space management is used, Oracle ignores the storage parameters PCTUSED, FREELISTS, and FREELIST GROUPS when creating objects.

Using SQL Developer is a very handy way to create a tablespace—and to learn the various clauses of creating a tablespace using the DDL tab. Figure 10.3 shows the Create Tablespace screen.

FIGURE 10.3 The Create Tablespace screen of SQL Developer

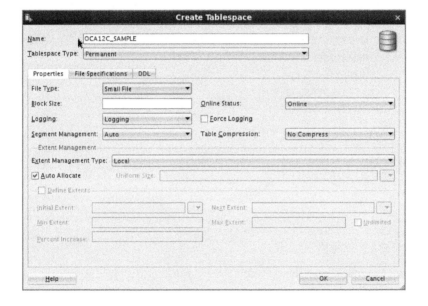

 Although the term *segment space management* sounds similar to extent management, it is quite different and can be more accurately regarded as block space management.

Choosing Other Tablespace Options

Several options are available to use when you are creating a tablespace. You learned to create bigfile and smallfile tablespaces and use the EXTENT MANAGEMENT and SEGMENT SPACE MANAGEMENT options in the previous sections. In this section, you will learn the other options available while creating a tablespace:

- Specifying nondefault block size
- Specifying default storage characteristics
- Specifying logging and flashback clauses
- Creating offline tablespaces

The following example shows the optional clauses you can use while creating a dictionary-managed tablespace:

```
CREATE TABLESPACE APPL_DATA
   DATAFILE '/disk3/oradata/DB01/appl_data01.dbf'
      SIZE 100M
   DEFAULT STORAGE (
                    INITIAL 256K
                    NEXT 256K
                    MINEXTENTS 2
                    PCTINCREASE 0
                    MAXEXTENTS 4096)
   BLOCKSIZE 16K
   MINIMUM EXTENT 256K
   LOGGING
   ONLINE
   FORCE LOGGING
   FLASHBACK ON
   EXTENT MANAGEMENT DICTIONARY
   SEGMENT SPACE MANAGEMENT MANUAL;
```

The following example shows the optional clauses you can use while creating a locally managed tablespace:

```
CREATE TABLESPACE APPL_DATA
   DATAFILE '/disk3/oradata/DB01/appl_data01.dbf'
      SIZE 100M
   DEFAULT STORAGE COMPRESS
   BLOCKSIZE 16K
   LOGGING
   ONLINE
   FORCE LOGGING
```

```
FLASHBACK ON
EXTENT MANAGEMENT LOCAL
SEGMENT SPACE MANAGEMENT AUTO;
```

Oracle manages the tablespace characteristics very efficiently with its default values; however, you can specify several clauses to obtain an even finer level of control. The clauses in the CREATE TABLESPACE command can specify the following:

DEFAULT STORAGE **Clause**   The DEFAULT STORAGE clause specifies the default storage parameters for new objects that are created in the tablespace. If an explicit storage clause is specified when an object is created, the tablespace defaults are not used for the specified storage parameters. The storage parameters are specified within parentheses; no parameter is mandatory, but if you specify the DEFAULT STORAGE clause, you must specify at least one parameter inside the parentheses. The storage parameters are valid only for dictionary-managed tablespaces; for locally managed tablespaces, you can specify only the COMPRESS option.

BLOCKSIZE **Clause**   You can specify block size that is different from the standard database block size when creating a new tablespace. The database block size is specified when you create the database using the initialization parameter DB_BLOCK_SIZE. This is the block size used for the SYSTEM tablespace and is known as the *standard block size*. The valid sizes of the nonstandard block size are 2KB, 4KB, 8KB, 16KB, and 32KB. If you do not specify a block size for the tablespace, the database block size is assumed. Multiple block sizes in the database are beneficial for large databases with Online Trasaction Processing (OLTP) and Decision Support System (DSS) data stored together and for storing large tables. The restrictions on specifying nonstandard block sizes along with the tablespace creation are discussed in the "Using Nonstandard Block Sizes" section.

MINIMUM EXTENT **Clause**   The MINIMUM EXTENT clause specifies that the extent sizes should be a multiple of the size specified. You can use this clause to control fragmentation in the tablespace by allocating extents of at least the size specified; this clause is always a multiple of the size specified. In the CREATE TABLESPACE example, all the extents allocated in the tablespace would be multiples of 256KB. The INITIAL and NEXT extent sizes specified should be multiples of MINIMUM EXTENT. This clause is valid only for dictionary-managed tablespaces.

LOGGING/NOLOGGING **Clause**   The LOGGING/NOLOGGING clause specifies that the DDL operations and direct-load INSERT should be recorded in the redo log files. This is the default, and the clause can be omitted. When you specify NOLOGGING, data is modified with minimal logging, and hence the commands complete faster. Because the changes are not recorded in the redo log files, you need to apply the commands again in the case of a media recovery. You can specify LOGGING or NOLOGGING in the individual object creation statement, and it will override the tablespace default.

FORCE LOGGING **Clause**   You must specify this clause to log all changes irrespective of the LOGGING mode for individual objects in the tablespace. You can specify the NOLOGGING clause and FORCE LOGGING clause together when creating a tablespace. If you do, the objects will be created in NOLOGGING mode and will be overridden by the FORCE LOGGING mode. When you take the tablespace out of the FORCE LOGGING mode, the NOLOGGING attribute for objects will go into effect.

`ONLINE/OFFLINE` **Clause** This clause specifies that the tablespace should be made online or made available as soon as it is created. This is the default, and hence the clause can be omitted. If you do not want the tablespace to be available, you can specify `OFFLINE`.

`FLASHBACK ON/OFF` **Clause** `FLASHBACK ON` puts the tablespace in flashback mode and is the default. The `OFF` option turns flashback off, and hence Oracle will not save any flashback data. We will discuss flashback operations in Chapter 15, "Using Backup and Recovery."

The clauses related to encrypting the tablespace are not discussed here because they are beyond the scope of this book.

Using Nonstandard Block Sizes

The block size to be used while creating the database is specified in the initialization parameter using the `DB_BLOCK_SIZE` parameter. This is known as the *standard block size* for the database. You must choose a block size that suits most of your tables. In most databases, this is the only block size you will ever need. Oracle gives you the option of having multiple block sizes, which is especially useful when you're transporting tablespaces from another database with a different block size.

The `DB_CACHE_SIZE` parameter defines the buffer cache size that is associated with the standard block size. To create tablespaces with nonstandard block sizes, you must set the appropriate initialization parameter to define a buffer cache size for the block size. The initialization parameter is `DB_nK_CACHE_SIZE`, where *n* is the nonstandard block size. The *n* can have the values 2, 4, 8, 16, or 32, but it cannot have the size of the standard block size. For example, if your standard block size is 8KB, you cannot set the parameter `DB_8K_CACHE_SIZE`. If you need to create a tablespace that uses a different block size, say 16KB, you must set the `DB_16K_CACHE_SIZE` parameter. By default, the value for `DB_nK_CACHE_SIZE` parameter is 0MB.

The temporary tablespaces that are created should have the standard block size.

The `DB_nK_CACHE_SIZE` parameter is dynamic; you can alter its value using the `ALTER SYSTEM` statement.

Creating Temporary Tablespaces

Oracle can manage space for sort operations more efficiently by using *temporary tablespaces*. By exclusively designating a tablespace for temporary segments, Oracle eliminates the allocation and deallocation of temporary segments in a permanent tablespace. A temporary tablespace can be used only for sort segments. A temporary tablespace is used for temporary segments, which are created, managed, and dropped by the database as needed. These temporary segments are most commonly generated during sorting operations such as `ORDER BY`, `GROUP BY`, and `CREATE INDEX`. They are also generated during other operations such as hash joins or inserts into temporary tables.

You create a temporary tablespace at database creation time with the DEFAULT TEMPORARY TABLESPACE clause of the CREATE DATABASE statement or after the database is created with the CREATE TEMPORARY TABLESPACE statement, like this:

```
CREATE TEMPORARY TABLESPACE temp
TEMPFILE '/u01/oradata/12CR11/temp01.dbf' SIZE 1G;
```

Notice that the keyword TEMPFILE is used instead of DATAFILE. Temp files are available only with temporary tablespaces. They never need to be backed up, and they do not log data changes in the redo logs. The EXTENT MANAGEMENT LOCAL clause is optional and can be omitted; you can provide it to improve readability. If you do not specify the extent size by using the UNIFORM SIZE clause, the default size used will be 1MB.

 Although it is always good practice to create a separate temporary tablespace, it is required when the SYSTEM tablespace is locally managed.

Temporary tablespaces are created using temp files instead of data files. Temp files are allocated slightly differently than data files. Although data files are completely allocated and initialized at creation time, temp files are not always guaranteed to allocate the disk space specified. This means that on some Unix systems a temp file will not actually allocate disk space until a sorting operation requires it. Although this delayed allocation approach allows rapid file creation, it can cause problems down the road if you have not reserved the space that may be needed at runtime.

Each user is assigned a temporary tablespace when the user is created. By default, the default tablespace (where the user creates objects) is the SYSTEM tablespace and the temporary tablespace (where the user's sort operations are performed) is the SYSTEM tablespace as well as when SYSTEM tablespace is dictionary managed. No user should have SYSTEM as their default or temporary tablespace. This will unnecessarily increase fragmentation in the SYSTEM tablespace.

When creating a database, you can also create a temporary tablespace using the DEFAULT TEMPORARY TABLESPACE clause of the CREATE DATABASE statement. If the default temporary tablespace is defined in the database, all new users will have that tablespace assigned as the temporary tablespace by default when you do not specify another temporary tablespace. You can also designate a data tablespace for application tables during database creation using the DEFAULT TABLESPACE clause.

If there are multiple temporary tablespaces in a database and if you want to utilize the space in multiple temporary tablespaces for a user's sort operation, you can use the temporary tablespace groups. When creating the temporary tablespace, use the TABLESPACE GROUP clause as in the following example:

```
CREATE TEMPORARY TABLESPACE TEMP01
TEMPFILE '/u01/oradata/12CR11/temp01a.dbf' size 200M
EXTENT MANAGEMENT LOCAL UNIFORM SIZE 5M
TABLESPACE GROUP ALL_TEMPS;
```

In this example, the tablespace is made part of the ALL_TEMPS temporary tablespace group. Tablespace groups are applicable only to temporary tablespaces. If the group does not exist, Oracle will create the group and add the tablespace to the group.

> When creating a temporary tablespace, you can use only the EXTENT MANAGEMENT and TABLESPACE GROUP clauses along with the TEMPFILE clause. All other options are invalid for temporary tablespaces.

Creating Undo Tablespaces

An *undo tablespace* stores undo segments, which are used by the database for several purposes, including the following:

- Rolling back a transaction explicitly with a ROLLBACK statement
- Rolling back a transaction implicitly (for example, through the recovery of a failed transaction)
- Reconstructing a read-consistent image of data
- Recovering from logical corruptions

To create an undo tablespace at database creation time, set the initialization parameter UNDO_MANAGEMENT=AUTO (default) and include an UNDO TABLESPACE clause in your CREATE DATABASE statement, like this:

```
CREATE DATABASE "TEST1"
DATAFILE '/u01/app/oracle/oradata/TEST1/system01.dbf'
    SIZE 300M REUSE AUTOEXTEND ON NEXT 10240K MAXSIZE UNLIMITED
    EXTENT MANAGEMENT LOCAL
SYSAUX DATAFILE '/u01/app/oracle/oradata/TEST1/sysaux01.dbf'
    SIZE 120M REUSE AUTOEXTEND ON NEXT  10240K MAXSIZE UNLIMITED
SMALLFILE DEFAULT TEMPORARY TABLESPACE TEMP
    TEMPFILE '/u01/app/oracle/oradata/TEST1/temp01.dbf'
    SIZE 20M REUSE AUTOEXTEND ON NEXT  640K MAXSIZE UNLIMITED
SMALLFILE UNDO TABLESPACE "UNDOTBS1"
    DATAFILE '/u01/app/oracle/oradata/TEST1/undotbs01.dbf'
    SIZE 200M REUSE AUTOEXTEND ON NEXT  5120K MAXSIZE UNLIMITED
DEFAULT TABLESPACE "USERS"
    DATAFILE '/u01/app/oracle/oradata/TEST1/users01.dbf'
    SIZE 5M REUSE AUTOEXTEND ON NEXT  1280K MAXSIZE UNLIMITED
    EXTENT MANAGEMENT LOCAL SEGMENT SPACE MANAGEMENT  AUTO
CHARACTER SET UTF8
NATIONAL CHARACTER SET AL16UTF16
LOGFILE
```

```
    GROUP 1 ('/u01/app/oracle/oradata/TEST1/redo01.log') SIZE 51200K,
    GROUP 2 ('/u01/app/oracle/oradata/TEST1/redo02.log') SIZE 51200K,
    GROUP 3 ('/u01/app/oracle/oradata/TEST1/redo03.log') SIZE 51200K
SET DEFAULT SMALLFILE TABLESPACE
USER SYS IDENTIFIED BY mysupersekret
USER SYSTEM IDENTIFIED BY supersekret;
```

You can create an undo tablespace after database creation with the CREATE UNDO TABLESPACE statement, like this:

```
CREATE UNDO TABLESPACE undo
DATAFILE '/ORADATA/PROD/UNDO01.DBF' SIZE 2G;
```

When creating an undo tablespace, you can specify the undo retention clause. The RETENTION GUARANTEE option specifies that Oracle should preserve unexpired undo data until the period of time specified by the UNDO_RETENTION initialization parameter. This setting is useful for flashback query operations. RETENTION NOGUARANTEE is the default.

When you're creating undo tablespaces, the only tablespace clauses available to specify are EXTENT MANAGEMENT LOCAL and DATAFILE. Undo management and retention are discussed in Chapter 11, "Managing Data Concurrency and Undo."

 Although it is always good practice to create a separate undo tablespace, it is required when the SYSTEM tablespace is locally managed.

Removing Tablespaces

Tablespaces that are not needed in the database can be dropped. Once a tablespace is dropped, there is no rollback. Although you can drop a tablespace with objects in it, it may be safer to drop the objects first and then drop the tablespace. To remove a tablespace from the database, use the DROP TABLESPACE statement:

```
DROP TABLESPACE USER_DATA;
```

If the tablespace is not empty, you should specify the optional clause INCLUDING CONTENTS to recursively remove any segments (tables, indexes, and so on) in the tablespace, like this:

```
DROP TABLESPACE dba_sandbox INCLUDING CONTENTS;
```

If referential integrity constraints from the objects on other tablespaces refer to the objects in the tablespace that is being dropped, you must specify the CASCADE CONSTRAINTS clause:

```
DROP TABLESPACE USER_DATA INCLUDING CONTENTS CASCADE CONSTRAINTS;
```

When you drop a tablespace, the control file is updated with the tablespace and data file information.

Dropping a tablespace does not automatically remove the data files from the file system. Use the additional clause `INCLUDING CONTENTS AND DATAFILES` to remove the underlying data files as well as the stored objects, like this:

`DROP TABLESPACE hr_data INCLUDING CONTENTS AND DATAFILES;`

If the Oracle Managed Files feature is used for the tablespace, such files will be removed automatically when you drop the tablespace. For files that are not Oracle managed, if you need to free up the disk space, you can use OS commands to remove the data files belonging to the dropped tablespace or you can use the `AND DATAFILES` clause.

You cannot drop the `SYSTEM` tablespace. You can drop the `SYSAUX` tablespace connected using `SYSDBA` system privilege when the database is started in UPGRADE mode.

Modifying Tablespaces

Use an `ALTER TABLESPACE` statement to modify the attributes of a tablespace. These are some of the actions you can perform on tablespaces:

- Change the default storage clauses and the `MINIMUM_EXTENT` of a dictionary-managed tablespace.
- Change the extent allocation and `LOGGING/NOLOGGING` modes.
- Change the availability of the tablespace.
- Make the tablespace read-only or read-write.
- Coalesce the contiguous free space.
- Add more space by adding new data files or temporary files.
- Resize the data files or temporary files.
- Rename a tablespace or rename files belonging to the tablespace.
- Shrink temporary files or shrink space in the tablespace.
- Change flashback on or off and change retention guarantee.
- Begin and end a backup.

The following sections detail common modifications you can perform on the tablespaces.

Changing Storage Defaults

Changing the default storage or `MINIMUM_EXTENT` or `LOGGING/NOLOGGING` does not affect the existing objects in the tablespace. The `DEFAULT STORAGE` and `LOGGING/NOLOGGING` clauses are applied to the newly created segments if such a clause is not explicitly specified when creating new objects. For example, to change the storage parameters, use the following statement:

```
ALTER TABLESPACE APPL_DATA
DEFAULT STORAGE (INITIAL 2M NEXT 2M);
```

Only the `INITIAL` and `NEXT` values of the default `STORAGE` are changed; the other storage parameters such as `PCTINCREASE` or `MINEXTENTS` remain unaltered.

Adding a Data File to a Tablespace

Smallfile tablespaces can have multiple data files and can, therefore, be spread over multiple file systems without engaging a logical volume manager. To add a data file to a smallfile tablespace, use an ADD clause with the ALTER TABLESPACE statement. For example, the following statement adds a 2GB data file on the /u02 file system to the RECEIVABLES tablespace:

```
ALTER TABLESPACE receivables ADD DATAFILE
  '/u02/oradata/ORA10/receivables01.dbf'
  SIZE 2G;
```

Taking a Tablespace Offline or Online

You can control the availability of certain tablespaces by altering the tablespace to be offline or online. When you make a tablespace offline, the segments in that tablespace are not accessible. The data stored in other tablespaces is available for use. When making a tablespace unavailable, you can use these four options:

NORMAL   This is the default. Oracle writes all the dirty buffer blocks in the SGA to the data files of the tablespace and closes the data files. All data files belonging to the tablespace must be online. You need not perform a media recovery when bringing the tablespace online. For example:

```
    ALTER TABLESPACE USER_DATA ONLINE;
```

TEMPORARY   Oracle performs a checkpoint on all online data files. It does not ensure that the data files are available. You may need to perform a media recovery on the offline data files when the tablespace is brought online. For example:

```
    ALTER TABLESPACE USER_DATA OFFLINE TEMPORARY;
```

IMMEDIATE   Oracle does not perform a checkpoint and does not make sure that all data files are available. You must perform a media recovery when the tablespace is brought back online. For example:

```
    ALTER TABLESPACE USER_DATA OFFLINE IMMEDIATE;
```

FOR RECOVER   This makes the tablespace offline for point-in-time recovery. You can copy the data files belonging to the tablespace from a backup and apply the archive log files. For example:

```
    ALTER TABLESPACE USER_DATA OFFLINE FOR RECOVER;
```

You cannot make the SYSTEM tablespace offline because the data dictionary must always be available for the functioning of the database. If a tablespace is offline when you shut down the database, it remains offline when you start up the database. You can make a tablespace offline by using the following statement:

```
    ALTER TABLESPACE USER_DATA OFFLINE
```

When a tablespace is taken offline, SQL statements cannot reference any objects contained in that tablespace. If there are unsaved changes when you take the tablespace offline, Oracle saves rollback data corresponding to those changes in a deferred rollback segment in the SYSTEM tablespace. When the tablespace is brought back online, Oracle applies the rollback data to the tablespace, if needed.

Making a Tablespace Read-Only

If a tablespace contains static data, it can be marked read-only. Tablespaces that contain historic or reference data are typical candidates for read-only. When a tablespace is read-only, it does not have to be backed up with the nightly or weekly database backups. One backup after being marked read-only is all that is needed for future recoveries. Tables in a read-only tablespace can only be selected from; their rows cannot be inserted, updated, or deleted.

You cannot make the SYSTEM tablespace read-only. When you make a tablespace read-only, all the data files must be online, and the tablespace can have no active transactions. You can drop objects such as tables or indexes from a read-only tablespace, but you cannot create new objects in a read-only tablespace.

Use a READ ONLY clause with an ALTER TABLESPACE statement to mark a tablespace read-only. For example, to mark the SALES2007 tablespace read-only, execute the following:

```
ALTER TABLESPACE sales2007 READ ONLY;
```

If you need to make changes to a table in a read-only tablespace, make it read writable again with the keywords READ WRITE, like this:

```
ALTER TABLESPACE sales2007 READ WRITE;
```

Oracle normally checks the availability of all data files belonging to the database when starting up the database. If you are storing your read-only tablespace on offline storage media or on a CD-ROM, you might want to skip the data file availability checking when starting up the database by setting the parameter READ_ONLY_OPEN_DELAYED to TRUE. Oracle checks the availability of data files belonging to read-only tablespaces only at the time of access to an object in the tablespace. A missing or bad read-only file will not be detected at database startup time.

Putting a Tablespace in Backup Mode

If you perform non-RMAN online backups, sometimes called *user-managed backups*, you will need to put a tablespace in backup mode before you begin to copy the data files using an operating-system program. While the tablespace is in backup mode, the database will continue to write data to the data files (checkpoints occur), but the occurrences of these checkpoints will not be recorded in the header blocks of the data files. This omission will tell the database that recovery may be needed if the database instance gets terminated abruptly.

While a tablespace is in backup mode, some additional information is written to the redo logs to assist with recovery, if needed.

 See Chapter 15 for more information on backups and recovery.

Some companies perform backups by splitting a third mirror, mounting these mirrored file systems onto another server, and then copying them to tape. To safely split the mirror, alter all your tablespaces into backup mode, make the split, and then alter all the tablespaces out of backup mode. Put them into backup mode like this:

```
ALTER TABLESPACE system BEGIN BACKUP;
```

Use the keywords `END BACKUP` to take a tablespace out of backup mode, like this:

```
ALTER TABLESPACE system END BACKUP;
```

If you forget to take a tablespace out of backup mode, the next time you bounce your database, it will see that the checkpoint number in the control file is later than the one in the data file headers and report that media recovery is required.

Obtaining Tablespace Information

DBAs often need to determine how much space is being used and how much is available in a tablespace, as well as query the tablespace characteristics. The data dictionary is the place to go for tablespace information. You can use the command-line utility SQL*Plus to query the information from data dictionary tables, or you can use Enterprise Manager Grid Control. We will review both in this section.

Obtaining Tablespace Information Using SQL*Plus

Many data dictionary views can provide information about tablespaces in a database, such as the following:

- `DBA_TABLESPACES`
- `DBA_DATA_FILES`
- `DBA_TEMP_FILES`
- `V$TABLESPACE`

The `DBA_TABLESPACES` view has one row for each tablespace in the database and provides the following information:

- The tablespace block size
- The tablespace status: online, offline, or read-only
- The contents of the tablespace: undo, temporary, or permanent
- Whether it uses dictionary-managed or locally managed extents
- Whether the segment space management is automatic or manual
- Whether it is a bigfile or smallfile tablespace

To get a listing of all the tablespaces in the database, their status, contents, extent management policy, and segment management policy, run the following query:

```
SELECT tablespace_name, status,contents
     ,extent_management extents
     ,segment_space_management free_space
FROM dba_tablespaces
```

TABLESPACE_NAME	STATUS	CONTENTS	EXTENTS	FREE_SPACE
SYSTEM	ONLINE	PERMANENT	LOCAL	MANUAL
UNDOTBS1	ONLINE	UNDO	LOCAL	MANUAL
SYSAUX	ONLINE	PERMANENT	LOCAL	AUTO
TEMP	ONLINE	TEMPORARY	LOCAL	MANUAL
USERS	ONLINE	PERMANENT	LOCAL	AUTO
EXAMPLE	ONLINE	PERMANENT	LOCAL	AUTO
DATA	ONLINE	PERMANENT	LOCAL	AUTO
INDX	ONLINE	PERMANENT	LOCAL	AUTO

The V$TABLESPACE view also has one row per tablespace, but it includes some information other than DBA_TABLESPACES, such as whether the tablespace participates in database flashback operations:

```
SELECT name, bigfile, flashback_on
FROM v$tablespace;
```

NAME	BIGFILE	FLASHBACK_ON
SYSTEM	NO	YES
UNDOTBS1	NO	YES
SYSAUX	NO	YES
USERS	NO	YES
TEMP	NO	YES
EXAMPLE	NO	YES
DATA	NO	YES
INDX	NO	YES

See Chapter 15 for more information on flashback operations.

The DBA_DATA_FILES and DBA_TEMP_FILES views contain information on data files and temp files, respectively. This information includes the tablespace name, filename, file size, and autoextend settings.

```
SELECT tablespace_name, file_name, bytes/1024 kbytes
FROM dba_data_files
UNION ALL
SELECT tablespace_name, file_name, bytes/1024 kbytes
FROM dba_temp_files;
```

```
TABLESPACE FILE_NAME                                  KBYTES
---------- ----------------------------------------- -------
USERS      C:\ORACLE\ORADATA\ORA12\USERS01.DBF        102400
SYSAUX     C:\ORACLE\ORADATA\ORA12\SYSAUX01.DBF       256000
UNDOTBS1   C:\ORACLE\ORADATA\ORA12\UNDOTBS01.DBF       51200
SYSTEM     C:\ORACLE\ORADATA\ORA12\SYSTEM01.DBF       460800
EXAMPLE    C:\ORACLE\ORADATA\ORA12\EXAMPLE01.DBF      153600
INDX       C:\ORACLE\ORADATA\ORA12\INDX01.DBF         102400
TEMP       C:\ORACLE\ORADATA\ORA12\TEMP01.DBF          51200
```

Generating DDL for a Tablespace

Another way to quickly identify the attributes of a tablespace is to ask the database to generate DDL to re-create the tablespace. The CREATE TABLESPACE statement that results contains the attributes for the tablespace. Use the PL/SQL package DBMS_METADATA to generate DDL for your database objects. For example, to generate the DDL for the USERS tablespace, execute this:

```
SET LONG 32000
SELECT DBMS_METADATA.GET_DDL('TABLESPACE','USERS')
FROM dual;
```

The output from this statement is a CREATE TABLESPACE statement that contains all the attributes for the USERS tablespace:

```
CREATE TABLESPACE "USERS" DATAFILE
SIZE 104857600
AUTOEXTEND ON NEXT 104857600 MAXSIZE 32767M
LOGGING ONLINE PERMANENT BLOCKSIZE 8192
EXTENT MANAGEMENT LOCAL AUTOALLOCATE DEFAULT
NOCOMPRESS  SEGMENT SPACE MANAGEMENT AUTO
```

In addition to the data dictionary, you can obtain tablespace information from several sources. Some of these sources are the DDL and the Enterprise Manager.

Obtaining Tablespace Information Using the EM Database Express

Instead of querying the data dictionary views with a command-line tool such as SQL*Plus, you can use the interactive GUI tool EM Database Express (or SQL Developer) to monitor and manage database structures, including tablespaces. EM Database Express is an alternative to a command-line interface.

Choose Tablespaces under the Storage drop-down menu, and the screen in Figure 10.4 will appear.

FIGURE 10.4 The Enterprise Manager Tablespaces screen

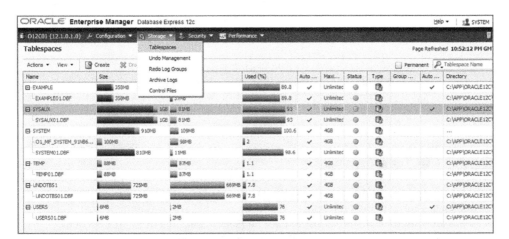

Using EM Database Express, you can create a new tablespace, modify the properties of a tablespace, change the status of a tablespace, add more data files, resize a tablespace, and drop a tablespace.

Managing Data Files

Data files (or temporary files) are made when you create a tablespace or when you alter a tablespace to add files. If you are not using the OMF feature, you will need to manage data files yourself. The database will create or reuse one or more data files in the sizes and locations that you specify whenever you create a tablespace. A data file belongs to only one tablespace and only one database at a time. Temp files are a special variety of data file that are used in temporary tablespaces. When the database creates or reuses a data file, the operating-system file is allocated and initialized—filled with a regular pattern of mostly binary zeros. This initialization will not occur with temp files.

Performing Operations on Data Files

Operations that you may need to perform on data files include:

- Resizing them
- Taking them offline or online
- Moving (renaming) them

Sizing Files

You can specify that the data file (or temporary file) will grow automatically whenever space is needed in the tablespace. This is accomplished by specifying the AUTOEXTEND clause for the file. This functionality enables you to have fewer data files per tablespace and can simplify the administration of data files. The AUTOEXTEND clause can be ON or OFF; you can also specify file size increments. You can set a maximum limit for the file size; by default, the file size limit is UNLIMITED. You can specify the AUTOEXTEND clause for files when you run the CREATE DATABASE, CREATE TABLESPACE, ALTER TABLESPACE, and ALTER DATAFILE commands. For example:

```
CREATE TABLESPACE APPL_DATA
DATAFILE '/disk2/oradata/DB01/appl_data01.dbf'
SIZE 500M
AUTOEXTEND ON NEXT 100M MAXSIZE 2000M;
```

The AUTOEXTEND ON clause specifies that the automatic file-resize feature should be enabled for the specified file; NEXT specifies the size by which the file should be incremented, and MAXSIZE specifies the maximum size for the file. When Oracle tries to allocate an extent in the tablespace, it looks for a free extent. If a large-enough free extent cannot be located (even after coalescing), Oracle increases the data file size by 100MB and tries to allocate the new extent.

The following statement disables the automatic file-extension feature:

```
ALTER DATABASE
DATAFILE '/disk2/oradata/DB01/appl_data01.dbf'
AUTOEXTEND OFF;
```

If the file already exists in the database, and you want to enable the autoextension feature, use the ALTER DATABASE command. For example, you can use the following statement:

```
ALTER DATABASE
DATAFILE '/disk2/oradata/DB01/appl_data01.dbf'
AUTOEXTEND ON NEXT 100M MAXSIZE 2000M;
```

You can increase or decrease the size of a data file or temporary file (thereby increasing or decreasing the size of the tablespace) by using the RESIZE clause of the ALTER DATABASE DATAFILE command. For example, to redefine the size of a file, use the following statement:

```
ALTER DATABASE
DATAFILE '/disk2/oradata/DB01/appl_data01.dbf'
RESIZE 1500M;
```

When decreasing the file size, Oracle returns an error if it finds data beyond the new file size. You cannot reduce the file size below the high-water mark in the file. Reducing the file size helps reclaim unused space.

Making Files Online and Offline

Sometimes you may have to make data files unavailable to the database if a file is corrupted. You can use the ONLINE and OFFLINE clauses of the ALTER DATABASE statement to take a data file online or offline. You can specify the filename or specify the unique identifier number that represents the data file. This identifier can be found in the FILE# column of V$DATAFILE or the FILE_ID column of the DBA_DATA_FILES view.

To take a data file offline, use the OFFLINE clause. If the database is in NOARCHIVELOG mode, then you must specify the FOR DROP clause along with the OFFLINE clause. The data file will be taken offline and marked with status OFFLINE. You can remove the data file using OS commands, if you want to get rid of the data file. If the database is in ARCHIVELOG mode, you don't need to specify the FOR DROP clause when taking a data file offline. When you're ready to bring the data file online, Oracle performs media recovery on the data file to make it consistent with the database. Also, the FOR DROP clause is ignored if the database is in ARCHIVELOG mode. Here is an example of taking a data file offline:

```
ALTER DATABASE DATAFILE '/u01/oradata/12CR11/tools02.dbf' OFFLINE;
```

The following statement brings the data file online:

```
ALTER DATABASE DATAFILE '/u01/oradata/12CR11/tools02.dbf' ONLINE;
```

Renaming Files

You can rename data files using the RENAME FILE clause of the ALTER DATABASE command as in the previous version of Oracle or using the newly introduced MOVE DATAFILE clause. You can also rename data files by using the RENAME DATAFILE clause of the ALTER TABLESPACE command. The RENAME or MOVE functionality is used to logically move tablespaces from one location to another. To rename or relocate data files belonging to a non-SYSTEM tablespace, you should follow certain steps. Consider the following example.

Your tablespace USER_DATA has three named data files, such as the following:

▪ /disk1/oradata/DB01/user_data01.dbf

▪ /disk1/oradata/DB01/userdata2.dbf

▪ /disk1/oradata/DB01/user_data03.dbf

Renaming a Data File in Online Mode

If you need to rename one of these, say the second file, use the MOVE DATAFILE clause of the ALTER DATABASE command.

```
ALTER DATABASE MOVE DATAFILE
'/disk1/oradata/DB01/userdata2.dbf' TO
'/disk1/oradata/DB01/user_data02.dbf';
```

The MOVE DATAFILE clause takes care of copying the file from the source directory to the destination directory (or to the ASM diskgroup) and deleting the file from the source location after the copy. If you do not want Oracle to remove the file from the source location, use the KEEP clause, as in the following example. ASM is discussed in Chapter 18, "Using Grid Infrastructure and Management Tools."

```
ALTER DATABASE MOVE DATAFILE
'/disk1/oradata/DB01/userdata2.dbf' TO
'+ORADATA' KEEP;
```

If for some reason the destination file already exists and is not part of the database, you can overwrite the file using the REUSE clause.

```
ALTER DATABASE MOVE DATAFILE
'/disk1/oradata/DB01/userdata2.dbf' TO
'/disk4/oradata/DB01/user_data02.dbf' REUSE;
```

The TO *<data file>* in the MOVE DATAFILE clause is optional. When TO is not specified, Oracle moves the file to the location specified by the DB_CREATE_FILE_DEST parameter as an Oracle Managed File.

Renaming a Data File in Offline Mode

The following steps are discussed only for completeness. There is really no need to use this approach when you are moving or renaming one file at a time (you can repeat the move datafile statement multiple times to move multiple files):

1. Take the tablespace offline:

```
ALTER TABLESPACE USER_DATA OFFLINE;
```

2. Copy or move the file to the new location, or rename the file by using operating-system commands.

3. Rename the file in the database by using one of the following two commands:

```
ALTER DATABASE RENAME FILE
'/disk1/oradata/DB01/userdata2.dbf' TO
'/disk1/oradata/DB01/user_data02.dbf';
```

or

```
ALTER TABLESPACE USER_DATA RENAME DATAFILE
'/disk1/oradata/DB01/userdata2.dbf' TO
'/disk1/oradata/DB01/user_data02.dbf';
```

4. Bring the tablespace online:

```
ALTER TABLESPACE USER_DATA ONLINE;
```

Because the SYSTEM tablespace cannot be taken offline, the ALTER DATABASE RENAME FILE clause cannot be used on files belonging to SYSTEM tablespace. But the ALTER DATABASE MOVE DATAFILE can be used on files belonging to SYSTEM tablespace.

Relocating a Tablespace

You may also determine that you need to relocate the tablespace from disk 1 to disk 2. If so, you should follow the same steps as when renaming a data file. If more than one data file is in a tablespace, you can rename all the files in the tablespace by using a single command. The steps are as follows:

1. Take the tablespace offline:

```
ALTER TABLESPACE USER_DATA OFFLINE;
```

2. Copy the file to the new location by using OS commands on the disk.

3. Rename the files in the database by using one of the following two commands. The number of data files specified before the keyword TO should be equal to the number of files specified after the keyword.

```
ALTER DATABASE RENAME FILE
'/disk1/oradata/DB01/user_data01.dbf',
'/disk1/oradata/DB01/userdata2.dbf',
'/disk1/oradata/DB01/user_data03.dbf'
 TO
'/disk2/oradata/DB01/user_data01.dbf',
'/disk2/oradata/DB01/user_data02.dbf',
'/disk2/oradata/DB01/user_data03.dbf';
```

or

```
ALTER TABLESPACE USER_DATA RENAME DATAFILE
'/disk1/oradata/DB01/user_data01.dbf',
'/disk1/oradata/DB01/userdata2.dbf',
'/disk1/oradata/DB01/user_data03.dbf'
```

```
    TO
    '/disk2/oradata/DB01/user_data01.dbf',
    '/disk2/oradata/DB01/user_data02.dbf',
    '/disk2/oradata/DB01/user_data03.dbf';
```

4. Bring the tablespace online:

```
ALTER TABLESPACE USER_DATA ONLINE;
```

 Oracle Database 12*c* Release 1 supports moving one data file at a time when using the ALTER DATABASE MOVE DATAFILE syntax. The ALTER DATABASE RENAME FILE syntax allows moving multiple files at a time, but does not support online operation.

Renaming or Relocating Files Belonging to Multiple Tablespaces

If you need to rename or relocate files belonging to multiple tablespaces, you can follow these steps (or use move data file multiple times):

1. Shut down the database. A complete backup is recommended before making any structural changes.

2. Copy or rename the files on the disk by using OS commands.

3. Start up and mount the database (STARTUP MOUNT).

4. Rename the files in the database by using the ALTER DATABASE RENAME FILE command.

5. Open the database by using ALTER DATABASE OPEN.

Using the Oracle Managed Files Feature

The Oracle Managed Files feature is appropriate for databases on disks using Logical Volume Manager (LVM) or using Oracle ASM. LVM software is available with most disk systems and is used to combine partitions of multiple physical disks into one logical volume. LVM can use mirroring, striping, RAID 5, and so on. Using the OMF feature has the following benefits:

Error Prevention   Because Oracle manages all aspects of the files associated with the tablespace, the DBA cannot accidentally remove a file belonging to an active tablespace.

Standard Naming Convention   The files created using the OMF method have unique and standardized filenames.

Space Retrieval   When tablespaces are dropped, Oracle removes the files associated with the tablespace, immediately freeing up space on the disk.

Easy Script Writing   Application vendors need not worry about the syntax for specifying directory names in the scripts when porting the application to multiple platforms. The same script can be used to create tablespaces on different OS platforms.

 **Real World Scenario**

Moving a Data File from the H Drive to the G Drive

Your operating-system administrator said that he sees a lot of contention on the H drive and would like options to move some of the reads off the H drive and to G drive. As a DBA, you can move one of the hot files belonging to the RECEIVABLES tablespace to the G drive.

You do not need to take the application or database offline to perform the data file move operation. You can move the data file from one location to another using a single command.

Move the data file:

```
ALTER DATABASE MOVE DATAFILE
    'H:\ORACLE\ORADATA\ORA12\RECEIVABLES02.DBF'
  TO 'G:\ORACLE\ORADATA\ORA12\RECEIVABLES02.DBF' ;
```

To be on the safe side, you might want to use the KEEP clause so the original file is not deleted by Oracle. You must delete the file outside of Oracle using OS utilities to save space.

```
ALTER DATABASE MOVE DATAFILE
    'H:\ORACLE\ORADATA\ORA12\RECEIVABLES02.DBF'
  TO 'G:\ORACLE\ORADATA\ORA12\RECEIVABLES02.DBF' KEEP;
```

The OMF feature can be used to create files and to remove them when the corresponding object (redo log group or tablespace) is dropped from the database. For managing OMF-created files, such as renaming or resizing, you will need to use the traditional methods.

Enabling the Oracle Managed Files Feature

To enable the creation of Oracle-managed data files, you need to set the parameter DB_CREATE_FILE_DEST. You can specify this parameter in the initialization-parameter file or set/change it using the ALTER SYSTEM or ALTER SESSION statement. The DB_CREATE_FILE_DEST parameter defines the directory where Oracle can create data files. Oracle must have read-write permission on this directory. The directory must exist on the server where the database is located. Oracle will not create the directory; it will create only the data file.

You can use the OMF feature to create data files when using the CREATE DATABASE, CREATE TABLESPACE, and ALTER TABLESPACE statements. In the CREATE DATABASE statement, you don't need to specify the filenames for the SYSTEM, UNDO, or TEMPORARY tablespaces.

In the CREATE TABLESPACE statement, you can omit the DATAFILE clause. In the ALTER TABLESPACE ADD DATAFILE statement, you can omit the filename.

The data files created using the OMF feature will have a standard format. For data files, the format is ora_%t_%u.dbf. For temp files, the format is ora_%t_%u.tmp, where %t is the tablespace name and %u is a unique eight-character string derived by Oracle. If the tablespace name is longer than eight characters, only the first eight characters are used. The filenames generated by Oracle are reported in the alert log file.

You can also use the OMF feature for the control files and redo log files of the database. Because these two types of files can be multiplexed, Oracle provides another parameter to specify the location of files, DB_CREATE_ONLINE_LOG_DEST_*n*, where *n* can be 1, 2, 3, 4, or 5. These initialization parameters also can be altered using ALTER SYSTEM or ALTER SESSION. If you set the parameters DB_CREATE_ONLINE_LOG_DEST_1 and DB_CREATE_ONLINE_LOG_DEST_2 in the parameter file when creating a database, Oracle creates two control files (one in each directory) and creates two online redo log groups with two members each (one member each in both directories).

The redo log file names will have the format ora_%g_%u.log, where %g is the log group number and %u is an eight-character string. The control file will have a format of ora_%u.ctl, where %u is an eight-character string.

In the following sections, you will see examples using the OMF feature while creating a database as well as creating additional tablespaces in a database.

In all SQL statements where you reference an existing data file by name, you can replace it with the file number. This is especially useful when dealing with Oracle Managed Files, typically with long names. Querying FILE# column in V$DATAFILE generates the file number.

Creating Databases Using the OMF Feature

Let's consider an example of creating a database. The following parameters are set in the initialization-parameter file:

```
UNDO_MANAGEMENT = AUTO
DB_CREATE_ONLINE_LOG_DEST_1 = '/ora1/oradata/MYDB'
DB_CREATE_ONLINE_LOG_DEST_2 = '/ora2/oradata/MYDB'
DB_CREATE_FILE_DEST = '/ora1/oradata/MYDB'
```

You do not have the CONTROL_FILES parameter set. Create the database using the following statement:

```
CREATE DATABASE MYDB
DEFAULT TEMPORARY TABLESPACE TEMP;
```

The following files will be created: the SYSTEM tablespace data file in /ora1/oradata/MYDB; the TEMP tablespace temp file in /ora1/oradata/MYDB; one control file in /ora1/

oradata/MYDB and another control file in /ora2/oradata/MYDB; one member of the first redo log group in /ora1/oradata/MYDB, and a second member in /ora2/oradata/MYDB; and one member of second redo log group in /ora1/oradata/MYDB, and a second member in /ora2/oradata/MYDB. Because you specified the UNDO_MANAGEMENT clause and did not specify a name for the undo tablespace, Oracle creates the SYS_UNDOTBS tablespace as an undo tablespace and creates its data file in /ora1/oradata/MYDB. If you omit the DEFAULT TEMPORARY TABLESPACE clause, Oracle will not create a temporary tablespace.

When using the OMF feature to create control files, you must get the names of control files from the alert log and add them to the initialization-parameter file using the CONTROL_FILES parameter for the instance to start again.

Creating Tablespaces Using the OMF Feature

Let's consider another example that creates two tablespaces. The data file for the APP_DATA tablespace will be stored in the directory /ora5/oradata/MYDB. The data file for the APP_INDEX tablespace will be stored in the directory /ora6/oradata/MYDB. Both data files will be of default size 100M.

```
ALTER SESSION SET DB_CREATE_FILE_DEST = '/ora5/oradata/MYDB';
CREATE TABLESPACE APP_DATA;
ALTER SESSION SET DB_CREATE_FILE_DEST = '/ora6/oradata/MYDB';
CREATE TABLESPACE APP_INDEX;
```

If you do not specify the DB_CREATE_ONLINE_LOG_DEST_*n* parameter when creating a database or when adding a redo log group, the OMF feature creates one control file and two groups with one member each for redo log files in the DB_CREATE_FILE_DEST directory. If the DB_CREATE_FILE_DEST parameter is not set and you did not provide filenames for data files and redo logs, Oracle creates the files in a default directory (mostly $ORACLE_HOME/dbs), but they will not be Oracle-managed. This is the default behavior of the database.

Overriding the Default File Size

If you want to have different sizes for the files created by the OMF feature, you can specify the DATAFILE clause without a filename. You can also turn off the autoextensible feature of the data file. The following statement creates a tablespace of size 10MB and turns off the autoextensible feature:

```
CREATE TABLESPACE PAY_DATA DATAFILE SIZE 10M
AUTOEXTEND OFF;
```

Here is another example that creates multiple data files for the tablespace. The second and third data files are autoextensible.

```
CREATE TABLESPACE PAY_INDEX
DATAFILE SIZE 20M AUTOEXTEND OFF,
SIZE 30M AUTOEXTEND ON MAXSIZE 1000M,
SIZE 1M;
```

The following example adds files to an existing tablespace:

```
ALTER SYSTEM SET DB_CREATE_FILE_DEST = '/ora5/oradata/MYDB';
ALTER TABLESPACE USERS ADD DATAFILE;
ALTER SYSTEM SET DB_CREATE_FILE_DEST = '/ora8/oradata/MYDB';
ALTER TABLESPACE APP_DATA
ADD DATAFILE SIZE 200M AUTOEXTEND OFF;
```

Once created, Oracle Managed Files are treated like other database files. You can rename and resize them and must back them up. Archive log files cannot be managed by OMF.

Creating a Database and Its Associated Tablespaces with OMF

You have been asked by the vendor to create a test database for a new application your company just bought. The database is to be used for testing the functionality of the application. The vendor told you it needs four tablespaces: SJC_DATA, SJC_INDEX, WKW_DATA, and WKW_INDEX. The system administrator has provisioned an LVM disk and mounted it as /oradata.

You decide to use the Oracle Managed Files feature, which makes your life easier by creating and cleaning the files belonging to the database.

Make sure you include the following in the parameter file:

```
UNDO_MANAGEMENT = AUTO
DB_CREATE_FILE_DEST = /oradata
DB_CREATE_ONLINE_LOG_DEST_1 = /oradata
DB_CREATE_ONLINE_LOG_DEST_2 = /oradata
```

Create the database using the following statement:

```
CREATE DATABASE SJCTEST
LOGFILE SIZE 20M
DEFAULT TEMPORARY TABLESPACE TEMP
TEMPFILE SIZE 200M
```

```
EXTENT MANAGEMENT LOCAL UNIFORM SIZE 2M
UNDO TABLESPACE UNDO_TBS SIZE 200M;
```

The previous code creates a database called SJCTEST. The SYSTEM tablespace, undo tablespace, and temporary tablespace are created in /oradata. The SYSTEM tablespace has the default size of 100MB, and the undo tablespace and temporary tablespace will have the size of 200MB. Because you do not want each log file member to be 100MB, you specify a smaller size for online redo log members.

Two control files are created, and redo log files with two members are created. Both members are stored in /oradata.

After running the necessary scripts to create the catalog and packages, you create the tablespaces for the application:

```
CREATE TABLESPACE SJC_DATA DATAFILE SIZE 800M AUTOEXTEND ON NEXT 50M MAXSIZE 8G;
CREATE TABLESAPCE WKW_INDEX
EXTENT MANAGEMENT LOCAL UNIFORM SIZE 512K
DATAFILE SIZE 500M AUTOEXTEND ON NEXT 50M MAXSIZE 8G;
CREATE TABLESPACE WKW_DATA AUTOEXTEND ON NEXT 50M MAXSIZE 8G;
CREATE TABLESPACE SJC_INDEX
EXTENT MANAGEMENT LOCAL UNIFORM SIZE 512K
DATAFILE SIZE 500M AUTOEXTEND ON NEXT 50M MAXSIZE 8G;
```

All data files for application tablespaces are created with the autoextend option, and the file increments by 50M, up to 8GB.

Querying Data File Information

Similar to the way you gather tablespace information, you can use SQL*Plus as well as the EM Grid Control to obtain information about data files and temporary files. In the following sections, you will query a few dictionary views that hold data-file and temporary-file information. You can obtain the same information using the EM Grid Control by drilling down the tablespaces shown in Figure 10.4. You can query data file and temporary-file information by using the following views.

V$DATAFILE

This view shows data file information from the control file:

```
SELECT FILE#, RFILE#, STATUS, BYTES, BLOCK_SIZE
FROM V$DATAFILE;
```

```
     FILE#    RFILE# STATUS       BYTES BLOCK_SIZE
---------- ---------- ------- ---------- ----------
         1          1 SYSTEM  734003200       8192
         2          2 ONLINE  883818496       8192
         3          3 ONLINE  225443840       8192
         4          4 ONLINE    5242880       8192
         5          5 ONLINE  104857600       8192
         6          6 ONLINE  209715200       8192
         7          7 ONLINE  209715200       8192
         8          8 ONLINE  104857600       8192
```

V$TEMPFILE

Similar to V$DATAFILE, this view shows information about the temporary files:

```
SELECT FILE#, RFILE#, STATUS, BYTES, BLOCK_SIZE
FROM V$TEMPFILE;
```

```
     FILE#    RFILE# STATUS       BYTES BLOCK_SIZE
---------- ---------- ------- ---------- ----------
         1          1 ONLINE   49283072       8192
```

DBA_DATA_FILES

This view displays information about the filenames, associated tablespace names, size, and status:

```
SELECT TABLESPACE_NAME, FILE_NAME, BYTES,
       AUTOEXTENSIBLE
FROM DBA_DATA_FILES;
```

```
TABLESPACE FILE_NAME                                    BYTES AUT
---------- --------------------------------------- ---------- ---
USERS      /u01/app/oracle/oradata/12CR11/users01.d   5242880 YES
           bf
UNDOTBS1   /u01/app/oracle/oradata/12CR11/undotbs01 225443840 YES
           .dbf
SYSAUX     /u01/app/oracle/oradata/12CR11/sysaux01. 883818496 YES
           dbf
SYSTEM     /u01/app/oracle/oradata/12CR11/system01. 734003200 YES
           dbf
EXAMPLE    /u01/app/oracle/oradata/12CR11/example01 104857600 YES
           .dbf
```

```
APPL_DATA   /u01/app/oracle/oradata/12CR11/appl_data  209715200 NO
            01.dbf
APPL_DATA   /u01/app/oracle/oradata/12CR11/appl_data  209715200 NO
            02.dbf
HR_DATA     /u02/oradata/12CR11/12CR11/datafile/o1_m  104857600 YES
            f_hr_data_46n3ck5t_.dbf
```

DBA_TEMP_FILES

This view displays information similar to that of DBA_DATA_FILES for the temporary files in the database:

```
SELECT TABLESPACE_NAME, FILE_NAME, BYTES,
       AUTOEXTENSIBLE
FROM DBA_TEMP_FILES;


TABLESPACE FILE_NAME                                      BYTES AUT
---------- ---------------------------------------- ---------- ---
TEMP       /u01/app/oracle/oradata/12CR11/temp01.dbf   49283072 NO
```

The maximum number of data files per tablespace is OS-dependent, but on most operating systems, it is 1,022. The maximum number of data files per database is 65,533. The MAXDATAFILES clause in the CREATE DATABASE and CREATE CONTROLFILE statements also limits the number of data files per database. The maximum data file size is OS-dependent. There is no limit on the number of tablespaces per database. Because only 65,533 data files are allowed per database, you cannot have more than 65,533 tablespaces, because each tablespace needs at least one data file.

A useful technique for managing disk space used by data files is to enable AUTOEXTEND for application tablespaces, which tells the database to automatically enlarge a data file when the tablespace runs out of free space. The AUTOEXTEND attribute applies to individual data files and not to the tablespace.

To resize a data file manually, use the ALTER DATABASE DATAFILE statement, like this:

```
ALTER DATABASE DATAFILE
   '/u01/app/oracle/oradata/12CR11/example01.dbf' RESIZE 2000M;
```

To configure a data file to automatically enlarge as needed by adding 100MB at a time up to a maximum of 8,000MB, execute the following:

```
ALTER DATABASE DATAFILE
   'C:\ORACLE\ORADATA\ORA10\DATA01.DBF'
AUTOEXTEND ON NEXT 100M MAXSIZE 8000M;
```

WARNING   If you plan to use the AUTOEXTEND option for the data files, use MAXSIZE to limit the file size to the disk space available. Also, enabling AUTOEXTEND for temporary and undo tablespaces is not advised because user errors can fill up the available disk space.

Now that you've learned the basics and the details of logical and physical tablespace storage, let's look at the space management features of Oracle Database 12*c* in the next section.

Managing Space

In this section, we will discuss the various space management options and features of Oracle Database 12*c*. We saw most of these options in the earlier sections of the chapter and when using SQL*Plus commands. We will illustrate the features using SQL*Developer and/or EM Database Express wherever applicable.

Automatic Space Management Features

The automatic space management features of the database include the following characteristics.

- Using EXTENT MANAGEMENT LOCAL when creating tablespaces. It is better to create the SYSTEM tablespace as locally managed—hence all tablespaces are automatically created as locally managed.

- Using SEGMENT SPACE MANAGEMENT AUTO when creating tablespaces.

- Using AUTOEXTEND ON for data files, when creating tablespaces or adding files to tablespaces.

- Using Oracle Managed Files to automate file management. OMF automates the creation and deletion of files as needed.

- When tables or indexes are created, the segments are not allocated until the first row is inserted into the table. Packaged applications like ERP install thousands of tables, but most are not used. The delayed segment creation speeds up the application installation and saves on storage for empty tables.

- Using automatic undo management to eliminate the complexities of managing rollback segments. Undo is discussed in Chapter 11, "Managing Data Concurrency and Undo."

- Oracle Database 12*c* automatically monitors free space and generates alerts based on default thresholds. Server-generated alerts are discussed in Chapter 14, "Maintaining the Database and Managing Performance."

Creating a tablespace using EM Database Express is easy and error free. Select Tablespaces from the Storage drop-down menu of EM Database Express. Click the Create button; the Create Tablespace screen will appear, as shown in Figure 10.5. In this screen, name the tablespace and click OK to create a tablespace with all defaults.

FIGURE 10.5   Create a tablespace using EM Database Express.

Creating a Locally Managed Tablespace

The Create Tablespace screen has other configurable options. Figure 10.6 shows the extent management options for a tablespace found under the Space section of the Create Tablespace screen. When you input the size in the Extent Size box, follow this format: ***numberunit***. The number variable needs to be an integer, and the unit variable needs to be one of the following only: K, M, or G. For example, you would enter **512K**. EM Database Express does not support creating dictionary-managed tablespaces.

FIGURE 10.6   The Create Tablespace screen's space options

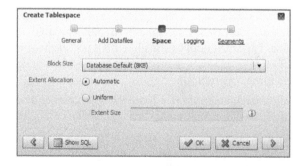

SQL Developer gives the option to create tablespaces as dictionary managed or locally managed. The Create Tablespace dialog box of SQL Developer is shown in Figure 10.7. For Local Extent Management, you can check the Auto Allocate check box for automatic extent allocation or provide Uniform Size for extent management. For Dictionary Extent

Management, you can check the Define Extents check box and manually enter the storage properties.

FIGURE 10.7   Create a tablespace using SQL Developer.

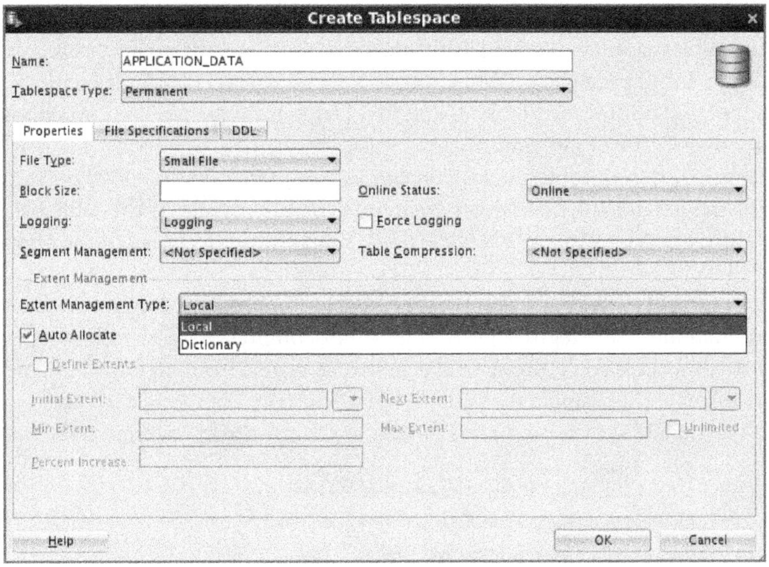

Choosing Automatic Segment Space Management

Segment space management is another configurable option of Create Tablespace using EM Database Express. Figure 10.8 shows the segment space management options for tablespaces, which are found under the Segments section of the Create Tablespace screen. The Segment Space Management setting lets you specify whether Oracle Database 12c should track the used and free space in the segments in the tablespace using free lists or bitmaps. For using free lists to manage free space, use segment space management setting MANUAL, and to use more efficient bitmaps use the AUTOMATIC setting. For bigfile tablespaces, segment management has to be automatic.

FIGURE 10.8   The Create Tablespace screen's segments options

In the SQL Developer Create Tablespace screen shown in Figure 10.7, you specify this option by choosing Auto from the drop-down menu beside Segment Management.

Using Compression

Oracle Database 12*c* has a compression feature that reduces the storage footprint of the database. Basic compression in an Oracle database has been available since version 9*i*. When you create a new tablespace, NOCOMPRESS is the default, which means no *compression* on the blocks. The Create Tablespace using EM Database Express screen shown in Figure 10.8 also shows the compression options available. Using EM Database Express, you can choose either basic compression or OLTP compression.

When creating or altering tablespaces, you can set the COMPRESS or NOCOMPRESS option. They will act as the default for the objects created in the tablespace. If the table or index definition has different COMPRESS or NOCOMPRESS options, those options will be applied for the object.

COMPRESS tells Oracle to use basic compression. Basic compression compresses data loaded using the direct-load method. Regular DML data is not compressed. The following example shows how to create a table structure with the COMPRESS clause from an existing table, how to load data into the new table using a direct-load operation, and compress the loaded data. The APPEND hint in the INSERT statement directs Oracle to use the direct-load method.

```
SQL> CREATE TABLE bookings_comp COMPRESS NOLOGGING
     AS SELECT * FROM bookings WHERE 1=2;
SQL> INSERT /*+ APPEND */ INTO bookings_comp
     SELECT * FROM bookings;
```

Compression for OLTP compresses the data in the data block. The compression happens at a block level, not when rows are inserted into the table. The rows are inserted as uncompressed during normal DML operations. OLTP Table Compression has no negative impact on read operations. Oracle compresses blocks in batch mode rather than compressing data every time a DML operation takes place. A block is initially uncompressed until data in the block reaches an internally controlled threshold. When a transaction causes the data in the block to reach this threshold, all contents of the block are compressed. When more data is added and this threshold is reached again, the compression operation happens again. This process is repeated until the highest level of compression is achieved.

The following is an example of creating the table for OLTP compression and loading data in a conventional method.

```
SQL> CREATE TABLE bookings_oltp COMPRESS FOR OLTP
     AS SELECT * FROM bookings WHERE 1=2;
SQL> INSERT INTO bookings_oltp
     SELECT * FROM bookings;
```

More compression options are available in Oracle Database 12*c*. Figure 10.9 shows the compression options available for Create Tablespace using SQL Developer.

FIGURE 10.9 The SQL Developer Compress options available when creating a tablespace

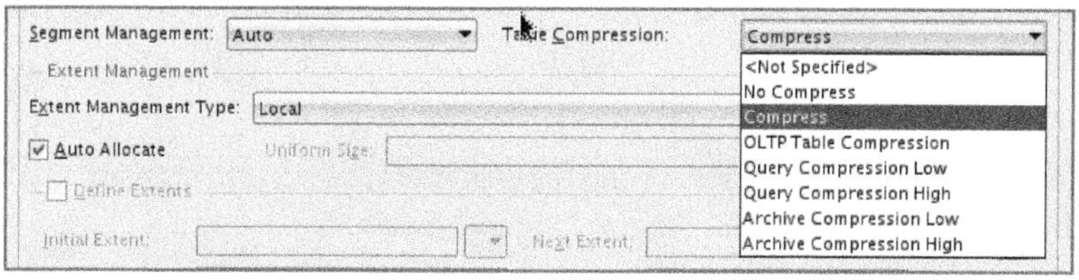

The additional compress options displayed in the screen are applicable only to Exadata machines.

Monitoring Tablespace Free Space

You can determine the tablespace space allocated and the amount of used space by utilizing dictionary views. You learned about obtaining tablespace and data file information earlier in the chapter under the "Obtaining Tablespace Information Using SQL*Plus" and "Querying Data File Information" sections. The DBA_DATA_FILES, DBA_TEMP_FILES, DBA_FREE_SPACE, and DBA_SEGMENTS dictionary views provide comprehensive information about tablespace space usage. DBA_FREE_SPACE has information about the free segments in a tablespace, and DBA_SEGMENTS is used to find the size of the objects in the database. The following query shows space usage information from data tablespaces (not including undo and temp-type tablespaces).

```
WITH
ts_free AS (SELECT tablespace_name, round(sum(bytes)/1048576) free_mb
       FROM dba_free_space GROUP BY tablespace_name),
ts_alloc AS (SELECT tablespace_name, round(sum(bytes)/1048576) alloc_mb
       FROM dba_data_files GROUP BY tablespace_name)
SELECT tablespace_name, status, alloc_mb,
       free_mb, alloc_mb-free_mb used_mb
FROM   dba_tablespaces
JOIN   ts_alloc USING (tablespace_name)
JOIN   ts_free USING (tablespace_name)
/
```

TABLESPACE_NAME	STATUS	ALLOC_MB	FREE_MB	USED_MB
SYSAUX	ONLINE	11370	547	10823
MYAPPDATA	ONLINE	100	99	1
USERS	ONLINE	5	2	3

SYSTEM	ONLINE	440	3	437
RENT	ONLINE	300	298	2

When data files are set to AUTOEXTEND, the query needs to be modified to take that into account. See the following query for an example.

```
WITH
ts_free AS (SELECT tablespace_name, round(sum(bytes)/1048576) free_mb
       FROM dba_free_space GROUP BY tablespace_name),
ts_alloc AS (SELECT tablespace_name,
       round(sum(decode(autoextensible, 'YES', maxbytes, bytes))/1048576)
alloc_mb
       FROM dba_data_files GROUP BY tablespace_name)
SELECT tablespace_name, status, alloc_mb, free_mb, alloc_mb-free_mb used_mb
FROM   dba_tablespaces t
JOIN   ts_alloc a USING (tablespace_name)
JOIN   ts_free f USING (tablespace_name)
/
```

In Figure 10.10, the tablespace information is obtained using EM Database Express. Checking the Permanent check box will show only permanent tablespaces, leaving out the temporary and undo tablespaces.

FIGURE 10.10   EM Database Express tablespace usage

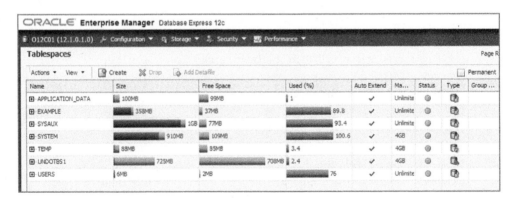

SQL Developer also displays tablespace usage information. See Figure 10.11. The Files tab shows the details of data files associated with the tablespaces. The Free Space tab shows the free-space detail by tablespace.

FIGURE 10.11   SQL Developer tablespace usage

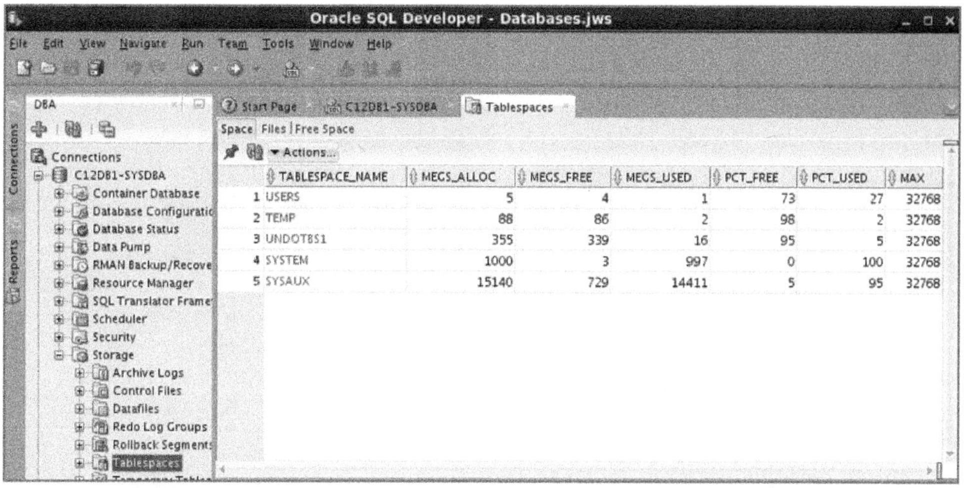

	TABLESPACE_NAME	MEGS_ALLOC	MEGS_FREE	MEGS_USED	PCT_FREE	PCT_USED	MAX
1	USERS	5	4	1	73	27	32768
2	TEMP	88	86	2	98	2	32768
3	UNDOTBS1	355	339	16	95	5	32768
4	SYSTEM	1000	3	997	0	100	32768
5	SYSAUX	15140	729	14411	5	95	32768

You can use OEM Cloud Control or DBMS_SPACE package to plan the capacity for database objects. You can also use them to estimate the amount of space the table and index will use, as well as growth trends.

Proactive Space Management

Space management used to be a very time-consuming task for DBAs. Now Oracle Database 12*c* monitors its space consumption, alerts administrators about potential problems, and recommends possible solutions. The database does nonintrusive and timely monitoring of space usage. The space-monitoring functionality of the database is set up automatically without any measurable performance impact.

By default, Oracle monitors tablespace space usage. It generates a warning at 85 percent and a critical alert at 97 percent. You can access the information by querying the DBA_THRESHOLDS view. In Figure 10.12, the DBA_THRESHOLDS are queried using SQL Developer Worksheet. The first three lines in the Query Result are for undo and temporary tablespaces, where the metric is set to Do Not Check.

DBA_THRESHOLDS is part of Oracle's server-managed alerts framework. The DBMS_SERVER_ALERT.SET_THRESHOLD procedure is used to add or make changes to threshold values. Oracle Enterprise Manager Cloud Control proactively monitors free space in tablespace and sends alerts to administrators when a space threshold is reached. EM Database Express does not have a built-in alerting mechanism.

FIGURE 10.12 The DBA_THRESHOLDS contents

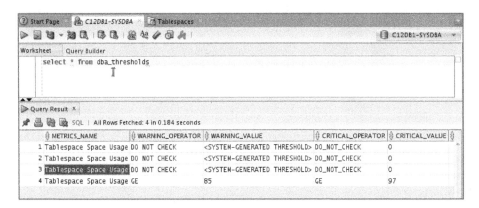

You will learn more about server-generated alerts in Chapter 14.

The server-managed threshold alerts for tablespace space usage will not be generated for dictionary-managed tablespaces. They are supported for locally managed bigfile and smallfile tablespaces, and for undo and temporary tablespaces.

Using Segment Advisor

When large amounts of updates and deletes are performed on tables, pockets of empty space (known as fragmented space) are created in the segment that cannot be reused efficiently. The *Segment Advisor* identifies whether a segment is a good candidate for a shrink operation based on the level of fragmentation within the segment. The advisor also keeps track of historical growth of the segment, which can be used for capacity planning. Segments that can be shrunk are those that the Segment Advisor has found to need less space than they are currently allocated. By shrinking or compressing these segments, space is returned to the database for use by other objects, and the total number of I/Os needed to access these objects is reduced, potentially improving the performance of SQL statements that access these objects.

Segment Advisor utilizes the growth statistics in the Automatic Workload Repository (AWR) and samples the data in the segment for its recommendations. It is configured to run during maintenance windows as an automated maintenance task. You may also run it manually using the DBMS_ADVISOR package. The Segment Advisor automated maintenance task is known as the Automatic Segment Advisor.

Segment Advisor recommendations can be accessed using OEM Cloud Control 12*c*; to access them, select Administration ➪ Storage ➪ Segment Advisor. Figure 10.13 shows the Segment Advisor screen.

FIGURE 10.13   The Segment Advisor Recommendations screen

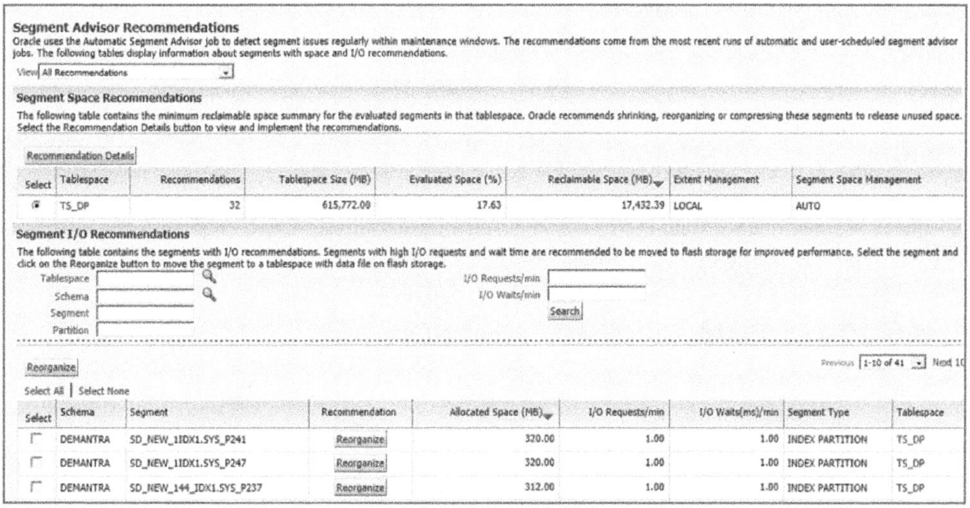

Clicking on the Recommendation Details shows the individual objects in the tablespace and how much space could be reclaimed with the recommended operation. See Figure 10.14.

FIGURE 10.14   The Segment Advisor Recommendation Details screen

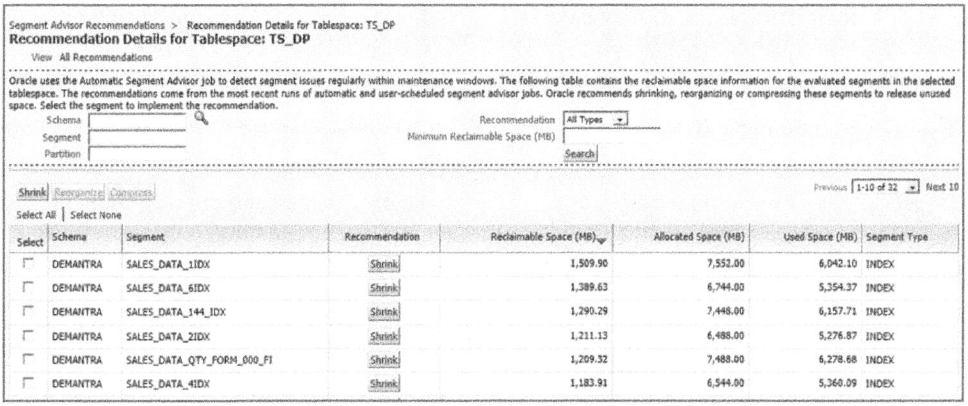

Automatic Segment Advisor Job is set up automatically in the database to run the Segment Advisor during the maintenance window (AUTO_SPACE_ADVISOR_JOB). The Segment Advisor results can be queried directly from the database using the DBA_ADVISOR_% views. The following views are available in Oracle Database 12c Release 1.

DBA_ADVISOR_FINDINGS: Shows the findings of Segment Advisor.

DBA_ADVISOR_RECOMMENDATIONS: Shows the recommendations of Segment Advisor based on the findings. The recommendations are shrink, reorganize, or compress the object.

DBA_ADVISOR_ACTIONS: Shows the actions or SQL to perform against the recommendations.

DBA_ADVISOR_OBJECTS: Shows the objects and the recommendations.

Shrinking Space Usage of Objects

In Figure 10.14, notice the Shrink button against each object as well as on top. You can select the objects you want to reclaim the space from and submit a job to shrink the space. When you click Shrink, you will be presented with two options as in Figure 10.15.

FIGURE 10.15   The Shrink Segment Options screen

The Compact Segments And Release Space option will first compact the segments and then release the recovered space to the tablespace. During the short space-release phase, any cursors referencing this segment may be invalidated and queries on the segment could be affected. The Compact Segments option will compact segment data without releasing the recovered space. After the data is compacted, the recovered space can be quickly released by running Compact Segments And Release Space.

The Segment Shrink option is available only to the segments belonging to tablespaces with automatic segment space management. Segment shrink is an online operation, and other DML operations on the object can continue.

You can use SQL*Plus to perform the shrink space of objects. The ALTER TABLE and ALTER INDEX statements have the SHRINK SPACE clause to accomplish this. You can manually shrink space in a table, index-organized table or its overflow segment, index, partition, subpartition, LOB segment, materialized view, or materialized view log. By default, Oracle Database 12c compacts the segment, adjusts the high-water mark, and releases the recuperated space immediately.

The ROW MOVEMENT option should be enabled on the object so that the segment compacting is performed. When rows move, any ROWID-based triggers will fire, so it is better to disable such triggers before performing the shrink space operation on tables. The SHRINK

SPACE clause can be followed by COMPACT and CASCADE options. Using the COMPACT option is similar to choosing the Compact Segments in Figure 10.15. The CASCADE option performs the operation on all dependent indexes. Even if the CASCADE option is not specified, the dependent indexes are not left in UNUSABLE state after the shrink operation on the table.

Specifying ALTER INDEX ... SHRINK SPACE COMPACT is equivalent to specifying ALTER INDEX ... COALESCE.

 **Real World Scenario**

Using Segment Advisor and Shrink Space in SQL*Plus

Here is a working example that invokes Segment Advisor to analyze a table and uses the Shrink option to reclaim the unused space. Table XX_DATA is a table with several inserts and deletes, thus prone to fragmentation. Let's run Segment Advisor on this table to determine if there is any reclaimable space.

Running Segment Advisor involves four DBMS_ADVISOR procedures. First, define the task, then add objects to the task, then define expected recommendations, and finally execute the task.

```
SQL> EXEC DBMS_ADVISOR.CREATE_TASK (advisor_name=>'Segment Advisor',
 task_name=> 'XX_DATA_SEG_ADV');

PL/SQL procedure successfully completed.

SQL> DECLARE
objid NUMBER;
BEGIN
DBMS_ADVISOR.CREATE_OBJECT (task_name=> 'XX_DATA_SEG_ADV',
object_type=> 'TABLE',
attr1 => 'SYSTEM',
attr2 => 'XX_DATA',
attr3 => NULL,
attr4 => 'NULL',
attr5 => NULL,
object_id => objid);
```

```
END;
/

PL/SQL procedure successfully completed.

SQL>
SQL> EXEC DBMS_ADVISOR.SET_TASK_PARAMETER (task_name => 'XX_DATA_SEG_ADV',
 parameter => 'RECOMMEND_ALL', value => 'TRUE');

PL/SQL procedure successfully completed.

SQL>
SQL> EXEC DBMS_ADVISOR.EXECUTE_TASK (task_name => 'XX_DATA_SEG_ADV');

PL/SQL procedure successfully completed.
```

Now, query DBA_ADVISOR_FINDINGS for the findings.

```
SQL> SELECT message, more_info
     FROM DBA_ADVISOR_FINDINGS
     WHERE task_name = 'XX_DATA_SEG_ADV';

MESSAGE
MORE_INFO
--------------------------------------------------------------------------------
Enable row movement of the table SYSTEM.XX_DATA and perform shrink, estimated
savings is 252134195 bytes.
Allocated Space:503316480: Used Space:251182285: Reclaimable Space :252134195

SQL>
SQL> SELECT benefit_type
     FROM dba_advisor_recommendations
     WHERE task_name = 'XX_DATA_SEG_ADV';

BENEFIT_TYPE
--------------------------------------------------------------------------------
Enable row movement of the table SYSTEM.XX_DATA and perform shrink, estimated
savings is 252134195 bytes.

SQL>
```

So our expectation was correct. The XX_DATA table does have some reclaimable space.
Validate the current allocated space and then perform the Shrink Space operation.

```
SQL> SELECT bytes FROM dba_segments
     WHERE segment_name = 'XX_DATA';

     BYTES
----------
 503316480

SQL>
```

Now, follow the recommendation. First, we will perform the COMPACT to show the impact on allocated space, and then we will perform a shrink.

```
SQL> ALTER TABLE xx_data ENABLE ROW MOVEMENT;

Table altered.

SQL> ALTER TABLE xx_data SHRINK SPACE COMPACT;

Table altered.

SQL> SELECT bytes FROM dba_segments
     WHERE segment_name = 'XX_DATA';

     BYTES
----------
 503316480

SQL> ALTER TABLE xx_data SHRINK SPACE;

Table altered.

SQL> SELECT bytes FROM dba_segments
     WHERE segment_name = 'XX_DATA';

     BYTES
----------
 212598784

SQL>
```

Avoiding Out-of-Space Errors

During OLTP insert or update operations and bulk data-load operations, when all the blocks in the segment are used, Oracle will try to add a new extent from the tablespace free space to the segment and continue the DML operation. If no free space is available in the tablespace, Oracle will look for data files with autoextensible turned on. Such files will be extended to give more free space to the tablespace, which in turn will satisfy the new extent addition to the segment; therefore, the DML operation will not fail.

If all the data files in the tablespace are not autoextensible, or if there is no room left in the ASM diskgroup or file system, the tablespace cannot grow; therefore, the DML operation requiring a new extent added to the segment will fail. The user will get an error, which is not a good thing. To avoid space-related errors, Oracle Database 12c has the *resumable space allocation* feature. Resumable space allocation can suspend a session when one of the following conditions occurs in the database, and prevent the session from getting an error.

- Out-of-space condition (ORA-01653, ORA-01654)
- Maximum extents reached condition (ORA-01631, ORA-01632)
- Space quota exceeded condition (ORA-01536)

These conditions can occur and are resumable for the following operations:

- Queries involving sorting and causing an out-of-space condition in a temporary tablespace
- DML statements such as INSERT, UPDATE, DELETE, MERGE
- Import, SQL*Loader data load
- DDL statements such as

      CREATE TABLE ... AS SELECT

      CREATE INDEX

      ALTER INDEX ... REBUILD

      ALTER TABLE ... MOVE PARTITION

      ALTER TABLE ... SPLIT PARTITION

      ALTER INDEX ... REBUILD PARTITION

      ALTER INDEX ... SPLIT PARTITION

      CREATE MATERIALIZED VIEW

      CREATE MATERIALIZED VIEW LOG

Once the error condition is rectified by the DBA within a predefined timeframe, the suspended session will resume its operation.

> One quick way to remember the operations that are resumable is to know the operations that could create an extent for all type of segments.

Setting Up Resumable Space Allocation

A statement executes in resumable mode if the RESUMABLE_TIMEOUT initialization parameter is set to a nonzero value and the ALTER SESSION ENABLE RESUMABLE statement is issued during the user session. If the parameter is not set, resumable mode can be enabled in the user session using ALTER SESSION ENABLE RESUMABLE TIMEOUT *timeout_value*, where *timeout_value* is nonzero. The *timeout_value* for the session or in the parameter is specified in seconds.

If the suspended error condition is not rectified within the time specified by the *timeout_value* or RESUMABLE_TIMEOUT parameter, an error is returned to the user session. A resumable statement can be suspended and resumed multiple times during its execution. The timeout can be modified using the DBMS_RESUMABLE.SET_TIMEOUT procedure as well as ALTER SESSION ENABLE RESUMABLE TIMEOUT *timeout_value.*

Notifying on Session Suspend

When a resumable exception condition is raised in the session, the following actions are taken by Oracle.

- The error is reported in the alert log; DBA_RESUMABLE view is populated with suspended session, statement, and error information; the EVENT column in V$SESSION_WAIT is updated with "Statement suspended, wait error to be cleared" status.

- A resumable session suspended alert is triggered.

- The AFTER SUSPEND system event trigger, if it exists, is fired. You may use this trigger to automatically perform the corrective action if needed.

When a resumable session is suspended, an alert log entry similar to the following is generated.

```
statement in resumable session 'User SYSTEM(8), Session 268, Instance 1' was
suspended due to
    ORA-01653: unable to extend table SYSTEM.XX_DATA1 by 128 in tablespace TEST1
```

The DBA_RESUMABLE view can be queried to view this information as well.

```
SQL> SELECT user_id, session_id, status, timeout, suspend_time,
  2  error_number, sql_text
  3  FROM DBA_RESUMABLE
  4  /

   USER_ID SESSION_ID STATUS       TIMEOUT SUSPEND_TIME          ERROR_NUMBER
SQL_TEXT
---------- ---------- --------- ---------- -------------------- ------------
         8        264 SUSPENDED        300 11/05/13 16:53:46            1653
insert into xx_data1 select * from dba_objects
```

If no action is taken to fix the error condition, the user session will receive the error after the timeout period.

```
SQL> alter session enable resumable timeout 300;
SQL> insert into xx_data1 select * from dba_objects;
```

```
insert into xx_data1 select * from dba_objects
              *
ERROR at line 1:
ORA-30032: the suspended (resumable) statement has timed out
ORA-01653: unable to extend table SYSTEM.XX_DATA1 by 128 in tablespace TEST1
```

If action taken to fix the error condition before the timeout expires, the user session will not receive an error or message. The alert log will have the following information:

```
Tue Nov 05 17:09:49 2013
statement in resumable session 'User SYSTEM(8), Session 38, Instance 1' was
suspended due to
    ORA-01653: unable to extend table SYSTEM.XX_DATA2 by 128 in tablespace TEST2
Tue Nov 05 17:10:22 2013
alter tablespace test2 add datafile size 10m autoextend on next 10m
Completed: alter tablespace test2 add datafile size 10m autoextend on next 10m
statement in resumable session 'User SYSTEM(8), Session 38, Instance 1' was
resumed
Tue Nov 05 17:10:29 2013
```

If you would like to be notified by email, you can write the appropriate code in the AFTER SUSPEND event trigger, as in the following example:

```
CREATE OR REPLACE TRIGGER alert_on_resumable_error
AFTER SUSPEND ON DATABASE
DECLARE
  -- Declare any variables
BEGIN
  -- Add space allocation code
  -- Code to Notify DBA.
  COMMIT;
END;
/
```

If you use OEM Cloud Control, you will be notified when a resumable session suspended event occurs. So that the DBA has time to respond and fix the issue, keep the timeout value large.

Summary

This chapter discussed the most important aspect of Oracle Database 12*c*: storing data. You learned to create both tablespaces and data files. You found out how to create and manage tablespaces, as well as how Oracle stores some schema objects as segments that are comprised of extents and data blocks. A data block is the minimum unit of I/O in an Oracle database. Every data block has an internal structure known as the block format to track the data stored in the block as well as the free space still available in the block.

A data file belongs to one tablespace, and a tablespace can have one or more data files. The size of the tablespace is the total size of all the data files belonging to that tablespace. The size of the database is the total size of all tablespaces in the database, which is the same as the total size of all data files in the database. Tablespaces are logical storage units used to group data depending on their type or category. The relationship between data files and tablespaces is important to understand for the certification exam.

Tablespaces can manage the extents through the Oracle dictionary or locally in the data files that belong to the tablespace. Locally managed tablespaces can have uniform extent sizes; this reduces fragmentation and wasted space. You can also make Oracle perform the entire extent sizing for locally managed tablespaces.

A temporary tablespace is used for sorting operations; no permanent objects can be created in a temporary tablespace. Only one sort segment will be created for each instance in the temporary tablespace. Multiple transactions can use the same sort segment, but one transaction can use only one extent. Although temporary files are part of the database, they do not appear in the control file, and the block changes do not generate any redo information because all the segments created on locally managed temporary tablespaces are temporary segments.

The locally managed tablespaces eliminate the extent management activities from the DBA, and the automatic segment space management feature eliminates the need to manage free lists by using bitmaps. Tablespace data files can be set to extend automatically whenever space is needed in the tablespace. Tablespace storage can be monitored using data dictionary views or using tools like Oracle Enterprise Manager.

You also learned about using the compression options when creating a tablespace and during object creation. Basic compression is applicable only for direct-load operations, whereas OLTP compression compresses blocks based on a block full algorithm. Exadata systems have additional hyper columnar compression features. The Segment Advisor can be used to get advice on reclaimable space in segments. Such segment space can be reclaimed online using the SHRINK SPACE clause in SQL or using OEM.

When tablespaces reach out-of-space or a segments-cannot-extent situation arises, the resumable space allocation feature can suspend the session and resume after the space condition is rectified, thereby avoiding an error. When a session is suspended, it is written to the alert log and an event trigger is fired.

Exam Essentials

Know the relationship between data files and tablespaces.   Tablespaces are built on one or more data files. Bigfile tablespaces are built on a single data file, and smallfile tablespaces are built on one or more data files.

Understand the statements needed to create, modify, and drop tablespaces.   Use a CREATE TABLESPACE, ALTER TABLESPACE, or DROP TABLESPACE statement to create, modify, or drop a tablespace, respectively.

Know how to take tablespaces offline and understand the consequences the OFFLINE IMMEDIATE **option poses.**   Use an ALTER TABLESPACE statement to take a tablespace offline or bring it online. If you use the OFFLINE IMMEDIATE option, you must perform media recovery when you bring it back online.

Understand the default tablespaces for the database.   When the database is created, if you do not specify the DEFAULT TABLESPACE and DEFAULT TEMPORARY TABLESPACE clauses, the SYSTEM tablespace will be the default for user objects and temporary segments.

Know how to use EM Database Express to view tablespace information.   The EM Database Express or Cloud Control can be used to view tablespace information, as well as perform various administrative tasks. A working knowledge of this tool is required.

Know the difference between segment space management and extent management.   Extent management deals with segment-level space allocations, and segment space management deals with data block-level space allocations.

Know which initialization parameter controls OMF placement.   The DB_CREATE_FILE_DEST parameter tells the database where to place Oracle Managed Files.

Understand the compression options.   The default compression option can be set at the tablespace level, and individual objects can override the compression option.

Know the events that invoke a session suspension when a space condition is reached.   Out-of-space, extents-reaching-maximum, and space-quota-exceeded conditions invoke session suspension. Session suspended lasts until the timeout value in seconds is reached.

Learn how Segment Advisor can be invoked and apply its recommendation.   Segment Advisor analyses space usage of segments and recommends reclaimable space. Learn the options available to reclaim such space.

Review Questions

1. Which of the following statements about tablespaces is true?

    A. A tablespace is the physical implementation of a logical structure called a namespace.

    B. A tablespace can hold the objects of only one schema.

    C. A bigfile tablespace can have only one data file.

    D. The SYSAUX tablespace is an optional tablespace created only if you install certain database options.

2. Automatic segment space management on the tablespace causes which of the following table attributes in that tablespace to be ignored?

    A. The whole storage clause

    B. NEXT and PCTINCREASE

    C. BUFFERPOOL and FREEPOOL

    D. PCTFREE and PCTUSED

3. Which is not a type of segment that is stored in a tablespace?

    A. Undo

    B. Redo

    C. Permanent

    D. Temporary

4. Which allocation unit is the smallest?

    A. Data file

    B. Extent

    C. Data block

    D. Segment

5. You performed the following statement in the database. What actions can you perform on the CUST_INFO table in the CUST_DATA tablespace. (Choose all that apply.)

    ALTER TABLESPACE CUST_DATA READ ONLY;

    A. ALTER TABLE CUST_INFO DROP COLUMN xx;

    B. TRUNCATE TABLE CUST_INFO;

    C. INSERT INTO CUST_INFO VALUES (…);

    D. DROP TABLE CUST_INFO;

    E. RENAME CUST_INFO TO CUSTOMER_INFO;

6. If the tablespace is offline, which statements should be executed to make the USERS tablespace read-only? (Choose all that apply.)

    A. ALTER TABLESPACE USERS READ ONLY

    B. ALTER DATABASE MAKE TABLESPACE USERS READ ONLY

    C. ALTER TABLESPACE USERS ONLINE

    D. ALTER TABLESPACE USERS TEMPORARY

7. How would you add more space to a tablespace? (Choose all that apply.)

    A. ALTER TABLESPACE *<TABLESPACE NAME>* ADD DATAFILE SIZE *<N>*

    B. ALTER DATABASE DATAFILE *<FILENAME>* RESIZE *<N>*

    C. ALTER DATAFILE *<FILENAME>* RESIZE *<N>*

    D. ALTER TABLESPACE *<TABLESPACE NAME>* DATAFILE *<FILENAME>* RESIZE *<N>*

8. The database is using automatic memory management. The standard block size for the database is 8KB. You need to create a tablespace with a block size of 16KB. Which initialization parameter should be set?

    A. DB_8K_CACHE_SIZE

    B. DB_16K_CACHE_SIZE

    C. DB_CACHE_SIZE

    D. None of the above

9. Which data dictionary view can be queried to obtain information about the files that belong to locally managed temporary tablespaces?

    A. DBA_DATA_FILES

    B. DBA_TABLESPACES

    C. DBA_TEMP_FILES

    D. DBA_LOCAL_FILES

10. How would you drop a tablespace if the tablespace were not empty?

    A. Rename all the objects in the tablespace, and then drop the tablespace.

    B. Remove the data files belonging to the tablespace from the disk.

    C. Use ALTER DATABASE DROP *<TABLESPACE NAME>* CASCADE.

    D. Use DROP TABLESPACE *<TABLESPACE NAME>* INCLUDING CONTENTS.

11. Which command is used to enable the autoextensible feature for a file if the file is already part of a tablespace?

    A. ALTER DATABASE.

    B. ALTER TABLESPACE.

    C. ALTER DATA FILE.

    D. You cannot change the autoextensible feature once the data file is created.

12. Which statement is true regarding the SYSTEM tablespace?

    A. It can be made read-only.

    B. It can be offline.

    C. Data files can be renamed.

    D. Data files cannot be resized.

13. The default critical threshold for a tablespace is set at 97 percent, and you think that is too low. Which two options can you use to change the threshold value to 90 percent for tablespace *APPS_DATA*?

    A. Use Oracle Enterprise Manager Database Express.

    B. Use Oracle Enterprise Manager Cloud Control.

    C. Use DBMS_SERVER_ALERT package.

    D. Use DBMS_SPACE package.

14. Choose the statements that are resumable. (Choose three.)

    A. ALTER TABLE … SPLIT PARTITION

    B. SELECT

    C. INSERT INTO … SELECT

    D. CREATE TABLESPACE

    E. ALTER TABLE … SHRINK SPACE

15. How do you ensure you are notified when a resumable session is suspended? (Choose two.)

    A. You'll be notified by email at the address registered in database properties.

    B. Write a custom script to look for "statement in resumable session * was suspended" in the alert log and notify the DBA.

    C. Create an AFTER SUSPEND trigger and a code notification.

    D. A suspended session displays a message on the screen.

16. Which statement regarding reclaiming wasted space is true?

    A. Segment shrink is accomplished using the ALTER TABLE … MOVE and ALTER INDEX … REBUILD statements.

    B. Segment shrink and reorganize are similar operations.

    C. When a table segment shrink operation is completed, the dependent indexes are in invalid state and need to be rebuilt.

    D. A segment shrink operation is applicable only on tablespaces with automatic segment space management.

17. Which compression option should be specified to compress blocks of tables that are used by the OLTP application?

    A. COMPRESS

    B. NOCOMPRESS

    C. COMPRESS FOR OLTP

    D. COMPRESS FOR ONLINE DML

18. Choose the best option regarding extents.

    A. An extent is a grouping of Oracle blocks.

    B. An extent is a grouping of OS blocks.

    C. An extent is a grouping of segments.

    D. An extent is allocated when a table is created.

19. You issue the statement CREATE TABLESPACE X;. Which of the following is the best option?

    A. The statement fails because mandatory properties are not defined.

    B. The 100MB tablespace is created.

    C. The mandatory DATAFILE clause is missing.

    D. The tablespace name should be at least three characters long.

20. Choose the information that is not part of a ROWID.

    A. Data object number

    B. Relative file number

    C. Segment ID where the block belongs

    D. Block number in the file

Chapter

11

Managing Data Concurrency and Undo

ORACLE DATABASE 12c: OCA EXAM OBJECTIVES COVERED IN THIS CHAPTER:

✓ **Managing Undo Data**

- Explain DML and undo data generation.
- Monitor and administer undo data.
- Describe the difference between undo data and redo data.
- Configure undo retention.

✓ **Managing Data Concurrency**

- Describe the locking mechanism and how Oracle manages data concurrency.
- Monitor and resolve locking conflicts.

Data Manipulation Language (DML) is used to manage data in any relational database. When data is changed, it must be tracked somewhere until the user decides to save the change permanently. Oracle Database 12c uses the redo mechanism to track all changes and the undo mechanism to store the previous image of the changed block in case the user decides to discard the change. Redo can be transferred to a remote site to build disaster recovery systems. Undo can also be used to construct a before-image to compare, change, or retrieve old data.

A transaction is a logical unit of work that contains one or more SQL statements. It takes the database from one consistent state to the next. A transaction begins with the first SQL statement and ends with a commit or rollback. In this chapter, you will learn about transactions and how Oracle ensures data consistency and concurrency.

Before reading this chapter, you must be familiar with the DML statements in Oracle Database 12c. Please familiarize yourself with DML statements and make sure to read the introduction to transaction control in Chapter 6, "Manipulating Data."

Managing Data Changes Using DML

A change in the database is made using Data Manipulation Language (DML). Data Definition Language (DDL) and Data Control Language (DCL) statements also make changes, but to the data dictionary. INSERT, DELETE, UPDATE, and MERGE are the DML statements available to make changes to application data.

A transaction is a logical unit of work. All the changes made by the SQL statements in a transaction commit or rollback at the same time to ensure data consistency in the database. The use of transactions is one of the important ways in which a database management system differs from a file-based system. In the database management system, a transaction must obey *ACID* properties. ACID stands for atomicity, consistency, isolation, and durability.

Atomicity   The entire sequence of action must be either committed or rolled back. There cannot be partial success in a transaction. For example, if a bank transfer includes crediting an account and debiting another account, the entire set of actions to credit and debit must be committed or rolled back as a transaction.

Consistency Consistency ensures that the result of the query indicates the state of the data when the query started. For example, if you are querying a large table that normally takes 30 minutes to read all records, and someone changed a few rows of the table 15 minutes into the query, the query should still show you consistent information as it existed when the query started.

Isolation Isolation mandates that unsaved (not committed) information is not visible to other users in the database. The session that is making changes to the data must see only the uncommitted changes, not other transactions in the database. Changes should be visible to other sessions when the transaction making the change is committed.

Durability The changes made by the committed transactions are saved and the system must not lose the change, even if there is a system failure. The database must guarantee that a committed change is never lost.

The redo and undo mechanism of Oracle Database 12*c* ensures ACID properties of the Oracle Database 12*c* database. Let's review what happens when a user session makes changes to a table in Oracle Database 12*c*.

Understanding "Change"

With the first DML statement in a session, a transaction is initiated and it ends when the change is saved (COMMIT) or when the change is discarded (ROLLBACK). When a change is made to the database, it is not immediately visible to other sessions in the database. The change is visible only after the change-initiated session performs a commit. Until the change is committed or rolled back, the before-image of change is saved in the *undo segments* of the database. A consistent view of the data is provided to other sessions by using the data from the undo blocks, as long as the change is not saved. Oracle also writes the changes to undo blocks and data blocks to log buffer and is flushed to disk, to the online redo log files. The redo data keeps track of change, so that if needed the change can be reapplied, or so that during instance recovery the change can be rolled back if the transaction was not committed.

Figure 11.1 shows how a change is made in the database in the simplest form. All the block changes are made after reading the block into the buffer cache. Let's assume user X issues UPDATE tabx SET namef = 'ABCD'. Oracle optimizer determines the fastest way to get to the block based on statistics and indexes on the table. Once the block(s) with row(s) namef = 'ABCD' are identified, the server process reads the blocks from the data file to buffer cache (1). Before making changes to the block, the row is written to the undo segment, to re-create the original state if needed (2). The change that was made to the data is written to the log buffer, to repeat the change if needed (3). Since the undo block also changed, the undo change is written to the log buffer as well (3). When the log buffer is one-third full, or after 3 seconds or after a commit in the database, the log buffer is written to the online redo log files by the LGWR process. When a checkpoint happens, the data and undo blocks (dirty blocks) are written to the disk by the DBW*n* process. To remind you how often and when the LGWR and DBW*n* processes write, please refer to Chapter 8, "Introducing Oracle Database 12*c* Components and Architecture."

FIGURE 11.1 Making a change in the database

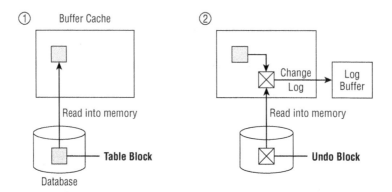

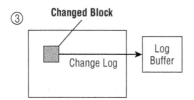

The log buffer is flushed when one of the following conditions is met:

- The log buffer is one-third full.
- The log buffer has 1MB of redo data.
- Three seconds have passed since the last flush.
- A commit has been performed.
- A database checkpoint occurs.

Differentiating Undo and Redo

Although undo and redo both track changes, they serve totally different purposes, and both are essential for a transaction in the database operation. As the names suggest, undo data is used to "undo" a change and redo data is used to "redo" a change. The undo space is dynamic, and segments and extents are allocated as and when required, whereas the redo log buffer is a fixed size.

Undo data is the old value of data when a process or user changes data in a table. Undo data serves four purposes in an Oracle database:

- Rollback of a transaction
- Read consistency of DML operations and queries
- Instance recovery operations (undo data from the redo log file is used for instance recovery)
- Flashback functionality

Redo data is written to the online redo log files, and the information is used to reproduce a change. Redo data is used primarily for recovery by the database in the following situations:

- Roll forward a change during instance recovery
- Archive the redo data in archive log files and use for point-in-time recovery of database
- Use log miner to read the redo (online or archived) log files and reapply the change or undo the change

Let's look at the undo operations in detail in the following sections. Chapter 15, "Using Backup and Recovery," discusses how log files are archived and how redo log files are used in database recovery operations.

 All DML operations generate undo and redo data. Rolling back the change (DML) also generates redo data.

Using Undo for Transaction Rollback

At the user-session level, there may be one or hundreds of DML commands (such as DELETE, INSERT, UPDATE, or MERGE) within a particular transaction that need to be undone. Undoing the changes within a transaction is called rolling back part or all of the transaction. The undo information needed to roll back the changes is called, appropriately, the *rollback information* and is stored in a special type of tablespace called an *undo tablespace*.

When an entire transaction is rolled back, Oracle uses the saved undo information in the undo tablespace to undo all the changes since the beginning of the transaction, releases any locks on rows involved in the transaction, and ends the transaction.

If a failure occurs on the client or a network, abnormally terminating the user's connection to the database, undo information is used in much the same way as if the user explicitly rolled back the transaction, and Oracle undoes all the changes since the beginning of the transaction, using information saved in the undo tablespace.

 When a DML SQL statement fails, only the changes made by the failed DML statement are rolled back and not the entire transaction.

Undo and Redo Application During Instance Recovery

When a database is shut down cleanly (not using SHUTDOWN ABORT), a full checkpoint happens and, therefore, all the dirty blocks from the buffer cache are written to the data files. As a result, when the database starts, there is no need for any kind of recovery. If the database was shut down using SHUTDOWN ABORT or if the instance crashed for some reason, then during the instance startup both redo and undo data are required to put the database in a consistent state. This operation is known as instance recovery, or crash recovery.

As you learned in previous chapters, Oracle keeps many changes in memory to improve performance, and it writes changes to files only at periodic intervals or at specific events. This behavior improves database operational performance. Therefore, when the database instance crashes or is brought down abruptly, Oracle has the responsibility to perform a cleanup and bring the database to a consistent state.

In order to ensure that no committed change is lost, Oracle writes the redo log buffer to redo log files immediately after a commit. As such, any change in the database is captured in the log file, but not necessarily in the data file. Changed data blocks (dirty buffer) from the buffer cache are written to the data files only during checkpoints. *Instance recovery* is a two-phase operation consisting of cache recovery (or rolling forward) and transaction recovery (or rolling back). Cache recovery uses redo information, and transaction recovery uses undo information.

During cache recovery, Oracle replays the transactions from the online redo log files since the last checkpoint. During this roll forward operation, both committed and uncommitted changes are applied to the data files. At the end of the roll-forward operation, the data files will have committed changes, uncommitted changes that were written to the data files to free up buffer cache space and uncommitted changes applied by the roll-forward operation. The database can be opened as soon as cache recovery is complete. See Figure 11.2.

FIGURE 11.2 Instance recovery using undo and redo

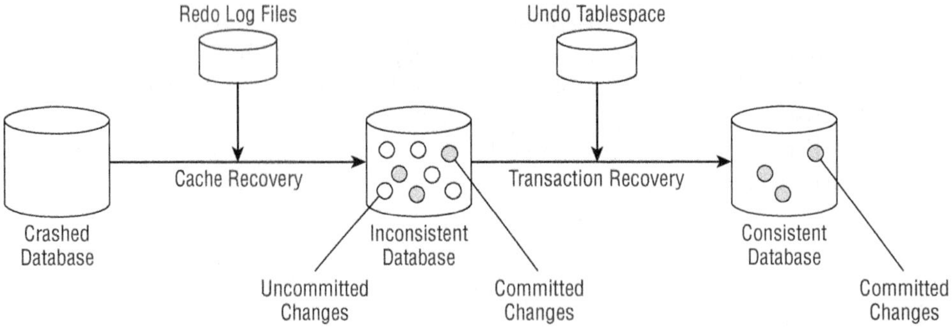

After the cache is recovered, the database is inconsistent; the database includes both committed and uncommitted changes. To clean up the mess, Oracle uses the undo segments from the undo tablespace. In the transaction-recovery phase of instance recovery, Oracle applies undo blocks to roll back uncommitted changes in data blocks that were either written before the instance crash or made by the roll-forward operation during cache recovery.

When a user session abnormally terminates due to a network issue or desktop crash, the PMON process will detect the session failure and perform the transaction rollback. During instance recovery, the SMON process is responsible for performing the transaction recovery by rolling back the uncommitted changes.

Achieving Read Consistency

Undo also provides read consistency for users who are querying rows involved in a DML transaction by another user or session. When one user starts to make changes to a table after another user has already begun a query against the table, the user issuing the query will not see the changes to the table until after the query has completed and the user issues a new query against the table. Undo segments in an undo tablespace are used to reconstruct the data blocks belonging to the table to provide the previous values of the rows for any user issuing SELECT statements against the table before the DML statements' transaction commits.

For example, the user JOSEPHJ begins a transaction at 3:00 P.M. that contains several long-running DML statements against the EMPLOYEES table; the statements aren't expected to finish until 3:15 P.M. As each DML command is issued, the previous values of each row are saved in the transaction's undo segment. At 3:05 P.M., the user SARAR issues a SELECT against the EMPLOYEES table; none of the changes made so far by JOSEPHJ are visible to SARAR. The undo tablespace provides the previous values of the EMPLOYEES table to SARAR and any other users querying the EMPLOYEES table between 3:00 P.M. and 3:15 P.M. Even if SARAR's query is still running at 3:20 P.M., the query still appears as it did at 3:00 P.M., before JOSEPHJ started making changes.

INSERT statements use little space in an undo segment; only the pointer to the new row is stored in the undo tablespace. To undo an INSERT statement, the pointer locates the new row and deletes it from the table if the transaction is rolled back.

In a few situations, either SARAR's query or JOSEPHJ's DML statements might fail, because the undo tablespace is not sized correctly or because the undo retention period is too short.

You can also apply read consistency to an entire transaction instead of just a single SELECT statement by using the SET TRANSACTION statement as follows:

```
SQL> set transaction read only;
Transaction set.
```

Until the transaction is either rolled back or committed, all queries in the transaction see only those changes to other tables that were committed before the transaction began. Only the following statements are permitted in a read-only transaction:

- SELECT statements without the FOR UPDATE clause
- LOCK TABLE

- SET ROLE
- ALTER SESSION
- ALTER SYSTEM

In other words, a read-only transaction cannot contain any statement that changes data in a table, regardless of where the table resides. For example, although an ALTER USER command does not change data in the USERS or any other non-SYSTEM tablespace, it does change the data dictionary tables and, therefore, cannot be used in a read-only transaction.

Undo data is kept in undo segments. In the next section, you will learn how to configure and monitor undo.

> User-initiated transaction rollback and commit are applicable only to DML statements. DDL statements end the active transaction by performing a commit before the DDL and a commit after the DDL. Therefore, DDL statements cannot be rolled back.

Configuring and Monitoring Undo

Compared with configuring rollback operations in releases prior to Oracle9i, managing undo in later versions of Oracle requires little DBA intervention. However, two particular situations will trigger intervention: either not enough undo space to handle all active transactions or not enough undo space to satisfy long-running queries that need undo information for read consistency. Running out of undo space for transactions generates messages such as ORA-01650: Unable to extend rollback segment; long-running queries whose undo entries have been reused by current transactions typically receive the ORA-01555: Snapshot too old message.

In the following sections, you will learn how to configure the undo tablespace using two initialization parameters: UNDO_MANAGEMENT and UNDO_TABLESPACE. You will also learn about the methods available for monitoring the health of the undo tablespace, as well as using EM Database Express Undo Advisor to size or resize the undo tablespace. Using the dynamic performance view V$UNDOSTAT, you can calculate an optimal size for the undo tablespace if the Undo Advisor is not available. Finally, you will see how to guarantee that long-running queries will have undo entries available, even if it means that a DML transaction fails, by using the RETENTION GUARANTEE option.

> Multiple active transactions can write simultaneously to the same current extent or to different current extents in the same undo segment. Within an undo extent, a data block contains data for only one transaction.

Configuring the Undo Management

Manual undo management is not recommended, although it is still available in Oracle Database 12*c*. Automatic undo management is the default for the Oracle Database 12*c*. To configure automatic undo management, use the initialization parameters UNDO_MANAGEMENT, UNDO_TABLESPACE, and UNDO_RETENTION.

UNDO_MANAGEMENT

The parameter UNDO_MANAGEMENT specifies the way in which undo data is managed in the database: either manually using rollback segments or automatically using a single tablespace to hold undo information.

The allowed values for UNDO_MANAGEMENT are MANUAL and AUTO. To change the undo-management mode, you must restart the instance. This parameter is not dynamic, as you can see in the following example:

```
SQL> alter system
     set undo_management = manual;

set undo_management = manual
    *
ERROR at line 2:
ORA-02095: specified initialization parameter cannot be modified
```

If you are using an spfile, you can change the value of this parameter in the spfile and then restart the instance for the parameter to take effect, as follows:

```
SQL> alter system
     set undo_management = manual scope=spfile;
System altered.
```

Manual undo management is specified by setting the parameter UNDO_MAN-AGEMENT to MANUAL. You must then create appropriately sized rollback segments and make them available to the database using another parameter, ROLLBACK_SEGMENTS. Using manual undo management is not recommended, because automatic undo management reduces DBA intervention and provides undo tuning information as well as flashback query capabilities.

UNDO_TABLESPACE

The UNDO_TABLESPACE parameter specifies the name of the undo tablespace to use for read consistency and transaction rollback when in automatic undo management mode.

You can create an undo tablespace when the database is created; you can resize it or create a new one later. In any case, only one undo tablespace can be active at any given time, unless the value of UNDO_TABLESPACE is changed while the old undo tablespace still contains active transactions. In this case, the old undo tablespace remains active until the last transaction using the old undo tablespace either commits or rolls back; all new transactions use the new undo tablespace.

If UNDO_TABLESPACE is not defined but at least one undo tablespace exists in the database, the first undo tablespace discovered by the Oracle instance at startup is assigned to UNDO_TABLESPACE. You can find out the name of the current undo tablespace with the SHOW PARAMETER command, as in the following example:

```
SQL> show parameter undo_tablespace

NAME                     TYPE         VALUE
------------------------ ----------- --------------------
undo_tablespace          string       UNDOTBS1
```

For most platforms, if an undo tablespace is not explicitly created in the CREATE DATABASE command, Oracle automatically creates one with the name SYS_UNDOTBS.

Here is an example of how you can switch the undo tablespace from UNDOTBS1 to UNDO_BATCH:

```
SQL> show parameter undo_tablespace

NAME                     TYPE         VALUE
------------------------ ----------- --------------------
undo_tablespace          string       UNDOTBS1

SQL> alter system set undo_tablespace=undo_batch;
System altered.

SQL> show parameter undo_tablespace

NAME                     TYPE         VALUE
------------------------ ----------- --------------------
undo_tablespace          string       UNDO_BATCH
```

 In Real Application Cluster database, each instance must have dedicated undo tablespace configured using the UNDO_TABLESPACE parameter.

UNDO_RETENTION

The UNDO_RETENTION parameter specifies, in seconds, how long undo information that has already been committed should be retained until it can be overwritten. This is not a guaranteed limit: if the number of seconds specified by UNDO_RETENTION has not been reached and if a transaction needs undo space, already committed undo information can be overwritten.

```
SQL> show parameter undo

NAME                                 TYPE          VALUE
------------------------------------ ------------- ------------------------------
temp_undo_enabled                    boolean       FALSE
undo_management                      string        AUTO
undo_retention                       integer       900
undo_tablespace                      string        UNDOTBS1
SQL>
```

 To guarantee undo retention, you can use the RETENTION GUARANTEE keywords for the undo tablespace, as you will see later in this chapter in the "Guaranteeing Undo Retention" section.

Setting UNDO_RETENTION to zero turns on automatic undo retention tuning. Oracle continually adjusts this parameter to retain just enough undo information to satisfy the longest-running query to date. If the undo tablespace is not big enough for the longest-running query, automatic undo retention retains as much as possible without extending the undo tablespace. In any case, automatic undo retention attempts to maintain at least 900 seconds, or 15 minutes, of undo information.

Regardless of how long undo information is retained, it falls into one of three categories:

Uncommitted Undo Information   Uncommitted or *active undo* is undo information that still supports an active transaction and is required in the event of a ROLLBACK or a transaction failure. This undo information is never overwritten.

Committed Undo Information   Also known as *unexpired undo*, this is undo information that is no longer needed to support an active transaction but is still needed to satisfy the undo retention interval, as defined by UNDO_RETENTION. This undo can be overwritten, however, if an active transaction needs undo space.

Expired Undo Information   *Expired undo* is undo information that is no longer needed to support an active transaction and is overwritten when space is required by an active transaction.

Here is an example of how you can change undo retention from its current value to 12 hours:

```
SQL> show parameter undo_retention

NAME                 TYPE          VALUE
-------------------- ------------- -----------------------
undo_retention       integer       600
```

```
SQL> alter system set undo_retention = 43200;
System altered.

SQL> show parameter undo_retention

NAME                 TYPE        VALUE
-------------------- ----------- ------------------------
undo_retention       integer     43200
```

Unless you use the SCOPE parameter in the ALTER SYSTEM command, the change to UNDO_RETENTION takes effect immediately and stays in effect the next time the instance is restarted.

If the undo tablespace data file is C, Oracle retains undo for at least the time specified in UNDO_RETENTION, and tunes the undo retention period to satisfy the undo requirements of the queries. For fixed-size undo tablespaces, Oracle automatically tunes undo retention for the maximum possible period, based on undo tablespace size and usage history, and ignores the UNDO_RETENTION setting.

Undo and Flashback Operations

Oracle flashback features let you see the state of data, object, and database as they existed in the past. The following flashback operations depend on automatic undo management and undo data.

Flashback Query   This provides the ability to query data as it existed in the past. How far back you can query depends on the size of the undo tablespace and the undo retention.

Flashback Version Query   This provides the ability to query the versions of rows in a table that existed at a specific time interval.

Flashback Transaction   This backs out a transaction and its dependent transactions.

Flashback Transaction Query   This provides the ability to view all of the changes made to the database at the transaction level.

Flashback Table   This provides point-in-time recovery of an individual table.

The flashback features are discussed in detail in Chapter 15.

Guaranteeing Undo Retention

By default, undo information from committed transactions (unexpired undo) is overwritten before a transaction fails because of a lack of expired undo. If your database requirements are such that you want long-running queries to succeed at the expense of DML in a transaction, such as in a data warehouse environment where a query can run for hours or even days, you can set the RETENTION GUARANTEE parameter for the undo tablespace.

This setting is not available as an initialization parameter. You can set a retention guarantee using ALTER TABLESPACE at the SQL*Plus command line, as in the following example:

```
SQL> alter tablespace undotbs1 retention guarantee;
Tablespace altered.
```

Turning off the setting is just as easy, as you can see in the next example:

```
SQL> alter tablespace undotbs1 retention noguarantee;
Tablespace altered.
```

Different undo tablespaces can have different settings for RETENTION. As expected, you cannot set RETENTION for a tablespace that is not an undo tablespace. The following example attempts to change the RETENTION setting for the USERS tablespace and generates an error message:

```
SQL> select tablespace_name, contents,
  2  retention from dba_tablespaces;

TABLESPACE_NAME                 CONTENTS  RETENTION
------------------------------- --------- -----------
SYSTEM                          PERMANENT NOT APPLY
SYSAUX                          PERMANENT NOT APPLY
UNDOTBS1                        UNDO      NOGUARANTEE
TEMP                            TEMPORARY NOT APPLY
USERS                           PERMANENT NOT APPLY

SQL> alter tablespace users retention guarantee;

alter tablespace users retention guarantee
*
ERROR at line 1:
ORA-30044: 'Retention' can only be specified for undo tablespace
```

Monitoring the Undo Tablespace

Undo tablespaces are monitored just like any other tablespace: if a specific set of space thresholds is not defined for undo tablespace, the database default values are used; otherwise, a specific set of thresholds can be assigned. When an undo tablespace's data files do not have the AUTOEXTEND attribute set, transactions can fail because too many transactions are vying for too little undo space.

Although you can allow the data files in your undo tablespace to autoextend initially, you should turn off autoextend on its data files once you believe that the undo tablespace has been sized correctly. This prevents a single user from accidentally using up large amounts of disk space in the undo tablespace by neglecting to commit transactions as frequently as possible.

Figure 11.3 shows the Automatic Undo Management screen in EM Database Express (choose Undo Management under Storage drop-down). There are six sections in the Undo Management Details screen, three each under Configuration and Statistics groups.

FIGURE 11.3 The Undo Management Details screen in EM Database Express

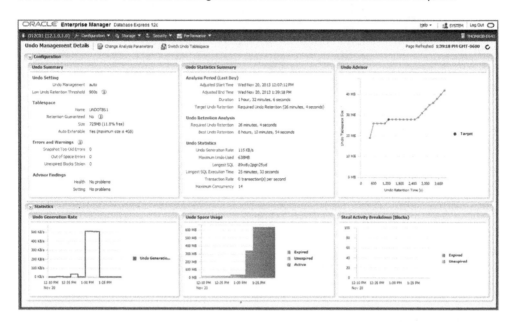

The sections in the screen are self-explanatory and show the undo configuration and usage details. The Undo Summary section needs further explanation. The Undo Summary section shows the following:

Undo Setting The value of undo-related initialization parameters. You can modify the undo retention by clicking on the value, which takes you to the Initialization Parameter Modification screen.

Tablespace This shows details of the active undo tablespace. Along with size of the tablespace, you can see the Retention Guarantee setting and determine if the tablespace data file is set to autoextend. Notice the Switch Undo Tablespace option on the top section; use this to change the active undo tablespace for the database. Switching changes the UNDO_TABLESPACE parameter.

Errors and Warnings This shows any errors related to an undo reported in the database. Transaction-stealing unexpired undo blocks can lead to Snapshot too old errors or can prevent flashback database to a desired point in time.

Advisor Findings This section shows any findings from the ADDM runs related to undo. ADDM is discussed in Chapter 14, "Maintaining the Database and Managing Performance."

The Undo Statistics Summary section shows the following:

Analysis Period The analysis period can be changed by using the Change Analysis Parameters button shown in the top section of Figure 11.3. The period can be changed to Last Hour, Last Week, or Last Day, as shown in Figure 11.4. You can also provide the undo retention value to use for the analysis. You can specify the Target Undo Retention value or the database can pick the minimum required time based on database activity.

FIGURE 11.4   The Undo Management Change Analysis Period

Undo Retention Analysis   This shows the undo retention based on the undo configuration and available data from the database.

Undo Statistics   This shows the undo generation rate, the longest running SQL information.

The Undo Advisor shows a graph of undo size against retention time; the blue dot shows the current undo_retention value. When you move the mouse over to any point on the graph, it shows the size of the undo used against the retention time. Use this information to properly size the undo tablespace. In Figure 11.3, the screen shows an analysis of the undo tablespace based on the longest-running query in the analysis period. If you don't expect your undo usage to increase or you don't expect to need to retain undo information longer than the current longest one, you can drop the size of the undo tablespace to around 45MB from the current size of 4GB.

On the other hand, if you expect to need undo information for more than the current longest-running query, you can see the impact of this increase by entering a new value for undo retention by using the Change Analysis Parameters.

EM Database Express uses the data dictionary view V$UNDOSTAT to calculate the undo usage rate and provide recommendations. V$UNDOSTAT collects 10-minute snapshots of the undo space consumption and, in conjunction with UNDO_RETENTION and the database block size, can provide an optimal undo tablespace size.

Running out of space in an undo tablespace can also trigger an ORA-01555: Snapshot too old error. Long-running queries that need a read-consistent view of one or more tables can be at odds with ongoing transactions that need undo space. Unless the undo tablespace is defined with the RETENTION GUARANTEE parameter, ongoing DML can use undo space that is needed for long-running queries. As a result, a Snapshot too old error is returned to the user executing the query, and an alert is generated.

The Snapshot too old error alert can be triggered independently of the space available in the undo tablespace if the UNDO_RETENTION initialization parameter is set too low.

SQL Developer is a good place to view the details as well as modify tablespaces, especially the undo tablespace. The Details tab shows properties such as retention guarantee. The Datafiles tab shows the files associated with the undo tablespace and indicates if they are autoextensible. The Objects tab shows the undo segments in the tablespace. The SQL tab shows the SQL used to create the undo tablespace. See Figure 11.5 showing the undo segments of UNDOTBS1 undo tablespace.

FIGURE 11.5 Undo tablespace information using SQL Developer

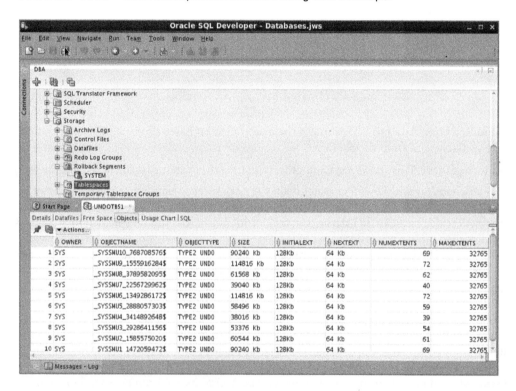

Managing Data Concurrency

Most databases will have many users using the tables and making changes simultaneously. At times, multiple users may be making changes to the same data concurrently. Oracle Database 12c has several locking mechanisms to minimize conflict and ensure data integrity.

Undo on Temporary Table Operations

By default, undo information on global temporary-table DML operations are stored in the undo tablespace, similar to undo operations on persistent tables. Oracle Database 12*c* introduced a new feature, where the undo information generated by DML operations on temporary tables is stored in the temporary tablespace; therefore, no redo is generated for the undo operation. This is accomplished by setting the database initialization parameter TEMP_UNDO_ENABLED to TRUE or setting the parameter in the user session. The temporary undo feature provides the following benefits:

Reduces the amount of undo data stored in the undo tablespaces.

Reduces the amount of redos generated. Operations on temporary tables do not generate redo.

Temporary undo can be enabled or disabled in a session before making any changes to temporary tables in the session by using the ALTER SESSION statement.

As a DBA, you will eventually have to deal with locking conflicts when two or more users try to change the same row in the database. In the following sections, we'll present an overview of how locking works in the Oracle Database 12*c*, how users are queued for a particular resource once it is locked, and how Oracle classifies lock types in the database. Then we'll show you a number of ways to detect and resolve locking issues; we'll also cover a special type of lock situation: the deadlock.

Understanding Locks and Transactions

Locks prevent multiple users from changing the same data at the same time. Before one or more rows in a table can be changed, the user executing the DML statement must obtain a lock on the row or rows; a *lock* gives the user exclusive control over the data until the user has committed or rolled back the transaction that is changing the data.

In Oracle Database 12*c*, a transaction can lock one row, multiple rows, or an entire table. Although you can manually lock rows, Oracle can automatically lock the rows needed at the lowest possible level to ensure data integrity and minimize conflicts with other transactions that may need to access other rows in the table.

In Table 11.1, both updates to the EMPLOYEES table return to the command prompt immediately after the UPDATE because the locks are on different rows in the EMPLOYEES table and neither session is waiting for the other lock to be released.

TABLE 11.1   Concurrent Transactions on Different Rows of the Same Table

Session 1	Time	Session 2
update employees set salary = salary * 1.2 where employee_id = 102;	11:29	update employees set manager = 100 where employee_id = 109;
commit;	11:30	commit;

 Real World Scenario

Packaged Applications and Locking

The Human Resources (HR) department recently purchased a benefits-management package that interfaced well with our existing employee-management tables; however, once HR started using the application, other users who accessed the employee tables started complaining of severe slowdowns in updates to the employee information.

Reviewing the CPU and I/O usage of the instance did not reveal any problems. It wasn't until we looked at the locking information that we noticed a table lock on the employees table whenever the benefits-management features were being used. The benefits-management application was written to work on a number of database platforms, and the least capable of those platforms did not support row locking. As a result, no one could make changes to the employees table when an employee's benefits were being changed, and everyone had to wait for the benefits changes to complete. Fortunately, the parameter file for the benefits-management package had an option to specify Oracle as the target platform; after setting the specific database version in the package's parameter file, the package was smart enough to use row locking instead of table locking whenever the employee table needed to be updated.

Queries never require a lock. Even if another transaction has locked several rows or an entire table, a query always succeeds, using the prelock image of the data stored in the undo tablespace.

If multiple users require a lock on a row or rows in a table, the first user to request the lock obtains it, and the remaining users are enqueued using a first-in, first-out (FIFO) method. At a SQL> command prompt, a DML statement (INSERT, UPDATE, DELETE, or MERGE) that is waiting for a lock on a resource appears to hang, unless the NOWAIT keyword is used in a LOCK statement.

The WAIT and NOWAIT keywords are explained in the next section, "Maximizing Data Concurrency."

At the end of a transaction, when either a COMMIT or a ROLLBACK is issued (either explicitly by the user or implicitly when the session terminates normally or abnormally), all locks are released.

Oracle Database 12c Locking Behavior

- A row is locked only when it is updated or deleted. A row can also be locked using SELECT … FOR UPDATE statement. Only modified rows are locked. There is no lock escalation—for example, a row lock does not become a table lock after certain time period or after a certain number of rows are locked in a table.

- A session (A) making changes to a row already changed by another session (B) waits until transaction B ends. This prevents one row from being modified by two sessions at the same time.

- A SELECT statement (reader) never blocks any other sessions—readers or writers. The exception is the SELECT … FOR UPDATE statement.

- A SELECT statement (reader) is never blocked by readers or writers. When a row read is changed by a writer (update or delete statements), Oracle gets the data from undo segments for the reader.

Maximizing Data Concurrency

Rows of a table are locked either explicitly by the user at the beginning of a transaction or implicitly by Oracle, usually at the row level, depending on the operation. If a table must be locked for performance reasons (which is rare), you can use the LOCK TABLE command, specifying the level at which the table should be locked.

In the following example, you lock the EMPLOYEES and DEPARTMENTS tables at the highest possible level, EXCLUSIVE:

```
SQL> lock table hr.employees, hr.departments
     in exclusive mode;
Table(s) Locked.
```

Until the transaction with the LOCK statement either commits or rolls back, only queries are allowed on the EMPLOYEES and DEPARTMENTS tables.

In the following sections, we will review the lock modes and discuss how to avoid the lock enqueue process and terminate the command if the requested resource is already locked.

Lock Modes

Lock modes provide a way for you to specify how much and what kinds of access other users have on rows and tables that you are using in DML commands. There are two types of locks: exclusive and shared. Exclusive lock mode prevents the associated resource (table or row) from being shared. A transaction obtains an exclusive lock when it modifies data, and it is the only transaction that can alter the resource until the exclusive lock is released. Share lock mode allows the associated resource to be shared. Multiple users reading data can share the data, each holding a share lock to prevent concurrent access by a writer who needs an exclusive lock. Multiple transactions can acquire share locks on the same resource (table or row).

DML locks guarantee the integrity of data when multiple users concurrently access and update the data. DML statements such as INSERT, UPDATE, and DELETE always acquire row locks in exclusive mode (RX), to prevent another transaction from modifying the same row, and table lock in RX mode to prevent other transactions from running DDL on the table.

In Table 11.2, you can see the types of locks that can be obtained at the table level.

TABLE 11.2 Table Lock Modes

Table Lock Mode	Description
ROW SHARE (RS)	Permits concurrent access to the locked table but prohibits other users from locking the entire table for exclusive access.
ROW EXCLUSIVE (RX)	Same as ROW SHARE but also prohibits locking in SHARE mode. This type of lock is obtained automatically with standard DML commands such as UPDATE, INSERT, or DELETE.
SHARE (S)	Permits concurrent queries but prohibits updates to the table; this mode is required to create an index on a table and is automatically obtained when using the CREATE INDEX statement.
SHARE ROW EXCLUSIVE (SRX)	Used to query a whole table and to allow other users to query the table but prevents other users from locking the table in SHARE mode or updating rows.
EXCLUSIVE (X)	The most restrictive locking mode; permits queries on the locked table but prohibits DML by any other users. This mode is required to drop the table and is automatically obtained when using the DROP TABLE statement.

Manual lock requests wait in the same queue as implicit locks and are satisfied in a FIFO manner as each request releases the lock with an implicit or explicit COMMIT or ROLLBACK.

You can explicitly obtain locks on individual rows by using the SELECT … FOR UPDATE statement, as you can see in the following example:

```
SQL> select * from hr.employees
     where manager_id = 100 for update;
```

Not only does this query show the rows that satisfy the query conditions, but it also locks the selected rows and prevents other transactions from locking or updating these rows until a COMMIT or ROLLBACK occurs.

 Oracle never escalates locks. Row locks are not escalated to table lock, even if all rows in the table are modified by a transaction. A transaction holds exclusive row locks for all rows inserted, updated, or deleted within the transaction.

NOWAIT Mode

Using NOWAIT in a LOCK TABLE statement returns control to the user immediately if any locks already exist on the requested resource, as you can see in the following example:

```
SQL> lock table hr.employees
     in share row exclusive mode
     nowait;
lock table hr.employees
             *
ERROR at line 1:
ORA-00054: resource busy and acquire with NOWAIT specified or timeout expired

SQL>
```

This is especially useful in a PL/SQL application if an alternative execution path can be followed if the requested resource is not yet available. NOWAIT can also be used in the SELECT … FOR UPDATE statement.

WAIT Mode

You can tell Oracle to wait a specified number of seconds to acquire a DML lock. If you do not specify a NOWAIT or WAIT clause, the database waits indefinitely if the table is locked by another user. In the following example, Oracle will wait for 60 seconds to acquire the lock. If the lock is not acquired within 60 seconds, an error is returned.

```
SQL> lock table hr.employees
     in share row exclusive mode wait 60;
```

DDL Lock Waits

A DDL lock protects the definition of a schema object when a DDL operation is performed on the object. Only individual schema objects that are modified are locked during DDL operations.

When DML statements have rows locked in a table or if the table is manually locked by a user, DDL statements on the table fail with the ORA-00054 error. To have the DDL statements wait for a specified number of seconds before throwing the ORA-00054 error, you can set the initialization parameter DDL_LOCK_TIMEOUT. The default value is 0, which means the error is issued immediately. You can specify a value up to 1,000,000 seconds.

```
SQL> alter table hr.employees modify salary number (15,2);
alter table hr.employees modify salary number (15,2)
              *
ERROR at line 1:
ORA-00054: resource busy and acquire with NOWAIT specified or timeout expired

SQL> show parameter ddl_lock
NAME                                 TYPE        VALUE
------------------------------------ ----------- ------------------------------
ddl_lock_timeout                     integer     0
SQL>
```

Detecting and Resolving Lock Conflicts

Although locks are a common and sometimes unavoidable occurrence in many databases, they are usually resolved by waiting in the queue. In some cases, you may need to resolve the lock problem manually (such as if a user makes an update at 4:59 P.M. and does not perform a COMMIT before leaving for the day).

In the next few sections, we will describe in more detail some of the reasons that lock conflicts occur and how to detect lock conflicts, and we'll discuss a more specific and serious type of lock conflict: a deadlock.

Understanding Lock Conflicts

In addition to the proverbial user who makes a change at 4:59 P.M. and forgets to perform a COMMIT before leaving for the day, other more typical lock conflicts are caused by long-running transactions that perform hundreds, thousands, or even hundreds of thousands of DML commands in the overnight batch run but are not finished updating the tables when the normal business day starts. The uncommitted transactions from the overnight batch jobs may lock tables that need to be updated by clerical staff during the business day, causing a lock conflict.

Another typical cause of lock conflicts is using unnecessarily high locking levels. In the "Packaged Applications and Locking" sidebar earlier in this chapter, we described a third-party application that routinely locked resources at the table level instead of at the row level to be compatible with every SQL-based database on the market. Developers may unnecessarily code updates to tables with higher locking levels than required by Oracle.

Real World Scenario

Detecting Lock Conflicts Using SQL Developer

Detecting locks in Oracle Database 12c using SQL Developer makes your job easy; you don't need to query against V$SESSION, V$TRANSACTION, V$LOCK, and V$LOCKED_OBJECT to see who is locking what resource. Also, you can learn the various data dictionary views involved in identifying a session and locks in this exercise.

Let's lock some tables for demonstration purposes. Log in to the database as HR user and lock some tables.

```
SQL> show user
USER is "HR"

SQL> lock table employees in exclusive mode;
Table(s) Locked.

SQL> lock table departments, locations in share mode;
Table(s) Locked.
```

Find the session in SQL Developer using Monitor Session from the Tools menu. To remove the clutter, filter the user column by clicking on the funnel icon for user HR. See the following graphic, which shows the Monitor Session screen of SQL Developer.

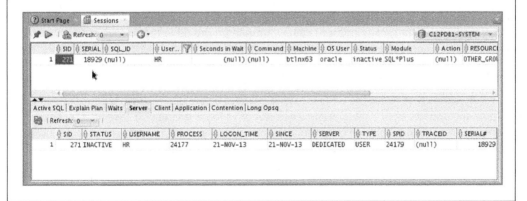

Now, using another SQL Plus or SQL Developer connection, log in to the database as HR. When you refresh the Monitor Session screen, there should be two sessions from HR. Execute the following SQL statement:

```
SELECT * FROM employees;
```

Although employees table is locked in exclusive mode (the highest lock mode in Oracle), we can still query the table. Let's try to update.

```
UPDATE employees SET salary = salary + 100;
```

The statement waits indefinitely. Let's use SQL Developer to find out what is happening. In the following graphic, the session by Samuel OS user is active and executing an UPDATE statement.

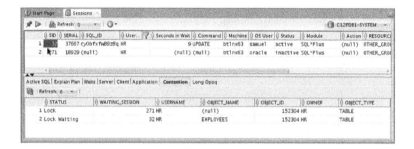

The Contention tab in the bottom portion shows the locked table and why the HR session from user Samuel is waiting.

Click on the third icon at the top (Run Report in SQL Worksheet), just before the Refresh. This action will copy the SQL statement executed by the SQL Developer tool to find the session and lock information to a worksheet window. Review this SQL to learn the columns in V$SESSION view.

Cancel the UPDATE statement and issue a new update on the table that is locked in share mode.

```
UPDATE locations SET country_id = country_id;
```

The result is the same. Once the table is locked in share or exclusive mode, we cannot perform any updates on the table. Issue a commit or rollback on the first session, thereby ending the transaction. This will clear the lock and make the UPDATE successful.

Perform the two update statements, one each in two different sessions. Do both of the statements succeed, or does the second one wait for the first update to either commit or roll back?

```
UPDATE employees set salary=salary WHERE employee_id = 206;
UPDATE employees set first_name = first_name WHERE employee_id = 206;
```

The Reports section of SQL Developer also has useful lock- and blocking-lock-related information. Select the Report menu option under View to get the reports available in SQL Developer. Under the Database Administration folder, choose Locks. The following graphic shows the Blocking Lock screen, with the SQL statement that is waiting. In this screen, you can see the sessions and SQL statements by the waiter and blocker.

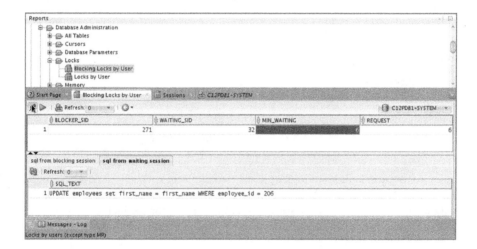

Click the Run Report in SQL Worksheet icon to display the underlying SQL code for this screen, which you can use to investigate the V$LOCK columns.

Understanding and Resolving Deadlocks

To resolve a lock conflict, the user holding the lock can either COMMIT or ROLLBACK the current transaction. If you cannot contact the user and it is an emergency, you can select the session holding the lock and click the Kill Session button on the Monitor Session screen of SQL Developer (refer to the graphic in the "Detecting Lock Conflicts Using SQL Developer" sidebar, earlier in this chapter). The next time the user whose session has been killed tries to execute a command, the error message ORA-00028: Your session has been killed will be returned. Again, this is an option of last resort: the user will lose all the statements executed in the session since the last COMMIT.

A more serious type of lock conflict is a deadlock. A *deadlock* is a special type of lock conflict in which two or more users are waiting for a resource locked by the other users. As a result, neither transaction can complete without some kind of intervention: the session that first detects a deadlock rolls back the statement waiting on the resource with the error message ORA-00060: Deadlock detected while waiting for resource. Oracle automatically resolves deadlocks without user/DBA intervention.

In Table 11.3, two sessions are attempting to update a row locked by the other session.

TABLE 11.3 Deadlock Scenario

Session 1	Time	Session 2
update employees set salary = salary * 1.2 where employee_id = 102;	11:29	update employees set manager = 100 where employee_id = 109;
update employees set salary = salary * 1.2 where employee_id = 109;	11:44	
	11:50	update employees set manager = 100 where employee_id = 102;

Prior to 11:44, session 1 and session 2 updated two different rows in the database and did not commit the transaction. At 11:44, session 1 issued an UPDATE statement against the same row locked by session 2. This causes session 1 to hang, waiting for the lock to be released by session 2. The lock held by session 2 will be released only when session 2 performs a commit or rollback. At 11:50, when session 2 is trying to update a row already locked by session 1, you have a deadlock situation: session 1 waiting on session 2 and session 2 waiting on session 1. When this situation occurs, Oracle throws out the ORA-00060 error and fails the statement. Remember, the transaction is not rolled back, because only the statement is in error. In this example, session 2 will get the ORA-00060 error when the update at 11:50 is issued, but session 1 will wait until session 2 commits or rolls back.

Deadlocks often occur when transactions explicitly override the default locking mechanism of Oracle Database 12c by using LOCK TABLE. With Oracle's default locking mechanism, Oracle Database 12c does not escalate locks and does not use read locks for queries but uses row-level locking; therefore, deadlocks are often avoided.

The data dictionary view DBA_LOCK is a very handy way for the DBA to look for locks and determine whether any session is blocking other users. A session with a value of Blocking in the BLOCKING_OTHERS column may have to be manually terminated using the ALTER SYSTEM KILL SESSION statement. DBA_WAITERS is another view that shows only the sessions that are waiting on a lock. This view shows the holding session and the waiting session.

Summary

In this chapter, you learned how undo is managed and how locks work in Oracle Database 12*c*. The undo tablespace is important for two types of database users: those who want to query a table and receive consistent results and those who want to make changes to a table and have the option to roll back the data to its original state when the transaction started. Using undo data, Oracle retrieves only committed changes in the database for a query and gives writers the ability to not block the readers.

You can configure an undo in the database with a handful of initialization parameters. UNDO_MANAGEMENT defines the mode in which undo is managed and can be either MANUAL or AUTO. UNDO_TABLESPACE identifies the current undo tablespace, which can be switched while the database is open to users; however, only one undo tablespace can be active at a time. UNDO_RETENTION specifies the desired minimum amount of time for which undo should be retained, to help long-running queries and flashback operations.

You can use EM Database Express to both proactively monitor and resize the undo tablespace. For databases whose long-running queries have priority over successful DML transactions, you can specify that an undo tablespace retain expired undo information at the expense of failed transactions.

Although Oracle usually manages locks at the minimum level to ensure that two sessions do not try to simultaneously update the same row in a table, you can explicitly lock a table at a number of levels. In addition, you can lock a subset of rows in a table to prevent updates or locks from other transactions with the FOR UPDATE clause in the SELECT statement. Readers never block other readers or writers; writers never block readers.

You learned some reasons that lock conflicts occur and how to resolve them; a special kind of lock conflict, a deadlock, occurs when two users are waiting on a resource locked by the other user. Deadlocks, unlike other types of lock conflicts, are resolved quickly and automatically by Oracle long before any manual lock resolution is attempted.

Exam Essentials

List the features supported by undo data in an undo tablespace.   Enumerate the four primary uses for undo data: rollback, read consistency, database recovery, and flashback operations. Show how the rollback requirements for users who perform long transactions can interfere with read consistency required for query users. Be able to identify and use the method to preserve expired undo at the expense of transactions.

Understand when undo and redo are generated.   Undo is generated whenever data is changed in the database, and the change is written to redo as well. Undo writing will also generate redo. Rollback of a transaction also generates redo.

Summarize the steps for monitoring, configuring, and administering the undo tablespace.   Set the initialization parameters required to use an undo tablespace. Be able to review the status of the undo tablespace using EM Database Express, and use the Undo Advisor to resize the undo tablespace when conditions warrant it. Alter the initialization parameter UNDO_RETENTION to configure how long undo information needs to be retained for long-running queries.

Know the purpose of the Undo Advisor. Optimize the UNDO_RETENTION parameter as well as the size of the undo tablespace by using Undo Advisor. Use the graph on the Undo Advisor screen to perform what-if analyses given the undo retention requirements.

Learn how undo data is used to produce consistent query results. When long-running queries run, data in the underlying table might change. Oracle produces a consistent query result by obtaining the prechange data from the undo segments to build the query result.

Know when the ORA-01555 Snapshot too old error happens. When Oracle could not constitute a consistent view of the data as it existed at the start of the query, the error is produced. Tuning UNDO_RENTENTION can help avoid the error.

Be able to monitor locking and resolve lock conflicts. Identify the reasons for database lock conflicts, and explain how to resolve them. Show an example of a more serious type of lock conflict, a deadlock.

Understand the WAIT options for acquiring a lock. The LOCK TABLE statement includes the WAIT clause to specify how long to wait to acquire a lock. You can set the initialization parameter DDL_LOCK_TIMEOUT to specify the number of seconds to wait when trying to acquire a DDL lock.

List the types of lock modes available when locking a table. Identify the locks available, from least restrictive to most restrictive. Be able to request a lock with either a LOCK or SELECT statement and return immediately if the lock is not available.

Be clear on when locks happen and who is affected. Oracle locks only the row changed for DML operations. Other rows in the table are available for writers, and all rows are available for readers.

Review Questions

1. Changes made with an UPDATE statement in a transaction are permanent in the database and visible to other users after what occurs?

   A. DBWR flushes the changes to disk.

   B. You issue a SAVEPOINT statement.

   C. You issue a COMMIT statement.

   D. A checkpoint occurs.

2. Which of the following commands returns an error if the transaction starts with SET TRANSACTION READ ONLY?

   A. ALTER SYSTEM

   B. SET ROLE

   C. ALTER USER

   D. None of the above

3. Guaranteed undo retention can be specified for which of the following objects?

   A. A tablespace

   B. A table

   C. The database

   D. A transaction

   E. The instance

4. Which of the following lock modes permits concurrent queries on a table but prohibits updates to the locked table?

   A. ROW SHARE

   B. ROW EXCLUSIVE

   C. SHARE ROW EXCLUSIVE

   D. All of the above

5. Select the statement that is *not* true regarding undo tablespaces.

   A. Undo tablespaces will not be created if they are not specified in the CREATE DATABASE command.

   B. Two undo tablespaces can be active if a new undo tablespace was specified and the old one contains pending transactions.

   C. You can switch from one undo tablespace to another while the database is online.

   D. UNDO_MANAGEMENT cannot be changed dynamically while the instance is running.

6. To resolve a lock conflict, which of the following methods can you use? Choose all that apply.

   A. Oracle automatically resolves the lock after a short but predefined time period by killing the session that is holding the lock.

   B. The DBA can kill the session holding the lock.

   C. The user can either roll back or commit the transaction that is holding the lock.

   D. Oracle automatically resolves the lock after a short but predefined period by killing the session that is requesting the lock.

7. Two transactions occur at the wall clock times in the following table. What happens at 10:05?

Session 1	Time	Session 2
update customer set region = 'H' where state='WI' and county='GRANT';	9:51	
	9:59	update customer set mgr=201 where state='IA' and county='JOHNSON';
update customer set region='H' where state='IA' and county='JOHNSON';	10:01	
	10:05	update customer set mgr=201 where state='WI' and county='GRANT';

   A. Session 2 will wait for session 1 to commit or roll back.

   B. Session 1 will wait for session 2 to commit or roll back.

   C. A deadlock will occur, and both sessions will hang unless one of the users cancels their statement or the DBA kills one of the sessions.

   D. A deadlock will occur, and Oracle will cancel one of the statements.

   E. Neither session is updating the same column, so no waiting or deadlock will occur.

8. If all extents in an undo segment fill up, which of the following occurs next? Choose all that apply.

    A. A new extent is allocated in the undo segment if all existing extents still contain active transaction data.

    B. Other transactions using the segment are moved to another existing segment with enough free space.

    C. A new undo segment is created, and the transaction that filled up the undo segment is moved in its entirety to another undo segment.

    D. The first extent in the segment is reused if the undo data in the first extent is not needed.

    E. The transaction that filled up the undo segment spills over to another undo segment.

9. Which of the following commands returns control to the user immediately if a table is already locked by another user?

    A. `LOCK TABLE HR.EMPLOYEES IN EXCLUSIVE MODE WAIT DEFERRED;`

    B. `LOCK TABLE HR.EMPLOYEES IN SHARE MODE NOWAIT;`

    C. `LOCK TABLE HR.EMPLOYEES IN SHARE MODE WAIT DISABLED;`

    D. `LOCK TABLE HR.EMPLOYEES IN EXCLUSIVE MODE NOWAIT DEFERRED;`

10. Undo information falls into all the following categories except for which one?

    A. Uncommitted undo information

    B. Undo information required in case an instance crash requires a roll forward operation when the instance is restarted

    C. Committed undo information required to satisfy the undo retention interval

    D. Expired undo information that is no longer needed to support a running transaction

11. Undo segments are owned by which user?

    A. SYSTEM

    B. The user who initiated the transaction

    C. SYS

    D. The user who owns the object changed by the transaction

12. The EM Database Express Undo Advisor uses what to recommend the new size of the undo tablespace?

    A. The value of the parameter `UNDO_RETENTION`

    B. The number of `Snapshot too old` errors

    C. The current size of the undo tablespace

    D. The desired amount of time to retain undo data

    E. The most recent undo generation rate

13. Choose the option that is true regarding locks in Oracle Database 12*c*.

   A. When session 1 has a table locked using the `LOCK TABLE…EXCLUSIVE MODE` statement, all DML statements and queries wait until session 1 does a `COMMIT` or `ROLLBACK`.

   B. When `SELECT…FOR UPDATE` is performed, the table is locked.

   C. The `DDL_LOCK_TIMEOUT` parameter can be set to `TRUE` to not return the `ORA-00054` error.

   D. The `LOCK TABLE` statement can include the `WAIT` clause to specify the number of seconds to wait for acquiring the lock.

14. The following table shows the timestamp and actions by two users. Choose the best option that describes the outcome of the actions.

Time	John	Sara
10:14	`Select * from hr.employees`	
10:15		`Update hr.employees set salary = 100 where employee_id = 206`
10:16	`Commit;` `Select * from hr.employees`	
10:18		`Commit;`
10:20	`Select * from hr.employees;` `Commit;`	

   A. John's query will return the same results all three times it is executed as they are run in the same session.

   B. John's queries run at 10:16 and 10:20 produce the same result, which is different from the one at 10:14.

   C. John's query run at 10:16 waits until 10:18 to produce results, waiting for the commit to happen.

   D. John's queries run at 10:14 and 10:16 produce the same result, which is different from the one at 10:20.

15. Which statement is true regarding the locking behavior of Oracle Database 12*c*?

   A. Readers block writers.

   B. Writers block readers.

   C. Readers block writers.

   D. Writers do not block readers.

16. Identify the operation that does not generate redo.

    A. An INSERT statement reading from a global temporary table into a persistent table

    B. An INSERT statement reading from a persistent table into a global temporary table

    C. Roll back an UPDATE operation

    D. Writing undo records during a DML operation

17. User Maria just called to let you know that the long-running query she runs every week just received a Snapshot Too Old error. What is the best action you can take?

    A. Tell Maria to rerun the query.

    B. Increase Undo Retention.

    C. The materialized view used in the query is stale and needs to be refreshed.

    D. Increase the undo tablespace size.

18. Which two statements regarding undo and transactions are true?

    A. Multiple active transactions can write concurrently to the same extent in an undo segment.

    B. Multiple active transactions can write concurrently to the same undo segment.

    C. Each transaction acquires an extent in the undo segment and does not share the extent.

    D. Each transaction acquires a segment in the undo tablespace and does not share the segments.

19. Which statement ends a transaction?

    A. UPDATE

    B. ALTER TABLE

    C. ALTER SESSION

    D. ALTER SYSTEM

20. Which statement regarding lock is true?

    A. A developer must lock the row before performing an update to prevent others from changing the same row.

    B. When a row in a table is locked, the table is locked and no other transactions can update the table.

    C. When two sessions try to update the same row at the same time, both sessions fail.

    D. When a session tries to update the row already updated by another session, it waits until the other session does a commit or rollback.

Chapter

12

Understanding Oracle Network Architecture

ORACLE DATABASE 12c: OCA EXAM OBJECTIVES COVERED IN THIS CHAPTER:

✓ **Configuring the Oracle Network Environment**

- Configure Oracle Net Services.

- Use tools for configuring and managing the Oracle network.

- Configure client-side network.

- Understand database resident connection pooling.

- Configure communication between databases.

Networks have evolved from simple terminal-based systems to complex multitiered systems. Today's networks can comprise many computers on multiple operating systems using a wide variety of protocols and communicating across wide geographic areas. Although networks have become increasingly complex, they also have become easier to use and manage. For instance, we all take advantage of the Internet without knowing or caring about the components that make this communication possible because the complexity of this huge network is completely hidden from us.

The experienced Oracle database administrator has seen this maturation process in the Oracle network architecture as well. From the first version of SQL*Net to the latest releases of Oracle Net, Oracle has evolved its network strategy and infrastructure to meet the demands of the rapidly changing landscape of network communications.

This chapter highlights the areas you need to consider when implementing an Oracle network strategy and when managing an Oracle Database 12c network. We'll also discuss the most common network configurations. This chapter introduces the features of Oracle Net—the connectivity-management software that is the backbone of the Oracle network architecture. We'll explain how to configure the main client- and server-side components of Oracle Net, and we'll discuss the tools you have at your disposal to perform these tasks.

As the number of users connecting to Oracle databases in the enterprise grows, the system requirements of the servers increase—particularly the memory and process requirements. When a system starts to encounter these capacity issues, you need to know which alternatives are available within the Oracle environment that can address the problem. A configuration alternative that may help to overcome this capacity problem is Oracle Shared Server or using Database Resident Connection Pooling (DRCP).

Introducing Network Configurations

When designing an Oracle infrastructure, you can select from three basic types of network configurations:

- Single-tier
- Two-tier
- *n*-tier

Single-tier is the simplest type. It has been around for years and is characterized by the use of terminals for serial connections to the Oracle server. The two-tier configuration is also referred to as the *client/server* architecture, and more recently the *n*-tier architecture has been introduced. Let's take a look at each of these configuration alternatives.

Single-Tier Architecture

Single-tier architecture was the standard for many years before the birth of the personal computer. Applications using single-tier architecture are sometimes referred to as green-screen applications because most of the terminals that used them, such as the IBM 3270, had green screens. Single-tier architecture is commonly associated with mainframe-type applications.

This architecture is still in use today for many mission-critical applications, such as order processing and fulfillment and inventory control, because it is the simplest architecture to configure and administer. Because the terminals are directly connected to the host computer, the complexities of network protocols and multiple operating systems don't exist.

When single-tier architecture is used—for example, in mainframes—users interact with the database using terminals, which are nongraphical, character-based devices. In this type of architecture, client terminals are directly connected to larger server systems such as mainframes. All the intelligence exists on the mainframe, and all the processing takes place there. Simple serial connections also exist on the mainframe. Although no complex network architecture is necessary, a single-tier architecture is somewhat limiting in terms of scalability and flexibility (see Figure 12.1). The user PC makes a direct connection (using tools like Putty) to the database server to use the database (using tools like SQL*Plus).

FIGURE 12.1   Single-tier architecture

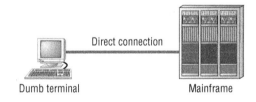

Dumb terminal   Mainframe

Two-Tier Architecture

Two-tier architecture gained popularity with the introduction of the personal computer and is commonly referred to as *client/server* computing. In a two-tier environment, clients connect to servers over a network using a network protocol, which is the agreed-upon method for the client to communicate with the server. Transmission Control Protocol/ Internet Protocol (TCP/IP) is a popular network protocol and has become the de facto standard of network computing. Whether you choose TCP/IP or some other network protocol, both the client and the server must be able to understand it. Figure 12.2 shows an example of two-tier architecture.

FIGURE 12.2 Two-tier architecture

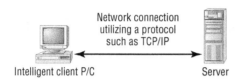

Intelligent client P/C   Server

This architecture has definite benefits over single-tier architecture. First, client/server computing introduces the graphical user interface (GUI). This interface is easier to understand and learn, and it offers more flexibility than the traditional character-based interfaces of the single-tier architecture. Also, two-tier architecture allows the client computer to share the application process load. To a certain degree, this reduces the processing requirements of the server.

The two-tier architecture does have some faults, even though at one time, this configuration was thought to be the panacea of all networking architectures. Unfortunately, the main problem—that being scalability—persists. Notice that the term *client/server* contains a slash (/). The slash represents the invisible component of the two-tier architecture and the one that is often overlooked—the network! The limitation of client/server computing is one of scalability.

When prototyping projects, many developers fail to consider the network component and soon find out that what worked well in a small environment does not scale effectively to larger, more complex systems. The two-tier architecture model is subject to a great deal of redundancy because application software is required on every PC. As a result, many companies end up with bloated computers and large servers that still do not perform adequately. What is needed is a more scalable model for network communications. That is what *n*-tier architecture provides.

n-Tier Architecture

The next logical step after two-tier architecture is *n-tier architecture*. Instead of dividing application processing work between a client and a server, you divide the work among three or more machines. The *n*-tier architecture introduces *middleware* components, such as application servers or web servers, situated between the client and the database server, which can be used for a variety of tasks, including the following:

- Moving data between machines that work with different network protocols

- Serving as firewalls that can control client access to the servers

- Offloading processing of the business logic from the clients and servers to the middle tier

- Executing transactions and monitoring activity between clients and servers to balance the load among multiple servers

- Acting as a gateway to bridge existing systems to new systems

The Internet is an example of the ultimate *n*-tier architecture, with the user's browser providing a consistent presentation interface. This common interface means less training of staff and also increases the potential reuse of client-side application components.

This is part of the reason *n*-tier architecture is rapidly becoming the architecture of choice for enterprise networks. This model is scalable and divides the tasks of presentation, business logic and routing, and database processing among many machines, which means that this model accommodates large applications. Many factors are driving *n*-tier computing, such as the Internet and Oracle cloud computing, which uses a large number of back-end processors to scale database services and connectivity.

By reducing the processing load on the database servers, those servers can do more work with the same number of resources. Also, the transaction servers can balance the flow of network transactions intelligently, and application servers can reduce the processing and memory requirements of the client (see Figure 12.3).

FIGURE 12.3   Connection requests in *n*-tier architecture

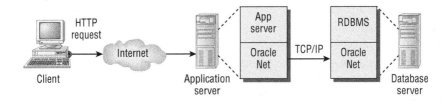

An Overview of Oracle Net Features

Oracle Net is the glue that bonds the Oracle network together. It is responsible for handling client-to-server and server-to-server communications, and it can be configured on the client, the middle-tier application, web servers, and the Oracle server. Oracle Net manages the flow of information in the Oracle network infrastructure. First, it establishes the initial connection to the Oracle server, and then it acts as the messenger, passing requests from the client back to the server or passing them between two Oracle servers. Oracle Net handles all negotiations between the client and server during the client connection.

In addition to functioning as an information manager, Oracle Net supports the use of middleware products such as Oracle Application Server and Oracle Connection Manager. These products allow *n*-tier architectures to be used in the enterprise, which increases the flexibility and performance of application designs. To provide a further explanation of the features of Oracle Net, the following sections discuss in detail the five categories of networking solutions that Oracle Net addresses:

- Connectivity
- Manageability
- Scalability
- Security
- Accessibility

Connectivity

A client can interact with an Oracle database in many ways. A client can be running a PC-based application or a dumb terminal application, or perhaps the client is connecting to the database via the Internet. Let's take a look at how Oracle supports connectivity to the database through these and other interfaces:

Multiprotocol Support Oracle Net supports a wide range of industry-standard protocols such as TCP/IP and named pipes. This support is handled transparently and allows Oracle Net to connect to a wide range of computers and a wide range of operating environments.

Multiple Operating Systems Oracle Net can run on many operating systems, from Windows to all variants of Unix to large mainframe-based operating systems. This range allows users to bridge existing systems to other Unix or PC-based systems, which increases the data access flexibility of the organization without making wholesale changes to the existing systems.

Java and JDBC Applications written in Java can take advantage of the Java Database Connectivity (JDBC) drivers provided with Oracle to connect to an Oracle server. The two basic types of JDBC drivers are JDBC Oracle Call Interface (OCI) and JDBC thin.

The JDBC OCI driver is a client-side installed driver that is used if the Java application is resident on a client computer. It uses OCI to interact with the Oracle Net infrastructure. Figure 12.4 shows how a client and server communicate when using a JDBC OCI connection.

FIGURE 12.4 Oracle JDBC OCI connection

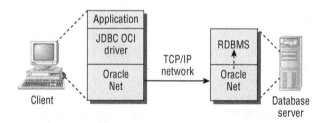

In this example, the Java application installed on the client uses the JDBC OCI driver and Oracle database server. When an application makes a database request, it uses the JDBC OCI driver to translate the JDBC calls and send them to Oracle Net. Oracle Net is used on both the client and the server to broker all communications between the two end points.

The JDBC thin driver is written entirely in Java and, as such, is platform independent. It does not have to be installed on a client computer (which is why it's called a thin driver). The driver interfaces directly with a layer of the Oracle Net infrastructure called the two-task common layer.

Manageability

Oracle Net provides a variety of features that allow you to manage the components of an Oracle network. Let's review the key manageability features of Oracle Net.

Web Applications

Oracle Net supports a variety of connectivity solutions from a web browser interface. Connections can be made through a middle-tier web or application server or directly from a web browser to an Oracle service.

When a middle-tier solution is used, the web browser uses HTTP to contact a database service and request information. Typically, an application or web server receives this request and hands it off to Oracle Net, which manages the connection between the web server and the database server. Once the database server receives the connection request, the request is processed and passed back to the web server. The web server then sends the response to the client's web browser. This type of request fulfillment requires that the middle-tier application server be loaded with the Oracle Net software, but the client does not require any additional software.

Oracle also supports web connectivity directly from a web client. For example, a Java applet running within a web browser can use a JDBC driver to connect directly to an Oracle server without the need for an application or web server.

Location Transparency

Oracle Net provides the infrastructure to manage the database location. This is important especially in large organizations that support many databases and clients. Each database in the organization is represented as one or more services. Database services are defined by one or more service names. The actual definition of the service names is managed within Oracle Net. The definition holds information about the type and location of the service on the network. This layer of abstraction provides location transparency to the client and centralizes the management of connection information within Oracle Net, which simplifies the job of managing the network.

Directory Naming

Directory naming allows service names to be resolved through a centralized naming repository. The central repository takes the form of a Lightweight Directory Access Protocol (LDAP)–compliant server. LDAP is a protocol and language that defines a standard method for storing, identifying, and retrieving services. It provides a simplified way to manage directories of information, whether this information is about users in an organization or Oracle services connected to a network. The LDAP server allows for a standard form of managing and resolving names in an Oracle environment. The quality of these services excels because LDAP provides a single, industry-standard interface to a directory service such as Oracle Internet Directory (OID). By using OID, you ensure the security and reliability of the directory information because information is stored in the Oracle database.

Scalability

Many enterprise systems are growing rapidly, supporting larger and larger databases and user communities. Your network capabilities need to be able to support this growth. Oracle Net provides features that allow you to expand your network reach and maximize your system resources to meet these demands.

Oracle Shared Server

Oracle Shared Server is an optional configuration of the Oracle server that allows support for a large number of concurrent connections without increasing physical resource requirements. This is accomplished by sharing resources among groups of users.

 Oracle Shared Server is discussed in detail later in the chapter in the section "An Overview of Oracle Shared Server."

Database Resident Connection Pooling

Database Resident Connection Pooling (DRCP) is an optional configuration of the Oracle server, enhancing middle-tier connection pools that share connections between threads in a middle-tier process. This architecture significantly reduces the resource required to support many client connections.

 Database Resident Connection Pooling is discussed in detail later in the chapter in the section "Using Database Resident Connection Pooling."

Connection Manager

Oracle Connection Manager is a middleware solution that provides three additional scalability features. It usually resides on a computer separate from the database server and client computers. Oracle Connection Manager is a proxy server that forwards connection requests to databases or other proxy servers. To a user running Oracle Net, the Connection Manager looks like a database server. An application can connect to a Connection Manager machine and have the Connection Manager redirect the Oracle Net packets to an Oracle database server running on a different machine.

Multiplexing Connection Manager can group many client connections and send them as a single multiplexed network connection to the Oracle server. This reduces the total number of network connections that the server has to manage.

Network Access You can configure Connection Manager with rules that restrict access by IP address. You can set up this rules-based configuration to accept or reject client connection requests. Also, connections can be restricted by point of origin, destination server, or Oracle server.

Cross-Protocol Connectivity This feature allows clients and servers that use different network protocols to communicate. Connection Manager acts as a translator, providing two-way protocol conversion.

Oracle Connection Manager is controlled by a set of background processes that manage the communications between clients and servers. Figure 12.5 provides an overview of the Connection Manager architecture.

FIGURE 12.5   The Connection Manager architecture

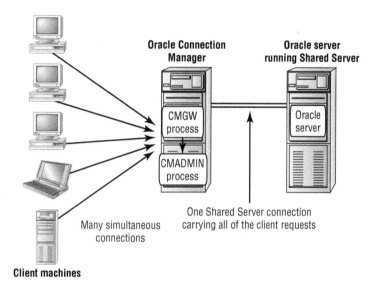

Security

The threat of data tampering and database security is an issue of major concern in many organizations as network systems continue to grow in number and complexity and as users gain increasing access to systems. Sensitive business transactions are being conducted with greater frequency and, in many cases, are not protected from unauthorized tampering or message interception. Oracle Net is capable of providing organizations with a secure network environment to conduct business transactions. Many tools and options are available in Oracle Database 12*c* to protect sensitive information.

Advanced Security

Oracle Advanced Security not only provides the tools necessary to ensure secure transmissions of sensitive information, but it also provides mechanisms to mask data in the Oracle enterprise. Oracle Advanced Security in Oracle Database 12*c* comprises Oracle Database Transparent Data Encryption (TDE) and Oracle Data Redaction.

TDE helps to encrypt data so that only authorized users are able to read it. TDE allows applications to continue working seamlessly as before, and does not require any application modification. It automatically encrypts data when it is written to disk, and then automatically decrypts the data when applications access it.

Oracle Data Redaction masks column data. Data Redaction performs the redaction at application runtime, when the user tries to view the data.

Firewall Support

Firewalls are an important security mechanism in corporate networks. Firewalls are generally a combination of hardware and software that is used to control network traffic and prevent intruders from compromising corporate network security. Firewalls fall into two broad categories:

IP-Filtering Firewalls   IP-filtering firewalls monitor the network packet traffic on IP networks and filter out packets that either originated or did not originate from specific groups of machines. The information contained in the IP packet header is interrogated to obtain this information. Vendors of this type of firewall include Network Associates and Axent Communications.

Proxy-Based Firewalls   Proxy-based firewalls prevent information from outside the firewall from flowing directly into the corporate network. The firewall acts as a gatekeeper, inspecting packets and sending only the appropriate information to the corporate network. This prevents any direct communication between clients outside the firewall and applications inside the firewall. Check Point Software Technologies and Cisco are examples of vendors that market proxy-based firewalls.

Oracle works closely with the vendors of both types of firewalls to ensure support of database traffic through these types of mechanism. Oracle supplies the Oracle Net Application Proxy Kit to the firewall vendors. This product can be incorporated into the firewall architecture to allow database packets to pass through the firewall and still maintain a high degree of security.

 **Real World Scenario**

Know Thy Firewall

It is important to understand your network infrastructure, the network routes you are using to obtain database connections and the type of firewall products you are using. In more than one situation, we've seen firewalls cause connectivity issues between a client and an Oracle server.

For instance, a small patch was applied to a firewall when a friend was working as a DBA for one of his former employers. In this case, employees started experiencing intermittent disconnects from the Oracle database. After many days of investigation and network tracing, the team pinned down the exact problem. The database team then contacted the firewall vendor, who sent a new patch that corrected the problem.

In another instance, the development staff started experiencing a similar connection problem. It turned out that the networking routes for the development staff had been modified to connect through a new firewall, with connections timing out after 20 minutes. This timeout was too short for this department. Increasing the timeout parameter solved the problem.

These are examples of the types of network changes you need to be aware of to avoid unnecessary downtime and to avoid wasting staff time and resources.

Accessibility

In many organizations, workers need to be able to communicate across a variety of systems and databases. They spend a lot of time bringing together data from different systems. The accessibility features of Oracle Net have capabilities that allow you to communicate with non-database data sources. This ability opens up new opportunities to provide customers with accurate and timely information. In this section, we'll discuss the options available in Oracle Database 12*c* to access data that resides in a non-Oracle database and to execute programs that are not SQL or PL/SQL.

Heterogeneous Services

The Heterogeneous Services component provides the ability to communicate with non-Oracle databases and services. These services allow organizations to leverage and interact with their existing data stores without having to necessarily move the data to an Oracle server.

   The suite of Heterogeneous Services comprises the Oracle Transparent Gateway and Generic Connectivity. These products allow Oracle to communicate with non-Oracle data sources in a seamless configuration. Heterogeneous Services also integrates existing systems with the Oracle environment, which allows you to leverage your investment in those systems. These services also allow for two-way communication and replication from Oracle data sources to non-Oracle data sources.

External Procedures

In some development efforts, interfacing with procedures that reside outside the database may be necessary. These procedures are typically written in a third-generation language, such as C. Oracle Net provides the ability to invoke such external procedures from Oracle PL/SQL callouts. When a call is made, a process is started that acts as an interface between Oracle and the external procedure. This callout process defaults to the name extproc. The listener is then responsible for supplying information, such as a library or procedure name and any parameters, to the called procedure. These programs are then loaded and executed under the control of the extproc process.

Configuring Oracle Net on the Server

Now that you understand the basic features Oracle Net provides, you need to understand how to configure the major components of Oracle Net. You must configure Oracle Net on the server in order for client connections to be established. The following sections will focus on how to configure the network elements of the Oracle server. It will also describe the types of connection methods that Oracle Net supports. We will then discuss how to manage Oracle Net on the server and troubleshoot connections from the server if clients experience connection problems.

Understanding the Oracle Listener

The Oracle *listener* is the main server-side Oracle networking component that allows connections to be established between client computers and an Oracle database. You can think of the listener as a big ear that listens for connection requests to Oracle services.

The type of Oracle service being requested is part of the connection descriptor information supplied by the process requesting a connection, and the service name resolves to an Oracle database. The listener can listen for any number of databases configured on the server, and it is able to listen for requests being transported on a variety of protocols. A client connection can be initiated from the same machine that the listener resides on, or it may come from some remote location.

The listener is controlled by a centralized file called listener.ora. Typically, only one listener.ora file is configured per machine; there may be numerous listeners on a server, and this file contains all the configuration information for every listener configured on the server (multiple listener.ora files are possible per machine, but as best practice, are not recommended). If multiple listeners are configured on a single server, they are usually set up for failover purposes or to balance connection requests and minimize the burden of connections on a single listener.

> The content and structure of the listener.ora file is discussed later in this chapter in the section "Managing Oracle Listeners."

Every listener is a named process that runs on the database server. The default name of the Oracle listener is LISTENER, and it is typically created when you install Oracle. If you configure multiple listeners, each must have a unique name. Now that you have a basic understanding of the Oracle listener, let's explore the main function of the listener, which is responding to client connection requests.

How Do Listeners Respond to Connection Requests?

A listener can respond to a client request for a connection in several ways. The response depends on several factors, such as how the server-side network components are configured and what type of connection the client is requesting. The listener then responds to the connection request in one of two ways.

The listener can spawn a new process and pass control of the client session to the process. In a *dedicated server* environment, every client connection is serviced by its own server-side process. Server-side processes are not shared among clients. Two types of dedicated connection methods are possible: direct and redirect. Each method results in a separate process that handles client processing, but the mechanics of the actual connection-initiation process are different. For remote clients to use dedicated connections, the listener process must be running on the same physical server as the database or databases for which it is listening.

The listener can also pass control of a connection request to a dispatcher. This type of connection takes place in an Oracle Shared Server environment. There are also two types of connection methods when using Oracle Shared Server: direct and redirect. DRCP complements middle-tier connection pools or applications that do not have application connection pools to share resources, and scale the connections supported to multiple fold.

Let's take a look at each of these connection-method types.

Dedicated Connections: Direct Handoff Method

Direct handoff connections are possible when the client and database exist on the same server. For example, a direct handoff method is used when the client connection request originates from the same machine on which the listener and database are running.

The following steps, which show the connection process for the bequeath connections, are illustrated in Figure 12.6:

FIGURE 12.6   Dedicated connections: direct handoff method

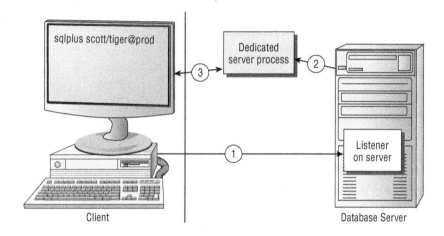

1. The client contacts the Oracle listener after resolving the service name.
2. The listener starts a dedicated process, and the client connection inherits the dedicated-server-process network-connect end point from the listener.
3. The client now has an established connection to the dedicated server process.

Dedicated Connections: Redirect Method

Redirect connections occur in a dedicated server environment when the client exists on a machine that is separate from the listener and database server. The listener must inform the client of the address of the spawned process in order for the process to contact the newly created dedicated server process.

The following steps, which show the connection process for redirect connections in a dedicated server environment, are illustrated in Figure 12.7:

1. The client contacts the Oracle listener after resolving the service name.
2. The listener starts a dedicated process.

3. The listener sends an acknowledgment back to the client with the address of the dedicated-server-connect end point on the database server to which the client will connect.

4. The client establishes a connection to the dedicated-server-connect end point.

FIGURE 12.7 Dedicated connections: redirect method

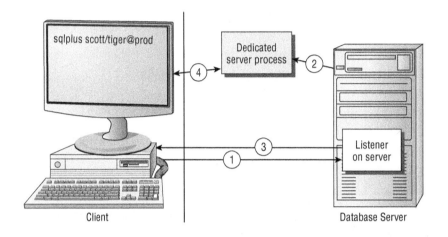

Oracle Shared Server: Direct Handoff Method

When you are using Oracle Shared Server, the client connection can also be established using a direct handoff method. This would be the case, for example, when the client request originates from the same machine on which the listener and database are running. Figure 12.8 outlines the connection steps when using Oracle Shared Server and the direct handoff method:

1. The client contacts the Oracle listener after resolving the service name.

2. The Oracle listener passes the connection request to the dispatcher with least load.

3. The client now has an established connection to the dispatcher process.

4. LREG (process monitor) sends information to the listener about the number of connections being serviced by the dispatchers.

Oracle Shared Server: Redirect Method

The listener can also redirect the user to a server process or a dispatcher process when using Oracle Shared Server. This type of connection can occur when the operating system does not directly support direct handoff connections or the listener is not on the same physical machine as the Oracle server.

FIGURE 12.8   Oracle Shared Server: direct handoff method

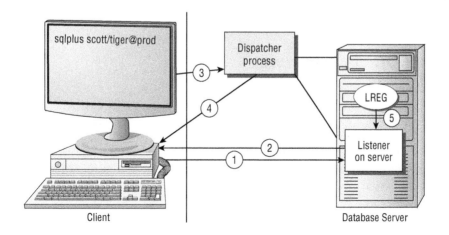

The following steps are illustrated in Figure 12.9:

1. The client contacts the Oracle server after resolving the service name.

2. The listener sends information to the client, redirecting the client to the dispatcher port. The original network connection between the listener and the client is disconnected.

3. The client then sends a connect signal to the server or dispatcher process to establish a network connection.

4. The dispatcher or server process sends an acknowledgment to the client.

5. LREG sends information to the listener about the number of connections being serviced by the dispatchers. The listener uses this information to maintain consistent loads between the dispatchers.

FIGURE 12.9   Oracle Shared Server: redirect connection method

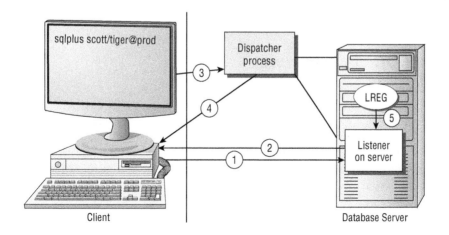

Database Resident Connection Pooling

For DRCP, the connection request typically originates from the application server. The following steps are illustrated in Figure 12.10.

1. The client (or middle-tier application) contacts the Oracle server after resolving the service name.

2. The listener sends information to the client, redirecting the client to the DRCP connection broker.

3. When an application wants to communicate with the database, the pooled-server process connection to the connection broker is handed off to the client.

4. The application then sends a connect signal to the server process to establish a network connection. The server process sends an acknowledgment to the application (client). At this point, the connection behaves like a dedicated session.

5. After the request is finished, the server process is released into the pool. The connection from the client is restored to the broker.

FIGURE 12.10 Database Resident Connection Pooling

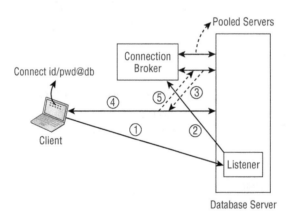

Managing Oracle Listeners

You can configure the server-side listener files in a number of ways. As part of the initial Oracle installation process, the installer prompts you to create a default listener (see Figure 9.15 in Chapter 9, "Creating and Operating Oracle Database 12c"). This creates a basic listener configuration file (listener.ora).

You can administer and manage the Oracle network file configurations by using Oracle Net Manager, Oracle Enterprise Manager Cloud Control, the server control utility srvctl, or the command-line facility lsnrctl. In the next few sections, you will learn to configure and manage the listener and service name files using these tools.

Managing Listeners with Oracle Net Manager

Oracle Net Manager is a tool you can use to create and manage most client- and server-side configuration files. Oracle Net Manager has evolved from the Oracle 7 tool, Network Manager, to the latest Oracle Database 12c version. Throughout this evolution, Oracle has continued to enhance the functionality and usability of the tool.

If you are using a Windows environment, you can start Oracle Net Manager by choosing Start ➢ Programs ➢ *Your Oracle 12c Programs choice* ➢ Configuration and Migration Tools ➢ Net Manager. In a Unix environment, you can start it by running netmgr from your $ORACLE_HOME/bin directory.

Figure 12.11 shows an example of the Oracle Net Manager opening screen.

FIGURE 12.11 The Oracle Net Manager opening screen

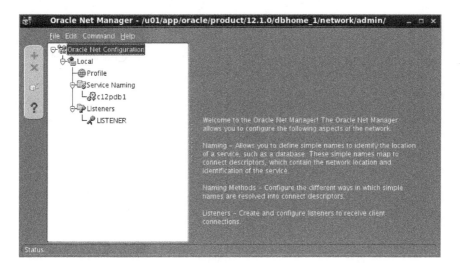

 A simplistic version of Net Manager is available as a tool named NetCA (Network Configuration Assistant). This can be invoked on Windows by using the Net Configuration Assistant program or on Unix by running $ORACLE_HOME/bin/netca. You can add, modify, and delete simple listener configurations using this tool. Because this tool has only a subset of features offered in Net Manager, NetCA is not discussed in detail here. However, we do encourage you to invoke and explore the tool.

Configuring Listener Services Using Oracle Net Manager

Oracle Net Manager provides an easy-to-use graphical interface for configuring most of the network files you will be using. By using Oracle Net Manager, you can ensure that the files are created in a consistent format, which will reduce the potential for connection problems.

When you first start Oracle Net Manager, the opening screen displays a tree structure with a top level called Oracle Net Configuration. If you click the plus (+) sign next to this icon, you will see the Local folder. The choices under the Local folder relate to different network configuration files. Here are the network file choices and what each configures:

Icon	File Configured
Profile	sqlnet.ora
Service Naming	tnsnames.ora
Listeners	listener.ora

Creating the Listener

Earlier we said that, by default, Oracle creates a listener called LISTENER when it is initially installed. The default settings that Oracle uses for the listener.ora file are as follows:

Section of the File	Setting
Listener name	LISTENER
Port	1521
Protocols	TCP/IP and IPC
Hostname	Default Host Name
SID name	Default Instance

You can use Oracle Net Manager to create a nondefault listener or change the definition of existing listeners. Oracle Net Manager has a wizard interface for creating most of the basic network elements, such as the listener.ora and tnsnames.ora files.

Follow these steps to create the listener:

1. Click the plus (+) sign next to the Local icon.

2. Click the Listeners folder.

3. Click the plus sign icon, or choose Edit ⇨ Create to open the Choose Listener Name dialog box.

4. Oracle Net Manager defaults to LISTENER or to LISTENER1 if the default listener is already created. Click OK if this is correct, or enter a new name and then click OK to open the Listening Locations screen, as shown in Figure 12.12.

FIGURE 12.12   The Listening Locations screen

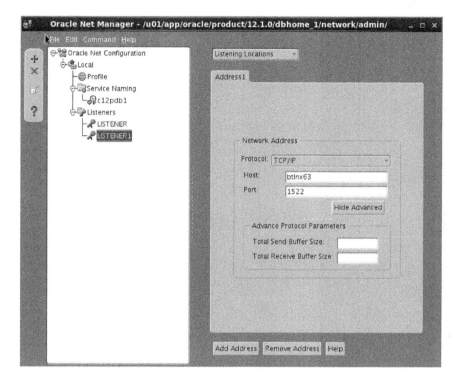

5. To configure the listening locations, click the Listening Locations drop-down list, and make your selection. Then click the Add Address button at the bottom of the screen to open a new window.

The prompts on this screen depend on your protocol. By default, TCP/IP information is displayed. If you are using TCP/IP, the Host and Port fields are filled in for you. The *host* is the name of the machine in which the listener is running, and the *port* is the listening location for TCP/IP connections. The default value for the port is 1521.

6. To save your information, choose File ⇨ Save Network Configuration, and then look in the directory where the file was saved.

You can also add listeners by following these steps. Listeners must have unique names and listen on separate ports, so assign the listener a new name and a new port (1522, for example). You also must assign service names to the listener. You'll see how to add service information in the next section.

Oracle Net Manager actually creates three files during this process: listener.ora, tnsnames.ora, and sqlnet.ora. The tnsnames.ora file does not contain any information.

The sqlnet.ora file may contain a few entries at this point, but you can ignore them for the time being. The listener.ora file contains information, as shown in the following code:

```
# listener.ora Network Configuration File: /u01/app/oracle/product/12.1.0/
dbhome_1/network/admin/listener.ora
# Generated by Oracle configuration tools.

LISTENER1 =
  (DESCRIPTION =
    (ADDRESS = (PROTOCOL = TCP)(HOST = btlnx63)(PORT = 1522))
  )

ADR_BASE_LISTENER1 = /u01/app/oracle

LISTENER =
  (DESCRIPTION_LIST =
    (DESCRIPTION =
      (ADDRESS = (PROTOCOL = TCP)(HOST = btlnx63)(PORT = 1521))
    )
    (DESCRIPTION =
      (ADDRESS = (PROTOCOL = IPC)(KEY = EXTPROC1521))
    )
  )

ADR_BASE_LISTENER = /u01/app/oracle
```

To figure out where the files are stored, just look at the top banner of the Oracle Net Manager screen.

Adding Service-Name Information to the Listener

After you create the listener with the name, protocol, and listening location information, you can define the network services to which the listener is responsible for connecting. This is called *static service registration*, because Oracle is not automatically registering the service with the listener. In releases of Oracle prior to Oracle8*i*, static service registration was the only method to associate services with a listener.

A listener can listen to an unlimited number of network service names. Follow these steps to add the service name information:

1. To select the listener to configure, click the Listeners icon, and highlight the name of the listener that you want to configure.

2. From the drop-down list at the top right of the screen, select Database Services.

3. Click the Add Database button at the bottom of the screen. This opens the window that allows you to add the database (see Figure 12.13).

FIGURE 12.13   The Database Services screen

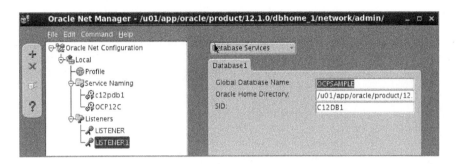

4. Enter values in the Global Database Name, Oracle Home Directory, and SID fields. The entries for SID and Global Database Name are the same if you are using a flat naming convention.

5. Choose File ➪ Save to save your configuration.

Here is an example of the completed `listener.ora` file:

```
# listener.ora Network Configuration File: /u01/app/oracle/product/12.1.0/
dbhome_1/network/admin/listener.ora
# Generated by Oracle configuration tools.

LISTENER1 =
  (DESCRIPTION =
    (ADDRESS = (PROTOCOL = TCP)(HOST = btlnx63)(PORT = 1522))
  )

SID_LIST_LISTENER1 =
  (SID_LIST =
    (SID_DESC =
      (GLOBAL_DBNAME = OCPSAMPLE)
      (ORACLE_HOME = /u01/app/oracle/product/12.1.0/dbhome_1)
      (SID_NAME = C12DB1)
    )
  )

ADR_BASE_LISTENER1 = /u01/app/oracle
```

Table 12.1 describes each of the listener.ora parameters for the Listening Location section of the listener.ora file.

TABLE 12.1   Parameters for the Listening Location Section of listener.ora

Parameter	Description
Listener_Name	Indicates the starting point of a listener definition. This is actually the name of the listener being defined. The default name is LISTENER.
DESCRIPTION	Describes each of the listening locations.
ADDRESS	Contains address information about the locations where the listener is listening.
PROTOCOL	Designates the protocol for this listening location.
HOST	Holds the name of the machine on which the listener resides.
PORT	Contains the address on which the listener is listening.
SID_LIST_Listener	Defines the list of Oracle services for which the listener (named LISTENER) is configured.
SID_DESC	Describes each Oracle SID.
GLOBAL_DBNAME	Identifies the global database name. This entry should match the SERVICE_NAMES entry in the init.ora file for the Oracle service.
ORACLE_HOME	The Oracle Home location on the server.
SID_NAME	Oracle SID name for the Oracle instance.

Optional listener.ora Parameters

You can set optional parameters that add functionality to the listener. To do so, select a parameter from the General Parameters drop-down list at the top right of the screen. Table 12.2 describes these parameters and where you can find them in Oracle Net Manager.

TABLE 12.2 Optional `listener.ora` Parameter Definitions

Net Manager Prompt	`listener.ora` Parameter	Description
Startup Wait Time	STARTUP_WAIT_TIME	Defines how long a listener will wait before it responds to a STATUS command in the `lsnrctl` command-line utility.
(Not available in Net Manager)	INBOUND_CONNECT_TIMEOUT	Defines how long a listener will wait for a valid response from a client once a session is initiated. The default is 10 seconds.
Save Configuration On Shutdown	SAVE_CONFIG_ON_STOP	Specifies whether modifications made during an `lsnrctl` session should be saved when exiting.
Enable ADR	ADR_BASE	Specify if log and trace files are written to Automatic Diagnostic Repository location. If checked, cannot specify the location for trace and log location.
Log File	LOG_FILE. Will not be in the `listener.ora` file if the default setting is used. By default, listener logging is enabled with the log created in the default location.	Specifies where a listener will write log information. This is ON by default and defaults to `$ORACLE_HOME/network/log/listener.log`.
Trace Level	TRACE_LEVEL. Not present if tracing is disabled. The default is OFF.	Sets the level of detail if listener connections are being traced. Valid values include Off, User, Support, and Admin.
Trace File	TRACE_FILE	Specifies the location of listener trace information. Defaults to `$ORACLE_HOME/network/trace/listener.trc`.
Require A Password For Listener Operations	PASSWORDS	Specifies password required to perform administrative tasks in the `lsnrctl` command-line utility.

Understanding Service Registration

Oracle Database 12c allows two types of service registration. Static service registration occurs when entries are added to the listener.ora file manually by using one of the Oracle tools. It is static because you are adding this information manually. Static service registration is necessary if you will be connecting to pre-Oracle8i instances using Oracle Enterprise Manager or if you will be connecting to external services.

Another way to manage listeners that does not require manual updating of service information in the listener.ora file is called *dynamic service registration*. Dynamic service registration allows an Oracle instance to automatically register itself with an Oracle listener. The benefit of this feature is that it does not require you to perform any updates of server-side network files when new Oracle instances are created. Dynamic service registration will be covered in more detail later in this chapter in the section "Dynamically Registering Services."

As you will see, you cannot add some parameters directly from the Oracle Net Manager and must do so manually. These optional parameters also have the listener name appended to them so that you can identify the listener definition to which they belong. For example, if the parameter STARTUP_WAIT_TIME is set for the default listener, the parameter created is STARTUP_WAIT_TIME_LISTENER.

Oracle EM Database Express cannot be used to manage a listener or services, but Oracle EM Cloud control can be used. You can add, stop, start, and configure the listener.

Managing Listeners with lsnrctl

You can also use a command-line interface, lsnrctl, to administer the listener. This tool gives you full configuration and administration capabilities. If you have been using Oracle, this tool should be familiar. This command-line interface has been around since the early releases of the Oracle product. Other Oracle network components, such as Connection Manager, also have command-line tools that are used to administer their associated processes.

In Windows, the listener runs as a service. Services are programs that run in the background in Windows. You can start the listener from the Windows Services panel. Choose Start ➢ Settings ➢ Control Panel ➢ Services. Then select the name of the listener service from the list of services. If the name of your listener is LISTENER, for example, look for an entry such as OracleOraDB12Home1TNSListenerO12C01_LISTENER. Select the listener name, and click Start.

To invoke the command-line utility, type **lsnrctl** at the command line. The following code shows a resulting login screen:

```
$ lsnrctl

LSNRCTL for Linux: Version 12.1.0.1.0 - Production on 28-NOV-2013 15:35:53

Copyright (c) 1991, 2013, Oracle.  All rights reserved.

Welcome to LSNRCTL, type "help" for information.

LSNRCTL>
```

The listener has commands to perform various functions. You can type **help** at the LSNRCTL> prompt to display a list of these commands. The SET command is used to set configuration parameters, and the SHOW command displays the current value.

```
LSNRCTL> help
The following operations are available
An asterisk (*) denotes a modifier or extended command:

start           stop          status          services
version         reload        save_config     trace
spawn           quit          exit            set*
show*

LSNRCTL> help show
The following operations are available after show
An asterisk (*) denotes a modifier or extended command:

rawmode                       displaymode
rules                         trc_file
trc_directory                 trc_level
log_file                      log_directory
log_status                    current_listener
inbound_connect_timeout       startup_waittime
snmp_visible                  save_config_on_stop
dynamic_registration          enable_global_dynamic_endpoint
oracle_home                   pid
connection_rate_limit         valid_node_checking_registration
registration_invited_nodes    registration_excluded_nodes
remote_registration_address
```

```
LSNRCTL> help set
The following operations are available after set
An asterisk (*) denotes a modifier or extended command:
```

rawmode	displaymode
trc_file	trc_directory
trc_level	log_file
log_directory	log_status
current_listener	inbound_connect_timeout
startup_waittime	save_config_on_stop
dynamic_registration	enable_global_dynamic_endpoint
connection_rate_limit	valid_node_checking_registration
registration_invited_nodes	registration_excluded_nodes

```
LSNRCTL>
```

You can perform a variety of functions from within the lsnrctl utility. Let's take a look at the most common functions you'll perform on the listener using this utility.

Starting the Listener

To start the default listener named LISTENER, type **start** at the prompt. To start a different listener, type **start** and then that listener name. For example, typing **start listener1** starts the LISTENER1 listener.

The following code shows the results of starting the default listener:

```
LSNRCTL> start listener1
Starting /u01/app/oracle/product/12.1.0/dbhome_1/bin/tnslsnr: please wait...


TNSLSNR for Linux: Version 12.1.0.1.0 - Production
System parameter file is /u01/app/oracle/product/12.1.0/dbhome_1/network/admin/
listener.ora
Log messages written to /u01/app/oracle/product/12.1.0/dbhome_1/network/log/
listener1.log
Trace information written to /u01/app/oracle/product/12.1.0/dbhome_1/network/
trace/listener1.trc
Listening on: (DESCRIPTION=(ADDRESS=(PROTOCOL=tcp)(HOST=btlnx63)(PORT=1522)))


Connecting to (DESCRIPTION=(ADDRESS=(PROTOCOL=TCP)(HOST=btlnx63)(PORT=1522)))
STATUS of the LISTENER
------------------------
Alias                    listener1
Version                  TNSLSNR for Linux: Version 12.1.0.1.0 - Production
Start Date               28-NOV-2013 15:39:03
```

```
Uptime                        0 days 0 hr. 0 min. 0 sec
Trace Level                   support
Security                      ON: Local OS Authentication
SNMP                          OFF
Listener Parameter File       /u01/app/oracle/product/12.1.0/dbhome_1/network/admin/
listener.ora
Listener Log File             /u01/app/oracle/product/12.1.0/dbhome_1/network/log/
listener1.log
Listener Trace File           /u01/app/oracle/product/12.1.0/dbhome_1/network/trace/
listener1.trc
Listening Endpoints Summary...
  (DESCRIPTION=(ADDRESS=(PROTOCOL=tcp)(HOST=btlnx63)(PORT=1522)))
Services Summary...
Service "OCPSAMPLE" has 1 instance(s).
  Instance "C12DB1", status UNKNOWN, has 1 handler(s) for this service...
The command completed successfully
LSNRCTL>
```

This listing shows a summary of information, including the services that the listener is listening for, the log locations, and whether tracing is enabled for the listener.

Reloading the Listener

If the listener is running and modifications are made to the listener.ora file manually, with Oracle Net Manager or with Enterprise Manager, you must reload the listener to refresh the listener with the most current information. The reload command rereads the listener.ora file for the new definitions. As you can see, it is not necessary to stop and start the listener to reload it. Although stopping and restarting the listener can also accomplish a reload, using the reload command is better because the listener is not actually stopped, which makes this process more efficient. The following code shows an example of the reload command:

```
LSNRCTL> reload listener1
Connecting to (DESCRIPTION=(ADDRESS=(PROTOCOL=TCP)(HOST=btlnx63)(PORT=1522)))
The command completed successfully
LSNRCTL>
```

Reloading the listener has no effect on clients connected to the Oracle server.

In the previous code example, Oracle reread the listener.ora file and applied any changes you made to the file against the currently running listener process. You can see the address, protocol, and port designation of the default listener. Notice that this listener is listening on port 1522. Security best practices advice you not run the listener on the default known ports.

Showing the Status of the Listener

You can display the status of the listener by using the status command. The status command shows whether the listener is active, the locations of the logs and trace files, how long the listener has been running, and the services for the listener. This is a quick way to verify that the listener is up and running with no problems.

The following code shows the result of the lsnrctl status command. Note that no listener name is specified; therefore, the status of default listener listener is shown:

```
LSNRCTL> status
Connecting to (DESCRIPTION=(ADDRESS=(PROTOCOL=TCP)(HOST=btlnx63)(PORT=1521)))
STATUS of the LISTENER
------------------------
Alias                     LISTENER
Version                   TNSLSNR for Linux: Version 12.1.0.1.0 - Production
Start Date                28-NOV-2013 12:36:14
Uptime                    0 days 3 hr. 5 min. 2 sec
Trace Level               off
Security                  ON: Local OS Authentication
SNMP                      OFF
Listener Parameter File   /u01/app/oracle/product/12.1.0/dbhome_1/network/admin/
listener.ora
Listener Log File         /u01/app/oracle/diag/tnslsnr/btlnx63/listener/alert/
log.xml
Listening Endpoints Summary...
  (DESCRIPTION=(ADDRESS=(PROTOCOL=tcp)(HOST=btlnx63)(PORT=1521)))
  (DESCRIPTION=(ADDRESS=(PROTOCOL=tcps)(HOST=btlnx63)(PORT=5500))(Security=(my_
wallet_directory=/u01/app/oracle/admin/C12DB1/xdb_wallet))(Presentation=HTTP)
(Session=RAW))
Services Summary...
Service "C12DB1" has 1 instance(s).
  Instance "C12DB1", status READY, has 1 handler(s) for this service...
Service "C12DB1XDB" has 1 instance(s).
  Instance "C12DB1", status READY, has 1 handler(s) for this service...
Service "bt1pdb" has 1 instance(s).
  Instance "C12DB1", status READY, has 1 handler(s) for this service...
Service "c12pdb1" has 1 instance(s).
  Instance "C12DB1", status READY, has 1 handler(s) for this service...
The command completed successfully
LSNRCTL>
```

This code example depicts a listener that has recently been started. You also see what the log file and parameter file locations are for the listener. This is a good facility to use to get a quick listing of vital information for the listener.

Use `lsnrctl status` to see how long the listener was up. Look for `Uptime`.

Listing the Services for the Listener

The `lsnrctl services` command displays information about the services, such as whether the services have any dedicated, prespawned server processes or dispatched processes associated with them, and how many connections have been accepted and rejected per service. Use this method to check whether a listener is listening for a particular service.

The following code shows an example of running the `services` command:

```
LSNRCTL> services listener1
Connecting to (DESCRIPTION=(ADDRESS=(PROTOCOL=TCP)(HOST=btlnx63)(PORT=1522)))
Services Summary...
Service "OCPSAMPLE" has 1 instance(s).
  Instance "C12DB1", status UNKNOWN, has 1 handler(s) for this service...
    Handler(s):
      "DEDICATED" established:0 refused:0
        LOCAL SERVER
The command completed successfully
LSNRCTL>
```

In this example, you can see that the listener is listening for connections to the service OCPSAMPLE. The line `"DEDICATED" established:0 refused:0` shows you how many connections to this service have been accepted or rejected by the listener. One reason why a listener may reject servicing a request is if the database is not available.

Other Commands in `lsnrctl`

You can run other commands in `lsnrctl`. Table 12.3 summarizes these other commands. Type the command at the LSNRCTL> prompt to execute it.

TABLE 12.3 A Summary of the `lsnrctl` Commands

Command	Definition
change_password	Allows a user to change the password needed to stop the listener.
exit	Exits the `lsnrctl` utility.
quit	Performs the same function as `exit`.
save_config	Copies the `listener.ora` file called `listener.bak` when changes are made to the `listener.ora` file from `lsnrctl`.

TABLE 12.3 A Summary of the lsnrctl Commands *(continued)*

Command	Definition
services listener	Lists a summary of services and details information about the number of connections established and the number of connections refused for each protocol service handler.
start listener	Starts the named listener.
status listener	Shows the status of the named listener.
stop listener	Stops the named listener.
trace	Turns on tracing for the listener.
version	Displays the version of the Oracle Net software and protocol adapters.

Using the set Commands in lsnrctl

The lsnrctl utility also has commands called set commands. To issue these commands, type **set** *commandname* at the LSNRCTL> prompt. You use the set commands to modify the listener.ora file. For example, you can use this command to set up logging and tracing. You can set most of these parameters using the Oracle Net Manager.

To display the current setting of a parameter, use the show command, which displays the current settings of the parameters set using the set command. Table 12.4 lists the most commonly used lsnrctl set commands. Type **set** or **show** to display a listing of all the commands (shown earlier in this section).

TABLE 12.4 A Summary of the lsnrctl set Commands

Command	Description
current_listener	Sets the listener to modify or show the name of the current listener.
displaymode	Sets the display for the lsnrctl utility to RAW, COMPACT, NORMAL, or VERBOSE.
log_status	Shows whether logging is on or off for the listener.
log_file	Shows the name of the listener log file.
log_directory	Shows the log directory location.

Command	Description
rawmode	Shows more detail on STATUS and SERVICES when set to ON. Values are ON or OFF.
startup_waittime	Sets the length of time that a listener will wait to respond to a status command in the lsnrctl command-line utility.
spawn	Starts external services that the listener is listening for and that are running on the server.
save_config_on_stop	Saves changes to the listener.ora file when exiting lsnrctl.
trc_level	Sets the trace level to OFF, USER, ADMIN, or SUPPORT.
trc_file	Sets the name of the listener trace file.
trc_directory	Sets the name of the listener trace directory.
inbound_connect_timeout	Sets the time in seconds for the client to complete the connection request.
valid_node_checking_registration	When set to on, only local IP address connections are allowed.

Stopping the Listener

To stop the listener, you must issue the lsnrctl stop command. This command stops the default listener. To stop a nondefault listener, include the name of the listener. For example, to stop LISTENER1, type **lsnrctl stop listener1**. If you are in the lsnrctl> facility, you will stop the current listener defined by the current_listener setting. To see what the current listener is set to, use the show command. The default value is LISTENER.

Stopping the listener does not affect clients already connected to the database. It only means that no new connections can use this listener until the listener is restarted.

The following code shows what the stop command looks like:

```
$ lsnrctl stop listener1

LSNRCTL for Linux: Version 12.1.0.1.0 - Production on 28-NOV-2013 15:52:10
Copyright (c) 1991, 2013, Oracle.  All rights reserved.
Connecting to (DESCRIPTION=(ADDRESS=(PROTOCOL=TCP)(HOST=btlnx63)(PORT=1522)))
The command completed successfully
```

The listener writes status, trace, startup, shutdown, and connection information to a listener log file named listener.log. This file can be found under <ADR>/diag/tnslsnr/ listener/trace.

Dynamically Registering Services

Oracle databases can automatically register their presence with an existing listener. The instance registers with the listener defined on the local machine. Dynamic service registration allows you to take advantage of other features, such as load balancing and automatic failover. The LREG process is responsible for registering this information with the listener.

When dynamic service registration is used, you will not see the service listed in the listener.ora file. To see the service listed, run the lsnrctl services command. Be aware that if the listener is started after the Oracle instance, there may be a time lag before the instance actually registers information with the listener.

For an instance to automatically register with a listener, the listener must be configured as a default listener, or you must specify the init.ora parameter LOCAL_LISTENER. The LOCAL_LISTENER parameter defines the location of the listener with which you want the Oracle server to register. You may specify the connection description for the parameter or use a tns alias resolved by the tnsnames.ora file.

When an instance starts, LREG polls the listener to determine whether it is running. If the listener is running, then LREG passes its relevant parameters. If it is not running, then LREG periodically attempts to contact it. You can register the instance with the listener by executing ALTER SYSTEM REGISTER.

You must configure two other init.ora parameters to allow an instance to register information with the listener. Two parameters are used to allow automatic registration: INSTANCE_NAME and SERVICE_NAMES.

The INSTANCE_NAME parameter is set to the name of the Oracle instance you want to register with the listener. The SERVICE_NAMES parameter is a combination of the instance name and the domain name. The domain name is set to the value of the DB_DOMAIN initialization parameter. For example, if your DB_DOMAIN is set to BJS.COM and your Oracle instance is DBA, set the parameters as follows:

```
Instance_name = DBA
Service_names = DBA.BJS.COM
```

If you are not using domain names, set the INSTANCE_NAME and SERVICE_NAMES parameters to the same values.

One optional parameter to configure for dynamic registration is the REMOTE_LISTENER. A remote listener is a listener residing on one computer that redirects connections to a database instance on the same or different computer. Remote listeners are typically used in an Oracle Real Application Clusters (Oracle RAC) environment, or when local and SCAN listeners are used in the environment. The syntax for configuring REMOTE_LISTENER is the same as LOCAL_LISTENER.

Dynamic service registration is configured in the database initialization file. It does not require any configuration in the `listener.ora` file. However, listener configuration must be set to listen on the ports named in the database initialization file.

Oracle Net Logging and Tracing on the Server

If a network problem persists, you can use logging and tracing to help resolve it. Oracle generates information into log files and trace files that can assist you in tracking down network connection problems. You can use logging to find general information about the success or failure of certain components of the Oracle network. You can use tracing to get in-depth information about specific network connections.

By default, Oracle produces logs for clients and the Oracle listener.

- Logging records significant events, such as starting and stopping the listener, along with certain kinds of network errors. Errors are generated in the log in the form of an error stack. The listener log records information such as the version number, connection attempts, and the protocols for which it is listening. You can enable logging at the client, middle-tier, and server locations.

- Tracing, which you can also enable at the client, middle-tier, or server location, records all events that occur on a network, even when an error does not occur. The trace file provides a great deal of information that logs do not, such as the number of network round-trips made during a network connection or the number of packets sent and received during a network connection. Tracing enables you to collect a thorough listing of the actual sequence of the statements as a network connection is being processed. This gives you a much more detailed picture of what is occurring with connections that the listener is processing.

Use Oracle Net Manager to enable most logging and tracing parameters. Many of the logging and tracing parameters are found in the `sqlnet.ora` file. Let's take a look at how to enable logging and tracing for the various components in an Oracle network.

Server Logging

By default, the listener is configured to enable the generation of a log file. The log file records information about listener startup and shutdown, successful and unsuccessful connection attempts, and certain types of network errors. Here's what everything means by default:

- The listener log location is `<DIAGNOSTIC_DEST>/diag/tnslsnr/<hostname>/listener/trace` on Unix.

- The default name of the file is `listener.log`.

- The XML version of the listener log is under <*DIAGNOSTIC_DEST*>/diag/
  tnslsnr/<*hostname*>/listener/alert, and the filename is log.xml.

- If the DIAGNOSTIC_DEST parameter is not defined, Oracle defaults it to $ORACLE_BASE.

 Real World Scenario

Use Tracing Sparingly

Use tracing only as a last resort if you are having connectivity problems between the client and server. Complete all the server-side checks described earlier before you resort to tracing. The tracing process generates a significant amount of overhead, and depending on the trace level set, it can create some rather large files. This activity will impede system I/O performance because of all the information that is written to the logs, and if left unchecked, it could fill your disk or file system.

We were once involved with a large project that was using JDBC to connect to the Oracle server. We were having difficulty with connections being periodically dropped between the JDBC client and the Oracle server. We enabled tracing to try to find the problem. We did eventually correct the problem (it was with how our DNS names server was configured), but the tracing was left on inadvertently. When the system eventually went into production, the trace files grew so large that they filled the disk where tracing was being collected. To prevent this from happening, periodically ensure that the trace parameters are not turned on, and if they are, turn them off.

Information in the listener.log file contains information about connection attempts, the name of the program executing the request, and the name of the client attempting to connect. The last field contains a zero if a request was successfully completed.

Server Tracing

As mentioned earlier, tracing gathers information about the flow of traffic across a network connection. Data is transmitted back and forth in the form of packets. A packet contains sender information, receiver information, and data. Even a single network request can generate a large number of packets.

In the trace file, each line starts with the name of the procedure executed in one of the Oracle Net layers and is followed by a set of hexadecimal numbers. The hexadecimal numbers are the actual data transmitted. If you are not encrypting the data, sometimes you will see the actual data after the hexadecimal numbers.

If you are doing server-to-server communications and have a sqlnet.ora file on the server, you can enter information in the Server Information section located on the Tracing tab of the Profile screen in Oracle Net Manager tracing. This provides tracing information for server-to-server communications.

Enabling Server Tracing

You can enable server tracing from the same Oracle Net Manager screens shown earlier. Simply click the Tracing Enabled radio button. The default trace file location is $DIAGNOSTIC_DEST/diag/tnslsnr/*hostname*/listener/trace in Unix. You can set the trace level to OFF, USER, ADMIN, or SUPPORT. The USER level detects specific user errors. The ADMIN level contains all the user-level information along with installation-specific errors. SUPPORT is the highest level and can produce information that might be beneficial to Oracle Support personnel. This level also can produce large trace files.

The following example shows a section of the listener.ora file with the logging and tracing parameters enabled:

```
TRACE_LEVEL_LISTENER = ADMIN
TRACE_FILE_LISTENER = LISTENER.trc
LOGGING_LISTENER = ON
LOG_FILE_LISTENER = LISTENER.log
```

Configuring Oracle Net for the Client

Once the Oracle server is properly configured, you can focus on configuring the clients to allow for connectivity to the Oracle server. It is important to understand how to configure Oracle clients because without proper knowledge of how to do this, you are limited in your connection choices to the server. As a DBA, you must understand the network needs of the organization, the type of connectivity that is required, and client/server connections versus *n*-tier connectivity, for example, in order to make the appropriate choices about client-side configuration. This section should help clarify the client-side connectivity options available to you and show you how to troubleshoot client connection problems.

Client-Side Names Resolution Options

When a client needs to connect to an Oracle server, the client must supply three pieces of information: their user ID, password, and net service name. The net service name provides the necessary information, in the form of a connect descriptor, to locate an Oracle service in a network.

This connect descriptor describes the path to the Oracle server and its service name, which is an alias for an Oracle database. The location where this information is kept depends on the names resolution method you choose. The five methods of net service name resolution are Oracle Internet Directory, external naming, host naming, Oracle Easy Connect, and local naming. Normally, you choose just one of these methods, but you can use any combination.

Oracle Internet Directory is advantageous when you are dealing with complex networks that have many Oracle servers. When you choose this method, you can configure and manage net service names and connect descriptor information in a central location.

External naming uses a non-Oracle facility to manage and resolve Oracle service names. For example, if an organization uses an external names resolution method such as Network Information Service (NIS), the database service information could be stored in this external location and used by clients to resolve service names.

 You need to be only casually familiar with the Oracle Internet Directory and the external-naming resolution options. For a more detailed description of how to configure and use external naming, please consult "Oracle® Database Net Services Administrator's Guide 12c Release 1 (12.1) Part Number E17610-09." You can find the Oracle documentation at http://tahiti.oracle.com.

In the following sections, we will take a closer look at the host naming, Oracle Easy Connect, and local naming methods.

The Host Naming Method

In small networks with few Oracle servers to manage, you can take advantage of the *host naming method*. Host naming is advantageous when you want to reduce the amount of configuration work necessary. Host naming saves you from configuring the clients, although it does have limitations. The following are the four prerequisites to using host naming:

- You must use TCP/IP as your network protocol.
- You must not use any advanced networking features, such as Oracle Connection Manager.
- You must have an external naming service, such as DNS, or a HOSTS file available to the client.
- The listener must be set up with the GLOBAL_DBNAME parameter equal to the name of the machine.

Now let's discuss how to configure this naming method.

Configuring the Host Naming Method

By default, Oracle attempts to use the host naming method from the client only after it attempts connections using local naming. To override this default search path for resolving names, set the NAMES.DIRECTORY_PATH parameter in the sqlnet.ora file on the client so that it searches for host naming only. The following is an example of the sqlnet.ora file:

```
# SQLNET.ORA Network Configuration File:
# Generated by Oracle configuration tools.

NAMES.DEFAULT_DOMAIN = bjs.com
NAMES.DIRECTORY_PATH= (HOSTNAME)
```

The host naming and the Oracle Easy Connect methods do not require any client-side configuration files. We'll discuss these connection methods later in this section.

You can check TCP/IP connectivity from the client using the TCP/IP utility ping. The ping utility attempts to contact the server by sending a small request packet. The server responds in kind with an acknowledgment.

The server must be configured with a listener running TCP/IP, and the listener must be listening on the default port 1521. If the instance has not been dynamically registered with the listener, you must configure the listener with the GLOBAL_DBNAME parameter.

The Oracle Easy Connect Method

The Oracle Easy Connect method is a connection resolution technique introduced in Oracle 10*g*. This method is similar to the host naming method described in the previous section but adds parameters that allow for a port and service-name specification. By default, the Oracle Easy Connect names resolution method is configured when Oracle Net is installed.

Like the host naming method, the Oracle Easy Connect method eliminates the need for any connection information to be configured on the client. This makes for less setup and administrative work. It enhances the host naming method by allowing for a port and service specification. Remember from the previous section that the host naming method requires a listener to be listening on the default port 1521. Allowing a port specification addresses one of the limitations of the host naming method. Using the Oracle Easy Connect method requires that certain conditions be met:

- Oracle Net Services (version 10*g* or higher) must be installed on the client.
- Oracle Net TCP/IP services must be enabled and supported on both the client and the server.
- No advanced connection descriptor features are allowed such as connection pooling or external procedure calls.

Table 12.5 describes the connect descriptor components when you are using the Oracle Easy Connect method. Here is the syntax to use Easy Connect method.

```
CONNECT username/password@[//]host[:port][/service_name][:server][/instance_name]
```

TABLE 12.5 Easy Connect Components

Syntax Component	Description
//	Optional: Used when you are connecting via a URL.
Host	Required: The host or IP address to connect to.
Port	Optional: The port to connect to. The default is 1521.
Service Name	The service name for the database. The default is the hostname of the computer on which the database resides. If the database name is different from the hostname, enter the service name or specify the default service name in the listener.ora file using the DEFAULT_SERVICE_*listener_name* parameter.
Server	Optional: Specify the type of server to use: dedicated, shared, or pooled.
Instance Name	Optional: Specify an instance name to connect to, typically applicable for RAC instances.

Here is an example of how to connect to a database using the Easy Connect method:

```
CONNECT scott/tiger@btlnx63:1522/DB12C1
```

The example shows how a user connects to the database service DB12C1 that is running on the btlnx63 server and has an Oracle listener listening for TCP/IP connections on port 1522. As stated previously, this method is configured automatically when you install Oracle Net. If you want the Oracle Easy Connect method to be the first method chosen by a client when a connection request is made, you can modify the NAMES.DIRECTORY_PATH parameter in the sqlnet.ora file. The following discussion shows how to do this.

You can use the Oracle Net Manager tool to configure the Easy Connect method as the default names resolution method. Start the Oracle Net Manager tool, and then follow these steps:

1. Choose Local ⇨ Profile Pane in the Navigator pane.
2. Select Naming from the panel on the right.
3. Select the Methods tab.
4. Select EZCONNECT in the Selected Methods list. You can click the promote arrows to move EZCONNECT to the top of the Selected Methods list.
5. Choose File ⇨ Save Network Configuration to save your changes.

   When you check your sqlnet.ora file, you should see the following entry:

   ```
   NAMES.DIRECTORY_PATH=(EZCONNECT,TNSNAMES)
   ```

Web applications can connect to the Oracle database using JDBC Connection syntax. `jdbc:oracle:thin:@<hostname>:<port>/<service_name>`. For example, to connect to database name sales on server sal01 as database user Scott with password tiger, use the connect string `connection = DriverManager.getConnection ("jdbc:oracle:thin:@sal01:1521:sales", "scott", "tiger");`.

The Local Naming Method

The *local naming method* is probably the most widely used and well-known method for resolving net service names. Most users know this method as the `tnsnames.ora` method because it uses the `tnsnames.ora` file.

To use the local naming method, you must configure the `tnsnames.ora` file, which can be in any location, as long as the client can get to it. The default location for the `tnsnames.ora` file and the `sqlnet.ora` file is `%ORACLE_HOME%\network\admin` in Windows and `$ORACLE_HOME/network/admin` in Unix systems. If you want to change the location of this file, set the environmental variable `TNS_ADMIN`. In Unix-based systems, you can `export TNS_ADMIN` to the user's shell environment or in the user's profile. In Windows, this setting is in the registry. The Windows registry key that stores the `TNS_ADMIN` depends on your particular setup. Generally, it is somewhere under `Hkey_local_machine/software/oracle`, but it may be at a lower level, depending on your configuration, or set as an environment variable.

Most installations probably keep the files in these default locations on the client and server. Some users create shared disks and place the `tnsnames.ora` and `sqlnet.ora` files in this shared location to take a centralized approach to managing these files. If server-to-server communication is necessary, these files need to be on the server. The default location on the server is the same as the default location on the client.

Now that you understand the local naming method, we will discuss how to configure this method using Oracle Net Manager.

Configuring the Local Naming Method Using Oracle Net Manager

To configure the local naming method, you may use Oracle Net Manager. To start this configuration, open Net Manager, and select Service Naming on the Local tab. Click the plus sign (+) on the left side of the screen, or choose Edit ➪ Create.

The Oracle Net Manager starts the Net Service Name Wizard, which guides you through the process of creating the net service names definition. The following steps detail how to configure the local naming method:

1. When you configure a client to use the local naming method, you must first choose a *net service name*. This is the name that users enter when they are referring to the location to which they want to connect. The name you supply here should not include the domain portion if you are using the hierarchical naming mode. Figure 12.14 shows an example of choosing the net service name. Click the Next button to continue.

2. The next step is to enter the type of protocol that the client should use when they connect to the server for this net service name. By default, TCP/IP is chosen (see Figure 12.15). The list of protocols depends on your platform. Click the Next button to continue.

3. The next step is to choose the hostname and port. This step depends on the protocol you chose in the previous step. If you chose TCP/IP, you are prompted for the hostname and the port number. The hostname is the name of the machine on which the listener process is running. The port number is the listening location for the listener. The default port is 1521 (see Figure 12.16).

FIGURE 12.14 Choosing a net service name

FIGURE 12.15 Choosing a network protocol

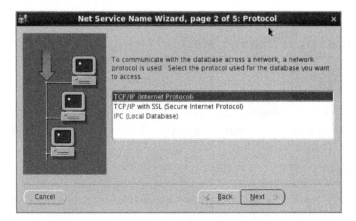

4. The next step is to define the service name. For Oracle Database 12c, the service name does not have to be the same as the ORACLE_SID because a database can have

multiple service names. This is the service name that is supplied to the listener, so the listener has to be listening for this service. You can also select the connection type from one of these choices:

- Database Default
- Shared Server
- Dedicated Server
- Pooled Server

FIGURE 12.16   Choosing a hostname and a port

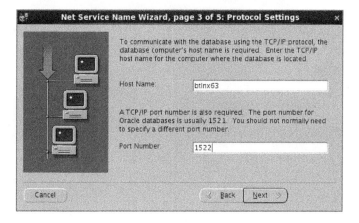

Figure 12.17 shows an example of the Oracle Net Manager service name screen.

FIGURE 12.17   Choosing the service name

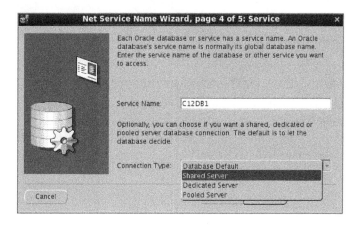

5. The last step is to test the net service name and verify that all the connection information entered is correct. Click the Test button to test the network connection.

Click the Finish button to create the tnsnames.ora entry. You can edit the entry, as shown in Figure 12.18.

After you complete all this, save your changes by choosing File ➢ Save Network Configuration. This creates and saves the tnsnames.ora file.

FIGURE 12.18   The Oracle Net Manager tnsnames.ora Wizard

Contents and Structure of the tnsnames.ora File

You created the tnsnames.ora file using the Oracle Net Manager, so open the tnsnames.ora file to view its contents. The tnsnames.ora file is located in the same location as the TNS_ADMIN variable setting, which defaults to the $ORACLE_HOME/network/admin directory. Here is an example of the tnsnames.ora file:

```
OCP12C =
  (DESCRIPTION =
    (ADDRESS_LIST =
      (ADDRESS = (PROTOCOL = TCP)(HOST = btlnx63)(PORT = 1522))
    )
```

```
(CONNECT_DATA =
  (SERVER = DEDICATED)
  (SERVICE_NAME = C12DB1)
  (INSTANCE_NAME = C12DB1)
  )
)
```

Table 12.6 summarizes the parameters in the tnsnames.ora file.

TABLE 12.6   The tnsnames.ora Parameters

Parameter	Description
DESCRIPTION	Starts the connect descriptor section of the file.
ADDRESS_LIST	Starts a list of all connect descriptor address information.
ADDRESS	Specifies the connect descriptor for the net service name.
PROTOCOL	Specifies the protocol used, such as TCP/IP.
HOST	Specifies the name of the machine on which the listener is running. An IP address can also be specified in TCP/IP.
PORT	Specifies the listening location of the listener specific to TCP/IP.
CONNECT_DATA	Starts the services section for this net service name.
SERVICE_NAME	Defines which service to connect to, which can be the same as the ORACLE_SID or the global database name. Databases can now be referred to by more than a single service name.
INSTANCE_NAME	Specifies the instance name to connect to.

The Easy Connect string btlnx63:1522/DB12C1:SHARED/DB12C11 can be translated to the following local naming connect:

```
(DESCRIPTION=
  (ADDRESS=(PROTOCOL=tcp)(HOST=btlnx63)(PORT=1522))
  (CONNECT_DATA=
    (SERVICE_NAME=DB12C1)
    (SERVER=SHARED)
    (INSTANCE_NAME=DB12C11)))
```

Although it is not recommended, you can edit the tnsnames.ora, listener.ora, and sqlnet.ora files using your favorite editor and add or modify entries. Using a tool like Net Manager will prevent errors in these files.

Troubleshooting Client-Side Connection Problems

Connection problems can also occur from the Oracle client. Several areas affect the ability of a client to connect successfully to the server. The client must be able to contact both the computer on which the Oracle server is located and the listener listening for connections to the Oracle server. The client must also be able to resolve the net service name. Let's look at the checks to perform on the client to verify connectivity to the Oracle server and to detect and troubleshoot client-side connection problems. Use the following list to help you systematically check various aspects of the client connection process:

- Verify that the client can contact the server.
- Determine the network route that the client is taking to the server.
- Verify local naming configuration files.
- Check for multiple-client network configuration files.
- Check network file locations.
- Check the NAMES.DIRECTORY_PATH parameter.
- Check the NAMES.DEFAULT_DOMAIN parameter.
- Check the client protocol adapters installed.
- Check for any common client-side error codes.

Oracle provides the tnsping utility to verify that the local naming entry defined in the tnsnames.ora file can talk to the service name defined in the listener.ora file. You can find tnsping in the $ORACLE_HOME/bin directory. It also provides the time it took to reach the listener in milliseconds.

Checking Network File Locations

One of the most common problems encountered is clients moving network files and not setting the TNS_ADMIN environmental variable to the new file location. Oracle expects the tnsnames.ora and sqlnet.ora files to be in the default location. If it cannot locate the files and you have not set TNS_ADMIN, you will receive an ORA-12154 error message. You will also receive this error if the supplied net service name is invalid or the NAMES.DEFAULT_DOMAIN value is mismatched in tnsnames.ora and sqlnet.ora files. The following code shows an example of this error message:

```
$ sqlplus system@ocp12c1
```

```
SQL*Plus: Release 12.1.0.1.0 Production on Sat Nov 30 01:06:07 2013
Copyright (c) 1982, 2013, Oracle.  All rights reserved.


Enter password:
ERROR:
ORA-12154: TNS:could not resolve the connect identifier specified
```

 If you decide to move network files, be sure to set the TNS_ADMIN environmental variable to the location of the files. Oracle first searches the default
location for the files and then searches the TNS_ADMIN location for the files.

Checking NAMES.DIRECTORY_PATH

Make sure the client has the proper names resolution setting. The NAMES.DIRECTORY_PATH
parameter in the sqlnet.ora file controls the order in which the client resolves net service
names. If the parameter is not set, the default is local naming, OID, and then host naming.

If this parameter is set incorrectly, the client may never check the appropriate names
resolution type. For example, if you are using local naming and the parameter is set to
HOSTNAMES, the tnsnames.ora file will never be used to resolve the net service name. You
will receive an ORA-12154 "Could Not Resolve the Connect Identifier Specified"
error message.

Checking NAMES.DEFAULT_DOMAIN

NAMES.DEFAULT_DOMAIN is another common error. It was more common in older releases of
Oracle because the parameter defaulted to the value WORLD. Check the client sqlnet.ora file
to see whether the parameter is set. If the parameter has a value and you are using unqualified net service names, the parameter value is appended to the end of the net service name.
An unqualified service name is a service name that does not contain domain information.

For example, if you entered **sqlplus matt/casey@PROD** and the NAMES.DEFAULT_DOMAIN
is set to WORLD, Oracle appends .WORLD to the net service name; as a result, Oracle passes
the command as sqlplus matt/casey@PROD.WORLD. You will receive an ORA-12154 "Could
Not Resolve the Connect Identifier Specified" error message if the service name
should not include the .WORLD domain extension. You use this parameter only if you are
using a hierarchical naming convention.

Checking for Client-Side Error Codes

You should next check for client-side error codes. Here is a summary of some of the common client-side Oracle error messages you might encounter. They are discussed in detail in
the following sections.

```
ORA-12154 "TNS: Could not resolve connect identifier specified"
ORA-12198 "TNS: Could not find path to destination"
```

```
ORA-12203 "TNS: Unable to connect to destination"
ORA-12533 "TNS: Illegal address parameters"
ORA-12541 "TNS: No listener"
```

ORA-12154 This indicates that the client cannot find the service listed in the tnsnames.ora file. Some of the causes of this were previously described, such as the file is not in the proper directory or the TNS_ADMIN variable is not specified or specified incorrectly.

ORA-12198 and **ORA-12203** These indicate that the client found an entry for the service in the tnsnames.ora file but the service specified was not found. Check to make sure the service specified in the tnsnames.ora file actually points to a valid database service.

ORA-12533 This indicates that you have configured the ADDRESS section of the tnsnames.ora file incorrectly. Check to make sure the syntax is correct or re-create the definition using the Oracle Net Manager tool.

ORA-12541 This indicates that the client contacted a server that does not have a listener running on the specified port. Make sure the listener is started on the server and that the listening port specifications on the client and the server match.

An Overview of Oracle Shared Server

Oracle Shared Server is an optional configuration of Oracle Server that allows the server to support a larger number of concurrent connections without increasing physical resource requirements. It does so by sharing resources among groups of users.

Shared Server is suitable for high-think applications. High-think applications are composed of small transactions with natural pauses in the transaction patterns, which makes them good candidates for Oracle Shared Server connections. Many web-based applications fit this model. These types of applications are typically form-based and involve submissions of small amounts of information to the database with small result sets returned to the client.

Oracle manages dedicated server and shared server connections differently. As a DBA, you need to be able to identify these differences. This knowledge will help you better understand the advantages and disadvantages of Oracle Shared Server and when it might be advantageous to use Oracle Shared Server in your environment.

Dedicated Server vs. Shared Server

If you have ever gone to an upscale restaurant, you may have had your own personal waitperson. That waitperson is there to greet you and escort you to your seat. They take your order for food and drinks and even help prepare your order. No matter how many other patrons enter the restaurant, your waitperson is responsible for serving only your requests. Therefore, your service is consistent—if the person is a good waitperson.

A *dedicated server* environment works in much the same way. Every client connection is associated with a dedicated server process, sometimes called a *shadow process,* on the machine where the Oracle server exists. No matter how many other connections are made to the server, the same dedicated server is always responsible for processing only your requests. You use the services of that server process until you disconnect from the Oracle server.

Most restaurants operate more like shared servers. When you walk in, you are assigned a waitperson, but they may be responsible for serving many other tables. This is good for the restaurant because they can serve more customers without increasing the staff. It may be fine for you as well, if the restaurant is not too busy and the waitperson is not responsible for too many tables. Also, if most of the orders are small, the staff can keep up with the requests, and the service will be as good as if you had your own waitperson.

In a diner, things work slightly differently; the waitperson takes your order and places it on a turnstile. If the diner has multiple cooks, the order is picked up from the turnstile and prepared by one of the available cooks. When the cook completes the preparation of the dinner, it is placed in a location where the waitperson can pick it up and bring it to your table.

This is how an Oracle Shared Server environment works. In an Oracle Shared Server environment, *dispatcher* processes are responsible for servicing client requests. These processes are capable of handling requests from many clients. This is different from the dedicated server environment, where a single client process is handled by a single server process. Like the waitperson in the diner, a dispatcher can be responsible for taking the orders of many clients.

 When using Oracle Shared Server, idle connections can be reused and allow several users to connect to the database, thus improving scalability.

When you request something from the server, it is the dispatcher's responsibility to take your request and place it in a location called a *request queue*. The request queue functions like the turnstile in the diner analogy. All dispatcher processes place their client requests in one request queue, which is a structure contained in the system global area (SGA).

Shared Server processes, like cooks in a diner, are responsible for fulfilling the client requests. The Oracle Shared Server process executes the request and places the result into an area of the SGA called a *response queue*. Every dispatcher has its own response queue. The dispatcher picks up the completed request from the response queue and returns the results to the client. Figure 12.19 illustrates the following processing steps for a Shared Server request:

1. The client passes a request to the dispatcher serving it.
2. The dispatcher places the request on a request queue in the SGA.
3. One of the Shared Server processes executes the request.
4. The Shared Server places the completed request on the dispatcher's response queue of the SGA.
5. The dispatcher picks up the completed request from the response queue.
6. The completed request is passed back to the client.

 Requests placed in the request queue are processed on a first-in, first-out basis (FIFO). Currently, there is no way to prioritize requests within the queue.

FIGURE 12.19   Request processing in Shared Server

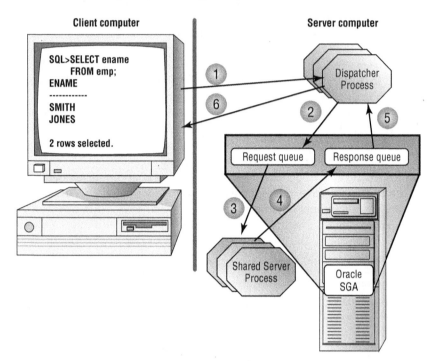

Advantages and Disadvantages of Shared Server

Oracle Shared Server is used when server resources, such as memory and active processes, become constrained. People tend to throw more hardware at problems such as these; this will likely remedy the problem, but it may be an unnecessary expense.

If your system is experiencing these problems, Oracle Shared Server allows you to support the same number or a greater number of connections without requiring additional hardware. As a result, Oracle Shared Server tends to decrease the overall memory and process requirements on the server. Because clients are sharing processes, the total number of processes is reduced. This translates into resource savings on the server.

Shared Server also allows for connection pooling. Connection pooling enables the database server to disconnect an idle Oracle Shared Server connection to service an incoming request. The idle connection is still active and is re-enabled once the client makes the next request. The connection pooling feature of Oracle Shared Server allows it to handle a larger number of requests without having to start additional dispatcher processes. You configure connection pooling by adding attributes to one of the Oracle Shared Server parameters.

See the section "Configuring Connection Pooling with the Dispatch-ers Parameter" later in this chapter to see how connection pooling is configured.

Shared Server is also required to take advantage of certain network options, such as connection multiplexing and client access control, which are features of Oracle Connection Manager. Oracle Connection Manager is a facility provided by Oracle that controls access to database services and multiplex connections in an Oracle environment. The access control component of Oracle Connection Manager allows you to configure rules that allow or disallow fulfillment of a connection request. The multiplexing component acts as a concentrator feature. It funnels multiple client sessions through a shared network connection from the Oracle Connection Manager server to the database server.

Oracle Shared Server also has some disadvantages. Applications that generate a significant amount of network traffic or result in large result sets are not good candidates for Shared Server connections. Think of the earlier diner analogy. Your service is fine until two parties of twelve people show up. All of a sudden, the waitperson is overwhelmed with work from these two other tables, and your service begins to suffer. The same thing would happen in a Shared Server environment. If requests for large quantities of information start going to the dispatchers, the dispatchers can become overwhelmed, and you can see performance suffer for the other clients connected to the dispatcher. This, in turn, increases your response times. Dedicated processes better serve these types of applications.

Some functions are not allowed when you are using an Oracle Shared Server connection. You cannot start up, shut down, or perform certain kinds of recovery of an Oracle server when you are connected via a shared server.

Also, you should not perform certain administrative tasks using Oracle Shared Server connections, including bulk loads of data, index and table rebuilds, and table analysis. These types of tasks deal with manipulating large datasets and should use dedicated connections.

Oracle Shared Server is a scalability enhancement option, not a performance enhancement option. If you are looking for a performance increase, Shared Server is not what you should be configuring. Use Shared Server only if you are experiencing the system constraint problems discussed earlier in this chapter. You will always have equal or better performance in a dedicated server environment.

Oracle Shared Server Infrastructure

As described in the previous section, you manage client connections quite differently when using Oracle Shared Server as opposed to using a dedicated server. To accommodate the change, several modifications take place inside the internal memory structures of the Oracle server. The way in which the database and listener interact is also affected when using Oracle Shared Server. It is important to understand these changes when configuring and managing Oracle Shared Server.

Certain changes are necessary to the memory structures within Oracle to provide the Shared Server capability. Let's see what changes within the Oracle infrastructure are needed to provide this support.

PGA and SGA Changes When Using Oracle Shared Server

When Oracle Shared Server is configured, Oracle adds two new types of structures to the SGA: request queues and response queues. These structures do not exist in a dedicated server environment. There is one request queue for all dispatchers, but each dispatcher has its own response queue. Therefore, if you have four dispatchers, you will have one request queue and four response queues. The request queue is located in the SGA where the dispatcher places client requests. A Shared Server process executes each request and places the completed request in the dispatcher's response queue.

In a dedicated server environment, each server has a memory segment called a *program global area* (PGA). The PGA is an area of memory where information about each client session is maintained. This information includes bind variables, cursor information, and the client's sort area. In an Oracle Shared Server environment, this information is moved from the PGA to an area of the SGA called the *user global area* (UGA). You can configure a special area of the SGA called the *large pool* to accommodate the bulk of the UGA.

Each connection being serviced by a dispatcher is bound to a shared memory segment and forms a *virtual circuit*. The dispatcher uses the shared memory segment to manage communications between the client and the Oracle database. The Oracle Shared Server processes use the virtual circuits to send and receive information to the appropriate dispatcher process.

> To limit the amount of UGA memory a session can allocate, set the PRIVATE_SGA resource limit in the user's profile.

The Role of the Listener in an Oracle Shared Server Environment

The listener plays an important role in the Oracle Shared Server environment. The listener supplies the client with the address of the dispatcher to connect to when a user requests connections to an Oracle Shared Server. The listener maintains a list of dispatchers available from the Oracle Shared Server. The Oracle background process LREG notifies the listener as to which dispatcher is responsible for servicing each virtual circuit. The listener is then aware of the number of connections that the dispatcher is managing. This information allows the listener to take advantage of dispatcher load balancing.

Load balancing allows the listener to make intelligent decisions about which dispatcher to redirect client connections to so that no one dispatcher becomes overburdened. When the listener receives a connection request, it looks at the current connection load for each dispatcher and redirects the client connection request to the least-loaded dispatcher. The listener determines the least-loaded dispatcher for all nodes if Real Application Clusters (RAC) are being used, followed by the least-loaded instance for the node, and finally by the least-loaded dispatcher for the instance. By doing so, the listener ensures that connections are evenly distributed across dispatchers.

The listener can either redirect the client connection to an available dispatcher or directly hand off the request to the dispatcher. The latter is performed whenever possible and is done typically when the listener and database service exist on the same node. When the listener and database service exist on different nodes, the redirection method is used.

When a client connection terminates, the listener is updated to reflect the change in the number of connections that the dispatcher is handling.

Configuring the Oracle Shared Server

You can configure Oracle Shared Server in a number of ways. You can configure it at the time the database is created, you can use Enterprise Manager to configure it after the database has been created, or you can manually configure it by editing initialization parameters. We'll discuss the parameters necessary to configure Oracle Shared Server. We'll also give examples of how to configure Shared Server at database creation or after the database is created using EM.

Defining the Shared Server Parameters

You configure Oracle Shared Server by adding parameters to the Oracle initialization file. These parameters identify the number and type of dispatchers, the number of shared servers, and the name of the database you want to associate with Shared Server.

One advantage of Oracle Database 12c is that all the parameters necessary to manage Oracle Shared Server can be changed dynamically. This fulfills one of your primary goals of ensuring the highest degree of database availability possible. Let's take a look at the parameters used to manage Oracle Shared Server.

Using the DISPATCHERS Parameter

The DISPATCHERS parameter defines the number of dispatchers that should start when the instance is started. This parameter specifies the number of dispatchers and the type of protocol to which the dispatchers can respond. If you configured your database using the Database Configuration Assistant, this parameter may already be configured.

You can add dispatchers dynamically using the ALTER SYSTEM command.

The DISPATCHERS parameter has a number of optional attributes. Table 12.7 describes several of them. You need to specify only ADDRESS, DESCRIPTION, or PROTOCOL for a DISPATCHERS definition. All the attributes for this parameter can be abbreviated.

TABLE 12.7   Summary of DISPATCHER Attributes

Attribute	Abbreviations	Description
ADDRESS	ADD or ADDR	Specifies the network protocol address of the end point on which the dispatchers listen.
CONNECTIONS	CON or CONN	The maximum number of network connections per dispatcher. The default value varies by operating system.

TABLE 12.7 Summary of DISPATCHER Attributes *(continued)*

Attribute	Abbreviations	Description
DESCRIPTION	DES or DESC	The network description of the end point where the dispatcher is listening, including the protocol being listened for.
DISPATCHERS	DIS or DISP	The number of dispatchers to start when the instance is started. The default is 1.
LISTENER	LIS or LIST	The address of the listener to which LREG sends connection information. This attribute needs to be set only when the listener is nonlocal, it uses a port other than 1521, the default port and the LOCAL_LISTENER parameter have not been specified, or the listener is resident on a different network node.
PROTOCOL	PRO or PROT	The network protocol for the dispatcher to listen for. This is the only required attribute.
SESSIONS	SES or SESS	The maximum number of network sessions allowable for this dispatcher. This will vary by operating system but predominantly defaults to 16KB.
SERVICE	SER or SERV	The Oracle net service name that the dispatcher registers with the listener. If it is not supplied, the dispatcher registers with the services listed in the SERVICE_NAMES initialization parameter.
POOL	POO	Provides connection pooling capabilities to provide the ability to handle a larger number of connections.

The two main attributes are DISPATCHERS and PROTOCOL. For example, if you want to configure three TCP/IP dispatchers and two IPC dispatchers, you set the parameter as follows:

```
DISPATCHERS = "(PRO=TCP)(DIS=3)(PRO=IPC)(DIS=2)"
```

You must consider several factors (discussed in the following section) when determining the appropriate setting for the DISPATCHERS parameter.

DETERMINING THE NUMBER OF DISPATCHERS TO START

The number of dispatchers you start depends on your particular configuration. Your operating system may place a limit on the number of connections that one dispatcher can handle. Consult your operating-system documentation to obtain this information.

When determining the number of dispatchers to start, consider the type of work that the database sessions will be performing and the number of concurrent connections that your database will be supporting. The more data-intensive the operations and the larger the number of concurrent connections, the fewer sessions each dispatcher should handle. Generally speaking, a starting point is to allow 50 concurrent sessions for each dispatcher.

You can use the following formula to determine the number of dispatchers to configure initially:

```
Number of Dispatchers = CEIL  (maximum number of concurrent sessions /
  connections per dispatcher)
```

For example, if you have 500 concurrent TCP/IP connections and you want each dispatcher to manage 50 concurrent connections, you need 10 dispatchers. You set your DISPATCHERS parameter as follows:

```
DISPATCHERS = "(PRO=TCP)(DIS=10)"
```

You can determine the number of concurrent connections by querying the V$SESSION view. This view shows you the number of clients currently connected to the Oracle server. Here is an example of the query:

```
SQL> select sid,serial#,username,server,program from v$session
  2  where username is not null;
    SID   SERIAL# USERNAME   SERVER    PROGRAM
--------- --------- ---------- --------- ---------------
      7        13     SCOTT   DEDICATED SQLPLUS.EXE
      8        12     SCOTT   DEDICATED SQLPLUS.EXE
      9         4    SYSTEM   DEDICATED SQLPLUS.EXE
```

In this example, three users are connected to the server. You can ignore any sessions that do not have a username because these would be the Oracle background processes such as PMON and SMON. If you take a sampling of this view over a typical work period, you get an idea of the average number of concurrent connections for your system. You can then use this number as a guide when you establish the starting number of dispatchers.

MANAGING THE NUMBER OF DISPATCHERS

You can start additional dispatchers or remove dispatchers dynamically using the ALTER SYSTEM command. You can start any number of dispatchers up to the MAX_DISPATCHERS setting, which is discussed next. Here is an example of adding three TCP/IP dispatchers to a system configured with two TCP/IP dispatchers:

```
ALTER SYSTEM SET DISPATCHERS="(PRO=TCP)(DIS=5)";
```

Notice that you set the number to the total number of dispatchers you want, not to the number of dispatchers you want to add.

You use additional attributes to the DISPATCHERS parameter to configure connection pooling.

CONFIGURING CONNECTION POOLING WITH THE DISPATCHERS PARAMETER

Connection pooling gives Oracle Shared Server the ability to handle a larger volume of connections by automatically disconnecting idle connections and using the idle connections to service incoming client requests. If the idle connections become active again, the connection to the dispatchers is automatically reestablished. This provides added scalability to Oracle Shared Server. If you manage applications that have a large number of possible client connections but also have a large number of idle connections, you might want to consider configuring this Oracle Shared Server option. Web applications are good candidates for connection pooling because they are typically composed of a large client base with small numbers of concurrent connections.

You enable connection pooling by adding attributes to the DISPATCHERS parameter. The POOL attribute specifies that a dispatcher is allowed to perform connection pooling. Set this attribute to the value ON to enable connection pooling for a dispatcher. You also need to specify the TICK attribute, which sets the number of 10-minute increments of inactivity for a connection to be considered idle.

Here is an example that turns on connection pooling:

```
DISPATCHERS="(PROTOCOL=tcp)(DISPATCHERS=1)(POOL=on)(TICK=1)
    (CONNECTIONS=500)(SESSIONS=1000)"
```

In this example, you want to turn on connection pooling. An idle connection is considered any connection with 10 minutes of inactivity. You want the TCP/IP dispatcher to handle a maximum of 500 concurrent connections and a maximum of 1,000 sessions per dispatcher.

Using the MAX_DISPATCHERS Parameter

You should set the MAX_DISPATCHERS parameter to the maximum number of dispatchers you anticipate needing for Oracle Shared Server. In Oracle Database 12*c*, this parameter can be set dynamically using the ALTER SYSTEM command. The maximum number of processes that a dispatcher can run concurrently is operating-system dependent. Use the following formula to set this parameter:

```
MAX_DISPATCHERS = (maximum number of concurrent sessions/connections
    per dispatcher)
```

Here is an example of the parameter and adjusting the parameter using the ALTER SYSTEM command:

```
ALTER SYSTEM SET MAX_DISPATCHERS=10;
```

In the ALTER SYSTEM example, the MAX_DISPATCHERS parameter is being set to 10. This will be the maximum number of dispatchers that Oracle Shared Server can start simultaneously.

Using the SHARED_SERVERS Parameter

The SHARED_SERVERS parameter specifies the minimum number of shared servers to start and retain when the Oracle instance is started. A setting of 0 or no setting means that shared servers will not be used. If dispatchers have been configured, the default value of SHARED_SERVERS is 1. This parameter can be changed dynamically, so even if shared servers are not configured when the instance starts, they can be configured without bringing the Oracle instance down and restarting it.

The number of servers necessary depends on the type of activities your users are performing. Oracle monitors the response queue loads, starts additional shared servers as needed, and removes these shared servers when the servers are no longer needed. Generally, for the types of high-think applications that will be using shared server connections, 25 concurrent connections per shared server should be adequate. If the users are going to require larger result sets or are doing more intensive processing, you'll want to reduce this ratio.

Here is an example of setting the SHARED_SERVERS parameter:

```
SHARED_SERVERS = 3
```

You can start additional Oracle shared servers or reduce the number of Oracle shared servers dynamically using the ALTER SYSTEM command. You can start any number of Oracle shared servers up to the MAX_SERVERS setting. Here is an example of adding three additional Oracle shared servers to a system initially configured with two shared servers:

```
ALTER SYSTEM SET SHARED_SERVERS = 5;
```

Notice that you set the number to the total number of Oracle shared servers you want, not to the number of Oracle shared servers you want to add.

Using the SHARED_SERVER_SESSIONS Parameter

The SHARED_SERVER_SESSIONS parameter specifies the total number of Oracle Shared Server sessions that are allowed for the Oracle instance. If the number of Oracle Shared Server client connections reaches this limit, any clients that attempt to connect via an Oracle Shared Server connection will receive the following error message:

```
ERROR:
ORA-00018 maximum number of sessions exceeded
```

Once the number of Oracle Shared Server connections falls below this number, additional Shared Server connections can be established. Using this parameter limits the total number of Shared Server sessions. Dedicated server connections are still allowed if this limit is reached. This parameter can be set in the Oracle initialization file and can be modified dynamically using the ALTER SYSTEM command. Here is an example of how you specify the initialization parameter:

```
SHARED_SERVER_SESSIONS = 2
```

Here is an example of how to dynamically modify the parameter using the ALTER SYSTEM command:

```
ALTER SYSTEM SET SHARED_SERVER_SESSIONS = 5;
```

Using the MAX_SHARED_SERVERS Parameter

The MAX_SHARED_SERVERS parameter sets the maximum number of Oracle shared servers that can be running concurrently. This number can be modified dynamically using the ALTER SYSTEM command. Generally, you should set this parameter to accommodate your heaviest work times. If no value is specified for MAX_SHARED_SERVERS, the number of Oracle shared servers that can be started is unlimited, which is also the default setting.

The V$SHARED_SERVER_MONITOR view can assist in determining the maximum number of Oracle shared servers that have been started since the Oracle instance was started.

Here is an example of the parameter and the ALTER SYSTEM command that will change the value MAX_SHARED_SERVER to 20:

```
ALTER SYSTEM SET MAX_SHARED_SERVERS = 20;
```

Using the CIRCUITS Parameter

The CIRCUITS parameter manages the total number of virtual circuits allowed for all incoming and outgoing network sessions. There is no default value for this parameter, and it does influence the total size of the SGA at system startup. Generally, you do not manually configure this parameter unless there is a need to specifically limit the number of virtual circuits.

Here is an example of the parameter:

```
CIRCUITS = 200
```

You can also use the ALTER SYSTEM command to change the parameter as follows:

```
ALTER SYSTEM SET CIRCUITS = 300;
```

Now that you understand the parameters that are needed to use the Oracle Shared Server, you need to know how to configure these parameters.

Managing a Shared Server

If the Oracle Shared Server parameters were configured dynamically using the ALTER SYSTEM command or at database creation, it isn't necessary to stop and start the server. After you configure the Oracle Shared Server parameters, you need to understand how to view information about Oracle Shared Server. Oracle provides a set of dynamic performance views that you can use to gather information about the Oracle Shared Server configuration and the performance of Oracle Shared Server. You can also gather information about Oracle Shared Server connections by using the lsnrctl utility.

In the following sections, we will explain how to display information about Oracle Shared Server connections using the listener utility and discuss the various dynamic performance views used to manage Shared Server.

Displaying Information about Shared Server Connections Using the Listener Utility

You can use the lsnrctl command-line listener utility to display information about the dispatcher processes. Remember from the previous section that the Oracle background process LREG registers dispatcher information with the listener. The listener keeps track of the current connection load for all the dispatchers.

Use the `lsnrctl services` query to view information about dispatchers. The following example shows a listener listening for two TCP/IP dispatchers:

```
$ lsnrctl services

LSNRCTL for Linux: Version 12.1.0.1.0 - Production on 30-NOV-2013 01:48:43
Copyright (c) 1991, 2013, Oracle.  All rights reserved.

Connecting to (DESCRIPTION=(ADDRESS=(PROTOCOL=TCP)(HOST=btlnx63)(PORT=1521)))
Services Summary...
Service "C12DB1" has 1 instance(s).
  Instance "C12DB1", status READY, has 2 handler(s) for this service...
    Handler(s):
      "DEDICATED" established:3 refused:0 state:ready
         LOCAL SERVER
      "D000" established:3 refused:0 current:0 max:500 state:ready
         DISPATCHER <machine: btlnx63, pid: 32320>
         (ADDRESS=(PROTOCOL=tcp)(HOST=btlnx63)(PORT=13370))
Service "C12DB1XDB" has 1 instance(s).
  Instance "C12DB1", status READY, has 0 handler(s) for this service...
Service "bt1pdb" has 1 instance(s).
  Instance "C12DB1", status READY, has 2 handler(s) for this service...
    Handler(s):
      "DEDICATED" established:3 refused:0 state:ready
         LOCAL SERVER
      "D000" established:3 refused:0 current:0 max:500 state:ready
         DISPATCHER <machine: btlnx63, pid: 32320>
         (ADDRESS=(PROTOCOL=tcp)(HOST=btlnx63)(PORT=13370))
Service "c12pdb1" has 1 instance(s).
  Instance "C12DB1", status READY, has 2 handler(s) for this service...
    Handler(s):
      "DEDICATED" established:3 refused:0 state:ready
         LOCAL SERVER
      "D000" established:3 refused:0 current:0 max:500 state:ready
         DISPATCHER <machine: btlnx63, pid: 32320>
         (ADDRESS=(PROTOCOL=tcp)(HOST=btlnx63)(PORT=13370))
```

Notice that the listing displays how many connections each dispatcher is managing, the listening location of the dispatcher, and the process ID of the dispatcher. The display also shows how many total client connections were established and how many were refused by each dispatcher since the time it was started. This summary information can be helpful when looking at how well the connections are balanced across all the dispatchers. It also can be helpful to see how many connections were refused. A connection can be refused if a user supplies an invalid user ID or password or reaches the MAX_SHARED_SERVER limit.

Requesting a Dedicated Connection in a Shared Server Environment

You can configure Oracle Shared Server connections and dedicated server connections to connect to a single Oracle server. This is advantageous if you have a mix of database activity. Some types of activities are well suited to Oracle Shared Server connections, and other types of activities are better suited to dedicated connections.

By default, if Oracle Shared Server is configured, a client is connected to a dispatcher unless the client explicitly requests a dedicated connection. As part of the connection descriptor, the client has to send information requesting a dedicated connection. Clients can request dedicated connections if the names resolution method is local naming. You cannot use this option with host naming. If local naming is being used, you can make the necessary changes to the tnsnames.ora file to allow dedicated connections. You can make these changes manually, or you can use Oracle Net Manager.

Configuring Dedicated Connections Manually

If you are using local naming, you can add a parameter to the service-name entry in the tnsnames.ora file. The parameter (SERVER=DEDICATED) is added to the DBA net service name. Here is an example of the entry in the tnsnames.ora file:

```
ORCL4DBA =
  (DESCRIPTION =
    (ADDRESS = (PROTOCOL = TCP)(HOST = XYZ01)(PORT = 1521))
    (CONNECT_DATA =
      (SERVICE_NAME = orcl)
      (SERVER = DEDICATED)  # Request a dedicated connection for DBA
    )
  )
```

You can accomplish the same thing using the Easy Connect method as well:

```
XYZ01:1521/ORCL:DEDICATED
```

Configuring Dedicated Connections Using Oracle Net Manager

You can use Oracle Net Manager to modify the connection type for a service. In Windows, Oracle Net Manager is a tool; in Unix, you open Oracle Net Manager by executing netmgr.

After you start Oracle Net Manager, follow these steps:

1. Under Service Naming in the left pane, select the service name you want to modify.

2. Click the Connection Type drop-down list in the Service Identification section, and choose Dedicated Server.

Choosing the Appropriate Connection Method Makes a Difference

As a DBA, you've configured Oracle Shared Server and are monitoring the dispatchers and Shared Server performance daily. The Shared Server environment has been running smoothly for months, but your monitoring starts to indicate that the wait times have increased significantly over the past week. You are also starting to receive complaints from the user community regarding system response time.

You start to investigate whether there have been any significant changes to the hardware, the network, or the database application. You confer with the systems administration and network group and find that no changes have taken place. Then your discussion with the applications group reveals that a new ad hoc reporting utility has been installed and a small number of administrators are starting to use the tool. These users are connecting via Oracle Shared Server and are requesting large datasets via the ad hoc reporting tool.

You suggest to the applications team that the administrators connect to the database using dedicated connections to alleviate the load on the shared servers. After modifying the appropriate network files, you again monitor the Shared Server wait times and discover that the waits have fallen back in line with what you were seeing prior to the deployment of the ad hoc reporting tool.

Understanding Database Resident Connection Pooling

DRCP was introduced in Oracle Database 11g to address scalability requirements where there are large numbers of connections to the database with minimal resource usage. DRCP has a set of dedicated database server processes known as *pooled servers* that can be shared across multiple applications. A pooled server is a combination of server process and database session. A connection broker process manages the pooled servers at the database instance level. DRCP configuration can coexist with a database running dedicated or shared server architecture.

Database Resident Connection Pooling allows multiple Oracle clients to share a server-side pool of sessions. To share the pool, the user ID must be the same. Clients can connect and disconnect without the overhead of creating a new server side session. DRCP is most suitable for applications that connect and disconnect frequently, but use the same database credentials for all connections—most PHP applications behave this way.

Configuring DRCP

DCHP is started or enabled using the Oracle supplied package DBMS_CONNECTION_POOL. To start the pool, execute the START_POOL procedure after logging into the database using SYSDBA connection as follows:

```
SQL> execute dbms_connection_pool.start_pool;
```

Once the pool is started, it remains active until it is explicitly shut down using the STOP_POOL procedure. The pool is automatically restarted during the database cycle, if the pool was active during shutdown.

When users or applications are connecting to the database, it must use the POOLED server type in the connection, by using:

Easy Connect: host:port/service_name:POOLED

Local Naming: Use SERVER = POOLED in the CONNECT_DATA section.

JDBC: jdbc:oracle:thin:@//host:port/service_name:POOLED

When the pool is started, the default configuration and status of the pool can be viewed by querying the DBA_CPOOL_INFO dictionary view as follows:

```
SQL> select * from dba_cpool_info;
```

```
CONNECTION_POOL         : SYS_DEFAULT_CONNECTION_POOL
STATUS                  : ACTIVE
MINSIZE                 : 4
MAXSIZE                 : 40
INCRSIZE                : 2
SESSION_CACHED_CURSORS  : 20
INACTIVITY_TIMEOUT      : 300
MAX_THINK_TIME          : 120
MAX_USE_SESSION         : 500000
MAX_LIFETIME_SESSION    : 86400
NUM_CBROK               : 1
MAXCONN_CBROK           : 40000
```

 The previous code output is formatted using Tom Kyte's print_ table procedure, for readability of the output. The print_table procedure can be found at http://asktom.oracle.com/pls/ apex/f?p=100:11:0:::::P11_QUESTION_ID:1035431863958.

The configuration parameters can be modified using the DBMS_CONNECTION_POOL .CONFIGURE_POOL procedure. The procedure changes the configuration of all parameters, either with the supplied new value in the procedure or by using default value for the parameter. The parameters to the procedure are pretty much the same columns in the DBA_CPOOL_INFO view.

```
DBMS_CONNECTION_POOL.CONFIGURE_POOL (
    pool_name               IN VARCHAR2 DEFAULT 'SYS_DEFAULT_CONNECTION_POOL',
    minsize                 IN NUMBER   DEFAULT 4,
    maxsize                 IN NUMBER   DEFAULT 40,
    incrsize                IN NUMBER   DEFAULT 2,
    session_cached_cursors  IN NUMBER   DEFAULT 20,
    inactivity_timeout      IN NUMBER   DEFAULT 300,
    max_think_time          IN NUMBER   DEFAULT 120,
    max_use_session         IN NUMBER   DEFAULT 500000,
    max_lifetime_session    IN NUMBER   DEFAULT 86400,
    num_cbrok               IN NUMBER   DEFAULT 1,
    maxconn_cbrok           IN NUMBER   DEFAULT 40000);
```

When you want to change only one parameter at a time and do not want to impact the other parameters, use the procedure ALTER_POOL instead of CONFIGURE_POOL. For example, if you want to change the increment number of pooled servers when pooled servers are unavailable at application request time, use the code as follows:

```
SQL> EXECUTE dbms_connection_pool.alter_param('','incrsize',5);
```

To restore all of the configuration parameters to their default values, use the procedure RESTORE_DEFAULTS as in:

```
SQL> EXECUTE dbms_connection_pool.restore_defaults();
```

Even though all of the procedures in DBMS_CONNECTION_POOL accept the pool name as a parameter, as of Oracle Database 12c Release 1, only one pool can be configured, and its name must be SYS_DEFAULT_CONNECTION_POOL if specified. The first parameter to all of the procedures is the pool name, which defaults to SYS_DEFAULT_CONNECTION_POOL.

Comparing Connection Architectures

To understand more about DRCP, let's compare the architecture with dedicated and shared server architecture. Figure 12.20 details the architectural differences between a dedicated connection, shared connection, and pooled connection. This section describes Figure 12.20 and gives a summary review of the architectures.

FIGURE 12.20 Comparing Oracle connection architectures

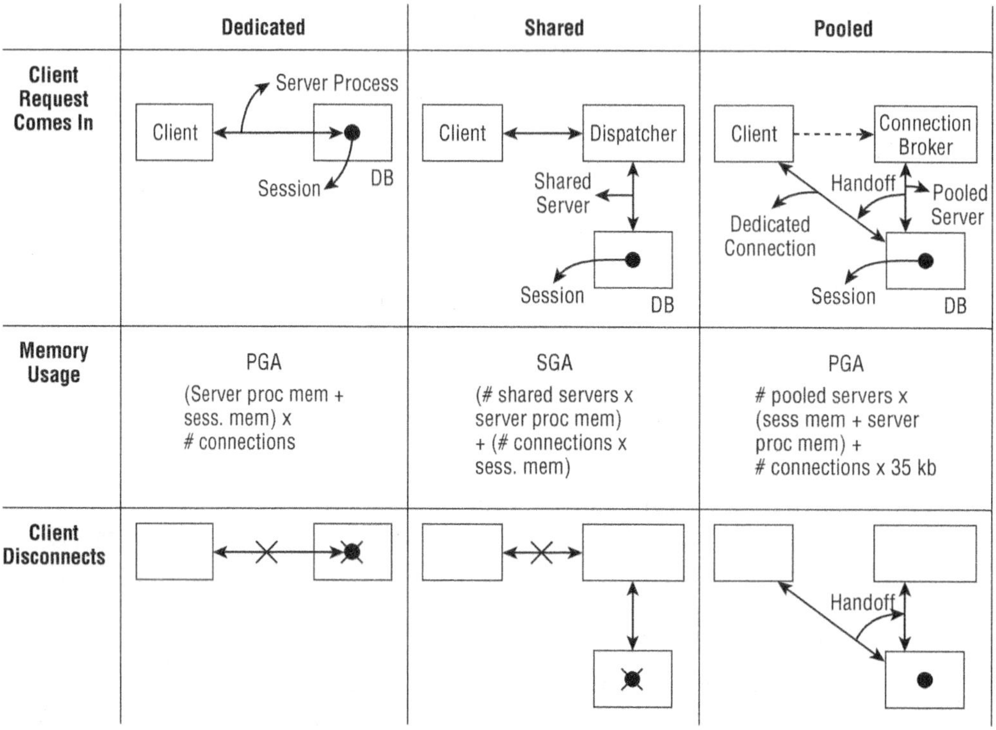

As shown in Figure 12.20, when a new connection request from a client is made, a dedicated server process is started and a dedicated session is created. The client communicates directly with the database using the dedicated server process. All the requests from the client are processed by this process. The session memory is allocated from PGA, and database server memory usage is in direct proportion to the number of connections. Each client connection has a process and session. When the client disconnects, the session and server process are terminated, and memory resources are given back to the server.

In the shared server architecture, a predefined number of server processes are started as defined by the SHARED_SERVERS initialization parameter. When a new connection request from a client is made, the listener redirects the connection to the dispatcher. When a request from a client is made, it goes to the request queue, and an available shared server process satisfies the request and gives the result to the response queue. From there, the result is given to the client by the dispatcher. The session memory is allocated from SGA, and the database memory usage is proportional to the number of shared server processes started. Each client has a dedicated session but no dedicated process. The request is fulfilled by any available process. When the client disconnects, the session is terminated and the dispatcher process is either terminated or given back to the session multiplexing pool.

In the pooled server architecture, when the connection broker is started, it starts the dedicated server processes and session. When a new connection request from a client is made, the listener directs the connection to the connection broker. The connection broker hands off an already established server process and session to the client. At this point, the connection is similar to a dedicated server. The session memory is allocated from PGA, similar to a dedicated server. The database memory usage is proportional to the number of pooled servers started. When the client disconnects, the process is handed back to the connection broker, which could be reused by a subsequent connection request with the same database user ID. If PHP application is used, the application server retains a network connection to the connection broker.

Oracle Shared Server and pooled server architectures require Oracle Net, even if the client is on the same machine as the database. A dedicated session can connect to the database directly without Oracle Net on the database machine.

Deciding on the Connection Method

Deciding which connection method to use depends on the applications that use the database and the amount of resources you have on the database server. The following may be used as a general guideline.

Use a dedicated connection when:

- The resources on the database server are not constrained.
- Clients connect from various sources, connect with different database user IDs, or stay connected for a long time.
- You are running a batch job, where no idle time is involved.
- You are running RMAN backups or performing certain database administrative tasks such as database startup and shutdown.
- You are connecting to the database without using Oracle Net.
- Certain applications like Oracle EBS do not support the use of shared servers, or the application holds the connection from the application server to database.

Use a shared server when:

- The resources on the database server are constrained.
- You are increasing the scalability of applications without any application architectural change.
- You are increasing the number of clients simultaneously connected to the database.

Use DRCP when:

- There are many connection requests to the database and most connections use the same database account.

- The connections are short, like typical PHP applications.
- You are sharing resources between multiple client applications and middle-tier application servers.
- You are reducing resource usage on the database host and increasing scalability.

Communicating Between Databases

So far in this chapter you have learned how an application or user connects to the database, how the components communicate, how the various connection architectures work. In this section, you will learn how an Oracle database can communicate with another database and share information. Communication between Oracle databases is facilitated through *database link* and the configuration known as *distributed database system*. A distributed database system allows applications to access data from local and remote databases. In a *homogenous distributed database system*, each database is an Oracle database. In a *heterogeneous distributed database system*, at least one of the databases is not an Oracle database.

Any heterogeneous distributed database system that connects to a non-Oracle database from an Oracle database uses Oracle transparent gateways. The transparent gateway has agents specific to the type of database. If the non-Oracle database supports protocols such as ODBC or OLE, then generic connectivity instead of transparent gateways can be used. Heterogeneous communication is beyond the scope of the OCA test.

Introduction to Database Links

A database link is the main component in the distributed database system. The database link helps a user access data from two databases as if the data is local to the database. Database links establish a connection from a source database to a target database, and this connection is always one-way. If you need two-way communication, another database link must be created with the source and target destination reversed.

There are two types of database links: private and public. A *private database link* is owned by a user, and the link is visible and accessible only to that user. You must log in as the user or schema to the database to create a private database link, meaning you cannot qualify the database link with a schema name and create the link under that user. A *public database link* is owned by the PUBLIC user and is accessible to all users in the database.

The database link configuration includes the username, the password, and the Oracle Net connection information used to connect to the remote database. To access a table or view from the remote database, you have to add *@database_link_name* to the table or view name. For example, if you are connected to the sales database in Chicago and want to see the sales information from Boston using a database link with the name *SALES_BOSTON*, you may do the following query:

```
SQL> SELECT 'CHICAGO' location, sum(amount) FROM OM.ORDERS_SUMMARY
     UNION ALL
     SELECT 'BOSTON' location, sum(amount) FROM OM.ORDERS_SUMMARY@SALES_BOSTON;
```

There is one database initialization parameter that determines how the database links are named. If the GLOBAL_NAMES parameter is set to TRUE, the database link name must be the same as the database name to which it connects.

Creating Database Links

A private database link is created using the CREATE DATABASE LINK statement, and the public database link is created using the CREATE PUBLIC DATABASE LINK statement. The rest of the syntax for both statements is exactly the same, as shown here:

```
CREATE [PUBLIC] DATABASE LINK dblink_name
[CONNECT TO user_name IDENTIFIED BY password]
USING connect_string;
```

The name of the database link is *dblink_name*. If the database link name does not have the domain name appended or it does not have any part separated by a dot (.), Oracle automatically appends the domain name to the database link name. For example, if the database domain name is BJS.COM, then if you specify the dblink name as SALES, Oracle creates the dblink name as SALES.BJS.COM. If the dblink name specified is SALES.BOSTON, then the link name created is also SALES.BOSTON, irrespective of the domain name.

> Objects in the remote database are referenced as schema.schema_object@
> database_link_name. A private or public synonym may be created to mask
> the link name or to improve readability and portability of code.

The CONNECT TO clause specifies the username and password to connect to the remote database. This is known as a *fixed user database link*. The user_name and password portion may be omitted in order to use the same credentials that were used to connect to the local database to connect to the remote database. This type of dblink is called *connected user database link*. The database link privileges depend on the user connecting to the remote database. It is not a good practice to use fixed user public database links that can update information on the remote database because the public link is accessible to every user in the local database.

Current user database links use the keywords CONNECT TO CURRENT_USER, and they recognize invoker rights in stored programs. Current user database links use a global user authenticated by an X.509 certificate and must be available on both databases. If the PL/SQL procedure or function owned by user JOHN is created with invoker rights, and if user MARY tries to execute the PL/SQL program, the database link used in the program will connect to the remote database using the ID and password of MARY. If the PL/SQL program is not created with invoker rights (default), then the database link in the program will connect as the owner of the program (JOHN) to the remote database.

The CONNECT TO clause specifies the Oracle Net connect information. You can provide a connection alias resolved by a tnsnames.ora file, the easy connection syntax, or the detailed Oracle Net connection syntax.

Table 12.8 shows a few examples of database link-creation statements to clarify the definitions.

TABLE 12.8   Database Link Examples

Code	Explanation
create database link sales.boston connect to om identified by ompwd using 'bostondb';	A private fixed user database link. The Oracle Net alias *bostondb* will be resolved using the tnsnames.ora file entry.
create public database link sales .boston connect to om identified by ompwd using 'bs1svr:1522/bosdb';	A public fixed user database link. No tnsnames.ora is required to connect to a remote database as Easy Connect information is used to create the link. Connect to service name *bosdb* on host *bs1svr* through listener listening on port *1522*.
create public database link sales .boston using '(DESCRIPTION = (ADDRESS_LIST = (ADDRESS = (PROTOCOL = TCP)(HOST = bs1svr)(PORT = 1522))) (CONNECT_DATA = (SERVICE_NAME = bosdb)))';	A public connected user database link. The ID and password used to connect in the database link will be the same ID and password used to connect to the local database. No tnsnames .ora is required, as Oracle Net connect information is provided in the link definition.

Summary

This chapter provided the foundation of knowledge you will need when you are designing, configuring, and managing the Oracle network infrastructure. Oracle Net manages the flow of information from client computers to Oracle servers and forms the foundation of all networked computing in the Oracle environment. Oracle Net provides services that can be divided into five main categories: connectivity, directory services, scalability, security, and accessibility.

Oracle Net provides support to *n*-tier architecture, where middleware components such as application servers are situated between the client and database server.

The listener is the main server-side component in the Oracle Net environment. Listener configuration information is stored in the listener.ora file, and you manage the listener using the lsnrctl command-line utility. You configure the listener by using the Oracle Net Manager. The Oracle Net Manager provides a graphical interface for creating most of the Oracle Net files you will use for Oracle, including the listener.ora file. If multiple listeners are configured, each one has a separate entry in the listener.ora file.

Depending on your network environment, the client configuration setups can vary from no work to configuring a number of files on the client. Local naming is the most popular of the names resolution methods, and it uses the tnsnames.ora file, which is typically located on each client, to resolve net service names. The client looks up the net service name in the tnsnames.ora file and uses the resulting connection descriptor information to connect to the Oracle server.

Shared Server is a configuration of the Oracle server that allows you to support a greater number of connections without the need for additional resources. In this configuration, user connections share processes called *dispatchers*. Dispatchers replace the dedicated server processes in a dedicated server environment. The Oracle Server is also configured with shared server processes that can process the requests of many clients. You add a number of parameters to the init.ora file to configure Shared Server. You can add dispatchers and shared servers dynamically after the Oracle server is started. You can add more shared servers and dispatchers up to the maximum value specified.

Database Resident Connection Pooling architecture improves the scalability and performance of web applications that connect to the database for a short duration and has large amounts of connections. The connection broker is started with a specified number of server processes. When clients connect, the server process is handed off to the client.

Communication between databases is achieved through database links. An object from the remote database is accessed using schema.schema_object@database_link_name. A database link can be private or public. Private links are accessible only to the user who owns the link. A fixed user link hard codes the user ID and password to connect to the remote database in the configuration definition. A connected user link uses the ID and password used to connect to the local database to connect to the remote database.

Exam Essentials

Understand what Oracle Net is and the functionality it provides.   Be able to list the categories of functionality that Oracle Net provides and explain the functionality that falls into each category. Also understand what functionality the Oracle Shared Server, Oracle Connection Manager, and Database Resident Connection Pooling options provide. In addition, be able to define Oracle Advanced Security and know when to use it.

Be able to define the main responsibilities of the Oracle listener.   To fully understand the function of the Oracle listener, you should understand how the listener responds to client connection requests.

Be able to define the `listener.ora` file and the ways in which the file is created.   To understand the purpose of this file, know its default contents and how to change it using the various Oracle tools. In addition, be able to define the sections of the file and know the definitions of the optional parameters it contains. Also understand the structure of the listener.ora file when one or more listeners are configured.

Understand how to use the `lsnrctl` command-line utility.   To start up and shut down the listener, know how to use the lsnrctl command-line utility. Be able to explain the command-line options for the lsnrctl utility, such as services, status, and reload. When using this utility, also know the options available to you, and be able to define the various set commands.

Understand the concepts of static and dynamic service registration.   Be able to define the difference between static service registration and dynamic service registration, and know the advantages of using dynamic service registration over static service registration. Also, be aware of the situations in which you have to use static service registration. Lastly, be familiar with the initialization parameters that you will need to set in order to enable dynamic service registration.

Define the Oracle client-side names resolution options.   Be able to define the Oracle client-side names resolution options. Know in which situations to use local naming, Oracle Easy Connect, host naming, and OID.

Define the local naming method.   In addition to knowing the meaning of the local naming method and what it does, understand how to use the Oracle Net Manager to configure this names resolution method. Understand the primary file used in the local naming method, the tnsnames.ora file.

Define the contents and structure of the `tnsnames.ora` file.   Be able to describe the tnsnames.ora file and the various sections of the file and to explain how the file is used. Understand the contents of the tnsnames.ora file so that you can identify syntax problems with the structure of entries in the file. Be familiar with the common locations of this file and how to set the TNS_ADMIN parameter to override the default location of this and the other client-side network files.

Define and correct client-side errors.   Understand the types of client-side connection errors that can occur. Be able to define these errors and understand the situations in which a client might encounter them.

Define Oracle Shared Server.   Be able to list the advantages of Shared Server compared to a dedicated server and when it is appropriate to consider both options.

Define Oracle Database Resident Connection Pooling.   Be able to list the advantages of DRCP compared to a dedicated server or shared server and when it is appropriate to consider DRCP.

Understand the changes that are made in the SGA and the PGA.   Make sure you understand that in a Shared Server environment, many PGA structures are moved in the large pool inside the SGA. This means the SGA will become larger and that the large pool will need to be configured in the init.ora file.

Know how to configure Oracle Shared Server.   Be able to define each of the parameters involved in the configuration of Oracle Shared Server. Know what parameters can be dynamically modified and what parameters require the Oracle instance to be restarted to take effect.

Know how to configure clients for different connection methods.   Be able to configure clients that need a dedicated connection to Oracle if it is running in Shared Server mode. Know how to connect to DRCP pool.

Learn the various methods a database link can be configured.   Understand the difference between private and public database links. Know how to configure fixed user database links and connected user database links.

Review Questions

1. Which of the following files must be present on the Oracle server to start a nondefault Oracle listener?

    A. listener.ora

    B. lsnrctl.ora

    C. sqlnet.ora

    D. tnsnames.ora

2. Which of the following is the correct way to start a listener called LISTENER?

    A. lsnrctl startup listener

    B. lsnrctl start

    C. netca start

    D. netmgr start listener

3. When dynamic service registration is used, you will not see the service listed in which of the following files where it would normally be located?

    A. sqlnet.ora

    B. tnsnames.ora

    C. listener.ora

    D. None of the above

4. Connection Manager provides which of the following?

    A. Multiplexing

    B. Cross-protocol connectivity

    C. Network access control

    D. All of the above

5. Which is a requirement for using host naming?

    A. You must use tnsnames.ora on the client.

    B. You must be using TCP/IP.

    C. You must have an OID present.

    D. You must have a sqlnet.ora file present on the client.

    E. None of the above.

6. Which statements regarding Database Resident Connection Pooling (DRCP) are true? (Choose two.)

   A. When a DRCP pooled server connection is made by an application, it is equivalent to a dedicated server connection.

   B. When a database has DRCP enabled, all connections default to a pooled connection unless `DEDICATED` server is explicitly specified in the connect string.

   C. When an application using the DRCP connection disconnects, the server connection (process) is handed off to the broker.

   D. When using the Oracle Net Easy Connect method, it is not possible to utilize DRCP.

7. A client receives the following error message:

   `"ORA-12154 TNS:could not resolve the connect identifier specified"`

   Which of the following could be possible causes of the error? Choose all that apply.

   A. The listener is not running on the Oracle server.

   B. The user entered an invalid net service name.

   C. The user supplied the correct net service name, but the net service name is misspelled in the `tnsnames.ora` file on the client file.

   D. The listener is not configured to listen for this service.

8. What portion of the `tnsnames.ora` file specifies the name or IP address of the server where the listener process is listening?

   A. `CONNECT_DATA`

   B. `SERVER`

   C. `SERVICE_NAME`

   D. `HOST`

9. A client wants to connect to the database service dbprod.com located on the dbprod.com server through a nondefault port (1522) using Oracle Easy Connect. Which of the following connect strings are the choices for the client to use? (Choose two.)

   A. `CONNECT scott/tiger@dbprod.com:1522`

   B. `CONNECT scott/tiger@1522:dbprod.com/dbprod.com`

   C. `CONNECT scott/tiger@//dbprod.com/1522:dbprod.com`

   D. `CONNECT scott/tiger@dbprod.com:1522/dbprod.com`

10. All of the following are reasons to configure the server using Shared Server *except* which one?

    A. Overall memory utilization is reduced.

    B. The system is predominantly used for decision support with large result sets returned.

    C. The system is predominantly used for small transactions with many users.

    D. The number of idle connections on the server is reduced.

11. Which of the following is true about Shared Server?

    A. Dedicated connections cannot be made when Shared Server is configured.

    B. It is recommended that DSS type batch jobs be performed when connected via Shared Server.

    C. The database can be started when connected via Shared Server.

    D. The database cannot be stopped when connected via Shared Server.

12. The administrator wants to allow a user to connect via a dedicated connection into a database configured in Shared Server mode. Which of the following options accomplishes this?

    A. `(SERVER=DEDICATED)`

    B. `(CONNECT=DEDICATED)`

    C. `(INSTANCE=DEDICATED)`

    D. `(MULTITHREADED=FALSE)`

    E. None of the above

13. In which of the following files would you find the Shared Server configuration parameters?

    A. `listener.ora`

    B. `mts.ora`

    C. `init.ora`

    D. `tnsnames.ora`

    E. `sqlnet.ora`

14. What is the first step that the dispatcher performs after it receives a request from the user?

    A. Pass the request to a shared server.

    B. Place the request in a request queue in the PGA.

    C. Place the request in a request queue in the SGA.

    D. Process the request.

15. When configured in Shared Server mode, which of the following is contained in the PGA?

    A. Cursor state

    B. Sort information

    C. User session data

    D. Stack space

    E. None of the above

16. Which of the following is false about request queues?

    A. They reside in the SGA.

    B. They are shared by all the dispatchers.

    C. Each dispatcher has its own request queue.

    D. The shared server processes remove requests from the request queue.

17. What is the process that notifies the listener after a database connection is established?

    A. SMON

    B. PMON

    C. LREG

    D. LGWR

18. Which network architecture connection uses session memory from the SGA?

    A. Dedicated Server

    B. Shared Server

    C. Database Resident Connection Pooling

    D. All of the above

19. Communication between two Oracle databases is configured using:

    A. Database Resident Connection Pooling

    B. Database link

    C. Connection Manager

    D. Oracle Net Manager

20. DBA user MIKE ran the SQL statement CREATE DATABASE LINK SCOTT.SALES_LINK .BJS.COM CONNECT TO SALES_INT IDENTIFIED BY SALESPWD1 USING 'ocasvr:1522/ ocadb'. Choose the option that is true.

    A. Use of 'ocasvr:1522/ocadb' is invalid in database link definition.

    B. A private database link is created under user MIKE.

    C. A private database link is created under user SCOTT.

    D. If the SALES_INT user does not exist or its password is not SALESPWD1, the database link will not be created.

Chapter

13

Implementing Security and Auditing

ORACLE DATABASE 12*c*: OCA EXAM OBJECTIVES COVERED IN THIS CHAPTER:

✓ **Administering User Security**

- ▪ Create and manage database user accounts.
- ▪ Grant and revoke privileges.
- ▪ Create and manage roles.
- ▪ Create and manage profiles.

✓ **Implementing Oracle Database Auditing**

- ▪ Explain DBA responsibilities for security and auditing.
- ▪ Enable standard database auditing and unified auditing.

One of the key functions of a DBA is to protect the data and database by controlling database access; DBAs must also keep track of key database activities. They must maintain the security, integrity, performance, and availability of their databases. In this chapter, you will learn about managing database security, including how to manage user accounts; implement password expiration and complexity rules; and configure security policies using object, system, and role privileges. To further enhance your ability to monitor and manage database access, you will also learn how to use auditing mechanisms to fine-tune your security policy, identify attempts to access areas of your database that a user is not authorized to visit, and identify intrusion attempts.

Creating and Managing User Accounts

One of the most basic administrative requirements for a DBA is to identify and manage the users. The first step to doing this is to make sure each user who connects to the Oracle Database 12*c* database has an *account*. An account shared between many users is difficult to troubleshoot and audit and is, therefore, a poor security practice that should be avoided.

You create a new database account with the CREATE USER statement. When you create a new account, at a minimum the user should have a unique username and authentication method. You can optionally assign additional attributes to the user account with the CREATE USER statement. To change or assign new attributes to an existing user account, use the ALTER USER statement.

The terms *user account*, *account*, *user*, and *schema* are all interchangeable and refer to a database user account. A *schema* is a user who owns objects. All schemas are users, but not all users are schemas.

The following is an example of the CREATE USER statement with common optional clauses:

```
SQL> CREATE USER james
     IDENTIFIED BY mia0101
     DEFAULT TABLESPACE users
     TEMPORARY TABLESPACE temp
     QUOTA UNLIMITED ON users
```

```
        PROFILE default
        PASSWORD EXPIRE
        ACCOUNT UNLOCK;

User created.

SQL>
```

The username must adhere to the database object-naming convention. It must begin with a letter, have no more than 30 characters, and be comprised of only letters, numbers, and $, #, _. In the following sections, you'll learn about the clauses presented in the CREATE USER statement.

> At the time of this writing, multitenant databases are not part of the OCA exam objectives. When creating users in multitenant databases, you may use the CONTAINER=ALL clause to create a common user in all pluggable databases connected to the root container. Common usernames must begin with C##. To create a local user in a pluggable database, use the CONTAINER=CURRENT clause connected to the pluggable database.

Configuring Authentication

When a user connects to an Oracle database instance, the user account must be authenticated. *Authentication* involves validating the identity of the user and confirming that the user has the authority to use the database. Oracle offers three authentication methods for your user accounts: password authentication (the most common), external authentication, and global authentication.

We'll cover each of these authentication methods in the following sections.

Password-Authenticated Users

When a user with password authentication attempts to connect to the database, the database verifies that the username is a valid database account and that the password supplied matches that user's password as stored in the database.

Password-authenticated user accounts are the most common and are sometimes referred to as *database-authenticated* accounts. With a password-authenticated account, the database stores the encrypted password in the data dictionary. For example, to create a password-authenticated user named rajesh with a password of welcome, you execute the following:

```
SQL> CREATE USER rajesh IDENTIFIED BY welcome;
```

The keywords IDENTIFIED BY *password* (in this case, the *password* is welcome) tell the database that this user account is a password-authenticated account.

> The user passwords in Oracle 11g databases and later versions are case
> sensitive. In earlier releases of Oracle, user passwords were case insensi-
> tive. The default value of the SEC_CASE_SENSITIVE_LOGON parameter is
> TRUE; to disable case sensitivity for passwords, change the value to FALSE.

Externally Authenticated Users

When an externally identified user attempts to connect to the database, the database
verifies that the username is a valid database account and trusts that the operating system has performed authentication.

Externally authenticated user accounts do not store or validate passwords in the database. These accounts are sometimes referred to as *OPS$ accounts*, because when Oracle
introduced them in Oracle 6, the account had to be prefixed with the keyword OPS$. With
all releases of the database since then, including Oracle Database 12c, you can configure this
OS_AUTHENT_PREFIX in the initialization file or spfile. For example, to create an externally
authenticated user named oracle using the default OS_AUTHENT_PREFIX, you would execute
the following:

```
CREATE USER ops$oracle IDENTIFIED EXTERNALLY;
```

The keywords IDENTIFIED EXTERNALLY tell the database that this user account is an
externally authenticated account. If you log in to the server as user *oracle*, you can log in
to the database without providing a username or password, as shown here:

```
SQL> show parameter os_authent_prefix

NAME                                 TYPE          VALUE
------------------------------------ ------------- -------------
os_authent_prefix                    string        ops$

SQL> host id
uid=5000(oracle) gid=5001(oinstall) groups=5001(oinstall),5000(dba),54323(oper),
54324(backupdba),54325(dgdba),54327(asmdba),54328(asmoper),54329(asmadmin) conte
xt=system_u:unconfined_r:unconfined_t:s0

SQL> create user ops$oracle identified externally;
User created.

SQL> grant connect to ops$oracle;
Grant succeeded.

SQL> connect /
Connected.
```

```
SQL> show user
USER is "OPS$ORACLE"
SQL>
```

Externally authenticated accounts are frequently used for administrative scripts so that a password does not have to be embedded in a human-readable script.

Globally Authenticated Users

When a globally identified user attempts to connect to the database, the database verifies that the username is valid and passes the connection information to the advanced security option for authentication. The advanced security option supports several mechanisms for authentication, including biometrics, X.509 certificates, Kerberos, and RADIUS.

Globally authenticated user accounts do not store or validate passwords in the database as a password-authenticated account does. These accounts rely on authentication provided by a service supported through the advanced security option.

The syntax for creating a globally authenticated account depends on the service called, but all use the keywords IDENTIFIED GLOBALLY, which tells the database to engage the advanced security option for authentication. Here is an example:

```
CREATE USER spy_master IDENTIFIED GLOBALLY AS 'CN=spy_master, OU=tier2,
   O=security, C=US';
```

Assigning Tablespaces and Quotas

Every user is assigned a default tablespace. When a user creates tables or indexes, they are created on the tablespace specified by the TABLESPACE clause. If the TABLESPACE clause is not provided, the segments will be created on the user's *default tablespace*. If you execute a CREATE TABLE statement and do not explicitly specify a tablespace, the database uses your default tablespace.

If you do not explicitly assign a default tablespace to a user at the time you create the user, the database assigns the database's default tablespace to the new user account. To assign a default tablespace to either a new user via a CREATE USER statement or an existing user, use the keywords DEFAULT TABLESPACE *tablespace_name*, like this:

```
CREATE USER rajesh IDENTIFIED BY welcome
DEFAULT TABLESPACE users;
```

Or use an ALTER USER statement:

```
ALTER USER rajesh
DEFAULT TABLESPACE users;
```

By default, the database default tablespace is SYSTEM. If the database was created using DBCA, the default tablespace would be USERS. To change the database default tablespace (the value that users inherit if no default tablespace is provided), use the ALTER DATABASE statement, like this:

```
ALTER DATABASE DEFAULT TABLESPACE users;
```

Assigning a Temporary Tablespace

Every user is assigned a temporary tablespace in which the database stores temporary segments. Temporary segments are created during large sorting operations, such as ORDER BY, GROUP BY, SELECT DISTINCT, MERGE JOIN, or CREATE INDEX.

Temporary segments are also used when a temporary table is used. The database creates and drops temporary segments transparently to the user. Because of the transitory nature of temporary segments, you must use a dedicated tablespace of type TEMPORARY for your user's temporary tablespace setting.

If you do not explicitly assign a temporary tablespace when the user is created, the database assigns the database default temporary tablespace to the new user account. Use the keywords TEMPORARY TABLESPACE *tablespace_name* to assign a temporary tablespace either to a new user via the CREATE USER statement:

```
CREATE USER rajesh IDENTIFIED BY welcome
DEFAULT TABLESPACE users
TEMPORARY TABLESPACE temp;
```

or to an existing user via an ALTER USER statement:

```
ALTER USER rajesh
TEMPORARY TABLESPACE temp;
```

If the SYSTEM tablespace is locally managed at the time of database creation, you're required to provide a non-SYSTEM temporary-type tablespace as the database default temporary tablespace. To change the database default temporary tablespace, use the ALTER DATABASE statement, like this:

```
ALTER DATABASE DEFAULT TEMPORARY TABLESPACE temp;
```

 You can query the data dictionary view DATABASE_PROPERTIES to see the current default tablespace and temporary tablespace assignment for the database. You may also use the OEM Database Express 12c option "Current Database Properties" under the Configuration drop-down menu.

Assigning Space Quotas

By default, Oracle Database 12c does not allocate a *space quota* in any tablespace when the user is created. To create segments (tables, indexes, and so on) in any tablespace, the user must have a quota of space allotted on the tablespace. Tablespace quotas limit the amount of disk space a user can consume. The default quota is none. You can assign a space usage quota at the same time you create a user with the CREATE USER statement:

```
CREATE USER dchip IDENTIFIED BY "Seek!r3t"
QUOTA 100M ON USERS;
```

Or you can assign the quota after the user has been created. Just use the ALTER USER statement:

```
ALTER USER bart
QUOTA UNLIMTED ON USERS;
```

The special keyword UNLIMITED tells the database that the user should not have a preset limit on the amount of space their objects can consume.

The user can create objects in any tablespace if the user has the UNLIMITED TABLESPACE system privilege. You will learn about system privileges later in the chapter in the "Granting System Privileges" section.

A feature called deferred segment creation was introduced in Oracle 11g Release 2. So when a new table is created, no space quota is needed because the segment is created only when the first row is inserted. This means that a quota of zero does not automatically prevent tables from being created in a schema, as was the case in previous releases. Here is an example to show this scenario: user Simon is created with database defaults (default permanent tablespace, temporary tablespace, profile) and granted privileges in one statement. Simon is able to create the table, but is not able to insert a row, because at row insert, the segment is created in the tablespace and has no quota.

```
SQL> GRANT CREATE SESSION, CREATE TABLE to simon IDENTIFIED BY simonpwd;
Grant succeeded.

SQL> CONNECT simon/simonpwd
Connected.

SQL> CREATE TABLE T1 (C1 NUMBER);
Table created.

SQL> INSERT INTO T1 VALUES (4);
INSERT INTO T1 VALUES (4)
            *
ERROR at line 1:
ORA-01950: no privileges on tablespace 'USERS'
```

NOTE The encrypted user password is stored in the dictionary table USER$. The password column has the 10g hash, and the spare4 column has the 11g hash. You may use the encrypted value directly in the CREATE USER or ALTER USER statement to use the same password for the user. This is useful when you duplicate user in another database or when you drop and recreate. The syntax is CREATE USER btsj IDENTIFIED BY VALUES 'FD6C945489780TER72C'.

Assigning a Profile and Account Settings

In addition to default and temporary tablespaces, every user is assigned a profile. A profile serves two purposes:

- It can limit the usage of some resources.
- It can enforce password-management rules.

The default profile is appropriately named default. To explicitly assign a profile to a user, include the keywords PROFILE *profile_name* in the CREATE USER or ALTER USER statement. For example, to assign the profile named adminuser_profile to the new user jiang as well as to the existing user hamish, execute the following SQL code:

```
CREATE USER jiang IDENTIFIED BY "kneehow.ma"
DEFAULT TABLESPACE users
TEMPORARY TABLESPACE temp
PROFILE adminuser_profile;

ALTER USER hamish
PROFILE adminuser_profile;
```

If you want users to change their passwords the first time they log in to the database, you can set the PASSWORD EXPIRE option. Every user will be forced to change their password at the first login. Here is an example of creating a user with an expired password:

```
SQL> CREATE USER shelly IDENTIFIED BY welcome
     PASSWORD EXPIRE;

User created.

SQL> GRANT CONNECT TO shelly;
SQL> connect shelly/welcome
ERROR:
ORA-28001: the password has expired

Changing password for shelly
```

```
New password:
Retype new password:
SQL> SHOW user
SQL> USER is "SHELLY"
```

By default, the user account is unlocked at creation. To lock the user account, use the `ACCOUNT LOCK` option.

To create and manage user accounts using EM Database Express, choose Users under the Security drop-down menu, as shown in Figure 13.1.

FIGURE 13.1   The EM Database Express Users screen

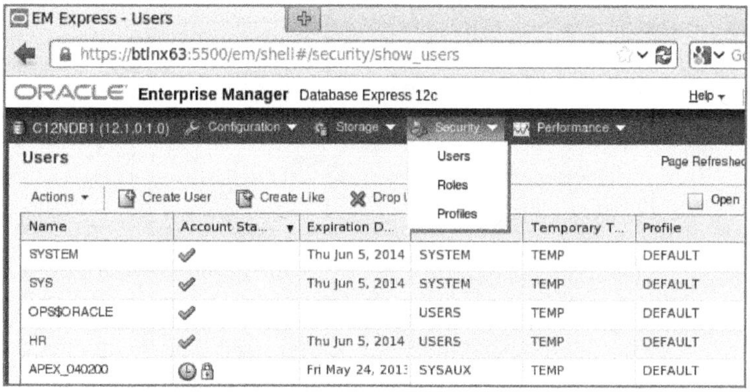

The screen shows all users in the database, with information such as account status, password expiration date, default and temporary tablespaces, and profile assignment. Clicking the Create User button on this screen opens the screen to create a new user, as shown in Figure 13.2. The Create Like button can duplicate a user account.

The Create User option has three dialog screens. The Show SQL button shows the SQL code used to create the user and privileges. Here is an example of SQL code generated by the dialogue:

```
create user "OCATRAIN1" identified by ******* profile "DEFAULT" password expire
account unlock default tablespace  "USERS" temporary tablespace "TEMP";

grant SELECT ANY TABLE to "OCATRAIN1";
grant "CONNECT" to "OCATRAIN1";
grant "RESOURCE" to "OCATRAIN1";
grant "SELECT_CATALOG_ROLE" to "OCATRAIN1";
```

The Actions drop-down menu in the Users screen (see Figure 13.1) provides the options to Create User, Drop User, View Details Of User, Alter The Properties Of User, Alter Tablespace Assignments, Alter Privileges And Roles, and Manage Object Privileges.

Removing a User from the Database

You use the DROP USER statement to remove a user from the database. You can optionally include the keyword CASCADE to tell the database to recursively drop all objects owned by that user.

To drop both user rajesh and all the objects he owns (this action also purges any Recycle Bin objects), execute the following:

```
DROP USER rajesh CASCADE;
```

FIGURE 13.2 The Grid Control's Create User screen

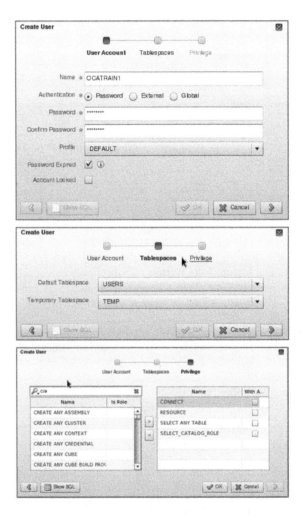

If a user is currently connected to the database, the user cannot be dropped. Dropping a user implicitly drops any object privileges (but not role or system privileges) for which the user was the grantor. The data dictionary records both the grantee and the grantor for object privileges, but only the grantee is recorded for role and system privileges.

Managing Default User Accounts

The SYS and SYSTEM user accounts are always created when an Oracle database is created. Other special accounts can be created to support installed products, such as Recovery Manager (RMAN) or XMLDB. When created via the DBCA, these special accounts are locked and expired, leaving only SYS and SYSTEM open. The SYS and SYSTEM accounts are the data dictionary owner and an administrative account, respectively.

If your database is created via any means other than the DBCA, ensure that the accounts are locked and expired and that the default passwords are changed. You expire and lock an account using the ALTER USER statement like this:

```
ALTER USER mdsys PASSWORD EXPIRE ACCOUNT LOCK;
```

Depending on the functionality installed in your Oracle database, you may need to lock and expire several default user accounts. The data dictionary view DBA_USERS_WITH_DEFPWD shows the database user accounts created by Oracle and having a default password.

Granting and Revoking Privileges

Privileges allow a user to access database objects or execute stored programs that are owned by another user. Privileges also enable a user to perform system-level operations, such as connecting to the database, creating a table, or altering the database. A user has complete privileges on the objects it owns, the privileges are required only on objects owned by some other user (schema).

Privileges are assigned to a user, to the special user PUBLIC, or to a role with the GRANT statement, and they can be rescinded with the REVOKE statement.

The Oracle Database 12*c* database has three types of privileges:

Object Privileges   These include permissions on schema objects such as tables, views, sequences, procedures, and packages. To use a schema object owned by another user, you need privileges on that object.

System Privileges   These include permissions on database-level operations, such as connecting to the database, creating users, altering the database, consuming unlimited amounts of tablespace, and querying all tables in the database.

Role Privileges   These include permissions granted to a user by way of a role. A *role* is a named group of privileges. Object and system privileges can be granted to a role.

We'll cover each of these privileges and how to grant them in the following sections.

Granting Object Privileges

Object privileges bestow upon the grantee the permission to use a schema object owned by another user in a particular way. As you'll see, there are several types of object privileges, some of which apply only to certain schema objects. For example, the INDEX privilege applies only to tables, and the SELECT privilege applies to tables, views, and sequences.

The following object privileges can be granted individually, can be granted grouped in a list, or can be granted with the keyword ALL to implicitly grant all available object privileges for a particular schema object.

 Be careful when using ALL. It may implicitly grant powerful privileges.

Table Object Privileges

Oracle Database 12*c* provides several object privileges for tables. These privileges give the table owner considerable flexibility in controlling how schema objects are used and by whom.

Commonly Granted Privileges

The following privileges are commonly granted, and you should know them well:

SELECT   This is the most commonly used privilege for tables. With this privilege, the table owner permits the grantee to query the specified table with a SELECT statement.

INSERT   This permits the grantee to create new rows in the specified table with an INSERT statement.

UPDATE   This permits the grantee to modify existing rows in the specified table with an UPDATE statement.

DELETE   This permits the grantee to remove rows from the specified table with a DELETE statement.

Powerful Administrative Privileges on Tables

The following are powerful administrative privileges on tables; grant them cautiously:

ALTER   This permits the grantee to execute an ALTER TABLE statement on the specified table. This privilege can be used to add, modify, or rename columns in the table, to move the table to another tablespace, or even to rename the specified table.

DEBUG   This permits the grantee to access, via a debugger, the PL/SQL code in any triggers on the specified table.

INDEX   This permits the grantee to create new indexes on the table. These new indexes will be owned by a user other than the one that owns the table, which is an unusual practice. In most cases, the indexes on a table are owned by the same user who owns the table. The owner of the table does not need the INDEX privilege to create an index.

REFERENCES   This permits the grantee to create foreign key constraints that reference the specified table.

Real World Scenario

Viewing Object Privileges

Object privileges can be queried from the database using the dictionary view DBA_TAB_PRIVS (or using ALL_TAB_PRIVS or USER_TAB_PRIVS; if you're using a multitenant database, you may use CDB_TAB_PRIVS as well). Let's find out what privileges are included when ALL privilege is granted.

User HR executes the following SQL code to grant ALL privileges on EMPLOYEES table to user OE.

```
SQL> grant all on hr.employees to oe;
```

To view the privileges granted to OE by this action, query DBA_TAB_PRIVS, like this:

```
SQL> col grantee format a7
SQL> col grantor format a7
SQL> col privilege format a20
SQL> SELECT grantee, grantor, privilege
     FROM dba_tab_privs
     WHERE owner = 'HR'
     AND table_name = 'EMPLOYEES';

GRANTEE GRANTOR PRIVILEGE
------- ------- --------------------
OE      HR      FLASHBACK
OE      HR      DEBUG
OE      HR      QUERY REWRITE
OE      HR      ON COMMIT REFRESH
OE      HR      REFERENCES
OE      HR      UPDATE
OE      HR      SELECT
OE      HR      INSERT
OE      HR      INDEX
OE      HR      DELETE
OE      HR      ALTER

11 rows selected.

SQL>
```

View Object Privileges

Oracle Database 12*c* offers a smaller set of object privileges for views than it does for tables:

SELECT   This is the most commonly used privilege for views. With this privilege, the view owner permits the grantee to query the view.

INSERT   This permits the grantee to execute an INSERT statement on the specified view to create new rows.

UPDATE   This permits the grantee to modify existing rows in the specified view with an UPDATE statement.

DELETE   This permits the grantee to execute a DELETE statement on the specified view to remove rows.

DEBUG   This permits the grantee to access, via a debugger, the PL/SQL code in the body of any trigger on this view.

REFERENCES   This permits the grantee to create foreign key constraints on the specified view.

Sequence Object Privileges

Oracle Database 12*c* provides only two object privileges for sequences:

SELECT   This permits the grantee to access the current and next values (CURRVAL and NEXTVAL) of the specified sequence.

ALTER   This lets the grantee change the attributes of the specified sequence with an ALTER statement.

Stored Functions, Procedures, Packages, and Java Object Privileges

Oracle Database 12*c* provides only two object privileges for stored PL/SQL programs:

DEBUG   This permits the grantee to access, via a debugger, all the public and private variables and types declared in the specified program. If the specified object is a package, both the specification and the body are accessible to the grantee. The grantee can also use a debugger to place breakpoints in the specified program.

EXECUTE   This permits the grantee to execute the specified program. If the specified object is a package, any program, variable, type, cursor, or record declared in the package specification is accessible to the grantee.

How to Grant Privileges

You use the GRANT statement to confer object privileges on either a user or a role. The optional keywords WITH GRANT OPTION additionally allow the grantee to confer these privileges on other users and roles. For example, to give SELECT, INSERT, UPDATE, and

DELETE privileges on the table CUSTOMERS to the role SALES_MANAGER, execute the following statement while connected as the owner of table CUSTOMERS:

```
GRANT SELECT, INSERT, UPDATE, DELETE ON customers TO sales_manager;
```

If you grant privileges to the special user PUBLIC, you make them available to all current and future database users. For example, to give all database users the SELECT privilege on table CUSTOMERS, execute the following while connected as the owner of the table:

```
GRANT SELECT ON customers TO public;
```

When you extend a privilege to another user or role, you can also extend the ability for that grantee to turn around and grant the privilege to others. To extend this extra option, include the keywords WITH GRANT OPTION in the GRANT statement. For example, to give the SELECT privilege on table SALES.CUSTOMERS to the user SALES_ADMIN together with the permission for SALES_ADMIN to grant the SELECT privilege to others, execute the following:

```
GRANT SELECT ON sales.customers TO sales_admin WITH GRANT OPTION;
```

You can include the WITH GRANT OPTION keywords only when the grantee is a user or the special account PUBLIC. You cannot use WITH GRANT OPTION when the grantee is a role.

If you grant an object privilege using the WITH GRANT OPTION keywords and later revoke that privilege, the revoke cascades, and the privileges created by the grantee are also revoked. For example, Mary grants SELECT privileges on her table clients to Zachary with the WITH GRANT OPTION keywords. Zachary then creates a view based on the table mary.clients and grants the SELECT privilege on it to Rex. If Mary revokes the SELECT privilege from Zachary, the revoke cascades and removes the privilege from Rex. See Figure 13.3 for an illustration of this example.

FIGURE 13.3   Revoking an object privilege will cascade.

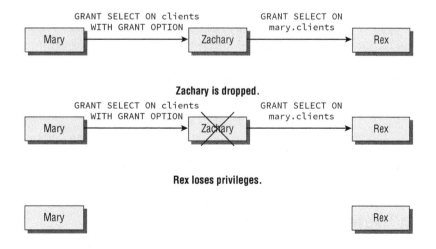

With object privileges, the database records both the grantor and the grantee. Therefore, a grantee can obtain a privilege from more than one grantor. When this multiple grant of the same privilege occurs, revoking one of these grants does not remove the privilege. To remove the privilege, all grants must be revoked, as shown in Figure 13.4.

FIGURE 13.4   Revoking an object privilege with multiple grant paths

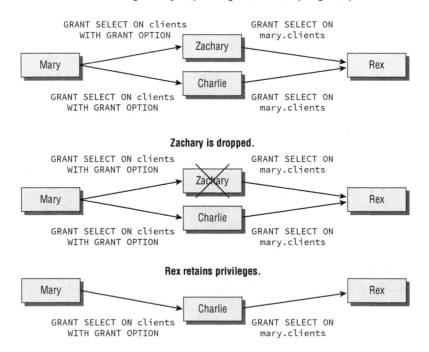

Continuing with our example, Mary has granted SELECT privileges on her table clients to Zachary using WITH GRANT OPTION. Zachary has then granted SELECT on mary.clients to Rex. Mary has also granted SELECT on her table clients to Charlie, who has in turn granted to Rex. Rex now has the SELECT privilege from more than one grantee. If Zachary leaves and his account is dropped, the privilege from Charlie remains, and Rex can still select from mary.clients.

 SQL Developer provides a very good interface for managing users and privileges. From the DBA menu, choose Security and then Users. You can then view object privileges, system privileges, and the roles assigned to a user.

Granting System Privileges

In general, *system privileges* permit the grantee to execute Data Definition Language (DDL) statements—such as CREATE, ALTER, and DROP—or Data Manipulation Language (DML)

statements system-wide. Oracle Database 12*c* has more than 200 system privileges, all of which are listed in the data dictionary view SYSTEM_PRIVILEGE_MAP.

 You will not be required to know all these privileges for the certification exam (thank goodness!), because many are for features that fall outside the scope of the exam. Pay attention to the database-related and table-related system privileges.

You should be familiar with the following groups of privileges.

Database

Oracle Database 12*c* gives you the following database-oriented system privileges:

ALTER DATABASE   This permits the grantee to execute the ALTER DATABASE statement.

ALTER SYSTEM   This permits the grantee to execute the ALTER SYSTEM statement.

AUDIT SYSTEM   This permits the grantee to execute AUDIT and NOAUDIT statements to perform statement auditing.

AUDIT ANY   This permits the grantee to execute AUDIT and NOAUDIT statements to perform object auditing on objects in any schema.

CREATE PLUGGABLE DATABASE   This permits the grantee to create pluggable databases in a multitenant database.

Debugging

Oracle Database 12*c* gives you two debugging-oriented system privileges.

DEBUG CONNECT SESSION   This permits the grantee to connect the current session to a debugger.

DEBUG ANY PROCEDURE   This permits the grantee to debug all PL/SQL and Java code in the database. This system privilege is equivalent to granting the object privilege DEBUG for every applicable object in the database.

Indexes

Oracle Database 12*c* gives you three system privileges related to indexes:

CREATE ANY INDEX   This permits the grantee to create an index in any schema.

ALTER ANY INDEX   This permits the grantee to alter indexes in any schema.

DROP ANY INDEX   This permits the grantee to drop indexes from any schema.

Job Scheduler

Oracle Database 12c gives you several system privileges related to the job scheduler:

CREATE JOB   This permits the grantee to create jobs, programs, or schedules in their own schema.

CREATE ANY JOB   This permits the grantee to create jobs, programs, or schedules in any schema.

 The CREATE ANY JOB privilege gives the grantee the ability to execute programs using any other user's credentials. Grant it cautiously.

EXECUTE ANY PROGRAM   This permits the grantee to use any program in a job in their own schema.

EXECUTE ANY CLASS   This permits the grantee to specify any job class for jobs in their own schema.

MANAGE SCHEDULER   This permits the grantee to create, alter, or delete any job class, window, or window group.

Procedures

Oracle Database 12c gives you several system privileges related to stored procedures:

CREATE PROCEDURE   This permits the grantee to create procedures in their own schema.

CREATE ANY PROCEDURE   This permits the grantee to create procedures in any schema.

ALTER ANY PROCEDURE   This permits the grantee to recompile any procedure in the database.

DROP ANY PROCEDURE   This permits the grantee to remove procedures from any schema.

EXECUTE ANY PROCEDURE   This permits the grantee to run any procedure in any schema.

Profiles

Oracle Database 12c gives you three system privileges related to user profiles:

CREATE PROFILE   This permits the grantee to create profiles. Causing a profile to be used requires an ALTER USER statement (which requires the ALTER USER privilege).

ALTER PROFILE   This permits the grantee to modify existing profiles.

DROP PROFILE   This permits the grantee to drop profiles from the database.

Roles

Oracle Database 12c gives you several system privileges related to roles. Because roles deal with security, some of these privileges are very powerful.

CREATE ROLE   This permits the grantee to create new roles.

ALTER ANY ROLE   This permits the grantee to change the password for any role in the database.

DROP ANY ROLE   This permits the grantee to remove any role from the database.

GRANT ANY ROLE   This permits the grantee to grant any role to any user or revoke any role from any user or role.

> The GRANT ANY ROLE privilege permits grantees to assign or rescind powerful administrative roles, such as SCHEDULER_ADMIN and IMP_FULL_DATABASE, to or from any user, including themselves or other DBAs. Grant it cautiously.

Sequences

Oracle Database 12*c* gives you several system privileges to manage sequences:

CREATE SEQUENCE   This permits the grantee to create new sequences in their own schema.

CREATE ANY SEQUENCE   This permits the grantee to create new sequences in any schema.

ALTER ANY SEQUENCE   This permits the grantee to change the characteristics of any sequence in the database.

DROP ANY SEQUENCE   This permits the grantee to remove any sequence from any schema in the database.

SELECT ANY SEQUENCE   This permits the grantee to select from any sequence.

Sessions

Oracle Database 12*c* gives you four session-oriented system privileges:

CREATE SESSION   This permits the grantee to connect to the database. This privilege is required for user accounts but may be undesirable for application owner accounts.

ALTER SESSION   This permits the grantee to execute ALTER SESSION statements to enable and disable SQL_TRACE.

ALTER RESOURCE COST   This permits the grantee to change the way Oracle calculates resource cost for resource restrictions in a profile.

> For more information on managing resource consumption, see the "Controlling Resource Usage by Users" section later in this chapter.

RESTRICTED SESSION   This permits the grantee to connect when the database has been opened in RESTRICTED SESSION mode, typically for administrative purposes. User accounts should not normally be granted this privilege.

Synonyms

Oracle Database 12*c* gives you several system privileges related to synonyms:

CREATE SYNONYM   This permits the grantee to create new synonyms in their own schema.

CREATE ANY SYNONYM   This permits the grantee to create new synonyms in any schema.

CREATE PUBLIC SYNONYM   This permits the grantee to create new public synonyms, which are accessible to all users in the database.

DROP ANY SYNONYM   This permits the grantee to remove any synonyms in any schema.

DROP PUBLIC SYNONYM   This permits the grantee to remove any public synonym from the database.

Tables

Oracle Database 12*c* gives you several system privileges for managing tables:

CREATE TABLE   This permits the grantee to create new tables in their own schema.

CREATE ANY TABLE   This permits the grantee to create new tables in any schema.

ALTER ANY TABLE   This permits the grantee to alter existing tables in any schema.

DROP ANY TABLE   This permits the grantee to drop tables from any schema.

COMMENT ANY TABLE   This permits the grantee to assign table or column comments to any table or view in any schema.

SELECT ANY TABLE   This permits the grantee to query any table or view in any schema.

INSERT ANY TABLE   This permits the grantee to insert new rows into any table in any schema.

UPDATE ANY TABLE   This permits the grantee to modify rows in any table in any schema.

DELETE ANY TABLE   This permits the grantee to delete rows from tables in any schema.

LOCK ANY TABLE   This permits the grantee to execute a LOCK TABLE statement to explicitly lock a table in any schema.

FLASHBACK ANY TABLE   This permits the grantee to execute a SQL flashback query, using the AS OF syntax, on any table or view in any schema.

> See Chapter 15, "Using Backup and Recovery," for more information on using flashback queries.

Tablespaces

Oracle Database 12*c* gives you the following system privileges to control tablespace management:

CREATE TABLESPACE   This permits the grantee to create new tablespaces.

ALTER TABLESPACE   This permits the grantee to alter existing tablespaces with the ALTER TABLESPACE statement.

DROP TABLESPACE   This permits the grantee to delete tablespaces from the database.

MANAGE TABLESPACE   This permits the grantee to alter a tablespace with the ONLINE, OFFLINE, BEGIN BACKUP, or END BACKUP command.

UNLIMITED TABLESPACE   This permits the grantee to consume unlimited disk space in any tablespace. This system privilege is equivalent to granting an unlimited quota in each tablespace to the specified grantee.

Triggers

Oracle Database 12c gives you several system privileges to control trigger management:

CREATE TRIGGER   This permits the grantee to create new triggers on tables in their own schema.

CREATE ANY TRIGGER   This permits the grantee to create new triggers on tables in any schema.

ALTER ANY TRIGGER   This permits the grantee to enable, disable, or compile existing triggers on tables in any schema.

DROP ANY TRIGGER   This permits the grantee to remove triggers from tables in any schema.

ADMINISTER DATABASE TRIGGER   This permits the grantee to create new ON DATABASE triggers. The grantee must also have the CREATE TRIGGER or CREATE ANY TRIGGER privilege before they can create an ON DATABASE trigger.

Users

Oracle Database 12c gives you several system privileges to control who can manage user accounts:

CREATE USER   This permits the grantee to create new database users.

ALTER USER   This permits the grantee to change the authentication method or password and assign quotas, temporary tablespaces, default tablespaces, or profiles for any user in the database. All users can change their own password without this privilege.

WARNING   The ALTER USER privilege allows the grantee to change the authentication method or password for any user (and also change it back). This makes it possible for the grantee to masquerade as another user. Grant this privilege cautiously.

DROP USER   This permits the grantee to remove users together with any objects they own from a database.

Views

Oracle Database 12c gives you several system privileges to manage views. Note that some of these privileges include the word TABLE and not VIEW. These privileges apply to either tables or views.

CREATE VIEW   This permits the grantee to create new views in their own schema.

CREATE ANY VIEW   This permits the grantee to create new views in any schema.

DROP ANY VIEW   This permits the grantee to remove views from any schema.

COMMENT ANY TABLE   This permits the grantee to assign table or column comments to any table or view in any schema.

FLASHBACK ANY TABLE   This permits the grantee to execute a SQL flashback query, using the AS OF syntax, on any table or view in any schema.

Administrative Privileges

Oracle Database 12c gives you five system privileges for administering your database that are very powerful. These privileges should not be granted lightly. The administrative privileges are "special" system privileges in that administrators who are granted these privileges can access a database instance even if the database is not open and perform administrative operations without having any other privileges.

SYSDBA   The most powerful system privilege, this permits the grantee to create, alter, drop, start up, or shut down databases; enable ARCHIVELOG and NOARCHIVELOG mode; recover a database; and create an spfile; in addition to having all the system privileges the database has to offer, including RESTRICTED SESSION. When this privilege is used, the user connected to the database is SYS.

SYSOPER   Only slightly less powerful than SYSDBA, this privilege permits the grantee to start up, shut down, alter, mount, back up, and recover a database. The grantee can create or alter an spfile and enter restricted session mode. When this privilege is used, the user connected to the database is PUBLIC.

SYSBACKUP   Use this privilege to perform RMAN backup and recovery operations from RMAN or through SQL. This privilege also gives the grantee the ability to start and stop the database instance, create an spfile, create or drop a database, and create control files. When this privilege is used, the user connected to the database is SYSBACKUP.

SYSDG   The SYSDG administrative privilege allows the grantee to perform Data Guard operations with Data Guard Broker or the DGMGRL command-line interface. When this privilege is used, the user connected to the database is SYSDG.

SYSKM   The SYSKM administrative privilege allows the grantee to manage transparent data encryption wallet operations. When this privilege is used, the user connected to the database is SYSKM.

Similar to the SYSDBA privilege, the SYSASM privilege is very powerful and used to administer an Automatic Storage Management (ASM) instance.

 Database administrative users SYSBACKUP, SYSDG, and SYSKM cannot be dropped.

Others

Oracle Database 12*c* gives you several system privileges for managing your database that don't fit into the earlier categories. These privileges include powerful administrative capabilities and should not be granted lightly.

ANALYZE ANY   This permits the grantee to execute an ANALYZE statement on tables, indexes, or clusters in any schema.

PURGE DBA_RECYCLEBIN   This permits the grantee to purge objects owned by any user from dba_recyclebin.

GRANT ANY OBJECT PRIVILEGE   This permits the grantee to assign object privileges on any object in any schema.

GRANT ANY PRIVILEGE   This permits the grantee to assign any system privilege to other users or roles.

GRANT ANY ROLE   This permits the grantee to assign any role to other users or roles. This privilege also gives the grantee permission to revoke any role.

SELECT ANY DICTIONARY   This permits the grantee to select from the SYS-owned data dictionary tables, such as TAB$ or SYSAUTH$.

How to Grant System Privileges

As with object privileges, you use the GRANT statement to confer system privileges on either a user or a role. Unlike object privileges, the optional keywords WITH ADMIN OPTION are required to additionally allow the grantee to confer these privileges on other users and roles. For example, to give the CREATE USER, ALTER USER, and DROP USER privileges to the role APPL_DBA, you execute the following statement:

```
GRANT create user, alter user, drop user TO appl_dba;
```

 System and role privileges require the wording WITH ADMIN OPTION; object privileges require the wording WITH GRANT OPTION. Because the function is so similar but the syntax is different, be sure you know when to use ADMIN and when to use GRANT—a question involving this subtle difference may appear on the exam.

As with object privileges, you can grant system privileges to the special user PUBLIC. Granting privileges to PUBLIC allows anyone with a database account and the CONNECT privilege to exercise this privilege. In general, because system privileges are more powerful than object privileges, take care when granting a system privilege to PUBLIC. For example, to give all current and future database users the FLASHBACK ANY TABLE privilege, execute the following:

```
GRANT flashback any table TO public;
```

To give the INDEX ANY TABLE privilege to the role APPL_DBA, together with the permission to allow anyone with the role APPL_DBA to grant this privilege to others, execute the following:

```
GRANT index any table TO appl_dba WITH ADMIN OPTION;
```

If you grant a system privilege WITH ADMIN OPTION and later revoke that privilege, the privileges created by the grantee will not be revoked. Unlike object privileges, the revocation of system privileges does not cascade. Think of it this way: WITH GRANT OPTION includes the keyword GRANT and so implies that a revoke cascades, but WITH ADMIN OPTION does not mention GRANT, so a revoke has no effect. Here's an example. Mary grants the SELECT ANY TABLE privilege to new DBA Zachary with ADMIN OPTION. Zachary then grants this privilege to Rex. Later, Zachary gets promoted and leaves the department, so Mary revokes the SELECT ANY TABLE privilege from Zachary. Rex's privilege remains unaffected. You can see this in Figure 13.5.

This behavior differs from object privileges, because the database does not record both grantor and grantee for system privileges—only the grantee is recorded.

FIGURE 13.5   Revoking system privileges

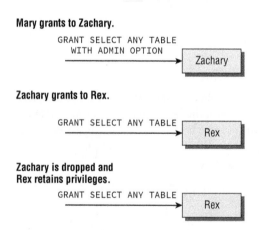

Mary grants to Zachary.

```
GRANT SELECT ANY TABLE
     WITH ADMIN OPTION
```
→ Zachary

Zachary grants to Rex.

```
GRANT SELECT ANY TABLE
```
→ Rex

**Zachary is dropped and
Rex retains privileges.**

```
GRANT SELECT ANY TABLE
```
→ Rex

The database only records the privilege granted, not who granted it.

The data dictionary view DBA_SYS_PRIVS lists all the system privileges granted in the database.

Role Privileges

Role privileges confer on the grantee a group of system, object, and other role privileges. Users who have been granted a role inherit the privileges that have been granted to that role. Roles can be password protected, so users may have a role granted to them yet not be able to use that role in all database sessions. We'll cover roles and role privileges—including how to grant them—in the following section, "Creating and Managing Roles."

Creating and Managing Roles

A *role* is a tool for administering privileges. Privileges can be granted to a role, and then that role can be granted to other roles and users. Users can, therefore, inherit privileges via roles. Roles serve no other purpose than to administer privileges.

To create a role, use the CREATE ROLE statement. You can optionally include an IDENTIFIED BY clause that requires users to authenticate themselves before enabling the role. Roles requiring authentication are typically used inside an application, where a user's activities are controlled by the application. To create the role APPL_DBA, execute the following:

```
CREATE ROLE appl_dba;
```

To enable a role, execute a SET ROLE statement, like this:

```
SET ROLE appl_dba IDENTIFIED BY seekwrit;
```

The data dictionary view DBA_ROLE_PRIVS lists all the role privileges granted in the database.

How to Grant Role Privileges

As with object and system privileges, you use the GRANT statement to confer role privileges on either a user or another role. Also, like system privileges, the optional keywords WITH ADMIN OPTION allow the grantee to confer these privileges on other users and roles. For example, to give the OEM_MONITOR role to user charlie, execute the following:

```
GRANT oem_monitor TO charlie;
```

As with the other privileges, you can grant role privileges to the special user PUBLIC. Granting privileges to PUBLIC allows anyone with a database account to exercise this privilege. For example, to give all current and future database users use of the plustrace role, execute the following:

```
GRANT plustrace TO public;
```

To give the INDEX ANY TABLE privilege to the role APPL_DBA, together with the permission to allow anyone with the role APPL_DBA to grant this privilege to others, execute the following:

```
GRANT index any table TO appl_dba WITH ADMIN OPTION;
```

When it comes to granting a role WITH ADMIN OPTION, roles behave like system privileges, and subsequent revocations do not cascade.

If the role granted to a user is not the default role, the user must enable the role in the session to be able to use the role. In the following sections, you will learn to work with roles in a session.

Enabling Roles

Roles can be enabled—or disabled, for that matter—selectively in each database session. If you have two concurrent sessions, the roles in effect for each session can be different. Use the SET ROLE *role_list* statement to enable one or more roles. *role_list* is a comma-delimited list of roles to enable. This list can include the keyword ALL, which enables all the roles granted to the user. You can optionally append a list of roles to exclude from the ALL list by specifying ALL EXCEPT *exclusion_list*.

If a role has a password associated with it, the keywords IDENTIFIED BY *password* must immediately follow the role name in the *role_list*.

For example, to enable the password-protected role HR_ADMIN, together with the unprotected role EMPLOYEE, execute the following:

```
SET ROLE hr_admin IDENTIFIED BY "my!seekrit", employee;
```

To enable all roles except HR_ADMIN, run this:

```
SET ROLE ALL EXCEPT hr_admin;
```

You can enable as many roles as have been granted to you, up to the MAX_ENABLED_ROLES initialization parameter.

Identifying Enabled Roles

The roles that are enabled in your session are listed in the data dictionary view SESSION_ROLES. To identify these enabled roles for your session, run the following:

```
SELECT role FROM session_roles;
```

These roles include the roles that have been granted to you, the roles that have been granted to the special user PUBLIC, and the roles that you have inherited by way of other roles. To identify the roles granted to either user or the special user PUBLIC, run the following:

```
SELECT granted_role FROM user_role_privs
WHERE username IN (USER, 'PUBLIC');
```

The role DBA includes the role SCHEDULER_ADMIN, which in turn has system privileges (such as CREATE ANY JOB). A user who has been granted the DBA role inherits the SCHEDULER_ADMIN role indirectly. To identify the roles that are both enabled in your session and granted directly to you or PUBLIC, but not those roles that you inherited, run this:

```
SELECT role FROM session_roles
INTERSECT
SELECT granted_role FROM user_role_privs
WHERE username IN (USER, 'PUBLIC');
```

In your sessions, you can disable only these directly granted and public roles.

Disabling Roles

Roles can be disabled in a database session either en masse or by exception. Use the SET ROLE NONE statement to disable all roles. Use the SET ROLE ALL EXCEPT role_list statement to enable all roles except those in the comma-delimited role_list.

There is no way to selectively disable a single role. Also, you cannot disable roles that you inherit by way of another role without disabling the parent role. For example, if you have been granted the DBA, RESOURCE, and CONNECT roles, you inherit several roles through the DBA role when it is enabled. If you want to disable the SCHEDULER_ADMIN role you inherited through the DBA role, you cannot do that. The options you have are that you can disable the DBA role or you can create a new role similar to the DBA role without the SCHEDULER_ADMIN role and use that role.

Setting Default Roles

Roles that are enabled by default when you log on are called *default roles*. You do not need to specify a password for default roles and do not have to execute a SET ROLE statement to enable a default role. Change the default roles for a user account with an ALTER USER DEFAULT ROLE role_list statement. The role_list can include the keywords ALL, NONE, and EXCEPT, in the same manner as with a SET ROLE statement.

Including a password-protected role in the role_list defeats the purpose of password protecting the role because it is automatically enabled without the password. When you create a role, you are implicitly granted that role with the admin option, and it is configured as a default role for your account.

For example, to create the role EMPLOYEE, grant it to user scott, and configure all of scott's roles except PLUSTRACE as default roles, run the following:

```
CREATE ROLE employee;
GRANT employee TO scott;
ALTER USER scott DEFAULT ROLE ALL EXCEPT plustrace;
```

Because the creator of a role automatically has that role assigned as a default role, administrative users (such as SYS or SYSTEM) who create many roles may need to alter their default role list. If you attempt to log on with more default roles than allowed by the MAX_ENABLED_ROLES initialization parameter, you will raise an exception, and your logon will fail.

> ⊕ **Real World Scenario**
>
> ### A Password-Protected Role
>
> Lucinda works in HR and needs to be able to modify an employee's salary after they have a review and their raise is approved. The HR application ensures that the raise is approved and falls within corporate guidelines. Although Lucinda needs to be able to change employee salaries, she should be allowed to do so only from within the HR application, because it ensures that business rules are followed.
>
> You wisely choose to use a password-protected role to satisfy these requirements. Update privilege on the salary table is granted to the password-protected role salary_admin. Lucinda is then granted the salary_admin role, but she is not told the password for it. The HR application has the password encoded within it, so when Lucinda runs the HR application, unknown to her, a SET ROLE salary_admin IDENTIFY BY *password* statement is executed, enabling the role and allowing her to change the salary.
>
> If Lucinda tries to execute an UPDATE statement on the salary table from SQL*Plus, she will get an insufficient privileges error.

Default Database Roles

When you create a new database, Oracle Database 12*c* creates several roles in the database based on the options you chose at the database creation. The following are a few of the important roles that are created automatically during database creation:

CONNECT This role has only one privilege, CREATE SESSION.

RESOURCE This role has the privileges required to create common objects in the user's schema.

DBA This is the most powerful role in the database. Only database administrators should be given this role. This role has all the system privileges and several administrative privileges.

SELECT_CATALOG_ROLE This role gives the user access to query the data dictionary views.

EXECUTE_CATALOG_ROLE This role gives the user privileges to execute the packages and procedures in the data dictionary.

DELETE_CATALOG_ROLE This role gives the user the ability to delete records from the standard audit table (SYS.AUD$).

To list all the roles defined in the database, query the data dictionary view DBA_ROLES. To view the system privileges granted to a role, query the DBA_SYS_PRIVS dictionary view. For example, the following query lists the system privileges granted to the RESOURCE role:

```
SQL> SELECT grantee, privilege, admin_option
     FROM dba_sys_privs
     WHERE grantee = 'RESOURCE';


GRANTEE              PRIVILEGE            ADM
-------------------- -------------------- ---
RESOURCE             CREATE TRIGGER       NO
RESOURCE             CREATE SEQUENCE      NO
RESOURCE             CREATE TYPE          NO
RESOURCE             CREATE PROCEDURE     NO
RESOURCE             CREATE CLUSTER       NO
RESOURCE             CREATE OPERATOR      NO
RESOURCE             CREATE INDEXTYPE     NO
RESOURCE             CREATE TABLE         NO
```

Applying the Principle of Least Privilege

The principle of least privilege states that each user should be given only the minimal privileges needed to perform their job. This principle is a central tenet to the initially closed philosophy whereby all access is initially closed or unavailable and access is opened on a need-to-know basis. Highly secure environments typically operate under an initially closed philosophy. The contrasting philosophy is an initially open philosophy, whereby all access is by default open to all users and only sensitive areas are closed. Academic or learning environments typically operate under an initially open philosophy.

Many IT organizations want the most secure policies for production systems, which calls for the initially closed approach to security. To support the need for administrators and programmers to quickly learn new technology, these shops frequently create "sandbox" systems that follow the initially open philosophy. These sandbox systems afford their limited users the learning benefit of the initially open approach, while not storing or giving gateway access to any sensitive information elsewhere in the enterprise.

To implement the principle of least privilege on your production or development systems, you should take several actions, or best practices, while setting up or locking down the database. Let's take a look at these:

Protect the data dictionary.   Ensure that users with the SELECT ANY TABLE privilege cannot access the tables that underlie the data dictionary by setting O7_DICTIONARY_ACCESSIBILITY = FALSE. This is the default setting.

Revoke unnecessary privileges from PUBLIC.   By default, several packages and roles are granted to the special user PUBLIC. Review these privileges, and revoke the EXECUTE privilege from PUBLIC if not necessary. Some of these packages include the following:

UTL_TCP   This permits the grantee to establish a network connection to any waiting TCP/IP network service. Once a connection is established, arbitrary information can be sent and received directly from the database to and from the other TCP services on your network. If your organization is concerned about information exchange over TCP/IP, revoke the EXECUTE privilege on this package from PUBLIC. Grant privileges on this package only to those users who need it.

UTL_SMTP   This permits the grantee to send arbitrary email. If your organization is concerned about information exchange via email, revoke the EXECUTE privilege on this package from PUBLIC. Grant privileges on this package only to those users who need it.

UTL_HTTP   This permits the grantee to send and receive arbitrary data via the HTTP protocol. If your organization is concerned about information exchange via HTTP, revoke the EXECUTE privilege on this package from PUBLIC. Grant privileges on this package only to those users who need it.

UTL_FILE   This permits the grantee to read and write text data to and from arbitrary operating-system files that are in the designated directories. UTL_FILE does not manage concurrency, so multiple user sessions can step on each other, overwriting changes via UTL_FILE. Consider revoking the EXECUTE privilege on this package from PUBLIC.

DBMS_OBFUSCATION_TOOLKIT and **DBMS_CRYPTO**   These permit the grantee to employ encryption technologies. In a managed environment using encryption, the keys are stored and managed. If encryption keys are lost, the encrypted data is undecipherable. Consider revoking the EXECUTE privilege on these packages from PUBLIC.

You can revoke the EXECUTE privileges like this:

```
REVOKE EXECUTE ON utl_tcp FROM PUBLIC;
REVOKE EXECUTE ON utl_smtp FROM PUBLIC;
REVOKE EXECUTE ON utl_http FROM PUBLIC;
REVOKE EXECUTE ON utl_file FROM PUBLIC;
REVOKE EXECUTE ON dbms_obfuscation_toolkit FROM PUBLIC;
REVOKE EXECUTE ON dbms_crypto FROM PUBLIC;
```

You can query the data dictionary to see what other packages may need to be locked down by revoking the EXECUTE privilege from PUBLIC. Here is a query to list the packages, owned by user SYS, that have the EXECUTE privilege granted to PUBLIC:

```
SELECT * FROM DBA_TAB_PRIVS
WHERE GRANTEE = 'PUBLIC'
AND PRIVILEGE = 'EXECUTE'
AND OWNER = 'SYS';
```

Limit the users who have administrative privileges. Grant administrative privileges to user accounts cautiously. Some powerful administrative privileges and roles to exercise caution with include the following:

SYSDBA This gives the grantee the highest level of privileges with the Oracle Database 12*c* software. A clever user with the SYSDBA role can circumvent most database security measures. There is usually no good reason to grant this role to any account except SYS, and the SYS password should be both cautiously guarded and changed regularly. Also, guard operating-system accounts carefully. If you are logged on to the database server using a privileged operating-system account, you might be able to connect to the database with SYSDBA authority and no password by entering connect / as sysdba in SQL*Plus.

DBA This permits the grantee to assign privileges and manipulate data throughout the database. A clever user with the DBA role can circumvent most database security measures. Grant this role only to those users who need it.

The ANY system privileges SELECT ANY TABLE, GRANT ANY ROLE, DELETE ANY TABLE, and so on, permit the grantee to assign privileges and manipulate data throughout the database. A malicious user with one of these roles can wreak havoc in your database. Grant these privileges only to those users who need them.

Do not enable REMOTE_OS_AUTHENT. The default setting for the initialization parameter REMOTE_OS_AUTHENT is FALSE. There is rarely a reason to enable this feature. When set to TRUE, this parameter tells the database to trust any client to authenticate externally authenticated accounts. For example, if you have an externally identified account named ORACLE that has DBA privileges for use in administrative scripts running on the database server (a common practice), setting this parameter to TRUE will allow someone with a notebook or desktop PC and a locally created ORACLE account to connect to your database with DBA credentials and no password.

Identifying Unused Privileges

A major concern in existing databases and applications is that users have excessive privileges because over granting privileges is easier than identifying what is really required. This is not a problem as long as the user uses only the application to connect to the database. Direct connection to the database provides an opportunity to misuse the privileges.

To achieve the least privilege principle, unused privileges need to be identified and revoked. Oracle Database 12*c* offers a DBMS_PRIVILEGE_CAPTURE package to identify user privileges. The procedures available in this package are

- CREATE_CAPTURE
- ENABLE_CAPTURE
- DISABLE_CAPTURE
- GENERATE_RESULT
- DROP_CAPTURE

We will give a brief overview of the privilege-capture functionality. As the subprograms or procedure names indicate, you must first define a policy using the CREATE_CAPTURE procedure. The policy can be at the database level analysis, at the role level, or it can be based on a context. Once policy is created, it is not enabled by default. Use the ENABLE_CAPTURE program to enable the policy.

After enabling capture, run the application or the programs while connected as the user in review and perform all necessary functions. After the analysis period, you disable the policy using the DISABLE_CAPTURE program. Once the policy is disabled, you are ready to generate the results using the GENERATE_RESULT program. The DROP_CAPTURE, as the name indicates, is to drop the capture policy. The capture must be disabled before it can be dropped. You provide a name for the policy when creating it, and that name is the parameter for all the other programs.

By running the GENERATE_RESULT, the following data dictionary views are populated:

DBA_USED_*xxx*

DBA_USED_*xxx*_PATH

DBA_UNUSED_*xxx*

DBA_UNUSED_*xxx*_PATH

The DBA_USED_ views show the privileges used by the user for the policy. The DBA_UNUSED_ views show the privileges that are assigned to the user, but are not used. The _PATH views show the privilege path (how the privilege was given to the user and through which role).

The following code shows a simple example using the procedures and the dictionary views mentioned in this section. User OE has obtained privileges on certain objects owned by HR, and you want to identify the privileges used by OE and revoke the unused privileges.

As SYSTEM user (or user with CAPTURE_ADMIN role), you create and enable the capture.

```
SQL> show user
USER is "SYSTEM"
SQL> exec SYS.DBMS_PRIVILEGE_CAPTURE.CREATE_CAPTURE ( -
      name => 'REVIEW_OE_PRIV', -
      description => 'Review OE privileges', -
      type => dbms_privilege_capture.g_context, -
      condition => 'SYS_CONTEXT(''USERENV'',''SESSION_USER'' ) = ''OE'' ');

PL/SQL procedure successfully completed.

SQL>
SQL> exec SYS.DBMS_PRIVILEGE_CAPTURE.ENABLE_CAPTURE ( -
      name => 'REVIEW_OE_PRIV');

PL/SQL procedure successfully completed.

SQL>
```

Now as OE user, you perform a few actions.

```
SQL> show user
USER is "OE"
SQL> select count(*) from hr.employees;
  COUNT(*)
----------
       107


SQL> update hr.employees set salary = salary where employee_id = 120;
1 row updated.
```

Next, you connect back as SYSTEM user and disable the capture. Then you generate the results to query the views.

```
SQL> show user
USER is "SYSTEM"
SQL> exec SYS.DBMS_PRIVILEGE_CAPTURE.DISABLE_CAPTURE ( -
      name => 'REVIEW_OE_PRIV');

PL/SQL procedure successfully completed.

SQL> exec SYS.DBMS_PRIVILEGE_CAPTURE.GENERATE_RESULT ( -
      name => 'REVIEW_OE_PRIV');

PL/SQL procedure successfully completed.
```

Then you review which system privileges were used by OE during the analysis period.

```
SQL> SELECT username, sys_priv
    FROM dba_used_sysprivs;

USERNAME   SYS_PRIV
---------- --------------------
OE         CREATE SESSION
```

Then review which object privileges were used by OE during the analysis period. DBA_USED_PRIVS view shows both the system and the object privileges used.

```
SQL> SELECT username, object_name, obj_priv
    FROM dba_used_objprivs;
```

USERNAME	OBJECT_NAME	OBJ_PRIV
OE	EMPLOYEES	SELECT
OE	ORA$BASE	USE
OE	DUAL	SELECT
OE	PRODUCT_PRIVS	SELECT
OE	DUAL	SELECT
OE	DBMS_APPLICATION_INFO	EXECUTE
OE	EMPLOYEES	UPDATE

The DBA_UNUSED_PRIVS view shows the privileges that are unused and potentially revoked from OE. Part of the output is truncated in the following.

```
SQL> SELECT username, sys_priv, obj_priv, object_owner, object_name
     FROM dba_unused_privs;
```

USERNAME	SYS_PRIV	OBJ_PRIV	OBJECT_	OBJECT_NAME
OE		REFERENCES	HR	EMPLOYEES
OE		ALTER	HR	EMPLOYEES
OE		DELETE	HR	EMPLOYEES
OE		INDEX	HR	EMPLOYEES
OE		INSERT	HR	EMPLOYEES
OE		EXECUTE	SYS	DBMS_STATS
OE		SELECT	HR	COUNTRIES
OE		REFERENCES	HR	COUNTRIES
OE		SELECT	HR	LOCATIONS
OE		REFERENCES	HR	LOCATIONS
... ...				
OE	CREATE DATABASE LINK			
OE	UNLIMITED TABLESPACE			
... ...				
OE	CREATE TRIGGER			
OE	CREATE TYPE			
OE	CREATE OPERATOR			
OE	CREATE INDEXTYPE			
OE		DELETE	XDB	APP_USERS_AND_ROLES
OE		INSERT	XDB	APP_USERS_AND_ROLES

After you are satisfied with the analysis, drop the capture.

```
SQL> exec SYS.DBMS_PRIVILEGE_CAPTURE.DROP_CAPTURE ( -
      name => 'REVIEW_OE_PRIV');

PL/SQL procedure successfully completed.
```

Controlling Resource Usage by Users

Oracle Database 12*c* lets you limit some resources that your user accounts consume. Disk-space limits are governed by tablespace quotas (discussed in "Assigning Tablespace and Quotas" earlier in the chapter); CPU and memory limits are implemented with *profiles.*

CPU and session-oriented resource limits are managed through profiles. Profiles let you set limits for several resources, including CPU time, memory, and the number of logical reads performed during a user session or database call. A database call is either a parse, an execute, or a fetch. Usually, the database implicitly performs these calls for you. You can explicitly make these database calls from Java, PL/SQL, or Oracle Call Interface (OCI) programs.

A logical read is a measure of the amount of work the database performs while executing SQL statements. Statements that generate more logical reads require the database to perform more work than statements generating fewer logical reads. Technically, a logical read is counted for each row accessed via ROWID (index access) and for each data block accessed via a multiblock read (full-table scan or index fast-full scan).

To enable resource limit restrictions with profiles, first enable them in the database by setting the initialization parameter resource_limit to TRUE, like this:

```
ALTER SYSTEM SET resource_limit = TRUE SCOPE = BOTH;
```

To assign resource limits to a profile, use the CREATE PROFILE or ALTER PROFILE statement with one or more of the kernel resource parameters. The following is an example of the CREATE PROFILE statement, with all the resources that can be controlled. A resource value of DEFAULT indicates that the value is derived from the DEFAULT profile. Initially, the DEFAULT profile has all the system resources set to UNLIMITED.

```
CREATE PROFILE "TEST1" LIMIT
CPU_PER_SESSION DEFAULT
CPU_PER_CALL DEFAULT
CONNECT_TIME DEFAULT
IDLE_TIME 10
SESSIONS_PER_USER DEFAULT
LOGICAL_READS_PER_SESSION DEFAULT
LOGICAL_READS_PER_CALL 250000
PRIVATE_SGA 25000
COMPOSITE_LIMIT DEFAULT;
```

Each resource is explained here:

CONNECT_TIME   This limits any session established by a user having this profile set to the specified number of minutes. Connection time is sometimes called wall clock time to differentiate it from CPU time. When a session exceeds the specified number of minutes, the database rolls back any uncommitted changes and terminates the session. The next call to the database raises an exception. You can use the special value UNLIMITED to tell the database that there is no limit to a session's duration. Set this parameter in a CREATE PROFILE or ALTER PROFILE statement like this:

```
CREATE PROFILE agent LIMIT CONNECT_TIME 10;
ALTER PROFILE data_analyst LIMIT CONNECT_TIME UNLIMITED;
```

CPU_PER_CALL   This limits the amount of CPU time that can be consumed by any single database call in any session established by a user with this profile. The specified value is in hundredths of a second and applies to a parse, an execute, or a fetch call. These calls are implicitly performed by the database for any SQL statement executed in SQL*Plus and can be explicitly called from OCI, Java, and PL/SQL programs. When this limit is breached, the statement fails and is automatically rolled back, and an exception is raised. The user can then commit or roll back any uncommitted changes in the transaction. Set this parameter in a CREATE PROFILE or ALTER PROFILE statement like this:

```
CREATE PROFILE agent LIMIT CPU_PER_CALL 3000;
ALTER PROFILE data_analyst LIMIT CPU_PER_CALL UNLIMITED;
```

CPU_PER_SESSION   This limits the amount of CPU time that can be consumed in any session established by a user with this profile. The specified value is in hundredths of a second and applies to a parse, an execute, or a fetch. When this limit is breached, the current statement fails, the transaction is automatically rolled back, and an exception is raised. The user can then commit or roll back any uncommitted changes in the transaction before logging off. Set this parameter in a CREATE PROFILE or ALTER PROFILE statement like this:

```
CREATE PROFILE agent LIMIT CPU_PER_CALL 30000;
ALTER PROFILE data_analyst LIMIT CPU_PER_CALL UNLIMITED;
```

IDLE_TIME   This limits the duration of time between database calls to the specified number of minutes. If a user having this profile exceeds this setting, the next statement fails, and the user is allowed to either commit or roll back any uncommitted changes before logging off. Long-running statements are not affected by this setting. Set IDLE_TIME in a CREATE PROFILE or ALTER PROFILE statement like this:

```
CREATE PROFILE agent LIMIT IDLE_TIME 10;
ALTER PROFILE daemon LIMIT IDLE_TIME UNLIMITED;
```

LOGICAL_READS_PER_CALL   This caps the amount of work that any individual database call performs to the specified number of logical reads. The database call is either a parse, an execute, or a fetch. If the limit is exceeded, the database rolls back the statement, returns an error to the calling program, and allows the user to either commit or roll back any uncommitted changes. Logical reads are computed as the sum of consistent gets plus current mode gets. Set this parameter in a CREATE PROFILE or ALTER PROFILE statement like this:

```
CREATE PROFILE agent LIMIT LOGICAL_READS_PER_CALL 2500;
ALTER PROFILE data_analyst LIMIT LOGICAL_READS_PER_CALL 1000000;
```

LOGICAL_READS_PER_SESSION   This limits the amount of database work that a user's session can consume to the specified number of logical reads. When the limit is exceeded, the current statement fails and an exception is raised, and the user must either commit or roll back the transaction and end the session. Logical reads are computed as the sum of consistent gets plus current mode gets. Set this parameter in a CREATE PROFILE or ALTER PROFILE statement like this:

```
CREATE PROFILE agent LIMIT LOGICAL_READS_PER_SESSION 250000;
ALTER PROFILE data_analyst
    LIMIT LOGICAL_READS_PER_SESSION 35000000;
```

PRIVATE_SGA   This limits the amount of system global area (SGA) memory in bytes that a user connecting with shared servers (via a multi-threaded server [MTS]) can allocate to the persistent area in the program global area (PGA). This area contains bind information among other items. Set this parameter in a CREATE PROFILE or ALTER PROFILE statement like this:

```
CREATE PROFILE agent LIMIT PRIVATE_SGA 2500;
ALTER PROFILE data_analyst LIMIT PRIVATE_SGA UNLIMITED;
```

SESSIONS_PER_USER   This restricts a user with this profile to the specified number of database sessions. This setting can be useful to discourage DBAs from all connecting to a shared administrative account to do their work when corporate policy indicates that they should be connecting to their individual accounts. Set this parameter in a CREATE PROFILE or ALTER PROFILE statement like this:

```
CREATE PROFILE admin_profile LIMIT SESSIONS_PER_USER 2;
ALTER PROFILE data_analyst LIMIT SESSIONS_PER_USER 6;
```

COMPOSITE_LIMIT   This limits the number of service units that can be consumed during a user session. Service units are calculated as the weighted sum of CPU_PER_SESSION, LOGICAL_READS_PER_SESSION, CONNECT_TIME, and PRIVATE_SGA values. The weightings are established with the ALTER RESOURCE COST statement and can be viewed from the RESOURCE_COST data dictionary view. This COMPOSITE_LIMIT allows you to cap the resource consumption of user groups in more complex ways than a single resource limit. Set this parameter in a CREATE PROFILE or ALTER PROFILE statement like this:

```
CREATE PROFILE admi_profile LIMIT COMPOSITE_LIMIT UNLIMITED;
ALTER PROFILE data_analyst LIMIT COMPOSITE_LIMIT 100000;
```

To enforce the resource limits established with profiles, you must enable them by setting the initialization parameter RESOURCE_LIMIT to TRUE. The default setting is FALSE. Set this parameter with the ALTER SYSTEM statement, like this:

```
ALTER SYSTEM SET resource_limit = TRUE SCOPE=BOTH;
```

You can also use profiles to manage passwords, which is discussed in the next section.

Implementing Password Security Features

For users who are configured for database authentication, password-security rules are enforced with profiles and password complexity rules with verification functions. Profiles have a set of standard rules that define how long a password can remain valid, the elapsed time, the number of password changes before a password can be reused, the number of failed login attempts that will lock the account, and how long the account will remain locked.

If you want a parameter to inherit the setting from the DEFAULT profile, set the parameter's value to the keyword DEFAULT. Explicitly assign password rules to a profile using the CREATE PROFILE or ALTER PROFILE statement. The following is an example of the CREATE PROFILE statement, with all the password features that can be controlled:

```
CREATE PROFILE "TEST2" LIMIT
PASSWORD_LIFE_TIME 60
PASSWORD_GRACE_TIME 7
PASSWORD_REUSE_MAX 2
PASSWORD_REUSE_TIME 4
PASSWORD_LOCK_TIME DEFAULT
FAILED_LOGIN_ATTEMPTS 5
PASSWORD_VERIFY_FUNCTION DEFAULT;
```

Each option is discussed in detail here with examples:

FAILED_LOGIN_ATTEMPTS and PASSWORD_LOCK_TIME   The FAILED_LOGIN_ATTEMPTS parameter specifies how many times in a row the user can fail password authentication. If this limit is breached, the account is locked for PASSWORD_LOCK_TIME days. If the PASSWORD_LOCK_TIME parameter is set to UNLIMITED and a user exceeds FAILED_LOGIN_ATTEMPTS, the account must be manually unlocked. You can set these parameters in a CREATE PROFILE or ALTER PROFILE statement like this:

```
-- lock account for 10 minutes if 3 consecutive logins fail
CREATE PROFILE agent LIMIT
    FAILED_LOGIN_ATTEMPTS 3
    PASSWORD_LOCK_TIME 10/1440;

-- remove failed login restrictions
ALTER PROFILE student LIMIT FAILED_LOGIN_ATTEMPTS UNLIMITED;
```

```
-- manually unlock an account
ALTER USER scott ACCOUNT UNLOCK;
```

The default value for FAILED_LOGIN_ATTEMPTS in Oracle Database 12c is 10 and for PASSWORD_LOCK_TIME is 1 day.

PASSWORD_LIFE_TIME and PASSWORD_GRACE_TIME   The PASSWORD_LIFE_TIME parameter specifies the maximum number of days that a password can remain in force, and PASSWORD_GRACE_TIME is the number of days after the first successful login following password expiration during which the user will be reminded to change their password but allowed to log in. After the PASSWORD_GRACE_TIME limit is reached, the user must change their password. If you set PASSWORD_LIFE_TIME to a value and set PASSWORD_GRACE_TIME to UNLIMITED, users will be reminded to change their password every time they log in but never forced to actually do so. You can set these two parameters in a CREATE PROFILE or ALTER PROFILE statement like this:

```
-- limit the password lifetime to 90 days
-- during the last 14 days the user will be reminded
-- to change the password
CREATE PROFILE agent LIMIT
    PASSWORD_LIFE_TIME 90 - 14
    PASSWORD_GRACE_TIME 14;

-- set no limit to password lifetime
ALTER PROFILE student LIMIT
    PASSWORD_LIFE_TIME UNLIMITED
    PASSWORD_GRACE_TIME DEFAULT;
```

The default value for PASSWORD_LIFE_TIME in Oracle Database 12c is 180 days and for PASSWORD_GRACE_TIME is 7 days.

PASSWORD_REUSE_TIME and PASSWORD_REUSE_MAX   The PASSWORD_REUSE_TIME parameter specifies the minimum number of days that must transpire before a password can be reused. PASSWORD_REUSE_MAX specifies the minimum number of password changes that must occur before a password can be reused. If you specify a value for one of these two parameters and UNLIMITED for the other, passwords can never be reused. If you set both PASSWORD_REUSE_TIME and PASSWORD_REUSE_MAX to UNLIMITED (the default), these parameters are essentially disabled. You can set these password parameters in a CREATE PROFILE or ALTER PROFILE statement like this:

```
-- require at least 4 password changes and 1 year
-- before a password may be reused.
CREATE PROFILE agent LIMIT
    PASSWORD_REUSE_TIME 365
    PASSWORD_REUSE_MAX 4;
```

```
-- remove password reuse constraints
ALTER PROFILE student LIMIT
   PASSWORD_REUSE_TIME UNLIMITED
   PASSWORD_REUSE_MAX UNLIMITED;
```

 Real World Scenario

Setting Password Lock Time to Two Hours

Several password attributes are durations expressed in days. These durations are normally set with integer values, such as 1, 15, 30, 90, or 365 days.

The default password lock time for Oracle Database 12c is 1 day, and the unit used to express the lock time is in days. A few of the clients we've worked for needed the password lock to go away after two hours if the user tried to enter an incorrect password too many times. How do you set the value in hours or minutes when the unit is in days?

All these password profile attributes take fractional values as well; therefore, you can represent hours and minutes. Because there are 1,440 minutes in a day, you can represent 5 minutes as 5/1,440 days and represent 5 seconds as 5/86,400 days. The following code sets the password lock time to two hours:

```
ALTER PROFILE student LIMIT PASSWORD_LOCK_TIME 2/24;
```

You can represent the value using decimal numbers; for example, the following code sets the password lock time to six hours:

```
ALTER PROFILE student LIMIT PASSWORD_LOCK_TIME .25;
```

Using a fractional number of days is a great way to try combinations of values and observe the results of setting these password rules.

PASSWORD_VERIFY_FUNCTION   The PASSWORD_VERIFY_FUNCTION parameter lets you codify additional rules that will be verified when a password is changed. These rules usually verify password complexity such as minimal password length or check that a password does not appear in a dictionary. The PL/SQL function used in the PASSWORD_VERIFY_FUNCTION parameter must be created under the user SYS and must have three parameters of type VARCHAR2. These parameters must contain the username in the first parameter, the new password in the second, and the old password in the third. You can set this parameter in a CREATE PROFILE or ALTER PROFILE statement like this:

```
-- use a custom password function
CREATE PROFILE agent LIMIT PASSWORD_VERIFY_FUNCTION my_function;
```

```
-- disable use of a custom function
ALTER PROFILE student LIMIT PASSWORD_VERIFY_FUNCTION DEFAULT;
```

 **Real World Scenario**

Implementing a Corporate Password-Security Policy

Many companies have security policies requiring that several password complexity rules be followed. For your Oracle database, these rules can be incorporated into a password verify function. This real-world scenario highlights an example of three password complexity requirements and how they are satisfied through a password verify function named MY_PASSWORD_VERIFY.

The first rule specifies that the password must be at least six characters in length. The second rule disallows passwords containing some form of either the username or the word *password*. The third rule requires the password to contain at least one alphabetic character, at least one digit, and at least one punctuation character. If the new password fails any of these tests, the function raises an exception, and the password change fails.

After creating this function as user SYS, assign it to a profile, like this:

ALTER PROFILE student LIMIT password_verify_function my_password_verify;

Any user having the student profile will need to abide by the password rules enforced by the my_password_verify function:

```
CREATE OR REPLACE FUNCTION my_password_verify
    (username VARCHAR2
    ,password VARCHAR2
    ,old_password VARCHAR2
    ) RETURN BOOLEAN
IS

BEGIN
    -- Check for the minimum length of the password
    IF LENGTH(password) < 6 THEN
        raise_application_error(-20001
            ,'Password must be at least 6 characters long');
    END IF;

    -- Check that the password does not contain any
    -- upper/lowercase version of either the user name
    -- or the keyword PASSWORD
```

```
    IF (    regexp_like(password,username,'i')
       OR regexp_like(password,'password','i')) THEN
        raise_application_error(-20002
            ,'Password cannot contain username or PASSWORD');
    END IF;

    -- Check that the password contains at least one letter,
    -- one digit and one punctuation character
    IF NOT(    regexp_like(password,'[[:digit:]]')
          AND regexp_like(password,'[[:alpha:]]')
          AND regexp_like(password,'[[:punct:]]')
          ) THEN
        raise_application_error(-20003
            ,'Password must contain at least one digit '||
            'and one letter and one punctuation character');
    END IF;

    -- password is okey dokey
    RETURN(TRUE);
END;
/
```

Oracle Database 12c provides the PL/SQL code to create a password complexity verify function. The script is called `utlpwdmg.sql` and is in the `$ORACLE_HOME/rdbms/admin` directory. The name of the function created using this script is called `ora12c_verify_function`. This script also creates `ora12c_strong_verify_function` for stringent password check requirements.

OEM Database Express can be used to create and manage profiles. Choose Profiles from the Security drop-down menu. Figure 13.6 shows the Create Profile screen.

Auditing Database Activity

Auditing involves monitoring and recording specific database activity. Oracle Database 12c Traditional Auditing supports four levels of auditing:

- Statement
- Privilege
- Object
- Fine-grained access

FIGURE 13.6   Creating a profile with Database Express

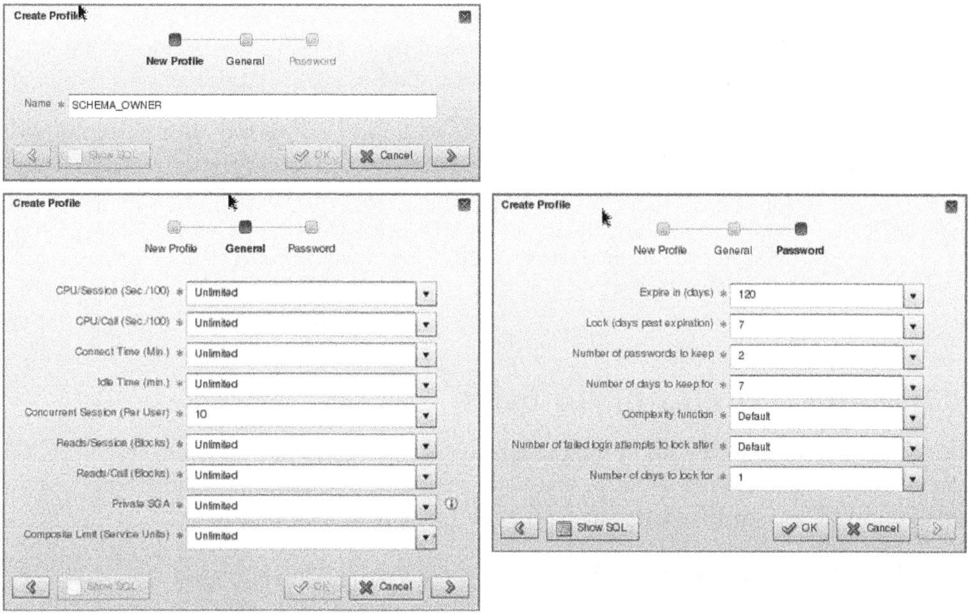

These afford you two locations for recording these activities. Audit records can be stored in either of these locations:

- Database
- Operating-system files

You tell the Oracle Database 12*c* where to record audit-trail records by setting the initialization parameter `audit_trail`. The default is DB, as in AUDIT_TRAIL=DB (that is, if the database was created using DBCA, otherwise the auditing is disabled), which tells the database to record audit records in the database. AUDIT_TRAIL=DB,EXTENDED tells the database to record audit records in the database together with bind variables (SQLBIND) and the SQL statement triggering the audit entry (SQLTEXT). AUDIT_TRAIL=OS tells the database to record audit records in operating-system files. You cannot change this parameter in memory, only in your pfile or spfile. For example, the following statement will change the location of audit records in the spfile and will be in effect after a database restart:

```
ALTER SYSTEM SET audit_trail=DB SCOPE=SPFILE;
```

The `audit_trail` parameter can also have the values XML and XML,EXTENDED. With these two options, audit records are written to OS files in XML format. The value of NONE disables auditing.

After changing the `audit_trail` parameter, you will need to bounce (shut down and start up) your database instance for the change to take effect.

When recorded in the database, most audit entries are recorded in the SYS.AUD$ table. On Unix systems, operating-system audit records are written into files in the directory specified by the initialization parameter audit_file_dest (which is set to $ORACLE_BASE/admin/$ORACLE_SID/adump if the database is created using DBCA). On Windows systems, these audit records are written to the Event Viewer log file.

The four levels of auditing are described in the following sections.

Certain database activities are always recorded in the OS audit files. Database connections using administrator privileges such as SYSDBA and SYS-OPER are recorded. Database startup and shutdown are also recorded in the OS audit files.

Managing Statement Auditing

Statement auditing involves monitoring and recording the execution of specific types of SQL statements. In the following sections, you will learn how to enable and disable statement auditing as well as identify what statement auditing options are enabled.

Enabling Statement Auditing

You enable auditing of specific SQL statements with an AUDIT statement. For example, to audit the SQL statements CREATE TABLE, DROP TABLE, and TRUNCATE TABLE, use the TABLE audit option like this:

```
AUDIT table;
```

To record audit entries for specific users only, include a BY *USER* clause in the AUDIT statement. For example, to audit CREATE, DROP, and TRUNCATE TABLE statements for user juanita only, execute the following:

```
AUDIT table BY juanita;
```

Frequently, you want to record only attempts that fail—perhaps to look for users who are probing the system to see what they can get away with. To further limit auditing to only these unsuccessful executions, use a WHENEVER clause like this:

```
AUDIT table BY juanita WHENEVER NOT SUCCESSFUL;
```

You can alternatively specify WHENEVER SUCCESSFUL to record only successful statements. If you do not include a WHENEVER clause, both successful and unsuccessful statements will trigger audit records.

You can further configure non-DDL statements to record one audit entry for the triggering session or one entry for each auditable action during the session. Specify BY ACCESS or BY SESSION in the AUDIT statement, like this:

```
AUDIT INSERT TABLE BY juanita BY ACCESS;
```

There are many auditing options other than TABLE or INSERT TABLE. Table 13.1 shows common statement-auditing options.

TABLE 13.1   Statement-Auditing Options

Statement-Auditing Option	Triggering SQL Statements
ALTER SEQUENCE	ALTER SEQUENCE
ALTER TABLE	ALTER TABLE
DATABASE LINK	CREATE DATABASE LINK DROP DATABASE LINK
DELETE TABLE	DELETE
EXECUTE PROCEDURE	Execution of any procedure or function or access to any cursor or variable in a package
GRANT PROCEDURE	GRANT on a function, package, or procedure
GRANT SEQUENCE	GRANT on a sequence
GRANT TABLE	GRANT on a table or view
INDEX	CREATEINDEX
INSERT TABLE	INSERT into table or view
LOCK TABLE	LOCK
NOT EXISTS	All SQL statements
PROCEDURE	CREATE FUNCTION DROP FUNCTION CREATE PACKAGE CREATE PACKAGE BODY DROP PACKAGE CREATE PROCEDURE DROP PROCEDURE
PROFILE	CREATE PROFILE ALTER PROFILE DROP PROFILE

TABLE 13.1 Statement-Auditing Options *(continued)*

Statement-Auditing Option	Triggering SQL Statements
ROLE	CREATE ROLE ALTER ROLE DROP ROLE SET ROLE
SELECT SEQUENCE	SELECT on a sequence
SELECT TABLE	SELECT from table or view
SEQUENCE	CREATE SEQUENCE DROP SEQUENCE
SESSION	LOGON
SYNONYM	CREATE SYNONYM DROP SYNONYM
SYSTEM AUDIT	AUDIT NOAUDIT
SYSTEM GRANT	GRANT REVOKE
TABLE	CREATE TABLE DROP TABLE TRUNCATE TABLE
TABLESPACE	CREATE TABLESPACE ALTER TABLESPACE DROP TABLESPACE
TRIGGER	CREATE TRIGGER ALTER TRIGGER (to enable or disable) ALTER TABLE (to enable all or disable all)
UPDATE TABLE	UPDATE on a table or view

Statement-Auditing Option	Triggering SQL Statements
USER	CREATE USER
	ALTER USER
	DROP USER
VIEW	CREATE VIEW
	DROP VIEW

Identifying Enabled Statement-Auditing Options

You can identify the statement-auditing options that have been enabled in your database by querying the DBA_STMT_AUDIT_OPTS data dictionary view. For example, the following example shows that SESSION auditing is enabled for all users, NOT EXISTS auditing is enabled for all users, and TABLE auditing WHENEVER NOT SUCCESSFUL is enabled for user juanita:

```
SELECT audit_option, failure, success, user_name
FROM dba_stmt_audit_opts
ORDER BY audit_option, user_name;


AUDIT_OPTION          FAILURE     SUCCESS     USER_NAME
--------------------  ----------  ----------  -------------

CREATE SESSION        BY ACCESS   BY ACCESS
NOT EXISTS            BY ACCESS   BY ACCESS
TABLE                 BY ACCESS   NOT SET     JUANITA
```

You can enable administrator auditing by setting the initialization parameter AUDIT_SYS_OPERATIONS=TRUE. All the activities performed connected as SYS or SYSDBA/SYSOPER privileges are recorded in the OS audit trail.

Disabling Statement Auditing

To disable auditing of a specific SQL statement, use a NOAUDIT statement, which allows the same BY and WHENEVER options as the AUDIT statement. If you enable auditing for a specific user, specify that user in the NOAUDIT statement as well. However, it is not necessary to include the WHENEVER NOT SUCCESSFUL clause in the NOAUDIT statement.

For example, to disable the three audit options in the previous section, execute the following three statements:

```
NOAUDIT session;
NOAUDIT not exists;
NOAUDIT table BY juanita;
```

Examining the Audit Trail

Statement, privilege, and object audit records are written to the SYS.AUD$ table and made available via the data dictionary views DBA_AUDIT_TRAIL and USER_AUDIT_TRAIL. These data dictionary views cannot contain values for every record because these views are used for three different types of audit records. For example, you can view the user, time, and type of statement audited for user juanita by executing the following:

```
SELECT username, timestamp, action_name
FROM dba_audit_trail
WHERE username = 'JUANITA';
```

```
ORA USER          TIMESTAMP               ACTION_NAME
---------------   ---------------------   -------------
JUANITA           15-Jun-2004 18:43:52    LOGON
JUANITA           15-Jun-2004 18:44:19    LOGOFF
JUANITA           15-Jun-2004 18:46:01    LOGON
JUANITA           15-Jun-2004 18:46:40    CREATE TABLE
```

If you enable AUDIT SESSION, the database creates one audit record when a user logs on and updates that record when the user logs off successfully. These session audit records contain some valuable information that can help you narrow the focus of your tuning efforts. Among the information recorded in the audit records are the username, logon time, logoff time, and the number of physical reads and logical reads performed during the session. By looking for sessions with high counts of logical or physical reads, you can identify high-resource-consuming jobs and narrow the focus of your tuning efforts.

Managing Privilege Auditing

Privilege auditing involves monitoring and recording the execution of SQL statements that require a specific system privilege, such as SELECT ANY TABLE or GRANT ANY PRIVILEGE. You can audit any system privilege. In the following sections, you will learn how to enable and disable privilege auditing as well as identify which privilege-auditing options are enabled in your database.

Enabling Privilege Auditing

You enable privilege auditing with an AUDIT statement, specifying the system privilege that you want to monitor. For example, to audit statements that require the system privilege CREATE ANY TABLE, execute the following:

```
AUDIT create any table;
```

To record audit entries for specific users only, include a BY *USER* clause in the AUDIT statement. For example, to audit SQL statements made by user juanita that require the CREATE ANY TABLE privilege, execute the following:

```
AUDIT create any table BY juanita;
```

Just as you do with statement auditing, you can further configure non-DDL privileges to record one audit entry for the triggering session or one for each auditable action during the session by specifying BY ACCESS or BY SESSION in the AUDIT statement, like this:

```
AUDIT DELETE ANY TABLE BY juanita BY ACCESS;
```

Identifying Enabled Privilege-Auditing Options

You can report on the privilege auditing that has been enabled in your database by querying the DBA_PRIV_AUDIT_OPTS data dictionary view. For example, the following report shows that ALTER PROFILE auditing is enabled for all users and that ALTER USER and DELETE ANY TABLE auditing is enabled for user juanita:

```
SELECT privilege, user_name
FROM dba_priv_audit_opts
ORDER BY privilege, user_name;

PRIVILEGE            USER_NAME
-------------------- -----------------
ALTER PROFILE
DELETE ANY TABLE     JUANITA
ALTER USER           JUANITA
```

Disabling Privilege Auditing

To disable auditing of a system privilege, use a NOAUDIT statement. The NOAUDIT statement allows the same BY options as the AUDIT statement. If you enable auditing for a specific user, you need to specify that user in the NOAUDIT statement. For example, to disable the three audit options in the previous section, execute the following three statements:

```
NOAUDIT alter profile;
NOAUDIT delete any table BY juanita;
NOAUDIT alter user BY juanita;
```

Managing Object Auditing

Object auditing involves monitoring and recording the execution of SQL statements that require a specific object privilege, such as SELECT, INSERT, UPDATE, DELETE, or EXECUTE. Unlike either statement or system privilege auditing, schema object auditing cannot be restricted to specific users—it is enabled for all users or no users. In the following sections, you will learn how to enable and disable object-auditing options as well as identify which object-auditing options are enabled.

Enabling Object Auditing

You enable object auditing with an AUDIT statement, specifying both the object and object privilege that you want to monitor. For example, to audit SELECT statements on the HR.EMPLOYEE_SALARY table, execute the following:

```
AUDIT select ON hr.employee_salary;
```

You can further configure these audit records to record one audit entry for the triggering session or one for each auditable action during the session by specifying BY ACCESS or BY SESSION in the AUDIT statement. This access/session configuration can be defined differently for successful or unsuccessful executions. For example, to make one audit entry per auditable action for successful SELECT statements on the HR.EMPLOYEE_SALARY table, execute the following:

```
-- one audit entry for each triggering statement
AUDIT select ON hr.employee_salary
   BY ACCESS WHENEVER SUCCESSFUL;
```

Another example, to make one audit entry for all unsuccessful SELECT access in the session on the HR.EMPLOYEE_SALARY table.

```
-- one audit entry for the session experiencing one or more
-- triggering statements
AUDIT select ON hr.employee_salary
   BY SESSION WHENEVER NOT SUCCESSFUL;
```

Identifying Enabled Object-Auditing Options

The object-auditing options that are enabled in the database are recorded in the DBA_OBJ_AUDIT_OPTS data dictionary view. Unlike the statement and privilege _AUDIT_OPTS views, the DBA_OBJ_AUDIT_OPTS data dictionary view always has one row for each auditable object in the database. There are columns for each object privilege that auditing can be enabled on, and in each of these columns, a code is reported that shows the auditing options. For example, the following report on the HR.EMPLOYEES table shows that no auditing is enabled, for the INSERT object privilege and that the SELECT object privilege has auditing enabled with one audit entry for each access when the access is successful and one audit entry for each session when the access is not successful:

```
SELECT owner, object_name, object_type, ins, sel
FROM dba_obj_audit_opts
WHERE owner='HR'
```

```
AND    object_name='EMPLOYEE_SALARY';

OWNER          OBJECT_NAME                OBJECT_TY INS SEL
-----------    -------------------------  --------- --- ---
HR             EMPLOYEE_SALARY            TABLE     -/-  A/S
```

The coding for the object privilege columns contains one of three possible values: a hyphen (-) to indicate no auditing is enabled, an A to indicate BY ACCESS, or an S to indicate BY SESSION. The first code (preceding the slash) denotes the action for successful statements, and the second code (after the slash) denotes the action for unsuccessful statements.

Disabling Object Auditing

To disable object auditing, use a NOAUDIT statement, which allows the same WHENEVER options as the AUDIT statement. For example, to disable the auditing of unsuccessful SELECT statements against the HR.EMPLOYEES table, execute the following:

```
NOAUDIT select ON hr.employee_salary  WHENEVER NOT SUCCESSFUL;
```

Using SQL Developer for Audit Management

You can also use SQL Developer to enable and disable auditing. Under the DBA menu, choose Security and then Audit Settings, as shown in Figure 13.7.

FIGURE 13.7   The SQL Developer Audit Settings screen

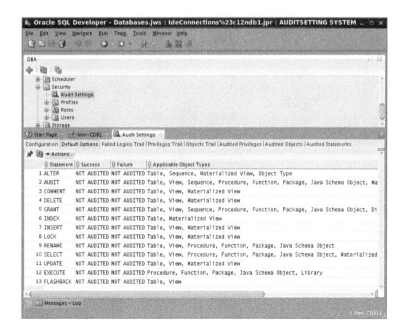

The Actions drop-down menu has three options. The Edit Audited Privileges option enables or disables the auditing of privileges. Figure 13.8 shows the Audited Privileges screen.

FIGURE 13.8 The SQL Developer Edit Audited Privileges screen

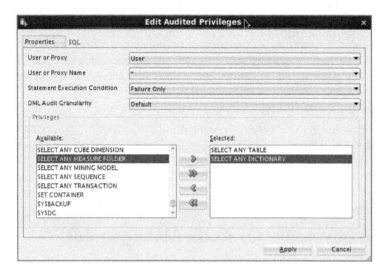

The Edit Audited Objects screen is shown in Figure 13.9. Object privilege auditing is managed using this screen.

FIGURE 13.9 SQL Developer Edit Audited Objects screen

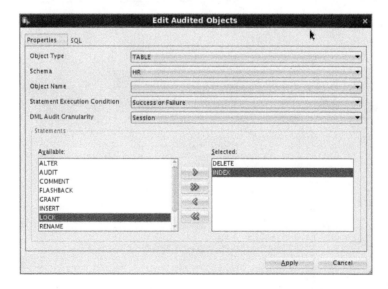

The Edit Audited Statements screen is shown in Figure 13.10. Statement privilege auditing is managed using this screen.

FIGURE 13.10 The SQL Developer Edit Audited Statements screen

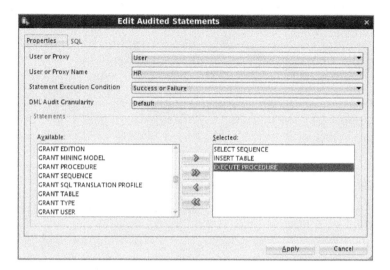

Purging the Audit Trail

Database audit records for statement, privilege, and object auditing are stored in the SYS.AUD$ table. Depending on how extensive your auditing and retention policies are, you will need to periodically delete old audit records from this table. The database does not provide an interface to assist in deleting rows from the audit table, so you will need to do so yourself. To purge audit records older than 90 days, execute the following as user SYS:

```
DELETE FROM sys.aud$ WHERE timestamp# < SYSDATE -90;
```

You might want to copy the audit records into a different table for historical retention or export them to an operating-system file before removing them. It is a good practice to audit changes to the AUD$ table so that you can identify when changes were made.

Only the user SYS, a user with the DELETE ANY TABLE privilege, or a user to whom SYS granted the DELETE privilege on SYS.AUD$ can delete the audit-trail records from the SYS.AUD$ table.

Oracle Database 12c audits all DML statements against the SYS.AUD$ table. The INSERT, UPDATE, MERGE, and DELETE statements against the SYS.AUD$ table are not deleted from the SYS.AUD$ table. You have to truncate the SYS.AUD$ table to remove such records.

Moving SYS.AUD$ to Another Tablespace

For space management purposes, Oracle supports moving the SYS.AUD$ table out of the SYSTEM tablespace to another tablespace. A PL/SQL package is available for audit-trail management. The following code shows the location of the audit-trail table, and using the DBMS_AUDIT_MGMT package to move the table to SYSAUX tablespace.

```
SQL > select tablespace_name
      from   dba_tables
      where  table_name = 'AUD$';


TABLESPACE_NAME
------------------------------
SYSTEM



SQL> execute DBMS_AUDIT_MGMT.SET_AUDIT_TRAIL_LOCATION( -
     AUDIT_TRAIL_TYPE               => DBMS_AUDIT_MGMT.AUDIT_TRAIL_AUD_STD, -
     AUDIT_TRAIL_LOCATION_VALUE  => 'SYSAUX');

PL/SQL procedure successfully completed.

SQL>
SELECT tablespace_name
FROM   dba_tables
WHERE  table_name = 'AUD$';


TABLESPACE_NAME
------------------------------
SYSAUX
```

Using the Audit Management Framework

Purging OS audit files, AUD$ and FGA_LOG$ records can be automated and completed in a secure and documented procedure using the audit-trail management framework. If you already have procedures set to delete records from AUD$, you may continue to use them, as they may be tuned over years for better management and customized record deletions. To be able to utilize the Oracle Database 12*c* audit-record purging feature, you need to do the following:

1. Initialize the audit cleanup infrastructure using INIT_CLEANUP.
2. Optionally, set the archive timestamp using SET_LAST_ARCHIVE_TIMESTAMP. By default, records older than this timestamp are deleted when purge job is invoked.

3. Purge the records using CLEAN_AUDIT_TRAIL.

4. Optionally, set up a job to clean records periodically using CREATE_PURGE_JOB.

If you are archiving records to another table, database, or location, you must do that outside of this framework and use the SET_LAST_ARCHIVE_TIMESTAMP procedure to set the archive date. Thus, records older than this are deleted when the job runs next time. If you do not need to archive audit records, but delete them after a certain age, you must still use this procedure to set the archive timestamp. If you do not intend to keep any records in the audit trail when the purge job runs, use the "use_last_arch_timestamp => FALSE" parameter for the purge job.

The following dictionary views are used to support the audit management framework:

DBA_AUDIT_MGMT_CONFIG_PARAMS   This shows the current parameters values.

DBA_AUDIT_MGMT_LAST_ARCH_TS   This shows the last archive timestamp set for audit-trail purges.

DBA_AUDIT_MGMT_CLEANUP_JOBS   This shows current cleanup jobs.

DBA_AUDIT_MGMT_CLEAN_EVENTS   This shows the history of purge events. The DBA needs to manually purge records from this view if it grows too large.

The following query shows the audit management configuration parameters.

```
SQL>
SELECT *
FROM    DBA_AUDIT_MGMT_CONFIG_PARAMS;


PARAMETER_NAME              PARAMETER_VALUE AUDIT_TRAIL
-------------------------- --------------- --------------------
DB AUDIT TABLESPACE        SYSAUX          STANDARD AUDIT TRAIL
DB AUDIT TABLESPACE        SYSAUX          FGA AUDIT TRAIL
AUDIT FILE MAX SIZE        10000           OS AUDIT TRAIL
AUDIT FILE MAX SIZE        10000           XML AUDIT TRAIL
AUDIT FILE MAX AGE         5               OS AUDIT TRAIL
AUDIT FILE MAX AGE         5               XML AUDIT TRAIL
DB AUDIT CLEAN BATCH SIZE  10000           STANDARD AUDIT TRAIL
DB AUDIT CLEAN BATCH SIZE  10000           FGA AUDIT TRAIL
OS FILE CLEAN BATCH SIZE   1000            OS AUDIT TRAIL
OS FILE CLEAN BATCH SIZE   1000            XML AUDIT TRAIL
DEFAULT CLEAN UP INTERVAL  24              STANDARD AUDIT TRAIL
```

"DEFAULT CLEAN UP INTERVAL" appears only for Standard Audit Trail because cleanup is enabled only for AUD$ in this database. When Unified Auditing (discussed later) is enabled in the database, more parameters will appear in this view.

Managing Fine-Grained Auditing

Fine-grained auditing (FGA) lets you monitor and record data access based on the content of the data. With FGA, you define an audit policy on a table and optionally a column. When the specified condition evaluates to TRUE, an audit record is created, and an optional event-handler program is called. You use the PL/SQL package DBMS_FGA to configure and manage FGA.

In the following sections, you will learn how to create, drop, enable, and disable fine-grained auditing policies.

Creating an FGA Policy

To create a new FGA policy, use the packaged procedure DBMS_FGA.ADD_POLICY. This procedure has the following parameters:

object_schema   This is the owner of the object to be audited. The default is NULL, which tells the database to use the current user.

object_name   This is the name of the object to be monitored.

policy_name   This is a unique name for the new policy

audit_condition   This is a SQL expression that evaluates to a Boolean. When this condition evaluates to either TRUE or NULL (the default), an audit record can be created. This condition cannot directly use the SYSDATE, UID, USER, or USERENV functions; it cannot use subqueries or sequences; and it cannot reference the pseudocolumns LEVEL, PRIOR, and ROWNUM.

audit_column   This is a comma-delimited list of columns that the database will look to access. If a column in audit_column is referenced in the SQL statement and the audit_condition is not FALSE, an audit record is created. Columns appearing in audit_column do not have to also appear in the audit_condition expression. The default value is NULL, which tells the database that any column being referenced should trigger the audit record.

handler_schema   This is the owner of the event handler procedure. The default is NULL, which tells the database to use the current schema.

handler_module   This is the name of the event handler procedure. The default NULL tells the database to not use an event handler. If the event handler is a packaged procedure, the handler_module must reference both the package name and the program, using dot notation, like this:

```
UTL_MAIL.SEND_ATTACH_RAW
```

enable   This is a Boolean that tells the database whether this policy should be in effect. The default is TRUE.

statement_types   This tells the database which types of statements to monitor. Valid values are a comma-delimited list of SELECT, INSERT, UPDATE, and DELETE. The default is SELECT.

audit_trail   This parameter tells the database whether to record the SQL statement and bind variables for the triggering SQL in the audit trail. The default value DBMS_FGA .DB_EXTENDED indicates that the SQL statement and bind variables should be recorded in the audit trail. Set this parameter to DBMS_FGA.DB to save space by not recording the SQL statement or bind variables in the audit trail.

audit_column_ops   This parameter has only two valid values: DBMS_FGA.ALL_COLUMNS and DBMS_FGA.ANY_COLUMNS. When set to DBMS_FGA.ALL_COLUMNS, this parameter tells the database that all columns appearing in the audit_column parameter must be referenced in order to trigger an audit record. The default is DBMS_FGA.ANY_COLUMNS, which tells the database that if any column appearing in the audit_column also appears in the SQL statement, an audit record should be created.

To create a new disabled audit policy named COMPENSATION_AUD that looks for SELECT statements that access the HR.EMPLOYEES table and references either SALARY or COMMISSION_PCT, execute the following:

```
DBMS_FGA.ADD_POLICY(object_schema=>'HR' -
   ,object_name=>'EMPLOYEES' -
   ,policy_name=>'COMPENSATION_AUD' -
   ,audit_column=>'SALARY, COMMISSION_PCT' -
   ,enable=>FALSE -
   ,statement_types=>'SELECT');
```

Enabling an FGA Policy

Use the procedure DBMS_FGA.ENABLE_POLICY to enable an FGA policy. This procedure will not raise an exception if the policy is already enabled. For example, you can enable the COMPENSATION_AUD policy added in the previous section like this:

```
DBMS_FGA.ENABLE_POLICY(object_schema=>'HR' -
   ,object_name=>'EMPLOYEES' -
   ,policy_name=>'COMPENSATION_AUD');
```

WARNING   If you use direct path inserts, be careful with FGA. If an FGA policy is enabled on a table participating in a direct path insert, the auditing overrides the hint, disabling the direct path access and causing conventional inserts. As with all hints, the database does not directly tell you that your hint is being ignored.

Disabling an FGA Policy

To turn off an FGA policy, use the DBMS_FGA.DISABLE_POLICY procedure. Here is an example:

```
DBMS_FGA.DISABLE_POLICY(object_schema=>'HR' -
   ,object_name=>'EMPLOYEES' -
   ,policy_name=>'COMPENSATION_AUD');
```

Dropping an FGA Policy

To remove an FGA policy, use the DBMS_FGA.DROP_POLICY procedure. For example, to drop the COMPENSATION_AUD policy used in this section, run this:

```
DBMS_FGA.DROP_POLICY(object_schema=>'HR' -
   ,object_name=>'EMPLOYEES' -
   ,policy_name=>'COMPENSATION_AUD');
```

Identifying FGA Policies in the Database

Query the DBA_AUDIT_POLICIES data dictionary view to report on the FGA policies defined in your database. For example, the following report shows that the policy named COMPENSATION_AUD on the column SALARY in the table HR.EMPLOYEES is defined but not enabled:

```
SELECT policy_name ,object_schema||'.'||
      object_name object_name
      ,policy_column
      ,enabled ,audit_trail
FROM dba_audit_policies;


POLICY_NAME        OBJECT_NAME   POLICY ENABLED AUDIT_TRAIL
---------------- ------------- ------ ------- -----------
COMPENSATION_AUD HR.EMPLOYEES SALARY NO      DB_EXTENDED
```

Audit records from this policy, when enabled, capture the standard auditing information as well as the text of the SQL statement that triggered the auditing (DB_EXTENDED).

Reporting on the FGA Audit-Trail Entries

The DBA_FGA_AUDIT_TRAIL data dictionary view is used in reporting on the FGA audit entries that have been recorded in the database. The following example shows audit-trail entries for the COMPENSATION_AUD policy, listing the database username and the timestamp of the audit record and computer from which the database connection was made:

```
SELECT db_user, timestamp, userhost
FROM dba_fga_audit_traiL
WHERE policy_name='COMPENSATION_AUD'


DB_USER      TIMESTAMP             USERHOST
------------ -------------------- --------------------
CHIPD        10-Jun-2004 09:48:14 XYZcorp\CHIPNOTEBOOK
JUANITA      19-Jun-2004 14:50:47 XYZcorp\HR_PC2
```

Implementing Unified Auditing

The various audit statements and view audit-trail information discussed so far in this section are also available in versions prior to Oracle Database 12*c*. The traditional auditing architectures involve many audit-trail locations and tables to review information for the auditors, and do not follow a standard. Every new product introduced in the database had to essentially have a new audit table because the AUD$ table is limited. The Oracle *Unified Audit* feature introduced in Oracle Database 12*c* addresses these issues and gives a standard interface and single location for the audit trail.

Unified Auditing is a database option and is not enabled by default. The following query shows if Unified Auditing is enabled or not.

```
SQL> SELECT VALUE FROM V$OPTION
     WHERE PARAMETER = 'Unified Auditing';


VALUE
----------
FALSE
```

To enable Unified Auditing, shut down the database and listener, and then relink the oracle executable using the following options:

```
cd $ORACLE_HOME/rdbms/lib
make -f ins_rdbms.mk uniaud_on ioracle ORACLE_HOME=$ORACLE_HOME
```

Unified Auditing is managed by creating and enabling audit policies. Unified audit-trail records can be read using the UNIFIED_AUDIT_TRAIL view. This view includes audit records from standard and fine-grained auditing, along with auditing of data pump, SQL loader, database vault, label security, recovery manager, and real application security products.

Oracle Database 12*c* has two roles to support Unified Auditing. The AUDIT_ADMIN role has privileges to create, alter, and drop audit policies. It also has privileges to enable or disable audit policies for each business requirement, to view audit records, and to clean up the audit trail. The AUDIT_VIEWER role is for users who only need to view the audit-trail contents. Unified Auditing is owned by AUDSYS user, not SYS user.

 Traditional auditing and Unified Auditing can coexist in an Oracle Database 12*c* database. Both audit-trail locations are populated based on the audits enabled. It is recommended to migrate or use only pure Unified Audit facilities to avoid the cost of writing audit records to multiple locations.

Privilege auditing in traditional auditing has to be enabled by setting the AUDIT_SYS_OPERATIONS=true. The audit records are written to operating system files. With Unified Auditing, privilege audit is enabled by default and can be queried using the same UNIFIED_AUDIT_TRAIL view. In a unified audit database, the following actions are audited mandatorily without any policy:

CREATE AUDIT POLICY

ALTER AUDIT POLICY

DROP AUDIT POLICY

AUDIT

NOAUDIT

EXECUTE of DBMS_FGA

EXECUTE of DBMS_AUDIT_MGMT

When Unified Auditing is enabled, the following audit-related initialization parameters are ignored: AUDIT_TRAIL, AUDIT_FILE_DEST, AUDIT_SYS_OPERATIONS, and AUDIT_SYSLOG_LEVEL. Fine-grained auditing still uses DBMS_FGA.

Creating a Unified Audit Policy

To create an audit policy, the AUDIT SYSTEM system privilege or the AUDIT_ADMIN role is required. The high-level syntax of the CREATE AUDIT POLICY statement is

```
CREATE AUDITY POLICY policy_name   audit_clauses
[WHEN 'audit_condition'
EVALUATE PER [STATEMENT | SESSION | INSTANCE]]
```

The *audit_clauses* have different options and syntax based on whether privilege, statement, or role is audited. The *audit_condition* specifies a condition that determines if the unified audit policy is enforced. If *audit_condition* evaluates to TRUE, then the policy is enforced. If FALSE, then the policy is not enforced.

Audit policy can be based on privileges, actions, or roles. The privilege audit option audits all events that exercise the specified system privilege. The Action Audit option indicates which RDBMS action should be audited. The Role Audit option audits the use of all system or object privileges granted directly to the role. Let's demonstrate how to create an audit policy with a few examples.

Create a policy to audit the system privilege use of SELECT ANY TABLE and ALTER SESSION. System privileges can be audited from the SYSTEM_PRIVILEGE_MAP view. Here is an example:

```
SQL> CREATE AUDIT POLICY ocatrain_syspriv_1
     PRIVILEGES SELECT ANY TABLE, ALTER SESSION;

Audit policy created.
```

Create a policy to audit a system-wide database action when EXECUTE or ALTER DATABASE LINK actions are performed. A list of auditable system-wide options is available in the AUDITABLE_SYSTEM_ACTIONS table. Instead of auditing a specific action, the ALL clause can be used to audit all system actions for the database, as in the following example:

```
SQL> CREATE AUDIT POLICY ocatrain_action_sys_priv_1
     ACTIONS execute, alter database link;
```

Audit policy created.

Create a policy to audit the use of all system or object privileges granted directly to the roles RESOURCE and OLAP_DBA, as in this example:

```
SQL> CREATE AUDIT POLICY ocatrain_role_audit_1
     ROLES olap_dba, resource;
```

Audit policy created.

There is no need to create separate policies for each type of policy. A policy can have privileges, actions, and roles, as in the following example:

```
SQL> CREATE AUDIT POLICY ocatrain_multi_1
     PRIVILEGES SELECT ANY TABLE, ALTER SESSION
     ACTIONS execute, alter database link
     ROLES olap_dba, resource;
```

Audit policy created.

Auditing is not limited to system-wide auditing; an individual object or a group of objects can be audited using ACTIONS. The ON clause specifies the objects; the ALL ON clause instructs Oracle database to audit all actions on the specified object. Let's review a few examples of object-specific auditing.

Create a policy to audit the delete and insert operations on an HR.DEPARTMENTS table as follows:

```
SQL> CREATE AUDIT POLICY ocatrain_obj1_hr
     ACTIONS delete, insert ON hr.departments;
```

Audit policy created.

Unified Auditing has a lot of flexibility regarding what to audit and how to avoid unnecessary audit records. The WHEN and EVALUATE clauses add lots of flexibility to auditing. The following audit policy looks for suspicious change activity from ODBC users to the database on tables hr.employees and hr.departments. The ODBC users in the database follow a standard naming convention that requires names to begin with ODBC (for example, John's ID in the database is ODBCJOHN). In the WHEN condition, LIKE 'ODBC%' would have been easier, but LIKE is not one of the operators allowed.

```
SQL> CREATE AUDIT POLICY ocatrain_hr_odbc_1
     ACTIONS delete, insert, update ON hr.employees,
            delete, insert, update ON hr.departments
     WHEN 'INSTR(SYS_CONTEXT (''USERENV'', ''SESSION_USER''), ''ODBC'') = 1'
     EVALUATE PER SESSION;


Audit policy created.
```

At the time of this writing, Oracle Database 12*c* Release 1 allows only a very limited set of functions in the WHEN clause. The WHEN clause's audit condition must be enclosed in quotes; therefore, if the condition itself involves quotes, they must be quoted properly with two consecutive single quotes.

The EVALUATE clause has three options:

PER STATEMENT specifies to evaluate the *audit_condition* for each auditable statement.

PER SESSION specifies to evaluate the *audit_condition* once during the session. The *audit_condition* is evaluated for the first auditable statement that is executed during the session.

PER INSTANCE specifies to evaluate the *audit_condition* once during the lifetime of the instance.

Using Component Auditing

With Unified Auditing, you can adjust standard RDBMS components as well as additional components. The components and actions that can be audited are viewable by querying the auditable_actions_items view. The following query shows how many actions can be audited in each component:

```
SQL> SELECT component, count(*) actions
     FROM auditable_system_actions
     GROUP BY component
     ORDER BY component;


COMPONENT              ACTIONS
-------------------- ----------

Database Vault            13
Datapump                   3
Direct path API            2
Label Security            18
Standard                 166
XS                        47
```

If an audit policy is created outside of standard database functionality, the COMPONENT keyword must follow ACTIONS, and it must identify the component. DATAPUMP, DIRECT_LOAD, OLS, XS, and DV are valid components. The following example creates a policy to audit datapump export actions:

```
SQL> CREATE AUDIT POLICY datapump_exp_aud
     ACTIONS COMPONENT=datapump export;


Audit policy created.
```

 RMAN backup, restore, and recover operations are audited by default by the unified audit. There is no need to create a policy or enable the policy.

Enabling and Disabling Audit Policies

Policy auditing is enabled by using the AUDIT POLICY statement. The syntax is

```
AUDIT POLICY policy
    [ { BY user [, user]... } | { EXCEPT user [, user]... } ]
    [ WHENEVER [ NOT ] SUCCESSFUL ]
```

With a simple syntax, you can apply the audit policy to all users in the database, only certain users in the database by using the BY clause, all users except a few users using the EXCEPT clause, audit only successful executions, audit only unsuccessful executions, or audit all executions.

Let's use the policies created in the earlier examples, and enable some of them. Enable the object auditing policy *ocatrain_hr_odbc_1* for all users in the database (remember the policy has filtering to monitor only ODBC users) as follows:

```
SQL> AUDIT POLICY ocatrain_hr_odbc_1;


Audit succeeded.
```

Enable the actions policy *ocatrain_action_sys_priv_1* for users bthomas and joshua whenever the action fails, and enable policy *ocatrain_obj1_hr* for all users except jenna when the action succeeds, as follows:

```
SQL> AUDIT POLICY ocatrain_action_sys_priv_1
     BY bthomas, joshua WHENEVER NOT SUCCESSFUL;


Audit succeeded.


SQL> AUDIT POLICY ocatrain_obj1_hr
```

```
        EXCEPT jenna WHENEVER SUCCESSFUL;
```

Audit succeeded.

To disable an audit policy, use the NOAUDIT POLICY statement. Here is an example:

```
SQL> NOAUDIT POLICY ocatrain_action_sys_priv_1;
```

Noaudit succeeded.

Predefined Unified Audit Policies

In Oracle Database 12c, the predefined unified audit policy ORA_SECURECONFIG is enabled by default. This policy audits all Oracle Database 12c secure configuration audit options. There are two other predefined policies created by Oracle: ORA_ACCOUNT_MGMT (audits events for the user account and privilege management) and ORA_DATABASE_PARAMETER (audits the changes made to the database parameters settings). They are not enabled by default.

To understand what the Oracle Database 12c audits by default with the ORA_SECURECONFIG policy enabled, view the results of this query:

```
select POLICY_NAME, AUDIT_OPTION
from   AUDIT_UNIFIED_POLICIES
where  policy_name =  'ORA_SECURECONFIG'
order by AUDIT_OPTION;
```

Querying Audit Information and Audit Policies

For all types of audits, the information is queried from a single source: UNIFIED_AUDIT_TRAIL. This view has several columns. This section mentions a few, and we encourage you to create and enable several audit policies, and query the information in this view to understand it better. The following query shows the audit information from the audit policies created and enabled in this chapter:

```
  select UNIFIED_AUDIT_POLICIES, DBUSERNAME,
         ACTION_NAME, SYSTEM_PRIVILEGE_USED
  from unified_audit_trail
  where  UNIFIED_AUDIT_POLICIES like 'OCATRAIN%';
```

DBUSERNAME, ACTION_NAME, UNIFIED_AUDIT_POLICIES, EVENT_TIMESTAMP, OBJECT_SCHEMA, and OBJECT_NAME are the most commonly used columns to query and filter. There are many more useful columns in UNIFIED_AUDIT_TRAIL, such as DBLINK_INFO, STATEMENT_ID, SCN, and so on.

When querying for component audit information, look for the columns prefixed with the component name. For example, to query the datapump operations, you may use the following query:

```
select DBUSERNAME, DP_TEXT_PARAMETERS1, DP_BOOLEAN_PARAMETERS1
from   UNIFIED_AUDIT_TRAIL
where  DBUSERNAME = 'SYSTEM';
```

Similarly, to query the RMAN operations, you may use the following:

```
select OS_USERNAME, RMAN_OBJECT_TYPE, RMAN_OPERATION
from UNIFIED_AUDIT_TRAIL
where RMAN_OPERATION is not null;
```

AUDIT_UNIFIED_POLICIES lists information on the policies created in the database. The following query shows the policies created using examples in this chapter:

```
SQL> SELECT policy_name, audit_option, audit_option_type, audit_condition
  2  FROM audit_unified_policies
  3* WHERE policy_name like 'OCA%';
```

POLICY_NAME	AUDIT_OPTION	AUDIT_OPTION_TYPE
AUDIT_CONDITION		
OCATRAIN_SYSPRIV_1	SELECT ANY TABLE	SYSTEM PRIVILEGE
NONE		
OCATRAIN_SYSPRIV_1	ALTER SESSION	SYSTEM PRIVILEGE
NONE		
OCATRAIN_MULTI_1	SELECT ANY TABLE	SYSTEM PRIVILEGE
NONE		
OCATRAIN_MULTI_1	ALTER SESSION	SYSTEM PRIVILEGE
NONE		
OCATRAIN_ACTION_SYS_PRIV_1	ALTER DATABASE LINK	STANDARD ACTION
NONE		
OCATRAIN_ACTION_SYS_PRIV_1	EXECUTE	STANDARD ACTION
NONE		
OCATRAIN_MULTI_1	ALTER DATABASE LINK	STANDARD ACTION
NONE		
OCATRAIN_MULTI_1	EXECUTE	STANDARD ACTION
NONE		
OCATRAIN_OBJ1_HR	DELETE	STANDARD ACTION
NONE		
OCATRAIN_HR_ODBC_1	INSERT	STANDARD ACTION
instr(SYS_CONTEXT ('USERENV', 'SESSION_USER'), 'ODBC') = 1		

```
OCATRAIN_HR_ODBC_1              DELETE              STANDARD ACTION
instr(SYS_CONTEXT ('USERENV', 'SESSION_USER'), 'ODBC') = 1
OCATRAIN_HR_ODBC_1              UPDATE              OBJECT ACTION
instr(SYS_CONTEXT ('USERENV', 'SESSION_USER'), 'ODBC') = 1
OCATRAIN_HR_ODBC_1              UPDATE              OBJECT ACTION
instr(SYS_CONTEXT ('USERENV', 'SESSION_USER'), 'ODBC') = 1
OCATRAIN_OBJ1_HR               INSERT              OBJECT ACTION
NONE
OCATRAIN_ROLE_AUDIT_1     OLAP_DBA                 ROLE PRIVILEGE
NONE
OCATRAIN_ROLE_AUDIT_1     RESOURCE                 ROLE PRIVILEGE
NONE
OCATRAIN_MULTI_1          OLAP_DBA                 ROLE PRIVILEGE
NONE
OCATRAIN_MULTI_1          RESOURCE                 ROLE PRIVILEGE
NONE
```

The AUDIT_UNIFIED_ENABLED_POLICIES query lists the policies that are enabled in the database as follows:

```
SQL> SELECT user_name, policy_name, enabled_opt, success, failure
  2* FROM audit_unified_enabled_policies;


USER_NAME  POLICY_NAME                   ENABLED_ SUC FAI
---------- --------------------------- -------- --- ---

BTHOMAS    OCATRAIN_ACTION_SYS_PRIV_1  BY       YES YES
JOSHUA     OCATRAIN_ACTION_SYS_PRIV_1  BY       YES YES
JENNA      OCATRAIN_OBJ1_HR            EXCEPT   YES NO
ALL USERS  ORA_SECURECONFIG            BY       YES YES
ALL USERS  OCATRAIN_HR_ODBC_1          BY       YES YES
```

Purging Unified Audit Records

Unlike SYS.AUD$, UNIFIED_AUDIT_TRAIL cannot be deleted using DML statements. Trying to do so will result in the following error:

```
SQL> delete from unified_audit_trail;
delete from unified_audit_trail
            *
ERROR at line 1:
ORA-02030: can only select from fixed tables/views
```

Records from a unified audit trail are deleted using the DBMS_AUDIT_MGMT.CLEAN_AUDIT_ TRAIL procedure. You learned about using this procedure and other related procedures in the "Using the Audit Management Framework" section earlier in the chapter.

The following code segment shows how to manually purge unified audit logs as well as how to schedule a job to purge periodically, keeping only 60 days of audit records in the database:

```
REM Enable Automated Audit Trail Cleanup - 60 days
set serveroutput on
REM Set Archive TimeStamp - delete records older than 60 days
begin
        dbms_audit_mgmt.set_last_archive_timestamp(
          audit_trail_type => dbms_audit_mgmt.AUDIT_TRAIL_UNIFIED,
          last_archive_time => systimestamp-60);
end;
/
REM Onetime Manual Purge
begin
        dbms_audit_mgmt.clean_audit_trail(
          audit_trail_type => dbms_audit_mgmt.AUDIT_TRAIL_UNIFIED,
          use_last_arch_timestamp => true);
end;
/
REM Create Purge Job for Automated Purging
begin
        dbms_audit_mgmt.create_purge_job(
          audit_trail_type => dbms_audit_mgmt.AUDIT_TRAIL_UNIFIED,
          audit_trail_purge_interval => 24 /* 1 day */ ,
          audit_trail_purge_name => 'PURGE_DB_AUDIT_RECORDS',
          use_last_arch_timestamp => true);
end;
/
REM Schedule a Job for adjusting the archived date
REM Records are not archived, but need deleted after 60 days
begin
        dbms_scheduler.create_job (
          job_name => 'SET_AUDIT_ARCHIVE_DATE',
          job_type => 'PLSQL_BLOCK',
          job_action => 'DBMS_AUDIT_MGMT.set_last_archive_timestamp(
            audit_trail_type => DBMS_AUDIT_MGMT.AUDIT_TRAIL_AUD_STD,
            last_archive_time => SYSTIMESTAMP-60);',
          start_date => systimestamp,
          repeat_interval => 'freq=daily; byhour=20',
```

```
            end_date => null,
            enabled => true,
            comments => 'Job to support automatic audit trail purge');
end;
/
```

In the code, notice the `audit_trail_type` value `DBMS_AUDIT_MGMT.AUDIT_TRAIL_AUD_STD`. Table 13.2 shows the types of audit trails you can use to purge different types of records.

TABLE 13.2   Types of Audit Trails

Constant Name	Audit Trail Identified
AUDIT_TRAIL_ALL	All audit trails (standard, unified, OS, XML)
AUDIT_TRAIL_AUD_STD	Audit records in the SYS.AUD$ table
AUDIT_TRAIL_DB_STD	Both standard audit (SYS.AUD$) and FGA audit (SYS.FGA_LOG$) records
AUDIT_TRAIL_FGA_STD	Fine-grained auditing (FGA) records in the SYS.FGA_LOG$ table
AUDIT_TRAIL_FILES	Both operating system (OS) and XML audit trails
AUDIT_TRAIL_OS	Audit records stored in operating system files
AUDIT_TRAIL_UNIFIED	Unified audit trail
AUDIT_TRAIL_XML	Audit records stored in XML files

Unified Auditing Internals

In standard auditing, the records are written to either the AUD$ or the FGA_LOG$ table, just like any other table in the database. This causes performance overhead on the database when auditing is enabled. To overcome the performance challenge, Oracle Database 12*c* uses the SGA queues to store the audit records when Unified Auditing is used so the audit records are written to memory and flushed to AUDSYS table, similar to the redo log buffer architecture. When the SGA queue is full, the audit information is flushed by the background process GEN0.

Because the records are written to SGA first and stay there until the queue is full, there is a possibility that the audit date might be lost if there is an instance crash. If audit data is more critical than performance, you can enable immediate write mode for the database by setting the audit-trail property.

To change the audit engine to write records immediately to disk and to avoid losing records, set the audit-trail property using the following code. This comes with a performance cost.

```
SQL> EXEC DBMS_AUDIT_MGMT.SET_AUDIT_TRAIL_PROPERTY(-
    DBMS_AUDIT_MGMT.AUDIT_TRAIL_UNIFIED, -
    DBMS_AUDIT_MGMT.AUDIT_TRAIL_WRITE_MODE, -
    DBMS_AUDIT_MGMT.AUDIT_TRAIL_IMMEDIATE_WRITE);
```

To change back to the default queued write mode, perform the following:

```
SQL> EXEC DBMS_AUDIT_MGMT.SET_AUDIT_TRAIL_PROPERTY(-
    DBMS_AUDIT_MGMT.AUDIT_TRAIL_UNIFIED, -
    DBMS_AUDIT_MGMT.AUDIT_TRAIL_WRITE_MODE, -
    DBMS_AUDIT_MGMT.AUDIT_TRAIL_QUEUED_WRITE);
```

Sometimes, you might be looking for current audit information, and Oracle won't have written the information to AUDSYS table yet. To flush the information from the SGA memory to AUDSYS table, use the following procedure:

```
SQL> EXEC SYS.DBMS_AUDIT_MGMT.FLUSH_UNIFIED_AUDIT_TRAIL;
```

The AUDSYS user is a special user; you cannot use the AUDSYS user to log in to the database. Also, the table that is written is a special one that is read only.

```
SQL> connect audsys/ocatest1
ERROR:
ORA-46370: cannot connect as AUDSYS user

SQL> SELECT table_name FROM dba_tables
    WHERE owner = 'AUDSYS';

TABLE_NAME
-----------------------
CLI_SWP$5b64e236$1$1
```

Summary

Oracle Database 12*c* gives you a well-stocked toolkit for managing users and securing the database. You create and manage user accounts with the CREATE, ALTER, and DROP USER statements. User passwords in Oracle Database 12*c* are case sensitive. You can assign tablespace resources to be used for sorting (temporary tablespace) that are different than those for tables or indexes (default permanent tablespace). By employing tablespace quotas and kernel resource limits in user profiles, you can limit the I/O, CPU, and memory resources your users consume. Profiles are also used to enforce password complexity and password policies.

To protect data from unwanted access or manipulation, you can employ object and system privileges. You can create and use roles to make managing these database privileges easier. System privileges allow users to perform DDL operations on the database or to perform DML operations database wide. Object privileges provide access to read and modify objects owned by another user. Role privileges give access to a role.

You can enable object, statement, privilege, and fine-grained auditing to help you monitor and record sensitive database activity. In addition to traditional standard auditing, Oracle Database 12*c* has a unified audit trail. All of the audit records are stored in UNIFIED_AUDIT_TRAIL.

The Oracle Database 12*c* database has several powerful features (user accounts and packages) that will need to be locked down in your production systems. In this chapter, you learned which user accounts need to be locked, as well as which standard packages should be locked down to better protect your company's data. You also learned to use the privilege-capture feature to identify both used and unused privileges to help enforce the principle of least privilege.

Exam Essentials

Be familiar with the authentication methods.   Database accounts can be authenticated by the database (identified by password), by the operating system (identified externally), or by an enterprise security service (identified globally).

Know how to assign default and temporary tablespace to users.   Assign default and temporary tablespaces with either a CREATE USER statement or an ALTER USER statement. Understand which tablespace would be assigned if you omitted the DEFAULT TABLESPACE clause when creating a user.

Be able to identify and grant object, system, and role privileges.   Know the difference between these types of privileges and when to use each type.

Know the differences between the WITH ADMIN OPTION and WITH GRANT OPTION keywords.   The ADMIN option applies to role or system privileges, but the GRANT option applies to object privileges.

Know how to enable roles.   Know when a role needs to be enabled and how to enable it.

Be able to secure your database.   Make sure you know how to lock down your database. Know how to use the privilege-capture feature to identify the used and unused privileges for a user.

Know how to implement password security. Oracle Database 12c gives you several standard password-security settings. Know what is available in a profile and what needs to be implemented in a password-verifying function.

Know how to enable, disable, and identify standard auditing options. Be able to describe the types of auditing, how to enable them, and how to report on the audit trail.

Learn how to implement Unified Auditing. Unified Auditing provides one unified location to look for audit records. Know how to create audit policies, where to look for audit records, and how to find out the policies and actions defined.

Review Questions

1. Which of the following statements create an Oracle account but let the operating system authenticate logons? (Choose two.)

   A. `create user ops$admin identified by os;`

   B. `create user ops$admin identified externally;`

   C. `create user ops$admin nopassword;`

   D. `create user ops$admin authenticated by os;`

2. If you want to capture the SQL statement and bind variables when performing a standard statement audit, which value should the `AUDIT_TRAIL` parameter have?

   A. `NONE`

   B. `DB`

   C. `DB,EXTENDED`

   D. `OS`

   E. `OS,EXTENDED`

3. Which of the following statements give user desmond the ability to alter table `gl.accounts`?

   A. `grant alter on gl.accounts to desmond;`

   B. `grant alter to desmond on gl.accounts;`

   C. `grant alter table to desmond;`

   D. `allow desmond to alter table gl.accounts;`

4. Which of the following statements has the correct syntax and gives the ability to grant the privilege to other users?

   A. `grant alter any table with grant option to desmond;`

   B. `grant alter on gl.accounts to desmond with admin option;`

   C. `grant alter any table to desmond with grant option;`

   D. `grant alter any table to desmond with admin option;`

5. Examine the CREATE USER statement and choose which of the following options best applies.

```
CREATE USER JOHN IDENTIFIED BY JOHNNY
DEFAULT TABLESPACE INDEX01
PASSWORD EXPIRE
QUOTA UNLIMITED ON DATA01
QUOTA UNLIMITED ON INDEX01;
GRANT CONNECT TO JOHN;
```

   A. JOHN will not be able to log in to the database using SQL*Plus until the DBA changes his password.

   B. JOHN is authenticated by the database.

   C. When tables are being created, if JOHN did not specify the TABLESPACE clause, the table will be created on the DATA01 tablespace.

   D. Specifying unlimited space quota on INDEX01 is a redundant step because INDEX01 is JOHN's default tablespace.

6. User system granted the SELECT privilege on sh.products to user ian using WITH GRANT OPTION. Ian then granted SELECT on sh.products to user stuart. Ian has left the company, and his account has been dropped. What happens to Stuart's privileges on sh.products?

   A. Stuart loses his SELECT privilege on sh.products.

   B. Stuart retains his SELECT privilege on sh.products.

   C. Stuart loses his SELECT privilege if Ian was dropped with the CASCADE REVOKE option.

   D. Stuart retains his SELECT privilege if Ian was dropped with the NOCASCADE REVOKE option.

7. User system granted the SELECT ANY TABLE privilege to user ian using WITH ADMIN OPTION. Ian then granted SELECT ANY TABLE to user stuart. Ian has left the company, and his account has been dropped. What happens to Stuart's privileges?

   A. Stuart loses his privileges.

   B. Stuart retains his privileges.

   C. Stuart loses his privileges if Ian was dropped with the CASCADE REVOKE option.

   D. Stuart retains his privileges if Ian was dropped with the NOCASCADE REVOKE option.

8. Which of the following system privileges should be granted judiciously because they can allow the grantee to masquerade as another user?

   A. CREATE ANY JOB

   B. ALTER USER

   C. CREATE ANY PROCEDURE

   D. All of the above

9. Which of the following statements enables the role user_admin in the current session?

   A. `alter session enable role user_admin;`

   B. `alter session set role user_admin;`

   C. `alter role user_admin enable;`

   D. `set role user_admin;`

10. Which of the following SQL statements allows user augustin to use the privileges associated with the password-protected role info_czar that has been granted to him?

    A. `set role all;`

    B. `alter user augustin default role all;`

    C. `alter session enable role info_czar;`

    D. `alter session enable info_czar identified by brozo;`

11. By default, how much space can any account use for a new table?

    A. None

    B. Up to the current free space in the tablespace

    C. Unlimited space, including autoextends

    D. Up to the default quota established at tablespace creation time

12. Which of the following SQL statements disconnects a session after it has been idle for 30 minutes?

    A. `alter session set idle_timeout=30;`

    B. `alter session set idle_timeout=1800;`

    C. `alter profile default limit idle_time 30;`

    D. `alter profile default set idle_timeout 30;`

13. Which of the following options prevents a user from reusing a password when they change their password?

    A. Setting the initialization parameter NO_PASSWORD_REUSE to TRUE

    B. Altering that user's profile to UNLIMITED for PASSWORD_REUSE_TIME and 1 for PASSWORD_REUSE_MAX

    C. Altering that user's profile to UNLIMITED for both PASSWORD_REUSE_TIME and PASSWORD_REUSE_MAX

    D. Using a password verify function to record the new password and comparing the new passwords to those recorded previously

14. Examine the code, and choose the option that best describes the reason for error.

```
CREATE USER JOHN IDENTIFIED BY JOHN1;
CREATE ROLE HR_QUERY;
GRANT CONNECT, OEQUERY, SELECT ANY TABLE TO HR_QUERY;
ALTER USER JOHN DEFAULT ROLE ALL EXCEPT HR_QUERY;
GRANT HR_QUERY TO JOHN;
CONNECT JOHN/JOHN1
SELECT COUNT(*) FROM HR.EMPLOYEES;
Error: ORA-01031: insufficient privileges
```

    A. John needs the SELECT_CATALOG_ROLE privilege.

    B. HR_QUERY is not a default role for John.

    C. The SELECT privilege on the HR.EMPLOYEES table is not granted to JOHN or HR_QUERY.

    D. John should enable the role using the SET ROLE statement and a password.

15. You created a database user using the following statement. Which option will connect the user successfully to the database?

```
CREATE USER JOHN IDENTIFIED BY John1;
GRANT CONNECT TO JOHN;
```

    A. CONNECT JOHN/JOHN1

    B. CONNECT JOHN/john1

    C. CONNECT john/John1

    D. All of the above

16. Which of the following SQL statements limits attempts to guess passwords by locking an account after three failed logon attempts?

    A. alter profile default limit failed_login_attempts 3;

    B. alter system set max_logon_failures = 3 scope=both;

    C. alter user set failed_login_attempts = 3;

    D. alter system set failed_login_attempts = 3 scope=both;

17. User JAMES has a table named JOBS created on the tablespace USERS. When you issue the following statement, what effect will it have on the JOBS table?

```
ALTER USER JAMES QUOTA 0 ON USERS;
```

    A. No more rows can be added to the JOBS table.

    B. No new blocks can be allocated to the JOBS table.

    C. No new extents can be allocated to the JOBS table.

    D. The table JOBS cannot be accessed.

    E. The table is truncated.

18. How do you manage fine-grained auditing?

    A. With the AUDIT and NOAUDIT statements

    B. With the DBMS_FGA package

    C. With the GRANT and REVOKE statements

    D. With the DBMS_AUDIT_MGMT package and CREATE_POLICY procedure

19. Of the following privileges, which is the least privilege required to create and manage Unified Auditing in a database, including purging of audit trail?

    A. SYSDBA

    B. DBA

    C. AUDIT_ADMIN

    D. AUDIT ANY

20. Which statement regarding Unified Auditing is true?

    A. Unified Auditing is enabled by setting the parameter AUDIT_TRAIL=UNIFIED.

    B. Unified Auditing writes audit records to the table owned by user AUDSYS.

    C. You have to log in as SYSDBA to purge the unified audit-trail records.

    D. Audit records for RMAN and Datapump are written to audit tables in SYS schema.

Chapter

14

Maintaining the Database and Managing Performance

ORACLE DATABASE 12*c*: OCA EXAM OBJECTIVES COVERED IN THIS CHAPTER:

✓ **Performing Database Maintenance**

- ▪ Manage the Automatic Workload Repository (AWR).
- ▪ Use the Automatic Database Diagnostic Monitor (ADDM).
- ▪ Describe and use the advisory framework.
- ▪ Set alert thresholds.
- ▪ Use automated tasks.

✓ **Managing Performance**

- ▪ Use Enterprise Manager to monitor performance.
- ▪ Use Automatic Memory Management.
- ▪ Use the Memory Advisor to size memory buffers.

✓ **Managing Performance: SQL Tuning**

- ▪ Manage optimizer statistics.
- ▪ Use the SQL Tuning Advisor.
- ▪ Use the SQL Access Advisor to tune a workload.

Successful database administrators are always on the lookout for potential database problems that could adversely impact the availability or performance of the systems they manage. They are always looking for ways to prevent performance issues and system outages. Fortunately, Oracle Database 12c comes with an array of proactive performance monitoring features and an alert mechanism to help get ahead of potential issues to prevent them from impacting business. Such issues can often be identified and fixed before users even notice. Appropriate thresholds can be set based on business requirements for alert and failure notifications.

Oracle Database 12c periodically collects statistics on database objects and uses those statistics to find the best execution plan for an SQL statement. Accurate statistics with data distribution and value range are important so that the optimizer can figure out the most optimal data-access path. The Automatic Workload Repository collects, analyzes, and maintains the performance statistics of the database. Oracle Database 12c also offers several advisors that help DBAs fine-tune the database components. Automatic Memory Management greatly simplifies memory management so that the DBA doesn't need to size the various memory components in the SGA and PGA. In this chapter, you will learn about all the database-management and performance-management tools available to DBAs for better database management and for keeping the database healthy. All of these tools can be accessed using SQL*Plus, SQL Developer, or Enterprise Manager.

This chapter is packed with a lot of information, so please take the time to understand the material and practice. The examples use Oracle Enterprise Manager Cloud Control extensively. We recommend that you install EM Cloud Control and supplement your reading with topics from the Oracle documentation found on http://docs.oracle.com.

Proactive Database Maintenance

You can monitor your systems for management and performance problems in essentially two ways:

- *Reactive monitoring* involves monitoring a database environment after a performance or management issue has arisen. For example, you start gathering performance statistics using third-party tools, EM, or homegrown scripts after users call to tell you that the system is slow. Obviously, this type of monitoring leaves a lot to be desired because a problem has already arisen and the system users are already impacted. You can use the techniques discussed in this chapter for reactive monitoring, but they are most effective when used to perform proactive monitoring.

- *Proactive monitoring* allows you to identify and respond to common database-performance and management issues before they occur. Most of the features in Enterprise Manager Cloud Control are geared toward proactive monitoring.

The database maintenance framework in Oracle Database 12c consists of proactive tools to help the database administrator keep the database functioning at its best:

- Automated tasks, such as collecting optimizer statistics
- Automatic Workload Repository
- Advisory Framework
- Server alerts and thresholds

The Automatic Diagnostic Repository, where the alert log and trace information are kept, is used for reactive database maintenance.

The monitoring tools available in Enterprise Manager collect their information from a variety of sources, including data dictionary views, dynamic performance views, and the operating system. Oracle Database 12c also makes extensive use of the cost-based optimizer statistics for its proactive monitoring. However, discussing all the database-maintenance and performance options available is not in the scope of this book; it is a large topic that warrants its own book. In the following sections, you will instead learn the database-maintenance options available in Oracle Database 12c that are relevant to the OCA certification exam. We encourage you to install Oracle Enterprise Manager Cloud Control and explore through the items listed under the Performance menu to learn and understand Oracle Database performance better. Let's start with an important component in database performance: optimizer statistics.

Managing Optimizer Statistics

Optimizer statistics are a collection of important statistical data that describe the contents of the database. The query optimizer uses the optimizer statistics to find the best execution plan to get to the row of data the query wants to find. The database collects statistics on objects that have segments allocated as well as overall system statistics. The optimizer uses the statistics to decide how to do the following:

- Access data and determine which indexes to use
- Join tables
- Evaluate expressions and conditions

The *cost-based optimizer* (CBO) uses these statistics to formulate efficient execution plans for each SQL statement that is issued by application users. For example, the CBO may have to decide whether to use an available index when processing a query. The CBO can make an effective guess at the proper execution plan only when it knows the number of rows in the table, the size and type of indexes on that table, and how many rows the CBO expects to be returned by a query. Because of this, the statistics gathered and stored in the data dictionary views are called optimizer statistics.

The following are some of the statistics collected:

- Table and index statistics
    - Total number of rows in a table and average row length
    - Total number of blocks used
    - Levels, clustering factor, and number of leaf blocks for indexes
- Column statistics
    - Number of distinct values in a column
    - Number of NULL values
    - Low value and high value for a column
    - Data distribution and data skew
- System statistics
    - Disk I/O performance
    - CPU performance

You can use the DBMS_STATS package to collect optimizer statistics in the database. DBMS_STATS has several subprograms (procedures and functions) to collect and manage statistics. In the following sections, you will learn how to collect optimizer statistics and what management options are available to maintain the statistics.

 Optimizer statistics are a snapshot of statistical information at a specific point in time. They are persistent across instance restarts because they are stored in the data dictionary tables.

Collecting Statistics

In an Oracle Database 12c database, you'll rarely need to manually collect statistics. The default collection frequency and options are good for most of the database environments. You may have to collect statistics manually when you bulk-load data into a table or when you delete several rows from the table. Sometimes you may have to create *histograms* for the optimizer to be able to make better execution plans based on the query.

When you create the database using DBCA, gathering optimizer statistics is automatically set up and enabled using the *Automated Maintenance Tasks* (AutoTask) infrastructure. AutoTask schedules maintenance tasks to run automatically, using the Oracle Scheduler, during predefined maintenance windows. An automatic optimizer statistics-collection job collects statistics on objects that have no statistics collected or have stale statistics. Oracle Database 12c considers statistics stale when more than 10 percent of data in the table has changed since statistics were last gathered on the table. This procedure also prioritizes the objects that need the statistics collected and processes them first.

You can enable and disable automatic optimizer statistics gathering by using the DBMS_ AUTO_TASK package. To disable automatic statistics gathering, use the DISABLE subprogram, as shown here:

```
BEGIN
  DBMS_AUTO_TASK_ADMIN.DISABLE (
      client_name=>'auto optimizer stats collection',
      operation=>NULL, window_name=>NULL);
END;
```

If you disable automatic statistics gathering, make sure you collect statistics manually so that the optimizer produces intelligent execution plans. To enable automatic statistics gathering, use the ENABLE subprogram as follows:

```
BEGIN
  DBMS_AUTO_TASK_ADMIN.ENABLE (
      client_name=>'auto optimizer stats collection',
      operation=>NULL, window_name=>NULL);
END;
```

To view the status of AutoTask jobs, you can run the following query:

```
SQL> SELECT client_name, status FROM dba_autotask_client;
```

```
CLIENT_NAME                                 STATUS
----------------------------------------- --------
auto optimizer stats collection            ENABLED
auto space advisor                         ENABLED
sql tuning advisor                         ENABLED
```

You can collect statistics manually by using the DBMS_STATS procedure from SQL*Plus or by using Enterprise Manager Cloud Control.

Manually Collecting Stats Using SQL*Plus

Collecting statistics manually can be useful for tables and indexes with storage characteristics that change frequently or that need to be analyzed outside the normal analysis window. Statistics may also need to be collected manually if the data in the table is highly volatile, such as when you truncate and load the table often. For such tables, you can collect the statistics when the table is fully loaded and lock the statistics so that subsequent statistics-gathering jobs do not override the statistics. The following example collects statistics on a table and locks the statistics:

```
BEGIN
  DBMS_STATS.GATHER_TABLE_STATS('HR','EMPLOYEES');
  DBMS_STATS.LOCK_TABLE_STATS('HR','EMPLOYEES');
END;
```

Procedures are available to collect optimizer statistics at the database, schema, table, or index level. Table 14.1 shows the optimizer's statistics-gathering procedures.

TABLE 14.1   DBMS_STATS Statistics-Gathering Procedures

Procedure Name	Purpose
GATHER_TABLE_STATS	Collects table, column, and index stats
GATHER_INDEX_STATS	Collects index stats
GATHER_SCHEMA_STATS	Collects stats on all objects in the schema
GATHER_DATABASE_STATS	Collects stats on all objects in all schemas of the database
GATHER_DICTIONARY_STATS	Collects statistics on SYS-owned dictionary objects
GATHER_FIXED_OBJECTS_STATS	Collects stats on the dynamic performance tables (fixed objects)
GATHER_SYSTEM_STATS	Collects the runtime system statistics with workload

The following example collects statistics on all objects owned by the HR schema, sampling 50 percent of rows for the statistics gathering:

```
SQL> EXEC DBMS_STATS.GATHER_SCHEMA_STATS('HR',estimate_percent=>50);
PL/SQL procedure successfully completed.
SQL>
```

For complete details on the many options available in the DBMS_STATS package, see Chapter 153 of the "Oracle Database PL/SQL Packages and Types Reference 12c Release 1 (12.1) Part E17602-14" documentation, available at http://docs.oracle.com.

Four constants are used with the GATHER_*_STATS procedures. These constants tell Oracle to choose the automatic option, using internal algorithms, and they are the default values for their respective parameters. The constants available in the DBMS_STATS package are

- AUTO_CASCADE: Lets Oracle decide whether to collect statistics for indexes when table stats are collected.
- AUTO_DEGREE: Lets Oracle choose the best degree of parallelism based on the number of CPUs available and the size of the object.

- AUTO_INVALIDATE: Lets Oracle decide whether to invalidate dependent cursors during statistics collection.

- AUTO_SAMPLE_SIZE: Lets Oracle decide the best sample size for the table. Auto sample size is generally recommended because the internal algorithms used by Oracle are very good and generate a collection accuracy close to 100 percent sample.

Although each GATHER_*_STATS procedure has several parameters, the most commonly used ones are discussed here.

- OWNNAME: The schema owner name.

- ESTIMATE_PERCENT: The percentage of rows to sample to get the statistics; 100 provides accurate statistics, but collecting 100 percent on a large database is a very expensive operation. Using auto sample size would be the best choice in this situation.

- METHOD_OPT: Use this procedure to tell Oracle to collect column statistics or to collect histograms, etc.

- CASCADE: This parameter tells whether to collect index stats when table stats are collected.

- OPTIONS: Tells how the statistics should be collected: full or only stale stats.

- NO_INVALIDATE: When stats are collected on base tables, the SQL cursor can be invalidated; therefore, a new plan can be generated if needed during the next run. This parameter specifies if it is required to invalidate or not.

- DEGREE: The parallelism degree to be used for statistics collection.

Manually Collecting Stats Using EM Cloud Control 12*c*

You can use the EM Cloud Control Optimizer Statistics Wizard to manually collect statistics for individual segments, schemas, or the database as a whole. To start the Wizard, choose SQL from the Performance drop-down menu, and choose the Optimizer Statistics menu option. Figure 14.1 shows the menu items available in the Manage Optimizer Statistics screen of Oracle Enterprise Manager.

You can choose from several options in addition to gathering optimizer statistics, as shown on the Manage Optimizer Statistics screen (Figure 14.1). Whenever you collect statistics, existing statistics are saved to history tables and preserved for 31 days. You can click the Restore Optimizer Statistics link to restore old statistics. You can also lock, unlock, and delete statistics. Similar to all EM management screens, once you choose the options, you can view the SQL code that was used, which will help you to understand the options and syntax better.

The Related Links section of the Manage Optimizer Statistics screen has links you can use to query and manage optimizer preferences and options. The Object Statistics link is useful for determining the status of statistics on a particular object, if the stats are current or stale, when it was analyzed, sample size used for analysis, and so on. The Global Statistics Gathering Options and Object Level Statistics Gathering Preferences links let you change the default options and set your own. The Job Scheduler and Automated Maintenance Tasks links let you customize when the stats gathering jobs run.

Click the Gather Optimizer Statistics link on the Manage Optimizer Statistics screen. You can collect statistics at the database, schema, object, or system level. Choose the options needed to collect statistics, as shown in Figure 14.2.

FIGURE 14.1 Manage Optimizer Statistics in OEM Cloud Control

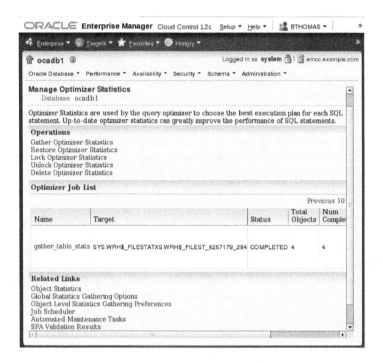

You will be taken through scope, objects, options, schedule, and review screens. The Objects screen is shown in Figure 14.2. The scope you select in the previous screen will determine the objects that are presented. For example, in Figure 14.2, the scope is Schema; therefore, you will be presented the option to pick the schemas for statistics collection (see Figure 14.3).

If you have chosen to customize the options as shown in Figure 14.2, you will get a screen similar to Figure 14.4 for choosing options. Select the options you'll need for the statistics collection.

You can collect the statistics immediately or at a later time using a schedule. Figure 14.5 shows the next screen, where you'll select the scheduling options.

The final screen shows a summary of options chosen for you to review. Clicking the Submit button will schedule the stats collection job to run. By clicking the Show SQL button, you can also view the SQL behind the options you have chosen. Figure 14.6 shows the code behind a statistics-gathering job for the options shown on the screen.

In the next section, you will learn how to set preferences for statistics gathering.

Defining Statistics Preferences

The default staleness percentage for statistics gathering is 10; if you want to change this and other default options, you can set the preferences for statistics gathering using Enterprise Manager or using DBMS_STATS directly. In this section, you will learn how to set preferences using EM Cloud Control, and using the Show SQL option, you can see the DBMS_STATS code behind it.

FIGURE 14.2 The Gather Optimizer Statistics screen in EM Cloud Control

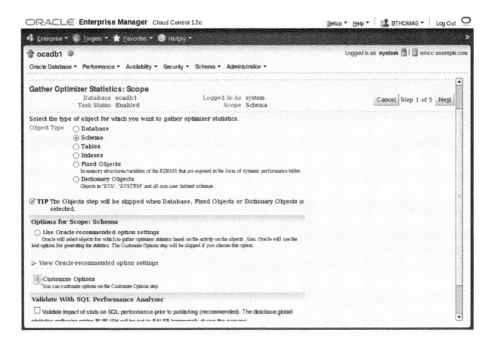

FIGURE 14.3 The Objects screen in Gather Optimizer Statistics

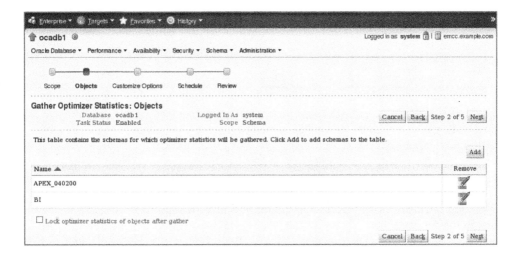

FIGURE 14.4 The options for Gather Optimizer Statistics

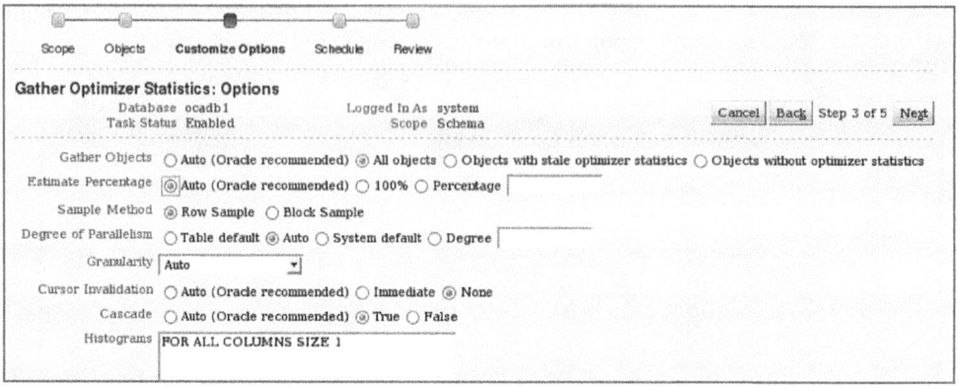

FIGURE 14.5 The scheduling options for Gather Optimizer Statistics

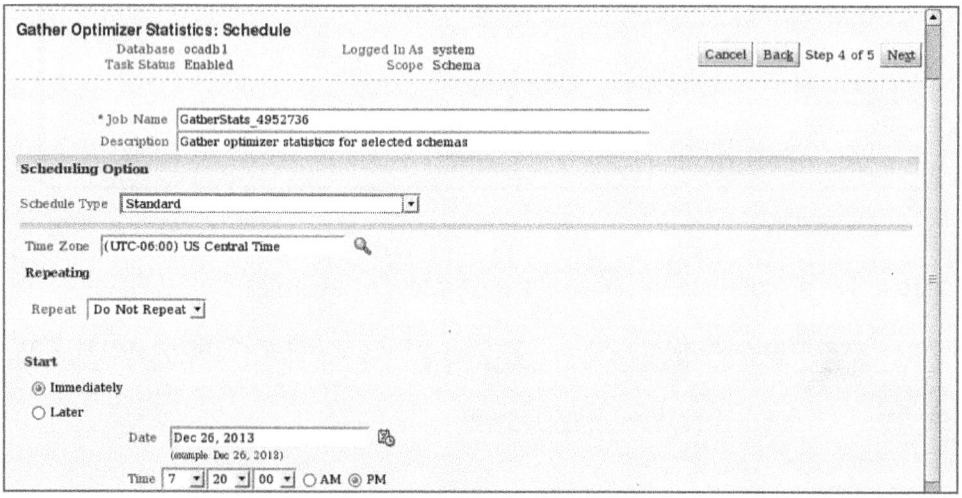

On the EM Cloud Control Manage Optimizer Statistics screen (shown earlier in Figure 14.1), you can click the Global Statistics Gathering Options and Object Level Statistics Gathering Preferences links.

Figure 14.7 shows the Global Statistics Gathering Options screen. Using this screen, you can set the preferences at a global level, which is applicable to all the objects in all the schemas, unless specific schema or object-level preferences are set.

Here you can change the retention period for how long the optimizer statistics history is kept in the database (DBMS_STATS.ALTER_STATS_HISTORY_RETENTION), as well as other default options (DBMS_STATS.SET_GLOBAL_PREFS). Table 14.2 shows the EM Cloud Control option and its corresponding preference name when using DBMS_SQL.

FIGURE 14.6   Show SQL for the Gather Optimizer Statistics

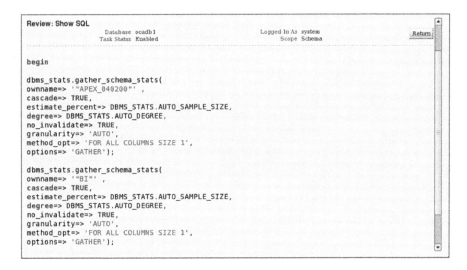

FIGURE 14.7   The Global Statistics Gathering Options screen in EM Cloud Control

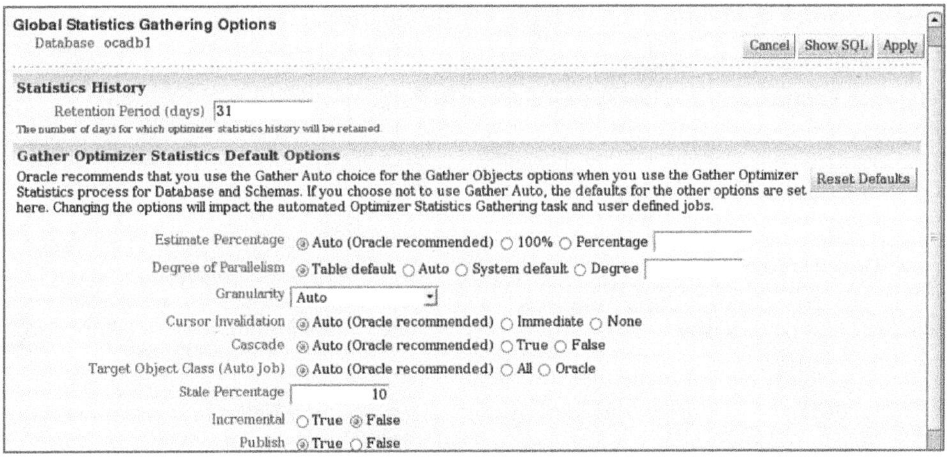

If you want to minimize the time required to collect table statistics for partitioned tables, you can set the global preference INCREMENTAL to TRUE, where only statistics on a (new) partition are gathered and the table statistics are adjusted accordingly:

```
EXEC DBMS_STATS.SET_GLOBAL_PREFS ('INCREMENTAL', 'TRUE');
```

The code generated using EM Cloud Control for the same is shown here. This displays the default values for all preference settings without much explanation, except for INCREMENTAL, which was modified.

```
DECLARE
estimate VARCHAR2(100) := ;
degreeValue VARCHAR2(100) := ;
currentGranularity VARCHAR2(100) := AUTO;
targetObjectClass VARCHAR2(100) := AUTO;
cascade VARCHAR2(100) := DBMS_STATS.AUTO_CASCADE;
invalidateCur VARCHAR2(100) := DBMS_STATS.AUTO_INVALIDATE;
createHist VARCHAR2(100) := FOR ALL COLUMNS SIZE AUTO;
retentionPeriod VARCHAR2(100) := 31;
stalePercentage VARCHAR2(100) := 10;
incremental VARCHAR2(100) := TRUE;
publish VARCHAR2(100) := TRUE;

BEGIN
dbms_stats.set_global_prefs('incremental', incremental);
END;
```

TABLE 14.2   DBMS_STATS.SET_GLOBAL_PREFS Preferences

Preference Parameter	EM Cloud Control Option	Purpose
ESTIMATE_PERCENT	Estimate Percentage	Sets the percentage of rows in the table to consider when estimating statistics
DEGREE	Degree of Parallelism	Specifies how many parallel processes are used to gather stats
GRANULARITY	Granularity	Determines granularity of statistics to collect for partitioned tables
NO_INVALIDATE	Cursor Invalidation	Determines whether dependent cursors should be made invalid
CASCADE	Cascade	Determines whether index statistics should be gathered when table statistics are gathered
AUTOSTATS_TARGET	Target Object Class	Determines which objects are considered for automatic statistics collection

Preference Parameter	EM Cloud Control Option	Purpose
STALE_PERCENT	Stale Percent	Sets the percentage of rows that need to change before statistics are gathered again
INCREMENTAL	Incremental	Gives global stats on the partitioned table without doing a full scan
PUBLISH	Publish	Determines whether newly gathered stats are published immediately
METHOD_OPT	Histograms	Sets options for collecting histograms

Similar to the global stats preferences, you can also set preferences on a table or schema. Click the Object Level Statistics Gathering Preferences link on the Manage Optimizer Statistics screen (Figure 14.1). Figure 14.8 shows the Object Level Statistics Gathering Preferences screen when Edit Table Preferences is chosen.

FIGURE 14.8 Object Level Statistics Gathering — The Add Table Preferences screen

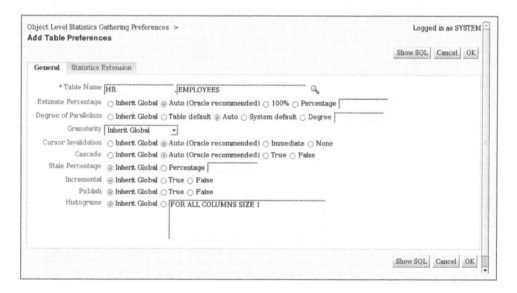

To view the tables where preferences are set, enter the filters, if any (schema and/or table name), and click Go. You have the following options on this screen:

- Click Add Table Preferences to set the table preferences on a new table (this runs DBMS_STATS.SET_TABLE_PREFS).

- Click Edit Schema Preferences to add/edit schema preferences (this runs DBMS_STATS .SET_SCHEMA_PREFS).

- Select existing tables, and click Edit Preferences to edit (this runs DBMS_STATS.SET_TABLE_PREFS).

- Select existing tables, and click Inherit Global to remove preferences (this runs DBMS_STATS.DELETE_TABLE_PREFS).

The code related to the preferences set in Figure 14.8 is shown here.

```
BEGIN
dbms_stats.set_table_prefs('"HR"', '"EMPLOYEES"', 'ESTIMATE_PERCENT', DBMS_
STATS.AUTO_SAMPLE_SIZE);
dbms_stats.set_table_prefs('"HR"', '"EMPLOYEES"', 'DEGREE', DBMS_STATS.AUTO_
DEGREE);
dbms_stats.set_table_prefs('"HR"', '"EMPLOYEES"', 'NO_INVALIDATE', 'DBMS_STATS
.AUTO_INVALIDATE');
dbms_stats.set_table_prefs('"HR"', '"EMPLOYEES"', 'CASCADE', 'DBMS_STATS.AUTO_
CASCADE');
END;
```

Figure 14.9 shows the Object Level Statistics Gathering Preferences for Schema. Here you choose the schema and set the preferences that are applicable to all objects in the schema.

FIGURE 14.9 Object Level Statistics Gathering — The Edit Schema Preferences screen

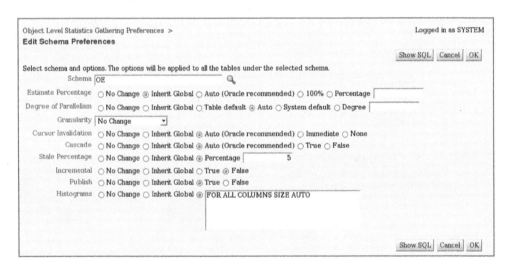

The code used to set the preferences shown in Figure 14.9 is shown here:

```
BEGIN
dbms_stats.delete_schema_prefs('"OE"', 'ESTIMATE_PERCENT');
dbms_stats.set_schema_prefs('"OE"', 'DEGREE', DBMS_STATS.AUTO_DEGREE);
dbms_stats.set_schema_prefs('"OE"', 'NO_INVALIDATE', 'DBMS_STATS.AUTO_
INVALIDATE');
```

```
dbms_stats.set_schema_prefs('"OE"', 'CASCADE', 'DBMS_STATS.AUTO_CASCADE');
dbms_stats.set_schema_prefs('"OE"', 'STALE_PERCENT', '5');
dbms_stats.set_schema_prefs('"OE"', 'INCREMENTAL', 'FALSE');
dbms_stats.set_schema_prefs('"OE"', 'PUBLISH', 'TRUE');
dbms_stats.set_schema_prefs('"OE"', 'METHOD_OPT', 'FOR ALL COLUMNS SIZE AUTO');
END;
```

The data dictionary view DBA_TAB_STAT_PREFS (or ALL_ or USER_) displays the tables with a preference set. Remember, when you use the SET_SCHEMA_PREFS procedure, DBMS_STATS adds an entry to this view for each table under the schema. When you use the SET_DATABASE_ PREFS procedure, DBMS_STATS adds an entry to this view for each table in the database except system tables. To include system tables, set the third parameter to TRUE.

Let's explore two key features of Oracle statistics gathering using table preferences.

Pending Statistics

In Oracle Database 12c, statistics gathering is divided into two steps: collect the statistics and then publish them. By default, the statistics will be available (published) to all users as soon as the stats are gathered. If you want to test the implications of the new statistics before making them available to all users in the database, you can do so. It can be very helpful to test new statistics to make sure they do not affect the database negatively.

To test the new statistics before making them available to all users, perform these steps:

1. Set the table preference parameter PUBLISH to FALSE. If you're working with a lot of tables, you can use the SET_SCHEMA_PREFS, SET_DATABASE_PREFS, or SET_GLOBAL_PREFS procedure as appropriate. For demonstration purposes, the statistics on the HR.EMPLOY- EES table are deleted in this example:

```
SQL> exec dbms_stats.delete_table_stats('HR','EMPLOYEES');
SQL> select table_name, num_rows, last_analyzed from dba_tables
  2  where owner = 'HR' and table_name = 'EMPLOYEES';
TABLE_NAME NUM_ROWS   LAST_ANAL
---------- ---------- ---------
EMPLOYEES

SQL> select dbms_stats.get_prefs('PUBLISH','HR','EMPLOYEES')
     from dual;
DBMS_STATS.GET_PREFS('PUBLISH','HR','EMPLOYEES')
-----------------------------------------------------------
TRUE

SQL> exec dbms_stats.set_table_prefs('HR','EMPLOYEES','PUBLISH','FALSE');
PL/SQL procedure successfully completed.
```

2. Using the DBMS_STATS package, gather table statistics as you normally would. Because the PUBLISH preference is set to FALSE, you do not see the statistics:

```
SQL> exec dbms_stats.gather_table_stats('HR','EMPLOYEES');
PL/SQL procedure successfully completed.

SQL> select num_rows, last_analyzed from dba_tables
  2  where owner = 'HR' and table_name = 'EMPLOYEES';
  NUM_ROWS LAST_ANAL
---------- ---------
```

3. You can verify the pending statistics by querying DBA_TAB_PENDING_STATS:

```
SQL> select table_name, num_rows, blocks, sample_size
  2  from dba_tab_pending_stats;
TABLE_NAME           NUM_ROWS     BLOCKS SAMPLE_SIZE
------------------ ---------- ---------- -----------
EMPLOYEES                 107          5         107
```

4. Test your SQL code by making the pending statistics visible:

```
SQL> alter session set optimizer_use_pending_statistics = true;
```

5. When you're ready to publish the statistics, execute the following:

```
SQL> exec dbms_stats.publish_pending_stats('HR','EMPLOYEES');
PL/SQL procedure successfully completed.

SQL> select num_rows, last_analyzed from dba_tables
  2  where owner = 'HR' and table_name = 'EMPLOYEES';
  NUM_ROWS LAST_ANAL
---------- ---------
       107 15-FEB-08

SQL> select table_name, num_rows, blocks, sample_size
  2  from dba_tab_pending_stats;
no rows selected
```

The PUBLISH_PENDING_STATS procedure accepts the schema name and the table name as the first two parameters. If you specify NULL for the schema name, the default user's schema will be used. If you specify NULL for the table name, all pending stats on all tables in the schema will be published.

Changing the Default Staleness Threshold

Since Oracle10*g*, tables have had the default MONITORING enabled. The statistics-collec-tion job looks for staleness of 10 percent or more for it to reanalyze the table. In Oracle Database 12*c*, you can specify the threshold value for each table if you want to override the 10 percent default using SET_TABLE_PREFS. Here's an example:

```
SQL> exec dbms_stats.set_table_prefs('SH','CUSTOMERS','STALE_PERCENT','20');
PL/SQL procedure successfully completed.

SQL> DESCRIBE dba_tab_stat_prefs
 Name                            Null?    Type
 ------------------------------  -------- --------------------------------
 OWNER                           NOT NULL VARCHAR2(30)
 TABLE_NAME                      NOT NULL VARCHAR2(30)
 PREFERENCE_NAME                          VARCHAR2(30)
 PREFERENCE_VALUE                         VARCHAR2(1000)

SQL> SELECT table_name, preference_name, preference_value
     FROM dba_tab_stat_prefs;

TABLE_NAME      PREFERENCE_NAME         PREFERENCE_VALUE
--------------  ----------------------  --------------------

CUSTOMERS       STALE_PERCENT                20
```

You can also use the function GET_PREFS to verify the preference value. The function returns the custom-defined preference value. If no such value is defined, it returns the default.

```
SQL> SELECT dbms_stats.get_prefs('STALE_PERCENT','SH','CUSTOMERS')
     FROM dual;

DBMS_STATS.GET_PREFS('STALE_PERCENT','SH','CUSTOMERS')
-------------------------------------------------------------

20

SQL> SELECT dbms_stats.get_prefs('STALE_PERCENT','HR','EMPLOYEES')
     FROM dual;

DBMS_STATS.GET_PREFS('STALE_PERCENT','HR','EMPLOYEES')
-------------------------------------------------------------

10
```

Extended Statistics

In Oracle Database 12c, you can tell the optimizer the relationship between columns by using the *extended statistics* feature (multicolumn statistics). The extended statistics feature also includes statistics on columns where a function is applied (function-based statistics). By collecting extended statistics on columns, the optimizer will be able to estimate the selectivity better.

By using EM Cloud Control, you can set extended statistics in the Add Table Preferences screen, shown in Figure 14.8. Click on the Statistics Extension tab and provide the relevant information.

To collect multicolumn statistics (extended histograms), use the GATHER_TABLE_STATS procedure with the METHOD_OPT option, just as you would collect normal histogram statistics.

To create multicolumn statistics and function-based statistics, follow these two steps:

1. Create an extended statistics group using the DBMS_STATS.CREATE_EXTENDED_STATS function. The function returns the name of the extended stat group created. This function has three arguments: the owner, the table name, and the extension. The "extension" could be a combination of columns, up to 32, or an expression on a column (for function-based statistics, discussed later).

2. Collect histogram statistics on the table using the GATHER_TABLE_STATS procedure. FOR ALL COLUMNS SIZE SKEWONLY is a good option because Oracle collects histograms only on columns with large data distribution.

 Real World Scenario

Collecting Extended Table Statistics: An Example

Here we'll demonstrate the extended statistics feature of Oracle Database 12c with an example. The CUSTOMERS table is populated and has about 91,000 rows. Statistics are collected on the table with the FOR ALL ROWS SIZE AUTO option:

```
SQL> select column_name, num_distinct, histogram
  2  from dba_tab_col_statistics
  3  where owner = 'BTHOMAS' and table_name = 'CUSTOMERS';

COLUMN_NAME                    NUM_DISTINCT HISTOGRAM
------------------------------ ------------ ---------------
CUST_COUNTRY                              3 FREQUENCY
CUST_STATE                               6 FREQUENCY
CUST_NAME                            47692 NONE
SQL>
SQL> set autotrace traceonly explain
SQL> select * from customers where cust_country = 'India' and cust_state = 'TN';
```

```
--------------------------------------------------------------------------
| Id  | Operation          | Name      | Rows | Bytes | Cost (%CPU)| Time     |
--------------------------------------------------------------------------
|   0 | SELECT STATEMENT   |           | 1447 | 41963 | 137    (1)| 00:00:02 |
|*  1 |  TABLE ACCESS FULL| CUSTOMERS | 1447 | 41963 | 137    (1)| 00:00:02 |
--------------------------------------------------------------------------

Predicate Information (identified by operation id):
---------------------------------------------------

   1 - filter("CUST_STATE"='TN' AND "CUST_COUNTRY"='India')


SQL> set autotrace off
SQL> SELECT dbms_stats.create_extended_stats('BTHOMAS','CUSTOMERS',
               '(CUST_COUNTRY, CUST_STATE)') EXTSTAT
     FROM dual;

EXTSTAT
-------------------------------
SYS_STUZVS6GX30A0GN_5YRYSD2LPM

SQL>
SQL> exec dbms_stats.gather_table_stats(null, 'customers',
        method_opt=>'for all columns size skewonly');

PL/SQL procedure successfully completed.

SQL> select column_name, num_distinct, histogram
  2  from user_tab_col_statistics
  3* where table_name = 'CUSTOMERS'
SQL> /

COLUMN_NAME                    NUM_DISTINCT HISTOGRAM
------------------------------ ------------ ---------------
CUST_NAME                             47692 HEIGHT BALANCED
CUST_STATE                                6 FREQUENCY
CUST_COUNTRY                              3 FREQUENCY
SYS_STUZVS6GX30A0GN_5YRYSD2LPM            8 FREQUENCY
SQL> set autotrace traceonly explain
SQL> select * from customers where cust_country = 'India' and cust_state = 'TN';
```

```
----------------------------------------------------------------------------
| Id  | Operation          | Name      | Rows | Bytes | Cost (%CPU)| Time     |
----------------------------------------------------------------------------
|   0 | SELECT STATEMENT   |           |   86 |  2580 |  137    (1)| 00:00:02 |
|*  1 |  TABLE ACCESS FULL| CUSTOMERS |   86 |  2580 |  137    (1)| 00:00:02 |
----------------------------------------------------------------------------

Predicate Information (identified by operation id):
--------------------------------------------------

   1 - filter("CUST_STATE"='TN' AND "CUST_COUNTRY"='India')
```

As you can see in the example, before extended statistics were collected, the estimated number of rows was 1,447; whereas after the extended statistics were collected, the number of rows the optimizer estimated to return was 86.

To drop the extended statistics, use the DROP_EXTENDED_STATISTICS procedure:

```
SQL> exec dbms_stats.drop_extended_stats(null,'CUSTOMERS',
        '(CUST_COUNTRY, CUST_STATE)');
PL/SQL procedure successfully completed.
SQL>
```

To define the extension and collect statistics in one step, you can do the following:

```
SQL> exec dbms_stats.gather_table_stats(null, 'customers',
        method_opt=>'for all columns size skewonly
        for columns (cust_country, cust_state)');
PL/SQL procedure successfully completed.

SQL> select extension_name, extension from user_stat_extensions
  2  where table_name = 'CUSTOMERS';

EXTENSION_NAME                      EXTENSION
----------------------------------  -----------------------------
SYS_STUZVS6GX30A0GN_5YRYSD2LPM      ("CUST_COUNTRY","CUST_STATE")
```

In the next section, you'll learn how to enable and disable automatic statistics collection as well as perform other AutoTask jobs.

Configuring Automated Maintenance Tasks Using EM

Automated maintenance tasks are tasks that are started automatically at predefined intervals to do proactive maintenance operations on the database in order to keep the database healthy. The following are three automated maintenance tasks (known as AutoTask):

Gathering Optimizer Statistics   Collects optimizer statistics for all schema objects in the database for which there are no statistics or that have stale statistics.

Running the *Segment Advisor*   Identifies table and index segments that have space available for reclamation, and makes recommendations on how to reclaim the space.

Running the *SQL Tuning Advisor*   Analyzes high-load SQL statements and makes recommendations to tune the SQL code, with the option to automatically implement *SQL Profiles*.

You can enable and disable AutoTask jobs using EM Cloud Control. Click on Automated Maintenance Tasks in the Manage Optimizer Statistics screen (Figure 14.1). Figure 14.10 shows the Automated Maintenance Tasks screen.

FIGURE 14.10   The Automated Maintenance Tasks screen

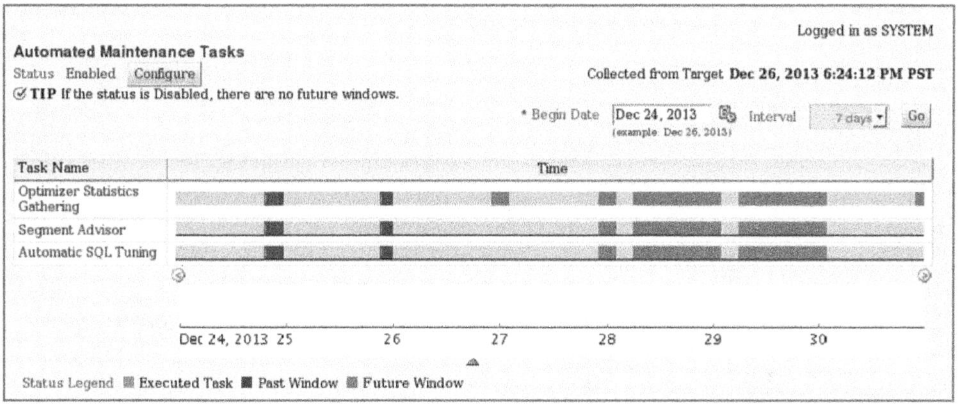

SQL Profiles

A SQL profile is created by SQL Tuning Advisor, which contains auxiliary statistics specific to a SQL statement. When profiling a SQL statement, SQL Tuning Advisor uses a set of bind values as input and compares the optimizer estimate with values obtained by executing fragments of the statement on a data sample. When significant variances are found, SQL Tuning Advisor bundles corrective actions together in a SQL profile and then recommends its acceptance. When SQL profiles are used, no changes to the application source code are necessary. The use of SQL profiles by the database is transparent to the user and, therefore, is a very good SQL performance-improvement tool considered to be a magic wand.

By clicking the Configure button, you can enable or disable the default AutoTask jobs, as well as adjust the days on which these tasks are run, as shown in Figure 14.11.

FIGURE 14.11   The Configure Automated Maintenance Tasks screen

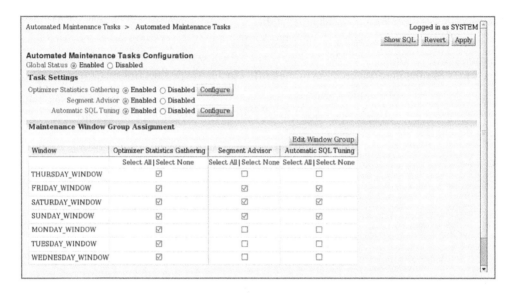

The SQL code behind the options chosen in Figure 14.11 is shown here:

```
BEGIN
dbms_auto_task_admin.disable(client_name => 'auto space advisor', operation =>
NULL, window_name => 'THURSDAY_WINDOW');
dbms_auto_task_admin.disable(client_name => 'sql tuning advisor', operation =>
NULL, window_name => 'THURSDAY_WINDOW');
dbms_auto_task_admin.disable(client_name => 'auto space advisor', operation =>
NULL, window_name => 'MONDAY_WINDOW');
dbms_auto_task_admin.disable(client_name => 'sql tuning advisor', operation =>
NULL, window_name => 'MONDAY_WINDOW');
dbms_auto_task_admin.disable(client_name => 'auto space advisor', operation =>
NULL, window_name => 'TUESDAY_WINDOW');
dbms_auto_task_admin.disable(client_name => 'sql tuning advisor', operation =>
NULL, window_name => 'TUESDAY_WINDOW');
dbms_auto_task_admin.disable(client_name => 'auto space advisor', operation =>
NULL, window_name => 'WEDNESDAY_WINDOW');
dbms_auto_task_admin.disable(client_name => 'sql tuning advisor', operation =>
NULL, window_name => 'WEDNESDAY_WINDOW');
END;
```

To completely disable any of the automated maintenance tasks, leave the operation and window as NULL. The code to disable the SQL Tuning Advisor is shown here:

```
BEGIN
  dbms_auto_task_admin.disable(
```

```
      client_name => 'sql tuning advisor',
      operation   => NULL,
      window_name => NULL);
END;
```

 By default, there are seven predefined maintenance windows, each one representing a day of the week. The weekend maintenance windows, *SATURDAY_WINDOW* and *SUNDAY_WINDOW*, are longer in duration than the weekday maintenance windows. The window group *MAINTENANCE_WINDOW_ GROUP* consists of these seven windows. Job scheduling and windows are discussed in detail in Chapter 16, "Controlling Resources and Jobs."

Gathering Performance Statistics

Oracle Database 12*c* generates several performance statistics that are used for self-tuning purposes and are available for administrators to better tune the database. Most of the performance statistics information is available through V$ dictionary views (also known as dynamic performance views). The information in the V$ views is not persistent—that is, information is lost when the database is shut down. *Automatic Workload Repository* (AWR) saves the performance information in system tables and is made available for analysis through Enterprise Manager and other third-party tools. AWR information is persistent across database shutdowns.

The AWR data is captured at a system or database level, and session-level information is captured using another mechanism called the Active Session History (ASH). You will learn about AWR and ASH in the following sections.

Using Automatic Workload Repository

Two background processes are responsible for collecting the performance statistics: Manageability Monitor (MMON) and Memory Monitor Light (MMNL). These processes work together to collect performance statistics directly from the system global area (SGA). The MMON process does most of the work by waking up every 60 minutes and gathering statistical information from the data dictionary views, dynamic performance views, and optimizer, and then storing this information in the database. The tables that store these statistics are the Automatic Workload Repository. These tables are owned by the user SYS and are stored in the SYSAUX tablespace.

To activate the AWR feature, you must set the pfile/spfile's parameter STATISTICS_LEVEL to the appropriate value. The values assigned to this parameter determine the depth of the statistics that the MMON process gathers. Table 14.3 shows the values that can be assigned to the STATISTICS_LEVEL parameter.

TABLE 14.3 Specifying Statistics Collection Levels

Collection Level	Description
BASIC	Disables the AWR and most other diagnostic monitoring and advisory activities. Few database statistics are gathered at each collection interval when operating the instance in this mode.
TYPICAL	Activates the standard level of collection activity. This is the default value and is appropriate for most environments.
ALL	Captures all the statistics gathered by the TYPICAL collection level, plus the execution plans and timing information from the operating system.

Once gathered, the statistics are stored in the AWR for the default duration of eight days. However, you can modify both the frequency of the snapshots and the duration for which they are saved in the AWR. One way to modify these intervals is by using the Oracle-supplied package DBMS_WORKLOAD_REPOSITORY. The following SQL command shows the DBMS_WORKLOAD_REPOSITORY package being used to change the AWR collection interval to 1 hour and the retention period to 30 days:

```
SQL> execute dbms_workload_repository.modify_snapshot_settings
             (interval=>60,retention=>43200);
PL/SQL procedure successfully completed.
```

The 30-day retention value shown here is expressed in minutes: 60 minutes per hour × 24 hours per day × 30 days = 43,200 minutes.

You can also change the AWR collection interval, retention period, and collection depth using EM Cloud Control. Choose AWR from the Performance drop-down menu and select AWR Administration (see Figure 14.12).

Click the Edit button to change the settings, as shown in Figure 14.13.

In Figure 14.13, the retention period for statistics gathered by the MMON process is set to 30 days, and statistics are collected every 30 minutes. You can also modify the depth at which statistics are collected by the AWR by clicking the Collection Level link. Clicking this link opens the Initialization Parameters screen, where you can specify any of the three predefined collection levels shown in Table 14.3. If you want to perform the same change using SQL*Plus, the following code can be used:

```
SQL> EXEC DBMS_WORKLOAD_REPOSITORY.MODIFY_SNAPSHOT_SETTINGS(43200,30);
```

Take care when specifying the AWR statistics collection interval. Gathering snapshots too frequently requires additional space in the SYSAUX tablespace and adds database overhead each time the statistics are collected. AWR does not use any space in the SGA.

FIGURE 14.12 AWR Administration using EM Cloud Control

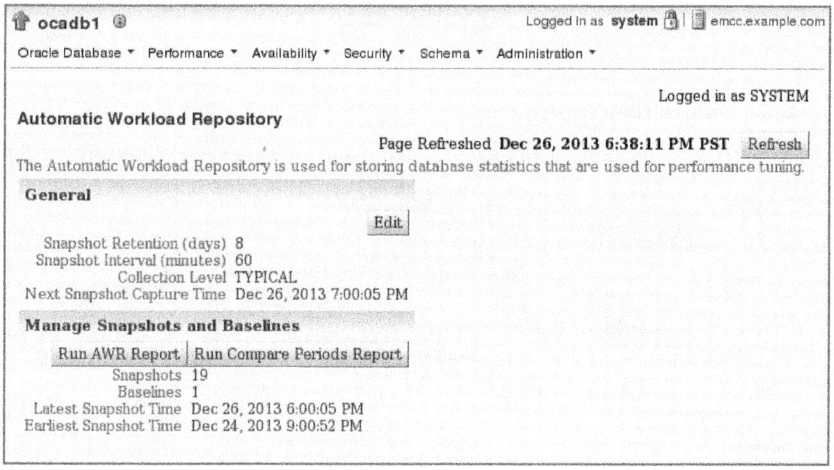

FIGURE 14.13 Changing AWR statistics collection and retention using EM

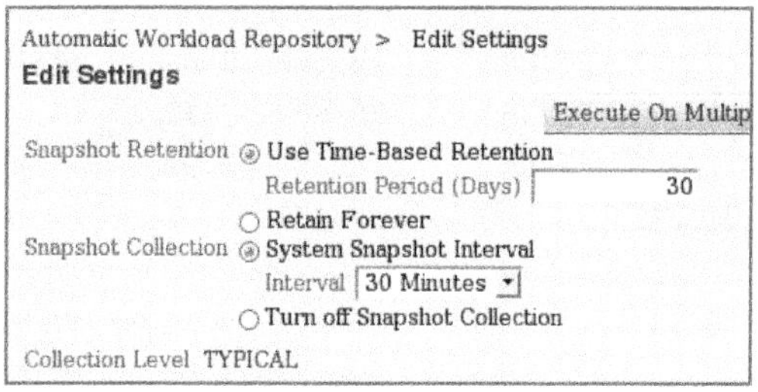

Using EM Cloud Control, you can view the AWR report. Click the Run AWR Report button on the Automatic Workload Repository screen shown earlier in Figure 14.12. You can get the same report using SQL*Plus by running the script $ORACLE_HOME/rdbms/admin/awrrpt.sql. You have the option to get a text report or HTML report.

The Run Compare Periods Report button on the Automatic Workload Repository screen (shown in Figure 14.12) is useful for comparing the AWR report from two different time-frames. For example, if you are experiencing a performance issue today, and if you want to compare the health and activity in the database to a week earlier, you could do so using the Compare Periods report. The two time periods selected in an AWR Compare Periods report can be of different durations because the report normalizes the statistics by the amount of time spent on the database for each time period, and presents statistical data ordered by the largest difference between the time periods. The compare period report can be invoked from SQL*Plus using script $ORACLE_HOME/rdbms/admin/awrddrpt.sql.

You can manage the AWR snapshots with SQL*Plus by utilizing the DBMS_WORKLOAD_REPOSITORY package, as described in the next section.

AWR data resides in the SYSAUX tablespace objects owned by SYS schema. You can use the dynamic performance view V$SYSAUX_OCCUPANTS to identify what else resides in the SYSAUX tablespace.

Managing AWR Snapshots Manually

You can create AWR snapshots by using the CREATE_SNAPSHOT procedure, as shown here:

```
SQL> EXECUTE DBMS_WORKLOAD_REPOSITORY.CREATE_SNAPSHOT ();
PL/SQL procedure successfully completed.
SQL>
```

You can use the DROP_SNAPSHOT_RANGE procedure to delete a range of snapshots, and you can query valid snapshot IDs from the DBA_HIST_SNAPSHOT view. The following example shows how to query the DBA_HIST_SNAPSHOT view:

```
SQL> SELECT snap_id, begin_interval_time, end_interval_time
  2  FROM dba_hist_snapshot
  3  ORDER BY snap_id;

  SNAP_ID BEGIN_INTERVAL_TIME            END_INTERVAL_TIME
---------- ------------------------------ ------------------------------
        1 24-SEP-13 02.06.11.000 AM      24-SEP-13 03.00.14.156 AM
        2 25-SEP-13 12.06.26.000 AM      25-SEP-13 12.17.55.437 AM
        3 25-SEP-13 12.17.55.437 AM      25-SEP-13 01.00.51.296 AM
        4 25-SEP-13 01.00.51.296 AM      25-SEP-13 02.00.22.109 AM
... ... ...
       27 27-SEP-13 07.03.17.375 PM      29-SEP-13 04.03.47.687 AM
       28 29-SEP-13 04.03.47.687 AM      29-SEP-13 05.00.39.437 AM
       29 29-SEP-13 05.00.39.437 AM      29-SEP-13 05.42.13.718 AM
```

To delete snapshots in the range 5–15, you can execute the following code. Note that the ASH (discussed in the next section) data is also purged between the time periods specified by the snapshot range.

```
SQL> BEGIN
  2    DBMS_WORKLOAD_REPOSITORY.DROP_SNAPSHOT_RANGE (5, 15);
  3  END;
  4  /
PL/SQL procedure successfully completed.
SQL>
```

Once AWR snapshots are taken and stored in the database, the Automatic Database Diagnostic feature uses the AWR data, as described in the "Automatic Database Diagnostic Monitoring" section.

Active Session History

Active Session History (ASH) is data sampled at specified intervals from the current state of all active sessions. The data is collected in memory and can be accessed by V$ views. The ASH information is also written to a persistent store by the AWR snapshots.

The V$ACTIVE_SESSION_HISTORY provides the information collected by the ASH sampler. The sessions are sampled every second by the MMNL process and are stored in a circular buffer in SGA. Each session is stored as a row. The current and historical information is available in the data dictionary view DBA_HIST_ACTIVE_SESS_HISTORY. ASH information also includes the execution plan for each SQL captured.

Oracle provides a script to generate an ASH report, $ORACLE_HOME/rdbms/admin/ashrpt .sql. You will be prompted for the report type (HTML or text), the begin time in minutes prior to SYSDATE, the duration in minutes for the report, and a name for the report. You can also use EM Cloud Control to generate the ASH report.

On the EM Cloud Control screen, select Performance Home from the Performance drop-down menu and click the Run ASH Report button, as shown in Figure 14.14.

FIGURE 14.14   Performance Home in EM Cloud Control

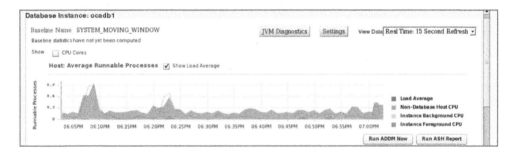

The screen shown in Figure 14.15 captures parameters for the ASH report. Specify the start time and end time for the report, and click the Generate Report button.

FIGURE 14.15   ASH report parameters

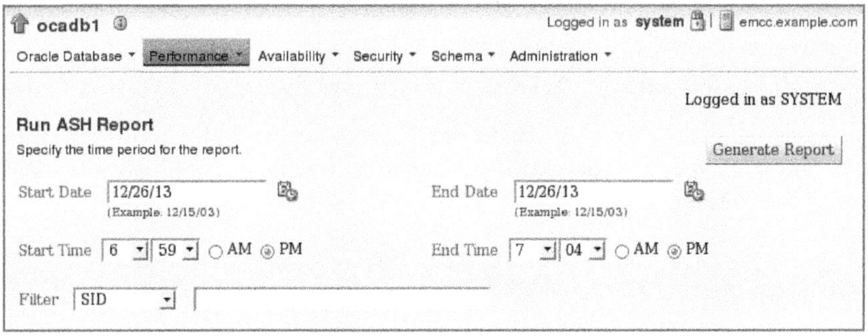

The ASH report using SQL*Plus can be generated using the script $ORACLE_HOME/rdbms/admin/ashrpt.sql. Similar to the AWR report, you can generate a text report or HTML report.

> Any session that is connected to the database and does not wait for a wait event that belongs to the idle wait class is considered an active session.

AWR Baselines

It is a good practice to baseline your database when everything is working as expected. When things go south, you can use this baseline to compare system statistics and performance metrics. *AWR baselines* contain performance data from a specific time period that is preserved for comparison when problems occur. This baseline data is excluded from the AWR purging process.

You can create two types of baselines: a *single* baseline and a *repeating* baseline. A single baseline is captured at a single fixed-time interval, such as October 5 between 10 A.M. and 1 P.M. A repeating baseline repeats during a time interval for a specific period, such as every Friday between 10 A.M. and 1 P.M. You can create and delete AWR baselines using EM Cloud Control or SQL*Plus.

Managing AWR Baselines Using SQL*Plus

To create a single baseline, use the CREATE_BASELINE procedure as shown in the following code. You can include the optional expiration parameter to automatically delete the snapshot after the specified number of days.

```
SQL> BEGIN
    DBMS_WORKLOAD_REPOSITORY.CREATE_BASELINE(
      start_snap_id => 27,
      end_snap_id => 29,
      baseline_name => 'OCP Example',
      expiration => 21);
    END;
SQL> /
PL/SQL procedure successfully completed.
SQL>
```

To drop a baseline, use the DROP_BASELINE procedure as shown in the following code. The cascade parameter specifies that only the baseline should be dropped, not the snapshots associated with the baseline.

```
SQL> BEGIN
    DBMS_WORKLOAD_REPOSITORY.DROP_BASELINE(
      baseline_name => 'OCP Example',
```

```
        cascade => FALSE);
    END;
SQL> /
PL/SQL procedure successfully completed.
SQL>
```

You can create a baseline for the future date and time. These are called *baseline templates*. The following code creates a baseline template:

```
SQL> BEGIN
    DBMS_WORKLOAD_REPOSITORY.CREATE_BASELINE_TEMPLATE(
        start_time => TO_DATE('01-JAN-15 05.00.00','DD-MON-YY HH.MI.SS'),
        end_time => TO_DATE('01-JAN-15 08.00.00','DD-MON-YY HH.MI.SS'),
        baseline_name => 'baseline_150101',
        template_name => 'template_150101',
        expiration => 21);
    END;
SQL> /
PL/SQL procedure successfully completed.
SQL>
```

A repeating baseline is created using the following code. The example shows a baseline captured every Friday at 9 A.M. for two years. The duration of the baseline is 9 A.M. to 12 P.M. The baselines will have a prefix of *baseline_FRI*, and they expire in 60 days.

```
SQL> BEGIN
    DBMS_WORKLOAD_REPOSITORY.CREATE_BASELINE_TEMPLATE(
        day_of_week => 'friday', hour_in_day => 9,
        duration => 3, expiration => 60,
        start_time => SYSDATE+1,
        end_time => ADD_MONTHS(SYSDATE, 24),
        baseline_name_prefix => 'baseline_FRI_',
        template_name => 'template_FRI');
    END;
SQL> /
PL/SQL procedure successfully completed.
SQL>
```

AWR baselines and baseline templates are never dropped automatically (or purged) from the database unless explicitly dropped by the DBA or the expiration period ends.

Managing AWR Baselines Using EM Cloud Control

Using EM Cloud Control to create, rename, and drop AWR baselines is easier than using SQL*Plus, and it is error free. From the Performance drop-down menu, select Adaptive Thresholds, and click the AWR Baselines link under Related Links. The current baselines are displayed, as shown in Figure 14.16.

FIGURE 14.16   The AWR Baselines screen

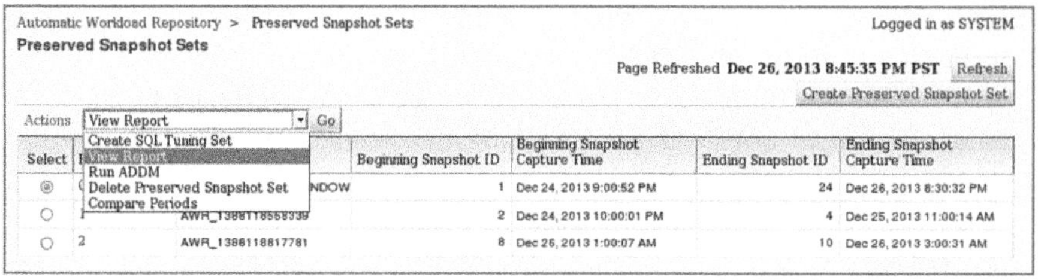

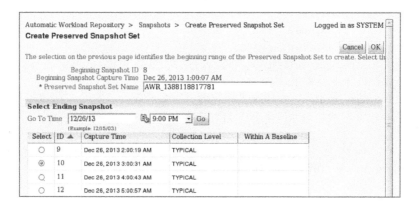

Click the Create Preserved Snapshot Set button to create a new baseline. You will be presented with the option to create a baseline as shown in Figure 14.17. Enter the name of the baseline. You can specify the snapshots to include in the baseline by using the snapshot IDs.

The Actions drop-down menu (shown in Figure 14.16) has an option to view the AWR Report. You can drop a baseline by choosing the Delete Preserved Snapshot Set option. The AWR Compare Periods report can be produced as well using the saved snapshots.

FIGURE 14.17   The AWR Create Preserved Snapshot screen

Automatic Database Diagnostic Monitoring

Following each AWR statistics-collection process, the *Automated Database Diagnostic Monitoring* (ADDM) feature proactively analyzes the gathered statistics and compares them to the statistics gathered by the previous two AWR snapshots. It is a self-advisor built in the database. By comparing the current statistics to two previous snapshots, the ADDM can easily identify potential database problems such as these:

* CPU and I/O bottlenecks
* Resource-intensive SQL or PL/SQL or Java execution
* Lock contention
* Utilization of Oracle's memory structures within the SGA
* RAC-specific issues
* Issues with Oracle Net configuration
* Data-concurrency issues

Based on these findings, the ADDM may recommend possible remedies. The goal of these recommendations is to minimize DB Time. DB Time is composed of two types of time measures for active database users: CPU time and wait time. This information is stored as the cumulative time that all database users have spent either using CPU resources or waiting for access to resources such as CPU, I/O, or Oracle's memory structures. High or increasing values for *DB Time* indicate that users are requesting increasingly more server resources and may also be experiencing waits for those resources, which can lead to less than optimal performance. In this way, minimizing DB Time is a much better way to measure overall database performance than Oracle's old ratio-based tuning methodologies.

To help you understand the concept of DB Time, Table 14.4 shows an example of how DB Time is calculated for four sessions in the database for four seconds.

TABLE 14.4 DB Time Calculation Example

Clock Time	Session 1	Session 2	Session 3	Session 4	DB Time
3:00:01	Active - Using CPU	Idle	Active - Wait on I/O	Active - Using CPU	1+0+1+1=3
3:00:02	Active - Using CPU	Active - Wait on Lock	Idle	Active - Wait on I/O	1+1+0+1=3
3:00:03	Active - Using CPU	Active - Wait on I/O	Idle	Idle	1+1+0+0=2
3:00:04	Active - Using CPU	Active - Using CPU	Active - Using CPU	Active - Using CPU	1+1+1+1=4
Total Elapsed Clock Time =4 Seconds					Total DB Time=12

The database takes a snapshot of the sessions every second. In the snapshot taken at 3:00:01, Sessions 1, 3, and 4 are active; session 2 is idle. So the DB Time is 1+0+1+1=3 seconds. In the next snapshot at 3:00:02, three sessions are active. After 4 seconds of wallclock time, the database has spent 12 seconds DB Time. Remember, DB Time is not how much time the database spent, since only three seconds have passed. It's the cumulative time of all active sessions. After 4 seconds of wallclock time, the DB Time is 12 seconds.

DB Time is calculated by combining all the times from all active user sessions into one number. Therefore, it is possible for the DB Time value to be larger than the total time that the instance has been running. The goal of database performance tuning is to reduce the DB Time of the system for a given workload.

Once ADDM completes its comparison of the newly collected statistics to the previously collected statistics, the results are stored in the AWR. You can use these statistics to establish baselines against which future performance will be compared, and you can use deviations from these baseline measures to identify areas that need attention. In this manner, ADDM allows you to not only better detect and alert yourself to potential management and performance problems in the database, but also allows you to automatically take corrective actions to rectify those problems quickly and with little or no manual intervention.

The following sections introduce the interfaces, features, and functionality of ADDM and explain how you can use this utility to monitor and manage database storage, security, and performance. We'll begin by examining the EM Cloud Control tools you can use to view the results of ADDM analysis.

Set the initialization parameter CONTROL_MANAGEMENT_PACK_ACCESS to either DIAGNOSTIC+TUNING (default) or DIAGNOSTIC to enable Automatic Database Diagnostic Monitoring. Setting CONTROL_MANAGEMENT_PACK_ ACCESS to NONE disables ADDM. Setting STATISTICS_LEVEL to BASIC also disables ADDM.

Using EM Cloud Control to View ADDM Analysis

EM Cloud Control graphically displays the results of the ADDM analysis. ADDM can be invoked at various screens in EM Cloud Control.

- Select Advisor Home from the Performance menu, and choose ADDM.
- Click the Run ADDM button on the Performance home screen.

In the following sections, you'll see sample output from each of the EM Cloud Control screens.

Running ADDM from Advisor Home Screen

When ADDM is invoked from the Advisor Central screen, you are given the option to analyze current performance or past performance. Current performance analysis captures an AWR snapshot and compares the newly created snapshot to the previous one for analysis. For past period analysis, you choose a start snapshot and an end snapshot for comparison. Figure 14.18 shows the Run ADDM screen when invoked from Advisor Central.

FIGURE 14.18   The Run ADDM screen from Advisor Central in EM

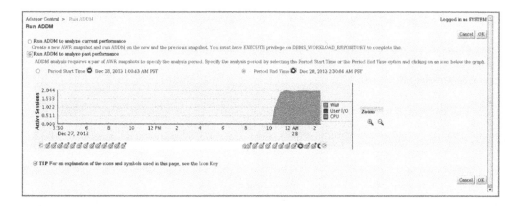

As stated earlier, the ADDM automatically compares the most recent AWR snapshot to previous AWR snapshots when formulating its recommendations. However, you can use the Run ADDM To Analyze Past Performance option to manually select any two AWR snapshot times and formulate ADDM recommendations for activity that occurred between those two points in time. To start this process, click the Period Start Time radio button, and then select a start date and time by clicking the point in the graph's timeline that corresponds to the beginning period that you want to use. Repeat this process to specify the end-process timestamp. In Figure 14.18, notice that the past period performance is chosen to analyze the database performance between December 28, 1 A.M. and 2:30 A.M. Click the OK button to see the findings.

ADDM analysis of I/O performance partially depends on DBIO_EXPECTED. It describes the expected performance of the I/O subsystem (the average time it takes to read a single database block, in microseconds). Oracle Database 12c uses the default value of 10,000 microseconds. This parameter can be modified using the DBMS_ADVISOR.SET_DEFAULT_TASK_PARAMETER procedure or from the Advisor Central screen of EM Cloud Control by clicking the Change Default Parameters link.

Running ADDM from Performance Home

Clicking the Run ADDM Now button on the Performance Home screen brings up the same dialogue screen you get when the first option on Figure 14.18 is chosen (Run ADDM To Analyze Current Performance). Once you confirm the creation of a new snapshot dialogue by clicking Yes, you will be presented with the analysis as shown in Figure 14.19. The output of past performance analysis (Figure 14.18) has the same format and content as well.

FIGURE 14.19   ADDM Performance Analysis findings

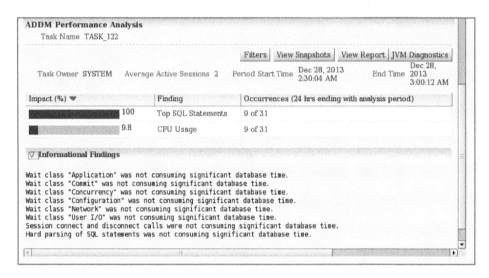

Click the View Snapshots button to view various statistics between the two snapshots, including CPU, I/O, and memory performance. You can also view a detailed AWR report between the two snapshots. The View Report button brings up the ADDM findings and analysis report in text form. The text report can be obtained by running $ORACLE_HOME/rdbms/admin/addmrpt.sql as well. The result of addmrpt.sql run, with its findings and recommendations, is shown here:

```
ADDM Report for Task 'TASK_123'
-------------------------------


Analysis Period
---------------
AWR snapshot range from 66 to 67.
Time period starts at 28-DEC-13 02.30.05 AM
Time period ends at 28-DEC-13 03.00.12 AM

Analysis Target
---------------
Database 'OCADB1' with DB ID 6257179.
Database version 12.1.0.1.0.
ADDM performed an analysis of instance ocadb1, numbered 1 and hosted at
ocasvr1.bj.com.
```

Activity During the Analysis Period

Total database time was 3629 seconds.
The average number of active sessions was 2.01.

Summary of Findings

	Description	Active Sessions Percent of Activity	Recommendations
1	Top SQL Statements	2.01 | 100	2
2	CPU Usage	.2 | 9.81	2

~~~~~~

~~~~~~

            Findings and Recommendations

Finding 1: Top SQL Statements
Impact is 2.01 active sessions, 100% of total activity.

SQL statements consuming significant database time were found. These
statements offer a good opportunity for performance improvement.

    Recommendation 1: SQL Tuning
    Estimated benefit is 1 active sessions, 50% of total activity.

    Action
        Run SQL Tuning Advisor on the SELECT statement with SQL_ID
        "5m8ggahzwr3ja".
        Related Object
           SQL statement with SQL_ID 5m8ggahzwr3ja.
           select count(*) from dba_segments, dba_tables, dba_synonyms
    Rationale
        The SQL spent 100% of its database time on CPU, I/O and Cluster waits.
        This part of database time may be improved by the SQL Tuning Advisor.
    Rationale

Database time for this SQL was divided as follows: 100% for SQL
execution, 0% for parsing, 0% for PL/SQL execution and 0% for Java
execution.

Recommendation 2: SQL Tuning
Estimated benefit is 1 active sessions, 50% of total activity.

Action
   Run SQL Tuning Advisor on the SELECT statement with SQL_ID
   "ahdm8cswnuqfg".
   Related Object
      SQL statement with SQL_ID ahdm8cswnuqfg.
      select count(*) from dba_synonyms, dba_segments, dba_views
Rationale
   The SQL spent 100% of its database time on CPU, I/O and Cluster waits.
   This part of database time may be improved by the SQL Tuning Advisor.
Rationale
   Database time for this SQL was divided as follows: 100% for SQL
   execution, 0% for parsing, 0% for PL/SQL execution and 0% for Java
   execution.

Finding 2: CPU Usage
Impact is .2 active sessions, 9.81% of total activity.

Host CPU was a bottleneck and the instance was consuming 99% of the host CPU.
All wait times will be inflated by wait for CPU.
Host CPU consumption was 99%.

   Recommendation 1: Application Analysis
   Estimated benefit is 2.01 active sessions, 100% of total activity.

Action
   Look at the "Top SQL Statements" finding for SQL statements consuming
   significant time on CPU. For example, the SELECT statement with SQL_ID
   "5m8ggahzwr3ja" is responsible for 50% of CPU usage during the analysis
   period.

   Recommendation 2: Host Configuration
   Estimated benefit is .2 active sessions, 9.81% of total activity.

```
     --------------------------------------------------------------
Action
   Consider adding more CPUs to the host or adding instances serving the
   database on other hosts.
Action
   Also consider using Oracle Database Resource Manager to prioritize the
   workload from various consumer groups.




~~~~~~~~~~~~~~~~~~~~~~~~~~~~~~~~~~~~~~~~~~~~~~~~~~~~~~~~~~~~~~~~~~~~~~~~~~~~
~~~~~~~~~~~~~~~~~~~~~~~~~~~~~~~~~~~~~~~~~~~~~~~~~~~~~~~~~~~~~~~~~~~~~~~~~~~~



        Additional Information
        ----------------------


Miscellaneous Information
-------------------------
Wait class "Application" was not consuming significant database time.
Wait class "Commit" was not consuming significant database time.
Wait class "Concurrency" was not consuming significant database time.
Wait class "Configuration" was not consuming significant database time.
Wait class "Network" was not consuming significant database time.
Wait class "User I/O" was not consuming significant database time.
Session connect and disconnect calls were not consuming significant database
time.
Hard parsing of SQL statements was not consuming significant database time.


End of Report
Report written to addmrpt_1_66_67.txt
```

> You can also manually perform an ADDM analysis without EM Cloud Con-
> trol by using the addmrpt.sql script located in the $ORACLE_HOME/rdbms/
> admin directory. Specify the period to analyze using the snapshot IDs.

You can use the DBMS_ADDM package to manually analyze AWR snapshots. Table 14.5 shows some of the subprograms in DBMS_ADDM that can be used to manually manage ADDM analysis.

TABLE 14.5 Partial List of DBMS_ADDM Subprograms

Procedure Name	Description
ANALYZE_DB	Creates an ADDM analysis by specifying the begin and end AWR snapshot IDs
DELETE	Deletes an ADDM task
INSERT_FINDING_DIRECTIVE	Excludes certain findings from ADDM reporting
INSERT_SEGMENT_DIRECTIVE	Excludes a certain schema, object, or segment from ADDM reporting (do not run Segment Advisor on these segments)
INSERT_SQL_DIRECTIVE	Excludes certain SQL from ADDM reporting

The DBA_ADVISOR_FINDINGS, DBA_ADVISOR_RECOMMENDATIONS, and DBA_ADVISOR_ACTIONS dictionary views have a column named FILTERED. If the value for this column is Y, the row in the view is filtered by a directive and is not reported.

Although using EM Cloud Control to create and view ADDM results is by far the simplest way to review ADDM recommendations, you can also query the ADDM data dictionary views directly. We'll discuss some of these data dictionary views in the following section.

Using Data Dictionary Views to View ADDM Analysis

You can use more than 20 data dictionary views to examine the results of ADDM's activities. Table 14.6 describes five commonly used ADDM views that store the recommendation information you saw in the EM Cloud Control pages.

TABLE 14.6 ADDM Data Dictionary Views

View Name	Description
DBA_ADDM_TASKS	Displays executed advisor tasks
DBA_ADDM_FINDINGS	Describes the findings identified by the ADDM analysis
DBA_ADVISOR_OBJECTS	Describes the objects that are referenced in the ADDM findings and recommendations

View Name	Description
DBA_ADVISOR_RECOMMENDATIONS	Describes the recommendations made based on ADDM findings
DBA_ADVISOR_RATIONALE	Describes the rationale behind each ADDM finding

DBA_ADDM_TASKS, DBA_ADDM_INSTANCES, and DBA_ADDM_FINDINGS are extensions of the corresponding DBA_ADVISOR_ views but are specific for ADDM tasks and findings.

The following SQL statement shows a sample query on the DBA_ADVISOR_FINDINGS data dictionary view that identifies the type of performance problem that is causing the most impact on the database:

```
SQL> SELECT task_id, type, message
    FROM dba_advisor_findings
    WHERE impact= (select MAX(impact) FROM dba_advisor_findings);

TASK_ID TYPE      MESSAGE
------- --------- -----------------------------------------------------
    114 PROBLEM   SQL statements consuming significant database time were found.
                  These statements offer a good opportunity for performance
                  improvement.
```

The output from this query shows that SQL statements being executed in the database are contributing to the poor database performance. By itself, the DBA_ADVISOR_FINDINGS table does not identify which SQL statements are consuming the database time. Instead, these are shown in the DBA_ADVISOR_OBJECTS data dictionary view and are identified by the TASK_ID value shown in the query on DBA_ADVISOR_FINDINGS. A query on that view, using the TASK_ID of 114 returned by the ADDM session that had the potential for the greatest database impact, returns the SQL statements shown here:

```
SQL> SELECT attr4
    FROM dba_advisor_objects
    WHERE task_id = 114;

ATTR4
----------------------------------------------------------------
select count(*) from dba_segments, dba_tables, dba_synonyms
select count(*) from dba_synonyms, dba_segments, dba_views
```

This query shows all the SQL statements that were captured by the AWR during the snapshot period and that were used in the ADDM analysis for that same period.

The DBA_ADVISOR_ACTIONS data dictionary view shows the ADDM recommendations for each finding. If you want to see the rationale behind each of the actions shown in DBA_ADVISOR_ACTIONS, query the DBA_ADVISOR_RATIONALE data dictionary view. The DBA_ADVISOR_RATIONALE view stores the ADDM recommendations that ADDM has formulated based on the AWR data, like those stored in DBA_ADVISOR_FINDINGS and DBA_ADVISOR_OBJECTS. The following example shows a sample query on the DBA_ADVISOR_RATIONALE view using the TASK_ID of 114 identified earlier:

```
SQL> SELECT message
    FROM dba_advisor_rationale
    WHERE task_id = 114;


MESSAGE
-----------------------------------------------------------------------
The SQL spent 99% of its database time on CPU, I/O and Cluster waits. This part
of database time may be improved by the SQL Tuning Advisor.
Database time for this SQL was divided as follows: 100% for SQL execution, 0%
for parsing, 0% for PL/SQL execution and 0% for Java execution.
The SQL spent 100% of its database time on CPU, I/O and Cluster waits. This part
of database time may be improved by the SQL Tuning Advisor.
Database time for this SQL was divided as follows: 100% for SQL execution, 0%
for parsing, 0% for PL/SQL execution and 0% for Java execution.
```

> As you can see from the complexity of these examples, examining the ADDM results via EM Cloud Control is much easier than accessing the data dictionary views via SQL. From a practical standpoint, you would run SQL queries against these ADDM views only if EM Cloud Control were unavailable.

Real-Time ADDM

Real-Time ADDM is a feature available in Oracle EM Cloud Control 12c. Real-Time ADDM runs through a set of predefined criteria to analyze the current performance of the database. After analyzing the problem, Real-Time ADDM identifies potential issues such as deadlocks, hangs, shared pool connections, and other exception situations. It also helps to resolve the problems without having to restart the database. Figure 14.20 presents the results of a Real-Time ADDM analysis that shows the components verified by Real-Time ADDM. You will have to provide a SYSDBA connection to the database and operating system access to the server to be able to resolve the issues through Real-Time ADDM.

To gain further insight into the recommendations and information gathered by the ADDM, Oracle Database 12c also provides several advisor utilities in EM Cloud Control. We will discuss these advisors in the next section.

FIGURE 14.20   Real-Time ADDM results

The Advisory Framework

Oracle Database 12*c* comes with several advisors to help you proactively manage the database. Figure 14.21 shows the Advisors Home screen, and the top portion shows the advisors available in Oracle Database 12*c* and how to invoke them. Advisors provide recommendations that are key for a DBA to manage the database effectively.

FIGURE 14.21   Advisor Home screen

The advisors can be classified into the following:

- Memory
    - SGA Advisor
    - PGA Advisor
    - Shared Pool Advisor
    - Buffer Cache Advisor
- SQL
    - SQL Tuning Advisor
    - SQL Access Advisor
    - SQL Repair Advisor
- Automatic Undo Management
    - Undo Advisor
- Recovery
    - MTTR Advisor
    - Data Recovery Advisor
    - Maximum Availability Architecture Advisor
- Space
    - Segment Advisor
- Streams
    - Streams Performance Advisor
- Testing
    - SQL Performance Analyzer

You can click each advisor's link on the Advisor Central screen and familiarize yourself with the contents and recommendations. The advisors perform the following functions:

SQL Advisors   The SQL Tuning Advisor and SQL Access Advisor provide recommendations and advice. They are discussed in the next section.

Memory Advisors   Memory advisors provide the optimal size for various memory parameters for Automatic Memory Management (AMM) and Automatic Shared Memory Management (ASMM). AMM and ASMM are discussed later in the chapter.

Segment Advisor   The Segment Advisor identifies whether a segment is a good candidate for a shrink operation based on the level of fragmentation within the segment. The advisor also keeps historical growth of the segment, which can be used for capacity planning. The Segment Advisor is discussed in Chapter 10, "Understanding Storage and Space Management."

Undo Advisor (Automatic Undo Management)   The Undo Advisor recommends the optimal size for the undo tablespace based on the undo retention and flashback requirements. Undo Advisor is discussed in Chapter 11, "Managing Data Concurrency and Undo."

MTTR Advisor The MTTR Advisor provides the optimal value for the FAST_START_ MTTR_TARGET initialization parameter. This parameter determines the amount of time required by the instance to start in the event of an instance crash. MTTR Advisor is discussed in Chapter 15, "Using Backup and Recovery."

Data Recovery Advisor The Data Recovery Advisor helps diagnose and repair data failures and corruptions. It analyzes the failure based on the symptoms and determines the repair strategies. Data Recovery Advisor is discussed in Chapter 15.

Maximum Availability Architecture Advisor The MAA advisor is a collection of tools to ensure your data is safe and recoverable. Click on the link to find out how you can ensure safety of the database and prevent data loss in the event of failures and disasters.

Streams Performance Advisor Oracle Streams enable information sharing, using messaging technology between databases or within a database. Streams are heavily used in data replication and data warehouse environments, and provide data availability during upgrade and maintenance operations. The Streams Performance analyzer captures and advises on various streams components.

SQL Repair Advisor Run the SQL Repair Advisor after a SQL statement fails with a critical error. The advisor analyzes the statement and advises if a patch is available to repair the statement. Critical errors are mostly the errors that produce error code ORA-00600 or ORA-07445. SQL Repair Advisor can be run from SQL*Plus using the subprograms in the DBMS_SQLDIAG package.

SQL Performance Analyzer SQL Performance Analyzer is used to test various scenarios when a change is made to the system. The change could be an upgrade, hardware change, parameter change, exadata migration, etc. The workload is captured from the production (source) system and played in the target system to analyze the impact.

SQL tuning is an important component to help keep the database performing at its best. A few bad SQL codes could bring the database to its knees. Oracle depends on optimizer statistics to find the best execution plan for the SQL code. The SQL Advisors go a step further and perform deep analysis of the SQL statements to recommend alternative execution plans and additional indexes. Let's briefly explore the SQL Tuning Advisor and SQL Access Advisor in the next sections.

SQL Tuning Advisor

The *SQL Tuning Advisor* provides SQL tuning advice. You can use the top activity or current session's graphs to drill down to the SQL statement to tune. You can tune one statement or multiple statements; however, the Tuning Advisor does not understand the interdependencies between the statements. Advice can include restructuring SQL statements, creating additional indexes, using materialized views, partitioning tables, refreshing the optimizer statistics, creating SQL Profile with better execution plan, or reusing a better plan found in the AWR.

The SQL Tuning Advisor can be accessed through either EM Cloud Control under Performance menu or in EM Cloud Control wherever SQL statement information is provided, such as on the Top Activity page, the Historical SQL page, the ADDM SQL findings, and so on. Figure 14.22 shows the SQL Tuning Advisor screen when accessed from EM Cloud Control Performance menu.

FIGURE 14.22 The SQL Tuning Advisor screen

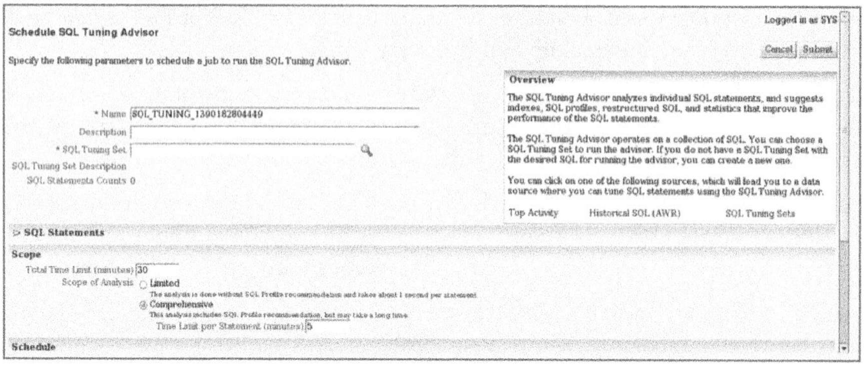

From the Top Activity page, click on the SQL ID to view more information on the SQL statement, and in the Actions drop-down menu, choose SQL Tuning Advisor to tune the SQL statement. Figure 14.23 shows an example analysis and recommendations from the Tuning Advisor.

In Figure 14.23, you can see three recommendations. The first one is to gather optimizer statistics for the optimizer to build a better plan. The second recommendation is to create a SQL profile. The Tuning Advisor also explains the benefits of each recommendation, so you can determine if the recommendation is worth implementing. For many recommendations, Tuning Advisor also provides the plan comparison. The third recommendation you see is to restructure the SQL statement, because there is a Cartesian join. From a practical standpoint, restructuring SQL to fix the missing join condition and collecting optimizer statistics would be the best way to solve this SQL performance issue.

FIGURE 14.23 Tuning Advisor recommendations

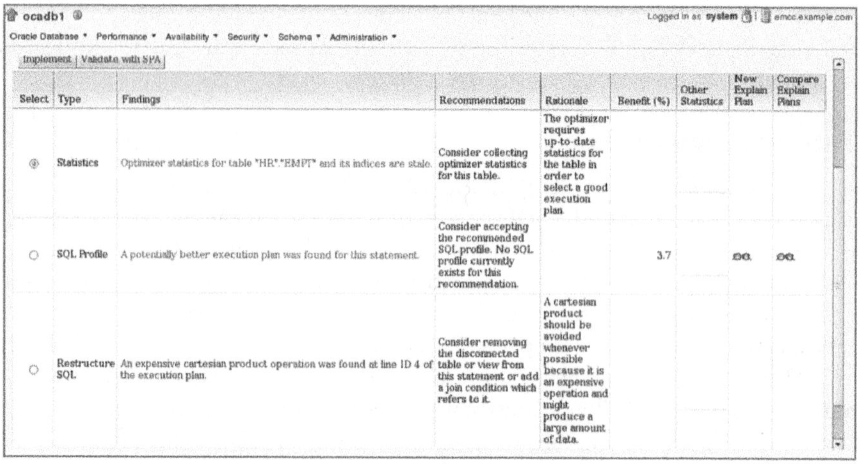

As you learned in the section "Configuring Automated Maintenance Tasks Using EM," the SQL Tuning Advisor is automatically scheduled and enabled when the database is created using DBCA or upgraded using DBUA. Automatic SQL tuning information can be accessed from EM Cloud Control using the Automated Maintenance Tasks menu item under Oracle Scheduler in the Administration menu. Figure 14.24 shows the Automated SQL Tuning Result Summary screen. Here you can configure automated SQL tuning options, such as enable or disable tasks, and decide whether the SQL profile recommendations made by the Tuning Advisor should be automatically implemented.

In the screen, you can also see a summary of recommendations, which you can review and implement.

WARNING The SQL Tuning task status and any recommendations are visible on the Advisor Central page. When a SQL Tuning task is running, you can click the Interrupt button to end the task. Note that closing the page or clicking Cancel will not stop the advisor task that is running in the database.

SQL Access Advisor

The *SQL Access Advisor* provides recommendations on schema modifications to optimize data access paths. Specifically, it recommends how database performance can be improved through partitioning, materialized views, indexes, and materialized view logs. SQL Access Advisor is also accessed through the SQL menu item under Performance in EM Cloud Control. Figure 14.25 shows the SQL Access Advisor screen. In this screen, you choose the workload source and the SQL statements to analyze.

FIGURE 14.24 Automated SQL tuning results

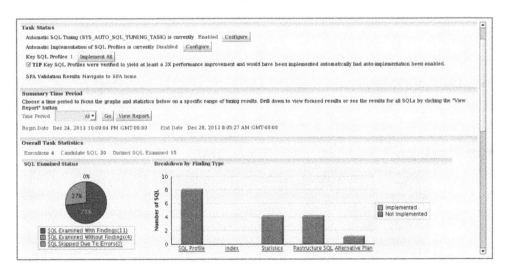

Figure 14.26 shows the Access Advisor recommendations. Here you can specify the type of structures, such as indexes or materialized views, that should be considered for recommendation. You can also specify either a limited analysis or comprehensive analysis. Comprehensive analysis requires more resources and takes longer.

The next two screens are used for scheduling and review. Once scheduled, the Access Advisor will run, and the results can be accessed from Advisor Central.

 The Advisor Central screen shown in Figure 14.20 has another tab, named Checkers, next to the Advisors tab. Don't forget to review it so that you'll understand the various integrity checks performed by the database.

In the next section, you'll learn about another tool that will help you proactively monitor the Oracle Database 12c database with timely alerts.

FIGURE 14.25   The SQL Access Advisor

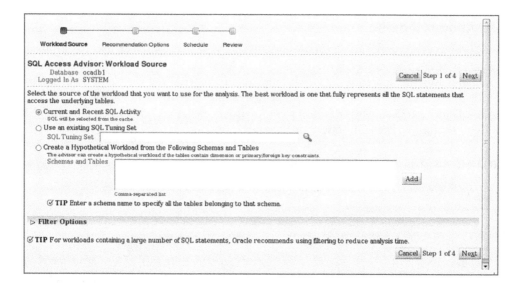

Monitoring Server-Generated Alerts

In addition to monitoring and making recommendations on SQL, memory, mean time to recover, segments, and undo activity, an Oracle Database 12c database can also proactively monitor itself for other types of problems related to configuration, security, and space management. To do so, you use the server-generated alerts feature.

A *server-generated alert* is an alert from Oracle Database 12c that says it suspects a problem with the database. These alerts are also an integral part of the ADDM architecture. They notify you when a management or performance issue occurs and begin taking corrective actions—if you configured such actions. By default, the alert notifications are sent to a pre-defined persistent queue named ALERT_QUE owned by SYS. EM Cloud Control reads this queue.

FIGURE 14.26   SQL Access Advisor recommendations

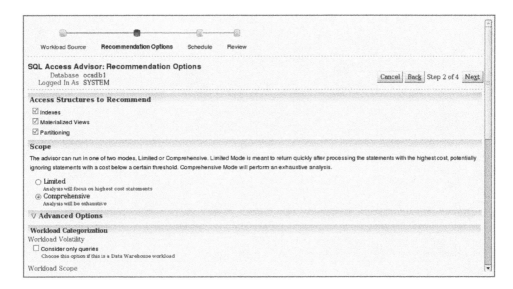

There are two types of server-generated alerts: threshold based and event based. *Threshold alerts* are triggered when a specified threshold is met, such as when a tablespace has reached a certain capacity. Threshold alerts can be fired at a warning level (for example, 85 percent tablespace capacity) or at a critical level (for example, 97 percent tablespace capacity). *Event alerts* are triggered when a specified event occurs, such as a database error.

Viewing and Configuring Alerts Using EM Cloud Control

The EM Cloud Control Database home page displays the alerts when they are triggered. Alerts can be reviewed using the Alert History menu item under Monitoring in the Administration drop-down menu. The All Metrics menu item also shows alerts and metric violations. You can also see the alert history by clicking the Alert link from the Oracle Database 12*c* home page. You can configure the alerts by clicking the Metric and Collection Settings menu, as shown in Figure 14.27.

Each alert can have two levels of severity: Warning and Critical. These two alert levels allow you to achieve greater granularity. For example, you might want two thresholds set up with regard to the archive destination. One might be a warning threshold that triggers an alert when the archive destination is 80 percent full—causing a message to be displayed on the EM Cloud Control main screen. In addition, you might want to set up a critical threshold so that you receive an email whenever the archive destination device is 90 percent full. In this manner, you can escalate a potential problem from an EM Cloud Control console message to an email alert to a text alert as the problem gets worse.

FIGURE 14.27   The Metric and Collection Settings screen

You can also use warning and critical alerts to distinguish between lower-severity problems, such as statistics indicating temporary poor performance, and higher-severity problems, such as ORA-0600 error messages in the database alert log. You can achieve this by defining warning thresholds only for lower-severity alerts and defining warning and critical alerts for higher-severity problems.

Viewing and Configuring Alerts Using SQL

You can use SQL*Plus to configure the alert thresholds and to view the alerts. The DBMS_SERVER_ALERT package has the subprograms to define and query the thresholds. The SET_THRESHOLD procedure is used to define the threshold, and the GET_THRESHOLD procedure is used to retrieve threshold information.

You can also query the thresholds from the DBA_THRESHOLDS dictionary view. The following is an example:

```
SQL> SELECT metrics_name, warning_value, critical_value
    FROM dba_thresholds
    WHERE metrics_name like 'Tablespace%'
SQL> /
```

```
METRICS_NAME                         WARNING_VA CRITICAL_V
----------------------------------   ---------- ----------
Tablespace Bytes Space Usage             0          0
Tablespace Space Usage                   85         97
SQL>
```

Threshold alerts are written to DBA_OUTSTANDING_ALERTS. Nonthreshold alerts are written only to DBA_ALERT_HISTORY. Entries from DBA_OUTSTANDING_ALERTS are cleared when the alert condition is cleared. The following is a query from the DBA_OUTSTANDING_ALERTS view:

```
SQL> SELECT reason FROM dba_outstanding_alerts;
REASON
--------------------------------------------------------
db_recovery_file_dest_size of 4395630592 bytes is 97.27%
used and has 119794176 remaining bytes available.

Metrics "Database Time Spent Waiting (%)" is at 36.84571
for event class "Concurrency"
```

The V$METRIC view shows system-level metric values. Metric history is saved in the V$METRIC_HISTORY view.

So far, you have seen several tools that help DBAs proactively monitor the database. They cannot possibly identify all the potential issues and how to proactively avoid them. Errors and database corruptions do happen. Oracle Database 12*c* has a reporting mechanism to analyze the problem reactively and take measures to avoid issues in the future. You'll learn about the Automatic Diagnostic Repository in the next section.

Understanding Automatic Diagnostic Repository

The *Automatic Diagnostic Repository* (ADR) is a file-based repository for database diagnostic data such as alert log files, trace files, core dump files, health monitor reports, and so on. ADR replaces the BACKGROUND_DUMP_DEST, CORE_DUMP_DEST, and USER_DUMP_DEST locations. The parameter, DIAGNOSTIC_DEST, specifies the base directory for the ADR. The default for DIAGNOSTIC_DEST is $ORACLE_BASE if available; otherwise, it's $ORACLE_HOME/log. ADR is a vast topic and is not covered here in its entirety.

Within *ADR base*, there can be multiple *ADR homes*. Each ADR home is the base directory for all the files belonging to an instance. The ADR home directory for an instance is $DIAGNOSTIC_DEST/diag/rdbms/<dbname>/<instance name>.

The subdirectories under the DIAGNOSTIC_DEST are as follows:

```
DIAGNOSTIC_DEST/diag              DIAGNOSTIC_DEST/diag
    rdbms                             tnslsnr
       <db_name>                         <machine_name>
          <instance_name>                   <listener_name>
             alert                             alert
```

```
cdump                          cdump
hm                             incident
incident                       incpkg
incpkg                         lck
ir                             metadata
lck                            stage
metadata                       sweep
stage                          trace
sweep
trace
```

In Oracle Database 12*c*, an alert log file is written in XML format as well as in text format. The XML-format file is under the `alert` directory, whereas the text-format file is under the `trace` directory. The values for _DUMP_DEST parameters are ignored by Oracle Database 12*c* databases. The new view V$DIAG_INFO gives file locations:

```
SQL> SELECT name, value FROM v$diag_info;

NAME
VALUE
----------------------------------------------------------------
Diag Enabled
TRUE
ADR Base
/u01/app/oracle
ADR Home
/u01/app/oracle/diag/rdbms/ocadb1/ocadb1
Diag Trace
/u01/app/oracle/diag/rdbms/ocadb1/ocadb1/trace
Diag Alert
/u01/app/oracle/diag/rdbms/ocadb1/ocadb1/alert
Diag Incident
/u01/app/oracle/diag/rdbms/ocadb1/ocadb1/incident
Diag Cdump
/u01/app/oracle/diag/rdbms/ocadb1/ocadb1/cdump
Health Monitor
/u01/app/oracle/diag/rdbms/ocadb1/ocadb1/hm
Default Trace File
/u01/app/oracle/diag/rdbms/ocadb1/ocadb1/trace/ocadb1_ora_14885.trc
Active Problem Count
0
Active Incident Count
0
```

The standard directory structure and diagnostic framework enables DBAs to package and send trace-file and log information to Oracle Support for timely resolution to issues. The ADR command interface (ADRCI) is a command-line tool available to view the ADR information and to package incident and problem information into a ZIP file.

Internal errors ORA-00600 and ORA-07445 are considered critical errors. Other errors considered as critical are listed in the view V$DIAG_CRITICAL_ERROR.

Using ADRCI to View the Alert Log File

You invoke the ADRCI command-line tool with the executable *adrci*, and you use the show alert command to view the alert log file. You can use options such as -tail to view the end of the file or -P to filter the output. You can also use the SPOOL command similar to SQL*Plus to write the output to a file.

The help command in adrci displays all the available commands in ADRCI. Invoke ADRCI using the adrci.exe executable on Windows or using the adrci executable on Unix/Linux platforms.

```
$ adrci

ADRCI: Release 12.1.0.1.0 - Production on Sat Dec 28 10:05:05 2013
Copyright (c) 1982, 2013, Oracle and/or its affiliates.  All rights reserved.
ADR base = "/u01/app/oracle"

adrci> help
HELP [topic]
   Available Topics:
        CREATE REPORT
        ECHO
        EXIT
        HELP
        HOST
        IPS
        PURGE
        RUN
        SET BASE
        SET BROWSER
        SET CONTROL
        SET ECHO
        SET EDITOR
        SET HOMES | HOME | HOMEPATH
        SET TERMOUT
```

```
SHOW ALERT
SHOW BASE
SHOW CONTROL
SHOW HM_RUN
SHOW HOMES | HOME | HOMEPATH
SHOW INCDIR
SHOW INCIDENT
SHOW LOG
SHOW PROBLEM
SHOW REPORT
SHOW TRACEFILE
SPOOL
```

```
There are other commands intended to be used directly by Oracle, type
"HELP EXTENDED" to see the list
adrci>
```

To find out the purpose and get detailed syntax information on a specific command, do help <command>:

```
adrci> help show alert

  Usage: SHOW ALERT [-p <predicate_string>]  [-term]
                   [ [-tail [num] [-f]] | [-file <alert_file_name>] ]
  Purpose: Show alert messages.

  Options:
    [-p <predicate_string>]: The predicate string must be double-quoted.
    The fields in the predicate are the fields:
        ORIGINATING_TIMESTAMP       timestamp
        NORMALIZED_TIMESTAMP        timestamp
        ORGANIZATION_ID             text(65)
        COMPONENT_ID                text(65)
        HOST_ID                     text(65)
        HOST_ADDRESS                text(17)
        MESSAGE_TYPE                number
        MESSAGE_LEVEL               number
        MESSAGE_ID                  text(65)
        MESSAGE_GROUP               text(65)
        CLIENT_ID                   text(65)
        MODULE_ID                   text(65)
        PROCESS_ID -                text(33)
```

```
THREAD_ID                        text(65)
USER_ID                          text(65)
INSTANCE_ID                      text(65)
DETAILED_LOCATION                text(161)
UPSTREAM_COMP_ID                 text(101)
DOWNSTREAM_COMP_ID               text(101)
EXECUTION_CONTEXT_ID             text(101)
EXECUTION_CONTEXT_SEQUENCE       number
ERROR_INSTANCE_ID                number
ERROR_INSTANCE_SEQUENCE          number
MESSAGE_TEXT                     text(2049)
MESSAGE_ARGUMENTS                text(129)
SUPPLEMENTAL_ATTRIBUTES          text(129)
SUPPLEMENTAL_DETAILS             text(4000)
PROBLEM_KEY                      text(65)
```

[-tail [num] [-f]]: Output last part of the alert messages and
output latest messages as the alert log grows. If num is not specified,
the last 10 messages are displayed. If "-f" is specified, new data
will append at the end as new alert messages are generated.

[-term]: Direct results to terminal. If this option is not specified,
the results will be open in an editor.
By default, it will open in emacs, but "set editor" can be used
to set other editors.

[-file <alert_file_name>]: Allow users to specify an alert file which
may not be in ADR. <alert_file_name> must be specified with full path.
Note that this option cannot be used with the -tail option

Examples:
  show alert
  show alert -p "message_text like '%incident%'"
  show alert -tail 20

adrci>

Similar to `tail -f` in Unix, where the output appended to a file is continuously displayed, you can use `tail -f` in adrci as well to continuously
show the alert log when messages are added to it.

Using EM to View the Alert Log File

You can also use EM Cloud Control to view the alert log contents. On the Cloud Control home page, click the Alert Log Contents link under Related Links. You can view the last 50, 100, or up to 2,000 lines of the alert log. See Figure 14.28 showing the various menu options to view alert log content under the Oracle Database menu.

FIGURE 14.28 Alert log viewing options

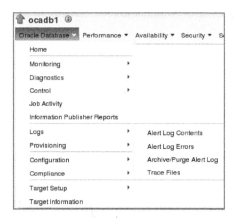

In addition to viewing the alert log content and errors, there is an option to purge or archive the alert log.

In the next section, you will learn the tools available to monitor the performance of the database.

Managing Performance

Although AWR, ADDM, advisors, and ADR all help you proactively monitor and manage your databases, you can use additional performance-specific features of EM Cloud Control to further enhance the performance of your database. When thinking about tuning, you should consider the following areas:

- Memory-allocation issues
- I/O contention (disk/SAN configuration)
- CPU contention
- Network issues
- SQL problems (bad SQL, optimizer plans)

Several dictionary and dynamic performance views are available in Oracle Database 12*c* that help you tune and gather system information. When it comes to tuning, managing the instance memory is very important. How much memory should you allocate for all the various SGA components? In the following sections, you will learn how Oracle Database 12*c* can help you take the guesswork out of database administration and tune the database.

Sources of Tuning Information

EM Cloud Control provides a wealth of information for improving database monitoring and management, but you also need to be aware of several other sources of information about database performance, including the following:

- The alert log
- Background and user trace files
- Dynamic performance views
- Data dictionary views

The Alert Log

The Oracle alert log records informational and error messages for a variety of activities that have occurred against the database during its operation. These activities are recorded in chronological order from the oldest to most recent. You can find the alert log in the ADR directory that you learned about earlier.

The alert log frequently indicates whether gross tuning problems exist in the database. Tables that are unable to acquire additional storage, sorts that are failing, and problems with rollback segments are all examples of tuning problems that can show up as messages in the alert log. Most of these messages are accompanied by an Oracle error message.

Background and User Trace Files

Oracle trace files are text files that contain session information for the process that created them. Trace files can be generated by the Oracle background processes, through the use of trace events, or by user server processes. These trace files can contain useful information for performance tuning and system troubleshooting. Trace files are also located in the ADR directories.

You can generate user trace files for a particular session by using the DBMS_MONITOR package. Many subprograms are available in this package to enable and disable trace; the most common ones are SESSION_TRACE_ENABLE to start the tracing and SESSION_TRACE_DISABLE to stop the tracing.

To use the SESSION_TRACE_ENABLE procedure, you must know the SID and SERIAL# on the session, which you can get by querying the V$SESSION view. The third argument to the procedure is waits, which is TRUE by default. The fourth argument is binds, which is FALSE by default. By enabling the waits, the wait information is written to the trace file. By enabling the binds, the bind variable values are also written to the trace file. Once you have the SID and SERIAL# , you can enable trace for the session by doing the following:

```
SQL> BEGIN
        DBMS_MONITOR.SESSION_TRACE_ENABLE(session_id=>324,
```

```
                        serial_num=>54385,
                        waits=>TRUE,
                        binds=>TRUE);
   END;
```

To stop tracing, you have to pass in the SID and SERIAL# as parameters:

```
SQL> BEGIN
        DBMS_MONITOR.SESSION_TRACE_DISABLE(session_id=>324,
                                    serial_num=>54385);
     END;
```

You can also use EM Cloud Control to enable and disable trace. To see the sessions in the instance, you can choose any of the following links under the Additional Monitoring Links on the Performance tab in Database Control (see Figure 14.29):

- Top Consumers
- Instance Locks
- Instance Activity

FIGURE 14.29 Additional Monitoring Links section on the Performance home screen

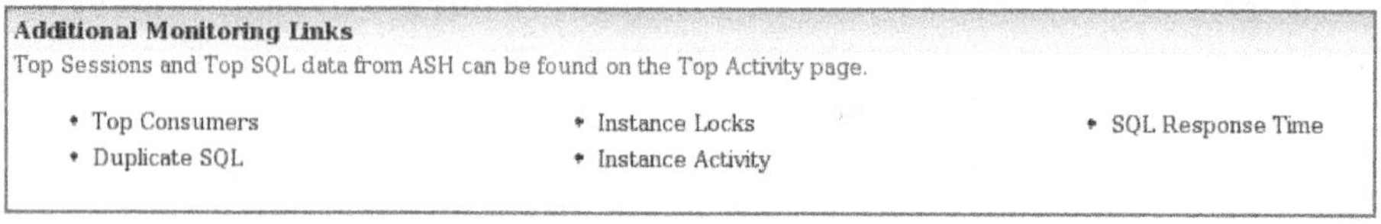

When you click the Top Consumers link, you will get an overview of the consumers. Click the Top Sessions link to view the sessions in the instance. The session can be searched by specifying filter criteria using the Search Sessions menu under the Performance tab. You can also view the Blocking Sessions menu under the Performance tab, where you have the option to trace as well. You can use the Enable SQL Trace and Disable SQL Trace buttons on these screens to enable and disable tracing.

Session trace files are written to the trace directory under the ADR home screen. Oracle Database 12c provides multiple tools to analyze trace files. The standard tool to convert the trace file to a readable format is known as *tkprof*. It works on a single file, and provides the SQL statements, execution and elapsed times, as well as explains the plan. Oracle Support also provides the Trace Analyzer tool for download, which produces HTML output and is filled with a lot of useful information.

End-to-end application tracing and analysis of multiple trace files are made possible with *trcsess* utility. It consolidates trace output from selected trace files based on criteria such as Session ID, Client ID, Service name, Action name, and Module name. After trcsess merges the trace information into a single output file, the output file can be processed by tkprof or Trace Analyzer.

The 10046 trace event, which can be activated at the instance or session level, is particularly useful for finding performance bottlenecks. See Note 171647.1 at http://metalink.oracle.com for a discussion of using the 10046 trace event as a tuning technique. Through EM Cloud Control, you can enable trace capturing the waits and binds information. Another trace event helpful to analyze optimizer behavior is 10053.

Dynamic Performance Views

As described in Chapter 8, "Introducing Oracle Database 12*c* Components and Architecture," Oracle Database 12*c* contains several dynamic performance views. Table 14.7 contains a partial listing of some of the V$ views that are frequently used in performance tuning and troubleshooting.

TABLE 14.7   A Partial Listing of Dynamic Performance Views

Name	Description
V$SGAINFO	Shows information about the size of the SGA's components.
V$PGASTAT	Shows information about PGA memory usage.
V$EVENT_NAME	Shows database events that may require waits when requested by the system or by an individual session.
V$SYSTEM_EVENT	Shows events for which waits have occurred for all sessions accessing the system.
V$SESSION_EVENT	Shows events for which waits have occurred, individually identified by session.
V$SESSION_WAIT	Shows events for which waits are currently occurring, individually identified by session.
V$STATNAME	Matches the name to the statistics listed only by number in V$SESSTAT and V$SYSSAT.
V$SYSSTAT	Shows overall system statistics for all sessions, both currently and previously connected.
V$SESSTAT	Shows statistics on a per-session basis for currently connected sessions.
V$SESSION	Shows current connection information on a per-session basis.
V$WAITSTAT	Shows statistics related to block contention.

TABLE 14.7   A Partial Listing of Dynamic Performance Views *(continued)*

Name	Description
V$LOCK	Lists the locks currently in the database.
V$PARAMETER	Shows the initialization-parameter values that are currently in effect.
V$SPPARAMETER	Shows the contents of the server parameter file (spfile); look for value TRUE in column ISSPECIFIED to see if the parameter was explicitly specified in the spfile, as opposed to default values.
V$FILESTAT	Shows number of reads/writes and timing statistics for data files.
V$DATAFILE	Shows data file properties.
V$TEMPFILE	Shows temporary file properties.
V$TEMPSEG_USAGE	Displays temporary segment usage by session.

In general, queries that incorporate V$SYSSTAT show statistics for the entire instance since the time it was started. By joining this view to the other relevant views, you get the overall picture of performance in the database. Alternatively, queries that incorporate V$SESSTAT show statistics for a particular session. These queries are better suited for examining the performance of an individual operation or process. EM Cloud Control makes extensive use of these views when creating performance-related graphs.

Data Dictionary Views

Depending on the features and options installed, an Oracle database has hundreds of data dictionary views. Table 14.8 contains a partial listing of some of the DBA views that are used when you tune performance on a database.

TABLE 14.8   A Partial Listing of Data Dictionary Views for Tuning and Troubleshooting

Name	Description
DBA_TABLES	Table storage, row, and block information.
DBA_INDEXES	Index storage, row, and block information.
INDEX_STATS	Index depth and dispersion information.
DBA_DATA_FILES	Data file location, naming, and size information.
DBA_SEGMENTS	General information about any space-consuming segment in the database.

Name	Description
DBA_HISTOGRAMS	Table and index histogram definition information.
DBA_OBJECTS	General information about all objects in the database, including tables, indexes, triggers, sequences, and partitions.
DBA_WAITERS	Shows sessions that are waiting for another session to release a lock.
DBA_TABLESPACES	Shows tablespaces in the database and their properties.
DBA_FREE_SPACE	Shows the free space available in all tablespaces in the database.
DBA_HIST_*	Views beginning in DBA_HIST_ show AWR historic information.

Important Performance Metrics

Throughput is another example of a statistical performance metric. *Throughput* is the amount of processing that a computer or system can perform in a given amount of time—for example, the number of customer deposits that can be posted to the appropriate accounts in four hours under regular workloads. Throughput is an important measure when considering the scalability of the system. *Scalability* refers to the degree to which additional users can be added to the system without system performance declining significantly. New features such as Oracle Database 12*c*'s Grid Computing capabilities make Oracle one of the most scalable database platforms on the market.

 Performance considerations for transactional systems usually revolve around throughput maximization.

Another important metric related to performance is response time. *Response time* is the amount of time it takes for a single user's request to return the desired result when using an application—for example, the time it takes for the system to return a listing of all the customers who purchased products that require service contracts.

 Performance-tuning considerations for decision-support systems usually revolve around response time minimization.

You can use EM Cloud Control to both monitor and react to sudden changes in performance metrics such as throughput and response time.

In the next section, we will revisit memory configuration and learn more about tuning memory components.

Tuning Memory

In Chapter 8, you learned about the architecture of Oracle Database 12*c*. An Oracle instance consists of memory structures and background processes. The memory structure comprises SGA and PGA, and it is important to size the SGA and PGA appropriately for better database performance.

Fortunately, Oracle Database 12*c* provides a variety of automatic options to tune memory so that DBAs don't need to worry about tuning the individual memory components such as the Java pool and the shared pool. In the following sections, you will revisit the memory components and learn the options available to tune and manage.

Memory Components

The two primary memory components are SGA and PGA. SGA consists of the following components. The parameters that control these pools are also provided for your reference.

- Shared pool: SHARED_POOL_SIZE
- Database buffer cache: DB_CACHE_SIZE
- Large pool: LARGE_POOL_SIZE
- Java pool: JAVA_POOL_SIZE
- Streams pool: STREAMS_POOL_SIZE
- Log buffer: LOG_BUFFER
- Result Cache: RESULT_CACHE_SIZE
- Database keep buffer cache: DB_KEEP_CACHE_SIZE
- Database recycle buffer cache: DB_RECYCLE_CACHE_SIZE
- Buffer cache for nonstandard block size: DB_nK_CACHE_SIZE
- Unified auditing queue size: UNIFIED_AUDIT_SGA_QUEUE_SIZE

    The parameters that can be configured to manage the PGA are as follows:

- SORT_AREA_SIZE
- HASH_AREA_SIZE
- BITMAP_MERGE_AREA_SIZE
- CREATE_BITMAP_AREA_SIZE

As you can see from the previous components and parameters, correctly sizing these pools and memory parameters can become complicated. Oracle Database 12*c* takes the pain away from DBAs by providing these automatic memory-tuning options:

- Automatic SGA tuning using SGA_TARGET
- Automatic PGA tuning using PGA_AGGREGATE_TARGET
- Automatic Memory tuning (PGA and SGA) using MEMORY_TARGET

The following advisors views are available in Oracle Database 12*c* to tune the individual components of memory:

- `V$DB_CACHE_ADVICE` to size the database buffer cache
- `V$SHARED_POOL_ADVICE` to size the shared pool
- `V$JAVA_POOL_ADVICE` to size the Java pool
- `V$STREAMS_POOL_ADVICE` to size the streams pool

Because of the multitenant architecture in Oracle Database 12*c*, most dynamic performance views have a column named `CON_ID`. `CON_ID` will have a value of 0 for a single-tenant database (known as non-CDB); in the case of CDB, it indicates an item that pertains to the entire CDB. Value 1 indicates it is for root CDB, and any other number identifies the container ID of the container database.

Automatic Shared Memory Management

Automatic Shared Memory Management (ASMM) was introduced in Oracle 10*g* and can automatically tune five important SGA components as well as the area required (fixed size) for internal allocations:

- `SHARED_POOL_SIZE`
- `DB_CACHE_SIZE`
- `LARGE_POOL_SIZE`
- `JAVA_POOL_SIZE`
- `STREAMS_POOL_SIZE`

To enable ASMM, you set the `SGA_TARGET` parameter, where you specify the total size for the SGA. You still have to manually size the other SGA components, which in most cases do not need much tuning. These components are as follows:

- `LOG_BUFFER`
- `DB_KEEP_CACHE_SIZE`
- `DB_RECYCLE_CACHE_SIZE`
- `DB_nK_CACHE_SIZE`

`SGA_TARGET` is a dynamic parameter; you can increase it to the maximum size specified by the static parameter `SGA_MAX_SIZE`.

You can change a dynamic initialization parameter by using the ALTER SYSTEM statement, whereas you should change static parameters in the spfile or init.ora file first. The instance needs to be restarted for the new value to take effect.

You can still specify sizes for the five pools when using ASMM. Oracle will use the values specified as the minimum size for the components. To get full automatic tuning, the five SGA components must be set to zero or not specified in the initialization file.

 The STATISTICS_LEVEL parameter must be set to TYPICAL or ALL for the Automatic Shared Memory Management feature to function.

You can tune the appropriate size of SGA_TARGET using the advisor view V$SGA_TARGET_ADVICE. The V$SGAINFO view shows the sizes of various SGA components. Notice the granule size. All SGA components allocate and deallocate space in units of *granules*.

```
SQL> SELECT name, bytes FROM v$sgainfo;

NAME                                    BYTES
-------------------------------- ----------
Fixed SGA Size                        2287864
Redo Buffers                          8859648
Buffer Cache Size                   318767104
Shared Pool Size                    419430400
Large Pool Size                      33554432
Java Pool Size                       16777216
Streams Pool Size                    16777216
Shared IO Pool Size                  50331648
Data Transfer Cache Size                    0
Granule Size                         16777216
Maximum SGA Size                   1252663296
Startup overhead in Shared Pool     125410800
Free SGA Memory Available           436207616

SQL> SELECT * FROM v$sga_target_advice;
```

The V$SGA_TARGET_ADVICE view has the following columns and shows the impact on the database when the SGA size is reduced from the current level; it also indicates what performance gains can be expected when SGA size is increased. The SGA_SIZE and SGA_SIZE_FACTOR columns show the hypothetical size of SGA.

- SGA_SIZE
- SGA_SIZE_FACTOR
- ESTD_DB_TIME

- ESTD_DB_TIME_FACTOR
- ESTD_PHYSICAL_READS
- ESTD_BUFFER_CACHE_SIZE
- ESTD_SHARED_POOL_SIZE
- CON_ID

The V$SGA_RESIZE_OPS view has a circular history of the last 800 SGA resize requests, both manual and automatic. V$SGA_CURRENT_RESIZE_OPS displays information about SGA resize operations that are currently in progress.

Automatic SQL Execution Memory Management

You can use Automatic SQL Execution Memory Management to tune the PGA using the PGA_AGGREGATE_TARGET and WORKAREA_SIZE_POLICY parameters. Both parameters can be dynamically modified.

PGA_AGGREGATE_TARGET specifies the target amount of memory available to the instance (PGA memory) for all server processes. Setting a nonzero value for PGA_AGGREGATE_TARGET automatically sets the WORKAREA_SIZE_POLICY parameter to AUTO, which means the _AREA_SIZE parameters are automatically sized.

You can tune PGA performance by using the advisor view V$PGA_TARGET_ADVICE. The advice is generated by simulating past workload.

Automatic Memory Management

Automatic Memory Management (AMM) further eases memory management. AMM automatically tunes the SGA and PGA components. All you have to do is specify the total memory available to the instance by using the MEMORY_TARGET parameter.

When AMM is used, Oracle automates the sizing of SGA and PGA, and it causes the indirect transfer of memory from SGA to PGA, and vice versa, as required by the workload. The default for SGA is 60 percent, and the default for PGA is 40 percent allocation when the instance is started.

MEMORY_TARGET is a dynamic parameter; you can increase it up to the maximum specified by the static parameter MEMORY_MAX_TARGET. By default, AMM is not enabled—the default value for MEMORY_TARGET is zero.

You still can set SGA_TARGET, PGA_AGGREGATE_TARGET, and the various SGA pool parameters in the initialization file. Oracle will use these values as the minimum when configuring the various pools. Table 14.9 shows some rules when you have configured the AMM and ASMM memory parameters.

TABLE 14.9   Memory-Tuning Parameters Dependency

MEMORY_TARGET (MT)	SGA_TARGET (ST)	Result
MT=0 AMM is disabled.	ST=0 ASMM is disabled.	Must specify values for individual pools.
MT=0 AMM is disabled.	ST>0 ASMM is enabled.	Individual pools will be automatically tuned. SGA and PGA memory will be treated separately.
MT>0 AMM is enabled.	ST=0 ASMM is disabled.	Full automatic tuning of SGA and PGA.
MT>0 AMM is enabled.	ST>0 ASMM is enabled.	Automatic tuning of SGA and PGA, but SGA will keep the minimum value specified by ST.

You can adjust the MEMORY_TARGET parameter size after reviewing the advisor view V$MEMORY_TARGET_ADVICE:

```
SQL> SELECT memory_size, memory_size_factor, estd_db_time, estd_db_time_factor
     FROM v$memory_target_advice;

MEMORY_SIZE MEMORY_SIZE_FACTOR ESTD_DB_TIME ESTD_DB_TIME_FACTOR
----------- ------------------ ------------ -------------------
        900                .75        37040              1.0005
       1200                  1        37021                   1
       1500               1.25        37017               .9999
       1800                1.5        37017               .9999
       2100               1.75        37017               .9999
       2400                  2        37017               .9999
```

If you want to know the size of all the AMM memory components, you can query the V$MEMORY_DYNAMIC_COMPONENTS view:

```
SQL> SELECT component, current_size, min_size, max_size
     FROM v$memory_dynamic_components;

COMPONENT                         CURRENT_SIZE   MIN_SIZE   MAX_SIZE
------------------------------    ------------ ---------- ----------
shared pool                         419430400  184549376  419430400
large pool                           33554432   33554432  150994944
java pool                            16777216   16777216   16777216
```

streams pool	16777216	16777216	16777216
SGA Target	822083584	822083584	822083584
DEFAULT buffer cache	268435456	268435456	503316480
KEEP buffer cache	0	0	0
RECYCLE buffer cache	0	0	0
DEFAULT 2K buffer cache	0	0	0
DEFAULT 4K buffer cache	0	0	0
DEFAULT 8K buffer cache	0	0	0
DEFAULT 16K buffer cache	0	0	0
DEFAULT 32K buffer cache	0	0	0
Shared IO Pool	50331648	50331648	50331648
Data Transfer Cache	0	0	0
PGA Target	436207616	436207616	436207616
ASM Buffer Cache	0	0	0

The V$MEMORY_RESIZE_OPS view has a circular history of the last 800 memory resize requests, both manual and automatic. V$MEMORY_CURRENT_RESIZE_OPS displays information about memory resize operations that are currently in progress.

Managing Memory Using EM Cloud Control

You can use EM Cloud Control to enable and disable various memory-tuning options as well as monitor the memory components and their performance. You can use the information on this screen to decide whether your Oracle Database 12c database needs more memory allocated for better performance. Figure 14.20 shows the Advisor Central screen; choose Memory Advisors from this screen. You will be presented with the screen shown in Figure 14.30.

FIGURE 14.30   The Memory Advisors screen in EM

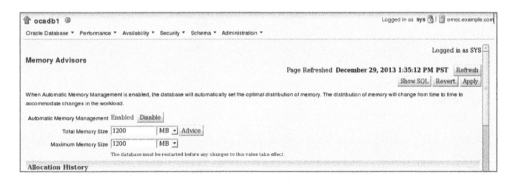

The Memory Advisors screen shows the current status of memory usage and provides the option to enable or disable Automatic Memory Management. Click the Advice button, and you can view the memory size suggestions.

If you disable AMM using the Disable button, EM automatically enables ASMM, as shown in Figure 14.31.

FIGURE 14.31 The ASMM screen in EM

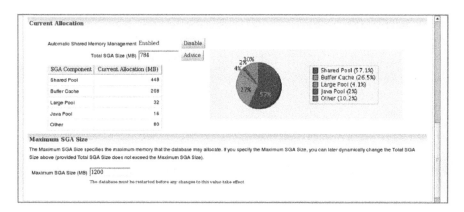

If you disable ASMM, EM will prompt you to provide the sizes for individual components, as shown in Figure 14.32.

FIGURE 14.32 The Memory Components screen in EM

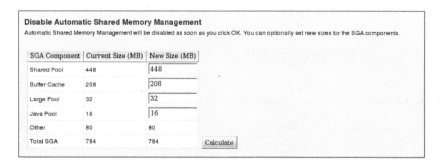

When you scroll down the Memory Advisors screen (Figure 14.30), a section will display the SGA and PGA allocations. When using manual or ASMM, you can configure PGA as well as see the PGA memory usage details under the PGA tab.

EM also shows several important performance metrics, discussed in the next section.

Review Figures 9.20 to 9.23 in Chapter 9, "Creating and Operating Oracle Database 12c," to revisit the memory configuration options available when you create a database using DBCA.

Summary

Oracle Database 12*c* provides many tools for proactively identifying and fixing potential performance and management problems in the database. In this chapter, you learned about tools such as AWR, ADDM, ADR, AMM, and ASMM.

At the core of the monitoring system is the Automatic Workload Repository (AWR), which uses the MMON background process to gather statistics from the SGA and store them in a collection of tables owned by the user SYS.

Following each AWR statistics-collection interval, the Automatic Database Diagnostic Monitoring (ADDM) feature examines the newly gathered statistics and compares them to previous AWR statistics to establish baselines in an attempt to identify poorly performing components of the database. The ADDM then summarizes these findings on the EM Cloud Control main screen and Performance tab. Using these screens, you can identify and examine the SQL statements that are contributing the most to DB Time. You can further explore the opportunities for improving the performance or manageability of your database using the EM Cloud Control advisors, which include the SQL Tuning Advisor, SQL Access Advisor, Memory Advisor, Mean Time To Recover Advisor, Segment Advisor, Undo Management Advisor, and so on.

In addition to alerts, you can find indicators of database performance in the database alert log, user and background trace files, data dictionary views, and dynamic performance views. Some data dictionary views do not contain accurate information about the segments in the database until after optimizer statistics are collected on those objects. Oracle Database 12c has automated tasks to manage optimizer stats, to analyze SQL statements for performance improvement, and to look for ways to reclaim unused space in objects.

Memory tuning is simplified in Oracle Database 12c using Automatic Memory Management. AMM is configured using the MEMORY_TARGET parameter. If other memory parameters are specified, they will be considered as the minimum for those components. If you do not want to completely automate memory, the next level is to automate shared Memory Management using the SGA_TARGET parameter.

EM Cloud Control summarizes several important performance metrics on the EM Cloud Control Performance home screen. These metrics include performance statistics for the host server, user sessions, and instance throughput.

Exam Essentials

Understand the Automatic Workload Repository.   Describe the components of the AWR and how they are used to collect and store database performance statistics. Understand the sections of the AWR report.

Describe the role of Automatic Database Diagnostic Monitor.   Know how ADDM uses the AWR statistics to formulate tuning recommendations using historical and baseline metrics.

Explain how each advisor is used to improve performance.   Describe how you can use each of the EM Cloud Control advisors shown on the Advisor Central screen to improve database performance and manageability.

Describe how alerts are used to monitor performance.   Show how you can configure the EM Cloud Control alert system to alert you via the console or via email whenever a monitored event occurs in the database.

Remember the location of the alert log file.   The alert log file location is determined by the DIAGNOSTIC_DEST parameter. Learn the location of the text alert log file and XML alert log file.

Know how to manage the automated tasks.   Know the automated tasks of Oracle Database 12c, and how to enable and disable those tasks. Learn the various options to collect optimizer statistics.

Understand Automatic Memory Management.   Know the parameters that control the memory management and how the pools are allocated.

Learn to configure Automatic Shared Memory Management.   Know the parameters that control Shared Memory Management and how the pools are allocated. Learn how to provide minimum values for each pool when ASMM is used.

Understand the sources of tuning information.   Know in which dynamic performance views, data dictionary views, and log files, tuning information can be found outside the EM Cloud Control monitoring system.

Review Questions

1. Which of the following components of the Oracle architecture stores the statistics gathered by the MMON process?

   A. ADDM

   B. AWR

   C. ASMM

   D. ADR

2. Which of the following options for the pfile/spfile's STATISTICS_LEVEL parameter turns off AWR statistics gathering and ADDM advisory services?

   A. OFF

   B. TYPICAL

   C. ALL

   D. BASIC

3. Which parameter is used to enable Automatic Memory Management?

   A. AMM_TARGET

   B. MEMORY_TARGET

   C. SGA_TARGET

   D. AUTOMATIC_MEMORY

4. Which two parameters configure automatic PGA memory management?

   A. SGA_TARGET

   B. PGA_AGGREGATE_TARGET

   C. WORKAREA_SIZE_POLICY

   D. PGA_AGGREGATE_LIMIT

5. Suppose you have used EM Database Control to drill down into ADDM findings and have found that a single SQL statement is causing the majority of the I/O on your system. Which of the following advisors is best suited to troubleshoot this SQL statement?

   A. SQL Tuning Advisor

   B. SQL Access Advisor

   C. Both A and B

   D. Neither A nor B

6. Which SGA component cannot be dynamically changed after instance startup?

   A. SHARED_POOL

   B. JAVA_POOL_SIZE

   C. LOG_BUFFER

   D. None of the above

7. Which procedure is used to tell Oracle that the statistics gathered should not be published?

   A. DBMS_STATS.PUBLISH_STATS

   B. DBMS_STATS.SET_TABLE_PREFS

   C. DBMS_STATS.PENDING_STATS

   D. DBMS_STATS.GATHER_TABLE_STATS

8. Which data dictionary view contains information explaining why ADDM made its recommendations?

   A. DBA_ADVISOR_FINDINGS

   B. DBA_ADVISOR_OBJECTS

   C. DBA_ADVISOR_RECOMMENDATIONS

   D. DBA_ADVISOR_RATIONALE

9. Which of the following advisors determines if the space allocated to the shared pool, large pool, or buffer cache is adequate?

   A. SQL Tuning Advisor

   B. SGA Tuning Advisor

   C. Memory Advisor

   D. Pool Advisor

10. Which initialization parameter can disable memory advisors and Automatic Shared Memory Management? (Choose the best answer.)

    A. CONTROL_MANAGEMENT_PACK_ACCESS

    B. STATISTICS_LEVEL

    C. MEMORY_TARGET

    D. Memory advisors cannot be disabled.

11. Which statement regarding SGA_MAX_SIZE is true?

    A. SGA_MAX_SIZE is modifiable after an instance is started, only when Automatic Memory Management is used.

    B. SGA_MAX_SIZE is not dynamically modifiable.

    C. SGA_MAX_SIZE is ignored when MEMORY_TARGET > 0.

    D. SGA_MAX_SIZE must be specified when SGA_TARGET > 0.

12. When you configure an alert, which of the following types of alert thresholds can you use to monitor a tablespace for diminishing free space?

    A. Warning threshold

    B. Critical threshold

    C. Both A and B

    D. Neither A nor B

13. Multiple baseline metrics can be gathered and stored in the AWR. Why might you want more than one metrics baseline?

    A. You might want a separate baseline metric for each user.

    B. You might want a separate baseline metric for daytime usage versus off-hours usage.

    C. You might want a separate baseline metric for each schema.

    D. You would never want more than one baseline metric, even though it is possible to gather and store them.

14. When does ADDM run? (Choose two.)

    A. When an AWR snapshot is taken automatically by the MMON process

    B. When an AWR snapshot is taken automatically by the MMNL process

    C. When an AWR snapshot is taken manually by DBA

    D. When the AutoTask process runs hourly to take workload snapshots

15. Which statement about the MEMORY_TARGET parameter is not true?

    A. It is a dynamic initialization parameter.

    B. It represents the total maximum memory that can be allocated to the instance memory (PGA and SGA combined).

    C. Its default value is zero.

    D. You will not get an error when SGA_TARGET and PGA_AGGREGATE_TARGET parameters are set to nonzero values.

16. Which of the following is a performance metric that could be defined as "the amount of work that a system can perform in a given amount of time"?

    A. Response time

    B. Uptime

    C. Throughput

    D. Runtime

17. Which parameter determines the location of the alert log?

   A. CORE_DUMP_DEST

   B. BACKGROUND_DUMP_DEST

   C. ALERT_LOG_DEST

   D. DIAGNOSTIC_DEST

18. By default, how long will database statistics be retained in the AWR?

   A. 8 days

   B. 30 days

   C. 7 hours

   D. Indefinitely

19. Your users have called to complain that system performance has suddenly decreased markedly. Which is the most likely place to look for the cause of the problem in EM Database Control?

   A. The Main screen

   B. The Performance tab

   C. The Administration tab

   D. The Maintenance tab

20. Using EM Database Control, you've identified the following SQL statement as the source of a lot of disk I/O:

```
SELECT NAME, LOCATION, CREDIT_LIMIT FROM CUSTOMERS
```

What should you do first to try to improve performance?

   A. Run the SQL Tuning Advisor.

   B. Run the SQL Access Advisor.

   C. Check the EM Database Control main screen for alerts.

   D. Click the Alert Log Content link in the EM Database Control main screen.

Chapter

15

Using Backup and Recovery

ORACLE DATABASE 12*c*: OCA EXAM OBJECTIVES COVERED IN THIS CHAPTER:

✓ **Backup and Recovery Concepts**

- ▪ Identify the importance of checkpoints, redo log files, and archive log files.

✓ **Backup and Recovery Configuration**

- ▪ Configure the Fast Recovery Area.
- ▪ Configure ARCHIVELOG mode.

✓ **Performing Database Backups**

- ▪ Create consistent database backups.
- ▪ Back up your database without shutting it down.
- ▪ Create incremental backups.
- ▪ Automate database backups.
- ▪ Manage backups.

✓ **Performing Database Recovery**

- ▪ Determine the need for performing recovery.
- ▪ Use Recovery Manager (RMAN) and the Data Recovery Advisor to perform recovery of the control file, redo log file, and data file.

The most important commitment a DBA has is to protect all transaction data the business has generated and not lose it. In other words, as a DBA you want to configure your database to minimize downtime while being able to recover quickly and without losing any committed transactions when the database becomes unavailable for reasons beyond your control. Fortunately, Oracle Database 12c makes it easy to configure a database to be highly available and reliable.

First, we'll look at the failures that can occur in an Oracle database and explore how they can occur because of user or DBA mistakes or because of hardware or software failures beyond your direct control. Each of these failures can require little or no action whatsoever, as in the case of an instance failure, but at the other end of the spectrum, they may require a recovery effort, as in the case of a disk crash containing the SYSTEM tablespace.

In this chapter, you will learn about the components you will use to minimize or eliminate data loss in your database while at the same time keeping availability high. Next, you will learn how to configure your database for recovery. This will include a discussion of ARCHIVELOG mode and other required initialization parameters. Once your environment is configured, you will need to know how to actually back it up, using the RMAN utility. You will also learn how to automate and manage your backups as well as how to monitor one of the key components in your backup strategy: the Fast Recovery Area.

Similar to backups, Oracle Database 12c makes it easy for you to recover from a number of database failures. To balance performance with recoverability, you will learn how to tune instance recovery to minimize the amount of time Oracle requires to recover from an instance failure while still providing a reasonable response time for ongoing transactions. In a nutshell, your job is to increase the *mean time between failures* (MTBF) by providing redundant components where possible and leveraging other Oracle high-availability features such as Real Application Clusters (RAC) and Streams (an advanced replication technology). Hand in hand with increasing MTBF is decreasing the *mean time to recovery* (MTTR) to ensure compliance with any service-level agreements you have in place. Last, but certainly not least, these efforts should help you minimize data loss in such a way that committed transactions are never lost.

The Data Recovery Advisor was introduced in Oracle 11g, which automates most of the recovery tasks and is integrated with Enterprise Manager (EM) Cloud Control. Oracle's administration tool, EM Cloud Control, makes configuring and performing backups and recovery easier. Most, if not all, of the functionality available with the command-line interface is available in a graphical user interface to save time and make backup and recovery operations less error-prone.

Understanding and Configuring Recovery Components

As a database administrator, your primary goal is to keep the database open and available for users, usually 24 hours a day, seven days a week. Your partnership with the server's system administrator includes the following tasks:

- Proactively solving common causes of failures
- Increasing the mean time between failure (MTBF)
- Ensuring a high level of hardware redundancy
- Increasing availability by using Oracle options such as Real Application Clusters (RAC), Oracle Streams (an advanced replication technology), and Oracle Data Guard (a disaster recovery solution)
- Decreasing the mean time to recover (MTTR) by setting the appropriate Oracle initialization parameters and ensuring that backups are readily available in a recovery scenario
- Minimizing or eliminating loss of committed transactions by using redo application, replication, and Oracle Data Guard

A number of structures and events in the database directly support backup and recovery operations. The control files maintain the list of database files in the database, along with a record of the most recent database backups (if you are using RMAN for your backups). The checkpoint (CKPT) background process works in concert with the database writer (DBW*n*) process to manage the amount of time required for instance recovery; during instance recovery, the redo log files are used to synchronize the data files. For more serious types of failures, such as media failures, archived redo log files are applied to a restored backup copy of a data file to synchronize the data files and ensure that no committed transactions are lost. Finally, the Fast Recovery Area, introduced in Oracle 10*g*, is a common area for all recovery-related files that makes your job much easier when backing up or recovering your database.

To maximize your database's availability, it almost goes without saying that you want to perform regularly scheduled backups. Most media failures require some kind of restoration of a data file from a disk or tape backup before you can initiate media recovery.

In addition to regularly scheduled backups (see the section "Performing Backups" later in this chapter), you can configure a number of other features to maximize your database's availability and minimize recovery time, such as multiplexing control files, multiplexing redo log files, configuring the database in ARCHIVELOG mode, and using a Fast Recovery Area.

Understanding Control Files

The control file is one of the smallest, yet also one of the most critical, files in the database. Recovering from the loss of one copy of a control file is relatively straightforward; recovering from the loss of your only control file or all control files is more of a challenge and requires more-advanced recovery techniques.

In the following section, you will get an overview of the control file architecture. You will then learn how to maximize the recoverability of the control file in the section "Multiplexing Control Files."

Control File Architecture

The control file is a relatively small (in the megabyte range) binary file that contains information about the structure of the database. You can think of the control file as a metadata repository for the physical database. It has the structure of the database, meaning the data files and redo log files constitute a database. The control file is created when the database is created and is updated continuously with information required for recovery and configuration of the database.

The control file is updated continuously and should be available at all times. Don't edit the contents of the control file; only Oracle processes should update its contents. When you start up the database, Oracle uses the control file to identify and open the data files and redo log files. Control files play a major role when recovering a database.

The contents of the control file include the following:

- The database name to which the control file belongs. A control file can belong to only one database.
- The database-creation timestamp.
- The name, location, and online/offline status information of the data files.
- The name and location of the redo log files.
- Redo log archive information.
- Tablespace names.
- The current log sequence number, which is a unique identifier that is incremented and recorded when an online redo log file is switched.
- The most recent checkpoint information.
- The beginning and ending of undo segments.
- Recovery Manager's backup information. *Recovery Manager* (RMAN) is the Oracle utility you use to back up and recover databases.

The control file size is determined by the MAX clauses you provide when you create the database:

- MAXLOGFILES
- MAXLOGMEMBERS
- MAXLOGHISTORY
- MAXDATAFILES
- MAXINSTANCES

Oracle pre-allocates space for these maximums in the control file. Therefore, when you add or rename a file in the database, the control file size does not change. The control file tracks all structural changes to the database. When you add a new file to the database or relocate a file, an Oracle server process immediately updates the information in the control file. Back up the control file after any structural changes. The log writer (LGWR) process updates the control file with the current log sequence number. The checkpoint (CKPT) process updates the control file with the recent checkpoint information. When the database is in ARCHIVELOG mode, the archiver (ARC*n*) process updates the control file with information such as the archive log filename and log sequence number.

The control file contains two types of record sections: reusable and not reusable. RMAN information is kept in the reusable section. Items such as the names of the backup data files are kept in this section, and once this section fills up, the entries are reused in a circular fashion after the number of days specified by the initialization parameter CONTROL_FILE_RECORD_KEEP_TIME is reached. Therefore, the control file can continue to grow because of new RMAN backup information recorded in the control file before CONTROL_FILE_RECORD_KEEP_TIME is reached. By default, seven days history is kept in the control file.

You can query the control filenames and their status by using EM Database Express, as you have already seen in Chapter 8, "Introducing Oracle Database 12*c* Components and Architecture." The Control File Section (on the Server tab, under Storage) shows the record information from the control file. It shows the size used in the control file for each section, the total number of records that can be saved with the current size of the control file, and the number or records used.

Reading and writing the control file blocks is different from reading and writing data blocks. Oracle Database 12*c* reads and writes directly from the disk to the program global area (PGA) for control files. Each process allocates a small amount of its PGA memory for control file blocks.

Multiplexing Control Files

Because the control file is critical for database operation, at a minimum you must have two copies of the control file; Oracle recommends a minimum of three copies. You duplicate the control file on different disks either by using the multiplexing feature of Oracle or by using the mirroring feature of your operating system. If you have multiple disk controllers on your server, at least one copy of the control file should reside on a disk managed by a different disk controller.

If you use the Database Configuration Assistant (DBCA) to create your database, control files are multiplexed by default. The next section discusses how you can implement the multiplexing feature using an init.ora or using the server-side spfile.

The control filename can be queried from the database using V$CONTROLFILE; information about the control file record sections is stored in V$CONTROLFILE_RECORD_SECTION. The information found in V$DATABASE comes from the control file.

Multiplexing Control Files Using init.ora

Multiplexing means keeping a copy of the same control file on different disk drives and ideally on different controllers, too. To multiplex a control file, copy the control file to multiple locations and change the CONTROL_FILES parameter in the text-based initialization file init.ora to include all control filenames. The following syntax shows three multiplexed control files:

```
CONTROL_FILES = ('/ora01/oradata/MYDB/ctrlMYDB01.ctl',
                 '/ora02/oradata/MYDB/ctrlMYDB02.ctl',
                 '/ora03/oradata/MYDB/ctrlMYDB03.ctl')
```

By storing the control file on multiple disks, you avoid the risk of a single point of failure. When multiplexing control files, updates to the control file can take a little longer, but that is insignificant when weighed against the benefits. If you lose one control file, you can restart the database after copying one of the other control files or after changing the CONTROL_FILES parameter in the initialization file.

When multiplexing control files, Oracle updates all the control files at the same time but uses only the first control file listed in the CONTROL_FILES parameter for reading.

When creating a database, you can list the control filenames in the CONTROL_FILES parameter, and Oracle creates as many control files as are listed. You can have a maximum of eight multiplexed control file copies.

If you need to add more control file copies, follow these steps:

1. Shut down the database.

```
SQL> SHUTDOWN NORMAL
```

2. Copy the control file to more locations by using an operating-system command:

```
$ cp /u02/oradata/ord/control01.ctl /u05/oradata/ord/control04.ctl
```

3. Change the initialization-parameter file to include the new control filename(s) in the parameter CONTROL_FILES by changing this:

```
CONTROL_FILES=('/u02/oradata/ord/control01.ctl',
'/u03/oradata/ord/control02.ctl',
'/u04/oradata/ord/control03.ctl')
```

to this:

```
CONTROL_FILES=('/u02/oradata/ord/control01.ctl',
'/u03/oradata/ord/control02.ctl',
'/u04/oradata/ord/control03.ctl',
'/u05/oradata/ord/control04.ctl')
```

4. Start the instance:

```
SQL> STARTUP
```

This procedure is somewhat similar to the procedure for recovering from the loss of a control file.

After creating the database, you can change the location of the control files, rename the control files, or drop certain control files. You must have at least one control file for each database. To add, rename, or delete control files, you need to follow the preceding steps. Basically, you shut down the database, use the operating-system copy command (copying, renaming, or deleting the control files accordingly), modify the init.ora parameter file, and start up the database.

Multiplexing Control Files Using an spfile

Multiplexing using a binary spfile is similar to multiplexing using init.ora. The major difference is in how the CONTROL_FILES parameter is changed. Follow these steps:

1. Alter the spfile while the database is still open:

```
SQL> ALTER SYSTEM SET CONTROL_FILES =
       '/ora01/oradata/MYDB/ctrlMYDB01.ctl',
       '/ora02/oradata/MYDB/ctrlMYDB02.ctl',
       '/ora03/oradata/MYDB/ctrlMYDB03.ctl',
       '/ora04/oradata/MYDB/ctrlMYDB04.ctl' SCOPE=SPFILE;
```

The use of the SCOPE=SPFILE qualifier means this parameter change won't take effect until after the instance is restarted. The contents of the binary spfile are changed immediately, but the old specification of CONTROL_FILES is used until the instance is restarted.

2. Shut down the database:

```
SQL> SHUTDOWN NORMAL
```

3. Copy an existing control file to the new location:

```
$ cp /ora01/oradata/MYDB/ctrlMYDB01.ctl /ora04/oradata/MYDB/ctrlMYDB04.ctl
```

4. Start the instance:

```
SQL> STARTUP
```

 You can always create the spfile from the init file using the syntax CREATE SPFILE FROM PFILE.

Understanding Checkpoints

The CKPT process controls the amount of time required for instance recovery. During a checkpoint, CKPT updates the control file and the header of the data files to reflect the last successful transaction by recording the last system change number (SCN). The SCN, which is a number sequentially assigned to each transaction in the database, is also recorded in the control file against the data filename that is taken offline or made read-only.

A checkpoint occurs automatically every time a redo log file switch occurs, either when the current redo log file fills up or when you manually switch redo log files. The DBW*n* processes in conjunction with CKPT routinely write new and changed buffers to advance the checkpoint from where instance recovery can begin, thereby reducing the MTTR. It also ensures that the database regularly writes dirty buffers in the buffer cache to disk and the database writes all committed data to disk during a consistent database shutdown.

A full checkpoint (thread checkpoint) occurs when the DBA manually initiates a checkpoint using the ALTER SYSTEM CHECKPOINT statement, when the database is shut down in normal or immediate mode, or when an online redo log is switched. To avoid a large number of updates to data files during redo log switches, whenever the DBW*n* process writes dirty buffers to data files, it advances the checkpoint on those files. Therefore, during redo log switches, the CKPT writes the checkpoint position only in the control file and does not update the data file headers. This is known as an incremental checkpoint, which happens automatically. An incremental checkpoint occurs when DBW*n* wakes up every 3 seconds and if there are any dirty blocks to write to data file.

Note that the incremental checkpoint to the data file is written by the DBW*n* process and not the CKPT process.

Understanding Redo Log Files

A redo log file records all changes to the database, before the changes are written to the data files. The database maintains online redo log files to protect against data loss. To recover from an instance or a media failure, redo log information is required to roll data files forward to the last committed transaction. Ensuring that you have at least two members for each redo log-file group dramatically reduces the likelihood of data loss because the database continues to operate if one member of a redo log file is lost.

In the following sections, we will give you an architectural overview of redo log files, as well as show you how to add redo log groups, add or remove redo log group members, and clear a redo log group in case one of the redo log group's members becomes corrupted.

Redo Log File Architecture

Online redo log files are filled with redo records. A redo record, also called a *redo entry*, consists of a group of change vectors, each of which describes a change made to a single block in the database. Redo entries record data that you can use to reconstruct all changes made to the database, including the undo segments. When you recover the database by using redo log files, Oracle reads the change vectors in the redo records and applies the changes to the relevant blocks.

The LGWR process writes redo information from the redo log buffer to the online redo log files under a variety of circumstances:

- When a user commits a transaction, even if this is the only transaction in the log buffer.
- When the redo log buffer becomes one-third full.
- When the buffer contains approximately 1MB of changed records. This total does not include deleted or inserted records.
- When a database checkpoint is performed.
- When 3 seconds have elapsed since the last redo log buffer write.

 LGWR always writes its records to the online redo log file *before* DBW*n* writes new or modified database buffer cache records to the data files.

Each database has its own set of online redo log groups. A redo log group can have one or more redo log members (each member is a single file). If you have a RAC configuration, in which multiple instances are mounted to one database, each instance has one online redo thread, and at least two groups under each thread. That is, the LGWR process of each instance writes to the same online redo log files, and hence Oracle has to keep track of the instance from where the database changes are coming. Single-instance configurations will have only one thread, and that thread number is 1. The redo log file contains both committed and uncommitted transactions. Whenever a transaction is committed, a system change number is assigned to the redo records to identify the committed transaction.

The redo log group is referenced by an integer; you can specify the group number when you create the redo log files—either when you create the database or when you create a redo log group after you create the database. You can also change the redo log configuration (adding, dropping, or renaming files) by using database commands. The following example shows a CREATE DATABASE command:

```
CREATE DATABASE "MYDB01"
... ... ...
LOGFILE '/ora02/oradata/MYDB01/redo01.log' SIZE 100M,
        '/ora03/oradata/MYDB01/redo02.log' SIZE 100M;
```

This example creates two log-file groups; the first file is assigned to group 1, and the second file is assigned to group 2. You can have more files in each group; this practice is known as the *multiplexing* of redo log files, which we'll discuss later in this chapter in the section "Multiplexing Redo Log Files." You can specify any group number—the range will be between 1 and the initialization parameter MAXLOGFILES. Oracle recommends that all redo log groups be the same size. The following is an example of creating the log files by specifying the group number:

```
CREATE DATABASE "MYDB01"
… … …
LOGFILE GROUP 1 '/ora02/oradata/MYDB01/redo01.log' SIZE 100M,
        GROUP 2 '/ora03/oradata/MYDB01/redo02.log' SIZE 100M;
```

V$LOG shows the redo log groups, size, SCN number, and status. V$LOGFILE shows the members in each group. V$LOG_HISTORY shows, as the name suggests, the log history, which includes the sequence number, SCN number, and time associated with each log.

Log Switch Operations

The LGWR process writes to only one redo log-file group at any time. The file that is actively being written to is known as the current log file. The log files that are required for instance recovery are known as the active log files. The other log files are known as inactive. Oracle automatically recovers an instance when starting up the instance by using the online redo log files. Instance recovery can be needed if you do not shut down the database cleanly or if your database server crashes.

The log files are written in a circular fashion. A log switch occurs when Oracle finishes writing to one log group and starts writing to the next log group. A log switch always occurs when the current redo log group is completely full and log writing must continue. You can force a log switch by using the ALTER SYSTEM command. A manual log switch can be necessary when maintenance is performed on the redo log files using the ALTER SYSTEM SWITCH LOGFILE command.

Whenever a log switch occurs, Oracle allocates a sequence number to the new redo log group before writing to it. As stated earlier, this number is known as the *log sequence number*. If there are lots of transactions or changes to the database, the log switches can occur too frequently. Size the redo log files appropriately to avoid frequent log switches. Oracle writes to the alert log file whenever a log switch occurs.

Redo log files are written sequentially on the disk, so the I/O will be fast if there is no other activity on the disk. (The disk head is always properly positioned.) Keep the redo log files on a separate disk for better performance. If you have to store a data file on the same disk as the redo log file, do not put the SYSTEM, UNDOTBS, SYSAUX, or any very active data or index tablespace file on this disk. A commit cannot complete until a transaction's information has been written to the redo logs, so maximizing the throughput of the redo log files is a top priority.

Database checkpoints are closely tied to redo log file switches. You learned about check-points earlier in the chapter in the section "Understanding Checkpoints." A checkpoint is an event that flushes the modified data from the buffer cache to the disk and updates the control file and data files. A checkpoint is initiated when the redo log file is filled and a log switch occurs; when the instance is shut down with NORMAL, TRANSACTIONAL, or IMMEDIATE; when a tablespace status is changed to read-only or put into BACKUP mode; or when other values specified by certain parameters (discussed later in this section) are reached.

You can force a checkpoint if needed, as shown here:

```
ALTER SYSTEM CHECKPOINT;
```

Forcing a checkpoint ensures that all changes to the database buffers are written to the data files on disk.

Another way to force a checkpoint is by forcing a log-file switch:

```
ALTER SYSTEM SWITCH LOGFILE;
```

The size of the redo log affects the checkpoint performance. If the size of the redo log is smaller and the transaction volume is high, a log switch occurs often, and so does the checkpoint. The DBW*n* process writes the dirty buffer blocks whenever a checkpoint occurs. This situation might reduce the time required for instance recovery, but it might also affect the runtime performance. You can adjust checkpoints primarily by using the initialization parameter FAST_START_MTTR_TARGET. It is used to ensure that recovery time at instance startup (if required) will not exceed a certain number of seconds.

You can use the FAST_START_MTTR_TARGET parameter to tune checkpoint frequency; its value determines how long an instance can take to start after an instance crash.

Multiplexing Redo Log Files

You can keep multiple copies of the online redo log file to safeguard against damage to these files. When multiplexing online redo log files, LGWR concurrently writes the same redo log information to multiple identical online redo log files, thereby eliminating a single point of redo log failure. All copies of the redo file are the same size and are known as a *redo group,* which is identified by an integer. Each redo log file in the group is known as a *redo member.* You must have at least two redo log groups for normal database operation.

When multiplexing redo log files, keeping the members of a group on different disks is preferable so that one disk failure will not affect the continuing operation of the database. If LGWR can write to at least one member of the group, database operation proceeds as normal; an entry is written to the alert log file. If all members of the redo log-file group are not avail-able for writing, Oracle hangs, crashes, or shuts down. An instance recovery or media recovery can be needed to bring up the database, and you can lose committed transactions.

You can create multiple copies of the online redo log files when you create the database. For example, the following statement creates two redo log-file groups with two members in each:

```
CREATE DATABASE "MYDB01"
... ... ...
LOGFILE
  GROUP 1 ('/ora02/oradata/MYDB01/redo0101.log',
          '/ora03/oradata/MYDB01/redo0102.log') SIZE 500M,
  GROUP 2 ('/ora02/oradata/MYDB01/redo0201.log',
          '/ora03/oradata/MYDB01/redo0202.log') SIZE 500M;
```

The maximum number of log-file groups is specified in the clause MAXLOGFILES, and the maximum number of members is specified in the clause MAXLOGMEMBERS. You can separate the filenames (members) by using a space or a comma.

In the following sections, you will learn how to create a new redo log group, add a new member to an existing group, rename a member, and drop a member from an existing group. In addition, we'll show you how to drop a group and clear all members of a group in certain circumstances.

Redo Log Troubleshooting

In the case of redo log groups, it's best to be generous with the number of groups and the number of members for each group. After estimating the number of groups that would be appropriate for your installation, add one more. The slight additional work involved in maintaining either additional or larger redo logs is small in relation to the time needed to fix a problem when the number of users and concurrent active transactions increase.

The space needed for additional log-file groups is minimal and is well worth the effort up front to avoid the undesirable situation in which writes to the redo log file are waiting on the completion of writes to the database files or the archived log file destination.

Creating New Groups

You can create and add more redo log groups to the database by using the ALTER DATABASE command. The following statement creates a new log-file group with two members:

```
ALTER DATABASE ADD LOGFILE
  GROUP 3 ('/ora02/oradata/MYDB01/redo0301.log',
          '/ora03/oradata/MYDB01/redo0302.log') SIZE 100M;
```

If you omit the GROUP clause, Oracle assigns the next available number. For example, the following statement also creates a multiplexed group:

```
ALTER DATABASE ADD LOGFILE
    ('/ora02/oradata/MYDB01/redo0301.log',
     '/ora03/oradata/MYDB01/redo0302.log') SIZE 100M;
```

To create a new group without multiplexing, use the following statement:

```
ALTER DATABASE ADD LOGFILE
    '/ora02/oradata/MYDB01/redo0301.log' REUSE;
```

You can add more than one redo log group by using the ALTER DATABASE command—just use a comma to separate the groups.

> If the redo log files you create already exist, use the REUSE option and don't specify the size. The new redo log size will be the same as that of the existing file.

Adding a new redo log group is straightforward using EM Database Express. You can view the current redo log groups and add another redo log group using the Create Group button, on the Redo Log Groups screen (see Chapter 8).

Adding New Members

If you forgot to multiplex the redo log files when creating the database (multiplexing redo log files is the default when you use DBCA) or if you need to add more redo log members, you can do so by using the ALTER DATABASE command. When adding new members, you do not specify the file size, because all group members will have the same size.

If you know the group number, use the following statement to add a member to group 2:

```
ALTER DATABASE ADD LOGFILE MEMBER
'/ora04/oradata/MYDB01/redo0203.log' TO GROUP 2;
```

You can also add group members by specifying the names of other members in the group, instead of specifying the group number. Specify all the existing group members with this syntax:

```
ALTER DATABASE ADD LOGFILE MEMBER
 '/ora04/oradata/MYDB01/redo0203.log' TO
('/ora02/oradata/MYDB01/redo0201.log',
 '/ora03/oradata/MYDB01/redo0202.log');
```

Renaming Log Members

If you want to move the log file member from one disk to another or just want it to have a more meaningful name, you can rename it. Before renaming the online redo log member, the new (target) online redo file should exist. The SQL commands in Oracle change only the internal pointer in the control file to a new log file; they do not change or rename the operating-system file. You must use an operating-system command to rename or move the file. Follow these steps to rename a log member:

1. Shut down the database.

2. Copy/rename the redo log file member to the new location by using an operating-system command.

3. Start up the instance, and mount the database (`STARTUP MOUNT`).

4. Rename the log file member in the control file. Use `ALTER DATABASE RENAME FILE 'old_redo_file_name' TO 'new_redo_file_name';`.

5. Open the database (`ALTER DATABASE OPEN`).

6. Back up the control file.

Another way to achieve the same result is to add a new member to the group and then drop the old member from the group, as discussed in the "Adding New Members" section earlier in this chapter and the "Dropping Redo Log Groups" section, which is next.

Dropping Redo Log Groups

You can drop a redo log group and its members by using the `ALTER DATABASE` command. Remember that you should have at least two redo log groups for the database to function normally. The group that is to be dropped should not be the active group or the current group—that is, you can drop only an inactive log-file group. If the log file to be dropped is not inactive, use the `ALTER SYSTEM SWITCH LOGFILE` command.

To drop log-file group 3, use the following SQL statement:

```
ALTER DATABASE DROP LOGFILE GROUP 3;
```

When an online redo log group is dropped from the database, the operating system files are deleted if you use Oracle Managed Files, otherwise you must delete the files manually. The control files of the associated database are updated to drop the members of the group from the database structure. After dropping an online redo log group, make sure the drop is completed successfully, and then use the appropriate operating-system command to delete the dropped online redo log files.

Dropping Redo Log Members

In much the same way that you drop a redo log group, you can drop only the members of an inactive redo log group. Also, if there are only two groups, the log member to be dropped should not be the last member of a group. Each redo log group can have a different number of members, though this is not advised. For example, say you have three log groups, each with two members. If you drop a log member from group 2 and a failure occurs to the sole member of group 2, the instance will hang, crash, and potentially cause the loss of committed transactions when attempts are made to write to the missing redo log group, as we discussed earlier in this chapter. Even if you drop a member for maintenance reasons, ensure that all redo log groups have the same number of members.

To drop a redo log member, use the DROP LOGFILE MEMBER clause of the ALTER DATABASE command:

```
ALTER DATABASE DROP LOGFILE MEMBER
'/ora04/oradata/MYDB01/redo0203.log';
```

The operating-system file is not removed from the disk; only the control file is updated. Use an operating-system command to delete the redo log file member from disk.

 If a database is running in ARCHIVELOG mode, redo log members cannot be deleted unless the redo log group has been archived.

Clearing Online Redo Log Files

Under certain circumstances, a redo log group member (or all members of a log group) can become corrupted. To solve this problem, you can drop and add the log-file group or group member again. It is much easier, however, to use the ALTER DATABASE CLEAR LOGFILE command. The following example clears the contents of redo log group 3 in the database:

```
ALTER DATABASE CLEAR LOGFILE GROUP 3;
```

Another distinct advantage of this command is that you can clear a log group even if the database has only two log groups and only one member in each group. Additionally, by using the UNARCHIVED keyword, you can clear a log-group member even if it has not been archived. In this case, it is advisable to do a full database backup at the earliest convenience because the unarchived redo log file is no longer usable for database recovery.

You can clear the redo logs by choosing Clear Logfile from the Actions drop-down box in EM Cloud Control. The other options available in the drop-down box are as follows:

- Create Like
- Force Checkpoint
- Generate DDL
- Sizing Advice
- Switch Logfile

Understanding Archived Redo Log (ARCHIVELOG) Files

If you use only online redo log files, your database is protected against instance failure but not media failure. Although saving the redo log files before they are overwritten takes additional disk space and management, the increased recoverability of the database outweighs the additional overhead and maintenance costs.

In the following sections, we will present an overview of how archived redo log files work, how to set the location for saving the archived redo log files, and how to enable archiving in the database.

Archived Redo Log File Architecture

An *archived redo log* file is a copy of a redo log file before it is overwritten by new redo information. Because the online redo log files are reused in a circular fashion, you have no way of bringing a backup of a data file up to the latest committed transaction unless you configure the database in ARCHIVELOG mode.

The process of copying is called archiving. The ARC*n* background processes do this archiving. By archiving the redo log files, you can use them later to recover a database, update a standby database, or use the LogMiner utility to audit the database activities.

When an online redo log file is full and LGWR starts writing to the next redo log file, ARC*n* copies the completed redo log file to the archive destination. It is possible to specify more than one archive destination. The LGWR process waits for the ARC*n* process to complete the copy operation before overwriting any online redo log file. As with LGWR, the failure of one of the ARC*n* backup processes will cause instance failure, but no committed transactions will be lost because the "Commit Complete" message is not returned to the user or calling program until LGWR successfully records the transaction in the online redo log-file group.

When the archiving process is copying the redo log files to another destination, the database is said to be in ARCHIVELOG mode. If archiving is not enabled, the database is said to be in NOARCHIVELOG mode. In production systems, you cannot afford to lose data and should, therefore, run the database in ARCHIVELOG mode so that in the event of a failure, you can recover the database to the time of failure or to a point in time. You can achieve this ability to recover by restoring the database backup and applying the database changes by using the archived log files.

The LOG_MODE column in V$DATABASE shows if the database is in ARCHIVELOG mode. As best practice, all production databases must run in ARCHIVELOG mode for recoverability.

Setting the Archive Destination

You specify the archive destination in the initialization-parameter file. To change the archive destination parameters during normal database operation, you use the ALTER SYSTEM command. The following sections cover some of the parameters associated with archive log destinations and the archiving process. You can find a complete list of initialization parameters in the Oracle documentation "Oracle Database 12*c* Reference" at http://tahiti.oracle.com.

LOG_ARCHIVE_DEST_n

Using this parameter, you can specify, at most, 31 archiving destinations. These locations can be on the local machine or on a remote machine where the standby database is located. Archive destinations 1 to 10 are available for local or remote locations, and archive destinations 11 to 31 are available for remote locations only. The syntax for specifying this parameter in the initialization file is as follows:

```
LOG_ARCHIVE_DEST_n =  "null_string" |
```

```
((SERVICE = tnsnames_name |
  LOCATION = 'directory_name')
 [MANDATORY | OPTIONAL]
 [REOPEN [= integer]])
```

The following example specifies a location for the archive log files on the local machine at /archive/MYDB01. The MANDATORY clause specifies that writing to this location must succeed.

```
LOG_ARCHIVE_DEST_1 = 'LOCATION=/archive/MYDB01 MANDATORY'
```

Here is another example, which applies the archive logs to a standby database on a remote computer:

```
LOG_ARCHIVE_DEST_2 = 'SERVICE=STDBY01 OPTIONAL REOPEN 60';
```

In this example, STDBY01 is the Oracle Net connect string used to connect to the remote database. Because writing is optional, the database activity continues even if ARC*n* could not write the archive log file. It tries the writing operation again because the REOPEN clause is specified. The REOPEN clause specifies when the next attempt to write to this location should be made if the first attempt does not succeed. The default value is 300 seconds.

> The V$ARCHIVE_DEST dictionary view shows all archive destinations configured in the database.

You can also use EM Cloud Control to configure the backup and recovery settings by choosing the Availability menu shown in Figure 15.1.

FIGURE 15.1 The Availability menu of EM Cloud Control

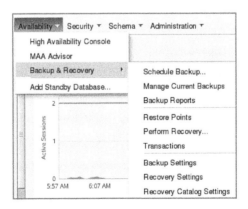

The Recovery Settings screen under the Availability menu has three sections. Figure 15.2 shows the Media Recovery section, which is basically configuring the ARCHIVELOG mode and the destinations. For the database shown in the example, only one archive location is set up.

FIGURE 15.2   The Recovery settings — Media Recovery screen

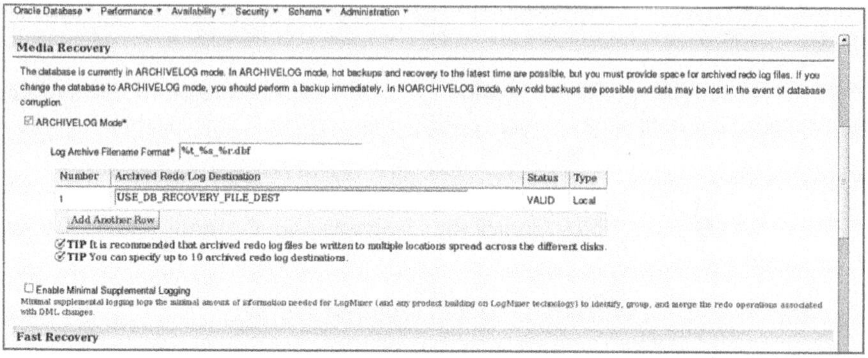

The archive location specified is the Fast Recovery Area using the string USE_DB_RECOVERY_FILE_DEST. If none of the log_archive_dest_n parameters are set, the archive location defaults to USE_DB_RECOVERY_FILE_DEST. The SQL statement to set a specific archive location to use Fast Recovery Area for ARCHIVELOG files is

```
SQL> ALTER SYSTEM SET log_archive_dest_1 = "LOCATION=USE_DB_RECOVERY_FILE_DEST";
```

> **NOTE**   The Fast Recovery Area is discussed in the section "Understanding the Fast Recovery Area," later in this chapter.

LOG_ARCHIVE_MIN_SUCCEED_DEST

This parameter specifies the minimum number of destinations the ARC*n* process should successfully write to continue overwriting the online redo log files. The default value of this parameter is 1. This parameter cannot exceed the total number of enabled destinations. If this parameter value is less than the number of MANDATORY destinations, the parameter is ignored.

LOG_ARCHIVE_FORMAT

This parameter specifies the format in which to write the filename of the archived redo log files. To ensure that the log files are not overwritten, you use predefined substitution variables to construct the name of each archived redo log file. You can provide a text string and any of the predefined substitution variables. The variables are as follows:

- %s: This is the log sequence number.
- %t: This is the thread number.
- %r: This is the reset log's ID, which ensures uniqueness even after using advanced recovery techniques that reset the log sequence numbers.
- %d: This is the database ID.

The format you provide must include at least %s, %t, and %r. If you use the same archived redo log location for multiple databases, you must also use %d. In Figure 15.1, shown previously, the log archive filename format is defined as %t_%s_%r.dbf.

 Data dictionary view V$ARCHIVE_PROCESSES shows the status of each ARC*n* process. The parameter log_archive_max_processes determines the maximum number of ARC*n* processes created.

Setting ARCHIVELOG

Specifying the LOG_ARCHIVE* parameters does not automatically initialize the process of writing the archive log files. To enable archiving of the redo log files, place the database in ARCHIVELOG mode. You can specify the ARCHIVELOG clause while creating the database. However, you might prefer to create the database first and then enable ARCHIVELOG mode. To enable ARCHIVELOG mode, follow these steps:

1. Shut down the database.
2. Set up the appropriate initialization parameters.
3. Start up and mount the database; you can change ARCHIVELOG mode only when the database is in the MOUNT state.
4. Enable ARCHIVELOG mode by using the command ALTER DATABASE ARCHIVELOG.
5. Open the database by using ALTER DATABASE OPEN.
6. Back up the database.

To disable ARCHIVELOG mode, follow these steps:

1. Shut down the database.
2. Start up and mount the database.
3. Disable ARCHIVELOG mode by using the command ALTER DATABASE NOARCHIVELOG.
4. Open the database by using ALTER DATABASE OPEN.

The dynamic performance view V$DATABASE tells you whether or not you are in ARCHIVELOG mode, as you can see in this query:

```
SQL> SELECT dbid, name, created, log_mode FROM v$database;

    DBID NAME      CREATED   LOG_MODE
---------- --------- --------- ------------
 6257179 OCADB1    24-DEC-13 ARCHIVELOG
```

Using EM Cloud Control, you can enable and disable ARCHIVELOG mode by checking the ARCHIVELOG Mode check box (shown in Figure 15.2). Any changes require a database restart, and EM Cloud Control will do the database restart after you confirm the restart. You must be logged into EM Cloud Control with SYSDBA privileges to be able to enable or disable ARCHIVELOG mode.

Resolving Archive-Logging Space Issues

After you configure the database for ARCHIVELOG mode, your job is only half complete. You need to continually make sure there is enough room for the archived log files. Otherwise, the database will hang. At least once in your DBA career, you will get a phone call from someone saying that the database is "hung." You won't discover that the archiving process can't find disk space for a newly filled log file until you check the alert log.

There should be enough space available for online archived redo log files to recover and roll forward from the last full backup of each data file that is also online; the remaining archived logs and any previous data file backups can be moved to another disk or to tape.

Remembering your zero-transaction-loss strategy (which should be every DBA's strategy), make sure you do not misplace or delete an archived log file before it is backed up to tape; otherwise, you will not be able to perform a complete recovery from a media failure.

If you use RMAN and the Fast Recovery Area for all your backup files, you can further automate this process by directing RMAN to maintain enough backups to satisfy a recovery-window policy (number of days) or a redundancy policy (multiple copies of each backup). Once an archived log or other backup file is no longer needed for the policy, the files will be deleted automatically from the Fast Recovery Area.

Understanding the Fast Recovery Area

As the price of disk space drops, the difference in its price compared to the price of tape is offset by the advantages of using a disk as the primary backup medium. Even a slow disk can be accessed randomly faster than a tape drive. This rapid access means that any database-recovery operation takes only minutes instead of hours.

Using disk space as the primary medium for all database-recovery operations is the key component of the Oracle database's *Fast Recovery Area*. The Fast Recovery Area is a single, unified storage area for all recovery-related files and recovery activities in an Oracle database.

The Fast Recovery Area can be a single directory, an entire file system, or an Automatic Storage Management (ASM) disk group. To further optimize the use of disk space for recovery operations, a Fast Recovery Area can be shared by more than one database.

In the following sections, we will cover all the major aspects of a Fast Recovery Area: what can and should be kept in the Fast Recovery Area and how to set up a Fast Recovery using initialization parameters and SQL commands. Also, as with other aspects of Oracle Database 12c, we will show how you can manage most parts of the Fast Recovery Area using EM Cloud Control, and we'll introduce some of the more advanced management techniques.

Fast Recovery Area Occupants

All of the files needed to recover a database from a media failure or a logical error are contained in the Fast Recovery Area. The Fast Recovery Area can contain the following:

Control Files A copy of the control file is created in the Fast Recovery Area when the database is created. This copy of the control file can be used as one of the mirrored copies of the control file to ensure that at least one copy of the control file is available after a media failure.

Archived Log Files When the Fast Recovery Area is configured, archive log location is automatically set to the Fast Recovery Area location. The corresponding ARC*n* processes create archived log files in the Fast Recovery Area or any other defined LOG_ARCHIVE_ DEST_*n* locations.

Flashback Logs If Flashback Database is enabled, its flashback logs are stored in the Fast Recovery Area.

Control File and Spfile Autobackups The Fast Recovery Area holds the control file and spfile autobackups generated by RMAN if RMAN is configured for control file autobackup. When RMAN backs up data file 1, which is part of the SYSTEM tablespace, the control file is automatically included in the RMAN backup.

Data File Copies For RMAN BACKUP AS COPY image files, the Fast Recovery Area is the default destination for the data file copies.

RMAN Backup Sets By default, RMAN uses the Fast Recovery Area for both backup sets and image copies. In addition, RMAN puts restored archived log files from tape into the Fast Recovery Area in preparation for a recovery operation.

The data dictionary view V$RECOVERY_AREA_USAGE gives information on space used by each type of files in the Fast Recovery Area.

```
SQL> SELECT file_type, percent_space_used psu,
    percent_space_reclaimable psr, number_of_files nf
    FROM v$recovery_area_usage;


FILE_TYPE                   PSU         PSR          NF
----------------------  ----------  ----------  ----------
CONTROL FILE                  0           0           0
REDO LOG                      0           0           0
ARCHIVED LOG                  0           0           1
BACKUP PIECE              16.57           0           4
IMAGE COPY                    0           0           0
FLASHBACK LOG              3.42           0           7
FOREIGN ARCHIVED LOG          0           0           0
AUXILIARY DATAFILE COPY       0           0           0
```

Configure Fast Recovery Area Using SQL Commands

You must define two initialization parameters to set up the Fast Recovery Area: DB_ RECOVERY_FILE_DEST_SIZE and DB_RECOVERY_FILE_DEST. Because both of these are dynamic parameters, the instance doesn't need to be shut down and restarted for the Fast Recovery Area to be usable.

DB_RECOVERY_FILE_DEST_SIZE, which must be defined before DB_RECOVERY_FILE_DEST, defines the size of the Fast Recovery Area. To maximize the benefits of the Fast Recovery Area, it should be large enough to hold a copy of all data files, incremental backups, online redo logs, archived redo logs not yet backed up to tape, control files, and control file auto-backups. At a bare minimum, you need enough space to hold the archived log files not yet copied to tape.

Here is an example of configuring DB_RECOVERY_FILE_DEST_SIZE:

```
SQL> ALTER SYSTEM SET
     db_recovery_file_dest_size = 80g SCOPE=both;
```

The size of the Fast Recovery Area will be 80GB, and because this example uses the SCOPE=BOTH parameter in the ALTER SYSTEM command, the initialization parameter takes effect immediately and stays in effect even after a database restart.

The parameter DB_RECOVERY_FILE_DEST specifies the physical location where all Fast Recovery files are stored. The ASM disk group or file system must have at least as much space as the amount specified with DB_RECOVERY_FILE_DEST_SIZE, and it can have significantly more. DB_RECOVERY_FILE_DEST_SIZE, however, can be increased on the fly if more space is needed and the file system where the Fast Recovery Area resides has the space available.

The following example uses the directory /OraFlash for the Fast Recovery Area, like so:

```
SQL> ALTER SYSTEM SET
     db_recovery_file_dest = '/OraFlash' SCOPE=both;
```

Clearing the value of DB_RECOVERY_FILE_DEST disables the Fast Recovery Area; the parameter DB_RECOVERY_FILE_DEST_SIZE cannot be cleared until the DB_RECOVERY_FILE_ DEST parameter has been cleared.

 Even after files in the Fast Recovery Area are obsolete (based on retention time), they are not deleted until space is needed for new files.

Configure Fast Recovery Area Using EM Cloud Control

Using the Recovery Settings screen, you can create and maintain the Fast Recovery Area with EM Cloud Control. Figure 15.3 shows the Fast Recovery section.

In the Fast Recovery section, the Fast Recovery Area has been configured for a database in the file system /u01/app/oracle/flash_recovery_area, with a maximum size of 10GB. Just under 2GB of space is currently used in the Fast Recovery Area. Flashback logging is also enabled for this database.

FIGURE 15.3 The Fast Recovery section of the Recovery Settings screen

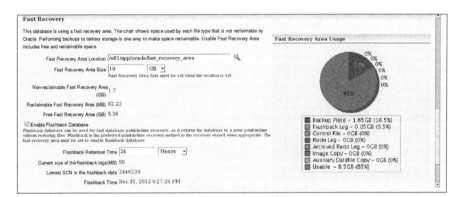

You can enable flashback logging by selecting the Enable Flashback Database box. Oracle's flashback features complement the media-recovery options in the database. Using the FLASHBACK DATABASE command in RMAN, you can revert the data file contents to a state at a prior time. This operation is much faster than recovering from a full database backup and applying the archive logs to recover the database to a point in time. The flashback logs contain the past versions of the data blocks.

You can enable Flashback Database using SQL*Plus. The steps are as follows:

1. Make sure the database is in ARCHIVELOG mode and the Fast Recovery Area is configured using the DB_RECOVERY_FILE_DEST and DB_RECOVERY_FILE_DEST_SIZE parameters.

2. Optional: Specify the length of desired flashback window using the DB_FLASHBACK_ RETENTION_TARGET parameter. The default is 1,440 minutes.

3. Enable the Flashback Database feature using the ALTER DATABASE FLASHBACK ON statement.

The background process RVWR writes flashback data to Flashback Database logs in the Fast Recovery Area.

Managing the Fast Recovery Area

Because the space in the Fast Recovery Area is limited by the initialization parameter DB_RECOVERY_FILE_DEST_SIZE, the Oracle database keeps track of which files are no longer needed on disk so that they can be deleted when there is not enough free space for new files. Each time a file is deleted from the Fast Recovery Area, a message is written to the alert log.

A message is also written to the alert log in other circumstances. If no files can be deleted and the recovery area's used space is at 85 percent, a warning message is issued. When the space used is at 97 percent, a critical warning is issued. These warnings are recorded in the alert log file, can be viewed in the data dictionary view DBA_OUTSTANDING_ ALERTS, and are available on the main screen of Enterprise Manager.

When you receive these alerts, you have a number of options. If your retention policy can be adjusted to keep fewer copies of data files or reduce the number of days in the recovery window, this can help alleviate the space problems in the Fast Recovery Area. Assuming your retention policy is sound, you should instead add more disk space or back up some of the files in the Fast Recovery Area to another destination, such as another disk or a tape device.

If the Fast Recovery Area is full, Oracle Database 12c will write ORA-19809 and ORA-19804 errors to the alert log file. The Fast Recovery Area is automatically cleared based on the retention specified. To manually clear the Fast Recovery Area, you must perform BACKUP RECOVERY AREA to back up the Fast Recovery Area files and to delete the files. The options to reduce the Fast Recovery Area size are

1. Make a backup of the Fast Recovery Area using RMAN.

2. Change the RMAN retention policy.

3. Adopt a more aggressive RMAN archived-log deletion policy.

4. Delete files from the Fast Recovery Area using RMAN.

If none of the above action clears enough space in the Fast Recovery Area, you should increase the DB_RECOVERY_FILE_DEST_SIZE.

The archive log location is implicitly set to point to the Fast Recovery Area if no archive log locations have been set and the database is in ARCHIVELOG mode with a Fast Recovery Area defined.

Performing Backups

Your backup strategy depends on the activity of your database, the level of availability required by your service-level agreements (SLAs), and how much downtime you can tolerate during a recovery effort.

In this section, we'll first review some terminology and then we'll show you a way to back up the control file to a text file that you can edit and use in case all the control files are lost. We will then discuss how to back up the database using OS utilities. Finally, we will introduce Recovery Manager and show you how to make some of the backups described in the terminology review.

Understanding Backup Terminology

You can make a *whole* backup, which backs up the entire database, or you can back up only part of the database, which is called a *partial* backup. Whole backups and partial backups are known as Oracle *backup strategies*. The backup type can be divided into two general categories: *full* backups and *incremental* backups. Depending on whether you make your database backups when the database is open or closed, backups can be further categorized into the backup modes known as *consistent* backup and *inconsistent* backup.

Your backups can be managed using operating-system and SQL commands or entirely by RMAN. Many backup types are available using only RMAN, such as incremental backups; unless you have some specific requirements, we highly recommended that you use RMAN to implement your backup strategy.

The following definitions are for whole database backups, partial database backups, full backups, incremental backups, consistent backups, and inconsistent backups:

Whole Database   A whole database backup includes all data files, at least one control file, archived log files, and a server parameter file. Online redo log files are never backed up; restoring backed-up redo log files and replacing the current redo log files will result in loss of data during media recovery. Only one of the control files needs to be backed up; all copies of the control file are identical.

Partial Database   A partial database backup includes zero or more tablespaces, which in turn includes zero or more data files; a control file is optional in a partial database backup.

Full   A full backup includes all blocks of every data file backed up in a whole or partial database backup.

Incremental   An incremental backup makes a copy of all data blocks that have changed since a previous backup. Although Oracle Database 12*c* supports five levels of incremental backups from 0 to 4, 0 and 1 are the most commonly used. An incremental backup at level 0 is considered a baseline backup; it is the equivalent of a full backup and contains all data blocks in the data file(s) that are backed up. Although incremental backups can take less time, the potential downside is that you must first restore the baseline backup and then apply incremental backups performed since the baseline backup.

Consistent   A consistent backup, also known as an *offline backup*, is performed while the database is not open. These backups are consistent because the SCN in the control file matches the SCN in every data file's header. Although recovering using a consistent backup requires no additional recovery operation after a failure, you reduce your database's availability during a consistent backup, as well as risk the loss of committed transactions performed since the consistent backup.

Inconsistent   Although the term *inconsistent backup* may sound like something you might avoid in a database, it is a way to maintain the availability of the database while performing backups. An inconsistent backup, also known as an *online backup*, is performed while the database is open and available to users. The backup is inconsistent because the SCN in the control file is most likely out of sync with the SCN in the header of the data files. Inconsistent backups require recovery when they are used for recovering from a media failure, but they keep availability high because the database is open while the backup is performed.

Backups can be performed using two methods: user-managed backup or Oracle's backup and recovery tool called Recovery Manager. RMAN backups are easier to create, and the recovery operations are pretty much automated. We discuss RMAN backups in the section "Using RMAN to Perform Backups."

In the next sections, you will learn to back up the control file, back up the database, and use Recovery Manager.

Backing Up the Control File

In addition to multiplexing the control file, you can guard against the loss of all control files by backing up the control file. You can back up the control file using three methods:

- An editable text file; this backup is called a *backup to trace*.
- A binary backup of the control file.
- An RMAN backup of the control file.

Performing a Text Backup of Control File

The text backup is created using the ALTER DATABASE BACKUP CONTROLFILE TO TRACE statement, and the file is created in the trace directory under <ADR_HOME>/trace. The trace file format is *sid_ora_pid*.trc, where *sid* is the ORACLE_SID and *pid* is the process ID of the user creating the trace backup. This special backup of the control file is not a trace file per se; in other words, it is not a dump file or an error report for a failed user or system process. It is a proactive rather than reactive report of the contents of the control file, and the report happens to end up in a directory with other trace files.

Back up the control file to trace after any change to the structure of the database, such as adding or dropping a tablespace or creating a new redo log-file group. Using the command line to create a backup of the control file is almost as easy as clicking the Backup to Trace button in EM Database Express. (See Chapter 8. A similar option is available in EM Cloud Control as well in the Administration menu ➢ Storage ➢ Control Files.)

```
SQL> alter database backup controlfile to trace;
Database altered.
```

If you want to name the control file backup rather than using an Oracle-generated trace filename, you can do this:

```
SQL> alter database backup controlfile to trace as '/tmp/mydbcontrol.txt';
Database altered.
```

The control file create statements are created in the file */tmp/mydbcontrol.txt*. To save space, output of control file backup as text file is not shown. After you generate the backup file, remember to review the content of the trace file and understand each section.

Performing a Binary Backup of Control File

Another way to back up your control file is to make a binary copy of it using the ALTER DATABASE command, as in the following example:

```
SQL> alter database backup controlfile to
             '/ora_backup/11GR11/ctlfile20040911.bkp';
Database altered.
```

You can then copy the binary backup of the control file to a backup device.

Using RMAN to Back Up a Control File

Using RMAN, you can back up the control file using the BACKUP CURRENT CONTROLFILE statement, as shown here. This backup is also a binary backup.

```
RMAN> BACKUP CURRENT CONTROLFILE;

Starting backup at 31-DEC-13
using target database control file instead of recovery catalog
allocated channel: ORA_DISK_1
channel ORA_DISK_1: SID=35 device type=DISK
channel ORA_DISK_1: starting full datafile backup set
channel ORA_DISK_1: specifying datafile(s) in backup set
including current control file in backup set
channel ORA_DISK_1: starting piece 1 at 31-DEC-13
channel ORA_DISK_1: finished piece 1 at 31-DEC-13
piece handle=/u01/app/oracle/fast_recovery_area/OCADB1/backupset/2013_12_31/o1_
mf_ncnnf_TAG20131231T224419_9d7gb4nb_.bkp tag=TAG20131231T224419 comment=NONE
channel ORA_DISK_1: backup set complete, elapsed time: 00:00:03
Finished backup at 31-DEC-13

RMAN>
```

 To perform backup and recovery tasks with RMAN, you must connect to the database as a user with the SYSDBA or SYSBACKUP privilege. The SYSBACKUP privilege is new in Oracle Database 12c and encompasses all the privileges required to back up and recover the database. SYSBACKUP privileges are a subset of the privileges included in the SYSDBA administrative privilege.

Backing Up the Database

An Oracle Database 12c database can be backed up using different modes, depending on the ARCHIVELOG setting of the database. If the database is in ARCHIVELOG mode, you can perform an online database backup (also known as an *inconsistent* or *hot* backup) or an offline database backup (also known as a *consistent* or *cold* backup). If the database is in NOARCHIVELOG mode, you can perform only an offline backup.

You can use OS utilities to perform the database backup or use RMAN. Using RMAN is the preferred and easier method of backup. In the following sections, you will learn how to back up the database using OS utilities (user-managed backups). RMAN backups are discussed in the subsequent section.

Performing User-Managed Cold Backups

Cold backups are performed after shutting down the database. Shut down the database cleanly using the SHUTDOWN IMMEDIATE or SHUTDOWN TRANSACTIONAL statement, and copy all control files and data files to another location or to your tape management system using OS commands. You can also copy the redo logs, but this is not necessary if the database shutdown is clean. You also need to back up the parameter file (init file or spfile) and password file.

You can identify the control files in the database using the dynamic performance view V$CONTROLFILE. The data files that need to be backed up can be identified by using the view V$DATAFILE.

Performing User-Managed Hot Backups

To perform a hot backup, the database must be in ARCHIVELOG mode. Before starting to copy the data files belonging to a tablespace, you must place the tablespace in backup mode using the BEGIN BACKUP clause. For example, if you want to back up the USERS tablespace, perform the following:

```
SQL> ALTER TABLESPACE users BEGIN BACKUP;
```

When a tablespace is placed in backup mode, data-block changes are written to the redo log files. After you take the tablespace out of backup mode, the database advances the data file checkpoint SCN to the current database checkpoint SCN.

When a tablespace is in backup mode, use OS utilities to copy the data files belonging to the tablespace to another location or to the tape management system. To take the tablespace out of backup mode, use the END BACKUP clause as in the following example:

```
SQL> ALTER TABLESPACE users END BACKUP;
```

If your database is small or if you plan to place all the tablespaces in backup mode for the hot backup, instead of placing each tablespace in backup mode, you can use the ALTER DATABASE statement to put the whole database in backup mode, as in the following example:

```
SQL> ALTER DATABASE BEGIN BACKUP;
```

> You cannot perform incremental backups using user-managed backups. You must use RMAN for incremental backups.

Using RMAN to Perform Backups

RMAN is the primary component of the Oracle database used to perform backup and recovery operations. You can use RMAN to back up all types: whole or partial databases, full or incremental, and consistent or inconsistent. RMAN is closely integrated with EM Cloud Control.

RMAN has a command-line interface for advanced configuration and backup operations; the most common backup functions are available within EM Cloud Control. It includes a scripting language to make it easy to automate backups, and it can back up the most critical types of files in your database except for online redo log files (which you should not back up anyway), password file, and text-based init.ora file. Data files, control files, archived log files, and spfiles can be backed up using RMAN. In other words, RMAN is a "one-stop shopping" solution for all your backup and recovery needs.

Because of the relatively static nature of password files and text-based init.ora files, they can be included in the regular operating-system backups, or you can back them up manually whenever they are changed.

In the following sections, we will explain the difference between image copies and backup sets and how RMAN handles each of these backup types. After explaining some of the RMAN configuration settings, we will show you some examples of how RMAN performs full and incremental backups, using both the command line and the graphical user interface.

Configuring RMAN Backup Settings

Configuring RMAN backup settings is straightforward using EM Cloud Control. On the Availability menu, click Backup Settings to open the Device tab screen, as shown in Figure 15.4.

FIGURE 15.4   The Backup Settings: Device screen

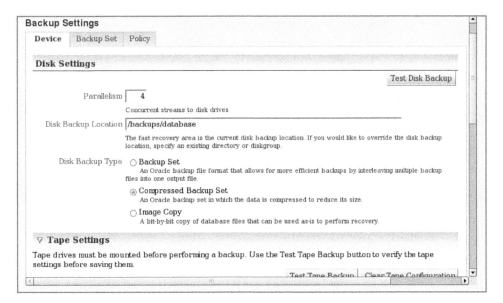

There is a separate section in this screen for your disk device, tape device, and Oracle Secure Backup. Under the Disk Settings section, you can control the following parameters:

Parallelism   To take advantage of multiple CPUs or disk controllers, increase the value of this parameter to reduce the overall backup time by performing different portions of the backup in parallel.

Disk Backup Location   If you are not backing up to the Fast Recovery Area, change this value to the location where you want the backups stored.

Disk Backup Type   You can choose Image Copy, Backup Set, or Compressed Backup Set.

Under the Tape settings, you can specify whether you want the backups to be written directly to the tape or media management tool. You also have the option to configure the Oracle Secure Backup (OSB) tool on this screen. OSB is a separately licensed product from Oracle to manage the backups and tape libraries. Using OSB, you can back up any type of OS files anywhere on the network.

Click the Backup Set tab, and specify the maximum size for a backup-set piece (a single backup file), as shown in Figure 15.5. In this case, set the maximum backup-set piece size to 4GB.

FIGURE 15.5   The Backup Settings: Backup Set screen

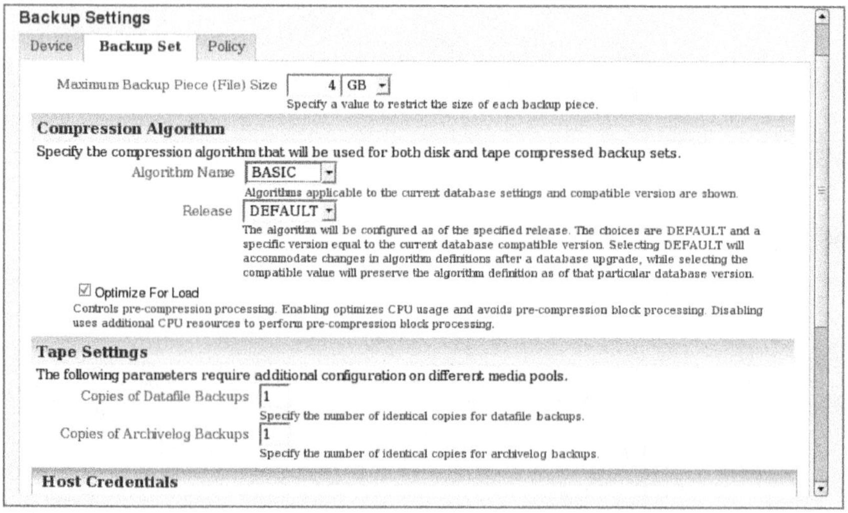

The default compression algorithm used for compressed backups is BASIC. If the database is configured with Advanced Compression Option, additional compression options are available.

You use the last tab on the Backup Settings screen, the Policy tab, to set a number of other default backup settings, such as automatically backing up the control file with each backup, skipping read-only and offline data files, and using a block-change tracking file. A block-change tracking file keeps track of changed blocks in each tablespace so that incremental backups need not read every block in every data file to determine which blocks need to be backed up during an incremental backup. Figure 15.6 shows an example of the Policy tab with a block-change tracking file specified.

FIGURE 15.6   The Backup Settings: Policy screen 1

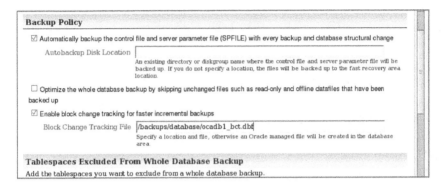

Always enable the automatic backup of control files and spfiles. This is an Oracle-recommended best practice.

The Policy tab also specifies the retention policy for backups and the deletion policy for archive logs. See Figure 15.7.

FIGURE 15.7   The Backup Settings: Policy screen 2

Infrequently used parameters, such as the control file autobackup filename format and the snapshot control file destination filename, are not available from the graphical user interface; you must use the RMAN command-line interface to change these values.

You can invoke the RMAN command line by using the executable rman. RMAN can optionally use a catalog database where the backup information is kept. RMAN always uses the database control file to record backup and recovery operations. The drawback to depending on the control file for backup information is that it can only hold values for the days specified by the CONTROL_FILE_RECORD_KEEP_TIME value.

The following RMAN command-line session uses the RMAN SHOW ALL command to display the RMAN backup settings:

```
$ rman target / nocatalog

Recovery Manager: Release 12.1.0.1.0 - Production on Tue Dec 31 23:35:28 2013
Copyright (c) 1982, 2013, Oracle and/or its affiliates.  All rights reserved.

connected to target database: OCADB1 (DBID=6257179)
using target database control file instead of recovery catalog

RMAN> show all;

RMAN configuration parameters for database with db_unique_name OCADB1 are:
CONFIGURE RETENTION POLICY TO REDUNDANCY 1; # default
CONFIGURE BACKUP OPTIMIZATION OFF; # default
CONFIGURE DEFAULT DEVICE TYPE TO DISK; # default
CONFIGURE CONTROLFILE AUTOBACKUP ON;
CONFIGURE CONTROLFILE AUTOBACKUP FORMAT FOR DEVICE TYPE DISK TO '%F'; # default
CONFIGURE DEVICE TYPE DISK BACKUP TYPE TO COMPRESSED BACKUPSET PARALLELISM 4;
CONFIGURE DEVICE TYPE DISK PARALLELISM 1 BACKUP TYPE TO BACKUPSET; # default
CONFIGURE DATAFILE BACKUP COPIES FOR DEVICE TYPE DISK TO 1; # default
CONFIGURE ARCHIVELOG BACKUP COPIES FOR DEVICE TYPE DISK TO 1; # default
CONFIGURE CHANNEL DEVICE TYPE DISK FORMAT   '/backups/database/%d_%U'
MAXPIECESIZE 4 G;
CONFIGURE MAXSETSIZE TO UNLIMITED; # default
CONFIGURE ENCRYPTION FOR DATABASE OFF; # default
CONFIGURE ENCRYPTION ALGORITHM 'AES128'; # default
CONFIGURE COMPRESSION ALGORITHM 'BASIC' AS OF RELEASE '12.1.0.0.0' OPTIMIZE FOR
LOAD TRUE;
CONFIGURE RMAN OUTPUT TO KEEP FOR 7 DAYS; # default
CONFIGURE ARCHIVELOG DELETION POLICY TO BACKED UP 1 TIMES TO 'SBT_TAPE';
CONFIGURE SNAPSHOT CONTROLFILE NAME TO '/u02/app/oracle/product/12.1.0/dbhome_1/
dbs/snapcf_ocadb1.f'; # default

RMAN>
```

You can enable block-change tracking (BCT) in the database by using the SQL statement `ALTER DATABASE ENABLE BLOCK CHANGE TRACKING`. Block change tracking helps to identify the block changes since the last backup so you do not have to scan the whole data file for incremental backups. The `V$BLOCK_CHANGE_TRACKING` view indicates if BCT is enabled and displays the change tracking filename.

Understanding Image Copies and Backup Sets

Image copies are duplicates of data files or archived redo log files, which means that every block of every file is backed up; you can use RMAN or operating-system commands to make image copies. In contrast, backup sets are copies of one or more data files or archived redo log files that are stored in a proprietary format readable only by RMAN; backup sets consist of one or more physical files and do not include never-used blocks in the data files being backed up. Backup sets can save even more space by using a compression algorithm designed specifically for the type of data found in an Oracle data file.

Another difference between image copies and backup sets is that image copies can be copied only to a disk location; backup sets can be written to disk or directly to a tape or other secondary storage device.

Creating Full and Incremental Backups

The Oracle-recommended backup strategy uses RMAN to make a one-time, whole-database, baseline incremental level 0 online backup and then a daily level 1 incremental backup. You can easily fine-tune this strategy for your own needs by making, for example, a level 2 incremental backup at noon during the weekdays if heavy Data Manipulation Language (DML) activity is occurring in the database.

Using RMAN, you can accomplish this backup strategy with just a couple of the RMAN commands that follow. First, here is the code for a baseline level 0 backup at the RMAN command prompt:

```
RMAN> backup incremental level 0
        as compressed backupset database;
```

This backs up the entire database using compression to save disk space in addition to the space savings already gained by using backup sets instead of image copies.

Starting with a baseline level 0 incremental backup, you can make level 1 incremental backups during the rest of the week, as in the following example:

```
RMAN> backup incremental level 1
        as compressed backupset database;
```

The options are the same as in the previous example, except that only the blocks that have changed since the last backup are copied to the backup set.

Another variation is to make an incrementally updated backup. An incrementally updated backup uses an incremental backup and updates the changed blocks in an existing image copy as if the entire image copy were backed up. In a recovery scenario, you can restore the image copy of the data file(s) without using an incremental backup; the incremental backup is already applied, saving a significant amount of time during a recovery operation. The following RMAN script shows how an incrementally updated backup works at the command line:

```
run
{
    recover copy of database with tag 'inc_upd_img';
    backup incremental level 1 for
        recover of copy with tag 'inc_upd_img' database;
}
```

This short and cryptic script demonstrates the advantages of using EM Cloud Control to perform incrementally updated backups (or you can use EM to generate the scripts and schedule using another job scheduler). A backup tag is a text string that identifies a backup, either uniquely or as part of a group of backups. All RMAN backups, including incremental backups, are labeled with a tag. In the code shown earlier, 'inc_upd_img' is the backup tag. If no explicit backup tag is specified, RMAN will assign a system-generated name as the backup tag. The Schedule Backup screen of EM Cloud Control is shown in Figure 15.8.

FIGURE 15.8   The Schedule Backup main screen

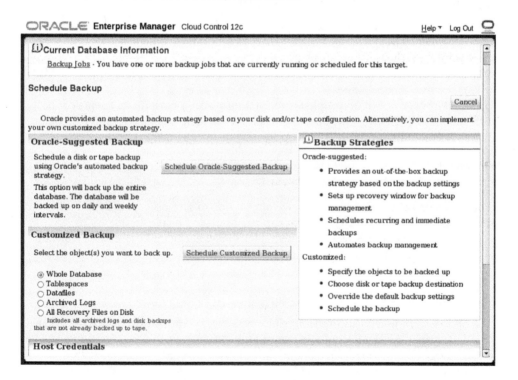

You have the option to schedule a backup based on the Oracle-suggested backup policy or using custom settings. If you want to enable an Oracle-suggested policy for backups, click the Schedule Oracle-Suggested Backup button. To customize the backups according to your company policy, click the Schedule a Customized Backup button.

An Oracle-suggested backup policy does the following:

- It creates a level 0 image backup (all blocks in all data files) on day 1 of the backup.

- It creates an incremental level 1 image backup (changed blocks in data files only) from day 2 onward.

- On day 3 and subsequent days, the incremental backup from day 1 is applied to the previous backup to make the data files roll forward. On the beginning of day m, the level 0 backup is updated with day m-1 incremental backup.

- If a recovery is required on day 2, the full backup plus archive logs generated on day 2 are used.

- If a recovery is required on day m, the incrementally updated backup as of day m-1 is used, plus any archive logs for day m.

Using EM Cloud Control to schedule the suggested backup is easy, and it generates the following script with the description: "*A full database copy will be performed during the first backup. Subsequently, an incremental backup to disk will be performed every day. The backups on disk will be retained so that you can always perform a full database recovery or a point-in-time recovery to any time within the past day.*"

```
Daily Script:
run {
allocate channel oem_disk_backup device type disk;
recover copy of database with tag 'ORA$OEM_LEVEL_0';
backup incremental level 1 copies=1 for recover of copy with tag 'ORA$OEM_
LEVEL_0' database;
}
```

The Schedule Customized Backup screen has the options to choose the whole database, tablespace, data file, archive log, and recover area files shown in Figure 15.8. Figure 15.9 shows screen 1 of 4 used in scheduling a customized backup. The first screen is used to specify the backup options.

On this screen, you can specify the backup type (full backup or incremental), backup mode (online or offline), and whether to back up archive logs and to delete archive logs after backup. Click the Next button to advance to the next screen, where you specify the backup settings. Specify whether you want to back up to disk or tape (see Figure 15.10). If you click the View Default Settings button, you will be taken to the screen shown in Figure 15.4.

You have the option to override the default settings, specific for this backup using the Override Default Settings button. If you do not want to change the default settings but do not want to use the default location for backups, you can click the Override Default Settings button. The Schedule screen gives you the option to perform the backup one time immediately, one time at a later time, or on a repeating basis. If you choose Repeating, you will be provided with the options to specify the backup repeating schedules, as shown in Figure 15.11. Automated backups are configured using the repeating schedule option.

FIGURE 15.9   The Schedule Customized Backup: Options screen

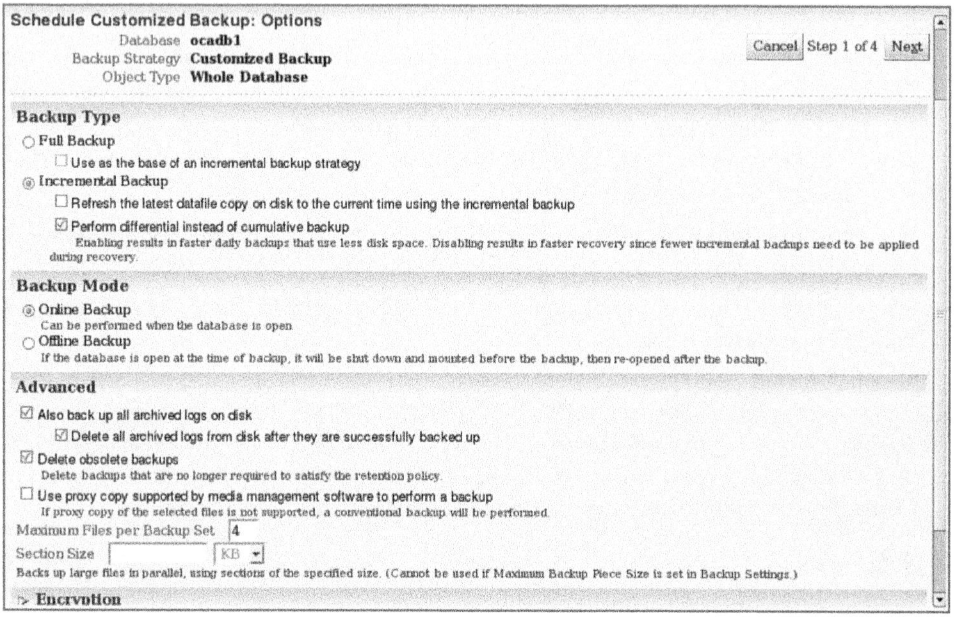

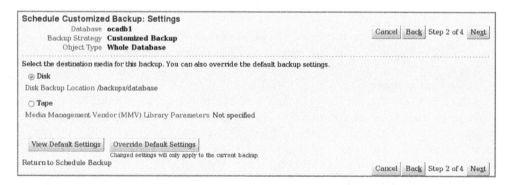

FIGURE 15.10   The Schedule Customized Backup: Settings screen

On the Review screen, you will be provided a summary of all the options you chose in the previous screens and the RMAN script that will be used to back up the database, as shown in Figure 15.12. You will also have the option to edit the RMAN script before scheduling the job.

After reviewing the backup settings, click the Submit Job button to schedule the backup. The backup script generated by the screens is shown here:

```
backup incremental level 1 device type disk tag '%TAG' database;
backup device type disk tag '%TAG' archivelog all not backed up delete all
input;
allocate channel for maintenance type disk;
delete noprompt obsolete device type disk;
release channel;
```

In the next section, you will learn about managing RMAN backups.

 In addition to the RMAN-specific commands, most SQL statements and the SQL*Plus DESCRIBE command are supported in RMAN. You can also use the STARTUP and SHUTDOWN commands.

FIGURE 15.11   The Schedule Customized Backup: Schedule screen

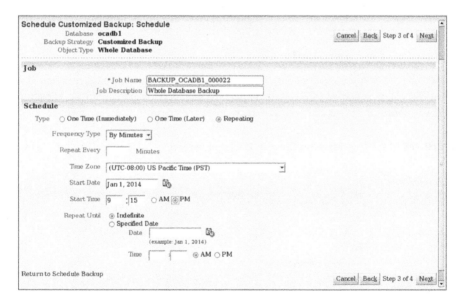

Managing Backups

Managing your database backups using EM Cloud Control is straightforward. In the following sections, you will get an overview of the RMAN backup- and catalog-maintenance commands, and you will learn how to monitor the Fast Recovery Area and automate backups using the Scheduler. Along with the OEM screens, we will also provide the RMAN commands so that you will know how to perform these actions from RMAN command prompt as well.

FIGURE 15.12   The Schedule Customized Backup: Review screen

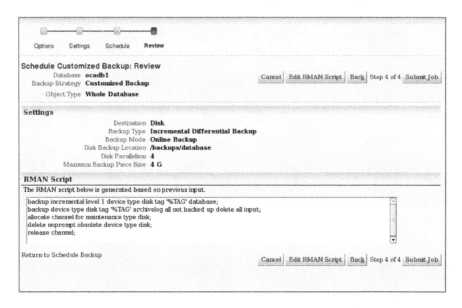

Maintaining Current Backups

A number of backup-management functions are available on the Manage Current Backups screen in EM Cloud Control (see Figure 15.13). To get there, from the screen shown in Figure 15.1, choose Manage Current Backups.

FIGURE 15.13   The Manage Current Backups screen

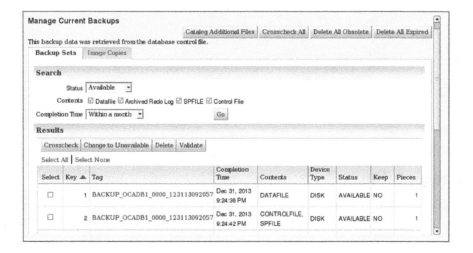

This screen shows you the current backups based on the search criteria entered. The four buttons at the top perform the following functions:

Catalog Additional Files   This button adds any image-copy backups made outside RMAN to the RMAN catalog. You can specify a file or a directory. The command used to catalog files is CATALOG START WITH 'file or directory'.

Crosscheck All   This button double-checks the backup files listed in the catalog (or control file) against the actual files on disk (or tape) to make sure they are all available. The commands used are CROSSCHECK BACKUPSET; CROSSCHECK COPY.

Delete All Obsolete   This button deletes all backup files not needed to satisfy the existing retention policy. The command used is DELETE NOPROMPT OBSOLETE.

Delete All Expired   This button deletes the catalog entry for any backups not found when a crosscheck was performed. The commands used are DELETE NOPROMPT EXPIRED BACKUP; DELETE NOPROMPT EXPIRED COPY.

After selecting a backup under the Results section, you can perform additional actions in this screen. The four options perform the following functions:

Crosscheck   Use this to crosscheck a backup set. The command used is CROSSCHECK BACKUPSET *n*;

Change to Unavailable   Use this to make the backup set unavailable. The command used is CHANGE BACKUPSET *n* UNAVAILABLE.

Delete   Use this to delete a backup set. The command used is DELETE NOPROMPT BACKUPSET *n*,

Validate   Use this to validate a backup set. The command used is VALIDATE BACKUPSET *n*,

Viewing Backup Reports

In EM Cloud Control under the Availability menu, as shown earlier in Figure 15.1, click the Backup Reports menu to show the View Backup Report screen. Click the name of the backup in the Backup Name column to display a detailed status report of the backup, including what is being backed up (data files, control files, spfiles), the size of the backup, the backup start and end times, and the backup pieces.

You can use the LIST command from RMAN command line to see the reports. The following example shows an example of LIST BACKUP output.

```
RMAN> list backup;

List of Backup Sets
===================

BS Key  Type LV Size       Device Type Elapsed Time Completion Time
------- ---- -- ---------- ----------- ------------ ---------------
1       Incr 0  1.57G      DISK        00:03:31     31-DEC-13
```

```
        BP Key: 1   Status: AVAILABLE  Compressed: NO  Tag: BACKUP_
OCADB1_0000_123113092057
        Piece Name: /u01/app/oracle/fast_recovery_area/OCADB1/
backupset/2013_12_31/o1_mf_nnnd0_BACKUP_OCADB1_0000_1_9d79g1b6_.bkp
  List of Datafiles in backup set 1
  File LV Type Ckp SCN    Ckp Time   Name
  ---- -- ---- ---------- --------- ----

   1   0   Incr 2445763    31-DEC-13 /u01/app/oracle/oradata/ocadb1/system01.dbf
   2   0   Incr 2445763    31-DEC-13 /u01/app/oracle/oradata/ocadb1/example01.dbf
   3   0   Incr 2445763    31-DEC-13 /u01/app/oracle/oradata/ocadb1/sysaux01.dbf
   4   0   Incr 2445763    31-DEC-13 /u01/app/oracle/oradata/ocadb1/undotbs01.dbf
   6   0   Incr 2445763    31-DEC-13 /u01/app/oracle/oradata/ocadb1/users01.dbf


BS Key  Type LV Size       Device Type Elapsed Time Completion Time
------- ---- -- ---------- ----------- ------------ ---------------
2       Incr 0  9.64M       DISK        00:00:01     31-DEC-13
        BP Key: 2   Status: AVAILABLE  Compressed: NO  Tag: BACKUP_
OCADB1_0000_123113092057
        Piece Name: /u01/app/oracle/fast_recovery_area/OCADB1/
backupset/2013_12_31/o1_mf_ncsn0_BACKUP_OCADB1_0000_1_9d79nt31_.bkp
  SPFILE Included: Modification time: 31-DEC-13
  SPFILE db_unique_name: OCADB1
  Control File Included: Ckp SCN: 2446054       Ckp time: 31-DEC-13
```

So far you have learned how backups work and how to perform backups. In the next sections, you will see how the backups can be used for recovery purposes and what other measures you can take to prevent failures in the database.

Understanding Types of Database Failures

Database-related failures fall into six general categories. Understanding which category a failure belongs in will help you more quickly understand the nature of the recovery effort you need to use to reverse the effects of the failure and maintain a high level of availability and performance in your database. The six general categories of failures are as follows:

Statement   A single database operation fails, such as a Data Manipulation Language (DML) statement—INSERT, UPDATE, and so on.

User Process   A single database connection fails.

Network   A network component between the client and the database server fails, and the session is disconnected from the database.

User Error   An error message is not generated, but the operation's result, such as dropping a table, is not what the user intended.

Instance   The database instance crashes unexpectedly.

Media   One or more of the database files is lost, deleted, or corrupted.

In the next six sections, we'll provide details on these failure types and suggest some possible solutions for each one. For one particular type of failure, media failure, we'll provide more detailed solutions for recovery later in this chapter.

Statement Failures

Statement failures occur when a single database operation fails, such as a single INSERT statement or the creation of a table. Table 15.1 shows the most common problems that occur when a statement fails, along with their solutions.

TABLE 15.1   Common Problems and Solutions for Statement Failures

Problem	Solution
Attempts to access tables without the appropriate privileges	Provide the appropriate privileges, or create views on the tables and grant privileges on the view.
Running out of space	Add space to the tablespace, increase the user's quota on the tablespace, or enable resumable-space allocation.
Entering invalid data	If constraints and triggers are not in place to enforce data integrity, entering bad data may succeed and cause application issues. DBAs need to work with users to validate and correct data.
Logic errors in applications	Work with developers to correct program errors or provide additional logic in the application to recover gracefully from unavoidable errors.

Although granting user privileges or additional quotas within a tablespace solves many of these problems, also consider whether there are any gaps in the user education process that might lead to some of these problems in the first place.

User-Process Failures

The abnormal termination of a user session is categorized as a *user-process failure*. After a user-process failure, any uncommitted transaction must be cleaned up. The PMON (process monitor) background process periodically checks all user processes to ensure that the session is still connected. If the PMON finds a disconnected session, it rolls back the uncommitted transaction and releases all locks held by the disconnected process. The causes of user-process failures typically fall into one of these categories:

- A user closes their SQL*Plus window without logging out.
- The workstation reboots suddenly before the application can be closed.
- The application program causes an exception and closes before the application can be terminated normally.

A small percentage of user-process failures are generally no cause for concern unless it becomes chronic. A failure may be a sign that user education is lacking—for example, training users to terminate the application gracefully before shutting down their workstation. A DBA intervention is not needed for user-process failures, but administrators must watch for trends, and if something happens too often, they need to investigate because there may be application problems or network issues that cause an excessive number of user-process failures. More information may be available in the alert log file showing whether the user process is hitting a bug and whether there are any trace files written.

Network Failures

Depending on the locations of your workstation and your server, getting from your workstation to the server over the network might involve a number of hops; for example, you might traverse several local switches and WAN routers to get to the database. From a network perspective, this configuration provides a number of points where failure can occur. These types of failures are called *network failures*.

In addition to hardware failures between the server and client, a listener process on the Oracle server can fail, or the network card on the server itself can fail. To guard against these kinds of failures, you can provide redundant network paths from your clients to the server, as well as additional listener connections on the Oracle server and redundant network cards on the server.

User-Error Failures

Even if all your redundant hardware is at peak performance and your users have been trained to disconnect from their Oracle sessions properly, users can still inadvertently delete or modify data in tables or drop an object in the database. This is known as a *user-error failure*. Although these operations succeed from a statement point of view, they might not be logically correct: the DROP TABLE command worked fine, but you really didn't want to drop that table!

If data was inadvertently deleted from a table and not yet committed, a ROLLBACK statement will undo the damage. If a COMMIT has already been performed, you have a number of options at your disposal, such as using data in the undo tablespace for a Flashback Query or using data in the archived and online redo logs with the LogMiner utility, available as a command-line interface or a graphical user interface.

You can recover a dropped table using Oracle's recycle-bin functionality. A dropped table is stored in a special structure in the tablespace and is available for retrieval as long as the space occupied by the table in the tablespace is not needed for new objects. Even if the table is no longer in the tablespace's recycle bin, depending on the criticality of the dropped table, you can use either *tablespace point-in-time recovery* (TSPITR) or *Flashback Database* recovery to recover the table, taking into consideration the potential data loss for other objects stored in the same tablespace for TSPITR or in the database if you use Flashback Database recovery.

 TSPITR and Flashback Database recovery are beyond the scope of this book but are covered in more detail in *OCP: Oracle Database 12c Administrator Certified Professional Study Guide* (Sybex, 2014).

If the inadvertent changes are limited to a small number of tables that have few or no interdependencies with other database objects, Flashback Table functionality is most likely the right tool to bring back the table to a certain point in time.

Later in this chapter, in the section "Performing Recovery Operations," we'll show you how to recover dropped tables from the recycle bin using the Flashback Drop functionality, retrieve deleted rows from a table using the Flashback Query functionality, use the Flashback Table functionality to bring a table back to a specific point in time along with its dependent objects, and use LogMiner to query online and archived redo logs for the previous state of modified rows.

 The Oracle Database 12c database provides flashback technology, which is aimed to recover from user errors.

Instance Failures

An *instance failure* occurs when the instance shuts down without synchronizing all the database files to the same system change number (SCN), requiring a recovery operation the next time the instance is started. Many of the reasons for an instance failure are out of your direct control; in these situations, you can minimize the impact of these failures by tuning instance recovery. You will learn how to tune instance recovery later in this chapter, in the section "Tuning Instance Recovery."

Here are a few causes of instance failure:

- A power outage
- A server-hardware failure
- Failure of an Oracle background process
- Emergency shutdown procedures (intentional power outage or SHUTDOWN ABORT)

In all these scenarios, the solution is easy: run the STARTUP command, and let Oracle automatically perform instance recovery using the online redo logs and undo data in the undo tablespace. If the cause of the instance failure is related to an Oracle background-process failure, you can use the alert log and process-specific trace files to debug the problem. EM Cloud

Control makes it easy to review the contents of the alert log and any other alerts generated right before the point of failure.

Media Failures

Another type of failure that is somewhat out of your control is media failure. A *media failure* is any type of failure that results in the loss of one or more database files: data files, control files, or redo log files. Although the loss of other database-related files such as an init.ora file or a server-parameter file (spfile) is of great concern, Oracle Corporation does not consider it a media failure. The database file can be lost or corrupted for a number of reasons:

- Failure of a disk drive
- Failure of a disk controller
- Inadvertent deletion or corruption of a database file

Following the best practices defined earlier—in other words, adequately mirroring control files and redo log files and ensuring that full backups and their subsequent archived redo log files are available—will keep you prepared for any type of media failure.

In the next section, we will show you how to recover from the loss of control files, data files, and redo log files.

Performing Recovery Operations

Once the inevitable database failure occurs, you can perform a relatively quick and painless recovery operation if you have followed the backup guidelines presented earlier in the chapter and clearly understand the types of failures that could happen in the system.

Before we show you how to perform *recovery*, however, it is important for you to understand how an Oracle instance starts up and what kinds of failures can occur at each startup phase. Understanding the startup phases is important, because some types of recovery operations must occur in a particular phase. Once a database is started, the instance will fail under a number of conditions that we will describe in detail.

Next, we will describe how instance recovery works and how to tune instance recovery, and then show you ways to easily recover from several types of user errors. Finally, we will show you how to recover from media failures due to the loss of both critical and non-system-critical data files.

Understanding Instance Startup

Starting up a database involves several phases, from being shut down to being open and available to users. If certain prerequisites are not present, the database startup halts, and you must take some kind of remedial action to permit the startup to proceed. In the following list are the four basic database states along with their prerequisites after you type the STARTUP command at the SQL*Plus prompt:

SHUTDOWN   No background processes are active. A STARTUP command is used when the database is in this state; the STARTUP command fails if you are in any other state, unless you are using STARTUP FORCE to restart an instance.

NOMOUNT   Also known as the STARTED state, the instance must be able to access the initialization-parameter file, either as a text-based init.ora file or as an spfile.

MOUNT   In this state, the instance checks that all control files listed in the initialization-parameter file are present and identical. Even if one of the multiplexed control files is unavailable or corrupted, the instance does not enter the MOUNT state and stays in the NOMOUNT state.

OPEN   Most of the time spent in the instance startup occurs during this phase. All redo log groups must have at least one member available, and all data files that are marked as online must be available.

You are notified in a number of ways that a redo log group member is missing or a data file is missing. If a data file is missing or corrupted, you will get a message while you are running the STARTUP command, as in this example:

```
SQL> startup
ORACLE instance started.
Total System Global Area  197132288 bytes
Fixed Size                   778076 bytes
Variable Size             162537636 bytes
Database Buffers           33554432 bytes
Redo Buffers                 262144 bytes
Database mounted.
ORA-01157: cannot identify/lock data file 4 - see DBWR trace file
ORA-01110: data file 4: '/u05/oradata/ord/users01.dbf'
```

The message in SQL*Plus shows only the first data file that needs attention. You will have to use the dynamic performance view V$RECOVER_FILE to list all the files that need attention. Here is a query against the view V$RECOVER_FILE and a second query joining V$RECOVER_FILE and V$DATAFILE given the previous STARTUP command:

```
SQL> select file#, error from v$recover_file;
    FILE# ERROR
---------- -----------------------------------------------
        4 FILE NOT FOUND
       11 FILE NOT FOUND
SQL> select file#, name from
        v$datafile join v$recover_file using (file#);
    FILE# NAME
---------- ---------------------------------------
        4 /u05/oradata/ord/users01.dbf
```

11 /u08/oradata/ord/idx02.dbf

If a data file is offline or taken offline, the instance can still start as long as the data file does not belong to the SYSTEM or UNDO tablespace. Once the instance is started, you can proceed to recover the missing or corrupted data file and subsequently bring it online. If all files are available but out of sync, automatic instance recovery is performed as long as the online redo log files can bring all data files to the same SCN. Otherwise, media recovery is required using archived redo log files.

If a redo log group member is missing, a message is generated in the alert log, but the database will still open.

Keeping an Instance from Failing

Media failures are not always critical, depending on which type of data file is lost. If any of the multiplexed copies of the control file are lost, an entire redo log group is lost, or any data file from the SYSTEM or UNDO tablespace is lost, the instance will fail. The instance also could crash due to an internal error.

In some cases, the instance becomes unavailable to users but will not shut down; in this case, you can use SHUTDOWN ABORT to force the instance to shut down without resynchronizing the data files with the control file. The next time the instance is started, instance recovery will be performed. If you plan on starting up the instance right after using SHUTDOWN ABORT, you can instead use STARTUP FORCE as shorthand for a SHUTDOWN ABORT and a STARTUP.

Later in this chapter, we will show you how to recover from the loss of a control file, a redo log file member, or one or more data files.

Recovering from Instance Failure

As we discussed earlier, in the section "Instance Failures," an instance failure is any kind of failure that prevents the synchronization of the database's data files and control files before the instance is shut down.

Oracle automatically recovers from instance failure during *instance recovery*. Instance recovery is initiated by simply starting up the database with the STARTUP command. Instance recovery is also known as *crash recovery*.

During a STARTUP operation, Oracle first attempts to read the initialization file, and then it mounts the control file and attempts to open the data files referenced in the control files. If the data files are not synchronized, instance recovery is initiated.

Instance recovery occurs in phases:

Phase 1 Find data files that are out of sync with the control file.

Phase 2 Use the online redo log files to restore the data files to the state before instance failure in a roll-forward operation. After the roll-forward, data files have committed and uncommitted data.

Phase 3 Open the database. Once the roll-forward operation completes, the database is open to users.

Phase 4 Oracle then uses the undo segments to roll back any uncommitted transactions. The rollback operation uses data in the undo tablespace; without a consistent undo tablespace, the rollback operation cannot succeed. After the rollback phase, the data files contain only committed data.

 Instance recovery is required when you perform database startup after an instance crash or after stopping the database using SHUTDOWN ABORT.

Tuning Instance Recovery

Before a user receives a "Commit complete" message, the new or changed data must be successfully written to a redo log file. At some point in the future, the same information must be used to update the data files; this operation usually lags behind the redo log file write because sequential writes to the redo log file are by nature faster than random writes to one or more data files on disk.

As we discussed earlier, checkpoints keep track of what still needs to be written from the redo log files to the data files. Any transactions not yet written to the data files are at an SCN after the last checkpoint.

The amount of time required for instance recovery depends on how long it takes to bring the data files up-to-date from the last checkpoint position to the latest SCN in the control file. To prevent performance problems, the distance between the checkpoint position and the end of the redo log group cannot be more than 90 percent of the size of the redo log group.

You can tune instance recovery by setting an MTTR target, in seconds, using the initialization parameter FAST_START_MTTR_TARGET. The default value for this parameter is zero; the maximum is 3,600 seconds (1 hour).

A setting of zero disables the target, which reduces the likelihood of redo logs waiting for writes to the data files. However, if FAST_START_MTTR_TARGET is set to a low nonzero value, writes to the redo logs most likely have to wait for writes to the data files. Although this reduces the amount of time it takes to recover the instance in the case of an instance failure, it affects performance and response time. Setting this value too high can result in an unacceptable amount of time needed to recover the instance after an instance failure.

Other parameters control instance recovery time:

LOG_CHECKPOINT_TIMEOUT This is the maximum number of seconds that any new or modified block in the buffer cache waits until it is written to disk.

LOG_CHECKPOINT_INTERVAL Specifies number of redo log file blocks that can exist between an incremental checkpoint and the last block written to the redo log. If the value exceeds the actual redo log-file size, checkpoints occur only when switching logs.

FAST_START_IO_TARGET This is similar to FAST_START_MTTR_TARGET, except that the recovery operation is specified as the number of I/Os instead of the number of seconds to finish instance recovery.

Setting any of these parameters overrides FAST_START_MTTR_TARGET. As part of the enhanced manageability features, setting FAST_START_MTTR_TARGET is the easiest and most straightforward way to define your database's recovery time given the time-based constraints included in most typical SLAs.

The EM Cloud Control interface makes it easy to adjust FAST_START_MTTR_TARGET. On the Availability screen of EM Cloud Control, choose Recovery Settings. Figure 15.14 shows the Instance Recovery setting, which you can find in the top section of the Recovery Settings screen.

FIGURE 15.14 Adjusting MTTR for instance recovery

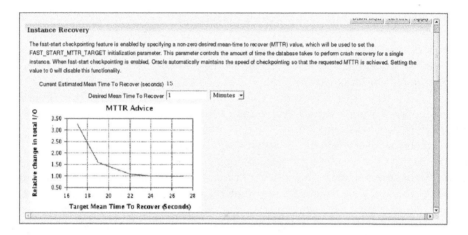

Enter the desired value using seconds or minutes. When you click the Apply button, the new value for FAST_START_MTTR_TARGET goes into effect immediately and stays in effect when the instance is restarted. The screen also shows the MTTR recommendations. The same information is available in the view V$MTTR_TARGET_ADVICE. For each possible value of FAST_START_MTTR_TARGET, the view displays details about how many cache writes would be performed under the workload tested for that value of FAST_START_MTTR_TARGET.

The V$INSTANCE_RECOVERY view displays instance-recovery-required blocks, estimated time, and various instance-recovery-related data. Use the column OPTIMAL_LOGFILE_SIZE to determine the best size of online redo logs.

Using the SQL*Plus command line, you can adjust the MTTR target by using the ALTER SYSTEM command, as in this example:

```
SQL> alter system set fast_start_mttr_target=60 scope=both;
System altered.
```

Using SCOPE=BOTH, the new value of the parameter takes effect immediately and stays in effect the next time the instance is restarted.

WARNING   You must remove the FAST_START_IO_TARGET, LOG_CHECKPOINT_INTERVAL, and LOG_CHECKPOINT_TIMEOUT initialization parameters when using FAST_START_MTTR_TARGET. Setting these parameters conflicts with the recovery time specified by FAST_START_MTTR_TARGET.

Recovering from User Errors

Earlier in this chapter, in the section "User-Error Failures," you learned a number of scenarios in which a user's data was inadvertently changed or deleted or a table was dropped. In the following sections, you'll learn quite a few helpful tasks, such as how to do the following:

- Use Flashback Query to retrieve selected rows from a previous state of a table.

- Recover a table using Flashback Drop and a tablespace's recycle bin.

- Bring an entire table and its dependent objects (such as indexes) back to a specific point in time using the Flashback Table functionality.

- Perform a table-level recovery from RMAN backup.

- Roll back a specific transaction and its dependent transactions using Flashback Transaction technology.

- Query previous transactions in the online and archived redo logs using the LogMiner utility.

NOTE   Flashback operations are not part of the Oracle Database 12c OCA exam topics, but they are included here to complete the recovery discussion. Explore the EM Cloud Control menu options under the Availability option to learn more.

Using Flashback Query

One of the features introduced in Oracle9i was called *Flashback Query*. It allows a user to "go back in time" and view the contents of a table as it existed at some point in the recent past. A Flashback Query looks a lot like a standard SQL SELECT statement, with the addition of the AS OF TIMESTAMP clause.

Before users can take advantage of the Flashback Query feature, the DBA must perform two tasks:

- Make sure there is an undo tablespace in the database that is large enough to retain changes made by all users for a specified period of time. This is the same tablespace that is used to support COMMIT and ROLLBACK functionality (discussed in Chapter 11, "Managing Data Concurrency and Undo").

- Use the initialization parameter UNDO_RETENTION to specify how long the undo information will be retained for use by flashback queries. This parameter is specified in seconds; therefore, if you specify UNDO_RETENTION=172800 (default is 900), the undo information for flashback queries can be available for up to two days.

The key to the Flashback Query functionality is using the AS OF TIMESTAMP clause in the SELECT statement; you can specify the timestamp as any valid expression that evaluates to a date or timestamp value. In the following example, you want to query the EMPLOYEES table as it existed 15 minutes ago:

```
SQL> SELECT employee_id, last_name, email
     FROM hr.employees
     AS OF TIMESTAMP (systimestamp - interval '15' minute)
     WHERE employee_id = 101;


EMPLOYEE_ID LAST_NAME            EMAIL
----------- -------------------- --------------------
        101 Kochhar              NKOCHHAR
```

You can just as easily specify an absolute time of day to retrieve the contents of the row at that time, as in this example:

```
SQL> SELECT employee_id, last_name, email
     FROM hr.employees
     AS OF TIMESTAMP
        (to_timestamp ('01-Jan-14 16:18:57.845993',
                       'DD-Mon-RR HH24:MI:SS.FF'))
     WHERE employee_id = 101;


EMPLOYEE_ID LAST_NAME            EMAIL
----------- -------------------- --------------------
        101 Kochhar              NTKOCHHAR
```

If your Flashback Query requires undo data that is no longer available in the undo tablespace, you will receive an error message:

```
SQL> SELECT employee_id, last_name, email
     FROM hr.employees
     AS OF TIMESTAMP (systimestamp - interval '10' month)
     WHERE employee_id = 101;


select employee_id, last_name, email
       *
ERROR at line 1:
ORA-08180: no snapshot found based on specified time
```

Real World Scenario

Using Flashback Query to Retrieve Missing Rows

Recently, an application administrator inadvertently deleted a bunch of rows from a database table and committed the transaction. He learned about the deletion, which was caused by the wrong WHERE clause, only when users started calling him about missing data and the various errors they were getting.

Panicked, the application administrator called his manager and told her what had happened. They planned an outage for the affected application and a couple of other applications hosted in the same database. As usual, the DBA was the last person to know about issues, and by the time the problem came to the DBA, it was a crisis.

The application administrator told the DBA team that there was a recovery situation and that he had arranged for all the outages and notifications. One of the DBAs asked the application administrator for the time of the data deletion and the table name. With that information, the DBA performed a query similar to the following to display the deleted records:

```
SELECT * FROM vms.dvbt606a
AS OF TIMESTAMP to_timestamp ('12-Sep-12 12:20', 'DD-Mon-RR HH24:MI');
```

Luckily, only a few transactions were occurring in the database, because users were getting errors and the changed rows were still available in the undo. If a lot of transactions had been processing, Oracle could have overwritten the committed transaction's rollback space (depending on the UNDO_RENTENTION setting).

After performing the query, the DBA got the WHERE clause from the administrator to filter out the rows the administrator had accidently deleted and inserted those rows into the original table using the following SQL statement:

```
INSERT INTO vms.dvbt606a
SELECT * FROM vms.dvbt606a
AS OF TIMESTAMP to_timestamp ('12-Sep-12 12:20', 'DD-Mon-RR HH24:MI')
WHERE TRANS_DATE BETWEEN TO_DATE('01-MAY-12','DD-MON-YY')
      AND TO_DATE('31-MAY-12','DD-MON-YY');
```

They did not have to take any applications offline, and the whole recovery operation took less than 15 minutes after the DBA was informed of the problem. They could have used the FLASHBACK TABLE feature instead, which would have made the recovery even quicker (and there would be no need to know the WHERE clause used for deletion), but nobody thought of it at the time.

Using Flashback Drop and the Recycle Bin

Another user-recovery flashback feature, *Flashback Drop*, lets you restore a dropped table without using tablespace point-in-time recovery. Although tablespace point-in-time recovery could effectively restore a table and its contents to a point in time before it was dropped, it is potentially time-consuming and has the side effect of losing work from other transactions that occurred within the same tablespace after the table was dropped.

In the following sections, we will talk about the new logical structure available in each tablespace—the recycle bin—and how you can query the recycle bin and retrieve dropped objects from it. We will also describe some minor limitations involved in using the recycle bin.

Recycle-Bin Concepts

The *recycle bin* is a logical structure within each tablespace that holds dropped tables and objects related to the tables, such as indexes. The space associated with the dropped table is not immediately available but shows up in the data dictionary view DBA_FREE_SPACE. When space pressure occurs in the tablespace, objects in the recycle bin are deleted in a first-in, first-out (FIFO) fashion, maximizing the amount of time that the most recently dropped object remains in the recycle bin.

The dropped object still belongs to the owner and still counts against the quota for the owner in the tablespace; in fact, the table itself is still directly accessible from the recycle bin, as you will see in subsequent examples.

Retrieving Dropped Tables from the Recycle Bin

You can retrieve a dropped table from the recycle bin at the SQL command line by using the FLASHBACK TABLE...TO BEFORE DROP command. In the following example, the user retrieves the table ORDER_ITEMS from the recycle bin after discovering that the table was inadvertently dropped:

```
SQL> select order_id, line_item_id, product_id
  2  from order_items
  3  where rownum < 5;
from order_items
     *
ERROR at line 2:
ORA-00942: table or view does not exist


SQL> flashback table order_items to before drop;

Flashback complete.

SQL> select order_id, line_item_id, product_id
  2  from order_items
  3  where rownum < 5;
```

```
ORDER_ID LINE_ITEM_ID PRODUCT_ID
---------- ------------ ----------
      2355            1       2289
      2356            1       2264
      2357            1       2211
      2358            1       1781
```

If the table ORDER_ITEMS was re-created after it was dropped, the RENAME TO clause in the FLASHBACK TABLE command would be added to give the restored table a new name, as in the following example:

```
SQL> drop table order_items;

Table dropped.

SQL> flashback table order_items to before drop
  2      rename to order_items_old_version;

Flashback complete.

SQL> select order_id, line_item_id, product_id
  2  from order_items_old_version
  3  where rownum < 5;

ORDER_ID LINE_ITEM_ID PRODUCT_ID
---------- ------------ ----------
      2355            1       2289
      2356            1       2264
      2357            1       2211
      2358            1       1781
```

If the table to be retrieved from the recycle bin was dropped more than once and you want to retrieve an incarnation of the table before the most recent one, you can use the name of the table in the recycle bin; you can query the view RECYCLEBIN or use the SHOW RECYCLEBIN command.

Recycle-Bin Considerations and Limitations

A few limitations are associated with the recycle bin:

- Only non-SYSTEM locally managed tablespaces can have a recycle bin. However, dependent objects in a dictionary-managed tablespace are protected if the dropped object is in a locally managed tablespace.

▪ A table's dependent objects are saved in the recycle bin when the table is dropped, except for bitmap join indexes, referential integrity constraints (foreign key constraints), and materialized view logs.

▪ Indexes are protected only if the table is dropped first; explicitly dropping an index does not place the index into the recycle bin.

Using Flashback Table

Flashback Table allows you to recover one or more tables to a specific point in time without having to use more time-consuming recovery operations such as tablespace point-in-time recovery or Flashback Database that can also affect the availability of the rest of the database. Flashback Table works in place by rolling back only the changes made to the table or tables and their dependent objects, such as indexes. Flashback Table is different from Flashback Drop; Flashback Table undoes recent transactions to an existing table, whereas Flashback Drop recovers a dropped table. Flashback Table uses data in the undo tablespace, whereas Flashback Drop uses the recycle bin.

The FLASHBACK TABLE command brings one or more tables back to a point in time before any number of logical corruptions have occurred on the tables. To be able to flash back a table, you must enable row movement for the table. Because DML operations are used to bring the table back to its former state, the row IDs in the table change. As a result, Flashback Table is not a viable option for applications that depend on the table's row IDs to remain constant.

In the following example, someone in the HR department has accidentally deleted all the employees in department 60, the IT department, along with the row for IT in the DEPARTMENTS table. Because this happened less than 15 minutes ago, you are sure there is enough undo information to support a Flashback Table operation.

Before running the FLASHBACK TABLE command, you confirm that the row in DEPARTMENTS for the IT department is still missing using this query:

```
SQL> SELECT * FROM hr.departments
    WHERE department_name = 'IT';
```

```
no rows selected
```

Next, you flash back the table to 15 minutes ago, specifying both tables in the same command, as follows:

```
SQL> FLASHBACK TABLE hr.employees, hr.departments
    TO TIMESTAMP systimestamp - interval '15' minute;
```

```
Flashback complete.
```

Finally, you check to see whether the IT department is truly back in the table:

```
SQL> SELECT * FROM hr.departments
    WHERE department_name = 'IT';
```

```
DEPARTMENT_ID DEPARTMENT_NAME   MANAGER_ID LOCATION_ID
------------- ------------------ ---------- -----------
          60 IT                        103        1400
```

If you flash back either too far or not far enough, you can simply rerun the FLASHBACK TABLE command with a different timestamp or SCN, as long as the undo data is still available.

Although the rest of the database is unaffected by a Flashback Table operation, the FLASHBACK TABLE command acquires exclusive DML locks on the tables involved in the flashback. This is usually not an availability issue, because the users who would normally use the table are waiting for the flashback operation to complete anyway!

Integrity constraints are not violated when one or more tables are flashed back; this is why you typically group tables related by integrity constraints or parent-child relationships in the FLASHBACK TABLE command. When a flashback operation is in progress, the triggers on the table are disabled. If you want the triggers to fire during the flashback operation, add the ENABLE TRIGGERS clause to the FLASHBACK TABLE statement, as in the following example.

```
SQL> FLASHBACK TABLE hr.employees
     TO TIMESTAMP TO_TIMESTAMP('02NOV12 22:00'. 'DDMONYY HH24:MI')
     ENABLE TRIGGERS;
```

To be able to perform a Flashback Table operation, the table must have ROW MOVEMENT enabled. Enable row movement using ALTER TABLE <name> ENABLE ROW MOVEMENT.

Using EM Cloud Control to Perform Table Recovery

You can perform recovery operations using EM Cloud Control. On the Availability menu, choose Perform Recovery under Backup/Recovery. On the Perform Recovery screen, choose Tables as the Recovery Scope, as shown in Figure 15.15.

FIGURE 15.15 The Perform Recovery screen

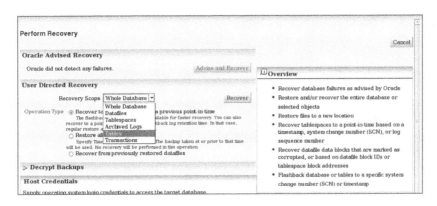

Choosing Tables as the Recovery Scope gives you two options:

- Flashback Existing Tables
- Flashback Dropped Tables

Choose Flashback Existing Tables to roll back the table to a previous state. Choose Flashback Dropped Tables to retrieve a table from the recycle bin.

Using Flashback Transaction

You can use the Flashback Transaction technology to undo a transaction and its dependent transactions. The DBMS_FLASHBACK.TRANSACTION_BACKOUT procedure is used to accomplish this task.

You must meet the following prerequisites to perform a Flashback Transaction on an Oracle Database 12c database:

- The database must be in ARCHIVELOG mode.
- Supplemental logging must be enabled in the database using ALTER DATABASE ADD SUPPLEMENTAL LOG DATA.
- A supplemental log data primary key should be created using the statement ALTER DATABASE ADD SUPPLEMENTAL LOG DATA (PRIMARY KEY) COLUMNS.
- The user performing the Flashback Transaction must have the SELECT ANY TRANSACTION privilege.
- The user should have the EXECUTE privilege on DBMS_FLASHBACK.
- The user should also have appropriate DML privileges on the tables (such as INSERT/UPDATE/DELETE).

Using EM Cloud Control, you can perform the Flashback Transaction. Choose Transactions from the Backup and Recovery menu under Availability.

Using LogMiner

Oracle *LogMiner* is another tool you can use to view past activity in the database. By using a set of PL/SQL procedures and functions, the LogMiner tool can help find changed records in redo log files. LogMiner extracts all DDL and DML activity from the redo log files for viewing via the dynamic performance view V$LOGMNR_CONTENTS. In addition to extracting the DDL and DML statements used to change the database, the V$LOGMNR_CONTENTS view also contains the DML statements needed to reverse the change made to the database. This is a good tool for not only pinpointing when changes were made to a table, but also for automatically generating the SQL statements needed to reverse those changes.

LogMiner works differently from Oracle's Flashback Query feature. The Flashback Query feature allows a user to see the contents of a table at a specified time in the past, while LogMiner can search a time period for all changes against the table. A Flashback Query uses the undo information stored in the undo tablespace; LogMiner uses redo logs, both online and archived. Both tools can be useful for tracking down how and when changes to database objects took place.

LogMiner does not actually undo the change; it only provides the statements that you can use to undo the change. You can extract and run any or all DML commands you find in the redo logs, keeping in mind any integrity constraints in place for the tables you are modifying.

Recovering from the Loss of a Control File

Losing one of the multiplexed control files immediately aborts the instance. Assuming you haven't lost every control file, recovering from this type of failure is fairly straightforward.

Here are the steps to recover from the loss of a control file:

1. If the instance is not shut down, use SHUTDOWN ABORT to force a complete shutdown.

2. Copy one of the good copies of the control file to the location of the corrupted or missing control file. If the corrupted or missing control file resided on a failed disk, copy it to another suitable location instead, and update the initialization-parameter file to update the control file reference. Alternatively, you can temporarily remove the reference from the initialization parameter file until you find a suitable location. However, it is highly desirable to have at least two, if not more, copies of the control file available in case of another media failure.

3. Start the instance with STARTUP.

In the following example, you use a server-parameter file (spfile) for initialization parameters, and you decide to temporarily do without a third multiplexed control file until the disk containing the lost control file is repaired. You'll change the initialization parameter CONTROL_FILES using the ALTER SYSTEM … SCOPE=SPFILE command when the instance is started in NOMOUNT mode. You cannot start in MOUNT mode because that mode checks for the existence of all copies of the control file, and as far as the spfile is concerned, you are still missing a control file.

The first step is to start the database in NOMOUNT mode, as you can see in this example:

```
SQL> startup nomount

ORACLE instance started.

Total System Global Area  188743680 bytes
Fixed Size                   778036 bytes
Variable Size             162537676 bytes
Database Buffers           25165824 bytes
Redo Buffers                 262144 bytes
SQL>
```

Looking at the dynamic performance view V$SPPARAMETER, you can see that you still have three copies of the control file referenced, but the disk containing the third copy has failed:

```
SQL> select name, value from v$spparameter
    where name = 'control_files';


NAME             VALUE
---------------  -------------------------------------------------
control_files    /u02/oradata/ord/control01.ctl
control_files    /u06/oradata/ord/control02.ctl
control_files    /u07/oradata/ord/control03.ctl
```

In the next step, you change the value of CONTROL_FILES in the spfile and restart the instance, as you can see here:

```
SQL> alter system set control_files =
    '/u02/oradata/ord/control01.ctl',
    '/u06/oradata/ord/control02.ctl'
    scope = spfile;

System altered.

SQL> shutdown immediate
ORA-01507: database not mounted
ORACLE instance shut down.

SQL> startup
ORACLE instance started.

Total System Global Area  188743680 bytes
Fixed Size                   778036 bytes
Variable Size             162537676 bytes
Database Buffers           25165824 bytes
Redo Buffers                 262144 bytes
Database mounted.
Database opened.
SQL>
```

Once the instance is restarted successfully, you confirm that the control file is no longer being referenced, as you can see in this query:

```
SQL> select name, value from v$spparameter
    where name = 'control_files';
```

```
NAME              VALUE
---------------   ---------------------------------------
control_files     /u02/oradata/ord/control01.ctl
control_files     /u06/oradata/ord/control02.ctl
```

You still have two multiplexed copies of the control file; therefore, you are covered in case of a media failure of the disk containing one of the remaining control files.

Using the Data Recovery Advisor

The *Data Recovery Advisor* (DRA) is a tool first introduced in the Oracle 11g database that automatically diagnoses database failures and determines the appropriate recovery options. In addition to recommending the recovery options available, it can perform the recovery after the DBA confirms the operation. DRA can proactively check for failures, before the database process detects corruption and signals an error.

DRA has user interfaces through the GUI of EM Cloud Control and through the command-line utility RMAN. You can invoke the Data Recovery Advisor from EM Cloud Control using any of the following methods:

- Using the Perform Recovery screen shown earlier in Figure 15.15. If any failures are detected, the Advise and Recover button will be enabled, as shown in Figure 15.16. It will also display a summary of failures with the failure description.

- Using the Support Workbench. Support Workbench is invoked from the Diagnostics menu under Oracle Database. The Checker Findings tab in Support Workbench shows the failures in the database, as shown in Figure 15.17. By clicking the Launch Recovery Advisor button, you can invoke DRA.

- Using the Advisor Central page by clicking the Data Recovery Advisor link under Advisors.

FIGURE 15.16   Invoking DRA from the Perform Recovery screen

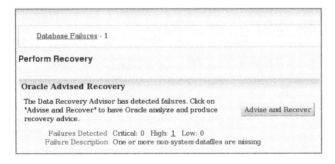

The *Health Monitor* (HM) tool in the Oracle Database 12c database proactively monitors the health of the database. It assesses data failures and reports to the Data Recovery Advisor. DRA consolidates the findings of HM into failures and assigns a priority based on the failure.

FIGURE 15.17   Invoking DRA from the Support Workbench screen

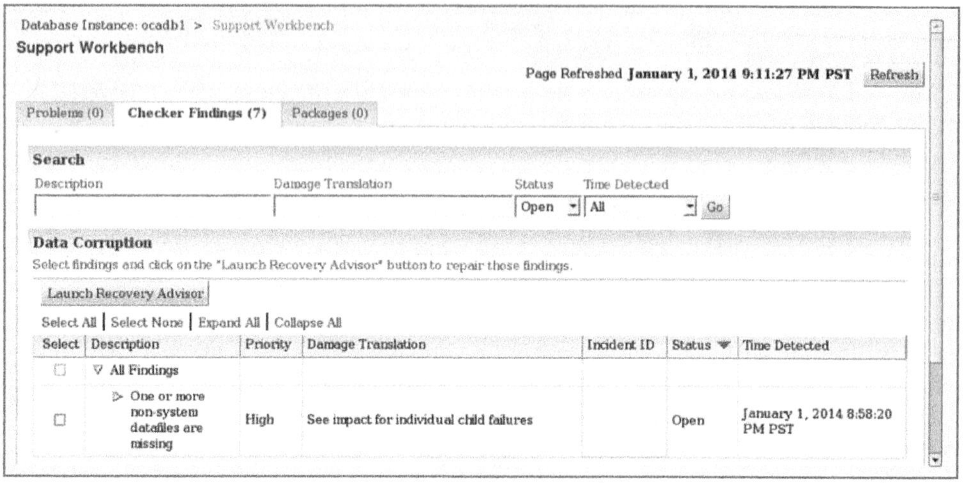

Failure checks in the database can be reactive or proactive. When an error occurs in the database, reactive checks are automatically executed. The following are examples of data failures where the DRA can analyze and suggest repair options:

- Missing data files
- Data files with incorrect OS permissions
- Offline tablespaces
- Corrupted data files (physical corruption)
- Corrupt index entry or dictionary entry (logical corruption)
- I/O failures
- Number of open files exceeded

In the following sections, you will look at the various scenarios of media-failure errors and see how DRA can help analyze and fix errors.

Recovering from the Loss of a Redo Log File

A database instance stays up as long as at least one member of a redo log group is available. The alert log records the loss of a redo log group member; as with most database status information, EM Cloud Control allows you to easily review the contents of the alert log.

The dynamic performance view V$LOGFILE provides the status of each member of each redo log file of each redo log group; the STATUS column is defined as follows:

INVALID   The file is corrupted or missing.

STALE   This redo log file member is new and has never been used.

DELETED   The file is no longer being used.

<blank>   The redo log file is in use and is not corrupted.

When you are aware of a missing or deleted redo log group member, follow these three steps to ensure that you maintain a maximum level of redundancy. Losing the remaining member(s) of the redo log group will cause the instance to fail.

1. Verify which redo log group member is missing.

2. Archive the redo log group's contents; if you clear this redo log group before archiving it, you must back up the full database to ensure maximum recoverability of the database in case of the loss of a data file. Use the command ALTER SYSTEM ARCHIVE LOG GROUP *groupnum*; to force the archive operation. (*groupnum* refers to the redo log group that you want to archive.)

3. Clear the log group to re-create the missing redo log file members using the command ALTER DATABASE CLEAR LOGFILE GROUP *groupnum*;. Alternatively, you can replace the missing member by copying one of the good group members to the location of the missing member; using ALTER DATABASE CLEAR LOGFILE GROUP has the advantage of being platform-independent.

In this example, you lose a redo log-file group member and check the status of the redo log-file groups using V$LOGFILE:

```
SQL> SELECT group#, member FROM v$logfile;

    GROUP# MEMBER
---------- -------------------------------------------
         1 /u01/app/oracle/oradata/ocadb1/redo01.log
         1 /u01/app/oracle/oradata/ocadb1/redo01b.log
         2 /u01/app/oracle/oradata/ocadb1/redo02b.log
         2 /u01/app/oracle/oradata/ocadb1/redo02.log
         3 /u01/app/oracle/oradata/ocadb1/redo03b.log
         3 /u01/app/oracle/oradata/ocadb1/redo03.log


SQL> ! rm /u01/app/oracle/oradata/ocadb1/redo02.log
```

The alert log quickly shows the issue of a missing redo log member:

```
Wed Jan 01 21:27:46 2014
Errors in file /u01/app/oracle/diag/rdbms/ocadb1/ocadb1/trace/ocadb1_arc1_23552.
trc:
ORA-00313: open failed for members of log group 2 of thread 1
ORA-00312: online log 2 thread 1: '/u01/app/oracle/oradata/ocadb1/redo02.log'
ORA-27037: unable to obtain file status
```

```
Linux-x86_64 Error: 2: No such file or directory
Additional information: 3
```

It appears that group number 2 has a missing member, so you want to archive group number 2 using the ALTER SYSTEM ARCHIVE command, if it requires archiving:

```
SQL> alter system archive log group 2;
```

Finally, you can re-create the missing redo log-file group member using the ALTER DATABASE command mentioned in step 3:

```
SQL> alter database clear logfile group 2;

Database altered.
```

By reviewing the contents of the alert log, you see that the issue is fixed:

```
ORA-00316: log 2 of thread 1, type 0 in header is not log file
ORA-00312: online log 2 thread 1: '/u01/app/oracle/oradata/ocadb1/redo02b.log'
Checker run found 3 new persistent data failures
Completed: alter database clear logfile group 2
Wed Jan 01 21:59:31 2014
Thread 1 advanced to log sequence 204 (LGWR switch)
  Current log# 2 seq# 204 mem# 0: /u01/app/oracle/oradata/ocadb1/redo02b.log
  Current log# 2 seq# 204 mem# 1: /u01/app/oracle/oradata/ocadb1/redo02.log
```

The Database Recovery Advisor knows about the failure. When you invoke DRA, you can see more details about these failures. You can increase or decrease the priority of a failure by using the Set Priority High and Set Priority Low buttons. If you have taken care of the issue or if you do not want to resolve a noncritical failure, you can use the Close button to close the failure incident.

 To fix a missing redo log group member, you can use the actions such as Switch Log File and Clear Log File on the Redo Log Groups screen.

Recovering from the Loss of a Non-System-Critical Data File

If you lose a non-system-critical data file (in other words, not the SYSTEM or UNDO tablespace), your options are similar to those for losing a system-critical data file, except that most of your recovery effort in ARCHIVELOG mode can occur while the database is open to users who can use tablespaces other than the one being recovered.

Loss in NOARCHIVELOG Mode

The loss of a non-system-critical data file in NOARCHIVELOG mode requires the complete restoration of the database, including the control files and all data files, not just the missing data files. As a result, you must reenter any changes made to the database since the last backup.

Loss in ARCHIVELOG Mode

The loss of a non-system-critical data file in ARCHIVELOG mode affects only objects that are in the missing file, and recovery can proceed while the rest of the database is online. Because you are in ARCHIVELOG mode, no committed transactions in the lost data file will have to be reentered.

Recovering from the loss of a non-system-critical data file is not quite as complicated as the recovery from a system-critical data file, which we will cover in the next section; the database is continuously available to all users, except for the data files being recovered.

We have mimicked a failure by removing a file belonging to the USER_DATA tablespace. Try to create a table in this tablespace and see the following error:

```
SQL> create table x2 tablespace user_data as select * from dba_tables;
create table x2 tablespace user_data as select * from dba_tables
                                             *

ERROR at line 1:
ORA-01110: data file 5:
'/u01/app/oracle/oradata/OCADB1/datafile/o1_mf_user_dat_9d9zcx06_.dbf'
ORA-01116: error in opening database file 5
ORA-27041: unable to open file
Linux-x86_64 Error: 2: No such file or directory
Additional information: 3
```

In the EM Cloud Control interface, invoke the Data Recovery Advisor. Choose the failure you want to fix, and click the Advice button. Figure 15.18 shows the Manual Actions screen.

FIGURE 15.18 The Manual Actions screen of DRA

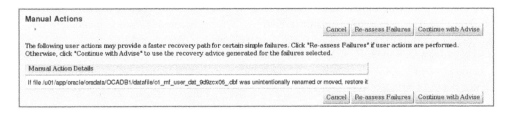

Click the Continue with Advise button to see the recovery advice. DRA generates an RMAN script to execute, as shown in Figure 15.19. You can run this script manually using the RMAN command line with no modification.

FIGURE 15.19   The Recovery Advice screen of DRA

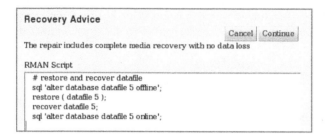

Click Continue to review and submit a job to start the restore and recovery.

You can also recover from the failure without using DRA. On the Perform Recovery screen, choose Datafiles as the Recovery Scope. You will be presented with four options to recover, as shown in Figure 15.20:

- Recover to Current Time: Restore the data file from backup, and recover the data file using archive log and redo log files.

- Restore Datafiles: No recovery is performed.

- Recover from Previously Restored Datafile: Continue recovery after the data file restore.

- Block Recovery: Recover the corrupted blocks in a data file.

FIGURE 15.20   User-directed recovery of a data file

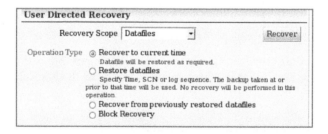

You have the option to restore the data file to its original location or to another location. You also have the option to edit the RMAN script generated. When you click Submit, the RMAN script is executed, and the data file is recovered. Because the database is in ARCHIVELOG mode, you will not lose any committed transactions in the USER_DATA tablespace.

You can run the RMAN statement LIST FAILURE at the RMAN command prompt, and you will see output similar to the following:

```
$ rman target /
```

```
Recovery Manager: Release 12.1.0.1.0 - Production on Wed Jan 1 22:19:48 2014
Copyright (c) 1982, 2013, Oracle and/or its affiliates.  All rights reserved.
```

```
connected to target database: OCADB1 (DBID=6257179)

RMAN> list failure;

using target database control file instead of recovery catalog
Database Role: PRIMARY

List of Database Failures
=========================

Failure ID Priority Status    Time Detected Summary
---------- -------- --------- ------------- -------
8          HIGH     OPEN      01-JAN-14     One or more non-system datafiles are
                                            missing

RMAN>
```

The ADVISE FAILURE command lists the failures. You can list all failures, or you can specify options such as CRITICAL, HIGH, and so on. Here is some output from the ADVISE FAILURE statement:

```
RMAN> advise failure all;

Database Role: PRIMARY

List of Database Failures
=========================

Failure ID Priority Status    Time Detected Summary
---------- -------- --------- ------------- -------
8          HIGH     OPEN      01-JAN-14     One or more non-system datafiles are
                                            missing

analyzing automatic repair options; this may take some time
allocated channel: ORA_DISK_1
channel ORA_DISK_1: SID=35 device type=DISK
allocated channel: ORA_DISK_2
analyzing automatic repair options complete

Mandatory Manual Actions
========================
no manual actions available
```

```
Optional Manual Actions
=======================
1. If file /u01/app/oracle/oradata/OCADB1/datafile/o1_mf_user_dat_9d9zcx06_.dbf
was unintentionally renamed or moved, restore it

Automated Repair Options
========================
Option Repair Description
------ -------------------

1       Restore and recover datafile 5
  Strategy: The repair includes complete media recovery with no data loss
  Repair script: /u01/app/oracle/diag/rdbms/ocadb1/ocadb1/hm/reco_488075229.hm

RMAN>
```

To fix the failures using DRA, you can use the command REPAIR FAILURE, as shown next. It asks for your confirmation before performing the restore and recovery. If you do not want the confirmation, include the NOPROMPT clause, which will automatically repair all HIGH and CRITICAL priority failures. The REPAIR FAILURE command can be executed only after performing the ADVISE FAILURE.

```
RMAN> repair failure;

Strategy: The repair includes complete media recovery with no data loss
Repair script: /u01/app/oracle/diag/rdbms/ocadb1/ocadb1/hm/reco_488075229.hm

contents of repair script:
   # restore and recover datafile
   sql 'alter database datafile 5 offline';
   restore ( datafile 5 );
   recover datafile 5;
   sql 'alter database datafile 5 online';

Do you really want to execute the above repair (enter YES or NO)? YES
executing repair script

sql statement: alter database datafile 5 offline

Starting restore at 01-JAN-14
using channel ORA_DISK_1
```

```
channel ORA_DISK_1: starting datafile backup set restore
channel ORA_DISK_1: specifying datafile(s) to restore from backup set
channel ORA_DISK_1: restoring datafile 00005 to /u01/app/oracle/oradata/OCADB1/
datafile/o1_mf_user_dat_9d9zcx06_.dbf
channel ORA_DISK_1: reading from backup piece /backups/database/
OCADB1_8not0nod_1_1
channel ORA_DISK_1: piece handle=/backups/database/OCADB1_8not0nod_1_1
tag=BACKUP_OCADB1_0000_010114095002
channel ORA_DISK_1: restored backup piece 1
channel ORA_DISK_1: restore complete, elapsed time: 00:00:03
Finished restore at 01-JAN-14

Starting recover at 01-JAN-14
using channel ORA_DISK_1
channel ORA_DISK_1: starting incremental datafile backup set restore
channel ORA_DISK_1: specifying datafile(s) to restore from backup set
destination for restore of datafile 00005: /u01/app/oracle/oradata/OCADB1/
datafile/o1_mf_user_dat_9db1g2rp_.dbf
channel ORA_DISK_1: reading from backup piece /backups/database/
OCADB1_8tot0nqk_1_1
channel ORA_DISK_1: piece handle=/backups/database/OCADB1_8tot0nqk_1_1
tag=BACKUP_OCADB1_0000_010114095112
channel ORA_DISK_1: restored backup piece 1
channel ORA_DISK_1: restore complete, elapsed time: 00:00:01

starting media recovery
media recovery complete, elapsed time: 00:00:00

Finished recover at 01-JAN-14

sql statement: alter database datafile 5 online
repair failure complete

RMAN>
```

When you run REPAIR FAILURE, the Data Recovery Advisor closes the failure after successfully repairing the failure. You can increase or decrease the priority of a failure by using the CHANGE FAILURE command in RMAN. You can also close a failure using this command.

```
RMAN> CHANGE FAILURE 2 PRIORITY LOW;
RMAN> CHANGE FAILURE 5 CLOSE;
```

Data Recovery Advisor Views

The Data Recovery Advisor added four new views to the Oracle Database 12c data dictionary. These views start with V$IR_.

- V$IR_FAILURE: List of all the failures in the database (the same result you see with the LIST FAILURE command)

- V$IR_MANUAL_CHECKLIST: List of the manual-actions section of ADVISE FAILURE

- V$IR_REPAIR: Repair recommendations as provided by the ADVISE FAILURE command

- V$IR_FAILURE_SET: Link between V$IR_REPAIR and V$IR_FAILURE

Recovering from the Loss of a System-Critical Data File

When you lose a system-critical data file (in other words, a file from the SYSTEM or UNDO tablespace), the kinds of recovery available depend on whether you are operating in ARCHIVELOG mode or NOARCHIVELOG mode. Oracle strongly recommends operating in ARCHIVELOG mode for any production database that is not read-only.

Loss in NOARCHIVELOG Mode

The loss of a system-critical data file in NOARCHIVELOG mode requires a complete restoration of the database, including the control files and all data files, not just the missing data files. As a result, you must reenter any changes made to the database since the last backup, which must have been a cold backup.

Loss in ARCHIVELOG Mode

The loss of a system-critical data file in ARCHIVELOG mode cannot proceed while the database is open; recovery must be performed while the database is in the MOUNT state. Because the database is operating in ARCHIVELOG mode, you will not have to reenter any committed transactions in the database.

When a system-critical data file is lost, such as the data file for the SYSTEM tablespace, the instance will abort. In the rare circumstance that this does not happen, shut down the database, and start it in MOUNT mode, as in this example:

```
SQL> shutdown abort
ORACLE instance shut down.
SQL> startup mount
ORACLE instance started.

Total System Global Area  197132288 bytes
Fixed Size                   778076 bytes
Variable Size             162537636 bytes
```

```
Database Buffers          33554432 bytes
Redo Buffers               262144 bytes
Database mounted.
SQL>
```

Once the database is mounted, you can restore and recover the missing data file. After the recovery is completed, open the database.

To use the Data Recovery Advisor for the recovery, invoke Perform Recovery from the Availability screen of EM Cloud Control. Select Datafiles as the recovery scope, choose Restore to Current Time, and add the files that need recovery. Submit the job to complete the recovery operation. After the recovery operation is completed, open the database using ALTER DATABASE OPEN.

Users are not required to reenter any data because the recovery is up to the time of the last commit in the database.

The difference between recovering from the loss of a system-critical data file and non-system-critical data file is the state of the database. To recover a system-critical data file, the database must be in MOUNT state, not OPEN.

Table Recovery Using RMAN

RMAN in Oracle Database 12*c* can recover a table using the available backups. In versions prior to Oracle Database 12*c*, recovering a table from an RMAN backup involved several steps such as:

- Provision resources to stand up an instance to restore and recover the database backup.
- Once the database is recovered, export the table.
- Import the table to the target database.
- Drop the temporary database created for recovery purposes.

In Oracle Database 12*c* RMAN does all the work for you when you give the command RECOVER TABLE. The following steps are performed by RMAN.

- Determines the backup pieces required for recovery based on the time specified in the RECOVER command.
- Creates a temporary database with just the required tablespaces and recovers the database.
- Creates a data pump export from the temporary database for the tables listed in the RECOVER command.
- Imports the table to the target database. The table can be imported in another name or to another schema.

To learn more about the table recovery feature of RMAN, read Chapter 22 "Recovering Tables and Table Partitions from RMAN Backups" in the Oracle documentation "Oracle Database Backup and Recovery User's Guide 12*c* Release 1 (12.1) Part E17630-14," found at http://docs.oracle.com.

Summary

In this chapter, you studied the database structures that are key elements to ensuring a smooth recovery in the event of a database failure: control files, online redo log files, and archived redo log files. You learned to back up the various pieces of the database, and you learned how to schedule and manage backups using EM Cloud Control.

The control files contain the metadata about every other structure in the database. The online redo log files provide performance benefits to ongoing transactions and ensure that no committed transactions are lost after an instance failure; being able to change the number of redo log groups and the number of members in each group enhances both the availability and performance of the database. Archived redo log files make copies of online redo log files to one or more destinations before they are overwritten by new transactions. The common thread through all three of these structures is multiplexing: creating redundant copies of database components or redundant archival locations to minimize the impact of a media failure.

You learned about the Fast Recovery Area and how it can be used as the central location for backups of all database files, control files, initialization-parameter files, and archived redo log files in the database. You can manage the Fast Recovery Area via the EM Cloud Control interface or by using a SQL command-line interface to set or change database initialization parameters that control its location and size.

Before making database backups, you must understand backup strategies, types, and modes. The ARCHIVELOG mode provides many benefits and few downsides, especially in a production environment; the NOARCHIVELOG mode, in many ways, restricts the types of backups you can make.

Recovery Manager, or RMAN, provides a number of benefits over manual backup methods using a combination of SQL and operating-system commands. You can access most RMAN functionality via EM Cloud Control or with a command-line version for advanced backup and recovery techniques. One of RMAN's many benefits is the ability to create compressed incremental backup sets, which not only skips unused blocks in database data files but also compresses the blocks before writing to the backup set, saving I/O bandwidth and disk space.

In addition to knowing how an instance fails, you need to know what is required to keep a database up and running: all control files, at least one member of each redo log group, and all data files for the SYSTEM and UNDO tablespaces. For instance failures, you want to know how long the database will take to recover. You can use the initialization parameter FAST_START_MTTR_TARGET to specify the target recovery time, making it easier to meet service-level agreements.

Also in this chapter, we presented scenarios of media failures and how to recover from such failures using the Data Recovery Advisor. If the database is in ARCHIVELOG mode, you can recover the database from these failures without losing any committed transactions. If the database is in NOARCHIVELOG mode, you can recover only to the last good, cold backup. RMAN includes several commands to support the Data Recovery Advisor.

Exam Essentials

Identify the purpose of the redo log files. Describe the redo log file architecture. Provide details about how to create new redo log-file groups and add new members to redo log-file groups. Be able to drop redo log group members. Know how to clear online redo log-file groups when a log file member becomes corrupted.

Be able to multiplex a control file. List the steps required to create additional copies of the control file, for both an init.ora file and an spfile.

Describe the basic differences between operating a database in ARCHIVELOG mode and in NOARCHIVELOG mode. Identify the initialization parameters and commands that control the archive process. Briefly describe how archive log information is recorded in the control file.

Identify and discuss backup terminology. Enumerate the backup strategies, the backup types, and the backup modes. Give examples of how you can combine the strategies, types, and modes in different scenarios.

List the benefits of using RMAN to create backups. Show how to configure RMAN backup settings via the EM Cloud Control interface. Differentiate image copies from backup sets. Provide examples of an incremental backup strategy.

Explain the benefits of the Fast Recovery Area. Show how you can access the characteristics and status of the Fast Recovery Area using EM Cloud Control, as well as via dynamic performance views. Describe the database components that can be stored in the Fast Recovery Area. Enumerate the initialization parameters that control the location and size of the Fast Recovery Area.

Identify the initialization parameters used to tune instance recovery. Be able to define the possible values for FAST_START_MTTR_TARGET, FAST_START_IO_TARGET, and LOG_CHECKPOINT_TIMEOUT. Show the relationship between these parameters and in which situations each is most appropriately used.

List the phases of instance startup. Show how the database instance moves from SHUTDOWN to NOMOUNT to MOUNT to OPEN, and describe the conditions required in each step before the instance can proceed to the next phase.

List the features supported by Oracle to help users fix their own errors. Describe each type of user-error recovery solution: Flashback Query, Flashback Table, Flashback Transaction, and Flashback Drop.

Understand how many control files and redo log members are required for the database to function. When you use multiplexed control files and redo log files, Oracle Database 12c requires all control files to be available and at least one member of the redo log group to be available for the database to function.

Understand the failures that can be identified and repaired by the Data Recovery Advisor. The Data Recovery Advisor can detect and repair all types of media failures and logical corruption. It cannot detect user errors or network issues.

Familiarize yourself with the commands you can use to identify and perform recovery using RMAN. RMAN commands such as LIST FAILURE, ADVISE FAILURE, REPAIR FAILURE, and CHANGE FAILURE are used to support the Data Recovery Advisor actions.

Review Questions

1. Among the failure events, which is the most serious and may cause data loss?

   A. The loss of an entire redo log-file group but no loss in any other group

   B. The loss of one member of each redo log-file group

   C. The failure of the ARC*n* background process

   D. The failure of the LGWR background process

2. When the database is in ARCHIVELOG mode, database recovery is possible up to which event or time?

   A. The last redo log file switch

   B. The last checkpoint position

   C. The last commit

   D. The last incremental backup using RMAN

3. Which is a true statement regarding image copies and backup sets.

   A. An image copy stores one data file per image copy, and a backup set can store many data files in a single file.

   B. An image copy stores one data file per image copy, and a backup set consists of one file per data file backed up.

   C. Both image copies and backup sets use a single file to store all objects to be backed up.

   D. A backup set stores each data file in its own backup file, but an image copy places all data files into a single output file.

4. Which of the following is not a step in configuring your database to archive redo log files?

   A. Place the database in ARCHIVELOG mode.

   B. Multiplex the online redo log files.

   C. Specify a destination for archived redo log files.

   D. Specify a naming convention for your archived redo log files.

5. Why are online backups known as inconsistent backups?

A. Because not all control files are synchronized to the same SCN until the database is shut down

B. Because both committed and uncommitted transactions are included in a backup when the database is online

C. Because a database failure while an online backup is in progress can leave the database in an inconsistent state

D. Because online backups make copies of data files while they are not consistent with the control file

6. Which of the following initialization parameters specifies the location where the control file trace backup is sent?

A. DIAGNOSTIC_DEST

B. BACKGROUND_DUMP_DEST

C. LOG_ARCHIVE_DEST

D. CORE_DUMP_DEST

7. Which of the following pieces of information is not available in the control file?

A. Instance name

B. Database name

C. Tablespace names

D. Log sequence number

8. Which statement adds a member /logs/redo22.log to redo log-file group 2?

A. ALTER DATABASE ADD LOGFILE '/logs/redo22.log' TO GROUP 2;

B. ALTER DATABASE ADD LOGFILE MEMBER '/logs/redo22.log' TO GROUP 2;

C. ALTER DATABASE ADD MEMBER '/logs/redo22.log' TO GROUP 2;

D. ALTER DATABASE ADD LOGFILE '/logs/redo22.log';

9. To place the database into ARCHIVELOG mode, in which state must you start the database?

A. MOUNT

B. NOMOUNT

C. OPEN

D. SHUTDOWN

E. Any of the above

10. Which of the following substitution-variable formats are always required for specifying the names of the archived redo log files? Choose all that apply.

    A. %d

    B. %s

    C. %r

    D. %t

11. Which of the following initialization parameters controls the mean time to recover the database, in seconds, after an instance failure?

    A. FAST_START_IO_TARGET

    B. LOG_CHECKPOINT_TIMEOUT

    C. FAST_START_MTTR_TARGET

    D. MTTR_TARGET_ADVICE

    E. FAST_START_TARGET_MTTR

12. Identify the statement that is not true regarding the loss of a control file.

    A. A damaged control file can be repaired by using one of the remaining undamaged control files, assuming there are at least two copies of the control file.

    B. The missing or damaged control file can be replaced while the instance is still active.

    C. You can temporarily run the instance with one fewer control file, as long as you remove one of the references to the missing control file in the spfile or init.ora file.

    D. An instance typically fails when one of the multiplexed control files is lost or damaged.

13. Which failures can be detected by the Data Recovery Advisor, which then provides repair recommendations? Choose all that apply.

    A. Instance failure

    B. Accidental deletion of a data file

    C. Disk containing one redo log member is offline

    D. User accidentally dropped a table

14. The instance can still be started even if some data files are missing; this rule does not apply to which tablespaces? (Choose all that apply.)

    A. USERS

    B. SYSTEM

    C. TEMP

    D. SYSAUX

    E. UNDO

15. Select the statement that is *not* true regarding media failure. A media failure occurs when:

   A. The network card on the server fails.

   B. The DBA accidentally deletes one of the data files for the SYSTEM tablespace.

   C. There is a head crash on all physical drives in the RAID controller box.

   D. A corrupted track on a CD containing a read-only tablespace causes a query to fail.

16. Choose the correct statement about the Data Recovery Advisor.

   A. The Data Recovery Advisor is a standalone tool.

   B. The Data Recovery Advisor does not support RAC databases.

   C. The CHANGE FAILURE command can be used in a SQL*Plus session.

   D. The REPAIR FAILURE command works only after LIST FAILURE.

17. Place the following events or actions leading up to and during instance recovery in the correct order.

   1. The database is opened and available.

   2. Oracle uses undo segments in the undo tablespace to roll back uncommitted transactions.

   3. The DBA issues the STARTUP command at the SQL*Plus prompt.

   4. Oracle applies the information in the online redo log files to the data files.

   A. 4, 3, 2, 1

   B. 3, 4, 1, 2

   C. 2, 1, 3, 4

   D. 2, 1, 4, 3

   E. 3, 2, 4, 1

   F. 3, 4, 2, 1

18. You've noticed that when an instance crashes, it takes a long time to start up the database. Which advisor can be used to tune this situation?

   A. The Undo Advisor

   B. The SQL Tuning Advisor

   C. The Database Tuning Advisor

   D. The MTTR Advisor

   E. The Instance Tuning Advisor

19. In ARCHIVELOG mode, the loss of a data file for any tablespace other than the SYSTEM or UNDO tablespace affects which objects in the database?

A. The loss affects only objects whose extents reside in the lost data file.

B. The loss affects only the objects in the affected tablespace, and work can continue in other tablespaces.

C. The loss will not abort the instance but will prevent other transactions in any tablespace other than SYSTEM or UNDO until the affected tablespace is recovered.

D. The loss affects only those users whose default tablespace contains the lost or damaged data file.

20. Which of the following conditions prevents the instance from progressing through the NOMOUNT, MOUNT, and OPEN states?

A. One of the redo log-file groups is missing a member.

B. The instance was previously shut down uncleanly with SHUTDOWN ABORT.

C. Either the spfile or init.ora file is missing.

D. One of the five multiplexed control files is damaged.

E. The USERS tablespace is offline, with one of its data files deleted.

Chapter

16

Controlling Resources and Jobs

ORACLE DATABASE 12*c*: OCA EXAM OBJECTIVES COVERED IN THIS CHAPTER:

✓ **Managing Resources Using Database Resource Manager**

- ※ Configure the Database Resource Manager.
- ※ Access and create resource plans.
- ※ Monitor the Resource Manager.

✓ **Automating Tasks by Using Oracle Scheduler**

- ※ Use Oracle Scheduler to simplify management tasks.
- ※ Use job chains to perform a series of related tasks.
- ※ Use Scheduler jobs on remote systems.
- ※ Use advanced Scheduler on remote systems.

Hardware resources can be shared and divided up in Oracle Database 12c using various components including resource consumer groups, resource plans, and resource plan directives.

Tasks are automated within Oracle Database 12c using the Oracle Scheduler, which is like the Windows Task Scheduler or cron jobs in Linux or Unix. The Scheduler will execute tasks automatically within the general scope of the functionality of an Oracle database.

This chapter focuses on configuring, accessing, using, and monitoring resources inside the Oracle Resource Manager components; basic scheduling; and some specialized scheduling. You will also learn about specialized scheduling functionality, which includes job chaining, working with remote systems, and setting priorities.

Resource Management with the Resource Manager

The Oracle Database 12c Resource Manager allows the workload on a database to be managed from within the database as opposed to outside the database from the operating system. The process of managing the resources in this way is called workload management—for example, where a database servicing a website needs small but fast operations to run during the day, but will need to process much larger transactions after hours when batch processing and reporting.

Resource management inside an Oracle database can be more effective than using the operating system, which tends to allocate processing on a generic basis; the Oracle Resource Manager is more precise with respect to Oracle Database 12c.

Functions of the Resource Manager

The Oracle Database 12c Resource Manager can manage the sharing of hardware resources from a database requirements perspective, where sessions (processes) within Oracle would benefit by being managed differently depending on the type and function of the session. The Resource Manager performs the following types of functions within Oracle:

- Gives specific sessions a required CPU allocation regardless of the load, to make sure that critical processing completes.

- Can allocate specific percentages of CPU time to different users and applications. For example, backups must complete within available time windows.

- Limits parallel processing, which is important because parallel processing can spread across and occupy all the processing power on a multiple-node Oracle RAC database, which can completely dominate a system and lock out other essential competing processing.

- Assigns processing priorities.

- Sets maximum limits of active sessions for groups of users.

- Records resource sharing statistics in V\$RSRC_ and GV\$RSRC_* (Oracle RAC) views.

- Runaway Sessions Management monitors limits on CPU use, I/O, buffer operations, and execution time. Runaway sessions can also be automatically terminated or passed to another resource consumer group, which allows processing to complete but with much less resource consumption.

- Controls execution of operations that, according to the optimizer, will exceed limitations.

- Limits session idle times, especially blocking sessions. For example, someone leaving an uncommitted transaction in an open window and going out for lunch.

- Resource plans that apply to different requirements can be changed manually or within the Oracle Scheduler, and with the database online.

Understanding Resource Manager Components

The Resource Manager consists of a number of components, each of which performs a specific function:

- *Resource consumer groups* put users together based on CPU requirements.

- *Resource plans* allocate resources to resource consumer groups. Subplans are assigned to plans to give subset allocation capabilities within a plan.

- *Resource plan directives* connect consumer groups and plans.

- *Resource allocation methods* apply varying CPU percentage allocations to consumer groups and their associated plans.

The functions of the various components of the Resource Manager are as shown in Figure 16.1.

The Resource Manager and its various components can be administered from Oracle Database 12*c* using two built-in PL/SQL packages called DBMS_RESOURCE_MANAGER and DBMS_RESOURCE_MANAGER_PRIVS. They also can be managed using OEM Cloud Control. Figure 16.2 shows the introduction screen when the Resource Manager menu is invoked.

Consumer Groups

Consumer groups or resource consumer groups are used to group user sessions together so that the different groups can be assigned different processing requirements. Therefore, daytime processing on a website-based Online Transaction Processing (OLTP) database could have a group that allows high CPU use, which cuts off most processing activity to a reporting or data warehousing group. At night, OLTP CPU resource requirements are lower, and that allows reporting and heavy I/O activity to dominate CPU cycles. This change can be performed automatically in an Oracle Scheduler process or in its simplest way, manually using an ALTER SYSTEM command on the resource_manager_plan Oracle Database parameter.

FIGURE 16.1 Resource Manager components and their functions

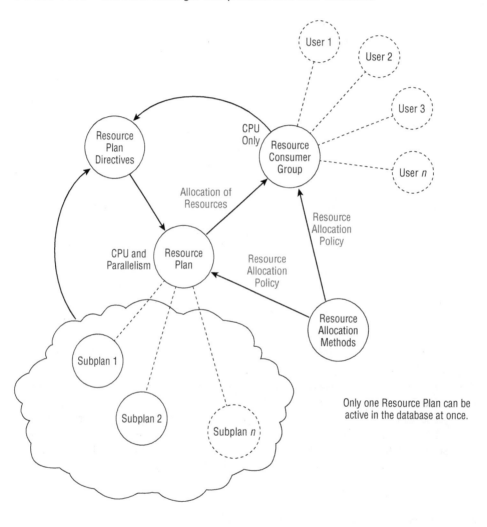

There are other more detailed methods of switching resource consumer groups, such as switching groups for specific sessions, which will be covered later in this chapter.

FIGURE 16.2   OEM – The Getting Started with Resource Manager screen

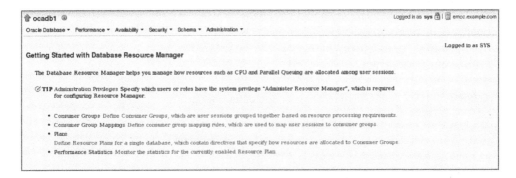

When a session connects to a database, it connects as part of the currently set resource consumer group, and thus the amount of resources it can use is determined by that current consumer group; this is in addition to the consumer groups that can be created by DBAs.

Figure 16.3 shows the Consumer Groups screen from OEM Cloud Control. Here you can edit or delete existing consumer groups, and add new consumer groups.

FIGURE 16.3   OEM – The Consumer Groups screen

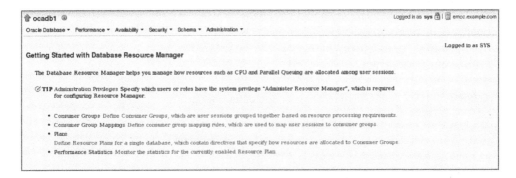

Resource Plans, Subplans, and Plan Directives

A resource plan includes possible subplans, plan directives, and consumer groups that are referenced by plan directives. Resource plan directives contain resource allocations such as CPU percentages and parallelism limitations. The directives are assigned to plans, which are in turn grouped into groups of users (resource consumer groups), all as shown in Figure 16.1.

The result is a parent-to-child relationship between plan and subplan (subplans apply vary-ing directives within a plan), as well as a parent-to-child relationship between a plan and its defined plan directives. It is, therefore, implied that a plan can have more than one directive, but only one directive can be allocated at once.

So, an active resource plan will have each of its plan directives allocate resources for different consumer groups, as shown in Figure 16.4.

FIGURE 16.4   Plans, plan directives, and consumer groups

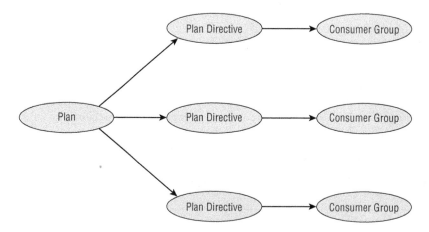

It is important to note that a group can use more resources than it is allocated as long as it does not take away resources from another group with higher priority.

Figure 16.5 shows the relationships between plans, subplans, and consumer groups (the objects that consume the allocated resources). Note that a plan can contain both consumer groups and other subplans, where the subplans further divide resources.

In Figure 16.6, the process is taken a little further, where specific percentages (such as CPU utilization) are assigned to plans, subplans, and consumer groups. As progress is made down through the levels from left to right, each percentage divides up the percentage passed from the parent. Also, note that with something like CPU use, leftover resources are passed down the stack as they are required, but also that areas above the current level can use high resource values when the child resource does not need all resources allocated.

Resource Allocation Methods (Resource Types)

Resource allocation methods include the types of resources that can be allocated to con-sumer groups and plans, as well as the methods by which those resources are allocated. The various types of resources that can be allocated and altered are as follows:

CPU   CPU resources can be divided up into directives using the management (MGMT_Pn) and utilization (UTILIZATION_LIMIT) attributes. Resources can be allocated from 1 to 8 levels with level 8 being the lowest. By implication, the lowest level only takes resources within its limit when levels above do not need the resources. Also, resources can be passed from higher levels in the stack when the lower levels can utilize them.

FIGURE 16.5   Plans, subplans, and consumer groups

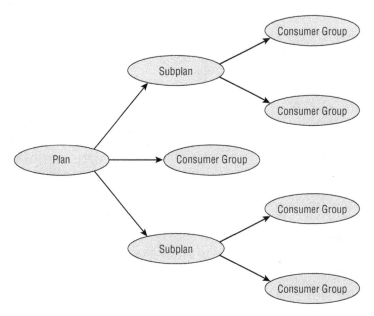

FIGURE 16.6   Simple resource allocation with plans and subplans

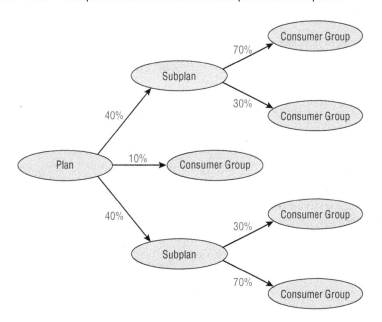

CPU resources get passed down the levels; but if a group or plan and a level have a specific utilization limit, that particular allocation will not go above the CPU utilization limit even when spare CPU resource capacity is available. The management attributes set the CPU values needed for a specific group or plan at a specific level, and the utilization limit will limit the maximum resources used regardless of how much is being used at higher priority levels.

Exadata I/O   This setting allows resource allocation for Exadata I/O only. I/O can be a very high consumer of CPU resources.

Parallel Execution Servers   Parallel execution is available in Oracle Database 12*c* and has been for years; however, one of the critical issues with parallel processing is uncontrolled use, usually as a result of misunderstanding how and when it can be used beneficially. In general, when Oracle interprets and executes a parallel operation, such as a query reading lots of data, the database starts separate specialized parallel processes to execute the operation. If too many processes are started at once, an operator can effectively swamp an entire multiple-node Oracle RAC database. For example, creating an uncontrolled parallel index on an empty table can drastically slow down all other sessions in a database, regardless of concurrency. Therefore, parallel processing sometimes has to be controlled at the database level. That can be done in a number of ways, one of which is to use the Resource Control Manager, which limits how much parallel processing is done by any particular session at any particular time.

The Degree of Parallelism Limit (PARALLEL_DEGREE_LIMIT_n) controls the maximum degree of parallel processing within a consumer group. In other words, if a query wants to execute on 32 parallel threads and the limit is 16, then that query will be able to work with only 16, not 32, degrees of parallelism.

The Parallel Server Limit (PARALLEL_SERVER_LIMIT) exerts a limitation on the parallel processing capacity of individual consumer groups.

Parallel Queue Timeout is applied when a database lacks the resources to execute a parallel statement, and it will be made to wait. The PARALLEL_QUEUE_TIMEOUT directive allows a processing request to wait until the timeout expires.

Runaway Queries   Sometimes a session can use up too many resources, including things like CPU, I/O, processing times, rollback, temporary sort space, and so on. Runaway queries can be detected and switched to other consumer groups with lower allocations, execution times can be limited, or SQL code can be cancelled and sessions can be terminated.

Active Session Pool with Queuing   This option can control the number of concurrent sessions that are active at a time within a resource consumer group.

Undo Pool   This option controls the amount of undo space that can be allocated for a transaction, limiting the amount and size of uncommitted transactions that can be maintained within a consumer group. Sometimes very large transactions can push a database to run out of undo space on disk and abort a transaction after a very long run, potentially wasting a lot of time.

Idle Time Limit   Idle sessions can be killed off as active sessions, and even blocking sessions can be controlled.

Configuring the Database Resource Manager

So far you have read about what can be done with the Database Resource Manager; the next step is to find out how to work with it.

Administration Privileges

Configuring the Resource Manager requires the ADMINISTER_RESOURCE_MANAGER privilege (granted through the DBA role), which gives execute privileges on all DBMS_RESOURCE_MANAGER procedures.

 DBMS_RESOURCE_MANAGER is a built-in Oracle Database package.

The DBMS_RESOURCE_MANAGER_PRIVS procedure is used to grant privileges to and from the DBMS_RESOURCE_MANAGER package; those procedures are listed in Table 16.1.

TABLE 16.1 DBMS_RESOURCE_MANAGER_PRIVS Procedures

Procedure	Description
GRANT_SWITCH_CONSUMER_GROUP	Grant resource consumer group switch
GRANT_SYSTEM_PRIVILEGE	Grant a system privilege
REVOKE_SWITCH_CONSUMER_GROUP	Revoke resource consumer group switch
REVOKE_SYSTEM_PRIVILEGE	System privilege revoke

When a user in a database called BOOKS is being examined, the following system privileges are available:

```
SQL> select * from dba_sys_privs where grantee='BOOKS';


GRANTEE    PRIVILEGE                               ADM COM
---------- --------------------------------------- --- ---
BOOKS      QUERY REWRITE                           NO  NO
BOOKS      UNLIMITED TABLESPACE                    NO  NO
```

If you grant the resource manager privilege to the BOOKS user, the result is shown in the form of the system privilege called ADMINISTER_RESOURCE_MANAGER:

```
BEGIN
DBMS_RESOURCE_MANAGER_PRIVS.GRANT_SYSTEM_PRIVILEGE
```

```
(GRANTEE_NAME=>'BOOKS',ADMIN_OPTION=>FALSE);
END;
/
```

PL/SQL procedure successfully completed.

```
SQL> select * from dba_sys_privs where grantee='BOOKS';
```

GRANTEE	PRIVILEGE	ADM	COM
BOOKS	QUERY REWRITE	NO	NO
BOOKS	ADMINISTER RESOURCE MANAGER	NO	NO
BOOKS	UNLIMITED TABLESPACE	NO	NO

The same privilege can then be revoked:

```
BEGIN
DBMS_RESOURCE_MANAGER_PRIVS.REVOKE_SYSTEM_PRIVILEGE
(REVOKEE_NAME=>'BOOKS');
END;
/
```

PL/SQL procedure successfully completed.

```
SQL> select * from dba_sys_privs where grantee='BOOKS';
```

GRANTEE	PRIVILEGE	ADM	COM
BOOKS	QUERY REWRITE	NO	NO
BOOKS	UNLIMITED TABLESPACE	NO	NO

```
SQL> grant ADMINISTER RESOURCE MANAGER to books;
```

Grant succeeded.

```
SQL> select * from dba_sys_privs where grantee='BOOKS';
```

GRANTEE	PRIVILEGE	ADM	COM
BOOKS	QUERY REWRITE	NO	NO
BOOKS	ADMINISTER RESOURCE MANAGER	NO	NO
BOOKS	UNLIMITED TABLESPACE	NO	NO

```
SQL> revoke ADMINISTER RESOURCE MANAGER from books;

Revoke succeeded.

SQL> select * from dba_sys_privs where grantee='BOOKS';

GRANTEE    PRIVILEGE                                ADM COM
---------- ---------------------------------------- --- ---
BOOKS      QUERY REWRITE                            NO  NO
BOOKS      UNLIMITED TABLESPACE                     NO  NO
```

According to the Oracle Database 12c manuals, the ADMINISTER RESOURCE MANAGER system privilege can be granted to roles, such as the DBA role— which is false. Additionally, the manuals clearly state that the ADMINIS- TER RESOURCE MANAGER system privilege is supported only when granted or revoked using the DBMS_RESOURCE_MANAGER_PRIVS procedure—which is also false. We have successfully granted and revoked the privilege using the GRANT and REVOKE commands, as shown in the following code. (However, this ability could change in a future Oracle patchset.)

Initial Resource Consumer Group

Two groups that are part of the default setup in Oracle cannot be removed or changed. They are

- The SYS_GROUP, which is the default setting for all SYS and SYSTEM use sessions. This group is essential for database maintenance.

- OTHER_GROUPS, which will be allocated to all sessions that have not been specifically allocated to a consumer group.

Mapping Rules and Priorities

Mapping rules are created between sessions and consumer groups, and priorities can be allocated to various mapping rules. A session gets an initial consumer group. A session can be switched to a different consumer group on the fly, depending on the circumstances. Also, different mapping rules can have different priorities; whereas a user connecting using a par- ticular consumer group can be overridden and have its consumer group switched. This is because another attribute changes the user's session to a higher priority.

Oracle has a built-in procedure that is used to manage consumer group mappings using name-value pairs, as in:

```
BEGIN
DBMS_RESOURCE_MANAGER.SET_CONSUMER_GROUP_MAPPING(
```

```
attribute=>'attrib'
,value=>'avalue'
,consumer_group=>'ETL_GROUP');
END;
/
```

The attributes can be a list of items including attributes that change behavior based on connected users, the service names users are connected to, and even the modules with which they are connecting to a database. Priorities are set for mapping groups using the following Oracle built-in procedure:

```
DBMS_RESOURCE_MANAGER.SET_CONSUMER_GROUP_MAPPING_PRI(
    explicit              IN NUMBER,
    oracle_user           IN NUMBER,
    service_name          IN NUMBER,
    client_os_user        IN NUMBER,
    client_program        IN NUMBER,
    client_machine        IN NUMBER,
    module_name           IN NUMBER,
    module_name_action    IN NUMBER,
    service_module        IN NUMBER,
    service_module_action IN NUMBER,
    client_id             IN NUMBER DEFAULT 11);
```

Each attribute is described in Table 16.2.

TABLE 16.2 Setting Consumer Mapping Privileges

Attribute	Description
Explicit	Explicit
oracle_user	Oracle user names
service_name	A service name
client_os_user	Username in the client operating system
client_program	Program running on the client
client_machine	Client machine

Attribute	Description
module_name	Application module
module_name_action	Application module and action
service_module	Service name plus application module
service/module_action	Service name, application module, and application mapping
client_id	The Client ID

Switching Consumer Groups

When a user or piece of software executes a process that overloads the CPU, quite often the session might have to be manually killed. One way to resolve this type of situation is to use the DBMS_RESOURCE_MANAGER procedures to switch a user's session to a different consumer group that perhaps limits CPU use to much less than 100 percent capacity. You can do this using either of the following two procedures:

- SWITCH_CONSUMER_GROUP_FOR_SESS uses a SID and SERIAL# combination as an ALTER SYSTEM KILL SESSION command, in order to move a session to a different consumer group.

- SWITCH_CONSUMER_GROUP_FOR_USER does the same thing, except that it switches all sessions for a specific user.

The SWITCH_CURRENT_CONSUMER_GROUP procedure inside the DBMS_SESSION package allows consumer groups to be switched.

Valued-based automatic consumer group switching is available when certain conditions are met, in order to automatically switch a session to a lower allocation consumer group where actions can be taken. Those actions can include dynamic consumer group switching, session termination, aborting a SQL statement, or even just logging information. A switch group and actions can be defined as part of a plan directive.

The privilege to grant and revoke switching of consumer groups can be authorized using the DBMS_RESOURCE_MANAGER package. The following commands grant and then revoke the switch privilege to and from a schema called CONCERTS:

```
BEGIN
DBMS_RESOURCE_MANAGER_PRIVS.GRANT_SWITCH_CONSUMER_GROUP(
grantee_name=>'CONCERTS'
,consumer_group=>'BATCH_GROUP'
,grant_option=>TRUE);
        DBMS_RESOURCE_MANAGER_PRIVS.REVOKE_SWITCH_CONSUMER_GROUP(
```

```
revokee_name=>'CONCERTS'
,consumer_group=>'BATCH_GROUP');
END;
/
```

Accessing and Creating Resource Plans

So far this chapter has covered the components of the Database Resource Manager, as well as the configuration of the Database Resource Manager. This section will go through the process of analyzing and using the stored procedures that are used to work with resource management in Oracle Database 12*c*.

Simple Resource Plans

There is a simple way to create a resource management plan and a more complex way. The simple method uses the following procedure:

```
DBMS_RESOURCE.CREATE_SIMPLE_PLAN();
```

The CREATE_SIMPLE_PLAN procedure only allows the CPU resource allocation method, using the default EMPHASIS CPU allocation policy, and each consumer group uses the default ROUND_ROBIN as a scheduling policy. A "round-robin queue" is a Unix term used to describe a process that allocates an equal amount of processing time to a number of concurrently running processes, where each process takes turns consuming a set amount of processing each time the round-robin process occurs. In a more complex model, the round-robin switching process can still allocate a chunk of time to each process one at a time, but the priorities of some processes can be higher than others; therefore, higher-priority processes simply get more processing time each time they are executed.

The CREATE_SIMPLE_PLAN procedure allows one procedure to create a simple setup very rapidly, defining one to eight consumer groups, each with a round-robin-like percentage of allocated CPU, as shown in Table 16.3.

TABLE 16.3 The CREATE_SIMPLE_PLAN Procedure

Parameter	Description
consumer_group1	Consumer group name
consumer_group2	Consumer group name
consumer_group3	Consumer group name

Parameter	Description
consumer_group4	Consumer group name
consumer_group5	Consumer group name
consumer_group6	Consumer group name
consumer_group7	Consumer group name
consumer_group8	OTHER_GROUPS includes all unmapped sessions
group1_percent	Resource % allocated to group
group2_percent	Resource % allocated to group
group3_percent	Resource % allocated to group
group4_percent	Resource % allocated to group
group5_percent	Resource % allocated to group
group6_percent	Resource % allocated to group
group7_percent	Resource % allocated to group
group8_percent	Resource % allocated to group
simple_plan	Resource plan name

A simple execution of the CREATE_SIMPLE_PLAN procedure would look something like this:

```
BEGIN
DBMS_RESOURCE_MANAGER.CREATE_SIMPLE_PLAN(
SIMPLE_PLAN=>'MYSIMPLEPLAN',CONSUMER_GROUP1=>'GROUP1'
,GROUP1_PERCENT=>50,CONSUMER_GROUP2=>'GROUP2'
,GROUP2_PERCENT=>30,CONSUMER_GROUP3=>'GROUP3'
,GROUP3_PERCENT=>20);
END;
/
```

Or, you could run the previous code nicely formatted and much more easily read by embedding it into a PL/SQL BEGIN END block:

```
BEGIN
        DBMS_RESOURCE_MANAGER.CREATE_SIMPLE_PLAN
```

```
        (
                SIMPLE_PLAN=>'MYSIMPLEPLAN'
              , CONSUMER_GROUP1=>'GROUP1',GROUP1_PERCENT=>50
              , CONSUMER_GROUP2=>'GROUP2',GROUP2_PERCENT=>30
              , CONSUMER_GROUP3=>'GROUP3',GROUP3_PERCENT=>20
        );
END;
/
```

As you see, it is possible to rapidly and easily create a simple plan, building a very simplistic resource plan using multiple groups where each group has a specific percentage of CPU allocated to it. Plans can also be much more complex, as you already know from previous information in this chapter. In order to create the more complex plans, you should follow these steps:

1. Create the pending area.
2. Create the consumer groups.
3. Create the session-to-consumer group mappings.
4. Create a complex resource plan.
5. Add the plan directives.
6. Validate and submit the pending area.

The next few sections will explain this set of steps.

Working with the Pending Area

A database cannot have a resource plan running that is incorrectly configured—the consequences could cause huge imbalances in a database system. To avoid any such problems, a pending area is used. The pending area is a staging area where resource plans are built before they are submitted to the database. It is essentially a process of verification where a new plan is prepared and verified before it replaces the existing resource management plan. The pending area is created as follows:

```
SQL> exec DBMS_RESOURCE_MANAGER.CREATE_PENDING_AREA();
```

The pending area is exclusive in that only one session can use the pending area at any one time, which means that it must be cleared before another session can create the pending area again. Only one can be used at a time because only one resource plan is used at a time.

After consumer groups, plans and anything else that has been created in the pending area will be submitted to the database—but first you must validate the pending area using the VALIDATE_PENDING_AREA procedure. Then you must submit the SUBMIT_PENDING_AREA procedure. Additionally, the pending area can be simply cleared out to start fresh using the CLEAR_PENDING_AREA procedure. The pending area validation procedure checks all the obvious semantic details on consumer resource management, which cannot otherwise be checked by individual DBMS_RESOURCE_MANAGER procedural details at the syntax level. The validation procedure checks for the following:

- That there are no loops
- That the plans, groups, and directives used actually exist
- That a plan's directives point to plans or groups
- That percentage sums aggregate to 100 percent
- That subplans are removed before top-level plans
- That the limit of 28 for groups and plan children is not exceeded
- That plans and groups do not have duplicate names
- That the OTHER_GROUPS group has an active plan
- That various other very detailed parameter checks are performed

Creating Resource Consumer Groups

A resource consumer group is created using the CREATE _CONSUMER_GROUP procedure, which has parameters as shown in Table 16.4.

TABLE 16.4   The CREATE_CONSUMER_GROUP Procedure

Parameter	Description
consumer_group	Consumer group
mgmt_mth	Named CPU allocation method
Category	Category for Exadata I/O purposes only

Here are a number of examples that clear and create the pending area, grant switch privileges, validate and submit the pending area, and finally set the initial consumer group called OLTP.

Some new Oracle schema/usernames along with specific privileges are needed first:

```
SQL> create user books identified by books;
SQL> create user concerts identified by concerts;
SQL> grant connect,resource to books,concerts;

BEGIN
DBMS_RESOURCE_MANAGER_PRIVS.GRANT_SYSTEM_PRIVILEGE
(GRANTEE_NAME=>'CONCERTS',ADMIN_OPTION=>FALSE);
DBMS_RESOURCE_MANAGER_PRIVS.GRANT_SYSTEM_PRIVILEGE
```

```
(GRANTEE_NAME=>'BOOKS',ADMIN_OPTION=>FALSE);
END;
/
```

Next is a single consumer group:

```
BEGIN
dbms_resource_manager.clear_pending_area();
dbms_resource_manager.create_pending_area();
dbms_resource_manager.create_consumer_group
(consumer_group=>'OLTP_GROUP');
dbms_resource_manager.validate_pending_area();
dbms_resource_manager.submit_pending_area();
END;
/
```

This code grants the switching privileges:

```
BEGIN
dbms_resource_manager.clear_pending_area();
dbms_resource_manager.create_pending_area();
dbms_resource_manager_privs.grant_switch_consumer_group
('CONCERTS', 'OLTP_GROUP', false);
dbms_resource_manager_privs.grant_switch_consumer_group
('BOOKS', 'OLTP_GROUP', false);
dbms_resource_manager.set_initial_consumer_group
('CONCERTS', 'OLTP_GROUP');
dbms_resource_manager.set_initial_consumer_group
('BOOKS', 'OLTP_GROUP');
dbms_resource_manager.validate_pending_area();
dbms_resource_manager.submit_pending_area();
END;
/
```

Session-to-consumer group mappings can be created using the SET_CONSUMER_GROUP_
MAPPING procedure and the SET_CONSUMER_GROUP_MAPPING_PRI procedure. The objective of

session mappings is to assign sessions to specific groups, as well as to assign varying priority levels to sessions that have various attributes, as described in Table 16.2.

Creating Complex Resource Plans

As opposed to the CREATE_SIMPLE_PLAN procedure, a complex resource plan is created using the CREATE_PLAN procedure utilizing parameters as shown in Table 16.5.

TABLE 16.5 The CREATE_PLAN Procedure

Parameter	Description
active_sess_pool_mth	ACTIVE_SESS_POOL_ABSOLUTE is the only available method, limiting the number of active sessions to 1.
parallel_degree_limit_mth	PARALLEL_DEGREE_LIMIT_ABSOLUTE limits the degree of parallelism.
queueing_mth	FIFO_TIMEOUT for queuing resources, controlling the order of queued inactive sessions.
mgmt_mth	General resource allocation amounts to a group or subplan. 1) EMPHASIS: distributes I/O to groups in multilevel plans. 2) RATIO: distributes I/O in single-level plans.
sub_plan	Not for use as a top plan if TRUE (subplans only).

Plans cannot be created yet because they have to be created at the same time as the plan directives. So, next we will look at resource plan directives followed by some examples of plans.

You can also use OEM Cloud Control to create resource plans. The Resource Plans screen is shown in Figure 16.7. This screen lists the resource plans that are available in the database.

By clicking the Create button, you can create a new resource plan. The initial screen for creating a new resource plan is shown in Figure 16.8

Implementing Resource Plan Directives

Plan directives are created using the CREATE_PLAN_DIRECTIVE procedure, including some of the less obscure parameters as shown in Table 16.6.

FIGURE 16.7   OEM – The Resource Plans screen

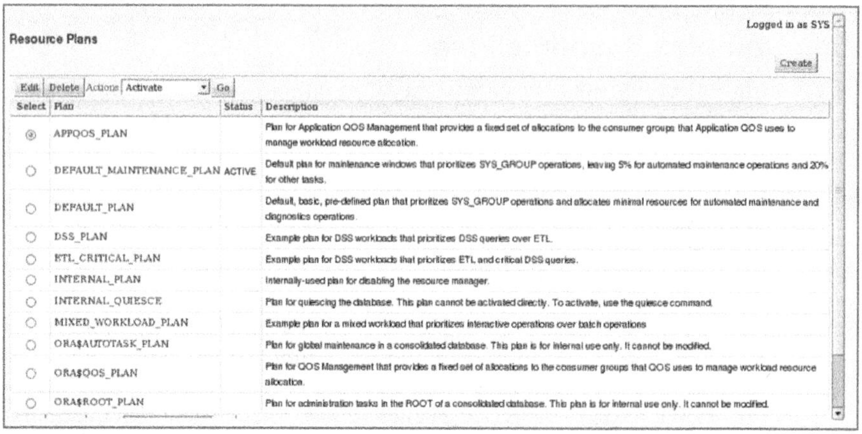

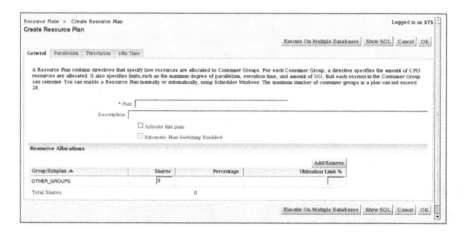

FIGURE 16.8   OEM – The Create Resource Plan screen

TABLE 16.6   The `CREATE_PLAN_DIRECTIVE` Procedure

Attribute	Description
group_or_subplan	Group or subplan name
active_sess_pool_p1	Maximum active sessions

Attribute	Description
parallel_degree_limit_p1	Limit on degree of parallelism
switch_group	Group to switch to
switch_time	CPU switch time
undo_pool	Undo limitation
max_idle_time	Idle time
max_idle_blocker_time	Block session idle time
mgmt_p1-8	General resource allocation amounts to a group or subplan
	1) EMPHASIS: distributes I/O to groups in multi-level plans
	2) RATIO: distributes I/O in single-level plans
parallel_queue_timeout	Query in group parallel statement queue before being timed out
parallel_server_limit	Parallel server limit that overrides utilization limit

All of the details are placed into the Resource Manager during the stage when plan directives are created. You can see the real meat and learn how resource management works by examining the following code. Begin with the pending area; follow with the OLTP plan and then the plan directives.

```
BEGIN
dbms_resource_manager.clear_pending_area();
dbms_resource_manager.create_pending_area();
dbms_resource_manager.create_plan(plan=>'OLTP_PLAN');
dbms_resource_manager.create_plan_directive(
plan => 'OLTP_PLAN'
,group_or_subplan => 'OLTP_GROUP',cpu_p1 => 80
, cpu_p2 => 40, cpu_p3 => 20, cpu_p4 => 10,cpu_p5 => 0
, cpu_p6 => 0, cpu_p7 => 0, cpu_p8 => 0
,parallel_degree_limit_p1 => 0);
dbms_resource_manager.create_plan_directive(
plan => 'OLTP_PLAN'
```

```
,group_or_subplan => 'SYS_GROUP',cpu_p1 => 10
, cpu_p2 => 25, cpu_p3 => 35, cpu_p4 => 40,cpu_p5 => 0
, cpu_p6 => 0, cpu_p7 => 0, cpu_p8 => 0
,parallel_degree_limit_p1 => 0);
dbms_resource_manager.create_plan_directive(
plan => 'OLTP_PLAN'
,group_or_subplan => 'BATCH_GROUP',cpu_p1 => 0
, cpu_p2 => 10, cpu_p3 => 10, cpu_p4 => 10,cpu_p5 => 0
, cpu_p6 => 0, cpu_p7 => 0, cpu_p8 => 0
,parallel_degree_limit_p1 => 0);
dbms_resource_manager.create_plan_directive(
plan => 'OLTP_PLAN'
,group_or_subplan => 'OTHER_GROUPS',cpu_p1 => 5
, cpu_p2 => 0, cpu_p3 => 0, cpu_p4 => 0,cpu_p5 => 0
, cpu_p6 => 0, cpu_p7 => 0, cpu_p8 => 0
,parallel_degree_limit_p1 => 0);
dbms_resource_manager.validate_pending_area();
dbms_resource_manager.submit_pending_area();
END;
/
```

Updating and Deleting Resources

Consumer groups, plans, and plan directives can be updated and deleted with the procedures described in this section. It makes sense to describe these various steps in the order in which they should be deleted: child objects first. Updates can be performed in any sequence as long as any dependencies are handled.

Updating and Deleting Plan Directives

You can update the plan directives using the following procedure. (Note that only the PLAN and GROUP_OR_SUBPLAN parameters must be specified in addition to one or more changes.)

```
DBMS_RESOURCE_MANAGER.UPDATE_PLAN_DIRECTIVE
(
    plan                          IN VARCHAR2,
    group_or_subplan              IN VARCHAR2,
    new_comment                   IN VARCHAR2 DEFAULT NULL,
    new_active_sess_pool_p1       IN NUMBER   DEFAULT NULL,
    new_queueing_p1               IN NUMBER   DEFAULT NULL,
    new_parallel_degree_limit_p1  IN NUMBER   DEFAULT NULL,
    new_switch_group              IN VARCHAR2 DEFAULT NULL,
    new_switch_time               IN NUMBER   DEFAULT NULL,
```

```
new_switch_estimate            IN BOOLEAN  DEFAULT FALSE,
new_max_est_exec_time          IN NUMBER   DEFAULT NULL,
new_undo_pool                  IN NUMBER   DEFAULT NULL,
new_max_idle_time              IN NUMBER   DEFAULT NULL,
new_max_idle_blocker_time      IN NUMBER   DEFAULT NULL,
new_mgmt_p1                    IN NUMBER   DEFAULT NULL,
new_mgmt_p2                    IN NUMBER   DEFAULT NULL,
new_mgmt_p3                    IN NUMBER   DEFAULT NULL,
new_mgmt_p4                    IN NUMBER   DEFAULT NULL,
new_mgmt_p5                    IN NUMBER   DEFAULT NULL,
new_mgmt_p6                    IN NUMBER   DEFAULT NULL,
new_mgmt_p7                    IN NUMBER   DEFAULT NULL,
new_mgmt_p8                    IN NUMBER   DEFAULT NULL,
new_switch_io_megabytes        IN NUMBER   DEFAULT NULL,
new_switch_io_reqs             IN NUMBER   DEFAULT NULL,
new_switch_for_call            IN BOOLEAN  DEFAULT NULL,
new_max_utilization_limit      IN NUMBER   DEFAULT NULL,
new_parallel_target_percentage IN NUMBER   DEFAULT NULL,
new parallel_queue_timeout     IN NUMBER   DEFAULT NULL,
new_parallel_server_limit      IN NUMBER   DEFAULT NULL,
new_utilization_limit          IN NUMBER   DEFAULT NULL,
new_switch_io_logical          IN NUMBER   DEFAULT NULL,
new_switch_elapsed_time        IN NUMBER   DEFAULT NULL,
new_shares                     IN NUMBER   DEFAULT NULL,
new_parallel_stmt_critical     IN VARCHAR2 DEFAULT NULL
);
```

Executing a procedure such as UPDATE_PLAN_DIRECTIVE with only NAME and GROUP_OR_SUBPLAN specified would change nothing.

Delete a plan directive as follows:

```
DBMS_RESOURCE_MANAGER.DELETE_PLAN_DIRECTIVE
(
    plan              IN VARCHAR2,
    group_or_subplan  IN VARCHAR2
);
```

When deleting a plan directive, all you need are the names of the plan and the group or subplan.

Updating and Deleting Resource Plans

Updating and deleting a plan is the next stage, which uses the UPDATE_PLAN procedure:

```
DBMS_RESOURCE_MANAGER.UPDATE_PLAN
(
    plan                            IN VARCHAR2,
    new_comment                     IN VARCHAR2 DEFAULT NULL,
    new_active_sess_pool_mth        IN VARCHAR2 DEFAULT NULL,
    new_parallel_degree_limit_mth   IN VARCHAR2 DEFAULT NULL,
    new_queueing_mth                IN VARCHAR2 DEFAULT NULL,
    new_mgmt_mth                    IN VARCHAR2 DEFAULT NULL,
    new_sub_plan                    IN BOOLEAN DEFAULT FALSE
);
```

And the DELETE_PLAN procedure:

```
DBMS_RESOURCE_MANAGER.DELETE_PLAN(plan IN VARCHAR2);
```

A special case of the DELETE_PLAN procedure is the DELETE_PLAN_CASCADE procedure, which will remove the plan and all its descendants, including plan, plan directives, subplans, and consumer groups:

```
DBMS_RESOURCE_MANAGER.DELETE_PLAN_CASCADE(plan IN VARCHAR2);
```

 Deletion of the active plan is not permitted.

Updating and Deleting Consumer Groups

Update a consumer group with the following procedure, where parameters that are not specified are not changed because all but the CONSUMER_GROUP name parameter are defaulted to null (DEFAULT NULL):

```
DBMS_RESOURCE_MANAGER.UPDATE_CONSUMER_GROUP
(
    consumer_group  IN VARCHAR2,
    new_comment     IN VARCHAR2 DEFAULT NULL,
    new_cpu_mth     IN VARCHAR2 DEFAULT NULL,
    new_mgmt_mth    IN VARCHAR2 DEFAULT NULL,
    new_category    IN VARCHAR2 DEFAULT NULL
);
```

Deleting a consumer group only requires the name of the consumer group to be removed:

```
DBMS_RESOURCE_MANAGER.DELETE_CONSUMER_GROUP (
    consumer_group IN VARCHAR2);
```

It is important to note that a consumer group cannot be deleted if it is referenced by any child objects, such as a plan directive; orphaned plan directives would be the result. Delete the plan and the consumer group as shown here:

```
SQL> select plan,status from DBA_RSRC_PLANS order by plan;
SQL> select consumer_group,status
        from DBA_RSRC_CONSUMER_GROUPS
        order by consumer_group;
BEGIN
        dbms_resource_manager.clear_pending_area();
        dbms_resource_manager.create_pending_area();
        dbms_resource_manager.delete_plan(plan=>'OLTP_PLAN');
        dbms_resource_manager.delete_consumer_group
                (consumer_group=>'OLTP_GROUP');
        dbms_resource_manager.validate_pending_area();
        dbms_resource_manager.submit_pending_area();
END;
/
```

Monitoring the Resource Manager

Monitoring the Resource Manager involves using specific database metadata (DBA_) and performance (V$_) views in order to determine how the Resource Manager is configured in an Oracle Database 12c. The easiest way to find the exact names for these types of views is to use the following query:

```
select table_name from dictionary
where table_name like 'DBA_RSRC%' order by 1;
```

These are the views that are most interesting:

```
DBA_RSRC_CONSUMER_GROUPS
DBA_RSRC_PLANS
DBA_RSRC_PLAN_DIRECTIVES
```

And these views are less interesting:

```
DBA_RSRC_CONSUMER_GROUP_PRIVS
DBA_RSRC_GROUP_MAPPINGS
```

```
DBA_RSRC_MANAGER_SYSTEM_PRIVS
DBA_RSRC_MAPPING_PRIORITY
```

 V$ views are also available in Oracle Database 12*c*, but they are generally used for monitoring performance as opposed to the DBA_ views, which are used for monitoring metadata.

The following queries can be used to work with simple additions and deletions of consumer groups, plans, and directives as shown in the previous two sections:

```
SQL> select plan,status from DBA_RSRC_PLANS order by plan;

PLAN                             STATUS
------------------------------   -------------------------

APPQOS_PLAN
DEFAULT_MAINTENANCE_PLAN
DEFAULT_PLAN
DSS_PLAN
ETL_CRITICAL_PLAN
INTERNAL_PLAN
INTERNAL_QUIESCE
MIXED_WORKLOAD_PLAN
ORA$AUTOTASK_PLAN
ORA$QOS_PLAN
ORA$ROOT_PLAN


SQL> select distinct plan from DBA_RSRC_PLAN_DIRECTIVES order by plan;

PLAN
------------------------------

APPQOS_PLAN
DEFAULT_MAINTENANCE_PLAN
DEFAULT_PLAN
DSS_PLAN
ETL_CRITICAL_PLAN
INTERNAL_PLAN
INTERNAL_QUIESCE
MIXED_WORKLOAD_PLAN
ORA$AUTOTASK_PLAN
ORA$QOS_PLAN
ORA$ROOT_PLAN
```

```
SQL> select consumer_group,status from DBA_RSRC_CONSUMER_GROUPS order by
consumer_group;

CONSUMER_GROUP                       STATUS
-----------------------------        -----------------------
BATCH_GROUP
DEFAULT_CONSUMER_GROUP
DSS_CRITICAL_GROUP
DSS_GROUP
ETL_GROUP
INTERACTIVE_GROUP
LOW_GROUP
ORA$APPQOS_0
ORA$APPQOS_1
ORA$APPQOS_2
ORA$APPQOS_3
ORA$APPQOS_4
ORA$APPQOS_5
ORA$APPQOS_6
ORA$APPQOS_7
ORA$AUTOTASK
OTHER_GROUPS
SYS_GROUP
```

You can also use OEM Cloud Control to monitor resource plans. Figure 16.9 shows the Resource Manager Statistics screen.

FIGURE 16.9   OEM – The Resource Manager Statistics screen

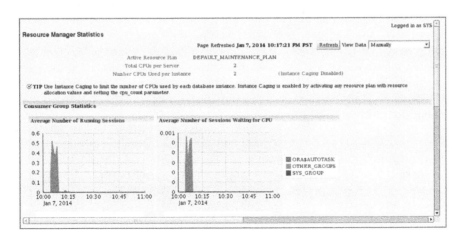

Task Automation with Oracle Scheduler

The Oracle Scheduler allows scheduled tasks (jobs) to be executed inside Oracle Database 12*c*, independent of the platform on which the database is running. The DBMS_SCHEDULER package contains all the procedures required to implement automated scheduling and the execution of tasks within a database.

Scheduled objects can be comprised of PL/SQL blocks (named or unnamed) or Java procedures inside Oracle. Objects can even run on remote databases; they can also be compiled executables that exist outside of the database.

Scheduling can occur as a result of time settings executing a job at a specific time, executing once, or repeating. Jobs can also be triggered by the Scheduler based on an event that has occurred inside the database, or even based on a dependency based on something like the completion of a previous task.

The Scheduler can also be used to execute jobs based on priorities, even grouping sets of jobs into groups called job classes. Individual jobs or classes of jobs are given prioritized access to resources, whereas critical jobs are allowed to use more hardware resources.

Oracle Database 12*c* can also monitor the Oracle Scheduler and jobs using various sources of information including DBA_ metadata views and V$ performance views.

> Using the DBMS_JOBS package and its associated procedures, processes, and views is an outdated method of managing scheduled processing inside Oracle databases. DBMS_JOBS is retained for backward compatibility.

Scheduler Architecture

The Oracle Job Scheduler contains a number of distinct parts and functions, including the job table, the coordinator process, the way in which jobs are executed, and the process that occurs after jobs have completed execution. Figure 16.10 shows the structure of the Oracle Database 12*c* Scheduler in general. The Job Coordinator determines when and where connections can trigger and execute jobs between multiple slave processes.

The job table contains all the scheduled jobs, visually available from the DBA_SCHEDULER_JOBS view. The Job Coordinator is a process that starts, stops, and manages the job slave processes, which execute the jobs. The following example shows two scheduled jobs (ora_cjq0_TESTSI and ora_cjq1_TESTSI), running on a database called TESTSI, where that database is running on a server called 64bit1:

```
oracle@64bit1.localdomain:[/home/oracle]
$ ps -ef | grep ora_cj | grep -v grep
oracle     6165     1  0 04:22 ?        00:00:00 ora_cjq0_TESTSI
oracle     6172     1  0 04:22 ?        00:00:00 ora_cjq1_TESTSI
```

FIGURE 16.10   The Oracle Database 12*c* Scheduler architecture

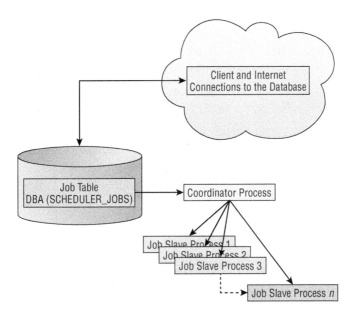

When jobs finish processing, the results are logged into the DBA_SCHEDULER_JOBS meta-data view, which indicates the completion status of the jobs and other information, such as if and when the job should be run again.

Granting Scheduler Privileges

Schedule administration tasks require the SCHEDULER_ADMIN role, by default part of the DBA role as granted to the SYS and SYSTEM users. The SCHEDULER_ADMIN privilege can be granted as follows:

```
GRANT SCHEDULER_ADMIN TO <user>;
```

The system privileges granted to the SCHEDULER_ADMIN role are listed here:

```
SQL> select grantee,privilege from dba_sys_privs where grantee='SCHEDULER_ADMIN';

GRANTEE               PRIVILEGE
------------------    ----------------------------------------
SCHEDULER_ADMIN       CREATE CREDENTIAL
SCHEDULER_ADMIN       CREATE ANY JOB
SCHEDULER_ADMIN       CREATE ANY CREDENTIAL
SCHEDULER_ADMIN       EXECUTE ANY CLASS
SCHEDULER_ADMIN       EXECUTE ANY PROGRAM
SCHEDULER_ADMIN       CREATE EXTERNAL JOB
```

```
SCHEDULER_ADMIN      MANAGE SCHEDULER
SCHEDULER_ADMIN      CREATE JOB
```

The following code lists the possible system privileges with names that contain the words JOB or SCHED. It indicates MANAGE SCHEDULER as an addition to the previously discussed system privileges, which are part of the SCHEDULER_ADMIN role:

```
SQL> select distinct privilege from dba_sys_privs where privilege like '%JOB%'
or privilege like '%SCHED%' order by 1;


PRIVILEGE
----------------------------------------
CREATE ANY JOB
CREATE EXTERNAL JOB
CREATE JOB
MANAGE SCHEDULER
```

The MANAGE SCHEDULER system privilege allows for maintenance of Scheduler objects including Scheduler windows, job classes, window groups, and Scheduler attributes, in addition to executing Scheduler log purging.

Specialized privileges used for scheduled job chains include those that work with specialized rules and contexts, including CREATE RULE, CREATE RULE SET, and CREATE EVALUATION CONTEXT.

Understanding Job States

The state of a job can be one of the following, which are based on the most recent execution (or failure) of that job—or its state during its current execution:

- **Disabled** Job is present but not scheduled to run.
- **Retry Scheduled** Failed or aborted but set to retry.
- **Scheduled** Scheduled to run at a specified time.
- **Running** Job is currently executing.
- **Completed** Job completed running successfully and is not set to run again; otherwise, it would be listed as **SCHEDULED** to run again.
- **Broken** Broken job that failed on last run and will not be executed until repaired because the maximum number of failures has been reached. Typically, a broken job is a job with some kind of an interpretive or compilation error, or perhaps even a dependency issue.
- **Failed** A failed job where all retries have consistently failed, regardless of the maximum number of retries.
- **Remote** Job is running remotely.
- **Succeeded** Job successfully ran.
- **Chain_Stalled** A chain-stalled process as a result of a dependency issue.

The following query shows the states of various jobs in a very simple, newly installed Oracle Database 12*c* database:

```
select owner, job_name, state from dba_scheduler_jobs;
```

OWNER	JOB_NAME	STATE
SYS	XMLDB_NFS_CLEANUP_JOB	DISABLED
SYS	FILE_WATCHER	DISABLED
SYS	PMO_DEFERRED_GIDX_MAINT_JOB	SCHEDULED
SYS	CLEANUP_NON_EXIST_OBJ	SCHEDULED
SYS	CLEANUP_ONLINE_IND_BUILD	SCHEDULED
SYS	CLEANUP_TAB_IOT_PMO	SCHEDULED
SYS	CLEANUP_TRANSIENT_TYPE	SCHEDULED
SYS	CLEANUP_TRANSIENT_PKG	SCHEDULED
SYS	CLEANUP_ONLINE_PMO	SCHEDULED
SYS	PURGE_LOG	SCHEDULED
SYS	ORA$AUTOTASK_CLEAN	SCHEDULED
SYS	HM_CREATE_OFFLINE_DICTIONARY	DISABLED
SYS	DRA_REEVALUATE_OPEN_FAILURES	SCHEDULED
SYS	BSLN_MAINTAIN_STATS_JOB	SCHEDULED
SYS	FGR$AUTOPURGE_JOB	DISABLED
SYS	RSE$CLEAN_RECOVERABLE_SCRIPT	SCHEDULED
SYS	SM$CLEAN_AUTO_SPLIT_MERGE	SCHEDULED
SYS	LOAD_OPATCH_INVENTORY	DISABLED
SYSTEM	TEST2	DISABLED
SYSTEM	MYJOB	DISABLED
SYSTEM	TEST	DISABLED
ORACLE_OCM	MGMT_CONFIG_JOB	SCHEDULED
ORACLE_OCM	MGMT_STATS_CONFIG_JOB	SCHEDULED

Understanding Scheduler Objects

The Oracle Database 12*c* Scheduler's constituent parts can be broken into more easily manageable objects, which presents a self-contained modular approach to working with schedules. The most important Scheduler component is the job, which is scheduled by the Scheduler; most of the other objects are used in support of jobs. Scheduler objects are as follows:

Jobs   A job is the sequence of steps executed by the Scheduler when a job is executed. Internal jobs run code inside a database, and an external job runs a job external to the database, such as an executable or a script. There are even jobs that are remote or externally remote. Jobs have applied actions as attributes, such as the name of the object to execute. To execute a job, the user must have the EXECUTE privilege granted to the schema user on the contents (the procedure) executed by the job. The schedule for a job defines when a job is run and how often, and what to do in the event of job failure. The destination of a job defines where a job is executed (locally or remotely).

Schedules   The schedule object defines when (time-based) or how (event-based) a job is executed.

Job Classes   Jobs are grouped into classes according to things they have in common, such as an attribute, resource allocation, prioritization within a class, or even divisions by application or functionality.

Groups   A list of Scheduler objects that can be passed to the Scheduler for execution of a group of related objects: (1) a database destination runs a group of jobs inside multiple remote databases, (2) an external destination group runs a group of external jobs on remote database servers, (3) works with a group windows objects.

Windows   A window creates a sliding time-window interval in which actions and events can occur. In the case of the Oracle Scheduler, those actions and events can be things like a job starting or a change in allocation of resources.

Destinations   A destination is a running job location, which is either an external (remote host name and IP address) or database destination (remote instance that runs a database job). If multiple destinations are required to run the same job, a destination group can be used (see Groups).

Chains   Chains link jobs together in interdependent links of related jobs, where jobs are triggered by other jobs depending on the results. The simplest chain is a sequential chain of two or more jobs, ranging through to more complex jobs chains containing hierarchical structures of inter-linked jobs. Each link in a chain of jobs can point to a chain, a nested chain (hierarchy), a piece of code (internal or external executable), an event, or a file watcher object.

File Watchers   These wait for a file to arrive on a server, which then triggers the Scheduler to execute a job on that file.

Credentials   Username and password pairs (where passwords are said by Oracle to be "obfuscated," which presumably means encrypted) are stored as credentials. Credential objects are used to execute remote and external jobs, and to access file watcher triggering files when those files arrive.

Programs   This is an executable set of instructions including PL/SQL blocks, scripts, or an executable outside of Oracle, and can even include parameters. A job can point to or include a program, but a program is still invoked using a job inside a Scheduler.

Using Oracle Scheduler

The DBMS_SCHEDULER package contains procedures used to work with the Oracle Scheduler inside Oracle Database 12c.

Working with Schedules

The CREATE_SCHEDULE procedure allows the creation of a schedule, where that schedule object determines how a process of some form is executed on a repetitive basis as shown here:

```
begin
  DBMS_SCHEDULER.CREATE_SCHEDULE
  (
      schedule_name=>'MYSCHEDULE'
    , start_date=>SYSDATE
    , repeat_interval=>'FREQ=HOURLY;BYMINUTE=45'
    , end_date=>SYSDATE+1
  );
END;
/
```

> The repeat_interval parameter of CREATE_SCHEDULE determines the frequency of the schedule and uses a rich calendaring syntax to enable you to define complex repeating schedules.

To drop that same schedule later, simply execute the DROP_SCHEDULE procedure:

```
exec dbms_scheduler.drop_schedule(schedule_name=>'MYSCHEDULE');
```

> The DBMS_SCHEDULER package procedures generally require the CREATE JOB or the CREATE ANY JOB privilege.

The DBMS_SCHEDULER.GET_SCHEDULER_ATTRIBUTE and SET_SCHEDULER_ATTRIBUTE procedures are used to change general attributes for the Oracle Database 12c Scheduler, with attribute-value pairs like this in the SET procedure:

```
BEGIN
DBMS_SCHEDULER.SET_SCHEDULER_ATTRIBUTE
(attribute=>'LOG_HISTORY', value=>'5');
END;
/
```

The GET_SCHEDULER_ATTRIBUTE procedure shows values:

```
SET SERVEROUTPUT ON;
DECLARE
      locVALUE INTEGER;
BEGIN
```

```
DBMS_SCHEDULER.GET_SCHEDULER_ATTRIBUTE('LOG_HISTORY',locVALUE);
DBMS_OUTPUT.PUT_LINE('LOG_HISTORY='||locVALUE);
END;

  /
```

Or similarly:

```
CREATE OR REPLACE FUNCTION TEST(parATTRIBUTE IN VARCHAR2)
RETURN VARCHAR2 IS
locVALUE INTEGER;
BEGIN
DBMS_SCHEDULER.GET_SCHEDULER_ATTRIBUTE(parATTRIBUTE,locVALUE);
RETURN locVALUE;
END;
/
SET SERVEROUTPUT ON;
exec DBMS_OUTPUT.PUT_LINE(TEST('current_open_window'));
exec DBMS_OUTPUT.PUT_LINE(TEST('email_sender'));
exec DBMS_OUTPUT.PUT_LINE(TEST('email_server'));
exec DBMS_OUTPUT.PUT_LINE(TEST('event_expiry_time'));
exec DBMS_OUTPUT.PUT_LINE(TEST('log_history'));
exec DBMS_OUTPUT.PUT_LINE(TEST('max_job_slave_processes'));
SET SERVEROUTPUT OFF;
```

Table 16.7 shows the various attributes that can be set and viewed with SET and GET_ SCHEDULER_ATTRIBUTE procedures. The explanations are mostly self-explanatory.

TABLE 16.7 The SET and GET_SCHEDULER_ATTRIBUTE Options

Attribute	Description
current_open_window	Name of the window currently open
default_timezone	Repeat interval's default timezone
email_sender	email address of the sender for job notifications
email_server	SMTP server address that the Scheduler uses to send email notifications
event_expiry_time	Time in seconds before an event expires
log_history	Retention in days

Working with Jobs

The DBMS_SCHEDULER.CREATE_JOB procedure is used to create a job, which can be executed directly or executed automatically on a scheduled basis inside the Oracle Scheduler. A simple job includes the following parameters:

```
CREATE OR REPLACE PROCEDURE THISIS IS
BEGIN
DBMS_OUTPUT.PUT_LINE('APROCEDURE');
END;
/
SET SERVEROUTPUT ON;
BEGIN
DBMS_SCHEDULER.CREATE_JOB(
job_name=>'test'
,job_type=>'STORED_PROCEDURE'
,job_action=>'THISIS'
);
END;
/
```

The parameters for the CREATE_JOB procedure are shown in Table 16.8.

TABLE 16.8 The CREATE_JOB Procedure

Attribute	Description
job_name	A unique job name.
job_type	PL/SQL_BLOCK, STORE_PROCEDURE, EXECUTABLE, CHAIN, EXTERNAL_SCRIPT, SQL_SCRIPT, BACKUP_SCRIPT (RMAN script).
job_action	The piece of code or the name of the object that is executed. Store procedure IN or OUT parameters are not allowed.
number_of_arguments	Number of job arguments.
program_name	Name of external executable.
start_date	First time of job execution.
repeat_interval	The time between each job repetition.
schedule_name	The name of the schedule, window, or window group associated with this job.

TABLE 16.8   The CREATE_JOB Procedure *(continued)*

Attribute	Description
job_class	The class associated with this job.
end_date	After the end date is passed, there are no more executions.
comments	This attribute specifies a comment about the job. By default, this attribute is NULL.
job_style	REGULAR or LIGHTWEIGHT (helps performance, but for short running jobs only).
credential_name	The default credential to use with the job.
destination_name	The database destination or external destination for the job, used only for remote database jobs and remote external jobs.
enabled	Job is enabled and can be executed. All jobs are created initially as disabled.
auto_drop	Drops the job after next execution.

The job_queue_processes parameter restricts the number of concurrently running job processes in an Oracle Database 12*c* database and is set to 1,000 by default.

 Setting the database parameter JOB_QUEUE_PROCESSES = 0 will disable the Oracle Database 12*c* Scheduler.

The SET_JOB_ARGUMENT_VALUE and SET_JOB_ANYDATA_VALUE procedures can be used for certain types of jobs in order to alter arguments of things executed by jobs—for example, changing the default value of a parameter executed by a procedure, which is executed within a job.

```
DBMS_SCHEDULER.SET_JOB_ARGUMENT_VALUE(
job_name=>'this is a job name'
,argument_position=>1
,argument_value=>'testing'
);
```

The RUN_JOB procedure is used to immediately run a job that has already been created, regardless of any schedule:

```
SQL> exec DBMS_SCHEDULER.RUN_JOB(job_name=>'test');
```

A second parameter, called USE_CURRENT_SESSION, implies that a job can be run as the owner of the job object, as opposed to the currently connected Oracle user, the latter being the default (TRUE).

The STOP_JOB procedure simply stops a currently running job:

```
SQL> exec DBMS_SCHEDULER.STOP_JOB(job_name=>'test');
```

Other parameters for the STOP_JOB procedure attempt to interrupt or retain the integrity of data. The FORCE parameter (defaulted to FALSE) uses a graceful method by not brutally terminating the job slave process. The FORCE option set to TRUE will terminate the job slave process (needs the MANAGE_SCHEDULER privilege). The COMMIT_SEMANTICS parameter allows a job to ABSORB_ERRORS or terminate when and if a STOP_ON_FIRST_ERROR occurs. In the example below, the job completed quickly before the STOP_JOB was executed. When the job is not in running status when stopped, you get the following error:

```
Error starting at line 2 in command:
exec DBMS_SCHEDULER.STOP_JOB(job_name=>'test')
Error report:
ORA-27366: job "SYSTEM"."TEST" is not running
ORA-06512: at "SYS.DBMS_ISCHED", line 216
ORA-06512: at "SYS.DBMS_SCHEDULER", line 674
ORA-06512: at line 1
27366. 00000 -  "job \"%s.%s\" is not running"
*Cause: An attempt was made to stop a job that was not running.
*Action: Verify the status of the job. If the job is running but this message is
still being returned, contact Oracle support.
```

The DROP_JOB procedure removes a job from the database:

```
SQL> exec DBMS_SCHEDULER.DROP_JOB(job_name=>'test');
```

Additional parameters for the DROP_JOB procedure are FORCE, DEFER, and COMMIT_SEMANTICS. When FORCE is TRUE, a STOP_JOB procedure will be executed to try to remove any executions cleanly. The DEFER parameter allows all currently running jobs to run to completion. The COMMIT_SEMANTICS parameter, in addition to the DROP_JOBS procedure, will allow the TRANSACTIONAL option, which will terminate on the first error and also rollback.

Figure 16.11 shows the Scheduler Jobs screen from OEM Cloud Control. Here you can view the scheduled jobs, modify jobs, run the job, or duplicate the job.

Job Classes

Job classes are created inside the SYS schema because they apply to all jobs for all users, classifying jobs into classes:

```
exec DBMS_SCHEDULER.CREATE_JOB_CLASS(job_class_name=>'sillyjobs');
```

The CREATE_JOB_CLASS procedure has the parameters shown in Table 16.9.

FIGURE 16.11   OEM – The Scheduler Jobs screen

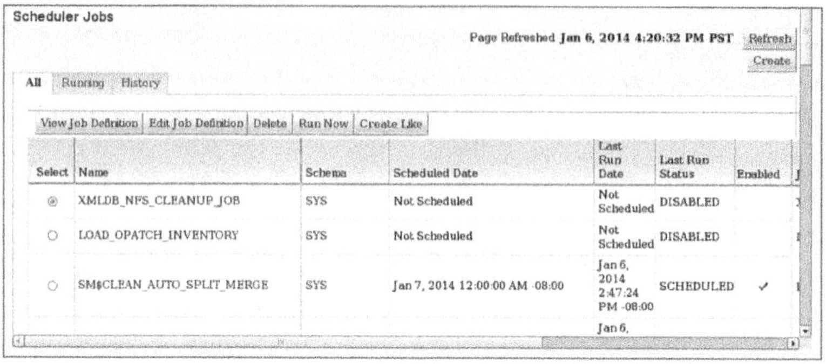

TABLE 16.9   The CREATE_JOB_CLASS Procedure

Attribute	Description
job_class_name	Name of the job class.
resource_consumer_group	A job class has an associated consumer group, allowing for controlled resource allocation, defaulting to the default consumer group if not set.
Service	A database service allows for specific access to a specific instance in a multiple instance Real Applications Cluster (RAC) database.
logging_level	Logging is switched off, when jobs run, or used for failed runs only.

Both the CREATE_JOB_CLASS and DROP_JOB_CLASS procedures require the MANAGE SCHEDULER privilege.

```
exec DBMS_SCHEDULER.DROP_JOB_CLASS(job_class_name=>'sillyjobs');
```

The DROP_JOB_CLASS has a force option, where jobs belonging to the class will not be dropped but set to disabled.

Groups

Groups can be created as groups of windows, destinations, or external destinations. The CREATE_GROUP command looks like this:

```
begin
DBMS_SCHEDULER.CREATE_GROUP(
```

```
group_name=>'things'
,GROUP_TYPE=>'DB_DEST'
,MEMBER=>'LOCAL'
);
end;
/
```

GROUP_TYPE is DB_DEST, EXTERNAL_DEST, or WINDOW. MEMBER is a comma-delimited list of group members, which can also be maintained after the fact using the ADD_GROUP_MEMBER procedure as a name and comma-delimited list-value pair, where the command-delimited list can consist of one or more items. Also, the REMOVE_GROUP_MEMBER procedure allows removal.

The DROP_GROUP procedure obviously drops a group, and setting the FORCE=TRUE drops the group even when jobs are referencing it; otherwise, the group will not be dropped.

 Real World Scenario

Special Statistics Gather

As you have seen in Chapter 14, "Maintaining the Database and Managing Performance," the AutoTask infrastructure runs the automatic optimizer statistics collection job daily. In one of my clients, there is a very critical table, where keeping the statics current is crucial for completing a business functionality within seconds. This table is loaded twice a day with data from an external source, and data is tailored for US business in one load and for India business in another load. So the following code was used to schedule and run the gather table statistics job twice a day. Note the job is created without an existing program or schedule.

```
BEGIN
 DBMS_SCHEDULER.CREATE_JOB (
    job_name        => 'xxobe.stats_on_wo_table',
    job_type        => 'PLSQL_BLOCK',
    job_action      => 'BEGIN
        DBMS_STATS.GATHER_TABLE_STATS(''xxobe'',''xxfmb01_wo_trans'');
        END;',
    start_date      => TRUNC(SYSDATE)+31/24,
    repeat_interval => 'FREQ=DAILY; BYHOUR=7,19',
    enabled         => TRUE,
    comments        => 'Gather statistics on wo_trans');
END;
/
```

Start date is specified as next day 7AM, and the job is scheduled to run at 7AM and 7PM daily.

Monitoring

The easiest way to work with character-based monitoring in Oracle Database 12*c* is to look for specific metadata and performance views in the DICTIONARY table. The following query will show all scheduler related dictionary views that you can use to find more information about jobs, programs, groups, windows, and schedules.

```
SELECT table_name FROM DICTIONARY
where TABLE_NAME like 'DBA_SCHED%' or table_name like 'V$SCHED%'
order by table_name;
```

The DBA_ views are metadata views that describe data about data (metadata), or the data that describes the logical structure of a database such as the tables, fields in the tables, indexes, and so on. The V$ views give information for monitoring the performance of a database in general, as opposed to the structure of the objects stored inside that database.

DBA_SCHEDULER_JOBS gives a list of jobs in a database, including recent executions, next executions, successes, failures, the contents of the jobs, what is executed, as well as all sorts of contextual details. Most of the names for the monitoring views are obvious, such as JOB_ARGS, JOB_CLASSES, JOB_DESTS, and so on.

Using OEM Cloud Control to create and manage Jobs is much easier for the DBA. Figure 16.12 shows the Create Job screen of OEM. You can get to this screen by clicking the Create Job Class button shown in Figure 16.12.

FIGURE 16.12 OEM – The Create Job screen

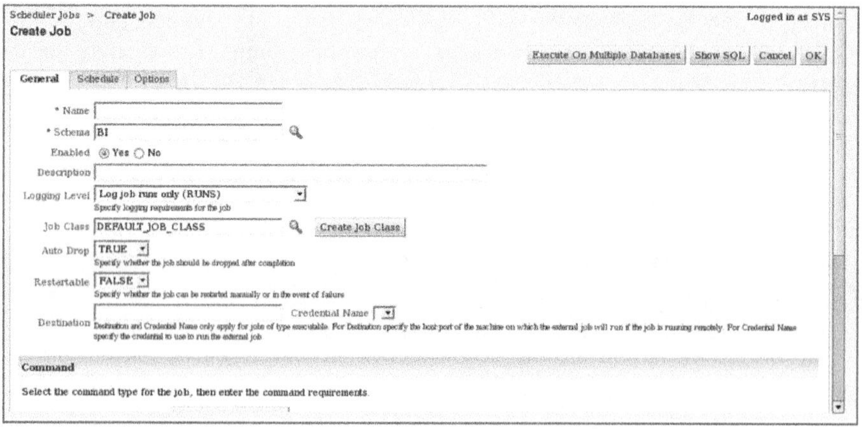

The Name and Schema fields under the job must be filled in for the job to be created; all other fields are optional. You determine the frequency at which to run the job in the next screen, under the Schedule tab. Figure 16.13 shows the Schedule tab.

You can define other options, such as Maximum Run Time, Maximum Failure, and so on before you save the job definition. Figure 16.14 shows the Options tab of the Create Job screen.

FIGURE 16.13   OEM – The Create Job - Schedule screen

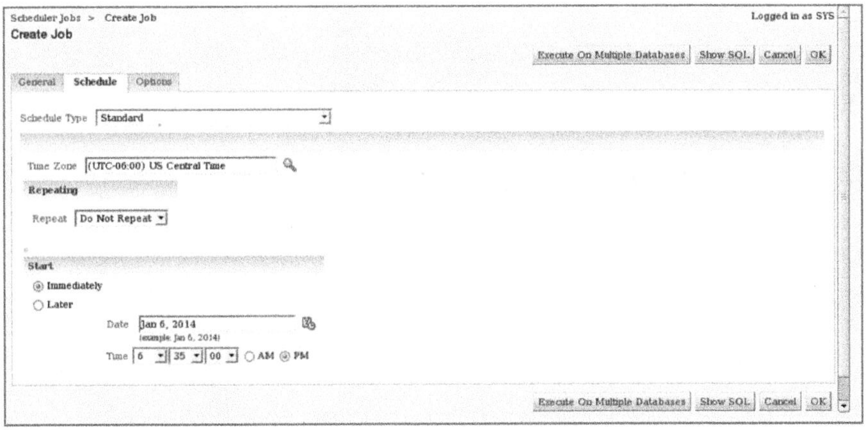

FIGURE 16.14   OEM – The Create Job - Options screen

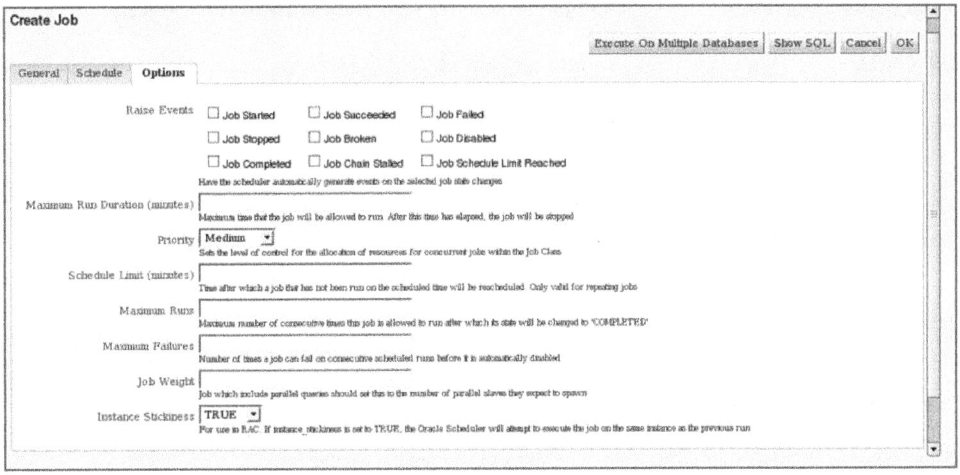

Relating Tasks with Job Chains

A job chain is a sequence of jobs that are dependent upon each other, as in jobs executed based on the results of previous jobs executed in the sequence. A number of logical steps are included in creating a job chain:

1. Create the chain object.

2. Set the chain steps.

3. Add rules to the chain and steps in the chain.

4. Set the chain as enabled.

5. Create a chain job.

In the process of building, operating, and managing job chains, there are a number of procedural functions that are used, including those shown in Table 16.10.

TABLE 16.10 Job Chains and the DBMS_SCHEDULER Package

Procedure	Function
CREATE_CHAIN	Create a chain.
ALTER_CHAIN	Alter a chain.
DROP_CHAIN	Drop a chain.
SET_ATTRIBUTE	Make changes to an existing job chain when the chain is not running.
ALTER_RUNNING_CHAIN	Change an existing job chain while it is running.
RUN_CHAIN	Execute a chained set of job steps.
DEFINE_CHAIN_RULE	Add or change a rule in an existing chain.
DROP_CHAIN_RULE	Drop a rule in a chain.
ENABLE or DISABLE	Enable or disable a DBMS_SCHEDULER object, including job chain objects.
DROP_CHAIN_STEP	Remove a step from a job chain.

The first step is to create a chain:

```
exec DBMS_SCHEDULER.CREATE_CHAIN(chain_name => 'chain1');
```

And then set some chain steps:

```
BEGIN
DBMS_SCHEDULER.DEFINE_CHAIN_STEP(chain_name => 'chain1'
, step_name => 'step1'
, program_name => 'program1');
DBMS_SCHEDULER.DEFINE_CHAIN_STEP(chain_name => 'chain1'
, step_name => 'step2'
, program_name => 'program2');
```

```
END;
/
```

And now adding a rule where SKIP is set to TRUE and will prevent the step from being executed, also assuming the step has already been executed:

```
exec DBMS_SCHEDULER.ALTER_CHAIN('chain1','step2','SKIP',TRUE);
```

A chain can be enabled or disabled using the following:

```
exec DBMS_SCHEDULER.ENABLE(name=>'chain1');
exec DBMS_SCHEDULER.DISABLE(name=>'chain1');
```

Examine and monitor existing chains in a database using the DBA_SCHEDULER_RUNNING_ CHAINS view as follows:

```
SQL> desc dba_scheduler_running_chains
Name                 Null     Type
-------------------- -------- ----------------------------
OWNER                NOT NULL VARCHAR2(128)
JOB_NAME             NOT NULL VARCHAR2(128)
JOB_SUBNAME                   VARCHAR2(128)
CHAIN_OWNER          NOT NULL VARCHAR2(128)
CHAIN_NAME           NOT NULL VARCHAR2(128)
STEP_NAME            NOT NULL VARCHAR2(128)
STATE                         VARCHAR2(15)
ERROR_CODE                    NUMBER
COMPLETED                     VARCHAR2(5)
START_DATE                    TIMESTAMP(6) WITH TIME ZONE
END_DATE                      TIMESTAMP(6) WITH TIME ZONE
DURATION                      INTERVAL DAY(9) TO SECOND(6)
SKIP                          VARCHAR2(5)
PAUSE                         VARCHAR2(5)
PAUSE_BEFORE                  VARCHAR2(5)
RESTART_ON_RECOVERY           VARCHAR2(5)
RESTART_ON_FAILURE            VARCHAR2(5)
STEP_JOB_SUBNAME              VARCHAR2(128)
STEP_JOB_LOG_ID               NUMBER
```

Lastly, you can create a job for a chain as follows:

```
BEGIN
DBMS_SCHEDULER.CREATE_JOB (
job_name => 'chainjob1'
,job_type => 'CHAIN'
```

```
,job_action => 'chain1'
,repeat_interval => 'freq=daily;byhour=12;byminute=0;bysecond=0'
,enabled => TRUE
);
END;
  /
```

 If you omit the REPEAT_INTERVAL parameter, the job will not be scheduled; therefore, the job will run immediately.

Run a chain using the RUN_CHAIN procedure:

```
BEGIN
DBMS_SCHEDULER.RUN_CHAIN(
chain_name=>'chain1'
,job_name=>'someofit'
,start_steps=>'step1, step2');
END;
/
```

Finally, drop a chain using the DROP_CHAIN procedure:
exec DBMS_SCHEDULER.DROP_CHAIN(chain_name=>'chain1',force=>TRUE);

 For a chain job to execute, at least one step in the chain must be enabled. Conversely, one step in a chain must have the END action set to TRUE; otherwise, the chain can stall.

A chain job can be stopped using the STOP_JOB procedure and dropped using the DROP_JOB procedure, as follows:

```
exec dbms_scheduler.stop_job(job_name=>'CHAINJOB1');
exec dbms_scheduler.drop_job(job_name=>'CHAINJOB1');
```

You can also drop an entire chain using the DROP_CHAIN procedure:

```
exec dbms_scheduler.drop_chain(chain_name=>'SYSTEM.CHAINJOB1');
```

Finally, chains can be monitored using the DBA%CHAIN metadata:

```
select table_name from dictionary
where table_name like 'DBA%CHAIN%' or table_name like 'V$%CHAIN%';
```

```
TABLE_NAME
--------------------------------------
DBA_SCHEDULER_CHAINS
DBA_SCHEDULER_CHAIN_RULES
DBA_SCHEDULER_CHAIN_STEPS
DBA_SCHEDULER_RUNNING_CHAINS
V$WAIT_CHAINS
```

Scheduling Jobs on Remote Systems

A job can be scheduled to execute on a remote system by specifying one or more destinations where the job will run. A single destination can be specified using a single job attribute, or by using a destination group that contains one or more destinations. Each destination can be either external (a remote host name and IP address) or a database destination (remote database instance); the destination allows a job to be executed on that remote database.

 If a destination group has a group member called LOCAL, the job is executed locally as well as remotely.

A destination can be created using the CREATE_DATABASE_DESTINATION procedure:

```
BEGIN
DBMS_SCHEDULER.CREATE_DATABASE_DESTINATION(
destination_name => 'my_other_database'
agent => 'agent_on_another_server'
tns_name => 'database_tns_name'
);
END;
/
```

 You can examine existing destinations using the metadata views:
DBA_SCHEDULER_DESTS
DBA_SCHEDULER_EXTERNAL_DESTS
DBA_SCHEDULER_DB_DESTS
DBA_SCHEDULER_JOB_DESTS

Connecting to a remote machine or a remote database requires credentials, which can be set up using the CREATE_CREDENTIAL procedure (the DATABASE_ROLE parameter is optional):

```
BEGIN
DBMS_SCHEDULER.CREATE_CREDENTIAL(
```

```
credential_name => 'myID'
username => 'mylogin'
password => 'my_encrypted_password'
database_role => SYSDBA
);
END;

  /
```

> **NOTE**   You can examine credentials using the metadata views:
>
> DBA_SCHEDULER_CREDENTIALS
>
> DBA_CREDENTIALS

Creating a group of items, such as a group of multiple destination objects, requires the use of the CREATE_GROUP procedure, as discussed previously in this chapter, where a group can be created as a DB_DEST (database destination), EXTERNAL_DEST (a remote machine identified by hostname and IP address), or as a WINDOW (Scheduler window object collection).

Creating a remote job with a single destination and credential requires one of each:

```
BEGIN
DBMS_SCHEDULER.CREATE_JOB(
job_name => 'test'
,job_type => 'STORED_PROCEDURE'
,job_action => 'THISIS'
,credential_name => 'myID'
,destination_name => 'my_other_database'
);
END;
/
```

Groups of items such as credentials and destinations can be found in the three metadata views for Scheduler groups (DBA_SCHEDULER_GROUPS, ALL_SCHEDULER_GROUPS, and USER_SCHEDULER_GROUPS) if needed.

Prioritizing Jobs with Oracle Scheduler

By applying varying priorities to jobs, you indicate that some jobs are more important than others, should run before others, or should have more hardware resources allocated to them than other jobs. You can prioritize jobs in Oracle Database 12c using job classes or windows (or windows groups), as well as by having the Resource Manager applied to specific jobs (covered earlier in this chapter).

> **NOTE**   Window and window groups are beyond the scope of this book.

A job can then use the Database Resource Manager to allocate resources to a job in a database resource consumer group. Additionally, job classes can be used to set priorities where jobs are assigned those prioritized job classes.

When using priorities in job classes, your first task is to create a job class using the CREATE_JOB_CLASS procedure. You begin by looking up resource consumer groups:

```
select table_name from dictionary
where table_name like 'DBA%CONSUMER%';
TABLE_NAME
----------------------------------
DBA_HIST_RSRC_CONSUMER_GROUP
DBA_RSRC_CONSUMER_GROUPS
DBA_RSRC_CONSUMER_GROUP_PRIVS
DBA_STREAMS_MESSAGE_CONSUMERS
```

Next, examine the various consumer groups:

```
BATCH_GROUP
ORA$AUTOTASK
INTERACTIVE_GROUP
OTHER_GROUPS
DEFAULT_CONSUMER_GROUP
SYS_GROUP
LOW_GROUP
ETL_GROUP
DSS_GROUP
DSS_CRITICAL_GROUP
ORA$APPQOS_0
ORA$APPQOS_1
ORA$APPQOS_2
ORA$APPQOS_3
ORA$APPQOS_4
ORA$APPQOS_5
ORA$APPQOS_6
ORA$APPQOS_7
```

Then create a job class, assigning the prioritization of the consumer group to the job class, ultimately assigning jobs to the job class:

```
BEGIN
DBMS_SCHEDULER.CREATE_JOB_CLASS(
job_class_name => 'jobclass1',     resource_consumer_group => 'ETL_GROUP'
);
```

```
END;
/
```

You could also use the SET_ATTRIBUTE procedure to assign a job priority to jobs within a job class, between priorities of 1 and 5:

```
BEGIN
DBMS_SCHEDULER.CREATE_JOB(
job_name=>'test'
,job_type=>'STORED_PROCEDURE'
,job_action=>'THISIS'
);
END;

 /
```

Next, assign the specific priority:

```
BEGIN
DBMS_SCHEDULER.SET_ATTRIBUTE (
name => 'test',
attribute => 'job_priority',
value => 1
);
END;
/
```

You can examine the job class priorities later in the DBA_SCHEDULER_JOBS metadata view:

```
select owner,job_name,program_name,job_priority
from dba_scheduler_jobs order by 4;
```

OWNER	JOB_NAME	PROGRAM_NAME	PRIORITY
SYSTEM	TEST		1
SYS	XMLDB_NFS_CLEANUP_JOB		3
SYSTEM	TEST2		3
SYSTEM	MYJOB	MYPROG	3

....

Summary

This chapter introduced resource management and scheduling in Oracle Database 12*c*. Resource management was broken into the basic metadata components of consumer groups, plans, and allocation methods, followed by configuration, creating and maintaining resource objects, and finally monitoring. Scheduling was divided into the general architecture of the Oracle Scheduler, followed by some work using the Scheduler and its various constituent components.

You completed this chapter by examining some specific scenarios that covered job chains, remote systems, and prioritization. You learned what resources and scheduling are, and all about how to create, manage, use, and maintain them.

Exam Essentials

Know the Resource Manager components.   Oracle divides resource management into parts including consumer groups, plans, plan directives, and methods of allocating resources. Understand what each part (object) is, what every part does, and how they link together.

Know about resource management configuration.   Learn about the Resource Manager–specific privileges, mapping rules, and mapping priorities. Know how to switch consumer groups.

Know about creating, updating, and deleting resource consumer objects.   Understand that resource consumer objects have interdependencies and that the sequence of creation, updating, and deletion is sometimes very important, depending on the Resource Manager object being used.

Know how to define and create schedules.   Understand that Oracle Scheduler has some basic components that include jobs, job classes, and groups, which all interlink and interrelate. Learn, however, that the most basic and commonly used component is just the job.

Know the basic metadata views.   Understand that resource management and scheduling metadata views.

Review Questions

1. Which of these is performed by the Resource Manager?

    A. Percentages of CPU time are split up.

    B. Percentages of memory are split up.

    C. Percentages of swap space in *nix and virtual memory in Windows are split up.

    D. Disk space is split up.

2. Which of these can be controlled by Resource Manager?

    A. Active session limits per user groups

    B. Assigning priorities

    C. Controlling runaway or out-of-control sessions

    D. Session idle time limits

    E. All of the above

3. Which of the following is the most significant and most effective allocation method controlled by the Resource Manager?

    A. Allocate CPU use between competing sessions

    B. Allocate CPU use between competing sessions based on priorities

    C. Limiting parallel processing

    D. Session idle time limits

4. How can runaway sessions be curtailed and prevented from overwhelming a system? (Choose two.)

    A. Automatically aborting a session when archive log space is filled

    B. Automatically aborting a session when rollback reaches an upper limit

    C. Automatically aborting a transaction inside a session when the transaction is too large

    D. Automatically changing the CPU use of a session to a consumer group with a lower priority

5. Which of these is a Resource Manager object?

    A. Plan direction

    B. Resource consumer plan

    C. Resource allocation method

    D. Subplan directive

6. Which of these packages are used to administer the Resource Manager? (Choose two.)

   A. DBMS_RESOURCE_MANAGER

   B. DBMS_RESOURCE_MANAGEMENT

   C. DBMS_RESOURCE_MANAGE

   D. DBMS_RESOURCE_MANAGER_PRIVS

   E. DBMS_RESOURCE_MANAGEMENT_PRIVS

7. A consumer group object can be assigned to which of the following? (Choose two.)

   A. A plan

   B. A subplan

   C. A consumer group

   D. None of the above

8. If a plan contains two subplans and one consumer group is below the subplan level, and each of the subplans is allocated 45 percent of CPU cycles each, what is the most that can be allocated to the consumer group, assuming that the subplans and plan are fully occupied?

   A. 11 percent

   B. 45 percent

   C. 5 percent

   D. 0 percent

   E. None of the above

9. Which of these can help prevent parallel processing limits from being exceeded, and help to prevent a database from being swamped by parallel executing queries?

   A. Degree of parallelism

   B. Parallel server processes

   C. Parallel queue timeouts

   D. All of the above

   E. None of the above

10. How many levels of utilization are there for CPU allocation in the Resource Manager?

   A. 0

   B. 1

   C. 15

   D. 8

   E. None of the above

11. Which database parameter has an impact on running the Scheduler jobs?

    A. PARALLEL_MAX_SERVERS

    B. JOB_QUEUE_PROCESSES

    C. AQ_TM_PROCESSES

    D. JOB_SCHEDULE_PROCESSES

12. Which of these are valid Resource Manager–specific privileges?

    A. GRANT_SYSTEM_PRIVS

    B. GRANT_SYSTEM_PRIVILEGES

    C. GRANT_SYS_PRIVS

    D. None of the above

13. Which of these are initial default resource consumer groups? (Choose two.)

    A. SYSTEM_GROUP

    B. OTHER_GROUP

    C. OTHER_SYSTEM_GROUP

    D. SYS_GROUP

    E. OTHER_GROUPS

14. With what types of resources does the CREATE_SIMPLE_PLAN procedure work?

    A. *nix cron jobs

    B. Oracle Scheduler job classes

    C. CPU resource allocations only

    D. Creates multiple plans

    E. None of the above

15. How many consumer groups, CPU percentages, and simple plans can the CREATE_SIMPLE_PLAN procedure create?

    A. 4, 4, and 1

    B. 8, 8, and 8

    C. 1, 1, and 8

    D. 8, 8, and 1

    E. None of the above

16. Why does the pending area exist? (Choose the best answer.)

    A. Because there is only one plan active at one time.

    B. Because there is only one plan active at one time, and changing the pending area changes the running plan.

    C. Because there is only one plan active at one time, and changing the pending area does not change the actively running plan.

    D. Because there is only one plan active at one time, and changing the pending area does not change the actively running plan until the pending area has been validated.

    E. None of the above.

17. How can you tell if a job is disabled in the Oracle Scheduler?

    A. Use the `DBA_SCHEDULER` view.

    B. Use the `DBA_SCHEDULER_JOBS` view.

    C. Use the `DBA_JOBS` view.

    D. All of the above.

    E. None of the above.

18. If a Scheduler job completes and it will run again in the future, what is its `STATE` setting?

    A. `COMPLETE`

    B. `RUNNABLE`

    C. `EDIBLE`

    D. `SCHEDULED`

19. If you create a job using the `CREATE_JOB` procedure, how many times can it be executed?

    A. Once

    B. As many times as it is scheduled

    C. Never

    D. Twice

    E. None of the above

20. Which query can be used to find the names of Oracle Scheduler metadata views?

    A. `SELECT table_name FROM dictionary WHERE table_name LIKE 'DBA%SCHED%';`

    B. `SELECT table_name FROM dictionary WHERE table_name LIKE 'DBA%PLAN%';`

    C. `SELECT table_name FROM dictionary WHERE table_name LIKE 'DBA%JOB%';`

    D. `SELECT table_name FROM dictionary WHERE table_name LIKE 'DBA%RSRC%';`

Chapter

17

Upgrading to Oracle Database 12*c*

ORACLE DATABASE 12*c*: OCA EXAM OBJECTIVES COVERED IN THIS CHAPTER:

✓ **Upgrading Oracle Database Software**

- ▨ Describe upgrade methods.

- ▨ Describe data migration methods.

- ▨ Describe the upgrade process.

✓ **Preparing to Upgrade to Oracle Database 12*c***

- ▨ Describe upgrade requirements when certain features or options are used in Oracle Database.

- ▨ Use the Pre-Upgrade Information tool before performing an upgrade.

- ▨ Prepare the new Oracle home prior to performing an upgrade.

✓ **Upgrading to Oracle Database 12*c***

- ▨ Upgrade the database to Oracle Database 12*c* by using the Database Upgrade Assistant (DBUA).

- ▨ Perform a manual upgrade to Oracle Database 12*c* by using scripts and tools.

✓ **Performing Post-Upgrade Tasks**

- ▨ Migrate to unified auditing.

- ▨ Perform post-upgrade tasks.

DBAs upgrade a database from one release to a higher release so that they can utilize new features and have a supported database version. Having a supported version of a database is important so that they can get bug fixes and security patches. Oracle typically announces the "de-support" date for a database version several months ahead of the date so that DBAs can plan and test the database upgrade. When you're ready to transform your pre-12*c* database to Oracle Database 12*c*, follow the database upgrade process. Before upgrading the production database, make sure you upgrade all nonproduction databases and that you thoroughly test all the application features.

Oracle Database 12*c* has several upgrade options. Depending on the version of the database and the required end state of the database, you can choose the best upgrade option. If you are looking for consolidation as part of your Oracle Database 12*c* migration strategy, you can use data-migration tools to move data from a pre-12*c* database to Oracle Database 12*c*.

Upgrading an Oracle database to Oracle Database 12*c* typically involves these tasks:

- Identify the supported upgrade options for the older database.
- Decide on the method to be used to upgrade the older database.
- Verify if the older database is ready for direct upgrade.
- Upgrade the older database.

In this chapter, you will learn the pre-upgrade tasks, the various methods to upgrade the database or to migrate data to a 12*c* database, and the post-upgrade tasks.

This chapter covers the upgrade topics specified by the OCA exam objectives. We highly recommend that you read and understand "Oracle Database Upgrade Guide 12*c* Release 1 (12.1) part E17642-14" or the latest release of the document found online at http://docs.oracle.com.

Determining the Database Upgrade Method

As a DBA, you will need to consider several factors before deciding on the best method for moving an application that uses an older version of Oracle to Oracle Database 12*c*. Although the terms *database upgrade* and *database migration* are often used synonymously, they present two different methods for moving to Oracle Database 12*c*. Database upgrade is the process of upgrading the Oracle database data dictionary and components to Oracle Database 12*c*. In the upgrade process, the actual data in the database is untouched—the application tables and tablespaces remain "as is." In database migration, the data from one database is moved or migrated to an already-created Oracle Database 12*c* database. The following options are available for the DBA to move to Oracle Database 12*c* from a prior release of Oracle database.

- Perform a direct upgrade using *Database Upgrade Utility (DBUA)*. DBUA is a GUI tool to upgrade an existing database to Oracle Database 12*c*. Using DBUA is the preferred and easiest method.
- Perform a direct upgrade by running scripts. (This is a manual upgrade.)
- Export/import utilities to copy data to a new Oracle Database 12*c* database.
- Copy data to a new Oracle Database 12*c* database using SQL tools.
- Use the transportable tablespace feature to move application tablespaces or an entire database to Oracle Database 12*c*.

Using Direct Upgrade

A *direct upgrade* gives you the option to upgrade the database to Oracle Database 12*c* without moving the database to another server or platform. This upgrade method is also known as an in-place upgrade. To be able to perform the direct upgrade, the Oracle database must be one of the following versions.

- Oracle Database 11g Release 2 – 11.2.0.2 or higher
- Oracle Database 11g Release 1 – 11.1.0.7
- Oracle Database 10g Release 2 – 10.2.0.5

If the source database is not at the proper patch level of the release, or if you are on a lower release, you will have to adopt the indirect upgrade method to upgrade to Oracle Database 12*c*. First, upgrade the database to a release supported by direct upgrade, and then upgrade to Oracle Database 12*c*. Alternatively, you can choose to perform a migration upgrade—that is, migrate the data to an Oracle Database 12*c* database. Figure 17.1 shows the direct upgrade path. As an indirect upgrade example, if the database version is 8.1.7.4, you must first upgrade to 10.2.0.5 before you can start the Oracle Database 12.1 upgrade.

A direct upgrade can be accomplished using two methods:

- Using Database Upgrade Assistant (DBUA)
- Performing a manual upgrade using scripts

DBUA is a GUI tool that performs the pre-upgrade checks, the upgrade, and the post-upgrade tasks for you after obtaining a few inputs from you. However, in the manual upgrade method, you have to perform each step manually and make sure you execute the scripts in the right order and monitor for errors.

FIGURE 17.1 The upgrade path to Oracle Database 12*c*

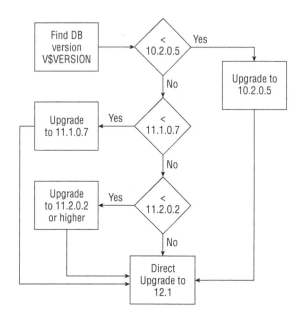

Oracle Release Numbers

Oracle Release numbers have five positions separated by dots, for example, 12.1.0.1.0. The first position indicates the major release number, the second position is the maintenance release number, the third position is applicable only for the application server release number, the fourth is the major patch release number, and the last position is the platform-specific release number. When you apply a Patch Set Update (PSU), the last position changes. To apply the major patch release (for example, 12.1.0.1.0 to 12.1.0.2.0), you will have to install Oracle software in a separate Oracle home directory.

The direct upgrade method at a high level includes the following steps.

- Run the *Pre-Upgrade Information tool* and review the results. Fix any issues or errors reported by the tool.
- In case the upgrade does not go well or encounters an error, to get back to where we started, backup the database before starting the upgrade.
- Install Oracle Database 12*c* software (you learned about this software install in Chapter 9, "Creating and Operating Oracle Database 12*c*").
- Start up the instance from the Oracle Database 12*c* home.

- Upgrade the database.
- Run the *Post-Upgrade Status tool* and review the status of the components.
- Recompile any invalid objects.
- Test the application.

When you use DBUA to perform the upgrade, the Pre-Upgrade Information tool script is run, and the results are shown for your review. DBUA upgrades the database and also runs the Post-Upgrade Status tool. We will show you the output from the Pre-Upgrade Information and Post-Upgrade Status tools later in the chapter.

Let's review the other options that are available if you are unable to or do not want to perform a direct upgrade.

Migrating to Oracle Database 12*c*

There may be situations where you cannot perform a direct upgrade of the database. Although a direct upgrade using DBUA is the easiest and safest upgrade method, you may have to use the migration method when:

- The database is not on one of the releases supported by a direct upgrade, and you do not want (or do not have the outage window) to perform a two-phased upgrade.
- You want to change the server hardware and/or operating system during the upgrade.
- You want to minimize the downtime required for the upgrade.

Migrating a database to Oracle Database 12*c* at a high level includes these steps.

- Install Oracle Database 12*c* software (you learned about doing a software install in Chapter 9).
- Create a new or use an existing Oracle Database 12*c* database.
- Copy database objects using the various migration methods available.
- Configure the application to use the new database.
- Test the application.

 NOTE   One great advantage of using an indirect upgrade of an Oracle database is that it provides the ability to easily roll back to an older database. The source database is kept intact, and the rollback process entails just starting up the old database and listener.

Oracle Database 12*c* supports the following migration methods.

- Using Data Pump Export and Import if the database is 10g or higher. For legacy databases, the traditional export/import method is supported. This method is suitable for databases that are not supported by the direct upgrade method, as well as for when you are planning a platform or server migration during the upgrade.

- Create table and copy data using the CREATE TABLE AS SELECT method through a database link. There are several restrictions when using this method, and it is not practical in many situations. For example, this method will not work if the table has a column of datatype LONG.

To reduce the downtime window, the following migration methods can be considered:

- Use the transportable tablespace feature to move the self-contained application tablespaces. This method can be used if you are considering a platform migration as well.

- Use Oracle Data Guard SQL Apply on a logical standby database to perform a rolling upgrade to Oracle Database 12c.

- Use Oracle Golden Gate to perform an online database upgrade to Oracle Database 12c.

- If the database is 11.2.0.3 or higher, use the transport database feature of Oracle Data Pump. If the target platform's endianness is different, the data file needs to be converted using RMAN.

Oracle Data Pump utilities and legacy exp/imp tools are discussed in Chapter 18, "Using Grid Infrastructure and Data Movement Tools."

The direct upgrade (DBUA or manual) and migration using Data Pump utilities are the most common methods used for database migration. Table 17.1 shows the pros and cons of each method.

TABLE 17.1 Comparison of Upgrade Methods

Method	Advantages	Disadvantages
Direct Upgrade Using DBUA	Guides you through the process. All tasks are automated. Supports RAC upgrade. Runs prerequisite script and fixes errors. Upgrades status report. Data file migration to different location or ASM possible.	Less control over the upgrade process. Must be on a specific release level. No hardware or operating system platform migration.
Manual Upgrade	More control over upgrade tasks.	Error prone. More work for the DBA. Manual error checks required. Must be on a specific release level. No hardware or operating system platform migration.

Method	Advantages	Disadvantages
Export/Import	Can be on any database release. Defragments data. Provides control over which tables are copied or not copied. Source database is intact and serves as backup or archive. Server hardware or platform migration possible.	May take a long time depending on database size. Import errors need to be fixed.
Full Transportable Export/Import	Exports all objects and data necessary to create a complete copy of database. Only metadata from objects residing in transportable tablespaces exported. Objects in nontransportable tablespaces (SYSTEM, SYSAUX) have both metadata and data exported. Server hardware or platform migration possible.	Works only on databases higher than 11.2.0.3.

Once you have decided to perform a direct upgrade of the database to Oracle Database 12*c*, you need to begin making preparations.

An Oracle database upgrade using Data Pump utilities is discussed in Chapter 18. This option entails nothing more than copying data from a lower version of Oracle database to Oracle Database 12*c*. Full Transportable Export/Import is also discussed in Chapter 18.

Preparing for a Database Upgrade

Updating a database from one version to another is a major activity that requires thorough testing of the application for functionality and performance. Preparation, testing, and practice help reduce errors and avoid unforeseen circumstances specific to your environment that might prevent the production upgrade from successfully completing. During the preparation stage, you also need to plan contingency measures in case the upgrade is not successful for some reason. To help the DBA prepare for the upgrade and avoid errors, Oracle provides a set of tools to prepare the database and software environment so they are ready for the upgrade. The primary tool is the Pre-Upgrade Information script, which has a series of checks and also provides a script to fix the errors.

Running the Pre-Upgrade Information Tool

The Pre-Upgrade Information tool is shipped with Oracle Database 12*c* software, which includes two scripts under the $ORACLE_HOME/rdbms/admin directory. You may copy these two scripts to any directory or run them from the rdbms/admin directory under the Oracle Database 12*c* home itself on the database that you want to upgrade to 12*c*. If the Oracle Database 12*c* software is not installed on the server where the current database is running, you can simply copy preupgrd.sql and utluppkg.sql scripts.

Invoke the preupgrd.sql connected as SYSDBA on the database you want to upgrade. This script loads utluppkg.sql (which defines the dbms_preup package) and then makes calls to the pre-upgrade package functions to determine the status of the to-be-upgraded database. You may pass two optional parameters to the script. The first parameter is TERMINAL or FILE, to indicate where the output goes. The second parameter is TEXT or XML, to indicate the type of output file. XML is used by DBUA. When you run the preupgrd.sql script without any parameters, the output goes to FILE in TEXT format.

If $ORACLE_BASE is defined, the generated scripts and log files are saved in $ORACLE_BASE/cfgtoollogs/db_unique_name/preupgrade directory. If $ORACLE_BASE is not defined, then the generated scripts and log files are created in $ORACLE_HOME/cfgtoollogs/db_unique_name/preupgrade. We recommend that you create the $ORACLE_BASE/cfgtoollogs/db_unique_name directory, if it does not exist, and define ORACLE_BASE before running the script.

Oracle uses DBMS_REGISTRY package to determine the components to be upgraded. In versions Oracle Database 10g and higher, the database and all the components have been integrated into the registry. DBA_REGISTRY displays information about all components in the database that are loaded into the component registry. The component registry tracks components that can be separately loaded into the Oracle database. If scripts are used to upgrade/downgrade the dictionary elements for the component, then those scripts also record status and version information.

The following is an example of running the preupgrd.sql script on an 11.2.0.4 database.

```
SQL> @preupgrd
Loading Pre-Upgrade Package...
Executing Pre-Upgrade Checks...
Pre-Upgrade Checks Complete.
Results of the checks are located at:
 /u01/app/oracle/cfgtoollogs/ocad11/preupgrade/preupgrade.log

Pre-Upgrade Fixup Script (run in source database environment):
 /u01/app/oracle/cfgtoollogs/ocad11/preupgrade/preupgrade_fixups.sql

Post-Upgrade Fixup Script (run shortly after upgrade):
 /u01/app/oracle/cfgtoollogs/ocad11/preupgrade/postupgrade_fixups.sql
        Fixup scripts must be reviewed prior to being executed.
               ====>> USER ACTION REQUIRED  <<====
 The following are *** ERROR LEVEL CONDITIONS *** that must be addressed
```

                    prior to attempting your upgrade.
          Failure to do so will result in a failed upgrade.
1) Check Tag: AUDSYS_USER_PRESENT
   Check Summary: Verify if a user or role with the name AUDSYS exists
   Fixup Summary:
    "The AUDSYS user or role must be dropped prior to upgrading."
   +++ Source Database Manual Action Required +++
2) Check Tag: AUDIT_VIEWER
   Check Summary: Verify if a user or role with the name AUDIT_VIEWER exists
   Fixup Summary:
    "The AUDIT_VIEWER role or user must be dropped prior to upgrading."
   +++ Source Database Manual Action Required +++
3) Check Tag: PURGE_RECYCLEBIN
   Check Summary: Check that recycle bin is empty prior to upgrade
   Fixup Summary:
    "The recycle bin will be purged."
          You MUST resolve the above errors prior to upgrade

The output shows the location of the log file and pre- and post-fix-up scripts. To help you understand what checks are performed and the issues identified by the tool, we'll show you the log file:

```
$ cat /u01/app/oracle/cfgtoollogs/ocad11/preupgrade/preupgrade.log
Oracle Database Pre-Upgrade Information Tool 01-11-2014 12:47:41
Script Version: 12.1.0.1.0 Build: 006
**********************************************************************
   Database Name:  OCAD11
         Version:  11.2.0.4.0
      Compatible:  11.2.0.4.0
       Blocksize:  8192
        Platform:  Linux x86 64-bit
   Timezone file:  V14
**********************************************************************
                    [Renamed Parameters]
             [No Renamed Parameters in use]
**********************************************************************
              [Obsolete/Deprecated Parameters]
--> log_archive_start         10.1      DESUPPORTED
--> max_enabled_roles         10.1      DESUPPORTED


     [Changes required in Oracle Database init.ora or spfile]
```

```
**********************************************************************
                          [Component List]
**********************************************************************
--> Oracle Catalog Views                [upgrade]  VALID
--> Oracle Packages and Types           [upgrade]  VALID
--> JServer JAVA Virtual Machine        [upgrade]  VALID
--> Oracle XDK for Java                 [upgrade]  VALID
--> Oracle Workspace Manager            [upgrade]  VALID
--> OLAP Analytic Workspace             [upgrade]  VALID
--> Oracle Enterprise Manager Repository [upgrade]  VALID
--> Oracle Text                         [upgrade]  VALID
--> Oracle XML Database                 [upgrade]  VALID
--> Oracle Java Packages                [upgrade]  VALID
--> Oracle Multimedia                   [upgrade]  VALID
--> Oracle Spatial                      [upgrade]  VALID
--> Expression Filter                   [upgrade]  VALID
--> Rule Manager                        [upgrade]  VALID
--> Oracle Application Express          [upgrade]  VALID
--> Oracle OLAP API                     [upgrade]  VALID
**********************************************************************
                           [Tablespaces]
ERROR: --> SYSTEM tablespace is not large enough for the upgrade.
       currently allocated size: 760 MB
       minimum required size: 1262 MB
       increase current size by: 502 MB
       tablespace is NOT AUTOEXTEND ENABLED.
ERROR: --> SYSAUX tablespace is not large enough for the upgrade.
       currently allocated size: 570 MB
       minimum required size: 1476 MB
       increase current size by: 906 MB
       tablespace is NOT AUTOEXTEND ENABLED.
--> UNDOTBS1 tablespace is adequate for the upgrade.
       minimum required size: 400 MB
--> TEMP tablespace is adequate for the upgrade.
       minimum required size: 60 MB
--> EXAMPLE tablespace is adequate for the upgrade.
       minimum required size: 310 MB
               [make adjustments in the current environment]
**********************************************************************
                        [Pre-Upgrade Checks]
**********************************************************************
```

```
WARNING: --> Process Count may be too low
      Database has a maximum process count of 150 which is lower than the
      default value of 300 for this release.
      You should update your processes value prior to the upgrade
      to a value of at least 300.
      For example:
         ALTER SYSTEM SET PROCESSES=300 SCOPE=SPFILE
      or update your init.ora file.

ERROR: --> A user or role with the name "AUDSYS" found in the database.

      This is an internal account used by Oracle Database Auditing.
      You must drop this user or role prior to upgrading.

ERROR: --> A user or role with the name "AUDIT_VIEWER" found in the database.

      This is an Oracle defined role.
      You must drop this role or user prior to upgrading.

WARNING: --> Enterprise Manager Database Control repository found in the
database

      In Oracle Database 12c, Database Control is removed during
      the upgrade. To save time during the Upgrade, this action
      can be done prior to upgrading using the following steps after
      copying rdbms/admin/emremove.sql from the new Oracle home
    - Stop EM Database Control:
     $> emctl stop dbconsole

    - Connect to the Database using the SYS account AS SYSDBA:

    SET ECHO ON;
    SET SERVEROUTPUT ON;
    @emremove.sql
      Without the set echo and serveroutput commands you will not
      be able to follow the progress of the script.

WARNING: --> Existing DBMS_LDAP dependent objects

      Database contains schemas with objects dependent on DBMS_LDAP package.
      Refer to the Upgrade Guide for instructions to configure Network ACLs.
      USER APEX_030200 has dependent objects.
```

WARNING: --> Database contains INVALID objects prior to upgrade

    The list of invalid SYS/SYSTEM objects was written to
    registry$sys_inv_objs.
    The list of non-SYS/SYSTEM objects was written to
    registry$nonsys_inv_objs unless there were over 5000.
    Use utluiobj.sql after the upgrade to identify any new invalid
    objects due to the upgrade.

INFORMATION: --> OLAP Catalog(AMD) exists in database

    Starting with Oracle Database 12c, OLAP is desupported.
    If you are not using the OLAP Catalog component and want
    to remove it, then execute the
    ORACLE_HOME/oraolap/admin/catnoamd.sql script before or
    after the upgrade.

INFORMATION: --> Older Timezone in use

    Database is using a timezone file older than version 18.
    After the upgrade, it is recommended that DBMS_DST package
    be used to upgrade the 11.2.0.4.0 database timezone version
    to the latest version which comes with the new release.
    Please refer to My Oracle Support note number 977512.1 for details.

ERROR: --> RECYCLE_BIN not empty.
    Your recycle bin contains 3 object(s).
    It is REQUIRED that the recycle bin is empty prior to upgrading.
    Immediately before performing the upgrade, execute the following
    command:
        EXECUTE dbms_preup.purge_recyclebin_fixup;
****
                [Pre-Upgrade Recommendations]
****

               ****
               ********* Dictionary Statistics *********
               ****

Please gather dictionary statistics 24 hours prior to
upgrading the database.

To gather dictionary statistics execute the following command
while connected as SYSDBA:
    EXECUTE dbms_stats.gather_dictionary_stats;

^^^ MANUAL ACTION SUGGESTED ^^^

****
                   [Post-Upgrade Recommendations]
****

                 ****
                 ******** Fixed Object Statistics ********
                 ****

Please create stats on fixed objects two weeks
after the upgrade using the command:
    EXECUTE DBMS_STATS.GATHER_FIXED_OBJECTS_STATS;

^^^ MANUAL ACTION SUGGESTED ^^^

****
                  *********** Summary ***********

5 ERRORS exist that must be addressed prior to performing your upgrade.
4 WARNINGS that Oracle suggests are addressed to improve database performance.
2 INFORMATIONAL messages that should be reviewed prior to your upgrade.

After your database is upgraded and open in normal mode you must run
rdbms/admin/catuppst.sql which executes several required tasks and completes
the upgrade process.

You should follow that with the execution of rdbms/admin/utlrp.sql, and a
comparison of invalid objects before and after the upgrade using
rdbms/admin/utluiobj.sql

If needed you may want to upgrade your timezone data using the process
described in My Oracle Support note 977512.1
                 ****

To fix the issues identified before the upgrade, you can run the preupgrade_fixups.sql script. This script uses the dbms_preup.run_fixup_and_report routine to fix the issues. Here is a sample of the script, with only a few lines shown.

```
$ cat /u01/app/oracle/cfgtoollogs/ocad11/preupgrade/preupgrade_fixups.sql
REM Pre-Upgrade Script Generated on: 2014-01-11 12:47:39
REM Generated by Version: 12.1.0.1 Build: 006
SET ECHO OFF SERVEROUTPUT ON FORMAT WRAPPED TAB OFF LINESIZE 750;
BEGIN
  dbms_output.put_line ('Pre-Upgrade Fixup Script Generated on 2014-01-11
12:47:39  Version: 12.1.0.1 Build: 006');
  dbms_output.put_line ('Beginning Pre-Upgrade Fixups...');
END;
/
BEGIN
dbms_preup.clear_run_flag(TRUE);
END;
/
BEGIN
-- ****************  Fixup Details **********************************
-- Name:        DEFAULT_PROCESS_COUNT
-- Description: Verify min process count is not too low
-- Severity:    Warning
-- Action:      ^^^ MANUAL ACTION REQUIRED ^^^
-- Fix Summary:
--     Review and increase if needed, your PROCESSES value.

dbms_preup.run_fixup_and_report('DEFAULT_PROCESS_COUNT');
END;
/
```

When you run the preupgrade_fixups.sql script, it fixes some of the trivial issues, but it does not fix the issues that could damage the database. For example, dropping Enterprise Manager Database Control, resizing tablespaces, dropping users and roles, gathering statistics, and so on must be fixed manually by the DBA. It will let you know to manually fix those issues before the upgrade. Here is the summary section shown after the script is run.

```
            ************ Fixup Summary ************

 1 fixup routine was successful.
 4 fixup routines returned INFORMATIONAL text that should be reviewed.
```

2 ERROR LEVEL checks returned INFORMATION that must be acted on prior to upgrade.

```
        ************************************************************
                   ====>> USER ACTION REQUIRED  <<====
        ************************************************************
```

1) Check Tag: AUDSYS_USER_PRESENT failed.
   Check Summary: Verify if a user or role with the name AUDSYS exists
   Fixup Summary:
   "The AUDSYS user or role must be dropped prior to upgrading."
   ^^^ MANUAL ACTION REQUIRED ^^^

2) Check Tag: AUDIT_VIEWER failed.
   Check Summary: Verify if a user or role with the name AUDIT_VIEWER exists
   Fixup Summary:
   "The AUDIT_VIEWER role or user must be dropped prior to upgrading."
   ^^^ MANUAL ACTION REQUIRED ^^^

```
        ****************************************************
        You MUST resolve the above errors prior to upgrade
        ****************************************************
```

The DBA must fix the errors identified in the script before proceeding with the upgrade. After running the preupgrade_fixups.sql, run the preupgrd.sql script again to verify that the database is ready. Manually fix all errors and informational notices in the script so that the upgrade goes smoother.

The tool also identifies certain best practices to complete after the upgrade. The postupgrade_fixups.sql script can be run after the upgrade. The first few lines of the script are shown here:

```
$ cat /u01/app/oracle/cfgtoollogs/ocad11/preupgrade/postupgrade_fixups.sql
REM Post Upgrade Script Generated on: 2014-01-11 12:47:39
REM Generated by Version: 12.1.0.1 Build: 006
SET ECHO OFF SERVEROUTPUT ON FORMAT WRAPPED TAB OFF LINESIZE 750;
BEGIN
  dbms_output.put_line ('Post Upgrade Fixup Script Generated on 2014-01-11
12:47:39  Version: 12.1.0.1 Build: 006');
  dbms_output.put_line ('Beginning Post-Upgrade Fixups...');
END;
/
BEGIN
```

```
dbms_preup.clear_run_flag(FALSE);
END;
/
BEGIN
-- ***************** Fixup Details ***********************************
-- Name:          INVALID_OBJECTS_EXIST
-- Description: Check for invalid objects
-- Severity:    Warning
-- Action:        ^^^ MANUAL ACTION REQUIRED ^^^
-- Fix Summary:
--      Invalid objects are displayed and must be reviewed.

dbms_preup.run_fixup_and_report('INVALID_OBJECTS_EXIST');
END;
/
BEGIN
-- ***************** Fixup Details ***********************************
-- Name:          OLD_TIME_ZONES_EXIST
-- Description: Check for use of older timezone data file
-- Severity:    Informational
-- Action:        ^^^ MANUAL ACTION REQUIRED ^^^
-- Fix Summary:
--      Update the timezone using the DBMS_DST package after upgrade is complete.

dbms_preup.run_fixup_and_report('OLD_TIME_ZONES_EXIST');
END;
/
```

> **WARNING**   Running the Pre-Upgrade Information tool prior to the manual database upgrade is mandatory; otherwise, the upgrade will terminate with errors. When you upgrade the database using DBUA, it runs this script for you automatically. We recommend that you still run the script and fix the errors before starting DBUA.

Additional Checks

The Pre-Upgrade Information tool checks for the following components and gives you guidance and fix-up scripts. The tool checks to determine:

- If the predefined users and roles required for Oracle Database 12*c* exist prior to upgrade. These roles and users must be dropped, because they are associated with the new features of the database. They are SYSDG, SYSBACKUP, SYSKM, AUDSYS, AUDIT_

VIEWER, AUDIT_ADMIN, CAPTURE_ADMIN, ORACLE_OCM. In addition, the tool checks for a few internal users such as APPQOSSYS.

- If OLAP Catalog (AMD) exists in the database. Starting with Oracle Database 12c, OLAP is desupported. The tool advises you to drop the catalog prior to the upgrade.
- If AWR data has inactive DBIDs.
- If the COMPATIBLE parameter is at 11.0.0 or higher.
- If the JOB_QUEUE_PROCESSES value is set too low.
- If the PROCESSES parameter is sufficiently high.
- If LOG_ARCHIVE_FORMAT has the required format.
- If there is a need to remove hidden parameters, depreciated parameters, and underscore events.
- If the timezone version needs to be updated or is newer. Oracle Dabase 12c 12.1.0.1 comes with version 18.
- If ORDSYS (Oracle Multimedia Domain Index) or UltraSearch is still used.
- If DMSYS schema still exists.
- If DBMS_LDAP dependent objects or manual network ACL configuration is required. Also, identifies schemas with network ACL.
- If Database Vault is enabled. It may recommend disabling, because it is a requirement to disable before the upgrade and enable after the upgrade if needed.
- If Enterprise Manager Database Control is present in the database.
- If it needs to drop sys.enabled$indexes, if it exists.
- If there are any unresolved distributed transactions.
- If information exists stating that the Expression Filter (EXF) and Database Rules Manager (RUL) features are desupported and will be removed during the upgrade process, if EXF or RUL are present in the database.
- If any files are in backup mode or in media-recovery-needed state.
- If SYS and SYSTEM users have SYSTEM as their default tablespace.
- If SYSTEM and SYSAUX tablespaces have enough free space for the upgrade.
- If there are INVALID objects in the database. The list of invalid SYS/SYSTEM objects are written to registry$sys_inv_objs. The list of non-SYS/SYSTEM objects are written to registry$nonsys_inv_objs. Use the utluiobj.sql script after the upgrade to identify any new invalid objects due to the upgrade.
- If the components in DBA_REGISTRY are valid.
- If the recycle bin needs to be purged.
- If any changes need to be made to the LOG_ARCHIVE_DEST_1 or LOG_ARCHIVE_DEST_10 parameters to satisfy the Oracle Database 12c archive destination rules.
- If the standby database is in sync with the primary.

- If all table data in the database has been updated to the latest type definitions.
- If recommendations are needed to run dictionary and fixed objects statistics.

In addition, as a best practice, you will need to perform the following:

- Drop or fix all invalid objects.
- Make sure sufficient space exists in the ASM disk group or file system where SYSTEM and SYSAUX files reside. It is better to have the data files belonging to these tablespaces in AUTOEXTEND mode.
- Check that the SGA value is at least the minimum required for Oracle Database 12c.
- Preserve the database performance statistics so that you can compare performance of queries and application before and after upgrade. The AWR data is automatically purged after certain days. Creates baselines so that the data is not purged. Also, you may export the AWR data.
- Preserve the operating system performance statistics.
- Make sure there is a good backup of the ORACLE_HOME and database.
- Determine the client versions of the users, application, and ODBC connecting to the database, and then upgrade the client versions.
- Disable cron jobs and jobs scheduled outside the database until the upgrade is completed.

If the database being upgraded has additional products or features installed, more preparation might be needed.

- If the database has Database Vault installed, disable it before the upgrade.
- If you have configured Oracle Label Security (OLS) with Database Vault, then you must run the OLS preprocess script, olspreupgrade.sql, to process the aud$ table contents. The OLS upgrade moves the aud$ table from the SYSTEM schema to the SYS schema.

The AWR compare-period reports are very helpful for comparing the performance of the database before and after the upgrade. Remember to capture periodic baselines before your upgrade to compare after the upgrade. For example, you may want to baseline month-end and quarter-end processing periods.

Preparing the Oracle Home

Before you upgrade a database to Oracle Database 12c, Oracle software must be installed in a different Oracle home on the same server. Make sure you verify the certification and minimum operating requirements before installing the software. Oracle Database 12c software installation was discussed in detail in Chapter 9. Once the software is installed, install the latest Patch Set Update (PSU). The PSU can be downloaded from My Oracle Support. Follow the readme document to apply the PSU.

If you use DBUA for the upgrade, the following activities are performed for you. For a manual upgrade, you need to perform the following activities.

- Copy and edit the parameter file. Perform `CREATE pfile FROM spfile` statement, and copy the text initialization parameter file from $ORACLE_HOME/dbs to the new Oracle Database 12*c* home directory under the dbs directory. Edit the parameter file to remove undocumented parameters and deprecated parameters. Make sure the SGA and other parameter values are appropriate.

- Copy the password file from the old $ORACLE_HOME/dbs directory to the Oracle Database 12*c* home.

- Copy the `tsnames.ora`, `sqlnet.ora` files from the old $ORACLE_HOME/network/admin directory to the Oracle Database 12*c* home. This is an important step, if the upgraded database uses database links that are resolved using the `tsnames.ora` file.

Reducing Upgrade Downtime

Various options are available to reduce the upgrade downtime required. They are as follows:

- Run the upgrade in parallel, making use of all available CPU resources.

- Run the gather dictionary statistics before the upgrade.

- The upgrade process drops the EM Database Control. You can run $ORACLE_HOME/rdbms/admin/emremove.sql from the Oracle Database 12*c* software install home to remove the EM before the upgrade.

- Back up (export or create another table) and truncate the SYS.AUD$ table.

- Keep the COMPATIBLE parameter at the current level until the database is tested after the upgrade (if upgrading from 10.2.0.5, the COMPATIBLE parameter must be changed to 11.0.0 or higher). If it is changed to 12.1, the database cannot be downgraded back to the old release. You will have to restore from the backup to go back to the old release.

- Make sure your redo logs are sufficiently sized and that you have at least four redo log groups.

- Run the upgrade using ARCHIVELOG mode, and use Flashback Database features to fall back if the upgrade does not go well.

Once all the pre-upgrade tasks are completed, you will be ready for the database upgrade.

Running the upgrade in ARCHIVELOG mode with Flashback Database enabled will have some performance impact on the upgrade. However, the flexibility this option gives, especially for a large database, outweighs the minor performance impact and storage required. If an error is encountered during the upgrade, the database can be rolled back to an earlier state quickly by using the flashback logs and guaranteed restore point.

Upgrading the Database

Upgrading an Oracle database to a new release is a major activity. We cannot stress enough the importance of planning and testing before upgrading the production database. Oracle's Database Upgrade Assistant (DBUA) is an easy-to-use, robust tool to upgrade an earlier Oracle database version to 12c. If you want to have more control over the upgrade process, you can perform a manual upgrade as well. In this section, you will learn about upgrading the database using DBUA and using the manual upgrade scripts.

Using Database Upgrade Assistant

DBUA is a graphical tool to upgrade a database in version 10.2.0.5, 11.1.0.7, 11.2.0.2, or higher to Oracle Database 12c. DBUA has a simple interface, with status reporting on the screen as well as to log files. DBUA is invoked by $ORACLE_HOME/bin/dbua on Unix. On Windows, choose Database Upgrade Assistant from the Configuration and Migration Tools tab under the Oracle Database 12c menu items.

On Unix systems, set the environment to Oracle Database 12c home. Make sure environment variables ORACLE_HOME, PATH, and LD_LIBRARY_PATH all point to Oracle Database 12c Oracle home. To help in setting up the environment, you may add a dummy entry in the /etc/oratab file with the new Oracle home path, as shown below with SID name *temp*, and use oraenv to set the environment.

```
$ cat /etc/oratab
# This file is used by ORACLE utilities.  It is created by root.sh
# and updated by either Database Configuration Assistant while creating
# a database or ASM Configuration Assistant while creating ASM instance.
# A colon, ':', is used as the field terminator.  A new line terminates
# the entry.  Lines beginning with a pound sign, '#', are comments.
# Entries are of the form:
#   $ORACLE_SID:$ORACLE_HOME:<N|Y>:
# The first and second fields are the system identifier and home
# directory of the database respectively.  The third field indicates
# to the dbstart utility that the database should, "Y", or should not,
# "N", be brought up at system boot time.
# Multiple entries with the same $ORACLE_SID are not allowed.
ocad11:/u01/app/oracle/db_home1/11.2.0:N
temp:/u01/app/oracle/db_home2/12.1.0:N
```

Set the environment using oraenv, and verify the variables.

```
$ . oraenv
ORACLE_SID = [oracle] ? temp
The Oracle base has been set to /u01/app/oracle
```

```
$ echo $ORACLE_HOME
/u01/app/oracle/db_home2/12.1.0

$ echo $LD_LIBRARY_PATH
/u01/app/oracle/db_home2/12.1.0/lib

$ which dbua
/u01/app/oracle/db_home2/12.1.0/bin/dbua
```

When you launch the DBUA application, the initial screen displayed is the Select Operation screen, as shown in Figure 17.2. DBUA gives you the option to upgrade the database or to move a database from one Oracle home to another home of the same release. Choose the Upgrade Oracle database option, and click Next.

FIGURE 17.2   DBUA – The Select Operation screen

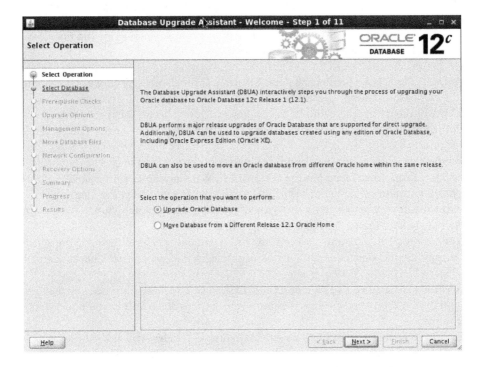

You will be presented with the Select Database screen, which allows you to select the database for the upgrade (Figure 17.3). Oracle lists the databases on the server based on the contents in /etc/oratab file. Choose the appropriate database for the upgrade. The screen shows the Source Database Oracle home directory and to which Oracle home the software is being upgraded.

FIGURE 17.3 DBUA – The Select Database screen

Database Upgrade Assistant - Upgrade Oracle Database - Step 2 of 11			

Select Database

ORACLE **12**c
DATABASE

- Select Operation
- **Select Database**
- Prerequisite Checks
- Upgrade Options
- Management Options
- Move Database Files
- Network Configuration
- Recovery Options

Select Database

Target Oracle Home · /u01/app/oracle/db_home2/12.1.0

Target Oracle Home Release · 12.1.0.1.0

Source Oracle Home · /u01/app/oracle/db_home1/11.2.0 ▼

Source Oracle Home Release · 11.2.0.4.0

Select	Name/SID	Release	Status	Type
⊙	ocad11	11.2.0.4.0	↑ Up	Single Instance

The oratab file is a control file maintained by the database configuration tools (DBCA or DBUA). The file is located under /etc/ on Linux and most Unix systems. On Solaris, the location is /var/opt/oracle. The file lists the databases installed on the server.

The screen also indicates whether the database is up. If the database is down, DBUA will bring up the database to run the prerequisite checks. If you have run the preupgrd.sql script and taken care of the issues, there will be only a few to address here. DBUA runs the Pre-Upgrade Information tool and shows you the results. The Prerequisite Check result screen is shown in Figure 17.4.

Click on the blue arrow beside Pre-Upgrade Utility Checks to view the checks that are failed. The Show drop-down menu has the options: All, Warnings and Failures, and Failures. The Action column shows what actions the DBUA can take: Fix Now, Fix Pre-Upgrade, Ignore, or Revalidate. Fix Now will fix the error when you click the Apply Action button, and Fix Pre-Upgrade will fix the error as part of the pre-upgrade tasks.

For certain errors, DBUA cannot perform the fix. It can only perform the revalidation. The fix has to be applied outside of DBUA. For example, in the Prerequisite Checks screen shown in Figure 17.4, the AUDSYS user and AUDIT_VIEWER role cannot be dropped using DBUA; they must be dropped by DBA, and the DBUA must revalidate the check by using the Check Again button. You may ignore errors and warning, but do so only if you understand the implications.

The next screen is the Upgrade Options screen (Figure 17.5). Here you can choose the number of CPUs to be used for the upgrade by specifying the parallelism. This option reduces the time needed to perform the upgrade based on the number of CPUs available to handle the running of scripts and processes. If you do not want a parallel upgrade, choose 1. You also have options to Recompile Invalid Objects, Upgrade Timezone Data, Gather Statistics Before The Upgrade, and to Set User Tablespaces To Read Only. When the user tablespaces are set to read only, only nonuser tablespaces (system, sysaux, and undo) will need to be restored in case of any failure.

FIGURE 17.4   DBUA – The Prerequisite Checks screen

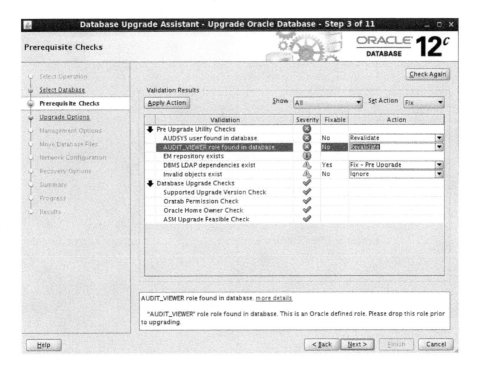

The Custom SQL Scripts tab is used for specifying custom SQL scripts that can be run before and after the upgrade.

You have the option to either configure the upgraded database with EM Database Express or to register with OEM Cloud Control, as shown in Figure 17.6. Oracle Enterprise Manager Database Express is a web-based database management application that is built into Oracle Database 12*c*. It replaces the DB Control component that was available in releases 10g and 11g.

DBUA also gives the option to migrate the storage of the database and Fast Recovery Area to another file system or to Automatic Storage Management (ASM). ASM is discussed in Chapter 18. Figure 17.7 shows the Move Database Files screen.

After Move Database Files options have been selected, click the Next button and the Network Configuration screen will be displayed as shown in Figure 17.8. The Listener Selection area of the Network Configuration screen shows a table with: Name, Port, Oracle Home, Status, and Migrate columns. To the left of the listener name is a box for selecting the listener. Select one or more listeners from the source Oracle home to be migrated to the new upgraded Oracle home. DBUA adds the selected listener to the listener.ora file of the target Oracle home and starts it. It also removes the entry of the upgraded database from the old listener.ora file. If you do not want to migrate the listener, create a new listener in the target Oracle home by specifying the listener name and port.

FIGURE 17.5   DBUA – The Upgrade Options screen

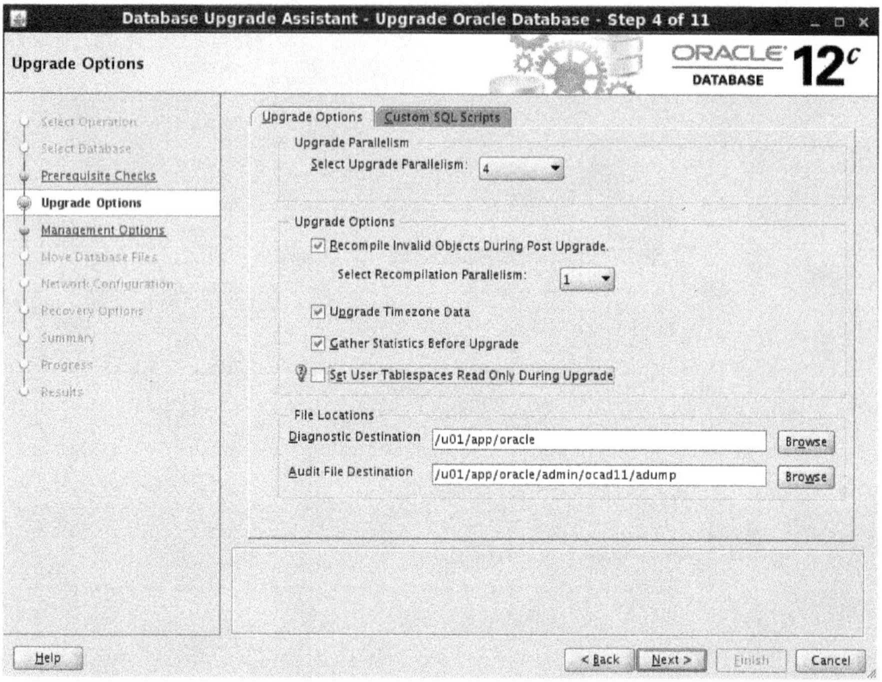

FIGURE 17.6   DBUA – The Management Options screen

The Recovery Options screen, shown in Figure 17.9, gives you options to backup the database.

You can choose from the following options:

- Create a New Offline RMAN Backup: Enter the full path for a location for the backup in the Backup Location field. DBUA performs a backup before the upgrade.

- Use Existing RMAN Backup: DBUA displays the timestamp for the latest RMAN backup that exists.

FIGURE 17.7   DBUA – The Move Database Files screen

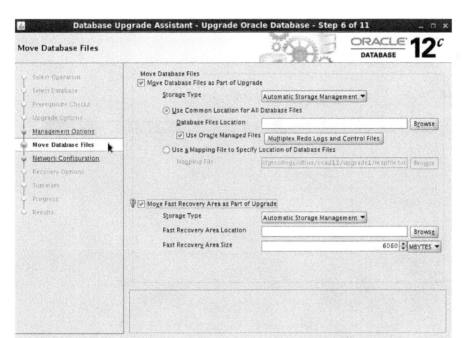

FIGURE 17.8   DBUA – The Network Configuration Screen

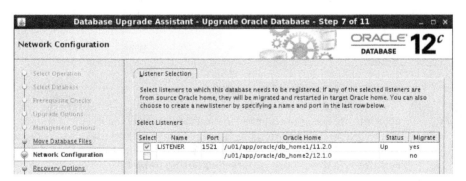

- Create a New Guaranteed Restore Point: If a Flash Recovery Area is currently configured, the current settings will be retained. DBUA also displays a screen to allow you to override these values if needed. DBUA automatically creates a restore point that you can revert back to in case of upgrade failure.

- Use Existing Guaranteed Restore Point: If a restore point was previously created, then select the existing restore point from the drop-down list.
- I Have My Own Backup and Restore Strategy: Use this option only if a customized backup procedure was used to back up the database. You should use customized restore procedures to restore the customized backup.

FIGURE 17.9   DBUA – The Recovery Options screen

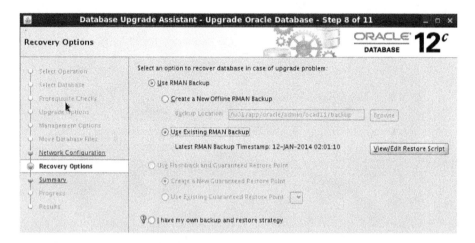

When you click Next on this screen, DBUA will check to see if the SYSTEM and SYSAUX data files are in auto-extend mode and if enough free space is available. DBUA at this time also checks to see if there is enough room to keep the archivelogs and flashback logs generated during the upgrade, and it warns you if there is not enough space.

Figure 17.10 shows the upgrade summary. It shows the source and target Oracle home directories, the checks ignored by DBA, which components of the database are upgraded, the initialization parameter changes, the versions of timezone upgrade, Enterprise Manager option, Recovery option, and Listener registration. Review this information carefully.

> The DBUA log files and scripts are written to $ORACLE_BASE/cfgtoollogs/ dbua/db_unique_name/upgradeN directory. Review the logs and scripts generated by DBUA during the upgrade to understand the upgrade process more fully. If you have chosen to back up the database using RMAN, you can also find a database restore script using RMAN.

The Progress screen shows the database upgrade status in detail (Figure 17.11). The progress is divided into three phases:

- Pre Upgrade Steps
- Database Upgrade Steps
- Post Upgrade Steps

FIGURE 17.10   DBUA – The Summary screen

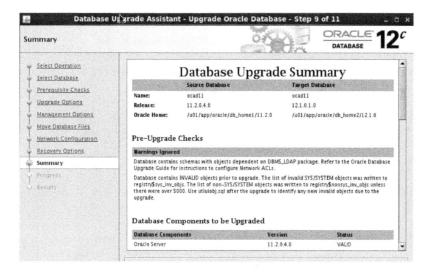

Each phase can be expanded to see the details. The timing for each step to take place is provided. The DBA can use the times to identify time-consuming steps during the test upgrade cycle.

The Progress screen also provides options to view the activity log and the alert log. The activity log shows the current action being performed; it shows the output of the trace.log file generated by DBUA. The alert log shows the alert log content. Monitoring the alert log for errors and messages is a best practice.

Monitoring the activity log shows the current phase of the upgrade, and whether the phase is run in parallel or serial. Oracle uses this information to restart an upgrade process. For example:

```
[Phase 23] type is 2 with 11 Files
catmetgrant1.sql catldap.sql       prvtocm.sql       prvtrepl.sql
catpstr.sql       prvthpci.plb      catilm.sql        catemxv.sql
catnaclv.sql      dbmsnacl.sql      dbmswlm.sql

... ... ...
Parallel Phase #:33 Files: 122    Time: 20s
Serial   Phase #:34 Files: 1      Time: 0s
Restart  Phase #:35 Files: 1      Time: 0s
Serial   Phase #:36 Files: 4      Time: 81s
Restart  Phase #:37 Files: 1      Time: 0s
Parallel Phase #:38 Files: 13     Time: 78s
Restart  Phase #:39 Files: 1      Time: 0s
Parallel Phase #:40 Files: 10     Time: 9s
Restart  Phase #:41 Files: 1      Time: 0s
```

FIGURE 17.11 DBUA – The Progress screen

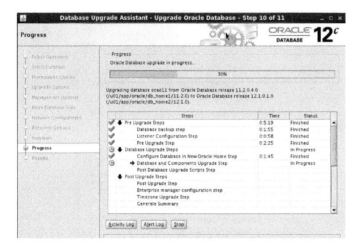

After the upgrade is completed, the Stop button on the Progress screen (Figure 17.11) becomes an Upgrade Results button. Click on the Upgrade Results button to view the results, as shown in Figure 17.12. You will get the option to Restore Database, which reverts the database back to its pre-upgraded state.

FIGURE 17.12 DBUA – The Update Results screen

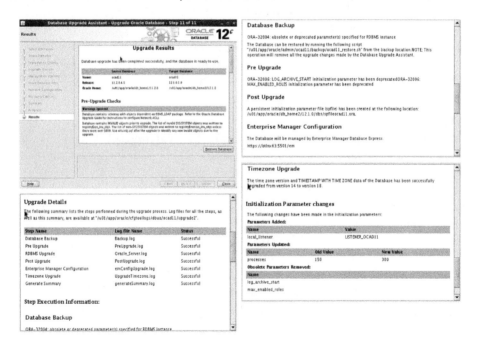

Review the information carefully so that you will understand the changes made by DBUA during the upgrade. The log files created by DBUA will be displayed so you can review them. The location of spfile created by DBUA will also be indicated.

Real World Scenario

Fixing a Stalled Database Upgrade

During one of the database upgrade activities, the DBA noticed that the Progress screen had not moved from one step to the next for a while. Clicking on the activity log did not reveal any errors or warnings. However, the Alert Log button displayed the following message, which kept repeating:

```
Errors in file /u01/app/oracle/diag/rdbms/p11d/p11d/trace/p11d_arc0_13863.trc:
ORA-19815: WARNING: db_recovery_file_dest_size of 4385144832 bytes is 99.55% used,
and has 19628032 remaining bytes available.
Errors in file /u01/app/oracle/diag/rdbms/p11d/p11d/trace/p11d_arc1_13865.trc:
ORA-19815: WARNING: db_recovery_file_dest_size of 4385144832 bytes is 99.55% used,
and has 19628032 remaining bytes available.
Sun Jan 12 18:36:41 2014
***********************************************************************
Sun Jan 12 18:36:41 2014
***********************************************************************
You have following choices to free up space from recovery area:

1. Consider changing RMAN RETENTION POLICY. If you are using Data Guard,1.
Consider changing RMAN RETENTION POLICY. If you are using Data Guard,then consider
changing RMAN ARCHIVELOG DELETION POLICY.   then consider changing RMAN ARCHIVELOG
DELETION POLICY.

2. Back up files to tertiary device such as tape using RMAN2. Back up files to
tertiary device such as tape using RMAN BACKUP RECOVERY AREA command.

3. Add disk space and increase db_recovery_file_dest_size parameter to3. Add disk
space and increase db_recovery_file_dest_size parameter to reflect the new space.
reflect the new space.

4. Delete unnecessary files using RMAN DELETE command. If an operating4. Delete
unnecessary files using RMAN DELETE command. If an operating system command was
used to delete files, then use RMAN CROSSCHECK and   system command was used to
delete files, then use RMAN CROSSCHECK and

   DELETE EXPIRED commands.   DELETE EXPIRED commands.
```

```
****************************************************************************
The DBA had ignored the warning of low space given by the DBUA. To fix the issue, the
DBA logged into the database using another session and increased the Fast Recovery
Area because enough space was available on the file system.

$ . oraenv
ORACLE_SID = [c12ndb1] ? temp
The Oracle base remains unchanged with value /u01/app/oracle
$
$ export ORACLE_SID=p11d
$ sqlplus '/ as sysdba'

SQL> alter system set db_recovery_file_dest_size=20g;

System altered.

SQL>
```

During an upgrade, make sure to monitor space usage, Fast Recovery Area usage, and
the alert log to avoid any problems. To avoid such issues and to improve upgrade performance, the database may be in NOARCHIVELOG mode, but you loose the ability to utilize
the flashback features to restore the database if the upgrade fails. So, it is a trade-off you
need to weigh.

Invoking DBUA in Silent Mode

DBUA can be invoked in silent mode with the `-silent` command-line option. In silent
mode, no user input is obtained. You can provide input in command line mode using
various options available. Invoking dbua with the `-help` option will display all the available command-line options.

```
$ dbua -help
dbua    [-silent] [<command> [options] ]*
Refer to the Oracle Database Upgrade Guide for details.
Following are the possible commands:

    [-sid <Specify System Identifier> ]
    [-oracleHome <Specify Source Database Oracle Home > ]
    [-oracleBase <Specify Database Oracle Base > ]
    [-diagnosticDest <Specify Database Diagnostic Destination > ]
```

```
    [-auditFileDest <Specify Database Audit File Destination > ]
    [-sysDBAUserName <user name  with SYSDBA privileges> ]
    [-sysDBAPassword <password for sysDBAUserName user name> ]
    [-autoextendFiles <Autoextend database files during upgrade. Datafiles will
be reverted back to their original autoextend settings after upgrade.> ]
    [-newGlobalDbName <Specify New Global Database Name> ]
    ... ... ...
    [-createGRP <To create a guaranteed restore point when database is in
archive log and flashback mode> ]
    [-useGRP <To restore the database using specified guaranteed restore point> ]
    [-useExistingBackup <To restore database using existing RMAN backup> ]
    [-listeners <To register the database with existing listeners, specify
listeners by comma separated listenerName:Oracle Home. Listeners from lower
release home are migrated to newer release home. Specifying  -listeners
lsnrName1,lsnrName2, DBUA searches specified listeners from GI home (if
configured), target home and source home.> ]
    [-createListener <To create a listener in newer release Oracle home specify
listenrName:lsnrPort> ]
    [-h | -help {Shows this usage help.}]


For example, the following command selects "orcl" database for upgrade:
    dbua -sid orcl


For example, the following command upgrades "orcl" database in silent mode:
    dbua -silent -sid orcl
```

Performing a Manual Upgrade

What happens during a manual upgrade is similar to what happens during a DBUA upgrade. However, during a manual upgrade, the DBA is responsible for reviewing the prerequisites before making the upgrade, for running the upgrade scripts, and for performing any post-upgrade tasks. The manual upgrade method can be used for database versions 10.2.0.5, 11.1.0.7, 11.2.0.2, and higher—the same as with a DBUA direct upgrade.

Similar to the DBUA upgrade, the manual upgrade also can be divided into three phases: pre-upgrade, upgrade, and post-upgrade.

Performing the Pre-Upgrade Tasks

The DBUA performs several checks and fixes for you before starting the upgrade. During the manual upgrade, the DBA is responsible for making sure the database and environment are ready for the upgrade. Although the manual upgrade allows more control for the DBA, the process is error prone and involves more work. The tasks to be taken care of before the upgrade can occur are as follows.

- Copy the Pre-Upgrade Information script preupgrd.sql and utluppkg.sql from the Oracle Database 12c $ORACLE_HOME/rdbms/admin directory to the $ORACLE_HOME/rdbms/admin directory of the source Oracle home. Run the Pre-Upgrade Information tool, and fix all errors and warnings.

  ```
  SQL> @$ORACLE_HOME/rdbms/admin/preupgrd.sql
  ```

- Complete all the steps and checks mentioned in the "Preparing for Database Upgrade" section. Make sure to prepare the Oracle home and create the parameter file and the password file.

- If you are using a cluster database (RAC), set the CLUSTER_DATABASE=FALSE parameter during the upgrade, and set it back to true after the upgrade.

- Run the Gather Dictionary Statistics job.

  ```
  SQL> EXEC DBMS_STATS.GATHER_DICTIONARY_STATS;
  ```

- Back up the source database. If desired, enable Fast Recovery Area and configure the restore point to use the Flashback Database.

- Purge the database recycle bin.

  ```
  SQL> PURGE DBA_RECYCLEBIN
  ```

- Confirm that SYS and SYSTEM users have SYSTEM as the default tablespace.

  ```
  SQL> ALTER user SYS default tablespace SYSTEM;
  SQL> ALTER user SYSTEM default tablespace SYSTEM;
  ```

- Remove the Enterprise Manager Database Control repository. Copy the emremove.sql script from the Oracle Database 12c $ORACLE_HOME/rdbms/admin to the source $ORALCE_HOME/rdbms/admin and then execute on the source database prior to the upgrade.

  ```
  $ emctl stop dbcontrol
  SQL> @?/rdbms/admin/emremove.sql
  ```

- Confirm that AUD$ table is owned by SYS and is in the SYSTEM tablespace. If there are too many rows in the AUD$ table, back up and truncate the AUD$ table, otherwise the upgrade process could run longer.

- If OLS(Lable Security) and/or DV(Database Vault) were already in the database prior to the upgrade, copy the olspreupgrde.sql script from the Oracle Database 12c $ORACLE_HOME/rdbms/admin to the source $ORALCE_HOME/rdbms/admin and then execute on the source database prior to the upgrade.

  ```
  SQL> @ ?/rdbms/admin/olspreupgrade.sql
  ```

Executing the Manual Upgrade Tasks

Once the pre-upgrade tasks and backup of the database are completed, you will be ready to upgrade the database. The upgrade tasks to be executed are as follows:

- Shut down the listener and database. Do not perform SHUTDOWN ABORT for any reason; it must be a graceful shutdown, where no instance recovery is needed during startup.

- Create a new listener or use an existing Oracle Database 12*c* listener. The listener must be running at the highest version of databases running on the server.

- If you are on Windows, stop the old version service and start a new service under Oracle Database 12*c* home.

  ```
  C:\> NET STOP OracleServiceSIDNAME
  C:\> ORADIM -DELETE -SID SIDNAME
  C:\> ORADIM -NEW -SID SID -INTPWD PASSWORD  -STARTMODE AUTO -PFILE %ORACLE_
  HOME%\DATABASE\INITSIDNAME.ORA
  ```

- Confirm that the environment variables point to Oracle Database 12*c* home.

  ```
  $ export ORACLE_HOME=<location of Oracle 12.1>
  $ export PATH=$ORACLE_HOME/bin:$PATH
  $ orabase
  /u01/app/oracle
  $ export ORACLE_BASE=/u01/app/oracle
  ```

- Edit the oratab file to add the instance name with Oracle Database 12*c* home, and comment out the instance with the prior version home.

  ```
  $ cat /etc/oratab
  #ocad11:/u01/app/oracle/db_home1/11.2.0:N
  ocad11:/u01/app/oracle/db_home2/12.1.0:N
  ```

- From Oracle Database 12*c* home, start up the database using STARTUP UPGRADE.

  ```
  $ cd $ORACLE_HOME/rdbms/admin
  $ sqlplus "/ as sysdba"
  SQL> startup UPGRADE
  ```

- Upgrade the database using catctl.pl script. In the earlier versions, the upgrade script catupgrd.sql was run directly from SQL Plus, which ran single threaded. The default parallelism for catctl.pl is 4. The upgrade script is provided as a parameter to the Perl script.

  ```
  $ cd $ORACLE_HOME/rdbms/admin
  $ $ORACLE_HOME/perl/bin/perl catctl.pl catupgrd.sql
  ```

The STARTUP UPGRADE Option

To upgrade the database to Oracle Database 12c, you must start the instance with the STARTUP UPGRADE option (introduced in Oracle9i Release 2). If you try to start the database in any other mode, you will get an error. This mode automatically handles certain system parameter values for the upgrade. It restricts logons to AS SYSDBA sessions, disables system triggers, and performs additional operations that prepare the environment for the upgrade. Also, this option suppresses the ORA-00942 error for the DROP TABLE statements in the upgrade script. When reviewing for errors, you will see only genuine errors in the log file. For a successful upgrade, there should be no ORA- or PLS- errors in the log file.

The Parallel Upgrade Script – catctl.pl

To upgrade the database to Oracle Database 12c, use the catctl.pl script, which runs in default parallelism of 4. To specify parallelism, use the -n option. Set to 0, the -n option runs the upgrade in serial mode. The maximum parallelism is 8. The -l option specifies the location of spool and log files. The default location is the current directory. The -p option lets you restart the upgrade from a specific phase. The log file shows which phases are completed and currently being executed.

The following example invokes the upgrade with six parallel threads and writes the log and output files to $ORACLE_BASE/admin/$ORACLE_SID/upgrade directory.

```
cd $ORACLE_HOME/rdbms/admin
$ORACLE_HOME/perl/bin/perl catctl.pl -n 6 -l $ORACLE_BASE/admin/$ORACLE_SID/
upgrade catupgrd.sql
```

If you want to run the catupgrd.sql directly from SQL*Plus, you may do so, but you have to use the parameter PARALLEL=NO, as in the following example:

```
SQL> @catupgrd.sql PARALLEL=NO
```

If you run catupgrd.sql by itself, then catuppst.sql does not run as part of the upgrade process. The catuppst.sql script must be run after catupgrd.sql completes.

- The upgraded database is shut down after running catctl.pl. Start up the instance. This database startup, following the database shutdown performed as part of the catctl.pl script, flushes all caches, clears buffers, and performs other housekeeping activities to ensure the integrity and consistency of the upgraded database.

  ```
  SQL> STARTUP;
  ```

- Run the Post-Upgrade Status tool to show a summary and status of the upgrade. If there are any errors or any component is INVALID, then troubleshoot to fix the error.

  ```
  SQL> connect / as sysdba
  SQL> @utlu121s.sql
  ```

- The Post-Upgrade script catuppst.sql (CATalog UPgrade PoST-upgrade actions) is run as part of the upgrade script. If the upgrade process had any errors, this script might not run. Look for the words *Started:catuppst.sql* in the upgrade log file. If you do not find the string, run the script manually. This script will migrate the baseline data on a pre-12*c* database to the 12*c* database.

  ```
  $ cd $ORACLE_HOME/rdbms/admin
  SQL> connect / as sysdba
  SQL> @catuppst.sql
  ```

- Recompile any invalid objects. You may specify parallelism for the script as a parameter.

  ```
  SQL> @utlrp 6
  ```

- Run the utluiobj.sql (UTility Upgrade Invalid OBJects tool) script to identify new invalid objects after the upgrade. This script will work only if you have run the preupgrd.sql script before the upgrade. It outputs the difference between the invalid objects that exist after the upgrade and invalid objects that existed prior to the upgrade. The invalid objects that existed prior to upgrade are available in the view registry$nonsys_inv_objs.

  ```
  $ cd $ORACLE_HOME/rdbms/admin
  SQL> connect / as sysdba
  SQL> @?/rdbms/admin/utluiobj.sql
  ```

The post-upgrade tasks are the same irrespective of the database upgrade method used: manual or using DBUA. They are discussed in the next section.

Completing the Post-Upgrade Tasks

Now that you've finished the upgrade, the majority of the work is done. Now that you have a newly upgraded Oracle Database 12*c* database, let's make sure the database is healthy and complete any post-upgrade tasks. To begin, make a database backup.

If you used DBUA to do the upgrade, most of the post-upgrade tasks are taken care of if you chose the appropriate options in the Upgrade options screen (see Figure 17.5 earlier).

Run the Post-Upgrade Status tool again to generate the status of the upgrade and to confirm that there are no issues.

```
SQL> connect / as sysdba
SQL> @?/rdbms/admin/utlu121s.sql
```

```
Oracle Database 12.1 Post-Upgrade Status Tool        01-13-2014 13:46:25

Component                        Current        Version  Elapsed Time
Name                             Status         Number   HH:MM:SS

Oracle Server
                                 VALID          12.1.0.1.0  00:25:11
JServer JAVA Virtual Machine
                                 VALID          12.1.0.1.0  00:04:13
Oracle Workspace Manager
                                 VALID          12.1.0.1.0  00:01:18
OLAP Analytic Workspace
                                 VALID          12.1.0.1.0  00:00:41
Oracle OLAP API
                                 VALID          12.1.0.1.0  00:00:19
Oracle XDK
                                 VALID          12.1.0.1.0  00:00:52
Oracle Text
                                 VALID          12.1.0.1.0  00:01:01
Oracle XML Database
                                 VALID          12.1.0.1.0  00:04:22
Oracle Database Java Packages
                                 VALID          12.1.0.1.0  00:00:12
Oracle Multimedia
                                 VALID          12.1.0.1.0  00:02:31
Spatial
                                 VALID          12.1.0.1.0  00:07:26
Oracle Application Express
                                 VALID          4.2.0.00.27 00:44:51
Final Actions
                                                            00:02:47
Total Upgrade Time: 01:36:10

PL/SQL procedure successfully completed.

SQL>
```

It is a good idea to run `utlrp.sql` and `utluiobj.sql` again and fix any newly invalidated objects.

```
SQL> @?/rdbms/admin/utlrp.sql
```

```
SQL> @?/rdbms/admin/utluiobj.sql
.
Oracle Database 12.1 Post-Upgrade Invalid Objects Tool 01-13-2014 13:48:44
.
This tool lists post-upgrade invalid objects that were not invalid
prior to upgrade (it ignores pre-existing pre-upgrade invalid objects).
.
Owner                     Object Name                    Object Type
PL/SQL procedure successfully completed.
SQL>
```

Review the environment setup files where you define the following variables, and verify that they are updated to point to the newly upgraded Oracle Database 12*c* home.

```
$ echo $ORACLE_BASE
$ echo $ORACLE_HOME
$ echo $PATH
$ echo $LD_LIBRARY_PATH
$ echo $SH_LIB_PATH
```

If you are not using spfile, maybe this is the time to start using spfile instead of pfile. You can create spfile from pfile using the following statement, and restart the database.

```
SQL> CREATE spfile FROM pfile;
```

If you performed a manual upgrade, all the Oracle-supplied user accounts have the default password and are unlocked. DBUA locks the Oracle-supplied user accounts as part of the post-upgrade by default. Lock the Oracle-created accounts and expire their passwords except for SYS and SYSTEM. The following SQL code can be used to identify the newly created users and their account status.

```
SQL> SELECT username, account_status, created
     FROM   dba_users
     ORDER BY created;
SQL> ALTER USER sysdg PASSWORD EXPIRE ACCOUNT LOCK;
```

If your timezone version is lower and the Pre-Upgrade Information tool advised you to upgrade the timezone, then you may upgrade timezone using the DBMS_DST package.

Once all the testing is completed and you are satisfied with the newly upgraded database, change the COMPATIBLE parameter to 12.1.0 (or the current release) to utilize the new features of the database. Once you make this change, the downgrade option will no longer be available. Restart the database for the change to take effect. To revert the COMPATIBLE value after restarting the database, you must restore the database from a backup before upgrade.

```
SQL> ALTER SYSTEM SET compatible = '12.1.0' SCOPE=spfile;
```

To be able to perform the RMAN backup using a catalog repository, you will have to upgrade the catalog to Oracle Database 12c as well.

You learned about Unified Auditing of Oracle Database 12c in Chapter 13, "Implementing Security and Auditing." Unified Auditing is not enabled by default after the upgrade. In the following section, we will show you what needs to be done to enable Unified Auditing after the upgrade.

> Even if you use DBUA to upgrade the database, it won't change the COMPATIBLE parameter from its original value (the exception is when you upgrade a 10.2.0.5 database, because the minimum COMPATIBLE must be 11.0.0 to upgrade the database to 12.1). After the upgrade is completed and the database is validated, make sure to change the COMPATIBLE parameter to 12.1.0 to utilize all features of Oracle Database 12c.

Migrating to Unified Auditing

In Unified Auditing, all of the audit trail information is combined into UNIFIED_AUDIT_TRAIL data dictionary view. See Chapter 13 to learn about the unified audit trail. After the database upgrade, the Unified Auditing option is not enabled; you have to manually enable the option by relinking the Oracle executable.

You have the option to remain on traditional pre-Oracle Database 12c auditing or to migrate to Oracle Database 12c Unified Auditing or to use both in mixed-mode. The mixed-mode Unified Auditing facility becomes available if you enable at least one of the Unified Auditing predefined audit policies. In mixed-mode, the traditional audit records are written to the AUD$ and other audit tables for those audits still enabled using the traditional audit statements. You can create and enable new audit policies and use the predefined audit policies. These records will be written to the unified audit trail.

The Unified Auditing option and all predefined audit policies are disabled after a database upgrade. You can review the status using the queries you learned in Chapter 13.

```
SQL> SELECT VALUE FROM V$OPTION
    WHERE PARAMETER = 'Unified Auditing';

SQL> SELECT user_name, policy_name, enabled_opt, success, failure
    FROM audit_unified_enabled_policies;
```

There are three predefined audit policies: ORA_SECURECONFIG, ORA_ACCOUNT_MGMT, and ORA_DATABASE_PARAMETER. You can enable these audit policies and create new policies.

To migrate to pure Unified Auditing and disable traditional audit trails for new audit records, you enable the Unified Auditing option by recompiling the Oracle executable. Shut down the database and the listener, and relink Oracle using the following syntax:

```
cd $ORACLE_HOME /rdbms/lib
make -f ins_rdbms.mk uniaud_on ioracle ORACLE_HOME=$ORACLE_HOME
```

For Windows, rename the %ORACLE_HOME%/bin/orauniaud12.dll.dbl file to %ORACLE_HOME%/bin/orauniaud12.dll.

After migrating to pure Unified Auditing, the traditional audit records will still be available in the old audit tables; they are not migrated to the new format. No new audit records write to the earlier audit trails. You may archive or purge those audit records. The audit configuration from the earlier release has no effect in the unified audit system. Only unified audit policies generate audit records inside the unified audit trail.

Configuring a Database for an Extended Datatype

Oracle Database 12c supports up to 32KB for VARCHAR2, NVARCHAR2, and RAW datatypes; however, to store over 4,000 bytes you must set the MAX_STRING_SIZE to EXTENDED. This change can be performed only when you start the database in UPGRADE mode. Once changed to EXTENDED, it cannot be changed back to STANDARD. The steps are

- Shut down the database.

- Start the database in UPGRADE mode.

- Change MAX_STRING_SIZE using ALTER SYSTEM SET MAX_STRING_SIZE = EXTENDED.

- Run the $ORACLE_HOME/rdbms/admin/utl32k.sql script as SYSDBA.

- Shut down and start the database for normal operation.

Downgrading to an Earlier Release

Sometimes it may be necessary to downgrade a database to its previous release because of issues with applications in the new database. Although the safe method to go back is to restore from the backup taken prior to upgrade, Oracle provides an option to downgrade the database to its earlier release. You cannot downgrade back to release 10.2.0.5 because the minimum compatibility setting for Oracle Database 12c is 11.0. The earliest release that you can downgrade back to is Oracle Database release 11.1.0.7. If the COMPATIBLE parameter of your Oracle Database 12c database is 12.1.0, you will not be able to downgrade.

During the upgrade, EM Database Control was removed. You will have to reinstall it (or if you have backup, reconfigure EM Database Control).

To downgrade the database, follow these steps:

1. From the Oracle Database 12c Oracle home, shut down the database, and then start up using the DOWNGRADE option.

```
SQL> SHUTDOWN IMMEDIATE;
SQL> STARTUP DOWNGRADE;
```

2. Run the downgrade script. The `catdwgrd.sql` script downgrades all Oracle Database 12*c* components in the database to the supported major release or patch release from which you originally upgraded.

```
$ cd $ORACLE_HOME/rdbms/admin
SQL> connect / as sysdba
SQL> @catdwgrd.sql
```

3. Shut down the instance.

```
SQL> SHUTDOWN IMMEDIATE;
```

4. Set the environment of the 11g database.

```
$ echo $ORACLE_HOME
$ echo $PATH
$ echo $LD_LIBRARY_PATH
```

5. Start up the database in `UPGRADE` mode.

```
SQL> STARTUP UPGRADE;
```

6. Reload the catalog using script `catrelod.sql`. The `catrelod.sql` script reloads the appropriate version for each of the database components in the downgraded database.

```
$ cd $ORACLE_HOME/rdbms/admin
SQL> connect / as sysdba
SQL> @catrelod.sql
```

7. Manually reload Apex using script `apxrelod.sql`.

```
SQL> @apxrelod.sql
```

8. Shut down the database and start up in `NORMAL` mode.

```
SQL> SHUTDOWN IMMEDIATE;
SQL> STARTUP;
```

9. Recompile any invalid objects.

```
SQL> @?/rdbms/admin/utlrp.sql
```

Summary

Performing an Oracle Database 12*c* upgrade is a major task that requires proper planning, testing, and practice. In this chapter, you learned the pre-upgrade, upgrade, and post-upgrade tasks associated with a database upgrade. Oracle supports the direct upgrade of the database to Oracle Database 12*c* if the current database version is 10.2.0.5, 11.1.0.7, 11.2.0.2, or higher. If you are on any other version, you will first need to get to these versions using an intermediate upgrade step before upgrading to Oracle Database 12*c*.

A lot of planning, preparation, and fixing may need to go into the pre-upgrade phase. The more careful you are in this phase and the better you complete all the tasks identified by the Pre-Upgrade Information tool (preupgrd.sql), the better and more error-free your upgrade will be. Running the preupgrd.sql script is a must for a manual upgrade of the database.

Upgrading a database to Oracle Database 12*c* is simplified by the use of a DBUA. DBUA does the pre-install tasks, backs up the database, adjusts parameters, upgrades the database, and does the post-upgrade status. It also can perform a few post-upgrade tasks such as upgrade a timezone and recompile invalid objects. Upgrade status and log files are provided by DBUA.

Upgrading the database using the manual method is accomplished by running the all-new Perl script catctl.pl. This script performs the upgrade in parallel, making use of the CPU resources available. In manual upgrade mode, the DBA has to take care of the pre-upgrade and post-upgrade tasks to complete the upgrade project successfully.

The Post-Upgrade Status tool (utlu121s.sql) shows the status of the components after upgrade. Another very useful post-upgrade tool is the utluiobj.sql. This tool lists the newly invalidated objects after the upgrade. After the upgrade, you may have to update the timezone version and migrate the database to Unified Auditing. Once you change the COMPATIBLE parameter of the database to 12.1.0, you won't be able to downgrade the database.

Exam Essentials

Learn which versions of Oracle can be upgraded directly to Oracle Database 12*c* and learn the upgrade path for other versions.   Oracle supports direct upgrade of the database to Oracle Database 12*c* from 10.2.0.5, 11.1.0.7, 11.2.0.2, or higher versions. For other database versions, you need to first upgrade to one of these releases before upgrading to Oracle Database 12*c*. You can also use data migration tools, such as Data Pump, to migrate data to an Oracle Database 12*c* database.

Understand the output files produced by the Pre-Upgrade Information tool.   The Pre-Upgrade Information tool is comprised of two scripts: preugrd.sql and utluppkg.sql. It produces three output files. preupgrade.log is the log file with detailed checks and status; preupgrade_fixups.sql is the script to fix trivial issues; postupgrade_fixups.sql script fixes issues after the upgrade.

Understand the advantages of using Database Upgrade Assistant to upgrade a database rather than a manual upgrade. Using DBUA automates the upgrade process. DBUA can back up the database, perform the pre-upgrade checks and fix issues, upgrade the database, and perform post-upgrade tasks. It also writes detailed log files.

Know the scripts involved in a manual upgrade of a database. The Perl script catctl.pl is used to upgrade the database. This script runs in parallel with the catupgrd.sql upgrade script. A catalog upgrade is performed by catuppst.sql script. The Post-Upgrade Status tool is invoked by running the script utlu121s.sql.

Understand the importance of the COMPATIBLE parameter in an upgrade. The COMPATIBLE parameter must be set to 11.0.0 or higher for the upgrade. Once you change the value to 12.1.0 on the upgraded database, you cannot downgrade the database.

Learn how to migrate a newly upgraded database to Unified Auditing. Unified Auditing and predefined audit policies are disabled after the upgrade. You can continue to use traditional auditing, migrate to Unified Auditing, or run in mixed-mode.

Review Questions

1. When you are upgrading a database to Oracle Database 12*c*, which of the following options are true?

   A. Any version of an Oracle 10g or Oracle 11g database can be upgraded to Oracle Database 12*c* using DBUA.

   B. Only the versions 10.2.0.5, 11.1.0.7, 11.2.0.2, 11.2.0.3, and 11.2.0.4 can be upgraded to 12.1.0.

   C. Once upgraded to Oracle Database 12*c*, the upgraded database can only be downgraded to Oracle 11g.

   D. When a 10.2.0.5 database is upgraded to Oracle Database 12*c*, it cannot be downgraded.

2. Which is the best option for upgrading an Oracle 10g R2 database that is in its terminal release to Oracle Database 12*c*?

   A. Use Data Pump utilities to export and import.

   B. Perform a direct upgrade using DBUA.

   C. Upgrade to 11g 11.1.0.7 or 11.2.0.2 using DBUA, and then upgrade the database to 12.1.0 using Oracle Database 12*c* DBUA.

   D. Run `catctl.pl` script on the Oracle 10g instance, and then start the instance in Oracle Database 12*c*.

3. When you're using DBUA to upgrade a database from Oracle 10g, which of the following activities are not performed by DBUA? (Choose two.)

   A. Perform the pre-upgrade steps.

   B. Change `listener.ora` to configure the new Oracle home directory information.

   C. Disable archiving during the upgrade.

   D. Back up the database after the upgrade.

   E. Recompile any invalid objects.

   F. Lock the new user accounts that were created.

   G. Adjust the initialization parameter values.

   H. Remove the deprecated initialization parameters.

4. When you're performing a manual upgrade to Oracle Database 12*c*, in what order are the following steps performed?

   1. Run `catctl.pl`.

   2. Run `preupgrd.sql`.

   3. Run `utlu121s.sql`.

   4. Start the database using the `STARTUP UPGRADE` option.

   5. Start the database using the `STARTUP NORMAL` option.

   A. 2, 5, 1, 4, 2

   B. 2, 4, 1, 5, 3

   C. 4, 2, 1, 5, 3

   D. 5, 2, 4, 1, 3

5. Which of the following statements regarding the Pre-Upgrade utility `preupgrd.sql` are correct? (Choose two.)

   A. It checks for space availability, user conflicts, role conflicts, initialization parameters, etc., and prepares fix-up scripts to take care of all issues.

   B. The Pre-Upgrade Information utility does not make any changes to the database, but merely reports results.

   C. `preupgrd.sql` is a standalone script and can be copied to another location to execute on the database to be upgraded.

   D. It recommends the amount of free space required in the `SYSTEM` and `SYSAUX` tablespaces.

6. Which two options are not true with the `STARTUP UPGRADE` mode instance startup?

   A. It initiates the upgrade process automatically after the instance is started.

   B. It suppresses spurious and unnecessary error messages, especially the `ORA-00942`.

   C. It handles certain system startup parameters that could interfere with the upgrade.

   D. This option is more of a documentation purpose when the database is started for upgrade. Its functionality is no different than the default `STARTUP` option.

7. When you click the Restore Database button on the Upgrade Results page, which options must be true to perform a complete restore?

   A. The database is upgraded from 11.2 release to Oracle Database 12*c*.

   B. The database must be backed up using DBUA.

   C. The `COMPATIBLE` parameter value must be 11.2.0.

   D. The database must be backed up prior to the upgrade.

8. Which of the following database options must be upgraded individually when you're upgrading the database using the manual method?

    A. JServer Java Virtual Machine

    B. Oracle Real Application Clusters

    C. Oracle XML Database

    D. All of the above

    E. None of the above

9. Which mechanism is used by Oracle to identify the components that need to be upgraded while upgrading a database?

    A. V$OPTION

    B. V$LICENSE

    C. DBMS_REGISTRY

    D. DBMS_OPTIONS

10. Before manually upgrading an 11.1.0.7 database, what should be the appropriate value of the COMPATIBLE parameter? The current value is the default and is not specified in the parameter file.

    A. 11.1.0.7

    B. 10.2.0.5

    C. 12.1.0

    D. Do not specify the COMPATIBLE parameter in the parameter file.

11. Which option provides the opportunity to defragment the database during the upgrade?

    A. Manual upgrade

    B. DBUA upgrade

    C. Data Pump Export/Import

    D. Transport Database

12. Complete the sentence. To run the Pre-Upgrade Information tool, the database must be started _____.

    A. From Oracle Database 12*c* home

    B. From the original database home

    C. With the STARTUP UPGRADE option

    D. With the STARTUP PREUPGRADE option

13. In your Oracle Database 11g environment, the ORACLE_SID is set to *my11g*, the ORACLE_BASE directory is set to /u01/app/oracle, and the ORACLE_HOME directory is set to /u01/app/oracle/db/11.2.0. When you run the Pre-Upgrade Information tool on this environment from the /home/dba/preup directory, to which location are the log file and fix-up scripts written?

    A. /u01/app/oracle/cfgtoollogs/my11g/preupgrade

    B. /u01/app/oracle/db/11.2.0/cfgtoollogs/my11g/preupgrade

    C. /home/dba/preup/cfgtoollogs/my11g/preupgrade

    D. /home/dba/preup

14. During an upgrade using DBUA, which task cannot be performed by DBUA?

    A. Configure listener.ora in the 12*c* Oracle home, if no listener.ora file exists.

    B. Register the database with an existing listener in the 12*c* Oracle home.

    C. Copy the tnsnames.ora file from an old Oracle home to the 12*c* Oracle home.

    D. Migrate the listener running in the old Oracle home to the 12*c* Oracle home.

15. Which statement about DBUA upgrade is true?

    A. You must shut down and start the source database using the UPGRADE option before invoking DBUA for upgrade.

    B. The new home of the database must be added to oratab file.

    C. DBUA displays the progress of the upgrade, but you have no way of knowing which step or phase is being executed.

    D. Space requirements are identified by DBUA in the Fast Recovery Area; the SYSTEM and SYSAUX tablespaces must be fixed manually outside DBUA.

16. Which option is not available for upgrading a database from 11.2.0.2 to 12.1.0?

    A. Full Database Export/Import using Data Pump.

    B. Full Transportable Export/Import.

    C. Manual upgrade using catctl.pl.

    D. DBUA upgrade.

    E. All of the above are available options.

17. Name the scripts used by the Pre-Upgrade Information and Post-Upgrade Status tools?

    A. preupgrd.sql, postupgrd.sql

    B. utlu121i.sql, utlu121s.sql

    C. utlu121i.sql, postupgrd.sql

    D. preupgrd.sql, utlu121s.sql

18. Which statement regarding Unified Auditing is true regarding a database after upgrade?

   A. The predefined Unified Auditing policies are disabled by default after a manual upgrade.

   B. Pre-12c audit configuration is disabled by default after the upgrade, and audit records are no longer written to the AUD$ table.

   C. One of the predefined Unified Auditing policies is enabled by default after a DBUA upgrade.

   D. Traditional pre-12c audit and 12c Unified Auditing policies cannot co-exist in the same database.

19. To improve upgrade performance and reduce the upgrade time, what tasks should be completed before starting the upgrade? (Choose two.)

   A. Run dbms_stats.gather_dictionary_stats.

   B. Run $ORACLE_HOME/rdbms/admin/emremove.sql.

   C. Run dbms_stats.gather_database_stats.

   D. Purge DBA_RECYCLEBIN.

20. You have a database in Oracle 8.1.7 .4 version. The database size is less than 5GB, including all tablespaces (user data, system, temp, and rollback). Which method would you choose to upgrade to Oracle Database 12c? (Choose the best answer.)

   A. A two-phased upgrade. Upgrade to 10.2.0.5 first, and then upgrade to 12.1.0.

   B. Use traditional export/import using exp/imp tools.

   C. Use the transportable tablespace feature to copy the user_data tablespace to an Oracle Database 12c database.

   D. Use DBUA to upgrade the 8.1.7.4 database directly to 12.1.0.

Chapter

18

Using Grid Infrastructure and Data Movement Tools

ORACLE DATABASE 12*c*: OCA EXAM OBJECTIVES COVERED IN THIS CHAPTER:

✓ **Moving Data**

- Describe ways to move data.

- Use SQL*Loader to load data from a non-Oracle database.

- Use external tables to move data via platform-independent files.

- Use Data Pump Export and Import to move data between Oracle databases.

✓ **Migrating Data by Using Oracle Data Pump**

- Migrate data by using Oracle Data Pump.

✓ **Installing Oracle Grid Infrastructure for a Standalone Server**

- Configure storage for Oracle Automatic Storage Management (ASM).

- Install Oracle Grid Infrastructure for a standalone server.

✓ **Using Oracle Restart**

- Use Oracle Restart to manage components.

As a DBA, you are often required to move data between databases, extract data, or load data received from external sources. Oracle Database 12*c* provides tools to move data. You can use these tools to back up data from a table or a schema before making changes for a quick recovery. Oracle Data Pump is a high-performance data movement tool that you can use to unload and load data between Oracle databases, and you can use the SQL*Loader tool to load data received from external sources such as flat files. External tables are another neat mechanism you can use to read or load flat-file data using the Oracle database.

In this chapter, you will also learn about Oracle's Grid Infrastructure for non-RAC installations as well as Oracle Restart. Learning about these features will complete your review based on the Oracle OCA objectives at the time of this writing. Be sure to complete the material available online after you complete this chapter.

Tools for Moving Data

Even though data movement tools are frequently used in data warehouse environments, OLTP databases also need to load data from external sources or send data to other applications. Oracle provides three major tools to migrate and load data to an Oracle database:

Data Pump   You can use Data Pump to copy data from one schema to another, between two databases, or within a single database. You can also use it to extract a logical copy of the entire database, a list of schemas, a list of tables, or a list of tablespaces to portable operating-system files. Data Pump can also transfer or extract the metadata (DDL statements) for a database, schema, or table. Data Pump is also commonly used to upgrade a database from its current version to 12*c*, especially when an operating system platform migration is planned along with the upgrade.

To support data transfer from legacy databases (versions older than 10g), Oracle Database 12*c* still supports the exp and imp tools. These tools are not enhanced to support new object types or new data types. They are maintained simply to help transfer data from an older-version database to Oracle Database 12*c*.

SQL*Loader   SQL*Loader loads data from flat files into the tables of an Oracle database. It has a powerful data-parsing engine that can read data in many formats. This tool is widely used to load data moved from other applications and external sources, as the source data is not in any proprietary format.

External Tables   External tables are tables with data that does not reside in the database. The external tables feature complements SQL*Loader to load data into the database with complex data manipulation. External tables also can be used to load and unload data from the database using the Data Pump engine.

Figure 18.1 shows the three tools and how they interact with the data when loading and migrating data.

FIGURE 18.1   Oracle data movement tools

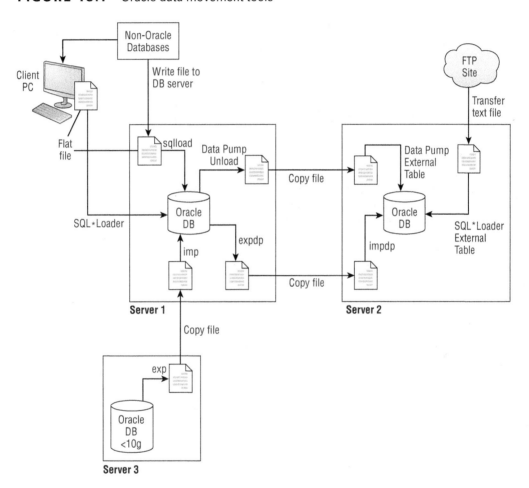

In the example, Data Pump is used to export data using expdp, transfer the binary dump file to the destination server, and import the file using impdp. Data Pump is available in Oracle databases from version 10g. Flat files generated from non-Oracle databases and other sources are transferred to the database server or on the client machine to load into the database using SQL*Loader. If data is to be transferred to the database from another Oracle database under version 10g, you will need to use the legacy exp/imp tools. An external table is used to read a flat file in the database using a SELECT statement, and the external table feature can be used to transfer data using the Data Pump engine between databases.

In the following sections, you will learn about each of these tools in detail. Let's start with Data Pump.

For Data Pump (expdp, impdp) and external tables, the data files need to be accessible on the server where the database is running; whereas SQL*Loader and exp/imp tools operate on files from the client machine. A client machine is another server or workstation different from the database server, or it could be the database server itself (client and server are the same machine).

Migrating Data Using Data Pump

The *Data Pump* facility is a high-speed mechanism for transferring data or metadata from one database to another or from operating-system files. Data Pump employs direct path unloading and direct path loading technologies. Unlike the older export and import programs (exp and imp), which operated on the client side of a database session, the Data Pump facility runs on the server. Therefore, you must use a database directory to specify dump-file and log-file locations.

You can call Data Pump from the command-line programs expdp and impdp or through the DBMS_DATAPUMP PL/SQL package, or you can invoke it from OEM Cloud Control or by using SQL Developer.

Data Pump Export extracts data and metadata from your database, and Data Pump Import loads this extracted data into the same database or into a different database, optionally transforming metadata along the way. These transformations let you, for example, copy tables from one schema to another or remap a tablespace from one database to another.

Some of the key features of Data Pump include:

- A fine-grained object selection using the INCLUDE and EXCLUDE options.

- An option to specify a lower-compatibility version so only supported object types are exported.

- The ability to perform export and import using parallel processes.

- The ability to detach and attach to a job from the client session, allowing the DBA to close the export/import session and yet have the ability to administer the jobs.

- An option to change target table names, tablespace names, and schema names.

- The ability to export views as tables and to export subset or transformed data.

- The option to compress metadata or data or both during export.

- The option to disable archive logging during import.

- The ability to export tablespace metadata to support the transportable tablespace feature of the database.

- Full transportable exports and imports to move an entire database using transportable tablespace technology.
- An option to append data to an existing table or to truncate and load data to an existing table.
- The automatic use of direct path export whenever possible.
- The ability to copy data from one database to another using a network.
- The ability to specify a sample percentage to unload only a subset of data.
- The ability to monitor job progress; job status can be queried from the database or using EM.
- An option to restart or terminate failed export and import jobs.
- The ability to audit Data Pump jobs with Unified Auditing.
- The option to perform an import in nologging mode to skip redo log generation.

Data Pump Architecture

In Oracle Data Pump, the database does all the work. This is a major deviation from the architecture of export/import utilities, which previously ran as clients and did the majority of the work. The dump files for export/import were stored at the client, whereas the Data Pump files are stored at the server. Figure 18.2 shows the Data Pump architecture.

FIGURE 18.2 The Data Pump architecture

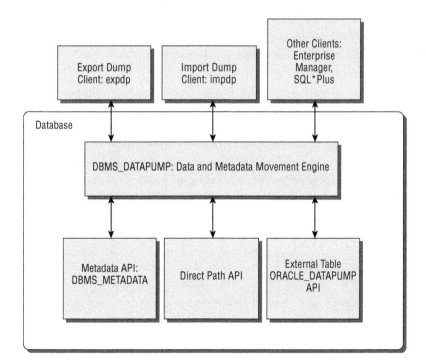

Data Pump Components

Data Pump consists of the following components:

Data Pump API   DBMS_DATAPUMP is the PL/SQL API for Data Pump, which is the engine. Data Pump jobs are created and monitored using this API.

Metadata API   The DBMS_METADATA API provides the database object definition to the Data Pump processes.

Client Tools   The Data Pump client tools expdp and impdp use the procedures provided by the DBMS_DATAPUMP package. These tools make calls to the Data Pump API to initiate and monitor Data Pump operations.

Data Movement APIs   Data Pump uses the Direct Path API (DPAPI) to move data. Certain circumstances do not allow the use of DPAPI; in those cases, the Oracle external table with the ORACLE_DATADUMP access driver API is used.

Data Pump Processes

Oracle Data Pump jobs, once started, are performed by various processes on the database server. The following processes are involved in the Data Pump operation:

Client Process   This process is initiated by the client utility—expdp, impdp, or other clients—to make calls to the Data Pump API. Because Data Pump is completely integrated into the database, once the Data Pump job is initiated, this process is not necessary for the progress of the job.

Shadow Process   When a client logs into the Oracle database, a foreground process is created (a standard feature of Oracle). This shadow process services the client data dump API requests. This process creates the master table and creates Advanced Queries (AQ) queues used for communication. Once the client process ends, the shadow process goes away, too.

Master Control Process (MCP)   The *master control process* controls the execution of the Data Pump job; there is one MCP per job. MCP divides the Data Pump job into various metadata and data-load or data-unload jobs and hands them over to the worker processes. The MCP has a process name of the format <ORACLE_SID>_DMnn_<PROCESS_ID>. It maintains the job state, job description, restart information, and file information in the master table.

Worker Process   The MCP creates the worker processes based on the value of the PARALLEL parameter. The workers perform the tasks requested by the MCP, mainly loading or unloading data and metadata. The worker processes have the format <ORACLE_SID>_DWnn_<PROCESS_ID>. The worker processes maintain the current status in the master table that can be used to restart a failed job.

Parallel Query (PQ) Processes   The worker processes can initiate parallel-query processes if an external table is used as the data-access method for loading or unloading. These are standard parallel-query slaves of the parallel-execution architecture.

Let's consider the example of an export Data Pump operation and see all the activities and processes involved. Say user A invokes the expdp client, which initiates the shadow process. The client calls the DBMS_DATAPUMP.OPEN procedure to establish the kind of export to be performed. The OPEN call starts the MCP process and creates two AQ queues.

The first queue is the status queue, used to send the status of the job, which includes logging information and errors. Clients interested in the status of the job can query this queue. This is strictly a unidirectional queue—the MCP posts the information to the queue, and the clients consume the information. The second queue is the command-and-control queue, which is used to control the worker processes established by the MCP and to perform API commands and file requests. This is a bidirectional queue where the MCP listens and writes. The commands are sent to this queue by the DBMS_DATAPUMP methods or by using the parameters of the expdp client.

Once all the components (parameters and filters) of the job are defined, the client (expdp) invokes DBMS_DATAPUMP.START_JOB. Based on the number of parallel processes requested, the MCP starts the worker processes. The MCP directs one of the worker processes to do the metadata extraction using the DBMS_METADATA API.

During the operation, a master table is maintained in the schema of the user who initiated the Data Pump Export. The master table has the same name as the name of the Data Pump job. This table maintains one row per object with status information. In the event of a failure, Data Pump uses the information in this table to restart the job. The master table is the heart of every Data Pump operation; it maintains all the information about the job. Data Pump uses the master table to restart a failed or suspended job. The master table is dropped (by default) when the Data Pump job finishes successfully.

The master table is written to the dump-file set as the last step of the export dump operation and is removed from the user's schema. For an import dump operation, the master table is loaded from the dump-file set to the user's schema as the first step and is used to sequence the objects being imported.

While the export job is underway, the original client who invoked the export job can detach from the job without aborting the job. This is especially useful when performing long-running data export jobs. Users can attach the job at any time using the DBMS_DATAPUMP methods and query the status or change the parallelism of the job.

WARNING   Because the master table is created in the Data Pump user's schema as a table, if there is an existing table in the schema with the Data Pump job name, the job fails. The user must have the appropriate privileges to create the table and have the appropriate tablespace quotas.

Data Access Methods

Data Pump chooses the most appropriate data-access method. Two methods are supported: direct path access and external table access. Direct path export has been supported since Oracle 7.3. External tables were introduced in Oracle9*i*, and support for writing to external tables has been available since Oracle 10g. Data Pump provides an external tables access driver (ORACLE_DATAPUMP) that can be used to read and write files. The format of the file is the same as the direct path methods; hence, it's possible to load data that is unloaded in another method. Data Pump uses the Direct Load API whenever possible. An external-tables method will be used for the following exceptions:

- Tables with fine-grained access control are enabled in insert and select operations.
- A domain index exists for a LOB column.
- A global index on a multipartition table exists during a single-partition load.
- A clustered table or table has an active trigger during import.
- A table contains BFILE columns.
- A referential integrity constraint is present during import.
- A table contains a VARRAY column with an embedded opaque type.
- Very large tables and partitions are loading and unloading, where the PARALLEL SQL clause can be used to an advantage.
- Tables that are partitioned differently at load time and unload time are loading.

Using Data Pump Clients

Oracle Database 12*c* comes with the expdp utility to invoke Data Pump for export and comes with impdp for import. The Data Pump Export utility (expdp) unloads data and metadata to a set of OS files called *dump files*. The Data Pump Import utility (impdp) loads data and metadata stored in an export dump file to a target database. expdp and impdp accept parameters that are then passed to the DBMS_DATAPUMP program. The command-line executable name for Data Pump Export is expdp and for Data Pump Import is impdp on Windows as well as Unix platforms. For a user to invoke expdp/impdp, they need to set up a directory where the dump files will be stored, and they must have appropriate privileges to perform Data Pump Export/Import. In the next section, we will discuss how to set up the export dump location.

Setting Up the Dump Location

Because Data Pump is server-based, directory objects must be created in the database where the Data Pump files will be stored. Directory objects are named directory locations on the database server, representing the physical location on the server's file system. Directories are used with several database features, including BFILEs, external tables, utl_file, SQL*Loader, and Data Pump.

The directory object contains the location of a specific operating-system directory. By using a named directory object, you do not have to hard-code the directory path in programs, and you get file-management flexibility.

Under Unix, you create directories with the CREATE DIRECTORY statement, like this:

```
CREATE DIRECTORY dump_dir AS '/oracle/data_pump/dumps';
CREATE DIRECTORY log_dir  AS '/oracle/data_pump/logs';
```

Under Windows, you create directories like this:

```
CREATE DIRECTORY dpump_dir  AS 'G:\datadumps';
```

Directories are not schema objects, like tables or synonyms, because they are not owned by a schema. Instead, directories are like profiles or roles, in that they are owned by the database. To control access to a directory, you need to grant the READ or WRITE object privilege on that directory, like this:

```
GRANT read,write ON DIRECTORY dump_dir TO HR;
```

To create directories, you must have the CREATE ANY DIRECTORY system privilege. By default, only the users SYSTEM and SYS have this privilege. Be careful in granting this system privilege to users, because the database employs the operating-system credentials of the database-instance owner.

 Directory objects are owned by the SYS user only; therefore, the directory names must be unique across the database.

The user executing Data Pump must have been granted permissions on the directory. READ permission is required to import, and WRITE permission is required to export and to create log files or SQL files.

Note that the *oracle* OS user (who owns the software installation and database files) must have read and write OS privileges on the directory. The user that connects to the database as SCOTT need not have the privileges on the OS directory for Data Pump to succeed.

A default directory can be created for Data Pump operations in the database. Privileged users (with the EXP_FULL_DATABASE or IMP_FULL_DATABASE privilege) need not specify a directory object name when performing the Data Pump operation. The name of the default directory must be DATA_PUMP_DIR. Also, the privileged users need not have explicit READ or WRITE permission on DATA_PUMP_DIR.

Using EM Cloud Control, you can create and edit directory objects. On the EM Cloud Control screen, choose Directory Objects from the Database Objects menu under Schema. Figure 18.3 shows the Directory Objects screen that appears.

Click the Edit button to change the physical directory. You can also use the Delete button to delete an existing directory and the Create button to create a new directory. The View button shows details about the directory, including the privileges.

Data Pump can write three types of files to the OS directory defined in the database. Remember that absolute paths are not supported; Data Pump can write only to a directory defined by a directory database object. The file types are as follows:

Dump Files   These contain data and metadata information.

Log Files   These record the standard output to a file and contain job progress and status information.

SQL Files   Data Pump Import can extract the metadata information from a dump file, which can be used to create database objects without using the Data Pump Import utility.

FIGURE 18.3 The Directory Objects screen of EM

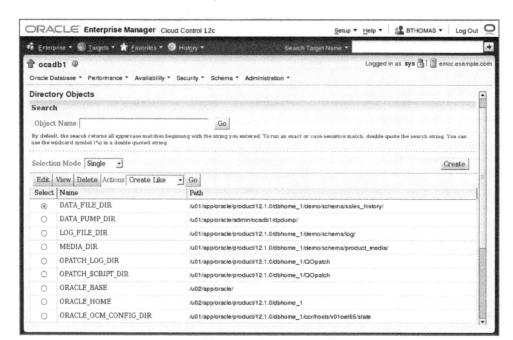

You can specify the location of the files to the Data Pump clients using three methods (given in the order of precedence):

- Prefix the filename with the directory name separated by a colon, for example, DUMPFILE=dumplocation:myfile.dmp.

- Use the DIRECTORY parameter on the OS environment.

- Define the DATA_DUMP_DIR directory in the database for privileged users.

The export and import performed using the expdp and impdp tools can have different modes based on the requirement. The next section discusses this.

Specifying Export and Import Modes

Export and import using the Data Pump clients can be performed in five different modes to unload or load different portions of the database. When performing the dump-file import, specifying the mode is optional; when no mode is specified, the entire dump file is loaded with the mode automatically set to the one used for export.

Table 18.1 describes the export and import modes.

TABLE 18.1 Data Pump Export and Import Modes

Mode	Description	Export	Import
Database	Performed by specifying the FULL=Y parameter.	The export user requires the EXP_FULL_DATABASE role.	The import user requires the IMP_FULL_DATABASE role.
Tablespace	Performed by specifying the TABLESPACES parameter.	Data and metadata for only those objects contained in the specified tablespaces are unloaded. The export user requires the EXP_FULL_DATABASE role.	All objects contained in the specified tablespaces are loaded. The import user requires the IMP_FULL_DATABASE privilege. The source dump file can be exported in database, tablespace, schema, or table mode.
Schema	Performed by specifying the SCHEMAS parameter. This is the default mode.	Only objects belonging to the specified schema are unloaded. The EXP_FULL_DATABASE role is required to specify a list of schemas.	All objects belonging to the specified schema are loaded. The source can be a database or schema-mode export. The IMP_FULL_DATABASE role is required to specify a list of schema.
Table	Performed by specifying the TABLES parameter.	Only the specified table, its partitions, and its dependent objects are unloaded. The export user must have the SELECT privilege on the tables.	Only the specified table, its partitions, and its dependent objects are loaded. This requires the IMP_FULL_DATABASE role to specify tables belonging to a different user.
Transport Tablespace	Performed by specifying the TRANSPORT_TABLESPACES parameter.	Only metadata for tables and their dependent objects within the specified set of tablespaces are unloaded. Use this mode to transport tablespaces from one database to another.	Metadata from a transport tablespace export is loaded.
Transport Database	Performed by specifying TRANSPORTABLE=ALWAYS and FULL=Y parameters. VERSION parameter must be 12.0 or higher.	Similar to transport tablespace for objects in non-SYSTEM/SYSAUX tablespaces. In addition, object data for other objects are exported.	Metadata and data for objects is loaded to build a complete database.

In a database-mode export, the entire database is exported to operating-system files, including user accounts, public synonyms, roles, and profiles. In a schema-mode export, all data and metadata for a list of schemas is exported. At the most granular level is the table-mode export, which includes the data and metadata for a list of tables. A tablespace-mode export extracts both data and metadata for all objects in a tablespace list as well as any object dependent on those in the specified tablespace list. Therefore, if a table resides in your specified tablespace list, all its indexes are included whether or not they also reside in the specified tablespace list. In each of these modes, you can further specify that only data or only metadata be exported. The default is to export both data and metadata.

With some objects, such as indexes, only the metadata is exported; the actual internal structures contain physical addresses and are always rebuilt on import.

The files created by a Data Pump Export are called dump files, and one or more of these files can be created during a single Data Pump Export job. Multiple files are created if your Data Pump job has a parallel degree greater than 1 or if a single dump file exceeds the `filesize` parameter. All the export dump files from a single Data Pump Export job are called a dump-file set.

Using expdp

You use the expdp utility to perform Data Pump Exports. Any user can export objects or a complete schema owned by the user without any additional privileges. Nonprivileged users must have WRITE permission on the directory object and must specify the DIRECTORY parameter or specify the directory object name along with the dump filename.

Here is an example to perform an export by user SCOTT. Because Scott is not a privileged user, he must specify the DIRECTORY object name.

```
$ expdp scott/tiger

Export: Release 12.1.0.1.0 - Production on Sat Jan 18 17:20:05 2014
Copyright (c) 1982, 2013, Oracle and/or its affiliates.  All rights reserved.

Connected to: Oracle Database 12c Enterprise Edition Release 12.1.0.1.0 - 64bit
Production
With the Partitioning, OLAP, Advanced Analytics and Real Application Testing
options
ORA-39002: invalid operation
ORA-39070: Unable to open the log file.
ORA-39145: directory object parameter must be specified and non-null
```

Let's create a directory for user SCOTT and grant read and write privileges on this directory:

```
SQL> CREATE DIRECTORY dumplocation AS '/u02/dpump';
Directory created.
```

```
SQL> GRANT READ, WRITE on DIRECTORY dumplocation TO scott;
Grant succeeded.
```

Now, let's try the export by specifying the directory:

```
$ expdp scott/tiger directory=dumplocation


Export: Release 12.1.0.1.0 - Production on Sat Jan 18 17:22:10 2014
Copyright (c) 1982, 2013, Oracle and/or its affiliates.  All rights reserved.


Connected to: Oracle Database 12c Enterprise Edition Release 12.1.0.1.0 - 64bit
Production
With the Partitioning, OLAP, Advanced Analytics and Real Application Testing
options
Starting "SCOTT"."SYS_EXPORT_SCHEMA_01":  scott/******** directory=dumplocation
Estimate in progress using BLOCKS method...
Processing object type SCHEMA_EXPORT/TABLE/TABLE_DATA
Total estimation using BLOCKS method: 192 KB
Processing object type SCHEMA_EXPORT/PRE_SCHEMA/PROCACT_SCHEMA
Processing object type SCHEMA_EXPORT/TABLE/TABLE
Processing object type SCHEMA_EXPORT/TABLE/COMMENT
Processing object type SCHEMA_EXPORT/TABLE/INDEX/INDEX
Processing object type SCHEMA_EXPORT/TABLE/CONSTRAINT/CONSTRAINT
Processing object type SCHEMA_EXPORT/TABLE/INDEX/STATISTICS/INDEX_STATISTICS
Processing object type SCHEMA_EXPORT/TABLE/CONSTRAINT/REF_CONSTRAINT
Processing object type SCHEMA_EXPORT/TABLE/STATISTICS/TABLE_STATISTICS
Processing object type SCHEMA_EXPORT/STATISTICS/MARKER
. . exported "SCOTT"."DEPT"                               6 KB       4 rows
. . exported "SCOTT"."EMP"                            8.75 KB      14 rows
. . exported "SCOTT"."SALGRADE"                      5.929 KB       5 rows
. . exported "SCOTT"."BONUS"                             0 KB       0 rows
Master table "SCOTT"."SYS_EXPORT_SCHEMA_01" successfully loaded/unloaded
******************************************************************************
Dump file set for SCOTT.SYS_EXPORT_SCHEMA_01 is: /u02/dpump/expdat.dmp
Job "SCOTT"."SYS_EXPORT_SCHEMA_01" successfully completed at Sat Jan 18 17:22:56
2014 elapsed 0 00:00:45
$
```

Because you did not specify any other parameters, expdp used default values for the filenames (expdat.dmp and export.log), performed a schema-level export (login schema), calculated dump file size estimation using the blocks method, used a default job name (SYS_EXPORT_SCHEMA_01), and exported both data and metadata.

Data Pump Export Parameters

You can use various parameters while invoking expdp. You can obtain a list of parameters by specifying the help option expdp help=y. The help description is self-explanatory, producing part of the output in a formatted list to show you the most commonly used options available in export dump client expdp. Default values are listed within square brackets. Be sure to check out all the parameters by executing expdp help=y.

- ATTACH: Attach to an existing job. For example, ATTACH=job_name.

- COMPRESSION: Reduce the size of a dump file.Valid keyword values are: ALL, DATA_ONLY, [METADATA_ONLY] and NONE.

- CONTENT: Specifies data to unload. Valid keyword values are: [ALL], DATA_ONLY and METADATA_ONLY.

- DIRECTORY: Directory object to be used for dump and log files.

- DUMPFILE: Specify list of destination dump file names [expdat.dmp]. For example, DUMPFILE=scott1.dmp, scott2.dmp, dmpdir:scott3.dmp.

- ESTIMATE: Calculate job estimates. Valid keyword values are: [BLOCKS] and STATISTICS.

- ESTIMATE_ONLY: Calculate job estimates without performing the export.

- EXCLUDE: Exclude specific object types. For example, EXCLUDE=SCHEMA:"='HR'".

- FILESIZE: Specify the size of each dump file in units of bytes.

- FLASHBACK_SCN: SCN used to reset session snapshot.

- FLASHBACK_TIME: Time used to find the closest corresponding SCN value.

- FULL: Export entire database [N].

- INCLUDE: Include specific object types. For example, INCLUDE=TABLE_DATA.

- JOB_NAME: Name of export job to create.

- LOGFILE: Specify log file name [export.log].

- NETWORK_LINK: Name of remote database link to the source system.

- NOLOGFILE: Do not write log file [N].

- PARALLEL: Change the number of active workers for current job.

- PARFILE: Specify parameter file name.

- QUERY: Predicate clause used to export a subset of a table. For example, QUERY=employees:"WHERE department_id > 10".

- REMAP_DATA: Specify a data conversion function. For example, REMAP_DATA=EMP.EMPNO:REMAPPKG.EMPNO.

- REUSE_DUMPFILES: Overwrite destination dump file if it exists [N].

- SAMPLE: Percentage of data to be exported.

- SCHEMAS: List of schemas to export [login schema].

- SERVICE_NAME: Name of an active Service and associated resource group to constrain Oracle RAC resources.

- STATUS: Frequency (secs) job status is to be monitored where the default [0] will show new status when available.
- TABLES: Identifies a list of tables to export. For example, TABLES=HR.EMPLOYEES,SH.SALES:SALES_1995.
- TABLESPACES: Identifies a list of tablespaces to export.
- TRANSPORTABLE: Specify whether transportable method can be used. Valid keyword values are: ALWAYS and [NEVER].
- TRANSPORT_TABLESPACES: List of tablespaces from which metadata will be unloaded.
- VERSION: Version of objects to export. Valid keyword values are: [COMPATIBLE], LATEST or any valid database version.
- VIEWS_AS_TABLES: Identifies one or more views to be exported as tables. For example, VIEWS_AS_TABLES=HR.EMP_DETAILS_VIEW.

The following commands are valid while in interactive mode. You can attach to the job and perform these actions.

- ADD_FILE: Add dumpfile to dumpfile set.
- CONTINUE_CLIENT: Return to logging mode. Job will be restarted if idle.
- EXIT_CLIENT: Quit client session and leave job running.
- FILESIZE: Default filesize (bytes) for subsequent ADD_FILE commands.
- KILL_JOB: Detach and delete job.
- PARALLEL: Change the number of active workers for current job.
- START_JOB: Start or resume current job. Valid keyword values are: SKIP_CURRENT.
- STATUS: Frequency (secs) job status is to be monitored where the default [0] will show new status when available.
- STOP_JOB: Orderly shutdown of job execution and exits the client. Valid keyword values are: IMMEDIATE.

FLASHBACK_SCN and FLASHBACK_TIME are mutually exclusive parameters.

The DUMPFILE parameter can specify more than one file. The filenames can be comma-separated, or you can use the %U substitution variable. If you specify %U in the DUMPFILE filename, the number of files initially created is based on the value of the PARALLEL parameter. Preexisting files that match the name of the files generated are not overwritten; an error is flagged. To forcefully overwrite the files, use the REUSE_DUMPFILES=Y parameter. The FILESIZE parameter determines the size of each file. Table 18.2 shows some examples.

You can specify all the parameters in a file and specify the filename with the PARFILE parameter. The only exception is the PARFILE parameter inside the parameter file. Recursive PARFILE is not supported.

TABLE 18.2   Data Pump DUMPFILE Examples

Parameter Examples	File Characteristics
DUMPFILE=exp%U.dmp FILESIZE=200M	Initially, the exp01.dmp file will be created; once the file is 200MB, the next file will be created.
DUMPFILE=exp%U_%U.dmp PARALLEL=3	Initially, three files will be created: exp01_01.dmp, exp02_02.dmp, and exp03_03.dmp. Notice that every occurrence of the substitution variable is incremented each time. Because there is no FILESIZE, no more files will be created.
DUMPFILE=DMPDIR1:exp%U.dmp, DMPDIR2:exp%U.dmp FILESIZE=100M	This method is especially useful if you do not have enough space in one directory to perform the complete export job. The dump files are stored in directories defined by DMPDIR1 and DMPDIR2.

The SAMPLE parameter is useful for unloading a subset of data from the source table. Specify the percentage of rows that need to be unloaded using this parameter. The SAMPLE parameter is not valid for network exports.

In the next section, we will discuss the impdp utility, which does the import from a dump file created using expdp.

The VERSION parameter of expdp is useful for exporting data from a database with the dump file compatible to a specific version. This is especially handy when the target database is at a lower version.

Using impdp

The Data Pump Import program impdp is the utility that can read and apply the dump file created by the expdp utility. The directory permission and privileges for using impdp are similar to those for expdp.

impdp has several modes of operation, including full, schema, table, tablespace, and transportable tablespace. In the full mode, the entire contents of an export file set are loaded. Full mode is also used for full transportable exports. In a schema-mode import, all content for a list of schemas in the specified file set is loaded. The specified file set for a schema-mode import can be from either a database or a schema-mode export. With a table-mode import, only the specified table and dependent objects are loaded from the export file set. With a tablespace-mode import, all objects in the export file set that were in the specified tablespace list are loaded. In transportable tablespace mode, the metadata from another database is loaded using a database link (specified with the NETWORK_LINK parameter) or by specifying a dump file that contains the metadata. The actual data files, specified by the TRANSPORT_DATAFILES parameter, must be made available from the source system for use in the target database, typically by copying them over to the target system.

With all these modes, the source can be a live database instead of a set of export files. Table 18.3 shows the supported mapping of export mode to import mode.

TABLE 18.3 Export to Import Modes

Source Export Mode	Import Mode
Database, Schema, Table, Tablespace, Live database	Full
Database, Schema, Live database	Schema
Database, Schema, Table, Tablespace, Live database	Table
Database, Schema, Table, Tablespace, Live database	Tablespace
Transportable tablespace	Transportable tablespace

The IMP_FULL_DATABASE role is required if the source is a live database or the export session required the EXP_FULL_DATABASE role.

The parameter VIEWS_AS_TABLES is new in the Oracle Database 12c expdp utility. This parameter lets you export the data in a view as if it were a table. This parameter is also available in impdp to use in the network mode of import.

Data Pump Import Parameters

You can use various parameters while invoking impdp. You can obtain a list of parameters by specifying impdp help=y. The help description is self-explanatory, producing part of the output in a formatted list to show you the most commonly used options available in import dump client impdp. Default values are listed within square brackets.

- ATTACH : Attach to an existing job.
- CONTENT : Specifies data to load. Valid keywords are: [ALL], DATA_ONLY and METADATA_ONLY.
- DIRECTORY : Directory object to be used for dump, log and SQL files.
- DUMPFILE : List of dump files to import from [expdat.dmp].
- ESTIMATE : Calculate job estimates.
- EXCLUDE : Exclude specific object types.
- FLASHBACK_SCN : SCN used to reset session snapshot.
- FLASHBACK_TIME : Time used to find the closest corresponding SCN value.

- FULL : Import everything from source [Y].
- INCLUDE : Include specific object types.
- JOB_NAME : Name of import job to create.
- LOGFILE : Log file name [import.log].
- NETWORK_LINK : Name of remote database link to the source system.
- NOLOGFILE : Do not write log file [N].
- PARALLEL : Change the number of active workers for current job.
- PARFILE : Specify parameter file.
- QUERY : Predicate clause used to import a subset of a table.
- REMAP_DATAFILE : Redefine data file references in all DDL statements.
- REMAP_SCHEMA : Objects from one schema are loaded into another schema.
- REMAP_TABLE : Table names are remapped to another table.
- REMAP_TABLESPACE : Tablespace objects are remapped to another tablespace.
- REUSE_DATAFILES : Tablespace will be initialized if it already exists [N].
- SCHEMAS : List of schemas to import.
- SERVICE_NAME : Name of an active Service and associated resource group to constrain Oracle RAC resources.
- SKIP_UNUSABLE_INDEXES : Skip indexes that were set to the Index Unusable state.
- SQLFILE : Write all the SQL DDL to a specified file.
- STATUS : Frequency (secs) job status is to be monitored where the default [0] will show new status when available.
- TABLE_EXISTS_ACTION : Action to take if imported object already exists. Valid keywords are: APPEND, REPLACE, [SKIP] and TRUNCATE.
- TABLES : Identifies a list of tables to import.
- TABLESPACES : Identifies a list of tablespaces to import.
- TRANSFORM : Metadata transform to apply to applicable objects. Valid keywords are: DISABLE_ARCHIVE_LOGGING, LOB_STORAGE, OID, PCTSPACE, SEGMENT_ATTRIBUTES, STORAGE, and TABLE_COMPRESSION_CLAUSE.
- TRANSPORTABLE : Options for choosing transportable data movement.
- VERSION : Version of objects to import.Only valid for NETWORK_LINK and SQLFILE.
- VIEWS_AS_TABLES : Identifies one or more views to be imported as tables.

The following commands are valid while in interactive mode. You can attach to the job and perform these actions.

- CONTINUE_CLIENT : Return to logging mode. Job will be restarted if idle.
- EXIT_CLIENT : Quit client session and leave job running.
- KILL_JOB : Detach and delete job.

- PARALLEL : Change the number of active workers for current job.
- START_JOB : Start or resume current job. Valid keywords are: SKIP_CURRENT.
- STATUS : Frequency (secs) job status is to be monitored where the default [0] will show new status when available.
- STOP_JOB : Orderly shutdown of job execution and exits the client.

You must include one parameter to specify the mode, either full, schemas, tables, or tablespaces. You can include several other parameters on the command line or place them in a file and use the parfile= parameter to instruct impdp where to find them. Here are some examples of imports:

- Read the dump file FULL.DMP and extract all DDL, placing it in the file FULL.SQL. Do not write a log file.

  ```
  impdp system/password full=y dumpfile=dumplocation:FULL.DMP
      nologfile=y sqlfile= dumplocation:FULL.SQL
  ```

- Read the data accessed via the database link PROD, and import schema HR into schema HR_TEST, importing only metadata, writing the log file to the database directory chap7, and naming this log file HR_TEST.imp. Include the timestamp for each step in the log file using the LOGTIME parameter.

  ```
  impdp system/password network_link=prod schemas="HR"
      remap_schema="HR:HR_TEST" content=metadata_only
      logfile= dumplocation:HR_TEST.imp logtime=ALL
  ```

Read the dump file HR.DMP, and write all the DDL to the SQL file HR_proc_give.sql to create any procedures with the name LIKE 'GIVE%'. Do not write a log file.

```
impdp system/password full=y dumpfile= dumplocation:HR.DMP
    nologfile=y sqlfile= dumplocation:HR_proc_give.SQL
    include=PROCEDURE:"LIKE 'GIVE%'"
```

The combinations of parameters you can use to copy data and metadata give you, the DBA, flexibility in administering your databases.

 When using the schema-level import with the SCHEMAS parameter, if the schema does not exist in the target database, the import operation creates it with the same attributes from the source. The schema created by the import operation will need to have the password reset.

You can use the CONTENT, INCLUDE, and EXCLUDE parameters in the impdp utility to filter the metadata objects. Their behavior is the same as in the expdp utility. We'll discuss them in detail in the "Data and Metadata Filters" section. In the next section, we will discuss methods to use a different target for tablespaces, schemas, and data files.

Import Transformations

While performing the import, you can specify a different target name for data files, tablespaces, or schemas. These transformations are possible because the object metadata is stored in the dump file as XML. The REMAP_ parameters are used to specify this. When any one of the three REMAP_ parameters is used, Data Pump transforms the metadata DDL during import. The IMP_FULL_DATABASE role is required to use these parameters. You can use these parameters multiple times if there is more than one transformation to be made, but the same source cannot be repeated more than once. To specify a different target name for each type of object, you can use the following parameters:

REMAP_DATAFILES   Using this parameter, you can specify a different name for the data file. The filename referenced could be in a CREATE TABLESPACE, CREATE LIBRARY, or CREATE DIRECTORY statement. REMAP_DATAFILES is especially useful when you're performing a full database import, when the tablespaces are being created by impdp and the source directories do not exist in the target database server, or when the source and target platforms are different (VMS, Windows, Unix). The syntax is as follows:

    REMAP_DATAFILE=source_datafile:target_datafile

REMAP_SCHEMA   Using this parameter, you can load all the objects belonging to the source schema to a target schema. Multiple source schemas can map to the same target schema. If the target schema specified does not exist, the import operation creates the schema and performs the load. The syntax is as follows:

    REMAP_SCHEMA=source_schema:target_schema

REMAP_TABLE   Using this parameter, you can rename a table while performing the import. Only the table is renamed; its dependent indexes, triggers, constraints, and columns are not renamed. The syntax is as follows:

    REMAP_TABLE=source_table:target_table

REMAP_TABLESPACE   Using this parameter, you can create the objects that belong to a tablespace in the source to another in the target. The syntax is as follows:

    REMAP_TABLESPACE=source_tablespace:target_tablespace

TRANSFORM   Using the TRANSFORM parameter, you can specify that the storage clause should not be generated in the DDL for import. This is useful if the storage characteristics of the source and target databases are different. TRANSFORM has the following syntax:

    TRANSFORM=name:boolean_value[:object_type]

The name of the transform can be either SEGMENT_ATTRIBUTES or STORAGE. STORAGE removes the STORAGE clause from the CREATE statement DDL, whereas SEGMENT_ATTRIBUTES removes physical attributes, tablespaces, logging, and storage attributes. boolean_value can be Y or N; the default is Y. The type of object is optional; the valid values are TABLE and INDEX.

For example, if you want to ignore the storage characteristics during the import and use the defaults for the tablespace, you can do the following:

```
impdp dumpfile=scott.dmp  transform=storage:N:table exclude=indexes
```

The next example will remove all the segment attributes; the import will use the user's default tablespace and its default storage characteristics:

```
impdp dumpfile=scott.dmp  transform=segment_attributes:N
```

In the next section, we will discuss how data can be copied from one database to another without using a dump file.

The FILESIZE parameter in expdp limits the size of a dump file. The parameter is often used when the DUMPFILE parameter includes the %U format, to assign numbers from 01 to 99 to the filename—for example, expdp dumpfile=myfile%U.dmp logfile=myfile.log filesize=2048m.

Disabling Logging During Import

Oracle Data Pump Import provides an option to disable logging for faster imports. Redo log information is not generated with this option; therefore, there are no archive log files to manage either. This option is very useful for large data loads or jobs that initially populate a database. A small amount of logging will still happen when the objects are created in the database. If the database is running in FORCE LOGGING mode, setting this parameter has no effect.

Logging is disabled by using the TRANSFORM parameter. The syntax is

```
TRANSFORM=DISABLE_ARCHIVE_LOGGING:Y|N[:TABLE|INDEX]
```

You can choose to disable logging for tables, indexes, or both. If you specify Y:TABLE, logging is disabled for table loads. If you specify Y:INDEX, logging is disabled only for index creation. If you do not specify TABLE or INDEX along with Y, logging is disabled for both tables and indexes. You may provide the TRANSFORM parameter multiple times. For example, the code shown here disables logging for TABLE using two different methods.

```
$ impdp DIRECTORY=dump_dir DUMPFILE=ex1.dmp LOGFILE=ex1.log SCHEMAS=basket
TRANSFORM=DISABLE_ARCHIVE_LOGGING:Y TRANSFORM=DISABLE_ARCHIVE_LOGGING:N:INDEX
```

```
$ impdp DIRECTORY=dump_dir DUMPFILE=ex2.dmp LOGFILE=ex2.log SCHEMAS=ball
TRANSFORM=DISABLE_ARCHIVE_LOGGING:N:TABLE
```

When impdp is invoked, job status is written to the import master table. These writes are logged even if you set TRANSFORM=DISABLE_ARCHIVE_LOGGING:Y.

Network-Mode Import

NETWORK_LINK enables the network-mode import using a database link. The database link must be created before the import is performed. The export is performed on the source database based on the various parameters; the data and metadata are passed to the source database using the database link and loaded. To get a consistent export from the source database, you can use the FLASHBACK_SCN or FLASHBACK_TIME parameter.

Using FLASHBACK_SCN, FLASHBACK_TIME, ESTIMATE, or TRANSPORT_TABLESPACES requires that the NETWORK_LINK parameter is also specified. Here is an example of how to copy the SCOTT schema in the source (remote) database to LARRY in the target (local) database. Scott's objects are stored in the USERS tablespace; in the target, you will create Larry's objects in the EXAMPLE tablespace. The database link name is NEW_DB.

```
$ impdp schemas=scott network_link=new_db remap_schema=scott:larry
        remap_tablespace=users:example
```

The network mode import is different from using SQL*Net to perform the import: impdp username/password@database.

In the next example, data is read via the database link PROD, and it imports only the data from HR.DEPARTMENTS into schema HR_TEST.DEPARTMENTS. Write a log file to file DEPT_DATA.log.

```
impdp system/password network_link=prod schemas="HR"
    remap_schema="HR:HR_TEST" content=data_only
include=TABLE:"= 'DEPARTMENTS'"
    logfile= dumplocation:HR_TEST.imp
```

Using Network Mode to Refresh Test Data from Production

Consider that you periodically refresh the Oracle test database with production data. Because you have to preserve all the grants on the test schema, you can perform the following steps using SQL*Plus and exp/imp tools to perform the data refresh:

1. Disable all the foreign keys.

2. Disable all the primary keys.

3. Drop the indexes so that the import goes faster.

4. Truncate the tables.

5. Export the data from the production database.

6. Import the data to the test database using parameters:

```
COMMIT=Y
BUFFERS=10485760
FROMUSER=SCHEMAPROD
TOUSER=SCHEMATEST
IGNORE=Y
GRANTS=N
```

You can achieve the same results in a single step using impdp with the following parameters (TEST_SCHEMA is the name of the database link, and it must exist):

```
SCHEMAS=SCHEMAPROD
NETWORK_LINK=TEST_SCHEMA
REMAP_SCHEMA=SCHEMAPROD:SCHEMATEST
TABLE_EXISTS_ACTION=REPLACE
EXCLUDE=OBJECT_GRANT
```

Data and Metadata Filters

The Data Pump provides fine-grained object selection to filter the metadata objects during export and import. You can specify the EXCLUDE and INCLUDE parameters with expdp and impdp clients to filter metadata objects. You can use the CONTENT parameter to specify whether you need to export/import just data, just metadata, or both. You can use the QUERY parameter to filter data rows.

The EXCLUDE and INCLUDE parameters are mutually exclusive. Also, when you specify either parameter, you cannot specify CONTENT=DATA_ONLY. The QUERY, EXCLUDE, and INCLUDE parameters have the following syntax:

```
QUERY=[schema.][table_name:]"query clause"
EXCLUDE=object_type[:"object names"]
INCLUDE=object_type[:"object names"]
```

Table 18.4 shows examples of data and metadata filter usage. The explanations in the Accomplishes column refer to unloading; however, they are applicable to loading also.

TABLE 18.4 Data Pump Metadata Filter Examples

Parameter Examples	Accomplishes
schemas=traing content=metadata_only	Unloads the metadata information for all objects owned by the TRAING schema. No data row will be unloaded.
content=data_only schemas=traing query=traing.student:"where ee_dept = 'IST'"	No metadata will be unloaded; only data rows will be unloaded. All data rows will be unloaded for all tables owned by TRAING, except the STUDENT table, where only the rows that belong to the IST department are unloaded.
content=data_only tables=traing. student query="where ee_dept = 'IST'"	Only rows in the STUDENT table that belong to the IST department are unloaded.
schemas=traing exclude=view,package, procedure,function,grant,trigger exclude=index:"like 'S%'"	Table rows will be unloaded. Metadata definitions for view, trigger, procedure, function, grants, packages, and indexes that begin with *S* are not unloaded.
Content=data_only schemas=hr include=table:"in ('EMPLOYEES', 'DEPARTMENTS')" query="where DEPARTMENT_ID = 10"	Only rows belonging to department 10 are unloaded from the EMPLOYEES and DEPARTMENTS tables.

You can obtain the parameter values for INCLUDE and EXCLUDE by querying the OBJECT_PATH column from the following data dictionary views:

- DATABASE_EXPORT_OBJECTS for full-database export parameters
- SCHEMA_EXPORT_OBJECTS for schema-level export parameters
- TABLE_EXPORT_OBJECTS for table-level export parameters

The following query generates the values that can be used with the INCLUDE/EXCLUDE parameters when performing a schema-level export that is related to packages:

```
SQL> select object_path, comments
     from schema_export_objects
     where object_path like '%PACKAGE%';


OBJECT_PATH        COMMENTS
------------------ -----------------------------------------------------
ALTER_PACKAGE_SPEC Recompile package specifications in the selected
                   schemas
PACKAGE            Packages (both specification and body) in
                   selected schemas and their dependent grants and audits
```

```
PACKAGE_BODY          Package bodies in the selected schemas
PACKAGE_SPEC          Package specifications in the selected schemas

... ... ...
SQL>
```

Data Pump has the ability to monitor jobs and make adjustments to those jobs. The jobs initiated by impdp and expdp can be monitored and modified by using the same clients. In the next section, we will discuss managing jobs using expdp and impdp.

Managing Data Pump Jobs

Data Pump clients expdp and impdp provide an interactive command interface. Because each export and import operation has a job name, you can attach to that job from any computer and monitor or adjust the job. Table 18.5 lists the parameters that can be used interactively.

TABLE 18.5   Data Pump Interactive Parameters

Parameter	Purpose
ADD_FILE	Adds another file or a file set to the DUMPFILE set.
CONTINUE_CLIENT	Changes mode from interactive client to logging mode.
EXIT_CLIENT	Leaves the client session and discontinues logging but leaves the current job running.
KILL_JOB	Detaches all currently attached client sessions and terminates the job.
PARALLEL	Increases or decreases the number of threads.
START_JOB	Starts (restarts) a job that is not currently running. The SKIP_CURRENT option can be used to skip the recent failed DDL statement that caused the job to stop.
STOP_JOB	Stops the current job; the job can be restarted later.
STATUS	Displays detailed status of the job; the refresh interval can be specified in seconds. The detailed status is displayed to the output screen but not written to the log file.

The data dictionary view DBA_DATAPUMP_JOBS shows the active job information along with its current state, the number of threads, and the number of client sessions attached. You can join this view with DBA_DATAPUMP_SESSIONS to get the SADDR column of the sessions attached, and you can join the SADDR column with V$SESSION to get more information. The V$SESSION_LONGOPS view also has an entry showing the progress of the job. Use the SID and SERIAL# columns from V$SESSOIN to query V$SESSION_LONGOPS.

The following example should help you understand the parameters more clearly. Say you have an export dump job to be performed. You start the job with the following parameters in a parameter file:

```
DIRECTORY=DUMPLOCATION
DUMPFILE=volest.dmp
LOGFILE=volest.exp.log
FULL=Y
JOB_NAME=VOLEST_EXP_TEST
```

A table named VOLEST_EXP_TEST is created in your schema. This is the master control table. Querying the DBA_DATAPUMP_JOBS view will show the status of the jobs running:

```
SQL> SELECT job_name, state
  2  FROM dba_datapump_jobs;


JOB_NAME                        STATE
------------------------------  ----------------
VOLEST_EXP_TEST                 EXECUTING

SQL>
```

By pressing Ctrl+C, you can stop the logging screen, and you can enter interactive mode. If you find that the job is halfway through and is consuming too many resources on the server, you can suspend the job and restart it later when the server is less busy:

```
Export> stop_job
Are you sure you wish to stop this job ([y]/n): y
$
```

Let's say you went home and logged back in to your company network. From home, you see the status of the job; the job is in suspended mode. Now, you may use more processing power available in the server to resume the job, so the first step is to attach to the job:

```
$ expdp bill/billthedba attach=VOLEST_EXP_TEST

Export: Release 12.1.0.1.0 - Production on Sat Jan 18 18:11:06 2014
Copyright (c) 1982, 2013, Oracle and/or its affiliates.  All rights reserved.


Connected to: Oracle Database 12c Enterprise Edition Release 12.1.0.1.0 - 64bit
Production
With the Partitioning, OLAP, Advanced Analytics and Real Application Testing
options


Job: VOLEST_EXP_TEST
```

```
Owner: BILL
Operation: EXPORT
Creator Privs: TRUE
GUID: F04A47517DC62C50E0430100007F9D57
Start Time: Saturday, 18 January, 2014 18:11:07
Mode: FULL
Instance: ocadb1
Max Parallelism: 1
Timezone: +00:00
Timezone version: 18
Endianness: LITTLE
NLS character set: AL32UTF8
NLS NCHAR character set: AL16UTF16
EXPORT Job Parameters:
Parameter Name      Parameter Value:
   CLIENT_COMMAND       bill/******** full=y dumpfile=volest.dmp
LOGFILE=volest.exp.log JOB_NAME=VOLEST_EXP_TEST
State: IDLING
Bytes Processed: 0
Current Parallelism: 1
Job Error Count: 0
Dump File: /u01/app/oracle/admin/ocadb1/dpdump/volest.dmp
  bytes written: 4,096

Worker 1 Status:
  Instance ID: 1
  Instance name: ocadb1
  Host name: emcc.example.com
  State: UNDEFINED

Export> parallel=4

Export> status=60

Job: VOLEST_EXP_TEST
  Operation: EXPORT
  Mode: FULL
  State: IDLING
  Bytes Processed: 0
  Current Parallelism: 4
```

```
Job Error Count: 0
Dump File: /u01/app/oracle/admin/ocadb1/dpdump/volest.dmp
  bytes written: 4,096

Worker 1 Status:
  Instance ID: 1
  Instance name: ocadb1
  Host name: emcc.example.com
  State: UNDEFINED

Export> start_job

Export> continue_client
```

After attaching to the job, you increased the threads to 4 from 1 (parallel=4), set up to display detailed status to the screen every minute (status=60), restarted the job (start_job), and let the output display on the screen (continue_client).

Multiple clients (sessions) can attach to a job.

You can use Enterprise Manager Grid Control or Database Control to perform the Data Pump Export and Import. You can also monitor the job using OEM. The next section discusses using the Data Pump Wizard in OEM.

 Real World Scenario

Using Fine-Grained Object Selection

The fine-grained object selection in Data Pump Export came as a real boon for DBAs. As DBAs, we perform daily exports on the OLTP database excluding certain large (maybe we should say "huge") tables. This particular database includes tables that are DSS in nature in addition to the OLTP tables.

We reorganized a tablespace to better group the tables and organized the tables into multiple tablespaces based on the expected size of the tables. The tablespaces have a naming convention of %LARGE, %MED, and %SMALL.

While performing the daily export dump using expdp, we simply use EXCLUDE=TABLESPACE:"like '%LARGE'", which excludes all the objects created in the %LARGE tablespaces.

Using the Data Pump Wizard

You can use EM Cloud Control as a menu-driven interface to Data Pump Export, Import, and transportable tablespace jobs. This interface takes you through the steps of several options and then shows you the PL/SQL code that it will execute. Therefore, you can also use EM to learn more about using the PL/SQL interface. The Database Export/Import menu under Schema has the data movement options, as shown in Figure 18.4.

The data movement options in EM

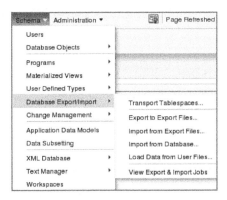

Click the Export to Export Files menu to start a Data Pump Export job. Export and import both support database, schema, table, and tablespace modes. On the first screen, you choose the mode of export. The screen shown in Figure 18.5 appears when you choose the export mode and the schemas to export. Here you have the option to estimate the disk space required for the dump file as well as the number of threads (PARALLEL) required.

You can expand the Show Advanced Options link to specify a data-only export or a metadata-only export, to include or exclude objects, to export a consistent view of data as of a timestamp or SCN, and to filter rows using a query. On the next two screens, you can specify the location of the dump file and job schedule. You have the option to run the job immediately, to run the job at a later time, or to repeatedly run the job. The final screen shows a review of the Data Pump Export, as shown in Figure 18.6. Click Submit Job to launch the Data Pump Export.

Click the Show PL/SQL link to see the PL/SQL code behind the export job. You can run this code using SQL*Plus. Here is an example:

```
declare
  h1    NUMBER;
begin
    h1 := dbms_datapump.open (operation => 'EXPORT', job_mode => 'SCHEMA', job_
name => 'EXPORT000062', version => 'COMPATIBLE');
    dbms_datapump.set_parallel(handle => h1, degree => 1);
```

```
    dbms_datapump.add_file(handle => h1, filename => 'EXPDAT.LOG', directory =>
'DUMPLOCATION', filetype => 3);
    dbms_datapump.set_parameter(handle => h1, name => 'KEEP_MASTER', value =>
0);
    dbms_datapump.metadata_filter(handle => h1, name => 'SCHEMA_EXPR', value =>
'IN(''BI'',''HR'')');
    dbms_datapump.add_file(handle => h1, filename => 'EXPDAT%U.DMP', directory
=> 'DUMPLOCATION', filetype => 1);
    dbms_datapump.set_parameter(handle => h1, name => 'INCLUDE_METADATA', value
=> 1);
    dbms_datapump.set_parameter(handle => h1, name => 'DATA_ACCESS_METHOD',
value => 'AUTOMATIC');
    dbms_datapump.set_parameter(handle => h1, name => 'ESTIMATE', value =>
'BLOCKS');
    dbms_datapump.start_job(handle => h1, skip_current => 0, abort_step => 0);
    dbms_datapump.detach(handle => h1);
end;
/
```

FIGURE 18.5   Data Pump Export – The Options screen in EM

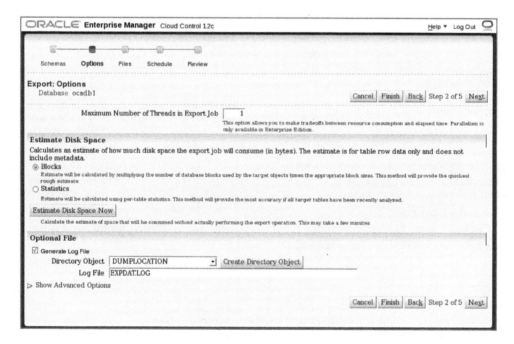

FIGURE 18.6   Data Pump Export – The Review screen in EM

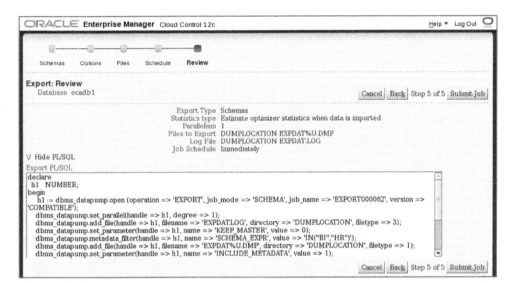

Once the Data Pump job is submitted, you can view its progress by clicking the Monitor Export and Import Jobs link on the Data Movement screen. In this screen, you have the option to increase the parallelism of the job; use the Change Job State button to stop or suspend the job. You also have the option to specify another location for the dump file.

Oracle Database 12c still supports the legacy export and import tools named exp and imp. These tools are not enhanced to include the new data types or new object types in the database. It is always better to use the expdp and impdp tools, if your database is higher than the 10.1 version. If you want to migrate data from a pre-10g database, you can use the exp and imp tools to perform the data migration.

Importing with EM Database Control

Click Import from the Export Files menu to invoke the Data Pump Import Wizard. Similar to Export, Import also has four modes: database, schema, table, and tablespace. After you choose the type of import, the next screen lets you choose the dump file from which to import. On the next screen, you have the option to remap the schema and tablespace. On the Re-Mapping screen shown in Figure 18.7, HR schema objects are imported to the JAMES schema, and the objects in the EXAMPLE tablespace are moved to the USERS tablespace.

FIGURE 18.7   Data Pump Import – The Re-Mapping screen

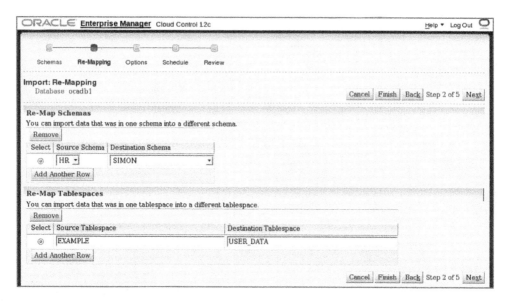

On the next screen, you can specify the number of parallel processes and the log-file destination directory. Similar to the way you export, you can specify to run the job immediately or at a later time. Save the job and schedule by clicking the Submit Job button on the Review screen of the import job. Similar to the way you export, clicking the Show PL/SQL link shows the PL/SQL code behind the import:

```
declare
  h1    NUMBER;
begin
    h1 := dbms_datapump.open (operation => 'IMPORT', job_mode => 'SCHEMA', job_
name => 'IMPORT000064', version => 'COMPATIBLE');
    dbms_datapump.set_parallel(handle => h1, degree => 1);
    dbms_datapump.add_file(handle => h1, filename => 'IMPORT.LOG', directory =>
'DATA_FILE_DIR', filetype => 3);
    dbms_datapump.set_parameter(handle => h1, name => 'KEEP_MASTER', value =>
0);
    dbms_datapump.add_file(handle => h1, filename => 'EXPDAT%U.DMP', directory
=> 'DUMPLOCATION', filetype => 1);
    dbms_datapump.metadata_remap(handle => h1, name => 'REMAP_SCHEMA', old_value
=> 'HR', value => 'SIMON');
    dbms_datapump.metadata_remap(handle => h1, name => 'REMAP_TABLESPACE', old_
value => 'EXAMPLE', value => 'USER_DATA');
    dbms_datapump.metadata_filter(handle => h1, name => 'SCHEMA_EXPR', value =>
'IN(''HR'')');
```

```
    dbms_datapump.set_parameter(handle => h1, name => 'DATA_ACCESS_METHOD',
value => 'AUTOMATIC');
    dbms_datapump.set_parameter(handle => h1, name => 'INCLUDE_METADATA', value
=> 1);
    dbms_datapump.set_parameter(handle => h1, name => 'SKIP_UNUSABLE_INDEXES',
value => 0);
    dbms_datapump.start_job(handle => h1, skip_current => 0, abort_step => 0);
    dbms_datapump.detach(handle => h1);
end;
/
```

If you are a DBA comfortable using the exp and imp tools, but have a hard time switching to expdp and impdp, Oracle Data Pump supports the use of legacy exp/imp parameters with expdp/impdp. The tools convert the legacy input to proper Data Pump parameters before executing the export and import. For example, if you specify GRANTS=N, Data Pump will convert this input to EXCLUDE=GRANT. This mode of operation is known as Data Pump legacy mode.

Upgrading an 11g R2 Database to 12*c* Using Full Transportable Export

The *full transportable export* feature in Oracle Database 12*c* makes it faster and easier to migrate an 11g database to 12*c*. This feature combines the benefits of a transportable tablespace with the full export/import option. Transportable tablespaces are usually the fastest method to move application data between databases. The data files belonging to the tablespace are copied from the source database to the target database. Moving the data file is much faster than exporting and importing individual tables. However, using transportable tablespaces to migrate an entire database is very complex.

The full transportable export option is easy to use, and it migrates the application data using the transportable tablespace feature and the rest of the data, such as metadata and system data, using the traditional export/import method. Like a conventional Data Pump Import, a full transportable import can be used to import a dump file or to import directly from a source database into a destination database over a database link

In order to use the full transportable feature, the databases involved must have the COMPATIBLE parameter set to 12.0.0 or higher. The full transportable option to migrate an 11g database to 12*c* is possible only if the version of the source database is higher than 11.2.0.3. In addition, the VERSION parameter in the expdp must also specify 12. We'll show you how to migrate an 11g R2 database to Oracle Database 12*c*. Just follow these steps:

1. For a transportable tablespace to work, the tablespaces must be self-contained—that is to say, there can be no dependencies between objects in the tablespace being transported

and the objects in tablespaces that are not being transported. For a full database migration, this may not be an issue, if you do not store application data in SYSTEM or SYSAUX tablespaces. Use the DBMS_TTS package to verify tablespaces. You must include all the tablespaces in the source database except SYSTEM, SYSAUX, UNDO, and TEMP.

```
SQL> EXECUTE DBMS_TTS.TRANSPORT_SET_CHECK('ts1, ts2, ts3', TRUE);
```

2. Confirm that there are no self-containment violations by querying the TRANSPORT_SET_VIOLATIONS view. If there are any violations, move the objects to remediate the violations.

3. Create a directory in the source database to point to the location where the export dump file will be written.

```
SQL> CREATE DIRECTORY datapump_exp_dir AS '/u01/app/oracle/dpump';
```

4. Make sure the tablespaces that will be transported to 12*c* database are in read-only mode. They must remain in read-only mode until the export is completed and the files are copied to their destination.

```
SQL> ALTER TABLESPACE ts1 READ ONLY; SQL> ALTER TABLESPACE ts2 READ ONLY;
SQL> ALTER TABLESPACE ts3 READ ONLY;
```

5. Perform a full transportable export. The VERSION=12 parameter must be specified because the source database is 11g. The export log file shows the data files that need to be copied to the destination database.

```
$ expdp FULL=y TRANSPORTABLE=always VERSION=12 \
DIRECTORY=datapump_exp_dir DUMPFILE=p11fullexp.dmp \
METRICS=y LOGFLIE=p11fullexp.log
```

6. Using the File Copy tools, copy the dump file and data files listed in the export log file to the destination database server.

> If the endianess of the source and destination database are different, you·
> must use the RMAN CONVERT command to convert them to an appropriate
> endian before you can copy the transportable tablespace database files to
> their destination.

7. To perform the import, create a directory in the 12*c* database pointing to the location of the dump file.

```
SQL> CREATE DIRECTORY datapump_imp_dir AS '/u01/app/oracle/dpump';
```

8. Perform a full import. Oracle Data Pump can determine whether a dump file was created by a conventional or full transportable export. The import only requires you to specify the dump-file name and the list of user tablespace data files to be transported using the

TRANSPORT_DATAFILES parameter. This parameter can use a comma-separated list of files, or it can be specified multiple times for multiple data files. Using parameter files will be helpful for the import. The following code shows imppar.txt as the parameter file with all its parameter values.

```
$ cat imppar.txt
 directory=datapump_imp_dir
 dumpfile=p11fullexp.dmp
 logfile=p11fullimp.log
 metrics=y
 transport_datafiles='/u01/app/oracle/oradata/p12cd/ts1.dbf'
 transport_datafiles='/u01/app/oracle/oradata/p12cd/ts2.dbf'
 transport_datafiles='/u01/app/oracle/oradata/p12cd/ts3.dbf'
$ impdp parfile=imppar.txt
```

9. After the import completes, the tablespaces transported will be in read-only mode. Make them read write.

```
SQL> ALTER TABLESPACE ts1 READ WRITE; SQL> ALTER TABLESPACE ts2 READ WRITE;
SQL> ALTER TABLESPACE ts3 READ WRITE;
```

 Oracle Data Pump cannot be used to load data into a database from data exported using the exp utility.

Loading Data with SQL*Loader

*SQL*Loader* is a program that reads data files in many possible formats, parses the data (breaks it into meaningful pieces), and loads the data into database tables. Like Data Pump, it has myriad options available, and a hefty book could be devoted to its use. The Oracle Database Utilities manual devotes several hundred pages of reference material to SQL*Loader alone. This section will not be so comprehensive, nor will we attempt to cram all possible uses of SQL*Loader into a few short pages. Instead, we will cover the basics and teach you what is necessary for the exam.

SQL*Loader uses the following file types:

Log This is a mandatory file. If you do not specify a log file, SQL*Loader will try to create one in the current directory with the name of your control file and a .log filename extension. If SQL*Loader cannot create the log file, execution is aborted. The log file contains a summary of the SQL*Loader session, including any errors that were generated.

Control   This is a mandatory file. This file tells SQL*Loader where the other files are, how to parse and load the data, and which tables to load the data into; this file can contain the data as well.

Data   Data files are optional and, if included, hold the data that SQL*Loader reads and loads into the database. The data can be located in the control file, so these files are optional.

Bad   This holds the "bad" data records—those that were not validated by either SQL*Loader or the database. Bad files are created only if one or more records fail validation. Just as with the log file, if you do not specify a bad file, the database will create one, with the name of your control file and a .bad filename extension.

Discard   This holds data records that did not get loaded because they did not satisfy the record-selection criteria in the control file. Discard files are created only if data records were discarded because they did not satisfy the selection criteria.

SQL*Loader provides a robust toolkit to build data-loading programs for your Oracle database. It can operate either on the database server or on a client machine.

The following section will show you how to employ SQL*Loader to load data into your database tables.

Specifying SQL*Loader Command-Line Parameters

To invoke the SQL*Loader program, use the command sqlldr followed by one or more command-line parameters. These parameters can be identified positionally on the command line or with a *keyword=value* pair. You can mix positional and keyword notation provided that all the keyword-notation parameters appear after all the positional parameters.

For example, to invoke SQL*Loader, telling it to use the connect string system/password and the control file regions.ctl, you can execute any of the following command lines:

```
sqlldr system/password regions.ctl
sqlldr control=regions.ctl userid=system/password
sqlldr system/password control=regions.ctl
```

The command-line parameters include those shown here, by executing the sqlldr command with no parameters:

```
$ sqlldr

SQL*Loader: Release 12.1.0.1.0 - Production on Sun Jan 19 00:36:27 2014
Copyright (c) 1982, 2013, Oracle and/or its affiliates.  All rights reserved.

Usage: SQLLDR keyword=value [,keyword=value,...]

Valid Keywords:
    userid -- ORACLE username/password
```

```
        control -- control file name
            log -- log file name
            bad -- bad file name
           data -- data file name
        discard -- discard file name
     discardmax -- number of discards to allow        (Default all)
           skip -- number of logical records to skip   (Default 0)
           load -- number of logical records to load   (Default all)
         errors -- number of errors to allow           (Default 50)
           rows -- number of rows in conventional path bind array or between direct
path data saves
                   (Default: Conventional path 64, Direct path all)
       bindsize -- size of conventional path bind array in bytes  (Default 256000)
         silent -- suppress messages during run (header,feedback,errors,discards,
partitions)
         direct -- use direct path                      (Default FALSE)
        parfile -- parameter file: name of file that contains parameter
specifications
       parallel -- do parallel load                     (Default FALSE)
           file -- file to allocate extents from
skip_unusable_indexes -- disallow/allow unusable indexes or index partitions
(Default FALSE)
skip_index_maintenance -- do not maintain indexes, mark affected indexes as
unusable  (Default FALSE)
commit_discontinued -- commit loaded rows when load is discontinued  (Default
FALSE)
       readsize -- size of read buffer                 (Default 1048576)
external_table -- use external table for load; NOT_USED, GENERATE_ONLY, EXECUTE
columnarrayrows -- number of rows for direct path column array  (Default 5000)
     streamsize -- size of direct path stream buffer in bytes  (Default 256000)
multithreading -- use multithreading in direct path
      resumable -- enable or disable resumable for current session  (Default FALSE)
 resumable_name -- text string to help identify resumable statement
resumable_timeout -- wait time (in seconds) for RESUMABLE  (Default 7200)
     date_cache -- size (in entries) of date conversion cache  (Default 1000)
no_index_errors -- abort load on any index errors  (Default FALSE)
          table -- Table for express mode load
    date_format -- Date format for express mode load
timestamp_format -- Timestamp format for express mode load
   terminated_by -- terminated by character for express mode load
     enclosed_by -- enclosed by character for express mode load
optionally_enclosed_by -- optionally enclosed by character for express mode load
```

```
characterset -- characterset for express mode load
degree_of_parallelism -- degree of parallelism for express mode load and
external table load
      trim -- trim type for express mode load and external table load
       csv -- csv format data files for express mode load
    nullif -- table level nullif clause for express mode load
field_names -- field names setting for first record of data files for express
mode load
dnfs_enable -- option for enabling or disabling Direct NFS (dNFS) for input data
files  (Default FALSE)
dnfs_readbuffers -- the number of Direct NFS (dNFS) read buffers  (Default 4)


PLEASE NOTE: Command-line parameters may be specified either by
position or by keywords.  An example of the former case is 'sqlldr
scott/tiger foo'; an example of the latter is 'sqlldr control=foo
userid=scott/tiger'.  One may specify parameters by position before
but not after parameters specified by keywords.  For example,
'sqlldr scott/tiger control=foo logfile=log' is allowed, but
'sqlldr scott/tiger control=foo log' is not, even though the
position of the parameter 'log' is correct.
$
```

Many of the command-line parameters can also appear in the control file. When they appear as both command-line parameters and in the control file, the command-line options take precedence.

Specifying Control File Options

The control file contains commands to tell SQL*Loader where to find the data, how to parse it, how to load it, what to do when errors occur, and what to do with records that fail validation. A control file has two or three main sections. The first contains session-wide information, such as log filename, bind size, and whether direct or conventional path loading will be used. The second section contains one or more INTO TABLE blocks. These blocks specify the target tables and columns. The third section, if present, is the actual data. Comments can appear anywhere in the control files (except in the data lines) and should be used liberally. The control file language can be somewhat cryptic, so generous use of comments is encouraged. Comments in a control file start with a double dash and end with a new line. The control file must begin with the line LOAD DATA or CONTINUE LOAD DATA and also have an INTO TABLE clause, together with directions on how to parse the data and load it into which columns.

The best way to learn how to construct a control file is to look at examples and then use variations of them to build your control file. This section gives you several examples but is certainly not a comprehensive sampling. Again, the intent is to present you with enough information to get you going.

For a comprehensive reference, see the Oracle manual "Oracle Database Utilities 12*c* Release 1."

The first example is rather simple and straightforward. The control file contains both control file commands and the data. The command line is as follows:

```
sqlldr hr/hr control=regions.ctl
```

The control file regions.ctl contains the following:

```
LOAD DATA
-- Control file begins with LOAD DATA
INFILE *
-- The * tells SQL*Loader the data is inline
INTO TABLE regions TRUNCATE
-- truncate the target table before loading
FIELDS TERMINATED BY ',' OPTIONALLY ENCLOSED BY '"'
-- how to parse the data
 (region_id, region_name)
-- positional mapping of data file fields to table columns
-- lines following BEGINDATA are loaded
-- no comments are allowed after BEGINDATA
BEGINDATA
1,"Europe"
2,"Americas"
3,"Asia"
4,"Middle East and Africa"
```

The LOAD DATA command tells SQL*Loader that you are beginning a new data load. If you are continuing a data load that was interrupted, specify CONTINUE LOAD DATA. The command INFILE * tells SQL*Loader that the data will appear in the control file. The table REGIONS is loaded. The keyword TRUNCATE tells SQL*Loader to truncate the table before loading it. Instead of using TRUNCATE, you can specify INSERT (the default), which requires the table to be empty at the start of the load. APPEND tells SQL*Loader to add the data to any existing data in the table. REPLACE tells SQL*Loader to issue a DELETE to empty out the table before loading. DELETE differs from a TRUNCATE; for DELETE, the DML triggers fire and DELETE can be rolled back.

The lines in the control file that follow the BEGINDATA command contain the data to parse and load. The parsing specification tells SQL*Loader that the data fields are comma-delimited and that text data can be enclosed by double quotation marks. These double quotation marks should not be loaded as part of the data. The list of columns enclosed in parentheses consists of the table columns that will be loaded with the data fields.

In the second example, the same data is loaded into the same table, but it is located in a standalone file called `regions.dat` and is in the following pipe-delimited, fixed format:

```
1|Europe                |
2|Americas               |
3|Asia                   |
4|Middle East and Africa |
The command line is as follows:
sqlldr hr/hr control=regions.ctl
The content of the control file is as follows:
LOAD DATA
INFILE  '/apps/seed_data/regions.dat'
BADFILE '/apps/seed_data/regions.bad'
DISCARDFILE '/apps/seed_data/regions.dsc'
OPTIONS (DIRECT=TRUE)
-- data file spec
INTO TABLE regions APPEND
-- add this data to the existing target table
(region_id   POSITION(1)    INTEGER EXTERNAL
,region_name POSITION(3:25) NULLIF region_name = BLANKS
) -- how to parse the data
```

The control file tells SQL*Loader where to find the data file (`INFILE`) as well as the bad and discard files (`BADFILE` and `DISCARDFILE`). The `OPTIONS` line specifies direct path loading. With fixed-format data, the column specification identifies the starting and ending positions. A numeric datatype can be identified as `INTEGER EXTERNAL`. The directive `NULLIF region_name = BLANKS` tells SQL*Loader to set the region_name column to `NULL` if the data field contains only white space.

You shouldn't have to know the minutiae of how to tell SQL*Loader precisely how to parse data—the options are far too arcane to expect you to recite them off the top of your head for an exam—but knowing the SQL*Loader capabilities of reading fixed-format and variable-format data is essential. More important to your job is understanding direct path loads and unusable indexes, which are discussed in the next section.

Oracle Database 12c introduced SQL*Loader Express Mode, where you can perform the load operation without a control file. This is suitable if the data file contains only scalar data and the columns are delimited. SQL*Loader uses the table definition to determine the input data types.

Using Direct Path Loading

Direct path loading is a SQL*Loader option that allows you, under certain conditions, to use the direct path interface to load data into a table. The direct path interface can be significantly faster than conventional path loading. With conventional loading, SQL*Loader loads data into a bind array and passes it to the database engine to process with an INSERT statement. Full undo and redo mechanisms operate on conventional path loads. Direct path loading is enabled by specifying the DIRECT=Y parameter.

With direct path loading, SQL*Loader reads data, passing it to the database via the direct path API. The API formats it directly into Oracle data blocks in memory and then flushes these blocks, en masse, directly to the data files using multiblock I/O, bypassing the buffer cache, as well as redo and undo mechanisms. Direct path loads always write to a table above the high-water mark; thus, they always increase the number of data blocks that a table is actually using.

The important thing to remember about direct path loading is that it is fast but has restrictions, including the following:

- Indexes are rebuilt at the end of a direct path load. If unique constraint violations are found, the unique index is left in an unusable state. To correct the index, you must find and remove the constraint violations and then rebuild the index.

Unusable indexes are a possible result of direct path loading. Make sure you know what causes an unusable index and how to fix it.

- Direct path loading cannot occur if active transactions against the table are being loaded.
- Triggers do not fire during direct path loads.
- Direct path loading into clustered tables is not supported.
- During direct path loads, foreign key constraints are disabled at the beginning of the load and then re-enabled after the load.
- Only primary key, unique, and NOT NULL constraints are enforced.
- Direct path loading prevents other users from making changes to the table while the direct load operation is in progress.

OEM Cloud Control and SQL Developer tools can also be used to load data with SQL*Loader. Figure 18.4 shows the menu item to invoke SQL*Loader using OEM Cloud Control.

Populating External Tables

External tables were introduced in Oracle9*i* and were read-only from the Oracle database. In Oracle 10g, external tables were made writable. In Oracle9*i*, ORACLE_LOADER was the only access driver available for external tables; Oracle 10g introduced the ORACLE_DATAPUMP access driver. The external tables that use the ORACLE_LOADER access driver are read-only—they read ASCII flat files from the OS. Only the external tables created with the ORACLE_DATAPUMP access driver can be written to. The resulting file is in proprietary format (Oracle native external representation, DPAPI), which only Data Pump can read. The data can, therefore, be read on any machine using ORACLE_DATAPUMP access driver and external tables, irrespective of the endianess of the source system. You can use this file to load data to another Oracle database as well.

You may wonder how this is beneficial. Why don't you use the Oracle Data Pump clients to generate the file? Well, although Oracle Data Pump can handle a certain level of filtering, join operations with another table are not possible. Using the external table ORACLE_DATAPUMP access driver, you can unload data that is derived from complex queries. This is useful in loading data marts from data warehouse or similar applications. Data from external tables can be used in SQL queries.

In the following sections, you will learn how to populate an external table using the ORACLE_DATAPUMP and ORACLE_LOADER DPAPI.

Loading External Tables Using Data Pump

You use the ORACLE_DATAPUMP access driver to unload data from an Oracle database to a flat file (DPAPI format) using the external table method. The external table must be created using the CREATE TABLE...AS SELECT... (CTAS) method. You can specify the PARALLEL clause when creating the table; the ORACLE_DATAPUMP access driver unloads data into multiple flat files at the same time. One parallel execution server will write to only one file at a time. Unloading data in the context of an external table means creating an external table using the CTAS method.

During the unload (or populate) operation, the data goes from the subquery to the SQL engine for the data to be processed, and it is extracted in the DPAPI format to write to the flat file. The external table to unload data can be created only using the CTAS method with the ORACLE_DATAPUMP access driver. The unload operation does not include the metadata for the tables. You can use the VERSION clause when unloading the data to make sure it loads correctly on the target database.

We'll demonstrate how to unload data using the ORACLE_DATAPUMP access driver. In this example, you will join the EMPLOYEES and DEPARTMENTS tables of the HR schema to unload data. The following statement creates the table in the database and creates two files, empl_comm1.dmp and empl_comm2.dmp, in the OS:

```
SQL> CREATE TABLE empl_commission
     ORGANIZATION EXTERNAL (TYPE ORACLE_DATAPUMP
```

```
      DEFAULT DIRECTORY work_dir
      LOCATION ('empl_comm1.dmp','empl_comm2.dmp'))
      PARALLEL 2
      AS
      SELECT employee_id,
             first_name || ' ' || last_name employee_name,
             department_name,
             TO_CHAR(hire_date,'DD-MM-YYYY') hire_date,
             salary * NVL(commission_pct, 0.5) commission
      FROM hr.employees JOIN hr.departments USING (department_id)
      ORDER BY first_name || ' ' || last_name
SQL> /

Table created.

SQL> SELECT department_name, sum(commission) total_comm
     FROM   empl_commission
     GROUP BY department_name;

DEPARTMENT_NAME                 TOTAL_COMM
------------------------------  ----------
Accounting                           10150
Finance                              25800
Human Resources                       3250
Marketing                             9500
Purchasing                           12450
Sales                                72640
Shipping                             78200
Administration                        2200
Executive                            29000
IT                                   14400
Public Relations                      5000
```

ORGANIZATION EXTERNAL specifies that the resulting table is an external table. TYPE ORACLE_DATAPUMP specifies that the Data Pump access driver should be used. DEFAULT DIRECTORY specifies the location of the dump files. The LOCATION parameter specifies the filenames. Most often when external tables are used, a very large amount of data is unloaded; hence, using the PARALLEL clause will speed up the operation. If the parallel clause is used, the number of files specified in the LOCATION clause must match the PARALLEL degree. If you did not specify enough files to match the degree of parallelism, Oracle decreases the parallelism to match the number of files provided.

Because the data is unloaded in a proprietary format, the files created using the ORACLE_ DATAPUMP access driver can be read only by Oracle database versions at or above 10g. You can use this method to move data from one database to another.

You can copy the dump files to another Oracle database and load them using the Data Pump utility, or you can create an external table on these dump files and load from it. Let's create an external table using these dump files and query it:

```
SQL> CREATE TABLE new_empl_commission (
     employee_id  NUMBER (6),
     employee_name VARCHAR2 (40),
     department_name VARCHAR2 (30),
     hire_date VARCHAR2 (10),
     commission NUMBER)
     ORGANIZATION EXTERNAL (TYPE ORACLE_DATAPUMP
     DEFAULT DIRECTORY work_dir
     ACCESS PARAMETERS (
     LOGFILE 'new_empl_commission.log')
     LOCATION ('empl_comm1.dmp', 'expl_comm2.dmp'));

Table created.
```

The data dictionary views DBA_EXTERNAL_TABLES and DBA_EXTERNAL_ LOCATIONS can be queried to view the characteristics, location, and file-names of external tables.

Loading External Tables Using Loader

You use the ORACLE_LOADER access driver to load data to an Oracle database from a flat file using the external table method. You can specify the PARALLEL clause when creating the table; the ORACLE_LOADER access driver divides the large flat file into chunks that can be processed separately. Loading data in the context of an external table means reading data from the external table (flat file) and loading to a table in the database using the INSERT statement.

Let's create an external table using the ORACLE_LOADER access driver; say the user already has the privilege to read from and write to the directory WORK_DIR. The source data file is employee.dat, which has fixed-column data (name, title, and salary). The following code shows the contents of the employee.dat file, creates the external table using the ORACLE_ LOADER driver, and queries the external table. You can use the data from this external table to load other tables using INSERT statements.

```
$ cat employee.dat
SMITH    CLERK    800
```

```
SCOTT    ANALYST   3000
ADAMS    CLERK     1100
MILLER   CLERK     1300
$

SQL> CREATE TABLE employees (
     ename  VARCHAR2 (10),
     title  VARCHAR2 (10),
     salary NUMBER (8))
     ORGANIZATION EXTERNAL (
     TYPE ORACLE_LOADER
     DEFAULT DIRECTORY WORK_DIR
     ACCESS PARAMETERS (RECORDS DELIMITED BY NEWLINE FIELDS (
     ename CHAR(10),
     title CHAR(10),
     salary CHAR(8)))
     LOCATION ('employee.dat'))
     PARALLEL
SQL> /

Table created.

SQL> SELECT * FROM employees;

ENAME       TITLE        SALARY
----------  ----------  ----------
SMITH       CLERK           800
SCOTT       ANALYST        3000
ADAMS       CLERK          1100
MILLER      CLERK          1300

SQL>
```

 Only SELECT statements are allowed on external tables; no INSERT, UPDATE, or DELETE operations are permitted on external tables.

You have learned to move data between databases using various tools. Next, let's do an overview of Grid Infrastructure and how Automatic Storage Management can help you manage some of Oracle database storage challenges.

Introducing Grid Infrastructure

Let's start with a little bit of history. The phrase "grid install" is usually associated with installing the Oracle cluster software for a Real Application Cluster (RAC) installation. Oracle *Automatic Storage Management* (ASM) was introduced in Oracle Database 10g. In 10g and 11g R1, the ASM could be installed and managed from Oracle database software home. For RAC installations in 10g, you had to install Grid software, which took care of the clustering and ASM management. In 10g and 11g R1, for non-RAC installations using ASM, there was no separate software to install; you just created an ASM instance to manage the ASM storage for the databases on the server. From Oracle Database 11g Release 2 onward, *Grid Infrastructure* (GI) is applicable to RAC and standalone server installations.

The Grid Infrastructure for a standalone server provides system support for Oracle systems, including database storage volume management, file system for applications, and automatic restart of various components in the system. To differentiate the GI for RAC from the GI for a standalone server, the GI for a standalone server is also known as *Oracle Restart*. Oracle Restart supports single-instance databases on one server, while Oracle Grid Infrastructure for a Cluster supports single-instance or Oracle RAC databases on a cluster.

Oracle ASM provides file system and volume manager capabilities built into the Oracle database kernel, and it provides a simple storage management interface across all server and storage platforms. ASM disks are managed and controlled by a special type of instance known as the *ASM instance*. The ASM instance does not have any data files or database associated with it; it has only the memory structures and processes. The ASM instance has a password file and a parameter file, though. The ASM instance manages the metadata for the disk groups. Database instances connect to ASM instance to create, delete, resize, open, or close files. Database instances read and write directly to the data files on ASM. The GI installation configures and starts the ASM instance. Figure 18.8 shows the relationship between the database instance, ASM instance, disk groups, and non-ASM file systems.

FIGURE 18.8 The ASM instance and disk groups

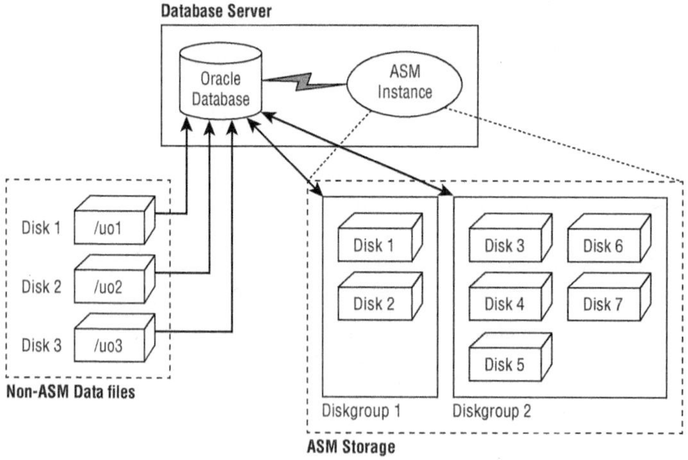

When ASM is managing the storage volume, the database instance is dependent on the ASM instance. The ASM instance manages the disk group and storage metadata. The database instance could have files on ASM storage and non-ASM disks.

In addition, ASM not only enhances performance by automatically spreading database objects over multiple devices, but increases availability by allowing new disk devices to be added to the database without shutting down the database. ASM automatically rebalances the distribution of files with no DBA intervention. Using ASM does not, however, preclude you from mixing ASM disk groups with file-system database files. But the ease of use and performance of ASM makes a strong case for converting all your storage to ASM *disk groups*.

> The ASM instance configured during the GI installation is named +ASM for a standalone installation. For a RAC installation, each node ASM instance will have the instance name +ASM1, +ASM2, and so on. The parameter INSTANCE_TYPE=ASM differentiates an ASM instance from a database instance.

Oracle ASM is a volume manager and storage system for Oracle database files, including RAC and non-RAC configurations. Oracle ASM also supports a general-purpose file system for application needs and Oracle database binaries.

Installing Oracle ASM or Grid Infrastructure is one of the first steps you perform on a server, if you plan on using ASM for database data file storage. This topic is covered toward the end of this book so that you will be familiar with databases before storage technologies are thrown into the mix. To be able to use Oracle Restart or Oracle ASM in Oracle Database 12*c*, you must install Oracle Grid Infrastructure for a standalone server. Before installing GI, you must prepare the storage area by creating disk partitions to mark as ASM disks.

> Oracle Automatic Cluster File System (ACFS) extends the Oracle ASM technology to support file systems for application files and Oracle binaries.

Installing Oracle Grid Infrastructure

The Grid Infrastructure software is delivered along with Oracle Database 12*c* Media Pack. Figure 18.9 shows the cloud edelivery.com software download page for Oracle Database 12*c* Release 1 (12.1.0.1.0) Media Pack v3 for Linux x86-64. There are two files for the Oracle Database 12*c* software and two files for the Grid Infrastructure install. Download and unzip them on the server where GI needs to be installed.

The GI software downloaded is the same for standalone and cluster installations. The type of installation is specified during the installation.

Oracle Database 11g Release 2 introduced the Grid Infrastructure Oracle home that includes Oracle Restart and ASM. To use ASM in Oracle Database 12*c*, you must install Grid Infrastructure. Before we install the ASM software, let's get the storage disks ready.

NOTE A discussion of storage types and how to set up storage are outside the scope of this book. We will demonstrate the storage setup using an example.

FIGURE 18.9 The Grid Infrastructure Installation Files Download screen

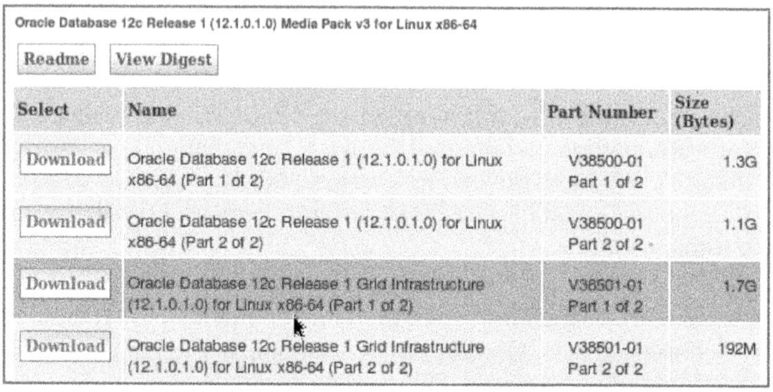

Oracle Database 12c Release 1 (12.1.0.1.0) Media Pack v3 for Linux x86-64			
Readme View Digest			
Select	**Name**	**Part Number**	**Size (Bytes)**
Download	Oracle Database 12c Release 1 (12.1.0.1.0) for Linux x86-64 (Part 1 of 2)	V38500-01 Part 1 of 2	1.3G
Download	Oracle Database 12c Release 1 (12.1.0.1.0) for Linux x86-64 (Part 2 of 2)	V38500-01 Part 2 of 2	1.1G
Download	Oracle Database 12c Release 1 Grid Infrastructure (12.1.0.1.0) for Linux x86-64 (Part 1 of 2)	V38501-01 Part 1 of 2	1.7G
Download	Oracle Database 12c Release 1 Grid Infrastructure (12.1.0.1.0) for Linux x86-64 (Part 2 of 2)	V38501-01 Part 2 of 2	192M

Preparing Storage for a Grid Infrastructure Install

Typically in organizations, storage is managed by a separate team or by the system administrator. The DBA requests specific disks or LUNs from the storage administrator, and gets the disk provisioned on the server to use for ASM storage. Oracle ASM uses *disk groups* to store data files; an Oracle ASM disk group is a collection of disks that Oracle ASM manages as a unit. During the GI install, one disk group is created; therefore, the disks need to be prepared before you install GI. Those disks must be partitioned to use for ASM.

The storage admin has provided three disks for you to use for ASM storage. On Linux, you can query the /proc/partitions to view the partitions.

```
# cat /proc/partitions
major minor  #blocks  name

    8       0   42991616 sda
    8       1     104391 sda1
    8       2   42885517 sda2
    8      16   41943040 sdb
    8      32    2155084 sdc
    8      48    2155084 sdd
  253       0   35717120 dm-0
  253       1    7143424 dm-1
```

Let's create partitions for disks sdc and sdd. Here is an example of creating a partition using fdisk for sdc.

```
# fdisk /dev/sdc
Device contains neither a valid DOS partition table, nor Sun, SGI or OSF disklabel.
Building a new DOS disklabel. Changes will remain in memory only,
until you decide to write them. After that, of course, the previous
content won't be recoverable.

Warning: invalid flag 0x0000 of partition table 4 will be corrected by w(rite)

Command (m for help): n
Command action
   e   extended
   p   primary partition (1-4)
p
Partition number (1-4): 1
First cylinder (1-268, default 1):
Using default value 1
Last cylinder or +size or +sizeM or +sizeK (1-268, default 268):
Using default value 268

Command (m for help): w
The partition table has been altered!

Calling ioctl() to re-read partition table.
Syncing disks.
```

Reading the partitions file again shows the new partitions sdc1 and sdd1 are created.

```
# cat /proc/partitions
major minor  #blocks  name

   8        0    42991616 sda
   8        1      104391 sda1
   8        2    42885517 sda2
   8       16    41943040 sdb
   8       32     2155084 sdc
   8       33     2152678 sdc1
   8       48     2155084 sdd
   8       49     2152678 sdd1
```

```
253        0   35717120 dm-0
253        1    7143424 dm-1
```

ASMLib is an optional support library for Oracle ASM that is included with the Oracle Linux unbreakable kernel. Using ASMLib is optional. One advantage to using ASMLib is that you can name the disks using the createdisk option.

```
# oracleasm createdisk ORAD1 /dev/sdc1
Writing disk header: done
Instantiating disk: done

# oracleasm createdisk ORAD2 /dev/sdd1
Writing disk header: done
Instantiating disk: done

# oracleasm listdisks
ORAD1
ORAD2

# ls -l /dev/oracleasm/disks
total 0
brw-rw---- 1 oracle dba 8, 33 Jan 25 00:20 ORAD1
brw-rw---- 1 oracle dba 8, 49 Jan 25 00:21 ORAD2
```

Notice that the disks are owned by the oracle software owner/user. Now the storage is ready for ASM installation, which is accomplished through the Grid Infrastructure for a standalone server installation, which is discussed in the next section.

 If you are not familiar with ASMLib or oracleasm, you can read more at http://www.oracle.com/technetwork/server-storage/linux/asmlib.

Installing Grid Infrastructure for a Standalone Server

After you download the GI software installation files and unzip them (Figure 18.9), the installation files will be under the grid folder. Similar to the Oracle Database 12c software installation you reviewed in Chapter 9, "Creating and Operating Oracle Database 12c," the GI is also installed by invoking runInstaller on Linux and Unix systems. When you invoke runInstaller, the first screen prompts you for software updates. You can choose to update the software, skip the software update, or provide a location if you have previously downloaded the software using runInstaller -downloadUpdates.

Figure 18.10 shows the Select Installation Option screen of Grid Infrastructure Install. The first option, Install and Configure Oracle Grid Infrastructure for a Cluster, is used for a GI cluster (RAC) installation. To install GI on a standalone server and to configure Oracle Restart, choose the second option: Install and Configure Oracle Grid Infrastructure for a Standalone Server. For this installation, choose this option, which will install the GI software and configure the ASM instance. This option can also upgrade an existing installation of ASM to GI, or an 11g R2 GI to 12c R1 GI.

FIGURE 18.10   GI Install – The Installation Option screen

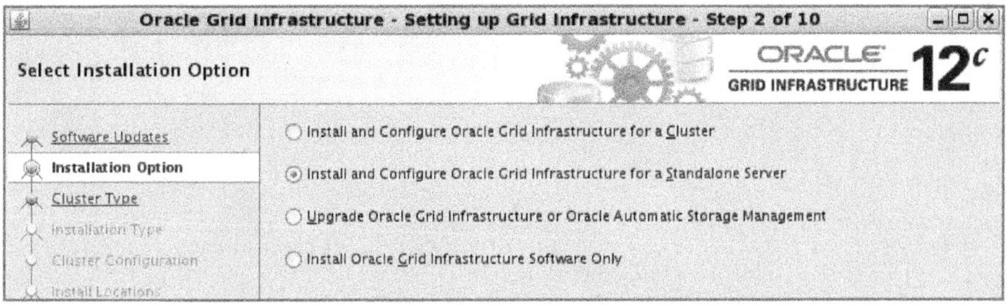

The third option in Figure 18.10 is used to upgrade the ASM or GI to the 12c version. You may also choose the Install Oracle Grid Infrastructure Software Only option to install only the GI software, but you will have to manually configure the GI components and ASM instance by running the `roothas.pl` script. If you are doing a software-only install, the disk partitions are required only when you create the ASM disk group.

The next screen is the Product Languages screen. Choose the languages you want to install in the GI home. By default, only English is chosen. Figure 18.11 shows the Create ASM Disk Group screen. We will be using the disks we prepared in the earlier section to create an ASM disk group.

In the Create ASM Disk Group screen, you can create only one ASM disk group. Additional disk groups can be created using the *Automatic Storage Management Configuration Assistant* (ASMCA) utility. Provide a name for the disk group; in the example, the disk group name is *ORADATA*. ASM allows three levels of redundancy when creating the disk group. Normal redundancy is two-way mirroring, which means you should allocate twice the number of storage disks required for the disk group. High redundancy is three-way mirroring. If the disks are from a storage array where RAID architecture is already implemented, you may tell Oracle ASM not to manage the redundancy in ASM, but rely on redundancy from the underlying storage system.

Best practice calls for at least a few disks in each disk group, and each disk in the disk group must be of the same size. This is because I/O activity is spread evenly across all available disks in a disk group to avoid hot spots. ASM also eliminates the need for over-provisioning a disk, because you can add or remove disks while the database is running without impacting the database. When a disk is added or removed from a disk group, ASM automatically redistributes blocks so that the utilized space in each disk is the same.

The smallest unit of storage in an ASM disk group is the *allocation unit* (AU). Oracle Database 12*c* permits sizes of 1, 2, 4, 8, 16, 32, or 64MB. An allocation unit is the size of the blocks allocated to a data file. The AU must be small enough not to create any hot spots and large enough for efficient sequential reads. The default is 1MB, and 4MB AU is recommended for most databases.

FIGURE 18.11 GI Install – The Create ASM Disk Group screen

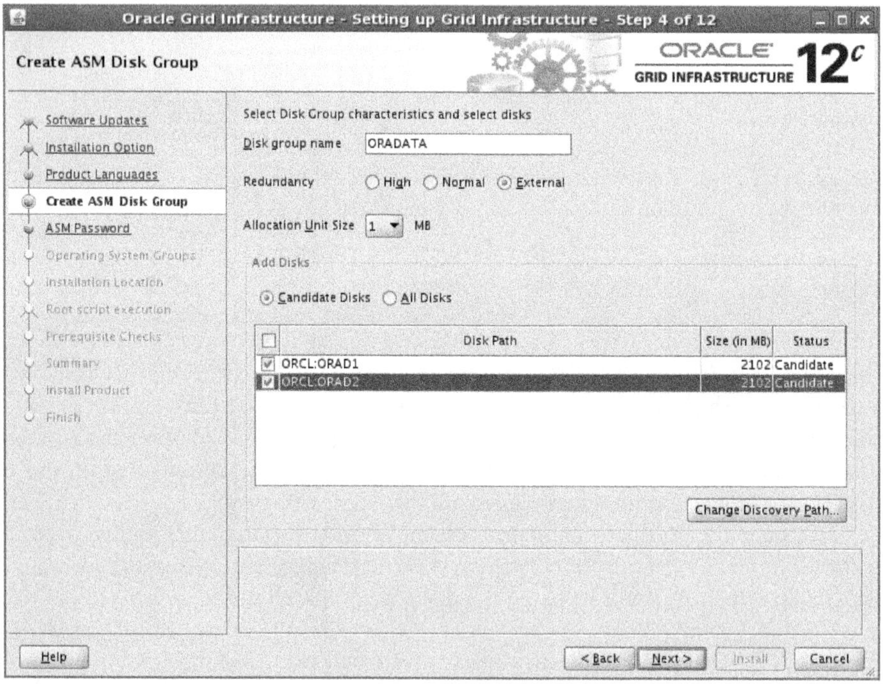

The Add Disks section in Figure 18.11 shows the disks partitioned and owned by GI software owner. Choose the disks you want to allocate to the disk group. You can add more disks or remove disks later using ASMCA or using SQL*Plus. When the disks are configured using ASMLib, the user-friendly names you used to create the ASMLib disks will appear. If you did not use ASMLib, the complete path name for disks will appear—for example, /dev/sdc1. If you want to change the search location for the disks from /dev/* to some other location—say /dev/did/rdisk, for example—you can click the Change Discovery Path button and enter the new location.

> The ASM_DISKSTRING parameter tells the ASM instance where the disk devices are located. If ASMLib is used, set ORCL: for the ASM_DISKSTRING parameter. The ASMLib interface is not required to run ASM; however, using it makes it easier to manage disk discovery and provisioning.

The next screen is used to assign passwords. Here you can assign passwords to SYS user and ASMSNP user. Similar to the database installation, you can choose two different passwords or the same passwords for these users. ASMSNMP user is similar to DBSNMP user for databases and is primarily used to monitor the instance through OEM Cloud Control. You can connect to the ASM instance using the SYSDBA or SYSASM privilege. The SYSASM privilege is required to manage disk groups. It separates the role of DBA from storage administrator for the ASM instance.

Figure 18.12 shows the Privileged Operating System Groups screen. Choose the appropriate OS groups that will have privileges on the ASM instance to connect without a password.

FIGURE 18.12   GI Install – The Privileged Operating System Groups screen

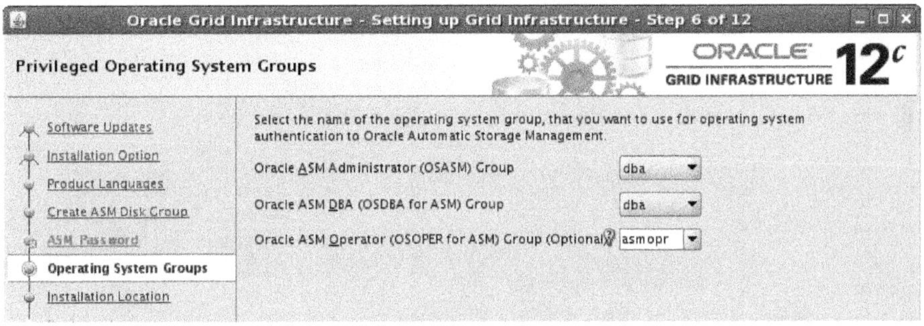

Oracle ASM Administrator (OSASM) group members are granted the SYSASM privilege, which gives full administrator privileges on the ASM instance, including storage administration. If you have created a group named asmadmin, then OUI picks that group as the default for the OSASM group. The Oracle ASM DBA (OSDBA) group members are granted only a subset of SYSASM privileges, such as stopping and starting the ASM instance. The Oracle ASM Operator (OSOPER) group members are granted read and write privileges on the files managed by ASM.

Figure 18.13 shows the location of the GI installation files. Specify the Oracle Base location and the GI home location.

The next screen is the Root Script Execution Configuration. If you have the root password handy, or if the GI software owner (usually *oracle* user) has the sudo privilege, you may choose the appropriate option. If you do not have root access, don't worry; at the end of installation, you can ask your system administrator to run the script to complete the ASM configuration.

OUI performs the prerequisite checks and lets you know of any issues that need your attention. Figure 18.14 shows the Perform Prerequisite Checks screen.

FIGURE 18.13   GI Install – The Specify Installation Location screen

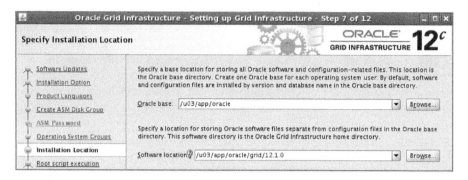

FIGURE 18.14   GI Install – The Perform Prerequisite Checks screen

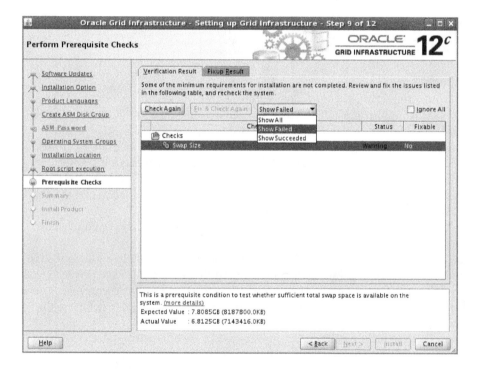

You can view the failed checks (by default), view all successful checks, or view all checks by selecting the appropriate option from the drop-down menu. You can use the Fix & Check Again button to correct any fixable errors. When you click on a reported issue, you will see

brief failure or success information at the bottom of the screen. Click the More Details link to learn more about the check and how to fix an issue. If you fixed an issue outside the OUI, you can click the Check Again button to validate the fix. If you think an issue reported is not applicable in your environment, you can click the Ignore All button and continue to the next screen.

The Summary screen, shown in Figure 18.15, summarizes the options chosen and the location of the install. It also shows the disk group being created.

FIGURE 18.15   GI Install – The Summary screen

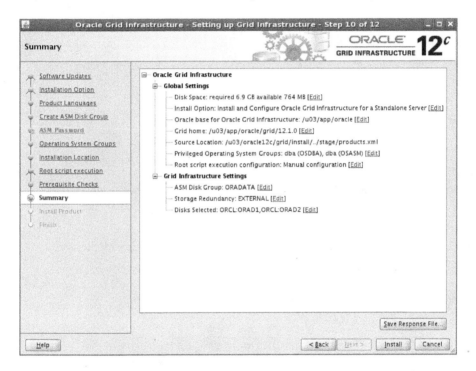

Click the Install button to begin the installation. The installation progress will be displayed. After the software installation completes, you will be prompted to run the root.sh script. A sample execution of the root.sh script is shown here.

```
# /u03/app/oracle/grid/12.1.0/root.sh
Performing root user operation for Oracle 12c

The following environment variables are set as:
    ORACLE_OWNER= oracle
    ORACLE_HOME=  /u03/app/oracle/grid/12.1.0
```

Entries will be added to the /etc/oratab file as needed by

Database Configuration Assistant when a database is created.

Finished running generic part of root script.

Now product-specific root actions will be performed.

Using configuration parameter file: /u03/app/oracle/grid/12.1.0/crs/install/
crsconfig_params

LOCAL ADD MODE

Creating OCR keys for user 'oracle', privgrp 'dba'..

Operation successful.

LOCAL ONLY MODE

Successfully accumulated necessary OCR keys.

Creating OCR keys for user 'root', privgrp 'root'..

Operation successful.

CRS-4664: Node emcc successfully pinned.

2014/01/25 15:15:34 CLSRSC-330: Adding Clusterware entries to file '/etc/
inittab'

emcc   2014/01/25 15:16:05   /u03/app/oracle/grid/12.1.0/cdata/emcc/
backup_20140125_151605.olr

2014/01/25 15:16:21 CLSRSC-327: Successfully configured Oracle Grid
Infrastructure for a Standalone Server.

#

After the root.sh script is executed, OUI will configure the Grid Infrastructure. Figure 18.16 shows the components configured by the GI install.

FIGURE 18.16   GI Install – The Component Install Status screen

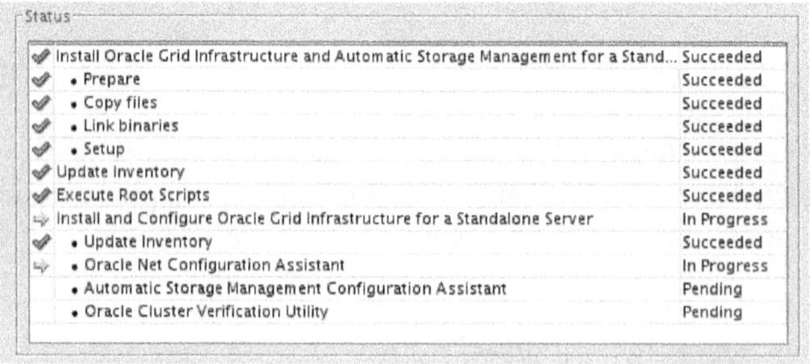

After the installation completes successfully, you will see several processes running out of the GI home. You will also see the process for the +ASM instance running. The ASM instance has fewer background processes than the database instance. The following are processes started by GI.

/etc/init.d/init.ohasd

/u03/app/oracle/grid/12.1.0/bin/ohasd.bin reboot

```
/u03/app/oracle/grid/12.1.0/bin/oraagent.bin
/u03/app/oracle/grid/12.1.0/bin/evmd.bin
/u03/app/oracle/grid/12.1.0/bin/evmlogger.bin -o /u03/app/oracle/grid/12.1.0/
log/[HOSTNAME]/evmd/evmlogger.info
/u03/app/oracle/grid/12.1.0/bin/tnslsnr LISTENER -no_crs_notify -inherit
/u03/app/oracle/grid/12.1.0/bin/cssdagent
/u03/app/oracle/grid/12.1.0/bin/ocssd.bin
```

You will learn more about stopping and starting these services in the "Using Oracle Restart" section.

In the 10g and 11g versions of Oracle ASM, each server must have a dedicated ASM instance to be able to use ASM storage for databases. In Oracle Database 12c, the Flex ASM feature eliminates this requirement for cluster installations.

Managing Oracle ASM Storage

ASMCA is the configuration tool used to manage ASM storage. In addition to managing ASM disk groups, ASMCA can also configure an ASM instance if there is no ASM instance running, and it can upgrade an ASM instance if the version of the ASM running is lower than 12.1. ASMCA is invoked by running asmca from the <GIHome>/bin directory. Figure 18.17 shows the ASMCA screen.

The Create button is used to create a new disk group. The Mount All button can be used to mount all the disk groups. You can choose a disk group and right-click to access additional menu actions that can be performed on the disk group. To increase the size of the disk group by adding more disks to it, use the Add Disks option. To reduce the size of the disk group, choose the Drop Disks option. The Edit Attributes option gives you the opportunity to adjust the compatibility parameters for the disk group. By default, the ASM Compatibility value is 12.1.0, meaning the minimum software version required for an ASM instance to mount this disk group (versions 10.1 and above). Database Compatibility by default is set to 10.1.0, and it is the minimum software version required for a database instance to use files in this disk group (versions 10.1 and above). You can also dismount and drop the disk group by choosing the appropriate menu options.

In the next section, you will learn to use SQL*Plus to manage the disk groups.

Managing Disk Groups

Because the data in the disk groups is distributed evenly among the disks, for better performance, you should allocate more than one disk for each disk group. A database should have at least two disk groups: one for database-related files and another for recovery-related files (for the fast recovery area). To manage the disk group storage, you should connect to the ASM instance with SYSASM privileges.

FIGURE 18.17 ASMCA – The Disk Groups tab

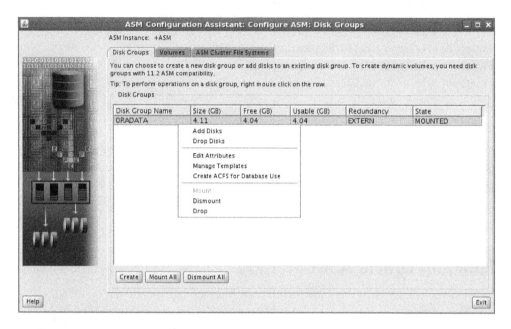

Creating and Dropping a Disk Group

The CREATE DISKGROUP statement is used to create a new disk group. The syntax for this statement is

```
CREATE DISKGROUP <dg_name> [ <redundancy_option> ]
[ <failure_group> ]
DISK <disk_path>
[ ATTRIBUTE <attribute_values> ]
```

The redundancy option by default is NORMAL, which means you should have at least two failure groups. A simple statement using external redundancy to create a disk group is shown here:

```
CREATE DISKGROUP fradisk EXTERNAL REDUNDANCY
DISK '/dev/rd/sd10c1', '/dev/rd/sd11c1';
```

This code creates a disk group named fradisk with two disks, and redundancy managed at the storage layer. Because no alias names are provided for the disks, ASM assigns a system-generated name.

Before defining the type of mirroring within a disk group, you must group the disks into failure groups. A failure group is one or more disks within a disk group that share a common resource such as a disk controller, whose failure would cause the entire set of disks to be unavailable to the group. In most cases, the ASM instance does not know the hardware and software dependencies for a given disk. Therefore, unless you specifically assign a disk to a failure group, each disk in the disk group is assigned to its own failure group. The following code creates a disk group with normal redundancy and two failure groups. Each failure group has two disks. Instead of using system-generated names, the disks are named. The allocation unit size defaults to 1MB, if not specified. In the example, AU is set to 4MB.

```
CREATE DISKGROUP datadisk NORMAL REDUNDANCY
FAILGROUP datadisk_fg1 DISK
'/dev/rd/sd10c1' NAME ddfg1a0,
'/dev/rd/sd11c1' NAME ddfg1a1
FAILGROUP datadisk_fg2 DISK
'/dev/rd/sd12c1' NAME ddfg2a0,
'/dev/rd/sd13c1' NAME ddfg2a1
ATTRIBUTE 'AU_SIZE'='4M';
```

When creating a disk group with HIGH REDUNDANCY, you must specify three failure groups. High redundancy uses three-way mirroring, with each extent getting two mirrored copies. HIGH REDUNDANCY disk groups can tolerate the loss of two failure groups.

To drop a disk group, use the DROP DISKGROUP statement. If the disk group being dropped contains any files, you must use the INCLUDING CONTENTS clause. For you to drop a disk group, the disk group must be in the mounted state. If errors prevent you from mounting the disk, you can use the FORCE option to drop the disk group. The following examples illustrate dropping an empty disk group, dropping a disk group with files, and force-dropping a disk group.

```
SQL> DROP DISKGROUP oradev;

SQL> DROP DISKGROUP oradev INCLUDING CONTENTS;

SQL> DROP DISKGROUP oradev FORCE  INCLUDING CONTENTS;
```

When specifying the disk while creating a disk group, you can use the wildcard *. The search string's matching disk should not be used by another ASM disk group. For example, you may use CREATE DISKGROUP ORADATA EXTERNAL REDUNDANCY DISK '/dev/md/sd1*c1'.

Adding and Dropping Disks

You can modify the disk group to add and drop disks. This action can be performed while the database using the disk group is running. The following example illustrates how to add disks to disk group datadisk, which was created using normal redundancy and two fail groups.

```
ALTER DISKGROUP datadisk ADD
FAILGROUP datadisk_fg1 DISK
```

```
'/dev/rd/sd14c1' NAME ddfg1a2
FAILGROUP datadisk_fg2 DISK
'/dev/rd/sd15c1' NAME ddfg2a2;
```

To add a disk to the fradisk created earlier, you can use the following code.

```
ALTER DISKGROUP fradisk ADD
DISK '/dev/rd/sd16c1';
```

The ALTER DISKGROUP statement can also be used to resize a disk allocated to a disk group. This action is not needed normally, because you will usually allocate the whole disk to a disk group.

If the ASMLib is configured, you should use ORCL:<diskname> instead of the device path when you're creating a disk group and adding a disk to a disk group. When you drop a disk from the disk group, you must use the disk name and not the path. For example, if you want to drop disk '/dev/rd/sd10c1' from *fradisk*, you must find the name of the disk from V$ASM_DISK and use that name to drop.

```
SQL> SELECT name, path
     FROM   v$asm_disk
     WHERE  path = '/dev/rd/sd10c1';

NAME          PATH
------------  ------------------------
FRADISK_000   /dev/rd/sd10c1

SQL> ALTER DISKGROUP fradisk DROP DISK fradisk_000;
```

 Real World Scenario

Disk Array Migration Using ASM Storage

When ASM is being used for storage, database migration from one disk array to another is as easy as attaching the new array to the server. To migrate the disk groups from one array to another, in versions before 12*c*, the following steps are performed.

1. Attach the new storage array to the database server.

2. Create partitions and prepare the LUNs for ASM storage on the new array.

3. Add disks from the new array to an existing disk group using the ALTER DISKGROUP ADD DISK statement.

4. Use the ALTER DISKGROUP DROP DISK statement to remove disks from the old array of the existing disk group.

5. Once the rebalancing operation completes, the disks from the old array will be removed from the disk group and can be detached from the database server.

In Oracle Database 12c, the ALTER DISKGROUP statement includes a new clause named REPLACE DISK. Steps 3 and 4 can be combined into one step using the REPLACE clause. The syntax of the REPLACE clause is

```
ALTER DISKGROUP diskgroup_name
  REPLACE DISK disk_name

  WITH 'path_name'

  [ POWER integer ] [ WAIT | NOWAIT ]
```

Disk Group Rebalancing

Disk group rebalancing happens automatically when you add a new disk to the disk group or remove a disk from the disk group. Oracle ASM redistributes data files evenly across all drives. No DBA intervention is required for the rebalance operation, but you may want to control the speed of the rebalance operation by adjusting the rebalancing power. There are two ways to adjust the rebalance speed.

The rebalance power at the instance level applicable to all disk groups in the ASM instance is managed by the initialization parameter ASM_POWER_LIMIT. The default value for this parameter is 1, but it has a range of values 0 to 1,024 and can be adjusted dynamically. The higher the power limit, the more quickly a rebalance operation can complete. Higher power values consume large amounts of I/O resources, which could impact database performance. Rebalancing takes longer with lower power values, but it consumes fewer processing and I/O resources.

If you do not want to change the ASM rebalancing power at the instance level, you can use the ALTER DISKGROUP statement to adjust the rebalancing power by disk group. You can change the rebalance power for an ongoing rebalancing operation, too. Here is an example:

```
ALTER DISKGROUP oradata REBALANCE POWER 8;
```

Data dictionary views with ASM information begin with V$ASM_. When a database is using ASM storage, these views are also available in the database, only showing the disk groups used by the database. V$ASM_DISKGROUP lists all disk groups. V$ASM_DISK shows all the disks discovered by the ASM instance. If the disk belongs to a disk group, the group_number column will identify the disk group. If the disk is not assigned to any disk group, the group number will be 0.

Using ASM Storage for a Database

In the earlier chapters, we discussed storage for database data files, redo log files, control files, the fast recovery area, and parameter files. Although ASM storage was an option on various occasions, we did not discuss in detail using ASM storage. ASM and Oracle Managed Files go together very well, eliminating all file management and I/O balancing activities from the DBA.

Using OMF with ASM

Oracle Managed Files (OMF) are best suited to use with an ASM disk group, by managing the file locations in the database initialization parameter file. Although you do not specify the plus sign (+) when creating a disk group, you must use + with the disk group when you're using the ASM disk group. This distinguishes the disk group name from the file system storage for the database. For example, to specify the archive location to +FRA, you can use the following ALTER SYSTEM statement.

```
ALTER SYSTEM log_archive_dest_1 = 'LOCATION=+FRA';
```

The following parameters can use the ASM disk group name as the value. Remember to specify the disk group name prefixed with a +.

DB_CREATE_FILE_DEST: Location to create database data files when CREATE TABLESPACE or ALTER TABLESPACE statements do not specify the file location.

DB_CREATE_ONLINE_LOG_DEST_1 to 5:   Location to create multiplexed online redo log files when the filename is not specified when adding a redo log group or member.

DB_RECOVERY_FILE_DEST: Location of the fast recovery area. By default archive logs and flashback log files go under the fast recovery area.

asmcmd is a command-line utility that you can use to manage Oracle ASM instances; disk groups and file access control for disk groups, files, and directories within disk groups; templates for disk groups; and volumes.

Migrating Files Between ASM and File System Storage

The online data-file move option can be used to migrate a file from the ASM disk group to another disk group, ASM to file system, or file system to ASM. The following example shows a non-OMF data file belonging to tablespace X1 migrated to ASM storage using OMF.

```
SQL> alter system set db_create_file_dest = '+ORADATA';
System altered.

SQL> SELECT file_name FROM dba_data_files
  2  WHERE tablespace_name = 'X1';
```

```
FILE_NAME
-------------------------------------------------------
/u01/app/oracle/oradata/ocadb1/x11.dbf


SQL> ALTER DATABASE MOVE DATAFILE '/u01/app/oracle/oradata/ocadb1/x11.dbf';
Database altered.


SQL> SELECT file_name FROM dba_data_files
  2  WHERE tablespace_name = 'X1';


FILE_NAME
------------------------------------------------
+ORADATA/OCADB1/DATAFILE/x1.257.837811593
```

When you perform a SHUTDOWN NORMAL or TRANSACTIONAL or IMMEDIATE on ASM instance, and if any database instance using the ASM instance is up, the ASM shutdown returns an error. If you perform SHUTDOWN ABORT (or STARTUP FORCE) on the ASM instance, the Oracle instances using the ASM instances are terminated.

Managing Tablespace Storage

When creating a tablespace or adding a data file to a tablespace, you can specify the disk group name using two different methods. If you omit the disk group name, the file will be created in the disk group specified in the DB_CREATE_FILE_DEST parameter. To create the data file in a specific disk group, you can provide the disk group name. The following code shows an example of each method.

```
SQL> CREATE TABLESPACE APPS_XX_DATA DATAFILE SIZE 100M;


SQL> ALTER TABLESPACE APPS_XX_DATA ADD DATAFILE '+MYPRODDISK' SIZE 50M;
```

When files are created in ASM disk group, ASM follows a standard naming convention and places the files under appropriate aliases (or subdirectories). Under each disk group, the directory is named with the value of DB_UNIQUE_NAME parameter. Under the database name level, subdirectories are named based on the file type. DATAFILE, CONTROLFILE, ONLINELOG, ARCHIVELOG, TEMPFILE, PARAMETERFILE, and FLASHBACK are some of the most common ASM file types.

Using Oracle Restart

Oracle Restart is a subset of Oracle clusterware services normally installed with an RAC setup. *Oracle High Availability Service* (OHAS) is the heart of Oracle Restart. The OHAS daemon ensures that Oracle components are started in the proper order, taking into account their dependencies. Oracle Restart is used only in standalone servers (non-RAC). Oracle Restart runs periodic check operations to monitor the health of these components. If a check operation fails for a component, the component is shut down and restarted, thus improving the availability of the Oracle database. Oracle Restart is more than just a database restart during server cycle or after a database crash. The components managed and automatically restarted by Oracle Restart are

- Database instances
- Non-default database services
- Oracle Net Listener
- Automatic Storage Management instance
- Mounting ASM disk groups
- Oracle Notification Services (ONS), where Data Guard is used

Oracle Restart includes the Server Control (srvctl) utility that you can use to manually start and stop Oracle Restart–managed components. Once you configure the components with Oracle Restart, we recommend that you use srvctl to manually start and stop the components.

 Grid Infrastructure is required to configure Oracle Restart. Oracle Restart is not part of the database software, although srvctl is included in the database home. You are not required to configure ASM to use Oracle Restart.

Registering Components with Oracle Restart

Oracle Restart maintains a list of all the components it manages and establishes dependency between the components. When a component is registered with Oracle Restart, the necessary configuration information is registered with the component. For example, when you register a listener, you have to provide the Oracle home directory and port number; when you register a database, you have to provide the Oracle home and spfile.

When you create an ASM instance, database, or listener using the wizard tools, they register the component with Oracle Restart if Grid Infrastructure is configured on the server. When you set up a new database server, installing GI is usually one of the first activities before you install a database.

The Server Control utility is available in the GI home and database home. Use the srvctl utility from GI home to stop and start the ASM instance, mount disk groups, and start and stop the listener from GI home and ONS. Use the srvctl from the database home to start and stop database and database services.

It is possible to manually stop the components using native utilities like sqlplus, lsnrctl, netca, or asmcmd; srvctl will not restart the services automatically, because these utilities are integrated into Oracle Restart. One advantage of using srvctl rather than native utilities is its ability to automatically stop and start the dependent services.

Use the add command of srvctl to add a component to Oracle Restart. The syntax is srvctl add *object options*. The *object* can be asm, database, diskgroup, filesystem, home, listener, service, and ons. You may use abbreviations for database, diskgroup, listener and service (db, dg, lsnr, serv, respectively). The *options* depend on the component being registered.

You can obtain help using srvctl -help. For help with a specific command on a component, such as adding a database, you can use srvctl add database -help.

```
$ srvctl
Usage: srvctl <command> <object> [<options>]
    commands: enable|disable|start|stop|status|add|remove|modify|getenv|
              setenv|unsetenv|config|upgrade|downgrade
    objects: database|service|asm|diskgroup|listener|home|ons
For detailed help on each command and object and its options use:
  srvctl <command> -help [-compatible] or
  srvctl <command> <object> -help [-compatible]
```

The following are a few examples of adding various components to Oracle Restart. The examples illustrate some of the most common and mandatory options. We encourage you to practice the other options by using the -help feature.

Registering a Listener

A listener is registered using the add listener option. When the listener is registered, Oracle Restart attempts to verify if the listener port is already in use. If the listener is already running, you can add the -skip option to skip checking the listener port.

Remove a listener by name *listener*, which is the default listener. Add a listener named *listenerasm* from the GI home.

```
$ srvctl remove listener -listener listener
```

Add a new listener from the GI home.

```
$ srvctl add listener -listener listenerasm -endpoints "TCP:1521" -oraclehome
$ORACLE_HOME
```

Verify the listener configuration using the config command.

```
$ srvctl config listener -listener listenerasm
Name: LISTENERASM
```

```
Home: /u03/app/oracle/grid/12.1.0
End points: TCP:1521
```

Check to see if the listener is running.

```
$ srvctl status listener -listener listenerasm
Listener LISTENERASM is enabled
Listener LISTENERASM is not running
```

Start the listener.

```
$ srvctl start listener -listener listenerasm
```

Check the status again.

```
$ srvctl status listener -listener listenerasm
Listener LISTENERASM is enabled
Listener LISTENERASM is running on node(s): emcc
```

Registering an ASM Instance

When you install GI with the Install and Configure Oracle Grid Infrastructure for a Standalone Server option, the ASM instance is registered with Oracle Restart by OUI, after creating the ASM instance. The following examples show how to register an ASM instance, list the configuration of ASM in Oracle Restart, modify the registration options, and remove the ASM instance from Oracle Restart. Because we installed ASM using GI (see the "Installing Oracle Grid Infrastructure" section), the ASM instance is already registered. But, for demonstration purposes, we are going to remove the ASM registration and add it again.

Before removing the existing ASM instance registration, obtain the configuration information.

```
$ srvctl config asm
ASM home: /u03/app/oracle/grid/12.1.0
Password file: +ORADATA/orapwasm
ASM listener:
Spfile: +ORADATA/ASM/ASMPARAMETERFILE/registry.253.837789509
ASM diskgroup discovery string:
```

Check the status of ASM.

```
$ srvctl status asm
ASM is running on emcc
```

Removing the ASM instance registration does not work because the instance is running. Let's remove the registration using the -force option, which will stop the running ASM instance.

```
$ srvctl remove asm
PRCR-1025 : Resource ora.asm is still running
$ srvctl remove asm -force
```

Register the ASM instance. Notice that not all configuration options are given.

```
$ srvctl add asm -listener listenerasm -spfile "+ORADATA/ASM/ASMPARAMETERFILE/
registry.253.837789509"
```

Verify the status of the registration. Notice the password file and ASM disk discovery string values.

```
$ srvctl config asm
ASM home: /u03/app/oracle/grid/12.1.0
Password file:
ASM listener: LISTENERASM
Spfile: +ORADATA/ASM/ASMPARAMETERFILE/registry.253.837789509
ASM diskgroup discovery string: ++no-value-at-resource-creation--never-
updated-through-ASM++
```

Use the modify option to add additional configuration options.

```
$ srvctl modify asm -pwfile "+ORADATA/orapwasm" -diskstring "ORCL:"
```

Verify the configuration.

```
$ srvctl config asm
ASM home: /u03/app/oracle/grid/12.1.0
Password file: +ORADATA/orapwasm
ASM listener: LISTENERASM
Spfile: +ORADATA/ASM/ASMPARAMETERFILE/registry.253.837789509
ASM diskgroup discovery string: ORCL:
```

Check the status of the ASM instance.

```
$ srvctl status asm
ASM is not running.
```

Start the ASM instance and verify the status again.

```
$ srvctl start asm

$ srvctl status asm
ASM is running on emcc
```

Registering a Database Instance

When you register a database with Oracle Restart, you'll have several configurable options. To view those options, execute srvctl add database -help. Unlike an ASM instance, you do not have to stop the database to remove a database registration from Oracle Restart (you will still have to use the -force option if the database is running, though), and removing the registration will not shut down the database.

Add database ocadb1 to Oracle Restart.

```
$ srvctl add database -db ocadb1 -oraclehome /u02/app/oracle/product/12.1.0/
dbhome_1 -spfile /u02/app/oracle/product/12.1.0/dbhome_1/dbs/spfileocadb1.ora
```

Verify the configuration.

```
$ srvctl config database -database ocadb1                    .
Database unique name: ocadb1
Database name:
Oracle home: /u02/app/oracle/product/12.1.0/dbhome_1
Oracle user: oracle
Spfile: /u02/app/oracle/product/12.1.0/dbhome_1/dbs/spfileocadb1.ora
Password file:
Domain:
Start options: open
Stop options: immediate
Database role: PRIMARY
Management policy: AUTOMATIC
Database instance: ocadb1
Disk Groups:
Services:
```

Add and verify an additional service named enccdb1 for the database ocadb1. Oracle Database 12*c* automatically adds and enables a service name as the database unique name. You cannot add a service name that is the same as the database's unique name to Oracle Restart.

```
$ srvctl add service -db ocadb1 -service emccdb1

$ srvctl config service -db ocadb1
Service name: emccdb1
Service is enabled
Cardinality: SINGLETON
Disconnect: false
Service role: PRIMARY
Management policy: AUTOMATIC
DTP transaction: false
```

```
AQ HA notifications: false
Global: false
Commit Outcome: false
Failover type:
Failover method:
TAF failover retries:
TAF failover delay:
Connection Load Balancing Goal: LONG
Runtime Load Balancing Goal: NONE
TAF policy specification: NONE
Edition:
Pluggable database name:
Maximum lag time: ANY
SQL Translation Profile:
Retention: 86400 seconds
Replay Initiation Time: 300 seconds
Session State Consistency:
```

Modify the database registration to add a password file and the disk groups associated with the database.

```
$ srvctl modify database -db ocadb1 -diskgroup ORADATA -pwfile /u02/app/oracle/
product/12.1.0/dbhome_1/dbs/orapwocadb1
```

You can use srvctl disable *component* to disable a component. When a component is disabled, it will no longer restart automatically and it cannot be started using srvctl. Use this option if you have to perform maintenance or repair a component. After the repair is made, the component can be enabled using srvctl enable.

Setting Environment Variables

You may need to set additional environment variables before you start a component. Use the setenv command to set the environment variables in Oracle Restart for the ASM instance, database, and listener. The getenv command can be used to display all the variable set for a component. To remove the environment variable, use the unsetenv command.

The -env option can be used to set one variable, and the -envs option can be used to set multiple variables. Here is an example of setting the environment variables for a database using setenv, and retrieving the variables using getenv.

```
$ srvctl setenv database -db ocadb1 -env ORACLE_BASE=/u03/app/oracle
```

```
$ srvctl setenv database -db ocadb1 -envs "ORA_NLS10=$ORACLE_HOME/nls/data,TNS_
ADMIN=/u03/app/oracle/tns_admin"
```

```
$ srvctl getenv database -db ocadb1
ocadb1:
TNS_ADMIN=/u03/app/oracle/tns_admin
ORA_NLS10=/u02/app/oracle/product/12.1.0/dbhome_1/nls/data
ORACLE_BASE=/u03/app/oracle
```

You can remove an environment variable using the unset command.

```
$ srvctl unsetenv database -db ocadb1 -envs TNS_ADMIN
```

```
$ srvctl getenv database -db ocadb1
ocadb1:
ORA_NLS10=/u02/app/oracle/product/12.1.0/dbhome_1/nls/data
ORACLE_BASE=/u03/app/oracle
```

Starting and Stopping Oracle Restart

Oracle Restart services or OHAS services are started and stopped using the Cluster Read Services Control utility (crsctl) from the GI home. You must be logged in to the server as the owner of GI software or the root user. Six commands are supported by crsctl to manage has: enable, disable, start, stop, check, and config.

The following examples show how to use these commands, which will help you better understand how the commands work.

Check to see if an automatic start of Oracle Restart is enabled. If you enable an automatic restart of has, Oracle Restart is automatically started when GI services are started after a server reboot.

```
$ crsctl config has
CRS-4622: Oracle High Availability Services autostart is enabled.
```

Check to determine if Oracle Restart is started.

```
$ crsctl check has
CRS-4638: Oracle High Availability Services is online
```

Stopping has will stop all the components registered in Oracle Restart. You can use the -f option to forcefully stop has.

```
[root@emcc bin]# pwd
/u03/app/oracle/grid/12.1.0/bin
[root@emcc bin]# ./crsctl stop has
CRS-2791: Starting shutdown of Oracle High Availability Services-managed
resources on 'emcc'
CRS-2673: Attempting to stop 'ora.ocadb1.emccdb1.svc' on 'emcc'
CRS-2673: Attempting to stop 'ora.LISTENERASM.lsnr' on 'emcc'
CRS-2677: Stop of 'ora.ocadb1.emccdb1.svc' on 'emcc' succeeded
```

```
CRS-2673: Attempting to stop 'ora.ocadb1.db' on 'emcc'
CRS-2677: Stop of 'ora.LISTENERASM.lsnr' on 'emcc' succeeded
CRS-2677: Stop of 'ora.ocadb1.db' on 'emcc' succeeded
CRS-2673: Attempting to stop 'ora.evmd' on 'emcc'
CRS-2673: Attempting to stop 'ora.ORADATA.dg' on 'emcc'
CRS-2677: Stop of 'ora.ORADATA.dg' on 'emcc' succeeded
CRS-2673: Attempting to stop 'ora.asm' on 'emcc'
CRS-2677: Stop of 'ora.asm' on 'emcc' succeeded
CRS-2677: Stop of 'ora.evmd' on 'emcc' succeeded
CRS-2673: Attempting to stop 'ora.cssd' on 'emcc'
CRS-2677: Stop of 'ora.cssd' on 'emcc' succeeded
CRS-2793: Shutdown of Oracle High Availability Services-managed resources on
'emcc' has completed
CRS-4133: Oracle High Availability Services has been stopped.
[root@emcc bin]#
```

To start Oracle Restart, use `crsctl start has`.

```
[root@emcc bin]# ./crsctl start has
CRS-4123: Oracle High Availability Services has been started.

[root@emcc bin]# ./crsctl check has
CRS-4638: Oracle High Availability Services is online
```

The status command shows the status of individual components. The -t option is used to display output in a tabular format.

```
[root@emcc bin]# ./crsctl status res -t
--------------------------------------------------------------------
Name            Target  State     Server          State details
--------------------------------------------------------------------
Local Resources
--------------------------------------------------------------------
ora.LISTENERASM.lsnr
                ONLINE  ONLINE    emcc            STABLE
ora.ORADATA.dg
                ONLINE  ONLINE    emcc            STABLE
ora.asm
                ONLINE  ONLINE    emcc            Started,STABLE
ora.ons
                OFFLINE OFFLINE   emcc            STABLE
--------------------------------------------------------------------
```

```
Cluster Resources
--------------------------------------------------------------------
ora.cssd
      1           ONLINE  ONLINE       emcc            STABLE
ora.diskmon
      1           OFFLINE OFFLINE                      STABLE
ora.evmd
      1           ONLINE  ONLINE       emcc            STABLE
ora.ocadb1.db
      1           ONLINE  OFFLINE      emcc            Instance Shutdown,ST
                                                       ARTING
ora.ocadb1.emccdb1.svc
      1           ONLINE  OFFLINE                      STABLE
--------------------------------------------------------------------
```

To display the output in list format, use the same command without the -t option—for example, crsctl status res.

Summary

In this chapter, we discussed how to move data using Oracle Data Pump, using SQL*Loader, and using external tables. You also learned how to install and use the Oracle Grid Infrastructure components.

Data Pump is a very high-speed utility for moving data and metadata. The client utilities expdp and impdp are used to unload and load data and metadata. The Data Pump architecture includes the data and metadata movement engine DBMS_DATAPUMP, the metadata API DBMS_METADATA, the external tables API, and the client utilities.

Data Pump Exports and Imports are performed on the server. You can attach to a job from any computer and monitor its progress or make resource adjustments. In the interactive mode, you can add a file to export a dump-file set, kill a job, stop a job, change the parallelism, and enable detailed status logging.

SQL*Loader is used to load ASCII files to the Oracle database. You can invoke Data Pump and SQL*Loader using EM Database Control or SQL Developer. You can also use external tables to move data. You can use the ORACLE_DATAPUMP access driver to write data to an external table, and you can use the ORACLE_LOADER access driver to read flat files into an Oracle database.

The Grid Infrastructure for a standalone server, also known as Oracle Restart, provides system support for Oracle systems, including database storage, volume management, file systems for applications, and automatic restart of various components in the system. Oracle Restart uses the ohas daemon to monitor and restart the components registered. Oracle Restart components include the ASM instance, database, listener, and database services.

The Server Control (srvctl) utility is used to register and configure the components of Oracle Restart. Oracle Restart itself is started and stopped by using the crsctl utility.

Exam Essentials

Know how to create database directory objects. Directory objects are required for use in the Data Pump Export and Data Pump Import programs.

Know that directory objects are not owned by an individual schema. Directory objects are not schema objects. Instead, they are owned by the database, just as roles or profiles are.

Be aware of the Data Pump Export and Import modes. Data Pump Export has database, schema, table, tablespace, and transport tablespace modes. Data Pump Import has full, schema, table, and tablespace modes. Although these modes sound similar, they differ between the two tools.

Be familiar with the Data Pump options that let you transfer both data and metadata from one schema to another. The content= parameter controls whether data, metadata, or both are copied. The remap_schema parameter allows you to transfer data from one schema to another.

Be aware of the limitations of SQL*Loader direct path mode, including unusable indexes. The SQL*Loader direct path mode has several limitations, the most prominent being that it locks the table in exclusive mode for the duration of the load. Unique indexes are marked unusable if unique violations are found after a direct path load. These unique violations must be resolved before the index can be rebuilt.

Know the external table access drivers. ORACLE_DATAPUMP and ORACLE_LOADER are the access drivers used with external tables. The ORACLE_DATAPUMP access driver can be used to read and write to an external table. The ORACLE_LOADER access driver is read-only.

Know which Data Pump option can be used to upgrade an 11g R2 database. Data Pump full export and transportable tablespace features are combined in the full transportable export feature, which can be used to migrate 11.2.0.3+ databases to 12.1.0.

Understand the installation options available for Grid Infrastructure. Grid Infrastructure can be installed for clustered environments and standalone servers. GI includes Oracle Restart and Oracle ASM.

Know the ASM disk group redundancy options. ASM disk groups have normal, high, and external redundancy. Learn how to specify and use fail groups.

Understand how Oracle Restart Components are registered. Oracle Restart understands the dependency between registered components. Oracle Restart automatically restarts a component if it detects failure.

Review Questions

1. Which two PL/SQL packages are used by Oracle Data Pump?

    A. UTL_DATAPUMP

    B. DBMS_METADATA

    C. DBMS_DATAPUMP

    D. UTL_FILE

    E. DBMS_SQL

2. Which of these options is not a benefit of Oracle Data Pump? (Choose two.)

    A. Data Pump supports fine-grained object selection using the EXCLUDE, INCLUDE, and CONTENT options.

    B. Data Pump has the ability to specify the target version of the database so that the objects exported are compatible. This is useful in moving data from Oracle 12c to Oracle 11g.

    C. Data Pump has the ability to specify the maximum number of threads to unload data.

    D. The DBA can choose to perform the export using a direct path or external tables.

    E. The Data Pump job can be monitored from another computer on the network.

3. The Data Pump job maintains a master control table with information about Data Pump. Choose the right statement.

    A. The master table is the heart of Data Pump operation and is maintained in the SYS schema.

    B. The master table contains one row for the operation that keeps track of the object being worked so that the job can be restarted in the event of failure.

    C. During the export, the master table is written to the dump-file set at the beginning of export operation.

    D. The Data Pump job runs in the schema of the job creator with that user's rights and privileges.

    E. All of the above.

4. When using the expdp and impdp clients, the parameters LOGFILE, DUMPFILE, and SQLFILE need a directory object where the files will be written to or read from. Choose the nonsupported method for nonprivileged users.

    A. Specify the DIRECTORY parameter.

    B. Specify the filename parameters with directory:file_name.

    C. Use the initialization parameter DATA_PUMP_DIR.

    D. None of the above (all are supported).

5. Which command-line parameter of expdp and impdp clients connects you to an existing job?

   A. CONNECT_CLIENT

   B. CONTINUE_CLIENT

   C. APPEND

   D. ATTACH

6. Which option unloads the data and metadata of the SCOTT user, except the tables that begin with TEMP? The dump file also should have the DDL to create the user.

   A. CONTENT=BOTH TABLES=(not like 'TEMP%')   SCHEMAS=SCOTT

   B. SCHEMAS=SCOTT   EXCLUDE=TABLE:"LIKE 'TEMP%'"

   C. INCLUDE=METADATA EXCLUDE=TABLES:"NOT LIKE 'TEMP%'" SCHEMAS=SCOTT

   D. TABLES="NOT LIKE 'TEMP%'" SCHEMAS=SCOTT

7. Which parameter is *not* a valid one for using the impdp client?

   A. REMAP_INDEX

   B. REMAP_TABLE

   C. REMAP_SCHEMA

   D. REMAP_TABLESPACE

   E. REMAP_DATAFILE

8. When do you use the FLASHBACK_TIME parameter in the impdp utility?

   A. To load data from the dump file that was modified after a certain time.

   B. To discard data from the dump file that was modified after a certain time.

   C. When the NETWORK_LINK parameter is used.

   D. FLASHBACK_TIME is valid only with expdp, not with impdp.

9. To perform a Data Pump import from a live database, which parameter needs to be set?

   A. db_link

   B. network_link

   C. dumpfile

   D. directory

10. When is it most appropriate to use an external table?

   A. When you need to read binary files (PDF and photos) into Oracle Database

   B. To query a large file without loading the data into the database

   C. When the expdp and impdp utilities are not licensed for use

   D. To load a large file into the database quickly

11. Choose the statement that is *not* true from the following about direct path load.

    A. Direct path load cannot occur if active transactions against the table are being loaded.

    B. Triggers do not fire during direct path loads.

    C. During direct path loads, foreign key constraints are disabled at the beginning of the load and then re-enabled after the load.

    D. Only primary key, unique, and `NOT NULL` constraints are enforced.

    E. Direct path load allows other users to perform DML operations on the table while the direct load operation is in progress.

12. Which two statements regarding the Grid Infrastructure are true?

    A. It is mandatory to create a disk group during the GI install using the Install and Configure Oracle Grid Infrastructure for a Standalone Server option.

    B. You can only create one disk group during the GI install.

    C. A disk group must have at least two disks.

    D. After a GI install, ASMCA must be run to configure an ASM instance.

13. What is the smallest unit of storage in an ASM disk group?

    A. Database block

    B. OS block

    C. Allocation unit

    D. Smallest disk in the disk group

14. Which privilege is required to start and stop an ASM instance?

    A. SYSDBA

    B. SYSASM

    C. SYSDBA or SYSASM

    D. SYSDBA or ASMOPER

15. What Oracle Restart utility that is used to start and stop ASM instances also starts the listener associated with the ASM?

    A. crsca

    B. asmca

    C. asmcmd

    D. srvctl

16. How many fail groups are required to configure a disk group with NORMAL redundancy?

    A. 0

    B. 1

    C. 2

    D. Fail groups are not applicable for NORMAL redundancy.

17. Review the following statement, and choose the SQL statement that successfully drops a disk from the disk group.

```
SQL> SELECT name, path
     FROM   v$asm_disk
     WHERE  group_number = 1;

NAME            PATH
------------    -----------------------
FRADISK_000     /dev/rd/sd10c1
FRADISK_001     /dev/rd/sd11c1
```

    A. `DROP DISK FRADISK_000`

    B. `ALTER DISKGROUP DROP DISK FRADISK_000`

    C. `ALTER DISKGROUP DROP DISK '/dev/rd/sd10c1'`

    D. `ALTER DISKGROUP DROP DISK FRADISK_000, FRADISK_001`

18. Which of the following statements can speed up the disk group rebalancing process? (Choose two.)

    A. `ALTER SYSTEM SET ASM_POWER_LIMIT=0`

    B. `ALTER SYSTEM SET ASM_POWER_LIMIT=100`

    C. `ALTER DISKGROUP oradata REBALANCE POWER 100`

    D. `ALTER DISKGROUP oradata ASM_POWER_LIMIT 100`

19. Choose the option that can be used to start an ASM instance.

    A. `sqlplus`

    B. `asmcmd`

    C. `asmca`

    D. `srvctl`

    E. All of the above

20. Which command registers an ASM instance in Oracle Restart?

    A. srvctl add asm

    B. srvctl config asm

    C. srvctl register asm

    D. srvctl start asm

Appendix
A

Answers to Review Questions

Chapter 1: Introducing Oracle Database 12c RDBMS

1. **B.** Because the relationship between MOVIES and CHARACTERS is represented through a solid line with a crowfoot at one end, the relationship is mandatory one-to-many, which means each movie must have one or more characters.

2. **D.** When the physical structure is being designed, an entity in the ER diagram may be mapped as a table in the database. An attribute may be mapped as a column, a relationship is the referential integrity, and a unique identifier is the primary key.

3. **A.** Object type lets you define structures that satisfy the business requirement. It can include built-in and user-defined types.

4. **D.** Oracle Database 12c has the multitenancy database feature, where multiple databases are plugged in. These pluggable databases share resources such as Oracle home, the memory area, processes, and the disk. Therefore, patching one pluggable database is not possible. Patches are applied to the container database.

5. **B.** SQL*Plus can be invoked with no parameters or with connection attributes. When connection attributes are provided, the <username> is mandatory. The <password> and <connect_string> commands are optional. When connection attributes are not provided, sqlplus prompts for username and password. If username is included in the command line, sqlplus prompts for password.

6. **B, C.** Oracle Enterprise Manager Cloud Control is a separate product to manage and administer various Oracle products including the database. TOAD is not an Oracle product.

7. **C.** The relationship between the entities is part of one or more constraints between the tables. The unique identifiers of an entity become the primary key of the table. The relationship between tables becomes the foreign key.

8. D. SQL Developer is Oracle's GUI interface to the database. It has menus and reports for DBAs, developers, and end users.

9. B. In RAC architecture, more than one instance communicates to the database. If an instance on one server fails, the remaining instances in the RAC pool remain active and service users.

10. B. Easy connect uses the information provided in the connect string to connect to the database directly, without looking for information in another source. Easy connect uses hostname, port, and the service name to connect to the database.

Chapter 2: Introducing SQL

1. C. Column alias names enclosed in quotation marks will appear as typed. Spaces and mixed case appear in the column alias name only when the alias is enclosed in double quotation marks.

2. A. Statements 1 and 2 will produce the same result. You can use the column name, column alias, or column position in the ORDER BY clause. The default sort order is ascending. For a descending sort, you must explicitly specify that order with the DESC keyword.

3. B. In the arithmetic evaluation, multiplication and division have precedence over addition and subtraction. Even if you do not include the parentheses, salary*0.1 will be evaluated first. The result is then divided by 2, and its result is added to 200.

4. A, C. Character literals in the SQL statement are enclosed in single quotation marks. Literals are concatenated using ||. Employee Name: is a character literal, and 10 is a numeric literal.

5. D. DISTINCT is used to display a unique result row, and it should follow immediately after the keyword SELECT. Uniqueness is identified across the row, not by a single column.

6. B. The WHERE clause is used to filter the rows returned from a query. The WHERE clause condition is evaluated, and rows are returned only if the result is TRUE. The ORDER BY clause is used to display the result in a certain order. The OFFSET and FETCH clauses are used to limit the rows returned.

7. B. There are three records belonging to DEPTNO 10: EMPNO 7934 (MILLER), 7839 (KING), and 7782 (CLARK). When you sort their names by descending order, MILLER is the first row to display. You can use alias names and columns that are not in the SELECT clause in the ORDER BY clause.

8. D. Here, a character column is compared against a string using the BETWEEN operator, which is equivalent to ename >= 'A' AND ename <= 'C'. The name CLARK will not be included in this query, because 'CLARK' is > 'C'.

9. C. Column alias names cannot be used in the WHERE clause. They can be used in the ORDER BY clause.

10. A. The IN operator can be used. You can write the WHERE clause as WHERE empno IN (7782, 7876);. Using the =ANY operator also produces the same result.

11. C. Because _ is a special pattern-matching character, you need to include the ESCAPE clause in LIKE. The % character matches any number of characters including 0, and _ matches a single character.

12. C. A CASE expression begins with the keyword CASE and ends with the keyword END.

13. B. The default sorting order for a numeric column is ascending. The columns are sorted first by salary and then by name, so the row with the lowest salary is displayed first. It is perfectly valid to use a column in the ORDER BY clause that is not part of the SELECT clause.

14. D. In the SELECT clause, the column names should be separated by commas. An alias name may be provided for each column with a space or by using the keyword AS. The FROM clause should appear after the SELECT clause. The WHERE clause appears after the FROM clause. The ORDER BY clause comes after the WHERE clause.

15. B. Column alias names cannot be used in the WHERE clause of the SQL statement. In the ORDER BY clause, you can use the column name or alias name, or you can indicate the column by its position in the SELECT clause.

16. C. The query will return an error, because the substitution variable is used without an ampersand (&) character. In this query, Oracle treats V_DEPTNO as another column name from the table and returns an error. Substitution variables are not case sensitive.

17. B, C. When a variable is preceded by double ampersands, SQL*Plus defines that variable. Similarly, when you pass values to a script using START *script_name arguments*, SQL*Plus defines those variables. Once a variable is defined, its value will be available for the duration of the session or until you use UNDEFINE *variable*.

18. D. % is the wild character to pattern-match for any number of characters. Option A is almost correct, except for the SORT keyword in the ORDER BY clause, which will produce an error because it is not a valid syntax. Option B will produce results but will sort them in the order you want. Option C will not return any rows because LIKE is the operator for pattern matching, not =. Option E has an error similar to Option A.

19. C. In the first SQL statement, the comm IN (0, NULL) will be treated as comm = 0 OR comm = NULL. For all NULL comparisons, you should use IS NULL instead of = NULL. The first SQL statement will return only one row where comm = 0, whereas the second SQL will return all the rows that have comm = NULL as well as comm = 0.

20. A. Option A is correct. It includes the OFFSET 3 clause to skip the first three rows and the FETCH 1 ROW clause to get the fourth row. The WITH TIES option retrieves all records if there is a tie for the fourth position. Option B SQL will error out because the SQL is missing the ONLY or WITH TIES clause—one should be specified. Even after the syntax is fixed, the result will be wrong. The sorting is performed in the reverse order. Option C is similar to Option A, but will retrieve the fifth position instead of the fourth. Option D will produce the wrong results—it is missing the DESC keyword as well as the OFFSET clause.

Chapter 3: Using Single-Row Functions

1. C. Double quotation marks must surround literal strings like "Week".

2. D. The TRUNC function removes the time portion of a date by default, and whole numbers added to or subtracted from dates represent days added or subtracted from that date. TRUNC(SYSDATE) –5 means five days ago at midnight.

3. C. The two statements are equivalent.

4. B. SUBSTR returns part of the string. INSTR returns a number. LPAD adds to a character string. LEAST does not change an input string.

5. C. Options A and B do not account for NULL surcharges correctly and will set the bonus to NULL where the surcharge is NULL. In option B, the NVL function is applied to the base_price column instead of the surcharge column. In option C, the LEAST function will return a NULL if surcharge is NULL, in which case BASE_PRICE * 1.05 would be returned from the COALESCE function.

6. B, D. ROUND does not accept character arguments. SUBSTR accepts only character arguments. SIGN accepts only numeric arguments.

7. A. The functions are evaluated from the innermost to outermost, as follows:

SIGN(ABS(NVL(-32,0))) = SIGN(ABS(-32)) = SIGN(32) = 1

8. D. The NVL function returns zero if the salary value is NULL, or else it returns the original value. The NVL2 function returns the second argument if the salary value is not NULL. If NULL, the third argument is returned.

9. A, B. RTRIM removes trailing (not leading) characters. INSTR returns a number. STRIP is not a valid Oracle function. SUBSTR, with the second argument greater than 1, removes leading characters from a string.

10. B. MOD returns the number remainder after division. The REMAINDER function is similar to MOD but will use the ROUND function in the algorithm; hence, the result of REMAINDER(11,4) would be –1. MOD uses FLOOR in the algorithm.

11. D. The SUBSTR function in option A would return the last two characters of the last name. These two characters are right-trimmed using the RTRIM function. The result would be the first portion of the last name and is concatenated to 'XX' only if the last two characters are not repeating (for example, Pululul will be PXX). Option B would replace all the occurrences of the last two characters. Option C would choose only the last two characters.

12. A. The CURRENT_TIMESTAMP function returns the session date, session time, and session time zone offset. The return datatype is TIMESTAMP WITH TIME ZONE.

13. C. Option A will result in NULL TOTAL_SALES for rows where there are NULL WARRANTY_SALES. Option B is not the correct syntax for NVL2, because it requires three arguments. With option C, if WARRANTY_SALES is NULL, then CAR_SALES is returned; otherwise, CAR_SALES+WARRANTY_SALES is returned. The COALESCE function returns the first non-NULL argument and could be used to obtain the desired results, but the first argument here is CAR_SALES, which is not NULL. Therefore, COALESCE will always return CAR_SALES.

14. C. The ADD_MONTHS function returns the date *d* plus *i* months. If <*d*> is the last day of the month or the resulting month has fewer days, then the result is the last day of the resulting month.

15. C. Statement 1 will result in 30-SEP-0007, and statement 2 will result in 30-SEP-2007. The RR and RRRR formats derive the century based on the current date if the century is not specified. The YY format will use the current century, and the YYYY format expects the century in the input.

16. B. The COALESCE function returns the first non-NULL parameter, which is the character string 'Oracle'.

17. E. Option A will not work if there is a February 29 (leap year) in the next 365 days. Option B will always add one year to the present date, except if the current date is February 29 (leap year). Option C will return the date one day later. NEW_TIME is used to return the date/time in a different time zone. ADD_MONTHS (SYSDATE,12) can be used to achieve the desired result.

18. A. LOCALTIMESTAMP does not return the time zone. CURRENT_DATE and SYSDATE return neither fractional seconds nor a time zone; they both return the DATE datatype.

19. D. CONVERT is used to change from one character set to another. EXTRACT works on date/time datatypes. TRANSLATE changes all occurrences of each character with a positionally corresponding character, so 'I like IBM' would become 'S like SUN'.

20. C. The INITCAP function capitalizes the first letter in each word. The REPLACE function performs search-and-replace string operations. There is no IFELSE function. The DECODE function is the one that implements IF...THEN...ELSE logic.

Chapter 4: Using Group Functions

1. **D.** Even though you do not have a `state` column in the `SELECT` clause, having it in the `GROUP BY` clause will group the results by state, so you end up getting two values (two columns) for each state.

2. **A.** All requirements are met. The gross-, net-, and earned-revenue requirements are satisfied with the `SELECT` clause. The second- and third-quarter sales requirement is satisfied with the first predicate of the `WHERE` clause—the sales date will be truncated to the first day of a quarter; thus, `01-Apr-1999` or `01-Jul-1999` for the required quarters (which are both between `01-Apr-1999` and `01-Sep-1999`). The state codes requirement is satisfied by the second predicate in the `WHERE` clause. This question is intentionally misleading, but so are some exam questions (and, unfortunately, some of the code in some shops is too).

3. **C.** Because the `department_id` column does not have any aggregate function applied to it, it must appear in the `GROUP BY` clause. To make the query work, the `ORDER BY` clause in the SQL instructions must be replaced with a `GROUP BY` clause.

4. **A.** Because group functions do not include `NULL` values in their calculations, you do not have to do anything special to exclude the `NULL` values. Only `COUNT(*)` includes `NULL` values.

5. **B.** An aggregate function is not allowed in the `WHERE` clause. You can have the `GROUP BY` and `HAVING` clauses in any order, but they must appear after the `WHERE` clause.

6. **D.** The SQL code will work fine and produce the desired result. Because group functions are nested, a `GROUP BY` clause is required.

7. **A.** It is perfectly all right to have one function in the `SELECT` clause and another function in the `HAVING` clause of the query. Options B and C are trying to use the alias name, which is not allowed. Option D has a group function in the `WHERE` clause, which is not allowed.

8. **D.** The query will return how many distinct alphabets are used to begin names in the `EMPLOYEES` table. You can nest a group function inside a single-row function, and vice versa.

9. **E.** All the queries will return the same result. Because `ORDER_NO` is the primary key, `NULL` values cannot be in the column. Hence, `ALL` and `DISTINCT` will give the same result.

10. **D.** Option A will display the highest salary of all the employees. Options B and E use invalid syntax keywords. Option C does not have a `GROUP BY` clause.

11. **B.** The first column in the first query counts the distinct `MGR` values in the table. The first column in the second query counts all `MGR` values in the table. If a manager appears twice, the first query will count her one time, but the second will count her twice. Both the first query and the second query select the maximum salary value in the table.

12. A, B. A group function is not allowed in GROUP BY or WHERE clauses, whether you use it as nested or not.

13. B. Both statements are valid. The first statement will produce the number of rows equal to the number of unique first_name values. The second statement will produce the number of rows equal to the unique number of first characters in the first_name column.

14. D. COUNT(*) will count all rows in the table. COUNT(salary) will count only the number of salary values that appear in the table. If there are any rows with a NULL salary, statement 2 will not count them.

15. A. A GROUP BY clause must contain the column or expressions on which to perform the grouping operation. It cannot use column aliasing.

16. A. You cannot place a group function in the WHERE clause. Instead, you should use a HAVING clause.

17. B. There is at least one column in the SELECT list that is not a constant or group function, so a GROUP BY clause is mandatory.

18. D. The HAVING clause filters data after the group function is applied. If an aggregate function is not used in the HAVING clause, the column used must be part of the SELECT clause.

19. C. The HAVING clause can be used in a SELECT statement only if the GROUP BY clause is present. The optional HAVING clause filters data after the rows are summarized.

20. C. The GROUP BY and HAVING clauses can appear in any order in the SELECT clause. If a WHERE clause is present, it must be before the GROUP BY clause. ORDER BY clause, if present, follows the GROUP BY clause – ORDER BY is recommended for consistent result order.

Chapter 5: Using Joins and Subqueries

1. C. When table aliases are defined, you should qualify the column names with the table alias only. In this case, the table name cannot be used to qualify column names. The line in option C should read WHERE e.deptno = d.deptno.

2. A. An outer join operator, (+), indicates an outer join and is used to display the records, even if there are no corresponding records in the table mentioned on the other side of the operator. Here, the outer join operator is next to the ORDERS table, so even if there are no corresponding orders from a customer, the result set will have the customer ID and name.

3. B. When an outer join returns values from a table that does not have corresponding records, a NULL is returned.

4. C. The join condition is specified in the ON clause. The JOIN clause specifies the table to be joined. The USING clause specifies the column names that should be used in the join. The WHERE clause is used to specify additional search criteria to restrict the rows returned.

5. B, D. Option A does not work because you cannot qualify column names when using a natural join. Option B works because the only common column between these two tables is DEPARTMENT_ID. The keyword OUTER is optional. Option C does not work, again because you cannot qualify column names when specifying the USING clause. Option D works because it specifies the join condition explicitly in the ON clause.

6. A, C. OR and IN are not allowed in the WHERE clause on the columns where an outer join operator is specified. You can use AND and = in the outer join.

7. A, C. Options A and B have an ORDER BY clause used in the subquery. An ORDER BY clause can be used in the subquery appearing in the FROM clause, but not in the WHERE clause. Options C and D use the GROUP BY clause in the subquery, and its use is allowed in FROM as well as WHERE clauses. Option D will give an error because the DEPARTMENT_ID in the SELECT clause is ambiguous and, therefore, doesn't need to be qualified as e.DEPARTMENT_ID. Another issue with option D is that since you used the USING clause to join, the column used in the USING clause cannot be qualified; e.hire_date in the SELECT clause should be hire_date.

8. B. The query fails because the d.DEPARTMENT_ID column is referenced before the DEPARTMENTS table is specified in the JOIN clause. A column can be referenced only after its table is specified.

9. D. Because DEPARTMENT_ID and MANAGER_ID are common columns in the EMPLOYEES and DEPARTMENTS tables, a natural join will relate these two tables using the two common columns.

10. B. There are two records in the STATE table with the ST_CODE value as 'TN'. Because you are using a single-row operator for the subquery, it will fail. Option C would be correct if it used the IN operator instead of = for the subquery.

11. A. The query will succeed, because there is only one row in the CITY table with the CTY_NAME value 'DALLAS'.

12. E. There is no error in the statement. The query will return the department number where the most employees are working and the number of employees in that department.

13. A. A subquery is correlated when a reference is made to a column from a table in the parent statement.

14. C. The subquery returns 91 to the main query.

15. D. You cannot have an ORDER BY clause in the subquery used in a WHERE clause.

16. C. The query will work fine, producing the difference between the employee's salary and the average salary in the department. You do not need to use the alias names, because the column names returned from the subquery are different from the column names returned by the parent query.

17. C. Because only one column is selected in the subquery to which you are doing the insert, only one column value should be supplied in the VALUES clause. The VALUES clause can have only CNT_CODE value (971).

18. B. When using set operators, the ORDER BY clause can appear only on the SQL at the very end. You can use the column names (or aliases) appearing in the top query or use positional columns.

19. B. All four queries produce the same result. The first query uses a scalar subquery in the SELECT clause. The rest of the queries use an inline view. All the queries display the last name, salary, and difference of salary from the highest salary in the department for all employees in department 20.

20. D. To find the top *n* rows, you can select the necessary columns in an inline view with an ORDER BY DESC clause. An outer query limiting the rows to *n* will give the result. ROWNUM returns the row number of the result row.

Chapter 6: Manipulating Data

1. D. When inserting from another table using a subquery, the VALUES clause should not be included. Options B and C are invalid syntaxes for the INSERT statement.

2. E. If a transaction is not currently open, any INSERT, UPDATE, MERGE, DELETE, SELECT FOR UPDATE, or LOCK statement will implicitly begin a transaction.

3. B, C. Option A will error out because when columns are used in SET, a subquery must be used as in option C. Option D is wrong because AND is used instead of a comma to separate columns in the SET clause.

4. A, D. COMMIT, ROLLBACK, and any DDL statement end a transaction—DDL is automatically committed. INSERT, UPDATE, and DELETE statements require a commit or rollback.

5. A. Option A uses a correlated subquery to match the correct employee. Option B selects all the rows in the subquery and, therefore, will generate an error. Option C is not valid syntax. Option D will update all the rows in the table because the UPDATE statement does not have a WHERE clause. The WHERE clause preset belongs to the subquery.

6. B. In an UPDATE statement, the WHERE clause should come after the SET clause.

7. D. When deleting a row from a table, do not use column names. To change column values to NULL, use the UPDATE statement.

8. C. The FROM keyword in the DELETE statement is optional. Statement 3 first builds a subquery with the necessary condition and then deletes the rows from the subquery.

9. B. When two savepoints are created with the same name, Oracle overwrites the older savepoint; therefore, only the newer savepoint will be available. In the code segment, the DELETE and the first INSERT are not rolled back.

10. C. When updating more than one column in a single UPDATE statement, separate the columns by a comma; do not use the AND operator.

11. D. Option A updates the wrong table. Option B has the right syntax but will update all the rows in the EMPLOYEE table because there is no WHERE clause for the UPDATE statement. Because the WHERE clause is in the subquery, all the rows that do not belong to department 22 will be updated with a NULL. Options C and D are similar, except for the AND keyword instead of WHERE.

12. D. The first INSERT statement and the last INSERT statement will be saved in the database. The ROLLBACK TO A statement will undo the second and third inserts.

13. B. Option B will raise an exception because there are not enough column values for the implicit column list (all columns).

14. B. Because the location_id column is defined with a default value of 99, statement 1 will insert 99 for location_id. In statement 2, a NULL is explicitly inserted into the location_id column; Oracle will not replace the NULL with the default value defined.

15. B. The FIRST clause tells Oracle to execute only the first WHEN clause that evaluates to TRUE for each row. Because no rows have a channel_id of C, no rows would be inserted into the catalog_sales table; 24,000 rows have a channel_id of I, so control would pass to the second WHEN clause 24,000 times, and the internet_sales table would get 24,000 rows. Because the second WHEN clause evaluates to TRUE and the INSERT FIRST option is specified, these rows would not make it to the third WHEN clause and would not be inserted into the new_channel_sales table. Had the INSERT ALL option been used, these 24,000 rows would also be inserted into the new_channel_sales table; 12,000 rows have a channel_id of T, so control would pass all the way to the third WHEN clause for these rows, and 12,000 rows would be inserted into new_channel_sales.

16. C. The TRUNCATE statement is DDL and performs an implicit commit. After the TRUNCATE statement is performed on the employees table, there will be 124 rows in the emp table. The one row that is inserted will be removed when the ROLLBACK statement is executed.

17. D. You must have the SET keyword in an UPDATE statement. The BETWEEN operator and any other valid operators are allowed in the WHERE clause.

18. D. When DML operations are performed, Oracle automatically locks the rows. You can query (read) the rows, but no other DML operation is allowed on those rows. When you read the rows, Oracle constitutes a read-consistent view using the undo segments.

19. B. The keywords INSERT INTO are required in single-table INSERT statements but are not valid in multiple-table INSERT statements.

20. D. The final rollback (to point_d) will roll the changes back to just after setting the salary to $1,500.

Chapter 7: Creating Tables and Constraints

1. B. When you create a table using CTAS (CREATE TABLE AS SELECT), only the NOT NULL constraints are copied.

2. B. A VARCHAR2 datatype should always specify the maximum length of the column.

3. C. The correct statement is C. When you are adding only one column, the column definition doesn't need to be enclosed in parentheses.

4. B, D. Only three special characters ($, _, and #) are allowed in table names along with letters and numbers.

5. C. All identifiers (column names, table names, and so on) must begin with an alphabetic character. An identifier can contain alphabetic characters, numbers, and the special characters $, #, and _.

6. C. The USER_TABLES view provides information on the tables owned by the user who has logged on that session. DBA_TABLES will have all the tables in the database, and ALL_TABLES will have the tables owned by you as well as the tables to which you have access. USR_TABLES is not a valid dictionary view.

7. D. When a default value is specified in the new column added, the column values for the existing rows are not populated with the default value; only the dictionary is updated.

8. B. In date arithmetic, adding 1 is equivalent to adding 24 hours. To add 6 hours to a date value with time, add 0.25.

9. D. If you do not specify a length for a CHAR column, the default length of 1 is assumed.

10. A. You can use the DROP COLUMN clause with the ALTER TABLE statement to drop a column. There is no separate DROP COLUMN statement or a REMOVE clause in the ALTER TABLE statement. The SET UNUSED clause is used to mark the column as unused. This column can be dropped later using the DROP UNUSED COLUMNS clause.

11. C, D, E. All actions that do not modify the data in the table are permitted on a read-only table. The actions of creating/dropping a constraint, creating/dropping an index, and dropping a table are allowed. Even though truncating is a DDL action, it is not permitted because the data in the table is affected.

12. C, D. The ALTER TABLE statement is used to create and remove constraints. CREATE PRIMARY KEY and CREATE CONSTRAINT are invalid statements. A constraint is always added to an existing table using the ALTER TABLE statement.

13. B, C. Check constraints cannot reference the SYSDATE function or other tables.

14. A, D, G. You cannot add two DATE datatypes, but you can subtract to find the difference in days. Multiplication and division operators are permitted only on INTERVAL datatypes. When you are adding or subtracting INTERVAL datatypes, both INTERVAL datatypes should be of the same category.

15. B. DEFERRABLE specifies that the constraint can be deferred using the SET CONSTRAINTS command. INITIALLY IMMEDIATE specifies that the constraint's default behavior is to validate the constraint for each SQL statement executed.

16. C. The default precision is six digits. The precision can range from 0 to 9.

17. C. Only TIMESTAMP WITH TIME ZONE stores the time-zone information as a displacement from UTC. TIMESTAMP WITH LOCAL TIME ZONE adjusts the time to the database's time zone before storing it.

18. C. You can disable a constraint by specifying its constraint name. You may enable the constraint after the load and avoid the constraint checking while enabling use of the ALTER TABLE ORDERS MODIFY CONSTRAINT FK_ORDERS ENABLE NOVALIDATE; command.

19. C. RENAME can be used to rename objects owned by the user. ALTER TABLE should be used to rename tables owned by another user. To do so, you must have the ALTER privilege on the table or the ALTER ANY TABLE privilege.

20. A. The table will be created without error. A table cannot have more than one LONG column, but LONG and multiple LOB columns can exist together. If a LONG or LONG RAW column is defined, another LONG or LONG RAW column cannot be used.

Chapter 8: Introducing Oracle Database 12c Components and Architecture

1. **B, C.** Database buffer cache, shared pool, and log buffer are required; they are configured automatically in every instance. It is better to use Automatic Memory Management or Automatic Shared Memory Management, so that the DBA does not need to tune individual components.

2. **D.** The control file is the most key file in an Oracle database. Due to its importance, it is a good practice to have two more copies of the file. A database must have at least one control file to start the database.

3. **A.** An Oracle database allows you to manage all memory components dynamically, except the redo log buffer. Redo log buffer is set at instance startup and is not dynamically alterable without restarting the instance.

4. **C.** Control file, data file, and redo log files are part of the Oracle database. The Oracle instance constitutes the memory structures and background processes.

5. **C.** The log writer (LGWR) process writes the redo log buffer information to the online redo log files. A commit operation is completed only after the redo buffer is written to online redo log files.

6. **D.** When a user issues a commit, the LGWR process makes sure the redo log buffer is written to the online redo log files. Database writer takes no action against the commit event.

7. **A.** With Real Application Clusters, multiple instances (known as *nodes*) can mount one database. One instance can be associated with only one database.

8. **C.** The shared SQL area is stored in the library cache in a shared pool and is shared between users. If a query is executed again before it is aged out of the library cache, Oracle will use the parsed code and execution plan from the library cache. The database buffer cache has the data blocks cached. The dictionary cache caches data dictionary information. There is no SGA component called the parse cache.

9. **A, D.** SMON is responsible for performing instance recovery using the online redo log files and for coalescing contiguous free space in tablespaces. The PMON is responsible for session cleanup and for freeing up all resources after a user session is terminated.

10. B. A table or index has a segment. A segment consists of one or more extents. A segment can belong to only one tablespace, but it can span across multiple data files.

11. C, D. MMON (Manageability Monitor) captures the AWR database and performs ADDM analysis. MMNL (Manageability Monitor Lite) performs tasks related to active session-history sampling and metrics computation. The ARC*n* (Archiver) process is responsible for writing redo log copies to the archive log location. This process is enabled only when the database is running in ARCHIVELOG mode. MMAN (Memory Manager) is responsible for resizing the memory components when required. This process is active only when Automatic Memory operations are configured.

12. D. The large pool is configured so that RMAN does not use the shared pool; therefore, the shared pool is totally dedicated to application space.

13. D. PMON is responsible for cleaning up failed user processes. It reclaims all the resources held by the user and releases all locks on tables and rows held by the user. No other process is involved in the session cleanup.

14. D. The LRU mechanism ensures that each user's server process can find free space in the shared pool and database buffer cache whenever they need it, but it also keeps frequently used objects cached in those memory areas.

15. A. The instance consists of the SGA and all the Oracle background processes. The database is composed of the control files, data files, and redo logs.

16. B. Multiple operating-system blocks make up database blocks, contiguous chunks of which make up extents. A segment consists of one or more extents.

17. D. PMON is one of the critical processes of Oracle Database 12*c*, and terminating that process will crash the database. During instance startup, Oracle will require the redo log files with status CURRENT as well as ACTIVE in order to perform instance recovery.

18. B. During an incremental database checkpoint, the control file is updated with the checkpoint position; data files are not updated. Data file headers are updated with checkpoint information by the DBW*n* process when dirty buffers are written to the files. During threaded checkpoint or full database checkpoint, all file headers are updated. This happens during a normal shutdown as well as during online log switch.

19. A, E, C, F, G, B. Data blocks are always changed in the memory, and the change vectors are written to redo the log buffer. LGWR writes the redo log buffers to redo the log files on disk as soon as the commit occurs. This guarantees recoverability. During a checkpoint, data files are updated with the changed blocks by the DBW*n* process.

20. A. Redo log groups with status CURRENT and ACTIVE are required during instance crash recovery.

Chapter 9: Creating and Operating Oracle Database 12*c*

1. C. When using ALTER SYSTEM to change parameter values, the change is made to the server parameter file (spfile) too, because the default for the SCOPE clause is BOTH. Option D would have been correct, if the pfile were used to start up the database. When a database is created using DBCA, the parameter file created is always spfile.

2. B. DIAGNOSTIC_DEST is the initialization parameter that determines where the Automatic Diagnostic Repository home is located. The alert log file would be in the *<diagnostic_dest>*/diag/rdbms/*<dbname>*/*<instancename>*/alert directory. A text version of the alert log is in the *<diagnostic_dest>*/diag/rdbms/*<dbname>*/*<instancename>*/trace directory. But BACKGROUND_DUMP_DEST shows the full path of the trace directory location.

3. C. V$PARAMETER shows information about the parameters and their current values in the database. V$SPPARAMTER shows the information as read from the spfile.

4. D. When creating a new database or creating a control file, the database should be in the NOMOUNT state.

5. B. The alert log file in Oracle Database 12*c* is saved in the $ORACLE_BASE/diag/rdbms/*<dbname>*/*<instancename>*/trace directory. The XML version of the alert log file is in the $ORACLE_BASE/diag/rdbms/*<dbname>*/*<instancename>*/alert directory.

6. C. The Custom template lets you choose the database block size in the DBCA. If the template includes data files, the block size of the template cannot be changed. The pre-defined templates that come with data files have the block size at 8KB.

7. A. The Database Configuration Assistant lets you create databases, manage templates, add database options, and delete databases. Although you can change initialization parameters when you are defining a database, this is not one of the management options available.

8. B. The runInstaller executable performs a preinstall check of the operating system and hardware resources before starting the OUI graphical tool.

9. D. While the Unix system administrator is responsible for creating volume groups and mount points, the DBA generally decides where the Oracle binaries will be installed—the location derived from $ORACLE_BASE or designated by the $ORACLE_HOME environment variable.

10. C. When starting the instance, Oracle looks for `spfileOCA12C.ora` file. If it cannot find that file, it looks for `spfile.ora`. If that file is not found, Oracle looks for the `initOCA12C.ora` file.

11. A. The block size of the database cannot be changed after database creation. The database name can be changed after the control file is re-created with a new name, and the `CONTROL_FILES` parameter can be changed after the control files are copied to the new location.

12. D. The `catalog.sql` script creates the data dictionary views, dynamic performance views, and synonyms.

13. B. The text-alert log file has the name `alert_<instancename>.log`. For most non-RAC databases, the instance name and database name would be the same.

14. B, D. `STARTUP FORCE` will perform a `SHUTDOWN ABORT` and `STARTUP` of the database. `SHUTDOWN ABORT` will terminate all sessions and processes and will shut down the instance.

15. C. The recovery of a database occurs when the database moves from the `MOUNT` mode to the `OPEN` mode. All these options attempt to start up and open the database except for option C, which only puts the database in `NOMOUNT` mode.

16. A. When you perform a `SHUTDOWN ABORT`, Oracle never performs a clean shutdown. All other types of shutdowns are considered clean shutdowns because Oracle will not have to perform a recovery on a subsequent database startup.

17. B. The `STARTUP RESTRICT` choice opens the database and allows only users with `RESTRICTED` database access to connect and use it.

18. C. An spfile is another term for a server-side binary file that Oracle reads when a database startup is performed. This binary file contains all the nondefault initialization parameters used at startup.

19. D. The Oracle alert log contains a chronological history of administrative events and actions and certain types of database errors that occur within the database. Adding a column to a user table is not an administrative action and is not recorded in the alert log. Adding a column will be written to alert log if the parameter `enable_ddl_logging` is set to TRUE; the default is FALSE.

20. B, C. A database cannot be started or stopped using OEM Database Express. The Database Control repository is not created when the `CREATE DATABASE` statement is executed. DBCA creates the Database Control repository and configures Database Control for you.

Chapter 10: Understanding Storage and Space Management

1. C. Bigfile tablespaces can have only a single data file. The traditional or smallfile tablespace can have many data files (the limit is OS-dependent, mostly 1022).

2. D. Segment space management refers to free-space management, with automatic segment space management using bitmaps instead of FREELISTS, PCTFREE, and PCTUSED.

3. B. Redo information is not stored in a segment; it is stored in the redo logs. Undo segments are stored in the undo tablespace; temporary segments are in the temporary tablespace; and permanent segments go into all the other tablespaces.

4. C. An extent is composed of two or more data blocks; a segment is composed of one or more extents; and a data file houses all these.

5. D, E. When a tablespace is read-only, DML operations and operations that affect data in the table are not allowed. TRUNCATE is not allowed, but the DROP operation is allowed. You can also rename the table using the RENAME statement or the ALTER TABLE statement.

6. C, A. To make a tablespace read-only, all the data files belonging to the tablespace must be online and available. So bring the tablespace online, and then make it read-only.

7. A, B. You can add more space to a tablespace either by adding a data file or by increasing the size of an existing data file. Option A does not have a filename specified; it uses the OMF feature to generate the filename.

8. B. DB_CACHE_SIZE doesn't need to be set for the standard block size because Automatic Memory Management is used. If you set DB_CACHE_SIZE, its value will be used as the minimum. DB_16K_CACHE_SIZE should be set for the nonstandard block size. You must not set the DB_8K_CACHE_SIZE parameter because the standard block size is 8KB.

9. C. Locally managed temporary tablespaces are created using the CREATE TEMPORARY TABLESPACE command. The data files (temporary files) belonging to these tablespaces are in the DBA_TEMP_FILES view. The EXTENT_MANAGEMENT column of the DBA_TABLESPACES view shows the type of tablespace. The data files belonging to locally managed permanent tablespaces and dictionary-managed (permanent and temporary) tablespaces can be queried from DBA_DATA_FILES. Locally managed temporary tablespaces reduce contention on the data dictionary tables.

10. D. The INCLUDING CONTENTS clause is used to drop a tablespace that is not empty. Oracle does not remove the data files that belong to the tablespace if the files are not Oracle-managed; you need to do it manually using an OS command. Oracle

updates only the control file. To remove the files, you can include the INCLUDING CONTENTS AND DATAFILES clause.

11. A. You can use the ALTER TABLESPACE command to rename a file that belongs to the tablespace, but all other file-management operations are done through the ALTER DATABASE command. To enable autoextension, use ALTER DATABASE DATAFILE *<FILENAME>* AUTOEXTEND ON NEXT *<INTEGER>* MAXSIZE *<INTEGER>*.

12. C. The data files belonging to the SYSTEM tablespace can be renamed when the database is in the MOUNT state by using the ALTER DATABASE RENAME FILE statement.

13. B, C. OEM Database Express does not have an option to adjust the server-managed alerts in Database 12*c* Release 1. OEM Cloud Control and DBMS_SERVER_ALERT.SET_THRESHOLD can be used to set the threshold for tablespaces.

14. A, B, C. ALTER TABLE … SPLIT PARTITION involves creating extents; therefore, it is resumable. However, ALTER TABLE … SHRINK SPACE does not create any new extents and is not resumable. The SELECT statement is resumable, because it could create sort extents. INSERT INTO … SELECT is resumable, as is any INSERT statement. CREATE TABLESPACE is not resumable, because it does not create any extents when a tablespace is created.

15. B, C. There is no out-of-the-box mechanism to notify a suspended resumable session. When a session is suspended, information is written to the alert log, an AFTER SUSPEND trigger is fired, and a resumable session suspended alert is issued.

16. D. ALTER TABLE … MOVE and ALTER TABLE … REBUILD are not online operations and will require an exclusive lock on the object. Segment shrink is accomplished using the SHRINK SPACE clause of ALTER TABLE and ALTER INDEX. A shrink operation does not invalidate dependent objects.

17. C. The COMPRESS option by itself enables basic compression, and it compresses only direct-load operations. NOCOMPRESS disables compression. COMPRESS for ONLINE DML is an invalid syntax.

18. A. An extent consists of one or more contiguous Oracle blocks. Option B is true if you extend the answer a little bit, that an Oracle block is a multiple of OS blocks. A segment consists of one or more extents, not the other way. An extent is not always allocated when a table is created; an extent is allocated when the first row is inserted into the table.

19. B. The tablespace *X* is created without any error and the syntax is correct. The tablespace created will have the default characteristics. It will use an Oracle Managed File of 100M, autoextensible up to 32GB. It will also have LOGGING, NOCOMPRESS, ONLINE, PERMANENT, EXTENT MANAGEMENT LOCAL AUTOALLOCATE, and SEGMENT SPACE MANAGEMENT AUTO properties.

20. C. Segment ID is not part of ROWID. ROWID includes the data object number, relative file number where the block is stored, the block number in the file, and the row number.

Chapter 11: Managing Data Concurrency and Undo

1. C. By ending the transaction, a commit makes pending DML changes permanent. A rollback also ends the transaction. When a checkpoint occurs, DBWR flushes dirty buffers to disk, which is independent of transaction boundaries.

2. D. When you use SET TRANSACTION READ ONLY, no data changes can be made in the transaction. You can make DDL changes though. A DDL statement does an implicit COMMIT and ends the transaction. ALTER USER is a DDL statement.

3. A. Guaranteed undo retention can be set at the tablespace level by using the RETENTION GUARANTEE clause with either the CREATE TABLESPACE or ALTER TABLESPACE command. Only undo tablespaces can have this attribute.

4. C. SHARE ROW EXCLUSIVE mode permits concurrent queries but prohibits updates to the locked table. SHARE mode is required to create an index on the table. ROW SHARE is the least restrictive mode of the table lock and allows updates on the table. ROW EXCLUSIVE locks the modified rows, but allows updates to the table for nonlocked rows. SHARE lock held by a transaction allows other transactions to query the rows, but updates are allowed when a single transaction holds the share table lock.

5. A. If an undo tablespace is not explicitly created in the CREATE DATABASE command, Oracle automatically creates one with the name SYS_UNDOTBS.

6. B, C. Locks are resolved at the user level by either committing or rolling back the transaction holding the lock. Also, the DBA can kill the session holding the lock as a last resort.

7. D. At 10:01, session 1 waits for session 2. At 10:05, a deadlock will occur; Oracle detects the deadlock and cancels one of the statements.

8. A, D. If a transaction fills up an undo segment, either a new extent is allocated for the undo segment or other extents in the segment are reused if the undo data in those extents is no longer needed by other transactions using the same undo segment. Transactions cannot cross segment boundaries in an undo tablespace, and they cannot move to another segment.

9. B. Regardless of the type of lock requested, NOWAIT is required if you want the command with the lock request to terminate immediately if a lock is already held on the table.

10. B. Undo information is required for instance recovery but only to roll back uncommitted transactions after the online redo logs roll forward. The redo is used for roll forward, and undo is used to roll back uncommitted transactions.

11. C. Undo segments are always owned by SYS.

12. D. The Undo Advisor uses the desired time period for undo data retention and analyzes the impact of the desired undo retention setting.

13. D. In Oracle, locks never block readers. Option A would be true, if it did not include the word *queries* in it. Only DML statements wait when the table is locked in exclusive mode. SELECT…FOR UPDATE locks only the rows returned by the SELECT clause; it does not lock the table. The DDL_LOCK_TIMEOUT parameter is used to specify the number of seconds to wait when DDL statements on locked objects are executed. The LOCK TABLE statement can include the WAIT clause to specify the number of seconds to wait to acquire the lock.

14. D. Because Sara did not perform the commit until 10:18, the changes she made are not visible to John. So the queries he ran at 10:14 and 10:16 have the same result. The query at 10:16 will read the undo segment to produce a consistent query result. The query run at 10:20 will have salary 100 for employee 206.

15. D. With the undo technology, Oracle is able to have readers access consistent data, irrespective of underlying data modified during or before the start of the query.

16. B. Global temporary tables are created in temporary tablespaces, and writing to temporary tablespace does not generate redo. Keep in mind that even this operation generates undo, and hence you can argue that redo is generated. In Oracle Database 12*c*, TEMP_UNDO_ENABLED can be set to TRUE to have the undo segments also created in the temporary tablespace; therefore, no redo is involved.

17. D. Option C is completely wrong and is unrelated to the Snapshot Too Old error. All other options are viable based on the situation, but increasing the tablespace size is the best. Once the tablespace is increased and its size is fixed, Oracle will keep the undo until it needs to expire for other transactions. Undo retention is applicable when the undo tablespace is not a fixed size (autoextensible). Sometimes running the query again is a solution, especially if you find out that the underlying table used by Maria was updated and committed during the query execution, causing the undo blocks to expire because the database was really busy with many transactions.

18. A, B. Multiple active transactions can write concurrently to the same undo segment or to different segments. Multiple active transactions can write simultaneously to the same current extent or to different current extents in the same segment. Within an undo extent, a data block contains data for only one transaction.

19. B. A DDL statement performs an implicit commit before the statement and ends the transaction. After the DDL, it does an implicit commit again; therefore, DDL can never roll back. UPDATE is DML and does not perform a commit. ALTER SESSION is a session-control statement, and ALTER SYSTEM is a system-control statement. Neither of them perform an implicit commit.

20. D. Oracle automatically acquires the minimum required lock appropriate for the DML operation. Developers need not and should not lock the rows. They should let Oracle manage the locks. When a row in the table is locked, it is locked in exclusive mode, and the table is locked in shared mode where other updates on the table on different rows are possible. When two sessions update the row at the same time, one will succeed and the other will wait until the first one commits or rolls back.

Chapter 12: Understanding Oracle Network Architecture

1. A. The listener is the process that manages incoming connection requests. The listener .ora file is used to configure the listener and must be configured to start a nondefault listener. The sqlnet.ora file is an optional client- and server-side file. The tnsnames.ora file is used for doing local naming resolution. There is no such file as lsnrctl.ora. You do not need the listener.ora file to start a default listener on port 1521.

2. B. Because the default listener name is LISTENER, simply enter **lsnrctl start**. The name LISTENER is assumed to be the listener to start in this case.

3. C. When services are dynamically registered with the listener, their information is not present in the listener.ora file.

4. D. Connection Manager is a middleware solution that provides for the multiplexing of connections, cross-protocol connectivity, and network access control. All the answers describe Connection Manager.

5. B. Host naming is typically used in small installations that have few Oracle databases. This is an attractive option when you want to minimize client-side configuration. TCP/IP is a requirement when you use host naming.

6. A, C. Even if DRCP is enabled in the database, the client or application connection must always request a pooled connection using SERVER=POOLED in connect syntax. To use Easy Connect and DRCP, the syntax is host:port/service_name:POOLED.

7. B, C. Supplying a net service name that is not contained in the tnsnames.ora file can cause this error. Problems with the tnsnames.ora file can cause this error, too. Listener problems will not cause this error.

8. D. The HOST portion specifies the name of the server to contact. CONNECT_DATA specifies the database service to connect to. The PORT portion specifies the location where the listener is listening on the HOST. Option C, SERVICE_NAME, is the name of the actual database service.

9. A, D. The correct syntax to use with the Oracle Easy Connect method when you are connecting to a non-URL location is `connect username/password@host:port/ service_name`. If the service name and the host are identical, you do not have to include the service name. If the port is any port other than the default port of 1521, it must be specified. Because you want to connect to a nondefault port where the database name and the hostname are the same, the best answer is A, but D is also correct.

10. B. Shared Server is a scalability option of Oracle. It provides a way to increase the number of supported user processes while reducing the overall memory usage. This configuration is well suited to high-volume, small-transaction-oriented systems with many users connected. Because users share processes, the number of overall idle processes is also reduced. It is not well suited for large data-retrieval-type applications such as decision support.

11. D. Users can still request dedicated connections in a Shared Server configuration. Bequeathed and dedicated connections are one and the same. The database cannot be stopped or started by the DBA when connected over a Shared Server connection.

12. A. A user must explicitly request a dedicated connection when a server is configured in Shared Server mode. Otherwise, the user gets a Shared Server connection. The correct parameter is `(SERVER=DEDICATED)`.

13. C. The Shared Server configuration parameters exist in the `init.ora` or the `SPFILE` file on the Oracle Server machine.

14. C. Once a dispatcher receives a request from the user process, it places the request on the request queue. Remember that in a Shared Server environment, a request can be handled by a shared server process. This is made possible by placing the request and user information in the SGA.

15. D. A small PGA is maintained even though most of the user-specific information is moved to the SGA (specifically called the UGA in the shared pool or the large pool). The only information left in the reduced PGA is stack space.

16. C. Request queues reside in the SGA, and there is one request queue per instance. This is where shared server processes pick up requests that are made by users. Dispatchers have their own response queues, but they *share* a single request queue.

17. C. The LREG process notifies the listener after a client connection is established. This is so that the listener can keep track of the number of connections being serviced by each dispatcher. In versions prior to Oracle Database 12c, the functions of LREG were performed by PMON.

18. B. Dedicated server uses session memory from PGA. A pooled server connection is similar to dedicated server once connected; therefore, the memory is coming from PGA as well. For a shared server, the server process is shared; therefore, the request and response information must be kept in the SGA.

19. B. Database links facilitate communication between databases. Using a database link access syntax (@dblink_name), data from a remote database is available locally.

20. B. Private database links are created under the user who executes the CREATE DATABASE LINK statement. You cannot create a database link under another schema. A link by the name SCOTT.SALES_LINK.BJS.COM is created under schema MIKE. You can use the Easy Connect syntax or the Oracle Net connect syntax, or you can resolve the alias name by using tnsnames.ora in the USING clause. During database link creation, a connection is not made to the target database to validate the connection or credentials.

Chapter 13: Implementing Security and Auditing

1. A, B. Authentication by the operating system is called external authentication, and the Oracle account name must match the operating-system account name prefixed with the OS_AUTHENT_PREFIX string. When a user is created with the OS_AUTHENT_PREFIX string, the password provided in option A is ignored, and the user is created as externally authenticated.

2. C. The AUDIT_TRAIL parameter with the value DB,EXTENDED enables you to capture SQL statements and bind variables in auditing. OS,EXTENDED is not a valid value for AUDIT_TRAIL.

3. A. Altering a table in another user's schema requires either the object privilege ALTER on that object or the system privilege ALTER ANY TABLE. Option A has the correct syntax for granting the object privilege on ALTER gl.accounts to user desmond. The alter table privilege in option C is invalid. CREATE TABLE implicitly gives the privilege to alter a table. One would need the ALTER ANY TABLE privilege to alter another user's table.

4. D. Conferring the ability to further grant the privilege requires the keywords WITH ADMIN OPTION for system or role privileges or the keywords WITH GRANT OPTION for object privileges. Only option D has both the correct syntax and the correct keywords. Option B would be correct if WITH GRANT OPTION were used. Option C would be correct if WITH ADMIN OPTION were used. Option A is not syntactically correct.

5. B. JOHN will be able to log in to the database using SQL*Plus, and Oracle will prompt for new password when John logs in the first time. Because John's default tablespace is INDEX01, the tables and indexes created will be on the INDEX01 tablespace if the TABLESPACE clause is omitted. Although INDEX01 is the default tablespace, to create objects on INDEX01 or any other tablespace, a specific space quota needs to be defined, or the user should have the UNLIMITED TABLESPACE system privilege.

6. A. When object privileges are granted through an intermediary, they are implicitly dropped when the intermediary is dropped. `CASCADE REVOKE` and `NOCASCADE REVOKE` are not part of the `GRANT` statement syntax.

7. B. When system privileges are granted through an intermediary, they are not affected when the intermediary is dropped. `CASCADE REVOKE` and `NOCASCADE REVOKE` are not part of the `GRANT` statement syntax.

8. D. The `CREATE ANY JOB` and `CREATE ANY PROCEDURE` system privileges allow the grantee to create and run programs with the privileges of another user. The `ALTER USER` privilege allows the grantee to change a user's password, connect as that user, and then change the password back. These are all powerful system privileges and should be restricted to as few administrative users as practical.

9. D. The `SET ROLE` statement enables or disables roles in the current session.

10. B. To enable a password-protected role, you need to either execute a `SET ROLE` statement specifying the password or alter the user to make the role a default role. Default roles do not require a `SET ROLE` statement or a password to become enabled.

11. A. By default, user accounts have no quota in any tablespace. Before a user can create a table or an index, you need to either give the user a quota in one or more specific tablespaces or grant the `UNLIMITED TABLESPACE` system privilege to give an unlimited quota (including autoextends) in all tablespaces.

12. C. Profiles limit the amount of idle time, CPU time, logical reads, or other resource-oriented session limits. Option C uses the correct syntax to limit idle time for a session to 30 minutes.

13. B. Although option D could also work, it involves storing the passwords in a table in the database, which could be a security concern. It also takes a lot more effort to configure and maintain. The better technique is to use the standard database profile features `PASSWORD_REUSE_TIME` and `PASSWORD_REUSE_MAX`. Setting one of these profile parameters to `UNLIMITED` and the other to a specific value prevents passwords from being reused. If both of these profile parameters are set to `UNLIMITED`, these parameters are essentially disabled. There is no initialization parameter called `NO_PASSWORD_REUSE`.

14. B. Because `HR_QUERY` has the `SELECT ANY TABLE` privilege, no other privilege is required to query user tables in the database. To avoid the error, `HR_QUERY` must be defined as a default role for John, or John should use the `SET ROLE` statement. A password is not needed for `SET ROLE` because the role is not password protected.

15. C. In Oracle Database 12*c*, user passwords are case sensitive. The username is not case sensitive if you did not enclose it in double quotes.

16. A. You limit the number of failed logon attempts with a profile.

17. C. When a space quota is exceeded or a quota is removed from a user on a tablespace, the tables remain in the tablespace, but no new extents can be allocated. New rows can be inserted into the table as long as the table does not require Oracle to allocate a new extent in the table.

18. B. Fine-grained auditing is managed using the DBMS_FGA package. The AUDIT and NOAUDIT statements are used to manage statement, privilege, and object auditing. The GRANT and REVOKE statements are used to manage system, object, and role privileges. FGA compliments Unified Auditing by enabling audit conditions to be associated with specific columns.

19. C. The AUDIT_ADMIN role is required to manage Unified Auditing in Oracle Database 12c. This role is granted to SYS and SYSTEM. An audit policy can be created using the AUDIT ANY privilege, but not other administrative actions. DBA and SYSDBA roles are not required, though those privileges work.

20. B. Audit records are written to a read-only table owned by AUDSYS user. The view UNIFIED_AUDIT_TRAIL shows the audit trail records.

Chapter 14: Maintaining the Database and Managing Performance

1. B. The MMON process gathers statistics from the SGA and stores them in the AWR. The ADDM process then uses these statistics to compare the current state of the database with baseline and historical performance metrics before summarizing the results on the EM Cloud Control screens.

2. D. Setting STATISTICS_LEVEL = BASIC disables the collection and analysis of AWR statistics. TYPICAL is the default setting, and ALL gathers information for the execution plan and operating-system timing. OFF is not a valid value for this parameter.

3. B. Automatic Memory Management is enabled by setting a nonzero value for the MEMORY_TARGET parameter. The default value for this parameter is zero. SGA_TARGET enables the ASSM (Automatic Shared Memory Management) feature. AMM_TARGET and AUTOMATIC_MEMORY are invalid parameters.

4. B, C. When the WORKAREA_SIZE_POLICY is set to AUTO, work areas used by memory-intensive operations are sized automatically, based on the PGA memory used by the system, and the target PGA memory set in PGA_AGGREGATE_TARGET. When WORKAREA_SIZE_POLICY is set to MANUAL, the *_AREA_SIZE parameters need to be configured manually.

5. C. You can use the SQL Tuning Advisor to determine if there is a better optimizer plan and use SQL Access Advisor to determine if creating an index or materialized view would improve performance. These tools together can be used to determine whether I/O can be minimized and overall DB Time reduced to the targeted SQL statement.

6. C. The log buffer cannot be dynamically resized once the instance is started. There is rarely a need to dynamically adjust the redo log buffer. All other components in the SGA can be dynamically modified.

7. B. The DBMS_STATS.SET_TABLE_PREFS procedure is used to set the PUBLISH preference to FALSE. To be able to use the pending statistics, the OPTIMIZER_USE_PENDING_STATISTICS parameter must be set to TRUE in the session.

8. D. DBA_ADVISOR_RATIONALE provides the rationale for each ADDM recommendation. The ADDM findings are stored in DBA_ADVISOR_FINDINGS. The objects related to the findings are shown in DBA_ADVISOR_OBJECTS. The actual ADDM recommendations are found in DBA_ADVISOR_RECOMMENDATIONS.

9. C. The Memory Advisor can help determine whether or not the overall size of the SGA is appropriate and whether or not memory is properly allocated to the SGA components.

10. B. Setting STATISTICS_LEVEL to BASIC disables Automatic Memory and Shared Memory Management as well as the memory advisors. CONTROL_MANAGEMENT_PACK_ACCESS specifies which of the Server Manageability Packs is active in the Enterprise Edition of Oracle Database 12c. MEMORY_TARGET enables Automatic Memory Management, but it does not disable Shared Memory Management or the memory advisors.

11. B. SGA_MAX_SIZE is not modifiable regardless of whether Automatic Memory Management is used or not. When either MEMORY_TARGET or MEMORY_MAX_TARGET is specified, the default value of SGA_MAX_SIZE is set to the larger of the two parameters and is not ignored. When SGA_TARGET is specified and SGA_MAX_SIZE is not specified, SGA_MAX_SIZE gets the value of SGA_TARGET.

12. C. You can specify both warning and critical thresholds for monitoring the available free space in a tablespace. In this situation, the warning threshold is generally a lower number than the critical threshold.

13. B. Because many transactional systems run batch processing during off-hours, having a relevant baseline for each type of usage pattern yields better results in terms of alerts and ADDM recommendations.

14. A, C. Whenever an AWR snapshot is taken, either automatically or manually, the ADDM is run. The MMNL process is responsible for ASH and not AWR. The MMON process is responsible for AWR. AutoTask manages only three components: optimizer statistics, Segment Advisor, and SQL tuning.

15. B. MEMORY_TARGET represents the total size allocated for SGA and PGA components. The maximum that can be allocated for these structures is determined by the MEMORY_MAX_TARGET parameter. You still can set the SGA_TARGET and PGA_AGGREGATE_TARGET parameters; Oracle will use these as the minimums.

16. C. Throughput is an important performance metric because it is an overall measure of performance that can be compared against similar measures taken before and after tuning changes are implemented.

17. D. An alert log is written to a subdirectory under DIAGNOSTIC_DEST. The location specified by DIAGNOSTIC_DEST is known as ADR Base. The *ADR_Base/rdbms/database/instance* directory is known as *ADR Home* for the instance. The Text alert log is written to *trace* directory under *ADR Home* and is named *alert_SID.log*. The XML alert log is written to *alert* directory under *ADR Home* and is named *log.xml*. _DUMP_DEST directories are ignored if they are set. If they are not explicitly set, they show the directory where trace files are written.

18. A. By default, database statistics are retained in the AWR for eight days. You can change the default duration using the EM Database Control Automatic Workload Repository link on the Performance tab or using the DBMS_WORKLOAD_REPOSITORY PL/SQL package.

19. B. The Performance tab of EM Database Control provides a quick overview of how the host system, user sessions, and throughput are impacted by the system slowdown. You can also drill down into any of these three areas to take a look at details about this slowdown.

20. A. Running the SQL Tuning Advisor provides the most information about how the performance of this SQL statement might be improved. The SQL Access Advisor is run only after the output from the SQL Tuning Advisor indicates that it will be useful. EM Database Control does not store detailed information about I/O activity in its alerts nor in the alert log.

Chapter 15: Using Backup and Recovery

1. A. Losing an entire redo log-file group can result in losing committed transactions that may not yet have been written to the database files. Losing all members of a redo log-file group except for one does not affect database operation and does not result in data loss. A message is placed in the alert log file. The failure of LGWR causes an instance failure, but you do not lose any committed transaction data. When an ARC*n* process fails or is manually terminated, Oracle spawns another one.

2. C. In ARCHIVELOG mode, recovering the database is possible up to the last COMMIT statement; in other words, no committed transactions are lost in ARCHIVELOG mode.

3. A. Image copies are duplicate data and log files in OS format. Backup sets are binary compressed files in Oracle proprietary format. In addition to storing multiple data files in a single output file, backup sets do not contain unused blocks.

4. B. Although it is recommended that you multiplex your online redo log files, it is not required to enable ARCHIVELOG mode of the database.

5. D. During an online backup, even if all data files are backed up at the same time, they are rarely, if ever, in sync with the control file.

6. A. The trace backup is created in a subdirectory under the location specified by the DIAGNOSTIC_DEST parameter—$DIAGNOSTIC_DEST/diag/<dbname>/<instancename>/ trace directory.

7. A. The instance name is not in the control file. The control file has information about the physical database structure.

8. B. When adding log-file members, specify the group number or specify all the existing group members.

9. A. To put the database into ARCHIVELOG mode, the database must be in the MOUNT state; the control files and all data files that are not offline must be available to change the database to ARCHIVELOG mode.

10. B, C, D. The substitution variable %d, which represents the database ID, is required only if multiple databases share the same archive log destination.

11. C. The parameter FAST_START_MTTR_TARGET specifies the desired time, in seconds, to recover a single instance from a crash or instance failure. The parameters LOG_CHECKPOINT_TIMEOUT and FAST_START_IO_TARGET can still be used in Oracle 12*c* but should be used only together with an advanced-tuning scenario or for compatibility with older versions of Oracle. MTTR_TARGET_ADVICE and FAST_START_TARGET_MTTR are not valid initialization parameters.

12. B. The instance must be shut down, if it is not already down, to repair or replace the missing or damaged control file.

13. B, C. Media failure, physical corruption, logical corruption, and missing data files all can be identified by the Data Recovery Advisor, which also provides recommendations for repair.

14. B, E. If a tablespace is taken offline because a data file is missing, the instance can still be started as long as the missing data file does not belong to the SYSTEM or UNDO tablespace.

15. A. If a network card fails, the failure type is network; the actual media containing the database files are not affected.

16. B. The Data Recovery Advisor in Oracle Database 12*c* Release 1 does not support RAC databases. It is integrated with EM Cloud Control and with RMAN. CHANGE FAILURE and other commands can be executed using RMAN. The ADVISE FAILURE command must be run before you can perform REPAIR FAILURE.

17. B. Instance recovery, also known as crash recovery, occurs when the DBA attempts to open the database but the files were not synchronized to the same SCN when the database was shut down. Once the DBA issues the STARTUP command, Oracle uses information in the redo log files to restore the data files (including the undo tablespace's data files) to the state before the instance failure. Oracle then uses undo data in the undo tablespace after the database has been opened and made available to users to roll back uncommitted transactions.

18. D. The MTTR Advisor can tell the DBA the most effective value for the FAST_START_MTTR_TARGET parameter. This parameter specifies the maximum time required in seconds to perform instance recovery.

19. B. The loss of one or more of a tablespace's data files does not prevent other users from doing their work in other tablespaces. Recovering the affected data files can continue while the database is still online and available.

20. D. All copies of the control files, as defined in the spfile or the init.ora file, must be identical and available. If one of the redo log-file groups is missing a member, a warning is recorded in the alert log, but instance startup still proceeds. If the instance was previously shut down with SHUTDOWN ABORT, instance recovery automatically occurs during startup. Only an spfile or an init.ora file is needed to enter the NOMOUNT state, not both. If a tablespace is offline, the status of its data files is not checked until an attempt is made to bring it online; therefore, it will not prevent instance startup.

Chapter 16: Controlling Resources and Jobs

1. A. The Resource Manager in Oracle can only divide up CPU usage as a way of spreading out resource power between different requirements.

2. E. All of the options are true, and the Resource Manager can do much more than this.

3. B. A is true, but unless some needs have higher priorities than others, there might be ill effects. Both C and D are correct, but they have far less impact overall than controlling and allocating the CPU cycles to the various tasks in a database.

4. B, D. With respect to A, aborting a session has nothing to do with archive logs and archive log space exhaustion. For C, transactions cannot be controlled but sessions

can. So a session can be aborted, but it can also have its allocation of CPU curtailed to reduce overhead by moving the session to a consumer group with less CPU cycles.

5. C. Resources are allocated to plan directives, which are assigned to plans and subplans, and grouped with consumers of those plan directives into resource consumer groups.

6. A, D. The packages are called `DBMS_RESOURCE_MANAGER` and `DBMS_RESOURCE_MANAGER_PRIVS`.

7. A, B. Plans and subplans contain the details of how resources are allocated. Consumer groups simply group together the consumers that will consume the details of the plans.

8. E. E is correct because the total must add up to 100 percent, where the consumer group can have a maximum of 10 percent.

9. D. All three of these settings are useful for controlling parallel processing. The degree of parallelism can be used to execute queries and some DML statements much faster. When a parallel process is started, it starts up multiple parallel servers to handle the separate parallel executed threads. Parallel queue timeouts force parallel processes to abort a little sooner. All of these settings will help to prevent overzealous parallel processing from becoming out of control parallel processing, which can swamp and drastically slow database performance.

10. D. Eight hierarchical layers of CPU utilization can be set for a multiple level hierarchy of plans, subplans, and consumer groups.

11. B. `JOB_QUEUE_PROCESSES` determines the number of slave processes available for the scheduled jobs to run. `DBMS_JOB` and Oracle Scheduler share the same job coordinator and job slaves. The default value for this parameter is 1,000. Setting `JOB_QUEUE_PROCESS` to 0 will disable Oracle Scheduler and `DBMS_JOB`.

12. D. The `GRANT_SYSTEM_PRIVILEGE` privilege is a privilege granted by the `DBMS_RESOURCE_MANAGER_PRIVS` procedure.

13. D, E. Options A, B, and C do not exist.

14. C. A and B are not resource management, and D is incorrect.

15. D. The `CREATE_SIMPLE_PLAN` allows a single CPU percentage allocation to be set for each of eight consumer groups, and it only creates a single plan at once.

16. D. D is the most complete and, therefore, the best answer.

17. B. The `DBA_SCHEDULER_JOBS.STATE` column will be set to `DISABLED`.

18. D. A `COMPLETE` job will not run again. B and C are nonsense. A job that will run again will be repeatable at a scheduled interval and will, therefore, be rescheduled to run again. `SCHEDULED` means it will run again.

19. A. A job can be executed once using the CREATE_JOB procedure. To execute a job more than once, a schedule has to be created using the CREATE_SCHEDULE procedure to configure the repetition.

20. A. The scheduler metadata views are named DBA%SCHED%. Option C is partially correct as the query will show the metadata views related to the scheduled jobs only.

Chapter 17: Upgrading to Oracle Database 12*c*

1. B. Oracle Database 12*c* gives the option to do a direct upgrade for all versions mentioned in option B, and not all versions as specified in option A. Option C is not correct because you cannot downgrade to any version of Oracle 11g. The lowest version you can downgrade to is 11.1.0.7 if you upgrade an 11g R1 or 10g R2 database. For 11.2 databases, you can downgrade to the version from which you upgraded. Although a 10.2.0.5 database cannot be downgraded back to 10.2.0.5, it can be downgraded to 11.1.0.7, which might not be useful for your business.

2. B. The terminal release of Oracle 10g R2 is 10.2.0.5. Oracle Database 12*c* supports a direct upgrade from the versions 10.2.0.5, 11.1.0.7, 11.2.0.2, and higher.

3. C, D. DBUA has an option to back up the database prior to the upgrade. It's up to you to back up the database after the upgrade is completed. There is no option to disable archiving during the upgrade. In fact, Oracle encourages you to run the database in ARCHIVELOG mode with flashback on, and DBUA can create a guaranteed restore point as a backup method during the upgrade.

4. B. The first step is to run the Pre-Upgrade Information utility preupgrd.sql. When you are ready to upgrade, start the database using STARTUP UPGRADE. The catctl.pl script performs the database upgrade and shuts down the database. Then start up the database and perform utlu121s.sql.

5. B, D. The Pre-Upgrade Information utility does not make any changes to the database. The utility creates a fix-up script that can be used to make trivial changes to the database. Not all issues can be fixed by the fix-up script; therefore, option A is not correct. The tool is comprised of preupgrd.sql and utluppkg.sql scripts, so you need to copy both scripts.

6. A, D. STARTUP UPGRADE is the only way you can bring up an instance prior to upgrading the database. You still need to upgrade the database using the upgrade scripts after starting up the database. This is not just for documentation; it differs from STARTUP NORMAL.

7. B. DBUA performs a restore from the backup it created prior to the upgrade; it restores the database files and configuration files from the backup location. For this, you should choose the Use RMAN backup option or the Use Flashback and Guaranteed Restore Point option in the Recovery Options screen (Figure 17.9).

8. E. Oracle Database 12*c* has a very simplified upgrade process that determines all the components of the database to be upgraded and automatically upgrades them. Oracle uses DBMS_REGISTRY to identify the components to be upgraded.

9. C. DBMS_REGISTRY is used by Oracle to keep the status of components loaded to the database. You can query DBA_REGISTRY to see all the components and their status. It also provides the schema owner of the component and the script to run if a component is invalid.

10. A. The minimum COMPATIBLE value for Oracle Database 12*c* is 11.0.0. Because the value is not set in the parameter file, the default value for the version of the database is 11.1.0. If you keep the parameter the same version as the upgraded database, you will have the opportunity to downgrade the database if something goes wrong after the upgrade; therefore, the best option is to keep the value at 11.1.0.7 during the upgrade. Option C and D are valid values, but you would lose the downgrade opportunity. The default value of the parameter is 12.0.0 if you do not specify the parameter explicitly.

11. C. The Data Pump Export/Import method copies data from the source database to an already-created Oracle Database 12*c* database. As the tables and indexes are newly created and data rows are inserted, there will be no fragmentation of space in the new database. The Transport Database option is available for databases 11.2.0.3 or higher, but it does not defragment tables.

12. B. The database must be running from the original Oracle database home. The Pre-Upgrade Information tool does not make any changes to the database or impact the application using the database. The Pre-Upgrade Information scripts (preupgrd.sql and utluppkg.sql) may be copied to another directory, and you can run preupgrd.sql to invoke the tool.

13. A. If $ORACLE_BASE is defined, the generated scripts and log files are saved in the $ORACLE_BASE/cfgtoollogs/db_unique_name/preupgrade directory. If $ORACLE_BASE is not defined, then the generated scripts and log files are created in $ORACLE_HOME/cfgtoollogs/db_unique_name/preupgrade.

14. C. DBUA can migrate, copy, and configure the listener in the new 12*c* Oracle home, depending on the choices you make in the Network Configuration screen of DBUA (Figure 17.8). It will also register the database with the listener by setting the LOCAL_LISTENER parameter.

15. D. DBUA takes care of most of the tasks for DBA during the upgrade, including running the Pre-Upgrade Information tool, performing the upgrade, configuring the network, performing a backup of the database before upgrade, recompiling invalids, adding the database to oratab, etc. It also provides a detailed upgrade progress report with the product component being upgraded and the upgrade phase. If DBUA identifies that there is a space deficiency in the tablespaces or in the fast recovery area, you must fix it manually outside DBUA.

16. B. The Full Transportable Export/Import option is available for database versions at or higher than 11.2.0.3.

17. D. Although the utlu121i.sql script is available in the $ORACLE_HOME/rdbms/admin directory, it does nothing. The Pre-Upgrade Information tool in Oracle Database 12*c* is invoked by running preupgrd.sql, which calls the utluppkg.sql script. The Post-Upgrade Status tool follows the naming convention of its predecessor versions and is named utlu121s.sql.

18. A. The predefined Unified Auditing policies are disabled after a database upgrade—both manual and DBUA. After the upgrade, the pre-12*c* audit configuration is maintained, and records are written to the AUD$ table. You can enable Unified Auditing policies and create new policies along with pre-12*c* audit configuration (mixed-mode). The two types of audits write information to different tables. For performance reasons, Oracle recommends that you switch to Unified Auditing Only mode by relinking the oracle executable with uniaud_on option.

19. A, B. Having current dictionary statistics helps the database upgrade. The upgrade does not touch or use the application tables; hence, there is no need to run full database statistics. In Oracle Database 12*c*, the EM Database Control is replaced with EM Database Express. During the upgrade, EM Database Control is dropped. This step can be completed prior to starting the upgrade in order to save upgrade time. RECYCLE_BIN must be purged before the upgrade is performed.

20. B. Because the database is small, exporting and importing to an existing or newly created Oracle Database 12*c* database is faster and cleaner.

Chapter 18: Using Grid Infrastructure and Data Movement Tools

1. B, C. The DBMS_METADATA package provides the database object definitions to the export worker processes in the order of their creation. The DBMS_DATAPUMP package has the API for high-speed export and import for bulk data and metadata loading and unloading.

2. B, D. Oracle Data Pump is known to versions 10g and newer; Oracle9*i* does not support Data Pump. Although Data Pump can perform data access using the direct-path or external-table method, Data Pump makes the decision automatically; the DBA cannot specify the data-access method. Data Pump also supports network mode to import directly from the source database and can estimate the space requirements for the dump file.

3. D. The master table is the heart of the Data Pump operation and is maintained in the schema of the job creator. It bears the name of the job, contains one row for each object and each operation, and keeps status. Using this information helps restart a failed job or suspend and resume a job. The master table is written to the dump file as the last step of the export and is loaded to the schema of the user as the first step of the import.

4. C. If a directory object is created with the name DATA_PUMP_DIR, the privileged users can use this location as the default location for Data Pump files. Privileged users are users with EXP_FULL_DATABASE or IMP_FULL_DATABASE roles. Using %U in the filename generates multiple files for parallel unloads, with each parallel process writing to one file.

5. D. The ATTACH parameter lets you attach or connect to an existing Data Pump job and places you in interactive mode. ATTACH without any parameters attaches to the currently running job, if there is only one job from the user. Otherwise, you must specify the job name when using the ATTACH parameter.

6. B. If the CONTENT parameter is not specified, both data and metadata will be unloaded. The valid values for CONTENT are METADATA_ONLY, DATA_ONLY, and ALL. If SCOTT is performing the export, SCHEMAS=SCOTT is optional.

7. A. REMAP_DATAFILE changes the name of the source data file to the target data filename in all DDL statements where the source data file is referenced. REMAP_SCHEMA loads all objects from the source schema into the destination schema. When using REMAP_TABLESPACE, all objects selected for import with persistent data in the source tablespace are remapped to be created in the destination tablespace. REMAP_TABLE changes the name of the table. Because the dump file is in XML format, Data Pump can make these transformations easily. REMAP_INDEX is an invalid parameter.

8. C. You can specify the FLASHBACK_TIME or FLASHBACK_SCN parameter only when performing a network import where the source is a database.

9. B. The network_link parameter specifies a database link to the source database.

10. B. External tables can be used to read ASCII flat files without loading them into the database. The external table must be created with the ORACLE_LOADER access driver.

11. E. While the direct path load is in progress, users cannot run any DML statements against the table. Only queries are allowed.

12. A, B. If you do not want to create a disk group during the GI install, you must choose the Software Only install option. Only one disk group can be created during the GI install. Additional disk groups can be created after the installation using ASMCA or SQL*Plus.

Although we recommend that you have more than one disk in each disk group, it is not mandatory. GI install configures the ASM instance and uses the disk group created during the install to save the parameter file and password file of ASM instance.

13. C. The smallest unit of storage in an ASM disk group is the allocation unit. Oracle Database 12*c* permits sizes of 1, 2, 4, 8, 16, 32, or 64MB. The allocation unit is the size of the blocks allocated to a data file. The AU must be small enough to keep hot spots from occurring and large enough for efficient sequential reads. 1MB is the default, and 4MB AU is recommended for most databases.

14. B. You must be connected to the ASM instance with the SYSASM privilege to start and stop the ASM instance.

15. D. Server control is used to start and stop all Oracle Restart components including ASM, listener, and database.

16. C. A NORMAL redundancy disk group requires two fail groups, and a HIGH redundancy disk group requires three fail groups.

17. B. Option A is an invalid statement. The disk path can be used only when adding a disk; when dropping a disk the disk name must be provided. Option C is using a disk path with the drop clause and is invalid. Option D is syntactically correct, but you cannot drop all disks from a disk group. A disk group must have at least one disk.

18. B, C. The rebalance speed at an instance level is adjusted using the ASM_POWER_LIMIT parameter. Rebalance power can be adjusted using the ALTER DISKGROUP statement as well. The higher the power limit, the more quickly a rebalance operation can complete. Higher power values consume more I/O resources, which could impact database performance. Rebalancing takes longer with lower power values, but it consumes fewer processing and I/O resources.

19. E. All of the tools listed in options A to D can be used to start an ASM instance. You have to explicitly provide start commands in sqlplus, asmcmd, and srvctl, but if asmca finds that the ASM instance is not started, it gets confirmation from you and starts the instance.

20. A. The Server Control utility (srvctl) is used to register a component during an Oracle Restart. The add command is used to register a component. The config command shows the configuration information. The start command starts the component after it is registered. The register command is not valid.

Appendix
B

About the Additional Study Tools

✓ **In This Appendix:**

   ▪ Additional study tools

   ▪ System requirements

   ▪ Using the study tools

   ▪ Troubleshooting

Additional Study Tools

The following sections are arranged by category and summarize the software and other goodies you'll find on the companion website. If you need help installing the items, refer to the installation instructions in the "Using the Study Tools" section of this appendix.

 You can find the additional study tools at www.sybex.com/go/oca12sg. You'll also find instructions on how to download the files to your hard drive.

Sybex Test Engine

The files contain the Sybex test engine, which includes bonus practice exams, as well as the assessment test and the chapter review questions, which are also included in the book.

Electronic Flashcards

These handy electronic flashcards are just what they sound like. One side has a question, and the other side shows the answer.

Bonus Author Materials

I've included some bonus Whitepapers on how to install an Oracle 12c database on Windows, how to create a non-CDB Oracle Database 12c on Windows, and how to install Oracle Enterprise Manager 12c on Virtual Box. I've also included all of the code from the book so you don't have to retype it.

PDF of Glossary of Terms

We have included an electronic version of the glossary in .pdf format. You can view the electronic version of the glossary with Adobe Reader.

Adobe Reader

We've also included a copy of Adobe Reader so you can view PDF files that accompany the book's content. For more information on Adobe Reader or to check for a newer version, visit Adobe's website at www.adobe.com/products/reader/.

System Requirements

Make sure your computer meets the minimum system requirements shown in the following list. If your computer doesn't meet these requirements, you may have problems using the software and files. For the latest and greatest information, please refer to the ReadMe file located in the download.

- A PC running Microsoft Windows XP or newer
- An Internet connection

Using the Study Tools

To install the items, follow these steps:

1. Download the .zip file to your hard drive, and unzip it to your desired location. You can find instructions on where to download this file at www.sybex.com/go/oca12sg.
2. Click the Start.EXE file to open the study tools file.
3. Read the license agreement, and then click the Accept button if you want to use the study tools.

   The main interface appears and allows you to access the content with just a few clicks.

Troubleshooting

Wiley has attempted to provide programs that work on most computers with the minimum system requirements. If a program does not work properly, the two likeliest problems are that you don't have enough memory (RAM) for the programs you want to use or you have other programs running that are affecting the installation or running of a program. If you get an error message such as "Not enough memory" or "Setup cannot continue," try one or more of the following suggestions and then try using the software again:

Turn off any antivirus software running on your computer.   Installation programs sometimes mimic virus activity and may make your computer incorrectly believe that it's being infected by a virus.

Close all running programs.   The more programs you have running, the less memory is available to other programs. Installation programs typically update files and programs, so if you keep other programs running, installation may not work properly.

Have your local computer store add more RAM to your computer.   This is, admittedly, a drastic and somewhat expensive step. However, adding more memory can really help the speed of your computer and allow more programs to run at the same time.

Customer Care

If you have trouble with the book's companion study tools, please call the Wiley Product Technical Support phone number at (800) 762-2974, or email them at `http://sybex.custhelp.com/`.

Index

Note to the Reader: Throughout this index **boldfaced** page numbers indicate primary discussions of a topic. *Italicized* page numbers indicate illustrations.

D

N

O

P

S

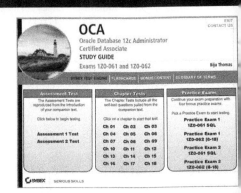